SOURCE READINGS IN MUSIC HISTORY

Source Readings in Music History, Revised Edition, is also available in separate paperbound volumes:

SOURCE READINGS IN

HISTORY

OLIVER STRUNK

EDITOR

Revised Edition
LEO TREITLER GENERAL EDITOR

 W · W · NORTON & COMPANY
New York · London

The text of this book is composed in Caledonia
with the display set in Bauer Bodoni and Optima
Composition and manufacturing by the Maple-Vail Book Manufacturing Group
Book design by Jack Meserole

The Library of Congress Cataloging-in-Publication Data:

Source readings in music history / Oliver Strunk, editor. — Rev. ed.
    / Leo Treitler, general editor.
        p.   cm.
    Also published in a 7 v. ed.
    Includes bibliographical references and index.
    ISBN 0-393-03752-5
    1. Music—History and criticism—Sources. I. Strunk, W. Oliver
(William Oliver), 1901–   . II. Treitler, Leo, 1931–   .
ML160.S89   1998
780′.9—dc20   94-34569
                                                 MN
W. W. Norton & Company, Inc.
500 Fifth Avenue, New York, N.Y. 10110
www.wwnorton.com

W. W. Norton & Company Ltd.
Castle House, 75/76 Wells Street, London W1T 3QT

34567890

CONTENTS

III   THE RENAISSANCE
Edited by GARY TOMLINSON

IV THE BAROQUE ERA
Edited by MARGARET MURATA

V   THE LATE EIGHTEENTH CENTURY
Edited by WYE J. ALLANBROOK

VI   THE NINETEENTH CENTURY
Edited by RUTH A. SOLIE

VII THE TWENTIETH CENTURY
Edited by ROBERT P. MORGAN

NOTES AND ABBREVIATIONS

Footnotes originating with the authors of the texts are marked [Au.], those with the translators [Tr.].

Years in the common era (A.D.) are indicated as C.E. and those before the common era as B.C.E.

Omissions in the text are indicated by five spaced bullets (• • • • •); three spaced bullets (• • •) indicate a typographical break in the original.

FROM THE FOREWORD TO THE
FIRST EDITION

*T*his book began as an attempt to carry out a suggestion made in 1929 by Carl Engel in his "Views and Reviews"—to fulfil his wish for "a living record of musical personalities, events, conditions, tastes . . . a history of music faithfully and entirely carved from contemporary accounts."[1] It owes something, too, to the well-known compilations of Kinsky[2] and Schering[3] and rather more, perhaps, to Andrea della Corte's *Antologia della storia della musica*[4] and to an evaluation of this, its first model, by Alfred Einstein.

In its present form, however, it is neither the book that Engel asked for nor a literary anthology precisely comparable to the pictorial and musical ones of Kinsky and Schering, still less an English version of its Italian predecessor, with which it no longer has much in common. It departs from Engel's ideal scheme in that it has, at bottom, a practical purpose—to make conveniently accessible to the teacher or student of the history of music those things which he must eventually read. Historical documents being what they are, it inevitably lacks the seemingly unbroken continuity of Kinsky and Schering; at the same time, and for the same reason, it contains far more that is unique and irreplaceable than either of these. Unlike della Corte's book it restricts itself to historical documents as such, excluding the writing of present-day historians; aside from this, it naturally includes more translations, fewer original documents, and while recognizing that the somewhat limited scope of the *Antologia* was wholly appropriate in a book on music addressed to Italian readers, it seeks to take a broader view.

That, at certain moments in its development, music has been a subject of widespread and lively contemporary interest, calling forth a flood of documentation, while at other moments, perhaps not less critical, the records are either silent or unrevealing—this is in no way remarkable, for it is inherent in the very nature of music, of letters, and of history. The beginnings of the Classical symphony and string quartet passed virtually unnoticed as developments without interest for the literary man; the beginnings of the opera and cantata, devel-

1. *The Musical Quarterly* 15, no. 2 (April 1929): 301.
2. *Geschichte der Musik in Bildern* (Leipzig, 1929; English edition by E. Blom, London, 1930).
3. *Geschichte der Musik in Beispielen* (Leipzig, 1931; English edition New York, 1950).
4. Two volumes (Torino, 1929). Under the title *Antologia della storia della musica della Grecia antica al' ottocento*, one volume (Torino, 1945).

opments which concerned him immediately and deeply, were heralded and reviewed in documents so numerous that, even in a book of this size, it has been possible to include only the most significant. Thus, as already suggested, a documentary history of music cannot properly exhibit even the degree of continuity that is possible for an iconographic one or a collection of musical monuments, still less the degree expected of an interpretation. For this reason, too, I have rejected the simple chronological arrangement as inappropriate and misleading and have preferred to allow the documents to arrange themselves naturally under the various topics chronologically ordered in the table of contents and the book itself, some of these admirably precise, others perhaps rather too inclusive. As Engel shrewdly anticipated, the frieze has turned out to be incomplete, and I have left the gaps unfilled, as he wished.

For much the same reason, I have not sought to give the book a spurious unity by imposing upon it a particular point of view. At one time it is the musician himself who has the most revealing thing to say; at another time he lets someone else do the talking for him. And even when the musician speaks it is not always the composer who speaks most clearly; sometimes it is the theorist, at other times the performer. If this means that few readers will find the book uniformly interesting, it ought also to mean that "the changing patterns of life," as Engel called them, will be the more fully and the more faithfully reflected. . . . In general, the aim has been to do justice to every age without giving to any a disproportionate share of the space.

It was never my intention to compile a musical Bartlett, and I have accordingly sought, wherever possible, to include the complete text of the selection chosen, or—failing this—the complete text of a continuous, self-contained, and independently intelligible passage or series of passages, with or without regard for the chapter divisions of the original. But in a few cases I have made cuts to eliminate digressions or to avoid needless repetitions of things equally well said by earlier writers; in other cases the excessive length and involved construction of the original has forced me to abridge, reducing the scale of the whole while retaining the essential continuity of the argument. All cuts are clearly indicated, either by a row of dots or in annotations.

Often, in the course of my reading, I have run across memorable things said by writers on music which, for one reason or another, were not suited for inclusion in the body of this book. One of these, however, is eminently suited for inclusion here. It is by Thomas Morley, and it reads as follows:

> But as concerning the book itself, if I had, before I began it, imagined half the pains and labor which it cost me, I would sooner have been persuaded to anything than to have taken in hand such a tedious piece of work, like unto a great sea, which the further I entered into, the more I saw before me unpassed; so that at length, despairing ever to make an end (seeing that grow so big in mine hands which I thought to have shut up in two or three sheets of paper), I laid it aside, in full determination to have proceeded no further but to have left it off as shamefully as it was foolishly begun. But then being admonished by some of my friends that it were pity to lose the fruits of the employment of so many good hours, and how justly I should be

condemned of ignorant presumption—in taking that in hand which I could not perform—if I did not go forward, I resolved to endure whatsoever pain, labor, loss of
time and expense, and what not, rather than to leave that unbrought to an end in the
which I was so far engulfed.[5]

OLIVER STRUNK
The American Academy in Rome

5. Thomas Morley, *A Plain and Easy Introduction to Practical Music*, ed. R. Alec Harman (New
York: Norton, 1966), p. 5.

FOREWORD TO THE REVISED EDITION

Hiding in the peace of these deserts
with few but wise books bound together
I live in conversation with the departed,
and listen with my eyes to the dead.
—Francisco Gómez de Quevedo
(1580–1645)

The inclusion here of portions of Oliver Strunk's foreword to the original edition of this classic work (to which he habitually referred ironically as his *opus unicum*) is already a kind of exception to his own
stricture to collect in it only "historical documents as such, excluding the writing of present-day historians." For his foreword itself, together with the book
whose purpose and principles it enunciates and the readings it introduces,
comes down to us as a historical document with which this revision is in a
conversation—one that ranges over many subjects, even the very nature of
music history.

This principle of exclusion worked for Strunk because he stopped his gathering short of the twentieth century, which has been characterized—as Robert Morgan observes in his introduction to the twentieth-century readings in this series—by "a deep-seated self-consciousness about what music is, to whom it should be addressed, and its proper role within the contemporary world." It is hardly possible to segregate historian from historical actor in our century.

For the collection in each of the seven volumes in this series the conversation begins explicitly with an introductory essay by its editor and continues with the readings themselves. The essays provide occasions for the authors to describe the considerations that guide their choices and to reflect on the character of the age in each instance, on the regard in which that age has been held in music-historical tradition, on its place in the panorama of music history as we construct and continually reconstruct it, and on the significance of the readings themselves. These essays constitute in each case the only substantial explicit interventions by the editors. We have otherwise sought to follow Strunk's own essentially conservative guidelines for annotations.

The essays present new perspectives on music history that have much in common, whatever their differences, and they present new perspectives on the music that is associated with the readings. They have implications, therefore, for those concerned with the analysis and theory of music as well as for students of music history. It is recommended that even readers whose interest is focused on one particular age acquaint themselves with all of these essays.

The opportunity presented by this revision to enlarge the book has, of course, made it possible to extend the reach of its contents. Its broader scope reflects achievement since 1950 in research and publication. But it reflects, as well, shifts in the interests and attitudes that guide music scholarship, even changes in intellectual mood in general. That is most immediately evident in the revised taxonomy of musical periods manifest in the new titles for some of the volumes, and it becomes still more evident in the introductory essays. The collections for "Antiquity and the Middle Ages" have been separated and enlarged. What was "The Greek View of Music" has become *Greek Views of Music* (eight of them, writes Thomas J. Mathiesen), and "The Middle Ages" is now, as James McKinnon articulates it, *The Early Christian Period and the Latin Middle Ages.* There is no longer a collection for "The Classical Era" but one for *The Late Eighteenth Century,* and in place of the epithet "The Romantic Era" Ruth Solie has chosen *The Nineteenth Century.* The replacements in the latter two cases represent a questioning of the labels "Classic" and "Romantic," long familiar as tokens for the phases of an era of "common practice" that has been held to constitute the musical present. The historiographic issues that are entailed here are clarified in Solie's and Wye Jamison Allanbrook's introductory essays. And the habit of thought that is in question is, of course, directly challenged as well by the very addition of a collection of readings from the twentieth century, which makes its own claims to speak for the present. Only the labels "Renaissance" and "Baroque" have been retained as period designations. But the former is represented by Gary Tomlinson as an age in fragmentation, for which "Renaissance" is retained only *faute de mieux*, and as to the latter, Margaret Murata places new emphasis on the indeterminate state of its music.

These new vantage points honor—perhaps more sharply than he would have expected—Strunk's own wish "to do justice to every age," to eschew the "spurious unity" of a "particular point of view" and the representation of history as a succession of uniform periods, allowing the music and music-directed thought of *each* age to appear as an "independent phenomenon," as Allanbrook would have us regard the late eighteenth century.

The possibility of including a larger number of readings in this revision might have been thought to hold out the promise of our achieving greater familiarity with each age. But several of the editors have made clear—explicitly or implicitly through their selections—that as we learn more about a culture it seems "more, not less distant and estranged from ours," as Tomlinson writes of the Renaissance. That is hardly surprising. If the appearance of familiarity has arisen out of a tendency to represent the past in our own image, we should hardly wonder that the past sounds foreign to us—at least initially—as we allow it to speak to us more directly in its own voice.

But these words are written as though we would have a clear vision of our image in the late twentieth century, something that hardly takes account of the link, to which Tomlinson draws attention, between the decline of our confidence about historical certainties and the loss of certainty about our own identities. Standing neck-deep in the twentieth century, surrounded by uncountable numbers of voices all speaking at once, the editor of this newest selection of source readings may, ironically, have the most difficult time of any in arriving at a selection that will make a recognizable portrait of the age, as Morgan confesses.

Confronted with a present and past more strange and uncertain than what we have been pleased to think, the editors have not been able to carry on quite in the spirit of Strunk's assuredness about making accessible "those things which [the student] must eventually read." Accordingly, this revision is put forward with no claim for the canonical status of its contents. That aim has necessarily yielded some ground to a wish to bring into the conversation what has heretofore been marginal or altogether silent in accounts of music history.

The sceptical tract *Against the Professors* by Sextus Empiricus, among the readings from ancient Greece, is the first of numerous readings that run against a "mainstream," with the readings gathered under the heading "Music, Magic, Gnosis" in the Renaissance section being perhaps the most striking. The passage from Hildegard's *Epistle* to the prelates of Mainz in the medieval collection is the first of many selections written by women. The readings grouped under the reading "Glimpses of Other Musical Worlds" in the Renaissance collection evince the earliest attention paid to that subject. A new prominence is given to performance and to the reactions of listeners in the collection from the Baroque. And the voices of North American writers and writers of color begin to be heard in the collection from the nineteenth century.

There is need to develop further these once-marginal strands in the representation of Western music history, and to draw in still others, perhaps in some future version of this series, and elsewhere—the musical cultures of Latin America for one example, whose absence is lamented by Murata, and the representation of the Middle Ages in their truly cosmopolitan aspect, for another.

This series of books remains at its core the conception and the work of Oliver Strunk. Its revision is the achievement of the editors of the individual volumes, most of whom have in turn benefited from the advice of numerous colleagues working in their fields of specialization. Participating in such a broadly collaborative venture has been a most gratifying experience, and an encouraging one in a time that is sometimes marked by a certain agonistic temper.

The initiative for this revision came in 1988 from Claire Brook, who was then music editor of W. W. Norton. I am indebted to her for granting me the privilege of organizing it and for our fruitful planning discussions at the outset. Her thoughts about the project are manifested in the outcome in too many ways to enumerate. Her successor Michael Ochs has been a dedicated and active editor, aiming always for the highest standards and expediting with expertise the complex tasks that such a project entails.

LEO TREITLER
Lake Hill, New York

$\mathcal{G}$REEK VIEWS OF MUSIC

Edited by THOMAS J. MATHIESEN

INTRODUCTION

*I*n the original edition of *Source Readings in Music History,* Oliver Strunk included only a brief sampling of early writings on ancient Greek music, no doubt for the primary purpose of introducing various themes recurring across the centuries in the later writings that made up the bulk of the volume. Strunk subtitled his little compendium—one technical treatise by Cleonides and four excerpts from the writings of Plato, Aristotle, Aristoxenus, and Athenaeus—"The Greek View of Music," quite properly recognizing that it represented only one of many ancient cultures. In the paperback edition of 1965, this preliminary section was too short to form a book by itself; accordingly, it joined the much larger group of writings from the early Christian period and the Middle Ages in a volume titled *Antiquity and the Middle Ages.*

Antiquity of course embraces more than Greek and Roman literature, but in a short paperback, it hardly seems advisable—or even possible—to include a reasonable sampling of materials of the ancient Near East, Egypt, Mesopotamia, China, India, and so on. In keeping with the spirit of Strunk's original conception, this new edition limits itself to Greek literature but expands the offerings. To afford a larger view of the themes and styles of Greek writers on music, Plato, Aristotle, Athenaeus, and Cleonides are now joined by Gaudentius, Aristides Quintilianus, and Sextus Empiricus. This group would still be too limited to warrant Strunk's original subtitle "*The* Greek View of Music," even if it did represent a unified view of music. In fact, as readers will perceive in the three complete treatises and five excerpts by a group of authors spanning eight centuries, the readings in this edition do not present a single view of music but rather, as the title suggests, eight *Greek Views of Music.*

Although Greek writers on music differ in their interests and approaches, some generalization about their views of music can be made. First of all, music (μουσική) was considered both an art and a science. It provided simple relaxation and entertainment, yet it also played a central role in the civic and religious life of the people. Plato recognized and employed music as a cosmological paradigm in the *Timaeus,* while still concerning himself in the *Republic* and the *Laws* with the specific issues of the influence of music on behavior and the types of music that should be allowed in an enlightened civilization. Aristotle considered the educational function of music in Book VIII of the *Politics* and pointed out its effect on the development of character. Several centuries later, at the twilight of the ancient world, Aristides Quintilianus provided a comprehensive description in his treatise *On Music:*

Music is a science, certainly, in which exists sure and infallible knowledge, for whether we speak of it in terms of problems or effects, it would never demonstrate any change or alteration. And indeed, we might also with reason call it an art, for it is both a composite of perceptions . . . and is not useless to life.[1]

This is not mere hyperbole. Music was used in all activities of Greek life: schooling, religious ceremony, mundane work, theatrical performance, the singing of poetry, and recreation.

Musical allusions and general descriptions of music appear to a greater or lesser degree in the *Iliad* and the *Odyssey,* in lyric poetry, and in dramatic works of ancient Greece. Moreover, nearly all this literature was sung, danced, and accompanied by musical instruments. The literature itself is therefore a part of the Greek musical heritage.

Music in this sense of a performing art was called melos (μέλος) by the Greeks. A distinction was made between melos in general, which might be no more than an instrumental piece or a simple song, and perfect melos (τέλειον μέλος), which comprised not only the melody and the text but also highly stylized dance movement.[2]

The process of selecting and applying the various components of melos and rhythm to create a complete composition came to be called melic composition (μελοποιία) and rhythmic composition (ῥυθμοποιία). Without explaining precisely how music produces its particular effects, Cleonides observes that any melos might be elevating (diastaltic), depressing (systaltic), or relaxing (hesychastic) in character, as appropriate. Aristides Quintilianus, too, seems to recognize three basic types of melos when he subdivides melic composition into three classes: dithyrambic, nomic, and tragic.[3] In fact, his parallel subdivision of rhythmic composition uses the same three terms Cleonides employed in describing the character of melos.

Although the treatises of Cleonides and Aristides Quintilianus are rather late, their systems of classification accord with the more general statements of earlier writers, and it is clear that from a very early period, the Greeks had developed a sophisticated musical typology. Forms might be typified by subject matter, rhythm and meter, large-scale structure, and so on. Plato's Athenian Stranger (*Laws* 3 [700a8-e4]) observes that the types were once distinct: a hymn would not be confused with a dirge, dithyramb, or paean. Nevertheless, he also clearly implies that this distinction was beginning to be lost by the middle of the fourth century B.C.E., and he laments that the mixing of forms and musical styles was leading to chaos. In Plato's *Republic* 4 (424b5-c6), Socrates argues against innovations in music because they threaten the fundamental structure of the state:

One must be cautious about changing to a new type of music as this risks a change in the whole. The modes [τρόποι] of music are never moved without movement of the greatest constitutional laws.

In both the *Republic* and the *Timaeus,* Plato makes use of the term "har-

1. See p. 48.
2. See p. 62.
3. Cf. p. 46, and pp. 65–66.

monia" (ἁρμονία) and its related forms, a term embodying the complexities of meanings and associations in the Greek view of music. In the *Timaeus*, on the one hand, it refers to the harmonious union of the disparate parts of the universal soul, all within the context of traditional Pythagorean musical ratios.[4] In the *Republic*, on the other hand, it is used in conjunction with the various ethnic characterizations of musical types—Dorian, Phrygian, Lydian, and so on—and it also refers to the harmonious state of the individual soul effected by the proper balance of music and gymnastics. As Socrates says:

> Then he who best blends gymnastics with music and applies them most suitably to the soul is the man whom we should most rightly pronounce to be the most musical and harmonious. . . .[5]

Plato's writings remind us once again that all the practical manifestations of music form only one part of the Greek concept of music. As both an art and a science, music occupied a prominent place in everyday life not only because it was amusing and socially valuable but also because it embodied larger universal principles and served as a vehicle for higher understanding.

In the *Politics*, Aristotle recognizes the claim of earlier writers that music has the power to amuse and relax, to instill ethical virtue, and to stimulate the intellect, but he intends to examine once again the validity of these claims and especially the importance of music in education. While Aristotle takes a somewhat more practical view of music, he still accepts the basic theoretical principles of music and certainly does not depart from Plato's concern about the power of music to influence behavior and its concomitant importance to society as a whole. For Aristotle, however, the propriety of music and education in music cannot be judged in purely absolute terms; rather, it is a relative matter, affected by time, place, purpose, age, and station.[6]

Later Epicurean and skeptic philosophers disagreed with the broad claims made for music by earlier writers such as Plato and Aristotle. In particular, the notion that music could, beyond the most basic level, affect character and influence behavior gradually lost favor until it was revived by the neo-Platonists. None, however, went as far as Sextus Empiricus in applying skeptic techniques of argument to demolish earlier technical, psychological, and metaphysical explanations of music, and in his collection of treatises *Against the Professors*, we have the best examples of systematic antidotes to dogmatism in any field.[7]

In addition to general discussions of music and music theory that abound in philosophy, considerable detail about the use, character, and value of music is contained in collections of anecdotes and similar types of literature. Historical, anecdotal, and lexicographical works such as Pausanias's *Description of Greece*, Athenaeus's *Sophists at Dinner*, Plutarch's *Table-Talk*, Photius's *Library*, the *Great Etymologicon*, the *Suda*, and Pollux's *Onomasti-*

---

4. See pp. 19–23
5. See pp. 18–19.
6. See pp. 32–34.
7. The sixth book of this collection, *Against the Musicians*, appears on pp. 94–109.

con[8] contain a wealth of valuable detail on matters as wide-ranging as the construction and use of musical instruments, the types of music and the occasions when they might be used, and the effect of music on behavior. The excerpt from Athenaeus included here exemplifies the type of musical lore that appealed to readers of the later Empire and so fascinated musicians and scholars when this material began to be published in Greek and in Latin translations in the sixteenth century.

Technical or systematic works that treat the theory of ancient Greek music are a particular type of literary source important to this subject. Like the other literary sources, these range over a wide period of time from the fourth century B.C.E. to the fourth century C.E.[9] Some of these treatises are simple technical manuals that provide valuable detail about the Greeks' musical system, including notation, the function and placement of notes in a scale, characteristics of consonance and dissonance, rhythm, and types of musical composition. This group includes, among others, the *Division of a Canon* (sometimes attributed to Euclid), the *Harmonic Introduction* by Cleonides, the *Manual of Harmonics* by Nicomachus of Gerasa, the *Harmonic Introduction* by Gaudentius, the *Musical Introduction* by Alypius, the *Introduction to the Art of Music* by Bacchius Geron, and the *Exposition of Mathematics Useful for Reading Plato* by Theon of Smyrna. By contrast, other treatises are long and elaborate books that show the way in which the science of music reveals universal patterns of order and thereby leads to the highest levels of knowledge and understanding. These longer books were written by well-known figures of antiquity: Aristoxenus, a principal disciple of Aristotle and aspirant to succeed him as head of the Lyceum; Claudius Ptolemy, the great Alexandrian astronomer; and Porphyrius and Aristides Quintilianus, associates of Plotinus and the neo-Platonists.

Modern scholarship commonly refers to this literature collectively as "ancient Greek music theory," but the phrase is not particularly apt. In the first place, most of it was written long after the time of Plato and Aristotle. With the exception of quotations in later literature,[10] the earliest surviving independent theoretical works are Aristoxenus's *Harmonics* and *Rhythmics*. Both of these are fragmentary, though the fragments are substantial. The *Division of a Canon* traditionally attributed to Euclid would be nearly contemporary if Euclid were the author,[11] but all the other treatises date from the end of the first century C.E. or later. In the second place, the modern pedagogical meaning of the phrase "mu-

---

8. Pausanias, Athenaeus, Plutarch, and Pollux are writers of the second and third centuries C.E.; Photius, the *Suda*, and the *Great Etymologicon* are later Byzantine sources.

9. Or even later, when works written in late antiquity and the Middle Ages in Latin, Greek, and Arabic are included. These writings, however, do not form part of the primary corpus of ancient Greek music theory but rather represent its transmission to later times.

10. Most of these are brief, and their authenticity can rarely be proven. The most extended quotation is the Aristotelian *De audibilibus*, which is preserved only in Porphyrius's commentary on Ptolemy's *Harmonics*.

11. For a new text and English translation, together with the most thorough study of this treatise and its authorship, see André Barbera, ed. and trans. *The Euclidean Division of the Canon: Greek and Latin Sources*, Greek and Latin Music Theory, vol. 8 (Lincoln: University of Nebraska Press, 1991).

sic theory" is foreign to these writings. With the possible exception of the rather late writer Alypius (fl. third or fourth century C.E.), it is quite unlikely that any of the authors intended his work for practicing musicians or was concerned with actual pieces of music. Readers who expect specific sorts of analytical details in a treatise on ancient Greek "music theory" and are then disappointed at their absence impose a concept on the treatises that is foreign to their purpose. The authors of these works are not primarily interested in analyzing pieces of music or explaining compositional or performance practice. This does not mean, of course, that the technical information cannot be applied to the surviving fragments, but it does mean that if the writings are to be properly assessed, they must be viewed within their own intellectual contexts, which differ among the treatises.[12]

Strunk's original edition included a brief excerpt from Aristoxenus's *Harmonics*—the beginning of the so-called second book. While there is no question of their tremendous importance, the surviving fragments of the *Harmonics* present a number of textual difficulties, and it is in any case very difficult to grasp the complexity and originality of his arguments in a short excerpt. In this new edition, Aristoxenus has been omitted, both in the interest of including some new material and because the *Harmonics* is better read as a whole. Moreover, two complete English translations of the treatise are readily available.[13]

The seven parts of harmonics outlined in Strunk's excerpt from Aristoxenus are more fully treated in the treatise ascribed to Cleonides, which presents the clearest and most concise summary of the basic technical system that by the second century C.E. had come to be regarded as Aristoxenian. Although this treatise was written at least five hundred years after the time of Aristoxenus, it was published in a Latin translation long before the first published Latin translation of Aristoxenus's own treatise. As such, it exerted considerable influence on the conceptions of ancient Greek music formed by later musical writers. In the treatise of Cleonides, the reader encounters all those technical terms and definitions associated with ancient Greek music theory: the names of all the notes, the definition of the pycnon, the various intervals that make up the six shades of the three genera, the octave species, the Greater and Lesser Perfect Scales (or systems), the thirteen tonoi, the three ethoses, and the basic devices of melic composition.

Like Cleonides, Aristides Quintilianus also explores the seven Aristoxenian parts of harmonics in his treatise *On Music*, yet their treatments are by no means identical. Cleonides provides no information about musical notation and makes no use of it in his treatise, perhaps in keeping with Aristoxenus's dis-

---

12. Many of the general observations in this introduction are adapted from my forthcoming book, *Apollo's Lyre: Greek Music and Music Theory in Antiquity and the Early Middle Ages*, to be published by the University of Nebraska Press.

13. Strunk's excerpt was drawn from *The Harmonics of Aristoxenus*, edited with translation, notes, introduction, and index of words by Henry S. Macran (Oxford: Clarendon, 1902; reprint, Hildesheim: G. Olms, 1974), and although the Greek text has since been improved and Macran's English style sounds somewhat old-fashioned today, it is still well worth reading. A new English translation has been published in Andrew Barker, *Greek Musical Writings*, vol. 2, *Harmonic and Acoustic Theory*, Cambridge Readings in the Literature of Music (Cambridge: Cambridge University Press, 1989), 126–84.

missal of notation as useless for understanding the principles of music.[14] Aristides Quintilianus, by contrast, includes several notational diagrams, illustrating among other things a series of purportedly early harmoniai, perhaps extending back to the time of Plato. Moreover, the section on harmonics in Aristides Quintilianus's treatise forms only a small portion of a large and elaborate musico-philosophical discourse. Prior to the discussion of harmonics, Aristides Quintilianus offers a preliminary definition of music as "knowledge of the seemly in bodies and motions" and presents his division of "the whole art of music" into the theoretical and the practical, each of which is further subdivided to produce categories encompassing the entire range of music from the natural and mathematical music of the universe to the most quotidian practical details. As a neo-Platonist, Aristides Quintilianus quite naturally sees music as a paradigm for the order of the soul and the universe.

The treatise of Gaudentius, published here for the first time in an English translation, represents another distinct approach to the subject of harmonics. Like Cleonides and Aristides Quintilianus, he includes technical detail from the Aristoxenian system, but in the middle of the treatise he turns his attention to the traditions of Pythagorean mathematics, including the famous story of Pythagoras's discovery of harmonic phenomena. Although later scholarship stressed the opposition of the supposed Aristoxenian and Pythagorean schools of music theory, such a clear distinction does not appear in the treatises themselves. Like Aristides Quintilianus's treatise, major sections of which were adopted by Martianus Capella in his *On the Marriage of Philology and Mercury,* Gaudentius's treatise apparently enjoyed some circulation in the very early Middle Ages; Cassiodorus mentions a Latin translation of the treatise and follows Gaudentius in accepting the interval of the eleventh (24:9) as consonant, even though it violates the more traditional Pythagorean restriction of consonance to multiple and superparticular intervals.[15]

Although readers should be able to understand the following translations without much background in the subject, some may find it helpful to read a brief overview before turning to the readings themselves. The following are particularly useful, succinct, and accessible:

> Barbera, André. "Greece." In *New Harvard Dictionary of Music,* ed. Don Michael Randel, 346–51. Cambridge: Belknap Press of Harvard University Press, 1986.
> Henderson, Isobel. "Ancient Greek Music." In *Ancient and Oriental Music,* ed. Egon Wellesz, 336–403. New Oxford History of Music, vol. 1. London: Oxford University Press, 1957.
> Winnington-Ingram, R. P. "Greece I (Ancient)." In *The New Grove Dictionary of Music and Musicians,* ed. Stanley Sadie, 7:659–72. 20 vols. London: Macmillan, 1980.

Following the model of Strunk's original edition, each translation is preceded by a brief preliminary note. In the translations themselves, however, I have provided somewhat more extensive annotation than Strunk tended to do.

14. See Macran, 194–95, or Barker, 155–57.
15. See pp. 143–48.

1 Plato

The great ancient Greek philosopher was born ca. 429 B.C.E. and died in 347. Although he may have derived his main ideas and method from the teachings of his eminent master Socrates (469–399 B.C.E.), Plato asked and answered enormously important questions about beauty and the arts, and his writings are fundamental to later aesthetic theory.

After Socrates's death, Plato devoted the next twelve years to extensive journeys, including perhaps Egypt but certainly Italy and Sicily in 387, where he met Dion of Syracuse and the Pythagorean Archytas of Tarentum. He then returned to Athens and began his career as a philosopher at the "Academy," located about a mile outside the city walls. A crowd of students and enthusiastic followers gathered around him, and in his writings, he attacked the fallacious ideas on education propagated by the sophists. Plato made two other visits to Syracuse, where he attempted unsuccessfully to put some of his political theories into practice.

Plato's chief philosophical writings are not arranged in systematic form but take the shape of highly poetic and often dramatically vivid dialogues. The important figures of Greek public life in Plato's time appear in them as representatives of their respective ideas. Socrates is regularly introduced as the moderator.

One of the most famous dialogues from Plato's middle period is the *Republic*. In this work, the philosopher expounds his ideas about the organization of the ideal state. In such a state, as Plato conceives it, education is paramount and art derives its main value as a means of attaining this educational ideal. In this connection, Plato regards music as highly important; its lofty purpose is to serve, not for superficial entertainment, but to help in building up a harmonious personality and in calming the human passions. Book III, a section of which is presented here, contains the most detailed discussion of music.

FROM THE *Republic*
3.9–13, 17–18 (398b–405a and 410a–412b)

"And now, my friend," said I, "we may say that we have completely finished the part of music that concerns speeches and tales. For we have set forth what

TEXT: English translation by Paul Shorey. Reprinted by permission of the publishers and the Loeb Classical Library from *Plato in Twelve Volumes*, vol. 5, *The Republic, Books I–V*, trans. Paul Shorey, Loeb Classical Library, vol. 237 (Cambridge, Mass.: Harvard University Press, 1969), 245–69 and 287–95. Shorey's original footnotes, where I have retained them, are followed by [Tr.]. In addition to providing explanatory comment on the text, my own footnotes will record any significant departures from Shorey's translation.

is to be said and how it is to be said." "I think so too," he replied.[1]

10. "After this, then," said I, "comes the manner of song and mele?"[2] "Obviously." "And having gone thus far, could not everybody discover what we must say of their character in order to conform to what has already been said?" "I am afraid that 'everybody' does not include me," laughed Glaucon; "I cannot sufficiently divine offhand what we ought to say, though I have a suspicion." "You certainly, I presume," said I, "have a sufficient understanding of this— that melos is composed of three things, the text, the harmonia, and the rhythm?"[3] "Yes," said he, "that much." "And so far as it is text, it surely in no manner differs from text not sung in the requirement of conformity to the patterns and manner that we have prescribed?" "True," he said. "And again, the harmonia and the rhythm must follow the text."[4] "Of course." "But we said we did not require dirges and lamentations in words." "We do not." "What, then, are the dirge-like harmoniai? Tell me, for you are a musician."[5] "The Mixolydian," he said, "and the intense Lydian, and others similar to them." "These, then," said I, "we must do away with. For they are useless even to women who are to make the best of themselves, let alone to men." "Assuredly." "But again, drunkenness is a thing most unbefitting guardians, and so is softness and sloth." "Yes." "What, then, are the soft and convivial harmoniai?"

---

1. Plato's use of dialogue makes his discussion of the educational value of music especially vivid. The dialogue is set around 410 B.C.E., on the day after the feast of Bendis. The principal speaker is Socrates, who leads the discussion with his companions. In Book III, Glaucon and Adeimantus, brothers of Plato, respond to Socrates's remarks and raise various questions.

2. The Greek term is μέλος (melos), here in the plural (mele). Shorey translated the term as "melodies," but melos is the whole complex of text, rhythm, and pitches and their functional relationships, as Plato himself explains just a few lines later in this paragraph. I have modified Shorey's various translations of this term to melos throughout the excerpt. On melos, cf. Aristides Quintilianus, On Music (De musica) 1.12 (see pp. 62–66).

3. Shorey: "the words, the tune, and the rhythm." "Harmonia" (ἁρμονία), however, has the much broader sense of an entire complex of relationships among pitches, commonly viewed by many writers as paradigmatic of larger universal relationships. Cf. Plato's own Timaeus (pp. 19–23). In the plural, "harmoniai" often refer to particular complexes associated with ethnic names (such as Dorian harmonia, Phrygian harmonia, and so on) or to particular scalar patterns (such as the Dorian octave species). Eventually, these begin to be closely associated with the so-called tonoi or tropoi (cf. Cleonides, Harmonic Introduction [Harmonica introductio; pp. 35–46], Aristides Quintilianus, On Music [pp. 47–66], and Gaudentius, Harmonic Introduction [Harmonica introductio; pp. 66–85]), which in turn evolve into the modes as explained by later Latin writers, including Boethius.

4. This point is reiterated in section 11. These remarks are frequently cited in the sixteenth and seventeenth centuries as arguments against what Monteverdi calls "The First Practice"; see pp. 535–43.

5. A musician (μουσικός) to the Greek writers was one who understood music in both its scientific and practical forms. Plato will later (3.18) draw a distinction between one who is most musical and one who is a mere artisan. Cf. Boethius's contrast between the musicus and the cantor in The Fundamentals of Music (De institutione musica) 1.34 (pp. 142–43). In the following passage, Socrates describes the harmoniai, rejecting four of them as unsuitable for education. Cf. the treatment in Aristotle's Politics (Politica; p. 29) and Sextus Empiricus's Against the Musicians (Adversus musicos; pp. 94–109).

"There are certain Ionian and also Lydian ones that are called relaxed." "Will you make any use of them for warriors?" "None at all," he said; "but it would seem that you have left the Dorian and the Phrygian." "I don't know the harmoniai," I said, "but leave us that[6] harmonia that would fittingly imitate the utterances and the accents of a brave man who is engaged in warfare[7] or in any enforced business, and who, when he has failed, either meeting wounds or death or having fallen into some other mishap, in all these conditions confronts fortune with steadfast endurance and repels her strokes. And another for such a man engaged in works of peace, not enforced but voluntary, either trying to persuade somebody of something and imploring him—whether it be a god, through prayer, or a man, by teaching and admonition—or contrariwise yielding himself to another who is petitioning or teaching him or trying to change his opinions, and in consequence faring according to his wish, and not bearing himself arrogantly, but in all this acting modestly and moderately and acquiescing in the outcome. Leave us these two harmoniai—the enforced and the voluntary—that will most beautifully imitate the utterances of men failing or succeeding, the temperate, the brave—leave us these." "Well," said he, "you are asking me to leave none other than those I just spoke of." "Then," said I, "we shall not need in our songs and mele polychordia or panharmonia."[8] "Not in my opinion," said he. "Then we shall not maintain makers of the trigona, the pektides, and all other instruments insofar as they are polychordic and polyharmonic."[9] "Apparently not." "Well, will you admit to the city makers and players of the aulos? Or is not the aulos the most polychordic of instruments and do not the panharmonic instruments themselves imitate it?"[10] "Clearly,"

6. ἐκείνην may mean, but does not say, Dorian, which the *Laches* (188d) pronounces the only true Greek harmonia. [Tr.]

7. Monteverdi tells us (p. 666) that this characterization of the harmonia suited to the brave man engaged in warfare prompted his discovery of the *stile concitato*.

8. Shorey translates πολυχορδίας γε οὐδὲ παναρμονίου as "instruments of many strings or whose compass includes all the harmonies." But it seems clear from the following sentences explaining the terms by applying them to various instruments that they should be retained as technical terms. Indeed, Shorey himself later (3.13) retained panharmonia as a technical term. "Polychordia" means "the use of many strings," which is naturally a violation of the more severe, restrained, and understated style Plato clearly admires. "Panharmonia" means "all of the harmoniai," and if only the Dorian and Phrygian harmoniai are to be retained, panharmonia too would naturally be undesirable and unnecessary.

9. Shorey: "Then we shall not maintain makers of triangles and harps and all other many-stringed and poly-harmonic instruments." The trigonon was a small triangular harp held upright in the lap and plucked with the fingers; in vase paintings of the instrument, it is generally shown with the shorter strings closer to the player's body. Some representations show the instrument with as many as thirty-two strings. The pektis, an instrument perhaps somewhat like the modern dulcimer, had many pairs of strings tuned in octaves. The feature of many strings would have made these instruments particularly flexible and well adapted to modulate from one harmonia to another. Both instruments were commonly associated with women.

10. Shorey translates αὐλός as "flute," a common mistranslation. The aulos, however, is an instrument played with a single beating-reed or a double reed. In sound, it is rather like the Romanian *taragato* (or, in terms of modern European instruments, perhaps most like an oboe in its

he said. "You have left," said I, "the lyre and the kithara.[11] These are useful in the city, and in the fields the shepherds would have a syrinx[12] to pipe on." "So our argument indicates," he said. "We are not innovating, my friend, in preferring Apollo and the instruments of Apollo to Marsyas and his instruments." "No, by heaven!" he said, "I think not." "And by the dog,"[13] said I, "we have all unawares purged the city which a little while ago we said was luxurious." "In that we show our good sense," he said.

11. "Come then, let us complete the purification. For upon harmoniai would follow the consideration of rhythms: we must not pursue complexity nor great variety in the basic movements, but must observe what are the rhythms of a life that is orderly and brave, and after observing them require the foot and the melos to conform to that kind of man's speech and not the speech to the foot and the melos. What those rhythms would be, it is for you to tell us as you did the harmoniai." "Nay, in faith," he said, "I cannot tell. For that there are some three species[14] from which the feet are combined, just as there are four in the notes of the voice[15] whence come all harmonies, is a thing that I have observed and could tell. But which are imitations of which sort of life, I am

---

lower register). It was commonly associated in Greek literature with the Phrygians (especially Marsyas), with extended and complex pieces of music, and with virtuosic performance (cf. the comments in Aristotle's *Politics* 8.7 [pp. 33–34]). As a reed instrument, it was capable of producing an extended scale, rapid changes of scalar pattern, and subtle variations of pitch. Plato suggests that the more complicated stringed instruments tried to copy the wider range and flexibility of the aulos.

11. Shorey: "the lyre and the either." As the instruments most strongly associated with Apollo, the lyre and the kithara are quintessentially Greek. Although "lyre" is a generic term that can imply any of the instruments of the lyre family (i.e., instruments played with a plectrum, such as the lyre itself, the kithara, the phorminx, the barbitos, etc.), in this context it probably refers to the small instrument built on a tortoise shell. This instrument, widely depicted in vase paintings, was the common instrument of everyday music-making. The kithara, by contrast, was a larger instrument associated with more formal musical occasions, such as religious ceremonies and the competitions of the Great Dionysia.

12. Shorey: "a little piccolo." The syrinx is a small reed pipe, and the term can be applied to a single pipe, a group of reeds of graduated length bound together—the Pan-pipe—or an aulos mouthpiece, which is made from the same type of reed, though cut and prepared in a different manner. It was commonly associated with Pan, the son of Hermes.

13. The so-called Rhadamanthine oath to avoid taking the names of the gods in vain. [Tr.]

14. Shorey translates εἴδη as "forms." Writers such as Cleonides and Gaudentius regularly use the terms εἶδος and σχῆμα almost as synonyms, and Aristoxenus states at the very end of the surviving fragments of his *Harmonics* (*Harmonica*) that both terms mean the same thing. Nevertheless, since the two terms are commonly used in close proximity in the technical treatises, I have routinely differentiated them in these translations by taking εἶδος as "species" and σχῆμα as "form." The three species of rhythm are the equal (i.e., those that can be divided into equal parts, such as dactyls [$-\smile\smile$], spondees [$--$], and anapests [$\smile\smile-$]); sesquialteran (i.e., those that can be divided into parts in a ratio of 3:2, such as the paeon diaguios [$-\smile-$], which is also commonly known as a cretic); and duple (i.e., those that can be divided into parts in a ratio of 2:1, such as the iamb [$\smile-$] and trochee [$-\smile$]). Aristides Quintilianus provides a fuller treatment of these species in *On Music* 1.13–19.

15. Perhaps the four notes of the tetrachord, which is the basic building-block of harmonic theory at the time of Plato, Aristotle, and Aristoxenus.

unable to say." "Well," said I, "on this point we will take counsel with Damon,[16] too, as to which are the feet appropriate to illiberality, and insolence or madness or other evils, and what rhythms we must leave for their opposites; and I believe I have heard him obscurely speaking of a foot that he called the enoplios,[17] a composite foot, and a dactyl and an heroic foot,[18] which he arranged, I know not how, to be equal up and down in the interchange of long and short,[19] and unless I am mistaken he used the term iambic, and there was another foot that he called the trochaic, and he added the quantities long and short. And in some of these, I believe, he censured and commended the tempo of the foot no less than the rhythm itself, or else some combination of the two; I can't say. But, as I said, let this matter be postponed for Damon's consideration. For to determine the truth of these would require no little discourse. Do you think otherwise?" "No, by heaven, I do not." "But this you are able to determine—that seemliness and unseemliness are attendant upon the good rhythm and the bad." "Of course." "And, further, that good rhythm and bad rhythm accompany, the one fair diction, assimilating itself thereto, and the other the opposite, and so of the harmonious and the disharmonious,[20] if, as we were just now saying, the rhythm and harmonia follow the text and not the text these." "They certainly must follow the text," he said. "And what of the manner of the diction, and the text?" said I. "Do they not follow and conform to the disposition of the soul?" "Of course." "And all the rest to the diction?" "Yes." "Good speech, then, good accord, and good grace, and good rhythm wait upon a good disposition, not that weakness of head which we euphemistically style goodness of heart, but the truly good and fair disposition of the ethos[21] and the mind." "By all means," he said. "And must not our youth pursue these everywhere if they are to do what it is truly theirs to do?" "They must

16. Damon, tutor of Pericles, was a highly regarded early authority on music. Although no writings by him survive, he is generally considered to be the source for many of the Greek theories about the ethical force of music. Socrates refers to him here, and in the *Republic* (*Respublica*) 4.3 (424c) Damon is credited with the maxim "the modes of music are never moved without movement of the greatest constitutional laws." He also appears in Plato's *Alcibiades I* (118c) and *Laches* (200b), and a major portion of the second book of Aristides Quintilianus's *On Music* (2.14) is based on his theory. For useful surveys of Damon and his thought, see Warren Anderson, "The Importance of Damonian Theory in Plato's Thought," *Transactions of the American Philological Association* 86 (1955): 88–102; his *Ethos and Education in Greek Music* (Cambridge, Mass.: Harvard University Press, 1966), 74–81; and Carnes Lord, "On Damon and Music Education," *Hermes* 106 (1978): 32–43.
17. A war-dance, but there is no scholarly agreement about the precise structure of its rhythm.
18. Possibly foot, possibly rhythm. δάκτυλον seems to mean the foot, while ἡρῷος is the measure based on dactyls but admitting spondees. [Tr.]
19. Cf. the discussion of warlike and peaceful dancing in the *Laws* (*Leges*) 7 (815e–816d).
20. Shorey translates the phrase τὸ εὐάρμοστον καὶ ἀνάρμοστον as "the apt and the unapt," but this obscures the various connections with harmonia that Socrates is drawing throughout this section of the *Republic*.
21. Shorey: "character." The Greek ἦθος conveys a much larger meaning than the modern English sense of "character," and I have retained it throughout this excerpt as the technical term "ethos." Aristotle expands on the relationship between music and ethos in the *Politics* (see pp.

indeed." "And there is surely much of these qualities in painting and in all similar craftsmanship—weaving is full of them and embroidery and architecture and likewise the manufacture of household furnishings and thereto the natural bodies of animals and plants as well. For in all these there is grace or gracelessness. And gracelessness and arhythmia[22] and disharmony are akin to evil speaking and the evil temper, but the opposites are the symbols and the kin of the opposites, the sober and good disposition." "Entirely so," he said.

12. "Is it, then, only the poets that we must supervise and compel to embody in their poems the semblance of the good ethos or else not write poetry among us, or must we keep watch over the other craftsmen, and forbid them to represent the evil disposition, the licentious, the illiberal, the graceless, either in the likeness of living creatures or in buildings or in any other product of their art, on penalty, if unable to obey, of being forbidden to practice their art among us, that our guardians may not be bred among symbols of evil, as it were in a pasturage of poisonous herbs, lest grazing freely and cropping from many such day by day they little by little and all unawares accumulate and build up a huge mass of evil in their own souls. But we must look for those craftsmen who by the happy gift of nature are capable of following the trail of true beauty and grace, that our young men, dwelling as it were in a salubrious region, may receive benefit from all things about them, whence the influence that emanates from works of beauty may waft itself to eye or ear like a breeze that brings from wholesome places health, and so from earliest childhood insensibly guide them to likeness, to friendship, to consonance[23] with beautiful reason." "Yes," he said, "that would be far the best education for them." "And is it not for this reason, Glaucon," said I, "that education in music is most sovereign, because more than anything else rhythm and harmonia find their way to the inmost soul and take strongest hold upon it, bringing with them and imparting grace, if one is rightly trained, and otherwise the contrary? And further, because omissions and the failure of beauty in things badly made or grown would be most quickly perceived by one who was properly educated in music, and so, feeling distaste rightly, he would praise beautiful things and take delight in them and receive them into his soul to foster its growth and become himself beautiful and good. The ugly he would rightly disapprove of and hate while still young and yet unable to apprehend the reason, but when reason came the man thus nurtured would be the first to give her welcome, for by this affinity he would know her." "I certainly think," he said, "that such is the cause of education in music." "It is, then," said I, "as it was when we learned our letters and felt that

---

26–30), and much of the second book of Aristides Quintilianus's *On Music* is devoted to the subject. Sextus Empiricus, on the other hand, sees nothing inherently affective or ethical about music (see pp. 94–109).

22. Shorey translates ἀρρυθμία as "evil rhythm."

23. Shorey translates ξυμφωνία as "harmony" (and related forms as "harmonious"), but the term is regularly found in the musical writings, where it clearly means "consonance."

we knew them sufficiently only when the separate letters did not elude us, appearing as few elements in all the combinations that convey them, and when we did not disregard them in small things or great and think it unnecessary to recognize them, but were eager to distinguish them everywhere, in the belief that we should never be literate and letter-perfect till we could do this." "True." "And is it not also true that if there are any likenesses of letters reflected in water or mirrors, we shall never know them until we know the originals, but such knowledge belongs to the same art and discipline?" "By all means." "Then, by heaven, am I not right in saying that by the same token we shall never be true musicians, either—neither we nor the guardians that we have undertaken to educate—until we are able to recognize the forms of soberness, courage, liberality, and high-mindedness and all their kindred and their opposites, too, in all the combinations that contain and convey them, and to apprehend them and their images wherever found, disregarding them neither in trifles nor in great things, but believing the knowledge of them to belong to the same art and discipline?" "The conclusion is inevitable," he said. "Then," said I, "when there is a coincidence of a beautiful disposition in the soul and corresponding and consonant beauties of the same type in the bodily form—is not this the fairest spectacle for one who is capable of its contemplation?" "Far the fairest." "And surely the fairest is the most lovable." "Of course." "The true musician, then, would love by preference persons of this sort, but if there were no conso-nance[24] he would not love this." "No," he said, "not if there was a defect in the soul; but if it were in the body he would bear with it and still be willing to bestow his love." "I understand," I said, "that you have or have had favorites of this sort and I grant your distinction. But tell me this—can there be any com-munion between soberness and extravagant pleasure?" "How could there be," he said, "since such pleasure puts a man beside himself no less than pain?" "Or between it and virtue generally?" "By no means." "But is there between plea-sure and insolence and license?" "Most assuredly." "Do you know of greater or keener pleasure than that associated with Aphrodite?" "I don't," he said, "nor yet of any more insane." "But is not the right love a sober and musical[25] love of the orderly and the beautiful?" "It is indeed," said he. "Then nothing of madness, nothing akin to license, must be allowed to come nigh the right love?" "No." "Then this kind of pleasure may not come nigh, nor may lover and beloved who rightly love and are loved have anything to do with it?" "No, by heaven, Socrates," he said, "it must not come nigh them." "Thus, then, as it seems, you will lay down the law in the city that we are founding, that the lover may kiss and pass the time with and touch the beloved as a father would a son, for honorable ends, if he persuade him. But otherwise he must so associate with the objects of his care that there should never be any suspicion of anything

---

24. Shorey translates ἀξύμφωνος as "disharmony."
25. Shorey translates μουσικῶς, an adverbial form, as "harmonious," but this confuses the analogy Plato is developing.

further, on penalty of being stigmatized for want of taste and true musical culture." "Even so," he said. "Do you not agree, then, that our discourse on music has come to an end? It certainly made a fitting end, for surely the end and consummation of all musical things[26] is the love of the beautiful." "I concur," he said.

13. "After music our youth are to be educated by gymnastics?" "Certainly." "In this too they must be carefully trained from boyhood through life, and the way of it is this, I believe; but consider it yourself too. For I, for my part, do not believe that a sound body by its excellence makes the soul good, but on the contrary that a good soul by its virtue renders the body the best that is possible. What is your opinion?" "I think so too." "Then if we should sufficiently train the mind and turn over to it the minutiae of the care of the body, and content ourselves with merely indicating the norms or patterns, not to make a long story of it, we should be acting rightly?" "By all means." "From intoxication we said that they must abstain. For a guardian is surely the last person in the world to whom it is allowable to get drunk and not know where on earth he is." "Yes," he said, "it would be absurd that a guardian should need a guard." "What next about their food? These men are athletes in the greatest of contests, are they not?" "Yes." "Is, then, the bodily habit of the athletes we see about us suitable for such?" "Perhaps." "Nay," said I, "that is a drowsy habit and precarious for health. Don't you observe that they sleep away their lives, and that if they depart ever so little from their prescribed regimen these athletes are liable to great and violent diseases?" "I do." "Then," said I, "we need some more ingenious form of training for our athletes of war, since these must be as it were sleepless hounds, and have the keenest possible perceptions of sight and hearing, and in their campaigns undergo many changes in their drinking water, their food, and in exposure to the heat of the sun and to storms,[27] without disturbance of their health." "I think so." "Would not, then, the best gymnastics be akin to the music that we were just now describing?" "What do you mean?" "It would be a simple and flexible[28] gymnastic, and especially so in the training for war." "In what way?" "One could learn that," said I, "even from Homer. For you are aware that in the banqueting of the heroes on campaign he does not feast them on fish, though they are at the sea-side on the Hellespont, nor on boiled meat, but only on roast, which is what soldiers could most easily procure. For everywhere, one may say, it is of easier provision to use the bare fire than to convey pots and pans along." "Indeed it is." "Neither, as I believe, does Homer ever make mention of sweetmeats. Is not that something which all men in training understand—that if one is to keep his body in good condition he must abstain from such things altogether?" "They are right," he said, "in that

26. Shorey translates τὰ μουσικά as "culture," again obscuring the musical analogy.
27. Perhaps in the context "cold." [Tr.]
28. Literally "equitable," if we translate ἐπιεικής by its later meaning, that is, not over-precise or rigid in conformity to rule. [Tr.]

they know it and do abstain." "Then, my friend, if you think this is the right way, you apparently do not approve of a Syracusan table and Sicilian variety of made dishes." "I think not." "You would frown, then, on a little Corinthian maid as the *chère amie* of men who were to keep themselves fit?" "Most certainly." "And also on the seeming delights of Attic pastry?" "Inevitably." "In general, I take it, if we likened that kind of food and regimen to melic composition[29] and song expressed in the panharmonia and in every variety of rhythm it would be a fair comparison." "Quite so." "And there variety engendered licentiousness, did it not, but here disease? While simplicity in music begets sobriety in the souls, and in gymnastic training it begets health in bodies." "Most true," he said. "And when licentiousness and disease multiply in a city, are not many courts of law and dispensaries opened, and the arts of chicanery and medicine give themselves airs when even free men in great numbers take them very seriously?" "How can they help it?" he said.

· · · · ·

"And so your youths," said I, "employing that simple music which we said engendered sobriety will, it is clear, guard themselves against falling into the need of the justice of the courtroom." "Yes," he said. "And will not our musician, pursuing the same trail in his use of gymnastics, if he please, get to have no need of medicine save when indispensable?" "I think so." "And even the exercises and toils of gymnastics he will undertake with a view to the spirited part of his nature to arouse that rather than for mere strength, unlike ordinary athletes, who treat diet and exercise only as a means to muscle." "Nothing could be truer," he said. "Then may we not say, Glaucon," said I, "that those who established an education in music and gymnastics had not the purpose in view that some attribute to them in so instituting, namely to treat the body by one and the soul by the other?" "But what?" he said. "It seems likely," I said, "that they ordained both chiefly for the soul's sake." "How so?" "Have you not observed," said I, "the effect on the disposition of the mind itself of lifelong devotion to gymnastics with total neglect of music? Or the disposition of those of the opposite habit?" "In what respect do you mean?" he said. "In respect of savagery and hardness or, on the other hand, of softness and gentleness?" "I have observed," he said, "that the devotees of unmitigated gymnastics turn out more brutal than they should be and those of music softer than is good for them." "And surely," said I, "this savagery is a quality derived from the high-spirited element in our nature, which, if rightly trained, becomes brave, but if overstrained, would naturally become hard and harsh." "I think so," he said. "And again, is not the gentleness a quality which the philosophic nature would yield? This if relaxed too far would be softer than is desirable but if rightly

---

29. Shorey translates μελοποιία simply as "music," but the term is distinct from the more general μουσική. Cf. Aristotle, *Politics* (p. 32); Cleonides, *Harmonic Introduction* 14 (p. 46); and Aristides Quintilianus, *On Music* 1.12 (pp. 62–66).

trained gentle and orderly?" "That is so." "But our requirement, we say, is that the guardians should possess both natures." "It is." "And must they not be harmonious to one another?" "Of course." "And the soul of the man thus harmonious[30] is sober and brave?" "Certainly." "And that of the disharmonious[31] is cowardly and rude?" "It surely is."

18. "Now when a man abandons himself to music to play upon him and pour into his soul as it were through the funnel of his ears those sweet, soft, and dirge-like harmoniai of which we were just now speaking, and gives his entire time to the warblings and blandishments of song, the first result is that the principle of high spirit, if he had it, is softened like iron and is made useful instead of useless and brittle. But when he continues the practice without remission and is spellbound, the effect begins to be that he melts and liquefies till he completely dissolves away his spirit, cuts out as it were the very sinews of his soul and makes of himself a 'feeble warrior.'" "Assuredly," he said. "And if," said I, "he has to begin with a spiritless nature he reaches this result quickly, but if a high-spirited, by weakening the spirit he makes it unstable, quickly irritated by slight stimuli, and as quickly quelled. The outcome is that such men are choleric and irascible instead of high-spirited, and are peevish and discontented." "Precisely so." "On the other hand, if a man toils hard at gymnastics and eats right lustily and holds no truck with music and philosophy, does he not at first get very fit and full of pride and high spirit and become more brave and bold than he was?" "He does indeed." "But what if he does nothing but this and has no contact with the Muse in any way, is not the result that even if there was some principle of the love of knowledge in his soul, since it tastes of no instruction nor of any inquiry and does not participate in any discussion or any other form of culture, it becomes feeble, deaf, and blind, because it is not aroused or fed nor are its perceptions purified and quickened?" "That is so," he said. "And so such a man, I take it, becomes a misologist[32] and a stranger to the Muses. He no longer makes any use of persuasion by speech but achieves all his ends like a beast by violence and savagery, and in his brute ignorance and ineptitude lives his life with arhythmia and ungraciousness."[33] "That is entirely true," he said. "For these two, then, it seems there are two arts which I would say some god gave to mankind, music and gymnastics for the service of the high-spirited principle and the love of knowledge in them—not for the soul and the body except incidentally, but for the harmonious adjustment of these two principles by the proper degree of tension and relaxation of each." "Yes, so it appears," he said. "Then he who best blends

30. Shorey translates ἡρμοσμένον as "attuned," but Plato is drawing an exact parallel to the previous question, where ἡρμόσθαι ("be harmonious") is used.
31. Shorey translates ἀνάρμοστος as "ill attuned."
32. A hater of rational discussion, as explained in *Laches* (188c), and the beautiful passage in the *Phaedo* (89d ff.). [Tr.]
33. Cf. the end of 3.11 (p. 14). Shorey translates ἀχαριστία as "gracelessness," but Plato is making a deliberate distinction here with ἀσχημοσύνη ("gracelessness"), which he used in 3.11.

gymnastics with music and applies them most suitably to the soul is the man whom we should most rightly pronounce to be the most musical and harmonious, far rather than the one who composes the strings one with another."[34] "That seems likely, Socrates," he said. "And shall we not also need in our city, Glaucon, a permanent overseer of this kind if its constitution is to be preserved?" "We most certainly shall."

34. Shorey: "most perfect and harmonious musician, far rather than the one who brings the strings into unison with one another." Plato, however, uses μουσικώτατος and εὐαρμοστότατος more as adjectives of general approbation for the type of person he is describing rather than as adjectives describing a type of musician. Plato does not, of course, mean that a performer brings the strings of a lyre or kithara into unison but rather that he knows how to compose the strings into a tune. On this contrast between the true musician and the performer, see n. 5.

2 Plato

The *Timaeus*, together with the *Sophist, Statesman, Philebus,* and the *Laws,* comes from Plato's last period. It describes an elaborate cosmogony in which the world is a single living thing. Humankind is present in this world, and human perceptions, the soul, and the body are shown as harmonious with larger universal structures. Although the dialogue made an enormous impression on later Platonists, its obscurity (and language) caused it to be known primarily through the numerous and extensive commentaries written about it throughout the Middle Ages and beyond. The section of the dialogue presented here describes the creation of the soul as a grand harmonious complex.

FROM THE *Timaeus*

34b–37c

SOUL IS PRIOR TO BODY

Now this soul, though it comes later in the account we are now attempting, was not made by the god younger than the body; for when he joined them

TEXT: English translation reprinted by permission of the publisher from Francis MacDonald Cornford, *Plato's Cosmology: The* Timaeus *of Plato Translated with a Running Commentary* (London: Routledge & Kegan Paul; New York: Humanities Press, 1937), 58–59, 66, 71–74, and 93–96. In addition to providing explanatory comment on the text, my own footnotes will record any significant departures from Cornford's translation.

together, he would not have suffered the elder to be ruled by the younger.[1] There is in us too much of the casual and random, which shows itself in our speech; but the god made soul prior to body and more venerable in birth and excellence, to be the body's mistress and governor.

The things of which he composed soul and the manner of its composition were as follows: (1) Between the indivisible Existence that is ever in the same state and the divisible Existence that becomes in bodies, he compounded a third form of Existence composed of both. (2) Again, in the case of Sameness and in that of Difference, he also on the same principle made a compound intermediate between that kind of them which is indivisible and the kind that is divisible in bodies. (3) Then, taking the three, he blended them all into a unity, forcing the nature of Difference, hard as it was to mingle, into union with Sameness, and mixing them together with Existence. And having made a unity of the three, again he divided this whole into as many parts as was fitting, each part being a blend of Sameness, Difference, and Existence.[2]

And he began the division in this way. First he took one portion from the whole, and next a portion double of this; the third half as much again as the second, and three times the first; the fourth double of the second; the fifth three times the third; the sixth eight times the first; and the seventh twenty-seven times the first.[3] Next, he went on to fill up both the double and the triple

1. Like the *Republic*, the *Timaeus* is presented as a dialogue, in this case between Socrates, Critias, Timaeus of Locri, Hermocrates of Syracuse, and a fourth unnamed person. Timaeus is the only speaker in this excerpt. The dialogue is supposed to take place in Athens on the day of the Panathenaia. As Hermocrates was killed in 407 B.C.E., the dramatic date of the dialogue may be assumed to be more or less contemporary with that of the *Republic*. Indeed, some of the principles of the *Republic* 2–5 are recapitulated at the beginning of the *Timaeus*.
2. A diagram may clarify the process:

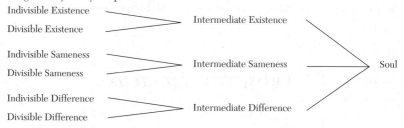

3. This produces the famous pattern commonly known as the "Pythagorean lambda" (because its shape is like the Greek capital Λ):

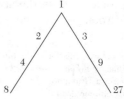

As a series of ratios, the numbers on the left can be envisioned as representing such musical intervals as the octave (2:1), double octave (4:1), and triple octave (8:1); the numbers on the

intervals, cutting off yet more parts from the original mixture and placing them between the terms, so that within each interval there were two means, the one exceeding the one extreme and being exceeded by the other by the same fraction of the extremes, the other exceeding the one extreme by the same number whereby it was exceeded by the other.[4]

These links gave rise to sesquialteran, sesquitertian, and sesquioctaval intervals within the original intervals. And he went on to fill up all the sesquitertian intervals with the sesquioctaval interval, leaving over in each a fraction. This remaining interval of the fraction had its terms in the numerical proportion of 256:243.[5] By this time the mixture from which he was cutting off these portions was all used up.

This whole fabric, then, he split lengthwise into two halves; and making the two cross one another at their centers in the form of the letter X, he bent each round into a circle and joined it up, making each meet itself and the other at a point opposite to that where they had been brought into contact.

---

right as representing the octave and a fifth (3:1), the triple octave and a tone (9:1), and the quadruple octave and a major sixth (27:1). But of greater importance to Plato's description of the development of the universe is the fact that the series on the left presents the duple ratios extending to the cube of the first even number, and the series on the right the triple ratios extending to the cube of the first odd number (the Pythagoreans did not consider 1 to be a number as such).

Aristides Quintilianus paraphrases this material (with credit to Plato's *Timaeus*) quite closely in *On Music* (*De musica*) 3.24, developing it with various neo-Platonic interpretations of the numbers and mathematical processes.

4. These are the harmonic and arithmetic means, both of which are described in a fragment attributed to Archytas (see p. 30, n. 16) and in various other manners by any of the later music theorists interested in the traditions of Pythagorean mathematics. Aristides Quintilianus, for example, discusses them in *On Music* 3.5 and Boethius in *The Fundamentals of Music* (*De institutione musica*) 2.14–17. To put Plato's explanations in numbers, 8 is the harmonic mean between 12 and 6, 9 is the arithmetic mean. 8 exceeds 6 by a third of six (i.e., 2), and 12 exceeds 8 by the same *fraction* (i.e., 4, a third of 12); 9 exceeds 6 by 3, and 12 exceeds 9 by the same *number*. Thus, the harmonic mean exceeds and is exceeded by the same fraction of the extremes, the arithmetic mean exceeds and is exceeded by the same number.

5. In this paragraph, Cornford converted the terms into their numerical equivalents 3:2, 4:3, and 9:8. I have preferred to retain the terms, since they are so commonly found in Greek and Latin music theory. In musical terms, the ratio of 3:2 is equivalent to a perfect consonant fifth, 4:3 to a perfect consonant fourth, and 9:8 to a whole tone. In equal temperament, of course, the fifth is flat by two cents, the fourth sharp by two cents, and the whole tone flat by 3.9 cents.

There are a number of possible interpretations of this paragraph, but it is commonly assumed that the numbers of the original series should be collapsed into 1, 2, 3, 4, 8, 9, and 27, and the means should then be inserted where not already represented in this series to produce the new series: 1, 1⅓, 1½, 2, 2⅔, 3, 4, 4½, 5⅓, 6, 8, 9, 13½, 18, and 27 (the fractions can, of course, also be expressed as ratios: 1, 4:3, 3:2, 2, 8:3, 3, 4, 9:2, 16:3, 6, 8, 9, 27:2, 18, and 27). 1⅓ and 1½ represent the harmonic and arithmetic means (and the ratios of 4:3 and 3:2) between 1 and 2, 2⅔ and 3 represent the same means and ratios between 2 and 4, and 5⅓ and 6 represent the same means and ratios between 4 and 8. 1½ and 2 represent the harmonic and arithmetic means between 1 and 3, 4½ and 6 represent the same means between 3 and 9, and 13½ and 18 represent the same means between 9 and 27. If each sesquitertian interval were separated into two sesquioctaval intervals (which added together equal the ratio 81:64), the remainder would indeed be the ratio of 256:243, a very small semitone (i.e., 9.8 cents flatter than an equal-tempered semitone).

He then comprehended them in the motion that is carried round uniformly in the same place, and made the one the outer, the other the inner circle. The outer movement he named the movement of the Same; the inner, the movement of the Different. The movement of the Same he caused to revolve to the right by way of the side; the movement of the Different to the left by way of the diagonal.

And he gave the supremacy to the revolution of the Same and uniform; for he left that single and undivided; but the inner revolution he split in six places into seven unequal circles, severally corresponding with the double and triple intervals, of each of which there were three.[6] And he appointed that the circles should move in opposite senses to one another; while in speed three should be similar, but the other four should differ in speed from one another and from the three, though moving according to ratio.[7] When the whole fabric of the soul had been finished to its maker's mind, he next began to fashion within the soul all that is bodily, and brought the two together, fitting them center to center. And the soul, being everywhere inwoven from the center to the outermost heaven and enveloping the heaven all round on the outside, revolving within its own limit, made a divine beginning of ceaseless and intelligent life for all time. Now the body of the heaven has been created visible; but she is invisible, and, as a soul having part in reason and harmonia,[8] is the best of things brought into being by the most excellent of things intelligible and eternal. Seeing, then, that soul had been blended of Sameness, Difference, and Existence, these three portions, and had been in due proportion divided and bound together, and moreover revolves upon herself, whenever she is in contact with anything that has dispersed existence or with anything whose existence is indivisible, she is set in motion all through herself and tells in what respect precisely, and how, and in what sense, and when, it comes about that something is qualified as either the same or different with respect to any given thing, whatever it may be, with which it is the same or from which it differs, either in the sphere of things that become or with regard to things that are always changeless.[9]

6. Recall the diagram in n. 3.
7. Plato is describing, but in deliberately vague terms, a kind of armillary sphere. The outermost sphere, the sphere of the Same, would correspond in Greek astrology to the sphere of the fixed stars. The movement of the Different, prior to being cut into seven circles, is the Zodiac. Cut into its seven circles, it corresponds to the orbits of the seven "planets," three of which (the Sun, Venus, and Mercury) move together in a similar speed, while the other four (the Moon, Mars, Jupiter, and Saturn) move at different speeds with respect to each other and with respect to the other three. It is important to note that Plato does not suggest here that the planets are *sounding* a "harmony of the spheres," but their numerical ratios do, of course, create a "harmonia of the spheres."
8. Cornford translates the term as "harmony." Here again, the term conveys the sense of large-scale universal relationships. Cf. p. 10, n. 3.
9. For an extensive commentary on the harmonic arrangement of this "world-soul," see Cornford, 66–94.

Now whenever discourse that is alike true, whether it takes place concerning that which is different or that which is the same, being carried on without speech or sound within the thing that is self-moved, is about that which is sensible, and the circle of the Different, moving aright, carries its message throughout all its soul—then there arise judgments and beliefs that are sure and true. But whenever discourse is concerned with the rational, and the circle of the Same, running smoothly, declares it, the result must be rational understanding and knowledge. And if anyone calls that in which this pair come to exist by any name but 'soul,' his words will be anything rather than the truth.[10]

10. This passage of the *Timaeus* was of considerable interest to Greek and Latin neo-Platonic writers well into the seventeenth century and has continued to intrigue commentators to the present day. For a useful collection of texts ranging from Plato to Albert von Thimus (and even later), see Joscelyn Godwin, ed., *The Harmony of the Spheres: A Sourcebook of the Pythagorean Tradition in Music* (Rochester, Vt.: Inner Traditions, 1993).

3 Aristotle

One of the most influential and versatile of thinkers, Aristotle was a philosopher, psychologist, political theorist, logician, biologist, and literary critic. The son of a physician, he was born in 384 B.C.E. in Stagirus, a Greek colonial town on the Aegean Sea. He became a pupil and later an independent scholar at Plato's Academy in Athens, remaining there until Plato's death in 347. In 343, he was invited by Philip of Macedonia to supervise the education of Philip's son Alexander. He probably resumed residence at Stagirus in 340, but in 335 after the death of Philip, he returned to Athens and founded there the so-called Peripatetic School in the Lyceum. After Alexander's death in 323, Aristotle left Athens for political reasons and died in 322 on his country estate near Chalcis on the island of Euboea.

Aristotle's extant works were probably written during the last twelve years of his life. They encompass nearly the entire range of the knowledge of his day. The *Politics* survives only as a fragment.

The influence of Aristotelian doctrine in the history of philosophy of the Western world has been immense. In the later Middle Ages, Aristotle became the supreme philosophical authority, until his influence began to be rivaled by a rebirth of Platonism in the early fifteenth century.

FROM THE *Politics*
8 (1337b4–1338b8 and 1339a11–1342b34)

II. It is therefore not difficult to see that the young must be taught those useful arts that are indispensably necessary; but it is clear that they should not be taught all the useful arts, those pursuits that are liberal being kept distinct from those that are illiberal, and that they must participate in such among the useful arts as will not render the person who participates in them vulgar. A task and also an art or a science must be deemed vulgar if it renders the body or soul or mind of free men useless for the employments and actions of virtue. Hence we entitle vulgar all such arts as deteriorate the condition of the body, and also the industries that earn wages; for they make the mind preoccupied and degraded. And even with the liberal sciences, although it is not illiberal to take part in some of them up to a point, to devote oneself to them too assiduously and carefully is liable to have the injurious results specified. Also it makes much difference what object one has in view in a pursuit or study; if one follows it for the sake of oneself or one's friends, or on moral grounds, it is not illiberal, but the man who follows the same pursuit because of other people would often appear to be acting in a menial and servile manner.

The branches of study at present established fall into both classes, as was said before. [3] There are perhaps four customary subjects of education, reading and writing, gymnastics, music, and fourth, with some people, drawing; reading and writing and drawing being taught as being useful for the purposes of life and very serviceable, and gymnastics as contributing to manly courage; but as to music here one might raise a question. For at present most people take part in it for the sake of pleasure; but those who originally included it in education did so because, as has often been said, nature itself seeks to be able not only to engage rightly in business but also to occupy leisure nobly; for—to speak about it yet again—this is the first principle of all things. For if although both business and leisure are necessary, yet leisure is more desirable and more fully an end than business, we must inquire what is the proper occupation of leisure. For assuredly it should not be employed in amusement,[1] since it would

TEXT: English translation by Harris Rackham. Reprinted by permission of the publishers and the Loeb Classical Library from Aristotle, *Politics,* trans. H. Rackham, Loeb Classical Library, vol. 264 (Cambridge, Mass.: Harvard University Press, 1959), 637–45 and 649–75. Numbers in brackets indicate the section divisions of the standard Berlin edition of the Greek text. In addition to providing explanatory comment on the text, my own footnotes will record any significant departures from Rackham's translation.

1. The distinction between "play," "sport," or "amusement" (παιδιά) and "pastime" or "entertainment" (διαγωγή) is essential to Aristotle's argument. "Amusement" is recreation, a restful and relaxing activity in spare time; "entertainment" is the employment of leisure. "Amusement" belongs to the worker, "entertainment" to the free man; "amusement" is useful, "entertainment" liberal. Rackham translates παιδιά in a variety of ways; I have taken the term uniformly as "amusement." The constant interplay in Aristotle's treatment between "amusement" (παιδιά) and "education" (παιδεία) is underscored in the Greek by the language itself.

follow that amusement is our end in life. But if this is impossible, and amusements should rather be employed in our times of business (for a man who is at work needs rest, and rest is the object of amusement, while business is accompanied by toil and exertion), it follows that in introducing amusements we must watch the right opportunity for their employment, since we are applying them to serve as medicine; for the activity of amusement is a relaxation of the soul, and serves as recreation because of its pleasantness. But leisure seems itself to contain pleasure and happiness and felicity of life. And this is not possessed by the busy but by the leisured; for the busy man busies himself for the sake of some end as not being in his possession, but happiness is an end achieved, which all men think is accompanied by pleasure and not by pain. But all men do not go on to define this pleasure in the same way, but according to their various natures and to their own characters, and the pleasure with which the best man thinks that happiness is conjoined is the best pleasure and the one arising from the noblest sources. So that it is clear that some subjects must be learnt and acquired merely with a view to the pleasure in their pursuit, and that these studies and these branches of learning are ends in themselves, while the forms of learning related to business are studied as necessary and as means to other things. Hence our predecessors included music in education not as a necessity (for there is nothing necessary about it), nor as useful (in the way in which reading and writing are useful for business and for household management and for acquiring learning and for many pursuits of civil life, while drawing also seems to be useful in making us better judges of the works of artists), nor yet again as we pursue gymnastics, for the sake of health and strength (for we do not see either of these things produced as a result of music); it remains therefore that it is useful as a pastime in leisure, which is evidently the purpose for which people actually introduce it, for they rank it as a form of pastime that they think proper for free men. For this reason Homer wrote thus:

> But him alone
> 'Tis meet to summon to the festal banquet;

and after these words he speaks of certain others

> Who call the bard that he may gladden all.[2]

And also in other verses Odysseus says that this is the best pastime, when, as men are enjoying good cheer,

> The banqueters, seated in order due
> Throughout the hall may hear a minstrel sing.[3]

III. It is clear therefore that there is a form of education in which boys should be trained not because it is useful or necessary but as being liberal and noble; though whether there is one such subject of education or several, and what these are and how they are to be pursued, must be discussed later, but as

2. These lines do not correspond exactly to *Odyssey* 17.383–85, but Aristotle may well be quoting from memory.
3. *Odyssey* 9.5–6.

it is we have made this much progress on the way, that we have some testimony even from the ancients, derived from the courses of education which they founded—for the point is proved by music. And it is also clear that some of the useful subjects as well ought to be studied by the young not only because of their utility, like the study of reading and writing, but also because they may lead on to many other branches of knowledge; and similarly they should study drawing not in order that they may not go wrong in their private purchases and may avoid being cheated in buying and selling furniture, but rather because this study makes a man observant of bodily beauty; and to seek for utility everywhere is entirely unsuited to men that are great-souled and free. And since it is plain that education by habit must come before education by reason, and training of the body before training of the mind, it is clear from these considerations that the boys must be handed over to the care of the wrestling-master and the trainer; for the latter imparts a certain quality to the habit of the body and the former to its actions.

•   •   •   •   •

[5] About music on the other hand we have previously raised some questions in the course of our argument, but it is well to take them up again and carry them further now, in order that this may give the key so to speak for the principles which one might advance in pronouncing about it. For it is not easy to say precisely what potency it possesses, nor yet for the sake of what object one should participate in it—whether for amusement and relaxation, as one indulges in sleep and deep drinking (for these in themselves are not serious pursuits but merely pleasant, and "relax our cares," as Euripides says;[4] owing to which people actually class music with them and employ all of these things, sleep, deep drinking, and music, in the same way, and they also place dancing in the same class); or whether we ought rather to think that music tends in some degree to virtue (music being capable of producing a certain quality of ethos[5] just as gymnastics are capable of producing a certain quality of body, music accustoming men to be able to rejoice rightly); or that it contributes something to intellectual entertainment and culture (for this must be set down as a third alternative among those mentioned). Now it is not difficult to see that one must not make amusement the object of the education of the young; for amusement does not go with learning—learning is a painful process. Nor yet moreover is it suitable to assign intellectual entertainment to boys and to the young; for a thing that is an end does not belong to anything that is imperfect. But perhaps it might be thought that the serious pursuits of boys are for the sake of amusement when they have grown up to be men. But if something

4. *Bacchae* 378.
5. Rackham: "character." The Greek ἦθος conveys a much larger meaning than the modern English sense of "character," and I have retained it throughout this excerpt as the technical term "ethos" (see pp. 13–14, n. 21).

of this sort is the case, why should the young need to learn this accomplishment themselves, and not, like the Persian and Median kings, participate in the pleasure and the education of music by means of others performing it? for those who have made music a business and profession must necessarily perform better than those who practice only long enough to learn. But if it is proper for them to labor at accomplishments of this sort, then it would also be right for them to prepare the dishes of an elaborate cuisine; but this is absurd. And the same difficulty also arises as to the question whether learning music can improve their ethoses; for why should they learn to perform edifying music themselves, instead of learning to enjoy it rightly and be able to judge it when they hear others performing, as the Spartans do? for the Spartans although they do not learn to perform can nevertheless correctly judge the good and bad characteristics of mele,[6] so it is said. And the same argument applies also if music is to be employed for refined enjoyment and entertainment; why need people learn to perform themselves instead of enjoying music played by others? And we may consider the conception that we have about the gods: Zeus himself does not sing and play the kithara for the poets.[7] But professional musicians we speak of as vulgar people, and indeed we think it not manly to perform music, except when drunk or for fun.

V. But perhaps these points will have to be considered afterwards; our first inquiry is whether music ought not or ought to be included in education, and what is its efficacy among the three uses of it that have been discussed—does it serve for education or amusement or entertainment? It is reasonable to reckon it under all of these heads, and it appears to participate in them all. Amusement is for the sake of relaxation, and relaxation must necessarily be pleasant, for it is a way of curing the pain due to laborious work; also entertainment ought admittedly to be not only honorable but also pleasant, for happiness is derived from both honor and pleasure; but we all pronounce music to be one of the pleasantest things, whether instrumental or instrumental and vocal music together (at least Musaeus[8] says, "Song is man's sweetest joy," and that is why people with good reason introduce it at parties and entertainments, for its exhilarating effect), so that for this reason also one might suppose that the younger men ought to be educated in music. For all harmless pleasures are not only suitable for the ultimate object but also for relaxation; and as it but

---

6. Rackham translated "nevertheless judge good and bad music correctly," but Aristotle is somewhat more specific in referring to melos (in the plural here). Cf. p. 10, n. 2. I have modified Rackham's various translations of this term to melos throughout the excerpt.
7. Rackham: "Zeus does not sing and harp to the poets himself." Aristotle uses the verb κιθαρίζει, which refers to the playing of a member of the lyre family, an instrument played with a plectrum, rather than to a harp-like instrument such as the trigonon, the strings of which were plucked directly by the fingers.
8. Pausanias refers to a number of early hymnographers in his *Description of Greece* (*Graeciae descriptio*), including Olen, Pamphus, Orpheus, Musaeus, and Homer. Orpheus and Musaeus are often related in legend, and both are associated with the lyre and with the cult of Apollo.

rarely happens for men to reach their ultimate object, whereas they often relax and pursue amusement not so much with some ulterior object but because of the pleasure of it, it would be serviceable to let them relax at intervals in the pleasures derived from music. But it has come about that men make amusements an end; for the end also perhaps contains a certain pleasure, but not any ordinary pleasure, and seeking this they take the other as being this because it has a certain resemblance to the achievement of the end of their undertakings. For the end is desirable not for the sake of anything that will result from it, and also pleasures of the sort under consideration are not desirable for the sake of some future result, but because of things that have happened already, for instance labor and pain. One might then perhaps assume this to be the reason which causes men to seek to procure happiness by means of those pleasures; but in the case of taking part in music, this is not because of this reason only, but also because performing music is useful, as it seems, for relaxation. But nevertheless we must examine whether it is not the case that, although this has come about, yet the nature of music is more honorable than corresponds with the employment of it mentioned, and it is proper not only to participate in the common pleasure that springs from it, which is perceptible to everybody (for the pleasure contained in music is of a natural kind, owing to which the use of it is dear to those of all ages and ethoses), but to see if its influence reaches also in a manner to the ethos and to the soul. And this would clearly be the case if we are affected in our ethoses in a certain manner by it. But it is clear that we are affected in a certain manner, both by many other kinds of music and not least by the mele of Olympus;[9] for these admittedly make our souls divinely suffused, and divine suffusion[10] is an affection of the ethos of the soul. And moreover everybody when listening to imitations is thrown into a corresponding state of feeling, even apart from the rhythms and mele themselves.[11] And since it is the case that music is one of the things that give pleasure, and that virtue has to do with feeling delight and love and hatred rightly, there is obviously nothing that is more needful to learn and become habituated to than to judge correctly and to delight in virtuous ethoses and noble actions;

9. The Ps. Plutarchean treatise On Music (De musica) identifies Polymnestus, Olympus, Mimnermus, and Sacadas as particularly skillful composer-performers. Several of the most famous compositions (nomoi) for solo aulos are attributed to Olympus, who was a Phrygian. Aristotle may very well have Phrygian mele in mind in this description.

10. Using cognates for the Greek ἐνθουσιαστικός and ἐνθουσιασμός, Rackham translates "souls enthusiastic, and enthusiasm is an affection," but the sense of the terms is rather different from the common sense of the English "enthusiasm." The influence of music on human affections or passions (πάθη) and its therapeutic power is described by Aristides Quintilianus in On Music (De musica) 2.5. Divine suffusion, which occurs in the rational part of the soul, is identified by him (On Music 3.25) as a primary cause of melody. Sextus Empiricus, on the other hand, takes a dim view of the notion that music has any inherently affective power (see pp. 99–103). I have modified Rackham's various translations of ἐνθουσιαστικός, ἐνθουσιασμός, and πάθος throughout the excerpt.

11. Unlike Plato, Aristotle considers purely instrumental music a legitimate "mode of imitation" (cf. Poetics [Poetica] 1.4–5 and Problems [Problemata] 19.27 [919b]).

but rhythms and mele contain representations of anger and mildness, and also of courage and temperance and all their opposites and the other ethical qualities, that most closely correspond to the true natures of these qualities (and this is clear from the facts of what occurs—when we listen to such representations we change in our soul); and habituation in feeling pain and delight at representations of reality is close to feeling them towards actual reality (for example, if a man delights in beholding the statue of somebody for no other reason than because of its actual form, the actual sight of the person whose statue he beholds must also of necessity give him pleasure); and it is the case that whereas the other objects of sensation contain no representation of ethoses, for example the objects of touch and taste (though the objects of sight do so slightly, for there are forms that represent character, but only to a small extent, and not all men participate in visual perception of such qualities; also visual works of art are not representations of ethoses but rather the forms and colors produced are mere indications of ethoses, and these indications are only bodily sensations in the affections; not but what in so far as there is a difference even in regard to the observation of these indications, the young must not look at the works of Pauson, but those of Polygnotus[12] and of any other ethical painter or sculptor), mele on the contrary do actually contain in themselves imitations of ethoses; and this is manifest, for even in the nature of the harmoniai[13] there are differences, so that people when hearing them are affected differently and have not the same feelings in regard to each of them, but listen to some in a more mournful and restrained state, for instance the so-called Mixolydian, and to others in a softer state of mind, for instance the relaxed harmoniai, but in a midway state and with the greatest composure to another, as the Dorian alone of the harmoniai seems to act, while the Phrygian makes men divinely suffused;[14] for these things are well stated by those who have studied this form of education, as they derive the evidence for their theories from the actual facts of experience. And the same holds good about the rhythms also, for some have a more stable and others a more emotional ethos, and of the latter some are more vulgar in their emotional effects and others more liberal. From these considerations therefore it is plain that music has the power of producing a certain effect on the ethos of the soul, and if it has the power to do this, it is clear that the young must be directed to music and must be educated in it. Also education in music is well adapted to the youthful nature; for the young owing to their youth cannot endure anything not sweetened by pleasure, and music is by nature a thing that has a pleasant sweetness. And we seem to have a certain affinity with the harmoniai and rhythms; owing

12. "Polygnotus represented men as better than they really were, Pauson as worse" (*Poetics* 2.1 [1448a]).
13. Rackham translates "harmonies," but Aristotle is using the term in its technical sense (see p. 10, n. 3).
14. This fourfold classification of the harmoniai according to their ethical character repeats the classification of Plato (Republic [*Respublica*] 3.10 [see pp. 10–11]).

to which many wise men say either that the soul is a harmonia or that it has harmonia.[15]

VI. [6] We ought now to decide the question raised earlier, whether the young ought to learn music by singing and playing themselves or not. It is not difficult to see that it makes a great difference in the process of acquiring a certain quality whether one takes a part in the actions that impart it oneself; for it is a thing that is impossible, or difficult, to become a good judge of performances if one has not taken part in them. At the same time also boys must have some occupation, and one must think Archytas's rattle[16] a good invention, which people give to children in order that while occupied with this they may not break any of the furniture, for young things cannot keep still. Whereas then a rattle is a suitable occupation for infant children, education serves as a rattle for young people when older. Such considerations therefore prove that children should be trained in music so as actually to take part in its performance; and it is not difficult to distinguish what is suitable and unsuitable for various ages, and to refute those who assert that the practice of music is vulgar. For first, inasmuch as it is necessary to take part in the performances for the sake of judging them, it is therefore proper for the pupils when young actually to engage in the performances, though when they get older they should be released from performing, but be able to judge what is beautiful and enjoy it rightly because of the study in which they engaged in their youth. Then as to the objection raised by some people that music makes people vulgar, it is not difficult to solve it by considering how far pupils who are being educated with a view to civic virtue should take part in the actual performance of music, and in what mele and what rhythms they should take part, and also what kinds of instruments should be used in their studies, as this naturally makes a difference. For the solution of the objection depends upon these points, as it is quite possible that some styles of music do produce the result mentioned. It is manifest therefore that the study of music must not place a hindrance in the way of subsequent activities, nor vulgarize the bodily frame and make it useless for the exercises of the soldier and the citizen, either for their practical pursuit now or for their scientific study later on. And this would come about in respect of their study if the pupils did not go on toiling at the exercises that aim at professional competitions, nor the wonderful and elaborate performances

15. Cf. Plato, *Republic* 3.12 (p. 15), 3.17, 4.17–18, and 8.9; *Timaeus* 34b–37c (pp. 19–23) and 47c–e; and *Phaedo* 85–95. Aristides Quintilianus expands on the notion to a considerable extent in *On Music* 3. For Aristotle's criticism, see his *On the Soul* (*De anima*) 1.4 (407b–409a); Sextus Empiricus (p. 103) also debunks this theory.

16. Archytas was a well-known Pythagorean and music theorist from Tarentum, a city at the southeastern tip of modern-day Italy that was also the birthplace of Aristoxenus. He flourished in the first half of the fourth century B.C.E. and was apparently known to Plato. As a music theorist, he is credited with a set of mathematical measurements for enharmonic, chromatic, and diatonic tetrachords, and a fragment attributed to him describes the harmonic, arithmetic, and geometric means.

which have now entered into the competitions and have passed from the competitions into education, but also only practiced exercises not of that sort until they are able to enjoy beautiful mele and rhythms, and not merely the charm common to all music, which even some lower animals enjoy, as well as a multitude of slaves and children. And it is also clear from these considerations what sort of instruments they should use. The auloi[17] must not be introduced into education, nor any other professional instrument, such as the kithara[18] or any other of that sort, but such instruments as will make them attentive pupils either at their musical education[19] or in their other lessons. Moreover the aulos is not an ethical but rather an exciting instrument,[20] so that it ought to be used for occasions of the kind at which attendance has the effect of purification rather than instruction. And let us add that aulos-music[21] happens to possess the additional property telling against its use in education that playing it prevents the employment of speech. Hence former ages rightly rejected its use by the young and the free, although at first they had employed it.[22] For as they came to have more leisure because of their wealth and grew more highspirited and valorous, both at a still earlier date and because after the Persian wars they were filled with pride as a result of their achievements, they began to engage in all branches of learning, making no distinction but pursuing research further. Because of this they even included aulos-playing among their studies; for in Sparta a certain chorus-leader himself played the aulos for his chorus, and at Athens it became so fashionable that almost the majority of freemen went in for aulos-playing, as is shown by the tablet erected by Thrasippus after having provided the chorus for Ecphantides.[23] But later on it came to be disapproved of as a result of actual experience, when men were more capable of judging what music conduced to virtue and what did not; and similarly also many of the old instruments were disapproved of, like the pektis and the barbitos and

---

17. Rackham: "flutes" (see pp. 11–12, n. 10).
18. Rackham: "harp" (see p. 12, n. 11).
19. Rackham: "training"; elsewhere, however, he translates this term (παιδεία) as "education." The modification distorts the careful distinctions Aristotle is attempting to draw, and I have accordingly modified his various translations of the term throughout the excerpt.
20. Rackham: "not a moralizing but rather an exciting influence."
21. Here, Aristotle uses the term αὔλησις which does not refer to the instrument (Rackham of course translates the term "flute") but rather to the type of music played on the instrument. This is another example of his careful use of terminology. The aulos itself does not, of course, prevent the employment of speech, but the nature of aulos-music precludes the close relationship between musical line and text because a single performer cannot play the aulos and simultaneously sing.
22. On this restriction of certain instruments as inappropriate for education, cf. Plato's *Republic* 3.10 (pp. 11–12).
23. Ecphantides was an Athenian comic poet. In Athens, a chorus-leader, such as Thrasippus, was the person who financed the training and presentation of the chorus (cf. Athenaeus, *Sophists at Dinner* [*Deipnosophistae*; p. 93]). It was common for the chorus-leader, or choregos, to set up monuments commemorating the names of the aulos-player, poet, and choregos responsible for a successful production.

the instruments designed to give pleasure to those who hear people playing them, the heptagonona, the trigona, and the sambykai,[24] and all the instruments that require manual skill. And indeed there is a reasonable foundation for the story that was told by the ancients about the auloi. The tale goes that Athena found a pair of auloi and threw them away. Now it is not a bad point in the story that the goddess did this out of annoyance because of the ugly distortion of her features; but as a matter of fact it is more likely that it was because education in aulos-music has no effect on the intelligence, whereas we attribute science and art to Athena.[25]

VII. And since we reject professional education in the instruments and in performance (and we count performance in competitions as professional, for the performer does not take part in it for his own improvement, but for his hearers' pleasure, and that a vulgar pleasure, owing to which we do not consider performing to be proper for free men, but somewhat menial; and indeed performers do become vulgar, since the object at which they aim is a low one, as vulgarity in the audience usually influences the music, so that it imparts to the artists who practice it with a view to suit the audience a special kind of personality, and also of bodily frame because of the movements required)—[7] we must therefore give some consideration to harmoniai and rhythms, and to the question whether for education we must employ all the harmoniai and all the rhythms or make distinctions, and next, whether for those who are working at music for education we shall lay down the same regulation, or ought we to establish some other third one (inasmuch as we see that music exists through melic composition and rhythm,[26] and it is important to notice what influence each of these has upon education), and whether we are to prefer music with a good melos or music with a good rhythm. Now we consider that much is well said on these matters by some of the musicians of the present day and by some of those engaged in philosophy who happen to be experienced in musical education, and we will abandon the precise discussion as to each of these matters for any who wish it to seek it from those teachers, while for the present let us lay down general principles, merely stating the outlines of the subjects. And since we accept the classification of mele made by some philosophers as ethi-

24. Rackham: "the septangle, the triangle, and the sambyc." The sambyke was most likely an instrument very similar to the trigonon (see p. 11, n. 9), but perhaps smaller and more delicate (as Aristides Quintilianus's *On Music* 2.16 states). On the other hand, Athenaeus says that "sambyke" is simply another name for the magadis, an instrument rather like the pektis. In any case, Aristotle's point is clear: these were instruments capable of producing the progressive "polychordia" and "panharmonia" that violated the austerity of the ancient style.

25. There are several stories about the invention of the aulos, the most famous of which involves the competition between the Greek Apollo and the Phrygian Marsyas. As the aulos became popular in Greek musical culture, legends began to attribute the discovery of the aulos to Athena. When she threw it away because it distorted her features, the instrument is supposed to have landed in Phrygia, thereby providing a neat way of linking the two traditions.

26. Rackham: "we see that the factors in music are melody and rhythm." On "melic composition," see p. 17, n. 29.

cal, practical, and divinely suffused,[27] distributing the various harmoniai among these classes as being in nature akin to one or the other, and as we say that music ought to be employed not for the purpose of one benefit that it confers but on account of several (for it serves the purpose both of education and of purgation—the term purgation we use for the present without explanation, but we will return to discuss the meaning that we give to it more explicitly in our treatise on poetry—and thirdly it serves for amusement, serving to relax our tension and to give rest from it), it is clear that we should employ all the harmoniai, yet not employ them all in the same way, but use the most ethical ones for education, and the practical and divinely suffused ones for listening to when others are performing (for any affection[28] that occurs violently in some souls is found in all, though with different degrees of intensity—for example pity and fear,[29] and also divine suffusion; for some persons are very liable to this form of emotion, and under the influence of sacred melos we see these people, when they use mele that violently arouse the soul, being thrown into a state as if they had received medicinal treatment and taken a purge; the same experience then must come also to the compassionate and the timid and the other affective people generally in such degree as befalls each individual of these classes, and all must undergo a purgation and a pleasant feeling of relief; and similarly also the purgative mele afford harmless delight to people). Therefore those who go in for theatrical music must be set to compete in harmoniai and mele of this kind (and since the audience is of two classes, one freemen and educated people, and the other the vulgar class composed of mechanics and laborers and other such persons, the latter sort also must be assigned competitions and shows for relaxation, and just as their souls are warped from the natural state, so those harmoniai and mele that are intense and irregular in coloration are deviations, but people of each sort receive pleasure from what is naturally suited to them, owing to which the competitors before an audience of this sort must be allowed to employ some such kind of music as this); but for education, as has been said, the ethical class of mele and of harmoniai must be employed. And of such a class is the Dorian harmonia, as we said before, but we must also accept any other harmonia that those who take part in the pursuit of philosophy and in musical education may recommend to us. Socrates in the *Republic* does not do well in allowing only the Phrygian harmonia along with the Dorian, and that when he has rejected the aulos among instruments,[30] for

27. Rackham translates "ethical melodies, melodies of action, and passionate melodies," but this does not fully convey Aristotle's larger distinction: the function of mele is to express or act on ethos, deed, or divine suffusion.

28. Rackham translates "experience," but this is the same term he has earlier translated as "affection" (see n. 10). I have accordingly modified his various translations of the term (and its related forms) throughout the excerpt.

29. In Aristotle's theory of drama (cf., e.g., *Poetics* 13–14), tragedy should effect a katharsis, or purgation, of pity and fear.

30. *Republic* 3.10 (p. 11).

the Phrygian harmonia has the same function[31] among harmoniai as the aulos among instruments—both are violently exciting and affective. This is shown by poetry, for all Bacchic meters[32] and all movement of that sort belongs particularly to the aulos among the instruments, and among the harmoniai, these meters are suitable in the Phrygian mele;[33] for example the dithyramb is admittedly held to be a Phrygian meter, and the experts on this subject adduce many instances to prove this, particularly the fact that Philoxenus when he attempted to compose a dithyramb, *The Mysians,* in the Dorian harmonia was unable to do so, but merely by the force of nature fell back again into the suitable harmonia, the Phrygian.[34] And all agree that the Dorian harmonia is more sedate and of a specially manly ethos. Moreover since we praise and say that we ought to pursue the mean between extremes, and the Dorian harmonia has this nature in relation to the other harmoniai, it is clear that it suits the younger pupils to be educated rather in the Dorian mele. But there are two objects to aim at, the possible as well as the suitable; for we are bound rather to attempt the things that are possible and those that are suitable for the particular class of people concerned; and in these matters also there are dividing lines drawn by the ages—for instance, those whose powers have waned through lapse of time cannot easily sing the intense harmoniai, but to persons of that age nature suggests the relaxed harmoniai. Therefore some musical experts also rightly criticize Socrates because he disapproved of the relaxed harmoniai for amusement,[35] taking them to have the character of intoxication, not in the sense of the function of strong drink, for that clearly has more the result of making men frenzied revellers, but as failing in power. Hence even with a view to the period of life that is to follow, that of the comparatively old, it is proper to engage in the harmoniai and mele of this kind too, and also such of the harmoniai as are suited to the age of boyhood because they are capable of being at once decorous and educative, which seems to be the nature of the Lydian most of all the harmoniai. It is clear therefore that we should lay down these three canons to guide education—moderation, possibility, and suitability.

31. Rackham translates δύναμις as "effect," but Aristotle is deliberately using the technical musical term here to suggest the functional arrangement of this harmonia or tonos in relation to all the others. I have accordingly modified his various translations of this term in the balance of the excerpt.
32. Rackham translates "versification."
33. Rackham translates "and these metres find their suitable accompaniment in tunes in the Phrygian mode among the harmonies."
34. Philoxenus and Timotheus of Miletus (fl. late fifth/early fourth century B.C.E.) were notorious for increasing the complexity of music through modulations and expansion of musical range. Dionysius of Halicarnassus (*On Literary Composition* [*De compositione verborum;* Roberts 194.23–196.7]) states that Philoxenus's dithyrambs (large-scale ecstatic compositions associated with the celebration of Dionysus) modulated across the Dorian, Phrygian, and Lydian harmoniai. Cf. Athenaeus, *Sophists at Dinner* (p. 89).
35. The manuscripts read παιδείαν, i.e., "education," but Rackham's edition emends it to παιδίαν [*sic*] (amusement).

4 Cleonides

Nothing is known of Cleonides; he is never cited by any other early author, although considerable portions of his treatise are appropriated by the Byzantine musicographer Manuel Bryennius in his *Harmonica* (written ca. 1300 C.E.). Cleonides's treatise is transmitted in thirty-nine manuscript codices, ten of which actually contain two separate copies of the treatise. Some of the manuscripts ascribe the treatise to Cleonides, some to Euclid. In a slightly different version, missing the first three sentences, some of the manuscripts ascribe the treatise to Pappus, an Alexandrian mathematician who flourished around 320 C.E. The principal reasons for assigning the treatise to Cleonides are: (1) in style and content, the treatise does not seem especially "Euclidean" or characteristic of Pappus; and (2) the name of Cleonides is assigned to the treatise in one of the two earliest and most important collections of ancient Greek music theory, a twelfth-century manuscript in the Biblioteca Apostolica Vaticana, Vaticanus gr. 2338.

The name of the author is, however, of little importance. The simple, straightforward style of the treatise and its content suggest that it was written no earlier than the second century and no later than the fourth century C.E. It is a kind of epitome of Aristoxenus's *Harmonics,* certainly one of the most important musical treatises of the fourth century B.C.E. Unfortunately, Aristoxenus's treatise survives only in fragmentary form, and Cleonides's little abstract is in effect a partial compensation for the loss.

The treatise was translated into Latin by Giorgio Valla and published in Venice in 1497, sixty-five years before the first printed edition of part of Aristoxenus's *Harmonics.* Thus, the treatise of Cleonides became an important source from which the musicians of the Renaissance drew their information about ancient Greek music.

Harmonic Introduction

1. Harmonics is the theoretical and practical science having to do with the nature of the harmonious. And the harmonious is made up of notes and inter-

TEXT: Strunk based his translation on the text of Karl von Jan (*Musici scriptores graeci. Aristoteles. Euclides. Nicomachus. Bacchius, Gaudentius. Alypius et melodiarum veterum quidquid exstat,* ed. Karl von Jan [Leipzig: B. G. Teubner, 1895; reprint, Hildesheim: G. Olms, 1962], 179–207). I have revised his translation, with further reference to the new critical text by Jon Solomon ("Cleonides: ΕΙΣΑΓΩΓΗ ΑΡΜΟΝΙΚΗ; Critical Edition, Translation, and Commentary" [Ph.D. dissertation, University of North Carolina–Chapel Hill, 1980]). Solomon included an English translation as part of his dissertation, and a free English translation by Charles Davy was published in 1787. The eminent French scholar of ancient Greek music, Charles-Emile Ruelle published his own modern French translation as part of his "collection of Greek musical authors" (*L'Introduction harmonique de Cléonide. La division du canon d'Euclide le géomètre. Canons harmoniques de Florence,* trans. C.-E. Ruelle, Collection des auteurs grecs relatifs à la musique, no. 3 [Paris: Firmin-Didot, 1884]).

vals having a certain order. The parts of harmonics are seven: on notes, intervals, genera, scales, tonoi, modulation, and melic composition.[1]

A note is a melodic incidence of the voice upon one pitch.

An interval is bounded by two notes differing as to height and depth.

Genus is a certain division of four notes.

A scale is made up of more than one interval.

A tonos is any position of the voice, receptive of a scale, and without breadth.

Modulation is the transposition of a similar thing to a dissimilar position.

Melic composition is the employment of the materials subject to harmonic practice with due regard to the requirements of each of the subjects under consideration.[2]

2. The things considered under quality of voice are these. It has two sorts of motions: one is called continuous and belongs to speech, the other is intervallic and belongs to melos. Continuous motion of the voice makes ascents and descents imperceptibly, and it is never at rest until it becomes silent. Intervallic motion of the voice moves oppositely to the continuous; it makes hesitations and distances between them, proceeding first in the one way, then in the other. The hesitations we call pitches, the passages from pitches to pitches we call intervals. The causes of the difference between pitches are ascent and descent, their effects are height and depth. The result of ascent is to lead to height, that of descent to depth. And height is the effect resulting from ascent, depth that resulting from descent. Pitches are also called notes. They are called "pitches" (τάσεις) from instruments with strings attached, because these are stretched (τετάσθαι); they are called "notes" (φθόγγοι) since they are produced by the voice (φωνή). To be stretched is a property of both. In respect to pitch, notes are infinite; in respect to function, there are eighteen in each genus.[3]

3. The genera are three: diatonic, color, and harmonia.[4] The diatonic is sung in descent by tone, tone, and semitone, and oppositely in ascent by semitone, tone, and tone. The color is sung in descent by trisemitone, semitone, and

---

1. In most of the manuscript sources, the treatise is followed by the *Division of a Canon* (*Sectio canonis*), a version of which is transmitted in Latin by Boethius in his *Fundamentals of Music* (*De institutione musica*) 4.1–2 and in Greek by Porphyrius in his commentary on Ptolemy's *Harmonics* (*Harmonica*) 1.5. The *Division* was commonly attributed to Euclid and exercised an enormous influence on later music theory, Greek and Latin. A new critical edition and translation of all three versions is presented in *The Euclidean Division of the Canon: Greek and Latin Sources*, ed. and trans. André Barbera, Greek and Latin Music Theory, vol. 8 (Lincoln: University of Nebraska Press, 1991).

2. These are the seven categories suggested in the surviving portions of Aristoxenus's *Harmonics* (*Harmonica*). Cf. Aristides Quintilianus, *On Music* (*De musica*) 1.4–5 (pp. 48–50) and the second sentence of Gaudentius's *Harmonic Introduction* (*Harmonica introductio;* p. 67).

3. Cf. Aristides Quintilianus, *On Music* 1.4–6 (pp. 48–53).

4. Cf. Aristides Quintilianus, *On Music* 1.9 (pp. 56–59) and Gaudentius, *Harmonic Introduction* 5 (p. 69). Although modern secondary literature commonly names the three genera diatonic, chromatic, and enharmonic, Greek writers often use these more general terms, reserving the adjectival forms for the description of a particular note or type of melos.

semitone, and oppositely in ascent by semitone, semitone, and trisemitone. The harmonia is sung in descent by ditone, diesis, and diesis, and oppositely in ascent by diesis, diesis, and ditone.

4. These are the notes in the diatonic, color, and harmonia:

Proslambanomenos	Proslambanomenos	Proslambanomenos
Hypate hypaton	Hypate hypaton	Hypate hypaton
Parhypate hypaton	Parhypate hypaton	Parhypate hypaton
Diatonic lichanos hypaton	Chromatic lichanos hypaton	Enharmonic lichanos hypaton
Hypate meson	Hypate meson	Hypate meson
Parhypate meson	Parhypate meson	Parhypate meson
Diatonic lichanos meson	Chromatic lichanos meson	Enharmonic lichanos meson
Mese	Mese	Mese
Trite synemmenon	Trite synemmenon	Trite synemmenon
Diatonic paranete synemmenon	Chromatic paranete synemmenon	Enharmonic paranete synemmenon
Nete synemmenon	Nete synemmenon	Nete synemmenon
Paramese	Paramese	Paramese
Trite diezeugmenon	Trite diezeugmenon	Trite diezeugmenon
Diatonic paranete diezeugmenon	Chromatic paranete diezeugmenon	Enharmonic paranete diezeugmenon
Nete diezeugmenon	Nete diezeugmenon	Nete diezeugmenon
Trite hyperbolaion	Trite hyperbolaion	Trite hyperbolaion
Diatonic paranete hyperbolaion	Chromatic paranete hyperbolaion	Enharmonic paranete hyperbolaion
Nete hyperbolaion	Nete hyperbolaion	Nete hyperbolaion

In the mixture of the genera, they are these:

Proslambanomenos
Hypate hypaton
Parhypate hypaton
Enharmonic lichanos hypaton
Chromatic lichanos hypaton
Diatonic lichanos hypaton
Hypate meson
Parhypate meson
Enharmonic lichanos meson
Chromatic lichanos meson
Diatonic lichanos meson
Mese

Trite synemmenon
Enharmonic paranete synemmenon
Chromatic paranete synemmenon
Diatonic paranete synemmenon
Nete synemmenon
Paramese
Trite diezeugmenon
Enharmonic paranete diezeugmenon
Chromatic paranete diezeugmenon
Diatonic paranete diezeugmenon
Nete diezeugmenon
Trite hyperbolaion
Enharmonic paranete hyperbolaion
Chromatic paranete hyperbolaion
Diatonic paranete hyperbolaion
Nete hyperbolaion[5]

Of the notes enumerated, some are stationary, others movable. The stationary notes are all those that do not migrate in the differences of the genera but remain on one pitch. The movable notes are all those in the opposite case; these are varied in the differences of the genera and do not remain on one pitch. The stationary notes are these eight: proslambanomenos, hypate hypaton, hypate meson, mese, nete synemmenon, paramese, nete diezeugmenon, and nete hyperbolaion; the movable notes are all those that lie between these.

Of the stationary notes, some are barypycnoi, others are apycnoi and bound the perfect scales. The barypycnoi are these five: hypate hypaton, hypate meson, mese, paramese, and nete diezeugmenon. The apycnoi, bounding the perfect scales, are these three: proslambanomenos, nete synemmenon, and nete hyperbolaion.

Of the movable notes, some are mesopycnoi, others are oxypycnoi, and others are diatonic. Mesopycnoi are these five: parhypate hypaton, parhypate meson, trite synemmenon, trite diezeugmenon, and trite hyperbolaion. Oxypycnoi are likewise five by genus: in the harmonia, the enharmonic oxypycnoi, in the color, the chromatic oxypycnoi; the diatonic does not share in the pycnon. In the harmonia, there are these: enharmonic lichanos hypaton, enharmonic lichanos meson, enharmonic paranete synemmenon, enharmonic paranete diezeugmenon, and enharmonic paranete hyperbolaion. In the color, there are these: chromatic lichanos hypaton, chromatic lichanos meson, chromatic paranete synemmenon, chromatic paranete diezeugmenon, and chro-

5. Assuming the conventional arrangement of the Greek system on A (but keeping in mind that the system has no absolute pitch), the sequence of notes would range from A to a'. Cf. Aristides Quintilianus, On Music 1.6 (pp. 51–53) for a fuller description of the meaning of the note names.

matic paranete hyperbolaion. In the diatonic, there are these: diatonic lichanos hypaton, diatonic lichanos meson, diatonic paranete synemmenon, diatonic paranete diezeugmenon, and diatonic paranete hyperbolaion.[6]

5. Of intervals, the differences are five: they differ from one another in magnitude, by genus, as consonant from dissonant, as composite from incomposite, and as rational from irrational. Difference by magnitude is that by which some intervals are greater and others lesser, for example, the ditone, tone, semitone, diatessaron, diapente, diapason, and the like. Difference by genus is that by which some intervals are diatonic, others chromatic, and others enharmonic. Difference of consonant from dissonant is that by which some intervals are consonant and others dissonant. Consonant intervals are the diatessaron, diapente, diapason, and the like. Dissonant intervals are all those lesser than the diatessaron and all those lying between the consonant intervals. Intervals lesser than the diatessaron are the diesis, semitone, tone, trisemitone,[7] and ditone; those lying between the consonant intervals are the tritone, the tetratone, the pentatone, and the like. Consonance is a blending of two notes, a higher and a lower; dissonance, on the contrary, is two unmixed notes, with the result that they do not blend but are rough to the hearing. Difference of composite from incomposite is that by which some intervals are incomposite and others composite. Incomposite intervals are those bounded by consecutive notes, for example, by hypate and parhypate and by lichanos and mese; the same applies to the remaining intervals. Composite intervals are those not bounded by consecutive notes, for example, by mese and parhypate, by mese and nete, and by paramese and hypate. Certain intervals are common to the composite and incomposite, namely, those from the semitone to the ditone. The semitone is composite in the harmonia but incomposite in the color and diatonic; the tone is composite in the color but incomposite in the diatonic; the trisemitone is incomposite in the color but composite in the diatonic; the ditone is incomposite in the harmonia but composite in the color and diatonic. All intervals lesser than the semitone are incomposite; likewise, all intervals greater than the ditone are composite. Difference of rational from irrational is that by which some intervals are rational and others irrational. Rational intervals are those whose magnitudes can be apportioned, such as the tone, semitone, ditone, tritone, and the like. Irrational intervals are those deviating from these magnitudes to a greater or lesser degree by some irrational magnitude.[8]

---

6. Cf. Aristides Quintilianus, *On Music* 1.9 (pp. 56–59) and Gaudentius, *Harmonic Introduction* 2, 8, and 17 (pp. 68, 72–73, and 78).

7. This interval does not appear in Jan's text, but it is reported in his critical apparatus as an addition in two manuscripts, M⁴ (i.e., one of the later hands that annotated Venice, Biblioteca Nazionale Marciana, app. cl. VI/3 [RISM BXI **270**]) and L (i.e., Leipzig, Universitätsbibliothek, Rep. I. fol. 2 [RISM BXI **39**]); Strunk included this reading in his translation and I have accordingly retained it.

8. Cf. Aristides Quintilianus, *On Music* 1.7 (pp. 53–54) and Gaudentius, *Harmonic Introduction* 3 (pp. 68–69).

6. The genera are the three already enumerated. Every melos will be either diatonic, chromatic, enharmonic, common, or a mixture of these. The diatonic genus is the one using diatonic division, the chromatic genus the one using chromatic division, the enharmonic genus the one using enharmonic division. The common genus is the one made up of stationary notes. The mixed genus is the one in which two or three generic characteristics reveal themselves, such as diatonic and color, diatonic and harmonia, color and harmonia, or even diatonic, color, and harmonia. The differences of the genera arise in connection with the movable notes, for the lichanos is moved within the whole-tone locus, the parhypate within that of a diesis. Thus the highest lichanos is that separated by a tone from the higher[9] of the notes bounding the tetrachord, the lowest that separated by a ditone. Likewise, the lowest parhypate is that separated by a diesis from the lower of the notes bounding the tetrachord, the highest that separated by a semitone.

7. A Shade is a specific division of a genus. There are six distinct and recognized shades: one of harmonia, three of color, and two of diatonic.

The shade of harmonia used the division of the genus itself, for it is sung by a diesis equivalent to a quarter-tone,[10] an equal diesis, and a ditone.

Of the chromatic divisions, the lowest is the shade of the soft color; it is sung by a diesis equivalent to a third-tone, an equal diesis, and an interval equal to a tone plus a half-tone plus a third-tone. The hemiolic color is sung by a diesis hemiolic to the enharmonic diesis, an equal diesis, and an incomposite interval of seven quarter-tone dieses. The whole-tone color used the shade of the genus itself, for it is sung by semitone, semitone, and trisemitone. And the aforesaid colors are so called from the pycna inherent to them: the whole-tone color from the tone inherent to it by arrangement, the hemiolic color from the dieses inherent to it, hemiolic to the enharmonic diesis; so too, the soft color is the one having the least pycnon, since the pycnon in it is relaxed and tuned down.

Of the diatonic divisions, one is called soft diatonic, the other intense. The shade of the soft diatonic is sung by semitone, an incomposite interval of three dieses, and likewise an incomposite interval of five dieses. The shade of the intense diatonic shares the division of the genus itself, for it is sung by semitone, tone, and tone.

The shades are also shown by numbers in this manner. The tone is assumed to be divided into twelve least parts, of which each one is called a twelfth-tone. The remaining intervals are also assumed analogous to the tone: the semitone

9. Jan's text reads ἑτέρου (one), but he reports ὀξυτέρου (higher) in his critical apparatus as the reading of M⁴ and L; as Strunk chose this reading in his translation, I have retained it.

10. Jan's text reads simply κατὰ δίεσιν (by a diesis), but he reports κατὰ δίεσιν τὸ τεταρτημό-ριον τόνου (a diesis equivalent to a quarter-tone) in his critical apparatus as the reading of M⁴ (two other manuscripts, B [i.e., Vatican City, Biblioteca Apostolica Vaticana, Barberinus gr. 265 (RISM BXI **238**)] and N [i.e., Naples, Biblioteca Nazionale, gr. 262 (III.C.4) (RISM BXI **203**)] are reported as having only τεταρτημόριον); as Strunk chose this reading in his translation, I have retained it.

into six twelfths, the quarter-tone diesis into three twelfths, the third-tone diesis into four twelfths, and the whole diatessaron into thirty twelfths. The harmonia will be sung by a magnitude of 3, 3, and 24 twelfths, the soft color by 4, 4, and 22, the hemiolic color by 4½, 4½ and 21, the whole-tone color by 6, 6, and 18, the soft diatonic by 6, 9, and 15, and the intense diatonic by 6, 12, and 12.[11]

8. Of scales, the differences are seven. Four are the same as in intervals: difference by magnitude, by genus, as consonant and dissonant, and as rational and irrational. Three differences are particular for scales: difference of consecutive and gapped, of conjunct and disjunct, and of immutable and modulating. In magnitude, the greater scales differ from the lesser, as the diapason differs from the tritone, diapente, diatessaron, or the like. In genus, the diatonic scales differ from the enharmonic or chromatic, or the chromatic or enharmonic from the others. As to the difference of consonant and dissonant, the scales bounded by consonant notes will differ from those bounded by dissonant notes. There are six consonant scales within the immutable scale: the smallest is the diatessaron, of two tones and a half, for example, the scale from hypate hypaton to hypate meson; the second is the diapente, of three tones and a half, for example, the scale from proslambanomenos to hypate meson; the third is the diapason, of six tones, for example, the scale from proslambanomenos to mese; the fourth is the diapason-and-diatessaron, of eight tones and a half, for example, the scale from proslambanomenos to nete synemmenon or diatonic paranete diezeugmenon; the fifth is the diapason-and-diapente, of nine tones and a half, for example, the scale from proslambanomenos to nete diezeugmenon; the sixth is the double diapason, of twelve tones, for example, the scale from proslambanomenos to nete hyperbolaion. The synemmenon scale extends only as far as the fourth consonant scale: within this scale, the first is the diatessaron, the second the diapente, the third the diapason, and the fourth the diapason-and-diatessaron. But the position of the voice is augmented to the eighth consonant scale, which includes the double diapason-and-diatessaron and the double diapason-and-diapente. The dissonant scales are those smaller than the diatessaron and all those between the aforesaid consonant scales.

9. Forms of the same magnitude and number arise—compounded of the same incomposite intervals—if their order is altered when a certain dissimilarity is inherent. There is no change made from entirely equal and similar forms.

Of the diatessaron, there are three species. The first is that bounded by barypycnoi, as is that from hypate hypaton to hypate meson; the second that bounded by mesopycnoi, as is that from parhypate hypaton to parhypate meson; the third that bounded by oxypycnoi, as is that from lichanos hypaton to lichanos meson. Thus, in the harmonia and color, the forms of the consonant scales are comprehended in accordance with the relationship of the pycnon.

---

11. Cf. Aristides Quintilianus, *On Music* 1.9 (pp. 56–59) and Gaudentius, *Harmonic Introduction* 5 (p. 69).

In the diatonic genus, the forms do not arise in connection with a pycnon, for this genus is divided into semitones and tones. In the consonance of the diatessaron, the form contains one semitone and two tones; likewise, in the diapente, it contains one semitone and three tones, and in the diapason, two semitones and five tones. In accordance with the relationship of the semitones, the forms are considered. Of the diatessaron, the first is the species in which the semitone lies at the bottom of the tones; the second, in which the semitone lies first at the top; the third, in which it lies between the tones. And these species—in like manner to the other genera—are from the same notes to the same notes.

Of the diapente, there are four forms. The first, bounded by barypycnoi, is the form in which the tone is first at the top, i.e., from hypate meson to paramese; the second, bounded by mesopycnoi, in which the tone is second from the top, i.e., from parhypate meson to trite diezeugmenon; the third, bounded by oxypycnoi, in which the tone is third from the top, i.e., from lichanos meson to paranete diezeugmenon; the fourth, bounded by barypycnoi, in which the tone is fourth from the top,[12] i.e., from mese to nete diezeugmenon or from proslambanomenos to hypate meson.

In the diatonic genus, the first is the form in which the semitone lies first at the bottom; the second, in which it lies first at the top; the third, in which it lies second from the top; and the fourth, in which it lies third from the top.[13]

Of the diapason, there are seven species. The first, bounded by barypycnoi, is the species in which the tone is first at the top, i.e., from hypate hypaton to paramese. It was called Mixolydian by the ancients.

The second, bounded by mesopycnoi, is the species in which the tone is second from the top, i.e., from parhypate hypaton to trite diezeugmenon. It was called Lydian.

The third, bounded by oxypycnoi, is the species in which the tone is third from the top, i.e., from lichanos hypaton to paranete diezeugmenon. It was called Phrygian.

The fourth, bounded by barypycnoi, is the species in which the tone is fourth from the top, i.e., from hypate meson to nete diezeugmenon. It was called Dorian.

The fifth, bounded by mesopycnoi, is the species in which the tone is fifth from the top, i.e., from parhypate meson to trite hyperbolaion. It was called Hypolydian.

12. Jan's text reads οὗ πρῶτος ὁ τόνος (ἐπὶ τὸ βαρύ), which Strunk translated as "in which the tone is at the bottom." While this is a perfectly correct description of the location of the tone in this form, the manuscripts actually read τέταρτος (fourth) instead of πρῶτος (first), some of them with the phrase ἐπὶ τὸ βαρύ (from the bottom), others with the phrase ἐπὶ τὸ ὀξύ (from the top). Since the other three forms use the top as the point of reference, there seems little reason to accept Jan's emendation.

13. The majority of the manuscripts preserving the treatise of Cleonides, including the earliest exemplars, do not include this paragraph (although a few of these do include the first few words, i.e., "In the diatonic genus, the first is the form").

The sixth, bounded by oxypycnoi, is the species in which the tone is sixth from the top, i.e., from lichanos meson to paranete hyperbolaion. It was called Hypophrygian.

The seventh, bounded by barypycnoi, is the species in which the tone is first at the bottom, i.e., from mese to nete hyperbolaion or from proslambanomenos to mese. It was commonly called Locrian or Hypodorian.

In the diatonic genus, the first is the species of diapason in which the semitone is first at the bottom but fourth from the top; the second, in which it is third from the bottom but first at the top; the third, in which it is second from either end; the fourth, in which it is first at the bottom but third from the top; the fifth, in which it is fourth from the bottom but first at the top; the sixth, in which it is third from the bottom but second from the top; and the seventh, in which it is second from the bottom but third from the top. These species are from the same notes to the same notes, just as in the harmonia and the color, and they were called by the same names.

10. As to the difference of rational and irrational, insofar as scales are compounded of rational intervals, they will differ from those compounded of irrational ones. Insofar as scales are compounded of rational intervals, they are rational, and insofar as they are compounded of irrational intervals, they are irrational.

As to the difference of consecutive and gapped, scales that are sung by consecutive notes will differ from those that are gapped.

As to the difference of conjunct and disjunct, insofar as scales are arranged from conjunct tetrachords, they will differ from those arranged from disjunct. Conjunction is the common note of two tetrachords, similar in form, sung consecutively; disjunction is the tone between two tetrachords, similar in form, sung consecutively. There are altogether three conjunctions: middle, highest, and lowest. The lowest is the conjunction of the tetrachords hypaton and meson; the common note hypate meson conjoins them. The middle is the conjunction of the tetrachords meson and neton synemmenon; the common note mese conjoins them. The highest is the conjunction of the tetrachords diezeugmenon and hyperbolaion; the common note nete diezeugmenon conjoins them. There is one disjunction: that of the tetrachords meson and neton diezeugmenon; the common tone disjoining them is the tone between mese and paramese.

There are two perfect scales, of which one is lesser, the other greater. The Lesser Perfect Scale is by conjunction from proslambanomenos to nete synemmenon. These three conjunct tetrachords are contained in it: hypaton, meson, and synemmenon—and the tone from proslambanomenos to hypate hypaton. It is defined by the consonant diapason-and-diatessaron.

The Greater Perfect Scale is by disjunction from the proslambanomenos to nete hyperbolaion. Four tetrachords are contained in it: disjunct by twos and conjunct one with another—hypaton and meson, and diezeugmenon and hyperbolaion—and moreover two tones, one from proslambanomenos to hypate hypaton, the other from mese to paramese. It is distinguished by the consonant double diapason.

Of the five tetrachords in the Immutable Scale, which is combined from both perfect scales, two are common to each of the perfect scales: the hypaton and meson. Particular to the scale by conjunction is the neton synemmenon; and particular to the scale by disjunction is the neton diezeugmenon and neton hyperbolaion.

11. As to the difference of immutable and modulating, scales will differ insofar as simple scales differ from those that are not simple. Simple scales are those harmonious with one mese, duple those harmonious with two, triple those harmonious with three, and multiple those harmonious with many. "Mese" is a function of a note whose property it is, by disjunction, to have an incomposite tone in ascent (when the scale is unchanged) and either a composite or incomposite ditone in descent;[14] by conjunction, as there are three conjunct tetrachords, its property is to be either the highest note of the middle tetrachord or the lowest note of the highest tetrachord. It is from the mese that the functions of the remaining notes are recognized, for how each of them functions becomes apparent in relation to the mese.[15]

12. "Tonos" is used in four senses: as note, interval, position of the voice, and pitch. Those speaking of a seven-toned phorminx use the word in the sense of "note," just as do Terpander and Ion. The former says:

> We will no longer love the four-voiced ode
> But will sing to thee new hymns with the seven-toned phorminx

the latter:

Eleven-stringed lyre, having a ten-step order, three consonant roads of harmonia,
Formerly all the Greeks raised a meager muse, strumming thee seven-toned by fours.

And not a few others have used the word. We use it in the sense of interval whenever we say that there is a tone from the mese to paramese.

We use it as a position of the voice whenever we say Dorian, Phrygian, Lydian, or any of the other tonoi. According to Aristoxenus,[16] there are thirteen tonoi:

Hypermixolydian, also called Hyperphrygian;
Two Mixolydians, a higher and a lower, of which the higher is also called Hyperiastian, the lower Hyperdorian;

14. Jan has rather heavily emended this sentence by changing the case of the parenthetical expression and adding the intervals "tone" and "trisemitone" to the possible descending intervals. He also rejects the phrase ἤτοι σύνθετον (either a composite). As Strunk seems to have ignored Jan's emendations, I have followed his reading.

15. On sections 8–11, cf. Aristides Quintilianus, *On Music* 1.8 (pp. 54–56) and Gaudentius, *Harmonic Introduction* 4, 6–7, 9, and 18–19 (pp. 69–73 and 78–79).

16. The philosopher and music theorist of the fourth century B.C.E. He had been a student of Aristotle and in fact anticipated succeeding him as head of the Lyceum. According to the *Suda*, he wrote 453 books, but only parts of the *Harmonics* and *Rhythmics* (*Rhythmica*) survive, as well as a number of small fragments.

Two Lydians, a higher and a lower, of which the lower is also called Aeolian;
Two Phrygians, a higher and a lower, of which the lower is also called Iastian;
One Dorian;
Two Hypolydians, a higher and a lower, the latter also called Hypoaeolian;
Two Hypophrygians, of which the lower is also called Hypoiastian;
Hypodorian.

Of these, the highest is the Hypermixolydian, the lowest the Hypodorian. From the highest to the lowest, the consecutive tonoi exceed one another by a semitone; the two parallel tonoi exceed by a tone; and every third tonos exceeds by a trisemitone;[17] this will proceed analogously for the distance of the remaining tonoi. The Hypermixolydian is a diapason higher than the Hypodorian.

"Tonos" is used as "pitch" when we speak of using a higher or lower or intermediate tone of voice.[18]

13. "Modulation" is used in four senses: by genus, by scale, by tonos, and by melic composition. Modulation by genus takes place whenever there is a modulation from diatonic into color or harmonia, or from color or harmonia into any of the rest. Modulation by scale takes place whenever there is a modulation from conjunction into disjunction or conversely. Modulation by tonos takes place whenever there is a modulation from Dorian into Phrygian; from Phrygian into Lydian, Hypermixolydian, or Hypodorian; or in general whenever there is a modulation from any of the thirteen tonoi to any of the rest. There are modulations beginning with the semitone and proceeding to the diapason, some of which are by consonant intervals, others by dissonant. Of these, the melodic are the ones by consonant intervals and by the whole-tone. For the rest, some are less melodic than unmelodic, others are more melodic.[19] Insofar as the commonality is greater, the modulations are more melodic, and insofar as the commonality is lesser, the modulations are more unmelodic, since it is necessary for every modulation to contain some common note, interval, or scale. But this commonality is determined by the similarity of the notes, for whenever similar notes fall on one another in modulations by participation in a pycnon, the modulation is melodic, but whenever the notes are dissimilar, the modulation is unmelodic.

Modulation by melic composition takes place whenever there is a modula-

---

17. Jan adds the phrase τόνον, οἱ δὲ τρίτοι (a tone, and every third tonos), but this was ignored by Strunk, who translated the passage as: "the distance between consecutive tones is a semitone, between two parallel tones a trisemitone." Jan's emendation is necessary, however, because the parallel tonoi (i.e., the high and low pairs) are indeed a tone apart; only every third tonos is separated by a trisemitone.

18. Cf. Aristides Quintilianus, *On Music* 1.10 (pp. 59–61) and Gaudentius, *Harmonic Introduction* 3 and 20–22 (pp. 68–69 and 79–85).

19. Jan has once again rather heavily emended this sentence, but the Greek in a number of the early sources is quite straightforward: τῶν δὲ λοιπῶν, αἱ μὲν ἐμμελεῖς ἧττον ἢ ἐκμελεῖς, αἱ δὲ μᾶλλον. Strunk originally translated Jan's Greek as: "Of the rest, some are more melodious than unmelodious, others less so."

tion from the diastaltic ethos to the systaltic or hesychastic, or from the hesy-chastic to any of the rest.[20] The diastaltic is the ethos of melic composition through which are revealed heroic deeds, the grandeur and loftiness of a manly soul, and an affection akin to these. It is most used in tragedy and in however many of the rest as border on this character. The systaltic is the ethos through which the soul is brought into dejection and an effeminate condition. Such a state will fit with erotic affections, dirges, expressions of pity, and things resem-bling these. The hesychastic is the ethos of melic composition by which qui-etude of soul and a liberal and peaceful state are accompanied. To it will fit hymns, paeans, encomia, counsels, and things similar to these.[21]

14. Melic composition is the use of the aforesaid parts of harmonics, which also have the function of precepts. Melic composition is accomplished by means of four things: sequence, succession, repetition, and prolongation. Sequence is the road of melos through consecutive notes; succession, the placement of intervals alternately side by side; repetition, the repeated stroke on one tone; and prolongation, a hesitation for an extended chronos on a single utterance of the voice.[22]

The Diagram is a plane form comprising the functions of the notes that are sung.[23]

Function is the order of the note in the scale; or, function is the order of the note, through which we recognize each of the notes.

Melic composition is the use of the precepts in the harmonic treatise, with reference to the propriety of each hypothesis.

This is the end of the treatise on the harmonious.[24]

20. Cf. the threefold classification of Aristotle's *Politics* (*Politica;* pp. 32–33).
21. Cf. Aristides Quintilianus, *On Music* 1.11–12 (pp. 61–66). For a brief discussion of these ethoses in the treatise of Cleonides, see Jon Solomon, "The Diastaltic Ethos," *Classical Philol-ogy* 76 (1981): 93–100.
22. Cf. Aristides Quintilianus, *On Music* 1.12 (pp. 62–66).
23. Diagrams of the notes of the so-called Greater or Lesser Perfect Scales are common in the treatises. Gaudentius himself includes one and refers to them on several occasions.
24. These final four paragraphs were not included in Strunk's translation. The Greek text appears in most manuscripts and in Jan's edition, but Strunk may have believed it was a gloss that should not be included.

5 Aristides Quintilianus

Little is known of Aristides Quintilianus the person, but it is reasonably certain that he was a neo-Platonist living in the late third and the early fourth century C.E. Preserved in fifty-nine manuscripts, his substantial treatise *On Music* is arranged in three books, but unlike the treatises of Cleonides and Gaudentius, it is not an introduction *(Eisagoge)* to the technique or science of music. Rather, a wide range of materials—musical, philosophical, medical, grammatical, metrical, and literary—are woven together into an intricate and elaborately unified philosophical discourse in which music provides a paradigm for the order of the soul and the universe. The language of the treatise is rigorous, systematic, and highly complex. This feature enables the author to develop implicit and explicit relationships across all three books and among all the disparate types of material.

The design of the treatise is stated in the first three sections of Book I: the first book will define music and its parts (i.e., harmonics, rhythmics, and metrics); Book II will explore music's role in education (paideia); and Book III, the culmination, will be devoted to an exegesis of number, the soul, and the order of the universe. The following excerpt presents the section on harmonics. It is largely Aristoxenian, perhaps derived in part from the treatise of Cleonides, but many points differ in specifics. Various notational diagrams are included, one of which purports to preserve a series of ancient scales, while another diagram lays out the fifteen tonoi in the shape of a wing. Later in Book I, Aristides Quintilianus again draws on Aristoxenus—as well as other theorists—in his treatments of rhythmics and metrics, carefully conjoining harmonics, rhythmics, and metrics in his vocabulary and development of definitions.

A substantial portion of Book I was paraphrased without credit by Martianus Capella in the ninth book of his *Marriage of Philology and Mercury* and was widely read in the Middle Ages in that form. At the turn the fifteenth century, both Franchino Gaffurio and Giorgio Valla made considerable use of Aristides Quintilianus in their several publications, and with Cleonides, Aristides Quintilianus came to be viewed by Renaissance musicians as one of the most important authorities on ancient Greek music theory.

FROM *On Music*

(1.4–12)

4. Music is a science of melos and of those things contingent to melos.[1] Some define it as follows: "the theoretical and practical art of perfect and instrumental melos";[2] and others thus: "an art of the seemly in sounds and motions." But we define it more fully and in accordance with our thesis: "knowledge of the seemly in bodies and motions."[3]

Music is a science, certainly, in which exists sure and infallible knowledge, for whether we speak of it in terms of problems or in terms of effects, it would never demonstrate any change or alteration.[4] And indeed, we might also with reason call it an art, for it is both a composite of perceptions (and these are practiced to gain accuracy) and is not useless to life, as the ancients discerned and our discourse will demonstrate.[5] And we might fairly speak of perfect melos, for it is necessary that melody, rhythm, and diction be considered so that the perfection of the song may be produced: in the case of melody, simply a certain sound; in the case of rhythm, the motion of sound; and in the case of diction, the meter. The things contingent to perfect melos are motion—both

TEXT: English translation by Thomas J. Mathiesen. Reprinted by permission of the publisher from *Aristides Quintilianus On Music in Three Books,* translation, with introduction, commentary, and annotations by Thomas J. Mathiesen, Music Theory Translation Series (New Haven, Conn.: Yale University Press, 1983), 74–93. Copyright © 1983 by Yale University. Only a small portion of the original annotations have been preserved in this excerpt, and the reader is advised to consult the original publication for fuller documentation and explanations.

1. As Aristides Quintilianus notes just below, the Greek term μέλος (melos; plural: mele) refers to the complete musical complex of melody, rhythm, and diction (i.e., in this context, text). At this point in the treatise, the phrase "things contingent" might seem to refer simply to other musical elements related to melos; just a few lines later, he defines these contingencies as motion, chronoi (units of time), and rhythm. In Books II and III, however, the sense of "contingency" is considerably expanded until it becomes clear (in Book III, section 26) that contingent things are necessary relationships predicated on one another.

2. "Perfect melos" is further defined below and in section 12. Cf. Cleonides, *Harmonic Introduction (Harmonica introductio;* p. 36).

3. Aristides Quintilianus's composite definition clearly signals his intention to pursue the discussion of music not in narrow technical terms but rather in a larger philosophical context. The four terms of his definition—"knowledge," "seemly," "bodies," and "motions"—function as refrains throughout the three books of the treatise and gradually take on complex meanings. Only at the end of the entire treatise does the reader realize the full significance of this definition: music as the palpable paradigm of the body and soul of the universe provides a model for learning the higher philosophical contemplation that leads the soul back to its original source.

4. Aristides Quintilianus's use of the term "knowledge" is Platonic. He makes the point here that music can be studied deductively (Problems) or inductively (Effects).

5. By treating music first as a science (ἐπιστήμη) and second as an art (τέχνη), Aristides Quintilianus emphasizes the epistemological quality over the technical. The union of the two aspects is important because of the distinctions between the two drawn by Greek philosophers. On the relationship of art and science to knowledge, see Aristotle, *Metaphysics (Metaphysica)* 1.1 and *Nicomachean Ethics (Ethica Nicomachea)* 6.3–8.

of sound and body[6]—and also chronoi and the rhythms based on these.[7] We might not unnaturally propose that art is a question of the seemly, for every contemptible thing has been deprived of the seemly and the seemly is the imparting—or the reciprocal concord—of beautiful and praiseworthy things by the superior things of the cosmos.[8]

Some declare that music is theoretical and practical for the following reasons. On the one hand, whenever it considers its own parts and discourses about division and technique, they say that it theorizes; on the other hand, whenever it operates in accord with its parts, composing in a useful and fitting manner, they declare that it practices.

Music's matter is sound and motion of body. Some say that sound is air having been struck, others that it is a striking of the air; the former define the affected body itself as sound, the latter—which is better—define its condition. Now surely motion exists in different chronoi, for a chronos is a measure of motion and stasis. Of motion, there is by nature the simple and the not simple,[9] and, of this latter, there is the continuous, the intervallic, and the medial. The continuous is sound that imperceptibly and with some speed descends and ascends, the intervallic is that which has apparent pitches—and the dimensions of these are imperceptible—,[10] and the medial is that which is compounded from both. It is the continuous in which we discourse, the medial in which we execute readings of poems, and the intervallic that produces between simple sounds certain intervals and hesitations, which kind is also called melodic.[11]

5. Of the whole art of music, one certain part is called theoretical, the other, practical. The theoretical is what discerns the technical rules of the art and the main categories and their parts and, moreover, examines its beginnings from on high, its natural causes, and its consonance with things as they are. The practical is what operates in accord with these technical rules and pursues its object—which, of course, is also called the educational.[12] The theoretical is

6. In the course of the treatise, the sense of "motion of sound and body" will be expanded from its limited musical and physical sense to the larger sense encompassing the shifting harmonic relationships of the universe and everything in it.

7. The chronos is the measure of time in rhythm. It may be a single short rhythmic duration—that of a short syllable—or it may be doubled, tripled, or quadrupled to produce rhythmic groupings. The various chronoi are studied in detail later in Book I (sections 14–19).

8. The subjects of seemliness and the superior things of the cosmos are treated in Books II and III.

9. The twofold distinction of simple and not simple or composite and incomposite is a basic mode of classification in Greek science and philosophy. This distinction will appear many times throughout Book I. Cf. Cleonides, *Harmonic Introduction* 5, 7, 9, and 11 (pp. 39–44).

10. This follows Aristoxenus, *Harmonics* (*Harmonica*) 1.3. Aristides Quintilianus wishes to propose that a pitch is like a point in geometry—it is indivisible and consequently without dimension (this very analogy is later drawn in the part of Book I devoted to rhythmics).

11. These types of motion are derived from the definitions of Aristoxenus (*Harmonics* 1.8–10, 12, 18–19). Cf. Cleonides, *Harmonic Introduction* 2 (p. 36) and Gaudentius, *Harmonic Introduction* (*Harmonica introductio*) 1 (pp. 67–68).

12. The practical part is the subject of most of Book II of the treatise, while music's beginning from "on high" and the phrase "things as they are" anticipate Aristides Quintilianus's metaphysical demonstrations of Book III (especially sections 9–11).

divided into the natural and the technical. Of these, with respect to the natural, the one part is the arithmetic and the other part has the same name as the class itself—the natural, which discourses about things as they are; and with respect to the technical, there are three parts: harmonic, rhythmic, and metric. The practical is parted into the application of the aforesaid categories and their expression. With respect to the application, the parts are melic composition, rhythmic composition, and poesy; and with respect to their expression, the parts are instrumental, odic, and theatric, in which, then, bodily motions homologous to the underlying mele are also employed.[13] Motion is the change of qualities in the same genus,[14] and of motion in sound, there are two species: manifold and indivisible. Concerning the manifold, there has already been mention; the indivisible and simple species of motion is named pitch. Pitch is a hesitation and stasis of sound, and there are two species of sound: descent and ascent. Descent is whenever the sound goes from a higher position to a lower, and ascent when it passes from a lower to a higher position. We name the positions arising from these motions low pitch and high pitch.[15] Low pitch occurs below a pouring forth of breath, high pitch above a forcing of breath. Now every simple motion of sound is pitch, which is in the specific melodic sense called a note.[16]

Concerning all this, let us then say, since we have now discussed these things, that of the whole science of harmonics there are seven parts: the first treats notes; the second, intervals; the third, scales; the fourth, genera; the fifth, tonoi; the sixth, modulations; and the seventh, melic composition.[17] Now let us speak first about notes, and if we use some names that are difficult to understand, this is excusable because the idiom is necessarily technical.

13. This description might be represented in terms of the following diagram:

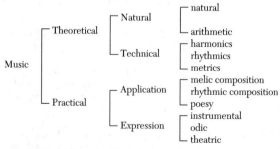

14. That is, *alteratio*. Cf. Plato, *Theatetus* 181c–d.
15. These definitions are Aristoxenian (cf. n. 11).
16. Aristides Quintilianus's description is vivid: when low pitches are sung, a good deal of air pours forth and the sound appears to come from within; when high pitches are sung, the breath is forced and the sound appears to come from the head. In Book II, section 14, these same vocal tones are related to ethos.
17. These are the seven categories suggested in the surviving portions of Aristoxenus's *Harmonics*. Cf. Cleonides, *Harmonic Introduction* (p. 36) and the second sentence of Gaudentius's *Harmonic Introduction* (p. 67).

6. A note is the smallest part of musical sound, and while there are certainly infinite functions of notes in nature, twenty-eight have been transmitted taking each of the genera collectively. For these, there are the following names: proslambanomenos, hypate hypaton, parhypate hypaton, enharmonic hypaton, chromatic hypaton, diatonic hypaton, hypate meson, parhypate meson, enharmonic meson, chromatic meson, diatonic meson, mese, trite synemmenon, enharmonic synemmenon, chromatic synemmenon, paranete synemmenon, nete synemmenon, paramese, trite diezeugmenon, enharmonic diezeugmenon, chromatic diezeugmenon, paranete diezeugmenon, nete diezeugmenon, trite hyperbolaion, enharmonic hyperbolaion, chromatic hyperbolaion, paranete hyperbolaion, and nete hyperbolaion.[18]

The proslambanomenos has been so termed because it does not share in any of the named tetrachords but is added[19] outside by consonance with the mese, having the whole-tone ratio to the hypate hypaton that the mese has to the paramese. The hypate hypaton has been so termed because it is placed first in the first tetrachord (for the ancients called what was first "hypaton") and the parhypate is situated beside it.[20] The enharmonic, chromatic, and diatonic hypaton of these genera are the expressive notes of the melody, for the disposition of the tetrachords is varied. These are generically called hyperhypatai.[21] The hypate meson is, in turn, the first of the middle tetrachord (this is considered only between the hypaton and the synemmenon).[22] The parhypate meson is after this, and the rest are similar to the hypatoids, which have also been named as a genus "lichanoi," homonymously named after the finger striking the string that sounds them.[23] The one after these is called the mese, for of the notes set forth in each mode, it is situated middlemost. After this, ascending by a semitone, is the trite synemmenon,[24] from which lowest string of the tetrachords after the mese we make our enumerations because it remains for us to reach the higher scales. The next after this are the enharmonic, chromatic, and diatonic for reasons which we previously discussed. These are called paranetai because they are situated preceding the nete. After these is the nete, that is to say, "ultimate," for the ancients called what was ultimate "neaton." The whole scale was called synemmenon because it was joined to the preceding perfect scale as far as the mese. Again, ascending by a tone from the mese, the string situated beside it is called the paramese. Those after this have their

---

18. Cf. Aristoxenus, *Harmonics* 1.28 and Cleonides, *Harmonic Introduction* 2 and 4 (pp. 36–39).
19. "Proslambanomenos" means "added."
20. The prefix "par[a]" means "beside."
21. The prefix "hyper" means "above." These notes stand respectively a half-step, a whole-step, or a minor third above the hypate and are therefore the chief expressive notes.
22. "Meson" means "middle," and the tetrachord stands between the hypaton and synemmenon tetrachords.
23. "Lichanos" means "forefinger."
24. "Synemmenon" means "joined" or "united"; this tetrachord is joined to the previous one at the mese.

names for similar reasons and in the same order as those in the synemmenon. This scale is called diezeugmenon,[25] for it is situated in different parts and is not equal to the scales preceding it. And then there is the trite hyperbolaion and those following it one after another, having their specific appellations in the same order and for the same reasons as the preceding. The generic appellation of these was termed hyperbolaion because, in reaching a limit in these strings, the power of the human voice is established.[26]

Of these notes, some are stationary and others movable; and some are barypycnoi, some mesopycnoi, some oxypycnoi, and some apycnoi. Now a pycnon is a certain disposition of three notes.[27] Barypycnoi are those that occupy the first positions of the pycnon, mesopycnoi the middle, and oxypycnoi the ultimate; and apycnoi are those that do not share in any position in the disposition of a tetrachord with a pycnon. Of these, the apycnoi and barypycnoi are stationary, which are also called hypatoid,[28] because they do not accept varied pitches; the rest of these notes are movable, because they show sometimes smaller, sometimes larger intervals in accord with certain compositions of the tetrachords. Of these movable notes, some are called parhypatoids and others lichanoids. Again, of the notes, some are consonant with another, some are dissonant; and some are in unison. Consonant notes are those where, when struck at the same time, the melos is no longer conspicuous in the higher or lower pitch; dissonant notes are those where, when struck at the same time, the individuality of the melos emerges from one or the other of the two; and unison notes are any of those that present a differing function of sound but a like pitch. There are further types of differences for notes: first, difference according to pitch in height and depth; second, difference according to participation in an interval, since some share in one interval and others are observed in more; third, difference according to scale, since some participate in one, others in two scales; fourth, difference according to position of the voice, since some are of greater and others are of lesser position—and what "the position of the voice" is, we shall discuss in the future;[29] and fifth,

25. "Diezeugmenon" means "disjunct"; this tetrachord is separated from the previous one by the whole tone (the tone of disjunction).

26. "Hyperbolaion" means "extreme." The limits of the human voice are discussed below in section 10 (see also Book II, section 14). On the names of the tetrachords, cf. section 8 below.

27. Actually, the pycnon is a group of three notes at the bottom of any tetrachord where the interval formed by the three notes collectively is smaller than the interval between the highest note of the pycnon and the highest note of the tetrachord (see Aristoxenus, *Harmonics* 1.24, 2.50). It is therefore possible for a pycnon to exist in the enharmonic or chromatic genera, but not in the diatonic. The genera are discussed in section 9 below.

28. This enumeration of the notes of the pycnon moves upwards from the bottom of the tetrachord. The hypatai are stationary notes. Cf. Cleonides, *Harmonic Introduction* 4 (pp. 37–39).

29. See section 12 below. The topic is also treated in Book II, section 14. On the "position of the voice," the definition of which is derived from Aristoxenus, *Harmonics* 1.7, cf. Cleonides, *Harmonic Introduction* 12 (pp. 44–45) and Gaudentius, *Harmonic Introduction* 1 (pp. 67–68).

difference according to ethos,[30] for some ethoses run upon the higher notes, others upon the lower, and some upon the parhypatoids, others upon the lichanoids.[31]

7. The term "interval" is used in two ways—in general and in particular: in general it is every magnitude defined by any limits; in particular in music, an interval is a magnitude of sound circumscribed by two notes. Of intervals, some are composite and some are incomposite.[32] The incomposite are those comprised of consecutive notes, the composite of notes not consecutive and which are able to resolve into more intervals in singing. Of these intervals, the smallest is—in melody—the enharmonic diesis; then—speaking roughly—the double of the diesis, the semitone; then the double of this, the tone; and then the double of this, the ditone. Again, of these, some are lesser and some greater; some are consonant and some dissonant; some are enharmonic, some chromatic, and some diatonic; and some are rational and some irrational—rational, where it is possible to speak of a certain ratio (I say "ratio" as a relationship one to another by number),[33] and irrational, where no ratio one to the other is discovered. The ratio of the fourth is sesquitertian, that of the fifth sesquialteran, that of the octave duple, and that of the tone sesquioctaval.[34] "Consonant and dissonant" we also speak of as in the case of notes. Concerning the enharmonic intervals and all the rest, we shall speak in due time. Some of the intervals are incomposite, such as the diesis; some are composite, such as the fourth; and some are both composite and incomposite, such as the semitone and the tone. Moreover, some of them are even and some odd: the even are divided into equal parts, such as the semitone and the tone, and the odd into unequal parts, such as three, five, or seven dieses. "Composition" is of the same nature: two dieses are placed one after the other, but no more than this; two semitones are placed one after the other, but no more; and two tones are placed one by one, but no more, for the whole interval is converted to a discord. Moreover, of intervals, some are in open order and some in close order: those in close order are the smallest, such as dieses; those in open order are the largest, such as the fourth. There are various divisions of the ditone: first, into twenty-four

---

30. On ethos (ἦθος), cf. Plato, *Republic* (*Respublica*) 3.11–12 (pp. 12–16) and Aristotle, *Politics* (*Politica;* pp. 26–30). Much of the second book of Aristides Quintilianus's *On Music* (*De musica*) is devoted to the subject of ethos. Sextus Empiricus, however, thoroughly debunks the theory of musical ethos (see pp. 94–109).

31. On this entire section, cf. Aristoxenus, *Harmonics* 1.4, 10–13; Cleonides, *Harmonic Introduction* 4 (pp. 37–39); and Gaudentius, *Harmonic Introduction* 2, 8 and 17 (pp. 68, 72–73, and 78).

32. See n. 9 above.

33. This parenthesis is added by Aristides Quintilianus because the term λόγος which means "ratio" here, has so many meanings. The author must tell his readers why he uses λόγος to define ῥητός (rational).

34. That is, respectively, 4:3, 3:2, 2:1, and 9:8. These numerical relationships will be of great importance in delineating the universal paradigm in Book III. On these ratios, cf. Plato, *Timaeus* (pp. 20–21) and Gaudentius, *Harmonic Introduction* 10–14 (pp. 74–76).

twelfth parts; second, into dieses or eight fourth parts of a tone; third, into six third parts; and fourth, into four semitones, that is, eight dieses.[35] In this way the ancients, too, constructed their scales, marking out each string in dieses.[36] Now the smallest interval of the voice was called diesis because this is the point of the dissolution of the voice; the first interval by magnitude stretching the voice was called the tone; and the half of the tone—or what is loosely about equal to a tone, for they do not say that the tone is cut into equal parts as if this can truly be done equally—was called the semitone.[37] The harmonia of the ancients is given below by dieses, the first octave carried out to twenty-four dieses, the second augmented by semitones.[38]

octave 1	✳	2	3	4	5	6	7	8	9	10	11	12
		-o	<	ϭ	U	9	L	⌐	λ	∇	E	Ⅎ
		o-	>	9	Π	ϭ	⌐	Γ	∇	λ	Ⅎ	E

	13	14	15	16	17	18	19	20	21	22	23	24
	⌐	⌐	Ч	Ⅎ	Є	Ⅴ	y	∝	>	<	ⅴ	Ⅴ
	⌐	⌐	μ	Є	Ⅎ	y	Ⅴ	∞	<	>	Ⅴ	Ⅴ

octave 2	26	28	30	32	34	36	38	40	42	44	46
	⊢	Ⅎ	-+	⌒	C	C	◡	-o	∈	λ	ſ
	⊣	F	⊁	ᴗ	Ɔ	Ɔ	⊱	o-	⊅	y	ſ

8. A scale is comprised of more than two intervals. Of scales, some differences are similar to those discussed in the case of intervals, but there are further

---

35. All this is Aristoxenian: cf. Aristoxenus, *Harmonics* 1.15–18, 21, 24–29; 2.53; 3.60–61; Cleonides, *Harmonic Introduction* 5 (p. 39); and Gaudentius, *Harmonic Introduction* 3 (pp. 68–69).

36. On this reference to the ancients, cf. Aristoxenus, *Harmonics* 1.7 and 28.

37. The term "diesis" is derived from the verb δίημι, which may mean "to dismiss" or "dissolve." The term "tone" (τόνος) is derived from the verb τείνω, which means "to stretch." Rationally, the tone, 9:8, cannot be divided into equal parts, though it can be by other means (for a useful introduction to the subject of Greek musical mathematics, see Richard Crocker, "Aristoxenus and Greek Mathematics," in *Aspects of Medieval and Renaissance Music: A Birthday Offering to Gustave Reese*, ed. Jan La Rue [New York: W. W. Norton, 1966], 96–110). Aristides Quintilianus is anticipating the mathematical objection to the "semi"-tone.

38. On the meaning of the term "harmonia," see p. 10, n. 3.
    The chart is frequently garbled in the manuscripts, and its precise reconstruction is a matter of some controversy (for a survey of the issues, see Mathiesen, *Aristides Quintilianus*, 18–20). Aristides Quintilianus's remarks introducing the chart bring to mind Aristoxenus's comment in *Harmonics* 1.28: "One must inquire if continuity is not as the Harmonicists attempt to give in their close-packed diagrams, where they mark as consecutive those notes that the smallest interval happens to separate one from another. For not only is it impossible for the voice to sing twenty-eight consecutive dieses, but it is also impossible even to place three dieses together by

differences, as follow. Some of them are continuous, such as those sung through consecutive notes, and some are gapped, such as those sung through notes that are not one after the other. Some are simple, which are posited in accord with a single mode, and some are not simple, which are in accord with a succession of more modes. So, some of the scales are conjunct, some disjunct, and some common: conjunct where one note is common, which are also termed congruent; disjunct where one note falls in the middle, separating both, which are also called parallel; and common where situated sometimes by conjunction, sometimes by disjunction.[39] Moreover, of scales, some are tetrachords, which are comprised of four notes situated in accord with nature, some are pentachords, and some are octachords; and it is necessary to perceive the same definition in the case of these. Of these, some are consonant, some dissonant. The consonant scales are those comprised of consonant notes, the discordant those not so structured. What "consonance of notes" is, we have previously discussed.[40] The display of the scales is produced from dissimilar intervals, such as diesis, semitone, and tone.[41] There is also a difference among the scales according to species: some are comprised of stationary notes, some of movable notes. Some of them are perfect, some not: the tetrachord and pentachord are imperfect, but the octachord is perfect, since every note after this is wholly similar to one of the foregoing. Now the tetrachord is called diatessaron[42] and is composed of two tones and a semitone, five semitones, ten dieses. The pentachord is called diapente[43] and is compounded of three-and-a-half tones, seven semitones, fourteen dieses. The octave is called diapason[44] and is disposed of six tones, twelve semitones, twenty-four dieses. Moreover, of the whole set of scales, some are in close order and some are in open order; and some are immutable (which have one mese), and some modulate (which have more mesai). Some are sung through consecutive notes, some through gapped notes. The various forms of these are considered from the authority or certain order

---

any effort." Perhaps Aristoxenus had just such a chart in mind. The symbols bear a striking resemblance to the symbols preserved in the tables of Alypius and Gaudentius's *Harmonic Introduction* 21–22 (pp. 80–85), but an absolutely certain reconstruction of the diagram is not possible. The most lucid attempt remains that of Friedrich Bellermann (*Die Tonleitern und Musiknoten der Griechen* [Berlin: Förstner, 1847; reprint, Wiesbaden: Sändig, 1969], 61–65), in which the two octaves do indeed ascend just as Aristides Quintilianus describes them, beginning at the point resembling a modern double-sharp and with only the first and final notes (1 and 48) missing from the diagram.

39. The hypaton and meson tetrachords would always be conjunct; the meson and diezeugmenon tetrachords would always be disjunct; and the meson tetrachord could be conjunct with the synemmenon or disjunct with the diezeugmenon. Likewise, the diezeugmenon and hyperbolaion tetrachords would always be conjunct.

40. See section 6 above.

41. That is, a notational diagram such as is found in section 9 below.

42. Because it moves "through four [strings]" (διὰ τεσσάρων).

43. Because it moves "through five [strings]" (διὰ πέντε).

44. Because it moves "through all [the strings]" (διὰ πασῶν).

of the intervals, for there is one semitone or two or three or whatever number. Now it happens that five tetrachords are considered by division in each tonos: hypaton, meson, synemmenon, diezeugmenon, and hyperbolaion; three consonant pentachords: meson, synemmenon, and diezeugmenon; and two octachords: synemmenon and diezeugmenon.[45] There are further species of these, determined by augmenting a parallel series from each note. By the ancients, however, the fourth was called syllabe; the fifth, dioxeion; and the octave, harmonia,[46] which also gained various names by species: the one from hypate hypaton was called Mixolydian; the one from parhypate, Lydian; the one from the diatonic [lichanos], Phrygian; the one from hypate meson, Dorian; the one from parhypate, Hypolydian; the one from the diatonic [lichanos], Hypophrygian; and the one from the mese, Hypodorian.[47] Surely from this it is apparent that by our having supposed the same initial point, which is named each time by a different function of note, it happens that the quality of the harmonia becomes apparent from the sequence of the notes one after another.[48] Now concerning scales, which the ancients also used to call the sources of the ethoses, let these things suffice.

9. A genus is a certain division of a tetrachord. There are three genera of melody: harmonia, color, and diatonic,[49] which take their differences from the narrowness or breadth of their intervals. The genus expanding by the smallest intervals is called harmonia from its having been harmoniously joined together;[50] the genus expanding by tones, diatonic, since the voice is stretched more excessively by this genus;[51] and the genus intensified through semitones,

---

45. These five fourths, three fifths, and two octaves will later be very important to Aristides Quintilianus's cosmology (e.g., in Book III, sections 14–17).

46. According to Nicomachus, *Manual of Harmonics* (*Manuale harmonices*) 9, which credits the terms to Philolaus, a Pythagorean from Tarentum, presumed to be a contemporary of Socrates.

47. These seven species represent the possible octave sequence of whole- and half-steps moving upwards from hypate hypaton. The eighth species (beginning with the paramese) would duplicate the first. Once again assuming the conventional arrangement of the Greek system on A (but keeping in mind that the system has no absolute pitch), the octave species would be distributed as follows:

Mixolydian	B–b
Lydian	c–c'
Phrygian	d–d'
Dorian	e–e'
Hypolydian	f–f'
Hypophrygian	g–g'
Hypodorian	a–a'

48. On this entire section, cf. Aristoxenus, *Harmonics* 1.17–18; 2.53; 3.58–62; Cleonides, *Harmonic Introduction* 8–11 (pp. 41–44); and Gaudentius, *Harmonic Introduction* 4, 6–7, 9, and 19 (pp. 69–73 and 78–79).

49. Cf. Cleonides, *Harmonic Introduction* 3 (p. 36, n. 4) and Gaudentius, *Harmonic Introduction* 5 (p. 69).

50. The term "harmonia" is derived from the verb ἁρμόζω, which means "to join together."

51. The term "diatonic" is derived from the verb διατείνω, which means "to stretch out."

color, for just as what is between white and black is called color, so also the
genus considered between both of the others is named color.[52] Each of these
is sung: the enharmonic by diesis, diesis, and incomposite ditone in ascent,
and contrariwise in descent; the color in ascent by semitone, semitone, and
trisemitone, and contrariwise in descent; and the diatonic by semitone, tone,
and tone in ascent, and contrariwise in descent. Of these, the diatonic is the
more natural, for it is singable by everyone, even by those altogether uneducated; the color is the more artistic, for it is sung only by men of education;
and the enharmonic is the more precise, for it has gained approval by those
most distinguished in music; but for the multitude, it is impossible. On this
account, some gave up melody by diesis because they assumed through their
own weakness that the interval was wholly unsingable.

We sing each of these genera in sequence and succession. There is sequence
when we compose melody through consecutive notes and there is succession
when we compose melody through notes taken by skip. Moreover, one type of
melody is called straight; another, returning; and another, revolving. Straight
melody is that from low to high pitch, returning melody is the opposite, and
revolving melody is modulating melody: for example, if a certain melody should
ascend the tetrachord by conjunction, the same melody would descend by disjunction.[53]

Again, of the generic scales, some are divided into specific types and some
are not. The enharmonic is indivisible, inasmuch as it is compounded from the
smallest dieses; the color will be divided into as many rational intervals as are
discovered between the semitone and the enharmonic diesis; and the diatonic,
of course, into so many as are considered rational intervals between the semitone and the tone. Therefore, there are three species of the color and two of
the diatonic, so that—when all these are added to the enharmonic—there are
six species of melody. The first is characterized by quarter-tone dieses and is
called enharmonic; the second by third-tone dieses and called soft color; the
third is characterized by dieses that are sesquialteran to the enharmonic diesis
and is called hemiolic color; the fourth is distinct in its constitution of the tone
from two incomposite semitones and is called whole-tone color; the fifth is
compounded from a semitone, three dieses, and five remaining over, and
is called soft diatonic; and the sixth has a semitone, a tone, and a tone, and is
termed intense diatonic.

So that what we say may be clear, we shall make a division in numbers,
supposing a tetrachord of sixty monads. The division of the enharmonic is
6 + 6 + 48; the division of the soft color is 8 + 8 + 44; of the hemiolic color,
9 + 9 + 42; of the whole-tone color, 12 + 12 + 36; of the soft diatonic,

52. The color is the intermediate genus because its pycnon is larger than that of the enharmonic
but smaller than the sum of the lower two intervals of the diatonic tetrachord.
53. This paragraph recalls Aristoxenus, *Harmonics* 1.29; cf. section 12 below and Cleonides, *Harmonic Introduction* 14 (p. 46).

12 + 18 + 30; and of the intense diatonic, 12 + 24 + 24.[54]

There are other tetrachordal divisions, which the exceedingly ancient peoples used for their harmoniai. Sometimes the divisions filled out a perfect octachord, but sometimes the scale was even greater than six tones, while often it was less, for they did not always employ all of the notes; we shall discuss the reason in the future.[55] They constructed the Lydian scale of diesis, ditone, tone, diesis, diesis, ditone, and diesis (and this was a perfect scale); the Dorian of tone, diesis, diesis, ditone, tone, diesis, diesis, and ditone (and this exceeded the octave by a tone); and the Phrygian of tone, diesis, diesis, ditone, tone, diesis, diesis, and tone (and this was a perfect octave). They constructed the Iastian of diesis, diesis, ditone, trisemitone, and tone (and this was short of the octave by a tone); the Mixolydian of two dieses situated consecutively, tone, tone, diesis, diesis, and three tones (and this was a perfect scale). The so-called intense Lydian was diesis, diesis, ditone, and trisemitone. Now one must understand in the case of all of these that the diesis is enharmonic. For the sake of clarity, let the diagram of the scales be written below. The divine Plato in the *Republic* surely calls these to mind when he says that both the Mixolydian and intense Lydian are threnodic, while the Iastian and the Lydian are convivial and exceedingly indulgent. And he thereafter concludes, saying: "it seems that you have the Dorian and Phrygian left over."[56] They used to make

---

54. These divisions follow Aristoxenus, *Harmonics* 1.22–27 and 2.50–52, with the tetrachord based on 60 units instead of the 30 implied by Aristoxenus's division. The following chart will illustrate the divisions. On section 9 up to this point, cf. Cleonides, *Harmonic Introduction* 6–7 (pp. 40–41) and Gaudentius, *Harmonic Introduction* 5 (p. 69).

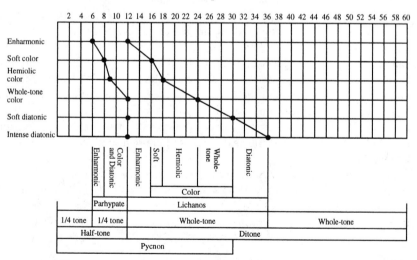

Each segment of the grid equals 1/12 of a whole-tone

55. I.e., in Book II, section 14.
56. Plato, *Republic* 3.10 (p. 11).

such displays of the harmoniai, arranging the qualities of the notes in relation to the preceding ethoses. We shall speak precisely about these things in the future.[57]

Lydian	Dorian
R Ⅴ C O Ξ N Z E	Φ C P Π Ι Z E Δ Θ
L ⅂ C K ⅄ ⟨Ж⟩ ⊏ ⊔ [F]	⟨F⟩ C ∪ Ɔ < ⊏ ⊔ ⊐ ∀
Phrygian	Iastian
Φ C P Π Ι Z E Δ ⅄	⅂ R Ⅴ C M Ι
F C ∪ ⟨Ɔ⟩ < ⊏ ⊔ ⟨⊐⟩ Z [Γ]	⟨Γ⟩ L ⅂ C Π <
Mixolydian	Intense Lydian
⅂ R Ⅴ Φ C P Π Z	⅂ R Ⅴ C M
Γ L ⅂ F C ∪ Ɔ ⊏	Γ L ⅂ C Π

10. Let us now speak about tonoi. In music, we call three things tonos: a pitch in the precise sense; a certain magnitude of sound, for example, by which the fifth exceeds the fourth; or a scalar mode, for example, Lydian or Phrygian. Concerning this last type, it is now proposed to speak. According to Aristoxenus, there are thirteen tonoi, the proslambanomenoi of which comprise an octave; according to the younger theorists, there are fifteen, the proslambanomenoi of which comprise an octave and a tone, reaching the tone by disjunction. Aristoxenus names them as follows: Hypodorian; two Hypophrygian, the one low, which is also called Hypoiastian, the other high; two Hypolydian, the one low, which is also called Hypoaeolian, the other high; one Dorian; two Phrygian, the one low, which is also called Iastian, the other high; two Lydian, the one low, which is now called Aeolian, the other high; two Mixolydian, the one low, which is now called Hyperdorian, the other high, which is now called Hyperiastian; and one Hypermixolydian, which is also called Hyperphrygian.

---

57. The matter of the relationship of differing scales and ethoses is taken up throughout Book II and the reasons for these relationships are studied in Book III. This diagram makes use of the symbols preserved in the tables of Alypius and Gaudentius's *Harmonic Introduction* 21–22 (pp. 80–85), and the scales can be transcribed as follows (assuming the conventional pitch):

Lydian	$e°$	f	a	b	$b°$	c'	e'	$e°'$	
Dorian	g	a	$a°$	$a\sharp$	d'	e'	$e°'$	f'	a'
Phrygian	g	a	$a°$	$a\sharp$	d'	e'	$e°'$	f'	g'
Iastian	e	$e°$	f	a	c'	d'			
Mixolydian	e	$e°$	f	g	a	$a°$	$a\sharp$	e'	
Intense Lydian	e	$e°$	f	a	c'				

($°$ = a quarter-tone ascent; c' is middle c)

For further comment on the significance of these scales, see Mathiesen, *Aristides Quintilianus*, 20–21.

To these are added by the younger theorists both the Hyperaeolian and the Hyperlydian, so that each tonos might have a low, medial, and high pitch.

Each of the tonoi will exceed the former by a semitone if we choose to begin from the lowest pitch, or will be lesser by a semitone if we make a beginning from the highest pitch. Their proslambanomenoi comprise, as I said, an octave and a tone.[58] On this account, they may also be determined by means of consonances, for if I begin from the lowest pitch and choose to ascend and in turn to descend by various intervals, I shall no doubt reach any one of their proslambanomenoi. Of these, some tonoi are sung in their entirety, some are not. The Dorian is sung in full because the voice serves us as far as twelve tones and because its proslambanomenos is in the middle of the Hypodorian octave. For the rest, those lower than the Dorian are sung as far as the note consonant with the nete hyperbolaion.[59]

58. On all of this section, cf. Cleonides, *Harmonic Introduction* 12 (pp. 44–45). Cleonides states (p. 44) that Aristoxenus identified thirteen tonoi, but there is nothing of this in the surviving portions of the *Harmonica,* except 2.37, where there are not thirteen tonoi and where Aristoxenus is not positing the tonoi himself but is once again paraphrasing the Harmonicists for purposes of refutation. It is very unlikely that Aristoxenus ever proposed thirteen tonoi. There are, however, fifteen tonoi preserved in the tables of Alypius. Assuming the conventional pitching for these tonoi (always recalling n. 47 above), the sequence would be as follows:

Aristoxenus		Proslambanomenos	"Younger theorists"
		g	Hyperlydian
		f♯	Hyperaeolian
Hypermixolydian (or Hyperphrygian)		f	
	Hyperiastian	e	
High and low Mixolydian	Hyperdorian	e♭	
	Lydian	d	
High and low Lydian	Aeolian	c♯	
	Phrygian	c	
High and low Phrygian	Iastian	B	
Dorian		B♭	
	Hypolydian	A	
High and low Hypolydian	Hypoaeolian	G♯	
	Hypophrygian	G	
High and low Hypophrygian	Hypoiastian	F♯	
Hypodorian		F	

59. All the notes of the Dorian may be sung because it has been defined that the voice can sing a full two octaves (twelve tones) and the Dorian proslambanomenos is the lower limit of the

So also we shall organize songs or cola[60] by the modes if in place of the deepest of the notes of the scale we should substitute one of the proslambano-menoi and then sing in descent from this. If we should not be able to descend further, this will be the Dorian because the first audible note has been defined by the proslambanomenos of the Dorian. But if a note should be audible, we shall try to perceive by how much it is higher than the Dorian proslambano-menos, that is, than the lowest note by nature, and that mode which is higher than the Dorian proslambanomenos shall be defined for us by the amount by which the deepest note of the melos was considered as higher than the deepest note by nature. If the lowest note of the song falls above the Dorian, beginning in a higher octave, we shall take it down an octave, and by using the aforesaid method, we shall without difficulty take note of the harmonia itself.[61]

11. Modulation is the alteration of the underlying scale and of the character of the sound. For if some certain type of sound accompanies each scale, it is evident that the species of melos will be altered together with the harmoniai. The various modulations in the tonoi arise in each of the intervals—both com-posite and incomposite—, but those taken from consonant intervals are more graceful, and the rest of these are not at all so. We are able to observe that the forms and successions of these modulate from a note by tone or semitone and—in short—by every interval, either odd or even and either descending or ascending. Commonalities among the tonoi also arise in tetrachords: some exceed the others by a semitone, some by a tone, some by intervals greater than these; and so it happens that the mesai of the deeper tetrachord become the hypatai of the higher tetrachord, or conversely, and so on consecutively.[62]

There are three tonoi by genus: Dorian, Phrygian, and Lydian. Of these, the Dorian is useful in relation to the lower activities of the voice, the Lydian to the higher, and the Phrygian to the middle.[63] The rest are considered more in instrumental compositions, for they are worked out in the longest scales. Since all of the tonoi are compounded inversely from the order of the twenty-four letters, after descending a tone from the lowest of all, the Hypodorian, we take the ⊐ as the beginning of the signs; thereafter the next sign presents an expres-

---

voice (cf. Book II, section 14). By definition, the tonoi lower than the Dorian can be sung only as high as their respective netai hyperbolaion because no higher notes exist in any tonos. In the next section, Aristides Quintilianus observes that the tonoi other than the Dorian, Phrygian, and Lydian are used chiefly in instrumental compositions, and this agrees with his observations at this point.

60. The cola are instrumental interludes. They are mentioned again in section 11 below.
61. The method described for determining the mode of a piece is not unlike that still taught in basic ear training courses for musicians.
62. Cf. Cleonides, *Harmonic Introduction* 13 (pp. 45–46). Some of the possible modulatory shifts can easily be seen by examining the "commonalities" in the diagram of the modes, which appears later in this section.
63. That is, there are three basic generic types of tonoi. All the others are hypertonoi, hypotonoi, or mixed tonoi (see n. 58 above).

sion of the diesis in the harmonia, and in the color and diatonic, of the semi-tone; and the next one after this; then we define that the fourth sign presents the tone. And having made a beginning of the deepest of the modes, we ascend again by a semitone and prescribe the proslambanomenos of the next mode; and by placing together the sequential notes by the same excesses, we fill out the number of the fifteen modes. Given below are the display of the letters by semitone, the display by tone, and then the modes derived from these. We have made the display of the signs double so that from the similarity of the signs written below we might consider the sequence of those above; so that we might characterize, with the signs below, the cola and the aulos interludes in songs or pure instrumental music, and with the signs above, the songs;[64] and so that we might calmly conceal the esoteric things in music, setting down instead of the letters in use those that have been written below in this display of the tonoi. The diagram of the modes is akin to a wing, explaining the excesses which the tonoi have one to another. These are set forth following the three genera and also comprise the concordances. There is concordance when, if two letters comprise two intervals in the enharmonic, only one of these in another genus signifies the two intervals united.[65]

[See figures on pp. 63–64.]

It remains necessary to speak about eklusis, spondeiasmos, and ekbole, for the ancients employed these intervals for the different types of harmoniai. A descent of three incomposite dieses was called eklusis; an ascent of the same interval, spondeiasmos; and an ascent of five dieses, ekbole. These were given names as modifications of intervals because of the scarcity of their use.[66]

12. Melos is, in the perfect sense, what is composed of harmonia, rhythm, and diction; and in the more specific sense—as in the science of harmonics—it is the succession of notes dissimilar in high and low pitch. Melic composition is a constructive function of melos. One type of melic composition is hypatoid, another mesoid, and another netoid in accord with the properties of the voice previously discussed by us.[67] The parts of melic composition are choice, mixing, and usage. It is choice through which it results that the musician discovers the scale it is necessary to make from a certain position of the voice—whether hypatoid or one of the rest. It is mixing through which we arrange the notes

64. The lower line shows the so-called instrumental notation; the upper, the so-called vocal. Cf. Gaudentius, *Harmonic Introduction* 21–22 (pp. 80–85).
65. For a summary explanation of these diagrams, see Mathiesen, *Aristides Quintilianus*, 21–24; and Bellermann, 69–77.
66. These intervals are also discussed in the Ps.-Plutarchean *On Music* (*De musica*) 11 and 29 (1135a–b and 1141b) and in Bacchius Geron, *Introduction to the Art of Music* (*Introductio artis musicae*) 37 and 41–42. There are several English translations of the Plutarchean dia-logue; for Bacchius, see Otto Steinmayer, "Bacchius Geron's *Introduction to the Art of Music*," *Journal of Music Theory* 29 (1985): 271–98.
67. I.e., in section 6.

DISPLAY BY SEMITONE

DISPLAY BY TONE

DIAGRAM OF MODES

SIGN	Hypodorian	Hypoiastian	Hypophrygian	Hypoaeolian	Hypolydian	Dorian	Iastian	Phrygian	Aeolian	Lydian	Hyperdorian	Hyperiastian	Hyperphrygian	Hyperaeolian	Hyperlydian

one to another or the positions of the voice or the genera of melody or the scales of modes. Usage is the certain execution of the melody. Of this in turn, there are three species: sequence, repetition, and succession. There are three species of sequence: straight, returning, and revolving. Straight sequence is that making an ascent through consecutive notes; returning is that bringing about depth through notes following each other; and revolving is that ascending by the synemmenon and descending by the diezeugmenon, or contrariwise; this last is observed in modulations. Succession is that emitting one tonos through gapped intervals of two notes or even more, determining beforehand either the low or the higher of these as producing the melos. And it is repetition by which we know which of the notes it is necessary to discard, which it is necessary to employ and how often each of them, and from which one it is necessary to begin and on which it is necessary to end. Repetition is also indicative of the ethos.[68]

Melic composition differs from melody: the latter is a recital of melos and the former is creative habit. The modes of melic composition are three in genus: dithyrambic, nomic, and tragic. The nomic mode is netoid; the dithyrambic, mesoid; and the tragic, hypatoid. But in species, more modes are discovered, which we are able by similarity to group under the generic types. Some are called erotic, among which the bridal songs are distinct; some comic; and some panegyric. These are termed modes because the ethos of the heart simultaneously appears in a certain way in the course of these mele.

Melic compositions differ from one another: in genus, as enharmonic, chromatic, diatonic; in scale, as hypatoid, mesoid, netoid; in tonos, as Dorian, Phrygian; in nomic or dithyrambic mode; in ethos, as we speak of the systaltic, through which we move the painful passions, the diastaltic, through which we awaken the spirit, and the medial, through which we bring the soul round to

---

68. A similar set of "compositional patterns" is described in Cleonides, *Harmonic Introduction* 14 (p. 46). Aristoxenus's *Harmonics* 1.29 is just beginning to describe "sequence" at the point where the surviving fragment breaks off. The patterns of sequence might be expressed in notation as follows:

and succession:

The devices of sequence and succession can in fact be seen in the famous Epitaph of Seikilos: the seventh colon exhibits sequence and the eighth, tenth, and eleventh cola exhibit succession (for a transcription, see Thomas J. Mathiesen, "Rhythm and Meter in Ancient Greek Music," *Music Theory Spectrum* 7 [1985]: 171–72; in the transcription, the seventh colon appears in the second line of music, and the remaining cola appear in lines 3–4). Aristides Quintilianus will later explain (in Books II–III) that repetition is important because each note carries a masculine, feminine, or mixed character; thus, the ethos of a piece of music is affected to some extent by the functional character of the notes.

quietude. These were called ethoses since the states of the soul were first observed and set right by them.[69] But not by them alone; rather these worked together as parts for the treatment of the passions, and that melos was perfect which also unceasingly applied paideia. For just as in the case of healing drugs, no one certain substance is naturally disposed to heal the sufferings of the body, but a substance commingled from many does good perfectly, so also here, the melody does little for right action, but perfect self-sufficiency is made up complete from every one of the parts.[70]

Now let this be sufficient for us on the harmonic class of music; and let us then pass on to rhythmic theory.

69. These ethical characters are also discussed in Cleonides, *Harmonic Introduction* 13 (p. 46 [see also n. 21]).
70. By introducing the notions of ethos and paideia (education) here, as well as the medical analogy, Aristides Quintilianus anticipates Book II and links this section to it. He is also making it clear that the melic composition alone is not responsible for proper morality (just as one drug does not heal an illness), but rather perfect self-sufficiency (an attribute of the philosopher, as in Aristotle's *Nicomachean Ethics* 1.7 [1097b8] and 10.7 [1177b1]) is the result of all its various parts.

6 Gaudentius

Little is known of Gaudentius, although unlike Cleonides, he is cited by another early author, Cassiodorus, who refers to him on two separate occasions in his *Fundamentals* (pp. 143–48). The *Harmonic Introduction* must therefore have been written prior to the sixth century C.E. His treatise, which is transmitted in thirty-one manuscripts, is unusual in its eclecticism: it begins as if Gaudentius were an Aristoxenian, moves abruptly in the middle section to the story of Pythagoras's discovery of harmonic phenomena, returns to a discussion of the various species of consonant intervals, and concludes with a section describing ancient Greek musical notation. This section breaks off in the middle of the Hypoaeolian tonos, but it is probable that the treatise originally included all fifteen tonoi. As the treatises survive today, only the tables of Alypius—an author also mentioned by Cassiodorus—provide a fuller treatment of ancient Greek notation. The consistency of the notational symbols as they appear in surviving fragments of Greek music (ranging in date from the third century B.C.E. to well into the Middle Ages) and in the treatises of Aristides Quintilianus, Gaudentius, and Alypius attests to the importance of musical notation in this very early period.

Gaudentius must have been known throughout the Middle Ages only as a tantalizing shadow in the references of Cassiodorus. In the sixteenth century, however, the treatise was known, no doubt in a new Latin translation, to Giovanni Del Lago and Gioseffo Zarlino, who specifically cites it in his *Istitutioni harmoniche* 3.5.

Harmonic Introduction

"I sing for the intelligent; uninitiated, close the door!" someone beginning a discourse on harmonics might justly say at the outset. This is a discourse on notes, intervals, and scales, and on tonoi, modulations, and melic composition in all the genera of harmonia.[1] It is necessary for one hearing a discourse on these matters to have already trained his hearing by experience to hear the notes exactly and to recognize the intervals, both consonant and dissonant, so that by consequently applying reason to a sense of the particular features of notes, he might practice a perfect science augmented by experience and reason. Whoever has come to hear the discourse but does not hear a note plainly and has not trained his hearing, let him go away and close the door on these sounds, for his ears—though present—will be stopped up by a sense that does not know beforehand the matters of this discourse.[2] As we begin, let us speak on the voice to those exactly trained by experience.

1. Position of the voice is an interval from depth to height and the converse. Within this position, every motion of the voice ranges, both the speaking voice and the intervallic voice, ascending and descending. On the one hand, in the speaking voice, with which we converse one with another, the notes pass over this position, continuous with themselves, nearly a stream in ascent and the converse, not stopping on one pitch. On the other hand, the so-called intervallic voice is in no way continuous with itself, nor is it nearly a stream, but by standing apart from itself and leaping silently over a small position, within the limits of the positions over which it leaps, it appears to stop and establishes its pitch clearly, remaining on those boundaries of the positions over which it

TEXT: The Latin translation of Gaudentius's treatise by Mutianus, to which Cassiodorus refers, is not known to have survived, but several later Latin translations do exist. The only modern-language translation of this treatise published heretofore is *Alypius et Gaudence, Bacchius l'Ancien*, trans. C.-E. Ruelle, Collection des auteurs grecs relatifs à la musique, no. 5 (Paris: Firmin-Didot, 1895). More than a decade ago, Professor Emeritus Walter Robert shared with me his unpublished English draft, but mine is an entirely new translation and restoration based on Jan's text (*Musici scriptores graeci*, 327–55) and my own review of all the manuscript sources.

1. These are the seven Aristoxenian divisions of harmonics, but Gaudentius has rearranged their presentation somewhat. Cf. Cleonides, *Harmonic Introduction* (*Harmonica introductio*) 1 (p. 36) and Aristides Quintilianus, *On Music* (*De musica*) 1.5 (p. 50). On the meaning of the term "harmonia," see p. 10, n. 3.
2. Gaudentius's emphasis on the importance of aural acuity combined with reason recalls Aristoxenus, *Harmonics* (*Harmonica*) 1.14–15 and especially 2.33–34 ("For the musician, exactness of sense has nearly the rank of a principle, for it is not possible for someone who senses poorly to speak well about things he does not sense in any way at all").

leaps. On this account, the intervallic voice had its name and was consequently so called by antithesis to the speaking voice.

Of the intervallic in particular, there is the melodic and unmelodic. The melodic uses rational intervals, and none falls short or overshoots; the unmelodic misses or overshoots the defined intervals by a small amount. Moreover, the melodic and the unmelodic appear to be opposite one to another.

The motion of the voice going from a lower to a higher position exists and is called ascent; the converse, descent. Ascent is productive of height; descent, of depth. Depth differs from descent and height from ascent not only because from each of the latter the former are achieved but also because when ascent ceases and no longer exists, height is generated and exists; and when descent ceases and no longer exists, likewise depth is generated and exists. Pitch, therefore, happens to be common to both, for both height and depth appear to have a certain pitch.[3]

2. *On the note.* A note is the falling of the voice upon one pitch; pitch is a tarrying and standing of the voice. Whenever the voice seems to stop on one pitch, we say that the voice is a note that can be ordered in melos.

Contingent to a note are shade, position, and chronos. It is chronos insofar as we sound longer notes in a greater chronos and shorter notes in a lesser chronos. Surely rhythm appears to have its locus here, for mele must be rhythmized by the chronos of the notes.

It is a position of the note insofar as we emit some lower and some higher. Notes that appear to be in the same position we say are unison; we speak of higher or lower notes as being in different positions.

It is shade by which notes appearing to be in the same position or chronos would differ one from another, e.g., the nature of the so-called melos in the voice and the like.[4]

3. *On the interval.* An interval is comprised of two notes. It is evident that the notes must differ one from another in pitch, for if they have the same pitch, there will not really be an interval since the voice appears to be in the same position. The difference, therefore, between the higher and lower note and between the lower and higher note should be spoken of as an interval.[5]

---

3. Gaudentius uses the phrases "position of the voice" and "motion of the voice" as if they were largely synonymous; this is close to Aristoxenus's own treatment (*Harmonics* 1.3) but rather different from the later Aristoxenian theorists. Gaudentius is also unusual in characterizing intervals as "melodic" or "unmelodic"; Aristoxenus (*Harmonics* 1.9, 27; 2.37; and especially 3.64–66) was very much concerned with identifying patterns that would be melodic or unmelodic, but the later Aristoxenian theorists largely ignore this subject. Cf. Cleonides, *Harmonic Introduction* 2 (p. 36) and Aristides Quintilianus, *On Music* 1.12 (pp. 62–66).

4. It is unusual for a *Harmonic Introduction* to include references to rhythm. Even Aristoxenus hardly mentions rhythm in his *Harmonics* (see 2.34), although he does write at least one separate treatise on the subject, only fragments of which survive. On the meaning of "chronos," see p. 49, n. 7. Gaudentius will return to the genera and the shades in section 5 and to the notes in section 17 below.

5. Cf. Cleonides, *Harmonic Introduction* 5 (p. 39) and Aristides Quintilianus, *On Music* 1.7 (pp. 53–54).

What is tonos? Tonos is a magnitude of interval and a difference of scales. "Tonos" is homonymous, but when it is spoken of as an interval, it is cut into semitones and dieses and is also combined with intervals that are larger than it, e.g., the trisemitone, the ditone, and the like. When it is used to name a difference of scales, it signifies what is the pitch of the entire scale.[6]

Some of the intervals are melodic, some unmelodic. Some of the melodic intervals are consonant, some inconsonant; some are greater, some lesser; some are primary and incomposite, some neither primary nor incomposite. It is for the hearing to distinguish melodic and consonant intervals or their opposites. The difference of consonant and dissonant notes—as well as melodic and unmelodic—lies for the most part in the difference of the sound; nevertheless, it lies to a small extent in reason (on which, there will be further comment).[7]

4. *On scales.* Intervals are incomposite when between the notes comprising the intervals, not even one note can be sung that is melodic with respect to the notes in the genus in which the incomposite interval is taken. Intervals are composite within which a note or notes are sung. These are also spoken of as scales, for a scale is simply an interval compounded of more than one interval. The incomposite and primary intervals in accord with each genus are the common measures of the rest of the intervals or scales in the same genus.[8]

5. *On genera.* Genus is a certain division and disposition of a tetrachord. There are three genera: diatonic, chromatic, and enharmonic. There are many species and shades of the genera. In the harmonic genus, the primary and incomposite interval is a quarter-tone, called the enharmonic diesis. In the chromatic genus, it is a third of a tone, called the least chromatic diesis. In the diatonic genus, which is most often called the intense, the semitone is primary and incomposite. The intense diatonic genus is sung in ascent by semitone, tone, tone; in descent, the obverse is evident. The chromatic genus uses many species as it is sung: one species, for example, is sung in ascent by semitone, semitone, trisemitone; in descent, the opposite. In the enharmonic genus, the melody proceeds by quarter-tone, quarter-tone, ditone.[9]

6. On the genera, the aforesaid is sufficient for now. Let us speak of them again when we take up the number, order, and intervals of the notes;[10] for now, we speak about one genus, the diatonic, for it is the only one of the three genera that is now generally sung. The use of the remaining two genera seems to have lapsed.

---

6. Cf. Cleonides, *Harmonic Introduction* 12 (pp. 44–45) and Aristides Quintilianus, *On Music* 1.10 (pp. 59–61). Gaudentius returns to the tonoi in sections 20–22.

7. See sections 8–10 below. Cf. Cleonides, *Harmonic Introduction* 5 (p. 39) and Aristides Quintilianus, *On Music* 1.7 (pp. 53–54).

8. Cf. Cleonides, *Harmonic Introduction* 8 (p. 41) and Aristides Quintilianus, *On Music* 1.8 (pp. 54–56). Gaudentius returns to the subject of scales in sections 6–7 and 18–19 below.

9. Cf. Cleonides, *Harmonic Introduction* 3 and 6–7 (pp. 36–37 and 40–41) and Aristides Quintilianus, *On Music* 1.9 (pp. 56–59).

10. I.e., sections 7 and 15–17.

Diagram of the Three Genera in One Tetrachord[11]

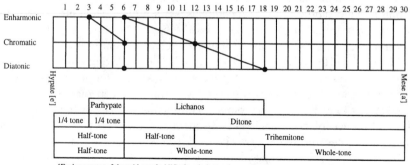

[Each segment of the grid equals 1/12 of a whole-tone]

The ancients called the lowest note of all, from which they made a beginning of harmonia in ascent, the proslambanomenos. They did not always take it as the lowest note by nature, but by position. The same note was not proslambanomenos for each of the modes, but in each it was another note, as will very soon be shown.[12] After it, they ordered the hypate hypaton, always standing apart from the proslambanomenos by a whole-tone interval in all the genera of harmonia. Following this, they placed the parhypate hypaton, a semitone higher than the hypate, then the lichanos hypaton, separated by a tone in ascent from the parhypate; in the diatonic genus, this was also called the diatonic hypaton. After this, the hypate meson was ordered, separated likewise by a tone from the lichanos (or diatonic), and at this point, the tetrachord scale of the hypaton was complete, beginning from the hypate hypaton and ending on the hypate meson. From this, they again made a beginning of the tetrachord of the meson; thus, the hypate meson is a common note in both tetrachords: it is the highest terminus of the first tetrachord, the hypaton; it is the lowest of the second tetrachord, the meson. After this, the parhypate meson is a semitone higher than the hypate, and after this, the lichanos meson or the diatonic meson is likewise higher by a tone than the parhypate. After this, the mese, and it too differs by a tone from the lichanos meson. At this point, they completed the second scale, the tetrachord of the meson. From there, they first appended the tetrachord of the synemmenon; again making the same mese the beginning of the following tetrachord (the so-called synemmenon) and on this account speaking of it as synemmenon. They then appended the tetrachord of the diezeugmenon; it did not have its beginning from the mese but from the

11. None of the surviving manuscripts preserves this diagram. Although the specific design of the diagram is of course unknown, I have reconstructed its content.
12. Gaudentius is alluding to the fact that the notes have no absolute pitch but are assigned positions in a spectrum of possible pitches according to their "tonos." Cf. section 20 below. Aristides Quintilianus, *On Music* 1.10 (pp. 59–61) describes this matter more fully, and the diagram on p. 64 represents the relationships. Both Aristides Quintilianus and Gaudentius use the term τρόπος (mode) more or less synonymously with the more technical τόνος (tonos).

so-called paramese. The paramese is always separated by a tone from the mese, and this is so in all the genera of melody.[13]

The ancients therefore made two perfect scales, calling one "by conjunction" and the other "by disjunction." When they made the scale by conjunction, they placed the trite synemmenon neton following the mese, separated from the mese by a semitone. Following the trite is the paranete synemmenon neton, a tone higher than the trite. Following these is the nete synemmenon neton, a tone higher than the paranete. They called this the tetrachord of the neton synemmenon: "neton" because it is the highest and boundary of progress in ascent; "synemmenon" because it does not stand apart from the meson but is conjoined to the preceding tetrachord by a common note, the mese. They spoke of the string next to the mese as the trite because it was the third string from the final terminus. The paranete was ordered following this, and the nete was the last because this is the boundary of motion in ascent, as we have said.

When they made the scale by disjunction, they ordered the paramese following the mese, always separated from the mese by a tone in all the genera, just as was said about the proslambanomenos and the hypate hypaton. They called this the tone of disjunction. From the paramese, they made a beginning of the tetrachord of the neton diezeugmenon, and in the same fashion, they ordered the trite diezeugmenon neton a semitone higher than the paramese, then the paranete diezeugmenon neton a tone higher than the trite, and following this, the nete diezeugmenon neton a tone higher. Again, they made this the beginning of the tetrachord of neton hyperbolaion; it was the final and highest string of the tetrachord of the neton diezeugmenon but the beginning and lowest string of the tetrachord of the neton hyperbolaion. Following it, they placed the trite hyperbolaion neton a semitone higher than it. Following this, they placed the paranete, separated by a tone from the trite; then the nete hyperbolaion neton, separated by a tone in ascent from the paranete. This was the boundary of the second scale, the so-called scale by disjunction.

7. In the lesser scale, the scale by conjunction, there are three tetrachords joined to one another by two common notes, the mese and the hypate meson; the proslambanomenos is outside. The functions of notes extend to eleven in number: proslambanomenos, hypate hypaton, parhypate hypaton, lichanos hypaton, hypate meson, parhypate meson, lichanos meson, mese, trite synemmenon neton, paranete synemmenon neton, and nete synemmenon neton. In the greater scale, the so-called scale by disjunction, there are four tetrachords: the tetrachord of the hypaton, the tetrachord of the meson, and the two tetrachords of the neton. Of these, the tetrachords of the hypaton and the meson are conjoined one to another by a common note, the hypate meson; they are disjunct from the rest by the tone from the mese to the paramese. The remaining two tetrachords are necessarily disjunct from the first by the same

13. Cf. Cleonides, *Harmonic Introduction* 4 (pp. 37–39) and Aristides Quintilianus, *On Music* 1.6 (pp. 51–53), but Gaudentius's identification of the note-names in conjunction with the names of the tetrachords is unusual.

tone; they are conjoined one to another, however, by a common note, the nete diezeugmenon neton. In a like manner to these, the proslambanomenos lies outside the tetrachords.[14] The functions of notes extend to fifteen in number: proslambanomenos, hypate hypaton, parhypate hypaton, lichanos hypaton, hypate meson, parhypate meson, lichanos meson, mese, paramese, trite diezeugmenon neton, paranete diezeugmenon neton, nete diezeugmenon neton, trite hyperbolaion neton, paranete hyperbolaion neton, and nete hyperbolaion neton. The functions of notes of both scales together extended to the number twenty-six, of which the eight functions up to the mese are common in both scales. All the remaining functions of notes are eighteen in number, in which everything is chanted or played on the aulos and kithara—or to say it all at once, sung.[15] The aforesaid will be more apparent from the posited diagram of the two scales, both conjunct and disjunct.[16]

Disjunct		Conjunct	
Proslambanomenos	[A]	Proslambanomenos	[A]
Hypate hypaton	[B]	Hypate hypaton	[B]
Parhypate hypaton	[c]	Parhypate hypaton	[c]
Lichanos hypaton	[d]	Lichanos hypaton	[d]
Hypate meson	[e]	Hypate meson	[e]
Parhypate meson	[f]	Parhypate meson	[f]
Lichanos meson	[g]	Lichanos meson	[g]
Mese	[a]	Mese	[a]
Paramese	[b]	Trite synemmenon neton	[b♭]
Trite diezeugmenon neton	[c′]	Paranete synemmenon neton	[c′]
Paranete diezeugmenon neton	[d′]	Nete synemmenon neton	[d′]
Nete diezeugmenon neton	[e′]		
Trite hyperbolaion neton	[f′]		
Paranete hyperbolaion neton	[g′]		
Nete hyperbolaion neton	[a′]		

This is the arrangement and order of the notes in the diatonic genus. These names are used for the notes in all the genera, except in the case of the notes movable by modulation of genus, where a particular name accrues to the common name in each genus, such as enharmonic parhypate, chromatic lichanos, and diatonic lichanos. The aforesaid will become clearer through the following.

8. Some of the melodic notes are unison, some are consonant, some are dissonant, and some are paraphonic. Unison notes are those that do not differ one from another in depth or height. Consonant notes are those where, when plucked or played on the aulos simultaneously, the melos of the lower note to

14. Cf. Cleonides, *Harmonic Introduction* 8 and 10 (pp. 41 and 43–44) and Aristides Quintilianus, *On Music* 1.8 (pp. 54–56).
15. Cf. Aristides Quintilianus, *On Music* 1.6 (pp. 51–53).
16. Here again, the diagram is omitted from the manuscripts, but I have restored it. The pitches indicated in brackets are, of course, merely conventional, and as always, it should be borne in mind that the system has no absolute pitch.

the high and the higher note to the low is always the same, or when a blend is revealed together in the utterance of two notes as if they were one; in this case, we say that they are consonant. Dissonant notes are those where, when plucked or played on the aulos simultaneously, it appears that none of the melos of the lower note to the high and the higher note to the low is the same, or when notes uttered simultaneously reveal no blend with respect to one another. Paraphonic notes are between consonant and dissonant but appear consonant in the plucking of strings (just as this appears in the three tones from parhypate meson to paramese and in the two tones from diatonic meson to paramese).[17]

9. The consonances in the perfect scale are six in number. The first is the diatessaron, the second the diapente, which exceeds the diatessaron by a tone. On this account, some defined the whole-tone interval as the difference in magnitude of the first two consonant intervals. The third consonance is a composite of both of these, the diapason. A diapente added to a diatessaron makes consonant extremes; this mode of consonance is called a diapason. The fourth consonance is the diapason together with the diatessaron. The fifth is the diapason together with the diapente. The sixth is the double diapason. It is possible to conceive of more consonances by combining these with others, but our instruments would not support the pitch. With respect to the function of instruments or the human voice, therefore, only six consonances altogether are posited for us. And so there are the diatessaron—consonant in every genus of melody—of four notes, three intervals, two-and-a-half tones, and five semitones; the diapente—likewise consonant in all the genera—of five notes, four intervals, three-and-a-half tones, and seven semitones; the consonant diapason of eight notes, seven intervals, six tones, and twelve semitones; the diapason-and-diatessaron of eleven notes, ten intervals, eight-and-a-half tones, and seventeen semitones; the diapason-and-diapente of twelve notes, eleven intervals, nine-and-a-half tones, and nineteen semitones; and the double diapason of fifteen notes, fourteen intervals, twelve tones, and twenty-four semitones.[18]

---

17. The first three definitions parallel Aristides Quintilianus, *On Music* 1.6 (p. 52), but Gaudentius adds a fourth, which clearly refers to the intervals of a ditone and a tritone. The definition is unique to Gaudentius. Theon of Smyrna (*Exposition of Mathematics Useful for Reading Plato* [*Expositio rerum mathematicarum ad legendum Platonem utilium*]) defines the paraphonic intervals as the diapente and the diatessaron, and Bacchius Geron (*Introduction to the Art of Music* [*Introductio artis musicae;* see p. 62, n. 66]) defines the noun form παραφωνία as "whenever two dissimilar notes are struck, the melos is no more in the higher note than in the lower." There is some evidence of a lacuna preceding the definition in Bacchius's text, but in any event, the definitions of Theon and Bacchius are quite different from Gaudentius's.

18. Gaudentius's description seems to be based on Aristoxenus's definition in *Harmonics* 1.20 and 2.45, although Aristoxenus states that there are eight magnitudes of consonance, with the largest practical consonant interval being the double-octave-and-a-fifth. Cf. Cleonides, *Harmonic Introduction* 8 (p. 41) and Aristides Quintilianus, *On Music* 1.8 (p. 55). Gaudentius's and Aristoxenus's acceptance of a compound interval such as the diapason-and-diatessaron (in the ratio 8:3) as consonant directly contradicts the Pythagorean principle that only multiple and superparticular ratios can be consonant. All the material up to this point in the treatise has been markedly Aristoxenian, but in sections 10–16, the treatise becomes decidedly Pythagorean.

10. The ratios of the consonances are discovered and exactly expressed in every way in numbers: the sesquitertia of the diatessaron, i.e., 24:18; the sesquialtera of the diapente, i.e., 24:16; the duple of the diapason, i.e., 24:12; the duple superbipartient of the diapason together with the diatessaron, i.e., 24:9; again, the triple of the diapason-and-diapente, i.e., 24:8; and the quadruple of the double diapason, i.e., 24:6.[19]

11. They tell the story that Pythagoras took the beginning of his discovery of these ratios from the chance that while passing by a smithy, he sensed that the strikings of the mallets upon the anvil were dissonant and consonant. Upon entering, he at once comprehended the reason for the difference of the strikings and for the consonances. He discovered this by concluding that as the hammers were of different weights, the ratios of the magnitudes of the weights were the cause both for the difference and the consonance of the noises. He discovered that the hammers having a sesquitertian ratio in their weights produced the consonance of a diatessaron in their noises; he perceived that the hammers weighing in a sesquialteran ratio resulted in a diapente consonance in their striking; and he sensed that the hammers duple in weight produced the consonance of a diapason in their sounds.

When he had made a beginning of the relationship of consonant intervals to numbers, he pursued the discovery in another fashion. After suspending two strings—equal and similar and of the same material—he attached on one a weight of three parts, on the other a weight of four parts; when he plucked both, he discovered that they were consonant in accord with the so-called diatessaron consonance. Again, after suspending sesquialteran weights and plucking both, he discovered that they produced a consonance one with another in accord with the diapente consonance. After that, he fastened a duple weight and discovered that the strings produced the consonance of a diapason; with a triple weight, he considered that the strings made a consonant diapason together with the diapente; and likewise for the rest.[20]

But not satisfied only with the experience of these things, he tested the method in another fashion. After stretching a string over a canon and dividing the canon into twelve parts, when he plucked first the whole string and then half of it—i.e., six parts—he discovered that the whole string to the half was consonant in accord with the diapason; just as in the first methods, he per-

19. These particular numbers, rather than the more common Pythagorean pattern of 12:9:8:6, are chosen because Gaudentius wants to include the diapason-and-diatessaron among the consonant intervals. Cassiodorus (*Fundamentals of Sacred and Secular Learning* [*Institutiones;* pp. 143–48]) uses Gaudentius's ratio of 24:9 (although the number 9 has been misrepresented as an 8 in the manuscript tradition) when describing the diapason-and-diatessaron, and similar extensions of the Pythagorean pattern to the number 24 appear in later medieval treatises such as the *Scholica Enchiriadis.* For a useful survey of ancient and medieval views of the diapason-and-diatessaron as a consonance, see André Barbera, "The Consonant Eleventh and the Expansion of the Musical Tetractys: A Study of Ancient Pythagoreanism," *Journal of Music Theory* 28 (1984): 191–223.

20. It is of course well known that this demonstration is invalid because string tensions increase pitch in proportion to the square root of the tension.

ceived it to be in duple ratio. Then, when he plucked the whole string and three parts of the whole, he observed the consonant diatessaron. When he struck the whole string and two parts of the whole, he discovered the consonance of the diapente, and likewise for the others. Then, when he had tested these things in many other fashions, he discovered the same ratios of the consonances exist in the aforesaid numbers.

12. From the aforesaid, it results that the whole-tone interval has the sesquioctaval ratio, for if it is a tone by which the consonant diatessaron differs from the diapente, let a diatessaron of the numbers 6 and 8 and a diapente of the numbers 6 and 9 be posited. The excess of the sesquialteran ratio with respect to the sesquitertian is the ratio, i.e., 8:9. The excess of the diatessaron with respect to the diapente is also a tone. The tone will therefore have this ratio, i.e., 8:9.[21]

13. The so-called semitone is not exactly a semitone. It is commonly called a semitone, but more particularly a "leimma," and it has a ratio, i.e., 243:256. First, it is necessary to consider that the so-called semitone has a ratio, i.e., 243:256; then, that 243:256 comprises an interval that is less than a semitone. Let a certain function of note be presented in the number 64, and let another note be presented next to this, separated by a tone, i.e., 72 in numbers. Then, let a third note be presented next to this, separated by a tone from the second, i.e., 81 in numbers. When a fourth note is taken for the completion of the tetrachord, since a diatessaron consonant with the first is necessary, it will have the sesquitertian ratio to 64, i.e., it will be 85⅓ in numbers. The fourth note to the third will therefore have a ratio of 85⅓ to 81, which in whole numbers is 256:243. In greater numbers, however much completes the remainder of the tetrachord after the two sesquioctaves will fill it out in accord with this ratio, i.e., 243:256.

14. Having considered this, we must say again that this ratio is less than a semitone, for 256:243 is less than 18:17. Combining two 18:17s does not complete a sesquioctave; thus, the ratio 18:17 falls short of being half a sesquioctave. As 256:243 also falls short of 18:17, it would fall even more short of being half a sesquioctave. Therefore, the so-called semitone is less than a true semitone, on which account it is called a leimma, and it has this ratio, i.e., 243:256.

After the leimma, the remainder in the completion of the tone is called "apotome," but it is commonly also called a semitone. So, of semitones, there

---

21. This account is similar though not identical to the account preserved in Nicomachus of Gerasa's *Manual of Harmonics* (*Manuale harmonices*) 6, which may be the source for the later accounts appearing in such treatises as Chalcidius, *Commentary on Plato's Timaeus* (*Commentarii in Platonis Timaeum*) 45; Iamblichus, *Life of Pythagoras* (*Vita Pythagorica*) 26; Censorinus, *On the Day of Birth* (*De die natali*) 10; Macrobius, *Commentary on the Dream of Scipio* (*Commentarii in somnium Scipionis*) 2.1.8; Boethius, *The Fundamentals of Music* (*De institutione musica*) 1.10–11; and Isidore of Seville, *Etymologies* (*Etymologiae*) 3.16.1. For a useful survey of the ancient literature on Pythagoras's discoveries, see Flora Rose Levin, "Nicomachus of Gerasa: *Manual of Harmonics*: Translation and Commentary" (Ph.D. dissertation, Columbia University, 1967), 143–48.

will be the greater and the lesser. The diatonic genus uses the lesser; the chromatic genus uses both.[22]

15. Now that these matters have been set down, let a diatonic diagram of the notes be presented, with the numbers distributed to the notes in the same diagram.[23]

2304	proslambanomenos	648
	9:8	
2048	hypate hypaton	729
	256:243	
1944	parhypate hypaton	768
	9:8	
1728	lichanos hypaton	864
	9:8	
1536	hypate meson	972
	256:243	
1458	parhypate meson	1024
	9:8	
1296	lichanos meson	1152
	9:8	
1152	mese	1296
	9:8	
1024	paramese	1458
	256:243	
972	trite diezeugmenon	1536
	9:8	
864	paranete diezeugmenon	1728
	9:8	
768	nete diezeugmenon	1944
	256:243	
729	trite hyperbolaion	2048
	9:8	
648	paranete hyperbolaion	2304
	9:8	
576	nete hyperbolaion	2592

22. The ratio of the apotome is 2187:2048. Discussion of the leimma and the apotome is best known as preserved in Boethius's *Fundamentals of Music* 3. If the first three or four books of Boethius's treatise are actually a paraphrase of Nicomachus's lost treatise *On Music* (*De musica*), as Calvin Bower has argued ("Boethius and Nicomachus: An Essay Concerning the Sources of *De Institutione Musica*," *Vivarium* 16 [1978]: 1–45), Gaudentius too may have drawn on it for these sections. The presence of this material in Gaudentius—albeit in a shorter and distinct form—may support Bower's argument. On the other hand, Cassiodorus remarks (pp. 143–48) that Gaudentius's treatise was translated into Latin by a certain Mutianus, and it is barely possible that Boethius may have derived his material at least in part from Gaudentius.
23. Once again, the diagram is omitted from the manuscripts, but it can be easily restored from the description that follows.

In the first diagram, when the proslambanomenos is placed on 2304, the hypate hypaton—separated by a tone from the proslambanomenos in accord with its ratio (i.e., 9:8)—is posited as 2048 in numbers. The parhypate hypaton—separated from the hypate by a semitone, which is properly referred to as a leimma, in accord with its ratio (i.e., 256:243)—is reasonably posited as 1944 in numbers. The remaining intervals are likewise presented in accord with the ratios of tones and semitones. In the second diagram, when the proslambanomenos is placed on 648 in numbers, the hypate hypaton is consequently posited as 729 in numbers; the parhypate hypaton is posited as 768 in numbers; and all the other intervals are consequently augmented by tones and semitones in like manner to the first, except that the numbers advance from lesser to greater.

16. Following this, I shall lay out a diagram of the intense chromatic genus that has the notes with the numbers distributed to them. In this, it becomes evident that the chromatic genus uses both semitones, the lesser and the greater, i.e., the leimma and the apotome. Its proslambanomenos begins with the greatest of the numbers, 20736, and the following.[24]

20736	proslambanomenos
	9:8
18432	hypate hypaton
	256:243
17496	parhypate hypaton
	2187:2048
16384	lichanos hypaton
	32:27
13824	hypate meson
	256:243
13122	parhypate meson
	2187:2048
12288	lichanos meson
	32:27
10368	mese
	9:8
9216	paramese
	256:243
8748	trite diezeugmenon
	2187:2048
8192	paranete diezeugmenon
	32:27
6912	nete diezeugmenon
	256:243

24. Here too, the diagram is omitted from the manuscripts, but it can be restored from the description.

6561	trite hyperbolaion
	2187:2048
6144	paranete hyperbolaion
	32:27
5184	nete hyperbolaion

17. Of the eighteen notes, some are stationary and some are movable. These are the stationary: proslambanomenos, hypate hypaton, hypate meson, mese, nete synemmenon, paramese, nete diezeugmenon neton, and nete hyperbolaion neton. These are the movable: the parhypatai and lichanoi and the tritai and paranetai, since in the modulations of the genera, these notes modulate their pitch. Therefore, they add to the common name a particular name, depending on the genus of each; that is to say, one is called enharmonic lichanos meson, chromatic lichanos meson, or diatonic lichanos meson. The same is said for the paranetai, parhypatai, and tritai.[25]

18. I will now take up scales. There are three species or forms of tetrachords. These arise whenever the same magnitude of tetrachords and number of scales is preserved, while only the order and arrangement are altered. The first species is that from hypate hypaton to hypate meson, in which the semitone is first in ascent.[26] The second species is that from parhypate hypaton to parhypate meson, in which the semitone is third in ascent. The third species is that from lichanos to lichanos, in which the semitone is in the middle. And the rest are like these.

There are four species or forms of the fifth. The first species is that from hypate meson to paramese, in which the semitone is first in ascent.[27] The second species is that from parhypate meson to trite diezeugmenon, in which the semitone is the final interval in ascent. The third species is that from lichanos meson to paranete diezeugmenon, in which the semitone is second from the end. The fourth species is from mese to nete diezeugmenon, in which the semitone is second from the beginning.

19. The species or forms of the eight-string diapason extend to twelve because there are three forms of the diatessaron, four forms of the diapente have been shown, and the diapason is combined from both of these. Nevertheless, there are but seven melodic and consonant species and forms of the diapason. We will explain the reason later. The first species is that from hypate hypaton to paramese, compounded of the first of the diatessarons and the first

---

25. With this section, the treatise returns to the largely Aristoxenian tone of sections 1–9. Cf. Cleonides, *Harmonic Introduction* 4 (pp. 37–39) and Aristides Quintilianus, *On Music* 1.6 (pp. 51–53).

26. Jan's text (345.19) reads ἐπὶ τὸ βαρύ, but I am emending it to ἐπὶ τὸ ὀξύ. In Cleonides's treatise these two phrases are used to mean, respectively, "at [*or* from] the bottom" and "at [*or* from] the top"; in this sense, the Greek would require no emendation. Nevertheless, it is clear from Gaudentius's usage elsewhere in the treatise that he takes the two phrases in their more common meaning of "in descent" and "in ascent," which would be incorrect here.

27. Here again, Jan's text (345.26) reads ἐπὶ τὸ βαρύ, and I am emending it to επὶ τὸ ὀξύ.

of the diapentes. The second species is that from parhypate hypaton to trite diezeugmenon, compounded of the second of the diatessarons and the second of the diapentes. The third species is that from lichanos hypaton to paranete diezeugmenon, compounded of the third of the diatessarons and the third of the diapentes. The fourth species is that from hypate meson to nete diezeugmenon, compounded of the first of the diapentes and the first of the diatessarons. The fifth species is that from parhypate meson to trite hyperbolaion, compounded of the second of the diapentes and the second of the diatessarons. The sixth species is that from lichanos meson to paranete hyperbolaion, compounded of the third of the diapentes and the third of the diatessarons. The seventh species is that from mese to nete hyperbolaion or from proslambanomenos to mese, compounded of the fourth of the diapentes and the first of the diatessarons or again of the third of the diatessarons and the fourth of the diapentes. The first species of the diapason is called Mixolydian; the second, Lydian; the third, Phrygian; the fourth, Dorian; the fifth, Hypolydian; the sixth, Hypophrygian; and the seventh is commonly called Locrian or Hypodorian.[28]

20. The ancients used names and letters—the so-called musical signs—for the signification of the eighteen notes; we must now speak on these.[29] The display of musical signs arose for the signing of notes so that the names would not have to be written for each note, and by one sign anyone would be able to recognize the note or sign it for himself. Since the notes move to a different pitch and do not remain altogether in the same position, there was a need not for just one sign in accord with each of the notes but different signs in order to signify its different pitch. In each mode or tonos, all the notes are different from all the others in pitch. For example, when the lowest note by nature is proslambanomenos,[30] as in the Hypodorian mode, we place the mese as antiphonic to it, and we name the other notes in accord with their relationship to these. When we place the mese—now antiphonic to the proslambanomenos—in order as proslambanomenos and hypothesize a mese as antiphonic to it and all the other notes analogously to these, we use the entire scale.[31] Often, when we adopt a certain note between the proslambanomenos and mese as the beginning of the scale, we use it as proslambanomenos, and we fit the pitch of the entire scale with respect to it. When many scales are laid out, it is necessary

28. On these species, cf. Cleonides, *Harmonic Introduction* 9 (pp. 41–43) and Aristides Quintilianus, *On Music* 1.8 (pp. 54–56).

29. By introducing a discussion of notation, Gaudentius departs once again from the Aristoxenian tradition. Aristoxenus states (*Harmonics* 2.39–41) that notation is not even a part of harmonics and that the signs are meaningless because the same sign can indicate completely different functions of notes. Indeed, the "wing diagram" in the treatise of Aristides Quintilianus (p. 64) demonstrates this quite clearly. Gaudentius, of course, recognizes that the same sign may indicate various notes and proceeds to explain the matter.

30. Cf. section 6 above.

31. The Hyperphrygian tonos would have a proslambanomenos equivalent in pitch to the mese of the Hypodorian tonos. Its mese would then be equivalent in pitch to the nete hyperbolaion of the Hypodorian tonos; thus, the "entire scale"—the two octaves—from F to f′ (using the conventional pitching of the fifteen tonoi) would have been used.

in each scale that mese be in relation to mese, or that proslambanomenos be in relation to proslambanomenos, so that every scale in relation to every scale has whichever of the homonymous notes in relation to its homonymous note.[32]

There was a need not for just one sign in accord with each of the notes but many and of sufficient quantity that each of the notes can be augmented by as many semitones as there are. The statement "each of the notes can be augmented by as many semitones as there are" is not easy to construe, for such things are defined in relation to the mechanisms of instruments and the function of the human voice; but from the diagrams in the Introductions to Music, one could easily learn how the augmenting is signified by the different signs.[33]

21. We must now consider the fashion by which the order of the signs by semitone is composed. Let a certain lowest and first-audible function of a note be posited. The ancients notated this with a half-phi on its side, and this was placed first as the beginning of the signs: ⊓.[34] It is evident that the sign should take proslambanomenos as its function and none of the other notes, for if it should take another note, where would proslambanomenos be in order, since the lowest function was posited as the half-phi? Following this note, let there be one a semitone higher. The ancients signified this with the sign tau T. It is evident that the pitch of the note will fit only with the proslambanomenos, for if it will fit with the hypate hypaton or any of the other notes, where will the proslambanomenos remain? Obliged to be a tone lower than the hypate hypaton, it is left with only the locus of a semitone in descent. Once again, let there be a note a semitone higher than the note in accord with T, which the ancients notated with a double sigma Ɛ. This can be proslambanomenos of a scale, and it can be hypaton hypaton; it is separated from the first and lowest note by a tone. Now, always likewise signing the note higher by a semitone than the preceding note, they continued until the thirtieth degree of semitones.[35] They signed the augmentation by semitone of the notes above these with the same signs over again by affixing an acute accent, beginning from the nineteenth degree, which has the sign omicron and kappa.[36] Double signs are placed on

32. These "commonalities" can be most easily seen in the "wing diagram" of Aristides Quintilianus's treatise (p. 64).

33. Cf., for example, the diagram in section 7 of Aristides Quintilianus's treatise (p. 54). It is possible that Gaudentius has in mind a complete set of notational tables, such as is preserved in the tables of Alypius (Jan, 367–406).

34. Cf. the diagram in section 22 below or section 11 of Aristides Quintilianus's treatise (p. 63), beginning with the third symbol in the upper row.

35. In other words, there are thirty pairs of signs indicating various functions of notes and thirty degrees of pitch (in terms of the conventional pitching of the Greek tonoi, from F to a♯′), each separated by a semitone.

36. Omicron and kappa (b, in conventional pitch) are the nineteenth pair of signs in the previous set of thirty. Noted with an acute accent, the pairs 19–27 are repeated after note 30, signifying the same degree an octave higher. Altogether, then, there are thirty-nine pairs of signs indicating various functions and thirty-nine degrees of pitch (F to g″, in conventional pitch). See the diagram in section 22 below.

each degree, of which the upper signifies the diction, the lower the plucking of strings. They also placed the so-called equivalent signs, which can be used indifferently in place of the others; it will make no difference which of the many equivalents is used for the signing. The equivalents have another use in addition: the dieses in the harmonic or chromatic genus are signed by the following placement of these. There is comment on them in the Introductions.[37]

22. Now let the signs be presented to us by semitone on a little canon, along with their equivalents, presenting the equivalents in the same column and the notes higher by semitone in the following column.[38]

The first degree of signs signifying the lowest function among the notes has the signs half-phi on its side ⊐ and reversed half-phi ⊓.

The second degree, higher by a semitone than the first note has the sign reversed upsilon on its side and upsilon on its side: Ⴈ. The equivalents to these, i.e., those signifying the same function among the notes, are reversed tau on its side and upright tau: T.

37. The very points made by Gaudentius can be seen in the diagram in section 22 below and section 11 of Aristides Quintilianus's treatise (p. 63), beginning with the third symbol in the upper row and extending to the end. The symbols in the middle and bottom rows represent the "equivalent signs."

38. As usual, the diagram is missing in the manuscripts, but I have restored it in accord with the tables preserved in the treatise of Aristides Quintilianus and the tables of Alypius. The conventional pitch equivalents are shown in brackets above the Greek symbols.

The third degree, higher than the second by a semitone in accord with the ratio of following degree, has the sign reversed double sigma and double sigma: $\overset{3}{\varepsilon}$.

The fourth degree has reversed rho and omega: $\overset{d}{\omega}$. Equivalent to these in the fourth degree are inverted pi and reversed double sigma: $\overset{\sqcup}{3}$.

The fifth, likewise higher than the fourth by a semitone—all the following degrees differ from the others by a semitone—, has the signs omicron with a downward stroke and eta: $\overset{\varphi}{H}$.

The sixth degree has reversed double xi and inverted double pi: $\overset{M}{H}$; equivalent to these are opposite-nu and double pi: $\overset{N}{A}$.

The signs of the Hypolydian mode in accord with the diatonic genus[39]

Proslambanomenos, omicron with a downward stroke and eta	$\overset{\varphi}{H}$
Hypate hypaton, inverted mu and defective eta	$\overset{W}{h}$
Parhypate hypaton, inverted alpha and supine defective eta	$\overset{\vee}{\mathsf{L}}$
Diatonic hypaton, defective zeta and tau on its side	$\overset{7}{\vdash}$
Hypate meson, reversed gamma and upright gamma	$\overset{\daleth}{\Gamma}$
Parhypate meson, defective beta and inverted gamma	$\overset{R}{L}$
Diatonic meson, phi and digamma	$\overset{\varphi}{F}$
Mese, sigma and sigma	$\overset{C}{C}$
Trite synemmenon, rho and inverted sigma	$\overset{P}{U}$
Diatonic synemmenon, mu and pi drawn outward	$\overset{M}{\sqcap}$
Nete synemmenon, iota and lambda on its side	$\overset{I}{<}$

39. It is probably no coincidence that Gaudentius begins his display with the Hypolydian because the Lydian tonoi most closely represent the "natural" form of the notational symbols, each of which is described in the simple terms of its letter shape. These same sorts of descriptions appear in the tables of Alypius. Gaudentius's treatise probably originally contained a full set of the notational tables, most likely identical or nearly identical to the tables of Alypius. In Jan's text, the symbols for the Aeolian and Hypoaeolian tonoi are missing, but they are indeed present in many of the manuscripts. Although this treatise and the tables of Alypius certainly date no earlier than the second century C.E., the notational symbols appear in surviving pieces of music beginning in the third century B.C.E.

Paramese, omicron and kappa O K

Trite diezeugmenon, xi and inverted kappa Ξ Λ

Diatonic diezeugmenon, iota and lambda on its side I <

Nete diezeugmenon, zeta and pi on its side Z Ⴑ

Trite hyperbolaion, square epsilon and inverted pi E �

Diatonic hyperbolaion, supine square omega and and zeta ᴗ Z

Nete hyperbolaion, phi on its side and careless eta Ⴔ Ɣ

The signs of the Hyperlydian mode in accord with the diatonic genus

Proslambanomenos, phi and digamma Ⴔ F

Hypate hypaton, sigma and sigma C C

Parhypate hypaton, rho and inverted sigma P ∪

Diatonic hypaton, mu and pi drawn outward M Ⴄ

Hypate meson, iota and lambda on its side I <

Parhypate meson, theta and inverted lambda Θ ᴠ

Diatonic meson, gamma and nu Γ N

Mese, supine square omega and and zeta ᴗ Z

Trite synemmenon, psi inclining downwards and right half-alpha ⅄ ↘

Diatonic synemmenon, inverted tau and right half-alpha inclining

   upwards ⊥ ↗

Nete synemmenon, mu and pi drawn outward, with an acute accent M′ Ⴄ′

Paramese, phi on its side and careless eta drawn outward Ⴔ Ɣ

Trite diezeugmenon, upsilon inclined downwards and left half-alpha

   inclined upwards ↓ ↖

Diatonic diezeugmenon, mu and pi drawn outward, with an acute accent   M′ Π′

Nete diezeugmenon, iota and lambda on its side, with an acute accent   I′ ＜′

Trite hyperbolaion, theta and inverted lambda, with an acute accent   Θ′ Ｖ′

Diatonic hyperbolaion, gamma and nu, with an acute accent   Γ′ Ｎ′

Nete hyperbolaion, square omega and and zeta, with an acute accent   Ц′ Ｚ′

The signs of the Aeolian mode in accord with the diatonic genus

Proslambanomenos, reversed defective eta and reversed square epsilon   ⅂ Ǝ

Hypate hypaton, inverted delta and inverted tau on its side   ⴸ ⊤

Parhypate hypaton, reversed gamma and upright gamma   ⅂ Γ

Diatonic hypaton, chi and right half-mu   Ⅹ ⅄

Hypate meson, tau and reversed digamma   ⊤ ⅎ

Parhypate meson, sigma and sigma   C C

Diatonic meson, omicron and kappa   O Κ

Mese, kappa and half-delta drawn outward   Κ ⋋

Trite synemmenon, iota and lambda on its side   I ＜

Diatonic synemmenon, zeta and pi on its side   Z ⊏

Nete synemmenon, alpha and grave accent   A ＼

Paramese, eta and reversed lambda on its side   H ＞

Trite diezeugmenon, zeta and pi on its side   Z ⊏

Diatonic diezeugmenon, alpha and grave accent   A ＼

Nete diezeugmenon, cancelled chi and half-alpha inclining downwards   ✕ ⟋

Trite hyperbolaion, phi on its side and careless eta drawn outward   ⴲ Ⴟ

Diatonic hyperbolaion, omicron and kappa, with an acute accent

$$\overset{\text{o}'}{\text{κ}'}$$

Nete hyperbolaion, kappa and half-delta drawn outward, with an acute

accent

$$\overset{\text{κ}'}{\text{λ}'}$$

The signs of the Hypoaeolian mode in accord with the diatonic genus

Proslambanomenos, inverted pi and reversed double sigma

Hypate hypaton, opposite-nu and double pi

Parhypate hypaton, inverted mu and defective eta

Diatonic hypaton, reversed defective eta and reversed square epsilon

Hypate meson, inverted delta and reversed tau on its side

7 Athenaeus

A Greek rhetorician and grammarian of Naucratis in Egypt, Athenaeus flourished in Rome about 200 C.E. As it survives, the *Deipnosophistae (Sophists at
Dinner)* is arranged in fifteen books, but there may originally have been thirty
books. It is an immense mine of information on matters connected with everyday life, the table, music, songs, dances, games, literature, and more. Its value
as source material cannot be overestimated, as it is filled with quotations from
writers whose works have not been otherwise preserved. In all, Athenaeus refers
to some 1,250 authors and quotes more than ten thousand lines of verse. The
work professes to be an account given by the author to his friend Timocrates of
twenty-three learned men dining together on several occasions at the house of
Laurentius, a scholar and wealthy patron of art.

FROM THE *Sophists at Dinner*
14 (623e–628c and 631e–633f)

On the subject of music there was daily conversation, some saying things recorded here, others saying other things, but all joining in praise of this kind of amusement,[1] and Masurius, in all things excellent and wise (for he is a jurist second to none, and he has always been devoted to music and has taken up the playing of musical instruments), said: The comic poet Eupolis, my friends, remarks: "Music is a matter deep and intricate," and it is always supplying something new for those who can perceive. Hence Anaxilas, also, says in *Hyacinthus:* "Music is like Libya, which, I swear by the gods, brings forth some new creature every year." To quote *The Harp-Singer* of Theophilus: "A mighty treasure, good sirs, and a constant one, is music for all who have learned it and are educated." For indeed it trains character, and tames the hot-tempered and those whose opinions clash. The Pythagorean Cleinias, for example, as Chamaeleon of Pontus records, whose conduct and character were exemplary, would always take his lyre and play on it whenever it happened that he was exasperated to the point of anger. And in answer to those who inquired the reason he would say, "I am calming myself down." So, too, the Homeric Achilles calmed himself with his kithara,[2] which was the only thing Homer grants to him out of the booty taken from Eëtion, and which had the power of allaying his fiery nature. He, at least, is the only one in the *Iliad* who plays this kind of music.[3] That music can also heal diseases Theophrastus has recorded in his work *On Inspiration:* he says that persons subject to sciatica would always be free from its attacks if one played the aulos[4] in the Phrygian harmonia[5] over the part affected. This harmonia was first discovered by the Phrygians and constantly used by them. For this reason, he says, aulos-players among the Greeks have names which are Phrygian and appropriate to slaves; such, for example, is Sambas, mentioned by Alcman, also Adôn and Têlus, and in Hippo-

---

TEXT: English translation by Charles Burton Gulick. Reprinted by permission of the publishers and the Loeb Classical Library from Athenaeus, *The Deipnosophists*, vol. 6, trans. Charles Burton Gulick, Loeb Classical Library, vol. 327 (Cambridge, Mass.: Harvard University Press, 1959), 361–87 and 409–19. Gulick's translation is extensively annotated, and the reader is advised to consult the original publication for fuller documentation of the various material quoted by Athenaeus. In addition to providing explanatory comment on the text, my own footnotes will record any significant departures from Gulick's translation.

1. On this term, see p. 24, n. 1.
2. Gulick translates "lyre" once again, but here the Greek reads τῇ κιθάρᾳ. See *Iliad* 9.186–88. Cf. Sextus Empiricus, *Against the Musicians* (*Adversus musicos*) 9 and 19 (pp. 97–98 and 101).
3. This, of course, is not true; see *Iliad* 3.54 and 18.570. [Tr.]
4. Gulick translates "flute," but I have translated the term as "aulos" (or the appropriate compound) throughout. See pp. 11–12, n. 10.
5. Gulick translates "mode," but I have translated the term as "harmonia" throughout. See p. 10, n. 3.

nax, Cion, Codalus, and Babys, who occasioned the proverb said of those whose aulos-playing grows ever worse and worse, "Babys is playing worse." Aristoxenus attributes its invention to the Phrygian Hyagnis.[6]

Heracleides of Pontus, however, says in the third book of his work *On Music* that the Phrygian should not be called a separate harmonia any more than the Lydian. For there are only three harmoniai, since there are also only three kinds of Greeks—Dorians, Aeolians, and Ionians. There is no small difference in the ethoses[7] of these three, for while the Lacedaemonians preserve better than all other Dorians the customs of their fathers, and the Thessalians (these are they who conferred upon the Aeolians the origin of their race) have always maintained practically the same mode of life, the great majority of the Ionians, on the other hand, have undergone changes due to barbarian rulers who have for the time being come in contact with them. Hence the style of melody which the Dorians constructed they called the Dorian harmonia, Aeolian they called the harmonia which the Aeolians sang, Ionian, they said of the third one, which they heard Ionians sing. Now the Dorian harmonia exhibits the quality of manly vigor, of magnificent bearing, not relaxed or merry, but sober and intense, neither varied nor complicated. But the Aeolian ethos contains the elements of ostentation and turgidity, and even conceit; these qualities are in keeping with their horse-breeding and their way of meeting strangers, yet this does not mean malice, but is, rather, lofty and confident. Hence also their fondness for drinking is something appropriate to them, also their love-affairs, and the entirely relaxed nature of their daily life. Wherefore they have the ethos of the Hypodorian harmonia, as it is called. This, Heracleides says, is in fact the one which they called Aeolian, as Lasus of Hermionê does in the *Hymn to Demeter of Hermion* in the following words: "I celebrate Demeter and Korê, wedded wife of Pluto, raising unto them a sweet-voiced hymn in the deep-toned Aeolian harmonia." These mele[8] are sung by all in the Hypodorian. Since, then, the melos is Hypodorian, it naturally follows that Lasus calls the harmonia Aeolian. Again, Pratinas says, I believe: "Pursue neither the intense Muse nor yet the relaxed Ionian, but ploughing rather the middle glebe play the melos in the Aeolian."[9] And in what follows he says more plainly: "Verily the Aeolian harmonia is the song that befits all the bold."[10] Formerly, then, as

6. Hyagnis was the father of Marsyas. Cf. Plato, *Republic (Respublica)* 3.10 (p. 12) and Aristotle, *Politics (Politica)* 8.5–6 (pp. 28 and 32). On Aristoxenus, see p. 44, n. 16.
7. Gulick translates "characters," but I have translated the term as "ethos" throughout. See pp. 13–14, n. 21.
8. Gulick translates "lyrics," but I have translated the term as "melos" (or "mele" in the plural) throughout. See p. 10, n. 2.
9. Gulick translates "play the Aeolian with your tune."
10. Since Dorian, Aeolian, and Ionian are the only harmoniai under discussion in this paragraph, we may perhaps take "the intense Muse" as referring to Dorian—or at least assume that the phrase was so understood by Heracleides or Athenaeus. But no matter how we take it and regardless of whether we understand the lines in a modal or in a tonal sense, the characterization of Aeolian as intermediate will be unintelligible unless we assume, as Gulick implies (6:369), that it refers not to pitch or structure but to ethical quality.

I have said, they called it Aeolian, but later Hypodorian, as some assert, because they thought that in the auloi it had a range below the Dorian harmonia.[11] But I believe that people who observed the turgid quality and pretence of nobleness in the ethoses of the Aeolian harmonia, regarded it not as Dorian at all, but something which somehow resembled the Dorian, hence they called it Hypodorian, just as we say that what resembles white is rather (hypo-) white, or what is not sweet, yet nearly sweet, rather (hypo-) sweet: in similar fashion they called Hypodorian that which was not quite Dorian.

Next in order let us examine the Milesians' ethos, which the Ionians illustrate. Because of their excellent physical condition they bear themselves haughtily, they are full of irate spirit, hard to placate, fond of contention, never condescending to kindliness nor cheerfulness, displaying a lack of affection and a hardness in their ethoses. Hence also the kind of harmonia known as the Ionian is neither bright nor cheerful, but austere and hard, having a seriousness which is not ignoble, and so their harmonia is well adapted to tragedy. But the ethoses of the Ionians today are more voluptuous, and the ethos of their harmonia is much altered. They say that Pythermus of Teos composed scolia mele in this kind of harmonia, and since the poet was an Ionian the harmonia was called Ionian. This is the Pythermus mentioned by Ananius or Hipponax in their *Iambic Verses:* . . . And in another passage as follows: "Pythermus speaks of gold as if other things were naught." In fact Pythermus does speak of it thus: "Other things, after all, are naught compared with gold." And so, considering also this saying of his, it is to be believed that Pythermus, being from Ionia, made the style of his mele fit the ethoses of the Ionians. Hence I assume that it was not the Ionian harmonia in which Pythermus composed, but a curious variation of the form of the harmonia.[12] So one should look with disdain on those who cannot see specific differences, but simply attend to the highness or lowness of notes, and assume a Hypermixolydian harmonia and again another higher than that. Nor can I see, in fact, that the Hyperphrygian has a special ethos of its own. And yet some persons assert that they have discovered another new, Hypophrygian, harmonia! But a harmonia must have a species of ethos or affection,[13] like the Locrian; this was once employed by some who flourished in the time of Simonides and Pindar, but it fell into disrepute again.[14]

These harmoniai, then, are three, as we said of them at the beginning, being as many as there are tribes of Greeks. The Phrygian and the Lydian harmoniai, originating with the barbarians, came to be known to the Greeks from the

11. See Aristoxenus, *Harmonics* (*Harmonica*) 2.37, where Aristoxenus explains that those predecessors of his who based their enumeration of the tonoi on the boring of the finger-holes on the auloi placed the Hypodorian tonos three dieses below the Dorian.

12. Gulick translates "variation of modal figure."

13. Gulick translates "specific character or feeling." On "species" and "affection" (εἶδος and πάθος), see p. 12, n. 14, and p. 28, n. 10.

14. This polemic against those who presume to add to the established harmoniai is well discussed by Reginald P. Winnington-Ingram in *Mode in Ancient Greek Music* (London: Cambridge University Press, 1936; reprint, Amsterdam: Hakkert, 1968), 20–21.

Phrygians and Lydians who emigrated to Peloponnesus with Pelops. The Lydians accompanied him because Sipylus was a city of Lydia; the Phrygians came not only because they lived on the borders of Lydia but also because Tantalus ruled over them. You may see everywhere in Peloponnesus, but especially in Lacedaemon, large mounds, which they call the tombs of the Phrygians who came with Pelops. These musical harmoniai, then, the Greeks learned from them. Hence also Telestes of Selinus says: "The first to sing the Phrygian nomos in honor of the Mountain Mother, amid the auloi beside the mixing-bowls of the Greeks, were they who came in the company of Pelops; and the Greeks struck up the Lydian hymn with the high-pitched twanging of the pektis."[15]

Polybius of Megalopolis says:[16] "One must not accept it as fact that music was introduced among men for purposes of deceit and quackery, as Ephorus asserts that it was, nor should one believe that the ancient Cretans and Lacedaemonians introduced the aulos and a marching rhythm into battle, instead of the salpinx,[17] without good reason; nor was it by chance that the earliest Arcadians carried music into their entire social organization, so that they made it obligatory and habitual not only for boys but also for young men up to thirty years of age, although in all other respects they were most austere in their habits of life. It is only among the Arcadians, at any rate, that the boys, from infancy up, are by law practiced in singing hymns and paeans, in which, according to ancestral custom, they celebrate their national heroes and gods. After these they learn the nomoi of Timotheus and Philoxenus[18] and dance them annually in the theatres with Dionysiac aulos-players, the boys competing in the boys' contests, the young men in the contests of adult males. And throughout their whole lives, in their social gatherings they do not pursue methods and practices so much with the aid of imported entertainments as with their own talents, requiring one another to sing each in his turn. As for other branches of training, it is no disgrace to confess that one knows nothing, but it is deemed a disgrace among them to decline to sing. What is more, they practice marching-songs with aulos accompaniment in regular order, and further, they drill themselves in dances and display them annually in the theatres with elaborate care and at public expense. All this, therefore, the men of old taught them, not to gratify luxury and wealth, but because they observed

15. On the pektis, see p. 11, n. 9. A "nomos" is a type of musical composition. Descriptions of specific nomoi that appear in various sources suggest a style of great complexity, associated with virtuoso performers. At least four types of nomoi can be identified: two are sung to the accompaniment of a kithara or an aulos, and two are performed by a solo kitharist or aulete.

16. *History* (*Historiae*) 4.20.5–21.9.

17. Gulick translates "trumpet." Pollux devotes considerable attention to the salpinx in his *Onomasticon*. He describes it as either straight or curved in form. The instrument is made of bronze and iron, with a bone mouthpiece. Its sound is described as booming, roaring, loud, clear, stout, powerful, deep, solemn, violent, frightening, terrifying, warlike and hostile, forceful, stark, weighty, rough, and troubling. Pollux also comments on the various signals played by the salpinx in its military role—such as encouragement, advance, and retreat—as well as its use for fanfares and other signals in various contexts.

18. See p. 34, n. 34.

the hardness in every one's life and the austerity of their ethoses, which are the natural accompaniment of the coldness of their environment and the gloominess prevailing for the most part in their abodes; for all of us human beings naturally become assimilated to the character of our abode; hence it is also differences in our national position that cause us to differ very greatly from one another in ethos, in build, and in complexion. In addition to the training just described, their ancestors taught the Arcadian men and women the practice of public assembly and sacrifice, also at the same time choruses of girls and boys, eager as they were to civilize and soften the toughness of their natures by customs regularly organized. But the people of Cynaetha came at the end to neglect these customs, although they occupied by far the rudest part of Arcadia in point of topography as well as climate; when they plunged right into friction and rivalry with one another they finally became so brutalized that among them alone occurred the gravest acts of sacrilege. At the time when they brought upon themselves the great massacre, into whatever Arcadian cities they went on their way through, all the others immediately barred them out by public proclamation, but the Mantinaeans, after their withdrawal, instituted a purification of their city, carrying the blood of slain animals round about their entire territory."

Agias, the musician,[19] has said that storax, which is burned as incense in the orchestras at the festival of Dionysus, produces a "Phrygian" odor to those who smell it.

In ancient times music was an incitement to bravery.[20] At any rate the poet Alcaeus, who certainly was very musical, if any one ever was, places deeds of bravery higher than the achievements of poetry, since he was more than ordinarily warlike. Wherefore, pluming himself on these activities, he says: "The great hall glistens with bronze, the whole roof is adorned by the War-god with shining helmets, and over them wave white plumes of horsehair, adornments for the heads of heroes, shining greaves of bronze, defence against the cruel missiles, hide the pegs on which they hang; corslets of new linen and hollow shields lie scattered on the ground, and beside them are Chalcidic swords, beside them, too, many sashes and tunics. These we must not forget, now that before all else we have set ourselves to this task." And yet it doubtless would have been more fitting for his house to be full of musical instruments. However, the men of old assumed that bravery is the highest of civic virtues, and to this they thought it right to allot most honors . . . not to other men. Archilochus, at any rate, who was an excellent poet, made it his first boast that he was able to take part in these civic rivalries, and only secondarily mentioned his poetic talents, saying: "I am the squire of the lord Enyalius, and I am versed, too, in the lovely gift of the Muses." Similarly Aeschylus also, for all the great repute which he enjoys because of his poetry, none the less thought it right to have

19. Gulick translates "the writer on music." See p. 10, n. 5.
20. But cf. Sextus Empiricus, *Against the Musicians* 18 (p. 100).

his bravery recorded by preference on his tomb, having composed this inscription: "Of his glorious might the grove at Marathon could tell, and the long-haired Medes—for they know!"

Hence it is that the brave Lacedaemonians march to battle with auloi, the Cretans with the lyre, the Lydians with syrinxes[21] and the auloi, as Herodotus records.[22] Many of the barbarians also conduct diplomatic negotiations to the accompaniment of the auloi and kithara to soften the hearts of their opponents. Theopompus, in the forty-sixth book of his *Histories,* says: "The Getae conduct negotiations holding kitharas in their hands and playing on them." Whence it is plain that Homer observes the ancient Greek system when he says: "and with the phorminx, which the gods have made companion to the bounteous feast,"[23] evidently because the art is beneficial also to those who feast. And this was the accepted custom, it is plain, first in order that every one who felt impelled to get drunk and stuff himself might have music to cure his violence and intemperance, and secondly, because music appeases surliness; for, by stripping off a man's gloominess, it produces good-temper and gladness becoming to a gentleman, wherefore Homer introduced the gods, in the first part of the *Iliad,* making use of music. For after their quarrel over Achilles, they spent the time continually listening "to the beautiful phorminx that Apollo held, and to the Muses who sang responsively with beautiful voice."[24] For that was bound to stop their bickerings and faction, as we were saying. It is plain, therefore, that while most persons devote this art to social gatherings for the sake of correcting conduct and of general usefulness, the ancients went further and included in their customs and laws the singing of praises to the gods by all who attended feasts, in order that our dignity and sobriety might be retained through their help. For, when the songs are enharmonic,[25] if discourse on the gods has been added it dignifies the mood of every one. Philochorus says that the ancients, in pouring libations, do not always sing dithyrambs, but when they pour libations, they celebrate Dionysus with wine and drunkenness,[26] but Apollo, in quiet and good order. Archilochus, at any rate, says: "For I know how to lead off, in the lovely song of lord Dionysus, the dithyramb, when my wits have been stricken with the thunder-bolt of wine." And Epicharmus, also, said in *Philoctetes:* "There can be no dithyramb when you drink water." It is plain, therefore, in

21. Gulick: "Pan's-pipes." See p. 12, n. 12.
22. *History* 1.17.
23. Athenaeus conflates *Odyssey* 8.99 and 17.270–71. Gulick translates: "(We have satisfied our souls with the equal feast) and with the lyre, which the gods have made the companion of the feast." "Phorminx" is used in early Greek literature as a general term for instruments of the lyre class. In more specific terms, it may refer to a lyre with a rounded base and straight, fairly substantial arms, such as is already depicted in painting and statuary prior to 800 B.C.E. The phorminx was strongly associated with Apollo and the Muses, the Homeric heroes, and the bards Phemius and Demodocus.
24. *Iliad* 1.603–4.
25. Gulick translates: "since the songs are sung in concert," but this ignores Athenaeus's obvious and appropriate technical description.
26. Cf. p. 34, n. 34.

the light of what we have said, that music did not, at the beginning, make its
way into feasts merely for the sake of shallow and ordinary pleasure, as some
persons think. As for the Lacedaemonians, if they studied music, they say nothing of it, but that they are able to judge the art well is admitted by them, and
in fact they assert that they have saved the art three times when it was threatened with debasement.[27]

. . . . .

In olden times the feeling for nobility was always maintained in music, and all
its elements skillfully retained the orderly beauty appropriate to them. Hence
there were auloi peculiarly adapted to every harmonia, and every player had
auloi suited to every harmonia used in the public contests. But Pronomus of
Thebes began the practice of playing all the harmoniai on the same auloi.
Today, however, people take up music in a haphazard and irrational manner.
In early times popularity with the masses was a sign of bad art; hence, when a
certain aulos-player once received loud applause, Asopodorus of Phlius, who
was himself still waiting in the wings, said "What's this? Something awful must
have happened!" The player evidently could not have won approval with the
crowd otherwise. (I am aware that some persons have narrated this story with
Antigeneidas as the speaker.) And yet the musicians of our day set as the goal
of their art success with their audiences. Hence Aristoxenus in his *Drinking-
Miscellany* says: "We act like the people of Poseidonia, who dwell on the Tyr-
rhenian Gulf. It so happened that although they were originally Greeks, they
were completely barbarized, becoming Tuscans or Romans; they changed their
speech and their other practices, but they still celebrate one festival that is
Greek to this day, wherein they gather together and recall those ancient words
and institutions, and after bewailing them and weeping over them in one
another's presence they depart home. In like manner we also, says Aristoxenus,
now that our theatres have become utterly barbarized and this prostituted
music has moved on into a state of grave corruption, will get together by ourselves, few though we be, and recall what music used to be." So much for what
Aristoxenus says.

In view of this it is plain to me also that music should be the subject of philosophic reflection. Pythagoras of Samos, with all his great fame as a philosopher,[28] is one of many conspicuous for having taken up music as no mere hobby;
on the contrary, he explains the very being of the universe as bound together by
musical principles. Taking it all together, it is plain that the ancient "wisdom" of
the Greeks was given over especially to music. For this reason they regarded
Apollo, among the gods, and Orpheus, among the demigods, as most musical

27. Cf. Aristotle, *Politics* 8.5 (p. 27). Athenaeus is presumably alluding to the abuses of Terpander,
   Timotheus, and Phrynis. Boethius (*The Fundamentals of Music* [*De institutione musica*] 1.1)
   transmits the famous Spartan decree expelling Timotheus for corrupting "the ears of our
   youth."
28. On Pythagoras, see pp. 74–75.

and most wise; and they called all who followed this art sophists, as Aeschylus has done: "Then the sophist wildly struck his tortoise-shell lyre with notes discordant." And that the men of old were disposed to treat music with the greatest familiarity is clear also from Homer; why, in setting all his poetry to music he often, without thought, composes verses which are "acephalous," or "slack," or even "taper off at the end." But Xenophanes, Solon, Theognis, Phocylides, also the Corinthian elegiac poet Periander and other poets who do not add melody to their poetry, finish off their verses in respect of the counting and the arrangement of the metrical feet, and see to it that not one of them is either acephalous or slack or tapering. Acephalous verses are those which have the quality of lameness at the beginning: "When they had come to the ships and to the Hellespont." "A strap lay stretched upon it, made of a slaughtered ox's hide." Slack verses are lame in the middle, as for example: "Then quickly Aeneas, dear son of Anchises." "Their leaders, again, were the two sons of Asclepius." Tapering verses limp at the close: "The Trojans shivered when they saw the wriggling snake." "Fair Cassiepeia, like unto the gods in form." "With this wine I filled a mighty goat-skin and carried it, with provisions as well."

Of all the Greeks the Spartans have most faithfully preserved music, employing it most extensively, and many composers of mele have arisen among them. Even to this day they carefully retain the ancient songs, and are very well taught in them and strict in holding to them. Hence Pratinas says: "The Spartan, that cicada ready for a chorus." Wherefore, also, their poets continually addressed songs in terms like these: "Leader of sweetest hymns," and "Mellifluous mele of the Muses." For people were glad to turn from the soberness and austerity of life to the solace of music, because the art has the power to charm. With good reason, therefore, the listeners enjoyed it.

Demetrius of Byzantium, in the fourth book of his work *On Poetry,* says that they used to employ the term *choregi,* not, as today, of the men who hired the choruses, but of those who led the chorus, as the etymology of the word denotes.[29]

Also, it was customary to practice good music and not violate the ancient rules of the art.

It happened that in ancient times the Greeks were music-lovers; but later, with the breakdown of order, when practically all the ancient customs fell into decay, this devotion to principle ceased, and debased fashions in music came to light, wherein every one who practiced them substituted effeminacy for gentleness, and license and looseness for moderation. What is more, this fashion will doubtless be carried further if some one does not bring the music of our forebears once more to open practice. For in ancient times it was the acts of heroes and hymns to the gods that the poets put to song. Homer, for example, says of Achilles: "And he was singing the glorious deeds of men,"[30] that is, of

29. Cf. Aristotle, *Politics* (p. 31).
30. *Iliad* 9.189.

heroes. And of Phemius he says: "He knoweth many charms for mortals, deeds of men and of gods, which minstrels celebrate."[31] This custom was kept up also among the barbarians, as Dinon declares in his *Persian History*. It was the singers, for example, that foresaw the courage of the first Cyrus and the war he was to wage against Astyages. "It was at the time (says Dinon) when Cyrus requested permission to visit Persia (he had previously been in charge of Asty-ages' rod-bearers, and later of his men-at-arms) and had departed; Astyages, therefore, celebrated a feast in company with his friends, and on that occasion a man named Angarês (he was the most distinguished of the singers) was invited, and not only began to sing other customary songs but also, at the last, he told how that a mighty beast had been let loose in the swamp, bolder than a wild boar; which beast, if it got the mastery of the regions round it, would soon contend against a multitude without difficulty. And when Astyages asked, 'What beast?' he replied, 'Cyrus the Persian.' Believing, therefore, that his sus-picion about him had been correct, he kept summoning him to return . . . it did no good."

Though I might say many things more on music, I hear the buzzing[32] of the auloi, and will therefore bring my long-winded discourse to a close, after repeating the lines from *The Aulos-Lover* of Philetaerus: "Zeus, it's indeed a fine thing to die to the music of the auloi. For only to such is it permitted in Hades to revel in love affairs, whereas those whose manners are sordid, having no knowledge of music, must carry water to the leaky jar."

31. *Odyssey* 1.337.
32. Gulick: "loud trill."

8 Sextus Empiricus

The writings of Sextus Empiricus, a physician and philosopher of the second century C.E., preserve the most complete treatment of ancient Pyrrhonian Skepti-cism, as well as an application of these methods to the three divisions of philos-ophy—logic, physics, and ethics—and the six cyclical studies of the ancient educational curriculum: grammar, rhetoric, geometry, arithmetic, astrology, and music. Today, Sextus Empiricus's skeptic examinations of these disciplines are known under the general title *Adversus mathematicos (Against the Professors)*. By deflating the dogmatic claims of the professors, Sextus Empiricus shows the impossibility of absolute knowledge. For the skeptic, this leads first to the sus-pension of judgment and ultimately to *ataraxia*—unperturbedness or quietude.

Adversus musicos (*Against the Musicians*), the sixth book of *Adversus mathe-maticos,* is preserved in twenty-eight manuscripts. The treatise is divided into two large sections, preceded by an introduction. In the first section, Sextus Empiricus considers and refutes the theoretical claims of musicians; in the second, he counters practical observations about music with arguments that suggest their inadequacy. Finally, by demonstrating that it is impossible to know either sound or time, he shows that there can be no science of music at all.

Many of the definitions and observations quoted or paraphrased by Sextus Empiricus will be familiar from the other writings in this collection, but Sextus Empiricus also draws on the Epicurean philosopher Philodemus of Gadara (fl. first century B.C.E.), the famous Latin rhetor Marcus Fabius Quintilianus (fl. first century C.E.), and the philosopher and biographer Plutarch (ca. 50–120 C.E.). Like a good physician, Sextus Empiricus supplies in his treatise a useful antidote to the other Greek views of music.

Against the Musicians

1. The term "music" is used in three manners:[1] according to one manner, it is a science concerned with melodies, notes, rhythmic compositions, and parallel subjects[2]—as we say that Aristoxenus,[3] the son of Spintharus, is a musician; according to another manner, it is the science concerned with instrumental experience,[4] as when we name those who use auloi and psalteries musicians and female harpers musicians.[5] Properly and among the many, "music" is used in accord with these very senses.

2. Sometimes, we are accustomed to refer—rather improperly—with the

---

TEXT: Translation reprinted from Sextus Empiricus, *Against the Musicians,* a new critical text and translation by Denise Davidson Greaves, Greek and Latin Music Theory, vol. 3 (Lincoln: University of Nebraska Press, 1986), 121–81. Copyright 1986 by the University of Nebraska Press. All the annotations (with the exception of cross-references to other parts of this volume) are by Greaves, but some of them have been shortened and only a portion of them have been preserved in this edition. The reader is advised to consult the original publication for much fuller documentation and explanations.

1. For definitions of music (μουσική), cf. Aristides Quintilianus, *On Music (De musica)* 1.4 (pp. 48–49) and Cleonides, *Harmonic Introduction (Harmonica introductio)* 1 (pp. 35–36).
2. The arrangement of the harmonic division of music into the seven parts of genera, intervals, notes, scales, tonoi, modulation, and melic composition is Aristoxenian. See Aristoxenus, *Harmonics (Harmonica)* 2.35–38; but cf. Cleonides, *Harmonic Introduction* 1 (p. 36) and Aristides Quintilianus, *On Music* 1.5 (pp. 49–50). In Aristides Quintilianus, *On Music* 1.13, rhythmics is divided into five parts: chronoi protoi, genera of metric feet, tempo, modulation, and rhythmic composition.
3. Cf. p. 44, n. 16.
4. In Graeco-Roman theory, music is generally divided into two main divisions: theoretical and practical. These broadly correspond to the first two uses of the term "music" that Sextus Empiricus offers here. Cf. Cleonides, *Harmonic Introduction* 1 (pp. 35–36) and Aristides Quintilianus, *On Music* 1.5 (pp. 49–50).
5. On various types of instruments, see pp. 11–12, nn. 9–10; and p. 32, n. 24.

same word to successful accomplishment in some subject. So, we say that something is musical even if it exists as a part of a painting and that the painter accomplished in this is musical.[6]

3. But even though music is conceived in so many manners, it is now proposed to make a refutation, by Zeus, not against any other music than that conceived in accord with the first sense. For this music, in comparison with the other senses of music, seems to have been established as most complete.[7]

4. The type of refutation, just as in the case of grammar, is twofold. Some undertook to teach rather dogmatically[8] that music is not a necessary subject of learning for good fortune[9] but is a harmful one rather, and they undertook to show this both by bringing into discredit things stated by the musicians and by claiming their leading arguments to be worthy of denial. Others, standing aloof in a more questioning fashion[10] from every such refutation, in shaking the principal suppositions of the musicians thought to abolish the whole of music.

5. For this reason, we too, so as not to seem to minimize anything of the elucidation, will methodically discuss rather systematically the character of each doctrine or subject,[11] neither going beyond the bounds into long expositions on extraneous matters nor falling short with respect to the display of pressing matters in the more necessary areas, but making the elucidation as moderate and measured as possible.

6. First in order, let us begin with the things customarily babbled about

---

6. On the painting analogy, cf. Aristides Quintilianus, *On Music* 2.4 and 3.8. Aristides Quintilianus, *On Music* 1.1 states that it is a function of music to organize harmoniously all things that have a nature. On the use of musical principles to judge things not musical in the proper sense, note Aristotle, *Politics* (*Politica*) 8.5 (p. 29). Music in its broad sense includes all the arts and sciences over which the Muses preside. Thus, the term "musical" (μουσικός) could be used to refer to someone educated generally, whereas "unmusical" (ἄμουσος) was used of one uneducated. Cf. Plato, *Republic* (*Respublica*) 3.18 (pp. 18–19).

7. The music that occupied the philosophers and was incorporated into the theory of paideia was a science rather than a practical art. Cf. Plato, *Republic* 7.12 (530d–531c) and Aristides Quintilianus, *On Music* 1.1, 2.1, and 3.27.

8. E.g., the Cynics in Diogenes Laertius 6.104; Epicurus in Sextus Empiricus *Against the Professors* (*Adversus mathematicos*) 1.1–5; and Philodemus, to sections of whose *On Music* (*De musica*) a significant portion of the first part of *Against the Professors* corresponds. For fuller detail, see Greaves, 24–26.

9. Εὐδαιμονία (good fortune) is important in the argument because it was the aim of some of the major philosophical schools that Sextus Empiricus is undertaking to refute throughout his writings. In connection with εὐδαιμονία, Sextus Empiricus mentions specifically the Epicurean, Stoic, and Peripatetic philosophies in *Against the Professors* 11.173ff.

10. On dogmatic vs. practical arguments, note Sextus Empiricus, *Outlines of Pyrrhonism* (*Hypotyposes*) 1.62ff. The dogmatic are those demonstrated in this treatise in sections 6–27, the practical in sections 28–50. In this first part (sections 6–27), Sextus Empiricus is using arguments of dogmatists to counter arguments of other dogmatists.

11. For the difference between doctrine (δόγμα) and subject (πρᾶγμα), see Sextus Empiricus, *Outlines of Pyrrhonism* 1.210. A doctrine is a dogmatic teaching; a subject is an observation based on practical experience.

music by the many. Now if, they say, we accept philosophy since it gives discretion[12] to human life and restrains the spiritual passions,[13] by much more do we accept music because it enjoins us not too violently, but with a certain enchanting persuasiveness prevails over the same effects as does philosophy.[14]

7. Pythagoras, when he once observed how lads who had been filled with Bacchic frenzy by alcoholic drink differed not at all from madmen, exhorted the aulete who was joining them in the carousal to play his aulos for them in the spondeic melos.[15] When he thus did what was ordered, they suddenly changed and were given discretion as if they had been sober even at the beginning.[16]

8. The Spartans, leaders of Hellas and famous for their manly spirit, would always do battle with music commanding them. And those who were subject to the exhortations of Solon drew up in battle order to the aulos and lyre, making the martial movement rhythmic.[17]

9. Just as music gives discretion to those who are frantic and turns the more cowardly toward a manly spirit,[18] so also it soothes those who are inflamed by anger. We see how Achilles, angry, according to the poet, is found by the ambassadors who were sent forth,

---

12. Discretion (σωφροσύνη) is one of the virtues and represents an ordering especially of the epithymetic (appetitive) part of the soul (see n. 61 below). Note Plato, *Republic* (*Respublica*) 4.8 (430e), where discretion is defined as a certain ordering and continence of certain pleasures and desires.

13. Cf. Plato, *Phaedrus* 34–38 (253c–257b), where an analogy is drawn between the rational part of the soul and the chariot driver trying to control two horses, which represent the thymic (spirited) and epithymetic (appetitive) part of the soul—both of which are irrational. The spiritual passions are irrational affects of the soul. The passions are often grouped into four general categories: pleasure, pain, fear, and desire.

14. Philosophy prevails over the rational part of the soul, music over the irrational. See, for example, Aristides Quintilianus, *On Music* 2.3 and Plutarch, *On Moral Virtue* (*De virtute morali*) 3 (441d–e). On the power of music to arouse or soften the passions, cf. Quintilian, *Fundamentals of Oratory* (*Institutio oratoria*) 1.10.21. On music's ability to gradually lead one into a correct condition, cf. *On Music* 2.5; and on the attempt of the ancients to restrain the motions of the soul by means of hearing and vision, cf. *On Music* 2.6. The idea of a close relationship between music and philosophy is attacked in Philodemus, *On Music* (Kemke 19.32.10 and 92.23.37).

15. The adjective is derived from the Greek word for libation and indicates a melos appropriate for religious occasions—solemn in character and dominated rhythmically by long time values. Cf. Aristides Quintilianus, *On Music* 1.15. On melos, cf. p. 10, n. 2.

16. For the story about Pythagoras, cf. Philodemus, *On Music* (Kemke 58.16–31) and Quintilian, *Fundamentals of Oratory* 1.10.32. This story became very popular and was embellished in the Middle Ages. For later versions of the story, see, for example, Boethius, *The Fundamentals of Music* (*De institutione musica*) 1.1; Iamblichus, *Life of Pythagoras* (*Vita Pythagorica*) 112; and Regino of Prüm, *Fundamentals of Harmonics* (*De harmonica institutione*) 6.

17. Pyrrhic rhythms and meters (characterized by short time values) were used in war dances and battles. Cf. Aristides Quintilianus, *On Music* 1.15, 2.6, and 2.15.

18. Cf. Philodemus, *On Music* (Kemke 55.77.15–17). Manly spirit (ἀνδρεία), one of the virtues, represents a proper ordering of the thymic (spirited) part of the soul (see n. 61 below).

> delighting his heart in a lyre, clear-sounding,
> splendid and carefully wrought, with a bridge of silver upon it
> which he won out of the spoils when he ruined Eetion's city.
> With this he was pleasuring his heart,[19]

as if clearly knowing that the musical pursuit is best able to prevail over his disposition.

10. Indeed, it was also customary for the other heroes—if they ever were away from home and set out on a long voyage—to leave behind musicians as the most faithful guardians and teachers of discretion to their wives. There was present with Clytemnestra a bard to whom Agamemnon gave many commands concerning her discreet conduct.[20] But Aegisthus, being a rogue, immediately

> took the singer and left him
> on a desert island for the birds of prey to spoil and feed on.[21]

Then Aegisthus, taking Clytemnestra thus unguarded, seduced her, after turning her to appropriate the sovereignty of Agamemnon.

11. Those who have great ability in philosophy, like Plato, say that the wise man is similar to the musician, since he has his soul organized by harmonia.[22] Accordingly, Socrates, although he had already come to great old age, was not ashamed to resort to Lampon the kitharist, and to one who reproached him for this, said that it is better to be brought into discredit for being late-learned than unlearned.

12. They say that one must not, of course, disparage the ancient music on the basis of the disreputable and enervating music of the present,[23] since even the Athenians, who gave much forethought to discreet conduct and also comprehended the dignity of music, handed this down to their descendants as a most necessary subject of learning.[24] A witness of this is the poet of the old comedy, who says

I will tell, therefore, of the life that I originally provided to mortals;
For it was necessary, first, that no one hear the voice of a muttering child;
Next, that one proceed in an orderly manner on the way to the place of the kitharist.[25]

19. *Iliad* 9.186–89 (translation by Richmond Lattimore).
20. *Odyssey* 3.267–68.
21. *Odyssey* 3.270–71 (translation by Richmond Lattimore).
22. On the soul being organized by harmonia, cf. Plato, *Republic* 3.17 (pp. 17–18) and *Timaeus* (pp. 19–23); Aristotle, *Politics* 8.5 (pp. 28–30); Aristides Quintilianus, *On Music* 2.17 and 3.24; and Philodemus, *On Music* (Kemke 31.23.1–6; 32.26.9–12). On "harmonia," cf. p. 10, n. 3. When applied to the soul, the term denotes that the parts of the soul—rational, thymic (spirited), and epithymetic (appetitive)—are properly proportioned one to another.
23. On the music of the ancients as compared with later corruptions, see Plato, *Laws* (*Leges*) 2 (669b–d) and 3 (700a–e) and Quintilian, *Fundamentals of Oratory* 1.10.31.
24. On music being handed down as a subject of education, cf. Ps. Plutarch, *On Music* (*De musica*) 27 (1140d). Education in ancient Athens was centered around music and gymnastics; note Plato, *Republic* 3.17–18 (pp. 17–19).
25. The first line of this quotation is from Telecleides fragment 1 (Kock). It is found in Athenaeus, *Sophists at Dinner* (*Deipnosophistae*) 6 (268b). The other two lines are from Aristophanes, *Clouds* (*Nubes*) 963–64.

For this reason, even if the music of today weakens the mind with certain fractured mele and effeminate rhythms,[26] this has nothing to do with the ancient and manly music.

13. If poetics is indeed useful for life and music seems to adorn this by arranging it into divisions and making it fit for singing, music will be needful.[27] Of course, the poets too are called makers of melos, and the epics of Homer in ancient times were sung to the lyre. In like manner are the mele and the stasima[28] by the tragedians, which contain a natural ratio,[29] such as the stasima so spoken:

> Greatest Earth and divine Ether,
> He is the begetter of men and gods;
> And she, while receiving water-bearing
> Drops of moisture, bears mortals;
> She bears food and races of beasts;
> Wherefore not unjustly is she esteemed
> As the mother of all.[30]

14. In general, music is heard not only from people who are rejoicing, but also in hymns,[31] feasts, and sacrifices to the gods. Because of this, it turns the heart[32] toward the desire for good things. But it is also a consolation to those who are grief-stricken; for this reason, the auloi playing a melody for those who are mourning are the lighteners of their grief.[33]

15. Such are the things on behalf of music. Against these things, first, it is said that it is not conceded offhand that by nature some of the mele are exciting to the soul and others are restraining, for such a thing is contrary to our opinion. Just as the crash of thunder—as the followers of Epicurus say—does not signify a manifestation of a god (but to the common people and the supersti-

---

26. On the characters of various rhythms, see Aristides Quintilianus, *On Music* 2.15.
27. On the relationship between music and poetics, note Aristotle, *Poetics (Poetica)* 1.4–12. Poetics as a whole includes musical accompaniment, though some specific forms may be without the melodic element. See Quintilian, *Fundamentals of Oratory* 1.10.10 and 1.10.29.
28. On stasimon, see Aristotle, *Poetics* 12 (1452b23): "a melos of the chorus that is without anapests and trochees"; and the scholiast on Aristophanes, *Frogs (Ranae)* 1281: "a species of melos, which the choral dancers sing while standing."
29. That is, a natural relationship between the text and the music that would accompany it.
30. Euripides fragment 839 (Nauck).
31. Cf. Aristides Quintilianus, *On Music* 2.4 and Quintilian, *Fundamentals of Oratory* 1.10.20. A hymn, in Graeco-Roman music, is an address to a deity in poetic form (usually hexameters) meant to be sung. Examples of hymns that survive from antiquity are the two Delphic Hymns to Apollo inscribed in stone and the Hymns of Mesomedes. Editions and transcriptions of these hymns can be found in Egert Pöhlmann, *Denkmäler altgriechischer Musik*, Erlanger Beiträge zur Sprach- und Kunstwissenschaft, no. 31 (Nuremberg: Hans Carl, 1970), 13–31 and 58–76.
32. The word "heart" is used throughout as a translation of διάνοια. It denotes the part of the mind that is moved by music and may be considered what might today be called the "feelings" or the emotional part of the intellect.
33. Cf. Aristides Quintilianus, *On Music* 2.4; Matthew 9.23; and Aristotle, *Problems (Problemata)* 19.1 (917b19–21).

tious it is supposed to be such) since when other bodies likewise strike one against another, a crash is similarly produced (just as when a millstone is turned round or hands clap), in the same manner, some of the mele of music are not by nature of one sort and others of another sort[34] but are presumed so to be by us. The same melos is exciting to horses but in no way to men when they hear it in theaters—and to the horses, perhaps it is not exciting but disturbing.

16. Second, even if the mele of music are such, music has not been established as useful for life because of this. It is not because it has the power of discretion that it restrains the heart,[35] but rather because it has the power of distraction. Consequently, when such mele are silenced in any way, the mind, as if it were not treated by them, reverts again to the former heart. In this same manner, sleep or wine do not relax grief but heighten it by producing torpor, feebleness, and forgetfulness; thus, a certain type of melos does not restrain a grief-stricken soul or a heart agitated by anger but—if it does anything at all—distracts them.

17. And Pythagoras, in the first place, was foolish in wishing to give discretion to those who were unseasonably intoxicated instead of turning from them.[36] In the second place, by correcting them in this manner, he concedes that the auletes have more power than the philosophers with respect to the correction of ethoses.[37]

18. That the Spartans do battle to the aulos and lyre is proof of what was said a short while before,[38] but not of music being useful for life.[39] Just as those who bear burdens or row or do some other of the toilsome works beat time in order to draw the mind away from the trial of the work, so also those who use auloi and salpinxes[40] in battles contrived this not because there was a certain melos stimulating to the heart and this melos was a cause of manly courage but because they were eager to draw themselves away from the agony and disorder (if indeed certain of the barbarians blow conches and do battle while beating on drums[41]). But none of these turns one toward a manly spirit.

---

34. On mele being a certain sort by nature, note Aristotle, *Politics* 8.5 (p. 28) and Philodemus, *On Music* (Kemke 12.1–16; 15.7–9; 71.7.25–35; 71.8.2–3).

35. Refutation of ¶6 above. On the "heart," see n. 32 above.

36. Refutation of ¶7 above.

37. An aulete, as a professional musician, would be considered a low character, hardly comparable to a philosopher; see Aristotle, *Politics* 8.4 and 8.7 (pp. 27 and 32–33). On the correction of ethoses, cf. Philodemus, *On Music* (Kemke 100.30.24) and Ps. Plutarch, *On Music* 32 (1142e–f). Ethos is the character of the soul and is influenced by music through mimesis; that is, the various elements of music have an ethos of their own, which may be transmitted to the soul of a person by a sort of sympathetic process (Aristides Quintilianus, *On Music* 2.18). Cf. pp. 13–14, n. 21; and see also n. 57 below.

38. I.e., that music distracts.

39. Refutation of ¶8 above.

40. See p. 89, n. 17.

41. This reflects a belief on the part of many Greeks that the barbarians, or non-Hellenes, were naturally inferior to those of Greek nationality. The argument here is that the barbarians would not have the capacity for manly spirit, one of the virtues. On this attitude in general, cf. Aristotle, *Politics* 1.5 and Aristides Quintilianus, *On Music* 2.6.

19. The same things must be said also of the angry Achilles.[42] And further, since he was amorous and intemperate,[43] it is not contrary to expectation for him to be eager about music.

20. But, by Zeus, even the heroes entrusted their wives to certain bards as guardians who were possessed of discretion, just as Agamemnon entrusted Clytemnestra![44] Yet this surely derives from men telling mythical tales—who then, immediately afterwards, convict themselves. For if music is indeed trusted for the correction of passions, how is it that Clytemnestra slew Agamemnon at his own hearth like an "ox at the manger"?[45] and how is it that Penelope received into the house of Odysseus a profligate throng of lads and, by always falsely luring and increasing their desires, stirred up for her husband the war in Ithaca more wretched and difficult than the expedition against Ilium?

21. Indeed, even if the followers of Plato accepted music,[46] one must still not say that it tends toward good fortune, since others, too, who are not wanting in trustworthiness on these things, such as the followers of Epicurus, deny this claim.[47] We say, conversely, that it is useless and

idle, fond of wine, careless of property.[48]

22. Simple-minded are those who confuse it with the use of poetics in respect to utility,[49] since one can, as we said in the book against the grammarians,[50] teach that poetics is without benefit and—not a lesser argument—show that music, since it is concerned with melos, is disposed by nature only to give delight, while poetics, since it is concerned with heart, can both be beneficial and give discretion.[51]

23. Such is the argument against the things that have been discussed. But it is also a leading argument in respect to music that if indeed it is needful, it is

42. Refutation of ¶9 above.
43. On the deleterious effects produced by the immoderate use of music, see Plato, *Republic* 3.18 (pp. 18–19) and Aristides Quintilianus, *On Music* 2.6. Cf. Ps. Plutarch, *On Music* 40 (1145d–f), where the story of Achilles playing his lyre to console himself is used as evidence that music is fitting for a man; and Aristides Quintilianus, *On Music* 2.10, where it is said that Achilles is singing nothing erotic, but is, on the contrary, pondering the feats in arms of former men and summoning his soul into a state of manliness.
44. Refutation of ¶10 above.
45. *Odyssey* 11.411.
46. Refutation of ¶11 above. Cf. Quintilian, *Fundamentals of Oratory* 1.10.15.
47. Plutarch (*That Epicurus Actually Makes a Pleasant Life Impossible* [*Non posse suaviter vivi secundum Epicurum*] 13 [1095c–e]) reports that Epicurus would go to the theatre to hear performers on the kithara and aulos but would not endure theoretical and philosophical discussions on music.
48. Euripides fragment 184 (Nauck).
49. Refutation of ¶13 above.
50. *Against the Professors* 1.280, 296–98.
51. If the usefulness of music rests on the usefulness of poetics, the usefulness of poetics must first be assumed. Poetics, since it uses words, is less abstract than music apart from words and may be more obvious in its sway of the feelings or disposition.

said to be useful in respect to the following: either insofar as one educated in music takes more delight—in comparison to the common people—from things heard musically,[52] or insofar as it is not the case that men become good if they have not received early training[53] under those educated in music, or because the same elements pertain to music and to the understanding of the subjects in philosophy[54] (such as we said above concerning grammar[55]), or because the cosmos is ordered in accord with harmonia[56] (just as the disciples of Pythagoras assert) and we need the musical theorems for the understanding of the whole universe, or because certain types of mele form the ethos of the soul.[57]

24. But music would not be said to be useful because musicians take more delight than the common people from the things heard. First the delight is not necessary for the common people, as are those delights that come from drink or warmth in a time of hunger or thirst or cold. Second, even if they are necessary delights, we are able to enjoy them without musical experience: infants are put to sleep when they listen to an emmelic cooing, and the irrational of the animals are charmed by the aulos and syrinx[58] (so dolphins, as the account goes, delighting in the melodies of auloi, swim toward ships as they are being rowed). Neither of these is likely to have experience or conception of music.[59]

25. And because of this, perhaps, in the same manner in which we enjoy tasting food or wine without the art of cookery[60] and the art of wine-tasting, so also without the art of music we would enjoy listening to delightful melos. Though on the one hand, the artists apprehend technically better than the common person, on the other, they gain nothing more of the pleasant passion.

26. So, music is not chosen insofar as it happens that those who have an understanding of it delight in it to a greater degree, and indeed, not because it prepares the soul beforehand for wisdom. Conversely, it beats back and goes

---

52. Cf. Aristotle, *Politics* 8.6 (p. 31).
53. On musical training at an early age, see Aristotle, *Politics* 8.6 (p. 30); Ps. Plutarch, *On Music* 41 (1146a–b); and Philodemus, *On Music* (Kemke 77.12.25–26).
54. The relationship of music to philosophy is one of the major themes of Aristides Quintilianus, *On Music;* note especially Book I, sections 1–2; Book III; and the introduction and commentary in Mathiesen, *Aristides Quintilianus,* 14–57.
55. *Against the Professors* 1.72.
56. The harmonic order of the cosmos is a concept developed especially by the Pythagoreans, according to which, the features of the cosmos (earth, moon, sun, planets, stars) are ordered by the same mathematical principles by which the harmonic division of music is ordered. This was believed by many to be an acoustical phenomenon as well as a physical arrangement (note Quintilian, *Fundamentals of Oratory* 1.10.12). Cf. Aristides Quintilianus, *On Music* 3.20 and Plato, *Timaeus* 35b–36c (pp. 20–22). Note also Archytas fragment 1 (Diels/Kranz 1:432.4–8) in which it is remarked that geometry, numbers, sphaeric, and music are kindred to astronomy.
57. Aristotle, *Politics* 8.5 (pp. 26–30). See Edward A. Lippman, "The Sources and Development of the Ethical View of Music in Ancient Greece," *Musical Quarterly* 49 (1963): 188–209; and Louis Harap, "Some Hellenic Ideas on Music and Character," *Musical Quarterly* 24 (1938): 153–68. See also n. 37 above.
58. See p. 12, n. 12.
59. Cf. Aristotle, *Politics* 8.6 (p. 31).
60. Cf. Aristotle, *Politics* 8.5 (p. 27).

against the desire for virtue,[61] rendering the young easily led into licentiousness and salaciousness, since indeed one educated in music

> Taking pleasure in song and dance, he pursues this always;
> He will be idle both at home and in the city;
> Even to friends a good-for-nothing, he goes away unseen,
> Whenever one is slave to sweet pleasure.[62]

27. In accord with these same things, the need for music must not adduce that music and philosophy are defined from the same elements,[63] as is immediately evident. It remains, therefore, to say that it happens to be needful for good fortune because the cosmos is ordered in accord with harmonia, or because one uses mele that form ethos. Of these, the last has already been brought into discredit as not being true.[64] That the cosmos is ordered in accord with harmonia is shown to be false in various ways; even if it is true, such a thing has no power in reference to happiness—just as neither does the harmonia in the instruments.[65]

28. Such is the manner of the first type of refutation against the musicians, but the second, assailing even the principles of music, consists rather of a more practical inquiry. So, since music is a science of the emmelic and ecmelic, the rhythmic and nonrhythmic,[66] especially if we show that neither do the mele have substance nor do the rhythms pertain to existent things, we shall have proven that music too is without substance. Let us speak first concerning mele and their substance, beginning with some brief preliminaries.

29. Sound is, as one would indisputably define it, the sense-object proper to

---

61. Cf. Philodemus, *On Music* (Kemke 78.28–32). On music and virtue, see Aristotle, *Politics* 8.5 (pp. 28–29). Aristotle's *Nicomachean Ethics* (*Ethica Nicomachea*) 1.13 (1102a5) claims that virtue is necessary for εὐδαιμονία (good fortune); this idea is found also among the Stoics. On good fortune, see n. 9 above. Virtue is a quality of the irrational, but it partakes of reason in the ordering and regulation of the irrational passions. It represents a moderation of the passions rather than a destruction or abolition. Four virtues commonly mentioned by the philosophers are judgment (φρονήσις), righteousness (δικαιοσύνη), discretion (σωφροσύνη), and manly spirit (ἀνδρεία), the latter two of which are frequently brought up in the first part of this treatise. Cf. Aristides Quintilianus, *On Music* 3.24; Plutarch, *On Moral Virtue* 2 (440e–441b); and Plato, *Laws* 1 (632e–633a).

62. Euripides fragment 187 (Nauck).

63. See n. 14 above.

64. Philodemus, *On Music* (Kemke 64.2.19–43).

65. On the refutation of the existence of a harmonia in the cosmos, cf. Philodemus, *On Music* (Kemke 100.30.6–19 and 101.31.10–24). Aristotle, *On the Heavens* (*De caelo*) 2.9 rejects the idea that the harmonia of the cosmos is an audible phenomenon, but see Aristides Quintilianus, *On Music* 3.20 for another explanation. The harmonia of instruments is discussed at some length in Aristides Quintilianus, *On Music* 2.17–19.

66. For definitions of emmelic and ecmelic, see Aristoxenus, *Harmonics* 2.36–38. Rhythmic is what is characterized by a regular pattern of chronoi ordered by arsis and thesis (see n. 91 below). Nonrhythmic has no such regular order. See Aristides Quintilianus, *On Music* 1.14, who also speaks of a rhythmoid type, which shares both in the order of the rhythmic and in the disorder of the nonrhythmic. In music, melody, diction, and bodily motion are organized by rhythmics (Aristides Quintilianus, *On Music* 1.13).

hearing. Just as it is the activity of sight alone to apprehend colors, and of smell alone to grasp what is sweet-smelling and ill-smelling, and—further—of taste to sense what is sweet or bitter, so sound would be the sense-object proper to hearing.

30. Of sound, one is sharp, another heavy, each of them taking the reference rather metaphorically from the sense-objects of touch. For just as the world refers to what stings and what cuts the touch as sharp, and what crushes and presses down as heavy, in the same manner too for sound, the one, as if it cut the hearing, is sharp; the other, as if it crushes (as it were), is heavy. It is not strange that, just as we call a sound gray and black and white[67] from the sense-objects of sight, so also we use some metaphors from the sense-objects of touch.

31. Whenever the sound is emitted evenly and on one pitch—when there occurs no distraction of the sense either toward the heavier or the sharper—then such a sound is called a note. Consequently, the musicians, describing in general, say "a note is a fall of emmelic sound on one pitch."[68]

32. Of notes, some are homophonous, others not homophonous; and homophonous are those that do not differ one from another in sharpness and heaviness;[69] not homophonous are those that are not so. Of the homophonous, as of the not homophonous, some are called sharp and others heavy; and again, of the not homophonous, some are referred to as dissonant, others as consonant. Dissonant are those that move the hearing irregularly and in a disjointed manner; consonant are those that do so more regularly and continuously.[70]

33. The property of each genus will be rather more clear when we use the transference from the qualities of taste. Just as, of the things that may be tasted, some have such a blend as to move the sense uniformly and smoothly—such as oenomel and hydromel—and others not in like manner nor similarly—like oxymel[71]—(for each of these mixed things imprints the proper quality on the taste) so, of the notes, dissonant are those that move the hearing irregularly and in a disjointed manner, and the consonant are more regular. Such is the difference of the notes according to the musicians.

---

67. For a similar color analogy, cf. Aristides Quintilianus, *On Music* 1.9 (p. 57).

68. Cf. ¶42 below. The definition of note as found in Aristoxenus, *Harmonics* 1.15 is the basis for the definition as found in the later minor theorists as well as Sextus Empiricus. Cf. Cleonides, *Harmonic Introduction* 1 (p. 36) and Gaudentius, *Harmonic Introduction* 2 (p. 68).

69. Cf. discussion by others on homophonous notes: in Gaudentius, *Harmonic Introduction* 8 (p. 72), they are, as in Sextus Empiricus, notes that do not differ from one another in height and depth. According to Ptolemy, *Harmonics* (*Harmonica*) 1.7, homophonous notes are those that impress upon the hearing the perception of only one sound, such as octaves and their compounds. Aristides Quintilianus, *On Music* 1.6 (p. 52) states that they are notes of equal pitch but differing function.

70. On consonant and dissonant, see Aristoxenus, *Harmonics* 2.44; Cleonides, *Harmonic Introduction* 5 (p. 39); Aristides Quintilianus, *On Music* 1.6 (p. 52); and Gaudentius, *Harmonic Introduction* 8 (pp. 72–73).

71. Oenomel is a mixture of honey and wine; hydromel, a mixture of honey and water; and oxymel, a mixture of honey and vinegar.

34. Some intervals[72] are outlined by these notes, in accord with which the sound moves, either ascending toward the sharper or descending toward the heavier. For this reason, by analogy, some of these intervals are referred to as consonant, others as dissonant. Consonant intervals are as many as are bounded by consonant notes; dissonant, as many as are bounded by dissonant notes. Of the consonant intervals,[73] the musicians refer to the fourth as the first and smallest, the fifth as the next greater one after this, and the octave as the one greater than the fifth. Again, of the dissonant intervals, the smallest and first is the so-called (by them) diesis; the second, the semitone, which is twice the diesis; the third, the tone, which is double the semitone.

35. Moreover, in this manner every interval in music has its substance in notes—so too every ethos. Ethos is a genus of melody. As of the human ethoses, some are sullen and stronger (they tell that such were those of the ancients) and others are easily yielding to love and drunkenness and lamentations and wailings, so one melody produces movements in the soul that are dignified and charming, another produces movements more base and ignoble. Melody of such a sort is commonly called by the musicians "ethos," from its being productive of ethos,[74] just as we call fear "pale" because it makes one pale, and the "south winds hard of hearing, hazy, headachy, sluggish, and relaxed" instead of effective of these.

36. Of this common melody, one type is termed "color," another "harmonia," and another "diatonic." Of these, the harmonia is somehow constructive of dignity and a severe ethos, the color is a shrill and mournful ethos, and the diatonic is a somewhat harsh and coarse ethos. Again, of those that are sung, the harmonic melos is undifferentiated, but the diatonic and the color have some more particular differences. The diatonic has two, the so-called difference of the soft diatonic and of the intense; the color has three, for of these, one is called tonal, another semitonal, and another soft.[75]

37. Moreover, it is evident from these things that every theory of melody

---

72. On the definition of intervals in general, see Aristoxenus, *Harmonics* 1.15; Cleonides, *Harmonic Introduction* 1 (p. 36); Aristides Quintilianus, *On Music* 1.7 (pp. 53–54); and Gaudentius, *Harmonic Introduction* 3 (p. 68).

73. The concept of consonant intervals was also influenced heavily by Pythagorean philosophy. According to the Pythagoreans, the consonant intervals are those that are represented by ratios whose terms are taken from the elements of the tetractys (1, 2, 3, 4), such as 4:3 (the fourth), 3:2 (the fifth), and 2:1 (the octave). The dissonant intervals are then derived from these by addition or subtraction. For instance, a tone is the difference between a fifth and a fourth; a semitone is the difference between a fourth and two tones. Aristoxenus accepts a like set of consonances and dissonances but posits empirical (as Sextus Empiricus does here) rather than purely mathematical criteria for their definition.

74. Three ethoses are regularly associated with music: systaltic, diastaltic, and hesychastic or medial. Cf. Cleonides, *Harmonic Introduction* 13 (p. 46) and Aristides Quintilianus, *On Music* 1.12 (pp. 65–66). According to Philodemus, *On Music* (Kemke 63.2.15–64.2.19), the distinctive ethoses are simply a matter of opinion.

75. On these three genera, cf. Aristoxenus, *Harmonics* 2.46–52; Cleonides, *Harmonic Introduction* 3 (pp. 36–37); Aristides Quintilianus, *On Music* 1.9 (pp. 56–59); and Gaudentius, *Harmonic Introduction* 5 (p. 69).

according to the musicians does not have its substance in any other thing except in the notes. And because of this, if they are abolished, music will be nothing. Now, how will one say that there are no notes? From the premise—we will say—that they are generically sound;[76] and that sound is nonexistent has been shown by us from the testimony of the dogmatists in our skeptic observations.[77]

38. The philosophers from Cyrene say that only the passions exist, but nothing else. For this reason, sound, since it is not a passion but productive of passion, does not arise from the existent things. Those who follow Democritus and Plato, in abolishing every sense-object, concomitantly abolish even sound, which seems to be a sense-object. In another way, if there is sound, it is either a body or not a body. But it is neither a body as the Peripatetics teach in many ways, nor is it not a body, as the Stoics teach.[78] There is, therefore, no sound.

39. But in yet another way, suppose one undertakes to say that unless there is a soul, there are no senses (for they exist as parts of the soul).[79] And unless there are senses, there are no sense-objects (for the substance of these is conceived with reference to the senses). And unless there are sense-objects, there is no sound (for it exists as a type of the sense-objects). But the soul is nothing, just as we showed in the observations on the soul.[80] There is, therefore, no sound.

40. Indeed, if sound is neither short nor long, there is no sound. But sound is neither long nor short, as we observed in our remarks against the grammarians, when questioning them on syllable and word.[81] There is, therefore, no sound.

76. On sound as the primary cause of music, see Euclid, *Division of a Canon* (*Sectio canonis;* proem); Gaudentius, *Harmonic Introduction* (p. 67); and Nicomachus, *Manual of Harmonics* (*Manuale harmonices*) 2, where a discussion on music is begun with the topic of sound.
77. Note Sextus Empiricus, *Against the Professors* 8.131, where a brief refutation of sound is made. The main points of the argument are as follows: every sound—if there is sound—is either coming into being or is being silenced. But there is not sound that is coming into being, because it has not yet been substantiated; and it is agreed that sound being silenced is no longer substantiated. There is, therefore, no sound.
78. According to Pythagoras, Plato, and Aristotle, sound is not a body, because sound is not the air but is a manifestation that occurs in accord with a striking of the air. As a similar example, when a rod is bent it is not the manifestation or appearance, but, rather, the matter that is bent. According to the Stoics, sound is a body, because everything that performs an action is a body; sound makes an imprint on the hearing as a finger does in wax. Everything that moves and annoys is a body; εὐμουσία (musicality) moves and ἀμουσία (want of musicality) annoys. Sound is moved and is reflected when it makes an echo.
79. In Aristotle, *On the Soul* (*De anima*) 2.2 (413b11–13), soul is the origin (ἀρχή) of the senses and is defined by them as well as nutrition, thought, and movement. Cf. Plato, *Timaeus* (43a–44b).
80. This is apparently a reference to a lost work.
81. On sound being neither long nor short, see Sextus Empiricus, *Against the Professors* 1.124–130. The argument may be summarized as follows. There is no short syllable, because there is no smallest chronos (see n. 92 below), since every chronos is divided *ad infinitum.* If the grammarians say that they call a syllable short and smallest not by nature but by sense, they will increase the difficulty, for what they call short is divisible by sense. Sextus Empiricus uses as an example here the syllable "ερ." This syllable is made of two elements and is, therefore,

41. Besides these things, sound is conceived neither as an effect nor as a substance, but rather as a coming-into-being and a temporal extension. What is conceived as coming-into-being is becoming but not yet is,[82] just as a house or a ship and other multitudinous things that are in a state of becoming are not said to be. So then, sound is nothing.

42. It is possible to use toward this end many other arguments, which, as I said, we went through in detail while making observations in the Pyrrhonea.[83] But now, since there is no sound, neither is there a note, which was said to be a fall of sound on one pitch.[84] Since there is no note, neither has a musical interval[85] been established nor consonance[86] nor melody nor the genera[87] derived from these. Because of this, there is no music, for it was said to be a science of the emmelic and the ecmelic.[88]

43. For this reason, it must be pointed out from another principle that even if we stand aloof from these things, music has still been established as nonsubstantial through the doubt that will be treated in connection with rhythmic composition. For if rhythm is nothing, neither will there be a science concerning rhythm. But indeed, rhythm is nothing, as we will prove. There is, therefore, no science of rhythm.[89]

44. As we have said many times, rhythm is a scale of feet,[90] and the foot is what has been composed of arsis and thesis. Arsis and thesis[91] are considered as a quantity of chronos:[92] the thesis contains some chronoi and the arsis others. Just as syllables are combined from elements and words from syllables, so

divisible and so cannot be short. A long syllable is also nonexistent. The grammarians say that it is dichronic, but two chronoi do not coexist with one another. For if they are two, one is in the present but the other is not, since one must be uttered before or after the other. Since the parts do not coexist, the syllable as a whole is not substantiated, but only a part of it. If only a part of the long syllable exists, it will not differ from the short syllable. And it is not possible to conceive something as compounded from parts if one part exists but the other does not. There is, therefore, no long syllable.

82. Being indicates a continuous and ongoing state without change; becoming implies a process in which a substantial change is taking place.

83. It is not evident to which work Sextus Empiricus is referring here, and it may be a lost work.

84. See ¶31 above.

85. See ¶34 above.

86. See ¶¶32–34 above.

87. See ¶36 above.

88. See ¶28 above.

89. Rhythmics is a part of the technical division of music, along with the harmonic and metric (Aristides Quintilianus, *On Music* 1.5 [pp. 49–50]).

90. On the definition of rhythm, cf. Aristoxenus, *Rhythmics* (*Rhythmica*) 2.7, 16–20 (see Lewis Rowell, "Aristoxenus on Rhythm," *Journal of Music Theory* 23 [1979]: 63–79) and Aristides Quintilianus, *On Music* 1.13. For a new consideration of the question of rhythm and meter in ancient Greek music, see Mathiesen, "Rhythm and Meter," 159–80.

91. On arsis and thesis, cf. Aristides Quintilianus, *On Music* 1.13. The terms "arsis" and "thesis" are derived from the dance movement that is a part of the music. Thesis is downward movement as in the placement of the foot, and arsis is upward movement as in the raising of the foot.

92. "Chronos" is a technical term used by the ancients to indicate a measure of rhythmic time (see p. 49, n. 7). The same term is also used in a more proper sense to indicate the phenomenon that approximates the denotation of the English word "time" in its primary sense. It is this

the feet come into being from the chronoi and the rhythms from the feet.

45. If we show that chronos is nothing, we will have concomitantly demonstrated that neither do feet exist, nor, because of this, do rhythms, since they take their composition from feet. It will follow from this that there is no science of rhythms. How so? That chronos is nothing we already proved in the Pyrrhonea,[93] but nevertheless, we will prove the things at hand up to a point.

46. If there is a chronos, either it has been limited or it is unlimited.[94] But it has not been limited, since we then say that at some time there has been a chronos when there was no chronos and that at some time there will be a chronos when there will be no chronos. Nor has it been established as unlimited: for part of it is past and present and future, in the case of each of which, if it is not, chronos has been limited; but if it is, there will be both the past and the future concurrently, which is absurd. There is, therefore, no chronos.

47. What has been composed from nonexistents is nonexistent. Chronos, since it is composed from what is past and no longer is and from what is future and is not yet,[95] will be nonexistent.[96]

48. In another way, if chronos is indivisible, how do we say that the past, the present, and the future are parts of it? If it is divisible, since everything that is divisible is measured by a part of itself (as a cubit by a palm, the palm by a finger), it will be necessary that chronos also be measured by one of its parts. Neither is it possible to measure the other chronoi with the present, since indeed the becoming and present chronos will be the same as the past and future (in respect to them)—past because it measures past chronos, future because it measures the future chronos, which is absurd.[97] So then, one must not measure the present by one of the remaining two. For this reason, it must not thus be said that there is a chronos.

49. Besides these things, chronos is tripartite, and one part is past, one present, and one future. Of these, the past is no longer, the future is not yet,[98] and the present is either indivisible or divisible. But it would not be indivisible, for in the indivisible, nothing divisible is able to come into being[99]—as Timon says—such as coming-into-being and perishing.[100]

---

ambiguity that Sextus Empiricus will play upon in the following sections. By proving the impossibility of the existence of "chronos" in one sense, the other is also abolished.

93. The discussion that will be found in sections 46–50 parallels discussion found in *Outlines of Pyrrhonism* 3.140–44 and *Against the Professors* 10.189–200.

94. The unlimited denotes in its original sense not only what is infinite in extent but also what has not been ordered or delimited by any internal arrangement or boundaries.

95. According to Parmenides (fr. 8 [Diels/Kranz 235.1–6]), everything is one and continuous; the acceptance of a past and a future implies the capacity of something to come-into-being or to perish. See n. 99 below.

96. The paragraph parallels Aristotle, *Physics* (*Physica*) 4.10 (217b33–218a3).

97. This parallels Aristotle, *Physics* 4.10 (218a6–8).

98. This parallels Aristotle, *Physics* 4.10 (217b33–34).

99. Parmenides (fr. 8 [Diels/Kranz 235.6–238.41]) denies the possibility of passing from nonbeing to being and vice versa.

100. On Timon, see Greaves, 7–8.

50. In another way, if indeed the present part of chronos is indivisible, it has neither a beginning from which it begins nor a limit at which it leaves off, nor, because of this, a middle, and so there will not be the present chronos. If it is divisible and if it is divided into the chronoi that are not, there will be no chronos; but if it is divided into the chronoi that are, the chronos will not be whole: rather, some of its parts will be and some will not be. So then, chronos is nothing, and because of this, neither are there feet, nor rhythms, nor the science of rhythms.

51. Having said so many things in a practical manner against the principles of music, with so many things we bring to completion the exposition against the subjects of learning.

THE EARLY CHRISTIAN PERIOD AND THE LATIN MIDDLE AGES

Edited by JAMES McKINNON

INTRODUCTION

*T*he pages that follow provide a representative selection of writings about music from the Early Christian period and from the Latin Middle Ages. The material appears in four sections of markedly different character. The first offers a sampling of passages from the rich literature of the Early Christian Church Fathers. These eminent fourth-century ecclesiastics from East and West—St. John Chrysostom, for example, and St. Augustine—express their views on the singing of psalms. In the second section, Boethius, Cassiodorus, and Isidore of Seville, the principal figures in the transmission of classical culture to the Middle Ages, illustrate the part that music played in that process. The third section provides a series of readings on early medieval ecclesiastical chant and its liturgical context. Included are descriptions of the Mass and the Office and conflicting accounts of an event in the history of Western music that is as puzzling as it is important—the transmission of Roman chant across the Alps to the Carolingian realm. The fourth and longest section is taken up with extended readings, in some cases entire short treatises, from the theoretical and pedagogical literature of the Middle Ages. Several of these selections deal with the development of modal theory, the central problem of earlier medieval musical theory, while others treat the rhythmic theory of thirteenth- and fourteenth-century polyphonic music.

Most of the Early Christian writing on music does not appear in works that are devoted entirely to music, but rather in occasional passages scattered throughout various types of religious literature. Three of the selections translated here represent an exegetical genre popular at the time, the psalm commentary, and another is taken from St. Augustine's celebrated autobiography *The Confessions*. Only one reading is drawn from a work that treats music exclusively, Niceta of Remesiana's unique sermon *On the Benefits of Psalmody*. There are, certainly, a considerable number of writings from the period that deal with music alone. For the most part these are theoretical treatises that explain music as one of the mathematical disciplines of the liberal arts. The authors of these tracts are for the most part pagans, but in the later fourth century, as the society of Late Antiquity comes to be increasingly Christianized, a figure such as St. Augustine can make his own contribution to the genre. His *De Musica* was intended as only one treatise in a series on the seven liberal arts. It deals with the rhythmic and metrical aspect of its subject, leaving the tonal aspect—what the ancients called harmonics—to a second work on music theory that was planned but never written. In the sixth and final book of the treatise, Augustine clothed his subject in the garb of Christian examples, using a hymn text to make his points about rhythm, but the work as a whole remains more a representative of the classical tradition than an exemplar of the Christian view of music.

Musica in Late Antiquity was not so much the everyday product of singing and playing that we call music today as it was the academic enterprise that we call music theory. Moreover, the music theory of the time was considerably more abstract than the effort that goes by that name in recent times; certainly it has little in common with the music theory that explains eighteenth- and nineteenth-century harmonic practice. In Late Antiquity the subject was permeated with Neoplatonic thinking, where ideas were considered to be real and where external manifestations of any sort—what we call reality—were mere shadows of those ideas. In this context the theoretical constructs themselves were the musical reality: good theory was the product of sophisticated mathematical calculation and the ingenious manipulation of tonal symmetries.

If, then, we are to understand the views of Augustine and his contemporaries on everyday music, we must turn from their writings on music as such to other types of literature, where they might have occasion to bring up the subject. In the case of Christian authors, the single genre of literature that speaks most often of music is the psalm commentary, a work in which the writer moves systematically through the 150 psalms, annotating nearly every verse of each one. The predominant style of the genre is the so-called allegorical method of exegesis. In this style the author is more concerned with the spiritual meaning of a passage than its literal or historical meaning. A reference, for example, to the hide that is stretched upon a frame to make a drum will lead the Church Father to comment on the mortification of the flesh rather than on percussive rhythms. Despite the extreme tendency of Late Antique intellectuals toward abstraction, ecclesiastical authors often lapse into remarks about everyday musical reality, even in the midst of a generally allegorical exegesis. To a Church Father, everyday musical reality was two things: the pagan musical practice that surrounded the Christian population on every side and the singing of psalms and hymns in church. The former was the subject of scathing denunciation because of its immoral associations, and the latter was generally approved as a beneficial, if sometimes suspect, practice. This second attitude is well exemplified by the readings presented here.

All three readings of the second section represent *musica* in the proper classical sense rather than music in its everyday sense. We observe the authors—Boethius, Cassiodorus, and Isidore—striving to provide a summary of the classical doctrine on music and doing so entirely without reference to the music of their own day. The example of Boethius is particularly interesting in this respect. We know that he was a Christian theologian who wrote a treatise on the Trinity, yet not once in his lengthy work on music does he mention the ecclesiastical music of his day. Even more remarkable perhaps is that while in prison awaiting execution, he wrote his *On the Consolation of Philosophy* without a single reference to his Christian faith. *Philosophia,* like *musica,* was an academic subject; each existed as a world unto itself, valued as a thing of the mind, and valued moreover because it was a microcosm within the system of classical education.

In the case of music, at least, this sort of intellectual compartmentalization appears to have been of benefit to medieval writers. The digests of classical music theory composed by these transitional authors provided their medieval successors with a theoretical vocabulary that they could apply to the music of their own time—not that Boethius, Cassiodorus, and Isidore thought of themselves as performing such a function (they certainly had no way of imagining their future medieval readership).

On the other hand they might very well have understood their relationship to their present and their past. They lived during what we look on as the twilight of Classical Antiquity. Although the Roman Empire had been swept by waves of barbarian invasion in the fifth century, these figures lived in circumstances of comparative stability. Boethius worked at Ravenna under the relatively benevolent Ostrogothic king Theodoric in earlier sixth-century Italy, and Isidore at Seville lived under similarly benevolent Visigothic sovereigns in earlier seventh-century Spain. The conditions under which Cassiodorus worked were different only in detail. He began his career in the same Ostrogothic court as did Boethius, but lived virtually until the end of the sixth century. He wrote his treatise on music many years after the death of Boethius, while in residence at his monastery of Vivarium in southern Italy. All three authors knew of no civilization other than that of the classical world. In spite of the intrusive barbarian presence, much of the external grandeur of that world—its public buildings, aqueducts, and circuses—was still in evidence, and its rich literature was still available. The literature was taught selectively, however, and to only a dwindling minority of the population. The three writers were surely aware that they represented a greatly weakened tradition, possibly even one in mortal peril. But they had no way of imagining themselves as transitional figures; more likely they saw their role as that of preserving a measure of their intellectual heritage and conveying it to their contemporaries.

The third section takes us to the world of *cantus,* the medieval term for all practical music, although the writings furnished here are confined to ecclesiastical chant and its liturgical context. The first reading presents the portion of St. Benedict's Rule that describes the early medieval monastic Office, that is, the series of eight services that occupied much of a medieval ecclesiastic's waking hours, from well before dawn until dusk. St. Benedict's was not the first monastic rule, but the same masterful clarity and succinctness that characterize his description of the Office are maintained throughout the entire document, contributing greatly to its near universal adoption by Western monasticism in later centuries. Benedict composed his Rule for his newly established community at Monte Cassino in about 530, just a few years after the death of Boethius, and only a few decades before Cassiodorus founded his own monastery at

Vivarium. Unlike Boethius and Cassiodorus, Benedict certainly did not see himself as preserving classical culture. In his youth he had been sent to Rome to further his education and had been appalled by the worldliness of that still impressive capital. But he shares with his Italian contemporaries the role of unwitting founder of medieval society. He designed his rule for his small band of monastic disciples at Monte Cassino, never dreaming that it would become one of the most influential books in the history of Western civilization.

Just as the reading from Benedict's Rule serves as a conveniently compact description of the medieval Office, so the excerpt from *Ordo romanus XVII* serves as a brief, virtually laconic, description of the medieval Mass. The *Exposition of the Ancient Gallican Liturgy*, however, is a document of different character. Its elaborately allegorical style is anything but compact or laconic, yet a relatively clear description of a Gallican Mass can be extracted from its fanciful symbolic explanation of that rite. At the same time, its very use of the allegorical style vividly exemplifies the method of allegorical exegesis, described above in connection with the Early Christian psalm commentary, that was applied here in the early Middle Ages to a genre different from that of biblical exegesis.

The following three readings deal with one of the central questions in the historiography of medieval music, how the chant fared in its transmission from Rome to the northern realm of the Carolingians. We know certain things about the process, for example, that Pope Stephen II brought Roman singers with him when he visited Pepin the Short in 754, and that the Franks were so impressed by the Roman chant that Pepin decided to replace the indigenous Gallican liturgy with that of the Romans. We also know that the Roman singers brought the texts of the chant in written form—certainly the texts of the Mass chants and quite possibly those of the Office—while the melodies, on the other hand, were somehow transmitted orally. And finally, we know that the melodies achieved a stable form by about 900 at the latest, because we have copies from that time in Frankish manuscripts with musical notation. But that leaves us with an immense gap in our knowledge. How much did the chant melodies change from their original orally transmitted Roman form to their final written Frankish form?

The three readings translated here form an important part of the evidence that scholars use to support their positions on this highly controversial question. The letter of Abbot Helisachar describes his efforts to establish a satisfactory antiphonary of the Office. It provides a sober and authoritative account by a contemporary witness on one important aspect of the transmission process. The passages from John the Deacon's life of Gregory the Great and from the Monk of St. Gall's life of Charlemagne provide sharply contrasting retrospective histories—the former from the Roman point of view and the latter from the Frankish—of how the Roman chant fared during its early years in Francia. Both documents, while entertainingly prejudiced and fanciful in style, are not without a measure of historical truth to be extracted by the careful reader.

The final reading of this section provides a touching and richly allusive passage from the writings of Hildegard of Bingen, in which she describes how her convent has been deprived of the consolation of the sung Office.

In the final section, on medieval music theory and pedagogy, we witness the marriage of *musica* and *cantus*. The Carolingian music theorists took the vocabulary and basic concepts of classical Greek music theory, chiefly as derived from Boethius, and applied them to their contemporary music, the so-called Gregorian chant. In doing so they distorted the original, but this is of little significance. What is important is that they and their successors developed a body of music theory that not only described their musical practice in a consistent and systematic way, but set Western music on its peculiarly rational course. In the earlier centuries of the discipline they rationalized music vertically, so to speak, in developing a theory of musical space—the system of eight ecclesiastical modes placed on a grid of intervals derived from mathematical ratios. And in later centuries, with the emergence of polyphonic music, they rationalized music horizontally with the development of increasingly complex ways of measuring musical duration. This twofold rationalization, to continue the argument, can be looked upon as having had a dual effect on Western classical music. It permitted the eventual composition of great architectonic musical structures like those of the later eighteenth and earlier nineteenth centuries, but it may have forced Western music to sacrifice much of the rhythmic and tonal nuance that characterizes the musics of certain other high cultures.

In any event, the merger of *musica* and *cantus* did take place, and the final section provides a generous selection from the resulting literature of medieval music theory. The first examples show the later Carolingians—in monastery, court, and cathedral—as they struggled to manipulate the Boethian tonal system into one that corresponded to the realities of contemporary ecclesiastical chant. There follows an interlude of inspired pedagogy as the great Guido of Arezzo and his Italian monastic contemporaries succeed admirably in applying the new theory to the task of teaching the chant, most notably with the use of the musical staff. And finally we witness the rapid development of rhythmic systems in the scholastic milieu of thirteenth- and fourteenth-century Paris. The so-called modal rhythm of the *Discantus positio vulgaris* is followed by the mensural rhythm of Franco's *Ars cantus mensurabilis*, which is followed, in turn, by the refinements of the fourteenth-century *ars nova* as summarized in Jehan des Murs's *Notitia artis musicae*, refinements which are then roundly denounced by the arch-conservative Jacques of Liège.

Finally one notes the intrusion of the later thirteenth-century Spanish cleric Aegidius of Zamora into this series of Parisian-based theorists on rhythm. He provides us with a colorful expansion on the medieval topos of the "inventors of music." His choice for the original inventor is the Bible's Jubal, who heard his brother Tubalcain ring out the musical consonances on his blacksmith's anvil. In his view, the Greeks engaged in deceit in claiming that Pythagoras made this discovery while one day passing by a smithy. Aegidius, who wrote on natural history as well as music theory, also describes a series of musical marvels in nature, ranging from the unsurprising musical feats of the nightingale to the somewhat unexpected accomplishments of musical dolphins. The reader will recognize in these tales about the musicians of nature the same impulse that underlies the medieval bestiaries. Indeed this entire selection from the literature on music, ranging from the fourth-century Church Fathers to the fourteenth-century scholastics, can be viewed as a microcosm of medieval literature in general.

•　　•　　•

I wish to express my gratitude to three scholars who came to my aid in the delicate task of reediting this portion of Oliver Strunk's classic work: Charles Atkinson, Richard Crocker, and Leo Treitler. The last named, especially, in his dual capacities as general editor and distinguished medievalist, gave wise counsel on every aspect of the revision, from details of annotation to the selection of new material. But my greatest debt is to Oliver Strunk himself, both for his original choice of material and for his translations. Even though I found it advisable to modernize the language to some degree—for example, in providing a less Latinate word order—throughout my work I continued to marvel at how he had wrestled the correct sense out of numerous obscure passages. In the choice of readings, his superb judgment remains clear after more than forty years of development in the field of medieval music. While all those I consulted could think of readings to add, there was little indeed from the original that they wished to replace. And in this area of selection I believe that I can claim unique help from Strunk. Some thirty years ago, as a graduate student engaged in the study of patristics and music, I met him and made bold to compliment him on his choice of readings from the Church Fathers. He modestly brushed aside my remarks and reproached himself instead for having omitted the Rule of St. Benedict. Needless to say, the present edition gratefully accepts his advice on this point.

ℰARLY CHRISTIAN
VIEWS OF MUSIC

9 St. Basil

St. Basil the Great, brother of St. Gregory of Nyssa and St. Macrina, was born at Caesarea, Cappadocia, about 330 C.E. Educated at Constantinople and Athens, he retired after extensive travels to his desert retreat at Pontus, where he wrote the two Rules that came to be influential in the development of eastern monasticism. He was named bishop of Caesarea in 370 and died in 379.

Although an influential opponent of the Arian heresy, he has been called a "Roman among the Greeks" because he is better characterized as a practical churchman than as a speculative theologian. In addition to his efforts to foster monasticism, he was an energetic builder of charitable institutions, an inspired preacher, a prolific writer of letters, and a liturgical innovator.

FROM *Homily on the First Psalm*

1. All scripture is inspired by God and is profitable;[1] it was composed by the Holy Spirit to the end that all we men, as in a common dispensary for souls, might each select the medicine for his own disease. For "medicine," it is said, "causes great offenses to cease."[2] The Prophets therefore teach certain things, the Histories others, the Law others, and the kind of counsel given in the Proverbs others. But the Book of Psalms embraces whatever in all the others is helpful. It prophesies things to come, it recalls histories to the mind, it gives laws for living, it counsels what is to be done. And altogether it is a storehouse of good instructions, diligently providing for each what is useful to him. For it heals the ancient wounds of souls and brings prompt relief to the newly wounded; it ministers to what is sick and preserves what is healthy; and it wholly removes the ills, howsoever great and of whatsoever kind, that attack souls in our human life; and this by means of a certain well-timed persuasion which inspires wholesome reflection.

For when the Holy Spirit saw that mankind was ill-inclined toward virtue and that we were heedless of the righteous life because of our inclination to pleasure, what did he do? He blended the delight of melody with doctrine in order that through the pleasantness and softness of the sound we might unawares receive what was useful in the words, according to the practice of wise physicians, who, when they give the more bitter draughts to the sick, often smear the rim of the cup with honey. For this purpose these harmonious melodies of the Psalms have been designed for us, that those who are of boyish age or wholly youthful in their character, while in appearance they sing, may in reality be educating their souls. For hardly a single one of the many, and

TEXT: Jacques Migne, ed., *Patrologia cursus completus. Series graeca*, vol. 29, cols. 209–13. Translation by William Strunk, Jr., and Oliver Strunk, revised by James McKinnon.

1. 2 Timothy 3:16.
2. Ecclesiastes 10:4.

even of the indolent, has gone away retaining in his memory any precept of the apostles or of the prophets, but the oracles of the Psalms they both sing at home and disseminate in the marketplace. And if somewhere one who rages like a wild beast from excessive anger falls under the spell of the psalm, he straightway departs, with the fierceness of his soul calmed by the melody.

2. A psalm is the tranquillity of souls, the arbitrator of peace, restraining the disorder and turbulence of thoughts, for it softens the passion of the soul and moderates its unruliness. A psalm forms friendships, unites the divided, mediates between enemies. For who can still consider him an enemy with whom he has sent forth one voice to God? So that the singing of psalms brings love, the greatest of good things, contriving harmony like some bond of union and uniting the people in the symphony of a single choir.

A psalm drives away demons, summons the help of angels, furnishes arms against nightly terrors, and gives respite from daily toil; to little children it is safety, to men in their prime an adornment, to the old a solace, to women their most fitting ornament. It populates the deserts, it brings agreement to the marketplaces. To novices it is a beginning; to those who are advancing, an increase; to those who are concluding, a confirmation. A psalm is the voice of the Church. It gladdens feast days, it creates the grief which is in accord with God's will, for a psalm brings a tear even from a heart of stone.

A psalm is the work of the angels, the ordinance of Heaven, the incense of the Spirit. Oh, the wise invention of the teacher who devised how we might at the same time sing and learn profitable things, whereby doctrines are somehow more deeply impressed upon the mind!

What is learned unwillingly does not naturally remain, but things which are received with pleasure and love fix themselves more firmly in our minds. For what can we not learn from the Psalms? Can we not learn the splendor of courage, the exactness of justice, the dignity of self-control, the habit of repentance, the measure of patience, whatsoever good things that you may name? Here is perfect theology; here is foretold the Incarnation of Christ; here are the threat of judgment, the hope of resurrection, the fear of punishment, the assurances of glory, the revelations of mysteries; all things are brought together in the Book of Psalms as in some great and common storehouse.

Although there are many musical instruments, the prophet made this book suited to the psaltery, as it is called, revealing, it seems to me, the grace from on high which sounded in him through the Holy Spirit, since this alone, of all musical instruments, has the source of its sound above. For the brass wires of the cithara and the lyre sound from below against the plectrum, but the psaltery has the origins of its harmonious rhythms above, in order that we may study to seek for those things which are on high and not be drawn down by the pleasantness of the melody to the passions of the flesh.[3] And I think that by

---

3. This comparison between the psaltery and the cithara is typical of the patristic allegorical exegesis of biblical musical instruments; see James W. McKinnon, "Musical Instruments in Medieval

reason of this structure of the instrument the words of the prophet profoundly and wisely reveal to us that those whose souls are attuned and harmonious have an easy path to things above. But now let us examine the beginning of the Psalms.

Psalm Commentaries and Psalters," *Journal of the American Musicological Society* 21 (1968), especially pp. 4–13.

10 St. John Chrysostom

St. John, born to a wealthy family in Antioch about 345 c.e., was thoroughly educated in rhetoric under the renowned teacher Libanius. A longtime admirer of the monastic life, he left the home of his widowed mother about 373 to live a life of severe privation as a hermit. With his health permanently impaired, he returned to Antioch to serve as deacon from 381 and then as priest from 386 to 398, the period when he delivered the bulk of his famous homilies.

In 398 he reluctantly consented to consecration as Patriarch of Constantinople. There his outspoken moralism made him a reproach to both clergy and court so that he was deposed in 404 and exiled to Cucusus, near Antioch. The people of Antioch flocked to hear their former spiritual guide, and he was exiled once again in 407, this time to a remote spot on the Black Sea. He died en route from the rigors of the journey. John was perhaps the most eloquent preacher of Christian antiquity; his sobriquet Chrysostom means the "golden-mouthed."

FROM *Exposition of Psalm 41*

When God saw that most men were slothful, that they came unwillingly to spiritual readings, and that they found the effort involved to be distasteful, wishing to make the labor more grateful and to allay its tedium he blended melody with prophecy in order that, delighted by the modulation of the chant, all might raise sacred hymns to him with great eagerness. For nothing so uplifts the mind, giving it wings and freeing it from the earth, releasing it from the prison of the body, affecting it with love of wisdom, and causing it to scorn all things pertaining to this life, as modulated melody and the divine chant composed of number.[1]

TEXT: Jacques Migne, ed., *Patrologia cursus completus. Series graeca*, vol. 55, cols. 155–59. Translation by Oliver Strunk, revised by James McKinnon.

1. In citing "modulated" melody, that is, properly measured melody, and chant composed of "number," John evokes typical ideas of classical Greek music theory, a subject that is characterized by a thoroughly mathematical conception of music.

To such an extent, indeed, is our nature delighted by chants and songs that even infants at the breast, if they be weeping or afflicted, are by reason of it lulled to slumber. Nurses, carrying them in their arms, walking to and fro and singing certain childish songs to them, cause their eyelids to close in sleep. For this reason travelers also sing as they drive their yoked animals at midday, thus lightening the hardships of the journey by their chants. And not only travelers, but peasants are accustomed to sing as they tread the grapes in the winepress, gather the vintage, tend the vine, and perform their other tasks. Sailors do likewise, pulling at the oars. Women, too, weaving and parting the tangled threads with the shuttle, often sing a particular melody, sometimes individually and to themselves, sometimes all together in concert. This they do—the women, travelers, peasants, and sailors—striving to lighten with a chant the labor endured in working, for the mind suffers hardships and difficulties more easily when it hears songs and chants.

Inasmuch as this kind of pleasure is thoroughly innate to our mind, and lest demons introducing lascivious songs should overthrow everything, God established the Psalms, in order that they might provide both pleasure and profit. From strange chants come harm, ruin, and many a dreadful thing, since what is lascivious and vicious in these songs settles in the recesses of the soul, making it softer and weaker; from the spiritual Psalms, however, proceeds much of value, much utility, much sanctity, and every inducement to philosophy, for the words purify the soul and the Holy Spirit descends swiftly upon the soul of the singer. For those who sing with understanding invoke the grace of the Spirit.

Hear what Paul says: "Be not drunk with wine, wherein is excess, but be filled with the Spirit." He adds, moreover, what the cause of this filling is: "Singing and making melody in your heart to the Lord."[2] What is the meaning of "in your heart"? With understanding, he says; not so that the mouth utters words while the mind is inattentive and wanders in all directions, but so that the mind may hear the tongue.

And as swine flock together where there is mud, and bees linger where there is aroma and incense, so demons congregate where there are licentious chants; but where there are spiritual ones there the grace of the Spirit descends, sanctifying mouth and soul. This I say, not only that you may yourselves sing praises, but also that you may teach your wives and children to do so, not merely to lighten the work while weaving, but especially at the table. For since Satan is wont to lie in wait at feasts, and to employ as allies drunkenness, gluttony, immoderate laughter, and an inactive mind; on these occasions, both before and after table, it is especially necessary to fortify oneself with the protection of the psalms and, rising from the feast together with one's wife and children, to sing sacred hymns to God.

2. Ephesians 5:18–19.

For if Paul—imprisoned, made fast in the stocks, and threatened with intolerable scourges—praised God along with Silas continually throughout the night (when sleep is most pleasant to everyone); and if neither the place, nor the hour, nor his anxieties, nor the tyrant's slumbers, nor the pain of his labors, nor anything else could bring him to interrupt his singing,[3] so much the more ought we, who live pleasantly and enjoy God's blessings, to give forth hymns that express thanks to him.

If something untoward be visited upon our souls because of drunkenness and gluttony, the arrival of psalmody will cause these evil and depraved counsels to retreat. And just as many wealthy persons wipe off their tables with a sponge filled with balsam, so that if any stain remain from the food, they may remove it and show a clean table; so should we also, filling our mouths with spiritual melody instead of balsam, so that if any stain remain in our mind from the abundance we may thereby wipe it away.

And let us all stand together and say: "For thou, Lord, hast made me glad by thy work; I will rejoice in the works of thy hands."[4] Then after the psalmody let there be added a prayer, in order that along with the soul we may also make holy the house itself.

And as those who bring comedians, dancers, and harlots into their feasts call in demons and Satan himself and fill their homes with innumerable contentions (among them jealousy, adultery, debauchery, and countless evils); so those who invoke David with his lyre call inwardly on Christ. Where Christ is, no demon would dare to enter, nor even to peep in; but peace, and charity, and all good things would flow there as from fountains. Those make their home a theater; you make yours a church. For where there are psalms, and prayers, and the dance of the prophets, and singers with pious intentions, no one will err if he calls such an assembly a church.

Even though the meaning of the words be unknown to you, teach your mouth to utter them; for the tongue is made holy by the words when they are spoken with a ready and eager mind. Once we have acquired this habit, we will not neglect so beautiful an office either deliberately or through carelessness; custom will compel us, even against our will, to carry out this worship daily. Nor will anyone, in such singing, be blamed if he be feeble from old age or too young, or have a harsh voice, or be totally lacking in the knowledge of rhythm.[5] What is sought for here is a sober spirit, an alert mind, a contrite heart, sound reason, and clear conscience; if having these you have entered into God's sacred choir, you may stand beside David himself.

Here there is no need for the cithara, or for stretched strings, or for the plectrum and technique, or for any musical instrument; but, if you like, you

---

3. Acts 16:25.
4. Psalm 91(92):4.
5. See note 1 above; rhythm is probably meant here more as the knowledge of durational proportions than the sensation of musical pulse.

may yourself become a cithara by mortifying the members of the flesh and making a full harmony of mind and body.[6] For when the flesh no longer lusts against the spirit,[7] but has submitted to its orders and has been led at length into the best and most admirable path, then will you create a spiritual melody.

Here there is no need for technique which is slowly perfected; there is need only for lofty purpose, and we shall become skilled in a brief decisive moment. Here there is no need for place or for season; in all places and at all seasons you may sing with the mind. For whether you walk in the marketplace, or begin a journey, or sit down with your friends you may rouse up your spirit or call out silently. So also Moses called out, and God heard him.[8] If you are an artisan, you may sing while sitting and working in your shop. If you are a soldier, or if you sit in judgment, you may do the very same. One may also sing without voice, as the mind resounds inwardly. For we sing, not to men, but to God, who can hear our hearts and enter into the silences of our minds.

In proof of this, Paul cries out: "Likewise the Spirit helps us in our infirmities. And he who searches the hearts of men knows what is the mind of the Spirit, because the Spirit intercedes for the saints according to the will of God."[9] This does not mean that the Spirit groans; it means that spiritual men—having the gifts of the Spirit, praying for their kinsmen, and offering supplications—do so with contrition and groanings. Let us also do this, daily conversing with God in psalms and prayers. And let us not offer mere words, but let us know the very meaning of our discourse.

6. Another instance of instrumental allegory; see p. 122, note 3.
7. Galatians 5:17.
8. Exodus 14:15.
9. Romans 8:26–27.

11 St. Jerome

Eusebius Sophronius Hieronymus, now known as St. Jerome, was born of wealthy Christian parents about 340 C.E. at Stridon in Dalmatia. He spent his teenage years in Rome studying Greek philosophy and Latin literature under the famed grammarian Donatus. Attracted to the ascetical life, he sojourned in Trier and Aquileia for a number of years in quasi-monastic communities. In about 374 he set out to visit Jerusalem, but was detained by illness at Antioch. During the next several years, living in Antioch, the nearby deserts, and in Constantinople, he perfected his Greek, became more deeply involved in the practice of asceticism, and began the study of Hebrew. From 382 to 385 he lived in Rome where he became the confidant and secretary of Pope Damasus, who commissioned him to revise the Latin texts of the Bible. In 386 Jerome settled in Bethlehem where he founded a monastery over which he presided as he continued his work of biblical translation and commentary until his death in 420.

Jerome, an irascible personality, was an aggressive theological polemicist and a rigorous spiritual advisor, but he is best remembered as a biblical scholar. He was unique among the Christians of his time in his command of Hebrew and his interest in biblical history and archeology. His translation of the Bible, the Vulgate, has endured into modern times as the standard Latin version.

FROM *Commentary on the Epistle of Paul to the Ephesians*

"Speaking to yourselves in psalms and hymns and spiritual canticles, singing and making melody in your heart to the Lord."[1] He who has kept himself from the drunkenness of wine, wherein is excess, and has thereby been filled with the Spirit, is able to accept all things spiritually—psalms, hymns, and canticles.[2] How the psalm, the hymn, and the song differ from one another we learn most fully in the Psalter. Here let us say briefly that hymns declare the power and majesty of the Lord and continually praise his works and favors, something that is done by all those psalms to which the word *Alleluia* is prefixed or appended. Psalms, moreover, properly affect the ethical seat, so that by this organ of the body we may know what ought to be done and what avoided. But he who treats of higher things, the subtle investigator who explains the harmony of the world and the order and concord of all creatures, this one sings a spiritual song. For surely, to speak more plainly than we might wish for the sake of the simple, the psalm is directed to the body and the canticle to the mind. We ought, then, to sing and to make melody and to praise the Lord more with the spirit than with the voice.

This, indeed, is what is written: "Singing and making melody in your heart to the Lord." Let youth hear this, let them hear it whose office it is to sing in the church: sing to God, not with the voice, but with the heart; not, after the fashion of tragedians, in smearing the throat with a sweet ointment, so that theatrical melodies and songs are heard in the church, but in fear, in work, and in knowledge of the Scriptures. And although a man be *kakophonos*, to use a common expression, if he have good works, he is a sweet singer before God. And let the servant of Christ sing so that he pleases, not through his voice, but

TEXT: Jacques Migne, ed., *Patrologia cursus completus. Series latina*, vol. 26, cols. 561–62. Translation by Oliver Strunk, revised by James McKinnon.

1. 2 Ephesians 5:19. See also Colossians 3:16.
2. Psalms, hymns, and canticles are not to be understood in the modern sense of psalms from the Psalter, newly-composed hymns, and biblical canticles; they are rather different categories of psalms, that are suggested by superscriptions in the Psalter. For other passages where patristic writers develop the same sort of distinctions, see James McKinnon, *Music in Early Christian Literature* (Cambridge: Cambridge University Press, 1987), items 272, 359, and 360.

through the words which he pronounces, in order that the evil spirit which was in Saul[3] may be cast out from those who are similarly possessed by it, and may not enter into those who would make of the house of God a popular theater.

3. 1 Samuel 16:23.

12 Niceta of Remesiana

Niceta was born in the Roman province of Dacia during the second quarter of the fourth century C.E. He was named bishop of Remesiana (present-day Bela Palanka in Serbia) about 370 and died there after 414. Although a churchman and theologian of some standing in his own time, his works came to be misattributed, with the result that he was forgotten until the twentieth century. His sermon on psalmody quoted here, for example, appears as the third item in Martin Gerbert's *Scriptores ecclesiastici de musica* (1784), but in a badly defective version attributed to the sixth-century Nicetius of Trèves. The sermon is one of a pair. In the first of the two, "Concerning Vigils," Niceta had promised to devote an entire sermon on the psalm-singing practiced at these ceremonies; he kept his promise with "On the Benefit of Psalmody," a remarkable summary of the early Christian doctrine on ecclesiastical song.

FROM *On the Benefit of Psalmody*

I know of some, not only in our region but in the East, who consider the singing of psalms and hymns to be an excess that is barely appropriate to divine religion; they consider it enough if a psalm is spoken in the heart, and frivolous if uttered aloud by the mouth. They appropriate to their view that passage which the Apostle wrote to the Ephesians: "Be filled with the Spirit, speaking in psalms, hymns, and spiritual canticles, singing and making melody to the Lord in your hearts."[1] Look, they say, the apostle makes it clear that a psalm is to be sung in the heart, not prattled like the tunes of an actor, because it is enough for God "who searches the heart"[2] if it is sung there in secret. Nevertheless, if truth be told, just as I do not censure those who "sing in the heart" (for it is always beneficial to meditate upon the things of God), so too do I commend those who honor God with the sound of the voice.

TEXT: Cuthbert Turner, "Niceta of Remesiana II. Introduction and text of *De psalmodiae bono*," *Journal of Theological Studies* 24 (1922–23): 233–41. Translation by James McKinnon.

1. Ephesians 5:18–19.
2. Romans 8:27.

Before I provide the testimony of numerous passages from Scripture, I shall, by reversing the interpretation of that very passage of the apostle that many use against singers, refute their foolishness. The Apostle says in fact: "Be filled with the Spirit as you speak," and I contend that the Spirit has freed our mouths, loosened our tongues, and opened our lips, for it is not possible for men to speak without these organs; and as heat differs from cold, so does silence from speaking. When, moreover, he adds, "speaking in psalms, hymns, and canticles," he would not have mentioned "canticles" *(canticorum)* if he had intended the singing to be altogether silent, because no one can sing *(cantare)* without making a sound. And when he says "in your hearts," he enjoins you not to sing only with the voice and without the heart, but as he says in another place, "I will sing with the Spirit, I will sing with understanding,"[3] that is, with both voice and thought.

• • • • •

If we enquire as to who first introduced this sort of song, we would find none other than Moses, who sang a splendid canticle to God after Egypt had been struck by the ten plagues, Pharoah had been drowned, and the people had been led along a miraculous pathway through the sea and into the desert; filled with gratitude he proclaimed, "Let us sing to the Lord, for he has triumphed gloriously."[4] For one ought not rashly to accept the volume called "The Inquiry of Abraham," where Abraham, along with animals, fountains, and the elements, is portrayed singing,[5] because this book is supported by neither faith nor any other authority. Moses, therefore, the leader of the tribes of Israel, was the first to establish choruses; he taught both sexes in separate groups to sing a triumphal canticle to God, while he and his sister went before them.[6] Afterwards one finds Deborah, an estimable woman, performing this ministry in the Book of Judges.[7] Again, Moses himself, as he was about to depart from his body, sang a fearsome song in the Book of Deuteronomy;[8] he left it to the people as a written testament, whereby the tribes of Israel would know what manner of deaths threatened them should they depart from the Lord . . .

After this you will find many, not only men but women as well, who were filled with the divine Spirit of God and sang of mysteries, this even before David, who, singled out by the Lord for this service from childhood, was found worthy to be a leader of singers and a treasury of song. While still a youth he played sweetly yet strongly upon the cithara and subdued the evil spirit that worked within Saul[9]—not because the cithara possessed such power, but

3. 1 Corinthians 14:15.
4. Exodus 15:1.
5. See the apocryphal Apocalypse of Abraham 17:6–18:14.
6. Miriam the prophetess, sister of Moses and Aaron, took a timbrel in hand and led the women in a canticle after the completion of Moses's canticle; see Exodus 15:20–21.
7. Judges 5:1–31.
8. Deuteronomy 32:1–43.
9. 1 Samuel 16:23.

because the image of Christ's cross was mystically exhibited in the wood and stretched strings of the instrument, and thereby it was the very Passion that was hymned and that overcame the spirit of the demon.

•   •   •   •   •

It would be tedious, dearly beloved, were I to recount every episode from the history of the Psalms, especially since it is necessary now to offer something from the New Testament in confirmation of the Old, lest one think the ministry of psalmody to be forbidden, inasmuch as many of the usages of the Old Law have been abolished. For those things that are carnal have been rejected, circumcision for example, and the observance of the Sabbath, sacrifices, discrimination among foods, as well as trumpets, citharas, cymbals, and tympana (all of which are now understood to reside in the bodily members of man, and there better to sound).[10] Daily ablutions, observance of new moons, the meticulous examination of leprosy, or whatever of this sort was necessary at the time for children,[11] have clearly ceased and gone their way. But the remaining practices that are spiritual, such as faith, piety, prayer, fasting, patience, chastity, and praise in song; these have been increased rather than diminished.

Hence you will find in the Gospels first Zacharias, father of the mighty John, to have voiced a prophetic hymn after his long silence.[12] Nor did Elizabeth, who had long been barren, cease to "magnify" God from her "soul" after her promised son had been born.[13] When Christ was born on earth a host of angels sang in praise of him, saying, "Glory to God in the highest," and proclaiming, "peace on earth to men of good will."[14] "The boys in the Temple cried out 'Hosanna to the son of David,' " nor did the Lord give in to the indignation of the loudly objecting Pharisees, and close the mouths of these innocents, but rather he opened them, saying, "Have you not read what was written, that 'Out of the mouth of babes and sucklings you have brought forth perfect praise,' "[15] and " 'if these were silent the very stones would cry out.' "[16] Finally, not to prolong this discourse, the Lord himself, a teacher in words and a master in deeds, in order to display his approval of the sweet ministry of hymns, "went out to the Mount of Olives with his disciples after singing a hymn."[17]

10. Still another example of instrumental allegorical exegesis; see note 3 above in the passage from St. Basil, p. 122.
11. The reference to the religious observances of the Hebrew Scriptures as necessary to hold the attention of spiritual children was a commonplace—not without its anti-Semitic dimension—of fourth-century historical exegesis; for a more explicit example, see McKinnon, *Music in Early Christian Literature,* items 229–31.
12. Luke 1:67–79.
13. Luke 1:46. A confusing reference; it was Mary, not her cousin Elizabeth, who sang "My soul magnifies the Lord" on the occasion of her visit to Elizabeth, and Elizabeth's son John was not yet born at the time.
14. Luke 2:13–14.
15. Matthew 21:15–16.
16. Luke 19:40.
17. Matthew 26:30 and Mark 14:26.

·　·　·　·　·

What could be more appropriate than this kind of benefit? For we are plea-sured by psalms, bedewed by prayers, and fed by the interspersed readings. Indeed, just as the honest guests at a banquet are delighted with a succession of courses, so are our souls nourished by a variety of readings and a display of hymns.

Then let us, dearly beloved, sing psalms with alert senses and awakened minds, as the hymnodist exhorts us: "Since God is King over all the earth, sing psalms with understanding,"[18] for a psalm is sung not only "in spirit," that is, with the sound of the voice, but also "in mind,"[19] so that we think of what we sing, rather than allow the mind, caught up in distractions (as often happens), to lose the fruit of its labor. Let the chant, then, be sung in a manner befitting holy religion; let it not display theatrical turgidity, but show a Christian simplic-ity in its melody, and let it not evoke the stage, but create compunction in the listeners. Our voices ought not to be dissonant, but concordant—not with one dragging out the song, and another cutting it short, while one sings too softly, and another too loudly—and all must seek to blend their voices within the sound of a harmonious chorus, not to project it outward in vulgar display like a cithara. It must all be done as if in the sight of God, not man, and not to please oneself.

We have a model and exemplar of this vocal consonance in those three blessed youths of whom the Book of Daniel speaks: "Then these three as if from one voice sang a hymn and glorified God in the furnace saying, 'Blessed art thou, the God of our Fathers.' "[20] You have it here on biblical authority that the three praised the Lord together "as if from one voice," just as all of us must exhibit the same intention and the same sounding melody as if from a single voice. Those, however, who are not able to blend and adapt themselves to the others, ought better to sing in a subdued voice than to create a great clamor; and thus will they fulfill their liturgical obligation and avoid disrupting the singing community. For it is not given to all to possess a supple and pleasant voice.

18. Psalm 46(47):8.
19. "I will sing with the spirit, and I will sing with the mind"; 1 Corinthians 15:15.
20. Daniel 3:51–52; the long passage that has the canticle of the three youths is present only in the Greek-Latin-Catholic textual tradition, not in the Hebrew-Protestant tradition.

13 St. Augustine

Aurelius Augustinus was born at Tagaste in North Africa in 354 C.E. to a pagan
father and Christian mother, the sainted Monica. In 384, after several years of
spiritual crisis and philosophical enquiry during which he lost his childhood
faith and maintained a relationship with the mistress who bore his son Adeoda-
tus, he settled in Milan as a professor of rhetoric. There he fell under the influence of St. Ambrose and was baptized in 387. Soon after, he returned to Africa
where, following a period of monastic seclusion, he was ordained priest in 391
and four years later was consecrated bishop of Hippo Regius, present-day
Annaba in Algeria. He died there in 430 while the city was under seige by the
Vandals.

Augustine may be the most important figure in the history of Christian
thought, seriously rivaled only by Thomas Aquinas. And while he is the author
of numerous exegetical and theological works, and more than 800 preserved
sermons, his intellectual influence is felt outside of the narrowly religious sphere
as well: his *De musica* moves beyond classical metrics to a philosophy of
rhythm; his *City of God* is a profound reflection on the nature of history; and his
Confessions is an autobiography marked by a quality of psychological probing
unknown before modern times. The passage from this last work that appears
below shows the saint torn between feelings of guilt at the pleasure he experiences in hearing music and the position that sacred song is ultimately a beneficial practice.

FROM THE *Confessions*

The delights of the ear had enticed me and held me in their grip, but you
have unbound and liberated me. Yet, I confess, I still surrender to some slight
pleasure in those sounds to which your words give life, when they are sung by
a sweet and skilled voice, but not so much that I cleave to them, unable to rise
above them when I wish. But yet, these chants, animated as they are by your
words, must gain entry to me and find in my heart a place of some dignity,
even if I scarcely provide them a fitting one. Sometimes it seems to me that I
grant them more honor than is proper, when I sense that the words stir my
soul to greater religious fervor and to a more ardent piety if they are thus sung
than if not thus sung, and when I feel that all the diverse affections of my soul
have their own proper measures in voice and song, which are stimulated by I

TEXT: Lucas Verheijen, ed., *Sancti Augustini Confessiones Libri XIII*, Corpus Christianorum
Series Latina 27 (Turnhout: Brepols, 1981), pp. 181–82. Translation of this selection (Book 10,
Chapter 33) by James McKinnon.

know not what hidden correspondences.[1] But the gratification of the flesh—to which I ought not surrender my mind to be enervated—frequently leads me astray, for the senses are not content to accompany reason by patiently following it, but after being admitted only for the sake of reason, they seek to rush ahead and lead it. I sin thus in these things unknowingly, but afterwards I do know.

Sometimes, however, overly anxious to avoid this particular snare, I err by excessive severity, and sometimes so much so that I wish every melody of those sweet chants to which the songs of David are set, to be banished from my ears and from the very church. And it seems safer to me what I remember was often told me concerning Bishop Athanasius of Alexandria, who required the reader of the psalm to perform it with so little inflection of voice that it resembled speaking more than singing.[2]

Yet when I recall the tears that I shed at the song of the Church in the first days of my recovered faith, and even now as I am moved not by the song but by the things which are sung—when chanted with fluent voice and completely appropriate melody—I acknowledge the great benefit of this practice. Thus I waver between the peril of pleasure and the benefit of my experience; but I am inclined, while not maintaining an irrevocable position, to endorse the custom of singing in church so that weaker souls might rise to a state of devotion by indulging their ears. Yet when it happens that I am moved more by the song than by what is sung, I confess to sinning grievously, and I would prefer not to hear the singer at such times. See now my condition! Weep with me and weep for me, you who cultivate within yourselves the good will whence good deeds proceed (for if you are not so disposed, my words will fail to move you). But you, my Lord and my God, give ear, look and see, have pity on me and heal me, you before whom I have become an enigma unto my self—and that is my very infirmity.

1. There is an echo of Platonic musical psychology in this latter clause that speaks of a causal relationship, almost physical and mechanical, between certain thoughts and feelings and certain musical melodies and rhythms. The belief in this sort of relationship is generally referred to as "ethos doctrine." See, for example, Plato's *Republic* 398–403 (pp. 9–16).
2. St. Athanasius was bishop of Alexandria intermittently from 328 to his death in 373; for examples of his somewhat severe ideas on psalmody see McKinnon, *Music in Early Christian Literature*, items 98–100.

MUSIC AS A
LIBERAL ART

14 Boethius

Anicius Manlius Severinus Boethius was born to a noble Roman family in about 480. Through a combination of his own birthright, his marriage into the powerful Symmachus family, and his extraordinary talents, he rose quickly in the political hierarchy of the time. He held the consulship in 510 and eventually became a friend and advisor of the Gothic king Theodoric. He fell under suspicion, however, of cooperating with Byzantine designs upon Gothic Italy; he was imprisoned at Pavia in 523 and executed sometime between 524 and 526.

Boethius is the primary figure in the transition between the intellectual worlds of Classical Antiquity and the Middle Ages. His works include treatises on the four mathematical arts of the quadrivium, on logic, and on various theological subjects, as well as his immensely popular *On the Consolation of Philosophy*, written during his imprisonment. His *Fundamentals of Music*, largely a translation and paraphrase of Nicomachus and Ptolemy, is one of the four quadrivial treatises; it had a far-reaching influence upon the development of medieval musical theory. Translated here are excerpts from the less technical portions of the work. (The entire treatise is translated by Calvin M. Bower, *Fundamentals of Music: Anicius Manlius Severinus Boethius* [New Haven: Yale University Press, 1989].)

FROM *Fundamentals of Music*

BOOK ONE

1. INTRODUCTION: MUSIC IS RELATED TO US BY NATURE AND CAN ENNOBLE OR CORRUPT THE CHARACTER

The perceptive power of all the senses is so spontaneously and naturally present in certain living creatures that to conceive of an animal without senses is impossible. Yet an inquiry by the mind will not provide to the same degree a knowledge and clear understanding of the senses themselves. It is easily understood that we use our senses to perceive sensible things, but the very nature of the senses by which we act, as well as the peculiar property of sensible things, is not so apparent or intelligible save by proper investigation and reflection upon the truth.

Sight is common to all mortals, but whether it results from images coming to the eye or from rays sent out to the object of sight is doubtful to the learned, though the vulgar are unaware that such doubt exists. Again, anyone seeing a triangle or square easily recognizes what he sees, but to know the nature of a square or triangle he must inquire of a mathematician.

TEXT: Gottfried Friedlein, ed., *Anicii Manliii Torquate Severini Boetii De Institutione Arithmetica Libri Duo De Institutione Musica Libri Quinque* (Leipzig, 1867), pp. 178–89, 223–25. Translation by William Strunk, Jr., and Oliver Strunk, revised by James McKinnon.

The same may be said of other matters of sense, especially of the judgment of the ear, whose power so apprehends sounds that it not only judges them and knows their differences, but is often delighted when the modes[1] are sweet and well-ordered, and pained when disordered and incoherent ones offend the sense.

From this it follows that, of the four mathematical disciplines, the others are concerned with the pursuit of truth, but music is related not only to speculation but to morality as well. Nothing is more characteristic of human nature than to be soothed by sweet modes and disturbed by their opposites. Nor is this limited to particular professions or ages; it is, rather, common to all professions, while infants, youth, and the old as well are so naturally attuned to musical modes by a kind of spontaneous feeling that no age is without delight in sweet song. From this may be discerned the truth of what Plato said, not idly, that the soul of the universe is united by musical concord.[2] For when we apprehend by means of what is well and fitly ordered in ourselves, that which is well and fitly combined in sounds—and take pleasure in this—we recognize that we ourselves are internally united by this congruity. For congruity is agreeable, incongruity hateful and contrary.

From this source, also, the greatest alterations of character arise. A lascivious mind takes pleasure in the more lascivious modes, and is often softened and corrupted by listening to them. Contrariwise, a sterner mind finds joy in the more stirring modes and is braced by them. This is why the musical modes are named after certain peoples, such as the Lydian and Phrygian; the mode takes the name of the nation that delights in it. For a people takes pleasure in modes resembling its own character, nor can it be that the soft should be joined to and delight the hard, or the hard delight the soft, but, as I have said, it is congruity which causes love and delight. For this reason Plato insists that any change in music of right moral tendency should be avoided, declaring that there could be no greater detriment to the morals of a community than a gradual perversion of modest and temperate music.[3] For the minds of the listeners are immediately affected and gradually go astray, retaining no trace of honesty and right, if either the lascivious modes implant in them something shameful or the harsher modes something savage and monstrous.

Discipline has no more open pathway to the mind than through the ear; when rhythms and modes gain access to the mind by this path, it is evident that they affect it and cause it to conform to their nature. One observes this among the nations. Ruder peoples delight in the harsher modes of the Thra-

---

1. Mode is a word with a wide variety of meanings in antiquity, although all of them, in keeping with the mathematical view of music predominating at the time, partake at least to some extent of the word's root meaning "measure." Here the word might convey something of the connotation of the Platonic *harmoniae* such as the Dorian and Phrygian, or it might simply refer to musical melody in a more general sense.
2. *Timaeus* 37a.
3. *Republic* 424b–424c.

cians, civilized peoples in more restrained modes; though in these days this almost never occurs. Since humanity is now soft and fickle, it is wholly captivated by the modes of the theater. Music was chaste and modest so long as it was played on simpler instruments, but since it has come to be performed in a protracted and confusing mixture of styles,[4] it has lost its grave and virtuous manner, descending virtually to depravity, and preserving only a trace of its ancient beauty.

This is why Plato prescribes that boys should not be trained in all modes, but only in those which are strong and simple.[5] And above all we should bear in mind that if something is altered even in the very slightest, it will—although not sensed at first—eventually make a considerable difference and will pass through the sense of hearing into the mind. Hence Plato holds that music which is carefully and modestly composed, so that it is chaste, simple, and masculine, not effeminate, savage, and inconsistent, is a great guardian of the commonwealth.[6]

•   •   •   •   •

It is well known indeed how often song has overcome anger, and how many wonders it has performed on the affections of the body and mind. Who is unaware that Pythagoras, by means of a spondaic melody, calmed and restored to self-control a youth of Taormina who had become intoxicated by the sound of the Phrygian mode? One night a harlot was shut up in the house of the youth's rival, and he in his frenzy was about to set fire to it. Pythagoras, observing the motion of the stars as was his custom, learned that the youth, agitated by the sound of the Phrygian mode, was deaf to the many pleas of his friends to desist from his crime; he ordered that the mode be changed, and thus reduced the youth's fury to a state of perfect calm.

Cicero, in his *De consiliis*, tells the story differently, in this manner: "But if I may, struck by some similarity, compare a trifling matter to a weighty one, it is said that when certain drunken youths, aroused, as is wont to happen, by the music of the tibia,[7] were about to break into the house of a modest woman, Pythagoras urged the player to perform a spondaic melody. When he had done this, the slowness of the measures and the gravity of the player calmed their wanton fury."[8]

To add a few brief illustrations in the same vein, Terpander and Arion of Methymna rescued the Lesbians and the Ionians from the gravest maladies by the aid of song. Then Ismenias the Theban, when the torments of sciatica

---

4. The Latin *tractatam varie et permixte* is cryptic; it seems to suggest the mixing of the musical genres, something that Plato considered to be the most serious of musical perversions; see the *Laws* 700a–701b.
5. *Republic* 399c. See p. 11.
6. *Republic* 401d. See p. 14.
7. The tibia is the Latin equivalent of the Greek aulos, the most common wind instrument of antiquity; it is frequently mistranslated flute although it was a reed instrument.
8. The passage does not appear to be from Cicero's *De consiliis*.

were troubling a number of Boeotians, is reported to have rid them of all their afflictions by his melodies. And Empedocles, when an infuriated youth drew his sword upon a guest of his who had passed sentence upon his father, is said to have altered the mode of the singing and thus to have tempered the young man's anger.

Indeed, the power of the musical art became so evident through the studies of ancient philosophy that the Pythagoreans used to free themselves from the cares of the day by certain melodies, which caused a gentle and quiet slumber to steal upon them. Similarly, upon rising, they dispelled the stupor and confusion of sleep by certain other melodies, knowing that the whole structure of soul and body is united by musical harmony.

·   ·   ·   ·   ·

Is it not evident that the spirit of warriors is roused by the sound of the trumpets? If it is true that a peaceful state of mind can be converted into wrath and fury, then beyond doubt a gentler mode can temper the anger and passionate desire of a perturbed mind. How does it happen that when someone willingly takes in a song with both the ears and the spirit, he is involuntarily turned to it, so that his body feigns some motion similar to that of the song heard, and how does it happen that his spirit picks out simply with its memory some previously heard melody. From all this it appears clear and certain that music is so much a part of our nature that we cannot do without it even if we wish to do so.

The power of the mind should therefore be directed to the purpose of comprehending by science what is inherent by nature. Just as in seeing, the learned are not content to behold colors and forms without investigating their properties, so they are not content to be delighted by melodies without learning what pitch ratios render them internally consistent.

2. THE THREE KINDS OF MUSIC, WITH A CONSIDERATION OF THE POWER OF MUSIC

A writer on music should therefore state at the beginning how many kinds of music those who have investigated the subject are known to have recognized. There are three kinds: the first, the music of the universe; the second, human music; the third, instrumental music, as that of the cithara or the tibia or the other instruments which serve for melody.

The first, the music of the universe, is especially to be studied in the combining of the elements and the variety of the seasons which are observed in the heavens. How indeed could the swift mechanism of the sky move silently in its course? And although this sound does not reach our ears (as must for many reasons be the case), the extremely rapid motion of such great bodies could not be altogether silent, especially since the courses of the stars are joined together by such mutual adaptation that nothing more equally compacted or united could be imagined. For some orbit higher and others lower, and all revolve by a common impulse, so that an established order of their circuits can be deduced from their various inequalities. For this reason an established order of modulation[9] cannot be lacking in this celestial revolution.

Now unless a certain harmony united the differences and contrary powers of the four elements, how could they form a single body and mechanism? But all this diversity produces the variety of seasons and fruits, yet thereby makes the year a unity. So if you could imagine any one of the elements that produce such a variety removed, all would perish, nor, so to speak, would they retain a vestige of consonance. And just as there is a careful adjustment of pitch in low strings lest the lowness descend to inaudibility, and an adjustment of tension in high strings lest, being too taut, they be broken by the rarified pitch, (while all remains congruous and fitting); similarly we perceive that in the music of the universe nothing can be so extreme as to destroy some other part by its own excess, but each part brings its own contribution or aids others to bring theirs. For what winter binds, spring releases, and what summer heats, autumn ripens; the seasons in turn bring forth their own fruits or help others to bring forth theirs. These matters will be discussed more searchingly later on.

What human music is, anyone may understand by examining his own nature. For what is that which unites the incorporeal activity of the reason with the body, unless it be a certain mutual adaptation and as it were a tempering of low and high sounds into a single consonance? What else joins together the parts of the soul itself, which in the opinion of Aristotle is a union of the rational and the irrational?[10] What causes the blending of the body's elements or holds its parts together in established adaptation? This also I shall take up later.

The third kind of music is that which is described as residing in certain instruments. This is produced by tension, as in strings, or by blowing, as in the tibia or in those instruments activated by water,[11] or by some kind of percussion, as in instruments where one beats upon a bronze concavity;[12] by such means various sounds are produced.

It seems best in this work to treat first of the music of instruments.[13] But enough of introduction. The elements of music themselves must now be discussed.

•   •   •   •   •

9. "Modulation" is a translation of *modulatio,* literally, measuring; it appears here to have the meaning of music in general, although, again, with mathematical connotation. At other places in this volume, *modulatio,* as suggested by the context, is translated "measurement."

10. *On the Soul* 423a.

11. Boethius has in mind here the hydraulis, or water organ, an instrument that he may have known only from literary references.

12. An apparent reference to the *cymbala* of antiquity, a pair of small cup-shaped cymbals.

13. Boethius moves on, then, not to a study of instrumental music, but to a study of pitch (the discipline of harmonics, that is) as demonstrated on instruments.

33. WHAT A MUSICIAN IS

It should be borne in mind that every art, and every discipline as well, has by nature a more honorable character than a handicraft, which is produced by the hand and labor of a craftsman.[14] For it is far greater and nobler to know what someone does than to accomplish oneself what someone else knows, for physical skill obeys like a handmaid while reason rules like a mistress. And unless the hand does what the mind sanctions, it acts in vain. How much more admirable, then, is the science of music in apprehending by reason than in accomplishing by work and deed! It is as much nobler as the body is surpassed by the mind, because the person destitute of reason lives in servitude. But reason reigns and leads to what is right; and unless its rule is obeyed, a work thus deprived of reason will falter. It follows, then, that reason's contemplation of working does not need the deed, while the works of our hands are nothing unless guided by reason.

How great the glory and merit of reason are can be understood from this: that those so-called physical craftsmen take their names, not from their discipline, but rather from their instruments. For the citharodist is named after the cithara, the aulodist after the tibia,[15] and the others after the names of their instruments. He however is a musician who has absorbed the science of singing by careful reflection, not by the servitude of work but by the rule of contemplation. We see the same thing in the erection of buildings and the waging of wars, namely in the contrary conferring of names: the buildings are inscribed and the triumphs held in the names of those by whose rule and reason they were begun, not of those by whose labor and servitude they were completed.

Thus there are three classes concerned with the art of music. One class has to do with instruments, another invents songs, a third judges the work of instruments and the song. But that class which is dedicated to instruments and there consumes its entire efforts, as for example the players of the cithara and those who show their skill on the organ and other musical instruments, are cut off from the understanding of musical science, since they are servants, as has been said, who do not make any use of reason, and are altogether lacking in thought. The second class having to do with music is that of the poets, which is attracted to song not so much by speculation and reason as by a certain natural instinct. Thus this class also is to be separated from music. The third is that which acquires the skill of judging, so that it weighs rhythms and melodies and the whole of song. And this class is rightly reckoned as musical because it relies entirely upon reason and speculation. And that person is a musician who possesses the faculty of judging—according to speculation and reason that is

14. There is more than an echo here of the classical prejudice, one with a long life in the Western European tradition, that the "liberal arts" are those practiced by individuals who have the leisure to cultivate the things of the mind, free as they are from the necessity to use their hands in making a living; see Aristotle, *Politics* 1337b–1338a. See pp. 24–26.

15. See note 7 above.

appropriate and suitable to music—of modes and rhythms, of the classes of melodies and their combinations,[16] of all those things about which there is to be discussion later on, and of the songs of the poets.

16. *Permixtionibus* is rendered "combinations" here because it seems to fit the context well even though the mixing of musical genres is forbidden by Plato; see note 4 above. Calvin M. Bower makes a plausible case for consonance; see his *Fundamentals of Music*, p. 51.

15 Cassiodorus

Flavius Magnus Aurelius Cassiodorus was born to a noble Roman family in about 490 C.E. at Squillace on the Ionian Sea. He served, as did Boethius, in the Gothic court of Theodoric, but managed to outlive his patron, who died in 526, not long after the execution of Boethius. Cassiodorus spent the dangerous years of the Gothic Wars in Constantinople, returning to Italy in 554 to settle at his monastery at Vivarium, near his native Squillace, where he died in about 583.

Cassiodorus, like Boethius, is one of the principal figures in the transmission of ancient culture to the Latin Middle Ages. Of musical interest among his works are the *Exposition of the Psalms,* written during his eastern sojourn, and the *Fundamentals of Sacred and Secular Learning,* written at Vivarium. The latter, intended as a primer for the monks under his charge, is divided into two books. The first is more directly concerned with religious studies, while the second provides brief summaries of the seven liberal arts. The section on music, given below, is much more superficial than Boethius's work, but was nonetheless influential in the formation of medieval musical thought, particularly in its earlier stages.

FROM *Fundamentals of Sacred and Secular Learning*

V. OF MUSIC

1. A certain Gaudentius, writing on music, says that Pythagoras found its beginning in the sound of hammers and the striking of stretched strings.[1] Muti-

TEXT: R. A. B. Mynors, ed., *Institutiones divinarum et saecularium litterarum* (Oxford: Clarendon Press, 1937), pp. 142–50. Translation by William Strunk, Jr., and Oliver Strunk, revised by James McKinnon.

1. On the topos of the "inventors of music" see James W. McKinnon, "*Jubal vel Pythagoras, quis sit inventor musicae:* Thoughts on Musical Historiography from Boethius to Burney," *The Musical Quarterly* 64 (1978): 1–28.

anus, a man of great eloquence, has translated the work of Gaudentius into Latin in a manner attesting his skill. Clement the Alexandrian priest declares in his *Exhortation to the Greeks* that music received its origin from the Muses, and takes pains to make clear for what reason the Muses themselves were invented: they were so named ἀπὸ τοῦ μῶσθαι, that is, "from inquiring," because, as the ancients would have it, they were the first to inquire into the power of songs and the modulation of the voice.[2] We find also that Censorinus, in his treatise *De die natali*, addressed to Quintus Cerellius, has written things not to be overlooked concerning the musical discipline, or the second part of mathematics,[3] hence it is profitable to read him so that these things are more deeply implanted in the mind by frequent meditation.

2. The discipline of music is diffused through all the actions of our life. First, it is true that if we perform the commandments of the Creator and with pure minds obey the rules he has laid down, then every word we speak, every pulsation of our veins, is related by musical rhythms to the powers of harmony. Music indeed is the knowledge of proper measurement.[4] If we live virtuously, we are constantly proved to be under its discipline, but when we commit injustice we are without music. The heavens and the earth, indeed all things in them which are directed by a higher power, share in this discipline of music, for Pythagoras shows that this universe was founded by and can be governed by music.

3. Music is closely bound up with religion itself. Witness the decachord of the Ten Commandments,[5] the tinkling of cithara and tympanum, the melody of the organ, the sound of cymbals.[6] The very Psalter is without doubt named after a musical instrument because the exceedingly sweet and pleasing melody of the celestial virtues is contained within it.

4. Let us now discuss the parts of music, as it has been handed down from the elders. Musical science is the discipline which treats of numbers in their relation to those things which are found in sounds, such as duple, triple, quadruple, and others said to be similar to these.[7]

---

2. In point of fact, Clement reports that Alcman derived the origin of the Muses from Zeus and Mnemosyne; he does not speak of the origin of music (see his *Exhoration to the Greeks* 2). As for the etymology of ἀπὸ τοῦ μῶσθαι, this is from Plato, *Cratylus* 406a.

3. *De die natali* 13.1.

4. *Musica quippe est scientia bene modulandi.* The definition is from Augustine, *De musica* 1.2. There is no completely adequate translation for *bene modulari*, a phrase that is rich not only in aesthetic connotation but ethical and mathematical connotation as well.

5. Cassiodorus repeats a commonplace of patristic instrumental allegory: the psaltery of ten strings (Psalm 32:2) is taken to symbolize the Ten Commandments.

6. See Psalm 150:3–5.

7. *Musica scientia est disciplina quae de numeris loquitur qui ad aliquid sunt his qui inveniuntur in sonis, ut duplum, triplum, quadruplum, et his similia quae dicuntur ad aliquid.* This definition is designed to indicate the relation of music to the other divisions of mathematics and is an expansion of one that Cassiodorus had already given (2.3.21) in introducing the subject of the quadrivium. "Mathematical science . . . is that which considers abstract quantity. By abstract quantity we mean that quantity which we treat in a purely speculative way, separating it intellec-

5. The parts of music are three: harmonics, rhythmics, metrics. Harmonics is the musical science which distinguishes the high and low in sounds. Rhythmics is that which inquires whether words in combination sound well or badly together. Metrics is that which by valid reasoning knows the measures of the various meters; for example, the heroic, the iambic, the elegiac.

6. There are three classes of musical instruments: instruments of percussion, instruments of tension, and wind instruments. Instruments of percussion include cup-shaped vessels of bronze and silver, and others whose hard metal, when struck, yields an agreeable ringing. Instruments of tension are made with strings, held in place according to the rules of the art, which upon being struck by the plectrum delightfully soothe the ear. Among these are the various species of cithara. Wind instruments are those which are actuated to produce a vocal sound when filled by a stream of air, as trumpets, reeds, organs, pandoria,[8] and others of this nature.

7. We have still to explain the symphonies.[9] Symphony is the fusion of a low sound with a high one or of a high sound with a low one, an adaptation effected either vocally or by blowing or striking. There are six symphonies:

1) diatessaron	4) diapason and diatessaron together
2) diapente	5) diapason and diapente together
3) diapason	6) disdiapason

I. The consonance of the diatessaron results from the epitrita ratio (4:3) and includes four pitches, hence its name.

II. The consonance of the diapente results from the emiola ratio (3:2) and includes five pitches.

III. The consonance of the diapason, also called diocto, results from the displasia or dupla ratio (2:1) and includes eight pitches, hence the names diocto and diapason. And since the citharas of the ancients had eight strings, this consonance, including as it does all sounds, is called diapason (literally, through all).[10]

---

tually from its material and from its other accidents, such as evenness, oddness, and the like. It has these divisions: arithmetic, music, geometry, astronomy. Arithmetic is the discipline of absolute numerable quantity. Music is the discipline which treats of numbers in their relation to those things which are found in sounds. Geometry is the discipline of immobile magnitude and of forms. Astronomy is the discipline of the course of the heavenly bodies." Cassiodorus's definition of music clearly influences the terse one that is common in the Middle Ages: *Musica est de numero relato ad sonos* ("music has to do with number as related to sounds").

8. By *pandoria* Cassiodorus appears to have in mind the Latin term *pandura*, which refers to a type of lute; see James McKinnon, "Pandoura," *The New Grove Dictionary of Music and Musicians*, vol. 14, p. 154.

9. Symphony is a term with a long and varied history in Western music; here it appears in its simple root meaning as a "sounding with" or consonance.

10. But see the Pseudo-Aristotelian *Problems* 720a: "Why is the octave called the 'diapason' instead of being called the diocto according to the number of the notes, in the same way as the terms used for the fourth and fifth? Is it because originally there were seven strings? Then

IV. The consonance of the combined diapason and diatessaron results from the ratio which the number 24 has to the number 8[11] and includes eleven pitches.

V. The consonance of the combined diapason and diapente results from the triplasia ratio (3:1) and includes twelve pitches.

VI. The consonance of the disdiapason, that is double diapason, results from the tetraplasia ratio (4:1) and includes fifteen pitches.

8. Key is a difference or quantity of the whole harmonic system, consisting in the intonation or level of the voice.[12] There are fifteen keys:

Hypodorian	Dorian	Hyperdorian
Hypoiastian	Iastian	Hyperiastian
Hypophrygian	Phrygian	Hyperphrygian
Hypoaeolian	Aeolian	Hyperaeolian
Hypolydian	Lydian	Hyperlydian

I. The Hypodorian key is the one sounding lowest of all, for which reason it is also called lower.

II. The Hypoiastian exceeds the Hypodorian by a semitone.

III. The Hypophrygian exceeds the Hypoiastian by a semitone, the Hypodorian by a tone.

IV. The Hypoaeolian exceeds the Hypophrygian by a semitone, the Hypoiastian by a tone, the Hypodorian by a tone and a half.

V. The Hypolydian exceeds the Hypoaeolian by a semitone, the Hypophrygian by a tone, the Hypoiastian by a tone and a half, the Hypodorian by two tones.

VI. The Dorian exceeds the Hypolydian by a semitone, the Hypoaeolian by a tone, the Hypophrygian by a tone and a half, the Hypoiastian by two tones, the Hypodorian by two tones and a half, that is, by the consonance diatessaron.

VII. The Iastian exceeds the Dorian by a semitone, the Hypolydian by a tone, the Hypoaeolian by a tone and a half, the Hypophrygian by two tones, the Hypoiastian by two tones and a half, that is, by the consonance diatessaron, the Hypodorian by three tones.

VIII. The Phrygian exceeds the Iastian by a semitone, the Dorian by a tone, the Hypolydian by a tone and a half, the Hypoaeolian by two tones, the Hypophrygian by two tones and a half, that is, by the consonance diatessaron, the

---

Terpander took away the trite and added the nete, and at that time it was called the diapason, not the diocto, for there were seven notes." (Translation by W. S. Hett, *Aristotle: Problems* (London: Loeb Classical Library, 1961), vol. 1, p. 397.)

11. The correct ratio is 24:9 or 8:3.

12. "Key" (*tonus*) is a difficult subject in ancient music theory. Some theorists of Late Antiquity seem not to have understood it very well themselves, reducing it to nothing more than fifteen transpositions by a half-step of the entire tonal system. Here Cassiodorus provides the *reductio ad absurdum* of the subject in an exposition that will remind the modern reader of "The Twelve Days of Christmas."

Hypoiastian by three tones, the Hypodorian by three tones and a half, that is, by the consonance diapente.

IX. The Aeolian exceeds the Phrygian by a semitone, the Iastian by a tone, the Dorian by a tone and a half, the Hypolydian by two tones, the Hypoaeolian by two tones and a half, that is, by the consonance diatessaron, the Hypophrygian by three tones, the Hypoiastian by three tones and a half, that is, by the consonance diapente, the Hypodorian by four tones.

X. The Lydian exceeds the Aeolian by a semitone, the Phrygian by a tone, the Iastian by a tone and a half, the Dorian by two tones, the Hypolydian by two tones and a half, that is, by the consonance diatessaron, the Hypoaeolian by three tones, the Hypophrygian by three tones and a half, that is, by the consonance diapente, the Hypoiastian by four tones, the Hypodorian by four tones and a half.

XI. The Hyperdorian exceeds the Lydian by a semitone, the Aeolian by a tone, the Phrygian by a tone and a half, the Iastian by two tones, the Dorian by two tones and a half, that is, by the consonance diatessaron, the Hypolydian by three tones, the Hypoaeolian by three tones and a half, that is, by the consonance diapente, the Hypophrygian by four tones, the Hypoiastian by four tones and a half, the Hypodorian by five tones.

XII. The Hyperiastian exceeds the Hyperdorian by a semitone, the Lydian by a tone, the Aeolian by a tone and a half, the Phrygian by two tones, the Iastian by two tones and a half, that is, by the consonance diatessaron, the Dorian by three tones, the Hypolydian by three tones and a half, that is, by the consonance diapente, the Hypoaeolian by four tones, the Hypophrygian by four tones and a half, the Hypoiastian by five tones, the Hypodorian by five tones and a half.

XIII. The Hyperphrygian exceeds the Hyperiastian by a semitone, the Hyperdorian by a tone, the Lydian by a tone and a half, the Aeolian by two tones, the Phrygian by two tones and a half, that is, by the consonance diatessaron, the Iastian by three tones, the Dorian by three tones and a half, that is, by the consonance diapente, the Hypolydian by four tones, the Hypoaeolian by four tones and a half, the Hypophrygian by five tones, the Hypoiastian by five tones and a half, the Hypodorian by six tones, that is, by the consonance diapason.

XIV. The Hyperaeolian exceeds the Hyperphrygian by a semitone, the Hyperiastian by a tone, the Hyperdorian by a tone and a half, the Lydian by two tones, the Aeolian by two tones and a half, that is, by the consonance diatessaron, the Phrygian by three tones, the Iastian by three tones and a half, that is, by the consonance diapente, the Dorian by four tones, the Hypolydian by four tones and a half, the Hypoaeolian by five tones, the Hypophrygian by five tones and a half, the Hypoiastian by six tones, that is, by the consonance diapason, the Hypodorian by six tones and a half.

XV. The Hyperlydian, the newest and highest of all, exceeds the Hyperaeolian by a semitone, the Hyperphrygian by a tone, the Hyperiastian by a tone and a half, the Hyperdorian by two tones, the Lydian by two tones and a half, that is, by the consonance diatessaron, the Aeolian by three tones, the Phrygian by three tones and a half, that is, by the consonance diapente, the Iastian by four tones, the Dorian by four tones and a half, the Hypolydian by five tones, the Hypoaeolian by five tones and a half, the Hypophrygian by six tones, that is, by the consonance diapason, the Hypoiastian by six tones and a half, the Hypodorian by seven tones.

From this it appears that the Hyperlydian key, the highest of all, exceeds the Hypodorian, the lowest of all, by seven tones. So useful, Varro observes, is the power displayed by these keys that they can compose distraught minds and also attract the very beasts, serpents even, and birds, and dolphins, to listen to their melody.

9. But the lyre of Orpheus and the songs of the Sirens, we will pass over in silence as fables. Yet what shall we say of David, who freed Saul from the unclean spirit by the discipline of wholesome melody, and by a new method, through the sense of hearing, restored the king to the health which the physicians had been unable to bestow by the virtues of herbs? Asclepiades the physician, according to the ancients a most learned man, is remembered for having restored a man from frenzy to his former sanity by means of melody. We read of many other miracles that have been wrought upon the sick by this discipline. It is said that the heavens themselves, as we have recalled above, are made to revolve by sweet harmony. And to summarize all in a few words, nothing in things celestial or terrestrial which is fittingly conducted according to the Creator's own plan is found to be exempt from this discipline.

10. This study, therefore, which both lifts up our senses to celestial things and pleases our ears with sweet melody, is most gratifying and useful. Among the Greeks Alypius, Euclid, Ptolemy, and others have written excellent treatises on the subject. Of the Romans the distinguished Albinus has treated it with compendious brevity. We recall obtaining his book in a library in Rome and eagerly reading it. If this work has been carried off in consequence of the barbarian invasion, you have here the Latin version of Gaudentius by Mutianus; if you read this with close attention it will open to you the courts of this science. It is said that Apuleius of Madaura also has brought together the doctrines of this book in a Latin work. Our father Augustine, moreover, wrote six books on music, in which he showed that human speech naturally has rhythmical sounds and a measured harmony in its long and short syllables. And Censorinus has treated with subtlety the accents of our speech, declaring that they have a relation to the discipline of music. Of this book, among others, I have left a transcript with you.

16 Isidore of Seville

Isidore was born, probably, in the southeastern Spanish town of Cartagena between 560 and 564, and came to Seville in early childhood. After the death of his parents, he was raised by his brother Leander, bishop of Seville. He suceeded Leander in that office in about 600, and thereafter figured prominently in the life of the Visigothic church and court until his death in 636.

Isidore, like Boethius and Cassiodorus, served as a mediary between the classical and medieval cultures. His most important work is the *Twenty Books of Etymologies or Origins,* a massive encyclopedia of ancient ecclesiastical and secular learning and lore, written in his later years. Its immense influence in the Middle Ages is attested to by its preservation in more than one thousand manuscripts. Its notorious penchant for fanciful etymologies is well illustrated by the portion devoted to music, which is given below. Of musical interest also is the chapter on the liturgical offices (Book 6, Chapter 19).

FROM THE *Etymologies*

BOOK THREE

15. OF MUSIC AND ITS NAME

Music is the art of measurement consisting in tone and song. It is called music by derivation from the Muses. The Muses were so named ἀπὸ τοῦ μῶσθαι, that is, "from inquiring," because, as the ancients would have it, they inquired into the power of songs and the measurement of pitch. The sound of these, since it is a matter of impression upon the senses, flows by into the past and is left imprinted upon the memory. Hence it was fabled by the poets that the Muses were the daughters of Jove and Memory. Unless sounds are remembered by man, they perish, for they cannot be written down.[1]

TEXT: W. M. Lindsay, ed., *Isidori Hispalensis Episcopi Etymologiarum sive Originum libri XX* (Oxford, 1962), Book 3, chapters 15–23 (no pagination). Translation by William Strunk, Jr., and Oliver Strunk, revised by James McKinnon.

1. The last sentence of this passage is taken by many as evidence that musical notation was not known in Isidore's time. The passage as a whole appears to be a simplification of Augustine, *De ordine* 2.14: "And since what the intellect perceives (and numbers are manifestly of this class) is always of the present and is deemed immortal, while sound, since it is an impression upon the sense, flows by into the past and is imprinted upon the memory. Reason has permitted the poets to pretend, in a reasonable fable, that the Muses were the daughters of Jove and Memory. Hence this discipline, which addresses itself to the intellect and to the sense alike, has acquired the name of Music."

16. OF ITS INVENTORS

Moses says that the inventor of the art of music was Tubal, who was of the race of Cain, before the Flood.[2] The Greeks say that Pythagoras found its beginnings in the sound of hammers and the striking of stretched strings. Others report that Linus the Theban and Zetus and Amphion were the first to become illustrious in the art of music. After their time this discipline gradually came to be well ordered and was expanded in many ways, so that not to know music was as disgraceful as to be unlettered. It was not only introduced into sacred rites, but was used in all festivals and on all joyful or mournful occasions. For as hymns were sung in the worship of the gods, so hymenaeal songs were sung at weddings, and threnodies and lamentations to the sound of tibias at funerals. At banquets the lyre or the cithara was passed from hand to hand, and festal songs were assigned to each guest in turn.

17. WHAT MUSIC CAN DO

Thus without music no discipline can be perfect, for there is nothing without it. The very universe, it is said, is held together by a certain harmony of sounds, and the heavens themselves are made to revolve by the modulation of harmony. Music moves the feelings and changes the emotions. In battles, moreover, the sound of the trumpet rouses the combatants, and the more furious the trumpeting, the more valorous their spirit. A chant likewise encourages the rowers, music soothes the mind so that it can endure toil, and song assuages the weariness encountered in any task. Music also composes distraught minds, as may be read of David, who freed Saul from the unclean spirit by the art of melody. The very beasts also, even serpents, birds, and dolphins, are enticed by music to listen to her melody.[3] Indeed every word we speak, every pulsation of our veins, is related by musical rhythms to the powers of harmony.

18. OF THE THREE PARTS OF MUSIC[4]

The parts of music are three: harmonics, rhythmics, and metrics. Harmonics is that which distinguishes the high and low in sounds. Rhythmics is that which inquires whether words in combination sound well or badly together. Metrics is that which by valid reasoning knows the measures of the various metres; for example, the heroic, the iambic, and the elegiac.

19. OF THE THREEFOLD DIVISION OF MUSIC

Moreover for every sound which forms the material of songs, there is a threefold nature. The first is the harmonic, which consists of singing; the sec-

---

2. Genesis 4:21. On the topos of music's "inventors" see above, note 1 to the reading from Cassiodorus, p. 143.
3. See the reference to Varro in Cassiodorus's *Fundamentals* 5.8, p. 148.
4. See above, Cassiodorus, *Fundamentals* 5.5, p. 145.

ond, the organic, which is produced by blowing; the third, the rhythmic, in which the music is produced by the impulse of the fingers. For sound is caused either by the voice, as with the throat, or by blowing, as with the trumpet or the tibia, or by an impulse, as with the cithara or with anything else which becomes resonant when struck.[5]

20. OF THE FIRST DIVISION OF MUSIC, CALLED HARMONIC

The first division of music, which is called the harmonic, that is, the modulation of the voice, is the affair of comedians, tragedians, and choruses and of all who sing. It produces motion of the mind and body, and from this motion sound; from this sound comes the music which in man is called voice.

Voice is air struck (*verberatus*) by the breath, whence words (*verba*) also receive their name. Voice is proper to man and to irrational animals. But sound in other things is called voice by a misuse and not properly, as, "The voice of the trumpet snarled," and "Broken voices by the shore."[6] For the proper locutions are that the cliffs of the shore should resound, and, "The trumpet with resonant brass gave forth a terrible sound from afar."[7]

Harmony is a modulation of the voice and a concordance or mutual adaptation of several sounds. Symphony is a fusion of the modulation of low and high concordant sounds, produced either vocally or by blowing or striking. Through symphony low and high sounds are concordant, in such a way that if any one of them is dissonant it offends the sense of hearing. The opposite of this is diaphony, that is, discrepant or dissonant sounds. Euphony is sweetness of the voice; it is also called melody, from the word *mel* (honey), because of its sweetness.

Diastema is an interval of the voice composed of two or more sounds. Diesis consists of certain intervals and diminutions of modulation and interpolations between one sound and another.

Key (*tonus*) is a raised enunciation of the pitch. It is the categorization and ranking of the *harmoniae* according to the intonation or level of the voice. Musicians have divided the varieties of keys into fifteen, of which the Hyperlydian is the newest and highest, and the Hypodorian the lowest of all.

Song is an inflecting of the voice, for sound is simple and moreover it precedes song. Arsis is a lifting up of the voice, that is, a beginning. Thesis is a lowering of the voice, that is, an end.

---

5. See Augustine, *De ordine* 2.xiv: "Reason has understood that the judgment of the ear has to do only with sound and that sound has three varieties: it consists either in the voice of an animate being, or in what blowing produces in instruments, or in what is brought forth by striking. The first variety it understands to be the affair of tragedians, comedians, choruses, and the like, and in general of all who sing. The second it understands to be allotted to the auloi and similar instruments. To the third it understands to be given the citharas, lyres, cymbals, and anything else which becomes resonant when struck."

6. Vergil, *Aeneid* 3.556.

7. *Aeneid* 9.503.

Sweet voices are fine, full, clear, and high. Penetrating voices are those which can hold a note an unusually long time, in such a way that they continuously fill the entire area, like the sound of trumpets. A thin voice is one lacking in breath, as the voice of children or women or the sick. This is similar to strings, for the finest strings emit subtle, thin sounds.

In thick voices, as those of men, much breath is emitted at once. A sharp voice is high and thin, as we see in strings. A hard voice is one which emits sound violently, like thunder, or like the sound of an anvil whenever the hammer is struck against the hard iron. A harsh voice is a hoarse one, which is broken up by minute, dissimilar impulses. A blind voice is one which is choked off as soon as produced, and once silent cannot be prolonged, as is the case with crockery when struck.

A pretty *(vinnola)* voice is soft and flexible; it is so called from *vinnus*, a softly curling lock of hair. The perfect voice is high, sweet, and clear: high, to be adequate to the sublime; clear, to fill the ear; sweet, to soothe the minds of the hearers. If any one of these qualities is absent, the voice is not perfect.

21. OF THE SECOND DIVISION OF MUSIC, THE ORGANIC

The second division is the organic, found in the instruments which come to life and produce a musical pitch when filled by a stream of air, such as trumpets, reeds, pipes, organs, pandoria, and similar instruments. Organ is the generic name of all musical vessels. The Greeks have another name for the kind of organ to which bellows are applied, but their common custom is to call it the organ.

The trumpet was invented by the Etruscans, of whom Virgil wrote: "And the clangor of Etruscan trumpets resounded on high."[8] The trumpet was employed not only in battles, but in all festivals of special praise giving or rejoicing. Wherefore it is also said in the Psalter: "Sound the trumpet at the beginning of the month, and on the day of your great solemnity."[9] For the Jews were commanded to sound the trumpet at the time of the new moon, as they still do.

Tibias are said to have been devised in Phrygia. For a long time they were used only at funerals, but afterward in the sacred rites of the heathen as well. It is thought that they are called tibias because they were first made from the leg-bones of deer and fawns, and that then, by a misuse of the term, the name was used of those not made of legbones. Hence there is also the term *tibicen,* that is, the song of tibias.[10]

The reed is the name of a certain tree, called *calamus* from *calendo,* that is,

---

8. *Aeneid* 8.526.

9. Psalm 80(81):3.

10. Isidore is correct in deriving *tibicen* from *tibia* and *canere* (to sing), but the term is properly applied to the player not the song itself.

giving out voice. The pipe some think to have been invented by Mercury; others, by Faunus, whom the Greeks call Pan; others by Daphnis, a shepherd of Agrigentum in Sicily. The pipe (*fistula*) is also named from sending forth a sound, for in Greek voice is called φῶς, and sent forth, στόλια.

The sambuca, among musicians, is a type of drum.[11] The word means a kind of fragile wood, from which tibias are made. The pandoria is named from its inventor, of whom Virgil says: "Pan first taught men to join reeds together with wax; Pan cares for sheep and for shepherds."[12] For among the heathen he was the god of shepherds, who first adapted reeds of unequal length to music and fitted them together with studious art.

22. OF THE THIRD DIVISION OF MUSIC, WHICH IS CALLED RHYTHMIC

The third division is the rhythmic, having to do with strings and striking, to which are assigned the different species of cithara, also the tympanum, the cymbal, the sistrum, vessels of bronze and silver, others whose hard metal yields an agreeable clanging when struck, and other instruments of this nature.[13]

Tubal, as was said before, is regarded as the inventor of the cithara and psaltery, but by the Greeks Apollo was believed to have first discovered the use of the cithara. According to their tradition, the form of the cithara was originally like that of the human chest, it received its name because it gives forth sound as the chest gives forth voice. In Doric, moreover, the chest was called κιθάρα. Gradually numerous species were invented, as psalteries, lyres, barbitons, phoenices, and pektises, and those which are called Indian citharas and are played by two musicians at once; also many others, some of square and others of triangular form. The number of strings was also increased and the shape altered. The ancients called the cithara *fidicula* and *fidicen,* because the strings are in good accord with each other, as befits men among whom there is trust (*fides*).[14]

The ancient cithara had seven strings; whence Virgil's phrase, "the seven distinctions of pitch,"[15] "distinctions" because no string gives the same note as its neighbor. There were seven strings because that number filled the range of the voice, and because the heavens sound with seven motions. The strings (*chordae*) are so called from *cor* (heart), because the striking of the strings of the cithara is like the beating of the heart in the breast. Mercury was their inventor; he was the first to draw sound from strings.

11. Here Isidore is simply wrong; the ancient sambuca was a kind of harp.
12. *Eclogues* 2.32.
13. Note the inclusion here within the same category of what we moderns distinguish as strings and percussion.
14. A good example of the fanciful sort of etymology for which Isidore's work is so well known.
15. *Aeneid* 6.646.

The psaltery, popularly called *canticum,* has its name from *psallendo* (singing), because the chorus answers its voice in consonance. It resembles a barbaric cithara in the form of the letter delta, but there is this difference between it and the cithara, that it has its wooden sound-box above, and the strings are struck below and sound above, while the cithara has the soundbox below. The Hebrews used a ten-stringed psaltery, because of the Ten Commandments of their law.

The lyre is so called ἀπὸ τοῦ ληρεῖν (from sounding folly), that is, from the variety of voices, because it produces dissimilar sounds. They say it was invented by Mercury in the following manner. When the Nile, retreating into its channels, had left various animals in the fields, a tortoise was among them. After it had putrefied and its sinews remained stretched within its shell, it gave out a sound on being struck by Mercury. He fashioned the lyre using this model and gave it to Orpheus, who applied himself studiously to it and is deemed not merely to have swayed wild beasts with his art, but to have moved rocks and forests with the measures of his song. Musicians have claimed in their fables that the lyre was placed among the constellations because of his love of study and the glory of his song.

The tympanum is a skin or hide stretched over one side of a wooden frame; it is a half-drum, shaped like a sieve. It is called tympanum because it is a half, for which reason a half-pearl is called a tympanum. It, like the drum, is struck with a stick. Cymbals are certain vessels which produce sound when struck together. They are called cymbals because they are struck together in time with dancing, since the Greeks call dancing συμβαλεῖν.

The sistrum is named from its inventress, for Isis, a queen of the Egyptians, is considered to have invented this species of instrument. Juvenal has: "Let Isis with angry sistrum blind my eyes."[16] Women use this instrument because a woman invented it. Among the Amazons the army of women was summoned to battle by the sistrum. The bell *(tintinnabulum)* is named from its sound, as are also the clapping *(plausus)* of hands and the creaking *(stridor)* of hinges. Drum *(symphonia)* is the ordinary name of a wooden frame covered on both sides with stretched skin, which the musicians strike in one place and another with small sticks; and there results a most delightful sound from the concord of low and high.

23. OF MUSICAL NUMBERS

You obtain musical numbers in this manner. Having set down the extreme terms, as say 6 and 12, you see by how many units 12 exceeds 6, and it is by 6 units. You square this: 6 times 6 is 36. You then add together those first extremes, 6 and 12; together they make 18. You then divide 36 by 18, which gives 2. Add this to the smaller number, that is, 6; this will give 8, which will be the harmonic mean between 6 and 12. From this it appears that 8 exceeds

16. *Satires* 13.931.

6 by 2 units, that is, by one third of 6, and 8 is exceeded by 12 by 4 units, one third of 12. By the same fraction that it exceeds, it is exceeded.[17]

But just as this ratio appears in the universe from the revolution of the spheres, so in the microcosm it is so inexpressibly potent that the man without its perfection and deprived of its harmony does not exist. And by the perfection of the same music, measures consist of arsis and thesis, that is, of raising and lowering.

17. This method for finding the harmonic mean between two extremes will give the correct answer only when the greater term is twice the lesser. Isidore's error lies in directing that the difference between the extremes be squared. It must be multiplied by the lesser term. With this correction, his method agrees with that given by Boethius, *The Fundamentals of Music* 2.17: "If we seek the harmonic mean, we add the extremes, for example 10 and 40, one to another, making 50. Their difference, which is 30, we multiply by the lesser term, that is 10, making 10 times 30, or 300. This we divide by 50, making 6. This we add to the lesser term, making 16. If now we place this number between 10 and 40, we have a harmonic proportion."

CHANT AND LITURGY IN THE EARLY MIDDLE AGES

17 St. Benedict of Nursia

St. Benedict was born to a prosperous family in the region of Nursia, near Spoleto, sometime in the later decades of the fifth century. As a young man, he cut short his education in Rome to devote himself to the monastic life. After a period of several years at Subiaco, east of Rome, spent at times in solitude and at other times in attempts at monastic organization, he journeyed south to Monte Cassino, a prominent hill near the town of Cassinum, halfway between Rome and Naples. Here he founded the monastery that would come to be looked upon as the mother house of Western monasticism. He died sometime after a meeting with the Gothic leader Totila in 546.

Benedict's significance lies in his Rule, which he composed for the community at Monte Cassino. Recommended by its clarity and reasonableness, it progressed from its obscure origins to become institutionalized during the Carolingian period as the universally observed Western monastic rule. Many would claim it to be the single most influential document written in the Middle Ages. Of musical relevance are the chapters, translated below, that describe the monastic Office.

FROM THE *Rule of St. Benedict*

VIII. CONCERNING THE DIVINE OFFICE AT NIGHT

In wintertime, that is, from the first of November until Easter, it seems reasonable to arise at the eighth hour of the night,[1] so that the brethren do so with a moderately full sleep after midnight and with their digestion completed. And whatever time remains after Vigils[2] should be devoted to the study of the psalms and lessons by those brothers who lack sufficient knowledge of them. And from Easter, in turn, to the first of November, let the hour of rising be postponed so that Lauds, which are celebrated as the light of day sets in, are separated from Vigils by a brief interval in which the brothers may attend to the necessities of nature.

TEXT: Adalbert de Vogüé, *La Règle de Saint Benoît*, vol. 2, Sources Chrétiennes 182 (Paris, 1972), pp. 508–36. Translation by James McKinnon.

1. Benedict's Rule follows the Roman *horarium*, which divides the day into twelve daylight hours and twelve night hours. During the winter, night hours are longer than daylight hours, while the opposite is true for the summer. At the latitude of Monte Cassino, a midwinter night hour is approximately one hour and twenty minutes of modern clock time. Thus Benedict's eighth hour of the night, two hours after midnight, would be about 2:40 A.M. on December 21. The summer time adjustments that Benedict calls for later in this chapter and in Chapter 10 are required by the shorter night hours of the summer.
2. Benedict's nighttime office, *vigiliae*, the equivalent of the misnamed medieval Matins, is translated "Vigils" here; while the service of morning praise, Benedict's *matutini*, is translated "Lauds."

IX. How Many Psalms Are to Be Said at the Night Offices

In the aforesaid wintertime, let there first be said, three times, the verse "O Lord, open thou my lips, and my mouth shall proclaim thy praise";[3] this is followed by Psalm 3 with the *Gloria* [*patri*] and after this Psalm 94 to be sung with the antiphon, or in any case to be sung. There follows next the Ambrosian hymn; then six psalms with antiphons. When these have been said,[4] and the versicle as well, let the abbot give the blessing. And after all are seated upon the benches three lessons are to be read in turn by brothers from the codex on the lectern, with three responsories sung between the lessons. Two of the responsories are to be sung without the *Gloria* but after the third lesson, whoever sings adds the *Gloria* and as soon as the singer begins this, all should rise from their seats out of honor and reverence for the Holy Trinity. The books to be read at Vigils are those with the divine authority of both Old and New Testaments, as well as commentaries upon them, that were composed by recognized and orthodox catholic Fathers. After these three readings with their responsories, there should follow the remaining six psalms to be sung with *Alleluia;* and after these the reading of the Apostle[5] recited by heart, a versicle, and the litany, that is, the *Kyrie eleison.* In this manner are the nocturnal Vigils to be brought to a close.

X. How the Nocturnal Praise is to Be Said in the Summer Time

From Easter to the first of November the same number of psalms as given above is to be maintained, although the lessons are not to be read from the codex because of the brevity of the night hours. In place of the three lessons one from the New Testament is to be recited from memory; this is followed by a brief responsory. And all the rest is done as described above, that is, never less than twelve psalms are to be recited at the nightly vigils, not counting Psalms 3 and 94.

XI. How Vigils Are to Be Said on Sundays

On the Lord's day we must rise earlier for Vigils. The following order should be observed in these Vigils: after the six aforementioned psalms and the versicle have been sung, and all are seated in proper order, the four lessons are to be read from the codex with their responsories, according to what we have said

---

3. Psalm 1:17.
4. The Latin *dicere* (to say) is translated here either "to say" or "to recite," while only *cantare* (to sing) is translated "to sing" or "to chant." But by no means is this meant to imply that psalms, which were in Benedict's language "said," were not in fact sung or chanted. In Early Christian literature *dicere* is used interchangeably with *cantare* in connection with the singing of psalms.
5. The term "Apostle," although referring specifically to St. Paul, is a generic early Christian term for a reading from the New Testament epistles.

above; the singer chants the *Gloria* only for the fourth responsory, and as soon as he begins it all should arise out of reverence. After these lessons the same order is followed: six more psalms with antiphons, and the versicle. Again four other lessons with their responsories are to be read following the above order. After these three canticles from the Prophets, selected by the abbot, are to chanted; these are sung with *Alleluia*. When the versicle has been recited, and the abbot has given the blessing, four other lessons, these from the New Testament, are to be read following the above order. But after the fourth responsory the abbot intones the hymn *Te deum laudamus*. When this is completed the abbot reads the lesson from the Gospel book, as all stand in awe and reverence. When this has been read let all respond *Amen*, and immediately the abbot follows with the hymn *Te decet laus;* then after he gives the blessing let them begin Lauds.

This order of Vigils is always to be observed on the Lord's day whether it be summer or winter, unless somehow the brothers should happen to arise late, in which case the lessons and responsories are to be shortened. We should take care that this does not happen, but if it does, he by whose neglect it came about, must make due satisfaction to God in the oratorio.

XII. How the Office of Lauds Is to Be Celebrated

Let Sunday Lauds begin with Psalm 66 said straight through[6] without antiphon. Then let Psalm 50 be recited with *Alleluia,* and after this Psalms 117 and 62; then the *Benedicite*[7] and the *Laudate* psalms,[8] one lesson by heart from the Apocalypse with responsory, an Ambrosian hymn, the versicle, the Gospel canticle, the litany—and all is done.

XIII. How Lauds Are to Be Said on Weekdays

On weekdays Lauds should be said in this way: let Psalm 66 be recited without antiphon, drawn out somewhat as on Sunday, so that all are assembled for Psalm 50, which is recited with antiphon. After this two other psalms are to be recited according to custom, that is, on Monday Psalms 5 and 35, on Tuesday Psalms 42 and 56, on Wednesdays Psalms 63 and 64, and on Thursday Psalms 87 and 89, on Friday Psalms 75 and 91, and on Saturday Psalm 142 and the canticle from Deuteronomy,[9] which is to be divided into two sections, each with closing *Gloria*. On the other days let a canticle from the Prophets be

6. Benedict's *in directum* is translated here as "straight through," that is, the psalm is sung straight through without the addition of antiphons.
7. *Benedicite* is the canticle of the three youths in the fiery furnace; it appears in Daniel 3:52–90 (but only in the Greek-Latin-Catholic textual tradition, not the Hebrew-Protestant).
8. The *Laudate* psalms, Psalms 148–50, were associated with Lauds from its Early Christian origins and give the service its name; they are so called because of their theme of praise; the first and last of them, in point of fact, begin with the word *laudate*.
9. The second canticle of Moses, *Audite coeli,* Deuteronomy 32.1–43.

recited, one proper to each day, as they are sung in the church of Rome. After this the *Laudate* psalms are to follow, then a lesson from the Apostle to be said by heart, a responsory, an Ambrosian hymn, a versicle, a Gospel canticle, the litany—and all is done.

Certainly the morning and evening offices must never be allowed to conclude without the prior saying the entire Lord's Prayer within the hearing of all, this, because of the thorns of contention that are liable to arise among the brethren; thus bound by the pledge that they give in this prayer, "Forgive us as we forgive," they purge themselves from this sort of failing. At the other offices only the last part of the prayer is to be said, so that all can respond, "But deliver us from evil."

XIV. HOW VIGILS ARE TO BE SAID ON THE FESTIVALS OF THE SAINTS

On the festivals of the saints and on all other solemn occasions, the Office should be performed as we described it for Sundays, except that psalms, antiphons, and lessons that are appropriate to the day are to be selected; the overall manner of execution, however, as given above, should be maintained.

XV. AT WHAT TIMES THE ALLELUIA SHOULD BE SAID

The *Alleluia* is to be said after both psalms and responsories, from the sacred Pasch to Pentecost without interruption. But from Pentecost to the beginning of Lent let it be said each night at the Nocturns only with the second group of six psalms. On every Sunday outside Lent let the canticles of Vigils and Lauds, and the psalms of Lauds, Prime, Terce, Sext, and None be sung with *Alleluia;* but at Vespers let there be an antiphon. Responsories, however, are never chanted with *Alleluia,* except from Easter to Pentecost.

XVI. HOW THE WORK OF GOD IS TO BE PERFORMED THROUGHOUT THE DAY

As the Prophet says: "Seven times during the day I have spoken thy praise."[10] This sacred number of seven is thus observed by us if we fulfil the obligations of our service at Lauds, Prime, Terce, Sext, None, Vespers, and Compline; since he says of these day hours, "Seven times during the day I have spoken thy praise." And of the nightly Vigils the very same prophet says: "I arose in the middle of the night to confess thee."[11] Therefore let us render praise to our Creator "for his just judgments" at these hours, that is, Lauds, Prime, Terce, Sext, None, Vespers, and Compline; and at night let us arise to confess him.

10. Psalm 118(119):164.
11. Psalm 118(119):62.

XVII. How Many Psalms Are to Be Said at These Hours

We have already established the order of psalmody at Vigils and Matins; now let us see to the remaining hours. At Prime three psalms should be sung, one by one, and not with only a single *Gloria;* the hymn for this hour comes after the verse *Deus in adjutorium,* before the psalms are begun. At the completion of the three psalms, let one lesson be read, then the versicle, the Kyrie eleison, and the dismissal. At Terce, Sext, and None, the same order of prayer is to be observed, that is, the hymn appropriate to the hour, three psalms, a lesson and versicle, Kyrie eleison, and the concluding prayers. If a larger group is present, the psalms are to be said with antiphons, but if a smaller one, they are sung straight through.

Let the service of Vespers be limited to four psalms with antiphons; after these psalms a lesson is to be read, then a responsory, an Ambrosian hymn, a versicle, a Gospel canticle, the litany, and the Lord's Prayer by way of conclusion. Compline is to be limited to the recitation of three psalms which are said straight through without antiphon; after these there follow the hymn of the hour, a lesson, a versicle, the *Kyrie eleison,* and by way of conclusion the blessing.

XVIII. In What Order the Psalms Are to Be Said

First let there be said the verse, "O God, incline thee to my aid, O Lord make haste to help me";[12] then the hymn appropriate to the hour. Then at Prime on Sunday, four chapters of Psalm 118 are to be said, and at the remaining hours, Terce, Sext, and None, three chapters each of the aforesaid Psalm 118. At Prime on Monday let three psalms be said, that is, Psalms 1, 2, and 6. And thus for each day at Prime, until Sunday, let three psalms be said in order up to Psalm 19, with Psalms 9 and 17 divided into two parts. And thus it happens that Sunday Vigils is always to begin with Psalm 20.

On Monday the remaining nine chapters of Psalm 118 should be said at Terce, Sext, and None, three at each hour. With Psalm 118 completed, then, in two days (Sunday and Monday), on Tuesday three psalms should be said at Terce, at Sext, and at None—Psalms 119 to 127, a total of nine. These psalms are always to be repeated in the same way at the same hours until Sunday; and the same arrangement of hymns, lessons, and versicles should be maintained for every day. Thus Sunday Prime will always begin with Psalm 118.

Vespers is to be sung every day with the chanting of four psalms. These should begin with Psalm 109 and extend to Psalm 147, omitting those which have been reserved for particular offices, namely, Psalms 117 to 127, and Psalms 133 and 142; all the rest should be sung at Vespers. And because there are three psalms too few, those of the aforesaid group that are longer should be divided, that is, Psalms 138, 143, and 144. But because Psalm 116 is short,

12. Psalm 69(70):2.

it should be joined to Psalm 115. With the order of Vesper psalms thus arranged, the rest of the service as determined above is to be completed, that is, the lesson, the responsory, the hymn, the versicle, and the canticle. At Compline the same psalms are to be repeated every day, namely, Psalms 4, 90, and 133.

The order of the daily psalmody thus arranged, all remaining psalms are to be distributed equally over the seven nightly Vigils; twelve can be assigned each night by dividing the longer psalms. We strongly recommend that whoever is not pleased with this distribution of the psalms, should arrange them in some other way that he considers to be better. But in any event let him see to it that every week the complete Psalter with its one hundred and fifty psalms is sung, always starting from the beginning at Sunday Vigils. For monks who sing less than the Psalter with its customary canticles in the course of a week display a lack of dedication and devotion, whereas we read of our holy fathers who arduously fulfilled in a single day what we tepid souls accomplish in an entire week.

XIX. ON THE DISCIPLINE OF PSALMODY

We believe that God is present everywhere and that "the eyes of the Lord look upon good men and evil in every place";[13] but we must believe without a shadow of doubt that this is especially so when we assist at the Divine Office. Let us always be mindful, then, of what the Prophet says: "Serve the Lord in fear";[14] and again, "Sing psalms wisely";[15] and, "I will sing to thee in the sight of the angels."[16] Hence we must consider how we are to comport ourselves in the sight of the Divinity and of his angels; and we must be thus instant in psalmody that our mind and voice are in harmony.

13. Proverbs 15:3.
14. Psalm 2:11.
15. Psalm 46:8 (the phrase appears only in the Greek-Latin text tradition).
16. Psalm 137.1.

18 Pseudo-Germanus

The "Exposition of the Ancient Gallican Liturgy" is the first of two letters formerly attributed to St. Germanus of Paris (d. 576). That they are considerably later is suggested by their apparent reliance upon the writings of Isidore of Seville (d. 636). Most scholars now believe them to have originated in the early eighth century somewhere in Burgundy, perhaps at Autun, where the manuscript containing them has long resided. (A. van der Mensbrugghe continues to argue for their authenticity in his "Pseudo-Germanus Reconsidered," *Studia Patristica*, vol. 5 [Texte und Arbeiten no. 80, 1962]: 172–84). The first letter, translated here, is a colorful explanation of the Gallican Mass in the style of allegorical exegesis. Although the central concern of the letter is clearly the symbolic significance of the liturgy, it is possible to extract from its text a fairly precise description of the various chants and ritual events that are the subject of its fanciful interpretations. The description refers, in all probability, to the Gallican Mass of only one time and place, perhaps Autun in the early eighth century, but it conforms in its more general features to what we know from other descriptive references to Gallican services (see William S. Porter, *The Gallican Rite* [London: 1958]). Most noteworthy is the dependence of the rite upon Eastern liturgies and the affinity with the contemporary Mozarabic Mass. The Gallican tendency to employ Ordinary hymnic chants stands in sharp contrast to Rome's use of Proper psalmic chants.

Exposition of the Ancient Gallican Liturgy

PREFACE. The Mass, first and greatest of spiritual gifts, is sung in commemoration of the Lord's death; the death of Christ becomes the life of the world, so that by this offering the salvation of the living and the eternal rest of the departed are secured.

1. BEFORE THE READINGS. The antiphon[1] before the readings is sung as a representation of those patriarchs, who before the Flood proclaimed the coming of Christ in mystic voices; like Enoch, of the seventh generation from Adam, who lifted up by God prophesied: "Behold the Lord cometh with thousands of his saints to exercise justice." The Apostle Jude, brother of James, preserves this testimony in his epistle.[2]

And just as in the prophesies of the patriarchs the hand of the Lord came over the Ark to withhold the fruits of the sacrifice from the evil ones, so too, as the clergy sings, the priest, in the image of Christ, proceeds from the sacristy, as if from heaven, into the Ark of the Lord, which is the Church, in order that, as much by encouragement as by warning, he may nourish good works among the people and root out evil.

2. THE SILENCE. The deacon proclaims the silence for two reasons, so that a quiet congregation may better hear the word of God, and so that our hearts may be deaf to any impure thoughts and thus better welcome the word of God.

3. The priest, then, blesses the people saying this, "The Lord be always with you." And he in turn is blessed by all, who reply, "And with thy spirit," He is

---

TEXT: Edward. C. Ratcliff, ed., *Expositio Antiquae Liturgiae Gallicanae* (London: Henry Bradshaw Society, 1971). Translation by James McKinnon.

1. There is no hint as to the character of this antiphon, except for the circumstance that it was sung by the clergy during the entrance of the celebrant.

2. Jude 14.

thus that much more worthy to bless the people since by the grace of God he receives a blessing from the mouth of the entire congregation.

4. THE AIUS.[3] The *Aius* is sung before the "Prophecy" in the Greek language for this reason: because the proclamation of the New Testament proceeded into the world through the Greek tongue, except for the Apostle Matthew, who was the first in Judea to compose the gospel of Christ in the Hebrew language. Thus was preserved the honor of the tongue which first took the gospel of Christ to its bosom, and which taught the first canticle in its literature. With the presiding priest[4] intoning, the church sings the *Aius,* chanting in Latin along with Greek,[5] so as to manifest the union of Old and New Testaments. The Amen that is recited is from the Hebrew, like that title which Pilate placed over the cross, at God's prompting in a trinity of languages, "Jesus of Nazareth, king of the Jews," thus proclaiming, while ignorant of the fact, that he was indeed the holy king.

5. The three boys who next sing the Kyrie eleison three times as from one mouth, do so as a representation of the threefold language of sacred law—Hebrew, Greek, and Latin—and after the three ages of the world, that is, before the Law, under the Law, and under the dispensation of grace.

6. THE PROPHECY [the *Benedictus*]. The canticle of Zachary the high priest is sung in honor of St. John the Baptist. For the beginning of salvation consists in the sacrament of baptism, which John received as his ministry from a generous God; and as the shadow of the Old Law receded and the brightness of the new Gospel emerged, John, intermediating as last of the prophets and first of the evangelists, shone as a lamp, indeed, before the face of the light. Thus the Church sings in alternate voices the "Prophecy" which his father sang at the news of his birth.

7. THE PROPHET AND THE APOSTLE [the Old Testament reading and the Epistle]. The prophetic reading, that of the Old Testament, maintains its place, chastising evil and announcing the future, so that we may understand that the God who thundered in prophecy is the very same who taught in the Apostle and who shone forth in the splendor of the Gospel. For what the Prophet says is to come, the Apostle teaches as already accomplished. The Acts of the Apostles and the Apocalypse of John are read for the renewal of Paschal rejoicing, maintaining the order of the calendar, just as the Old Testament histories are read in the Pentecostal season, and the acts of the holy confessors and martyrs on their festivals, so that the people will understand how greatly Christ, in

3. *Aius,* literally Greek for "holy." The *Aius* is the celebrated Trisagion chant, "Holy God, mighty God, holy immortal one, have mercy on us," that was sung in the Latin medieval liturgy only during the adoration of the cross on Good Friday. It was regularly sung in most Eastern liturgies, as here, before the readings.

4. *Praesul* is translated here "presiding priest," literally, in classical Latin, one who dances at the head of a procession; an equally plausible translation might be "cantor."

5. In the Western version of the chant, the Latin translation is interspersed after each phrase of the Greek; see the *Liber Usualis,* p. 705.

granting a sign of virtue to a servant, loved him whom the pious faithful claim as their patron.

8. THE HYMN [the *Benedicite* of the three youths]. The hymn of the three youths is sung following the readings as a representation of the holy ancients, who sitting in darkness, awaited the coming of the Lord. And just as a fourth being, an angel, joined the youths as they sang and overcame the flames with a cloud of dew;[6] so too did that very son of God, the angel of the great counsel, join those who awaited the messiah, and, breaking the rule of Tartarus and setting them free, brought them the joy of the resurrection, as the evangelist teaches.[7]

9. And for this reason the Church maintains an order of service in which no Collect is inserted between the hymn of the youths (*Benedictio*) and the gospel, but only the response (*Responsurium*),[8] which is sung by children as a representation of those Innocents whose deaths as companions of Christ in birth, are narrated in the gospel,[9] or of those children who cried out to the Lord in the temple, "Hosanna to the Son of David," as he drew near to his Passion— as the psalmist declares, "Out of the mouth of infants and of sucklings you have perfected praise."[10]

10. THE AIUS BEFORE THE GOSPEL. Then in anticipation of the holy gospel a cleric sings the *Aius* again with a clear voice, after the image of the angels at the gates of hell who cried out before the face of Christ: "Lift up your gates, ye princes, and ye the eternal gates shall be lifted up, and the Lord of powers, the king of glory, shall enter in."[11]

11. THE GOSPEL. The procession with the holy gospel book goes out, like the power of the triumphant Christ from death, with the melodies spoken of above [the *Aius*] and with seven lighted candelabras, which are the seven gifts of the Holy Spirit or the seven lights of the Law affixed to the mystery of the cross. The procession mounts the ambo, as if it were Christ attaining the seat of his royal Father, so that from there he might proclaim the gifts of life, while the clergy cries out, "Glory be to thee, O Lord," as a representation of the angels who appeared to the shepherds at the birth of the Lord and sang, "Glory to God in the highest."

12. THE SANCTUS AFTER THE GOSPEL. The Sanctus,[12] which is sung as the gospel book is returned, is chanted by a cleric as a representation of the saints who, following Jesus Christ as he returned from hell, sang a canticle of praise,[13]

---

6. See Daniel 3:49–50.
7. See the apocryphal Gospel of Nicodemus.
8. This would appear to be a responsorial psalm, in all probability the equivalent of the Roman gradual psalm.
9. See Matthew 2.16.
10. See Matthew 21.15–16.
11. Psalm 23.7.
12. This is the *Aius* in Latin, not the Sanctus that follows the Preface.
13. See the Gospel of Nicodemus.

or of the four and twenty elders commemorated by John in the Apocalypse, who cast down their crowns before the Lamb and sang a sweet song.[14]

13. THE HOMILIES. The homilies of the holy fathers that are read are substituted for the preaching of an individual, so that whatever the Prophet, the Apostle, or the gospel advised, this doctor or shepherd of the Church would relate to the people in plainer speech, exercising his art so that neither crudity of language would offend the learned nor honorable eloquence become obscure to the simple.

14. THE PRAYER. The chanting of the Prayer by deacons (levitas) had its origin in the Books of Moses, so that the deacons, after the preaching had been heard by the people, should pray for the people, and the priests, prostrate before the Lord, should intercede for the sins of the people. As the Lord said to Aaron: "You and your sons and all the tribe of Levi shall bear the sins of my people."[15]

15. THE CATECHUMENS. The deacon cries aloud, according to the ancient ritual of the Church, that the catechumens must go outside. So Jews as well as heretics and pagans under instruction, who, once proud, have come to be baptized and before that to be examined, should stay in the church to hear the counsel of the Old and New Testaments, after which the deacons pray for them, and the priest recites a collect after the prayer. But finally they must go out through the doors because they are not worthy to stay in the church while the sacrifice is offered. And outside before the entrance, prostrate on the earth, they should listen to the telling of God's wonders. This task falls to the deacon or the ostiary, for just as he should admonish them to go outside, he should see to it that no one unworthy lingers in the church. As the Lord says: "Give not that which is holy to dogs, and do not cast your pearls before the swine."[16] For what is holier on earth than to prepare the body and blood of Christ, and what more unclean than the dogs and pigs that provide an image for the person who has neither been cleansed by baptism nor fortified with the sign of the cross?

16. We are enjoined, in the spiritual sense, to stand at the entrance and to observe silence, that is, so that free from the confusion of words and vices we may place the sign of the cross before our face, lest concupiscence enter through the eyes or anger through the ear, or lest shameful speech pass through the lips; and let the heart pay heed to this alone, that it receive Christ unto itself.

17. THE SONUM [the Offertory chant]. The Sonum is that which is sung during the procession of the offerings.[17] It has its origin in this: the Lord com-

14. See the Book of Revelation 4:10–11.
15. See Numbers 18:23.
16. Matthew 7:6.
17. The elaborate procession described here, that brings in the eucharistic elements of bread and wine (referring to them as "body" and "blood" in anticipation of their consecration), is very similar to the Byzantine Great Entrance. Likewise the Gallican chant, the Sonum, would appear to be the celebrated Cherubicon Hymn, which was sung during the Great Entrance;

manded Moses to make trumpets of silver that the Levites would blow during the offering of the victim, and this would be a sign by which the people would understand at what hour the sacrifice would take place; and all would bow down and adore the Lord, until there appeared that column of fire and cloud that blessed the offering.[18] Now, however, the Church hymns with sweet melody the body of Christ as it approaches the altar, not with blameless[19] trumpets, but with spiritual voices proclaiming the brilliant wonders of Christ.

18. The body of the Lord is carried within towers,[20] because the tomb of the Lord was cut into the rock in the form of a tower, and within was the funeral couch where the body of the Lord rested, and whence he, the king of glory, arose in triumph. The blood of Christ, in particular, is offered in a chalice[21] because in such a vessel the mystery of the Eucharist was consecrated "on the day before he suffered," as he said himself, "this is the chalice of my blood, the mystery of faith which is poured out for many unto the remission of sins."[22]

·   ·   ·   ·   ·

20. [Conclusion of the *Sonum*]. The *Laudes* are the Alleluia which John in the Apocalypse heard sung in the heavens after the resurrection of Christ.[23] Therefore at that moment when the body of the Lord is covered by the pallium, just as Christ is covered by the heavens, the Church is wont to sing the angelic song, which has a first, second, and third *alleluia*, signifying the three ages: before the Law, under the Law, and under grace.

·   ·   ·   ·   ·

22. [The Kiss of Peace]. They extend the Peace of Christ to each other so that by a mutual kiss they may retain in themselves a sense of charity, and so that any discord might fade away and quickly revert to friendship and so that one might seek forgiveness from his neighbor and not, by giving a false Peace, achieve a traitorous relationship. And the reception of the Eucharist and the bestowal of the blessing will be all the more beneficial to the extent that Christ

---

the Cherubicon, like the Sonum, is an "angelic song," and it concludes in one version, as does the Sonum, with three *alleluias* (see paragraph 20 below).

18. A confused reminiscence of several Old Testament descriptions of sacrifice; see, for example, Numbers 10:2–10, Numbers 14:14, and Ecclesiasticus 50:19–20.

19. "Blameless" (*irreprensibilis*) trumpets would seem to refer to the circumstance that patristic authors found it necessary to justify God's allowing of the ancient Hebrews to use musical instruments at sacrifice; see McKinnon, *Music in Early Christian Literature*, items 173, 174, 229, 230, 231, and 232.

20. The bread is carried in a vessel fashioned in the likeness of a tower.

21. The wine, carried in a chalice, follows the bread in the procession.

22. The quotation is from the prayer of consecration, apparently the same as that of the Roman rite. Omitted from the remainder of the translation are several short paragraphs that refer to certain eucharistic vessels and cloths and to the consecration of the bread and wine that is to follow later in the service.

23. Book of Revelation 19:1–6.

sees their hearts to be at peace; for it was he himself who gave this command-
ment to his disciples before his ascension into the heavens: "My peace I leave
with you, my peace I give to you. I give you a new commandment, that you
love one another, and in this will all recognize that you are my disciples, if you
love one another."[24]

23. [The Preface]. "Lift up your hearts." Thus the priest admonishes that no
worldly considerations are to remain in our breasts. At the hour of the holy
sacrifice Christ will be that much the better received in the mind to the extent
that one's thoughts strive to fix upon him alone.

24a. [The Fraction]. The fraction and mingling of the body of the Lord was
manifested in ancient times to the holy fathers as an extraordinary mystery: as
the priest broke up the offering he appeared to be an angel of God who cut up
with a knife the limbs of a shining youth and caught his blood in the chalice,
so that they would believe the word of the Lord to be true when he said his
flesh was food and his blood was drink.[25]

24b. By this fraction the priest wishes to multiply the bread, and likewise he
adds [to the wine] so that heavenly things are mixed with earthly.[26] As the
priest prays the heavens are opened, and as he breaks the bread a suppliant
cleric sings the antiphon[27] because while the Lord endured the death agony all
the elements of the trembling earth joined in testimony.[28]

25. [The Lord's Prayer]. The Lord's Prayer is said, moreover, so that all of
our prayer is included within the prayer of the Lord.

26. [The Blessing]. The Lord commanded through Moses that the Blessing
of the People should be dispensed by the priests: "Say to Aaron and to his sons,
'Thus will you bless my people, *The Lord bless you and keep you, etc.*' "[29]

Aaron thus took the place of the bishop and his sons took the place of the
priests; the Lord therefore commanded both to bless the people, yet in order
to preserve the honor of the pontiff the sacred canons have ordained that the
bishop should give the longer blessing. And the priest should dispense the
shorter blessing in these words: "May the peace, faith, and love, and the communion of the body and blood of our Lord Jesus Christ be always with you." It
is allowed, then, that the priest give this blessing which God dictated to Moses,
and no one can contradict him because the Lord said: "Heaven and earth will
pass away, but my words will not pass away."[30] And for this reason is the bless-

---

24. John, 13:34–35.
25. There is a reference here to a curious episode told in the *Vitae Patrum* (Jacques Migne, ed.,
    Patrologia cursus completus, series latina, vol. 73, cols. 978–79); the vision of the slain boy was
    supposed to have converted a certain monk who had doubted the Real Presence.
26. By breaking the bread the priest multiplies it for distribution at Communion, and similarly he
    adds unconsecrated wine to the consecrated.
27. An antiphon of unknown character, not, in all probability, the Agnus dei, which was introduced
    at the Fraction of the Roman Mass only shortly before 700. The following reference to the
    trembling earth at Christ's death may offer a hint as to the content of its text.
28. See Matthew 27:51.
29. Numbers 6:22–27.
30. Luke 21:33; Mark 13:31.

ing given before the communion, so that the mystery of blessedness shall enter into a blessed vessel.

27. Christ shows how sweet is the sacred communion to soul and body in the words of the evangelist: "If you abide in me and my words abide in you, whatever you will ask the Father in my name shall be done for you."[31]

28. [The Communion chant]. The *Trecanum*[32] which is sung is a sign of the catholic faith. Proceding from a belief in the Trinity, its first part revolves to the second, its second to the third, then its third back to the second, and the second again to the first, just as in the mystery of the Trinity the Father is embraced within the Son, the Son within the Holy Spirit, and in return the Holy Spirit within the Son, and the Son again in the Father.

And now concludes the epistle in which the solemn liturgical order, briefly explained, is presented.

31. John 15:7.
32. The *Trecanum* is an unidentified Trinitarian chant. Johannes Quasten suggests that it might have been "The Holy Thing to the Holies," which is sung at this point in several Eastern liturgies; see his "Oriental Influence in the Gallican Liturgy," *Traditio* 1 (1943): 78.

19 Anonymous (8th Century)

Ordo romanus XVII is one of some fifty documents, the *Ordines romani,* that describe the papal liturgy of eighth-century Rome and its adaptation by the Franks. It was composed by an East Frankish monk sometime during the last two decades of the eighth century. Consisting of various liturgical prescriptions for the Mass and Office that cover the entire church year from Advent to the Sundays after Pentecost, it breaks off after the Christmas material to provide the description of the Mass that is translated here. The description provides a somewhat simplified version of the elaborate papal Mass of *Ordo romanus I* and offers a brief and fairly clear picture of the Mass as it was celebrated outside Rome throughout much of the Middle Ages. Its occasionally cryptic language is illuminated by reference to the more detailed descriptions of the earlier *ordines romani* upon which it is based.

Ordo romanus XVII

17. The manner and order of performing the solemnities of the Mass on that very day [Christmas] and on all important festivals is to be as follows. The

TEXT: Michel Andrieu, ed., *Les Ordines romani du haut moyen âge,* vol. 3, Spicilegium sacrum Lovaniense, no. 28 (Louvain, 1961), pp. 178–83. Translation by James McKinnon.

priests and deacons, when the hour draws near for them to begin the Mass, enter the sacristy, clothe themselves with the proper vestments for Mass, and arrange themselves according to rank,[1] as is the custom.

18. And the clergy begins the antiphon[2] proper to that day.

19. When they commence the first verse of the psalm,[3] the priests leave the sacristy according to the date of their ordination, first those priests who are not celebrating the public Mass on that day, walking together two by two.

20. Then there follow those holding the candelabras with lighted tapers, both the seven and the two,[4] walking in pairs, and those with the tower-shaped censers, processing before the priest.

21. And the priest who will celebrate the Mass follows, with deacons to his left and to his right.

22. And other deacons follow these, walking in pairs. Similarly the subdeacons follow after them, proceeding rather slowly, moving with trembling and reverence.

23. When they come before the altar, they separate and face the space before the priest, looking across at each other.

24. The celebrant inclines his head in prayer and gives the peace to one priest on the right and to all his deacons. In doing this he faces in such a direction that, after demonstrating peace and harmony to the entire order of priests and his clergy, he might draw near to offer the sacrifice to God with a pure heart.

25. Then he approaches the altar and, with his entire body prostrate upon the floor, he pours out prayers for himself and for the sins of the people, until they sing the introit antiphon with the psalm and the *Gloria patri* with the verses *ad repentendum.*[5]

26. Arising from prayer he kisses the holy gospel book that is placed on the altar, he and all the deacons as well.

27. He moves behind the altar with his deacons and looks out from the East;[6] while the deacons remain next to him, one group on the right and the other on the left, the other priests stand next to the altar, arranged by their rank.

1. *Per ordines* and similar phrases are translated "according to rank" here, that is, presumably, according to the date of a cleric's ordination (see "according to the date of their ordination," *sicut sunt ordinati*) in paragraph 19 below.
2. "Antiphon," that is, the Introit antiphon.
3. "The psalm," that is, the Introit psalm; a complete psalm was still sung at this time with the Introit antiphon.
4. *Aut septem aut duo* is translated here "both the seven and the two"; the cryptic Latin phrase seems to distinguish between the seven candle holders that are typical in the entry processions of the *Ordines romani,* and the two that are to accompany the gospel procession (see paragraph 35 below).
5. To sing the verses *ad repentendum* is a Frankish practice by which one or more psalm verses are repeated after the *Gloria patri.*
6. The church is oriented, that is, the chancel is in the East end and the main entrance in the West; here the celebrant goes behind the altar and turns to face west, literally "from the East," toward the congregation and the west end.

28. When the Introit antiphon and the ninefold Kyrie eleison are completed, the priest, facing the people, begins the Gloria in excelsis Deo. And when they arrive at the words *pax hominibus bonae voluntatis* they look again toward the East[7] until the Gloria in excelsis Deo is completed.

29. Then the priest turns to the people and says, "Peace to you," and all respond, "And with your spirit."

30. Then he looks to the East and says the proper prayer of the day.

31. The celebrating priest then sits in his chair behind the altar, while the deacons remain standing at his side, and the other priests sit on benches next to the altar.

32. The lector now enters to read the Apostle.[8]

33. And the subdeacons go up around the altar so that they are ready for all that the deacons might require of them.

34. After the lesson is read, so too is the response[9] sung and then the Alleluia.

35. The deacon then inclines his head toward the knees of the priest. After accepting the priest's blessing, the deacon proceeds to the altar, kisses the holy gospel book, and elevates it with his hands in great reverence. Going before him are two candelabras with lighted tapers, and the tower-shaped censer; he mounts the steps of the ambo, makes the sign of the cross on his forehead, looks up to heaven, and says, "The Lord be with you," and all respond, "And with your spirit." He then announces the gospel lesson and reads it.

36. When he has completed the reading, the priest says to him, "Peace to you." Next the priest says, "The Lord be with you," then, "Let us pray," and sits upon his chair.

37. Then an acolyte pours water on the hands of the priest, while the deacons dress the altar.

38. In a monastery where the people, including the women, are allowed to enter, the priest goes down from his chair with the deacons and accepts the offerings[10] from the people; he places these offerings in linen cloths which the acolyte is to carry before his breast.

39. Similarly the deacons accept the wine and place it in silver vessels, or chalices, which the acolytes are to carry.

40. After the reception of the offerings the priest returns to his chair and again washes his hands.

41. But in a monastery where women do not enter, after the first time the priest washes his hands, the priest and deacons go to the sacristy to receive the

---

7. The Latin has "from the East" (*ab oriente*), but it should be "to the east" (*ad orientem*); this is clear from the context, from the other *Ordines romani,* and from the universally-observed liturgical rubrics in this regard.

8. "The Apostle," referring to the Apostle Paul, is the standard early Christian and early medieval term for the epistle.

9. The "response" (*responsorium* here and *responsum* in certain other documents) is the contemporary term for the gradual.

10. That is, the bread.

gifts. They process then from the sacristy and the gifts are placed on the altar, while the brethren sing the offertory.

42. Then the priest goes to the altar and takes the proper offerings; he raises his eyes to heaven and his hands with the offerings, and prays to the Lord, then places the offerings on the altar.

43. Similarly he offers the wine.

44. The deacons go behind the priest and arrange themselves by rank, and the subdeacons go behind the altar and place themselves by rank, while the priests stand in order before the altar.

45. Then the celebrating priest, with the other priests on his right and left, offers a prayer.

46. He inclines his face to the earth and says the prayer in secret, with no one else able to hear it, until he arrives at the words: "through all ages of ages," and all reply, "Amen."

47. Immediately he says, "The Lord be with you," then, "Lift up your hearts," then, "Let us give thanks to the Lord our God," and then he commences the preface; he lifts his voice and proclaims the preface so that it may be heard by virtually all.

48. When he arrives at the words, "the dominations adore," all the priests and deacons incline their faces to the earth, and when he arrives at the words, "we sing in humble confession: *Sanctus*," the deacons bow again and the clergy with all the people.

49. As all proclaim the Sanctus with great reverence and trembling, the priest begins the canon,[11] in a contrastingly low voice.

50. The priests, deacons, and subdeacons remain bowed all the while up to the place where the priest says, "to us sinners also."

51. And when he arrives at the words, "deign to look upon us with a gracious and serence countenance," the priest inclines his head toward the altar and prays humbly until he says, "so that whatever from the participation in this sacrifice."

52. After the subdeacons arise, one of them goes and takes the paten from the acolyte and returns to where he stood in rank and holds the paten before his breast until the priest says, "all honor and glory."[12]

53. When the priest arrives at the words "through him and with him," he lifts the proper offerings from the altar and places them above the mouth of the chalice, which is held by the deacon who elevates it somewhat until the priest says, "through all ages of ages. Amen."

11. The canon (Latin for "rule") is the medieval term for the eucharistic prayer. Paragraphs 51–55 describe a series of inclinations and other actions that take place as the celebrating priest arrives at various points in the prayer. One notes that there is no elevation of host and chalice during the prayer; the elevation was not introduced until the early thirteenth century.

12. "All honor and glory" is the penultimate phrase of the canon; it is followed by "through all ages of ages. Amen." It is necessary to know this in order to follow the text of paragraphs 53–55, where the actions of the various ministers tend to overlap one another.

54. The priests and deacons remain continuously bowed in the same place except for the deacon who holds up the chalice.

55. The subdeacon who holds the paten gives it to the deacon at the point that the priest says, "all honor and glory." And the deacon holds it until the Lord's Prayer is finished and then hands it to the priest.

56. After the Lord's Prayer, the priest, while continuing to pray, takes the offerings and places them on the paten. He breaks off a small piece of the bread offering and places it in the chalice, makes the sign of the cross over it three times, and says: "The peace of the Lord be always with you."

57. And the people exchange the peace.

58. Then, if necessary, the priests first break up the bread offerings upon the altar, and then the deacons who are near the altar, as the subdeacon holds the paten before himself, break up these bread offerings [upon the paten], while the brethren sing *Agnus dei*.

59. Then the priests and the deacons receive communion according to their rank.

60. Afterwards the deacon takes the chalice to the right side of the altar, holding it up in his hands, and announces the festivals of the saints for the coming week in the following manner: "That approaching day is the feast of the holy Mary, or of a confessor, or of some other saint," whatever is to come according to the Martyrology.[13] And all respond: "Thanks be to God."

61. Then, after the singing of the communion antiphon, and the communion of all, the priest says the oration.

62. And the deacon sings, "Go the Mass is ended," and all reply, "Thanks be to God." And it is finished.

63. After this the priest returns to the sacristy with his ministers and all their paraphernalia, just as they previously exited from the sacristy. And they remove the vestments with which they celebrated the solemnities of the Mass. And now everything has been completed.

13. The Martyrology was a book, arranged by calendar, that listed the festivals of the martyrs and eventually other saints as well. It was used to announce the festivals of the coming week at a time when the clergy, let alone the laity, did not possess individual liturgical books.

20 Helisachar

The birth date of Helisachar, a Goth from the region of Septimania, is unknown. From 808 at latest he served in Aquitania as chancellor to Charlemagne's son Louis the Pious. After Louis became emperor in 814, Helisachar held the same post in the court at Aachen until about 817. He remained thereafter a figure of some importance in the court circle, working closely with Charlemagne's cousins Wala and Adalhard. Although a canon rather than a monk, who spent much of his career at court, he was appointed abbot of St. Aubin's of Angers and later of St. Riquier in Picardy, holding the latter position from 822 to 837.

Helisachar was an important figure in the Carolingian movement toward liturgical reform. He was probably the author of a preface and supplement to Alcuin's lectionary. The letter translated here, believed to have been written sometime between 819 and 822, describes his revision of an Office antiphonary.

Letter to Archbishop Nidibrius of Narbonne

I believe that your holy paternity recalls, when not long ago the command of the emperor bound me to service in his court at the palace in Aachen and held you there for the disposition of certain ecclesiastical affairs, that we often came together during the night hours for the celebration of the Divine Office, where the reading of holy scripture brought peace to our souls. But, as you frequently remarked, you were greatly troubled that the responsories were lacking in authority and reason,[1] and that the verses were inappropriately matched with certain of the responsories by both our cantors and yours.[2] You commissioned me, therefore, to explore the meadows of the sacred scriptures for appropriate verses, bringing to bear my experience and eagerness in compensation for my lack of native intelligence, and to match these verses suitably to responsories that have been authoritatively and rationally recorded. Granted that this task exceeds my powers, and that my ineptitude surpasses my ability to measure it; I could not presume, nevertheless, to neglect that which your holiness commands me to execute with absolute commitment. I placed my confidence in the gracious mercy of Him who has the power to satisfy your sacred wish through the agency of your weak and useless servant, and also to lend to my want of skill what is due to your merits and devotion.

Approaching this task, then, I first gathered from here and there antiphoners

---

TEXT: *Monumenta Germaniae Historica,* Epistolarum tomus V (Munich: MGH, 1978), pp. 307–309. Translation by James McKinnon.

1. Helisachar frequently uses the word authority *(auctoritas)* in this letter as a quality that liturgical chants ought to possess. In most cases the word seems to imply the authority derived from a biblical text, while at times it also seems to imply that such authority is conferred by the appearance of a chant in the majority of antiphoners.

2. One concludes from contemporary documents that the chief reason for this incongruity of verse and responsory is the result of the different manner of performing responsories at Rome and in Gaul. In Rome the entire response was repeated after the verse, but in Gaul only its latter portion, in most cases less than a complete sentence. This resulted, apparently, in numerous instances where there was a lack of coherence between the text of the verse and the text of the repeated portion of the response.

and cantors, and also an abundance of books and skilled readers, and then carefully set about to test the concordance of the antiphoners. Now, while they differed among themselves very little with respect to the chants of the Mass, which rest entirely upon the authority of the holy scriptures, few were found to manifest unity with respect to the chants of the Office,[3] even when these chants appear to have been derived from divine authority or from the writings of the Fathers. Some of the chants in these books were distorted by the error of scribes, some were removed at the whim of the unlearned, and some were jumbled together. It is altogether clear, then, that the antiphonary which was well edited with respect to the night offices by its author in the city of Rome, has been greatly corrupted by those who we mentioned above.

Although those who have the gift of understanding are able to choose that which should be approved and to reject that which should be disapproved, it was necessary, nonetheless, to obey your commands in every respect because of the simpleminded and the less intelligent. By means, therefore, of this persistent collecting and scrupulous examination of antiphoners, which revealed their numerous discrepancies, we have rejected those antiphons and responsories that were lacking in authority and reason and were thus unworthy to be sung in the praise of God. We have, moreover, assigned to their proper places those chants which are clearly authoritative, and we have to the best of our ability joined appropriate verses to them, calling upon that same authority which flows from the copious stream of books. Hence, as you have insisted yourself, a suitable verse is derived from the same source as was the responsory. There were actually some antiphons and responsories, altogether authoritative and suitable for the praise of God, which were unknown to both our cantors and yours. So I took care to call upon certain masters of the art of melody from whom our cantors and yours could eagerly learn these chants. Thus a sacred enterprise succeeds by dint of abundant grace, so that what has been justified by reason and authority is included in this work, and that what was lacking in these qualities is provided by the documentation of many books; and whatever was corrupted in various places by the negligence of scribes or the arrogance of cantors, or was omitted or added by the ignorant, is corrected by the zealous application of expertise and polished by the file of righteousness.

I humbly beg, then, that this project, carried out at your command and dedicated to your zeal, a work of singular necessity to our cantors and yours (even if not to others whom it may not please), be received favorably by you, my father, and be put to use with great devotion in the praise of God. Make available the work to those who will be content with it so that they may carefully copy it, but do not offer it to the fastidious and the ungrateful who are more inclined to criticize than to learn. And insist that those to whom it is lent will

3. Carolingian documents frequently refer to the Mass by the metonymy of "Gradual" (here *in gradali cantu*), and similar the Office by some form of the word "night" (here *in nocturnali* [*cantu*]). The latter usage stems from the circumstance that a large majority of the Office chants were sung at the night Office, commonly referred to today as Matins.

neither delete anything from it, nor add nor change anything, according to that adage of the blessed Jerome that there was nothing to be gained from the editing of books unless the emendation itself is preserved by the diligence of the scribes.

If there is anything in our work that can be faulted in any way (from a motive of arrogance rather than of humility), be assured that this is an instance of innocent dissimulation rather than something overlooked through carelessness or inexperience. For it was right that we approve by our silence, rather than presumptuously judge and tamper with, that which showed signs of wear from its long and devout use by many in the divine liturgy. Nothing of what your holiness finds arranged in this work, unless it be corrupted by subsequent neglect and carelessness, can be found guilty of improper admission to the praise of God; it was included either because it enjoyed scriptural authority, because it was composed from the sayings of the fathers, or because it was justified by the use of many in pious devotion over a long time.

Since we have deemed it appropriate to place this work before our cantors and yours, it is necessary that both the one group and the other take special care, since the verses have been properly placed and arranged, that they be sung accurately after the manner of the melodic art and that they be adapted at the right places in the responsories. It is necessary, moreover, that these chants—composed as they are according to the elegant standard of the melodic art and providing the cantors, as I have said, with a sterling example of something derived from that art—are well understood so that, by the careful observation of all this, there will be no straying in any way from the authority of the melodic art.

May the holy triune God keep you continually mindful of me in his holy service, my father, you who are to be venerated with honor and honored with veneration.

21 John the Deacon

John the Deacon, surnamed Hymonides, was probably a monk of Monte Cassino in the mid-eighth century. He resided for a while in the Frankish court of Charles the Bald (d. 877), and then returned to Italy, where he served in the administration of Pope John VIII (872–882). He died sometime before 882.

His biography of Gregory the Great, commissioned by John VIII, is a highly partisan work, glorifying both Gregory and Rome. Some of the details of the musical portion of the biography, translated here, are strikingly similar to those encountered in the reading from the Monk of St. Gall (even if their interpretation varies sharply). Perhaps both authors heard the same stories from members of the Frankish court.

FROM *Life of Gregory the Great*

6. Then, in the house of the Lord, after the manner of the most wise Solomon, the exceedingly diligent Gregory, motivated by the compunction[1] of musical sweetness, compiled a centonate antiphoner of chants,[2] a task of great usefulness. He also founded the *schola cantorum*, which still sings in the holy church of Rome according to its original instructions. And he built two dwellings for the *schola*, with the proceeds from some plots of land: one near the steps of the basilica of St. Peter the Apostle, and another near the lodgings of the Lateran palace,[3] where even today are preserved with fitting reverence, the bed on which Gregory lay while singing, the switch with which he threatened the boys, as well as the authentic antiphoner. He subdivided these dwellings through a series of injunctions subject to the penalty of anathema for the sake of the daily convenience of the ministry at both places.[4]

7. Of the various European peoples it was the Germans and the Gauls who were especially able to learn and repeatedly to relearn the suavity of the schola's song, but they were by no means able to maintain it without distortion, as much because of their carelessness (for they mixed in with the Gregorian chants some of their own) as because of their native brutishness. For Alpine bodies, which make an incredible din with the thundering of their voices, do not properly echo the elegance of the received melody, because the barbaric savagery of a drunken gullet, when it attempts to sing the gentle cantilena with its inflections and repercussions, emits, by a kind of innate cracking, rough tones with a confused sound like a cart upon steps. And so it disquiets the

---

TEXT: Jacques Migne, ed., *Patrologia cursus completus. Series latina*, vol. 75 (Paris, 1884), cols. 90–92. Translation by James McKinnon.

1. Compunction (*compunctio*), a highly favored word among medieval religious authors, connotes a sort of sweetly sorrowful remorse for one's sins.
2. "A centone antiphoner of chants" (*antiphonarium centonem cantorum*), a difficult and perhaps corrupt phrase; *centonem*, a substantive rather than adjective form, means, literally, something sewn together from patches.
3. The text has the dwelling at St. Peter's located *sub gradibus* and that at the Lateran, *sub domibus*. *Sub* can mean either "below" or "near"; "near," the more inclusive of the two meanings, is chosen here as a matter of caution. The steps at St. Peter's that John had in mind are most probably the prominent stairway that led from the great atrium at the east of the basilica to the plaza below.
4. This somewhat awkward sentence (what could be the meaning of subdividing dwellings through a series of injunctions?) has received little notice in the musicological literature. It is very significant in its suggestion that the *schola cantorum* sang both for papal ceremonies at the Lateran and for urban ceremonies at the basilica of St. Peter's, thus casting strong doubt on theories that there were separate papal and urban chant dialects in early medieval Rome.

spirits of those listeners that it should have mollified, irritating and disturbing them instead.

8. Hence it is that in the time of this Gregory, when Augustine went to Britain, cantors of the Roman school were dispersed throughout the West and instructed the barbarians with distinction. After they died the Western churches so corrupted the received body of chant that a certain John, a Roman cantor (together with Theodore, a Roman citizen yet also archbishop of York), was sent by bishop Vitalian[5] to Britain by way of Gaul; and John recalled the children of the churches in every place to the pristine sweetness of the chant, and preserved for many years, as much by himself as through his disciples, the rule of Roman doctrine.

9. But our patrician Charles,[6] the king of the Franks, disturbed when at Rome by the discrepancy between the Roman and the Gallican chant, is said to have asked—when the impudence of the Gauls argued that the chant was corrupted by certain tunes of ours, while on the contrary our melodies demonstrably represented the authentic antiphoner—whether the stream or the fountain is liable to preserve the clearer water. When they replied that it was the fountain, he wisely added: "Therefore it is necessary that we, who have up to now drunk the tainted water of the stream, return to the flowing source of the perennial fountain." Shortly afterward, then, he left two of his diligent clergymen with Hadrian, a bishop at the time, and, after they had been schooled with the necessary refinement, he employed them to recall the province of Metz to the sweetness of the original chant, and through her, to correct his entire region of Gaul.

10. But when after a considerable time, with those who had been educated at Rome now dead, that most sage of kings had observed that the chant of the other Gallican churches differed from that of Metz, and had heard someone boasting that one chant had been corrupted by the other; "Again," he said, "let us return to the source." Then Pope Hadrian, moved by the pleas of the king (as some today reliably confirm), sent two cantors to Gaul, by whose counsel the king recognized that all indeed had corrupted the suavity of the Roman chant by a sort of carelessness, and saw that Metz, in fact, differed by just a little, and only because of native savagery. Finally, even today, it is confirmed by those who love the simple truth, that as much as the chant of Metz cedes to the Roman, so much does the chant of the other Gallican and German churches cede to the church of Metz. I have mentioned all this by way of anticipation, lest I seem to pass over in silence the carelessness of the Gauls.

5. Theodore was in fact sent to Britain by Pope Vitalian (657–672) in 668, but John was sent a decade later, 678, by Pope Agatho (678–681).

6. Both Charles, and his father Pepin, were formally invested with the title "patrician of the Romans" by contemporary popes.

22 The Monk of St. Gall

A monk from the abbey of St. Gall composed a life of Charlemagne in about 884. At one point in the work he described himself as "toothless and stammering," a remark that suggests he might well be identified with Notker Balbulus ("Notker the stammerer"), a monk of St. Gall who lived from about 840 to 912.

The life is less a proper biography than a collection of anecdotes, many of them quite fanciful. The anecdotes are organized into an opening series on Charlemagne's "piety and his care for the Church" and a second series on his military exploits; a contemplated third series on his daily life was never written. Some see the story translated here as a direct reply to John the Deacon's unflattering remarks about Frankish chanting, but a comparison of the texts fails to establish such a connection between them. More likely, perhaps, is that both rely on the same source.

FROM *Life of the Emperor Charles the Great*

BOOK I

10. At this point I must relate a story that the men of our time might find difficult to believe, since even I who write it would still not entirely believe it—because of the great dissimilarity between our chant and that of the Romans—were it not that the veracity of the fathers is more credible than the flippant deceitfulness of the present generation. Charles, that tireless devotee of the divine liturgy, glad that his vow to do everything that he could for the discipline of letters had been fulfilled, yet sad that all the provinces, regions, and cities differed from one another in the divine praises, that is, in the melodies of the chant, took care to request from Stephen, pope of blessed memory, that he send additional clerics who were greatly skilled in the divine chant. It was Stephen who, after that wretched king of the Franks Childeric was deposed and had his head shorn, annointed Charles to the helm of kingship after the manner of the ancient fathers.[1] Stephen, benevolently disposed and

---

TEXT: Hans Haefele, ed. *Gesta Karoli Magni Imperatoris*, Monumenta Germaniae Historica, Scriptores rerum germanicarum, n.s., vol. 12 (Berlin: MGH, 1959), pp. 12–15. Translation by James McKinnon.

1. Pope Stephen II (752–757) annointed not Charles, but his father Pepin III, who reigned from 751 to his death in 768. Pepin, with the blessing of Pope Zacharias (741–752), deposed Childeric III in 751 and had him confined to a monastery.

inspired by his sacred studies as well,[2] gave assent and dispatched from the Apostolic See to Charles in Francia twelve clerics who were greatly learned in the chant, according to the number of the twelve apostles.

By Francia, incidentally, which I have just mentioned, I mean all the provinces beyond the Alps. For just as it is written, "In those days ten men from all the tongues of the nations shall hold fast the shirt of a man who is a Jew,"[3] at that time, because of the eminence of the glorious Charles, the Gauls and Aquitanians, the Aedui and Spaniards, the Germans and Bavarians, all prided themselves as greatly complemented if they merited to be called servants of the Franks.

When the above-mentioned clerics departed from Rome, they plotted among themselves (since all Greeks and Romans are ever consumed with envy of Frankish glory) how they could so alter the chant that its unity and harmony might never be enjoyed in a realm and province other than their own. So they came to Charles and were received with honor and dispersed to the most prestigious locations. And, in these various localities, everyone of them strove to sing, and to teach others to sing, as differently and as corruptly as they could possibly contrive. But the exceedingly clever Charles celebrated the feasts of Christmas and the Epiphany one year at Trier and Metz and very alertly and sharply comprehended the quality of the chants, indeed penetrated to their very essence, and then in the next year he followed the same festivals at Paris and Tours and heard nothing of that sound which he had experienced the year before in the above-mentioned places. Thus he discovered in the course of time how those he had sent to different places had come to differ from one another, and he conveyed the matter to Pope Leo of blessed memory, the successor to Stephen.[4] Leo, after recalling the cantors to Rome and condemning them to exile or to lifelong confinement, said to the illustrious Charles: "If I send others to you, they, blinded by envy like those before them, will not neglect to deceive you. Rather I will attempt to satisfy your wishes in this manner: give me two very intelligent clerics of your own, in such a way as not to alert my clergy that they belong to you, and they shall acquire, God willing, the total proficiency in this skill that you seek."

It was done in this way, and after a reasonable length of time Leo returned the clerics to Charles perfectly instructed. Charles kept one with himself, and sent the other, at the request of his son Drogo, bishop of Metz, to that church. The second cleric's industry not only held sway in that place, but came to be spread through all of Francia, to such an extent that now even among the

2. "Inspired by his sacred studies," more literally, "by his divinely inspired studies"; this appears to refer to a somewhat feeble instance of allegorical exegesis—the studious Stephen, inspired by reading of the scriptural twelve apostles, sends the same number of cantors from the Apostolic See.

3. Zacharias 8:23.

4. Leo, presumably Leo III (795–816), was not the immediate successor to Stephen; thirty-eight years and several popes intervened between their reigns.

people in those regions where they speak Latin, the ecclesiastical song is called the *mettensis*. Among us, however, who speak the Teutonic or Germanic language, it is called in the vernacular *met* or *mette,* or to use the word of Greek derivation, *mettisca*. Charles, moreover, the most benign emperor, sent the cantor who had been assigned to him, Peter by name, to stay for a while at the monastery of St. Gall; and since Charles was the powerful patron of St. Gall, he made the choir a gift of an authentic antiphoner and he took care that they be instructed so that they learned to sing in the Roman manner, as they do today.

23 Hildegard of Bingen

Hildegard was born in 1098 to noble parents near Spanheim in the Rhineland. She was dedicated to the Church from infancy and took the veil as a girl of fifteen at the Benedictine cloister of Disiboden, where she became superior in 1136. In about 1150 she founded her own convent on the Rupertsberg, in the Rhine Valley near Bingen. She remained there until her death in 1179, attracting a wide following through the fame of her prophetic visions. Known as the "Sibyl of the Rhine," her advice was sought by no less than popes, bishops, and kings. She was a person of extraordinarily varied talents; the author of mystical works, medical works, liturgical poetry set to music, and a morality play.

The excerpt translated here is from a letter she wrote near the end of her life to the hierarchy of Mainz. They had ordered—as punishment for Hildegard's alleged burying of an excommunicated individual in the consecrated ground of her convent's cemetery—that the nuns of the convent be deprived of the sacraments and that they be forbidden to celebrate the Office with music. Hildegard's letter, which recounts what she saw and heard in a vision, reveals at once the pain of being deprived of the sung Office, and her view of music's profoundly spiritual nature.

FROM *Epistle 47: To the Prelates of Mainz*

And I saw something beyond this—as in obedience to you we have until now given up the singing of the Divine Office, celebrating it only by quiet reading—and I heard a voice coming from the living light, telling of those various kinds of praise concerning which David speaks in the Psalms: "Praise him with the

TEXT: *Patrologia Latina* 197, cols. 219–21. Translation by James McKinnon.

sound of the trumpet, praise him with the psaltery and the cithara, praise him with the tympanum and the chorus, praise him with strings and the organ, praise him with the well-sounding cymbals, praise him with the cymbals of jubilation. Let every spirit praise the Lord."[1] In these words we are taught about inward concerns by external objects, how according to the makeup of material things (the properties of musical instruments) we ought best to convert and to refashion the workings of our interior man to the praise of the Creator. When we earnestly strive so to praise, we recall how man sought the voice of the living Spirit, which Adam lost through disobedience, he, who still innocent before his transgression, had no little concourse with the voices of angelic praise (which angels, who are always called spirits, thanks to the Spirit who is God, possess by reason of their spiritual nature). Thus Adam lost that likeness of an angelic voice which he had in Paradise, and thus he went to sleep in that musical science with which he was endowed before his sin. And upon awakening from his slumber he was rendered unaware and uncertain of what he had witnessed in his dreams, when deceived by a prompting from the Devil, and repudiating the will of his Creator, he became entangled in the darkness of inner ignorance because of his sin. But God, who restores the souls of the elect to their original state of bliss by the light of truth, wrought this in his wisdom: that when the Spirit renewed, with a prophetic infusion, the heart of however many, they recovered, by reason of this interior illumination, whatever had been lost from that which Adam possessed before the punishment for his derilection of duty.

But so that mankind, rather than recall Adam in his exile, be awakened to those things also—the divine sweetness and the praise which Adam had enjoyed before his fall—the same holy prophets, taught by that Spirit which they had received, not only composed psalms and canticles, which were to be sung in order to kindle the devotion of those hearing them, but also invented diverse instruments of the musical art, which would be played with a great variety of sound. They did so for this reason: so that the listeners would—as much from the construction and sound of these instruments, as from the meaning of the words sung to their accompaniment—be educated in interior matters, as said above, while being urged on and prodded by exterior objects. Wise and studious men imitated these holy prophets and invented numerous types of human instruments, so that they could make music for the delight of their souls, and adapt what they sang by the bending of their finger joints, as if recalling Adam who was formed by the finger of God (who is the Holy Spirit)— that Adam in whose voice, before he fell, resided the sound of all harmony and the sweetness of the entire musical art, and the power and sonority of whose voice (had he remained in that state in which he was created) the fragility of mortal men could not sustain.

1. Psalm 150.3–6.

But when his deceiver, the Devil, heard what man had begun to sing by the inspiration of God, and that man was invited by this to recall the sweetness of the songs of heaven, seeing that his cunning machinations had gone awry, he was so frightened that he was greatly tormented, and he continually busied himself in scheming and in selecting from the multifarious falsehoods of his iniquity, so that he did not cease to disrupt that affirmation and beauty of divine praise and spiritual hymnody, withdrawing it not only from the heart of man by evil suggestions, unclean thoughts, and various distractions, but even (wherever possible) from the heart of the Church, through dissension, scandal, and unjust oppression. Wherefore you and all other prelates must exercise the greatest care, and before you silence by your decrees the voice of some congregation that sings the praises of God, or before you suspend it from administering or receiving the sacraments, you must first air the reasons for doing this by the most meticulous investigation.

And pay heed that you are led to take such action by zeal for the justice of God, rather than by anger, by some unjust impulse, or by the desire for revenge, and always beware of being circumvented in your judgments by Satan, who deprived man of celestial harmony and the delights of Paradise. And consider, that just as the body of Jesus Christ was born of the Holy Spirit from the purity of the Virgin Mary, so too was the song of praise born in the Church according to celestial harmony through the Holy Spirit; for the body is in truth the clothing of the soul, which has a living voice, and thus it is fitting that the body, together with the soul, sing praises to God through its own voice. Whence the Prophetic Spirit proclaims symbolically[2] that God is to be praised on cymbals of jubilation and on other musical instruments, which clever and industrious men invented, since all the arts that contribute to the utility and need of mankind were discovered by some breath that God sent into the body of man.[3] Thus it is just that God be praised in everything. And since man sighs and moans with considerable frequency upon hearing some song, as he recalls in his soul the quality of celestial harmony, the prophet David, considering with understanding the nature of what is spiritual (because the soul is harmonious) exhorts us in the psalm, "Let us confess the Lord on the cithara, let us play to him on the psaltery of ten strings,"[4] intending that the cithara, which sounds from below, pertains to the discipline of the body; that the psaltery, which sounds from above, pertains to the striving of the spirit; and that the ten strings

2. *Per significationem* is translated "symbolically" here; this is an obvious reference to the standard allegorical treatment of musical instruments referred to above in note 3 of the reading from St. Basil (pp. 12–13) and note 6 of the reading from St. John Chrysostom (p. 16). In most circumstances such symbolical reference to musical instruments implies that actual musical instruments were not in use. However, by dwelling on the subject in the present reading, Hildegard creates the impression that the playing of instruments in her convent might very well have been a common practice, now forbidden by the Mainz hierarchy.
3. Compare Genesis 2.7.
4. Psalm 32(33).1.

refer to the contemplation of the Law.[5] Thus they who without the weight of sure reason impose silence upon a church in the matter of songs in praise of God, and thereby unjustly deprive God of the honor of his praise on earth, will be deprived themselves of the participation in the angelic praises heard in Heaven, unless they make amends by true regret and humble penitence.

5. There are three instances here of that symbolical treatment of biblical instruments referred to above in note 2; each of them is met with again and again in the exegetical literature of the patristic and medieval periods. The cithara (a type of lyre, with its sounding chamber at the bottom of the instrument) was taken to refer to the more mundane virtues, such as self-denial; the psaltery (probably understood by the Church Fathers as a triangular harp with its sounding chamber on its upper member) was taken to refer to the more spiritual virtues such as the practice of contemplation; while the ten strings of the psaltery were taken to refer to the Ten Commandments.

Music Theory and Pedagogy in the Middle Ages

24 Anonymous (9th Century)

The *Musica enchiriadis,* along with the *Scolica enchiriadis,* a short dialogue of related character that appears with it in most manuscripts, is of uncertain date and provenance. It is generally assumed to have been written toward the end of the ninth century somewhere in the north of the Carolingian realm. It has long been celebrated as the earliest surviving witness to Western polyphonic music, but the central focus of the treatise is on describing a tonal matrix for Gregorian chant. It shares this profoundly significant task with Hucbald's *De harmonica institutione* (translated in Claude Palisca, ed., *Hucbald, Guido, and John on Music* [New Haven: Yale University Press, 1978], 13–46), of slightly earlier date perhaps, and the anonymous *Alia musica,* thought to be compiled somewhat later.

At the core of the *Musica's* tonal system is a tetrachord corresponding to the modern notes D, E, F, and G, the four finals of the ecclesiastical modes. The tetrachord is repeated at various pitch levels to create a gamut that has scandalized some modern observers with its augmented octaves, but which matches the tonality of Gregorian chant better than the Boethian scale. It is expressed in a precise and ingenious—if rather ungainly—system of notation called daseian, from its use of the Greek aspirant (the *prosodia daseia,* ⊣ .)

FROM THE *Musica enchiriadis*

I. Beginning of the Handbook on Music

Just as letters are the elementary and indivisable parts of articulated speech, from which syllables and in turn verbs and nouns are formed to create the text of finished discourse, so too the pitches *(ptongi)*[1] of sung speech, which the Latins call sounds *(soni),* are themselves basic elements, and the totality of music is encompassed in their ultimate realization. From the combination of these sounds intervals are created, and from the intervals, in turn, scales *(systemata);* sounds are in truth the primary material of song. Pitches, however, are not just any kind of sound, but those which are suitable to melody by legitimate spacing between themselves. They have a certain natural order in their rise and fall so that a similarly constituted group of four pitches[2] appears

TEXT: Hans Schmid, ed., *Musica et scolica enchiriadis* (Munich: C. H. Beck, 1981), pp. 3–20. Translation by James McKinnon. (The entire treatise is translated by Raymond Erickson, *Musica enchiriadis and Scolica enchiriadis* [New Haven: Yale University Press, 1995].)

1. It would be comforting to the translator of medieval theory if there were unambiguous English equivalents to the Greek and Latin terms for musical pitches, but there are not. There is an attempt here to maintain consistency in translating *ptongus* as "pitch," *sonus* as "sound", and *nota* as "note" (the author of the *Musica enchiriadis* in fact offers definitions for the first two of these later in the paragraph). However, consistency of translation is not always possible, and there are passages later in this reading where it seems advisable to translate *sonus* as "note."
2. That is, a tetrachord.

four times in succession. But all four tetrachords, while dissimilar, are so internally homogeneous, that not only do they differ by height and depth, but it is in this very height and depth that they have the distinct quality of their nature, which is provided by a legitimate distance upwards or downward from each other.[3] To provide an example now, these are the notes *(notae)* of the tetrachord in their proper order:

t	*F*	The first and lowest, called *protos* or *archoos* by the Greeks;
s	*I*	The second or *deuterus,* separated from the protus by a tone;
t	*P*	The third or *tritus,* separated from the deuterus by a semitone;
	F	The fourth or *tetrardus,* separated from the tritus by a tone.

An unending succession of these sounds is created by their multiplication; it continues throughout the four tetrachords of similar make-up until they run out either by ascending or descending.

To illustrate:

As this little diagram shows, whether you trace the sounds in upward or downward order until the last note, the series of tetrachords of this sort does not cease. The quality of these four sounds, moreover, creates the power of the eight modes, as will be described later in the proper place. The complete agreement of these tetrachords is achieved by a sort of amiable diversity.

While, as has been said, their repetition leads to an immeasurable quantity, the logic of our discipline extracts a set number from this confusing multitude, confining its investigation to eighteen sounds. The first and lowest among them consists in the tetrachord of the *graves;* next to it comes the tetrachord of the *finales.* After these come the tetrachord of the *superiores,* and then of the *excellentes.* There remain two final sounds. A diagram of all this follows:

II. THE SYMBOLS OF THE PITCHES AND WHY THERE ARE EIGHTEEN

Since, as we have said, nature has decreed that there are four sets of four similarly related notes, so too are their symbols nearly identical. The difference between the tetrachords is indicated only by the various reversals of the characters.

3. This highly abstract sentence appears only to make the simple point that since each of the four tetrachords has the same configuration of half and whole steps, the four differ only by their higher or lower placement in the gamut.

The first final or end-note [D] has an inclined daseian F
                                        with S at its top, thus *F*
The second final [E] has a reversed C on top,   thus *F*
The third final [F] has a simple inclined I or *iota*,   thus *I*
The fourth final [G] has a half-C on top,   thus *F*
The *graves* reverse the finals,   thus Ⴣ Ⴣ N Ⴣ
The *superiores* invert the finals,   thus ↲ ↲ Ⴣ ↲
The *excellentes* invert the *graves*, thus Ⱡ Ⱡ Ⱡ Ⱡ

The third note is an exception to this: in the *graves* it has an inclined N *N*; in
the *superiores* a reversed and inclined N *�*; and in the *excellentes* a transfixed
iota *Ⱡ* . The two remaining signs have the recumbent forms of the protus and
deuterus ↴ ↴. There are eighteen notes all told, allowing each of them to
achieve its largest consonance, that is, the fifteenth, about which more later.[4]
There were many other signs created in antiquity for other sounds, but it
behooves us to begin with what is easier.

III. Why the Finals Are Named as Such

The finals or end-notes *(terminales soni)* are so called because it is necessary
that every melody end on one of them. Melodies of the first mode and of its
plagal *(subjugalis)* are ruled by and conclude on the low sound of the tetrachord *F*. The second mode and its plagal is ruled by and concludes on the
second sound *F*. The third mode and its plagal is ruled by and concludes on
the third sound *I*. The fourth mode and its plagal is ruled by and concludes
on the fourth sound *F*. The greater mode is called the authentic, the lesser,
the plagal.

IV. Why There Is Only One Tetrachord Below the Finals but Two Above

The finals or end-notes have one tetrachord beneath them, called *graves*,
but two above, the *superiores* and *excellentes* along with the two supernumerary notes. This is so because a natural and legitimate chant does not descend
lower than the fifth sound below its final: to be more specific, this distance in
the first and second modes is from low *F* [D] or the protus final to the corresponding note of the graves *Ⴣ* [G]; in the third and fourth modes it is from the
deuterus final *F* [E] to the corresponding note in the graves *Ⴣ* [A]; in the fifth
and sixth modes from the tritus final *I* [F] to the corresponding note in the
graves *N* [B]; and in the seventh and eighth modes from the tetrardus final *F*
[G] to the corresponding note in the graves *Ⴣ* [C]. On the other hand, a chant
may ascend from a given final to the third sound of the same name, that is,
into the excellentes.[5]

4. Whatever the precise intention of this statement, it is clear that not every note can have its
   fifteenth or double-octave within an eighteen-note system.
5. Thus it may ascend two tetrachords (to the "third" if one counts the tetrachord of the finals
   itself), or a ninth, above the final.

V. How the Authentic and Plagal Modes Differ

Since an authentic mode and the plagal beneath it are governed by and conclude on the same note, they are considered to be one mode; yet they differ in that the plagal *(minores)* modes ascend by lesser *(minora)* intervals, with a particular plagal mode going no higher than the fifth sound over its final, and even this is rare.

VI. On the Characteristics of the Notes and How Many Steps Separate Notes of the Same Character

Whoever finds pleasure in studying these questions should take care to distinguish the peculiar properties of an individual sound, and then immediately to grasp its pitch within a group of notes, relative to what is below it or above, so as clearly to see, by both its nature and its notational symbol, how far it is distant from a related note. Every musical note has at the fifth step in either direction a note of the same character, and at the third step on either side of it there is a similar note as well;[6] while the note that is a second away on this side or that, will be a fourth away on the other. To those little practiced in these pursuits, something more should be provided, something by which they can learn to detect the peculiar properties of the notes in any familiar melody and also to explore an unknown melody by the quality and order of the notes as revealed by the notational symbols. It is of no small benefit to this enquiry if the Greek names of the individual pitches are sung through the neighboring notes in order, as follows:

[DFED]	[ECDE]	[FEF]	[GbG]
ꟼI ꟼꟼ	ꟼꟼ ꟼꟼ	1 ꟼI	ꟼꟼ ꟼ
protus	deuterus	tritus	tetrardus[7]

VII. A Little Illustration of the Properties of The Notes for the Sake of Practice

Thus if any note is sung with its own name, one easily recognizes both the note and its name in the act of singing. By way of an example there follows a diagrammed song; it is sung by the musical symbols inscribed over each syllable, while the names of the notes are given above them in this way:

6. The notes a third step on either side are related to each other (they occupy the same position in their respective tetrachord), not to the central note.

7. This appears to be a kind of solmization, although one wonders about its practicality if the daseian symbols have to be translated into some sort of (presumably awkward) verbal code. (In reproducing this illustration, I have taken the liberty of choosing only four of six given examples, and of reordering these.)

Se	↗	tetrardos	Te	↗	tetrardos	Ty	↙	tetrardos	Rex cae	↙	tetrardos
ni	↗	tetrardos	hu	↗	tetrardos	ta	⅄	archoos	cae	⅄	archoos
be	↲	archoos	ni.	↲	archoos	nis	↘	deuteros	li:	↘	deuteros
as	↳	deuteros	les	↳	deuteros	ni.	↘	tritos	do	↘	tritos
fla	↯	tritos	fa	↯	tritos	ti.	↗	tetrardos	ni.	↗	tetrardos
g.	↯	tritos	nu	↯	tritos	ti:	↗	tetrardos	ne	↗	tetrardos
tant	↳	deuteros	ni:	↳	deuteros						
va	↗	tetrardos	no	↗	tetrardos						
ni.	↳	deuteros	du	↳	deuteros	ma	↲	archoos	squa	↲	archoos
is·	↲	archoos	lis	↲	archoos	ris·	↲	archoos	li:	↲	archoos
li:	↗	tetrardos	ve	↗	tetrardos	un	↗	tetrardos	ti:	↗	tetrardos
be	↲	archoos	ne	↲	archoos	ti:	↘	tritos	que	↘	tritos
ra	↗	tetrardos	ran	↗	tetrardos	so	⅄	archoos	so	⅄	archoos
re	↘	tritos	do	↘	tritos	ni.	↘	deuteros	li:	↘	deuteros
ma	⅄	archoos	ni.	⅄	archoos						
lis	↘	deuteros	is·	↘	deuteros						

But should there remain doubt about the pitch of any note, then one works through the notes in succession—guided by the placement of the semitones, which always separate the second and third note of a tetrachord—and it will quickly be revealed. This practice will make it possible to record and sing sounds no less easily than to copy and read letters. However all this has been phrased, it is intended to aid novices in their studies.

VIII. How All the Modes Are Derived from the Tetrachord

It must now be shown how the force of this tetrachord defines the modes (which we improperly call tones); the illustration will be arranged as follows. A series of quasi strings is set out in order with the notational symbols placed at their edge; the strings represent the pitches which the characters signify.

Between the strings a segment of some chant *(neuma)* is inserted, like this for example:

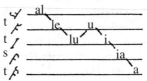

And now, in order to corroborate what has been said by both sight and sound, there follows another little diagram using the same *neuma*. After the strings have again been drawn from side to side, the *neuma* is inscribed within the strings in a fourfold series, with each of the four distinguished by its own color.[8] The first series begins at the note ⤷ [A] and ends on the note ⌐ [D]. The second starts at the note ⌐ [B] and concludes on the note ⌐ [E]. The third commences on the note ⌐ [c] and leaves off at the note ⌐ [F]. The fourth arises from the note ⌐ [d] and comes to a halt on the note ⌐ [G]. Thus:

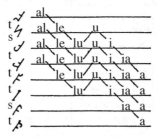

These four short examples, while separated from each other by only a tone or semitone (that is one step of the scale),[9] are transformed by that single step alone from one genus to another. When you sing the first series you can discern that the force of the first note ⌐ [D] creates the character of the first mode, what we call protus authentic. When you sing the second, you hear that the deuterus mode is governed by the second note ⌐ [E]. To take the third, you see again that the power of the tritus mode resides in the third note ⌐ [F]. And after you have sung the fourth, you will understand that the genus of the tetradus mode derives from the fourth note ⌐ [G].

Thus any melody of the first mode and its plagal can be treated like the first chant in the example below: and second mode melodies like the second, and third like the third, and fourth like the fourth. I have endeavored to make this especially clear by producing the examples in a dual format: by the precise placement of each notational symbol within the text, and graphically by the use of quasi strings.

8. One wonders if some manuscripts will exploit this opportunity to display attractive coloring.
9. The Latin has, "by an *armonico spacio*"; this refers, apparently, to the ancient science of harmonics, which concerns itself with the pitch relationships among the tones of the musical systems or scales. In the simplified medieval understanding of these systems, tones and semitones are the basic currency, whereas the ancients admitted a great variety of microtones.

A melody of the first mode and its plagal:

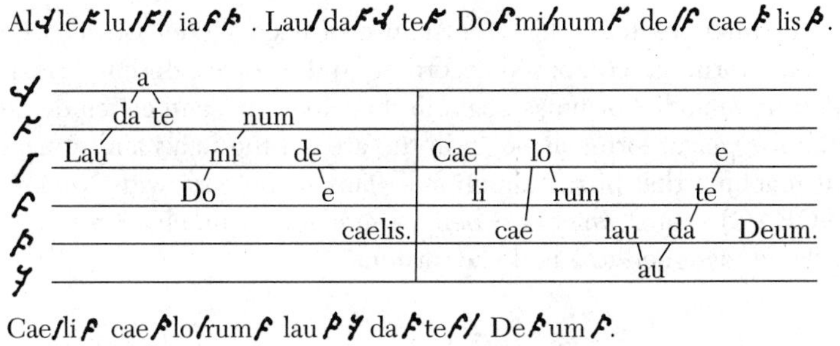
Al le lu ia . Lau da te Do mi num de cae lis .
a
da te num
Lau mi de Cae lo e
Do e li rum te
caelis. cae lau da Deum.
au
Cae li cae lo rum lau da te De um .

A melody of the second mode and its plagal:

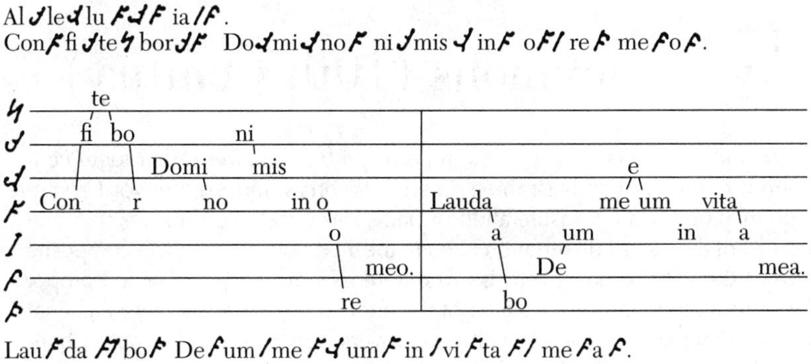
Al le lu ia .
Con fi te bor Do mi no ni mis in o re me o .
te
fi bo ni
Domi mis e
Con r no in o Lauda me um vita
o a um in a
meo. De mea.
re bo
Lau da bo De um me um in vi ta me a .

A melody of the third mode and its plagal:

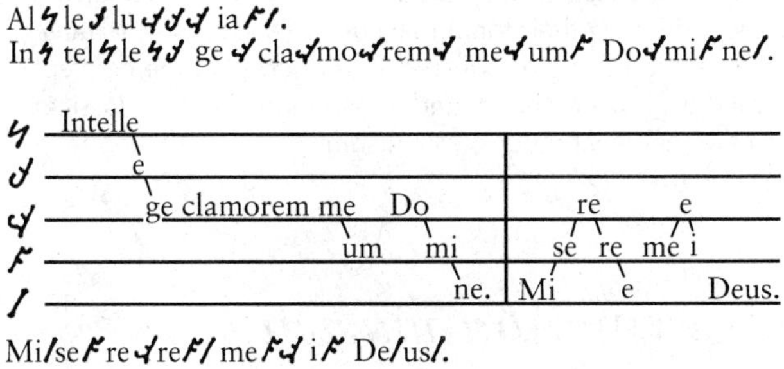
Al le lu ia .
In tel le ge cla mo rem me um Do mi ne .
Intelle
e
ge clamorem me Do re e
um mi se re me i
ne. Mi e Deus.
Mi se re re me i De us .

A melody of the fourth mode and its plagal:

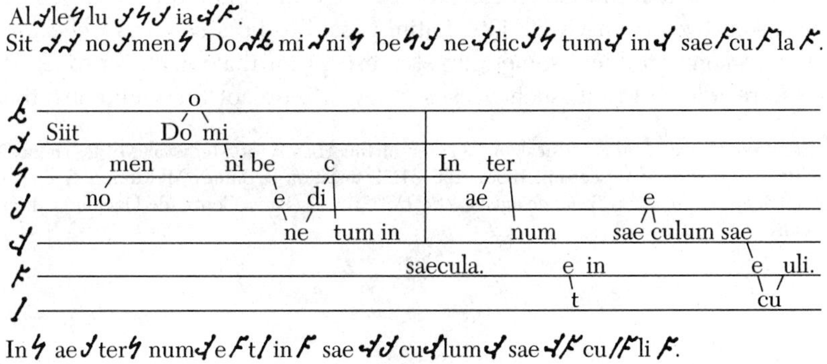
Al le lu ia .
Sit no men Do mi ni be ne dic tum in sae cu la .
o
Siit Do mi
men ni be c In ter
no e di ae e
ne tum in num sae culum sae
saecula. e in e uli.
t cu
In ae ter num e t in sae cu lum sae cu li .

In the same way, in order to explore the nature of each mode, we use the customary melodic formulas composed according to the corresponding principles. The authentic melodic formulas begin in the superiores and conclude on the finals; while the plagal formulas begin in the area of the finals and remain there, without reaching that of the superiores. This is the case with NOAN-NOEANE, NOEAGIS, etc. which we believe are not so much words with meaning as syllables assigned to a melodic formula.

25 Anonymous (10th Century)

The *Alia musica* is a compilation, completed probably in the earlier tenth century, from the work of at least three different theorists; indeed the word *alia* in its title may be a Latin transliteration of *halia,* the Greek word for compilation (see p. 19 of the Heard dissertation cited in the Text note below). The composite nature of the treatise has given rise to differences of opinion over the proper order of its material and over which of the anonymous theorists saw to its final form (the principal protagonists in this controversy are Heard and Jacques Chailley [see citation in the Text note below]).

Whatever the ultimate answer to such questions, the treatise adds up to a thorough treatment of the ecclesiastical modes, emphasizing in particular the arithmetical proportions underlying their tonal makeup. The section of it translated here is of special interest for two reasons: its introduction of the concept of octave species into medieval modal theory and its assignment of the classical Greek modal names to the medieval modes, establishing them permanently in spite of their obvious incongruity.

FROM THE *Alia musica*

Let us, now that these matters have been attended to, proceed to the system of eight tropes, which the Latins call modes. First off it should be known that a trope, taken over from Greek into Latin, is said to be a *conversio* because something is converted into something else, except for that which is proper to it. Tones are referred to as such because they are, except for semitones, the

TEXT: Edmund Heard, " 'Alia Musica': A Chapter in the History of Medieval Music Theory" (Ph.D. diss., University of Wisconsin, 1966), 125–31. Translation by James McKinnon. See also Jacques Chailley, *Alia musica (Traité de musique du IXème siècle)* (Paris: Centre de Documentation Universitaire, 1965), 105–110.

unique common currency of all the tropes. Modes also are referred to as such because each of the tropes must maintain its individual character *(modus)* and not exceed its proper measure *(mensura)*.[1]

Once a system has been established—one that is woven together from the duple, triple, quadruple, sesquialtera, and sesquitertial proportions,[2] with the notes of the fifteen strings interspersed[3]—it becomes necessary to name the eight tropes or modes.

The first mode, the lowest of all, will be called the Hypodorian; it uses the first species of octave and terminates on the middle string, called the mese [a].[4] The second mode is the Hypophrygian; it forms the second species of octave and terminates on the paramese [b]. The third mode is the Hypolydian, consisting in the third species of octave and ending on the string they call the trite diezeugmenon [c]. The fourth mode, the Dorian, reproduces the fourth species of octave and ends on the paranete diezeugmenon [d]. The fifth mode, the Phrygian, is confined to the fifth species of octave; its last string is the nete diezeugmenon [e]. The sixth mode, or Lydian, inescapably utilizes the sixth species of octave, terminating on the trite hyperbolaeon [f]. The seventh is the Mixolydian; it is formed from the seventh species of octave and comes to a close on the paranete hyperbolaeon [g].

A single doubling, that is, an octave, can accommodate no additional species because it is made up of eight pitches; this is so because every interval has one more pitch than it has species. (Hence Ptolemy added an eighth mode, the Hypermixolydian, forming it from the properties of the second and third modes.)[5] Thus the fourth has four strings and three species, the fifth has five strings and four species, and the octave has eight strings and seven species.

Finally, the first species of fourth has its semitone at its third step; the second species at its second step; and the third at its first.[6] And the same species always

1. There is something of a pun here: *modus* means both measure and character or manner.
2. The duple proportion (2:1) produces the octave; the triple (3:1), the tenth; the quadruple (4:1), the double octave; the sesquialtera (3:2), the fifth; and the sesquitertial (4:3), the fourth.
3. The "notes of the fifteen strings" refers to the fifteen notes of the Greek Greater Perfect System as it appears in Boethius; the notes were named for finger positions upon the strings of a lyre or kithara. The *Alia musica* uses these note names as did Hucbald's *De harmonica institutione;* in the present translation they will be followed by their letter equivalents in brackets, with upper case letters for the lower octave and lower case for the upper octave.
4. That is, it extends from A upward to a. The author of this portion of the treatise, which functions perhaps as an introduction to the whole, numbers the modes according to their ascending position on the Greek Greater Perfect System. In doing so the author is depending upon Boethius; in the main body of the treatise the modes are given their familiar medieval numbering.
5. The difficulty with an eighth mode within this context is, of course, that it has the same octave species as the first. The main body of the treatise, however, distinguishes between the first and eighth modes by their governing notes (their finals). Indeed the eighth mode is given the ambitus D to d, with a governing note of G, thus creating a proper tetrardus plagal; still Ptolemy's name for it, the hypermixolydian, is retained rather than the eventual hypomixolydian. See Heard, 65–67.
6. Counting downward, with the first species beginning on a.

returns at the fourth place, whether as a disjunct or conjunct tetrachord;[7] while the same species of fifth does not return at every fifth place.[8] It follows from this that by adding one whole tone the three species of fourth constitute the first three species of fifth; while the fourth species of fifth ends with a semitone (the first species begins at the nete diezeugmenon [e]).[9]

It remains only to examine the properties of the various octave species. The first species has its semitones at the third and sixth step;[10] the second at the fourth and seventh; the third at the first and fifth; the fourth at the second and sixth; the fifth at the third and seventh; the sixth at the first and fourth; the seventh at the second and fifth; and the eighth, as with the first species, at the third and sixth.

To return, in conclusion, to these same octave species, since the lichanos hypaton [D] is the proslambanomenos [D] of the Dorian,[11] the mese of the Dorian [a], which is the paranete diezeugmenon [a] of the Hypodorian, is an integral fourth higher than the mese [e] of the same Hypodorian. The difference between the Phrygian and Hypophrygian is similar, as is that between the Lydian and Hypolydian; while the Mixolydian differs from the Hypermixolydian by only a tone.

7. Chailley's punctuation, pp. 108–109, is preferred here to that of Gerbert and Heard, placing *quintis locis* with the following sentence. But Chailley's interpretation of the passage, which considers the author of the treatise guilty of absurdity, may be too complicated. The author's statement offers less difficulty when viewed within the context of the Greater Perfect System:

8. Obviously not, within a system that is made up of similar tetrachords.
9. The fourth species of fifth, from b to E, consists in a tritone plus a semitone.
10. That is, the third and the sixth step counting downward, etc.
11. The author's concern is with octave species species rather than fixed positions on the Greater Perfect System. Thus the proslambanomenos of the Dorian is (by affinity to A, the proslambanomenos of the Hypodorian) its lowest note, D; and, in the following clause, the paranete diezeugmenon of the Hypodorian is (by affinity to d, the paranete diezeugmenon of the Dorian) that mode's highest note, a.

26 Pseudo-Odo of Cluny

The *Dialogue on Music,* referred to also as the *Enchiridion musices* ("Musical Handbook"), was until recently attributed to the celebrated Benedictine abbot, Odo of Cluny (c. 878–942); the attribution stemmed from a reference in the treatise to a Dom Odo, now identified as the later-tenth-century Odo of Arezzo (see note 6). The *Dialogue* is the work of an anonymous theorist writing in the diocese of Milan sometime early in the eleventh century. The work is significant, among other reasons, for its use of letter notation with repeated octaves beginning on A, its paradigmatic description of the eight ecclesiastical modes, and its influence on Guido of Arezzo.

The treatise's Prologue, frequently appearing with it in manuscripts, is actually the work of another anonymous author. Originating in the same Italian milieu as the *Dialogue,* it was meant to serve as a preface to an antiphoner using an alphabetical notation similar to that advocated in the Dialogue; it, too, had a demonstrable influence upon Guido. Thus, the anonymous authors of the *Dialogue* and the Prologue, Odo of Arezzo, and the culminating figure of Guido, constitute an important Italian school of musical theorists.

Dialogue on Music

PROLOGUE

You have insistently requested, beloved brothers, that I should communicate to you a few rules concerning music, these to be only of a sort which boys and simple persons may understand and by means of which, with God's help, they may quickly attain to perfect skill in singing. You asked this, having yourselves seen and heard and having verified by certain evidence that it could be done. Indeed, when I lived among you, I instructed, with no help other than that of God, certain of your boys and young men in this art. Some of them after three days of training in it, others after four days, and others after a single week, were able to learn several antiphons and in a short time to sing them without hesitation, although they had not heard them sung by anyone, but were content simply with a copy written according to our rules. With the passage of not many more days they were singing at first sight, extempore, and without a mistake any written music, something which until now ordinary singers had never been able to do, with many of them continuing in vain to practice and study singing for fifty years.

When you earnestly and diligently inquired whether our doctrines would be of value for all melodies, I took as my helper a certain brother who seemed perfect in comparison with other singers, and I investigated together with him the Antiphoner of the blessed Gregory, where I found that nearly everything was accurately recorded. A few items, corrupted by unskilled singers, were corrected, both on the evidence of other singers and by the authority of the rules. But on very rare occasion within the longer melodies we found notes belonging to another mode, notes, that is, which contravened the rules by being too high or too low. Yet, since universal usage agreed in defending these

TEXT: The text of the Dialogue proper is from Martin Gerbert, ed., *Scriptores ecclesiastici de musica* (St. Blasien, 1784), vol. 1, pp. 25–59, 263–64; the text of the Prologue is from Michel Huglo, "Der Prolog des Odo zugeschriebenen 'Dialogus de Musica,'" *Archiv für Musikwissenschaft* 28 (1971): 138–39. Translation by William Strunk, Jr., and Oliver Strunk, revised by James McKinnon.

chants, we did not presume to emend them.[1] We marked them as unusual, however, in order that no one inquiring into the truth of the rule might be left in doubt.

This done, you were kindled by a greater desire and insisted, with passionate entreaties and urgings, not only that there be rules, but also that the whole Antiphoner should be written in practical notation and with the formulas of the tones,[2] to the honor of God and of his most holy mother Mary, in whose venerable monastery this project was proceeding.

Deriving confidence, therefore, from your entreaties, and complying with the orders of our common father, I am neither willing nor able to discontinue this work. There is among the learned of this age a very difficult and extensive doctrine of this art, but let whoever pleases cultivate and rework the field with great effort. He who of himself perceives our little gift of God will be satisfied with a simple fruit. And in order that you may better understand it and be adequately recompensed for your good will, let one of yours approach me to converse and ask questions. I shall not neglect to respond to him in so far as the Lord has given me the power.

1. OF THE MONOCHORD AND ITS USE

(Disciple) What is music?

(Master) The science of singing truly and the easy road to perfection in singing.

(D) How so?

(M) As the teacher first shows you all the letters on a slate, so the musician introduces all the sounds of melody on the monochord.

(D) What is the monochord?

(M) It is a long rectangular wooden chest, hollow within like a cithara; upon it is mounted a string, by the sounding of which you easily understand the varieties of sounds.

(D) How is the string itself mounted?

(M) A straight line is drawn down the middle of the chest, lengthwise, and points are marked on the line at a distance of one inch from each end. In the spaces outside these points two end-pieces are set, which hold the string so suspended above the line that the line beneath the string is of the same length as the string between the two end-pieces.

(D) How does one string produce many different sounds?

(M) The letters, or notes, used by musicians are placed in order on the line beneath the string, and when the bridge is moved between the line and the string, shortening or lengthening it, the string marvelously reproduces any chant by means of these letters. When the boys mark some antiphon with these

---

1. It is interesting indeed that the author appears to favor the preservation of the traditional chant melodies over the demands of modal theory.
2. For the "formulas of the tones," see David Hiley, *Western Plainchant: A Handbook* (Oxford: Clarendon Press, 1993), pp. 331–33.

letters, they learn it better and more easily from the string than if they heard some one sing it; and they are able after a few months' training to discard the string and sing by sight alone, without hesitation, music that they have never heard.

(D) What you say is truly marvelous; our singers have never aspired to such perfection.

(M) Instead, brother, they missed the right path, and failing to ask the way, they labored all their life in vain.

(D) How can it be true that a string teaches better than a man?

(M) A man sings as he will or can, but the string is divided with such art by very learned men, using the aforesaid letters, that if it is diligently observed and considered, it cannot mislead.

2. OF THE MEASUREMENT OF THE MONOCHORD

(D) I ask, then, what this art is.

(M) The measurement of the monochord, for if it is well measured, it never deceives.

(D) Can I possibly learn these measurements, simply and in a few words?

(M) Today, with God's help; only listen diligently.

At the first end-piece of the monochord, the point of which we have spoken above, place the letter Γ, that is, a Greek G (this Γ, since it is a letter rarely used, is by many not understood). Carefully divide the distance from Γ to the point placed at the other end into nine parts, and where the first ninth from Γ ends, write the letter A; we shall call this the first step. Then, similarly, divide the distance from the first letter, A, to the end into nine, and at the first ninth, place the letter B for the second step. Then return to the beginning, divide by four from Γ, and for the third step write the letter C. From the first letter, A, divide similarly by four, and for the fourth step write the letter D. In the same way, dividing by four from B, you will find the fifth step, E. The third letter, C, likewise reveals the sixth step, F. Then return to Γ, and from it and from the other letters that follow it in order, divide the line in two parts, that is, in the middle, until you have fourteen or fifteen steps not counting Γ.[3]

When you divide the sounds in the middle, you must mark them differently. For example, when you bisect the distance from Γ, instead of Γ, write G; for A bisected, set down a second a; for B, a second ♮; for C, a second c; for D, a second d; for E, a second e; for F, a second f; for G, a second g; and for a, a second ͣₐ; so that from the middle of the monochord forward, the letters will be the same as in the first part.[4]

3. The explanation is complete except for one detail. If one does not count Γ, then there are fifteen steps if one counts A, and fourteen if one does not.

4. One must not be misled here into thinking that the second octave, because it begins in the middle of the string, will fill the second half of the string. It will occupy only half the space of the first octave, thus leaving room for a theoretically infinite series of higher octaves, each higher octave taking up half of the remaining string length.

In addition, from the sixth step, F, divide into four, and before ♮, place a second round b; these two are taken as a single step, one being called the second ninth step; both are not regularly found together in the same chant.

The figures, both sounds and letters, are thus arranged in order:

		Γ	
First step	A	Eighth step	a
Second step	B	First ninth step	b
		Second ninth step	♮
Third step	C	Tenth step	c
Fourth step	D	Eleventh step	d
Fifth step	E	Twelfth step	e
Sixth step	F	Thirteenth step	f
Seventh step	G	Fourteenth step	g
		Fifteenth step	a

(D) Thanks be to God, I understand well, and I am confident that I shall now know how to make a monochord.

3. OF TONE AND SEMITONE

But why is it, I ask, that I see on the regularly measured monochord in one place smaller and in another place larger spaces and intervals between the steps?

(M) The greater space is called a tone; it is from Γ to the first step, A, and from the first step, A, to the second, B. The lesser space, such as that from the second step, B, to the third, C, is called a semitone and makes a more restricted rise and fall. By no measure or number may the space of a semitone amount to that of a tone, but when the divisions are made in their places by the calculations given above, tones and semitones are formed.

If you have marked all the tones to the very last step, you will marvel to find in every one of them a ninefold division just as you found it at first from Γ to the first step, A, and from the first step, A, to the second, B. Yet the first and second ninth steps, b and ♮, form with respect to one another neither a tone nor a semitone, but from the first ninth step, b, to the eighth, a, is a semitone and to the tenth, c, a tone; conversely, from the second ninth step, ♮, to the eighth, a, is a tone and to the tenth, c, a semitone. Thus one of them is always superfluous, and in any chant you accept one and reject the other in order not to seem to be making a tone and a semitone in the same place, which would be absurd.

(D) It is especially surprising that, although I did not divide by nine, except from Γ to the first step, A, and from the first step, A, to the second, B, I have found that all the tones are equally based on a ninefold division. But show me, if you please, whether there are other divisions of the monochord and whether they are found in all or in several places.

4. OF THE CONSONANCES

(M) Besides the division of the tone, there are three divisions that govern the natural position of sounds which I have spoken of above. The first is the quaternary division, as from the first step, A, to the fourth, D, so called because it is a division by four; this has four pitches and three intervals, namely, two tones and one semitone. Therefore, wherever you find two tones and a semitone between two pitches on the monochord, you will discover on trial that the interval formed by these two pitches maintains itself in quaternary division to the very end of the string; for this reason it is called *diatessaron* [fourth], that is, "of four."

The second is the ternary division, as from the first step, A, to the fifth, E, this contains five pitches and four intervals, namely, three tones and one semitone. Therefore, wherever you see three tones and one semitone between two pitches, the interval formed by these two pitches will be maintained to the end of the string by successive divisions of one-third. This interval is called *diapente* [fifth], that is, "of five," because it encloses five pitches.

The third is what is divided by two, or in the middle; it is called *diapason* [octave], that is, "of all." This, as was said above, you will plainly recognize from the likeness of the letters, as from the first step, A, to the eighth, a. It consists of eight pitches and seven intervals, namely, of five tones and two semitones, for it contains one fourth and one fifth, the interval from the first step, A, to the fourth, D, forming a fourth, that from the fourth step, D, to the eighth, a, forming a fifth. From the first step, A, to the eighth, a, the octave takes on this form: A, B, C, D, E, F, G, a.

(D) In a few words I have learned not a little about divisions. Now I wish to hear why the same letters are used both in the first and in the second part.
(M) The reason is, that since the sounds of the second part, beginning with the seventh step, G (but excepting the first ninth step, b), are formed from those of the first part by the octave, both parts so agree with each other that whatever letters form a tone, semitone, fourth, fifth, or octave in the first part will likewise be found to do so in the second part. For example, in the first part, from Γ to A is a tone, to B is a tone and a tone, that is, a *ditone* [major third], to C a fourth, to D a fifth, to G an octave; similarly, in the second part, from G to a is a tone, to ♮ is a tone and a tone, to c a fourth, to d a fifth, to g an octave. From this it follows that every melody is similarly sung in the first and in the second part. And the sounds of the first part sound in concord with those of the second part, as men's voices with those of boys.

(D) I consider that this has been wisely done. Now I expect to hear first how I may note down a chant so that I may understand it without a teacher and so that, when you give me examples of the rules, I may recognize the chant better and, if anything completely escapes my memory, have recourse to such notes with entire confidence.

(M) Place before your eyes the letters of the monochord as the melody ranges through them; then, if you do not fully recognize the force of the letters themselves, you may, by striking the string at the place of the letters, hear them and learn them, wonderful to relate, from a master without his knowing it.

(D) Indeed, I must say that you have given me a wonderful master, who, made by me, teaches me, and teaching me, knows nothing himself. Indeed, I fervently embrace him for his patience and obedience; he will sing to me whenever I wish, and he will never torment me with blows or abuse when provoked by the slowness of my sense.

(M) He is a good master, but he demands a diligent listener.

5. OF THE CONJUNCTIONS OF SOUNDS

(D) To what am I to direct especial diligence?

(M) To the conjunctions of sounds which form the various consonances, so that, just as they are various and different, you may be able to express each of them conveniently in a dissimilar and different manner.

(D) I ask that you teach me how many differences there are and that you demonstrate them to me by examples in everyday use.

(M) There are six, both in descent and in ascent. The first conjunction of sounds is that where we join two sounds between which there is one semitone, as from the fifth step, E, to the sixth, F, a consonance closer and more restricted than any other; for example, the first ascent of the antiphon *Haec est quae nescivit* or, in descent, conversely, *Vidimus stellam.* The second is that where there is a tone between two sounds, as from the third step, C, to the fourth, D; in ascent: *Non vos relinquam* and in descent: *Angelus Domini.* The third is that where a tone and a semitone make the difference between two sounds, as between the fourth step, D, and the sixth, F; in ascent: *Joannes autem* and in descent: *In lege.* The fourth is that where there are two tones between one sound and another, as from the sixth step, F, to the eighth, a; in ascent: *Adhuc multa habeo* and in descent: *Ecce Maria.* The fifth is that created by the fourth, as from the first step, A, to the fourth, D; in ascent: *Valde honorandus* and in descent: *Secundum autem.* The sixth is that created by the fifth, as from the fourth step, D, to the eighth, a, thus: *Primum quaerite,* or, in descent, from the seventh step, G, to the third, C, thus: *Canite tuba.* Other regular conjunctions of sounds are nowhere to be found.[5]

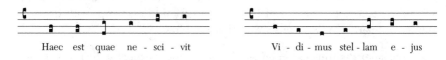

Haec est quae ne - sci - vit   Vi - di - mus stel - lam   e - jus

5. In Gerbert's edition, the incipits of the various melodies cited in this chapter are printed (sometimes incorrectly) in letters immediately above the textual incipits. Strunk replaced these with musical notation derived from modern chant books.

Non vos re - lin - quam

An - ge - lus Do - mi - ni nun - ti - a - vit

Jo - han - nes au - tem cum au - dis - set

In le - ge Do - mi - ni

Ad - huc mul - ta ha - be - o

Ec - ce Ma - ri - a ge - nu - it

Val - de ho - no - ran - dus est

Se - cun - dum au - tem si - mi - le est hu - ic

Pri - mum quae - ri - te re - gnum De - i

Ca - ni - te tu - ba in Sy - on

6. OF THE DISTINGUISHING OF TONE AND SEMITONE ACCORDING TO THE MODES

Mediocre singers often fall into the greatest error because they scarcely consider the qualities of tone and semitone and of the other consonances. Each of them chooses what first pleases his ear or appears easiest to learn and to perform, so that a considerable error is made with respect to the mode of many chants. (I use the term "mode" for the set of eight modes or tones, by the formulas of which all chants are arranged; for if I said "tone," it would be uncertain whether I was speaking of the tones of the formulas or of the tones formed by ninefold disposition and division.) These singers, if you question them about the mode of any chant, promptly reply with what they do not know as though they knew it perfectly. But if you ask them how they know it, they say falteringly: "Because at the beginning and end it is like other chants of the same mode," although they do not know the mode of any melody at all. They do not know that a dissimilarity in a single pitch forces the mode to change, as in the antiphon *O beatum Pontificem,* which, although in the second mode at the beginning and end, was most painstakingly emended to the first mode by Dom Odo,[6] merely because of the ascending interval on which are sung the words *O Martine dulcedo.* You can examine this more thoroughly in the antiphon *Domine qui operati sunt,* for if you begin, as many attempt to, on F, in the sixth mode, it will not depart from that mode until the semitone, at *in tabernaculo tuo,* on one syllable.[7] Yet since it is thus in use, and sounds well, it ought not to be emended.[8] But let us inquire whether it might not begin in another mode, in which all will be found consonant and in which there will be no need for emendation. Begin it, then, on G, that is, in the eighth mode, and you will find that it stands regularly in that mode. For this reason, some begin *Domine* as in *Amen dico vobis.*[9]

From this it is understood that the musician who lightly and presumptuously emends many melodies is ignorant unless he first goes through all the modes to determine whether the melody may perhaps not stand in one or another, nor should he care as much for its similarity to other melodies as for its fidelity to the rules. But if it conforms to no mode, let it be emended according to the one with which it least disagrees. This also should be observed: that the emended melody either sound better or depart little from its previous likeness. (D) You have warned me well against the error of unskilled singers and have also given me in few words no little knowledge of the careful investigation of the regulated monochord, of the verification of regular melodies and the emendation of false ones—all matters that provide a useful and appropriate exercise of one's mind.

7. OF THE LIMITS OF THE MODES

(D) Tell me, now, of how many sounds ought a melody to be formed.
(M) Some say eight, others nine, others ten.

6. The Odo in question here is not Odo of Cluny, but probably Odo of Arezzo, the later-tenth-century author of an antiphoner using alphabetic notation and of an explanatory treatise; see Michel Huglo, *Les Tonaires* (Paris: Société Française de Musicologie, 1971), 182–85.
7. The antiphon as it appears below in the version from the Worcester antiphoner illustrates the author's concern; if the antiphon begins on F, rather than transposed to c as it is here, the a and b-flat would appear as D and E-flat. The E-flat of course lies outside the contemporary gamut, and also creates an octave species on F identical to that normally found on G, thus violating modal theory in a fundamental way.

Do-mi-nè,   qui o - pe-ra - ti sunt ju - sti - ti-am, ha - bi - ta-bunt in ta-ber-na-cu - lo   tu - o,

8. See note 1 above.
9. The typical eighth mode version of *Amen [amen] dico vobis* begins thus:

8. G

A - men, a - men di - co vo - bis,   qui - a plo - rá - bi - tis et flé -

(D) Why eight?

(M) Because of the greater division, that is, the octave, or because the citharas of the ancients had eight strings.

(D) Why nine?

(M) Because of the double fifth, which is bounded by nine pitches. For since from Γ to the fourth step, D, is one fifth, and from this same fourth step to the eighth, a, is another; from Γ to the eighth step, a, there are nine pitches.

(D) Why ten?

(M) Because of the authority of David's psaltery, or because the triple fourth is found at the tenth pitch. For from Γ to the third step, C, is one fourth, from the third step, C, to the sixth, F, is a second, from the sixth step, F, to the first ninth, b, is a third; from Γ, therefore, to the first ninth step, b, one counts ten pitches.

(D) May there also be fewer sounds in a melody?

(M) There may indeed be five or four, so situated, however, that the five produce the fifth and the four the fourth.

(D) The reasoning you have adduced and the evidence of nearly all melodies proves that what you say is true. Now explain what tone is, that which you more often call mode.

8. WHAT MODE IS, AND WHENCE IT IS DETERMINED OR DISTINGUISHED

(M) A tone, or mode, is a rule which classifies every chant by its final. For unless you know the final you cannot know where the chant ought to begin or how far it ought to ascend and descend.

(D) What rule does the beginning take from the final?

(M) Every beginning ought to concord with its final in one of the before-mentioned six consonances. No note may begin a chant, unless it be the final itself or be consonant with it in some one of these six consonances. And whatever notes agree with the final by means of these same six consonances may also begin a melody having this final; with the exception that a melody ending on the fifth step, E, the first of the semitones in the third mode, is often found to begin on the tenth step, c, which is removed from the fifth step, E, by a fifth plus a semitone.

The distinctions, too, that is, the places at which we pause in a chant and at which we divide it, ought obviously to end in each mode on the same notes on which a chant in that mode may begin. And where each mode best and most often begins, there as a rule it best and most suitably begins and ends its distinctions. Several distinctions ought to end on the note which concludes the mode, the masters teach, for if more distinctions are made on some other note than on this one, they expect the chant to end on that other note and insist that it be changed from the mode in which it was. A chant, in other words, belongs for the most part to the mode in which the majority of its distinctions lie. The beginnings, too, are found most often and most suitably on the note which concludes the chant. You may confirm what has been said by the example of the antiphon *Tribus miraculis: Tribus miraculis* is the first distinction; *ornatum diem sanctum colimus* the second; *hodie stella Magos duxit ad praesepium* the third; *hodie vinum ex aqua factum est ad nuptias* the fourth; and *hodie a Joanne Christus baptizari voluit* is the last.[10] So you see that in a properly regulated chant several distinctions begin and end within its own mode and that chants begin and end on the same note.

9. ON THE RANGE OF THE MODES

(D) That these things are as you say is everywhere supported by the authority of singing masters. But continue: what rule with regard to ascent and descent does a chant take from its final?

(M) As for acute or high chants, as in the first, third, fifth, and seventh modes, none ought to ascend further above its final than to the eighth note, the pitch having the same letter as the final, and this because of the special quality of the division which we call the octave. A chant of this sort extends one note below its final. In lower chants, as in the second, fourth, sixth, and eighth modes, there should be no descent below the final to a note not joined to it by means of one of the six before-mentioned consonances; in ascent the range is from the final by means of these same six consonances to the fifth sound, indeed sometimes as far as the sixth. On what notes the chants of all modes most often begin (according to present usage), you will observe from their formulas.

10. THE EIGHT MODES

(D) Now that you have shown how the chants of all the modes are regulated by the final, it is time to explain how many modes, or tones, there are.

(M) Some count four modes.

(D) For what reason?

(M) Because every properly regulated chant ends on one of four pitches of the monochord.

(D) Which pitches are these?

(M) The fourth step, D, on which concludes the mode that we call *authentus protus,* that is, the first author or leader; the fifth step, E, on which concludes the mode that we call *authentus deuterus,* the second author or leader; the sixth step, F, on which concludes the *authentus tritus,* the third author or leader; and the seventh step, G, on which concludes the *authentus tetrardus,* the fourth author or leader. These four, moreover, are divided into eight.

---

10. Tribus miraculis is the *Magnificat* antiphon for second vespers of the Epiphany. It has six cadential points, the five interior ones given here and the one at the end of the final phrase, *ut salvaret nos alleluia;* in the Vatican editions it is a first mode chant with all of its phrases ending on D except for the one ending with the words *baptizari voluit.*

(D) For what reason?

(M) For the sake of high and low chants. For when a chant in the authentus protus is acute or high, we call the mode the authentus protus. But if in the same authentus protus it is grave or low, we call it the *plaga proti.*

(D) Why plaga proti?

(M) Plaga proti, or "a part of the first," because it ends on the same part, that is, on the same place or step of the monochord on which the authentus protus ended, the fourth, D. In a similar way, when a chant in the authentus deuterus is acute we call it the authentus deuterus, but if it is grave we call it the *plaga deuteri.* In the same manner, we say of the authentus tritus, *plaga triti,* and of the authentus tetrardus, *plaga tetrardi.* Common usage, however, has taught us to say first and second mode instead of authentus protus and plaga proti; third and fourth mode instead of authentus deuterus and plaga deuteri; fifth and sixth mode instead of authentus tritus and its plaga; and seventh and eighth mode instead of authentus tetrardus and its plaga. There are eight modes, then, by means of which every melody, proceeding by one of eight different sets of characteristics, is distinguished.

(D) In what way might I be able to to perceive their divergent and common qualities?

(M) By means of tones and semitones. For where tones and semitones occur in similar order, there also the remaining consonances are formed alike. Wherever there are two tones and a semitone, there will also be a fourth, and wherever three tones and a semitone are grouped together, there also the fifth will not be wanting. The remaining consonances are to be understood in a similar way.

· · · · ·

(D) Since I can hardly find even a few melodies which violate these rules, I have no doubt that their scarcity and, so to speak, furtive singularity are the work of presumptuous and corrupt singers.

(M) A rule, certainly, is a general mandate of any art; thus things that are singular do not obey the rules of art.

(D) But please add a few things more about the law of the modes, with respect to the position of each note.

(M) Your request deserves an answer, for with each note there is some affinity to one of the aforesaid modes.[11]

For example, Γ, since it has above it two tones, and after these a semitone and two tones and then a semitone and a tone, rightly bears a similarity to the seventh mode, for the final of the seventh mode sounds at the octave to Γ. Likewise the first step, A, since it has below it a tone, and above it a tone, a

11. There follows one of the earlier discussions of the so-called affinities, although the author uses the term *similitudo* rather than *affinitas;* on the history of the concept see Dolores Pesce, *The Affinities and Medieval Transposition* (Bloomington: Indiana University Press, 1987).

semitone, and two tones, observes the rule of the first mode and therefore is referred to with good reason as the first mode. And the second step, B, since one descends below it by two tones and ascends above it by a semitone and two tones, obeys the usual rule of the fourth mode. In addition, the third step, C, since it has below it a semitone and two tones, and above it two tones, a semitone, and then three tones, maintains the character of the fifth and sixth modes.

We say that the eighth step, a, occupies the first place in similarity to the first step, whose octave it is. On the other hand, if you consider it in connection with the first ninth step, b-flat, it will have in descent a tone, but in ascent a semitone and three tones, like the third mode. The first ninth step, b-flat, has below it a semitone and two tones, like the sixth mode, and above it—either because there are three tones in succession, or rather because it is not joined by any affinity to the following fourth (the principal consonance)—it has no regular resemblance to any mode. Nor can it form an octave with the notes that come after it; consequently you will find that neither a melody nor a distinction may begin or end with it, except by a fault.[12] The second ninth step, ♮, like the second step, B, resembles the fourth mode. The tenth step, c, like the third step, C, agrees with the fifth or sixth mode. But if it be deprived of the second ninth step, ♮, it will have below it a tone, a semitone, and two tones, and above it two tones and a semitone, like the eighth mode, from whose final it marks a fourth.

The remaining sounds are easily dealt with because of the similarity of their letters, as this diagram shows:

					III								
VII	I		V	I	III V	VII	I		V	I	III V	VII	I
Γ	A	B	C	D	E	F	G	a	♮	c	d	e	f	g	a / a
VIII	II	IV	VI	II	IV	VI	VIII	II	IV	VI	II	IV	VI	VIII	II
					VIII								

From what has been said, the diligent inquirer will, with the aid of divine grace, understand many other matters both concerning the modes and concerning the remaining rules of this art. But if he is negligent, or if he should presumptuously think that he understands them by the keenness of his wit and not by divine enlightenment, either he will comprehend them not at all or, so long as he does not return thanks to the Giver, he will become, God forbid, more the vassal of his pride than the servant of his Creator, who is blessed, world without end. Amen.

12. The language dealing with b-flat here is obscure, perhaps corrupt in places, but the overall sense is clear. There can be no affinities with the series of pitches beginning with b-flat at the ninth step of the gamut for two reasons: the first four steps of the series constitute a tritone, not a fourth, and the b-flat creates an octave with neither the B at the second step of the gamut, nor with any b-flat above, since the gamut runs out at aa.

27 Guido of Arezzo

Guido, born probably toward the end of the tenth century, was educated in the Benedictine Abbey of Pomposa on the Adriatic coast near Ferrara. There he and his colleague Michael began an antiphoner, now lost, that employed the unique style of notation described in the Prologue translated here. Around 1025 Guido moved to Arezzo to train the singers of its cathedral. His celebrated treatise, the *Micrologus,* was commissioned by Theodaldus, bishop of Arezzo between 1023 and 1036. Guido, by then a renowned pedagogue of ecclesiastical chant, was called to Rome by Pope John XIX around 1028; he left after a short stay and settled in a monastery near Arezzo, possibly the Camaldolese foundation at Avellana. His death date is unknown.

Although it may be an exaggeration to credit Guido with the invention of the staff, the Prologue to his Antiphoner makes it clear that he was at least a key figure in its early development; the precise date of the Prologue's composition is not known, but it is generally believed to have been written sometime after completion of the antiphoner, perhaps about 1030. A second famous innovation of Guido, the use of solmization syllables, is described in his *Epistolo de ignoto cantu,* the second reading to be translated here. The Epistle, which mentions the Prologue, was written sometime before the death of Pope John XIX in 1033. In subsequent centuries, Guido's reputation achieved mythic proportions, but there is no denying that he was a musical theorist of singular intelligence and originality.

Prologue to His Antiphoner

In our times singers are the most foolish of all men. For in any art those things which we know of ourselves are much more numerous than those which we learn from a master. Small boys know the meanings of all books as soon as they have read the Psalter attentively. Rustics grasp the science of agriculture unthinkingly, for he who knows how to prune one vineyard, to plant one tree, to load one ass, performs without hesitation in all cases just as he did in the one, or even better. But the wretched singers and their pupils, though they sing every day for a hundred years, will never sing by themselves without a master a single antiphon, not even a short one—thus losing time enough in singing to have learned thoroughly both sacred and secular letters.

And what is the most perilous of all evils, many clerics under religious rule[1]

TEXT: Joseph Smits van Waesberghe, ed., *Guidonis "Prologus in Antiphonarium,"* Divitiae Musicae Artis A.III (Buren: Frits Knuf, 1975). Translation by Oliver Strunk, revised by James McKinnon.

1. *Religiosi ordinis clerici,* an apparent reference to canons, that is, secular clergy who live under a quasi-monastic discipline, including the obligation to sing the daily Office.

and monks neglect the Psalms, the sacred readings, the nocturnal vigils, and the other works of piety that arouse and lead us on to everlasting glory, while they apply themselves with unceasing and most foolish effort to the science of singing which they can never master.

Who does not bewail this also, which is at once a grave error and a dangerous discord in Holy Church, that when we celebrate the Divine Office we are often seen rather to strive among ourselves than to praise God? One scarcely agrees with another, neither the pupil with his master, nor the pupil with his colleague. It is for this reason that the antiphoners are not one, nor yet a few, but rather as many as there are the masters in the various churches; and that the antiphoner is now commonly said to be, not Gregory's, but Leo's, or Albert's, or someone's else. And since to learn one is most difficult, there can be no doubt that to learn many is impossible.

Since the masters, then, change many things arbitrarily, little or no blame should attach to me if I depart only in the slightest from common use so that every chant may return uniformly to a common rule of art. And inasmuch as all these evils and many others have arisen from the fault of those who make antiphoners, I strongly urge and maintain that no one should henceforth presume to provide an antiphoner with neumes unless he understands this art and knows how to do it according to the rules laid down here. Otherwise, without having first been a disciple of truth, he will most certainly be a master of error.

Therefore I have decided, with God's help, to write this antiphoner in such a way that hereafter any intelligent and studious person may learn the chant by means of it; after he has thoroughly learned a part of it through a master, he will unhesitatingly understand the rest of it by himself without one. Should anyone doubt that I am telling the truth, let him come to learn and see that small boys can do this under our direction, boys who until now have been beaten for their gross ignorance of the Psalms and vulgar letters. Often they do not know how to pronounce the words and syllables of the very antiphon which they sing correctly by themselves without a master, something which, with God's help, any intelligent and studious person will be able to do if he tries to understand with what great care we have arranged the neumes.

The notes are so arranged, then, that each sound, however often it may be repeated in a melody, is found always in its own row. And in order that you may better distinguish these rows, lines are drawn close together, and some rows of sounds occur on the lines themselves, others in the intervening intervals or spaces. All the sounds on one line or in one space sound alike. And in order that you may understand to which lines or spaces each sound belongs, certain letters of the monochord are written at the beginning of the lines or spaces. And the lines are also gone over in colors, thereby indicating that in the whole antiphoner and in every melody those lines or spaces which have one and the same letter or color, however many they may be, sound alike throughout, as though all were on one line. For just as the line indicates complete identity of sounds, so the letter or color indicates complete identity of lines, and hence of sounds also.

Then if you find the second row of sounds everywhere distinguished by such a letter or colored line, you will also know readily that this same identity of sounds and neumes runs through all the second rows. Understand the same of the third, fourth, and remaining rows, whether you count up or down. It is then most certainly true that all neumes or sounds similarly positioned on lines of the same letter or color sound alike throughout, and they do so even if differently shaped so long as the line has the same letter or color; while on different lines or in different spaces even similarly formed neumes sound not at all alike. Hence, however perfect the formation of the neumes might be, it is altogether meaningless and worthless without the addition of letters or colors.

We use two colors, namely yellow and red, and by means of them I teach you a very useful rule that will enable you to know readily to what tone and to what letter of the monochord every neume and any sound belongs; that is, if— as is greatly convenient—you make frequent use of the monochord and of the formulas of the modes.

Now, as I shall show fully later on, the letters of the monochord are seven. Wherever, then, you see the color yellow, there is the third letter [C], and wherever you see the color red, there is the sixth letter [F], whether these colors be on the lines or between them. Hence in the third row beneath the yellow is the first letter [A], belonging to the first and second mode; above this, next to the yellow, is the second letter [B], belonging to the third and fourth mode; then, on the yellow itself, is the third letter or sound [C], belonging to the fifth and sixth mode; immediately above the yellow and third below the red is the fourth letter [D], belonging to the first and second mode; nearest the red is the fifth letter [E], belonging to the third and fourth mode; on the red itself is the sixth letter [F], belonging to the fifth and sixth mode; next above the red is the seventh letter [G], belonging to the seventh and eighth mode; then, in the third row above the red, below the yellow, is repeated the first letter [a], belonging, as already explained, to the first and second mode; after this all the rest are repeated, differing in no respect from the foregoing; all of which this diagram will teach you quite clearly.

VII	I	III	V	I	III	V	VII	I	III	V	I	III	V	VII	I	III	V	I
														a	♮		c	d
Γ	A	B	C	D	E	F	G	a	♮	c	d	e	f	g	a	♮	c	d
VIII	II	IV	VI	II	IV	VI	VIII	II	IV	VI	II	IV	VI	VIII	II	IV	VI	II

Although each letter or sound belongs always to two modes, the formulas of the second, fourth, six, and eighth modes agree much better and more frequently in the single neumes or sounds, for the formulas of the first, third, fifth, and seventh agree only when the melody, descending from above, concludes with a low note.[2]

Know, finally, that if you would make progress with these notes, you must learn by heart a fair number of melodies so that by the memory of these particular neumes, modes, and notes you will recognize all sounds, of whatever sort. For it is indeed quite another thing to recall something with understanding than it is to sing something by rote; only the wise can do the former while persons without foresight can often do the latter.

Let this suffice for a basic understanding of the neumes for the unsophisticated. As to how sounds are liquescent; whether they should be sung connected or separate; which are retarded and tremulous, and which hastened; how a chant is divided by distinctions; whether the following or preceding sound be higher, lower, or equal sounding; by a simple discussion all this is revealed in the very shape of the neumes, if the neumes are, as they should be, carefully composed.

2. To put it differently, the final will, as a rule, occur more frequently in plagal melodies than in authentic ones. Thus a given step will show a greater correspondence to the appropriate plagal formula than to the authentic formula with which it is paired.

28 Guido of Arezzo

Epistle Concerning an Unknown Chant

TO THE MOST BLESSED AND BELOVED BROTHER MICHAEL, GUIDO, BY MANY VICISSITUDES CAST DOWN AND STRENGTHENED.

Either the times are hard or the judgments of the divine ordinance are obscure when truth is trampled upon by falsehood and love is trampled upon by envy (which rarely ceases to accompany our order); thus the conspiring of the Philistines punishes the Israelitish transgression, so that if anything should turn out according to our wishes, the mortal soul would perish in its self-confidence. For our actions are truly good only when we ascribe to the Creator all that we are able to accomplish.

Hence it is that you see me banished from pleasant domains and yourself so choked by the snares of the envious that you can scarcely breathe. In this I find that we are much like a certain artisan who presented to Augustus Caesar an incomparable treasure, namely, flexible glass. Thinking that he deserved a

TEXT: Martin Gerbert, ed., *Epistola de ignoto cantu. Scriptores ecclestiastici de musica* (St. Blasien, 1784), vol. 2, pp. 42–46, 50. Translation by Oliver Strunk, revised by James McKinnon.

reward beyond all others because he could do something beyond the power of all others, he was by a cruel reversal of fortune sentenced to death, lest, if the glass could be made as durable as it was marvelous, the entire royal treasure, consisting of various metals, should suddenly become worthless. And so from that time on accursed envy has deprived mortals of this convenience, as it once deprived them of Eden. For since the jealousy of the artisan made him unwilling to teach anyone his secret, the envy of the king was able to destroy the artisan along with his art.[1]

Moved, then, by a divinely inspired charity, I have made available not only to you, but to as many others as possible, and as quickly and carefully as I could, a favor divinely bestowed on me, the most unworthy of men; so that those who come after us, when they learn with the greatest ease the ecclesiastical melodies which I and all my predecessors learned only with the greatest difficulty, will desire my eternal salvation as well as yours and that of my other helpers, and so that our sins will be remitted through God's mercy, or at least that some prayer for our souls will result from the gratitude of so many.

For if at present those who have succeeded in gaining only an imperfect knowledge of singing in ten years of study intercede most devoutly before God for their teachers, what do you think will be done for us and our helpers, who can produce a perfect singer in the space of one year, or at the most in two? And even if such benefits meet with ingratitude from the customary miserliness of mankind, will not a just God reward our labors? Or, since this is God's work and we can do nothing without him, shall we have no reward? Forbid the thought. For even the Apostle, though whatever is done is done by God's grace, sings none the less: "I have fought a good fight, I have finished my course, I have kept the faith. Henceforth there is laid up for me a crown of righteousness."[2]

Confident therefore in our hope of reward, we set about a task of such usefulness; and since after many storms the long-desired fair weather has returned, we must felicitously set sail.

But since you in your captivity are distrustful of liberty, I will set forth the situation in full. John, holder of the most high apostolic seat and now governing the Roman Church,[3] heard of the fame of our school, and because he was greatly curious as to how boys could, by means of our antiphoner, learn songs which they had never heard, he invited me through three emissaries to come to him. I therefore went to Rome with Dom Grunwald, the most reverend abbot, and Dom Peter, provost of the canons of the church of Arezzo, a most learned man by the standards of our time. The Pope was greatly pleased by my arrival, conversing much with me and inquiring of many matters. After repeatedly looking through our antiphoner as if it were some prodigy, and reflecting

---

1. See Petronius, *Satires* 51; there are variants of the story in Pliny, *Natural History* 36.26, and Dio Cassius, *Roman History* 57.21.
2. 2 Timothy 4:7–8.
3. John XIX, pope from 1024 to 1033.

on the rules prefixed to it, he did not give up or leave the place where he sat until he had satisfied his desire to learn a verse himself without having heard it beforehand, thus quickly finding true in his own case what he could hardly believe of others.

Need I say more? I was prevented by illness from remaining in Rome even a short time longer, as the summer heat in the marshy areas near the sea was threatening our demise. We finally came to the agreement that I should return later, at the beginning of winter, and at that time reveal this work of mine more fully to the Pope and his clergy, who had enjoyed a foretaste of it.

A few days after this, desiring to see our spiritual father Dom Guido, Abbot of Pomposa, a man beloved of God and men by the merit of his virtue and wisdom, and a dear friend as well, I paid him a visit. As soon as this man of penetrating intelligence saw our antiphoner, he tested it and found it credible. He regretted that he had once given countenance to our rivals and asked me to come to Pomposa, urging upon me, a monk, that monasteries were to be preferred to bishops' residences, especially Pomposa, because of its zeal for learning, which now by the grace of God and the industry of the most reverend Guido ranks foremost in Italy.

Swayed by the entreaties of so eminent a father, and obeying his instructions, I wish first with God's help to confer distinction upon so notable a monastery by this work and further to reveal myself to the monks as a monk. Since nearly all the bishops have been convicted of simony, I should fear to enter into relations with any of their number.

But since I cannot come to you at present, I am in the meantime addressing to you an excellent method of finding an unknown melody, recently given to us by God and found most useful in practice. Further, I greet especially our foremost helper Dom Martin, the prior of the holy congregation, and with the most earnest entreaties commend my miserable self to his prayers. I also remind Brother Peter, who nourished once by our milk now feeds on the coarsest barley, and who after bowls of golden wine now drinks a mixture of vinegar, to think of one who thinks of him.

To find an unknown melody, most blessed brother, the older and more common procedure is this.[4] You sound on the monochord the letters belonging to each neume, and by listening you will be able to learn the melody as if from hearing it sung by a teacher. But this procedure is childish, good indeed for beginners, but very bad for pupils who have made some progress. For I have seen many keen-witted philosophers who had sought out not merely Italian, but French, German, and even Greek teachers for the study of this art, but who, because they relied on this procedure alone, could never become, I will not say skilled musicians, but even choristers, nor could they duplicate the performance of our choirboys.

---

4. An apparent reference to the method recommended above in the *Dialogue on music* 1 of
Pseudo-Odo of Cluny, pp. 200–202.

We do not need to have constant recourse to the voice of a singer or to the sound of some instrument to become acquainted with an unknown melody, so that as if blind we should seem never to go forward without a leader; we need to implant deeply in memory the different qualities of the individual sounds and of all their descents and ascents. You will then have an altogether easy and thoroughly tested method of finding an unknown melody, provided there is someone present to teach the pupil, not merely from a written textbook, but rather by our practice of informal discussion. After I began teaching this procedure to boys, some of them were able before the third day to sing an unknown melody with ease, which by other methods would not have been possible in many weeks.

If, therefore, you wish to commit any note or neume to memory so that it will promptly recur to you whenever you wish in any known or unknown chant, and so that you will be able to sound it at once and with full confidence, you must concentrate upon that note or neume at the beginning of some especially familiar melody. And to retain in your memory any note, you must have at ready command a melody of this description which begins with that note. For example, let it be this melody, which, in teaching boys, I use from beginning to end:

C	D	F	DE D		D	D C	D	E E	
Ut	que-ant	la-xis			Re-so-na-re	fi-bris			

EEG E	D	EC D			F	G	a G	FEDD	
Mi-- ra	ge-sto-rum				Fa-mu-li	tu-o---rum,			

GaG FE F	G D		a	G a F	Ga a	GF ED	C E	D
Sol- ve pol-lu-ti			La-bi-i	re-a--tum,	san-cte	Jo-an-nes.[5]		

Do you not see how the six phrases each begin with a different note? If you, trained as I have described, know the beginning of each phrase so that you can begin any one you wish without hesitation, you will be able to sing these six notes in their proper qualities whenever you see them. Then, when you hear any neume that has not been written down, consider carefully which of these phrases is best adapted to the last note of the neume, so that this last note and the first note of your phrase are of the same pitch. And be sure that the neume ends on the note with which the phrase corresponding to it begins. And when you begin to sing an unknown melody that has been written down, take great care to end each neume so correctly that its last note joins well with the beginning of the phrase which begins with the note on which the neume ends. This rule will be of great use to you either in the competent singing of an unknown melody as soon as you see it written down, or in the accurate transcription of

---

5. This hymn melody is not in the earlier hymn collections; its unidiomatic character leads one to assume that it was composed by Guido in order to demonstrate his method.

an unwritten melody immediately upon hearing it.

I afterwards adapted short fragments of melody to the six notes in sequence. If you examine these phrases closely, you will be pleased to find at the beginning of them all the ascending and descending progressions of each note in turn. If you succeed in singing at will the phrases of each and every one of these fragments, you will have learned by means of a brief and easy rule the exceedingly difficult and manifold varieties of all the neumes. All these matters, which we can hardly explain in writing, we can easily lay bare by a simple discussion.

●   ●   ●   ●   ●

The few words on the form of the modes and neumes, which I have set down both in prose and in verse as a prologue to the antiphoner, will briefly and perhaps adequately open the portals to the art of music. And let the painstaking seek out our little book called the *Micrologus*[6] and also read the book *Enchiridion*,[7] composed with great clarity by the most reverend Abbot Odo. I have departed from his example only in the forms of the notes, since I have made concessions to the young, in this not following Boethius, whose treatise is useful to philosophers but not to singers.

6. For a translation of the *Micrologus,* see Claude V. Palisca, ed., *Hucbald, Guido, and John on Music* (New Haven: Yale University Press, 1978), pp. 57–83.
7. That is the *Dialogue on Music* of Pseudo-Odo of Cluny, this volume, pp. 198–210.

29 Anonymous (13th Century)

The *Discantus positio vulgaris,* originating about 1230, contains the earliest surviving description of modal rhythm, the first rhythmic system employed in Western polyphonic music. The short tract appears to be not so much an anonyomous treatise as a compilation of generally accepted doctrine, transmitted by oral tradition. It is preserved in the later-thirteenth-century *Tractatus de musica* of the Dominican friar Jerome of Moravia, where it stands as the first in a series of "positions" on mensural music. It was Jerome, apparently, who assigned it its title, which might be translated "the common or basic position on discant."

Discantus positio vulgaris

After understanding what discant is, it is necessary to look into certain pre-liminary considerations.[1] Now discant is a song that utilizes differing harmoni-ous sounds; and one must know also what an interval *(sonus)* is and how many intervals there are, what is measurable and what is beyond measure, what a ligature is and how it ought to be performed, and what consonance is and what dissonance.

An interval is the occurrence of two or more pitches at the same point or at differing points. There are nine intervals, namely, the unison, the semitone, the tone, etc.

That is measurable which is measured by one or more *tempora*.[2] That is beyond measure which is measured by less than one tempus or more than two, like semibreves which are written like this: ♦ ♦ ♦, and a long followed by a long, which has three tempora, like this: ❚ ❚ ❚.

A ligature is the binding together of several linked notes of differing pitch. Groups of two, three, and four notes are bound together according to the fol-lowing rules.

When two notes are bound in discant, the first is a breve and the second a long, unless the first is written larger than the second, like this: ◼◢. When three are bound, and preceded by a rest, the first is a long, the second a breve, and the third a long; but if preceded by a long, the first two are breves and the third a long; and when followed by a long, the third is longer than a long.[3] If four notes are bound, all are breves. If there are more than four, they do not follow precise rules, but are performed as one pleases, a practice that is partic-ularly appropriate to organum and conductus.

A consonance is the concord of different voice parts on the same pitch or on different pitches. Among concords three are better than others: the unison,

---

TEXT: Simon M. Cserba, ed., *Hieronymus de Moravia O.P. Tractatus de Musica* (Regensburg: Friedrich Pustet, 1935), pp. 189–94. Translation by James McKinnon.

1. On the problematic nature of this opening sentence, see Janet Knapp, "Two Thirteenth-Century Treatises on Modal Rhythm and Discant," *Journal of Music Theory* 6 (1962): p. 214; and Sandra Pinegar, "Textual and Conceptual Relationships among Theoretical Writings on Measurable Music of the Thirteenth and Early Fourteenth Centuries" (Ph.D. diss., Columbia University, 1991), p. 52.

   The present translation was compared with that in the Knapp article and has benefited from that scholar's expertise. Numerous points of chronology and substance involving this reading and those that follow are dependent upon Pinegar's work.

2. At this early point in the history of measured musical duration, a tempus, represented by the breve, is the basic short time value, generally transcribed today by the eighth note. With the gradual addition of shorter note values, the tempus, along with the breve, will come to represent a duration of some length and to have considerable internal division. See, for example, the table below in the reading from Jehan des Murs, p. 157.

3. That is, a long of three tempora, a note beyond measure.

fifth, and octave. The other intervals (modi) are more dissonant than consonant, although this is a matter of degree, with the interval of a single tone
seeming to be more dissonant than any other.

It should be noted, moreover, that every note of the plainchant is long
beyond measure, containing the measure of three tempora,[4] while every note
of the discantus[5] is measurable, either a proper breve or a proper long.[6]
Whence it follows that over any note of the cantus firmus at least two notes
should be sung, a long and a breve, or something of equal value, like four
breves or three with a plica brevis.[7] And the two voice parts should match each
other with one of the three consonances mentioned above.

Discant should move up and down in this way: every piece should ascend or
descend through one of the nine named intervals, or form a unison.

Let it be known further that all odd notes, when consonant, are more
consonant than even notes, and when dissonant, are less dissonant than even
notes.[8] Hence, if one ascends or descends from a fifth to a unison, one ought
to do so through a third. For example, if the cantus firmus has two successive notes of whatever pitch in unison, say lower F, and the discantus over
the first of them is at the fifth, that is upper c, and wishes to descend to
the unison at the second note by way of a third, that is upper a, it should so
descend, and it should ascend in reverse fashion.[9] If it descends from the
octave to the fifth over these same two notes of the same pitch, that is,
from upper f to upper c, it should do so by way of the third over the fifth,
that is, upper e, and it should ascend from the fifth to the octave in reverse
fashion.

If the cantus firmus ascends a semitone, for example, from lower E to lower
F, and the discantus is at the octave, upper e, it should descend a major third,
through a second,[10] and thus produce a fifth. And when the cantus firmus
reverses this process to descend a semitone, then the discantus, now at the
fifth, must ascend a major third to produce the octave. If the cantus firmus
ascends a tone, from C to D, with the discant at the octave, the discant should

---

4. This refers not to plainchant in general, but to the tenor part of a polyphonic composition
   which usually employs a segment of chant, the so-called cantus firmus.
5. While discantus is translated "discant" here when referring to the polyphonic genre as a whole,
   it is translated "discantus" when referring to the upper of the two polyphonic voices.
6. That is, a breve of one tempus and a long of two.
7. One would think three breves rather than four, or two with a plica brevis (a plica or nota
   plicata—literally a "folded note"—is one drawn with a tail that indicates the singing of a note
   in addition to the basic one, usually a passing tone to the following note).
8. This means that "odd notes," that is, the first, third, etc., notes of a first mode pattern should
   be more consonant than the second, fourth, etc., notes. In the examples of discant treatment
   that follow, the first interval, a perfect consonance, will generally pass to the third interval,
   another perfect consonance, by way of a lesser consonance.
9. Throughout this entire section that deals with discant treatment, the language is elliptical,
   omitting especially details of the reverse progressions. A minimum of such details is supplied
   in what follows.
10. "Through a second"; the text has per secundam a dupla.

descend a minor third by way of a second; and it should ascend in converse fashion when the cantus firmus descends a tone.

If the cantus ascends a minor third, the discantus should descend a tone, and ascend a tone when the discantus descends a minor third. If the cantus ascends a major third, the discantus should descend a semitone; and when the cantus returns by a major third, the discantus ascends a semitone.

If the cantus ascends a fourth, the discantus remains on the same note; and does the same when the cantus descends a fourth. If the cantus firmus ascends a fifth, the discantus moves from its interval of an octave to a fifth by either ascending a tone or descending an octave; and when the cantus firmus descends in return, the discantus ascends an octave.

If the cantus ascends a minor sixth, then the discantus ascends a minor third by way of a second or descends a duplex fourth;[11] and when the cantus descends a minor sixth, then the discantus descends a minor third or ascends a duplex fourth. If the cantus ascends a major sixth, the discantus ascends a major third by way of a second or descends a duplex fourth; and when the cantus returns by descending the like amount, then the discantus descends a major third or ascends a duplex fourth.

If the cantus ascends a duplex fourth, then the discantus descends a major sixth; and when the discantus ascends in reverse, so does the cantus descend. If the cantus ascends an octave, the discantus descends to the fifth; and it ascends in reverse when the cantus descends.

After all this has been observed and committed to memory one can come to possess the entire art of discant by putting it into practice.

One kind of discant is discant proper and another is organum, itself a twofold genre, comprising organum duplex and what is called pure organum. Other kinds of discantus include conductus, motet, and hocket.

Discant proper is a consonant song with different notes but the same text in each voice, as when some ecclesiastical chant is harmonized at the fifth, octave, and twelfth. Duplex organum has the same text but differing notes, with the notes of the tenor long and drawn out, while in the discantus there is a second consonant song differing from the first. Pure organum is that in which two notes of the discant, a long and a breve or something of equal value, correspond to each note beyond measure of the cantus firmus, as described above. Conductus is a consonant polyphonic song using a single poetic text; it employs imperfect consonances.

The motet is a consonant polyphonic song based on the predetermined notes of the cantus firmus, which are either measured or beyond measure; the motet has both diverse notes in each voice and diverse texts. The motet voice utilizes six rhythmic modes: the first consists of a long followed by a breve, the second of a breve followed by a long; the third of a long and two breves; the fourth of

---

11. This is true only if one takes the duplex fourth to mean a perfect fourth and a tritone; see the next situation where in fact two perfect fourths is the correct interval.

two breves and a long; the fifth entirely of longs; and the sixth entirely of breves and semibreves. The following rules govern their relationship to the tenor.

To begin with the first mode: at times the tenor corresponds to the motetus, as in *Virgo decus castitatis*,[12] so that every long of the motetus matches a long of the tenor, and similarly every breve matches a breve. A rest in either voice has the value of one breve, unless both voices pause together with the triplum,[13] and then the rests in the cantus firmus are held ad libitum. Sometimes the tenor consists entirely of longs, as does the tenor of the motet *O Maria maris stella*, and then a long and a breve of the motetus will always correspond to a long of the tenor.[14] The rest in each voice here is long, unless both pause together with the triplum, a situation treated as described previously.

In the second mode as well, the tenor sometimes corresponds to the notes of the motetus, as they do to some extent in *In omni fratre tuo sum* and in *Gaude chorus omnium*. Sometimes there is no such correspondence and the tenor consists entirely of longs; in that case everything is the opposite of the first mode. The rests of each voice also correspond.

Similarly in the third mode, when the tenor corresponds to the motetus, as in *O natio nephandi generis*, every long of the motetus matches every long of the tenor, and every breve matches every breve. But when the tenor consists entirely of long notes, as in *O Maria beata genitrix*, one long of the tenor has the same value as one long of the motetus, followed by a long of the tenor matching two breves of the motetus.[15] The rests of each ought to have this same value, unless both voices pause together with the triplum, and then they are as described before. In the fourth mode, whether the motetus corresponds to the tenor or not, everything maintains the opposite of the third mode, including the rests.

As for the fifth and sixth modes, whether their motetus parts match their tenors or not, it can be gathered from what has been said already how they must conform to the tenors at rests and even to the tripla of other modes.

A hocket is a concordant polyphonic song composed over a tenor, in one of the modes of the motets, but lacking words.[16]

---

12. See Knapp for manuscript references to the motets cited here.
13. The triplum (*tripla* here) is a third voice, added above the motetus.
14. Here the text adds the inexplicable phrase *et e converso* (and vice versa).
15. The sentence concludes with another confusing *et e converso*.
16. A hocket is a composition, or more often a passage within a composition, in which the melodic line is given in rapid distribution between two voice parts, so that when one sounds the other observes a rest. The term hocket is onomatopoetic, related etymologically to a variety of similar words, including the English language hiccup.

30 Johannes de Garlandia

Jerome of Moravia ended his transcription of the *Discantus positio vulgaris* with the following comment. "This is the first position. Since certain of the Nations [i.e., national student groups of thirteenth-century Paris] use it in common, and since it is older than the others, we refer to it as common *(vulgaris).* But because it is defective, we follow it with the position of Johannes de Garlandia." It is particularly defective, at least from the modern pedagogical point of view, in that it fails to explain how the six rhythmic modes are expressed in notation; and therefore the relevant chapter from the treatise attributed to Johannes is provided here.

The identity of this Johannes remains problematic (see Pinegar, "Textual and Conceptual Relationships," 78–102.) Among the factors complicating the question are the circumstances that the content of the treatise reflects musical practice from the first half of the century, and the existence of at least two figures named Johannes de Garlandia, one a poet and the other a music theorist, both of whom were late thirteenth-century figures. Perhaps the music theorist in question brought the treatise to Jerome's attention and was thus credited with its composition.

FROM *De musica mensurabili*

4. THE DEMONSTRATION OF THE MODES IN NOTATION

The first rule of the first mode calls for three notes in ligature at the beginning followed by two in ligature, and two more, etc., indefinitely. All ligatures must have both propriety and perfection:[1]

Angelus.

Angelus

TEXT: Erich Reimer, ed., *Johannes de Garlandia: De mensurabili musica*, Beihefte zum Archiv für Musikwissenschaft 10 (Wiesbaden: Franz Steiner, 1972), pp. 52–56. Translation by James McKinnon.

1. Propriety and perfection refer to the customary ways of writing the beginning and ending, respectively, of ligatures; see Franco of Cologne below for a full explanation and illustration.

A second rule of the first mode: three notes in ligature with a breve rest, etc., indefinitely. One can understand it as given here:

Angelus.

Angelus

The first rule of the second mode calls for two notes in ligature with propriety,[2] followed by two, etc., with three in ligature at the end without propriety and with perfection:

Balaam.

Balaam

A second rule of the same mode: a three-note ligature without propriety and with perfection followed by a long rest, a pattern repeated indefinitely as given here:

Balaam.

Balaam

The third mode is notated with an initial long note followed by a series of three-note ligatures with propriety:

2. It can be assumed here, and in each similar instance that follows, that a ligature described simply as "with propriety" is also to have perfection.

Cumque.

Cumque

The fourth mode is expressed by a series of three-note ligatures with propriety, concluded by a two-note ligature without perfection and a long rest:

Docebit.

Docebit

The fifth mode is expressed exclusively by long notes:

Eius.

Ejus

A second rule of the same mode: a continuous series of three-note ligatures with propriety and perfection, followed by a long rest. This is done for the sake of brevity and is not expressed properly; but it is used because it is accepted as such in the tenors of motets:

Et sperabit.

Et sperabit

The sixth mode is expressed in this way: a four-note ligature with propriety and plica, followed by a series of two-note ligatures with plica:

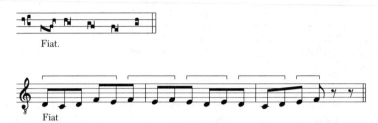

Fiat.

Fiat

A second rule of the same mode: it is not justified by this discipline, but it can be demonstrated by an example that one finds in the triplum of the Alleluia *Posui adjutorium,* namely, a four-note ligature with propriety, followed by a series of three-note ligatures with propriety, as given in the above-mentioned Alleluia:

31 Franco of Cologne

Although Franco of Cologne is a central figure in the history of European music theory, little is known for certain about his life. A fourteenth-century manuscript concludes the *Ars cantus mensurabilis* (The Art of Mensurable Music) by attributing it to "Franco, papal chaplain and preceptor of the Cologne Commandery of the Hospital of St. John of Jerusalem." Jacques of Liège, moreover, confirms Franco's German origins by calling him *Franco Teutonicus.* That Franco had moved to Paris where he was active in musical circles is strongly suggested by references to him in the writings of theorists with Parisian ties; in addition to the later Jacques of Liège there is the nearly contemporary Anonymous IV, who credits Franco with important rhythmic innovations. A fifteenth-century manuscript calls him "Magister Franco of Paris," pointing to a connection with the University of Paris.

The central innovation of his treatise, and one of the most fundamentally important in the history of Western notation, is the movement away from defining the rhythmic value of musical notes by their context—as in earlier modal notation—toward assigning fixed values to individual notes. It is true that a measure of relativity remains in his system; he defines all rhythmic values within the context of the so-called perfection, a unit of three short notes, but the break with the earlier thirteenth century is nonetheless decisive and irreversible. Recent scholarship tends to place the date of the *Ars cantus mensurabilis* quite late, about 1280, which might seem to detract from the originality of a work that summarizes mid-century musical practice. But the same scholarship confirms that Franco's treatise, whatever its date, is the first clear and coherent exposition of the principles underlying that practice.

Ars cantus mensurabilis

PROLOGUE

Now that the philosophers have treated sufficiently of plainsong and have fully explained it to us both theoretically and practically (theoretically above all Boethius, practically Guido Monachus, and, as to the ecclesiastical tropes, especially the blessed Gregory); we propose—in accordance with the entreaties of certain influential persons and without losing sight of the natural order—to treat of mensurable music, which plainsong, described so well by the philosophers cited above, precedes as does the principal the subaltern.

Let no one say that we began this work out of arrogance or merely for our own convenience; we began it rather out of evident necessity, for the ready apprehension of our readers, and the thorough instruction of all copiers of mensurable music. For when we see many, both moderns and ancients, saying sound things about mensurable music in their treatises on the arts but being on the other hand deficient and erroneous in many respects, especially in the details of the science, we think their views are to be supplemented, lest perchance as a result of their deficiency and error the science be exposed to harm.

We therefore propose to expound mensurable music in a compendium, in which we shall not hesitate to introduce things well said by others or to disprove and avoid their errors and, if we have discovered some new thing, to uphold and prove it with good reasons.

1. OF THE DEFINITION OF MENSURABLE MUSIC AND ITS SPECIES

Mensurable music is song measured by long and short units of time. To understand this definition, let us consider what measure is and what time is.

TEXT: Gilbert Reaney and André Gilles, eds., *Franconis de Colonia Ars Cantus Mensurabilis*, Corpus Scriptorum de Musica, no. 18 (Rome, 1974). Translation by Oliver Strunk, revised by James McKinnon.

Measure is an quantitative attribute showing the length and brevity of any mensurable melody. I say mensurable, because in plainsong this kind of measure is not present. Time is the measure of a sound's duration as well as of the opposite, the omission of a sound, commonly called a rest. I say rest is measured by time, because if this were not the case two different melodies—one with rests, the other without—could not be proportionately accommodated to one another.

Mensurable music is divided into wholly and partly mensurable. Music wholly mensurable is discant, because discant is measured by time in all its voice parts. Music partly mensurable is organum, because organum is not measured in all its voice parts. The word organum, be it known, is used in two senses—in its proper sense and in the sense commonly accepted. For organum in its proper sense is organum duplum, also called organum purum. But in the sense commonly accepted, organum is any ecclesiastical chant measured by time.

Since the simple precedes the complex, let us speak first of discant.

2. OF THE DEFINITION AND DIVISION OF DISCANT

Discant is a consonant combination of different melodies proportionately accommodated to one another by long, short, or still shorter sounds and expressed in writing as mutually proportioned by suitable figures. Discant is divided in this way: one kind is sounded simply; another, called hocket, is disconnected; another, called copula, is connected. Of these we must speak in turn, but since every discant proceeds by mode let us explain first about the modes and afterwards about their signs and figures.

3. OF THE MODES OF EVERY DISCANT

Mode is the knowledge of sound measured by long and short intervals of time. Different authorities count the modes and place them in order differently, some allowing six, others seven. We, however, allow only five, since to these five all others may be reduced.[1]

The first mode proceeds entirely by longs. With it we combine the one which proceeds by a long and a breve—for two reasons: first, because the same rests are common to both; second, to put a stop to the controversy between the ancients and some of the moderns. The second mode proceeds by a breve and a long, the third by a long and two breves, the fourth by two breves and a long, the fifth entirely by breves and semibreves.

1. Here Franco departs from the more familiar categorization of six modes as, for example, that seen above in both the *Discantus positio vulgaris* and in Johannes de Garlandia, 4, pp. 223–26. He does so by combining the first and fifth modes into one, with the first mode in the upper voice and the fifth in the tenor. See Pinegar, "Textual and Conceptual Relationships among Theoretical Writings on Measurable Music of the Thirteenth and Early Fourteenth Centuries," pp. 392–447, for a thorough discussion of the various thirteenth-century categorizations.

But since sounds are the cause and principle of the modes, and notes are the signs of sounds, it is obvious that we ought to explain about notes, or about figures, which are the same. And since discant itself is governed both by actual sound and by the opposite, that is, by its omission,[2] and since these two things are different, their signs will also be different because different objects require different signs. And since actual sound precedes its omission, just as "habit" precedes "privation,"[3] let us speak of figures, which represent actual sound, before speaking of rests, which represent its omission.

4. OF THE FIGURES OR SIGNS OF MENSURABLE MUSIC

A figure is a representation of a sound arranged in one of the modes. From this it follows that the figures ought to indicate the modes and not, as some have maintained, the contrary. Figures are either simple or composite. The composite figures are the ligatures. Of simple figures there are three species: long, breve, and semibreve, the first of which has three varieties—perfect, imperfect, and duplex.

The perfect long is said to be the first and principal, for in it all the others are included and all the others are reducible to it. It is called perfect because it is measured by three tempora, the ternary number being the most perfect number because it takes its name from the Holy Trinity, which is true and pure perfection. Its figure is quadrangular, with a descending tail on the right that represents length: ◗.

The imperfect long has the same figure as the perfect, but signifies only two tempora. It is called imperfect because it is never found except in combination with a preceding or following breve. From this it follows that those who call it proper *(recta)* are in error, for that which is proper can stand by itself.

The duplex long, formed in this way ◖, signifies two longs that are combined in one figure so that the line of plainsong in the tenor need not be broken up.

The breve, although it has two varieties, proper and altered, is represented in each case by a quadrangular figure without a tail: ■.

Of the semibreve one variety is major, the other minor, although both are represented by the same lozenge-shaped figure: ◆ .

5. OF THE MUTUAL ARRANGEMENT OF FIGURES

The valuation of simple figures is dependent on their arrangement with respect to one another. This arrangement is understood, moreover, in that after a long there follows either a long or a breve. And let it be observed that the

2. *Vox recta* is translated "actual sound" here and *vox amissa*, "its omission"; see Johannes de Garlandia 1.
3. For the philosophical terms "habit" and "privation" see Richard McKeon, *Selections from Medieval Philosophers*, vol. 2 (New York, Scribner's, 1930), Glossary.

same is true of the valuation of breves and semibreves.

If a long follows a long, then the first long, whether it be a figure or a rest, is measured under one accent by three tempora and called a perfect long:

But if a breve follows a long, the case is manifold, for there will be either a single breve or several of them.

If a single breve, then the long is of two tempora and called imperfect:

unless there be placed between the two, namely between the long and the breve, that little stroke that is called the "sign of perfection" by some and the "division of the mode" by others. In this case, the first long is perfect, and the breve makes the following long imperfect:

If several breves, the case is again manifold, for there might be two, three, four, five, or more than five.

If only two:

then then the long is perfect unless a single breve precedes it:

Of the two breves, the first, moreover, is called a breve proper, the second an altered breve. (A breve proper is one which contains one tempus only. An altered breve, while the same as the imperfect long in value, differs from it in form, for both, though differently figured, are measured by two tempora. What we call a tempus is the minimum duration to be sung in fullness of voice.) But if the stroke called division of the mode is placed between the aforesaid two breves:

then the first long is imperfect and the second also, while the breves will both be proper. This, however, is most unusual.

If only three breves stand between the two longs:

the case is the same as before, except that the one which we called altered breve in the first instance is here divided into two breves proper. But if between the first breve and the two following ones there is placed a division of the mode:

then the first long is made imperfect by the first breve, and of the two following breves the first becomes a breve proper while the last is altered. Observe also that three tempora, whether under one accent or under several, constitute a perfection.

If more than three breves:

then the first long is always imperfect unless the sign of perfection is added to it:

Of the following breves, all are proper that are found in counting by that ternary number which creates a perfection. But if at the end only two remain, the second is an altered breve:

while if only one remains, it will be proper and will make the final long imperfect:

The valuation of semibreves and breves is the same as in the rules already given. But observe that there cannot stand for a breve proper more than three semibreves (called minor semibreves, since they are the smallest parts of the breve proper):

or less than two (of which the first is called a minor semibreve, the second a major, since it includes in itself two minor ones):

But if three semibreves follow immediately after two standing for a breve proper, or vice versa:

then let a division of the mode be placed between three and two, or vice versa, as shown in the preceding example. For an altered breve, moreover, there cannot stand less than four semibreves:

or more than six:

for the altered breve includes within itself two breves proper. From this appears the mendacity of those who at one time replace the altered breve with three semibreves and at other times with two.

6. OF PLICAS IN SIMPLE FIGURES

Aside from these there are certain other simple figures, indicating the same things and called by the same names, but with the addition of what we call the plica.[4] Let us then consider what the plica is; it is a note dividing the same sound into low and high. Plicas are long, breve, and semibreve. But for the present we shall say nothing about the semibreve plica, for it cannot occur in simple figures, although, as will appear later on, it may be used in ligatures and groups of semibreves.

Plicas, further, are either ascending or descending. The long ascending plica is a quadrangular figure bearing on the right a single ascending stroke: ◼ or, more properly, bearing two strokes of which the right one is longer than the left: ◼. I say more properly, for it is from these two strokes that the plica takes its name. The long descending plica likewise has two strokes, but descending ones with the right stroke longer than the left, as before: ◥.

The breve ascending plica is that which has two ascending strokes, the left one, however, longer than the right: ◼. The descending breve plica has two descending strokes with the longer one on the left: ◤.

Observe also that these plicas have a force similar to that of the simple figures already mentioned and that they are similarly regulated as to value.

7. OF LIGATURES AND THEIR PROPERTIES

Now that simple figures have been discussed, let us speak about those that are composite or, what amounts to the same thing, bound together, those that are rightly called ligatures.

A ligature is a combination of simple figures arranged by the proper strokes of the pen. Ligatures are either ascending or descending. In an ascending ligature the second note is higher than the first; in a descending ligature the first note is higher than the second. Ligatures, moreover, are said to be "with propriety," "without propriety," or "with opposite propriety." And this is with respect to the beginning of the ligature. With respect to the end, however, they are said to be either "with perfection" or "without perfection."

Observe also that these differences are essential and specific to the ligature themselves. Hence a ligature with propriety differs essentially from one that is without, just as a rational being differs from an irrational one, and the same is true of the other differences we have mentioned. Species is subordinate to genus. Yet to the species themselves no name is given, but the differences we have mentioned and the genus to which they belong define them. This agrees

---

4. *Plica*, a fold, from *plicare*, to fold or double up.

with what occurs in other real genera: "animate body," for example, defines a certain species to which no name is given.

With respect to the middle notes of ligatures no essential difference is found, from which it follows that all the middle notes of a ligature agree in significance. Hence it appears that the position of those is false who hold that in one type of ternary ligature the middle note is a long,[5] even though it is a breve in all the others.

Now let us consider what is meant by with propriety, without propriety, and with opposite propriety, also by with perfection and without perfection, and what the significance of all these may be. Propriety applies to the first note of a ligature that retains its original form derived from plainsong; perfection means the same thing, but with respect to the final note. Whence follow the rules of the differences we have mentioned.

Every descending ligature having a stroke descending from the left side of the first note is called with propriety, being so figured in plainsong. If it lacks the stroke it is without propriety. Further, every ascending ligature is with propriety if it lacks the stroke. If, however, it has a stroke descending from the left side of the first note, or from the right side, which is more proper, it is without propriety.

Further, every ligature, whether ascending or descending, that has a stroke ascending from the first note, is with opposite propriety.

Now with respect to the final note of a ligature the following rules are given. Every ligature that has the final note immediately above the penultimate is perfect. A ligature is made imperfect in two ways: first, if the final note be rectangular, without a plica, the head turned away from (instead of being above) the penultimate; second, if the last two notes be combined in one ascending oblique form, or descending oblique form. In ascent, however, this last imperfection is out of use, nor is it necessary except, as will appear later on, when the final breve in an ascending ligature is to take a plica.

And let it be known that, just as one ligature differs from another in form by way of these differences, so also does it differ in value. Whence follow the rules of all ligatures. In every ligature with propriety the first note is a breve, in every one without propriety, a long. In every ligature with perfection the final note is a long, in every one without perfection, a breve. In every ligature with opposite propriety the first note is a semibreve, to which we add, and the following one, not in itself, but in consequence, for no semibreve may occur alone. Further, every middle note is a breve, except, as already explained, it be made a semibreve by opposite propriety. Be it also understood that in ligatures the longs are made perfect in the way that was explained under simple figures and that the breves in a similar way become proper or are altered.

---

5. See Johannes de Garlandia, 4, pp. 224–25, where his alternate forms of the second and fifth modes call for a long in the middle of a three-note ligature.

8. OF PLICAS IN COMPOSITE FIGURES

Aside from this let it be known that any ligature, whether perfect or imperfect, may take the plica, and this with respect to its end. (What a plica is, has already been explained under simple figures.) For perfect ligatures may take the plica in two ways, ascending or descending. Imperfect ligatures may also take the plica in two ways. And observe that imperfect ligatures always take the plica in oblique imperfection, ascending or descending. And in such a case, where an imperfect ligature is to take a plica, the oblique form must be used in ascending, because the final note is to be made a breve. For if the rectangular imperfection takes the plica, the plica will make it perfect, since it shares the rule of perfection.[6] Without the plica, the oblique imperfection is not to be used, for the rectangular form of imperfection suffices wherever there is no plica and is more proper and more usual. Thus are the plicas of all ligatures made clear.

There are also certain combinations of simple figures and ligatures which share the nature, in part of ligatures, in part of simple figures, and which cannot be called either the one or the other.[7] For the valuation of such combinations we can give no rules other than those already given for simple figures and ligatures. Besides, there are other arrangements of simple figures and ligatures, distinguished by the rules of simple figures alone, which supply the defect of the combinations not governed by rule.

9. OF RESTS AND OF HOW THROUGH THEIR AGENCY THE MODES ARE CHANGED FROM ONE TO ANOTHER

The signs signifying actual sound having been discussed, let us consider the rests, which represent its omission. A rest is an omission of actual sound in the quantity proper to some mode. Of rests there are six species: perfect long, imperfect long (under which is included the altered breve, since they both involve the same duration), breve proper, major semibreve, minor semibreve, and the double bar (*finis punctorum*).

The rest of a perfect long is the omission of a perfect actual sound, comprehending in itself three tempora. The rest of an imperfect long and altered breve is measured in a similar way by two tempora only. The rest of a breve is the omission of a breve proper, including in itself a single tempus. The major semibreve omits two parts of the breve proper, the minor a third part only. The double bar is called immensurable, for it occurs also in plainsong. This signifies simply that regardless of the mode the penultimate note is a long, even though it would be a breve if the mode were considered.

---

6. That is, the plica will give it the appearance of a long because it is to the right of the note as in the long plica.

7. Franco refers here to the so-called *conjuncturae*, notational combinations derived from the climacus and similar neumes of plain chant, which appeared to the theorists of his time to have mensural significance.

Further, these six rests are designated by six fine strokes, themselves referred to as rests. Of these the first, called perfect, touching four lines, covers three spaces, since it is measured by three tempora. For the same reason the imperfect rest, touching three lines, covers two spaces, the breve rest one space, the major semibreve rest two parts of one space, the minor semibreve rest one part only. The double bar, touching all lines, covers four spaces.

The forms for all these are shown in the following example:

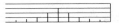

Observe also that rests have a marvelous power, for through their agency the modes are transformed from one to another. The proper rest of the first mode is the breve proper or perfect long; that of the second the imperfect long; the proper rests of the third and fourth are perfect longs, though, improperly, proper or altered breves; the fifth ought properly to have the breve or semibreve rest. Now if the first mode, which proceeds by long, breve, and long, has an imperfect long rest after a breve:

it is changed to the second. If the second mode has a breve rest after a long:

it is changed to the first.

The fifth mode, when combined with the first in any discant, is governed by the rests of the first and has a long note before a rest:

When combined with the second, it is governed by the rests of the second and has a breve at the end before the rest:

When it is neither the one nor the other, it is governed by its own rests:

Observe also that all the modes may run together in a single discant, for through perfections all are reduced to one. Nor need one attempt to determine the mode to which such a discant belongs, although it may be said to belong to the one in which it chiefly or frequently remains.

Let this be enough for the present of rests and of the changing of the modes.

10. HOW MANY FIGURES CAN BE BOUND AT ONE TIME?

Be it known that not to bind a figure that can be bound is a fault, but to bind a figure that cannot be bound a greater fault. Whence be it observed that longs cannot be bound together except in the binary ligature that is without propriety and with perfection. Nor is it a fault if even in this situation they are not bound, for nowhere else are longs bound together. From this it follows that those who occasionally bind three longs together, as in tenors, err exceedingly, as do those who bind a long between two breves, since, as we have seen, all middle notes become breves by rule.

Similarly, more than two semibreves cannot be bound together, and then only at the beginning of the ligature, a practice which is reserved to semibreves. Breves can be bound at the beginning, in the middle, and at the end of a ligature.

From these things it is evident that any mode written without words, except the mode which proceeds entirely by longs, can be bound. The first mode, which proceeds by long and breve, first binds three without propriety and with perfection, then two with propriety and perfection, and as many more twos as desired, so that it concludes with two of this species, unless the mode is changed.

Observe also, as already explained in the chapter on rests, that the modes can be changed in several ways. The second mode begins with a binary ligature with propriety and perfection, then two, two, and so forth, of the same species, a single breve remaining at the end, unless the mode is changed.

The third mode begins with a four-note ligature without propriety and with perfection, then three with propriety and perfection, then three, three, and so forth, unless the mode is changed.

The fourth mode first binds three with propriety and perfection, then three, three, and so forth, of the same species, concluding with two with propriety and without perfection, unless the mode is changed.

The fifth mode ought to be bound as far as possible, concluding with breves or semibreves, unless the mode is changed.

11. OF DISCANT AND ITS SPECIES

Now that figures and rests have been considered, let us speak of how discant ought to be made and of its species. But since every discant is governed by consonances, let us first consider the consonances and dissonances that are sounded at the same time and in different voice parts.[8]

By concord we mean two or more pitches so sounded at one time that the ear perceives them to agree with one another. By discord we mean the opposite, namely, two sounds so combined that the ear perceives them to be dissonant.

Of concords there are three species: perfect, imperfect, and intermediate. Concords are perfect when two sounds are so combined that, because of the consonance, one is scarcely perceived to differ from the other. Of these there are two: unison and diapason. Concords are imperfect when the ear perceives that two sounds differ considerably, yet are not discordant. Of these there are two: ditone and semiditone. Concords are intermediate when two sounds are so combined that they produce a concord better than the imperfect, yet not better than the perfect. Of these there are two: diapente and diatessaron. As to why one concord is more concordant than another, let this be left to plainsong.

Of discords there are two species: perfect and imperfect. Discords are perfect when two sounds are so combined that the ear perceives them to disagree with one another. Of these there are four: semitone, tritone, ditone plus diapente, and semitone plus diapente. Discords are imperfect when the ear perceives that two sounds agree with one another to a certain extent, yet are discordant. Of these there are three: tone, tone plus diapente, and semiditone plus diapente.

Observe also that both concords and discords can be endlessly extended, as in diapente plus diapason and diatessaron plus diapason, and similarly by adding the double and triple diapason, if it be possible for the voice. Be it also known that immediately before a concord any imperfect discord concords well.

Discant is written either with words or with and without words. If with words, there are two possibilities—with a single text or with several texts. Discant is written with a single text in the cantilena, in the rondellus, and in any ecclesiastical chant. It is written with several texts in motets which have a

---

8. Franco's treatment of concord and discord, although differing in some details, is clearly derived from that of Johannes de Garlandia, 9.

triplum and a tenor, for the tenor is the equivalent of some text. It is written with and without words in the conductus and in the ecclesiastical discant improperly called organum.

Observe also that except for the conductus the procedure is the same in all these forms, for in all except the conductus there is first heard some *cantus prius factus* (called tenor, since it supports the discant and has its place on its own). In the conductus, however, this is not the case, for cantus and discant are written by the same person. The term discant, however, is used in two senses—first, as meaning something sung by a number of persons; second, as meaning something based on a chant.

The following procedures are employed in discant. The discant begins either in unison with the tenor:

or at the diapason:

or at the diapente:

or at the diatessaron:

or at the ditone:

or at the semiditone:

proceeding then by concords, sometimes introducing discords in suitable places, so that when the tenor ascends the discant descends, and vice versa. Be it also known that sometimes, to enhance the beauty of a composition, the tenor and discant ascend and descend together:

Be it also understood that in all the modes concords are always to be used at the beginning of a perfection, whether this beginning be a long, a breve, or a semibreve.

In conductus the procedure is different, for he who wishes to write a conductus must first invent as beautiful a melody as he can, then, as previously explained, use it as a tenor is used in writing discant.

He who wishes to construct a triplum must have the tenor and discant in mind, so that if the triplum be discordant with the tenor, it will not be discordant with the discant, and vice versa. And let him proceed further by concords, ascending or descending now with the tenor, now with the discant, so that his triplum is not always with either one alone:

Dulcia

He who wishes to construct a quadruplum or quintuplum ought to have in mind the melodies already written, so that if it be discordant with one, it will be in concord with the others. Nor ought it always to ascend or descend with any one of these, but now with the tenor, now with the discant, and so forth.

Be it observed also that in discant, as also in tripla and so forth, the equivalence in the perfections of longs, breves, and semibreves ought always to be borne in mind, so that there may be as many perfections in the discant, triplum, and so forth, as there are in the tenor, and vice versa, counting both actual sounds and their omissions as far as the penultimate perfection, where such measure is not observed but rather a point of organum.

Let this be enough for the present of simple discant.

12. OF COPULA

A copula is a rapid, connected discant, either bound or unbound. A bound copula is one which begins with a simple long and proceeds by binary ligatures with propriety and perfection as in the second mode, although it differs from the second mode in notation and in performance. It differs in notation, since the second mode does not begin with a simple long as the copula does:

If a division of the mode is placed between the initial long and the following ligature, it is no longer a copula, but is said to be in the second mode:

A -   men

It differs from the second mode also in performance, since the second mode is performed with a proper breve and imperfect long, while the copula is performed quickly, as though with semibreve and breve, right through to the end.

An unbound copula resembles the fifth mode, although it differs from it in two respects—in notation and in performance. It differs in notation, since the fifth mode can be bound wherever there are no words, while the copula, although it is never used with words, is unbound:

In performance it differs also, since the fifth mode is performed with proper breves, while the copula is more quickly connected in performance.

Let this be enough of copula.

13. OF HOCKET

A truncation is a sort of music sounded in a broken way by actual sounds and their omissions. Be it known also that a truncation can be effected in as many ways as the long, breve, and semibreve can be divided. The long is divisible in a number of ways. First, it can be divided into long and breve, or breve and long, and from this division a truncation or hocket (for this is the same thing) is so effected that in one voice a breve is omitted and in the other a long:

(In seculum)

Then it can also be divided into three breves, or two, and into several semibreves, and from all these divisions a truncation is so sung by actual sounds and their omissions that when one voice rests, the other does not, and vice versa.

The breve, on the other hand, can be divided into three semibreves or two, and from this division a hocket is sung by omitting a semibreve in one voice and performing one in the other:

Be it observed that by way of these truncations, the omission and sounding of longs and breves, the vernacular hockets are sung. Be it observed also that in every case the equivalence of the tempora and the concord of the actual sounds must be borne in mind. And let it be known that every truncation must be based on a cantus prius factus, whether it is in the vernacular or Latin.

Let this suffice for hocket.

14. OF ORGANUM[9]

Organum, in the proper sense of the word, is a sort of music not measured in all its parts. Be it known that there can be no organum except over a single sustained note in the tenor, for when the tenor has several notes within a short space, discant is the immediate result:

[Constan - tes e - sto - te]

The longs and breves of organum are determined by three rules. The first is: whatever is written as a simple long note is long; as a breve, short; as a semibreve, still shorter. The second is: whatever is long requires concord with respect to the tenor; if a long occur as a discord, let the tenor be silent or render itself concordant:[10]

[Ju -   dea]

9. On this chapter, see Charles M. Atkinson, "Franco of Cologne on the Rhythm of Organum Purum," *Early Music History* 9 (1989): 1–26.

10. Thus the second note of the tenor is changed from an F, the original pitch of the chant from which it is derived, to an E in order to form a consonance with the upper voice.

The third is: Whatever occurs immediately before the rest which we call the double bar is long, for every penultimate note is long.

Be it observed also that in organum purum, whenever several figures occur over a sustained note, only the first is to be sung in measure, while all the rest are to observe the florid style.[11]

Of discant and its species, of signs (that is, of figures and rests), and of organum let what has been said here suffice.

Here ends the great "Art of music" of that reverend man, Dominus Franco, papal chaplain and preceptor of the Cologne Commandery of the Hospital of St. John of Jerusalem.

11. The translation of this difficult passage follows the interpretation of Atkinson, pp. 10–23.

32 Aegidius of Zamora

Aegidius was born at Zamora in northwestern Spain about 1240 and entered the Franciscan order in about 1270. He studied in Paris in the early 1270s and then returned to Spain, where he lived the rest of his long life as a scholar and ecclesiastical figure of some prominence. He worked, for example, at the court of Alphonso the Wise, for whom he compiled the celebrated *Cantigas de Santa Maria*. He was Minister of the Santiago province of the Franciscan Order from 1303 to 1318 and died some years later at an unknown date.

Aegidius dedicated his *Ars musica* to Jean Mincio de Murrovalle, Minister General of the Franciscan Order from 1296 to 1304. It is a conservative work that fails to mention polyphony and attempts rather to summarize the views of the traditional authorities on theoretical topics involving plainchant. One of the more original sections, Chapter II (translated here) deals with the exploits of musical animals, an area in which Aegidius, the author of a natural history, had special expertise. Another chapter frequently cited is the final one, in which he discourses at some length on musical instruments; unfortunately it is not known whether this is the work of Aegidius himself or if it was borrowed from Bartholomeus Anglicus.

FROM *Ars Musica*

CHAPTER I: ON THE ORIGINAL DISCOVERY OF THE MUSICAL ART

We read that, according to the diverse views of many savants, there were numerous discoverers of music. Others, however, have insisted that the philosopher Pythagoras, while passing by a smithy, heard a ringing sound produced by the beating of five hammers upon one anvil. He approached the place, led there by the sweet and melodious concord that arose from the diversity of sound, and carefully considered whether some secret of the musical art might lie hidden in the sound of these hammers. At this very spot, then, he set out immediately to weigh the hammers; one by one he briskly distinguished the various pitches from the ringing of the hammers, and thereby discovered the seven notes of the scale and the consonances.

Yet if we can assume from what has been said that the philosopher Pythagoras discovered something of this art by means of his alert intelligence, he was nevertheless not the very first inventor or founder of the art. As we are informed by the divinely inspired narratives in the Hebraic truth of Genesis, Chapter 4, and from the gloss on that passage, from Rhabanus, from the distinguished historiographer Josephus, and from the *Historia scholastica,*[1] Tubal, son of Lamech by his wife Ada, was the father of those who play upon the cithara and organ—but not the father of the instruments themselves, which were invented long afterwards. This man was the very first to discover the proportions and consonances of music, so that the work of a shepherd, which was so burdensome and debilitating to the body with its sleeplessness, exertions, and anxieties, would be rendered pleasurable. When Tubal heard, then, that Adam had prophesied concerning two judgments, one through water and a second through fire, he meticulously inscribed the science of music upon two pillars, thus transmitting the principles of this art in writing, lest what he had discovered be lost. Now one of these pillars was of marble, which could not be dissolved by the Flood, and the other was of brick, which could not be destroyed by fire. Indeed the marble one, according to Josephus, was later discovered in Syria.[2]

The above-mentioned Lamech fathered Tubalcain by his second wife Sella; Tubalcain was, as Chapter 4 of Genesis relates, a smith in every sort of bronze and ironwork. He was the original founder of the art of metalworking, and he

TEXT: Michel Robert-Tissot, ed., *Johannes Aegidius de Zamora: Ars musica,* Corpus Scriptorum de Musica, no. 20 (Rome, 1974), pp. 36–52. Translation by James McKinnon.

1. The *Historia scholastica, Liber Genesis XXVIII,* of Peter Comestor is a particularly important source for Aegidius in what follows.
2. Flavius Josephus, *Antiquitates Judaicae* 2.64.

expertly fashioned the tools of war. He also created sculptures in metal, that is, examples of metalwork that delighted the eye. Now as Tubalcain worked, Tubal (or Jubal), of whom we spoke before, was delighted by the sound of the hammers, as we read in the *Historia scholastica* histories, and he cleverly calculated (as told above) from the weights of the hammers the proportions and the consonances which arise from them. The Greeks falsely attributed this discovery to Pythagoras (again, as told above). Similarly it was in working with shrubbery that Tubalcain discovered how to fashion intriguing works in metal that delight the eye, like the consonances that delight the ear of musicians. For when the brothers had burned the brush in the fields so that the tender grass would sprout for the flocks, veins of metallic ore flowed into rivulets. According to Josephus, after these rivulets had formed into metal sheets and the brothers had lifted them up and supported them, they found the shapes of the places (in which the metal sheets had lain) impressed upon those very sheets.[3]

It should be noted, moreover, that Zoroaster (called Cham by some), the inventor of the magical arts, elegantly inscribed the seven liberal arts on fourteen pillars. Seven of the pillars were of bronze and seven of brick, to resist the Flood and fire mentioned above. But Ninus had his books consigned to the flames whence they perished. Abraham, who excelled in his knowledge of the stars, instructed this Zoroaster in the liberal arts. Still, Isidore states in the fifth book, second chapter, of his *Etymologies* that Tubal, the offspring of Cain, invented music before the Flood. The Greeks, however, according to Isidore, attributed this to Pythagoras, claiming that he discovered it in the sound of hammers and in the striking of stretched strings.[4]

Others, according to Isidore, say that the Theban philosopher Linus, or the philosophers Zethus and Amphion discovered music. After these, continues Isidore, there were further claims from time to time; as the poet would have it, "the new author must always make his own contribution." We read, accordingly, that music was discovered by the philosopher Asclepiades in the tinkling sound of gold; while some claim it was by some other philosopher from the song of birds, especially the nightingale, of which we shall have something to say in the next chapter. If indeed this is the case, the nightingale knows from natural instinct alone the various notes: the tractus, the subtractus, the contractus, and postractus; the high and the low; the plain, the joined, and the separate—and it teaches its art to the other small birds as they listen. Others say music was discovered from the buffeting of the wind in the vaulted forest, where there are certain sweet rustlings to be heard, especially at night. Others say from the sound of waters and the striking of wind upon cliffs and other rocky places: whence the line "his voice is as the voice of many waters." Others

3. Apparently the ultimate source (by way of Peter Comestor) is not Josephus, but Lucretius, *De rerum natura* 5.1252–61. This fact is of considerable interest since Lucretius was unknown for most of the Middle Ages until his rediscovery by Poggio in the early fifteenth century. I am indebted to Charles Segal of Harvard University for pointing out the Lucretian passage.
4. The passage appears in Isidore's *Etymologies* 3.16 (this volume, p. 150).

say it is clear from the Toledan tables that music originates from the violent motion of the peripheries of the heavens, that is, the revolution of the spheres either along their axes or in some manner along the shining rays of the sun.[5] Others, finally, say music originates from the stretched gut fibers of dead animals, separated from flesh and bone, particularly in flowing water or elsewhere.

Nonetheless one must agree with Hebraic truth that the original discoverer was Tubal, while various others, following him in both rank and lineage, up to the present time, produced new theories and findings, of which we shall speak below, and added these to the earlier discoveries, as is clear enough from other sciences. If indeed, as Priscian has it, while there are at first the elders, the youngers perceive with correspondingly greater penetration, as is clear from the ancient philosophers, then Socrates, then Plato, and finally Aristotle the Younger at the time of Alexander the Great.

CHAPTER II: ON THE BENEFITS THAT FOLLOW FROM THE INVENTION OF MUSIC

The ancients have made clear that the benefits of the musical art were so rich, that it would be, in the words of Isidore, as shameful to be ignorant of music as of letters. Hence music was never absent from sacrificial rites, from weddings, from banquets, or from war. And what was more remarkable, it was always present at burials. As blessed Isidore says, if the discipline of music be lacking, no discipline will be complete. Music stirs feeling, stimulates the senses, and animates warriors; indeed the more fierce the sound, the braver the soul in battle. Music gladdens the sorrowful, and it strikes fear in the guilty when the trumpet of the enemy sounds in their ears. Music lightens the labors of shepherds and of others, and braces those who languish; it calms agitated souls, banishes care and anxiety, and restrains and curbs violence. Moreover, to cite Isidore briefly, it miraculously draws beasts and snakes, birds and dolphins, to harken to its strains. And what is more marvellous, it casts out evil spirits from the body, banishing them by a certain miraculous and hidden divine power. If indeed, as we read, the Most High rightly allows demons to inhabit human bodies because of man's inclination to numerous vices, nevertheless when soothing melody moves the body to the opposite inclination, say, from severe depression to joy, the evil spirit departs. Whence the master of the *Historia scholastica* says that according to the magicians many demons cannot

---

5. This extremely difficult sentence compresses several elements of thirteenth-century Ptolemaic-Aristotelian astronomy. The Toledan tables, developed from Arabian astronomy, permitted one to calculate the position of the various heavenly bodies for every day of the year. The peripheries of the heavens (the supralunary spheres), in addition to their natural circular motion, have a "violent" motion, that is, one that is not natural but is caused by some agency such as a planetary intelligence. Musical sound is produced by the contrast between these two motions, the natural circular one and the "violent" one, which moves either inward along the axis of the universe to its earthly center or outward to the sun. I am indebted to Professor Catherine Tachau of the University of Iowa for her help with both the translation and the astronomical background.

endure harmony, and indeed none can when a fortuitous change in disposition is wrought through harmony in the bodies in which they dwell.[6] Whence the divinely inspired histories relate in the First Book of Kings, Chapter 15, that when the evil spirit vexed Saul, his servants said to him "take unto yourself a player (*psaltem*) who is skilled on the lyre" (by a *psaltes* one understands some-one skilled in music), "and you will be relieved."[7] And it happened, then, that David played before Saul on the lyre whenever Saul was vexed by the demon, and Saul was relieved and refreshed, and the evil spirit departed from him (he is a spirit by nature, but evil through his own fault). The philosopher Asclepi-ades also restored a certain crazed man to his originally healthy state of mind through concordant melody, as blessed Isidore attests.

What else? We know from observation that birds swiftly descend to hear a melody, and learn it gladly, and teach it to their pupils generously. Whence Pliny relates in Book 10 and Ambrose in the *Hexaemeron,* that the nightingale (also called the *luscinia* or *acredula*) is a bird rather small in body, but extraor-dinary in voice and song.[8] When she warms her eggs in the spring time, she consoles herself during the sleepless labor of the long night with pleasant mel-ody, so that she is able to bring life to the eggs on which she sits, no less by the sweet strains than by the warmth of her body. Usually the nightingale bears six eggs; thus, according to Pliny, she twitters away with her song for fifteen consecutive days and nights without letup, as the leafy twigs of the nest become compressed.

It is worthy of admiration that in so slight a body there thrives so tenacious a spirit. And it is admirable, too, that from one music of such perfection there flows such a variety of song, which is now drawn out, now varied in its inflec-tion, now clear and concise. It issues forth and it returns; it becomes faint, sometimes murmuring to itself; it is full, low, high, focused, repeated, and pro-longed. In so little a throat there is as much variation of song as in all the refined instruments that the art of man has invented. The song of each nightin-gale is like that of no other; it is her own unique song. Nightingales compete among themselves in a lively public contest. When conquered by death a night-ingale often gives up its life with its breath departing before its song. The younger birds study the sweetness of the nightingale's song, taking in songs which they imitate. The student listens with rapt attention and repeats the corrections, now by singing, now by listening in silence, and now by beginning the song again. The nightingale wastes little time in eating so that she can enjoy the beauty of her own song. Thus she dies sometimes from singing, and in dying sings. Occasionally she is observed to exchange the sweetness of her song with that of a musical instrument, and in order to sing more vigorously she frequently closes her eyes. But this exquisite music gradually begins to leave off after fifteen days, and the color of the nightingale, just like her song, is

6. Peter Comestor, *Historia scholastica, Liber I Regum, XVI.*
7. 1 Kings (1 Samuel) 16:14–16.
8. Pliny, *Historia naturalis* 10.43; Ambrose, *Hexaemeron* 6.24.

altered little by little. There is not to be seen in the winter what existed in the spring, as both song and coloring have changed. But when reared in the refined surroundings of the palace, she renders her melodies not only in spring, but also in winter, and not just by day but also by night, as she is instructed equally by artifice and by nature.

Melody gives pleasure not only to what flies, that is birds, and to what walks, that is, animals, but to what swims, that is fish. Whence learned men tell marvellous things about the attraction of music for fish, and especially dolphins. Thus blessed Isidore says in Book 12 of the *Etymologies* that dolphins are called *simones,* because they follow the voices of men, or because they come together in flocks to hear the sound of a musical instrument. And then Pliny in Book 9 says the dolphin is the fastest of all animals, not only of the sea but of the land as well. It is faster than a bird, swifter than an arrow; it flies past ships driven by the wind; no type of fish is able to escape it, nor can anything else delay it, unless it be because it always takes its prey while bent over backwards, since its mouth is on its belly and its eyes on its back. Its voice is like the sighing of humans, its tongue like that of a pig, while its spine is cartilaginous. Like the whale it does not produce eggs; nor does it manufacture gall. A dolphin lives for 140 years; this was learned from severing the tail of a particular dolphin at the proper time. But some live longer, and others not so long, as is the case with other animals.

A dolphin is pregnant for ten months, and the young dolphin grows for ten years. It breathes and snorts, which is contrary to the nature of other fish. It has its penis within, rather than projecting without. It does not have breasts above its genitalia, but near its joints,[9] while the organ in which the fetus lies is quite hidden (the dolphin gives birth only during the summer). It walks on the bed of the sea, with its young following behind. It takes in water through its nostrils like swimming things, and air through its lungs like land animals. Its food it takes bending over backwards. Its testicles are enclosed within, not protruding without, like other fish of great size. According to the *Physiologus,* they cry wildly when caught; it is by song that they are enticed and captured. They kill crocodiles, too, by guile and deceit. They sleep on the water's surface. They are charmed by music. Now it happened once when some sailors were about to cast the citharist Arion into the sea, that he gained the concession from them that he first be permitted to play. A flock of dolphins were attracted by his song, and when he leap towards the water, he was caught by one of them and carried to the shore. Dolphins answer to those who call them *simones,* and they hearken to the words of man quicker than to the breath of the north wind, even though they have no ears, but rather some sort of apertures, which are somehow blocked when the south wind blows.

Dolphins revel in the music of tibias, and whenever they hear musical instruments playing they immediately turn to hear them, according to Solinus the

---

9. This obscure sentence appears to be defective in the manuscript.

philosopher in his *Book of Marvels.* He adds that there is a particular species of dolphin in the Nile who have saw-toothed crests on their backs: "They eagerly entice crocodiles to swim, and by a clever ruse swimming underneath them themselves, they slash their tender bellies and so slay them."[10] Enough has been said about the character of these animals in our book *On Natural History* and in our book on the characteristics of whatever particular fish.

10. Solinus, *De Mirabilibus* 13 and 23.

33 Marchetto of Padua

Marchetto makes his first appearance in history as *maestro di canto* at Padua Cathedral between 1305 and 1308. He completed his influential treatise on plainsong, *Lucidarium in arte musicae planae,* at Verona in 1318, and his equally influential treatise on mensural music, with the colorful title of *Pomerium in arte musicae mensuratae* (The Garden of Mensural Music), at Cesena in 1326. He was aided in the composition of both by the Dominican friar Syphans da Ferrara, which accounts for the abstract scholastic tone so evident in the excerpt from the *Pomerium* translated here. Nothing is known of Marchetto's life after 1326 except that he wrote a brief practical summary of his doctrine on mensural music, the *Brevis compilatio in arte musica.*

The *Pomerium* explains the notational system that was unique to Italy. Its most basic characteristic is that the breve remains a stable unit that is broken down into numerous "divisions" of semibreves and minims in order to accommodate the new rhythms of the fourteenth century. In the section of the treatise translated here, Marchetto deals with the divisions of imperfect time.

FROM *Pomerium in arte musicae mensuratae*

BOOK TWO: OF IMPERFECT TIME

Since the discipline of music has to do with opposites, let us also, now that we have considered perfect time in mensurable music, treat the subject of imperfect time in a similar manner. And in doing so, let us proceed in the following order. We shall treat: first, of imperfect time in itself and absolutely,

TEXT: Joseph Vecchi, ed., *Marchetti de Padua Pomerium,* Corpus Scriptorum de Musica, no. 6 (Rome: American Institute of Musicology, 1961), pp. 157–81. Translation by Oliver Strunk, revised by James McKinnon. The music examples of the last chapter are those taken by Strunk from the *Brevis compilatio.*

insofar as the comprehension of its essence is concerned; second, of imperfect time in its application to notes according to its totality and multiplication; third, of imperfect time in its application to notes according to its partibility and division.

I. OF IMPERFECT TIME IN ITSELF AND ABSOLUTELY

1. WHAT IMPERFECT TIME IS, SPEAKING MUSICALLY

In the first place we say that imperfect musical mensurable time is that which is a minimum, not in fullness, but in semi-fullness of voice. We demonstrate this definition as follows. It is certain that just as the perfect is that which lacks nothing, so the imperfect is that which lacks something. But it is also certain, by the definition of perfect time already demonstrated, that perfect time is that which is a minimum in entire fullness of voice, formed in the manner there expounded.[1] It follows, therefore, that imperfect time, since it falls short of perfect, is not formed in entire fullness of voice.

But someone may say: you ought to derive the deficiency of imperfect time with respect to perfect, not from fullness of voice, but from a lesser degree of time; and you ought, then, to say that both times, perfect as well as imperfect, are formed in fullness of voice, but that fullness of voice is formed in less time when it is formed in imperfect time than when it is formed in perfect. Whence, so they say, that minimum which is formed in fullness of voice is imperfect time, not perfect.

But to this we reply that to be in fullness of voice and to be a minimum is necessarily perfect time, for perfect musical time is the first measure of all, so that the measure of imperfect time is derived from it by subtracting a part, as will presently be explained. Therefore, since the minimum in any genus is the measure of all other things within it, as previously observed,[2] we conclude that minimum time is always perfect of itself, provided it be formed in fullness of voice; for as soon as we subtract from fullness of voice, we subtract from the quantity of perfect time and thus create imperfect time. So it appears that to define time by fullness of voice is to define it by essential plenitude or deficiency. Therefore our definition stands, namely that imperfect time is that which is a minimum, not in fullness of voice, but in semi-fullness. So much for the first point.

2. HOW PERFECT AND IMPERFECT TIME ARE ESSENTIALLY OPPOSED

Perfect and imperfect time are essentially opposed in themselves, absolutely, and without reference to any division or multiplication of either. This is sufficiently clear from our definition, but we shall, nevertheless, demonstrate it also. It is certain that perfect and imperfect time are not entirely the same thing, for if they were, imperfect time could be called essentially perfect, and

1. See Vecchi, p. 77, where Marchetto names Franco as his authority for this definition.
2. See ibid., where Marchetto refers this statement to the authority of Aristotle.

vice versa. Therefore they differ essentially. Now if two things differ essentially they differ actually, for the one is not the other. In this case they are opposed through "privation," for the one actually has something that the other has not. And from this it follows also that they are contradictory, for the same thing can never be true of both at the same time. There can, then, be no time which could at once be essentially and actually perfect and imperfect.

And if someone says: there could be a sort of time which for various reasons was at once perfect and imperfect; we reply that something or nothing would correspond to these reasons. If nothing would correspond, so much for the objection; if something, then one thing would be two things at the same time, which is impossible. It is therefore impossible for any musical time to be at once actually and essentially perfect and imperfect, as some pretend, for this implies a manifest contradiction: it amounts to saying that someone is both man and not man. So much for the second point.

3. BY HOW MUCH IMPERFECT TIME FALLS SHORT OF PERFECT

Imperfect time falls short of perfect by a third part, something we demonstrate as follows. It is certain that imperfect time is not as great in quantity as perfect, for if it were, it would not be imperfect. It is therefore necessary that it fall short of it by some quantity. It can, moreover, not fall short by less than one part, for if you say by half a part, that half a part will be one part, even though it would be half of the remainder. Therefore, since the primary and principal parts of perfect time are three, for it was divided above in a ternary division to obtain what is primary and principal, imperfect time, if it falls short of perfect, cannot do so by less than a third part. It follows, therefore, that imperfect time comprehends in itself and essentially two parts of perfect time.

II. OF THE APPLICATION OF IMPERFECT TIME TO NOTES ACCORDING TO ITS TOTALITY AND MULTIPLICATION

Imperfect time, of itself and according to its totality and multiplication, is altogether and completely similar to perfect in its application to notes. Notes of three tempora, of two tempora, and of one tempus occur in the same way in imperfect time as in perfect and are also similarly notated. All accidents of music in imperfect time, such as rests, tails, and dots, are treated just as in perfect time.

The reason is this: since there can never be intellectual knowledge, nor even sensible perception, of imperfect things, except by comparison to what is perfect (for never, whether through the intellect or through the senses, can we know a thing to be imperfect unless we also know what is needed to make it perfect); so science, as regards those things that are apprehended either by the intellect or the senses, has always to do with the perfect. Music, therefore, both with regard to its notes and with regard to its accidents, has always to do primarily and principally with perfect time. But by a subtraction made by the intellect of a part of perfect time, music becomes a science of imperfect time.

For if imperfect time were to have its own notes and accidents, different from those of perfect time, it follows that there would be a proper science of imperfect things, principally one of sense perception with no relation to what is perfect, something which, as we have said, is impossible both according to the intellect and according to the senses.

And if you say: very well, I shall be guided by the perfect, namely by comparing to its notes and accidents those of imperfect time; we reply that this will be in vain, for in such a comparison you could work only with the notes and accidents of perfect time, namely by subtracting fullness and in consequence quantity from them. Thus you would create notes and accidents of imperfect time in vain.

But one might ask: how am I to know when music is in perfect time and when in imperfect if, as you say, they are completely alike both in their notes and in their accidents? We reply that this is to be left entirely to the judgment of the composer, who understands the science of music thoroughly. In order, however, that one may know when the composer wishes the music to be sung in perfect time and when in imperfect, we say that when they are combined some sign ought to be added at the beginning of the music so that by means of it the wish of the composer who has arranged this varied music might be known. For as concerns the figured music and the notes no natural difference can be discovered.

It has been demonstrated that any written composition can be sung in either perfect or imperfect time. This difference in the manner of singing is provided by the composer alone, for the sake of the harmony. And because it depends entirely upon the will of the composer, and not upon the nature of the music, a sign that indicates the difference need be added only when the composer so wishes, nor can any valid reason be found why one sign is preferable to another. For some use *p* and *i* to indicate the perfect and imperfect; others 3 and 2 to indicate the ternary and binary divisions of the tempus; others use other signs according to their good pleasure.

But since every composition of itself and naturally observes perfect time more than imperfect (since one is called perfect, the other imperfect), music is by its nature inclined, not toward imperfect time, but toward perfect. It is because of the wish of the composer for a particular manner of composition that music observes imperfect time, abandoning perfect; and for this reason it must be the composer who adds the sign indicating that he intends the music to be in imperfect rather than perfect time.

III. OF THE APPLICATION OF IMPERFECT TIME TO NOTES ACCORDING TO ITS PARTIBILITY AND DIVISION

1. INTO HOW MANY PRINCIPAL PARTS IMPERFECT TIME IS DIVIDED

According to its partibility and division, imperfect time is so applied to notes that by primary division it is divided into two parts. Nor can it be divided into more, something we demonstrate as follows. It was shown in our first book that perfect time is divided (by primary division) into three parts, no more, no less; we say by primary and perfect division for reasons already adduced. At the beginning of this second book it was also shown that imperfect time falls short of perfect and, as was likewise shown there, that it cannot fall short by less than a third part. There remain, then, two parts of imperfect time. It is clear, therefore, that by primary division imperfect time can be divided only into two parts, for otherwise it would in no respect fall short of perfect. And this is logical and appropriate, for just as the perfect division corresponds to perfect time, which is into three, no more, no less, and this division comprehends all others; so the imperfect division corresponds to imperfect time, which is into two. And just as imperfect division is a part constituted within the ternary division, so imperfect time is a part constituted within perfect time.

In the first division of imperfect time, then, two semibreves and not more are the standard [*the divisio binaria*]. They have the same value and significance as two of the three semibreves of the first division of perfect time [*the divisio ternaria*]. For this reason they ought to be similarly notated, like this ♦ ♦, for they are equal to one another in value and in nature.

2. OF THE SECONDARY DIVISION OF IMPERFECT TIME, CONSIDERED IN ONE WAY

But if either of the two semibreves is given a descending tail, ♦ ♦ = ♩ ♪, ♦ ♦ = ♪♩·, we go on to the second division of imperfect time [*division quaternaria*], which is the division of each of our two parts into two others and not into three. For we have already explained and shown that imperfect time first observes imperfect division. And if afterwards we were to divide our primary parts first into three, it would be necessary to return to twos; and wishing to show how twos relate to threes, it would be necessary to repeat what we have said about threes. First let us say, then, that our parts of imperfect time are initially divided into two others, making four. These four are equal in nature, and they equal eight parts of the twelve-part division of perfect time [*divisio duodenaria perfecta*]: ♦ ♦ ♦ ♦ = ♫♫ .

But if only three of the four be given, the Italian practice is that the final one, being the end, will equal the first two. But if either one of the others be given a tail, the final one and the one without a tail will retain their natural value, the one with a tail equaling, by art, the two others: ♦ ♦ ♦ = ♩ ♫, ♦ ♦ ♦ = ♪♩♩. With three notes, two cannot be given tails, for the second one with a tail would be meaningless. And with four notes, if we remain in this division, it is unnecessary to give tails to any; if it be done, the note with a tail will belong either to the secondary division of the primary parts, which is the division of each of two into three [*divisio senaria imperfecta*], or to the third division of imperfect time, which is the division of each of four into two [*divisio octonaria*]. In this case the proportion between the notes with ascending and descending tails and those without, and between the final notes and the preceding ones, both by art and by nature, is arrived at throughout as was amply demonstrated in our chapter on the semibreves of perfect time, and they will also be given the same names.

3. ON THE SECONDARY DIVISION OF IMPERFECT TIME CONSIDERED IN ANOTHER WAY

The principal parts of imperfect time, of which there are two, can each be divided into three, thus constituting six notes [*divisio senaria imperfecta*], and these six can again be divided in twos, making twelve [*divisio duodenaria imperfecta*], or in threes, making eighteen [*divisio octodenaria imperfecta*]. They are thus similar to the parts of the above described perfect time in the manner in which they are written and proportioned—in short, in all accidents, even in their names.

4. THE REFUTATION OF A CERTAIN ERROR

A serious error in mensurable music has arisen from what has just been stated. For some have maintained: you say that I can divide the two parts of imperfect time in threes and thus have six. But six also results from dividing the three parts of perfect time in twos. Therefore (our critics conclude) the *divisio senaria* is a mean between perfect and imperfect time.

We reply that, in dividing two things, a given number can always be found in both, and yet no part of either can ever be a mean between the one thing and the other; similarly, in dividing two lines by binary, ternary, and quaternary division, a given division can always be found in both, and yet no part of either can ever be a mean between the one line and the other. Thus, whenever you divide imperfect time into its parts, you hit upon the same number of parts as you will in dividing perfect time into its parts. Nevertheless, no part of imperfect time can ever be a mean between itself and perfect time, nor can all its parts together, because the nature of imperfect time differs from that of perfect time in itself and essentially, something that is altogether obvious in their performance.[3]

And if someone says: you claim that only the imperfect falls short of the perfect; we reply that this is true by the proportion of perfect time to imperfect, for in their essences the two times are distinct from one another, separate and opposite, as is clear from their opposed definitions, one being formed only in fullness of voice, the other in semi-fullness.

---

3. See ibid., 84, where Marchetto makes the same point, invoking the authority of Aristotle, *Meta-physics* 1057a.

5. ON THE GREAT DIFFERENCE BETWEEN THE SINGING OF THE FRENCH AND ITALIANS IN IMPERFECT TIME, AND ON WHO SINGS MORE RATIONALLY

Be it known that there is a great difference between the Italians and the French in the manner of proportioning notes when singing in imperfect time. The Italians always attribute perfection to the end, as results from proportioning the notes in the manner of singing in perfect time; while the French attribute perfection to the beginning. Thus the Italians say that the final note is more perfect, since it is the end, but the French say the opposite: they say that while this is true of perfect time, in imperfect time the final note is always less perfect, since it is the end.

Which nation, then, sings more rationally? The French, we reply. The reason is that just as in anything perfect its last complement is said to be its perfection with respect to its end (for the perfect is that which lacks nothing, not only with respect to its beginning, but also with respect to its end), so in anything imperfect its imperfection and deficiency is understood with respect to its end (for a thing is called imperfect when it lacks something with respect to its end). If, therefore, we wish to sing or proportion notes in the manner of singing in imperfect time, we ought rationally to attribute imperfection always to the final note, just as in the manner of singing in perfect time we attribute perfection to it. From this we conclude that in the manner of singing the French sing better and more reasonably than the Italians.

The manner of the Italians can, however, be supported by saying that they imitate perfection in so far as they can (which is reasonable enough), namely by always reducing the imperfect to the perfect. Then, since the proportion of imperfect time is reduced to the perfection of perfect time (which amounts to reducing the imperfect to the perfect), the singing of the Italians in imperfect time can be supported reasonably enough. Thus it must be maintained, for the reason already given, that the French sing better and more properly, but, again on the grounds already established, it is reasonable enough to accept the singing of the Italians.

6. OF THE NAMES AND PROPERTIES OF THE SEMIBREVES OF IMPERFECT TIME IN THE FRENCH AND THE ITALIAN MANNER.[4]

If two semibreves are taken for the imperfect tempus, in both the French and the Italian manners they are performed alike:

---

4. Marchetto's description in this section of the French manner of dividing the imperfect tempus agrees with that of Philippe de Vitry; see Gilbert Reaney, et al., eds., *Philippi de Vitriaco Ars Nova*, Corpus Scriptorum de Musica, no. 8 (Rome: American Institute of Musicology, 1964), p. 23.

And since they are parts of the first division of imperfect time [*divisio binaria*] they are called, by nature, major semibreves, because they are comparable to two semibreves of the first division of perfect time [*divisio ternaria*]. By art, however, one of them can be given a tail; and then, in the Italian manner, we go on to the second division of imperfect time [*divisio quaternaria*], which is the division into four equal semibreves. Since this second division of imperfect time is comparable in a partial way to the second division of perfect time [*divisio senaria perfecta*], which is the division into six, its four equal semibreves are called minor semibreves by nature. And the semibreve with a tail, which is called major by art, will contain three of four parts, while the one without a tail retains its natural value:

But in the French manner, if one is given a tail, we go on at once to the ternary division of imperfect time [*divisio senaria imperfecta*], which is the division into six equal semibreves. These are called minims in the first degree, because the semibreves have been divided beyond the division of minor semibreves. In this case the semibreve with a tail contains five of six parts by art, while the one without a tail retains its natural value.

If three semibreves are taken for the imperfect tempus, in the Italian manner the final one, since it is the end, will equal the two others in value:

But in the French manner, in order that the proportion and perfection of the whole measure may be preserved, the first note will contain three of six parts, the second will contain two, and the third one, the notes being called major semibreve, minor semibreve, and minim.

When there are four semibreves, in the Italian manner they are performed alike:

But in the French manner (for in dividing imperfect time the French do not go beyond the *divisio senaria,* even though they could) the first of these four contains two parts of six and the second contains one; while the other two make up the second half of the perfection, with the third containing two parts and the fourth one, which fills out the second half of the perfection. This way of proportioning four notes among the six parts of the tempus was altogether necessary in order that the French form might be observed. For, as will appear upon reflection, in no other way can such a proportion or perfection be worked out without an excess or deficiency of perfection. If each of the first two notes contained two parts of the tempus, and each of the remaining two contained only one, there would be no proportion between the parts, since in a division of this kind no mean proportion can ever rationally and naturally be found. This we refer to as by nature, for by art the same result can be obtained by adding the sign of art.

When there are five semibreves, in the Italian manner they belong to the fourth division of imperfect time [*divisio octonaria*], which is the division into eight, comparable in a partial way to the division of perfect time into twelve [*divisio duodenaria perfecta*]. The first two will be called minims in the second degree, while the others remain in the second division of imperfect time:

By art, however, these minims can be placed otherwise among the five:

But in the French manner the first three are equal minims by nature, while the fourth contains two parts, and the fifth one. For always when there are more than four semibreves, they take the first three minims for half of a tempus, and after this they place the more perfect immediately before the less perfect, proportioning them one to the other. Thus it ought always to be understood that the French attribute perfection to the beginning.

When there are six semibreves, in the Italian manner the first four are minims, measured as four of the eight parts of the tempus, while the last two remain in the second division:

But it is our wish that, however these minims are placed in the Italian manner, whether at the beginning or at the end, they always have tails added above:

The reason for this is that the Italians, as we said above, pass to the fourth division of the tempus, which is in eight, after the second division, which is in four, and never remain naturally in six.

But in the French manner all are equal and, as we have said before, they are called minims.

When there are seven semibreves, in the Italian manner the first six contain six parts of the tempus, while the last one remains in the second division:

unless it happens that the six are artificially distinguished:

When there are eight semibreves, all are performed alike as minims:

But in the French manner, if one wished to take more than six semibreves for the imperfect tempus, he would fall at once into its third division [*divisio duodenaria imperfecta*], which is the division of six into twelve, so that some of them would require ascending tails.

But someone might ask: how can I know which of the semibreves with ascending tails belong to the third division (in twelve), and which to the second division (in six), when with six also various notes are given ascending tails? We reply that this depends on whether the number of notes is less or greater than six.

And in order that it may be known which division of imperfect time we ought to follow in singing mensurable music, whether the French or the Italian, we say that at the beginning of any composition in the French manner, above the sign of imperfect time which appears there, one should place a G, denoting or indicating that the composition should be performed in the French manner (just as in plainsong the founders of music placed a gamma at the beginning of the Guidonian hand to show that we had music from the Greeks), for we had this division of the imperfect tempus from the French. And if a single composition in imperfect time be proportioned according to the French and Italian manners combined, we say that at the beginning of the part in the French manner there should be placed a G, but that in a similar way at the beginning of the part in the Italian manner there should be placed a Greek I [our Y], which is the initial of their name.

34 Jehan des Murs

Born in Normandy about 1300, Jehan is cited in 1318 as a baccalaureate student in the Faculty of Arts at Paris. He spent the next several years in Paris, until about 1325, completing his master's degree and writing the bulk of his works on music. He moved frequently during his well-documented but not particularly distinguished career, occupying ecclesiastical and academic positions occasionally in Paris but more often in cities of his native Normandy, and even in Avignon. The last firm date in his biography is 1345, suggesting that he died about mid-century.

Jehan wrote astronomical and mathematical works, but his treatises on music were considerably more influential. There are at least three genuine works and perhaps as many as six, copied in some 125 manuscripts of the fourteenth and fifteenth centuries. Jehan's exposition of the rhythmical innovations of the early fourteenth century, the so-called *ars nova,* was as authoritative for its subject as was that of Franco of Cologne for his. Translated here is the section of the *Notitia artis musicae (Ars novae musicae),* completed in 1321, which summarizes these innovations.

FROM *Notitia artis musicae*

BOOK TWO: MUSICA PRACTICA

Since we touched lightly and briefly on the theory of music in the preceding discourse, it now remains to inquire at greater length into its practice, that part which is mensurable, since different practitioners think differently about this. As was shown in Book 1, sound is generated by motion, because it belongs to the class of successive things.[1] For this reason it exists while it is being made, but it no longer exists once it has been made. Succession does not exist without motion. Time inseparably unites motion. Therefore it follows necessarily that time is the measure of sound. Time is also the measure of motion. But for us time is the measure of sound prolonged in one continuous motion, and we apply this same definition of time to the single *tempus.*

According to one account, there are two sorts of time—greater and lesser, greater time having longer motion, lesser time shorter. These do not, however, differ in species, for greater and lesser quantities do not alter species. Our predecessors reasonably attributed a certain mode of perfection to every tempus of measured sound; they prescribed the sort of tempus that would be subject to a ternary division, for they believed all perfection to be in the ternary number. Thus they established perfect time as the measure of all music, for they knew that it is unsuitable for the imperfect to be found in art. Yet certain moderns believe themselves to have discovered the opposite of this, which is not consistent. Their meaning will be more clearly set forth in what follows.

2. ON THE PERFECTION OF THE TERNARY NUMBER

That all perfection lies in the ternary number follows from many likely reflections. In God, who is most perfect, there is one substance, yet three per-

---

TEXT: Ulrich Michels, ed., *Johannis de Muris Notitia Artis Musicae,* Corpus Scriptorum de Musica, no. 17 (Rome: American Institute of Musicology, 1972), pp. 65–87; 106–107. Translation by Oliver Strunk, revised by James McKinnon.

1. See Michels, p. 50.

sons; he is threefold, yet one, and one, yet threefold. Very great, therefore, is the correspondence of unity to trinity. In knowledge, one finds (after God) in a ternary series: being, essence, and their composite. In the first of corporeal entities, the heavens, there are the thing that moves, the thing that is moved, and time. There are three attributes in the stars and the sun—heat, light, and splendor; in the elements—action, passion, and matter; in individuals—generation, corruption, and dissolution; in all finite time—beginning, middle, and end; and in all curable disease—rise, climax, and decline. There are three intellectual operations; three terms in the syllogism; three figures in argument; three intrinsic principles of natural things; three potentialities of the being that has not suffered privation; three loci of correlative distance; and three lines in the whole universe. The ternary number is the first uneven number (the first number is first and incomposite). Not two lines, but three, enclose a surface; the first of all polygonal figures is the triangle; and the first of all rectilinears is the triangular. Every object, if it is ever to stand, has three dimensions.

Now, since the ternary number is everywhere present in some form or other, it may no longer be doubted that it is perfect. And, by the contrary of this proposition, the binary number, since it falls short of the ternary and is of lesser repute, remains imperfect. But any composite number formed from these may properly be considered perfect because of its similarity and correspondence to the ternary. And time, since it belongs to the class of continuous things, is divisible not only by ternary numbers, but is endlessly divisible—to infinity.

Seeing, on the other hand, that sound measured by time consists in the union of two forms, namely the natural and the mathematical, it follows that because of the one its division never ceases, while because of the other its division must necessarily stop somewhere; for just as nature limits the magnitude and increase of all material things, so it also limits their minuteness and decrease. For natural things demonstrate that nature is limited by a maximum and a minimum. Sound, moreover, is in itself a natural form to which quantity is artificially attributed; it is necessary, therefore, for there to be limits of division beyond which no sound, however fractionable, may go. These limits we wish to apprehend by reason.

3. On the Limits of Dividing Sound

Prolonged sound measured by definite time is formed in the air not so much in the likeness of a point, line, or surface, as rather bodily and spherically (in the likeness of a sphere, as light is formed in free space), something which may be tested by six listeners placed according to the six differences of proportion. And since such a sound is set in motion by the force of the strike that produces it, which is finite since it proceeds from a finite body, its duration and continuation are necessarily limited, for a sound cannot be generated in infinity or in an instant. Its limits are disposed in the following way.

All music, especially mensurable music, is founded in perfection, combining in itself number and sound. The number, moreover, which musicians consider perfect in music is, as follows from what has been said, the ternary number. Music, then, takes its origin from the ternary number. The ternary number multiplied by itself produces nine; in a certain sense this ninefold number contains every other, for beyond nine there is always a return to the unit. Music, then, does not go beyond the nine-part number. Now the nine-part number again multiplied by itself produces 81, a product which is measured by the ternary number in three dimensions, just as sound is. For if we take three by three by three by three, or three threes nine times, with the products of three always multiplied by three; then, as 3 times 3 produces 9, and 3 times 9 produces 27, so 3 times 27 produces 81. From the unit, then, the third part of the ternary number, which is perfect, to 81, which is likewise perfect—these are said to be the maximum and minimum limits of any sound, for the entire duration of a sound is included between these extremes.

Within these limits, four distinct degrees of perfection may rationally be apportioned. They are the following. No musical perfection exceeds the ternary number; it embraces perfection within itself. A perfection is that according to which something is called perfect. Perfect is that which is divisible into three equal parts, or into two unequal ones, of which the larger is twice the smaller. Unity, moreover, is indivisible and may be called neutral. In these, then, is comprehended the genus of divisibility and likewise of indivisibility. Now, 81 is ternary and in this respect perfect; 54 is the corresponding binary number and in this respect imperfect; the corresponding unit is 27 which makes the perfect imperfect and the imperfect perfect. In these three numbers we distinguish the first degree of perfection; from 27 to 9 we distinguish the second; from 9 to 3 the third; and from 3 to 1 the fourth. In any one of these we find the ternary, the binary, and the unitary, that is, the perfect, the imperfect, and the neutral. There are then four degrees, no more, no less.

4. ON THE EXTENSION OF THE NOTATIONAL FIGURES

We have still to show by what figures, signs, or notes the things which we have said may be appropriately indicated or represented, and by what words or names they may be called, for at this very time our doctors of music dispute daily with one another about this. And although signs are arbitrary, yet, since all things should somehow be in mutual agreement, musicians ought to devise signs more appropriate to the sounds signified. In devising these, all the wiser ancients long ago agreed that geometrical figures should be the signs of musical sounds; and they wished to call them points, not, however, as if indivisible, but like a day, just as the physician does today.[2] The figure most suitable for writing

---

2. The difficult second clause of this sentence, along with two other passages that follow closely, were omitted by Strunk (see Michels, p. 109 on the subject of their authenticity). Its precise meaning eludes the present editor, who suggests only that Jehan, in contrasting something indivisible with a day, may have had in mind the principle that he stated in Chapter 2 above—that time is endlessly divisible.

music is the plane quadrilateral, for it is created by a single stroke of the pen. In it, every musical note shape coverges, as if within a genus, and through it, varied in its essential forms, every mode of any song is explained. When I say "by essential," I refer to the "natural" forms of the figure, after it has been named, or to the "essential" forms, that is, those of the essential shape of the note, the figure that expresses meaning.[3] The musical note is a quadrilateral figure arbitrarily representative of numbered sound measured by time. There are nine distinctions of this form: rectangularity, equilaterality, the tail, the dot, the position, the right side, the left side, the upward direction, and the downward direction as will be seen in the diagram to follow.

Now the ancients, while they wrote reasonably about the figures of the second and third degrees, had little to say about the first and fourth, although they made use of these remote degrees in their singing. For reasons which we shall pass over, their figures did not adequately represent what they sang. Nevertheless they gave us the means of accomplishing completely what they had incompletely accomplished. For they decided that the ternary and binary would be represented by the same figure, and the unit by a dissimilar one, inasmuch as the binary is closer to the ternary than the unit is. For the intellect takes those things that are close to be the same, and it passes more readily between things that have a common symbol[4] (and conversely). From the ternary to the binary, that is, from perfect to imperfect, and vice versa, one passes more readily than from the ternary to the unit; whatever the degree, therefore, the more similar figure ought to be common to those things the distinction between which is not perceived in themselves but is manifest rather in their relation to another thing.

In the second degree, according to our predecessors, the quadrilateral, equilateral, rectangular figure with a tail to the right, ascending or descending, represented perfect and imperfect alike, that is, the ternary and binary. The same figure without a tail represented the unit in the second degree, and the ternary and binary in the third degree; while the unit of the third degree was represented by the quadrilateral, equilateral, obtuse-angular figure.

As to the first degree, the earlier authorities spoke about the binary and the unit, omitting the ternary or representing it by a figure similar to the one denoting the binary. In the fourth they abandoned the unit entirely or figured

3. The second of the passages omitted by Strunk (beginning with "and through it"). The point of it appears to be a matter of fourteenth-century semiology derived from Roger Bacon. The different variations of the quadrilateral figure (the square shape of the breve, the lozenge shape of the semibreve, etc.) are not completely arbitrary; rather, they are signs chosen for some degree of innate (essential or natural) suitability. I am indebted to Catherine Tachau of the University of Iowa for this explanation.
4. The first clause of this sentence is the third of the passages omitted by Strunk; it offers no difficulties. As for the second clause, Strunk pointed out that it appears verbatim in Jacques of Liège (Roger Bragard, ed., *Jacobi Leodiensis Speculum Musicae,* Corpus Scriptorum de Musica, no. 3, Liber septimus [Rome, American Institute of Musicology, 1973], p. 72) in a different connection, suggesting that it might be a familiar axiom.

it implicitly in the ligatures. This is the last figure in the fourth degree, namely a quadrilateral, equilateral, obtuse-angular figure with a tail ascending. But in the first degree the first figure is similar to the second, namely a quadrilateral, non-equilateral, rectangular figure with a tail to the right, ascending or descending.

The differences of the first degree are between the non-equilateral figure and the equilateral; those of the second degree between the figure with a tail and the one without; those of the third between the rectangular figure and the obtuse-angular; those of the fourth between the obtuse-angular figure with a tail and the one without.

5. On Naming the Figures

We have still to speak about the names of the figures that we call notes. In the first degree we can name them triplex long, duplex long, and simplex long. In the second, following the terminology of the ancients, perfect long, imperfect long, and breve. In the third, after the fashion of the preceding degree, perfect breve, imperfect breve, and semibreve (so named not from equal division, but from being greater or lesser, so that the binary is called the greater part of three, the unit the lesser part, the lesser semibreve having been so called by the ancients also). In the fourth degree, following the terminology of the preceding ones, perfect semibreve, imperfect semibreve, and least semibreve.

Others name the notes differently while retaining the same sense. Omitting those of the first degree, which are named appropriately enough, there might be long, semilong, and breve; breve, semibreve, and minor; minor, semiminor, and minim. Or more appropriately (and beginning with the unit of the first degree): longa, longior, longissima (or magna, major, maxima); then, in the second degree, longa perfecta, longa imperfecta, and brevis; then, brevis, brevior, and brevissima (or parva); and then, parva, minor, and minima.

All this is clear from the following table [opposite]:

6. On the Perception of Perfection[5]

Perfection and imperfection are represented, as we have said, by the same figure, just as the same general material may appear in various forms; the authorities applied the distinction between them to five modes, as is evident in the second degree, the one about which they had the most to say. A long before a long is perfect, assigned the value of three *tempora;* so also is a long before two breves, before three breves, before a dot, and before a long rest. This distinction is called "from place or position." The imperfect long is recognized in two of these modes, by the preceding unit or by the following unit. What has been said of the second degree is to be understood of the other degrees in their own way.

5. Strunk's omission of three tables in this chapter is maintained in the present edition.

◼	3	81	longissima		first degree [maximodus]
◼	2	54	longior		
◼	1	27	longa	same	
◼	3	27	perfecta		second degree [modus]
◼	2	18	imperfecta		
◼	1	9	brevis	same	
◼	3	9	brevis		third degree [tempus]
◼	2	6	brevior		
◆	1	3	brevissima	same	
◆	3	3	parva		fourth degree [prolatio]
◆	2	2	minor		
◆	1	1	minima		

Five *species* of melody can be distinguished in any one of these degrees: one entirely in perfect notes or with the binary preceding and the unit following (with corresponding rests), as though in the first mode;[6] a second species with the unit preceding and the binary following; a third combining the first and second, that is, with the perfect note preceding and two units following (the second of which represents a binary value with a unitary form); a fourth made in the opposite way; and a fifth composed entirely of units and their divisions.

Of rests and ligatures new things might be said, but let what is found in the canons of the ancients be sufficient to them, except that rests may now be arranged in the four degrees.

7. ON PERFECT AND IMPERFECT TIME

At the end of this little work be it observed that music may combine perfect notes in imperfect time (for example, notes equal in value to three breviores) with imperfect notes in perfect time (for example, notes equal in value to two

---

6. These *species* are clearly the five rhythmic modes as defined above by Franco of Cologne, *Ars cantus mensurabilis*, section 3 (this volume, pp. 228–29).

breves), for three binary values and two ternary ones are made equal in multiples of six. Thus three perfect binary values in imperfect time are as two imperfect ternary ones in perfect, and alternating one with another they are finally made equal by equal proportion.[7] And music is sung with perfect notes in perfect time, or with imperfect ones in imperfect, whichever is fitting.

Again, it is possible to separate and disjoin perfections, not continuing them, as when a single breve occurs between two perfect notes, yet, when the breves have been gathered together, the whole produces a perfection.[8] For whatever can be sung can be written down, so long as the notes are whole and proper.

There are, moreover, many other new things latent in music which will appear altogether plausible to posterity.

Certain things are included in this *Ars musicae* of ours that are somewhat obscured by being left implicit; if they were to be made explicit, they might silence many of those who dispute with one another on various points. I should like, then, more from love of the disputants than for the sake of accuracy, to assert in a consistent and appropriate way certain conclusions regarding which there has been considerable controversy. And let no invidious critic rise up against us if we are obliged to state what was unspoken, while preserving the modes and other obvious points, and maintaining always the bounds set by the ancients.

8. Conclusions

1. The long may be made imperfect by the breve.
2. The breve may be made imperfect by the semibreve.
3. The semibreve may be made imperfect by the minim.
4. The long may be made imperfect by the semibreve.
5. The breve may be made imperfect by the minim.
6. The minim may not be made imperfect.
7. The altered breve may be made imperfect by the semibreve.
8. The altered semibreve may be made imperfect by the minim.
9. The tempus may be divided into any number of equal parts.

· · · · ·

15. Finis

In these nine stated conclusions there are implicit many other special ones that will be made clear to the student by their application.

If these few things which we have said include anything that seems to be inconsistent with the truth, we ask you, venerable musicians (you in whom we have delighted from earliest youth because of music, for no science is hidden from him who knows music well), how far, from love of this work, you will

---

7. Probably the first theoretical mention of the so-called *aequipollentiae;* the musical compositions of the fourteenth century generally represented this with red (or "colored") notes.
8. Probably the first theoretical mention of syncopation.

correct and charitably tolerate our defects. For it is not possible for the mind of one man, unless he have an angelic intellect, to comprehend the whole truth of any science. Perhaps in the course of time there will happen to us what is now happening to the ancients, who believed that they had spoken definitively about music. Let no one say that we have concealed the state of music or its immutable end. For knowledge and opinion move in cycles, revolving back upon themselves, as long as it pleases the supreme will of him who has freely created this world and of his own accord made discrete everything that is in it.

35 Jacques of Liège

Little is known of Jacques' life; he appears to have been born in Liège, perhaps about 1260, and to have studied at the University of Paris. He died in his native Liège, sometime after the completion of his *Speculum musicae* in about 1330. The *Speculum*, a profoundly conservative work, is the longest surviving medieval treatise on music, comprising seven books in 521 chapters. The first five books are devoted to *musica speculativa*, the sort of material dealt with in the Greek science of harmonics; here Boethius is Jacques' principal authority. The sixth book treats the ecclesiastical modes with Guido of Arezzo as principal authority, and the seventh treats discant and mensural music with Franco of Cologne serving in a similar capacity. It is in this final book, excerpted below, that Jacques engages in his famous attack on the innovations described by Jehan des Murs. Ironically, the *Speculum* was for many years attributed to Jehan.

FROM *Speculum musicae*

PROHEMIUM TO THE SEVENTH BOOK

In his commentary on the *Categories* of Aristotle, Simplicius says, by way of commending the ancients: "We are not at all adequate in our discernment of the true and the false, yet in this we delight—to attack our betters."[1]

Indeed, just as it is profitable and praiseworthy to imitate things well done by the ancients, so it is pleasant and commendable to approve things well said

TEXT: Roger Bragard, ed., *Jacobi Leodiensis Speculum Musicae*, Corpus Scriptrum de Musica, no. 3, Liber septimus (Rome, American Institute of Musicology, 1973), pp. 5–7; 86–95. Translation by Oliver Strunk, revised by James McKinnon.

1. *Commentaria in Aristotelem graeca*, 8.8

by them; rather than to attack them, which seems to be the custom of the young especially, for though the young are more inventive, the old are conceded to be more judicious. As the Master says in his *Histories,* young and inexperienced persons, pleased by new things (for novelty is congenial and enchanting to the ear), ought not so to prize the new that they bury the old. For as a rule new teachings, although they glitter outwardly upon first acquaintance, are revealed to lack solid inner foundations when carefully examined; they are dismissed and soon drop out of favor. If, moreover, it be unprofitable to accomplish by many means what can conveniently be accomplished by few, what profit can there be in adding to a sound old doctrine a wanton and curious new one, repudiating the former? As it is written, "You shall not remove your neighbor's landmark, which the men of old have set."[2]

Long ago venerable men, among them Tubalcain from before the Flood, and since his time many more whom we have already mentioned, have discoursed on plainsong; while many others, among whom Franco the German and another referred to as Aristotle[3] stand out, have written on mensurable music. Now in our day new and more recent authors have appeared, who write on mensurable music with little reverence for their ancestors, the ancient doctors; to the contrary, they change their sound doctrine in many respects, corrupting, criticizing, annulling, and protesting against it in word and deed, whereas the civil and ethical thing to do would be to imitate the ancients in what they have said well and, in doubtful matters, to explain and defend them.

I was grieved when I reflected upon these things in the modern manner of singing and still more in the modern writings, and decided, therefore, to write something about mensurable music with the defense of the ancients as my primary and principal purpose, although, afterwards, as a secondary purpose and from necessity, I turned to plainsong and to theoretical and practical music. Having with God's help completed what was incidental, let me now, if I can, carry out my original design.

I ask the benevolent reader to have pity on me, and I beg him to hear me with sympathy, for to my regret I am alone, while those whom I attack in this last satiric and controversial work are many. I do not doubt that the modern way of singing and what is written about it displease many worthy persons, but yet I have not observed anyone to have written against them. I still belong to the ancient company which some of the moderns call rude. I am old; they are young and vigorous. Those whom I defend are dead; those whom I attack still living. They rejoice in having found nine new conclusions about mensurable music;[4]

2. Deuteronomy 19:14.
3. Lambertus, who composed a treatise on mensural music, *Tractatus de musica,* in Paris about 1270.
4. An obvious reference to the nine new conclusions of Jehan des Murs; there are a number of further references to Jehan in what follows.

I am content to defend the traditional ones, which I deem reasonable. "Knowledge and opinion move in cycles," they say, borrowing from Aristotle's *Meteorology*;[5] for now it is dry where before there was water.

We are not to ascribe to presumption what is done from love of truth and from loyalty, when the moderns themselves claim that they write from love of truth. Where there are two friends it is most sacred to honor truth. "Socrates is my friend, but truth is still more my friend."[6] Whence St. Jerome, in his epistle against Rufinus, says on the authority of Pythagoras: "After God, let us cultivate truth, which alone brings men close to God."[7] For he who deserts truth deserts God, since God is truth.

It still seems pious to honor the ancients, who have given us a foundation in mensurable music; and pious to defend them in what they have said well and, in doubtful matters, to explain them, not to attack them; as it seems uncivil and reprehensible to attack good men after they are dead and unable to defend themselves. Let what I have said be my apology. For though in this work I am about to speak against the teachings of the moderns (insofar as they oppose the teachings of the ancients), I delight in their persons, and I have from my youth delighted in song and singers, music and musicians.

· · · · ·

45. A Comparison of the Old Art of Mensurable Music with the New, As Regards Perfection and Imperfection

As I near the end of this work, let me draw certain comparisons from what has already been said. Let none take offense; I have spoken and will continue to speak about things as I see them, without prejudice of any kind. The facts are in no way altered by any assertion or denial of mine. May what is reasonable or more reasonable and what accords more fully with this art be retained, and what is less reasonable be rejected. Since man lives by art and by reason, there must be a place in every man for what accords with art and reason. Reason follows the law of nature which God has implanted in rational creatures. But since imperfections have at last come to be discussed, let us now compare the ancient and modern arts of mensurable music with respect to perfection and imperfection.

To some, perhaps, the modern art will seem more perfect than the ancient, because it seems more subtle and more difficult. It appears to be more subtle because it reaches out further and makes many additions to the old art, as is evident in the notes and measures and modes (for the word subtle is used of that which is more penetrating, reaching out further). That it is more difficult

---

5. *Meteorology* 339b.

6. Proverbial, but ultimately derived from Aristotle, *Nicomachean Ethics* 1096a.

7. *Epistula adversus Rufinum* 39; pierre Lardet, ed., Corpus Christianorum Series Latina 79 (Turnhout: Brepols, 1982), p. 109.

may be seen in the manner of singing and of dividing the measure in the works of the moderns.

To others, however, the opposite seems true, for that art appears to be more perfect which follows its basic principle more closely and goes against it less. Now the art of mensural music is based on perfection, as not only the ancients but the moderns declare. Therefore whichever makes the greater use of perfection appears to be the more perfect; and this is true of the ancient art, the art of Master Franco.

For the new art, as we have seen, uses manifold and various imperfections in its notes, modes, and measures. Imperfection intrudes virtually everywhere: not content with imperfecting notes, modes, and measures, it extends itself to the tempus. For the new art has what it calls imperfect time, and has breves which it calls imperfect in regard to time, a thing unknown to the old art. And it applies an imperfection arising from time to the notes of the individual degrees: to simple, duplex, and also triplex longs; to breves, while some apply it even to semibreves.

The practitioners of this art are still inventing new ways of imperfecting what is perfect: by proximate or direct imperfection, when the perfect simple long is made imperfect by the breve; by remote, when the same note is made imperfect by the semibreve because it is the third part of a breve recta; and by more remote, when the same long is made imperfect by the minim. Nor are the moderns satisfied with making perfect notes imperfect and dragging them to imperfection; they must do this even with the imperfect notes, since they are not content with a single imperfection, but require many.

If the new art spoke of these imperfections only in a speculative way, it would be more tolerable; but not so, for they make excessive use of imperfection in practice. They employ more imperfect notes than perfect; more imperfect modes than perfect; and consequently more imperfect measures.

When it is said that the new art is more subtle than the ancient, it must be said also that, granting this, it is not therefore more perfect. For not all subtlety is proof of perfection, nor is greater subtlety proof of greater perfection. Subtlety has no place among the degrees or orders or species of perfection, as is made clear in the fifth book of the *Metaphysics*.[8] Nor is it sufficiently proven that the new art is more subtle than the old, even if we grant that it includes some new devices to which the old does not extend. That the new art includes many imperfections unknown to the old art does not prove it more perfect, but merely raises the question of which of the arts under discussion is the more perfect.

As to the further assertion that the modern art is more difficult than the ancient, this, it must be said, does not make it more perfect, for what is more difficult is not for that simple reason more perfect. Art, even if it is said to be concerned with what is difficult, is nevertheless concerned with what is good

8. Aristotle, *Metaphysics* 1021b.

and useful, since it is a virtue perfecting the soul through the medium of the intellect. For this reason authority says that the teaching of the wise is easy. But this will be discussed later on.

46. A COMPARISON OF THE OLD ART OF MENSURABLE MUSIC WITH THE NEW, AS REGARDS SUBTLETY AND RUDENESS

Some moderns regard those singers as rude, simpleminded, undiscerning, foolish, and ignorant who do not know the new art and who in singing follow the old art rather than the new; and in consequence they regard the old art as rude and, as it were, irrational, and the new as subtle and rational. But one might ask, what is the source of this subtlety in the moderns and this rudeness in the ancients? For if subtlety comes from a greater and more penetrating intellect, who are to be considered the more subtle: those who discovered the principles of this art and found out what things are contrary to them, but have scrupulously followed these principles, or those who protest their intention of following them but do not, and seem rather to combat them? Let the judicious observe without passion which party is offering a true judgment of this matter. And what is the value of subtlety, what the value of difficulty, without utility? What is the value of subtlety which is contrary to the principles of science? Are not the subtlety and difficulty involved in the many diverse imperfections in notes, times, modes, and measures which they have contrived, incompatible with a science which is based on perfection? Is it great subtlety to abound in imperfections and to dismiss perfections?

Should the ancients be called rude for using perfections, the moderns subtle for using imperfections? Should the moderns be called subtle for introducing triplex longs, for joining duplex longs in ligature, for using duplex longs profusely, for using semibreves singly, for providing them with tails, for giving them the power of making longs and breves imperfect and still another power which seems unnecessary to this art, and for many other innovations which seem to contradict its very foundation?

Should they be called subtle, moreover, for their new manner of singing, in which the words are lost, the effect of good concord is lessened, and the measure, as will be discussed later on, is confused? And who are those who use so many different sorts of music and manners of singing, who apply themselves to many distinct kinds of music and manners of singing? Do not the moderns use motets and chansons almost exclusively, except for introducing hockets into their motets? They have abandoned many other genres of music, not using them in their proper form as the ancients did; for example, measured organum, organum that is not measured throughout, and organum purum and duplum, which few of the moderns know; likewise the conductus, a song that is so beautiful and gives such pleasure, and which is similarly artful and delightful when duplex, triplex, or quadruplex; as is the case with duplex, contraduplex, triplex, and quadruplex hockets.

Among these types of song the singers of old divided their time in turn; these they made their foundation; in these they exercised themselves; and in these they delighted—not just in motets and chansons. Should they who understood and performed these kinds of music, or those who understand and perform them now, be called rude, foolish, and ignorant of the art of singing, because they do not sing the modern sorts of music or in the modern manner, and do not use the new art of the moderns? They would know that art if they were willing to give their hearts to it and sing in the modern manner; but the modern manner does not please them, only the ancient, for the reasons previously discussed or perhaps for others which might be discussed.

One modern doctor[9] says this: "The duplex long in the perfect mode takes up six tempora; in this, Franco, Petrus de Cruce, and all the others are wrong, since it should really take up nine." This doctor seems to be denouncing not merely the ancients, of whom he names two of great merit, but the moderns as well, since in that remark he says that not merely those two but all the others are wrong. He does not say, "the ancients," but says absolutely, "all the others," and in consequence says that he himself is wrong, since he too is numbered among "all." If all those who err are ignorant, that doctor, who reckons all to be ignorant in his statement, appears to speak with bad manners. Let him take care lest he, in that statement to which I just now replied and in others discussed earlier, commit a greater error. Still, I think that he, like all other doctors, believed himself to be speaking the truth.

The old art, it is clear, must not be considered rude and irrational: first, because the arguments brought against it and some of the additions made to it by the moderns have been shown already to be, respectively, contrary to reason or unnecessary to art; and secondly, because even if the moderns have made good additions to the ancient art, it does not follow that the ancient art, or its inventors and practitioners, are in themselves rude and irrational. Thus, granted that the doctors who have succeeded Boethius, such as the monk Guido and others, have made many good additions to the art of tones and modes which he transmitted to us, the art of Boethius and Boethius himself should not on that account be considered rude and irrational. For he laid the foundations of the art and furnished the principles from which others who follow him have drawn good and useful conclusions, consonant with the art and not contrary to or incompatible with those principles.

If the moderns make many distinctions and use many designations with regard to semibreves, the ancients, as has been mentioned, appear to use more insofar as substance is concerned, whatever might be the case with notational figures. For when the ancients used for the same equal tempus, that is, for the breve in its proper sense, now two unequal semibreves, now three, now four,

---

9. An otherwise unknown theorist whom Jacques had previously quoted and criticized in Chapters 26 and 27 of Book 7 of his *Speculum* (Bragard, pp. 54–57).

five, six, seven, eight, or nine equal ones, these could be called semibreves secundae when they used two, because two such were the equivalent of the breve; semibreves tertiae when they used three, because three such equalled the breve in value; semibreves quartae when they used four, for a similar reason; semibreves quintae, when five; semibreves sextae, when six; semibreves septimae, when seven; semibreves octavae, when eight; and (as explained above) semibreves nonae, when nine.[10] Though they made all these distinctions in semibreves, they never distinguished them in their shape and never gave them tails, but distinguished them sufficiently from each other by means of points.

47. A COMPARISON OF THE OLD ART OF MENSURABLE MUSIC WITH THE NEW AS REGARDS LIBERTY AND SERVITUDE

The modern art of singing seems to compare with the ancient art as a lady with a bondwoman or a housemaid, for now the new art appears to be the mistress, and the old art a servant; the new art reigns, the ancient is exiled. But is it reasonable that the art which uses perfections should be reduced to subjection and the art which uses imperfections should dominate, when the master should be more perfect than the slave?

Again, these arts seem to compare with one another as the Old Law with the New, except that in this comparison the art of the moderns seems to be in the position of the Old Law and the old music in that of the New Law. For the New Law is freer, plainer, more perfect, and easier to fulfill; it contains fewer precepts and is less burdensome to observe. Wherefore our Lord says in the Gospel: "My yoke is easy and my burden is light."[11] And St. James in his Epistle: "But he who looks into the perfect law, the law of liberty."[12] But the Old Law contained many and diverse moral, judicial, and ceremonial precepts which were difficult to fulfill. Whence St. Peter, in the Acts of the Apostles, speaking of the Old Law: "Why do you make trial of God by putting a yoke upon the neck of the disciples which neither our fathers nor we have been able to bear?"[13]

The teachings of the old law of measured music are few and clear compared with those of the new. It would take a long time to recount how many rules the moderns use for their various longs, breves, and semibreves; how many different measures and modes of singing; how many diverse instructions they lay down for causing imperfections; how many rules they use to distinguish their types of song. Nor are they completely in agreement about their doctrines. For

10. See Chapter 17 of Book 7 (Bragard, pp. 37–39, where Jacques gives examples from Petrus de Cruce and an anonymous composer, illustrating the use of from four to nine semibreves for the perfect breve.
11. Matthew 11:30.
12. James 1:25.
13. Acts 15:10.

some of them indicate perfect time in their music with a round circle, because the round form is perfect;[14] while others use three little strokes to indicate it. These three strokes must touch one line and project a little on each side, to distinguish them from the strokes that denote rests. And the prescriber of this rule upbraids those who are unaware of it, counting them as foolish and witless, for here resides great science, and great wisdom (and let these things be positive!).[15] Perfect and imperfect time, moreover, can be distinguished from each other in another way from these, indeed in many other ways, if combined with one another.

To indicate the perfect mode they draw a square enclosing three little strokes; but to indicate the imperfect mode, they draw a square enclosing two little strokes. Others indicate the imperfect by drawing a sign made up of two semicircles. By such a sign they denote both the time and the mode; as one of them says: "They do not know how to denote the one without the other." Others presume to prefix an M for the perfect mode and an N for the imperfect, saying that as O and C are used for variation of tempus, so M and N are used for recognition of the mode. Others, as if reversing matters, understand by O the perfect mode and perfect time, but by C the imperfect mode and imperfect time.

Others say that a circle enclosing three little strokes may be used for the perfect mode and time; but to designate the imperfect mode and time they use a semicircle enclosing two little strokes.

The moderns use these things and many others which the ancients never used, and thus they subject this art to many burdens, so that she who before was free from these burdens now seems a bondwoman in this respect. Whereas, according to Seneca, liberty is one of the greatest goods, whence the poetic saying: "Not for all the gold in the world were liberty well sold." Yet while the old art is free from such burdens, the moderns do not permit her to rule. But since that is not a proper regime where the free man who should be master is subject to him who is not free, the Philosopher, in his *Politics*, greatly disapproves of such government or rule.[16]

48. A COMPARISON OF THE OLD ART OF MENSURABLE MUSIC WITH THE MODERN AS REGARDS STABILITY, AND OF THE OLD MODE OF SINGING WITH THE NEW

One important difference, among others, between perfect and imperfect work is that the perfect work is more stable than the imperfect; for the perfect

14. A number of the symbols described here appear in Philippe de Vitry (Gilbert Reaney, André Gilles, and Jean Maillard, eds., *Philipp de Vitriaco Ars Nova*, Corpus Scriptorum de Musica, no. 8 [Rome, American Institute of Musicology, 1964], p. 27). Strunk's omission of the musical examples that illustrate the symbols is maintained in the present edition.

15. The last phrase, used clearly with ironic intent, is puzzling; perhaps there is some technical philosophic meaning involved.

16. Aristotle, *Politics* 1277b and 1279a.

work has no need of another; its existence does not depend on its being ordered with respect to something else; it has a firm foundation. That art, then, which is the more perfect of the two measured arts, the old and the modern, must be the one which is the more stable. Likewise, as has been mentioned above, we sometimes find certain new doctrines to be unstable. Although at first they are gladly and freely accepted because of their novelty, when they are carefully examined their lack of solid foundations causes them to displease and be rejected, and brings about a return to the more ancient teachings. Would that it were thus with the modern art of measured music and the old!

That the modern teachers are not fully in agreement with respect to the art of measured music in their treatises, is a sign of the instability of their art. For it is written: "Every kingdom divided against itself is laid waste";[17] for if one man oppose the other, how will their kingdom stand? Indeed if division spells evil and instability, then, according to the words of the prophet Hosea, "Their heart is divided; now shall they perish."[18]

Moreover, measured music seeks concord and shuns discord. It does not seek discordant teachers to attain these ends; indeed, all things accord together unto good. Would that it pleased the modern singers that the ancient music and the ancient manner of singing were again brought into use! For, if I may say so, the old art seems more perfect, more rational, more seemly, freer, simpler, and plainer. Have not the moderns rendered music lascivious beyond measure, when originally it was discreet, seemly, simple, masculine, and chaste? For this reason they have offended and continue to offend many judicious persons skilled also in music, just as Timotheus the Milesian offended the Spartans and Laconians, something mentioned in our first book.[19]

Let the judicious take heed and decide what is true. For what purpose have the old music and method of singing and the practice of the old art been banished in favor of the moderns and the modern method of singing? What wrong had they done? Were they banished because of their goodness? But they do not please the satraps, as King Achish said to David: "You are upright and good, but you do not please the satraps."[20]

It is illegal that anyone should be an exile from his country save for sure and just cause, and that he should be cut off from the fellowship of the faithful, as if excommunicated, save by his own fault. I do not deny that the moderns have composed much good and beautiful music, but this is no reason why the ancients should be maligned and banished from the fellowship of singers. For one good thing does not oppose another.

In a certain company in which some able singers and judicious laymen were assembled, and where new motets in the modern manner and some old ones were sung, I observed that even the laymen were better pleased with the

17. Luke 11:17.
18. Hosea 10:2.
19. See Bragard, Liber primus, p. 60.
20. 1 Samuel 29:6.

ancient motets and the ancient manner than with the new. And even if the new manner pleased when it was a novelty, it does so no longer, but begins to displease many. So let the ancient music and the ancient manner of singing be brought back to their native land; let them come back into use; let the rational art flourish once more. It has been in exile, along with its manner of singing; they have been cast out from the fellowship of singers with near violence, but violence should not be perpetual.

Wherein does this lasciviousness in singing so greatly please, this excessive refinement, by which, as some think, the words are lost, the harmony of consonances is diminished, the value of the notes is changed, perfection is brought low, imperfection is exalted, and measure is confused?

In a great company of judicious men, when motets in the modern manner were being sung, I observed that the question was asked, what language such singers were using, whether Hebrew, Greek, Latin, or some other, because what they were saying could not be made out. Thus, although the moderns compose good and beautiful texts for their songs, they waste them by their manner of singing, since they are not understood.

This is what it has seemed needful to say in support of the old art of measured music and in defense of those who practice it. And while I have not found any previous teachers who have written of this matter, may I find successors and helpers who will write of it and will fortify with better arguments what I have touched upon.

*T*HE
RENAISSANCE

Edited by GARY TOMLINSON

INTRODUCTION

*T*o write history is to strike at each moment a balance between continuity and revision. The Renaissance portrayed in the readings gathered here is both different from the one Oliver Strunk represented in his original *Source Readings in Music History* and also much in touch with it. At one level, the continuities are obvious enough. Strunk's primary concern was to exemplify the writings on music theory and practice that paralleled what he saw as the musical mainstream of the period, namely vocal polyphony. His most important secondary concerns were to give a glimpse of courtly society and the place of music in it, and to locate music in (mainly northern European) movements of religious reform. These broad themes, and many of the specific readings that embodied them for Strunk, have retained a prominent place in my revision of his work. More generally, the first two of these themes have continued to play a central role in the deliberations of Renaissance musicologists all told over the last forty years.

But continuities such as these operate here under the aegis of discontinuity, so to speak. They do so because the Renaissance has not grown straightforwardly more transparent over these last decades, despite our having exhumed and interpreted more and more traces of the literate musical cultures of Europe in the fifteenth and sixteenth centuries. Instead the period has taken on new, dark tints which, if not amounting to any total eclipse of our understanding, have at least caused us to see even once-familiar issues in new lights and colorations. From Strunk's day to our own, the Renaissance has grown immensely more problematic; in the same historiographic motion it has come to seem a culture more, not less, distant and estranged from ours. In the readings collected here, I have hoped to capture some of this complexity and distance.

Our sense of estrangement reflects in part our present-day concerns and the general shift in late twentieth-century intellectual life away from historical certainties toward a defamiliarization of ourselves and those whose histories we write. But it responds also to the traces of a fifteenth- and sixteenth-century European past. These convey an extraordinary ferment of recovery, discovery, and reform, and also the ambivalence and uncertainty attendant on it. Indeed, if there is any unifying thread that extends across European elite perceptions from, say, 1400 to 1600, it is probably the growing sense of the disunity and even disarray of knowledge that had once seemed more tractable and comprehensible. The Renaissance, we might say, forms a coherent historical epoch mainly through its sense of a breakdown of coherence. The estrangement of Renaissance culture, then, is not only a question of our historical relation with it but also of its relation to itself.

We may follow this self-estrangement in the three watchwords I have used above to capture the period. By *recovery* I allude to what has seemed to many the singular triumph of the thinkers of the period: the retrieval of a huge body of ancient thought, unearthing the achievement of Greek and Roman Antiquity in substantially the quantity and form we have today. This project of recovery, often referred to as "humanism" (the term also has useful broader applications in recent historical writing on the Renaissance), exerted a widespread and varied destabilizing force on European elite culture. In the first place, the new and expert philology that sprang up with the accelerating recovery brought many accepted beliefs into question—as when, to mention an exemplary instance, Lorenzo Valla proved the Donation of Constantine, the document on which the Pope's temporal power was founded, to be an eighth-century forgery. Such philology fostered a new awareness of historical contingency and change in languages, thought, and societies. In this way, whatever particular familiarities and connections with the ancient past it affirmed, it carried large and unsettling implications of cultural discontinuity and relativism.

In the second place, the sheer variety of newly accessible ancient authorities threatened once-stable structures of knowledge. For example, the imposing amalgam of Aristotelian and scriptural doctrine that scholastic thinkers had created in the twelfth and thirteenth centuries was challenged by the late fifteenth-century recovery of Plato and the ancient Neoplatonists; the new bodies of thought required that new compromises be struck between Christian and pre-Christian doctrine. Likewise, full knowledge of the ethical dimensions of ancient oratory that came with the full recovery especially of Cicero and Quintilian encouraged new conceptions of the polis and of political action. It also fostered a reorientation within educational curricula in which grammar, rhetoric, history, and ethics—the lightly regarded siblings of logic in the *studia humanitatis*, or "humanities"—could claim some of the prestige traditionally accorded the quadrivium of mathematical arts (arithmetic, geometry, astronomy, and music).

These broad tendencies played themselves out in musical culture as well. Increased philological expertise deepened knowledge of ancient music, often with contradictory results. Thus Heinrich Glarean's humanistic studies aided his overhaul of ecclesiastical modal theory and his application of it to polyphony, but Girolamo Mei's more extensive research into ancient music showed the accepted connection of ancient *tonoi* to modern modes to be misconceived and led him to question altogether the expressive efficacy of polyphony. The revival of Platonic and Neoplatonic philosophy encouraged a mathematical approach to harmonic proportions and temperaments, mainly derived from Boethius, that we might be tempted to see as musical rationalism or, in some of its forms, empiricism. But this mathematicism embodied a view of numbers different from ours; it was associated with views of magic, astrology, and mystical gnosis in which music played a central role (see section IV below). New oratorical modes of political engagement created a context that exacerbated distinctions between practice and its rationalization—what we tend today to call theory. These distinctions would concern and vex the writers of the time that we label music theorists (they are, for example, Pietro Aaron's starting point in the excerpt below [pp. 415–28] and a touchstone for Gioseffo Zarlino [pp. 436–62]).

Most important and most generally, the heightened esteem of grammar, rhetoric, history, and ethics helped exacerbate the dualism of the position that music had long occupied in Western structures of knowledge. In the fifteenth and sixteenth centuries, music did not give up its affiliations with the other mathematical arts: indeed, as I have said, the Neoplatonic resurgence could not help but reaffirm, in what we might call its "harmonic idealism," a transcendant mathematicism behind musical practice. But now the ties of music to the expressive and persuasive arts of poetry and rhetoric took on a novel ideological potency. Music was pulled with a new vigor in two different directions; it was, so to speak, estranged from itself. Its essential and uneasily reconcilable bonds both to pragmatic expressive force, on the one hand, and to idealized number, on the other, were set in an opposition more strenuous than they had known in the preceding centuries.

The readings collected here betray again and again the newly felt importance of music's affiliations with the humanities. They do so in their alignment of song with poetry and oratory, their detailing of the relations between words and notes, their frequent emphasis on solo song, their preoccupation with music's suasive force, and their description of the expressive gestures appropriate to individual genres. And they do so, most of all, in rehearsing, at every opportunity, examples of music's ethical powers culled from ancient writings and scripture. This review usually takes the form of an elaborate praise of music, a formula that was repeated so often as to become almost a standard starting point for musical discussion of the period (see the section "Praises and Dispraises of Music" and elsewhere). But in a late-Renaissance intellectual atmosphere touched by a revival of ancient skepticism and a new Christian fideism, it could also be voiced in negative terms—as a suspicion and denunciation of music's force (Agrippa [pp. 304–8]). Both gestures manifest the centrality of musical ethics in the elite thought of the period.

The fifteenth and sixteenth centuries were also, famously, a period of geographical, technological, and scientific *discovery;* this, too, contributed to the epistemological fragmentation of the era. In the first place, European navigators, soldiers, and missionaries brought back dizzying accounts of unsuspected lands and civilizations in Africa, America, and Asia. It is not too much to say that the distinctively Western project we have come to call ethnography is foreshadowed in such reports. They merged with and played upon the sense of cultural relativism already fostered by humanist historicism. And this sense in its turn made European efforts to familiarize and domesticate newly-known others more difficult. All told, the geographical and cultural discoveries eventually bred a widespread and uneasy fascination among literate Europeans, a fascination revealed in the immense popularity of proto-ethnographic travel narratives in the years around 1600 (witness, among the accounts here, the many editions and translations of Pigafetta (pp. 502–4) and Ricci (pp. 504–8) that quickly emerged).

These reports on other societies usually reserved room for comment on music (see the section "Glimpses of Other Musical Worlds"). In this they not only provide us with tantalizing traces of traditions of song, instrumental performance, and dance now mostly lost; they also afford a glimpse of European approaches to non-European others whose legacy we still live with in the quandaries of today's musical ethnography. They form a largely unexamined aspect of European musical estrangement in the era, of the nascent process by which Europeans grew more and more aware of distant, even incomprehensible musical practices in the geographical world around them and the historical world that had preceded them. And, not least, they reveal again the cultural centrality that music had assumed in the perceptions of literate Europeans, a centrality automatically projected onto others.

Meanwhile technologies of astounding novelty and monumental impact appeared. New navigational devices, such as the compass, aided the voyages of exploration, and gunpowder and other weapons technologies were crucial in the subjugation of indigenous peoples and colonization of their lands that usually followed quickly on the heels of discovery. More and more precise measurements of the heavens called into question hallowed ideas of cosmic order; they would receive their most impressive confirmation at the end of the period, when Galileo turned an odd Dutch contraption of tubes and lenses on the stars. And—most decisive technology of all, at least within Europe—from the second half of the fifteenth century on, thousands upon thousands of books printed with movable type poured forth from presses soon dispersed across Europe. This torrent of printed material conveyed the geographical and cultural discoveries, the newly accessible ancient writings, and knowledge of countless other sorts to larger readerships than had ever been reached in the past.

In music the technological difficulties of printing with movable type were solved only somewhat later, around 1500 and in the following decades. But the achievement resulted by the middle of the sixteenth century in a proliferation of printed scores of astounding extent. These vast quantities of music were not produced to answer the needs of only the most elite aristocratic circles. They also reached a growing bourgeoisie and touched its own aspirations to social distinction—touched them, that is, with the aid of oft-repeated admonishments, gleaned from ancient authors such as Plato and Quintilian, that music was an essential part of any "gentleman's" education and ethical formation (see here Zarlino [pp. 293–99], Ronsard [pp. 300–303], Castiglione [pp. 325–30], Peacham [pp. 346–51], and others).

The movements of *reform* that swept Europe throughout the sixteenth century may, finally, be understood in part as a widespread response to the subtle forces of disorientation that arose in a climate of discovery and recovery. The pressing need for reform was most obviously manifested in the religious schisms, strife, and doctrinal debate of the Protestant and Italian Reformations. Song, given its immense and central role in the Catholic liturgy, was inevitably implicated in these struggles (see the section "Music and Religion Reform"). But we need to remember that reform was not restricted to religious matters. A concern for it pervaded all aspects of life, and we might with some justification speak of reformations of secular society that gained powerful voice in the same decades that saw the first burgeonings of religious reformation. The immense popularity and influence of Castiglione's *Libro del cortegiano* bespeak a perceived need for clear social standards that might separate true (or, in Peacham's word, "compleat") gentlemen and gentlewomen from imposters. (Indeed the anxious discrimination of the genuine from the counterfeit is a topos that recurs with telling frequency in all sorts of connections from the late fifteenth century on—genuine versus sham religious faith, inspired versus contrived poetry, rational versus arbitrary learning and action, "honest" versus "meretricious" courtesans, and so forth.) The codes of behavior advocated by works like Castiglione's were derived from a courtly life of renewed vigor and self-consciousness that characterizes the late Renaissance as a whole. In their advocacy, these books came to enforce the codes on anyone who wished to gain admission to society's upper echelons. In a culture that emphasized music's rhetorical and ethical force, it is no surprise that such works usually saved an important place for a discussion of musical expertise and learning.

Given the new esteem for music's psychological force, it is also no surprise that some writers connected music with a female sexuality thought to be insufficiently controlled, thus renewing an association that had a long history in the West. But, in the context of heated debates on the place of women in elite society that were an important aspect of sixteenth-century social critique, voices opposing this view were also raised. Thus for every Castiglione who treats musical performance as a predominantly male pursuit; for every Bembo who impugns the virtue of young women who learn music; and for every Agrippa who repeats the age-old linkage of music to a misogynist view of effeminacy, there is a Doni who extols at once the virtuosity and the virtue of a female performer, a Stampa who sings her own Petrarchan love lyrics without joining the ranks of Venetian courtesans, and even a Casulana who purposefully infiltrates the male bastion of polyphonic composition and publication.

Which brings us back, finally, to Strunk's polyphonic mainstream. Where, in a rethought Renaissance, do we locate this tradition, whose reflection in theoretical writings formed the backbone of the original Renaissance *Source Readings?* Clearly it too is subject to the increased complexity and estrangement I have outlined here. In the first place we need to qualify thoroughly the central role we have accorded the polyphonic tradition. Writers on music who neither wrote polyphony nor discussed its theory tend to emphasize, as the centerpiece of their musical culture, not polyphony so much as practices of solo song (see Castiglione [pp. 325–30], Cortesi [pp. 316–21]). It is by now clear that these practices thrived not only after the great sixteenth-century efflorescence of printed polyphony but before and during it as well and that, indeed, they over-lapped in complex ways with polyphonic styles and genres. Unlike polyphony, solo song did not need to rely on print technology for its effective and wide-spread dissemination (see Calmeta [pp. 321–25]), so its small part in sixteenth-century musical prints is no reliable gauge of its prevalence. And it is clear also that the novelty of musical styles around 1600 was connected not with any unprecedented emphasis on solo singing but rather with the invention of new dramatic styles (i.e., recitative) within vigorous and deeply rooted solo tradi-tions (see Giustiniani [pp. 352–57]) and also with complex changes in musical practice, taste, and professional institutions that allowed solo-song composers to usurp, for a few decades, the print medium that polyphonists had domi-nated. All this needs to be taken into account even while we note the huge dispersion of printed polyphony across Europe through the late sixteenth cen-tury.

In the second place: monophonic repertories loomed at least as large as polyphonic ones in Reformation debates about music in worship. Thus while a Cirillo or an Agrippa might worry over the propriety of polyphony in the liturgy, major musical efforts of reformers north and south of the Alps concerned monophonic repertories and were aimed at either purging old bodies of liturgi-cal plainsong or creating new ones. Calvin banned polyphony from his church, worked with others to create a collection of melodies for his translated Psalter to be sung in the services, and left polyphonists such as Goudimel to harmonize these melodies for devotional singing at home. The moderate Erasmus permit-ted polyphony in church while cautioning that care must be taken to assure its appropriateness to worship; but a more urgent concern for him was the abuse of sequences, probably monophonic, whose length and complexity deformed the liturgy. Even in the case of Palestrina, the fabled savior of church polyph-ony, the most reliable evidence we have of his reform efforts concerns plainchant, not polyphony (see Pope Gregory XIII [pp. 374–76]). Again, the huge extent of polyphonic sacred repertories is not in question here, and nei-ther is the religious commitment of their composers (see Palestrina [pp. 373–74], Byrd [pp. 378–81]). But we need to understand better that these reperto-ries were not the primary music of worship across the whole of Europe and did not inevitably preoccupy those most intent on sacred musical reform.

In regard to Renaissance music theorists (the section "Writings on Poly-phonic Music") this reassessment of the old polyphonic mainstream cuts deeper still. Recent work by various musicologists (some of them cited in the annotations to the readings; see especially Tinctoris [pp. 401–7] and Aaron [pp. 415–28]) has greatly complicated our sense of the relation between theoretical writings on polyphony and polyphonic repertories themselves. It is increasingly evident that these writings, especially before the middle of the sixteenth century, were not in any unproblematic sense prescriptive of the polyphonists' compositional practices. Rather, they were something closer to ex-post-facto attempts to rationalize—by extending earlier theoretical systems—burgeoning practices whose novelty occasionally beggared the available vocabulary. Thus the whole discussion of mode in polyphony, at least up through Glarean, can be better understood as the theorists' attempt to match systems of tonality devised for plainchant to polyphony than as the laying-out of a set of precompositional choices that faced the composers themselves. Talk of *musica ficta* and the Guidonian compass of hexachords (see Ramis [pp. 407–14]) likewise represents a groping attempt to comprehend the freedoms of polyphonic practice through tools devised to theorize plainchant. And, most dramatically, Tinctoris's discussion of written and unwritten polyphony and of dissonance treatment reveals his own struggle to come to grips with fluctuating categories of music-making. Reading it suggests that we risk great anachronistic distortion in imposing any stable, reified senses of "counterpoint" or even "musical composition" on polyphonic practices of his time.

This particular sense of estrangement, at least, is greatly lessened by the end of the Renaissance. Zarlino's conceptions of "counterpoint" and "composition" are decisively closer to ours than Tinctoris's (though they too have their surprises). The fundamental change in the enterprise of music theory from 1470 to 1600 may be seen in hindsight as a shift from tentative *description* of what polyphonists were about to confident *prescription* of what one needed to do to be a competent polyphonist. The shift, put differently, is from an attempt to observe and rationalize current practice to an attempt to synthesize all permissible practice in a form that might be conveyed as a method or course of study. Certainly this sense of prescriptive law is the most important general achievement of Zarlino's *Istitutioni harmoniche,* the most influential of late-Renaissance music treatises, and in this his book is not so very different from Castiglione's in approach and tone.

One more word, on the question of retaining Strunk's "Renaissance" as the period designation for this collection. The term shows, at this late date, a mixture of neutrality and historiographic vested interest similar in kind to that built into other period labels historians still use out of convenience and for want of preferable alternatives. It is probably no worse than "Middle Ages" or "Romantic" in its difficulties, and it is a good deal better, I think, than "Baroque" and "Classic." I have avoided the most common alternative to it, "early-modern," for two reasons. First, as the foregoing discussion of estrangement makes evident, I am not happy with the confident continuities and teleologies between the sixteenth and later centuries that the term "early-modern" suggests. Second, "early-modern" may be helpful to those historians whose materials move outside the elite echelons of fifteenth- and sixteenth-century society—the echelons, that is, that have since the middle of the nineteenth century been associated with the term "Renaissance." But such non-elite materials are, for the music historian, exceedingly rare and play little role here (note that even the accounts that follow of music from Mexico, Peru, the Congo, and China speak of elite music-making). This restriction of materials also explains why more neutral and sweeping chronological designations such as "the fifteenth and sixteenth centuries" cannot serve. "Renaissance" continues to be, simply, the best label we have for the particular societal and cultural strands represented in this volume.

• • •

Lewis Lockwood, who had begun contemplating this revision before personal concerns induced him to withdraw, corresponded on the project with several leading scholars of Renaissance music, including Allan Atlas, Lawrence Bernstein, the late Howard M. Brown, Jessie Ann Owens, and Claude V. Palisca; this correspondence and Professor Lockwood's notes on it were helpful to me in my planning. I also have consulted with various colleagues on the project; among them, Martha Feldman and Cristle Collins Judd have been particularly helpful (the latter with invaluable assistance concerning the section "Writings on Polyphonic Music"). Leo Treitler has been a model general editor, patient, attentive, and full of thought-provoking queries. Marina Brownlee, Lance Donaldson-Evans, and Joseph Farrell looked over my translations from Spanish, French, and Latin respectively and saved me from more than one embarrassing gaffe (all the gaffes left over are my own). I wish also to salute Oliver Strunk himself; though I had read through his Renaissance *Source Readings* more than once before, I never fully appreciated the canniness and intelligence of his choices, translations, and annotations until I remade them. Finally, and by way of closing a circle of sorts, I dedicate this work to a man who had a hand in the first version of *Source Readings* and has had a hand in many fundamental musicological enterprises since: Joseph Kerman.

PRAISES AND
DISPRAISES OF
MUSIC

36 Johannes Tinctoris

Born around 1435 near the Flemish town of Nivelles, Johannes Tinctoris may have sung under Du Fay at Cambrai Cathedral. In the 1460s he was in charge of the choirboys at the Cathedral of Orleans and studied at the university there. By the early 1470s he had moved to Naples, where he served King Ferdinand and tutored Ferdinand's daughter Beatrice. In 1487 Tinctoris traveled in France and Germany in search of singers for Ferdinand's chapel. He died in 1511, a canon of Nivelles.

Tinctoris's principal writings include the treatise on harmonic proportions here excerpted; the *Terminorum musicae diffinitorium*, the first European dictionary of musical terms, written for his royal pupil before 1476 and published in 1495; the *Liber de natura et proprietate tonorum (Book on the Nature and Character of the Modes)*, dedicated in 1476 to his contemporaries Ockeghem and Busnois; and a book on the art of counterpoint, the *Liber de arte contrapuncti*, completed in 1477. The last work is particularly important for its guidelines concerning dissonance treatment in polyphony; it lays the groundwork for many later counterpoint treatises of the Renaissance. And it is particularly intriguing for its distinction between counterpoint sung from written polyphonic scores and counterpoint sung over books of plainchant without written-out parts (for these topics see no. 67 below, pp. 401–7).

In the forewords to his treatises and in remarks scattered through them, Tinctoris reveals himself to be a knowledgeable and shrewd observer of the contrapuntal styles of his day and of the immediately preceding generations. The dedication presented here shows this clearly enough, with its famous remark about the English "fount and origin" of contemporary Continental practices. It also exemplifies a rhetorical gesture—one whose antecedents reach back to ancient models—that would flourish through the Renaissance: the *laus musicae,* or praise of music, a mythological and historical sketch of music's antiquity, nobility, and power.

Proportionale musices

(1473–74)

THE PROPORTIONAL OF MUSIC, BY MASTER JOHANNES
TINCTORIS, LICENTIATE IN LAWS, CHAPLAIN TO THE
MOST SUPREME PRINCE FERDINAND, KING OF SICILY
AND JERUSALEM, BEGINS WITH GOOD OMEN

DEDICATION

To the most sacred and invincible prince, by the divine providence of the King of Kings and Lord of Lords, King of Sicily, Jerusalem, and Hungary,

TEXT: C. E. H. Coussemaker, *Scriptorum de medii aevi . . . nova series* (4 vols., Paris: A. Durand, 1864–76), vol. 4, pp. 153–55. Translation by Oliver Strunk.

Joannes Tinctoris, the least among professors of music and among his chaplains, proffers humble and slavish obedience, even to kissing his feet.

Although, most wise king, from the time of the proto-musician Jubal, to whom Moses has attributed so much, as when in Genesis he calls him the first of all such as handle the harp and organ,[1] many men of the greatest fame, as David, Ptolemy, and Epaminondas (princes of Judaea, Egypt, and Greece), Zoroaster, Pythagoras, Linus the Theban, Zethus, Amphion, Orpheus, Musaeus, Socrates, Plato, Aristotle, Aristoxenus, and Timotheus bestowed such labor upon the liberal art of music that, on the testimony of Cicero,[2] they attained a comprehension of almost all its powers and its infinite material, and although for this reason many of the Greeks believed that certain of these men, and especially Pythagoras, had invented the very beginnings of music; nevertheless we know almost nothing of their mode of performing and writing music. Yet it is probable that this was most elegant, for they bestowed on this science, which Plato calls the mightiest of all,[3] their highest learning, so that they taught it to all the ancients, nor was anyone ignorant of music considered an educated man. And how potent, pray, must have been that melody by whose virtue gods, ancestral spirits, unclean demons, animals without reason, and things insensate were said to be moved! This (even if in part fabulous) is not devoid of mystery, for the poets would not have feigned such things of music had they not apprehended its marvelous power with a certain divine vigor of the mind.

But, after the fullness of time, in which the greatest of musicians, Jesus Christ, in whom is our peace, in duple proportion made two natures one, there have flourished in his Church many wonderful musicians, as Gregory, Ambrose, Augustine, Hilary, Boethius, Martianus, Guido, and Jean de Muris, of whom some established the usage of singing in the salutary church itself, others composed numerous hymns and canticles for that purpose, others bequeathed to posterity the divinity, others the theory, others the practice of this art, in manuscripts now everywhere dispersed.

Lastly the most Christian princes, of whom, most pious King, you are by far the foremost in the gifts of mind, of body, and of fortune, desiring to augment the Divine Service, founded chapels after the manner of David, in which at extraordinary expense they appointed singers to sing pleasant and comely praise to our God[4] with diverse (but not adverse) voices. And since the singers of princes, if their masters are endowed with the liberality which makes men illustrious, are rewarded with honor, glory, and wealth, many are kindled with a most fervent zeal for this study.

At this time, consequently, the possibilities of our music have been so marvelously increased that there appears to be a new art, if I may so call it, whose

1. Genesis 4: 21.
2. *De oratore* 1.3.10
3. *Republic* 401d.
4. Psalm 147:1.

fount and origin is held to be among the English, of whom Dunstable stood forth as chief. Contemporary with him in France were Dufay and Binchois, to whom directly succeeded the moderns Ockeghem, Busnois, Regis, and Caron, who are the most excellent of all the composers I have ever heard. Nor can the English, who are popularly said to shout while the French sing,[5] stand comparison with them. For the French contrive music in the newest manner for the new times, while the English continue to use one and the same style of composition, which shows a wretched poverty of invention.

But alas! I have perceived that not only these, but many other famous composers whom I admire, while they compose with much subtlety and ingenuity and with incomprehensible sweetness, are either wholly ignorant of musical proportions or indicate incorrectly the few that they know. I do not doubt that this results from a defect in arithmetic, a science without which no one becomes eminent, even in music, for from its innermost parts all proportion is derived.

Therefore, to the purpose that young men who wish to study the liberal and honorable art of music may not fall into similar ignorance and error in proportions, and in praise of God, by whom proportions were given, and for the splendor of your most consecrated Majesty, whose piety surpasses that of all other pious princes, and in honor of your most well-proportioned chapel, whose like I cannot easily believe to exist anywhere in the world, I enter, with the greatest facility my powers permit, upon this work, which with appropriateness to its subject I conclude should be called the *Proportional of Music.* If I have ventured in it to oppose many, indeed nearly all famous musicians, I entreat that this be by no means ascribed to arrogance. Contending under the banner of truth, I do not order that my writings should necessarily be followed more than those of others. What in their writings I find correct, I approve; what wrong, I rebuke. If to my readers I seem to carry on this my tradition with justice, I exhort them to put their trust in me; if without justice, let them rather believe others, for I am as ready to be refuted by others as to refute them.

5. Compare Ornithoparcus, *Musice active micrologus* (Leipzig, 1516), 4.8, and Pietro Aaron, *Lucidario in musica* (Venice, 1545), fol. 31.

3 7 Gioseffo Zarlino

Gioseffo Zarlino was born at Chioggia, not far from Venice, in 1517. From 1541 his teacher was Adriano Willaert, choirmaster at St. Mark's from 1527 to 1562. In 1565, on the departure for Parma of Cipriano de Rore, Willaert's successor, Zarlino fell heir to his old teacher's position, which he occupied until his death in 1590. The *Istitutioni harmoniche,* or *Harmonic Institutes,* his principal work, was first published in 1558 and reprinted in 1562 and 1573. Other writings of his are the *Dimostrationi harmoniche* (1571) and the *Sopplimenti musicali* (1588), this last in reply to the stand taken by Vincenzo Galilei, a rebellious pupil who had attacked Zarlino's teaching on proportions, tuning, and other matters in his *Dialogo della musica antica, et della moderna* (1581; see no. 72 below, pp. 462–67).

In the *Istitutioni harmoniche* Zarlino sought to unite theoretical principles based on natural laws with practical rules for polyphonic composition. Many aspects of his approach are strikingly modern in tone: he grasped the full implications of just intonation and produced classical authority for it, dealt with harmony in terms of the triad rather than the interval, recognized the importance of the fundamental antithesis of major and minor, attempted a rational explanation of the old rule forbidding the use of parallel fifths and octaves, and isolated and described the effects of the false relation (for some of these topics, see no. 71 below, pp. 440–47). Zarlino's contrapuntal precepts were widely dispersed, long-lived, and hugely influential. They crystallized across the seventeenth century into the pedagogy that is still offered today in the "modal counterpoint" classes of many music departments. Zarlino's writings bear witness to the extraordinary range and depth of his reading; appropriately and no doubt with some pride, he recalled in the title *Istitutioni harmoniche* Quintilian's encyclopedic and systematic account of ancient rhetorical theory and practice, the *Institutio oratoria*. Something of Zarlino's ecumenical learning is reflected in the praise of music that follows.

FROM *Istitutioni harmoniche*
(1558)

BOOK 1
CHAPTER 2: ON THE PRAISES OF MUSIC

. . . The writings of ancient philosophers make it clear how much music was celebrated and held to be sacred. The Pythagoreans in particular believed that the world was composed musically, and that the heavens caused harmony in their revolutions, and that our soul is formed according to the same laws, and that it is awakened and its powers vivified by songs and instrumental music. Some Pythagoreans wrote that music was the prince of all the liberal arts, and some called it ἐγκυκλοπαιδεία, or "circle of the sciences," since it embraces (as Plato said) all disciplines.[1] We can see this to be true if we begin with grammar, first of the seven liberal arts, since we hear a great harmony in the proportionate juxtaposition and order of words. And if the grammarian departs

---

TEXT: The facsimile of the edition of 1573 (Ridgewood, N.J.: Gregg Press, 1966), pp. 7–11. Translation by Gary Tomlinson. Zarlino's postils are given here as author's notes.

1. *Laws* 1 [probably 642a; see also 2.654a–b]. [Au.]

from this he brings to our ears a displeasing sound in his phraseology, so much so that we listen to or read with difficulty prose or verse bereft of polished, beautiful, ornate, sonorous, and elegant order. Next, in dialectics, whoever considers the proportions of syllogisms will see that the truth is shown to be far from the false by means of a marvelous harmony greatly pleasing to our ears. The orator also gives marvelous delight to his listeners in his oration by using musical accents and appropriate rhythms. The great orator Demosthenes understood this best of all. He was asked three times what the principal part of oratory was, and three times he responded that enunciation mattered above all else.[2] Gaius Gracchus, a man of utmost eloquence, also knew this, as Cicero[3] and Valerius Maximus[4] relate: whenever he had to speak before the people he kept hidden behind him a servant musician who set the measure or voice or tone of his speech on an ivory flute, in a manner that relaxed him when he grew too excited and aroused him when he flagged.

Next, we can see that poetry is so closely joined with music that whoever would separate the two would be left, as it were, with a body separated from its soul. This is confirmed by Plato, who says in the *Gorgias* that anyone who removed harmony, number, and meter from poetry would be left with commonplace and impoverished speech.[5] Therefore we find that poets have employed the greatest diligence and marvelous artifice in accommodating their words to their verses and laying out the feet according to the requisites of speech. Virgil observed this throughout his *Aeneid,* matching all three sorts of speech found in his poem with appropriately sonorous verse, and doing it with such artifice that he seems to put the things he treats before our eyes by means of the sounds of his words. Thus where he speaks of love we find that he chose words sweet, pleasing, and gracious to the ears; where he needed to sing of wars and to describe naval battles or seafaring deeds or similar things, where the subjects are bloodletting, anger, hatred, vengeance, displeasing sentiments and all things hateful, he chose hard, bitter, and displeasing words that arouse fear in the speaking and hearing of them.[6] . . . All this is enough to conclude that poetry would be without any beauty if it were not made of harmonically ordered words.

Beyond this I will not speak of the close relations and similarities of arithmetic and geometry to music; I will say only that if an architect has no knowledge of music (as Vitruvius shows) he will not know how to balance machines, to place vases in theaters, and to arrange well and musically his buildings.[7] Astronomy, likewise, would not be able to judge the good and bad celestial influences

---

2. Related in Quintilian, *Institutio oratoria* 11.3.6.

3. *De oratore* 3 [i.e., 3.225] [Au.] See also Quintilian, *Institutio oratoria* 1.10.27.

4. *Factorum ac dictorum memorabilium libri IX* 8.10[.1] [Au.]

5. 502c.

6. Here follow several examples from the *Aeneid,* the *Georgics,* and the *Eclogues.*

7. *De architectura* 1.1. [Au.] The vases Zarlino mentions were vessels placed, according to Vitruvius, in an arrangement of musical porportion so as to amplify the speech from the stage.

if it were not aided by the fundamentals of harmony. Indeed I will go further: if the astronomer does not understand the concordance of the seven planets and when one is in conjunction or opposition with another, he will never predict future events. Similarly, does not natural philosophy, which takes as its task the rational discussion of the things produced or potentially produced by nature, confess that all things depend on the Prime Mover and are ordered so marvelously that there results in the universe a silent harmony? Thus heavy things take the lowest position, light things the highest, and things of middle weight, according to their nature, a middle place. Moreover, philosophers affirm that the revolving heavens make a harmony, which we do not hear because they revolve too fast, or are too far away from us, or for some other unknown reason. Medicine does not stand far from these subjects, since if the doctor does not understand music how will he mix in due proportion hot things with cold, according to their states? And how will he understand perfectly people's pulses, which the most wise Herophilus orders according to musical proportions?[8]

And to rise even higher among the disciplines, our theology divides the angelic spirits in the heavens into nine choruses and three hierarchies, as Dionysius the Areopagite writes. These gaze perpetually on the Divine Majesty and ceaselessly sing "Holy, holy, holy is the Lord of hosts," as it is written in Isaiah.[9] And not only these, but also the four beasts described by Saint John in his book of Revelations stand before the throne of God and sing the same song. There are also then the twenty-four ancients before the immaculate Lamb, who sing a new song to the highest God with the sound of harps and raised voices.[10] This song is also sung by the harpists playing their harps before the four beasts and twenty-four elders. The Bible is full of these and an almost infinite variety of other things relating to our subject, which in the interest of brevity I will pass over. It is enough to say in supreme praise of music that the Bible, without mentioning other sciences, places music in Paradise, where it is most nobly practiced. And just as happens in the heavenly court, called the Church Triumphant, so in our earthly one, the Church Militant, the Creator is praised and thanked with nothing so much as with music.

But let us leave the superior things aside and return to those produced by nature for the ornament of the world. Here we will see that everything is full of musical concord.[11] . . . But if so much harmony is found in celestial and terrestrial things—or, to put it better, if the world was composed by the Creator in such harmony—why should we believe man himself to be bereft of it? And if the soul of the world is (as some say) nothing other than harmony, could it be that our soul is not a cause of all our harmony and harmonically joined with

8. The *Anatomica* of Herophilus (4th–3rd century B.C.E.) has not survived. Zarlino takes his information from Martianus Capella, *De nuptiis Philologiae et Mercurii* 9.926–7.
9. *De coelestia hierarchia,* chaps. 7, 8, and 9; Isaias 6. [Au.]
10. Apocalypse [i.e., Revelations] 4, 5, 14, 15, and 19. [Au.]
11. Here follow examples of the musical qualities of the sea, air, earth, rivers, and springs.

the body? This is certainly reasonable to assume, especially since God created man according to the plan of the larger world, called by the Greeks *cosmos* (κόσμος), that is, "ornament" or "ornate," and made him similar to the world but of lesser quantity, whence he is called *microcosmos* (μικρὸκοσμος), or "small world." So that Aristotle, wanting to show the musical makeup of man, explained very well that the vegetative part of the soul has the same relation to the sensitive, and the sensitive to the intellective, as a triangle has to a rectangle.[12]

It is thus confirmed that there is no good thing that does not have a musical disposition. And truly music, beyond merely raising our spirits, leads man back to the contemplation of celestial things and has such power that it perfects everything it is joined to. Those people who are gifted in music are truly happy and blessed, as David affirmed saying "Blessed are they that know the joyful sound."[13] On the basis of that authority, the Catholic doctor Hilary, Bishop of Poitiers, speaking of the 65th psalm, was moved to say that music is necessary to Christians, since they find blessedness in its science.[14] Which emboldens me to say that those who do not have knowledge of this science must be numbered among the ignorant.

In ancient times, as Isidore reports, it was no less shameful to be unmusical than to be illiterate.[15] It is no wonder that the most famous and ancient poet Hesiod was excluded from poetic contests, as Pausanius narrates,[16] since he had never learned to play the harp or accompany himself with it. Even Themistocles, as Cicero reports,[17] was thought less wise and learned after he refused to play the lyre at a symposium. We read also the opposite: how Linus and Orpheus, both sons of gods, were held in great esteem because with sweet song they not only sweetened human souls, so to speak, but those of beasts and birds as well, and, what is more marvelous still, they moved the rocks from their usual places and rivers from their courses. Horace attributes this power also to Amphion, saying:

> Hence too the fable that Amphion, builder of Thebes's
>   citadel,
> moved stones by the sound of his lyre, and led them
> whither he would by his supplicating spell.[18]

Perhaps from this example the ancient Pythagoreans learned that musical sounds could soften ferocious animals, and Asclepiades likewise learned that music could quiet discord in the populace and that the sound of the trumpet

---

12. *On the soul* 2.3 [414b]. [Au.]
13. Psalm 88 [i.e. 89:15]. [Au.]
14. Hilary, *Tractatus in LXV psalmum* 1.
15. *Etymologiarum* [i.e., Isidore of Seville, *Etymologiarum sive originum libri XX*] 3.15. [Au.]
16. *Descriptio graeciae* 10 [i.e., 10.7.3]. [Au.]
17. *Tusculan Disputations* 1 [i.e., 1.2.4]. [Au.]
18. *Ars poetica* 11.394–396; trans. H. Rushton Fairclough, *Horace: Satires, Epistles and Ars Poetica* (Cambridge, Mass.: Harvard University Press, 1966), 483.

could restore hearing to the deaf.[19] Similarly, Damon the Pythagorean led with music several youths given to wine and pleasure back to a temperate and honest life.[20] Thus they who call music a certain law and rule of modesty speak well, since Theophrastes discovered certain musical modes that quiet perturbed spirits. But Diogenes the Cynic justly and wisely mocked the musicians of his time who had abandoned the customary harmonies and therefore, though they had well tuned harps, had discordant and discomposed souls.[21]

And if we can believe history, all that we have said thus far may seem as nothing, because it is a greater thing to be able to heal the sick than to correct the ways of dissolute youths. Indeed we read of Xenocrates who could restore sanity to the insane with the sound of the organ, or of Thaletas of Crete who expelled the plague with the sound of his harp. And we see today that music can do marvelous things, and that such is the force of sounds and dancing against the poison of the tarantula that in the shortest time those who have been bitten are healed (this is confirmed by experience every day in Apulia, a region in which such animals are abundant).[22] But turning from further secular examples, do we not read in the Bible that the prophet David quieted the evil spirit of Saul with the sound of his harp?[23] Because of this, I believe, this royal prophet ordered that songs and harmonies be used in the temple of God; he knew that they were able to lift the spirits and return people to the contemplation of celestial things.[24] And the prophets, when they wanted to prophesy (Ambrose says, commenting on psalm 118), asked that a good musician begin to play so that spiritual grace, summoned by that sweetness, might enter into them.[25] Eliseus did not want to prophesy to the King of Israel where he might find water for his parched troops until a musician was brought whose singing infused the divine spirit into him; then he foretold everything.[26]

But let us move on, because there are many examples. Timotheus, as St. Basil and many others relate, with music incited King Alexander to combat and then called him back to himself.[27] Aristotle tells in his book *History of Animals*[28] that deer are captured by the singing of hunters and that they delight

---

19. Zarlino took these examples, along with those that follow of Damon, Theophrastes, Xenocrates, and Thaletas, from Martianus, *De nuptiis* 9.923 and 926.
20. The story is usually told not of Damon but of Pythagoras; see, e.g., Quintilian, *Institutio oratoria* 1.10.32, Boethius, *De institutione musica* 1.1, and St. Basil, *To Young Men (Ad adolescentes)* 9.9.
21. See Diogenes Laertius's biographies of the Cynics Diogenes and Menedemus, specifically *Lives of Eminent Philosophers* 6.73 and 104.
22. Alessandro Alessandri [ca. 1461–1523], *Genialium dierum libri sex* 2.16 [Au.] For another early and influential account of this tarantism, see no. 29 below (Ficino), p. 111.
23. 1 Kings [i.e., 1 Samuel] 16. [Au.]
24. 1 Paralipomenon [i.e., Chronicles] 16. [Au.]
25. Ambrose, *In psalmum David CXVIII expositio* 7.26.
26. 4 [i.e., 2] Kings 3. [Au.]
27. Homily 54 *Ad adolescentes*. [Au.] I.e., *To Young Men* 8.7–8; see no. 10 below (Castiglione), pp. 48–49, n. 2.
28. 9.5 [611b]. [Au.]

greatly in the pastoral bagpipe as well as song (which Pliny confirms in his *Natural History*).[29] And so as not to go on any longer about this I will only say that I know people who have seen deer stop and stand attentively listening to the sound of a lyre or lute; and similarly we see everyday birds which, defeated and deceived by harmonic sounds, are captured by bird trappers. And Pliny narrates that music saved Arion from death when he threw himself into the sea; he was carried by dolphins to the shore of the island of Taenarum.[30] But let us set aside many other examples that we could adduce and say a little about good Socrates, master of Plato, who decided when he was old and full of wisdom to learn to play the harp; or about the old Chiron, who included music among the first arts he taught Achilles at a tender age, and who wanted him to play the harp before he dirtied his hands with Trojan blood.[31] Plato and Aristotle do not consider a man well formed who is without music. Indeed they persuade us with many reasons that music should be studied and show that its force in us is very great; and they think it should be taken up in childhood so that it can induce in us a new and good custom that will guide us to virtue and render our souls more capable of happiness.[32] Even the most severe Lycurgus, King of the Lacedaemonians, praised and approved of music among his very harsh laws, since he knew very well that it was most necessary for men and of great help in times of war. His armies, as Valerius tells us, never went to war without being first enflamed and animated by the music of pipes.[33] We still observe that custom in our own time, since of two armies one will not attack its enemy if it is not summoned by the sound of trumpets and drums or of some other musical instruments. And though there do not lack many other examples beyond those given here from which we can learn the dignity and excellence of music, in order not to go on too long, and since what has already been said is sufficient, I leave them aside.

29. 8.32 [i.e., 8.50.114]. [Au.]
30. *Natural History* 9.8 [.28] [Au.] Other sources of this famous story are Herodotus, *History* 1.23 and Plutarch *Moralia* 160e–162b.
31. For Socrates see Quintilian, *Institutio oratoria* 1.10.13–14; for Chiron see ibid. 1.10.30 and pseudo-Plutarch *De musica* 1145d–1146a.
32. *Laws* 3 [700–701]; *Politics* 8.3 [1337b–1338a]. [Au.]
33. *Factorum ac dictorum memorabilium libri IX* 2.1 [i.e., 2.6.2] [Au.] See also Quintilian, *Institutio oratoria* 1.10.15 and pseudo-Plutarch *De musica* 1140c. The Lacedaemonians were the Spartans.

38 Pierre de Ronsard

The great French poet was born in 1524 and died in 1585. Ronsard strived to bring about a rebirth of lyric poetry—in the ancient Greek sense of the term—as a musical expression of the soul in a state of emotion. As this ideal could be achieved only by a close cooperation of music and poetry, Ronsard set all his efforts in this direction. Thus, to the collected poems that appeared under the title *Les amours de Cassandre* (1552–53), he added a musical supplement containing settings of his poems by Marc-Antoine de Muret, Claude Janequin, Pierre Certon, and Claude Goudimel. Considering Ronsard's views on the union of music and poetry, it is not surprising that more than two hundred of his poems were set to music, some of them repeatedly, in the second half of the sixteenth century. There are entire collections of Ronsard's poems in settings by Philippe de Monte, Antoine de Bertrand, and other contemporary composers; and his verses are found in a great number of chanson collections by the composers named above, Orlando di Lasso, Claude Le Jeune, Guillaume Costeley, and others. Ronsard's dedication to Francis II of one such anthology, the *Livre des mélanges* published in 1560 by Le Roy and Ballard, rehearses many ancient examples, by now almost commonplaces, of the powers of music and the esteem in which it was held.

Livre des mélanges
(1560)

DEDICATION

Even, Sire, as by the touchstone one tries gold, whether it be good or bad, so the ancients tried by music the spirits of those who are noble and magnanimous, not straying from their first essence, and of those who are numbed, slothful, and bastardized in this mortal body, no more remembering the celestial harmony of heaven than the comrades of Ulysses, after Circe had turned them into swine, remembered that they had been men. For he, Sire, that hearing a sweet accord of instruments or the sweetness of the natural voice feels no joy and no agitation and is not thrilled from head to foot, as being delightfully rapt and somehow carried out of himself—'tis the sign of one whose soul is tortuous, vicious, and depraved, and of whom one should beware, as not fortunately born. For how could one be in accord with a man who by nature

TEXT: *Oeuvres complètes,* ed. Paul Laumonier (Paris: A. Lemerre, 1914–19), vol. 7, pp. 16–20. Translation by Oliver Strunk. Laumonier gives the text of 1572; Strunk translated the text of 1560, which he restored with the help of Laumonier's note (see n. 7 below, p. 302).

hates accord? He is unworthy to behold the sweet light of the sun who does not honor music as being a small part of that which, as Plato says, so harmoniously animates the whole great universe.[1] Contrariwise, he who does honor and reverence to music is commonly a man of worth, sound of soul, by nature loving things lofty, philosophy, the conduct of affairs of state, the tasks of war, and in brief, in all honorable offices he ever shows the sparks of his virtue.

Now to tell here what music is; whether it is governed more by inspiration than by art; to tell of its concords, its tones, modulations, voices, intervals, sounds, systems, and transformations; of its division into enharmonic, which for its difficulty was never perfectly in use; into chromatic, which for its lasciviousness was by the ancients banished from republics; into diatonic, which was by all approved, as approaching nearest to the melody of the macrocosm; to speak of the Phrygian, Dorian, and Lydian music; and how certain peoples of Greece went bravely into battle inspired by harmony, as do our soldiers today to the sounds of drums and trumpets; how King Alexander was roused to fury by the songs of Timotheus,[2] and how Agamemnon, going to Troy, left on purpose in his house I know not what Dorian musician, who by the virtue of the anapestic foot tempered the unbridled amorous passions of his wife Clytemnestra, inflamed with love of whom Aegisthus could never attain to enjoyment until he had wickedly put the musician to death;[3] to wish further to deduce how all things, as well in the heavens and in the sea as on the earth, are composed of accords, measures, and proportions; to wish to discuss how the most honorable persons of past ages, monarchs, princes, philosophers, governors of provinces, and captains of renown, were curiously enamored of the ardors of music; I should never have done; the more so as music has always been the sign and the mark of those who have shown themselves virtuous, magnanimous, and truly born to feel nothing vulgar.

For example I shall take solely the late King your father,[4] may God absolve him, who during his reign made it apparent how liberally Heaven had endowed him with all graces and with gifts rare among kings; who surpassed, not only in grandeur of empire, but in clemency, liberality, goodness, piety, and religion, not only all the princes his predecessors, but all who have ever lived that have borne that honorable title of king; who, in order to reveal the stars of his high birth and to show that he was perfect in all virtues, so honored, loved, and esteemed music that all in France who today remain well-disposed toward this art, have not, all combined, so much affection for it as he had alone.

You also, Sire, as the inheritor both of his realm and of his virtues, show that you are his son, favored by Heaven, in so perfectly loving this science and its accords, without which nothing of this world could remain whole.

1. The reference is probably to *Timaeus* 90d or 80b.
2. See no. 45 below (Castiglione), pp. 326–27, n. 2.
3. See *Odyssey* 3.267–272, as elaborated by Athenaeus, *Deipnosophists* 1.14, and later scholiasts.
4. Henri II.

Now to tell you here of Orpheus, of Terpander, of Eumolpus, of Arion, these are stories with which I do not wish to burden the paper, as things well known to you. I will relate to you only that anciently the kings most eminent for virtue caused their children to be brought up in the houses of musicians, as did Peleus, who sent his son Achilles, and Aeson, who sent his son Jason, to the venerated cave of the centaur Chiron to be instructed as well in arms as in medicine and in the art of music, the more so as these three professions, joined together, are not unbefitting the grandeur of a prince; and there were given by Achilles and Jason, who were princes of your age,[5] such commendable examples of virtue that the one was honored by the divine poet Homer as sole author of the taking of Troy, and the other was celebrated by Apollonius of Rhodes as the first who taught the sea to endure the unknown burden of ships; and after he had passed the rocks Symplegades and tamed the fury of the cold Scythian Sea, he returned to his country enriched by the noble fleece of gold. Therefore, Sire, these two princes will be to you as patrons of virtue, and when sometimes you are wearied by your most urgent affairs, you will imitate them by lightening your cares with the accords of music, in order to return the fresher and the better-disposed to the royal burden which you support with such adroitness.

Your Majesty should not marvel if this book of miscellanies, which is very humbly dedicated to you by your very humble and obedient servants and printers Adrian Le Roy and Robert Ballard, is composed of the oldest songs that can today be found,[6] because the music of the ancients has always been esteemed the most divine, the more so since it was composed in a happier age, less contaminated by the vices which reign in this last age of iron. Moreover, the divine inspirations of music, poetry, and painting do not arrive at perfection by degrees, like the other sciences, but by starts, and like flashes of lightning, one here, another there, appear in various lands, then suddenly vanish. And for that reason, Sire, when some excellent worker in this art reveals himself, you should guard him with care, as being something so excellent that it rarely appears. Of such men have arisen within six or seven score years Josquin Desprez, a native of Hainaut, and his disciples Mouton, Willaert, Richafort, Janequin, Maillard, Claudin, Moulu, Certon,[7] and Arcadelt, who in the perfec-

---

5. François II, husband of Mary Queen of Scots, was sixteen years old on January 19, 1560 and died on December 5 of that year. For Chiron and Achilles see no. 37 above (Zarlino), p. 299, n. 31; various ancient writers attest Jason's education with Chiron (see Pauly-Wissowa, *Real-Encyclopädie,* s.v. "Chiron"), but none that I have seen speaks specifically of musical training.
6. The composers most frequently represented are Willaert, Gombert, Lasso, Josquin, Leschenet, Arcadelt, Crequillon, Mouton, Certon, and Maillard.
7. For the remainder of this paragraph the edition of 1572 substitutes the following: "and Arcadelt, and now the more than divine Orlando [di Lasso], who like a bee has sipped all the most beautiful flowers of the ancients and moreover seems alone to have stolen the harmony of the heavens to delight us with it on earth, surpassing the ancients and making himself the unique wonder of our time."

tion of this art does not yield to the ancients, from being inspired by Charles, Cardinal of Lorraine, his Apollo.

Many other things might be said of music, which Plutarch and Boethius have amply mentioned. But neither the brevity of this preface, nor the convenience of time, nor the subject permits me to discourse of it at greater length. Entreating the Creator, Sire, to increase more and more the virtues of Your Majesty and to continue you in the kindly affection which you are pleased to have for music and for all those who study to make flourish again under your sway the sciences and arts which flourished under the empire of Caesar Augustus, of which Augustus may it be God's will to grant you the years, the virtues, and the prosperity.

39 William Byrd

Born in 1543, William Byrd, the foremost polyphonist of Elizabethan England, died at Stondon Massey, Essex, in 1623. Early on he studied with Thomas Tallis, and he assumed the position of organist and choirmaster at Lincoln Cathedral in 1563. Seven years later he was appointed Gentleman of the Chapel Royal in London, where also he served as organist (at first along with Tallis), and where he remained until around 1590. From then on, though he retained membership in the Chapel, he spent less time in London and more and more in Stondon Massey. Perhaps he distanced himself from London to avoid persecution for his recusancy: he remained Catholic in Anglican England throughout his life, seems to have taken part in some pro-Catholic initiatives, and probably escaped punishment on more than one occasion only by virtue of his considerable celebrity.

Composer of numerous English anthems, psalm settings, and consort songs, of three masses, and of a large body of instrumental music for consort and solo keyboard, Byrd nonetheless devoted himself especially to Latin sacred works. These seem to have answered best his religious convictions, and the more or less veiled Catholic protest of many of his early motets gave way to freely declared liturgical intent in the *Gradualia*, a huge collection of Mass Proper settings dating from 1605–7 (see below, no. 63, pp. 378–81).

This excerpt, from Byrd's *Psalmes, Sonets, & Songs of Sadnes and Pietie* of 1588, is in a different vein altogether. Far from the trials of Elizabethan recusancy, it is just as distant from the high-flown classicism of Tinctoris's, Zarlino's, and Ronsard's paeans. Here Byrd gives an earthy and plebeian assessment of music's advantages.

Psalmes, Sonets, & Songs of Sadnes and Pietie

(1588)

FRONTISPIECE

Reasons briefely set downe by th'auctor, to perswade every one to learne to sing.

First, it is a knowledge easely taught, and quickly learned where there is a good Master, and an apt Scoller.

2. The exercise of singing is delightfull to Nature & good to preserve the health of Man.

3. It doth strengthen all parts of the brest, & doth open the pipes.

4. It is a singuler good remedie for a stutting & stammering in the speech.

5. It is the best meanes to procure a perfect pronunciation, & to make a good Orator.

6. It is the onely way to know where Nature hath bestowed the benefit of a good voyce: which guift is so rare, as there is not one among a thousand, that hath it: and in many, that excellent guift is lost, because they want Art to expresse Nature.

7. There is not any Musicke of Instruments whatsoever, comparable to that which is made of the voyces of Men, where the voices are good, and the same well sorted and ordered.

8. The better the voyce is, the meeter it is to honour and serve God therewith: and the voyce of man is chiefely to be imployed to that ende.

Omnis spiritus laudet Dominum.

Since singing is so good a thing
I wish all men would learne to sing.

TEXT: Facsimile of the original frontispiece in *The Collected Works of William Byrd,* ed. Edmund H. Fellowes (20 vols., London: Stainer & Bell, 1937–50), vol. 12, p. xxxiv.

40 Henry Cornelius Agrippa

Skepticism—philosophical doubt as to human capacities to obtain any true or certain knowledge—grew in importance through the sixteenth century and finally found classic expression in works such as Montaigne's *Apology for Raymond Sebond.* In a general fashion, this growth reflects the erosion across the period of once-solid structures of knowledge. More specifically, it was nurtured by three forces: evangelical and Protestant emphasis on faith rather than knowledge or works as the road to salvation; the revival in Neoplatonic circles of certain forms of mystical gnosis dating from Late Antiquity but believed, in the sixteenth century, to be much older; and the recovery of the thought of the ancient Skeptics themselves, especially in the writings of Sextus Empiricus.

In 1530, the first two of these forces joined together in a famous skeptical diatribe by Henry Cornelius Agrippa. (The third force was less prominent; Sextus's works were not first published until 1562 and 1569, and Agrippa's knowledge of ancient Skepticism seems to have been fragmentary and indirect.) *De incertitudine et vanitate scientiarum et artium atque excellentia verbi Dei declamatio (Declamation of the Uncertainty and Vanity of the Sciences and Arts and of the Excellence of the Word of God)*, or *De vanitate*, as it is customarily called, devotes chapters to many different disciplines, doctrines, activities, social classes, and the like, ranging from ethics, religion, and mathematics to juggling, swordplay, and courtiers. In each case Agrippa depicts knowledge as a destroyer of innocence, an ally of sin, and a refuge of falsehood. In place of knowledge he advocates, at the end of his book, unquestioning faith in the scriptures. His chapter on music is typical. It begins with a review, reminiscent of nos. 1–3 above, of claims in favor of music (omitted here) and proceeds to demolish these claims with vitriol and counter-example. Though controversial, *De vanitate* clearly touched a chord dear to many contemporary readers: numerous editions appeared through the later sixteenth and seventeenth centuries, and the work was translated into Italian, English, French, Dutch, and German.

The itinerant scholar, magician, physician, and soldier Agrippa was born in 1486 in or near Cologne. He is also known for his huge treatise on magic, *De occulta philosophia*, drafted over a long period and published in 1533, two years before his death.

FROM *Declamation of the Uncertainty and Vanity of the Sciences and Arts*

(1530)

CHAPTER 17: OF MUSIC

. . . And although men confess that this Art hath much sweetness, yet the common opinion is, and also everyone may see it by experience, that it is the

---

TEXT: the first English edition: *Of the Vanitie and Uncertaintie of Artes and Sciences*, trans. James Sanford (London, 1569), fols. 28v–30r. A complete edition of this translation has been edited by Catherine M. Dunn (Northridge, Calif., 1974); where signaled below I have profited from her annotations in making my own. For a review of older interpretations of *De vanitate* and a helpful new reading, see Michael H. Keefer, "Agrippa's Dilemma: Hermetic 'Rebirth' and the Ambivalences of *De vanitate* and *De occulta philosophia*," *Renaissance Quarterly* 41 (1988): 614–53.

exercise of base men, and of an unprofitable and untemperate wit, which have no consideration of beginning nor ending, as it is read of Archabius the trumpeter, to whom men were glad to give more to make him cease, than to make him sing. Of which so unreasonable Musicians Horace speaketh:

> It is a fault, a common fault
>   that all our Minstrels use,
> The more you seem to crave a song
>   the more they will refuse.
> Request them not they never cease, etc.[1]

For this cause Music hath ever been wandering here and there for price and pence, and is the servant of bawdry which no grave, modest, honest, and valiant man ever professed: and therefore the Greeks with a common word called them the Artificers of Father Bacchus, or else (as Aristotle sayeth) *Dionisiaci technitae*,[2] that is the artificers of the Baccanalia, which for the most part, were always used to have lewd customs: leading for the most part, an unchaste Life: partly also in Misery, and Poverty, the which breedeth and encreaseth Vices. The Kings of the Persians, and Medes reckoned Musicians among Parasites, and Players, as they which take pleasure of their own doings, and make little account of the Masters. And Antisthenes that wise man, when he heard, that a certain man, called Ismenias, was a very good Trumpeter, he said, He is a Ribald, for if he were an honest man, he would not be a Trumpeter:[3] for as it is said, that is no sober, and honest man's Art, but the practice of Players and idle persons. This did Scipio Aemilianus, and Cato contemn, as far off from the Custom of the Romans. Augustus, and Nero were blamed, because they did over greedily follow Music. But Augustus being reproved did refrain: Nero coveting it more and more, was for this cause had in contempt, and little estimation. King Philip understanding that his Son had sweetly sung in a certain place, he reproved him, saying, art thou not ashamed, that thou knowest to sing so well? It is enough, and too much for a Prince, to have leisure to hear, when other sing.[4] Jupiter singeth not among the Greek Poets, nor soundeth the Harp. Learned Pallas doth detest the Flute. In Homer a Harper playeth, and Alcyone, and Ulysses give ear.[5] In Virgil Iopas doth sing and sound the Harp, Aeneas and Dido do harken.[6] When on a time Alexander the Great did sing, Antigonus his Master rent his Harp asunder, and cast it away, saying: It is now meet for thy age to Rule, and not to Sing.[7] And the Egyptians also, as

---

1. Horace, *Satires* 1.3.1–3 (see Dunn). I have not been able to locate the story of Archabius.
2. Pseudo-Aristotle, *Problems* 30.10.
3. Plutarch, *Lives, Pericles* 1.5.
4. Ibid.
5. *Odyssey* 8.72–103; it is Alcinous, not Alcyone, who listens with Ulysses (see Dunn).
6. *Aeneid* 1.740–46 (see Dunn).
7. I have not located this anecdote; for Alexander's awareness that music was beneath his station see Plutarch, *Moralia, On the Fortune or the Virtue of Alexander* 2.334c–335a.

Diodorus testifieth, did forbid their young men to learn Music, as that which doth effeminate the minds of men.[8] And Ephorus, (as Polybius witnesseth) said, that it was invented to no other end, but to deceive men.[9] But in very deed what is more unprofitable, more to be despised, and more to be eschewed, than these Pipers, Singers, and other sorts of Musicians? Which with so many, and diverse voices of songs, surpassing the chirping of all Birds, with a certain venomous sweetness, like to the Mermaids, with voices, gestures, and lascivious sounds, do destroy and corrupt men's minds. For the which thing the women of the Ciconians did persecute Orpheus unto the Death, because with his Music he corrupted their men.[10] But if there be any truth in Fables, a hundred eyes had Argus in his head, all which notwithstanding were brought asleep, and put out with the Harmony of one Bagpipe.[11] And yet for this, these Musicians do much boast, as though that they were more able to move the affections, than Rhetoricians are: which be so much misled by their madness, that they affirm moreover the Heavens themselves to sing, yet with voices never heard of any man, except perhaps they have come to the knowledge of those Musicians by means of their *Euouae,*[12] or through Drunkeness, or Dreaming. And yet in the mean season, there hath no Musician descended from Heaven, that hath known all the concordances of voices, and that hath found out all the measures of proportions. And for all that they say, that it is a very perfect Art, and which comprehendeth all Disciplines, and that it cannot be handled without the knowledge of all Learnings: attributing to it besides the force of Divination, whereby the plights of the body, the passions of the mind, the manners of men may thereby be judged. They say moreover, that it is an endless Art, and that it cannot be thoroughly learned with any wit: but that daily according to the capacity of every man, it giveth fresh melody. And therefore Anaxilas sayeth not amiss: By God sayeth he, Music is even like Affricke, it yearly bringeth forth some strange Beast.[13] Anathasius for the vanity thereof did forbid it the Churches: but Ambrose more desirous of Ceremony and Pomp, ordained in the Church the use of singing and playing on the Organs. But Augustine standing in doubt, sayeth in his *Confessions,* that hereof there grew to him a hard doubt:[14] but nowadays the unleeful liberty of Music, is so much used in Churches, that together with the Canon of the Mass, very filthy songs have like tunes in the Organs, and the Divine Service is sung by lascivious Musicians hired for a great stipend, not for the understanding of the hearers, but for the stirring up of the mind: But for dishonest lasciviousness,

8. Diodorus Siculus, *Library of History* 1.81.7 (see Dunn)
9. Polybius, *Histories* 4.20.5–6 (see Dunn); also quoted in Athenaeus, *Deipnosophists* 14.626. Polybius, it should be noted, cites Ephorus's view in order to dismiss it.
10. See especially Ovid, *Metamorphoses* 11.1–66.
11. Ovid, *Metamorphoses* 1.668–721 (see Dunn).
12. A shouted refrain at the Dionysiac orgies (see Dunn).
13. Reported in Athenaeus, *Deipnosophists* 14.623; Anaxilas was a Middle Comedian.
14. 10.33 (see Dunn).

not with manly voices, but with beastly skeeking, while the children bray the Discant, some bellow the Tenor, some bark the Counterpoint, some howl the Treble, some grunt the Bass, and cause many sounds to be heard, and no words and sentences to be understood, but in this sort the authority of judgment is taken both from the ears, and mind.

MUSIC IN
SECULAR
SOCIETY

41 Guillaume Du Fay

From June 1434 to April 1436, Pope Eugenius IV, beset by political and military troubles in Rome, resided in Florence. For the last half of this period, Guillaume Du Fay, the preeminent polyphonist of the mid-fifteenth century, joined him there, serving as singer and master of the papal chapel.

Du Fay's stay in Florence represents a convergence of personalities that is almost irresistible to the historian of Renaissance culture. During these twenty-two months, the composer struck up lasting relations with the banking family of the Medici, whose paterfamilias Cosimo was just then consolidating his control over the city; he composed an isorhythmic motet for the consecration of the cathedral of Santa Maria del Fiore, whose huge crossing Filippo Brunelleschi had just covered with his famous cupola; and he befriended the organist and composer Antonio Squarcialupi, who owned the chief manuscript repository of Italian polyphony from the preceding generations (the so-called Squarcialupi Codex).

Du Fay's ties to the Medici seem to have been especially cordial with Piero and Giovanni, Cosimo's music-loving sons. The composer's only surviving autograph letter, reproduced here, accompanied a gift of music he made to them in the mid-1450s. And as late as 1467 Squarcialupi could write a fulsome letter to Du Fay reporting the great enthusiasm for his music felt not only by Piero but also, now, by his son Lorenzo (later called "the Magnificent"). Perhaps these letters represent an occasional and opportunistic interaction (Squarcialupi sent a poem by Lorenzo, asking Du Fay to set it, while Du Fay may have been angling for patronage with his chansons), or perhaps they signal a more consistent relationship whose other traces are now lost.

Du Fay's surviving works include some of the latest isorhythmic motets, some of the earliest cycles of Mass Ordinaries, and many smaller liturgical works and secular chansons. He was born around 1400, probably near Cambrai, and died there in 1474.

Letter to Piero and Giovanni de' Medici
(1456?)

MAGNIFICENT AND NOBLE SIRS, ALL HUMBLE COMMENDATION BEFORE-HAND!

Since I well know that you have always taken pleasure in song and since, I believe, you have not changed your preferences, I have felt encouraged to send you some chansons which, at the request of some gentlemen of the King's

TEXT: Frank A. d'Accone, "The Singers of San Giovanni in Florence during the 15th Century," *Journal of the American Musicological Society [JAMS]* 14 (1961): 318–19. Translation by Frank A. d'Accone. Reprinted by permission of the American Musicological Society. For a facsimile of Du Fay's letter see David Fallows, *Dufay* (London: J. M. Dent, 1982), illustration 18.

court, I composed recently when I was in France with Monseigneur de Savoye. I also have some others which I shall send you at another time. In addition, in this past year I wrote four Lamentations for Constantinople[1] which are rather good: three of them are for four voices and the texts were sent to me from Naples. I do not know whether you have them there. If you do not have them, be so kind as to let me know and I shall send them to you. Furthermore, I am very much pleased with Francesco Sassetti[2] your representative here, for during the past year I was in need of something at the court of Rome and he helped me most magnanimously and treated me most graciously for which I extend my unceasing thanks. I understand that you now have some good people in your chapel at San Giovanni and because of this, if it pleases you, I should like to send you some of my little things more often than I have done in the past. I do this also out of my regard for Antonio,[3] your good friend and mine, to whom I beg you commend me cordially. Magnificent and noble sirs, if there is something which I can do here for your lordships, please let me know and I shall do it with all my heart through the aid of our Lord, who I hope will grant you a good and long life, and at the end paradise.

Written at Geneva, the 22nd of February[4]

Your humble chaplain and unworthy servant,
GUILLAUME DU FAY, Canon of Cambrai

1. Du Fay's four-voice "O tres piteulx de tout espoir fontaine / Omnes amici eius" is probably one of these laments; the other three are lost. Commentators have often speculated that one of the lost works may have been the lament performed at Philip the Good's Feast of the Pheasant in 1454 (see no. 42 below, pp. 315–16). For arguments against the connection see Fallows, *Dufay*, p. 287.
2. Francesco Sassetti was a member of a prosperous Florentine family of merchants, manager of the Medici bank in Geneva, and humanistic book-hunter. See Fallows, *Dufay*, p. 257.
3. Squarcialupi.
4. The letter bears no year, but it is now generally assigned to 1456; see Craig Wright, "Dufay at Cambrai: Discoveries and Revisions," *JAMS* 28 (1975): 175–229; p. 190.

42 Olivier de la Marche

Under a succession of dukes from the House of Valois, the Duchy of Burgundy sponsored through the fifteenth century one of the most sumptuous courts in all Europe. The high-water mark of its influence and power came during the reign of Philip the Good, which lasted almost half a century, from 1419 to 1467. Philip boasted a large and renowned musical establishment that included Gilles Binchois, Robert Morton, and other composers. Even Du Fay, who spent most of his last thirty-five years in Cambrai, a city under the sway of the Burgundian dukes, seems to have held some sort of appointment that brought him to the court at least once.

The famous Feast of the Pheasant, held on February 17, 1454, offers an unbridled introduction to the prominence of music in Renaissance court festivities. The feast was served up by Philip at Lille in order to inspire his Knights of the Golden Fleece to undertake a new crusade against the Turks, who had captured Constantinople the year before. Here the feast is described, in one of two surviving accounts, by Olivier de la Marche (ca. 1426–1502), a longtime member of the Duke's retinue and chronicler in his *Memoirs* of events at court. La Marche wrote his *Memoirs* mainly in the 1470s and '80s, well after the events described; they were first published at Lyon in 1562.

FROM *Memoir on the House of Burgundy*
(ca. 1471–92)

The hall where the banquet was held was large and beautifully hung with a tapestry depicting the life of Hercules. . . . In this hall were three covered tables, one medium-sized, another large, and another small. On the medium-sized table there was a skilfully made church with transept and windows, in which there were four singers and a ringing bell. . . . The second table, which was the largest, had on it (most conspicuously) a pastry in which there were twenty-eight living persons playing in turn various instruments. . . . The third table, smaller than the others, had on it a marvelous forest, like a forest of India, in which there were many strange and strangely made beasts that moved by themselves as if alive. . . .

When everyone was seated, in the manner described, a bell rang very loudly in the church on the principal table (it was the first course on that table). After the bell had stopped ringing, three little children and a tenor sang a very sweet chanson. And when they had finished, in the pastry (the first course on the long table, as noted above) a shepherd played a bagpipe in a very novel fashion. Hardly a moment after that there came in through the entrance to the room a horse walking backwards, richly covered with red silk. On it were two trumpeters seated back to back without a saddle. They were dressed in mantles of gray and black silk, with hats and masks; and they led the horse backwards up and down the length of the room, all the while playing a fanfare on their trumpets. To help in this action there were sixteen knights dressed as stablehands.

When this was finished an organ was played in the church and a German cornett was played, very strangely, in the pastry. Then a goblin entered the hall, a greatly disfigured monster with the hairy legs and feet and long talons of a griffin from the waist down and the form of a man above the waist. . . . When

TEXT: *Mémoire sur le maison de Bourgogne*, in *Choix de chroniques et mémoires sur l'histoire de France*, ed. J. A. C. Buchon, vol. 2 (Paris: Société du Panthéon Littéraire, 1842), pp. 490–96. Translation by Gary Tomlinson.

the goblin had departed, those in the church sang and in the pastry were played a shawm with another instrument; and a bit later four trumpets sounded a joyous and very loud fanfare. The trumpets were behind a green curtain hung over a large pedestal at one end of the hall. When the fanfare ended the curtain was suddenly drawn and a person playing the role of Jason, heavily armed, was spied on the pedestal. . . . After this mystery play [of Jason], organs in the church played a motet, and after them three sweet voices in the pastry sang a long chanson called "Sauvegarde de ma vie."[1]

Later, after the church and the pastry had each played four times, from the door where the other things had entered there came into the hall a stag, marvelously large and beautiful, all white with large antlers of gold, and covered, as far as I could tell, with red and green silk. On the stag rode a twelve-year-old girl dressed in a short robe of scarlet velvet, carrying on her head a black scalloped hood, and wearing lovely slippers. She held the stag's antlers in her hands. When she entered the room she began to sing loud and clear the upper part of a chanson; and the stag sang the tenor, without the participation of anyone else. The chanson they sang was named "Je ne vey onques le pareille, etc."[2] While they sang they walked down the chamber in front of the tables and then returned. This action seemed good to me, and it was well received. After this beautiful action of the white stag and the child, the singers sang a motet in the church and in the pastry a lute accompanied two good voices; in this manner the church and the pastry always did something between the plays.

After this, when those in the pastry had done their duty, on the pedestal where we had seen the play of Jason the four trumpets heard earlier played another fanfare. Then the curtain mentioned before was drawn back and Jason appeared again, richly armed as before. . . . [After this second play] the curtain was closed, organs were played in the church, and four minstrels in the pastry played flutes.

Then, high at one end of the hall, a fire-breathing dragon set out; it flew most of the length of the chamber and then went out, leaving us guessing what had become of it. After that those in the church sang, and some blind men in the pastry played hurdy-gurdies. Next, high in the air at one end of the room a heron flew in. Several people cried out at it, in the manner of falconers; and immediately a falcon set out from the side of the room, flying round and soaring in circles. And from the other side of the hall another falcon set out; it attacked with great ferocity and wounded the heron so grievously that it fell in the middle of the room. After another cry rang out, the heron was presented to Monsieur the Duke. Then once more there was singing in the church, and in the pastry three drums were played together.

Next the four trumpets were sounded on the pedestal, and after their fanfare the curtain was drawn and Jason appeared armed and fortified. . . . At the end

1. Jason was the mythological patron of Philip's Order of the Golden Fleece, founded in 1429.
2. This song might well be related to the three-voice *rondeau* "Je ne vis onques la pareille" that has come down to us in various manuscript sources. It is ascribed both to Du Fay and to Binchois.

of this third mystery play the organs in the church were heard and in the pastry they played a *chasse* so vivid it seemed there were little dogs yelping and hunters shouting and trumpets sounding, as if we were in a forest. With that *chasse* the role of the pastry ended.

Such were the secular entertainments of the banquet, and I will leave off speaking of them in order to recount a moving spectacle that seemed to me most special of all. It was this: From the door where all the other things had entered there came with great strides a huge giant, without any artifice that I could see, dressed in a long robe of green-striped silk. On his head he wore a turban in the manner of the Saracens of Granada, in his left hand he held an enormous, old-fashioned mace, and with his right hand he led an elephant draped with silk. On the elephant there was a castle, in which there was a woman dressed like a nun in white satin. Over this she wore a cloak of black cloth, and her head was bound with a white kerchief in the style of Burgundy or of a nun. As soon as she entered the hall and saw the noble company gathered there she said with some urgency to the giant who led her:

> Giant, I wish to stop here,
> because I see a noble company
> that I must speak to.
> Giant, I wish to stop here;
> I want to tell them and warn them
> about something that needs full well to be heard.
> Giant, I wish to stop here,
> for I see a noble company.

When the giant heard the lady speak, he looked at her in great fear, and he did not stop until he came before the table of the Duke. There were gathered many people marveling and wondering who the lady could be. As soon as her elephant had stopped she began a lament with the words written here:

> Alas! Alas! I am saddened,
> woebegone, far from pleasure, tormented,
> desolate, the most unhappy
>   of all!
> Each of you looks and sees me,
> yet none recognizes me;
> you all leave me in these straits
>   where I languish
> as no one living has ever languished before.
> My heart is pressed with bitterness and cruelty,
> my eyes melt and I grow pale,
>   as you can see.
> Hear my plaint, you whom I gaze upon;
> help me without dissembling;
> weep for my woe, for I am the Holy Church,
>   your Mother,
> brought to ruin and bitter sadness,
> trampled by harsh abuse;

and my awful grievances I bear, suffer, endure
on your behalf.

    •   •   •   •   •

O noble Duke of Burgundy,
son of the Church, brother to its children,
hear me, and consider my need!
Let your heart feel the shame,
the grieving remorse that I carry in my breast!
Infidels by hundreds and thousands
triumph in their damnèd land,
where once I was wont to be honored.

And you, powerful and honored princes,
grieve at my pain, weep at my sorrow!

    •   •   •   •   •

When I saw this action (that is, of Mother Church), and a castle on the back
of so strange a beast, I wondered whether I could fathom what it all meant. I
think it must be understood this way: The beast, exceedingly different and
strange to us, in leading the lady away signifies that she struggles against many
great adversities; in this she plays the role of Constantinople, whose adversities
we know well. Her castle signifies Faith. In addition, the armed giant leading
her gives us to understand that she fears the arms of the Turks who hunt her
and seek to destroy her.

43 Paolo Cortesi

Paolo Cortesi, born in Rome in 1465, grew up in a literary family and by the
age of seventeen had assumed a position at the papal court as "scriptor aposto-
licus." He remained in papal service until 1503, when he retired to a villa near
San Gimignano in Tuscany. There he died in 1510.

In the 1490s, Cortesi hosted at his house in Rome a loosely knit academy of
aristocratic literati in which music played an important role (see no. 44 below,
pp. 322–23). He corresponded with some of the most renowned humanistic
scholars of his day, including Ermolao Barbaro and Angelo Poliziano, wrote
poems in Italian and Latin, and produced Latin treatises and dialogues on subjects as diverse as astrology and Italian literary history. *Three Books on the Car-
dinalate,* published at Cortesi's villa in the months after his death, is a handbook
of comportment for cardinals—a kind of sacred analogue to Castiglione's
Cortegiano (see no. 45 below, pp. 325–30). It is written in a relentlessly pure
Ciceronian Latin that Poliziano, a more flexible and expert Latin stylist, criticized for its slavish adherence to Cicero's vocabulary. This adherence requires,
in Cortesi's discussion of the music appropriate for a cardinal's mealtime, elabo-

rate circumlocutions for modern names of instruments, musical genres, and so forth. Luckily, marginalia in the original edition explain many of these round-about expressions; where needed they are included in this translation in brackets.

Cortesi's musical categories are significant. In instrumental music he describes the different effects of various instruments. He categorizes vocal music in two ways: according to ancient doctrines of the differing effects of Dorian, Phrygian, and Lydian modes; and according to the bifurcated traditions of his own milieu, which separated polyphonic composition of masses and motets by composers such as Josquin, Jacob Obrecht, and Heinrich Isaac from the solo singing of vernacular poetry with instrumental accompaniment. Revealingly, Cortesi finds more compelling effects in the latter tradition than in the former.

FROM *Three Books on the Cardinalate*
(1510)

BOOK 2

. . . Since at this time those things must be sought after by which a cheerful mood is usually aroused, it may well be inquired whether the pleasure of music should be put to use particularly at this point, inasmuch as many, estranged from the natural disposition of the normal sense, not only reject it [music] because of some sad perversion of their nature, but even think it to be hurtful for the reason that it is somehow an invitation to idle pleasure, and above all, that its merriment usually arouses the evil of lust. On the opposite side, however, many agree to resort to it as to a certain discipline that is engaged in the knowledge of concordance and modes.

Indeed, we are convinced that music should be put to use at this time [after meals] for the sake not only of merriment, but also of knowledge and morals. . . . Music must be sought after for the sake of morals, inasmuch as the habit of passing judgment on what is similar to morals in its rational basis cannot be considered to be different from the habit of passing judgment on the rational basis of morals themselves, and of becoming expert in this latter judgment through imitation. Also, since the melodious modes of music appear to imitate all the habits of morals and all the motions of passions, there is no doubt that to be entertained by a temperate combination of modes would also mean to get in the habit of passing judgment on the rational basis of morals. This can

TEXT: *De cardinalatu libri tres* (Castel Cortesiano, 1510), fols. 72v–74v; in Nino Pirrotta, "Music and Cultural Tendencies in Fifteenth-Century Italy," *Journal of the American Musicological Society* 19 (1966): pp. 152–55. Translation by Nino Pirrotta. Reprinted by permission of the American Musicological Society.

also be proved, inasmuch as it is evident that all the habits and motions of the soul are found in the nature of the modes, in which nature the similarity to fortitude, or temperance, or anger, or mildness is exhibited, and it can easily be observed and judged that the minds of men are usually brought to those motions just as they are excited by the action of the modes. Nor can there be any doubt that things resembling each other are forced to be such in fact by the very closeness of their affinity.

But, since the kind of modes to be used is twofold, one that is produced by hand, and a second one consisting in the manner of singing, it must be understood that the senators must be engaged in listening to the kind of sounding things [instruments] in which the criterion in the combination of modes can be found more stable, and the mind is freer in its judgment. Concerning this, one must avoid, in those free moments devoted to music, those genres in which the sense of the ear seems to be stunned, and which are, too, most divergent from the rationale of morals. In this class *barbiti* and *pentades* are usually listed, which offend the discriminating ear with the aggressiveness of their notes and with an inordinate sound.[1] And so, those pneumatic genres [organs] can be more useful to the senators, in which tin pipes are usually assembled as it were in the shape of a castle; the which pipes, while they are made most apt to receive and emit the air, amplify the sounds, repeating them high and low. In touching them Isachius [Isaac of Byzantium], son of the peripatetic Argyropylos, stands out for his regular combination of modes. Those who admire most highly Dominicus Venetus or Daniel Germanus usually in their praise omit the fact that they make intemperate use of quick runs, by which the sense of the ear is filled with variety, but the artful modes cannot be knowingly discerned. Indeed, also those genres [clavichord] can be praised that are made out of wood in the shape of an ancient vase, out of which the pressure of the fingers extracts distinct sounds of strings. Which genres, however, are very far from the gravity of the pneumatic genres, because the percussion on them is sooner released, and ending produces a shorter sound. Most renowned in this genre is the precise agility of Laurentius Cordubensis.

Also in the same group are placed those genres [lutes] which can be considered as resembling certain fast ships, and are judged to have the most delightful impact on the ear; for those sure-fingered proceedings, now repetition, now stopping, now lessening and almost interlacing of sounds, are in the habit of creeping easily into the minds of men with their exquisite sweetness. Which genre, indeed, has been more knowingly revived into artistic perfection by our generation, and is acknowledged as the first genre of playing that can be praised for the way in which it is arranged and put together. They say that it was first established by Balthasar and Joannes Maria, both surnamed Ger-

---

1. The *barbiton* is a classic kithara-like instrument, but I have been unable to find any reference to *pentades;* unless this is a misreading for *pektides*, it is my suspicion, enhanced by Cortesi's outspoken dislike for the instrument, that it might be a Hellenization of *quinterne* or *guinterne*, unusual names (at least in Italy) for the popular guitar. [Tr.]

manus, so that the simple repetition in the high region used by the ancients would be joined by a connection of all single sounds from the lower region, and from the latter a combined symphony would flourish more richly. Before them, in fact, Petrus Bonus Ferrariensis,[2] and those who derived from him, often availed themselves of the repetition in the high region; nor was this mode of harmonizing all the individual sounds yet known, by which the sense of the ear can best be filled with perfect sweetness. Almost the same could be said of the Spanish lyre, were it not that its equal and soft sweetness is usually rejected by the satiety of the ear, and its uniformity is longer than it could be desired by the limits imposed by the ear.

The manner of singing, now, is divided into a tripartite description, according to which one manner is called Phrygian, the second Lydian, and the third Dorian. Phrygian is the one in which the spirits of the listeners are usually distracted by the fiercest straining of notes. Of which kind is that music of which French musicians make use by traditional rule in the palatine chapel on the holidays of Christmas and Easter. The Lydian one can be considered to be of two kinds, one that is called complex and the second simple. Complex is the one in which the souls are induced to weeping and compassion by a mode inflected toward sorrows; such may be considered the one in which the papal *novendilia*[3] or the senatorial *parentalia*[4] is customarily celebrated. Of this lugubrious manner of singing did the nation of the Spaniards always make use. Simple is that manner that results in a rather languid modulation; thus we saw to be inflected those verses of P. Maro, which used to be sung, on suggestion of Ferdinand II of Naples by the poet Caritheus.[5] And finally the Dorian manner is by far more restrained in plain moderation; such, as they say, is to be considered that manner that was established by Saint Gregory in the holy . . . (*aberruncatorium?*) in a stately rule of singing.

Concerning these things, our generation divides and distinguishes the whole manner of singing into propitiatory songs, precentorial songs, and sung poems. Propitiatory songs [masses] are those in which all kinds of modes, mensurations, and imitations are employed, and in which praise is given to the genus of musicians for devising the singing most admirably; hence, not without reason Cardinal Giovanni dei Medici, a knowledgeable man in the learned consideration of musical matters, believes that no one should be included in the number of the most eminent musicians, who is not very conversant with the making of the propitiatory mode. And so, just for this reason, they say that Josquin of France was the one who excelled among many, because more science was put

2. That is, Pietrobono dal Chitarrino, a lutenist-singer active in the mid-fifteenth century especially at the Ferrarese court.
3. Nine days of mourning for the death of a pope. [Tr.]
4. Annual memorial services for dead cardinals. [Tr.]
5. Maro is Publius Vergilius Maro, or Virgil. Caritheus, or (Il) Cariteo, is the poet-singer Benedetto Gareth, a leading literary figure and courtier in the Naples of Ferdinand of Aragon; on his participation in the academic scene there see no. 44 below (Calmeta), pp. 323–24.

by him in the propitiatory genres of singing than is usually put into it by the unskilled zeal of recent musicians. Then, those songs [motets] are called pre-centorial which, although mixed with the propitiatory singing, can be seen to be supernumerary and ingrafted, since for them there is free option of choice; and for this reason it happens, they say, that those modes all of one kind, on which the propitiatory songs unremittingly insist, are not preserved by them. In this genre Jacob Obrecht is considered great for varied subtlety, but more crude in the whole style of composition, and also he is considered to be the one by whom more of the sharpest agreeableness has been sowed among the musicians than would have been enough for the pleasure of the ear—like, in the field of taste, people who seem to like those things that taste of unripe juice better than sugar. For a similar inclination Heinrich Isaac of France is judged to be most apt to compose such precentorial songs; for, in addition to being much quicker than all the others in pouring forth this genre, his style of composition brightens the singing so floridly that it more than satiates the ordinary capacity of the ear. But, although he is the one who excels among many, nevertheless we know that it happens to be blamed on him that he uses in this genre *catachresis*[6] and repetition of modes more liberally than the most the ear can take without sensing annoyance because of uniformity in what it listens to. Nor are Alexander Agricola, Antonius Brumel, Loyset Compère, Jo. Spataro of Bologna far away from such musical praise; although one of them gets more credit than the other for either art or suavity in composing, and one is more acceptable than the other for his borrowing or novelty of paraphrase, all have expertly practiced in this precentorial genre, from which many things can be transferred for the use of the senator.

Finally, those modes usually listed as modes of sung poems that mainly consist of the measure of the octastics or ternaries.[7] Which genre Francesco Petrarca is said to have first established as he sang his exalted poems on the lute. But of late Seraphinus Aquilanus was the originator of the renewal of this genre, by whom such a controlled conjunction of words and songs was woven that there could be nothing sweeter than the manner of his modes. And so, such a multitude of imitative court singers emanated from him that whatever is seen to be sung in this genre in all Italy appears to be born out of the model of his sung poems and melodic modes. For which reason, it can be rightly said that the motions of the souls are usually appeased and excited with more vehemence by the *carmina* produced in this genre; for, when the rhythms of the words and sentences are combined with the sweetness of the melodic modes, nothing can prevent the audience from being exceedingly moved because of the power of the ear and the song's similarity to the soul. And this

6. Literally, improper use of words. [Tr.]

7. Cortesi's *ocstaticorum aut trinariorum ratio* must refer to two of the most prominent fixed forms of Italian sung poetry around 1500: *strambotti*, stanzas of eight eleven-syllable lines typically rhymed *abababcc;* and *capitoli*, stanzas of three eleven-syllable lines with the interlocking rhyme-scheme of Dante's *terza rima: aba bcb cdc* etc.

usually happens quite often when either vehement motions are represented in the singing by the verses, or souls are exhorted to the learning of morals and knowledge, on which human happiness is dependent.

44 Vincenzo Calmeta

Two of the courtiers who frequented Cortesi's academy in the early 1490s were Vincenzo Colli, called Calmeta (ca. 1460–1508), a poet and literary commentator of some stature, and Serafino Ciminelli, called Aquilano after his city of birth (1466–1500), the most renowned poet-singer of the waning fifteenth century. The two became fast friends, Serafino even living with Calmeta when he temporarily lost the support of his chief patron, Cardinal Ascanio Sforza. They were reunited in the mid-1490s at the glittering Milanese court of Lodovico Sforza ("il Moro"), where the Duchess Beatrice d'Este presided over a self-conscious revival of Italian poetry and oratory.

Serafino's untimely death inspired an outpouring of elegies that were collected in a commemorative volume of 1504, for which Calmeta prepared his brief biography. It also stimulated a rage for Serafino's poetry that saw some twenty editions of it published between 1502 and 1513. These show no glimpse of the musical settings, probably semi-improvised, that Serafino had provided for his words. Perhaps their style is reflected in the music setting several of Serafino's lyrics that survives in manuscript and print from around 1500. Or perhaps the excerpts here from Calmeta's *Life,* along with Cortesi's remarks on Serafino (no. 43 above, p. 320), are some of the broadest hints we have to fill this lacuna. Calmeta's *Life* also sketches a lively picture of professional emulation and competition among the singer-poets of the time.

FROM *Life of the Fertile Vernacular Poet Serafino Aquilano*
(1504)

Serafino Aquilano, descended from a very honorable family, was born in Aquila, a city of Abruzzo, in the year of our salvation 1466, when Paul II sat on the Pontifical Throne and Frederick reigned as Roman Emperor. Before he

TEXT: *Vita del facondo poeta volgare Serafino Aquilano,* in Vincenzo Calmeta, *Prose e lettere edite e inedite,* ed. Cecil Grayson (Bologna: Commissione per i testi di lingua, 1959), pp. 60–77. Translation by Gary Tomlinson.

even had the first rudiments of grammar[1] he was taken to the Kingdom of Naples by an uncle named Paul, who gave him to the Count of Potenza, governing there, to serve as page. This Count was an important prince who, though only in the flower of his youth, was so inclined to every virtue that all in his retinue, imitating their master, competed to see who could embody some new virtue. Amidst this praiseworthy school, with its varied pursuits, Serafino devoted himself to music under the tutelage of a certain Fleming named Guglielmo,[2] a most famous musician at that time. In a few years he made such progress that he excelled every other Italian musician in composing songs. Returning to his homeland of Aquila, where he stayed for three years,[3] he gave himself over to learning all the sonnets, canzoni, and *Trionfi* of Petrarch, which he not only knew extremely well but accompanied so beautifully with music that hearing him sing to his lute surpassed all other harmony. Moved then by a desire to seek his fortune he went to Rome. There he stayed in the house of a Bolognese Jerusalemite Knight named Nestor Malvezzo until he was taken into the service of Cardinal Ascanio Sforza. With him Serafino persevered for three years in anger and annoyance—since, their natures being different, the Cardinal (like most princes, and not unjustly) wanted Serafino to conform to his own ways, while the poet's forceful character suffered unwillingly such subjection.

•   •   •   •   •

It was necessary at that time[4] for Cardinal Ascanio to go to Lombardy, and while in Milan Serafino befriended a notable Neapolitan gentleman named Andrea Coscia, a soldier of Duke Lodovico Sforza, who sang sweetly to the lute in various styles including strambotti of Il Cariteo.[5] Serafino not only took this style from him, adding more polish to it, but devoted himself with such passion and labor to composing his own strambotti that he had the good fortune to win great fame in this style. He fell in love at this time with a woman of questionable virtue named Laura. She was the wife of the Milanese gentleman Pietro da Birago and was a very sweet and graceful singer; in his love for her he composed the airs and words of several strambotti. But, overindulging in such ways, he was seriously wounded in the face one night by an assailant whose identity and motive could not be discovered.

The wound healed after a short time, though it left a large scar, and Serafino returned to Rome with Cardinal Ascanio. Frequenting his usual haunts there, he not only seemed novel but aroused much admiration throughout Rome for having brought a new style of singing and raised the strambotto to a higher level. There flourished at the same time in Rome an academy in the house of

---

1. In 1478. I have taken this and the following dates from the entry "Ciminelli, Serafino," by Magda Vigilante, in the *Dizionario biografico degli italiani*.
2. This is Guglielmo Garnier, friend of Tinctoris and Gafori and active as a music teacher in Naples.
3. 1481–84.
4. 1490.
5. On Il Cariteo see No. 43 above (Cortesi) p. 319, n. 5.

Paolo Cortesi, a youth so much revered at court for his learning, status, and cordiality that his was rather called a center of eloquence and a refuge of all noble virtues than the mere home of a courtier. Every day a multitude of lofty spirits gathered there: Gianlorenzo Veneto, Pietro Gravina, Bishop Montepiloso, Agapito Gerardino, Manilio, Cornelio,[6] and many other erudite men, in whose shadows other younger men, eager to enlarge their own virtue, also lingered to enjoy themselves. Among vernacular poets the ardors of Aretino were held in greatest esteem, while my own fragments also enjoyed some little praise. Therefore Serafino, who spent more time with me than with anyone else, determined to participate in this academy, which afforded such recreation to its worthy members; thenceforth he often introduced the harmony of his music and wit of his strambotti into the arduous debates of those other literati. This only increased his reputation, as all those wise men strived to write strambotti with more recondite sentiments than his. And even though he had such a hurdle and paragon as Aretino to face, and such friendly emulation as Cortesi's and mine, nevertheless he was inferior to no poet of the present century in this style; what is more, there was a time when anyone who heard a new strambotto attributed it to Serafino no matter who had composed it, not out of ill will but admiration.

Many players and singers saw that Serafino's fame came from the force of his recitation more than from his composing, and that that style delighted princes, wise men, and beautiful women. So they set themselves to imitate him and by learning his airs learned his words as well; therefore in a short time his verses were scattered throughout Italy not only by himself but by many other *citaredi*.[7] But Serafino was not yet content with his Burchiellesque sonnets,[8] his ballate, and his strambotti and determined not only to sniff at but to taste and digest all other styles. During one Carnival season, having decided to leave Cardinal Ascanio, he wrote an eclogue that begins "Tell me, my Menander" in imitation of Jacopo Sannazaro, at that time the leader in bucolic verse. In his eclogue Serafino criticized behind a veil of poetic artifice the greed and other detestable vices of the court at Rome; he recited it during Carnival with the backing of Cardinal Colonna, and with it he aroused new admiration.

•   •   •   •   •

At that time[9] the governor of Abruzzo was Ferdinand of Aragon, later the second of that name to be King of Naples. News of Serafino's fame reached

---

6. For the identification of these various Roman prelates, church functionaries, literati, and academicians see Calmeta, *Prose e lettere*, ed. Grayson, "Indice de nomi."

7. With this classicizing term, referring to the ancient Greek lyre-like kithara, Calmeta no doubt embraces poets who accompanied themselves either on the lute or on the bowed *lira da braccio*. The latter instrument was also called *viola da braccio*; see no. 45 below (Castiglione), p. 328, n. 11.

8. The reference is to Domenico di Giovanni, called il Burchiello (1404–1449), author of a body of sonnets whose materials range from political satire and literary caricature to virtuosic nonsense-rhymes. His poems were first published in 1475 and reprinted many times over the following centuries.

9. 1493.

him and, being a prince of high ideals endowed with all the graces nature and good fortune can give, he turned his every thought to bringing Serafino to his court. There Serafino remained, in great favor and well rewarded, for three years. In Naples there flourished yet another academy of literati where Jacopo Sannazaro, Attilio Musefilo, Cariteo, and many other learned and perceptive minds gathered under the authority and reverence of Pontano in the Portico Antoniano.[10] But those who were foremost not only in Latin but in vernacular poetry were Sannazaro, Francesco Caracciolo, and Cariteo. Seeing that Serafino soothed with his poems not only common but learned ears as well, and suspecting perhaps that these poems when written down would not bear closer scrutiny, they studied and discussed in various manners his compositions. The result was always a positive verdict, praising Serafino's natural gifts more than his industry.

·　·　·　·　·

Seeing that amorous sonnets were prized, and thinking either that his facility would well enable him to follow that style or that he could with it better enflame the breasts of beautiful young women, Serafino decided to try his hand at some such sonnets in emulation of the ingenious poet Tebaldeo.[11] He won as much renown in these as he had in composing strambotti. I do not deny that they often did not measure up to Tebaldeo's in invention; nonetheless in their disposition they are so well accommodated to their subject matter that they deserve praise for this rather than blame for their weaknesses, if weaknesses they be. Indeed the prince of poets observed this same style of writing, as Macrobius describes at length in his *Saturnalia*.[12] Moreover Serafino's poems and Tebaldeo's cannot tell us whether or not he equalled Tebaldeo in this emulation, since where in the one we find more invention, doctrine, continuity and workmanship, in the other we discern more passion, grace, fullness of verse and natural gift.

·　·　·　·　·

Having attained the age of thirty-five, Serafino died of a pestiferous tertian fever, to the great sadness of the whole Roman court. Receiving the sacraments, he left his body on earth, and his soul returned whence it came on the day of San Lorenzo in the year of our salvation 1500.

---

10. Jacopo Sannazaro and Giovanni Pontano were the leading literary lights of the Neapolitan intelligentsia in the late fifteenth century. Sannazaro is chiefly remembered today for his Italian pastoral romance *L'Arcadia*, which spawned many imitations through the sixteenth century (including Sir Philip Sydney's huge *Arcadia*); Pontano was an expert Latinist who wrote treatises, dialogues, and poems on astrology, philosophy, politics, and other topics. The gathering place of the academy, the "Portico Antoniano," was named after its founder Antonio Panormita (see Giovanni Pontano, *Dialoge,* ed. Hermann Kiefer [Munich: W. Fink, 1984], p. 30).

11. The Petrarchan lyricist Antonio Tebaldeo (1463–1537), active chiefly at Ferrara and Mantua.

12. The reference is to Virgil; see *Saturnalia,* esp. bks. 3–6.

* * * * *

In reciting his poems he was so passionate and matched the music with the words so judiciously that he moved equally the souls of his listeners, whether wise or mediocre or plebeian or female. And though he competed with many poets, nevertheless he was not of a contentious or evil nature. . . . With this alone I conclude: I believe there never was another poet more successful than he in expressing his thoughts. All his efforts were bent on achieving fame in his lifetime, even if his repute reached only the mediocre and plebeian; and he had the great satisfaction of reaching his goal, giving great account of himself wherever he went. His death was widely lamented by contemporary poets, who thereby saw our age stripped of no small ornament. . . .

45 Baldassare Castiglione

Born in 1478 near Mantua, the descendant of an old and distinguished family, Baldassare Castiglione is one of the most influential figures of Renaissance court life. After an education in the Milan of Ludovico Sforza, he served successively at the courts of Mantua and Urbino (1499–1513) and, as ambassador of Urbino's Duke Francesco Maria della Rovere, at the papal court of Leo X. In 1525 he traveled to Spain as the pope's envoy to the court of Charles V. He died in Toledo in 1529.

Castiglione wrote poetry in Italian and Latin; vivid letters that reveal much about the society in which he moved; and a dramatic eclogue, *Tirsi,* that was staged at Urbino in 1506. His claim to lasting fame, however, rests on *Il libro del cortegiano (The Book of the Courtier).* The on-again off-again genesis of this work began soon after 1508 and ended around 1524. In the following years the book circulated in manuscript, and it was finally published in 1528 with the assistance of Pietro Bembo (see no. 47 below, pp. 332–33). In the *Cortegiano* Castiglione draws in lively dialogues a picture of the ideal courtier, the aristocratic woman, and the relations of courtier and prince. The book professes to be an account of discussions held at the ducal palace in Urbino on four evenings in 1507. The personages depicted are all more or less conspicuous historical figures, including Vincenzo Calmeta and Bembo. In their discussions about music, song, and dance, Castiglione leaves little doubt about the importance these activities assumed at the court of Urbino and in his view of Renaissance courtly society in general. In his specific opinions, Castiglione, like Paolo Cortesi, reserves the highest praise for solo singing with instrumental accompaniment.

FROM *Il libro del cortegiano*

(1528)

BOOK 1

CHAPTER 47

At this they all laughed. And the Count, beginning afresh:

"My lords (quoth he), you must think I am not pleased with the Courtier if he be not also a musician, and besides his understanding and cunning upon the book, have skill in like manner on sundry instruments. For if we weigh it well, there is no ease of labors and medicines of feeble minds to be found more honest and more praiseworthy in time of leisure than it. And principally in courts, where (beside the refreshing of vexations that music bringeth unto each man) many things are taken in hand to please women withal, whose tender and soft breasts are soon pierced with melody and filled with sweetness. Therefore no marvel that in the old days and nowadays they have always been inclined to musicians, and counted this a most acceptable food of the mind."

Then the Lord Gaspar:

"I believe music (quoth he) together with many other vanities is meet for women, and peradventure for some also that have the likeness of men, but not for them that be men indeed; who ought not with such delicacies to womanish their minds and bring themselves in that sort to dread death."

"Speak it not," answered the Count. "For I shall enter into a large sea of the praise of music and call to rehearsal how much it hath always been renowned among them of old time and counted a holy matter;[1] and how it hath been the opinion of most wise philosophers that the world is made of music, and the heavens in their moving make a melody, and our soul framed after the very same sort, and therefore lifteth up itself and (as it were) reviveth the virtues and force of it with music. Wherefore it is written that Alexander was sometime so fervently stirred with it that (in a manner) against his will he was forced to arise from banquets and run to weapon, afterward the musician changing the stroke and his manner of tune, pacified himself again and returned from weapon to banqueting.[2] And I shall tell you that grave Socrates when he was

TEXT: The reprint of the original edition of the translation of Sir Thomas Hoby (London, 1561), as published in *Tudor Translations* 23 (London: D. Nutt, 1900). In his notes Strunk made some use of those of Michele Scherillo's edition of *Il cortegiano* (Milan: U. Hoepli, 1928).

1. Quintilian, *Institutio oratoria* 1.10.9. From here to the end of Chapter 47 Castiglione follows, with many omissions and a few additions, *Institutio oratoria* 1.10.9–33.

2. Variously reported, although not in this form, by Seneca, Dio Chrysostom, Plutarch, and Suidas, the musician being sometimes Xenophantes, sometimes Timotheus, and sometimes Antigenedes. As told by Castiglione and other writers of his time, the story appears to come ultimately from St. Basil, *To Young Men (Ad adolescentes)* 8.7–8: "Once when he was playing the Phrygian mode to Alexander on his flute, he caused the prince, as it is said, to leap up and rush to his arms in the midst of a banquet, and then, by relaxing the harmony, brought him back again to

well stricken in years learned to play upon the harp.[3] And I remember I have understood that Plato and Aristotle will have a man that is well brought up, to be also a musician; and declare with infinite reasons the force of music to be to very great purpose in us, and for many causes (that should be too long to rehearse) ought necessarily to be learned from a man's childhood, not only for the superficial melody that is heard, but to be sufficient to bring into us a new habit that is good and a custom inclining to virtue, which maketh the mind more apt to the conceiving of felicity, even as bodily exercise maketh the body more lusty, and not only hurteth not civil matters and warlike affairs, but is a great stay to them. Also Lycurgus in his sharp laws allowed music.[4] And it is read that the Lacedemons, which were valiant in arms, and the Cretenses used harps and other soft instruments;[5] and many most excellent captains of old time (as Epaminondas) gave themselves to music; and such as had not a sight in it (as Themistocles) were a great deal the less set by.[6] Have you not read that among the first instructions which the good old man Chiron taught Achilles in his tender age, whom he had brought up from his nurse and cradle, music was one? And the wise master would have those hands that should shed so much Trojan blood to be oftentimes occupied in playing upon the harp?[7] What soldier is there (therefore) that will think it a shame to follow Achilles, omitting many other famous captains that I could allege? Do ye not then deprive our Courtier of music, which doth not only make sweet the minds of men, but also many times wild beasts tame; and whoso savoreth it not, a man may assuredly think him not to be well in his wits. Behold, I pray you, what force it hath, that in times past allured a fish to suffer a man to ride upon him through the tempestuous sea.[8] We may see it used in the holy temples to render laud and thanks unto God, and it is a credible matter that it is acceptable unto Him, and that He hath given it unto us for a most sweet lightening of our travails and vexations. So that many times the boisterous laborers in the fields in the heat of the sun beguile their pain with rude and carterlike singing. With this the unmannerly countrywoman that ariseth before day out of her sleep to spin and card, defendeth herself and maketh her labor pleasant. This is the most sweet pastime after rain, wind, and tempest unto the miserable mariners. With this do the weary pilgrims comfort themselves in their troublesome and long voyages. And oftentimes prisoners in adversity, in fetters, and in stocks. In like

---

his boon companions." Trans. Roy J. DeFerrari and Martin R. P. McGuire in *Saint Basil: The letters* (4 vols., Cambridge, Mass.: Harvard University Press, 1926–34). For the version of Suidas see no. 72 below (Galilei) p. 466, n. 10.

3. Quintilian, *Institutio oratoria* 1.10.13–14.

4. Ibid., 1.10.15.

5. Often reported; see Athenaeus, *Deipnosophists* 14.626.

6. Cicero, *Tusculan Disputations* 1.2.4. See also Quintilian, *Institutio oratoria* 1.10.19.

7. See no. 37 above (Zarlino) p. 299, n. 31.

8. The reference is to Arion's rescue by a musically inclined dolphin; see no. 37 above (Zarlino), p. 299, n. 30.

manner for a greater proof that the tunableness of music (though it be but rude) is a very great refreshing of all worldly pains and griefs, a man would judge that nature had taught it unto nurses for a special remedy to the continual wailings of sucking babes, which at the sound of their voices fall into a quiet and sweet sleep, forgetting the tears that are so proper to them, and given us of nature in that age for a guess of the rest of our life to come."[9]

CHAPTER 48

Here the Count pausing awhile the Lord Julian said:

"I am not of the Lord Gaspar's opinion, but I believe for the reasons you allege and for many others, that music is not only an ornament, but also necessary for a Courtier. But I would have you declare how this and the other qualities which you appoint him are to be practised, and at what time, and in what sort. Because many things that of themselves be worthy praise, oftentimes in practising them out of season seem most foolish. And contrariwise, some things that appear to be of small moment, in the well applying them are greatly esteemed."

BOOK 2

CHAPTER 13

. . . "Methink," answered Sir Frederick, "pricksong[10] is a fair music, so it be done upon the book surely and after a good sort. But to sing to the lute[11] is much better, because all the sweetness consisteth in one alone, and a man is much more heedful and understandeth better the feat manner and the air or vein of it when the ears are not busied in hearing any more than one voice; and beside, every little error is soon perceived, which happeneth not in singing with company, for one beareth out another. But singing to the lute with the ditty[12] (methink) is more pleasant than the rest, for it addeth to the words such a grace and strength that it is a great wonder. Also all instruments with frets[13] are full of harmony, because the tunes of them are very perfect, and with ease a man may do many things upon them that fill the mind with the sweetness of music. And the music of a set of viols[14] doth no less delight a man, for it is very sweet and artificial. A man's breast giveth a great ornament and grace to all these instruments, in the which I will have it sufficient that our Courtier have an understanding. Yet the more cunning he is upon them, the better it is for him, without meddling much with the instruments that Minerva and Alcibiades

---

9. St. John Chrysostom, *Exposition of Psalm XLI.*
10. That is, song from a "pricked" or written score. Castiglione has *il cantar bene a libro sicuramente e con bella maniera.*
11. Castiglione has *il cantare alla viola.* The instrument in question is the *viola* or *lira da braccio,* a bowed instrument favored in Italy around 1500 for the accompaniment of solo song.
12. Castiglione has *il cantare alla viola per recitare.*
13. Castiglione's *tutti gli strumenti di tasti* probably refers to fretted plucked string instruments, as Hoby interprets it, and not keyboard instruments, as modern Italian usage of *tasto* would suggest.
14. Castiglione has *quattro viole da arco.*

refused,[15] because it seemeth they are noisome. Now as touching the time and season when these sorts of music are to be practised, I believe at all times when a man is in familiar and loving company, having nothing else ado. But especially they are meet to be practised in the presence of women, because those sights sweeten the minds of the hearers and make them the more apt to be pierced with the pleasantness of music, and also they quicken the spirits of the very doers. I am well pleased (as I have said) they flee the multitude, and especially of the unnoble. But the seasoning of the whole must be discretion, because in effect it were a matter unpossible to imagine all cases that fall. And if the Courtier be a righteous judge of himself, he shall apply himself well enough to the time and shall discern when the hearers' minds are disposed to give ear and when they are not. He shall know his age, for (to say the truth) it were no meet matter, but an ill sight to see a man of any estimation being old, hoarheaded and toothless, full of wrinkles, with a lute in his arms[16] playing upon it and singing in the midst of a company of women, although he could do it reasonably well. And that because such songs contain in them words of love, and in old men love is a thing to be jested at, although otherwhile he seemeth among other miracles of his to take delight in spite of years to set afire frozen hearts."

Then answered the Lord Julian:

"Do you not bar poor old men from this pleasure, Sir Frederick, for in my time I have known men of years have very perfect breasts and most nimble fingers for instruments, much more than some young men."

"I go not about," quoth Sir Frederick, "to bar old men from this pleasure, but I will bar you these ladies from laughing at that folly. And in case old men will sing to the lute,[17] let them do it secretly, and only to rid their minds of those troublesome cares and grievous disquietings that our life is full of and to taste of that excellence which I believe Pythagoras and Socrates favored in music. And set case they exercise it not at all, for that they have gotten a certain habit and custom of it, they shall savor it much better in hearing than he that hath no knowledge in it. For like as the arms of a smith that is weak in other things, because they are more exercised, be stronger than another body's that is sturdy but not exercised to work with his arms, even so the ears that be exercised in music do much better and sooner discern it and with much more pleasure judge of it than other, how good and quick soever they be, that have not been practised in the variety of pleasant music; because those musical tunes pierce not, but without leaving any taste of themselves, pass by the ears not accustomed to hear them, although the very wild beasts feel some delight in melody. This is therefore the pleasure meet for old men to take in music. The selfsame I say of dancing, for indeed these exercises ought to be left of before age constraineth us to leave them whether we will or no."

---

15. The auloi (i.e., for Castiglione, wind instruments in general); for the story, see Plutarch, *Life of Alcibiades.*
16. Castiglione has *con una viola in braccio.*
17. Castiglione has *cantare alla viola.*

46 Francis I, King of France

The history of late Renaissance music is also—and fundamentally—a history of print technology and its impact. Beginning in 1501, when Ottaviano Petrucci released in Venice the first volume of music printed from movable type, thousands of collections of masses, motets, frottolas, chansons, madrigals, and other works poured forth from presses across Europe. The sheer volume of music that has come down to us in sixteenth-century prints dwarfs the repertory surviving in fifteenth-century manuscripts and no doubt exceeds the extant corpus from the seventeenth century, when economic decline across much of Europe shrank the music-printing industry along with many other commercial enterprises.

Petrucci's printing method, though it yielded beautiful results, was slow and costly: the staves, notes, and in some cases even the words of vocal works all required separate impressions on each sheet. Andrea Antico, Petrucci's first Italian competitor, chose another labor-intensive method: he did not use movable type at all, but engraved whole pages of music on wooden blocks and printed from them. It was left to Pierre Attaingnant (ca. 1494–1551 or 1552), the first French printer of music from movable type, to perfect a new, less expensive method in which staves, notes, and text could be printed in a single impression. Attaingnant's was the method of choice through the rest of the century.

Attaingnant brought out his first volume of chansons in April 1528; other volumes quickly followed. The next year he was granted a privilege from Francis I copyrighting the contents of his books. When it expired three years later, he petitioned for another, expanded privilege. The King's response was the six-year monopoly on music printing, dated June 18, 1531, that follows.

Royal Privilege for Music Printing to Pierre Attaingnant
(1531)

Francis, by the grace of God King of France, to the magistrates of Paris, bailiffs, seneschals, and to all other justices and officers or their lieutenants, greetings. Having received the humble supplication of our well-loved Pierre Attaingnant, printer-bookseller dwelling in the University of Paris, stating that heretofore no person in this our realm had undertaken to cut, found, and fashion notes and characters for the printing of figural music in *choses faictes* or tablatures for the playing of lutes, flutes, and organs, because of the intricate

TEXT: Daniel Heartz, "A New Attaingnant Book," *Journal of the American Musicological Society* 14 (1961): 22–23. Translation by Daniel Heartz. Reprinted by permission of the American Musicological Society.

conception, long consumption of time, and very great expenses and labors necessary to that purpose, the said suppliant, by protracted excogitation and mental effort and with very great expense, labor, and genius, has invented and brought to light the method and industry of cutting, founding, and printing the said notes and characters both of the said music and *choses faictes* as of the said tablatures for the playing of lutes, flutes, and organs, of which he has printed, has had printed, and hopes in the future to print, many books and quires of masses, motets, hymns, chansons, as well as for the said playing of lutes, flutes, and organs, in large volumes and small, in order to serve the churches, their ministers, and generally all people, and for the very great good, utility, and recreation of the general public. Nevertheless, he fears that after having brought to light his said invention and opened to other printers and booksellers the method and industry of printing the said music and tablatures, these printers and booksellers will similarly wish to attempt printing the said music in *choses faictes* and for the playing of lutes, flutes, and organs. And by this means the said suppliant would totally lose the merit of his labors and the recovery of expenses and investments which he has made and contracted for the invention and composition of the above said characters, unless he is patented and succored by us, having humbly sought our grace. Thus we, having considered these things, do not wish that the said suppliant's labors, application, expenses, and investments in the said affair go unrewarded. May he succeed in it and experience the benefit. From such causes and others stirring us to this we have willed and ordained: we will and ordain that for the time and term of six years to follow, starting with the date of this present day, other than the said suppliant or those having charge from him, may not print nor put up for sale the said books and quires of music in *choses faictes* and tablatures for the playing of lutes, flutes, and organs declared above. We charge and command therefore by these present orders that every person look to the said suppliant's enjoying and fully and tranquilly exercising the ordinance entreated from our present grace. Making strictures and prohibitions to all booksellers and other persons generally, whatever they may be, to print or put up for sale the said books and quires of music and tablature for the said time of six years without the express power and consent of the said suppliant. And this on great penalty to be levied by us and loss and confiscation of said books and quires. To the accomplishment of this all those to whom it may apply are constrained, that they may enforce it with all due ways and reasonable means. For such is our pleasure, all ordinances, restrictions, charges, or prohibitions to the contrary notwithstanding.

Given at St. Germain-en-Laye the eighteenth day of June, the year of grace fifteen hundred thirty-one, of our reign the seventeenth.

By the King, the Cardinal de Tournon, master of the Chapel of the said Seigneur, being present.

Signed

G. HAMELIN

47 Pietro Bembo

Born in Venice in 1470, Pietro Bembo was a humanist scholar, companion of Castiglione at Urbino, longtime literary lion in Padua and Venice, and finally a cardinal at Rome. He exerted a profound and lasting influence on Italian literary and courtly circles of the sixteenth century. His courtly influence sprang from his dialogues *Gli asolani* (*The Asolans,* referring to inhabitants of the town of Asolo, northeast of Venice), first published in 1505. In these dialogues he merged Neo-platonic theories of divine love from the late fifteenth century with an idealized chivalric love that had passed, via the lyrics of Dante and Petrarch, from earlier sources into Italian poetry. (The merger is eloquently summarized in the speech Castiglione had Bembo deliver in the closing pages of the *Cortegiano*.)

Bembo's literary influence emanated especially from his dialogues *Prose della volgar lingua,* first published in 1525. These "writings on the vernacular" exalted the Tuscan Italian of Petrarch (in poetry) and Boccaccio (in prose) as the preeminent Italian literary usages. The doctrines, temperament, and tastes of the *Prose* had an important impact on musical styles as well: they encouraged a decorous, motet-like demeanor and Petrarchan poetic orientation in the mid-century madrigal, an approach most monumentally embodied in Adriano Willaert's collection of madrigals and motets titled *Musica nova.*

Here Bembo writes, in a different and more pragmatic vein, to a daughter he considered overly given to musical pastimes and less than fully attentive to the domestic disciplines that would make her what, by his lights, she should aspire to be: a chaste and obedient wife. Bembo's short letter says much about the forces that circumscribed women's music-making throughout the Renaissance. These forces were complex and ambivalent. Male writers often enough associated women's singing and playing with a debilitating effeminacy or a threatening seductiveness (see for example no. 40 above [Agrippa], p. 307), but at the same time they could turn around and exalt its almost heavenly powers (no. 48 below [Doni], p. 334). Women musicians tended to be cast as either angels or sirens—or sometimes as a strange hybrid of the two.

Published books of letters were common through the sixteenth century; Bembo's began to appear in print in 1548, the year after his death, and saw several editions in the following decades. The present letter was first published in 1552.

Letter to His Daughter Elena

(1541)

I am pleased that you are well, as you relate, and that your brother attends diligently to his studies, which will all redound to his honor and profit. As to

TEXT: Pietro Bembo, *Opere in volgare,* ed. Mario Marti (Florence: Sansoni, 1961), pp. 877–78. Translation by Gary Tomlinson.

your request of me, that I give my blessing to your learning to play the mono-chord, I will explain to you something you are perhaps too young to know: playing music is for a woman a vain and frivolous thing. And I would wish you to be the most serious and chaste woman alive. Beyond this, if you do not play well your playing will give you little pleasure and not a little embarrassment. And you will not be able to play well unless you spend ten or twelve years in this pursuit without thinking of anything else. What this would mean to you you can imagine yourself without my saying more. Therefore set aside thoughts of this frivolity and work to be humble and good and wise and obedient. Don't let yourself be carried away by these desires, indeed resist them with a strong will. And if your companions want you to learn to play for their pleasure, tell them you don't wish to hear them laugh at your shame. Content yourself with writing and cooking; if you do these two pursuits well you will have accom-plished much. Thank the Sisters for their prayers for me, for which I am greatly indebted. Stay well, and greet Lucia.

December 10, 1541, Rome

48 Antonfrancesco Doni

Born in Florence in 1513, Antonfrancesco Doni spent most of his mature years in Venice and the Veneto. There (and, for a few years in the 1540s, also in Florence) he pursued a somewhat checkered career as a musician, printer, writer, academician, and general man-about-town. He died in 1574. His *Dia-logo della musica* of 1544 joins literary dialogue of the sort exemplified by Castiglione's *Cortegiano* with music printing. Its conversations are punctuated by madrigals and motets sung, in the fiction of the dialogue, by the interlocutors themselves. These characters include two Venetian madrigal composers, Giro-lamo Parabosco and Perissone Cambio.

Doni's dedicatory letter of the *Dialogo* describes his attendance at the kind of private concert that must have occurred often in aristocratic gatherings. The astoundingly novel music performed at this particular concert would appear in print fifteen years later in Willaert's *Musica nova*. We surmise this because the jealously guarded collection, circulating before its publication, was dubbed *La pecorina* after Polissena Pecorina, the singer Doni heard. Doni singles out the feature of Willaert's "new music" that was most striking to others as well: its extraordinary attention to the diction and declamation of its words.

As for Pecorina, she was a virtuosic participant of Venetian salons and musi-cal circles at least through the 1530s and '40s. She seems to have been, as Doni indicates, a respected aristocrat and not one of the numerous musically gifted courtesans for which some Venetian salons were famous. For Doni, then, music-making by a woman did not carry the stigma Bembo had attached to it in his letter to his daughter. It is ironic that Doni should effectively counter Bembo's view in the context of Willaert's most Bembian musical style.

Dialogo della musica
(1544)

DEDICATION

To Signor Annibale Marchese Malvicino

The music of lutes, instruments, pipes, flutes, and voices made in your house and that of the honorable M. Alessandro Colombo is most worthy, and the viols of San Guido della Porta are a miracle; but if you heard the divine sound I have tasted with the ears of my intellect here in Venice you would be astounded. Here there is a gentlewoman named Polissena Pecorina, wife of a citizen of my hometown, so virtuous and gentle that praises high enough to commend her cannot be found. I heard one night a concert of viols and voices in which she played and sang in the company of other excellent musicians, the flawless master of which was Adriano Willaert. The music, of his invention, in a style never before employed, was so concerted, so sweet, so just, and so miraculously appropriate to the words that I confessed never in my life to have known true harmony until that evening. The man most enthusiastic about such music, most enamored of such compositions, is a gentleman and most excellent spirit also from Florence named Neri Capponi. I was introduced to him by the nobleman Signor Francesco Corboli, and by his grace I felt, saw, and heard this divine music. This Neri spends hundreds of ducats a year on it. He keeps it close to his vest and would not give out a single song even to his father. Here, since I cannot give you that music, I give you this. I am truly sorry not to be able to demonstrate with greater means my friendship for you. Send my infinite regards to Pier'Antonio Burla, Signor Bartolomeo Cossad'occha, and all the other musicians.

April 7, 1544, Venice

Doni the Florentine

TEXT: Antonfrancesco Doni, *Dialogo della musica,* ed. Francesco Malipiero (Vienna: Universal Edition, 1964), p. 5. Translation by Gary Tomlinson. The standard account of the work is James Haar, "Notes on the 'Dialogo della musica' of Antonfrancesco Doni," *Music & Letters* 47 (1966), 198–224.

49 Gaspara Stampa

Across most of Europe, the Petrarchan and post-Petrarchan lyric poetry of the sixteenth century repeatedly plays upon the powers of music, its ability to inspire divine (or other) love, its consolations, and so forth. A theme often repeated was the male poet's praise of his beloved's singing or playing. This typical gender trajectory is reversed in the following sonnets, where it is the female poet who extols her beloved's song, but the deployment of the musical topos is otherwise entirely representative of the lyrics of the period.

Of a sizable group of women poets who achieved fame in the sixteenth century, including Vittoria Colonna, Veronica Franco, Marguerite of Navarre, and Louise Labé, Gaspara Stampa is one of the most gifted. She was born in 1523 in Padua, the daughter of a prosperous jeweler. Her father died in her childhood, and she moved with her mother to Venice. There she came to participate in the city's lively salon culture as both poet and musician. Stampa's *Rime* were first published in 1554, shortly after her premature death in the same year. They constitute a *canzoniere* of Petrarchan profile, celebrating, lamenting, and repenting of her troubled love for Collaltino di Collalto, Count of Treviso.

Two Sonnets

(1554)

HE SINGS WITH SWEETEST HARMONY

> In that noble and illustrious company
> of Graces who do make you, Count, immortal,
> one stands before the rest and spreads her wings:
> the most sweet harmony of song.
>   She every bitter, evil care in us
> can sweeten, and make light all vile things;
> she, when the harsh Euros most assails us,
> can quiet waves that just before were rough.
>   Pleasure, laughter, Venus and her Cupids
> are seen making the air around serene
> wherever her sweet accent echoes forth.
>   And I, if able to remain with you,
> would little care to make my return to
> the harmony of these celestial choirs.

TEXT: Gaspara Stampa and Veronica Franco, *Rime*, ed. Abdelkader Salza (Bari: G. Laterza, 1913), p. 20. Translation by Gary Tomlinson.

ON THE SAME THEME

She who does not know the heart's sweet rapture,
or how sweetly one forgets all pain,
or how sweetly all desires are calmed,
so that nothing still weighs on the soul,
　　Let her come, in all her best good fortune,
one time alone to listen to you, Count,
when you sweeten with your accustomed singing
the earth, the skies, and that which made all nature.
　　She'll see, at one sound of your amorous accents
the air grow quiet; and she'll see you stop
the proud waters, the tempests, and the winds.
　　And, having seen then all that you can do,
she will believe that tigers, bears, and serpents
Orpheus could have halted with his song.

50 Maddalena Casulana

The roles of women in aristocratic society and public culture were much debated in sixteenth-century Italy and France—if, usually, by men. While women could with some regularity achieve renown as poets and as performing musicians—through institutions of aristocratic prostitution such as Venetian courtesanship but also apart from them (see nos. 48 and 49 above)—it was much rarer for a woman to aspire to a professional, published career in polyphonic composition. In the dedication of the first of her three books of madrigals, Maddalena Casulana signals her awareness of this rarity and of the attitudes largely responsible for it.

Of Casulana's life we know little. She was prominent in the musical circles of Venice and Vicenza from the 1560s to the early 1580s. Already by 1568 her reputation was broad enough to extend beyond the Alps, for in that year Orlando di Lasso conducted an epithalamium of hers in Munich for the wedding of Wilhelm of Bavaria and Renée of Lorraine. Yet, if a report from Perugia in 1582 of a "Casolana famosa" who "sang divinely to the lute" refers to her, she was still young enough at that time to perform in public without censure.

The First Book of Madrigals
for Four Voices
(1568)

DEDICATION

To the Most Illustrious and Excellent Lady Donna Isabella de' Medici Orsina, Duchess of Bracciano

I truly know, Most Illustrious and Excellent Lady, that these first fruits of mine, because of their weakness, will not be able to produce the effect I desire, namely (beyond giving Your Excellency some testimony of my devotion) to expose to the world, insofar as it is given me to do so in the profession of music, the vain error of men who esteem themselves such masters of high intellectual gifts that they think women cannot share them too. In spite of their weakness, then, I have not refrained from publishing them, in the hope that the shining name of Your Excellency, to whom I dedicate them, will light them so brightly that they may enflame another, higher intellect than mine, inciting it to demonstrate clearly in practice what I have only been able to envision in my mind. Therefore, Your Excellency, welcome my candid attempt; and if from such unripe fruit I cannot gain the praise that rewards only virtuous efforts, at least grace me with the prize of your good will, so that I will be reputed most fortunate if not most skilled. I kiss Your Excellency's hand.

Venice, April 10, 1568
Your Excellency's Most Humble Servant, Maddalena Casulana

TEXT: *I madrigali di Maddalena Casulana*, ed. Beatrice Pescerelli (Florence: Leo S. Olschki, 1979), p. 7. Translation by Gary Tomlinson.

51 Charles IX, King of France; Jean-Antoine de Baïf and Joachim Thibault de Courville

The humanist impulse to emulate ancient models led to a number of Renaissance experiments with quantitative verse in modern languages. None of these was more influential than the *vers mesurés à l'antique* and accompanying *musique mesurée* pioneered from 1567 to 1570 by the poet Jean-Antoine de Baïf (1532–1589) and composer Joachim Thibault de Courville (d. 1581). Baïf believed that the fabled ethical effects of ancient music arose from the quantitative measuring of poetic lines and its reflection in musical rhythm. His measured verse in French assigned long or short values to each vowel according to certain orthographic rules; these values were to be conveyed in homophonic musical settings by rhythmic ratios of 2:1. The result in many settings was a freely additive rhythm, little constrained by metrical regularity, whose resonance can be heard in the early seventeenth-century *air de cour* and even in the recitative of later French opera.

Baïf translated the Psalter in measured verse and wrote at least three volumes of *chansonnettes mesurées*. In the years after 1575, settings of measured chansons by Courville (of whom only a few works survive), Claude le Jeune, Jacques Mauduit, and others appeared in print. Before that time, Baïf and Courville seem to have jealously guarded their musico-poetic innovations, as the restrictions in the statutes of their Academy of Poetry and Music suggest. The Academy first met at Baïf's home in May 1571. In 1574 it seems to have been transferred, under Henry III, to the Louvre as the Académie du Palais. It was defunct, probably a victim of French religious struggles and political turmoil, by 1584.

Letters Patent and Statutes for an Academy of Poetry and Music
(1570)

LETTERS PATENT

Charles, by the grace of God King of France, greets all present and future subjects. As we always consider it to be of particular importance, following the

TEXT: Frances Yates, *The French Academies of the Sixteenth Century* (London: The Warburg Institute, 1947), pp. 319–22. For Yates's discussion of the Letters Patent and Statutes see pp. 21–27. Translation by Gary Tomlinson.

example of the great and praiseworthy King Francis our ancestor (may God absolve him), to see letters and science flourish throughout our kingdom and likewise in our city of Paris, where there are many men who work on and study them each day; and as the opinion of many great men, including ancient rulers and philosophers, should not be gainsaid, the opinion, namely, that it is of great importance to the morals of the citizens of a city that the music current and heard there should be governed by certain laws, since the souls of most men conform to and behave in accord with it (so that where music is disordered morals are easily depraved, while where it is well ordered men are well chastened); because of these considerations and having seen the request of our Privy Counsel, presented by our dear and good friends Jean-Antoine de Baïf and Joachim Thibault de Courville, relating that for three years now those men have with great study and assiduous labor worked together to advance the French language, bringing both its poetic fashion and the measure and regulation of its music back to those of the ancient Greeks and Romans at the time when their nations flourished; and, as already in the short time they have spent on these matters they have made certain experiments of measured verse set to music, itself measured almost in accord with the laws of the masters of music of that great and ancient age; and as, finally, after this praiseworthy enterprise had reached this point they were not able to think of or find any better way to bring to light their happily successful experiments (desiring as they did not only to gather the fruits of their labors but also, following their first intentions, to multiply the grace God had afforded them) than by establishing in the manner of the ancients an Academy or Company composed both of composers, singers, and instrumentalists and of virtuous listeners to them; which Academy would not only be a school to serve as fertile soil from which one day would come poets and musicians instructed well in their art so as to give us pleasure, but would also profit the public as a whole; and which Academy could not be formed without the listeners subsidizing it through an appropriate fee for the maintenance of themselves and the composers, singers, and instrumentalists, or undertaken without our advice and consent: Let it be known that, having taken this matter under consideration and heard and followed the advice of our dearest and most honored Queen Mother, our most dear and beloved brothers the Dukes of Anjou and of Alençon, the Princes of our blood, and other great and notable counselors, we do now advise in favor of the establishment of the aforementioned Academy or Company. . . . And, as it is our intention that the said Academy should be attended and honored by the most noble men, we have freely accepted and do welcome the title of Protector and First Listener of it, since we wish and intend that all the activities there will be to the honor of God, the aggrandizement of our State, and the ornament of the name of the French People. . . . Such is our pleasure, in testimony of which we have signed this document with our hand and stamped it with our seal. Given at Faux-bourg Saint Germain in the month of November 1570, the tenth year of our reign. Signed CHARLES and, on the reverse, de Neufville for the King.

STATUTES

In order to bring the use of music back to its perfect state, which is to represent words in song made up of harmony and melody, themselves consisting of the choice and well arranged regulation of voice, sound, and concord so as to create the effects required by the sense of the words, constraining, freeing, or enlarging the soul; and in order to revive also the ancient fashion of composing measured verse to accord with song likewise measured according to the art of meter; and in order also that by this means the souls of listeners, accustomed and disposed to music in the very form of their faculties, might arrange themselves so as to be capable of higher knowledge, purging themselves of whatever barbarities may remain in them: we find it appropriate to establish, by pleasure of the King our sovereign master, an Academy or Company made up of musicians and listeners according to the laws and conditions that follow:

Neither the musicians nor the listeners will in any activities of the Academy contravene the public laws of this Realm.

The musicians will be required to sing and recite their measured words and music for two hours every Sunday, according to an order established among them, for the privilege of the listeners registered in the book of the Academy. In this book will be written the names, surnames, and titles of those who subscribe to the Academy, together with the sum they consent to pay; and likewise the names and surnames of the musicians and the conditions under which they are entered, received, and appointed.

None of the musicians will introduce anyone into the Academy without the consent of all the Company.

All the musicians will be required, unless they give a reasonable excuse, to come to the meeting room each day at an appointed time to rehearse the music each of them will have studied separately, which will have been distributed by the two Founders of the Academy, whom the musicians will be obliged to follow and obey in musical matters.

The musicians will swear not to give out any copy of the chansons of the Academy to anyone without the consent of the whole Company. And if one of them should withdraw, he will not be permitted to take away, openly or secretly, any of the books of the Academy or to copy either music or words from them.

No musician will be allowed to withdraw from the Academy without giving two months' prior notice to the Founders, whether the withdrawal is by their consent or because the time the musician agreed to remain in the Academy has expired.

Should one of the musicians fall ill, he will be cared for and treated solicitously until he recovers fully.

If a musician is not approved by the whole Academy for some occasion, he may be relieved of his duties with pay for the time he would have served.

A medallion will be struck carrying an emblem agreed upon by the members of the Academy, which the listeners will wear to gain entry.

If one of the listeners should pass from this life to the next, the heirs of the deceased will be required to return the medallion to the Academy. If this is not done in the months immediately after the death, the heirs will pay one hundred pounds to the treasury of the Academy.

No one will allow another person to enter with him or without him by means of loaning his medallion to him, unless through some special merit he is given the privilege of doing so by the Founders.

During the singing the listeners will not talk or make noise; they will remain as quiet as they can until the chanson being performed is finished. While a chanson is being sung neither will they knock on the doors of the room, which will be opened at the end of each chanson to admit listeners.

The listeners registered in the book of the Academy will pay the amount they have agreed to subscribe in semiannual installments, starting and finishing according to the day determined for the start of their attendance.

If a member, after having heard one or two concerts of the Academy, requests a refund of the money he has advanced, it will be returned to him and his name struck from the register. But if he has broken any of the laws of the Academy he will forfeit all the money he advanced.

No listener will touch or pass the barrier setting off the stage, and no one other than the musicians will enter there. Neither will anyone handle the book or the instruments; but, remaining off the stage, they will treat with respect everything that honors and serves the Academy, whether it be its book or its personnel.

If there is a dispute among any of the members of the Academy, musicians or listeners, they will not demand any satisfaction of word or deed within one hundred paces of the house where the Academy will be held.

Admission or refusal of anyone either to be registered in the book of the Academy or to be admitted as a listener ordinary or extraordinary will be at the sole discretion of the Founders.

Whoever breaks any of the above laws, whether musician or listener, will be excluded from the Academy and no longer allowed to enter there and will forfeit any monies paid for the maintenance of the Academy, except when, after the transgression has been repaired, the members of the Academy consent and agree otherwise.

Signed Baïf and Thibault

52 Balthasar de Beaujoyeulx

The *Balet comique de la royne (Ballet-Comedy of the Queen)* was presented at the Louvre on October 15, 1581. It was a high point in the so-called *Magnificences,* a two-week-long series of lavish spectacles sponsored by Henry III to commemorate a royal wedding and, more important, to celebrate his own power and grandeur at a time of religious and political instability. These spectacles involved countless poets, musicians, dancers, jousters, actors, painters, and sculptors, among them the poets Pierre de Ronsard and Jean-Antoine de Baïf and the composer Claude le Jeune. Balthasar de Beaujoyeulx himself (ca. 1535–ca. 1587), of Italian origin, was a dance master and violinist at the French court. He conceived and organized the *Balet comique,* directed the dancers, and wrote the description that was lavishly published a year after the performance. The music for the *Balet comique* was most likely composed by Lambert de Beaulieu, a follower of Baïf and Courville's Academy of Poetry and Music (see no. 51 above, pp. 338–41). The metrical freedoms of the vocal numbers in the commemorative volume reflect the influence of their *musique mesurée à l'antique* and contrast with the foursquare regularity of the instrumental dance music.

The *Balet comique* is noteworthy in its joining of music and dance with a coherent and continuous dramatic storyline. Beaujoyeulx showed his awareness of this novelty in a note to the reader at the beginning of the description.There he justifies, by ancient example and the magnificence of his king, his attempt to "make the balet speak and the comedy sing and resound," merging both in a single "well-proportioned body."

FROM *Le balet comique de la royne*
(1581)

As the nymphs arrived in front of the King, the whole party continued their ballet in two geometrical formations, each different from the other. During their last steps the strings played a very merry strain called la Clochette:

TEXT: The commemorative volume of the event, published in Paris 1582 and in a facsimile edition edited by Margaret M. McGowan (Binghamton, N.Y.: Center for Medieval & Early Renaissance Studies, 1982), fols. 22v–24v, 26v–27r, 30v–34v. Translation by Gary Tomlinson. I have omitted the music for the final chorus here, which is included along with the other musical numbers in the commemorative volume.

LE SON DE LA CLOCHETTE, AUQUEL CIRCE SORTIT DE SON JARDIN

Circe, still hidden in her garden behind a curtain, had hardly heard this music when she burst forth in great anger. Holding her golden wand high in her right hand she went the length of the hall to where the nymphs stood in a crescent formation facing Their Majesties. One after another she touched them with her golden wand, immediately rendering them as immobile as statues. She did the same to the viol players, who could no longer sing or play and indeed remained completely motionless. After that she returned to her garden, with a bold and happy expression one might see on a soldier who had won a glorious victory in some perilous and difficult enterprise. Indeed well might she take pride, having defeated so fierce and grand a courage as that of the nymphs.

When Circe had retired in glory to her garden, from high in the rafters, above the cloud, a great clap of thunder was heard that rumbled and murmured long afterward. When it stopped, suddenly the cloud (which I described before) began little by little to descend. In it was carried and enveloped Mercury, messenger of the god Jupiter, angrily coming to earth to break the spell of the sorceress Circe and deliver the nymphs from their enchantment with the juice of the moly root. Mercury was outfitted just as the poets describe him: dressed in red Spanish satin, painstakingly trimmed with gold, and wearing gilded boots with wings on their heels signifying the agility of his flight. On his head he wore a small, golden cap with wings on both sides. His cloak was of gold and purple cloth, and in his hand he carried the caduceus he once had used to put Argus to sleep for Jupiter.[1] While he descended, this god sang very gracefully the verses given below. He was played by Sir du Pont, a

1. See Ovid, *Metamorphoses* 1.668–721.

gentleman-servant of the King, and accompanied by many honorable musicians.[2]

> I am the messenger of all the gods,
> with winged heels, nimble and changeable,
> who, with his caduceus descended to the Fates
> in the deep abyss to steal away
> and revive dead souls; now that they are
> born again, I once more descend to earth.
>
> I taught men to obey the law;
> the sciences, arts, and cities come from me;
> among my treasures I grant eloquence;
> and, to heal souls robbed of reason,
> charmed away from virtue by pleasure,
> I carry the excellent root of moly.
>
> By its power I protected Ulysses, who reached
> the shores of Italy and did not became a swine
> through the enchanted arts of the sorceress Circe;[3]
> Circe who, in a castle she built in France,
> where she charmed the nymphs of the streams in
>   olden times,
> transformed many men into diverse beasts.
>
>   .   .   .   .   .
>
> I want to expose the art of her illusions;
> I have distilled the moly into water of forgetfulness,
> and by my stronger art would undo hers.
> I know how strong and powerful she is;
> but a great danger gives more pleasure afterwards
> to him who honors the name of a powerful foe.

CHANSON DE MERCURE

Je suis ___ de tous ___ les dieux le ___ com-mun mes-sa-ger Ai-lé par les ___ ta-lons, va-ri-a-ble et le-ger, Qui de ce ca - du-cée ___ à la ___ Par-que ___ fa-ta - le Dans l'a-bys-me pro-

2. Beaujoyeulx's French here, *accomply de beaucoup d'honorable parties*, is ambiguous. It probably refers to the musical accompaniment of Mercury's song, published in the commemorative volume only in its melody, but it could instead commend the many honorable traits and accomplishments of Sir du Pont himself.
3. For this episode see *Odyssey* 10.274–335.

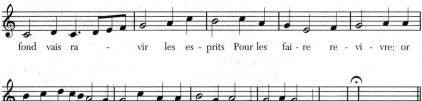

fond vais ra - vir les es - prits Pour les fai - re re - vi - vre: or

quand ⌣ ils ont ⌣ re - pris Nais-san-ce, a-pres en-core là bas je les de - va - le.

While Mercury was still in the air, a few feet above the nymphs, he finished his song and sprinkled the moly-root liquor, which he had in a gilded flask, on their heads. He splashed it so far that it reached even the string players who, barely moistened by that water, immediately began playing again; and the nymphs took up their dancing as they had before they were enchanted. Circe, thinking that Mercury had greatly offended her by interfering in her art, determined to show him how much she knew of magic and excercise her power on him and his caduceus as well. Leaving her garden once more, she ran as if in a fury to the middle of the hall; and, passing among that beautiful troupe of dancers as she had before, she touched them and the string players a second time, putting them back into the state from which Mercury had rescued them.

• • • • •

She approached Mercury, who was still enveloped in the cloud, and raising her golden wand struck him. As soon as he felt the blow he dropped his caduceus and was enchanted, and the cloud carried him motionless to the ground. Circe took him by the hand and led him into her garden, followed by the nymphs, who went gracefully, two by two, with no more movement than what seemed to be granted them by the power of Circe's magic. As they entered her garden they suddenly disappeared, without our being able to tell what had become of them. At that instant the drape that covered the garden of Circe fell away, and we saw clearly the beauty of this delightful garden, glimmering with a thousand torches and lights. We saw also Circe, on a throne at the entrance to her castle, with the trophies of her victory: at her feet, all topsy-turvy, lay Mercury, with no means of moving except by leave and permission of the enchantress. After the curtain was opened a great stag appeared. Leaving the garden it passed in front of Circe, followed by a dog, the dog by an elephant, the elephant by a lion, the lion by a tiger, the tiger by a swine, the swine by other beasts: all men transformed by her sorcery and by the force of her enchantment.

When this act ended, the second entr'acte began at the trellis on the other side of the hall. This new entr'acte was comprised of eight satyrs, seven of whom played flutes and one of whom, Sir de Saint Laurens, singer of the King's Chamber, sang. The harmony of that music was delightful to the King, Queen, Princes, Princesses, and indeed all the audience. Its music was novel in invention and full of gaiety. The satyrs made the round of the hall, continuing their chanson. And at the end of each strophe one of the ensembles in the starry vault above responded, as you can see:

> O Pan, angry Diana
> has left the forest
> along with the woodland nymphs
> who usually trample the grass
> with their dance to the rhythms
> of the sweet harmony of their voices.
>
> .   .   .   .   .

The response of the starry vault:

> Joy and unhappiness,
> fear and hope,
> follow their changeable order
> by an immutable destiny.

53 Henry Peacham

Born around 1576, Henry Peacham studied music in Italy with Orazio Vecchi, probably in 1603–4. He settled in London in 1612 and, apart from the following two years, when he traveled on the Continent, spent the rest of his life there. He had many friends in musical circles, among them the lutenist and composer John Dowland. His most important book, *The Compleat Gentleman,* appeared in 1622 and was reissued in 1626 and 1627. Peacham was an ardent supporter of the royal cause, but his book teaches a more or less Puritan concept of duty. Thus *The Compleat Gentleman* may be called an English Puritan counterpart to Castiglione's *Cortegiano.* Peacham's view of music shows this clearly enough: it is for him an extraordinarily praiseworthy and beneficial activity but should nevertheless not distract us overmuch from "more weighty employments." Peacham's last book was published in 1642, and he died soon thereafter.

FROM *The Compleat Gentleman*
(1622)

OF MUSIC

Music, a sister to Poetry, next craveth your acquaintance, if your genius be so disposed. I know there are many who are *adeo ἄμουσοι* [so far from the

TEXT: The Clarendon Press reprint of the 1634 edition (Oxford, 1906), pp. 96–104. Some of the postils of the original are given here as author's notes.

Muses, so lacking in harmony] and of such disproportioned spirits that they avoid her company (as a great cardinal in Rome did roses at their first coming in, that to avoid their scent he built him an house in the champaign, far from any town) or, as with a rose not long since, a great lady's cheek in England, their ears are ready to blister at the tenderest touch thereof. I dare not pass so rash a censure of these as Pindar doth,[1] or the Italian, having fitted a proverb to the same effect, "Whom God loves not, that man loves not music"; but I am verily persuaded they are by nature very ill disposed and of such a brutish stupidity that scarce anything else that is good and savoreth of virtue is to be found in them. Never wise man, I think, questioned the lawful use hereof, since it is an immediate gift of heaven, bestowed on man, whereby to praise and magnify his Creator; to solace him in the midst of so many sorrows and cares, wherewith life is hourly beset; and that by song, as by letters, the memory of doctrine and the benefits of God might be forever preserved (as we are taught by that song of Moses[2] and those divine psalms of the sweet singer of Israel, who with his psaltery[3] so loudly resounded the mysteries and innumerable benefits of the Almighty Creator) and the service of God advanced (as we may find in 2 Samuel vi:5, Psalm 33, 21, 43, and 4, 108, 3,[4] and in sundry other places of scripture which for brevity I omit).

But, say our sectaries, the service of God is nothing advanced by singing and instruments as we use it in our cathedral churches, that is, by "antiphony,[5] rests, repetitions, variety of moods and proportions, with the like."

For the first, that it is not contrary but consonant to the word of God so in singing to answer either, the practice of Miriam, the prophetess and sister of Moses, when she answered the men in her song,[6] will approve; for repetition, nothing was more usual in the singing of the Levites, and among the psalms of David the 136th is wholly compounded of those two most graceful and sweet figures of repetition, symploce and anaphora. For resting and proportions, the nature of the Hebrew verse, as the meanest Hebrician knoweth, consisting many times of uneven feet, going sometime in this number, sometimes in that (one while, as St. Jerome saith,[7] in the numbers of Sappho, another while, of Alcaeus), doth of necessity require it. And wherein doth our practice of singing and playing with instruments in his Majesty's chapel and our cathedral churches differ from the practice of David, the priests, and Levites?[8] Do we not make one sign in praising and thanking God with voices and instruments of all sorts? "Donec," as St. Jerome saith,[9] "reboet laquear templi"; the roof of the church echoeth again, and which, lest they should cavil at as a Jewish cere-

1. Pythian Odes 1.13–14.
2. Deuteronomy 32. [Au.]
3. It was an instrument three square, of 72 strings, of incomparable sweetness. [Au.]
4. Peacham's reference is not clear.
5. Answering one another in the choir. [Au.]
6. Exodus 15:20–21.
7. *Epistola* 53.8.
8. 2 Chronicles 5:12–13. [Au.]
9. Compare *Epistola* 77.11: *Et aurata Templorum tecta reboans.*

mony, we know to have been practiced in the ancient purity of the church. But we return where we left.

The physicians will tell you that the exercise of music is a great lengthener of the life by stirring and reviving of the spirits, holding a secret sympathy with them; besides, the exercise of singing openeth the breast and pipes. It is an enemy to melancholy and dejection of the mind, which St. Chrysostom truly calleth the Devil's bath;[10] yea, a curer of some diseases—in Apulia in Italy and thereabouts it is most certain that those who are stung with the tarantula are cured only by music.[11] Beside the aforesaid benefit of singing, it is a most ready help for a bad pronunciation and distinct speaking which I have heard confirmed by many great divines; yea, I myself have known many children to have been holpen of their stammering in speech only by it.

Plato calleth it "a divine and heavenly practice,"[12] profitable for the seeking out of that which is good and honest.

Homer saith musicians are "worthy of honor and regard of the whole world,"[13] and we know, albeit Lycurgus imposed most straight and sharp laws upon the Lacedaemonians, yet he ever allowed them the exercise of music.[14]

Aristotle averreth music to be the only disposer of the mind to virtue and goodness, wherefore he reckoneth it among those four principal exercises wherein he would have children instructed.[15]

Tully saith there consisteth in the practice of singing and playing upon instruments great knowledge and the most excellent instruction of the mind, and for the effect it worketh in the mind he termeth it "Stabilem thesaurum, qui mores instuit, componitque, ac mollit irarum ardores, &c."; a lasting treasure which rectifieth and ordereth our manners and allayeth the heat and fury of our anger, &c.[16]

I might run into an infinite sea of the praise and use of so excellent an art, but I only show it you with the finger, because I desire not that any noble or gentleman should (save at his private recreation and leisurable hours) prove a master in the same or neglect his more weighty employments, though I avouch it a skill worthy the knowledge and exercise of the greatest prince.

King Henry the Eighth could not only sing his part sure, but of himself composed a service of four, five, and six parts, as Erasmus in a certain epistle testifieth of his own knowledge.[17]

The Duke of Venosa, an Italian prince,[18] in like manner of late years hath

10. In *Liber de angore animi.* [Au.]
11. Compare no. 37 above (Zarlino) p. 298, and no. 64 below (Ficino) p. 389.
12. Δαιμόνιον πραγμα [*Republic* 531c]. [Au.]
13. τιμῆς ἔμμοροί εἰσι καὶ αἰδοῦς [*Odyssey* 8.480]. [Au.]
14. See no. 2 above (Zarlino) p. 21, n. 33.
15. *Politics* 1337b. [Au.]
16. Cicero, *Tusculan Disputations* 1. [Au.] Peacham evidently has in mind 1.2, though his quotation is not found there.
17. In *Farragine epistola* [i.e., *Farrago nova epistolarum* (Basel, 1519)]. [Au.]
18. Carlo Gesualdo, Prince of Venosa.

given excellent proof of his knowledge and love to music, having himself composed many rare songs which I have seen.

• • • • •

To deliver you my opinion, whom among other authors you should imitate and allow for the best, there being so many equally good, is somewhat difficult; yet as in the rest herein you shall have my opinion.

For motets and music of piety and devotion, as well for the honor of our nation as the merit of the man, I prefer above all others our phoenix, Mr. William Byrd, whom in that kind I know not whether any may equal, I am sure none excel, even by the judgment of France and Italy, who are very sparing in the commendation of strangers in regard of that conceit they hold of themselves. His *Cantiones sacrae*, as also his *Gradualia*, are mere angelical and divine, and being of himself naturally disposed to gravity and piety his vein is not so much for light madrigals or canzonets, yet his "Virginelle" and some others in his First Set cannot be mended by the best Italian of them all.

For composition I prefer next Ludovico de Victoria, a most judicious and a sweet composer; after him Orlando di Lasso, a very rare and excellent author who lived some forty years since in the court of the Duke of Bavaria. He hath published as well in Latin as French many sets; his vein is grave and sweet; among his Latin songs his *Seven Penitential Psalms* are the best, and that French set of his wherein is "Susanna un jour," upon which ditty many others have since exercised their invention.[19]

For delicious air and sweet invention in madrigals, Luca Marenzio excelleth all other whosoever, having published more sets than any author else whosoever, and to say truth hath not an ill song, though sometime an oversight (which might be the printer's fault) of two eights or fifths escaped him, as between the tenor and bass in the last close of "I must depart all hapless," ending according to the nature of the ditty most artificially with a minim rest. His first, second, and third parts of "Tirsi," "Veggo dolce mio bene," "Che fa hogg'il mio sole," "Cantava," or "Sweet singing Amaryllis," are songs the muses themselves might not have been ashamed to have had composed.[20] Of stature and complexion he was a little and black man; he was organist in the Pope's chapel at Rome a good while; afterward he went into Poland, being in displeasure with the Pope for overmuch familiarity with a kinswoman of his (whom the Queen of Poland sent for by Luca Marenzio afterward, she being one of the rarest women in

19. For Lasso's work see *Sämtliche Werke*, ed. Franz Haberl and Adolf Sandberger (21 vols., Leipzig: Breitkopf & Härtel, 1894–1926), vol. 14, pp. 29–33. For other works based on it see Ferabosco (*The Old English Edition*, vol. 11, no. 1), Byrd (*The English Madrigal School*, vol. 14, no. 29 and vol. 15, no. 8), Sweelinck (*Works*, vol. 7, no. 8), and Farnaby (*The English Madrigal School*, vol. 20, no. 12).

20. "Io partirò" ("I must depart all hapless"), "Tirsi," and "Che fa hogg'il mio sole" appeared with English text in Yonge's *Musica transalpina* (1588); "Cantava" and "Veggo dolce mio bene" appeared in Watson's *Italian Madrigals Englished* (1590). The parallel fifths at the end of "Io partirò" occur in Yonge's reprint but not in the original composition.

Europe for her voice and the lute). But returning, he found the affection of the Pope so estranged from him that hereupon he took a conceit and died.

Alphonso Ferabosco the father, while he lived, for judgment and depth of skill (as also his son yet living) was inferior unto none; what he did was most elaborate and profound and pleasing enough in air, though Master Thomas Morley censureth him otherwise.[21] That of his, "I saw my lady weeping," and the "Nightingale" (upon which ditty Master Byrd and he in a friendly emulation exercised their invention),[22] cannot be bettered for sweetness of air or depth of judgment.

I bring you now mine own master, Horatio Vecchi of Modena, beside goodness of air most pleasing of all other for his conceit and variety, wherewith all his works are singularly beautified, as well his madrigals of five and six as those his canzonets, printed at Nuremberg, wherein for trial sing his "Vivo in fuoco amoroso, Lucretia mia," where upon "Io catenato moro" with excellent judgment he driveth a crotchet through many minims, causing it to resemble a chain with the links. Again, in "S'io potessi raccor'i mei sospiri," the breaking of the word "sospiri" with crotchet and crotchet rest into sighs, and that "Fa mi un canzone, &c.," to make one sleep at noon, with sundry other of like conceit and pleasant invention.

Then that great master, and master not long since of St. Mark's chapel in Venice,[23] second to none for a full, lofty, and sprightly vein, following none save his own humor, who while he lived was one of the most free and brave companions of the world. His *Penitential Psalms* are excellently composed and for piety are his best.

Nor must I here forget our rare countryman Peter Philips, organist to their Altezzas at Brussels, now one of the greatest masters of music in Europe. He hath sent us over many excellent songs, as well motets as madrigals; he affecteth altogether the Italian vein.

There are many other authors very excellent, as Boschetto[24] and Claudio de Monteverdi, equal to any before named, Giovanni Ferretti, Stephano Felis, Giulio Rinaldi, Philippe de Monte, Andrea Gabrieli, Cipriano de Rore, Pallavicino, Geminiano, with others yet living, whose several works for me here to examine would be over tedious and needless; and for me, please your own ear and fancy. Those whom I have before mentioned have been ever (within these thirty or forty years) held for the best.

I willingly, to avoid tediousness, forbear to speak of the worth and excellency of the rest of our English composers, Master Doctor Dowland, Thomas Morley, Mr. Alphonso, Mr. Wilbye, Mr. Kirbye, Mr. Weelkes, Michael East, Mr.

---

21. See no. 75 below (Morley), p. 481.
22. Ferabosco's setting is reprinted in *The Old English Edition*, vol. 11, no. 9, Byrd's in *The English Madrigal School*, vol. 15, no. 9; both were prompted by Lasso's chanson "Le rossignol" (*Sämtliche Werke* 14.82), printed with English text in Yonge's *Musica transalpina*.
23. Giovanni Croce. [Au.]
24. Boschetto, his motets of 8 parts printed in Rome, 1594. [Au.]

Bateson, Mr. Deering, with sundry others, inferior to none in the world (however much soever the Italian attributes to himself) for depth of skill and richness of conceit.

Infinite is the sweet variety that the theorique of music exerciseth the mind withal, as the contemplation of proportion, of concords and discords, diversity of moods and tones, infiniteness of invention, &c. But I dare affirm there is no one science in the world that so affecteth the free and generous spirit with a more delightful and inoffensive recreation or better disposeth the mind to what is commendable and virtuous.

The commonwealth of the Cynethenses in Arcadia, falling from the delight they formerly had in music, grew into seditious humors and civil wars, which Polybius took especially note of,[25] and I suppose hereupon it was ordained in Arcadia that everyone should practise music by the space of thirty years.

The ancient Gauls in like manner (whom Julian[26] termed barbarous) became most courteous and tractable by the practise of music.

Yea, in my opinion no rhetoric more persuadeth or hath greater power over the mind; nay, hath not music her figures, the same which rhetoric? What is a revert but her antistrophe? her reports, but sweet anaphoras? her counterchange of points, antimetaboles? her passionate airs, but prosopopoeias? with infinite other of the same nature.[27]

How doth music amaze us when of sound discords she maketh the sweetest harmony? And who can show us the reason why two basins, bowls, brass pots, or the like, of the same bigness, the one being full, the other empty, shall stricken be a just diapason in sound one to the other; or that there should be such sympathy in sounds that two lutes of equal size being laid upon a table and tuned unison, or alike in the Gamma, G *sol re ut,* or any other string, the one stricken, the other untouched shall answer it?

But to conclude, if all arts hold their esteem and value according to their effects, account this goodly science not among the number of those which Lucian placeth without the gates of hell as vain and unprofitable, but of such which are πηγαὶ τῶν καλῶν, the fountains of our lives' good and happiness.[28] Since it is a principal means of glorifying our merciful Creator, it heightens our devotion, it gives delight and ease to our travails, it expelleth sadness and heaviness of spirit, preserveth people in concord and amity, allayeth fierceness and anger, and lastly, is the best physic for many melancholy diseases.

---

25. *Histories* 4.20. [Au.]
26. *Epistola* 71. [Au.]
27. For rhetorical thinking along similar (if more technical) lines, see no. 73 below (Burmeister), pp. 467–71.
28. The Greek is not from Lucian, but seems instead to recall Xenophon, *Cyropaedia* 7.2.13, where Croesus calls the τέχναι "πηγάς . . . τῶν καλῶν" (information from Joseph Farrell). This passage reads "arts and sciences, which be fountains of all good things" in William Barker's 1567 translation of the *Cyropaedia* (ed. James Tatum, New York: Garland, 1987, p. 169). I have not located the Lucianic passage alluded to by Peacham.

54 Vincenzo Giustiniani

Vincenzo Giustiniani was born of ancient Venetian stock on Chios, an island in the Aegean Sea, in 1564, and moved with his family to Rome when the Turks seized the island two years later. There he grew up amid the privileges of his high social status, circulating in the milieu of popes and cardinals and amassing a large art collection, a catalogue of which he published in 1631. He died in 1637.

Giustiniani's *Discourse on the Music of His Times (Discorso sopra la musica de' suoi tempi)* is the report of an informed amateur on Italian musical developments from the 1570s to the 1620s. It provides detailed observations on a new style of singing and composing inaugurated in the years after 1575. It is revealing that from his contemporary vantage point Giustiniani sees no such dramatic shift in musical style in the years around 1600. Rather he takes for granted the coexistence of solo song and polyphonic genres throughout the period he describes. And he incorporates into this varied musical landscape the recent "recitative style," by which he means not only dramatic recitative per se but also other manners of more or less declamatory song for one, two, or three voices with basso continuo.

FROM *Discourse on the Music of His Times*
(1628)

1. In my youth my father (of blessed memory) sent me to a school of music, and I observed that the compositions of Arcadelt, Orlando di Lasso, Striggio, Cipriano de Rore, and Filippo di Monte were in use and esteemed to be the best of those days, as in effect they were. In solo singing with instrumental accompaniment the fashion of *villanelle napolitane* was preferred, in imitation of which many were composed even in Rome, especially by a certain Pitio,[1] a great musician and eminent comedian.

TEXT: *Discorso sopra la musica de' suoi tempi*, in Angelo Solerti, ed., *Le origini del melodramma: testimonianze dei contemporanei* (Turin: Bocca, 1903), pp. 103–28. Translation by Gary Tomlinson. Where I have been able, I have identified the musicians mentioned who are not clearly named or included in standard reference works.

1. A bass singer especially known for his solo songs with lute accompaniment. See Anthony Newcomb, *The Madrigal at Ferrara 1579–97* (2 vols., Princeton: Princeton University Press, 1980), vol. 1, p. 47.

2. In a short time the taste in music changed and the compositions of Luca Marenzio and Ruggero Giovanelli appeared. Both those to be sung by many voices and those for solo voice and instrument were filled with inventions of delightful novelty. The excellence of this style consisted in a new sort of air, pleasing to the ears, with some easy runs and without extraordinary artifice. At the same time Palestrina, Soriano, and Giovanni Maria Nanino composed pieces to be sung in church. These were made effortlessly with a good, solid counterpoint, with a good air, and with suitable decorum, as is manifest in the fact that even today they are sung among the works of more modern composers (who have all learned from their elders their discipline, which they have sought to vary more often with pretty ornaments than with fundamental and substantial workmanship).

3. In the year of our Lord 1575 or a little after and for the following few years a new kind of singing appeared, very different from earlier kinds. It was especially apparent in solo song with instrumental accompaniment and in the examples of the Neapolitan Giovanni Andrea, Sig. Giulio Cesare Brancaccio, and the Roman Alessandro Merlo, who all sang bass with a range of three octaves and with a variety of runs new and pleasing to the ears of everyone.[2] These singers stimulated composers to write works, whether for many voices or for one over an instrument, imitating both their style and that of a certain woman named Femia,[3] but with greater invention and artifice. There resulted a style of mixed villanelle, halfway between florid madrigals and villanelle, which is seen today in many books of the above-named composers and of Orazio Vecchi and others. But just as these villanelle acquired greater perfection through this more skilled composition, so each composer sought to advance himself in writing for several voices so that his compositions would succeed in the general fashion. This was particularly true of Giaches de Wert in Mantua and Luzzasco in Ferrara, who were in charge of all the music of the dukes of those cities.[4] These dukes took the greatest delight in such music, especially in gathering many important gentlewomen and gentlemen to play and sing excellently. So great was their delight that they lingered sometimes for whole days in some little chambers they had ornately outfitted with pictures and tapestries for this sole purpose. There was a great rivalry between the women of Mantua and Ferrara, a competition not only in the timbre and disposition of their voices but also in ornamentation with exquisite runs joined opportunely and not excessively (from which excess Giovanni Luca, a falsettist from Rome who also served in Ferrara, often suffered).[5] There was competition

2. On Brancaccio, another renowned bass and a published military strategist, see Newcomb, *The Madrigal*, vol. 1, pp. 12–14 and 185–86; Merlo was a well-published composer as well as singer.

3. Probably Eufemia Jozola; see Newcomb, *The Madrigal*, vol. 1, p. 17, n. 50.

4. A selection of Luzzasco Luzzaschi's works of this type was later published as *Madrigali . . . per cantare, et sonare a uno, e doi, e tre soprani* (Rome, 1601).

5. That is, Giovanni Luca Conforto; see Vincenzo Giustiniani, *Discorso sopra la musica*, trans. Carol MacClintock (American Institute of Musicology, 1962), p. 69, and Newcomb, *The Madrigal*, vol. 1, p. 170.

even more in moderating or enlarging the voice, loud or soft, attenuating it or fattening it as was called for, now drawing it out, now breaking it off with the accompaniment of a sweet interrupted sigh, now giving out long runs, distinct and well followed, now turns, now leaps, now long trills, now short ones, now sweet runs sung quietly, to which sometimes one suddenly heard an echo respond; and more still in the participation of the face, and of the looks and gestures that accompanied appropriately the music and conceits of the poetry; and above all, without any indecorous motions of body, mouth, or hands that might have diminished the effect of their songs, in enunciating the words so well that each one could be heard down to the last syllable and was not interrupted or overwhelmed by the runs and other ornaments. And many other particular artifices could be observed in these singers and recorded by one more expert than I. And in such noble situations these excellent singers strove with all their might to win grace from their masters, the princes, and also fame for them—wherein lay their usefulness.

4. Following the example of these courts and of the two Neapolitan basses mentioned above, Roman composers began to vary their mode of composing both figured partsongs for several voices and songs for one or at most two voices with instrumental accompaniment. Prince Gesualdo of Venosa, who played excellently the lute and Neapolitan guitar, began to compose madrigals full of great artifice and exquisite counterpoint, with difficult and charming melodies in each part interwoven with such proportion that there was not in them a single superfluous note not contained in the initial melody, which itself was later sung in reverse. And because such exquisite discipline usually renders a work harsh and rough, Gesualdo tried with all his power and industry to choose melodies that were fluid, sweet, and smoothly shaped, even if they were the more difficult to compose. Indeed in singing them his melodies appeared to everyone easy to compose, but in the event they were found to be difficult and not for just any composer. In this style the Neapolitans Stella, Nenna, and Scipione de Ritici composed, following the abovementioned Prince of Venosa and also Count Alfonso Fontanelli.

5. At the same time Cardinal Ferdinando de' Medici, later Duke of Florence, stimulated by his own taste and by the examples of the princes mentioned above, excelled in finding excellent musicians. Among them above all was the famous Vittoria,[6] who almost originated the true female style of singing and was the wife of Antonio di Santa Fiore, named thus because he had been since childhood the excellent musician of the Cardinal of Santa Fiore. Following her example many others in Rome attempted her style of singing, so much so that they excelled all the other musicians of the places and princes mentioned above. Thus emerged Giulio Romano, Giuseppino, Giovanni Domenico and

6. That is, the singer Vittoria Concarini Archilei.

Rasi, who studied in Florence with Giulio Romano.[7] They all sang bass or tenor with a very wide range, with exquisite turns of phrase and runs, and with extraordinary feeling and a special talent for making the words audible. Beyond these, there were many sopranos, such as Giovanni Luca, Ottavio Durante, Simoncino, and Ludovico, who all sang falsetto, and many castrati of the Sistine Chapel, and others like Onofrio from Pistoia, a certain Mathias from Spain, Giovanni Gironimo from Perugia and many others whom I omit for the sake of brevity. Cardinal Montalto succeeded Cardinal Ferdinando de' Medici. He delighted in music no less than his predecessor, playing the cembalo excellently and singing in a sweet and affecting manner. In his household he kept many musicians who exceeded mediocrity, for example the Cavaliere del Leuto and Scipione Dentice del Cembalo, both excellent players and composers, and then Orazio, a virtuoso on the double harp. His singers included the castrato Onofrio Gualfreducci, Ippolita from Naples, the bass Melchior,[8] and many others to whom he gave generous provisions. With the example of these and all the others mentioned already music was revived, so that many papal relatives and other cardinals and princes could delight in it. Above all the chapelmasters undertook to train various castrati and other boys to sing with new and affecting runs and turns of phrase. Giovanni Bernardino Nanino, chapelmaster in San Luigi, and Ruggero Giovanelli had great success with their students who, because they are alive and many in number, I omit to name for now.

6. Just before the present time many composers, like Claudio Monteverdi, Giovanni Bernardino Nanino, Felice Anerio and others, without leaving behind the manner of Gesualdo, tried to sweeten and make more accessible the styles of composition. They composed especially works for church in various manners and scorings for as many as twelve choirs. This style is still in use today, and works are composed in it for large numbers of skilled singers. Indeed I might say that in our time music has been ennobled and made more illustrious than ever before, inasmuch as King Philip IV of Spain and both his brothers delight in it and often sing partsongs or play music for viols together (with the help of a few other musicians to fill out the consort, among whom Filippo Piccinini from Bologna, an excellent player of lute and pandora, stands

---

7. That is, Giulio Caccini; the Roman singer-composers Giovanni Domenico Puliaschi and, probably, Giuseppe Giamberti; and Francesco Rasi. All published books of song in the early seventeenth century.
8. On Onofrio Gualfreducci, singer at the Sistine Chapel, see Warren Kirkendale, *The Court Musicians in Florence during the Principate of the Medici* (Florence: Leo S. Olschki Editore, 1993), pp. 246–50. Ippolita is Hippolita Marotta Recupito; see *The Letters of Claudio Monteverdi*, ed. Denis Stevens (Cambridge: Cambridge University Press, 1980), pp. 75–77. Melchior is Melchior Palentrotti, famous for his roles in two Caccini music dramas of 1600, *Il rapimento di Cefalo* and *L'Euridice*. The double harpist is Orazio Michi; see Alberto Cametti, "Orazio Michi 'dell'Arpa,' virtuoso e compositore di musica della prima metà del seicento," *Rivista musicale italiana* 21 (1914): 203–7.

out).[9] Moreover the same king and his brothers compose works not only for their own delight but also for singing in the court chapel and other churches during the Office services. And this musical aptitude and taste of His Majesty will cause many noblemen to delight in music and many others to apply themselves to it, as the verse says: "The whole world is made in the image of the king."[10]

7. All these things confirm what I said before, that is, that the fashion and manner of singing changes from time to time according to the tastes of the noblemen and princes who delight in it, just as happens in styles of dress, whose fashions are always changing according to things introduced at important courts. . . .

8. . . . At the present time music is not much in use, not being practiced by gentlemen in Rome; neither do we hear the singing of partsongs as often as we used to, notwithstanding the fact that there are many opportunities to do so. It is true that music has been brought to an extraordinary and novel perfection through the practice of a great number of good musicians who, taught by the good masters mentioned before, offer much delight in their sweet and skilful song. Having left behind the older style, which was somewhat rough, and in particular the excessive runs with which it was ornamented, they mostly adhere now to a recitative style endowed with grace and ornaments appropriate to the words, with an occasional run sung clearly and with good judgment, and with just and varied consonances marking the end of each period—periods that in the works of today's composers bring such frequent cadences as to become tiresome. Above all in this recitative style the singer makes the words easily understood, applying to each syllable one note—quiet or loud, slow or fast— and displaying the thought that is sung by means of moderate and not excessive gestures and facial expressions. The songs are for one to three voices with the accompaniment of instruments appropriate to the circumstance: theorbo, guitar, harpsichord, or organ. Most often these songs are sung, with novel invention in their tunes and their ornaments, in the Spanish or Italian manner, the latter being similar to the former but with greater artifice and ornament. This is true whether they are sung in Rome, in Naples, or in Genoa, where the most prominent composers of them are il Todesco della Tiorba named Giovanni Geronimo[11] (in Rome), Gutierrez and later his son Pietro and Gallo and others (in Naples), and (in Genoa) a certain Cicco, who composes and sings and offers great delight to gentlemen in their academies and soirées, which are more popular there than elsewhere.

This recitative style was once customary in plays sung by ladies in Rome, and is still thus heard. But in these plays it is so crude and unvaried in conso-

---

9. Filippo Piccinini had earlier served with his father and brothers at the court of Ferrara. See Newcomb, *The Madrigal,* vol. 1, p. 179.

10. *Regis ad exemplum totus componitur orbis;* Claudianus, *De IV consolatu honorii* vol. 1, p. 299 (see Giustiniani, *Discorso,* trans. MacClintock, p. 72).

11. That is, Johann Hieronymus Kapsberger.

nance and ornament that if the boredom of listening was not moderated by the presence of the actors the audience would leave the seats and the room would be left empty.

Giulio Romano and Giuseppino were the ones who invented this style, as I said before, or at least who first shaped it well. After them it has grown more perfect from singer to singer to the point where it seems that little can be added to it in the future. And it has been introduced also for the singing of Latin verses, hymns, and odes full of holiness and devotion, in a sweet, decorous manner that clearly puts across the thoughts and words.

MUSIC AND RELIGIOUS REFORM

55 Martin Luther

Martin Luther, the famous German theologian and initiator of the Reformation, was born at Eisleben in 1483 and died there in 1546. From 1522 on he directed much of his attention toward recasting the services of the Roman Church so that the congregation would participate in them more fully. This plan did not at first involve a wholesale translation of the Latin Mass into German, but rather called for incorporating vernacular spiritual songs here and there in a reorganized Latin framework. In 1524, however, Luther worked out a fully German Mass, intended at first for smaller congregations with clergy not tutored in Latin, which substituted German devotional songs for the Latin Ordinary; it was published in 1526. In 1523–24 he began to write, translate, and arrange texts for songs that might be used in either service. Many of these were published, along with texts by others all set to music for four voices, in the *Wittemberg Gesangbuch* of 1524. Luther's precise role in the composition of the settings has remained obscure, although his extensive musical aptitude and training make him a plausible candidate for the task. Already by the end of the sixteenth century this sort of spiritual song was referred to as a chorale, the term we still use for it today.

Wittemberg Gesangbuch
(1524)

FOREWORD

That the singing of spiritual songs is a good thing and one pleasing to God is, I believe, not hidden from any Christian, for not only the example of the prophets and kings in the Old Testament (who praised God with singing and playing, with hymns and the sound of all manner of stringed instruments), but also the special custom of singing psalms, have been known to everyone and to universal Christianity from the beginning. Nay, St. Paul establishes this also, 1 Corinthians 14, and orders the Colossians to sing psalms and spiritual songs to the Lord in their hearts, in order that God's word and Christ's teaching may be thus spread abroad and practised in every way.

Accordingly, as a good beginning and to encourage those who can do better, I and several others have brought together certain spiritual songs with a view to spreading abroad and setting in motion the holy Gospel which now, by the grace of God, has again emerged, so that we too may pride ourselves, as Moses does in his song, Exodus 15, that Christ is our strength and song and may not know anything to sing or to say, save Jesus Christ our Savior, as Paul says, 1 Corinthians 2.

TEXT: Johann Walther, *Wittembergisch geistlich Gesangbuch von 1524*, ed. Otto Kade (Publikationen älterer praktischer und theoretischer Musikwerke 7 [Berlin, 1878]), preceding p. 1 of score. Translation by Oliver Strunk.

These, further, are set for four voices for no other reason than that I wished that the young (who, apart from this, should and must be trained in music and in other proper arts) might have something to rid them of their love ditties and wanton songs and might, instead of these, learn wholesome things and thus yield willingly, as becomes them, to the good; also, because I am not of the opinion that all the arts shall be crushed to earth and perish through the Gospel, as some bigoted persons pretend, but would willingly see them all, and especially music, servants of him who gave and created them. So I pray that every pious Christian may bear with this and, should God grant him an equal or a greater talent, help to further it. Besides, unfortunately, the world is so lax and so forgetful in training and teaching its neglected young people that one might well encourage this first of all. God grant us his grace. Amen.

56 Desiderius Erasmus

Irenics, the branch of Christian theology concerned with reconciliation among churches, found its greatest Renaissance advocate in the figure of Desiderius Erasmus of Rotterdam (ca. 1469–1536). Amid the firestorm of debate that sprang up in the wake of Luther's ninety-five theses, Erasmus maintained a stance of pragmatic moderation and compromise. This posture was not, in its day, wholly effective, earning him the enmity of both extremes: Roman prelates saw his writings as leaning toward Lutheranism while the reformers resented his clashes with Luther on the question of free will and other issues.

Erasmus's religious convictions urged him toward the personal piety and evangelicalism of the *Devotio moderna* rather than the theological disputation of the University of Paris (where he studied in the 1490s). His intellectual preference was for the careful philology and persuasive rhetoric of the humanists rather than the labyrinthine logic of the scholastics. These two facets, spiritual and scholarly, joined in his pathbreaking edition of the Greek New Testament (1516) and in his commentaries and treatises on religious issues, while his immense capacity for sardonic rhetorical wit came to the fore in the famous *Praise of Folly* (1511).

Erasmus's general stance is captured well in the following remarks on the Mass and its music. They come from a late work, *On Restoring the Harmony of the Church (Liber de sarcienda ecclesiae concordia*, 1533); it is an eloquent plea for Roman stalwarts and radical reformers to confine their doctrinal differences to synods and ecclesiastical councils and reunite their churches in a single devotion to Christ and the Gospels.

FROM *On Restoring the Harmony of the Church*

(1533)

If some superstition or impropriety has crept into the Mass, it is well to correct it. But I do not see why we should condemn the Mass through and through. It consists of psalmody (called the Introit), the Doxology, prayer, sacred songs, the recitation of the words of the prophets and apostles (called the Epistle), the recitation of the Gospel, the profession of Catholic faith, the giving of thanks (called the Eucharist), and the religious commemoration of the Lord's death; then more prayers, among them the Lord's Prayer; then follow the symbol of Christian peace, Communion, another sacred song, and prayer. Finally the priest commends to God the whole congregation, as a group under his guardianship, and enjoins it to go forth in a spirit of piety and charity. What is there in this that is not pious and worthy of veneration? Whoever is offended by the mean crowd of hired priests should expel the unworthy ones and keep the worthy. Whoever dislikes the sequences, especially the inept ones, may omit them; the Roman Church does not recognize any sequences.[1] Likewise the songs they sing these days in many churches after the consecration of the body and blood of the Lord—songs for peace or against pestilence or for a successful crop—may be omitted without any detriment to religion.[2] All this has been added onto the ancient usages.

· · · · ·

If modulated music[3] and song with musical instruments do not please you in church, they may be omitted with no prejudice to piety; if they do please you, you must take care that such music is worthy of a church of God. But what happens presently in some churches, where they omit or shorten important parts of the service for the sake of music of voices and instruments,

TEXT: *Liber de sarcienda ecclesiae concordia*, ed. R. Stupperich, in Desiderius Erasmus of Rotterdam, *Opera omnia*, ed. Conseil International pour l'Édition des Oeuvres Complètes d'Érasme, ordo 3, vol. 5 (Amsterdam: North-Holland Publishing Co., 1986), pp. 245–313; see pp. 307–8. Translation by Gary Tomlinson. For a translation of the complete *Liber,* see John P. Dolan, ed., *The Essential Erasmus* (New York: New American Library, 1964), pp. 327–88.

1. Erasmus reiterated this concern with the abuse of sequences elsewhere in his writings; see Clement A. Miller, "Erasmus on Music," *The Musical Quarterly* 51 (1966): 332–49; esp. pp. 336–37. In the decades after his death the use of sequences in the Mass would be sharply restricted at the Council of Trent.
2. Erasmus refers here to extraliturgical songs of various kinds, probably including polyphonic settings of votive antiphon texts and the like. On such music in the British Isles during this period see Frank Ll. Harrison, *Music in Medieval Britain* (London: Routledge and Paul, 1958), chaps. 6–7.
3. That is, polyphony.

is not right. Nearly an hour is spent on the sequence, while the Creed is shortened and the Lord's Prayer omitted. And they consume almost as much time
in those melismas sung at length on a single verse. It would be better not to
extend the solemn rite into tediousness with such gratuitous additions.

57 Jean Calvin

Jean Calvin (or Cauvin), the leading Franco-Swiss religious reformer, was born
at Noyon, France, in 1509 and died at Geneva in 1564. He lived first in Paris
but was forced to leave because of his leanings toward the cause of reformation.
He fled to Basle in 1534 and published there his great programmatic work of
religious reform, the *Christianae religionis institutio* (1536). Subsequently, Calvin settled and taught in Geneva, where he spent the rest of his life building up
a church community in accordance with his religious convictions. In regard to
music, these were more restrictive than Luther's or Erasmus's. They required
that polyphony be banned from church, since only monophonic singing by the
congregation assured the proper attentiveness to liturgical words. Marot and
Calvin's French translation of the Psalter, which in later, expanded editions was
to assume great importance for the service of the Calvinist Church, was published in Geneva in 1542.

The Geneva Psalter

(1542)

EPISTLE TO THE READER

Jean Calvin to all Christians and lovers of God's Word, Salutation:

As it is a thing indeed demanded by Christianity, and one of the most necessary, that each of the faithful observe and maintain the communion of the
Church in his neighborhood, attending the assemblies which are held both on
the Lord's day and on other days to honor and serve God, so it is also expedient
and reasonable that all should know and hear what is said and done in the
temple, to receive fruit and edification therefrom. For our Lord did not institute the order which we must observe when we gather together in his name
merely that the world might be amused by seeing and looking upon it, but

TEXT: *Oeuvres choisies. Publiées par la Compagnie des pasteurs de Genève* (Geneva, 1909), pp.
169–70, 173–76. Translation by Oliver Strunk.

wished rather that therefrom should come profit to all his people. Thus witnesseth Saint Paul,[1] commanding that all which is done in the Church be directed unto the common edifying of all, a thing the servant would not have commanded, had it not been the intention of the Master. For to say that we can have devotion, either at prayers or at ceremonies, without understanding anything of them, is a great mockery, however much it be commonly said. A good affection toward God is not a thing dead and brutish, but a lively movement, proceeding from the Holy Spirit when the heart is rightly touched and the understanding enlightened. And indeed, if one could be edified by the things which one sees without knowing what they mean, Saint Paul would not so rigorously forbid speaking in an unknown tongue and would not use the argument that where there is no doctrine, there is no edification.[2] Yet if we wish to honor well the holy decrees of our Lord, as used in the Church, the main thing is to know what they contain, what they mean, and to what end they tend, in order that their observance may be useful and salutary and in consequence rightly ruled.

Now there are in brief three things that our Lord has commanded us to observe in our spiritual assemblies, namely, the preaching of his Word, the public and solemn prayers, and the administration of his sacraments. I abstain at this time from speaking of preaching, seeing that there is no question thereof. . . . Of the sacraments I shall speak later.

As to the public prayers, these are of two kinds: some are offered by means of words alone, the others with song. And this is not a thing invented a little time ago, for it has existed since the first origin of the Church; this appears from the histories, and even Saint Paul speaks not only of praying by word of mouth, but also of singing.[3] And in truth we know by experience that song has great force and vigor to move and inflame the hearts of men to invoke and praise God with a more vehement and ardent zeal. It must always be looked to that the song be not light and frivolous but have weight and majesty, as Saint Augustine says,[4] and there is likewise a great difference between the music one makes to entertain men at table and in their homes, and the psalms which are sung in the Church in the presence of God and his angels.

Therefore, when anyone wishes to judge rightly of the form that is here presented, we hope that he will find it holy and pure, for it is entirely directed toward that edification of which we have spoken, however more widely the practice of singing may extend. For even in our homes and in the fields it should be an incentive, and as it were an organ for praising God and lifting up our hearts to him, to console us by meditating upon his virtue, goodness, wisdom, and justice, a thing more necessary than one can say. In the first place, it is not without reason that the Holy Spirit exhorts us so carefully by means of

1. 1 Corinthians 14:26.
2. 1 Corinthians 14:19.
3. 1 Corinthians 14:15.
4. *Epistola* 55.18.34.

the holy scripture to rejoice in God and that all our joy is there reduced to its true end, for he knows how much we are inclined to delight in vanity. Just as our nature, then, draws us and induces us to seek all means of foolish and vicious rejoicing, so, to the contrary, our Lord, to distract us and withdraw us from the enticements of the flesh and the world, presents to us all possible means in order to occupy us in that spiritual joy which he so much recommends to us.[5] Now among the other things proper to recreate man and give him pleasure, music is either the first or one of the principal, and we must think that it is a gift of God deputed to that purpose. For which reason we must be the more careful not to abuse it, for fear of soiling and contaminating it, converting it to our condemnation when it has been dedicated to our profit and welfare. Were there no other consideration than this alone, it might well move us to moderate the use of music to make it serve all that is of good repute and that it should not be the occasion of our giving free rein to dissoluteness or of our making ourselves effeminate with disordered pleasures and that it should not become the instrument of lasciviousness or of any shamelessness. But there is still more, for there is hardly anything in the world with more power to turn or bend, this way and that, the morals of men, as Plato has prudently considered.[6] And in fact we find by experience that it has a secret and almost incredible power to move our hearts in one way or another.

Wherefore we must be the more diligent in ruling it in such a manner that it may be useful to us and in no way pernicious. For this reason the early doctors of the Church often complain that the people of their times are addicted to dishonest and shameless songs, which not without reason they call mortal and Satanic poison for the corruption of the world. Now in speaking of music I understand two parts, namely, the letter, or subject and matter, and the song, or melody. It is true that, as Saint Paul says, every evil word corrupts good manners,[7] but when it has the melody with it, it pierces the heart much more strongly and enters within; as wine is poured into the cask with a funnel, so venom and corruption are distilled to the very depths of the heart by melody. Now what is there to do? It is to have songs not merely honest but also holy, which will be like spurs to incite us to pray to God and praise him, and to meditate upon his works in order to love, fear, honor, and glorify him. Now what Saint Augustine says is true—that no one can sing things worthy of God save what he has received from him.[8] Wherefore, although we look far and wide and search on every hand, we shall not find better songs nor songs better suited to that end than the Psalms of David which the Holy Spirit made and uttered through him. And for this reason, when we sing them we may be cer-

---

5. Here ends the preface in the first edition (1542). What follows is found only in the 1545 edition and in editions of the Psalter.
6. *Republic* 401d.
7. Ephesians 4:29.
8. *In Psalmum XXXIV enarratio* 1.1.

tain that God puts the words in our mouths as if himself sang in us to exalt his glory. Wherefore Chrysostom exhorts men as well as women and little children to accustom themselves to sing them, in order that this may be like a meditation to associate them with the company of angels.[9] Then we must remember what Saint Paul says—that spiritual songs cannot be well sung save with the heart.[10] Now the heart requires the intelligence, and therein, says Saint Augustine, lies the difference between the singing of men and of birds.[11] For a linnet, a nightingale, a parrot will sing well, but it will be without understanding. Now the peculiar gift of man is to sing knowing what he is saying. After the intelligence must follow the heart and the affection, which cannot be unless we have the hymn imprinted on our memory in order never to cease singing.

For these reasons the present book, even for this cause, besides the rest which has been said, should be in singular favor with everyone who desires to enjoy himself honestly and in God's way, that is, for his welfare and to the profit of his neighbors, and thus it has no need to be much recommended by me, seeing that it carries its value and its praise. But may the world be so well advised that instead of the songs that it has previously used, in part vain and frivolous, in part stupid and dull, in part foul and vile and consequently evil and harmful, it may accustom itself hereafter to sing these divine and celestial hymns with the good King David. Touching the melody, it has seemed best that it be moderated in the way that we have adopted in order that it may have the weight and majesty proper to the subject and may even be suitable for singing in church, according to what has been said.

Geneva, June 10, 1543.

9. *Exposition of Psalm XLI.*
10. Ephesians 5:19.
11. *In Psalmum XVIII enarratio* 2.1.

58 Claude Goudimel

Born at Besançon around 1515, the composer of chansons and sacred works Claude Goudimel was killed in 1572 in the St. Bartholomew's Day massacres at Lyon. His first compositions are found in the extensive collections of French chansons published in 1549 by Nicolas du Chemin in Paris. In 1557 and 1558 Goudimel published a Magnificat and four masses—his last music for the services of the Roman Church. In all, Goudimel published three distinct settings of the tunes in the Huguenot Psalters, one in contrapuntal style between 1551 and 1566 and two for four voices, simply harmonized, in 1564 and 1565.

The Geneva Psalter

(1565)

FOREWORD

To our readers:

To the melody of the psalms we have, in this little volume, adapted three parts, not to induce you to sing them in church, but that you may rejoice in God, particularly in your homes. This should not be found an ill thing, the more so since the melody used in church is left in its entirety, just as though it were alone.

TEXT: The facsimile of the original edition (Geneva, 1565) ed. Pierre Pidoux and Konrad Ameln (Kassel: Bärenreiter, 1935). Translation by Oliver Strunk.

59 Bernardino Cirillo

From humble beginnings in Aquila, where he was born in 1500, Bernardino Cirillo rose to become a prominent churchman in mid-sixteenth-century Rome. He was rector of Santa Casa of Loreto from 1535 to 1553, served as vicar of Fermo for the next two years, and reached Rome in late 1555 or early 1556. There he remained until his death in 1575, occupying various ecclesiastical posts and involving himself cautiously in the currents of reform swirling around the Roman Church in the years of the Council of Trent (1545–63). His surviving works include ecclesiastical and civil histories and many volumes of manuscript correspondence. Here, in a letter published during his lifetime, he attacks the expressive license he found in much church polyphony of his time from the somewhat incongruous perspective of ancient doctrines of modal ethos.

Letter to Ugolino Gualteruzzi[1]
(1549)

For many years my mind has been burdened with an idea that, for lack of ability to express it, has almost stopped the flow of my thoughts. Now I am determined to bear it no longer on my brain, and, as best I can, I propose to portray it for you in this letter with the aim and hope that you will read in it much more than I shall write to you, and that, thanks to your fine understanding, you will formulate my idea in your mind—for I cannot give a complete exposition of it, but can only sketch it out.

Now the subject is this—that music among the ancients was the most splendid of all the fine arts. With it they created powerful effects that we nowadays cannot produce either with rhetoric or with oratory in moving the passions and affections of the soul. With the power of song it was easy for them to drive a wise mind from the use of reason and bring it to a state of madness and willfulness. By this means it is said that the Lacedaemonians were incited to take up arms against the Cretans; that Timotheus was roused against Alexander; that a young man of Taormina was induced to set fire to the house in which his beloved was concealed; that in the sacrifices of Bacchus people were roused to frenzy; and similar effects.[2] And the mode or species that incited this state of mind was called Phrygian.

To this species there was opposed another, called Lydian, with which men could be easily withdrawn from the condition of frenzy and madness into which they had been plunged by the first kind of music.

The third was called Dorian, which attracted and moved the affections of the soul to gravity and modesty, and with so much strength and force that it was not only difficult, but almost impossible for anyone hearing it to bend his spirit toward a vicious or ignoble action. They say that Agamemnon, on going to the Trojan Wars, left a Dorian musician with his wife Clytemnestra, whose task it was, by means of his music, to charm her away from infidelity; and

TEXT: Aldo Manuzio, *Lettere volgari di diversi nobilissimi huomini . . . libro terzo* (Venice, 1564), pp. 114–18. Reprinted from Giovanni Pierluigi da Palestrina, *Pope Marcellus Mass*, A Norton Critical Score, ed. Lewis Lockwood (New York, 1975), by permission of W. W. Norton & Company, Inc. Translation by Lewis Lockwood.

1. In Cirillo's manuscript correspondence the recipient of the letter is erroneously identified as Cavaliere Ugolino Guastanezzo (see Pietro de Angelis, *Musica e musicisti nell'Arcispedale di Santo Spirito in Saxia* [Rome: Collana di studi storici in Saxia, 1950], p. 39).

2. For the Lacedaemonians (i.e., Spartans) and for Timotheus, see no. 37 above (Zarlino), p. 298, n. 27 and p. 299, n. 33. Cirillo has garbled the story of Timotheus, who was not roused against Alexander but instead with his music incited Alexander to take up arms; see no. 45 above (Castiglione), p. 326, n. 2. For the Taorminian youth and Bacchic frenzies, Quintilian, *Institutio oratoria* 1.10.32.

Aegisthus could not corrupt her until he had the musician murdered.[3] This kind of music was always highly valued and esteemed.

Then we have the fourth species, called Mixolydian, by which anyone hearing it was immediately moved to tears, cries, and lamentation; this was used for sad and mournful occasions.

See, my Lord, what a splendid thing this is! By means of the power of song a slow and lazy man becomes lively and active; an angry man is calmed; a dissolute man becomes temperate; an afflicted man is consoled; a miserable man becomes happy; and thus music governs human affections and has the power to alter them as need be. Now, where has this led?

I see and hear the music of our time, which some say has been brought to a degree of refinement and perfection that never was nor could be known before. And yet I neither see nor hear any of the aforesaid ancient modes, and testimony to this is given by the movements of the soul that arise from it (perhaps you will say to me, "Shoemaker, stick to your last"). This much is clear—that the music of today is not the product of theory, but is merely an application of practice. *Kyrie eleison* means "Lord, have mercy upon us." The ancient musician would have expressed this affection of asking the Lord's pardon by using the Mixolydian mode, which would have evoked a feeling of contrition in the heart and soul. And if it had not moved the listener to tears, at least it would have swayed each hardened mind to piety. Thus he would have used similar modes in accordance with the words, and would have made a contrast between Kyrie and Agnus Dei, between Gloria and Credo, Sanctus and Pleni, psalm and motet. Nowadays they sing these things in any way at all, mixing them in an indifferent and uncertain manner. And then, you see what they invariably do. They say, "Oh, what a fine mass was sung in chapel!" And what is it, if you please? It is *L'homme armé,* or *Hercules Dux Ferrariae* or *Philomena.*[4] What the devil has the Mass to do with the armed man, or with Philomena, or with the duke of Ferrara? What numbers, what intervals, what sounds, what motions of the spirit, of devotion, or piety can be gathered from them, and how can music agree with such subjects as the armed man or the duke of Ferrara? Now, my dear Lord, read what little I have said and draw your own conclusions, for what I say of the music of the church I say of all other music as well. When I reflect upon ancient music in comparison with music of today, I see nothing of value but the pavane and the galliard, at the sound of which those good ladies of San Rocco and of Piazza Lombarda begin their movements, and it almost seems that they are listening to the Dionysiac dithyramb.

---

3. See no. 38 above (Ronsard), p. 301, n. 3.

4. Cirillo's complaint concerns polyphonic Mass cycles incorporating nonliturgical material, whether the famous *L'homme armé* melody, employed by Du Fay, Josquin, Palestrina, and many others, the solmization tune Josquin derived from the name and title of his supporter "Hercules Dux Ferrariae," or the polyphony of Jean Richafort's motet *Philomena praevia.* See Lockwood, ed., *Pope Marcellus Mass,* p. 12 n. 4.

I consider the painting and sculpture of Michelangelo Buonarroti to be a miracle of nature; but when he decided to depict the scene of *Posteriora mea videbis* [roughly: see my behind] on the ceiling of the Sistine Chapel to show his ability in painting—and also so many nude figures, which he made in order to show off his skill—he might have done much better to paint them in the loggia of some garden, where it would have been more appropriate.[5] The quartered cloak was suitable attire for Captain Todeschino of the lancers when he was jousting, but when worn by our friend it is abominable; and nevertheless the cloak by itself is admirable. "The shoes are excellent, but they do not fit Socrates."

I should like, in short, when a mass is to be sung in church, the music to be framed to the fundamental meaning of the words, in certain intervals and numbers apt to move our affections to religion and piety, and likewise in psalms, hymns, and other praises that are offered to the Lord. And in the pavane and galliard, if the numbers and cadences they have are not sufficient, then let others be added to them so that they may be made to dance up to the very walls of the houses. Each mode should be adapted to its subject, and when one has a lullaby to sing, or a plaintive song, one should do likewise. Thus the musicians of today should endeavor in their profession to do what the sculptors, painters, and architects of our time have done, who have recovered the art of the ancients; and the writers, who have reclaimed literature from the hell to which it was banished by corrupt ages; and as the sciences have been explained and given in their purity to our times. Thus the musicians should seek to recover the styles and modes, and the power of the Phrygian, Lydian, Dorian, and Mixolydian compositions, with which they would be able to do what they wish. I do not say that they should try to recover the enharmonic, diatonic, and chromatic genera, for these were dismissed by the ancients themselves;[6] but that they should approximate as much as possible the four above-mentioned modes, and that they should lend beauty and individuality to sacred music. In our times they have put all their industry and effort into the writing of imitative passages, so that while one voice says "Sanctus," another says "Sabaoth," still another says "Gloria tua," with howling, bellowing, and stammering, so that they seem at times like cats in January or bulls in May. I hope that you will bear with me.

Now to conclude, for it is time. Again, where has this led? You, my Lord, are in Rome (Who knows? Sometimes things are first thought, then they are uttered, and at last at times they are even done), where it is imagined that

5. On the criticism by Cirillo and others of the nudity in Michelangelo's frescoes for the Sistine Chapel, see John Shearman, *Mannerism* (London: Penguin, 1967), pp. 167–69 (cited in Lockwood, *Pope Marcellus Mass*, p. 13).

6. Perhaps Cirillo refers loosely to pseudo-Plutarch, *De musica* 1137e–f and 1143e–f, or to various passages in Ptolemy, *Harmonics* 1.13–16 (a less likely source than pseudo-Plutarch for Cirillo to have known); but neither of these works simply "dismisses" the genera.

there are men gifted with all wisdom. See if you can find there some good, genial, and willing musician who is accustomed to reasoned discourse, and discuss this letter a bit with him. Impress upon him the idea of what the ancients achieved, and that today no such effects are known, for today everything follows a single mold, always in the same way. Thus let us see if certain corrupt practices could be banished from the church, and if some music could be introduced that would move men to religion, piety, and devotion. And if they should say that they are only guided by plainsong, I would not be concerned (be it said with sincerity and reverence) if they should depart from that kind of music, in which one recognizes less of that power but can add a great deal more if only one would apply himself to recovering the ancient art. I believe so strongly in the ingenuity of our men of today that it seems to me that they can penetrate wherever they will. And if anyone should say to me, "Your idea is not new, it has been said before by others and attempted by musicians," I would reply that I observe the world to be dedicated to that which it does, and not what it ought to do, and I believe that musicians follow the same path.

•   •   •   •   •

If this discourse seems to you reasonable, say a word on its behalf to Signor Beccadelli.[7] He, who has labored so much over his *Cosmography* for the benefit of the public, may labor too on this matter, to see to it that the praises of the Lord are sung well and in a manner different from those of secular texts. For this is all that stirs me: let them make their motets, chansons, madrigals, and ballate in their own way, as long as our church bends its own efforts to move men to religion and piety.

•   •   •   •   •

From Loreto
February 16, 1549

7. For Gualteruzzi's relations with the variously employed cleric Lodovico Beccadelli, and for a general discussion of Cirillo's letter, see Claude V. Palisca, "Bernardino Cirillo's Critique of Polyphonic Church Music of 1549: Its Background and Resonance," in *Music in Renaissance Cities and Courts: Studies in Honor of Lewis Lockwood,* ed. Jessie Ann Owens and Anthony M. Cummings (Warren, Mich.: Harmonie Park Press, 1997), pp. 281–92.

60 Giovanni Pierluigi da Palestrina

Giovanni Pierluigi da Palestrina was born in 1525 or early 1526 at Palestrina, not far from Rome. He received his early musical training in Rome and, after leaving to serve for seven years (ca. 1544–51) as organist and choirmaster of San Agapito in Palestrina, returned and spent the remainder of his career there. In 1551 he was appointed *maestro* of the Cappella Giulia and in 1555 member of the Cappella Sistina. He was dismissed from that position some months later with a change of popes, because his married status violated the chapel's statutes. For the next sixteen years he occupied various positions, including chapelmaster at San Giovanni in Laterano and Santa Maria Maggiore. In 1571 he returned to the Cappella Giulia, where he remained until his death in 1594.

Palestrina's huge output includes over one hundred masses, close to four hundred motets, and many other works. Probably the most famous of all these works is the *Pope Marcellus Mass,* published in 1567 in his Second Book of Masses. Since the early nineteenth century, scholars have debated, with equivocal results, whether this work was written in order to convince a commission of cardinals associated with the Council of Trent of the propriety of polyphonic Mass settings; the story that Palestrina's work "saved" polyphony for the Roman Church reaches back much further, at least to 1607. What seems undeniable is that the *Pope Marcellus Mass* reflects, in its emphasis on chordal texture and the resulting increase in the intelligibility of the words, the "new manner" of setting the Mass that Palestrina mentions in his dedication of the Second Book. In this it comes close to at least one of the ideals for church polyphony advocated by Bernardino Cirillo (see no. 59 above, p. 371).

Second Book of Masses
(1567)

DEDICATION

To Philip of Austria, Catholic and Invincible King:

Since the utility and pleasure afforded by the art of music is a gift of heaven greater than all human teachings, and since it is particularly valued and approved by the ancient and authoritative writings of holy scripture, so it

TEXT: *Joannis Petri Aloysi Praenestini Missarum liber secundus,* Rome, 1567. Reprinted from Giovanni Pierluigi da Palestrina, *Pope Marcellus Mass,* A Norton Critical Score, ed. Lewis Lockwood (New York, 1975), by permission of W. W. Norton & Company, Inc. Translation by Lewis Lockwood.

appears that this art can be properly exercised upon holy and divine subjects. I, therefore, who have been engaged in this art for many years, not wholly unsuccessfully (if I may rely on the judgment of others more than on my own), have considered it my task, in accordance with the views of most serious and most religious-minded men, to bend all my knowledge, effort, and industry toward that which is the holiest and most divine of all things in the Christian religion—that is, to adorn the holy sacrifice of the Mass in a new manner. I have, therefore, worked out these masses with the greatest possible care, to do honor to the worship of almighty God, to which this gift, as small as it may be, is offered and accommodated. And these products of my spirit—not the first, but, as I hope, the more successful—I decided to dedicate to your Majesty, who have taken your own name from the tradition of the Catholic faith, and who also guard the purity of the orthodox religion most ardently, and who honor and adorn the sacred services through the works and ministrations of most excellent musicians. Accept, then, most mighty and God-fearing king, these my labors as testimony of my perpetual loyalty toward your Majesty— and accept them with that kingly greatness of spirit with which you are wont to receive such gifts. If these labors should please you, then I would consider it their greatest success if they should satisfy your judgment. If they should not please you, then nonetheless my loyal affection will not waver toward the magnanimous and noble king whom may God, the bestower of kingdoms and giver of all good things, keep for Christendom in health and well-being as long as may be possible, and grant all good wishes of honorable men. Farewell, ornament and bulwark of all who bear the name of Christians.

Giovanni Petroaloysio Palestrina

61 Pope Gregory XIII

The brief of Gregory XIII, entrusting Palestrina and his colleague Annibale Zoilo with the revision of the music of the Roman Gradual and Antiphoner, was a natural outgrowth of the publication, in 1568 and 1570, of the reformed Breviary and Missal ordered by the Council of Trent and approved by Gregory's predecessor, Paul V. The aim of this proposed revision was twofold. On the one hand, it was to bring the choir books into agreement with the liturgical revisions already made official. On the other, it was to rid the plainsong melodies of what were deemed to be superabundant melismas, incorrect Latin accentuation, awkward melodic intervals, etc. (the "barbarisms, obscurities, contrarieties, and superfluities" Gregory alludes to). During the year 1578, as his correspondence shows, Palestrina was deeply preoccupied with this work of revision; later on, however, he seems to have set it aside, never to take it up again. In 1611, some years after his death, other hands were charged with the responsibility, and although it seems clear that the so-called Editio Medicaea, published in 1614, is not very different from the revised version that Palestrina must have had in mind, it is unlikely that it includes any work of his.

Pope from 1572 to 1585, Gregory XIII (Ugo Buoncompagno) inaugurated important changes in the musical arrangements at St. Peter's. His revision of the calendar once made his name a household word. To him Palestrina dedicated his Fourth Book of Masses (1582) and his motets on the Song of Solomon (Book V, 1584).

Brief on the Reform of the Chant
(1577)

TO PALESTRINA AND ZOILO

Beloved sons:

Greetings and apostolic benediction!

Inasmuch as it has come to our attention that the Antiphoners, Graduals, and Psalters that have been provided with music for the celebration of the divine praises and offices in plainsong (as it is called) since the publication of the Breviary and Missal ordered by the Council of Trent have been filled to overflowing with barbarisms, obscurities, contrarieties, and superfluities as a result of the clumsiness or negligence or even wickedness of the composers, scribes, and printers:[1] in order that these books may agree with the aforesaid Breviary and Missal, as is appropriate and fitting, and may at the same time be so ordered, their superfluities having been shorn away and their barbarisms and obscurities removed, that through their agency God's name may be reverently, distinctly, and devoutly praised; desiring to provide for this in so far as with God's help we may, we have decided to turn to you, whose skill in the art of music and in singing, whose faithfulness and diligence, and whose piety toward God have been fully tested, and to assign to you this all-important task, trusting confidently that you will amply satisfy this desire of ours. And thus we charge you with the business of revising and (so far as shall seem expedient to you) of purging, correcting, and reforming these Antiphoners, Graduals, and Psalters, together with such other chants as are used in our churches according to the rite of Holy Roman Church, whether at the Canonical Hours or at Mass or at other divine services, and over all of these things we entrust you for the present with full and unrestricted jurisdiction and power by virtue of our apostolic authority, and in order that you may pursue the aforesaid more quickly and diligently you have our permission to admit other skilled musicians as assis-

---

TEXT: Raphael Molitor, *Die nach-Tridentinische Choral-Reform zu Rom* (Leipzig: F. E. C. Leuckart, 1901–2), vol. 1, pp. 297–98. Translation by Oliver Strunk.

1. For Zarlino's view of barbarous misaccentuation in plainchant see no. 71 below, pp. 459–60.

tants if you so desire. The Apostolic Constitutions and any other regulations that may be to the contrary notwithstanding. Given at St. Peter's in Rome under Peter's seal this twenty-fifth day of October, 1577, in the sixth year of our pontificate.

To our beloved sons Giovanni Pierluigi da Palestrina and Annibale Zoilo Romano, musicians of our private chapel.

62 Thomas East

An important typographer and publisher, Thomas East (also Easte, Este) is remembered as the printer of much Elizabethan and Jacobean music. Starting with William Byrd's *Psalmes, Sonets, & Songs of Sadnes and Pietie* of 1588 (see no. 39 above, pp. 303–4), he printed a long series of works by Byrd, Nicholas Yonge, Thomas Watson, Thomas Morley, George Kirbye, John Wilbye, John Dowland, Robert Jones, and other composers. And he published three of the most famous Elizabethan music anthologies: the two volumes of *Musica transalpina* (1588 and 1597) and *The Triumphes of Oriana* (1601).

In 1592, East collected tunes for the English metrical Psalter, engaged a number of composers to harmonize them in four parts (including Kirbye, Dowland, John Farmer, and Giles Farnaby), and published the result as *The Whole Booke of Psalmes: with their Wonted Tunes, as they are song in Churches.* Unlike earlier English collections of harmonized psalms, East's book includes the full texts of the complete Psalter and presents the four musical lines of each setting on a single page opening instead of in separate partbooks. East's *Whole Booke* saw four editions, the last of them in 1611.

The Whole Booke of Psalmes
(1592)

DEDICATION

TO THE RIGHT HONORABLE SIR JOHN PUCKERING, KNIGHT, LORD KEEPER OF THE GREAT SEAL OF ENGLAND:

The word of God, Right Honorable, delighteth those which are spiritually minded; the art of music recreateth such as are not sensually affected; where

TEXT: The original edition (London, 1592). A reprint, ed. E. F. Rimbault, was published in 1844 as vol. 11 of the series brought out by the Musical Antiquarian Society.

zeal in the one and skill in the other do meet, the whole man is revived. The mercies of God are great provoking unto thankfulness; the necessities of man are great, enforcing unto prayer; the state of us all is such that the publishing of God's glory for the edifying one of another cannot be overslipped; in all these the heart must be the workmaster, the tongue the instrument, and a sanctified knowledge as the hand to polish the work. The Psalms of David are a paraphrasis of the Scriptures; they teach us thankfulness, prayer, and all the duties of a Christian whatsoever; they have such comfort in them that such as will be conversant in the same cannot possibly lose their labor. Blessed is that man which delighteth therein and meditateth in the same continually. He that is heavy hath the Psalms to help his prayer; he that is merry hath the Psalms to guide his affections; and he that hath a desire to be seriously employed in either of these duties hath this excellent gift of God, the knowledge of music, offered him for his further help; that the heart rejoicing in the word and the ears delighting in the notes and tunes, both these might join together unto the praise of God. Some have pleased themselves with pastorals, others with madrigals, but such as are endued with David's heart desire with David to sing unto God psalms and hymns and spiritual songs. For whose sake I have set forth this work that they busy themselves in the psalms of this holy man, being by men of skill put into four parts that each man may sing that part which best may serve his voice.

In this book the church tunes are carefully corrected and other short tunes added which are sung in London and other places of this realm. And regarding chiefly to help the simple, curiosity is shunned. The profit is theirs that will use this book; the pains theirs that have compiled it; the charges his who, setting it forth, respecteth a public benefit, not his private gain. Now having finished it, in most humble manner I present it unto Your Honor as to a maintainer of godliness, a friend to virtue, and a lover of music, hoping of Your Lordship's favorable acceptance, craving your honorable patronage and countenance, and praying unto God long to continue Your Lordship a protector of the just and the same God to be a protector of Your Lordship's welfare forever.

Your good Lordship's most humbly at command
Thomas East.

PREFACE

Although I might have used the skill of some one learned musician in the setting of these psalms in four parts, yet for variety's sake I have entreated the help of many, being such as I know to be expert in the art and sufficient to answer such curious carping musicians whose skill hath not been employed to the furthering of this work.[1] And I have not only set down in this book all the

---

1. East's contributors were John Farmer, George Kirbye, Richard Allison, Giles Farnaby, Edward Blancks, John Dowland, William Cobbold, Edmund Hooper, Edward Johnson, and Michael Cavendish.

tunes usually printed heretofore with as much truth as I could possibly gather among divers of our ordinary psalm books, but also have added those which are commonly sung nowadays and not printed in our common psalm books with the rest. And all this have I so orderly cast that the four parts lie always together in open sight. The which my travail, as it hath been to the furtherance of music in all Godly sort and to the comfort of all good Christians, so I pray thee to take it in good part and use it to the glory of God.

T. E.

63　William Byrd

Gradualia

(1605–7)

DEDICATIONS AND FOREWORD

To that Most Illustrious and Distinguished Man, and his
Right Honorable Lord, Henry Howard, Earl of North-
ampton, Warden of the Cinque Ports, and one of
the Privy Council of His Most Serene Majesty, James, King of Great Britain

The swan, they say, when his death is near, sings more sweetly. However little I may be able to attain to the sweetness of that bird in these songs which I have judged should be dedicated to you, most illustrious Henry, I have had two defences or incentives of no common rate for emulating that sweetness in some sort at least. The one was the sweetness of the words themselves, the other your worthiness. For even as among artisans it is shameful in a craftsman to make a rude piece of work from some precious material, so indeed to sacred words in which the praises of God and of the Heavenly host are sung, none but some celestial harmony (so far as our powers avail) will be proper. Moreover in these words, as I have learned by trial, there is such a concealed and hidden power that to one thinking upon things divine and diligently and earnestly pondering them, all the fittest numbers occur as if of themselves and freely offer themselves to the mind which is not indolent or inert. Truly your worthi-

TEXT: *Tudor Church Music* 7 (Oxford: Oxford University Press, 1927), facs. before pp. 3 and 209. Translation by Oliver Strunk.

ness is as great as that of your most ancient family, which, long beaten by bitter storms and stricken, as it were, by the frost of adverse fortune, now in part flourishes again in your own person, and in part, encouraged by the King's Most Serene Majesty, sends out, by your labor and merits, rays of its ancient splendor to the eager eyes of all Englishmen. Since you are also of the King's Privy Council, you always suggest, always further, those things which tend to the greater glory of God, to the greatness of this entire realm, now happily united under one sovereign, James, and most particularly to the honorable tranquillity and peace of all honest private men. In these things the praise due to you is the greater for that in their accomplishment you direct and aim all your efforts, not at popular favor, which you deem vain, nor at the desire of gain, which you consider base, but to the honor only of God, who sees in dark places. And these matters are indeed public, and truly honorable, such as not merely by any songs of mine, but by the mouth and pen of all, will be transmitted to our posterity and to foreign nations, among whom your name is renowned.

But private reasons also impelled me to use my utmost industry in this matter. I have had and still have you, if I err not, as a most benevolent patron in the distressed affairs of my family. You have often listened with pleasure to my melodies, which from men like yourself is a reward to musicians and, so to speak, their highest honorarium. At your plea and request, the Most Serene King has augmented me and my fellows who serve His Majesty's person in music with new benefits and with increases of stipend. For this reason I have resolved that this work of mine (if by chance it shall be of such desert) shall stand as an everlasting testimony of the gratitude of all our hearts to His Majesty and to yourself, distinguished patron, and of my affectionate wishes for those eminent men, whom I love and honor as I perform this office for them. You see, Right Honorable Earl, with what defenders I am provided and by what incentives I am prompted in wishing (if only I could) to imitate the swan.

With truly excellent judgment Alexander forbade any but Apelles or Lysippus to paint him or to sculpture him in bronze.[1] Nor has it been in any way granted to me to satisfy my task, save only that I have tried to ornament things divine with the highest art at my command and to offer nothing not wrought with care to so distinguished a man as yourself. If I have accomplished this, I shall declare these lucubrations of mine (for so without falsehood I may call the products of nightly toil) my swan songs. This they will surely be, if not for their sweetness, at least as proceeding from such age. While I indeed decided at the request of friends to work upon them and to spread them abroad, it was you alone that I set before me in my mind as shining above me like a star guiding me on a course beset with rocks. If in your judgment I have brought back wares not wholly without use, it will be the unique consolation of my old

---

1. The story is told in a number of ancient biographies of Alexander and in Pliny, *Natural History* 7.37.125 (Byrd's most likely source).

age to have brought into the light a work not unmeet for our Most Serene King, whose honor I have wished to augment in my epistle, nor for you, most generous Lord, skilled in the knowledge of human and divine letters, nor unworthy of my years, which I have all consumed in music. Farewell.

To your most Worshipful Honor,
William Byrd.

•   •   •

The Author
To the True Lovers of Music

For you, most high-minded and righteous, who delight at times to sing to God in hymns and spiritual songs, are here set forth for your exercising the Offices for the whole year which are proper to the chief Feasts of the Blessed Virgin Mary and of All Saints; moreover others in five voices with their words drawn from the fountain of Holy Writ; also the Office at the Feast of Corpus Christi, with the more customary antiphons of the same Blessed Virgin and other songs in four voices of the same kind; also all the hymns composed in honor of the Virgin; finally, various songs in three voices sung at the Feast of Easter. Further, to the end that they may be ordered each in its own place in the various parts of the service, I have added a special index at the end of the book; here all that are proper to the same feasts may easily be found grouped together, though differing in the number of voices.

If to these pious words I have set notes not unfitting (as I have wished and as they require), may the honor, as is just, be to God and the pleasure be yours. Howsoever this may be, give them fair and friendly judgment, and commend me to God in your prayers. Farewell.

To the Right Illustrious and Honorable
John Lord Petre of Writtle, his
most clement Maecenas,
Salutation

Since I have attained to such length of years, relying upon the divine mercy, that I have seen many of my pupils in music, men indeed peculiarly skillful in that art, finish their allotted time while I survived, and since also in my own house I consider that the benefits of the divine bounty have been directed toward me, indeed have been showered upon me, my mind is eager, remembering my faith, duty, and piety to God, to leave to posterity a public testimony, at least in some sort, of a heart grateful and referring all things, if this be counted a merit, to my Creator. Having attained to this age, I have attempted, out of devotion to the divine worship, myself unworthy and unequal, to affix notes, to serve as a garland, to certain pious and honeyed praises of the Christian rite to be sung by four, five, or six voices. These are adapted to the glorious

Nativity of Christ our Savior, the Epiphany, the Resurrection, and finally to the Feast of Saints Peter and Paul.

These songs, most Christian Sir, long since completed by me and committed to the press, should in my judgment be dedicated to you above all others, for you are held renowned for the harmony of virtues and letters and distinguished by your love for all the daughters of the Muses and of science. Inasmuch as these musical lucubrations, like fruits sprung from a fertile soil, have mostly proceeded from your house (truly most friendly to me and mine), and from that tempering of the sky have brought forth more grateful and abundant fruits, receive, then, Right Honorable Lord, these little flowers, plucked as it were from your gardens and most rightfully due to you as tithes, and may it be no burden to you to protect these my last labors, to the end that they may go forth to the public under the auspices of your most renowned name, to the glory of God the Greatest and Best, to the greatness of your honor, and finally for the pleasure of all who properly cultivate the Muses. Meanwhile I pray from my soul that all present things may be of good omen to you and all future things happy. Farewell.

The third day of April in the year of man's salvation restored 1607.

Your Honor's most dutiful
William Byrde.

MUSIC, MAGIC, GNOSIS

64 Marsilio Ficino

Marsilio Ficino (1433–99), physician, musician, magician, scholar, translator, Neoplatonic philosopher, and semi-official cultural leader in Florence through much of the late fifteenth century, is a figure also of broader and enduring cultural resonance. His central life's work consisted in translating into Latin and interpreting a huge body of ancient Greek writings previously inaccessible to western Europeans. He provided the first complete Latin version of the Platonic corpus and the first translations of many Neoplatonists of Late Antiquity: Plotinus, Porphyry, Proclus, Iamblichus, the so-called Hermes Trismegistus, and others. To these translations Ficino appended more or less extensive interpretive glosses. *De amore* (1468–1469), his lengthy commentary on Plato's *Symposium*, singlehandedly set the course of a large sixteenth-century literature on the psychology of love and stands behind both Pietro Bembo's and Baldassare Castiglione's conceptions of the subject. Ficino's translations and commentaries served as the bases for study and further translation for centuries after his death, and some of them continued to be republished well into the 1800s.

Three Books on Life (De vita libri tres) was first printed in 1489 and reappeared in almost thirty editions and translations over the next century and a half. It is in essence a work of therapeutic magic. Its third and largest book, titled *De vita coelitus comparanda (On Obtaining Life from the Heavens)*, started as a commentary on passages in Plotinus's *Enneads* and turns the medico-magical practices of the first two books in an astrological direction. Here in Chapter 21 Ficino discusses subjects always close to his heart: the heavenly sources of the powers of song, music's intimate relation to the human spirit (for Ficino a subtle intermediary between body and soul), and the ways to perform astrologically effective song.

FROM *Three Books on Life*
(1489)

BOOK 3

CHAPTER 21: ON THE POWER OF WORDS AND SONGS FOR CAPTURING CELESTIAL BENEFITS AND ON THE SEVEN STEPS THAT LEAD TO CELESTIAL THINGS

· · · · · ·

That a specific and great power exists in specific words is the claim of Origen in *Contra Celsum*, of Synesius and Al-Kindi where they argue about magic,

TEXT: *Marsilio Ficino: Three Books on Life*, ed. Carol V. Kaske and John R. Clark, Medieval & Renaissance Texts & Studies, vol. 57 (Binghamton, N.Y., 1989), pp. 354–63. Copyright by the Center for Medieval and Early Renaissance Studies, SUNY Binghamton. Translation by Carol V. Kaske. I have adapted and sometimes shortened Kaske's annotations.

and likewise of Zoroaster where he forbids the alteration of barbarian words, and also of Iamblichus in the course of the same argument.[1] The Pythagoreans also make this claim, who used to perform wonders by words, songs, and sounds in the Phoebean and Orphic manner.[2] The Hebrew doctors of old practiced this more than anyone else; and all poets sing of the wondrous things that are brought about by songs.[3] And even the famous and venerable Cato in his *De re rustica* sometimes uses barbarous incantations to cure the diseases of his farm animals.[4] But it is better to skip incantations. Nevertheless, that singing through which the young David used to relieve Saul's insanity—unless the sacred text demands that it be attributed to divine agency—one might attribute to nature.[5]

Now since the planets are seven in number, there are also seven steps through which something from on high can be attracted to the lower things. Sounds occupy the middle position and are dedicated to Apollo. Harder materials, stones and metals, hold the lowest rank and thus seem to resemble the Moon. Second in ascending order are things composed of plants, fruits of trees, their gums, and the members of animals, and all these correspond to Mercury—if we follow in the heavens the order of the Chaldeans.[6] Third are very fine powders and their vapors selected from among the materials I have already mentioned and the odors of plants and flowers used as simples, and of ointments; they pertain to Venus. Fourth are words, song, and sounds, all of which are rightly dedicated to Apollo whose greatest invention is music. Fifth are the strong concepts of the imagination—forms, motions, passions—which suggest the force of Mars. Sixth are the sequential arguments and deliberations of the human reason which pertain designedly to Jupiter. Seventh are the more remote and simple operations of the understanding, almost now disjoined from motion and conjoined to the divine; they are meant for Saturn, whom deservedly the Hebrews call "Sabbath" from the word for "rest."

Why all of this? To teach you that even as a certain compound of plants and

---

1. Origen, *Contra Celsum* 1.25; also 5.45 and 8.37; Synesius *De insomniis* 132c (section 3 in Ficino's translation; see the facsimile of the Basle, 1576 *Opera omnia*, ed. M. Sancipriano and Paul Oskar Kristeller [4 vols., Turin: Bottega d'Erasmo, 1959], p. 1969); Al-Kindi, *De radiis*, ed. M.-T. d'Alverny and F. Hudry in *Archives d'histoire doctrinale et littéraire du moyen âge* 41 (1974), chap. 6; Zoroaster, fragment no. 150 of *Oracles chaldaïques*, ed. Édouard des Places (Paris: Société d'edition "Les Belles Lettres," 1971), p. 103; Iamblichus, *De mysteriis* 7.4–5 (see Ficino, *Opera Omnia*, p. 1902). [Tr.]
2. See Iamblichus, *De vita pythagorica* 15.64–67 and 25.110–14, and Philostratus, *Vita Apollonii* 3.15. [Tr.]
3. For example, Virgil, *Aeneid* 4.487–91; Horace, *Epodes* 5.45–46. [Tr.]
4. Cato, *De agricultura* 160. [Tr.]
5. 1 Samuel 16:14–23. [Tr.] See also no. 37 above (Zarlino), p. 298.
6. For a diagram of Ficino's geocentric "Chaldaean" ordering of the heavens, also sometimes called "Ptolemaic," see the woodcut in no. 65 below (Gafori), p. 394. Note that throughout this chapter (and elsewhere) Ficino uses Apollo and Phoebus as synonyms for the middle "planet" in this order, the sun.

vapors made through both medical and astronomical science yields a common form of a medicine, like a harmony endowed with gifts from the stars; so tones first chosen by the rule of the stars and then combined according to the congruity of these stars with each other make a sort of common form, and in it a celestial power arises. It is indeed very difficult to judge exactly what kinds of tones are suitable for what sorts of stars, what combinations of tones especially accord with what sorts of constellations and aspects. But we can attain this, partly through our own efforts, partly by some divine destiny. . . .

We will apply three principal rules for this undertaking, provided you be warned beforehand not to think we are speaking here of worshipping the stars, but rather of imitating them and thereby trying to capture them. And do not believe that we are dealing with gifts which the stars are going to give by their own election but rather by a natural influence. We strive to adapt ourselves to this multifarious and occult influence by the same studied methods we use every day to make ourselves fit to receive in a healthy manner the perceivable light and heat of the Sun. But it is the wise man alone who adapts himself to the occult and wonderful gifts of this influence. Now, however, let us go on to the rules that are going to accommodate our songs to the stars. The first is to inquire diligently what powers in itself or what effects from itself a given star, constellation, or aspect has—what do they remove, what do they bring?— and to insert these into the meaning of our words, so as to detest what they remove and to approve what they bring. The second rule is to take note of what special star rules what place or person and then to observe what sorts of tones and songs these regions and persons generally use, so that you may supply similar ones, together with the meanings I have just mentioned, to the words which you are trying to expose to the same stars. Thirdly, observe the daily positions and aspects of the stars and discover to what principal speeches, songs, motions, dances, moral behavior, and actions most people are usually incited by these, so that you may imitate such things as far as possible in your song, which aims to please the particular part of heaven that resembles them and to catch an influence that resembles them.

But remember that song is a most powerful imitator of all things. It imitates the intentions and passions of the soul as well as words; it represents also people's physical gestures, motions, and actions as well as their characters and imitates all these and acts them out so forcibly that it immediately provokes both the singer and the audience to imitate and act out the same things. By the same power, when it imitates the celestials, it also wonderfully arouses our spirit upwards to the celestial influence and the celestial influence downwards to our spirit. Now the very matter of song, indeed, is altogether purer and more similar to the heavens than is the matter of medicine. For this too is air, hot or warm, still breathing and somehow living; like an animal, it is composed of certain parts and limbs of its own and not only possesses motion and displays passion but even carries meaning like a mind, so that it can be said to be a kind of airy and rational animal. Song, therefore, which is full of spirit and meaning—if it corresponds to this or that constellation not only in the things it signifies, its parts, and the form that results from those parts, but also in the disposition of the imagination—has as much power as does any other combination of things and casts it into the singer and from him into the nearby listener. It has this power as long as it keeps the vigor and the spirit of the singer, especially if the singer himself be Phoebean by nature and have in his heart a powerful vital and animal spirit. For just as the natural power and spirit, when it is strongest, not only immediately softens and dissolves the hardest food and soon renders harsh food sweet but also generates offspring outside of itself by the emission of the seminal spirit, so the vital and animal power, when it is most efficacious, not only acts powerfully on its own body when its spirit undergoes a very intense conception and agitation through song but soon also moves a neighboring body by emanation. This power influences both its own and the other body by a certain stellar property which it drew both from its own form and from the election of a suitable astrological hour. For this reason in particular many dwellers in the East and South, especially Indians, are said to have an admirable power in their words, as these peoples are for the most part Solar. I say that they are the most powerful of all, not in their natural, but in their vital and animal forces; and the same goes for all persons in other areas who are especially Phoebean.

Now song which arises from this power, timeliness, and intention is undoubtedly nothing else but another spirit recently conceived in you in the power of your spirit—a spirit made Solar and acting both in you and in the bystander by the power of the Sun. For if a certain vapor and spirit directed outwards through the rays of the eyes or by other means can sometimes fascinate, infect, or otherwise influence a bystander, much more can a spirit do this, when it pours out from both the imagination and heart at the same time, more abundant, more fervent, and more apt to motion. Hence it is no wonder at all that by means of song certain diseases, both mental and physical, can sometimes be cured or brought on, especially since a musical spirit of this kind properly touches and acts on the spirit which is the mean between body and soul, and immediately affects both the one and the other with its influence. You will allow that there is a wondrous power in an aroused and singing spirit, if you allow to the Pythagoreans and Platonists that the heavens are a spirit and that they order all things through their motions and tones.

Remember that all music proceeds from Apollo; that Jupiter is musical to the extent that he is consonant with Apollo; and that Venus and Mercury claim music by their proximity to Apollo. Likewise remember that song pertains to only those four; the other three planets have voices but not songs. Now we attribute to Saturn voices that are slow, deep, harsh, and plaintive; to Mars, voices that are the opposite—quick, sharp, fierce, and menacing; the Moon has the voices in between. The music, however, of Jupiter is deep, earnest, sweet, and joyful with stability. To Venus, on the contrary, we ascribe songs voluptuous with wantonness and softness. The songs between these two extremes we ascribe to the Sun and Mercury: if with their grace and smoothness they are reverential, simple, and earnest, the songs are judged to be Apollo's; if they are somewhat more relaxed, along with their gaiety, but vigorous and complex, they are Mercury's. Accordingly, you will win over one of these four to yourself by using their songs, especially if you supply musical notes that fit their songs. When at the right astrological hour you declaim aloud by singing and playing in the manners we have specified for the four gods, they seem to be just about to answer you like an echo or like a string in a lute trembling to the vibration of another which has been similarly tuned. And this will happen to you from heaven as naturally, say Plotinus and Iamblichus,[7] as a tremor re-echoes from a lute or an echo arises from an opposite wall. Assuredly, whenever your spirit—by frequent use of Jovial, Mercurial, or Venereal harmony, a harmony performed while these planets are dignified—singing at the same time most intently and conforming itself to the harmony, becomes Jovial, Mercurial, or Venereal, it will meanwhile become Phoebean as well, since the power of Phoebus himself, the ruler of music, flourishes in every consonance. And conversely when you become Phoebean from Phoebean song and notes, you at the same time lay claim to the power of Jupiter, Venus, and Mercury. And again, from your spirit influenced within, you have a similar influence on your soul and body.

Remember, moreover, that a prayer, when it has been suitably and seasonably composed and is full of emotion and forceful, has a power similar to a song. There is no use in reporting what great power Damis and Philostratus tell us certain Indian priests have in their prayers, nor in mentioning the words they say that Apollonius employed to call up the shade of Achilles.[8] For we are not now speaking of worshipping divinities but of a natural power in speech, song, and words. That there is indeed in certain sounds a Phoebean and medical power is clear from the fact that in Puglia everyone who is stung by the phalangium[9] becomes stunned and lies half-dead until each hears a certain sound proper to him. For then he dances along with the sound, works up a sweat, and gets well. And if ten years later he hears a similar sound, he feels a sudden urge to dance. I gather from the evidence that this sound is Solar and Jovial.

7. Plotinus, *Enneads* 4.3.12, 4.4.41; Iamblichus, *De mysteriis* 3.9 (see Ficino, *Opera omnia*, p. 1885). [Tr.] The sympathetic vibration of similarly tuned lute strings was a favorite Renaissance example of the wondrous (or magical) powers of music. For another mention of it see no. 53 above (Peacham), p. 351.
8. Philostratus, *Vita Apollonii* 4.16. [Tr.]
9. That is, the southern Italian wolf spider, commonly referred to as a tarantula. For other references to this musical tarantism see no. 37 (Zarlino), p. 298, and no. 53 (Peacham), p. 348.

65 Franchino Gafori

The music theorist and composer Franchino Gafori was born at Lodi in 1451. During an early stay at Naples, he befriended Tinctoris. After returning to Lodi, where he taught from 1480 to 1484, he was appointed chapelmaster of the Milan Cathedral. He remained in Milan for the rest of his life and died there in 1522.

At Milan in the 1490s, Gafori completed his three most important treatises. The *Theorica musicae* was published in 1492 and the *Practica musicae* in 1496; *De harmonia musicorum instrumentorum opus (A Work on the Harmony of Musical Instruments),* drafted by 1500, circulated in manuscript until its publication in 1518. All three treatises reveal Gafori's extensive knowledge of earlier music theorists, ancient and modern, and *De harmonia* in particular exploits Latin translations of Aristides Quintilianus and Ptolemy that Gafori himself commissioned. From these and other sources, and under the sway of Ficinian Platonism and Neoplatonism, Gafori indulged a tendency to speculate on musical cosmology stronger than that of most other Renaissance music theorists.

In Book 4, Chapter 12 of *De harmonia,* Gafori elaborates on correspondences between the modes and the planets advanced in the *Musica practica* of Bartolomé Ramis de Pareia (1.3). The author of the couplets here relating the Muses, modes, and planets is unknown; these verses reappeared some years later, no doubt culled from Gafori, in the magic treatise *De occulta philosophia* by Henry Cornelius Agrippa, the arch-magus of the Renaissance (for Agrippa see no. 40 above, pp. 304–8). The famous woodcut representing these correspondences first appeared, incongruously, as the frontispiece of *Practica musicae.* Perhaps it was prepared for a planned contemporaneous publication of *De harmonia* that was subsequently postponed.

FROM *De harmonia musicorum instrumentorum opus*

(1518)

BOOK FOUR

CHAPTER 12: THAT THE MUSES, STARS, MODES, AND STRINGS CORRESPOND TO ONE ANOTHER

There are those who believe that the Muses follow the order of the stars and the modes. Some count only three Muses, daughters of heaven and earth, while others have listed nine born of Jupiter and Mnemosyne. These nine Ovid calls

TEXT: facsimile of the edition of Milan, 1518 (New York: Broude Brothers, 1979), fols. 92–94. Translation by Gary Tomlinson. Gafori's postils add no new information to his account; I have omitted them.

the Mnemonides in Book 5 of the *Metamorphoses*, writing: "He said: 'O daughters of Mnemosyne'—for he knew us—'stay your steps.' "[1] And Diodorus Siculus in Book 5 famously interpreted them, almost describing the parts of the musical art associated with each one.[2] Homer also granted them extraordinary renown.[3] St. Augustine, moreover, named nine Muses in Book 2 of *De doctrina christiana*. He denied that they were daughters of Jupiter and Mnemosyne, accepting instead Varro's idea that three craftsmen made three statues each for the Temple of Apollo, which were then given names by Hesiod in his *Theogony*.[4] Just in this manner the ancients wished to give the Muses names to teach men good and useful things not known to the unlearned.

Some imagine the Muses to have sprung from Apollo's head, as this line from the poet expresses: "The power of Apollo's mind arouses Muses everywhere."[5] Others say they were taught by Apollo, on account of which they call Apollo himself a musician, as I described at length in Book 1 of my *Theorica musicae*.[6] Most agree that Apollo was depicted with a ten-stringed lyre, while others think it had seven, corresponding to the seven fundamental strings Virgil recounts with these lines from Book 6 of the *Aeneid*:

> There, too, the long-robed Thracian priest
> matches their measures with the seven clear notes.[7]

Moreover seven intervals come from these strings: the major third, minor third, fourth, fifth, major sixth, minor sixth, and octave. And the number seven is structured according to a certain perfection, since it is understood to make twenty-eight by the sum of itself and its individual parts, and twenty-eight is the only number between 10 and 100 that is the sum of its own aliquot parts.[8] They say that the Muse Clio invented history, Melpomene tragedy, Thalia comedy, Euterpe the music of pipes, Terpsichore the music of the psaltery, Erato geometry, Calliope writing, Urania astronomy, and Polyhymnia rhetoric. . . .

Callimachus, a poet of no mean authority among the Greeks, proclaimed the gifts of the Muses in this epigram:

> Calliope invented the wisdom of heroic song,
> Clio the sweet song of lovely dance and lyre,
> Euterpe the resounding voice of tragic chorus;

1. 5.280; trans. Frank Justus Miller, Ovid, *Metamorphoses* (2 vols., London: Heinemann, 1916), vol. 1, p. 257.

2. Gafori's reference to Book 5 is mistaken; see Diodorus Siculus, *Library of History* 4.7.2–4.

3. For example, *Iliad* 1.601–4, 11.218; *Odyssey* 8.487–88, 24.60–62.

4. See *De doctrina christiana* 2.17.27.

5. *Mentis Apollineae vis has movet undique musas.* The verse was thought in the Renaissance to be by Virgil, "the poet" Gafori refers to; it is now associated with Ausonius. See Edgar Wind, *Pagan Mysteries in the Renaissance* (New York: Norton, 1968), pp. 267–68.

6. See chap. 1, fol. aiir.

7. Ll. 645–46. Trans. H. Rushton Fairclough, *Virgil in Two Volumes* (London: Heinemann, 1922), vol. 1, p. 551. The priest of Thrace is, of course, Orpheus.

8. That is, 7 is numerologically significant because $7+6+5+4+3+2+1=28$; 28 in turn is important for numerologists because the sum of its factors (excluding 28 itself) $= 28$ (i.e., $1+2+4+7+14=28$). There are only six other numbers between 1 and 40,000,000 for which this is true (information from Victoria Kirkham).

> Melpomene gave the sweet knowledge of the lyre to
>   mortals;
> Terpsichore, obligingly, offered skilfully made pipes;
> Erato discovered the most delightful hymns to
>   immortals;
> erudite Polyhymnia found out the pleasures of dance
> and gave harmony to every song;
> Urania revealed the heavens and the dance
>   of the celestial stars;
> Thalia invented comedy and renowned mores.[9]

In addition to all this, we believe (and most others concur) that the Muses themselves correspond to the stars and modes such that we may assign them to the strings that begin the modes, one by one. First we put Thalia underground, as in subterrenean silence, as these verses express:

> In the first song Thalia, who lies quiet
> in the breast of the earth, sprouts nocturnal silence.

The comparison of the earth with silence because it is immobile occurs in Marcus Tullius;[10] they compare it to the three-headed, underground Cerberus lying at the feet of Apollo. The beginning of the hypodorian, the lowest mode, and the moon, the heaviest planet inhabiting only the house of Cancer (as astronomers say),[11] and Clio are assigned to the lowest string[12] by this poem:

> Persephone and Clio breath and the hypodorian
> is born; from this origin melody blossoms.

To the second string, called *hypate hypaton,* the beginning of the hypophrygian mode, Mercury in the houses of Gemini and Virgo and also Calliope are customarily assigned by this poem:

> The following string gives rise to hypophrygian,
> which Calliope and the messenger of the gods bring
>   forth.

The third string, called *parhypate hypaton,* Terpsichore consecrated to the hypolydian and to Venus in the houses of Libra and Taurus; whence the verses:

> The third string reveals the start of hypolydian;
> Terpsichore dances to it and kind Paphos rules it.

Melpomene and the sun in the house of Leo have granted the fourth string, *lychanos hypaton,* to the dorian mode by this poem:

9. Greek (i.e., Palatine) Anthology 9.504. There are many epigrams by Callimachus in this huge compilation, but this one on the Muses is no longer considered his work.

10. That is, Cicero; see Macrobius, *Commentarii in somnium Scipionis* 1.22–2.1 and Wind, *Pagan Mysteries,* p. 265.

11. The houses are the twelve regions of the zodiac, each associated with a constellation and its sign. In astrological teaching reaching back to Late Antiquity each planet is thought to exert its influence most strongly in one or two particular houses. These correspondences are given here by Gafori, starting with the moon and Cancer.

12. That is, *proslambanomenos* in Greek musical terminology. Gafori supplies the Greek names of the remaining strings in his text.

> Melpomene and Titan establish (I avow)
> the mode called dorian in the fourth position.

On the fifth string, called *hypate meson,* Erato and Mars in the houses of Aries and Scorpio have placed the phrygian mode. Hence the verses:

> Erato wants to prescribe the fifth string to phrygian,
> and Mars always loves war, not peace.

The sphere of Jupiter, holding steadfastly to the houses of Pisces and Sagittarius, and also Euterpe along with the lydian mode are included in the sixth string, *parhypate meson,* by this poem:

> The lydian mode governs Euterpe and Jupiter,
> which the sixth string, sweetly sounding, ordains.

On the seventh string, *lychanos meson,* Saturn in the houses of Aquarius and Capricorn and the Muse Polyhymnia have placed the mixolydian mode; hence the verses:

> On the seventh string live Saturn and also
> Polyhymnia; from it the mixolydian begins.

The eighth string, called *mese,* has consecrated Urania and the hypermixolydian to the starry sphere, as this poem declares:

> While the hypermixolydian contemplates the eighth
>   string,
> friendly to Urania, it turns the heavens well.

Aristides Quintilianus, at the end of Book II of his *De musica,* gave a correspondence of Muses and modes that is in some ways the opposite of this.[13] And Herodotus of Halicarnassus, who dedicated the nine books of his *Histories* to these same Muses, gave yet another order.[14] At Apollo's right side the Greeks usually placed the three young women called the Charities or Graces, attendants on Venus. Their names are Aglaia, meaning luster, Thalia, signifying youthful bloom, and Euphrosyne or joy.

All these things are shown in the following figure:[15]

---

13. 2.19. Here Gafori's understanding of Aristides was imperfect. Aristides names only three Muses, Polyhymnia, Erato, and Euterpe, and he associates them not with modes but with lesser forms of music for the kithara, lyre, and auloi respectively. See Aristides Quintilianus, *On Music,* trans. Thomas J. Mathiesen (New Haven: Yale University Press, 1983) pp. 155–56.

14. Gafori refers to the once conventional (but inauthentic) sectional division of Herodotus's *Histories* into nine "Muses." See *The Oxford Classical Dictionary* (Oxford: Clarendon Press, 1970), s.v. "Herodotus."

15. For interpretation of this famous woodcut beyond what Gafori makes explicit see esp. Wind, *Pagan Mysteries,* app. 6; James Haar, "The Frontispiece of Gafori's *Practica musicae* (1496)," *Renaissance Quarterly* 27 (1974): 7–22; and Claude Palisca, *Humanism in Italian Renaissance Musical Thought* (New Haven: Yale University Press, 1985), pp. 171–74.

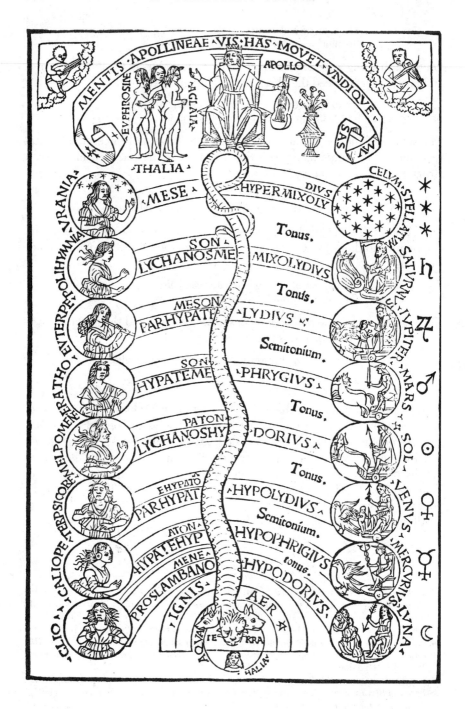

66 Pontus de Tyard

Among the Platonic themes dearest to Marsilio Ficino and his followers was the assertion (Plato, *Phaedrus* 265) that there were four sorts of divine madness by which the human soul might be seized and touched by divinity. One of these was the poetic furor or, as we might say, the furor of song or music. Ficino's writings on this topic gave rise to a literature extending through the sixteenth century on the heavenly sources of poetry and song. Pontus de Tyard's *First Solitaire or Prose on the Muses and Poetic Furor (Solitaire premier ou prose des Muses & de la fureur poétique)* elaborates this topic in the context of a work on music theory, often paraphrasing Ficino and occasionally taking over verbatim the views of his Florentine predecessor. The work takes the form of a dialogue between the Solitaire (representing Tyard himself) and his beloved Pasithée. The *Solitaire premier,* first published in 1552, was followed in 1555 by the *Solitaire second ou prose de la musique.* Both were reprinted in Tyard's *Discours philosophiques* in 1587.

In addition to his philosophical writings, Tyard is remembered for his poetry. Along with Ronsard and Baïf he was a member of the Pléiade, a circle of seven poets who strove to reform French literary usage and elevate the French lyric by imitating ancient models and Petrarch. Tyard was born in 1521 and died in 1605.

FROM *First Solitaire or Prose on the Muses and Poetic Furor*

(1552)

CHAPTER 3

. . . Platonic philosophers hold that when the soul descends into the body it is divided in various operations and loses the estimable unity that had enabled it to know and enjoy the sovereign one that is God. In this division and disunity its superior parts, sleeping and shrouded in a dull torpor, cede control to its inferior parts, which are always prey to perturbations. Therefore the whole soul lives full of a discord and disorder difficult to reconcile. So this is the task at

TEXT: Pontus de Tyard, *Oeuvres: Solitaire premier,* ed. Silvio F. Baridon (Geneva and Lille: Droz, 1950), pp. 12–13, 16–22. Translation by Gary Tomlinson. The first, fourth, and fifth paragraphs, and parts of the second and third as well, are virtual translations of Ficino's words in an account of divine furor he published twice with few alterations: first as his *Epitome* of Plato's *Ion* (mid-1460s; see *Opera omnia*, ed. M. Sancipriano and Paul Oskar Kristeller [4 vols., Turin: Bottega d'Erasmo, 1959] pp. 1281–84) and second as 7.13–14 of his commentary on Plato's *Symposium, De amore* (1468–69; *Opera omnia*, pp. 1361–62).

hand; this is where we must work to loosen the soul bogged in earthly mire and to lift it up to join with the sovereign one, restoring it to its earlier unity. Now, since the soul passes through four levels lowering itself into the body, it is likewise necessary that its elevation pass from low to high through the same four levels. As for the four levels of descent, the first and highest is angelic understanding, the second intellectual reason, the third opinion, and the fourth nature.[1]

•   •   •   •   •

Thus to move up again four levels are necessary, and these levels can be discerned in the illumination of the soul or elevation of the understanding . . . known as divine furor. Divine furor, Pasithée, is the only stairway by which the soul can find its way back to its original sovereign good and its ultimate happiness. . . . Man may be seized by divine furor in four ways. The first is by poetic furor, which comes from the gift of the Muses. The second is by the knowledge of the mysteries and secrets of religion, under the aegis of Bacchus. The third is by the ravishment of prophecy or vaticination or divination, under Apollo; and the fourth is by the violence of amorous affection, under Love and Venus. You must understand, Pasithée, that in these few words and these four types are hidden all the highest and most sacred things human understanding can aspire to, the true and certain knowledge of all disciplines that scholars seek through long (and often futile) study. For we must believe that, without the illumination of these divine rays, without the heat of this divine furor that lights the torch of the soul, we cannot attain in any other way the knowledge of sound doctrines and science. All the less can we elevate ourselves to a level of virtue, freed from the base, corporeal shadows whose dim light is nourished by the caprice of false and deceiving pleasures, where we could appreciate in our minds the sovereign good. . . . Now the lowest point the soul reaches in its descent is the body, to whose diverse and contrary parts it is so firmly attached that it is forced to separate and distribute its powers in diverse and contrary operations. Its superior part is asleep, stunned (as we might say) by so heavy a fall, and its inferior part is agitated and full of perturbations, from which arise a horrible discord, disorder, and unharmonious proportion. The soul seems incapable of any just action unless by some means this horrible discord is transformed into a sweet symphony and this impertinent disorder reduced to a measured equality, well ordered and proportioned. And to do this is the particular duty of poetic furor, awakening the sleeping part of the soul by the tones of music; comforting the perturbed part by the suavity of sweet harmony; then chasing away the dissonant discord by the well tuned diversity of musical

1. Ficino had adapted these ontological levels or grades of the universe from Plotinus; see Paul Oskar Kristeller, *The Philosophy of Marsilio Ficino,* trans. Virginia Conant (Gloucester, Mass.: Peter Smith, 1964), pp. 106–8.

accord; and finally reducing the disorder to a certain well and proportionately measured equality ordered by the graceful and grave facility of verses regulated by the careful observance of number and measure.

But this is, as yet, nothing; for it is necessary to efface the varying claims of diverse opinions caught up in the constant flux of a multitude of images and corporeal species; and it is necessary that the soul, now awakened and well ordered, call back into one its parts and powers so diversely diffused and separated. For this the holy communication of religious mysteries and secrets is needed, through whose purifications and devotional offices the soul gathers itself together and devotes itself completely to sacred dedication and utterly reverent intention, prostrating itself before the divinity it adores. When thus the diverse powers of the soul, formerly dispersed here and there in various exercises, are drawn up and gathered together in the single intention of rational understanding, the third furor is necessary to put aside such discursive intellectual ratiocinations concerning principles and conclusions and to lead the understanding back to union with the soul. This comes about through the ravishment of prophecies and divinations. Whoever is moved by the prophetic or divinatory furor is stolen away to interior contemplation and joins his soul and all his spirits together, rising high above all human apprehension and natural reason to draw from the most intimate, profound, and hidden secrets of divinity the prediction of things which must come to pass. Finally, when all that is in the essence and in the nature of the soul is made one, it must (in order to return to its source) suddenly withdraw itself into the sovereign one, above all essences. This the great and celestial Venus accomplishes by love, that is to say by a fervent and incomparable desire that the soul, so elevated, has of enjoying the divine and eternal beauty.

· · · · ·

CHAPTER 4

The poetic furor comes from the Muses . . . and is a ravishment of the docile and insuperable soul in which it is awakened, moved, and incited by songs and other poems for the instruction of man. By ravishment of the soul I mean that the soul is occupied and entirely directed toward and intent on the holy and sacred Muses, who have found it to be docile and ready to receive the form they impress on it. That is, they have found it well prepared to be taken by that ravishment, by which from its softness it becomes insuperable. Then it cannot be stained or overtaken by any base or worldly thing but instead rises above and beyond all such vileness. Moreover it is awakened from bodily torpor and sleep to intellectual vigilance; it is summoned back from the shadows of ignorance to the light of truth, from death to life, from a deep and stolid forgetfulness to a remembrance of divine and celestial things; so that finally it is moved, impelled, and incited to express in verses the things it foresees and contemplates. Therefore no one should undertake recklessly to knock at the doors of poetry; for whomever the Muses had not graced with their furor and whomever God had not looked upon propitiously and favorably would approach in vain and make cold and wretched verses.

WRITINGS ON POLYPHONIC PRACTICE

67 Johannes Tinctoris

FROM *Liber de arte contrapuncti*
(1477)

BOOK 2

CHAPTER 19: THAT COUNTERPOINT IS OF TWO SORTS, NAMELY SIMPLE AND DIMINISHED.

Because, as we said at the beginning of the preceding book,[1] dissonances are sometimes admitted in counterpoint, it should be noted first that there are two sorts of counterpoint, simple and diminished. Simple counterpoint is that which is made by simply placing against a note another note of the same value. . . . This counterpoint is called simple because it is fashioned simply through the proportion of equality without any flowering of diversity. Diminished counterpoint is that which is created by placing two or more notes against one, sometimes dividing that note equally, sometimes unequally. . . . Counterpoint of this sort is called diminished because in it full notes are divided into various smaller parts. Hence some people metaphorically call it florid, for just as diversity of flowers makes the fields most delightful, so variety of proportions renders counterpoint most pleasant.

CHAPTER 20: THAT BOTH SIMPLE AND DIMINISHED COUNTERPOINT ARE MADE IN TWO WAYS, NAMELY IN WRITING AND IN THE MIND, AND HOW A COMPOSED PIECE DIFFERS FROM A COUNTERPOINT.

Furthermore, both simple and diminished counterpoint are made in two ways, in writing and in the mind. Counterpoint that is written is usually called a "composed piece" *[resfacta]*. But that which we put together in the mind we call a "counterpoint" pure and simple, and those who do this are said in common parlance to "sing over the book" *[super librum cantare]*. A composed piece differs from a counterpoint above all in that all parts of a composed piece, whether three, four, or more, are mutually bound to one another, so that the ordering and rule of consonances of any one part must be observed with

TEXT: Johannis Tinctoris, *Opera omnia*, ed. Albert Seay (2 vols., American Institute of Musicology, 1975), vol. 2, pp. 105–41. Translation by Gary Tomlinson. I have profited from the recent interpretations of these chapters cited below and also from Claude Palisca's unpublished translation of most of the chapters here and Klaus Jürgen Sachs's discussion of them in *The New Grove Dictionary of Music and Musicians*, s.v. "Counterpoint." Tinctoris's music examples are long; I have omitted those that are not required to understand his discussion.

1. 1.1.

respect to each and all the others. . . . But when two, three, four, or more sing together over the book, one is not subject to the other. Indeed it is enough that each of them be consonant with the tenor in regard to the rule and ordering of consonances. However, I do not consider it blameworthy but rather most laudable if the singers prudently avoid similarity among themselves in their choice and succession of consonances. In doing so they will make their harmony much fuller and sweeter.[2]

· · · · ·

CHAPTER 22: HOW A COUNTERPOINT IS MADE ON A MEASURED MELODY.

A counterpoint is made on a measured melody when it is sung over a tenor measured in notes according to perfect or imperfect quantities. . . . A counterpoint resembling this is created on a plainchant when the notes of this plainchant are measured by means of the various quantities represented by the shapes of longs, breves, and semibreves. . . . There are still other counterpoints—though these are ever so rare—that are sung not only over a tenor but also over any other part of a composed piece. This sort of counterpoint requires much skill and practice. If it is done sweetly and expertly it deserves all the more praise for being so difficult.[3] Although all the preceding ways of making counterpoint, whether on a plainchant or on a measured melody, are examples of diminished counterpoint, it is possible in any of these ways to make simple counterpoint (that is, note against note of the same value). But to do this on a measured melody is altogether ridiculous and on a plainchant childish, except when the notes of the plainchant are sung more quickly as a semibreve of minor prolation, for then the words are distinctly enunciated and this kind of counterpoint yields great sweetness. . . .

2. This distinction between *res facta* and *cantare super librum* has in recent years stimulated much thought on the relations of written composition, performance of polyphony, and *contrapunctus* in the late fifteenth century; see esp. Margaret Bent, "*Resfacta* and *Cantare super librum,*" *Journal of the American Musicological Society* [*JAMS*] 36 (1983): 371–91; Bonnie J. Blackburn, "On Compositional Process in the Fifteenth Century," *JAMS* 40 (1987): 210–84; David E. Cohen, "*Contrapunctus,* Improvisation, and *Res facta,*" paper presented at the 1989 national meeting of the American Musicological Society, Austin, Texas; and Rob C. Wegman, "From Maker to Composer: Improvisation and Musical Authorship in the Low Countries," *JAMS* 49 (1996): 409–79. From all this a summary of Tinctoris's categories might be hazarded. In *cantare super librum* he describes a widespread practice of singing polyphony over a written melody, typically a plainchant or the tenor of a separate piece of polyphony. (The "book," then, refers to the place where the written melody is found; the other parts are, in principle at least, unwritten.) *Res facta* refers to a piece of polyphony in principle fully written out; it touches on a sense crystalizing around 1500 of such a piece as an autonomous entity termed *compositio*. *Contrapunctus,* finally, is a word increasingly caught between the two practices; it is not yet conceived only as a set of techniques and rules to guide voice-leading in the making of a composition but instead both overlaps with and stands independent of the emerging category *compositio*.

3. On this special kind of "singing over the book," apparently using two parts from the written source, see Bent, "*Resfacta,*" pp. 388–89, and Blackburn, "Compositional Process," p. 256.

CHAPTER 23: THAT DISSONANCES MUST NOT BE ADMITTED IN
SIMPLE COUNTERPOINT BUT ONLY IN DIMINISHED, AND FIRST,
ON DISSONANCES ON THE PARTS OF THE MINIM IN EITHER
PROLATION AND ON THE PARTS OF THE SEMIBREVE IN MINOR
PROLATION.[4]

In simple counterpoint dissonances are simply and absolutely prohibited, but in diminished counterpoint they are sometimes permitted in moderation. Here it should be known that I ignore the compositions of older musicians, in which there were more dissonances than consonances. Nearly all more recent composers and also singers over the book place a consonance over the first or other part of a minim in the tenor, both in major and minor prolation; and moreover in minor prolation they place it either over the first or another part of the semibreve. They employ a dissonance of the same or a smaller note value over what immediately follows.[5] On the other hand, a dissonance is almost always used in major or minor prolation on the first part of the first of two minims on the same pitch, joined together or separate, or of a single minim, and also on the first part of two semibreves in minor prolation, joined or separated, when these immediately precede some perfect quantity.[6] However, if the tenor descends to a perfect quantity through several minims in major or minor prolation or several semibreves in minor prolation, a syncopated dissonance is very frequently admitted on the first part of any of these minims or semibreves, as is clear from the following example:[7]

4. Prolation refers to the relationship in mensural notation between semibreve and minim; the semibreve is worth three minims in major prolation, two in minor. Major prolation is signaled by a dot in the mensuration sign, minor prolation by its absence.

5. For example, for major prolation: music example, m. 1, supremum, m. 3 supremum and contratenor; for minor prolation: m. 16, supremum.

6. This stipulation recognizes cadential suspensions. For two minims on the same pitch see m. 8 (major prolation) and m. 22 (minor prolation). For two minims "joined together" see m. 4 (major) and m. 20 (minor). For a single minim Tinctoris gives no examples other than those involved at the end of chains of syncopations; see n. 7 below. For two semibreves in minor prolation see m. 26; for two semibreves joined together see m. 24.

7. This is the syncopated descent to a cadence frequently encountered in mid- and late-fifteenth-century polyphony. For minims see m. 12 (major) and m. 28 (minor); for semibreves in minor prolation, m. 32.

CHAPTER 24: ON DISSONANCES ALLOWED ON PARTS OF THE NOTE
VALUES THAT DIRECT THE METER OF THE SONG AND ARE
SUBJECT TO BINARY PROPORTION AND IMPERFECT QUANTITY.

Although we have already spoken about the dissonances allowed on parts of
the semibreve in minor prolation, we must still explain how dissonances are
allowed on the parts of all the other note values in meters that divide them

evenly into two parts.[8] Concerning the parts of minims in either prolation in subduple proportion or where the tenor doubles its time, which amounts to the same thing; or concerning the parts of the breve in imperfect tempus and minor prolation in *cantus ad medium*[9] or in duple proportion, which are also the same thing; or in singing the parts of longs in the same tempus and prolation in imperfect minor mode but in quadruple proportion; or in singing the parts of maxims in the same tempus, prolation, and minor mode and in imperfect major mode in octuple proportion: when a consonance is placed over the first or other part of such notes sung according to the aforementioned modes, proportions, and quantities, then a dissonance of equal or lesser note value may be placed on what follows. If two of these notes on the same pitch, joined or separate, stand together before some perfect quantity, a dissonance is sometimes permitted on the first part of the first of these. However, when a descent is made into some perfect quantity through one or more of these aforementioned notes, any of these frequently permits a syncopated dissonance on its first part. . . .

*   *   *   *   *

CHAPTER 29: THAT MANY COMPOSERS NEVER EMPLOY A DISSONANCE THE LENGTH OF HALF THE NOTE VALUE THAT DIRECTS THE METER OF THE SONG BUT RATHER EMPLOY SHORTER DISSONANCES.

Many composers avoid dissonances so carefully that they never extend them over a full half of the note value that directs the meter but only over a third, fourth, or smaller part of it. In my opinion these composers should be imitated. . . .

*   *   *   *   *

CHAPTER 31: WHY SMALL DISSONANCES MAY BE USED BY MUSICIANS.

Nevertheless, in the manners described above small dissonances may sometimes be used by musicians, just as reasoned rhetorical figures are used by orators for the sake of embellishment and effect. For a song is embellished when it ascends or descends from one consonance to another by appropriate

8. That is, we must extend the rules of Chapter 23 to other note values, in mensurations that divide them in two, that might be brought by the use of proportion signs to take over the minim's or semibreve's usual role of carrying the beat. Thus in subduple proportion or where the tenor doubles its time (*crescit in duplo*) the minim carries the beat, in duple proportion the breve, in quadruple proportion the long, and in octuple proportion the maxim. Tinctoris's music example applies all these proportions to the tenor part only so that, for example, in the section showing octuple proportion the tenor's maxims have the same duration as semibreves in the other voices.
9. That is, cut time or *alla breve*.

means and by syncopations, which sometimes cannot be made without dissonances. These small dissonances do not present themselves so strongly to the
ear when they are placed over the last parts of notes in the tenor as they do
when placed over the first. . . .

CHAPTER 32: ON THE ARRANGEMENT OF ANY DISSONANCE.

Any dissonance should be arranged so that, whether ascending or descending, it comes after the consonance nearest to it, as for example a second after
a unison or a third, a fourth after a third or a fifth, a seventh after a fifth or an
octave, and so on. And any dissonance should be followed by a consonance that
is only one or, very rarely, two steps removed from it. . . .[10]

10. That is, dissonances should be approached and left by step and most often with oblique motion
between the parts. For exceptions to this rule in Tinctoris's music examples see Sachs, "Counterpoint."

68 Bartolomé Ramis de Pareia

The *Musica practica* of Bartolomé Ramis (or Ramos) de Pareia was printed in
Bologna in 1482. Of the life of its author we know little. That he came from
Baeza, near Madrid, and lectured in Bologna, after having previously lectured
in Salamanca, is set forth in his book. Other sources tell us that he left Bologna
sometime after 1484 and went to Rome, where he was still living in 1491. From
his pupil Giovanni Spataro we also learn that Ramis withheld parts of his book
from the printer with a view to lecturing on them publicly; as we have it, then,
the *Musica practica* is only a fragment. A completion of the work, in a companion treatise called *Musica theorica,* was written at least in part but never published.

Among other innovations in *Musica practica* Ramis challenges the solmization practices passed down from the Middle Ages and associated especially
with Guido of Arezzo. In place of the Guidonian system of six syllables matched
to the notes of a hexachord, Ramis proposes eight new syllables matched to the
octave. This does away with most of the mutations, or shifts of syllable (and
hence hexachord) on a single pitch, called for by the Guidonian system.
Although Ramis's syllables were never widely adopted, his system in general
stands behind modern "fixed *do*" approaches.

The increasing complexities of solmization resulted from the increasingly frequent use of half-steps in positions where they were not naturally found in the
three Guidonian hexachords (which started only on the notes C, F, and G).
Singing these new half-steps in the old system required a proliferation of *mi–fa*
mutations and hence a proliferation of new hexachords. (For example, to sing
a–c♯–d where a–c–d is written requires the syllables *ut–mi–fa* rather than *re–*

fa–sol and assigns *ut* to a non-Guidonian position on a.) Ramis outlines these difficulties in his discussion of *musica ficta.*

FROM *Musica practica*
(1482)

TRACTATE 1

CHAPTER 4: SUBTLE APPLICATION OF THE GIVEN FIGURE FOR THE PRACTICE OF SINGERS

By making use of a tetrachord Guido, perhaps a better monk than a musician, included all these twenty letters[1] when he developed the hexachord. And he was moved to create such a hexachord in this way because number six is called perfect by mathematicians, for its aliquot parts, namely 1, 2, 3, when added together make six, and each string of the hexachord receives a name from the first six syllables of six lines of the hymn of St. John the Baptist, namely: Ut queant laxis. Resonare fibris. Mira gestorum. Famuli tuorum. Solve polluti. Labii reatum. Sancte Johannes.

If we have examined correctly the first syllable after each period we will extract these six vocables: *ut, re, mi, fa, sol, la,* and when put in a successive order each is a whole tone from the next except *fa,* because it is a semitone from *mi.* So two whole tones will be above and two below the semitone. And with the first letter *g,* which is called Γ, the syllable *ut* is written, forming a unit called *gamma ut;*[2] from letter *a* and syllable *re* a unit is formed which is called *a re;* also from letter *b* and syllable *mi* comes *b mi,* from letter *c* and syllable *fa,* comes *c fa,* from *d* and *sol, d sol,* and from *e* and *la, e la.*

In order to follow the Boethian doctrine, which divides the entire tonal series by tetrachords,[3] when Guido comes to the fourth place, namely *c fa,* he again creates another hexachord, another offspring as it were. But if the syllable *ut* is joined to *c fa* the entire arrangement is called *c fa ut,* and it continues with *d sol re* and *e la mi,* where the first hexachord ends. Since *fa,* however, follows in the order of letters, the syllable *ut* is also joined to the second tetrachord's *fa,* which is the fourth tone of the second tetrachord. And so when *f fa* occurs *ut* will receive such a name by being joined to it, with *g sol re* and *a la*

TEXT: Bartolomé Ramis de Pareia, *Musica practica,* ed. Clement A. Miller (American Institute of Musicology, 1993), pp. 55–57, 64–66, 74–75, and 93–94. Reprinted by permission. Translation by Clement A Miller. I have made some minor alterations in Miller's translation by comparing it with the facsimile of the original edition (Bologna, 1482) published in Madrid, 1983.

1. That is, the pitch-letters Γ (gamma), representing our G, to e″ two octaves and a major sixth above it; this span is the medieval or Guidonian gamut of pitches.
2. The source, by contraction, of our word "gamut."
3. *De institutione musica* 1.20.

mi following. And so that he would not seem ignorant of the similitude of the outer limits of the octave[4] he again begins to form a hexachord. And since in the aforementioned two tetrachords, that is, the second and third, we place two syllables, namely *sol* and *re*, with letter *g*, by adding *ut* to them the unit is named *g sol re ut*, and it is followed by *a la mi re*, where the second hexachord is completed. And where two tones, namely *fa mi* are joined together, with the first as ♭ *fa* and the second as square ♮ *mi*, we recognize that the one is higher than the other, just as the letters and syllables are shown to be unequal.[5] And thus the whole tone is divided into two semitones, and is followed by *c sol fa ut*, for just as the second hexachord is joined to the first in the same place, the entire unit is named in this way, that is, *c sol fa ut*, and is followed by *d la sol re*, then *e la mi, f fa ut, g sol re ut, a la mi re*, and ♭ *fa* square ♮ *mi*, just as before.

Hexachords can be multiplied indefinitely according to the extent of the instrument, but since an end must be reached somewhere in all knowledge, the hexachords now stop repeating and therefore another *ut* is not placed with *c sol fa*, but we move to *d la sol*, where we leave the sixth hexachord, while the seventh ends on the syllable *e la*. And so he set down seven hexachords[6] because of seven different tones, as it had seemed to him, just as the following

4. That is, Γ to g. [Tr.]
5. This is the distinction in pitch between *fa* of the third hexachord (our b-flat) and *mi* of the fourth (our b-natural).
6. The full Guidonian hexachordal system, giving pitch names by letter and solmization syllables, may be represented as follows:

Hexachord:	1	2	3	4	5	6	7
Pitch (low to high):							
Γ (G)	ut						
A	re						
B	mi						
c	fa	ut					
d	sol	re					
e	la	mi					
f		fa	ut				
g		sol	re	ut			
a		la	mi	re			
b			fa	mi			
c′			sol	fa	ut		
d′			la	sol	re		
e′				la	mi		
f′					fa	ut	
g′					sol	re	ut
a′					la	mi	re
b′						fa	mi
c″						sol	fa
d″						la	sol
e″							la

figure will show. Do you see the true figure of Guido? Indeed he himself does not, but he shows it through joints of the fingers in this way.[7]

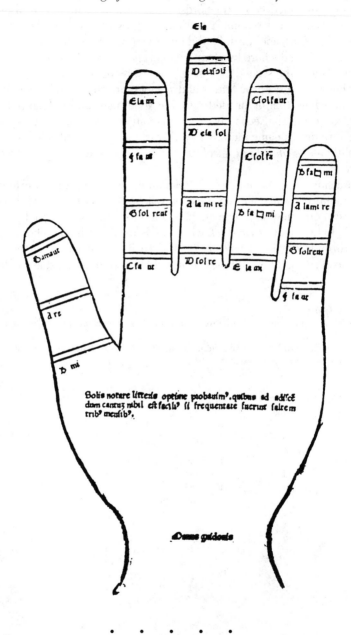

7. The text on the palm of the hand is: "We have shown that the best way to notate music is with letters alone; nothing is easier than learning how to sing with them if they have been practiced for at least three months." [Tr.]

CHAPTER 7: AN ACCURATE WAY OF CONNECTING A VOICE WITH AN INSTRUMENT

. . . In order, however, to memorize the sounds, each one is produced with a different name; this was customary among early writers. Odo said in the *Enchiriadis: noe, noananne, cane, agis,* which have no meaning.[8] Some used *tri, pro, de, nos, trite, ad,*[9] which indicated the bases of the modes, about which we will speak at the proper place. Others wrote only letters of the alphabet, namely: *a, b, c, d, e, f, g,* as Gregory, Augustine, Ambrose, and Bernard; but Guido used *ut, re, mi, fa, sol, la,* as we said earlier. Although he did not do this out of necessity, since he also showed all his examples with letters, his followers afterwards adhered so much to his syllables that they thought them entirely necessary to music, an idea which must be scorned.

We, therefore, who have labored a long time in nightly lucubrations and vigils to seek the truth of this art, arrange new syllables for individual strings and show the tones of the entire series,[10] so that on the lowest pitch *psal* is sung, on the next *li,* on the third *tur,* on the fourth *per,* on the fifth *vo,* on the sixth *ces,* on the seventh *is,* and on the eighth *tas.* And thus the connection of the syllables will be *psallitur per voces istas,*[11] for the entire series consists of eight syllables. We arrange them from low *c* to high *c* since they teach how to sing with perfection. Therefore they begin on letter *c* because the musical series begins on that letter, and the first semitone of two is included in the interval *r r* and the second sounds between the two *s s.* So the first is *e f* or *tur per.* But since the second semitone sometimes is formed from letter *a* to ♭, and sometimes from ♮ to high *c* on account of the synemmenon and diezeugmenon tetrachords,[12] because three semitones are located separately there, three places are indicated by letter *s,* that is, *ces, is, tas.* So with these syllables making sounds equivalent to the strings of an instrument we easily will be able to harmonize the natural instrument of voice with an instrument made by art. But if we wish to rise an octave higher we will place *psal* on the same sound as the first octave. Then one will have a dissyllabic *c,* namely, *tas-psal,*[13] and continue with *d li* and with *e tur* and the rest just as before. This must also be done in the low octave, because, as we often have said, a tone reappears after an octave,

---

8. These words occur in medieval treatises from the ninth century onward. For their relation to the modes see Michel Huglo, *Les tonaires* (Paris: Société française de musicologie, 1971), pp. 383–90; also "The Psalmodic Formula *Neannoe* and Its Origin," *The Musical Quarterly* 28 (1942): p. 93. [Tr.]

9. This version is based on an eleventh-century hymn. [Tr.]

10. A series that Ramis expanded and shifted from the Guidonian gamut to the three octaves from C to *c".*

11. "It is sung through these syllables."

12. That is, the conjunction of the c–f tetrachord with the tetrachord starting on f ("synnemenon") yields b-flat, while the disjunction of the c–f tetrachord from the tetrachord starting on g ("diezeugmenon") yields b-natural. The conception and terminology, if not the specific pitches associated with them, are from Boethius, *De institutione musica* 1.20.

13. This is the only mutation that remains in Ramis's system.

and whenever we ascend or descend more than an octave we repeat a tone; thus the teaching is correct only by using these eight syllables.[14]

• • • • •

TRACTATE 2

CHAPTER 2: AN EXPLANATION OF *MUSICA FICTA*.

In order to have a fuller understanding of these signs and notes[15] we will investigate some things about them in greater detail. For some signs are accustomed to be placed in songs through which unequal differences of intervals are heard; one of these is written as round ♭, the other as square ♮. The first sign is called soft or round ♭, the second square or hard ♮. Square ♮ and round ♭ are named from the nature of the sign, but soft ♭ or hard ♮ are so named because, when those singing with the letters of Gregory make a semitone from *a* to *b*, they call it soft *b*. For when a leap is made in arsis and thesis, the voice softens

14. In 2.7 Ramis supplied a picture of his alternative to the Guidonian hand:

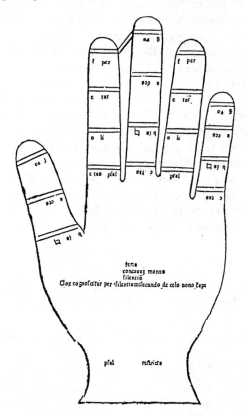

15. 2.1 discusses the notation of pitch with staves and clefs.

more in a semitone than in a whole tone, as for example from *a* to soft ♭ and from *a* to hard, square ♮. So also movement by a semiditone is softer than by a ditone, as *g* to soft ♭ and *g* to hard, square ♮; likewise a fourth is softer than a tritone, as *f* to soft ♭ and *f* to very hard, square ♮.

From these examples the error is clear of certain singers who say soft ♭ or square ♮. They err in two ways: first, because they sing with Guido's syllables and not Gregory's letters, thus saying neither soft ♭ or hard, square ♮ but *fa* or *mi;* second, they do not make the correct relationship, for when they say square ♮ they should correspondingly say round ♭ and when they say soft ♭ they should say hard ♮, and then the relationship will be correct. This was the custom among those singing with the letters of Gregory in early times; to them these letters are the proper names, just as synemmenon or diezeugmenon are proper to the Greeks. In our terminology the correct names in singing will be ♭ *is* in the conjunct tetrachord and *is* ♮ in the disjunct tetrachord; indeed, the syllables making a whole tone or semitone are common in all respects.

But elsewhere singers write whole tones or semitones with these signs not only on paramese,[16] for they say that wherever *fa* is found without *mi* then *mi* must be used, as in ♭ *fa* ♮ *mi.* The same occurs when *mi* is found without *fa.* Many call this musica ficta; of them Philipetus,[17] speaking rashly, says this: musica ficta is a single procedure. But he did not know that it should occur at least in two ways, for making *fa* from *mi* is different than making *mi* from *fa* (as will be shown a little later), since the tones do not correspond in the way in which they are naturally situated. Therefore, when *fa* is to be made from *mi,* they write with such a sign, namely, round ♭, but when *mi* is made from *fa* they write the sign, namely, square ♮ or else ♯.

Thus, according to them soft ♭ is located in five places, namely, on *b mi, e la mi,* the first *a la mi re,* high *e la mi,* and the second *a la mi re.* In these places we will say *fa* by lowering it a semitone from its original place. But we use ♮ or ♯ on *c fa ut, f fa ut, c sol fa ut,* high *f fa ut* and *c sol fa;* in those places we will say *mi* by raising it a semitone from its original position. They also call these procedures conjunctions, for just as when trite synemmenon is put after mese so that the whole tone of mese and paramese is to be divided into two semitones,[18] any whole tone located elsewhere should be divided in the same way. They add further that any of these conjunctions forms a hexachord, just as the others that were formed earlier; thus, just as after *f fa ut,* where *ut* is said, *g sol re ut* follows where *ut* is again placed, as already stated, so it occurs in each of the positions.[19] And they define a conjunction in this way: A conjunction is

16. For Ramis, the pitch b.
17. The reference is probably to Philippe de Vitry; see his *Ars contrapunctus* 2.1, in E. de Coussemaker, ed., *Scriptorum de musica medii aevi . . . nova series* (4 vols., Paris: A. Durand, 1864–76), vol. 3, p. 26.
18. That is, when the conjunct tetrachord f–b-flat calls for the interval a–b to be divided.
19. In other words, each mutation of *mi* to *fa* or *fa* to *mi* creates a hexachord beginning, respectively, a perfect fourth or major third beneath the pitch on which the mutation occurs.

making a whole tone from a semitone and a semitone from a whole tone, also a ditone from a semiditone and a semiditone from a ditone, and likewise with the other species. Here they speak correctly, because these conjunct hexachords occur in the manner of diezeugmenon and synemmenon tetrachords.

• • • • •

CHAPTER 7: REPROVING THE FOLLOWERS OF GUIDO AND SHOWING ACCURATELY THE TRUTH OF THE MATTER.

Having observed and examined the diversity of music, it now remains to be shown how whole tones may become semitones and the reverse. Regarding this it should be known, as John of Villanova[20] says, that a rising song desires the voice to be strengthened, and a descending song to become soft. Then he says that if a melody sounds *a c d* and does not return to *c*, although *re fa sol* should be said, as the order indicates, yet *ut mi fa* ought to be said, because *a c* is not the interval of a semiditone but of a ditone;[21] or if the melody is pronounced according to the other syllables, namely *re fa,* the ditone may be said to be understood. Again, if a melody may be formed as *g f g* and it does not return to *f*, a semitone is understood, even though *sol fa sol* or *re ut re* may be said. The same thing always holds true in forming synemmenon, when after a note placed on ♭ *fa* ♮ *mi* another note follows it on mese, whether it will have come from lower letters to synemmenon or will have reached it by descending from higher letters, especially if it will have repeated the same pitch many times.[22] It is also true if the melody will have made this movement *d b c d c d d,* and in its octaves; *b c* is a whole tone and *c d* is a semitone formed twice, and so either whole tones will replace semitones mentally or a mutation will be made of *mi* into *re,* which is a syllable of conjunctions.[23]

The same John also says a semiditone is made from a ditone in this way: if a melody may say *la fa sol sol* without returning to *fa,* either a semiditone will be mentally understood or a mutation may be made of *la* into *sol,* so that *lasol mi fa fa* may be said; in this way a diligent reader will be able to judge other syllables arranged in this manner. Such notes should be indicated with this sign, namely ♮ or ♯. For greater clarity, therefore, anyone who wishes to compose a song should zealously turn his attention to these things. . . .

20. Perhaps Ramis has Jehan des Murs in mind, though I cannot explain his association of Jehan with Villanova; the views that follow resemble Jehan's in his *Ars discantus* (see Coussemaker, *Scriptorum* vol. 3, pp. 71–73).
21. That is, the interval is not a minor but a major third. In modern terminology the c is altered to c-sharp, but note that for Ramis the interval a–c represents either our a–c or our a–c-sharp depending on the melodic context in which it is found and the syllables used to sing it.
22. That is, descending from b to a requires b-flat to be sung.
23. That is, a hexachord will be begun on a; in modern terms, the c's will be raised to c-sharps.

69 Pietro Aaron

Born about 1480 in Florence, Pietro Aaron (or Aron) was cantor at the Cathedral of Imola for a number of years until around 1522. Then he moved to Venice, where he seems to have remained until 1536. In that year he became a monk of the order of the Bearers of the Cross and entered the monastery of San Leonardo at Bergamo. He died about 1550.

Aaron's published works on music theory comprise the *Libri III de institutione harmonica* (1516), the *Toscanello in musica* (1523, with later revised editions), the *Treatise on the Nature and Recognition of All the Tones of Figured Song* (*Trattato della natura e cognitione di tutti gli tuoni di canto figurato*, 1525), the *Lucidario in musica* (1545), and the *Compendiolo di molti dubbi* (ca. 1549–50). The chapters from the *Trattato* given here take their general approach to identifying modes from the fourteenth-century *Lucidarium* of Marchetto of Padua and are anticipated in some particulars in treatises of Tinctoris. Nevertheless, they present the first systematic attempt to apply the modal theory of medieval plainsong to polyphonic repertories. In their numerous citations of individual pieces, they also reflect Aaron's familiarity with the printed collections of polyphony, especially those of Petrucci, that appeared in the first decades of the sixteenth century.

FROM *Treatise on the Nature and Recognition of All the Tones of Figured Song*
(1525)

I. AN EXPLANATION OF THE FINALS OF ALL THE TONES

Just as it is a credit and an honor to any artificer to comprehend and to know and to have a precise understanding of the parts and reasonings of his art, so it

TEXT: The original edition (Venice, 1525). Translation by Oliver Strunk. References to practical examples and certain parentheses of the original are given as author's notes. The many examples that Aaron cites are listed below in alphabetical order, with his attributions, the indications of the tones to which he assigns them, and references to the following contemporary editions in which the works appear: *Harmonice musices Odhecaton A* (RISM 1501), *Canti B* (RISM 1502[2]), *Misse Petri de La Rue* (RISM L718; 1503), *Motetti C* (RISM 1504[1]), *Missarum Josquin liber secundus* (RISM J670; 1505), *Motetti a cinque libro primo* (RISM 1508[1]), *Missarum Josquin liber tertius* (RISM J673; 1514), *Motetti de la corona. Libro primo* (RISM 1514[1]), *Motetti de la corona libro secondo* (RISM 1519[1]), *Motetti de la corona. Libro tertio* (RISM 1519[2]), *Motetti libro primo* (RISM 1521[3]).

| 6 A l'audience | Hayne | Odhecaton 93 |
| 6 Allez regretz | Agricola | Odhecaton 57 |

is a disgrace and a reproach to him not to know and to be in error among the articles of his faculty. Therefore, when I examined and considered the excellence and grandeur of many, many authors, ancient and modern, there is no manner of doubt that did not assail me inwardly as I reflected on this undertaking, especially since I knew the matter to be most difficult, sublime, and lofty

5	Alma redemptoris	Josquin	Corona III
7	Ascendens Christus	Hylaere	Corona I
8	Beata Dei genitrix	Anon	Motetti C
1 / 2	Beata Dei genitrix	Mouton	Corona I
3	Benedic anima mea	Anon	Corona II
6	Brunette	Stokhem	Odhecaton 5
8	C'est possible	Anon	Odhecaton 72
2	Ce n'est pas	La Rue	Canti B
–	Cela sans plus	Josquin	Odhecaton 61
6	Celeste beneficium	Mouton	Corona I
1	Clangat plebs flores	Regis	Motetti a 5
7	Comment peult	Josquin	Canti B
1	Congregati sunt	Mouton	Corona II
2	D'ung aultre amer	Orto	Canti B
2	D'ung aultre amer	Hayne	
2	De tous biens playne	Hayne	Odhecaton 20
8	Disant adieu madame	Anon	Odhecaton 89
8	E d'en revenez vous	Compère	Canti B
8	E la la la	Anon	Canti B
6	Egregie Christi	Févin	Corona I
1	Fors seulement	La Rue	Canti B
1	Gaude Barbara	Mouton	Corona I
1	Gaude Virgo	Festa	
8	Hélas hélas	Ninot	Canti B
1	Hélas qu'il est à mon gré	Japart	Odhecaton 30
5	Hélas que pourra devenir	Caron	Odhecaton 13
–	Hélas m'amour	Anon	
5	Illuminare Jerusalem	Mouton	Corona II
3	Interveniat pro rege nostro	Jacotin	Corona II
7	Je cuide si ce temps	Anon	Odhecaton 2
1	Je déspite tous	Brumel	Canti B
6	Je ne demande	Busnois	Odhecaton 42
8	Je suis amie	Anon	Canti B
1	Judica me Deus	Caen	Corona II
1	L'homme armé	Josquin	Canti B
8	Ne l'oserai je dire	Anon	Odhecaton 29
–	La dicuplaisant	Anon	
1	La plus des plus	Josquin	Odhecaton 64
5	La regretée	Hayne	Canti B
3	Laetatus sum	Eustachio	Corona I
–	Le serviteur	Anon	Odhecaton 35
7	Madame hélas	Anon	Odhecaton 66
3	Malheur me bat	Ockeghem	Odhecaton 63
7	Mes pensées	Compère	Odhecaton 59
3	Michael archangele	Jacotin	Corona II
3	Miserere	Josquin	Corona III

to explain. None the less I intend to relate it to you, most gracious reader, not in a presumptuous or haughty style, but speaking humanely and at your feet. And knowing it to be exacting and strange, I judge that it was abandoned by the celebrated musicians already referred to not through ignorance but merely because it proved otherwise troublesome and exacting at the time. For it is clear that no writers of our age have explained how the many different modes are to be recognized, although to their greater credit they have treated of matters which cannot be readily understood. I, therefore, not moved by ambition of any kind, but as a humble man, have undertaken this task, hoping that in humanity and kindliness my readers will all excuse whatever errors I may make. I show briefly what I know to be necessary, for I see that many are deceived

1 Missa Ave maris stella	Josquin	Missarum II
1 Missa D'ung aultre amer	Josquin	Missarum II
– Missa de Beata Virgine	Josquin	Missarum III
5, 7 Missa de Beata Virgine	La Rue	Missae
2 Missa Hercules dux Ferrariae	Josquin	Missarum II
7 Missa Ut sol	Mouton	
7 Mittit ad Virginem	Anon	Motetti C
8 Mon mari m'a diffamée	Orto	Canti B
7 Multi sunt vocati	Zanetto [Giovanni del Lago]	
8 Myn morgem ghaf	Anon	Canti B
1 Nobilis progenie	Févin	Corona I
1 Nomine qui Domini	Caen	Corona II
3 Nunca fué pena mayor	Anon	Odhecaton 4
6 O admirabile commercium	Josquin	Motetti I
4 O Maria rogamus te	Anon	Motetti C
8 O venus bant	Josquin	Odhecaton 78
– Peccata mea Domine	Mouton	Corona II
1 Pour quoy fut fuie cette emprise	Anon	Canti B
1 Pourtant si mon	Busnois	
5 Quaeramus cum pastoribus	Mouton	Motetti I
1 Rogamus te Virgo Maria	Jacotin	Corona II
6 Sancta Trinitas	Févin	Corona I
8 Si dedero	Agricola	Odhecaton 56
2 Si mieulx	Compère	Odhecaton 51
5 Si sumpsero	Obrecht	Canti B
5 Stabat mater	Josquin	Corona III
6 Tempus meum	Févin	Corona I
2 Virgo celesti	Compère	Canti B
6 Vostre bergeronette	Compère	Odhecaton 41
1 Vulnerasti cor meum	Févin	Corona I

For careful analysis of the chapters translated here see Harold Powers, "Is Mode Real? Pietro Aron, the Octenary System, and Polyphony," *Basler Jahrbuch für historische Musikpraxis* 16 (1992): 9–52, and Cristle Collins Judd, "Reading Aron reading Petrucci: The Music Examples of the *Trattato della natura et cognitione di tutti gli tuoni* (1525)," *Early Music History* 14 (1995): 121–52. I have made several changes in Strunk's chart by comparison with Judd's Tables.

about the true understanding, and regarding this I hope in some measure to satisfy them.

First I intend to explain what is meant by "final" and what by "species" and whether the final is always necessary and rational for the recognition of the tone or whether the tones are sometimes to be recognized from their species. Then I shall show what part the singer ought to examine and how composers ought to proceed in their compositions in accordance with their intentions, touching also on certain other secrets which will surely afford you no little delight.

I say, then, that the final being diverse, that is, regular or irregular, it follows that each tone has a similarly diverse form. From this it follows that at one time the final governs and at another time the species. "Final" I define in this way: a final is simply a magisterial ending in music, introduced in order that the tone may be recognized. Musicians conclude such an ending regularly or irregularly in order that the nature and form of each tone may be the better understood. Thus the positions D *sol re,* E *la mi,* F *fa ut,* and G *sol re ut* have been constituted regular finals or ending steps for the first and second, third and fourth, fifth and sixth, and seventh and eighth tones, while the steps Gamma *ut,* A *re,* ♮ *mi,* C *fa ut,* A *la mi re,* B *fa* ♮ *mi,* and C *sol fa ut* are called irregular. In accordance with this understanding, the final remains necessary, rational, and governing to every tone on the above-named regular steps.

The species, then, will govern sometimes regularly and sometimes irregularly. "Species" is simply the arrangement of the sounds of the genus, varied in definite prescribed ways, as shown in the example.

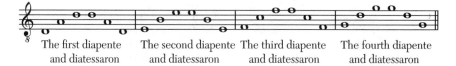

| The first diapente and diatessaron | The second diapente and diatessaron | The third diapente and diatessaron | The fourth diapente and diatessaron |

It follows, then, that the final is also necessary in the above-named irregular positions, namely A *la mi re,* B *fa* ♮ *mi,* and C *sol fa ut.* Here we shall consider it in two ways: first, with respect to confinality; second, with respect to the differences of the Saeculorum.[1] Thus, if a composition[2] ends in the position called A *la mi re* and there is no flat in the signature, the final will be common to the first and second tones with respect to confinality and also to the third with respect to difference, provided—as you will understand from what fol-

1. The confinals of the eight tones are, for Aaron, the pitches a fifth above (or a fourth below) the established finals. He seems not to have thought it necessary to list the differences. These are the variable formulas used to end the eight psalm tones associated with the eight modes of chant theory; see Powers, "Is Mode Real?", p. 25. Aaron calls them "the differences of the Saeculorum" because the last word of the Lesser Doxology that ends psalm recitations is *saeculorum.*
2. I speak always of masses, motets, canzoni, frottole, strambotti, madrigali, sonetti, and capitoli. [Au.]

lows—that the *processo* in the composition be suited and appropriate to confinality or difference.[3] But if the composition has a flat in the signature, the final will be in my opinion neither necessary nor rational with respect to confinality, for it is clear that the form will differ from its previous state. For this reason, such compositions are to be judged by their species. The same will obviously apply to compositions ending on B *fa* ♮ *mi*, C *sol fa ut,* and all other steps on which the species may occur.

Therefore, the cognition derived from species is necessary understanding and not arbitrary to music. First, because this cognition is by definition true and necessary. Besides this, understanding that is necessary has something essential about it; but the cognition of species is essential and therefore necessary. Besides this, that which demands necessary cognition is *per se;* but the cognition of species is cognition *per se* and therefore necessary. Nor is it an objection that we are for the most part accustomed to base our cognition of music on the final, for I reply that this has been for the sake of readier understanding, inasmuch as those things that are at the end are customarily more closely observed than those that are at the beginning and in the middle.

And that our conclusion is true, we may demonstrate with these and other similar arguments. We say that man is defined as an animal rational and mortal; it is certain that rational and mortal are two differences for knowing what man is; of these, one is final and considered according to the end of man, namely mortal—the other is formal and considered according to the specific and formal being of living man, namely rational; the latter makes the essence of man better known than the former, which considers him according to his end, namely that man is mortal, for this is common both to man and to the other animals. Thus the cognition of the end is not cognition *per se* and therefore not always necessary. And this is demonstrated by certain compositions which, having the ordinary and regular final, but lacking the ascent and descent of some of its species, are not said to be of any tone but (as was shown in Chapter 30 of the first book of another work of mine, *De institutione harmonica*) are merely called *Canti euphoniaci.*

---

3. As Aaron explains in Chapter 8, suitable and appropriate *processo* turns largely on the choice of proper steps for medial cadences. In Chapters 9 to 12 these are said to be as follows: for the first tone—D, F, G, and a; for the second—A, C, D, F, G, and a; for the third—E, F, G, a, ♮, and c; for the fourth—C, D, E, F, G, and a; for the fifth—F, a, and c; for the sixth—C, D, F, a, and c; for the seventh—G, a, ♮, c, and d; for the eighth—D, F, G, and c. *Processo* (Latin *processus*) is a difficult but important term in Medieval and Renaissance discussions of mode, and I have chosen to mark this complexity throughout Aaron's chapters here by leaving it untranslated. For Aaron, *processo* signifies in part the range or compass of a given tenor melody. But it also connotes less quantifiable elements: the way the melody moves through its range, the pitch areas it emphasizes, the medial cadential points it gravitates toward, and others. In this way the term cuts to the heart of Medieval and Renaissance conceptions of mode, which did not involve reified scales so much as manners of exploring and exploiting particular segments extracted from the Guidonian gamut of pitches.

2. How the Singer Ought to Judge the Tone

The tenor being the firm and stable part, the part, that is, that holds and comprehends the whole concentus of the harmony, the singer must judge the tone by means of this part only. For we see that when a tenor and its cantus are far apart it causes, not pleasure, but little sweetness to those who hear it, something which arises from the distance that lies between the cantus and the contrabassus. The tenor being for this reason better suited to the natural *processi* and more easily handled, every composition[4] is in my opinion to be judged by its tenor. For in the tenor the natural form is more readily considered than in the soprano, where, should you wish to form the seventh tone, you would need to find its diatessaron through the accidental course.[5] Thus we prescribe this manner and order for all compositions written at the composer's pleasure, whether upon a plainsong or without regard for one, also for compositions for five, six, seven, and more voices, in which it is usual to write a first and principal tenor. Each of the added parts will be governed by the nature of the tenor, and by means of the tenor the tone will be recognized unless the plainsong itself, which is primary and principal to such a recognition, be in some other part.[6]

3. Ways of Recognizing the Tone of Different Compositions

Reflecting alone for days and days, I recalled certain projects often in my mind. Wherefore, gracious reader, had not your gentle aspect and my eager wish for the desired end constrained me, I should more lightly have lowered the sails at the hard-won port. But since I think that you by no means blamed it, I wish to pursue the enterprise begun, not for those who turn a thing over and over, but solely for those unfamiliar with this fare. Thus, having reached this point, I am left somewhat in doubt. Yet I intend rather to go on reasoning

4. Whether Introit, Kyrie, Gloria, Gradual, Alleluia, Credo, Offertory, Sanctus, Agnus Dei, Postcommunion, Respond, Deo gratias, Psalm, Hymn, Magnificat, motet, canzone, frottola, bergerette, strambotto, madrigal, or capitolo. [Au.]

5. We see, in other words, that when a tenor and its cantus belong to the same tone—and unless this is the case, the cantus can have no bearing on the tonality of the composition—they will lie far apart and the resulting texture will be disagreeable, particularly in view of the disparity between the cantus and the contrabassus. Thus the usual thing will be to make the tenor authentic and the cantus plagal, or vice versa, leaving the tenor as the sole determining factor. Aside from this, "in view of the inconvenience of the upward range," the cantus will seldom ascend to the octave above the final in the seventh tone or (see chap. 5 below) in the transposed third. Aaron's "accidental course" refers to pitches above the Guidonian gamut.

6. Cf. Johannes Tinctoris, *Liber de natura et proprietate tonorum* 24: "When some mass or chanson or any other composition you please is made up of various parts, belonging to different tones, if you ask without qualification to what tone such a composition belongs, the person asked ought to reply without qualification according to the quality of the tenor, for in every composition this is the principal part and the basis of the whole relationship. But if it be asked specifically to what tone some single part of such a composition belongs, the person asked will reply specifically, 'To such and such a tone.'

with you, seeking a rule by means of which you may arrive at a clear understanding of each of the tones in question.

In so far as compositions end in the positions D *sol re,* E *la mi,* F *fa ut,* and G *sol re ut,* they are to be judged according to their finals, and by means of these their true and proper species[7] will be recognized. These are the steps called regular to the first, second, third, fourth, fifth, sixth, seventh, and eighth tones, and on these steps the final will be necessary, rational, and governing.

Let me explain this to you more fully. First consider those compositions that have their final on D *sol re* and that at the beginning or in their course proceed with the species of the third, fourth, fifth, sixth, seventh, or eighth tone; all these are in my opinion to be judged only from their proper and regular final, even though they contain contradictory and unsuitable *processi,* for no other tone has a difference ending on this step. And as to those ending on E *la mi,* these are in my opinion subject in the same way only to their own form. Such compositions are best said to belong to mixed tones *(toni commisti).*[8]

But those compositions that end in the position called F *fa ut* are in my opinion subject not only to their own final and species but also to the nature and form of the first and fourth tones, in view of the difference which these tones sometimes exhibit on this step. Understand, however, that this is when they proceed in the way suited to the first and fourth tones, for otherwise they will remain of the fifth or sixth. Certain others end on G *sol re ut;* these are in my opinion subject to the seventh and eighth tones and also to the first, second, third, and fourth, as you will understand from what follows.[9]

Certain other compositions end on the irregular steps A *la mi re,* B *fa ♮ mi,* and C *sol fa ut;* these we shall consider according to their *processo,* their species, and the differences of the Saeculorum, for these considerations will govern them and yield the true recognition of the tone.

Certain other compositions end on D *la sol re,* E *la mi,* F *fa ut,* and G *sol re ut;*[10] these steps are of the same nature as the regular steps previously named.

Certain other compositions, although they end regularly, have a flat signature; these are to be judged according to their species (excepting those ending on D *sol re* and F *fa ut,* etc.), for the final will now be neither necessary nor rational to the recognition of the tone.

Certain other compositions proceed at the beginning and in their course with the species suited to a given tone but end with species that contradict it;

7. Namely, from D *sol re* to the first A *la mi re* and from thence to D *la sol re,* from E *la mi* to B *fa ♮ mi* and from thence to high E *la mi,* from F *fa ut* to C *sol fa ut* and from thence to high F *fa ut,* and from low G *sol re ut* to D *la sol re* and from thence to the second G *sol re ut.* [Au.]

8. Cf. Johannes Tinctoris, *Terminorum musicae diffinitorium* 18: 'A *tonus commixtus* is one which, if authentic, is mixed with a tone other than its plagal, if plagal, with a tone other than its authentic."

9. Aaron does not refer again to the possibility of endings on F in the first and fourth tones or on G (as difference) in the first, second, and fourth; for the ending on G in the third, see chap. 5 below.

10. I.e., an octave above the regular finals D *sol re* etc.

these are to be judged according to the species and differences previously mentioned, excepting (as was noted above) those ending on the regular finals.

Certain other compositions have an irregular end and an inharmonious *processo* without any complete diapente by means of which their true form might be recognized; these are to be judged by means of some species of diatessaron or by their own finals.

One will also find compositions arbitrarily written without regard to form or regular manner, comparable indeed to players of the game called *alleta,* who agree upon a certain goal at which they will take refuge and, chasing one after another, run back to that place or goal and are safe; of the composers of such works as these we say that they turn aimlessly round and round, progressing and digressing beyond the nature and the primary order that they have in mind until, by some trick, they arrive at an end of their own. Such harmonies or compositions can in my opinion be judged only by means of the final, and then only when they end without a flat signature.

In certain other compositions this signature appears only in the contrabassus, in others only in the tenor; such an arrangement is in our opinion neither permissible nor suitable in a harmony or composition unless it is used deliberately and introduced with art.[11]

Certain other compositions have a flat signature on low E *la mi,* the first A *la mi re,* B *fa ♮ mi,* and high E *la mi;* whether they end regularly or irregularly, these are in my opinion to be judged according to the species, not according to the final.[12]

4. AN EXPLANATION OF THE FIRST AND SECOND TONES

Every composition in which the tenor ends on D *sol re* is unhesitatingly to be assigned to the first or second tone, the more readily if the soprano ends on D *la sol re* with the regular and rational final, clearly showing the natural form.[13] The same is also true of certain other compositions with a flat signature; the nature of these remains unchanged, in my opinion, for only the diatessaron,

11. As by the excellent Josquin in the Patrem of his Mass of Our Lady and in a similar way by the divine Alexander [Agricola] in many of his compositions. [Au.] As published in vol. 42 of *Das Chorwerk,* the Credo of Josquin's *Missa de Beata Virgine* has no signatures whatever. But it is clear from Aaron's comment and from the composition itself that the Tenor secundus, following the Tenor in canon at the fifth below, should have the signature one flat.

12. For example, "Cela sans plus" by Josquin, "Peccata mea Domine" by Jean Mouton (in the *Motetti de la corona*), "Le serviteur," "Hélas m'amour," "La dicuplaisant," &c. [Au.] Cf. Johannes Tinctoris, *Liber de natura et proprietate tonorum* 24: "If some one were to say to me, speaking in general, 'Tinctoris, I ask you to what tone the chanson *Le serviteur* belongs,' I would reply, 'Generally speaking, to the first tone irregular,' since the tenor, or principal part, of this chanson belongs to this tone. But if he were to ask specifically to what tone the superius or contratenor belongs, I would reply specifically that the one and the other belong to the second tone irregular. But there is no one who doubts that a specific question about the tenor is to be answered as was the general one."

13. As in the motets "Rogamus te virgo Maria" by Jacotin, "Judica me Deus" by A. Caen, "Congregati sunt" and "Beata Dei genitrix" by Jean Mouton, and "Clangat plebs flores" by Regis. [Au.]

formed by the interval A *la mi re* to D *la sol re,* is altered. Seeing then that the diapente primary and natural to the tone is left intact, such compositions are also to be assigned to the first tone.[14]

And if sometimes, as has become the custom, the composer prolongs his work, amusing himself with additional progressions, you will, in my opinion, need to consider whether the final, as altered by the composer, is suited to and in keeping or out of keeping with his composition, for if reason guides him in what is suited to the tone he will at least see to it that some one part (namely, the tenor or cantus) sustains the final, while the others proceed as required by the tone, regular or irregular, with pleasing and appropriate progressions like those shown below, or in some more varied manner according to his pleasure and disposition.

OPTIONAL ENDING FOR THE FIRST AND SECOND TONES:

But since some will say, perhaps, that the position D *sol re* is common also to the second tone, I shall tell you that in figured music you will very seldom find a tenor with the *processo* and downward range suited and appropriate to the second tone ended in this way. Nevertheless, a composer may wish to proceed in accordance with the nature of the second tone; he will then take care to proceed at the beginning and in the course of his composition with some regard for its proper form, as observed and comprehended in the psalms and the Magnificat, where he is restricted and subject to the manner and order proper to the second tone.

Certain other compositions end on the step G *sol re ut;* with a flat signature, these are in my opinion only to be understood as of the first or second tone, even though this is the step ordinary and regular to the seventh and eighth. For this signature (or figure) alters the form or structure proper and natural to the seventh and eighth tones; at the same time, having acquired the species belonging to the first and second, the final becomes inactive and on this step is left arbitrary and as it were regular *per se,* not suited to the seventh and eighth tones, but necessary to the first and second.[15]

Certain other compositions, ending on this same step, are said to be of the

14. As in the motet "Nomine qui Domini" by A. Caen, "Pour quoy fut fuie cette emprise," &c. [Au.]
15. This is demonstrated by the following masses and motets, which are of the first tone in view of their *processo,* structure, and complete diapason: *Ave maris stella* and *D'ung aultre amer* by Josquin, "Nobilis progenie" and "Vulnerasti cor meum" by Févin, &c. [Au.]

second tone; these are readily recognized by their extended downward range.[16] And if this consideration seems to you not always to the purpose, do not be surprised, for composers sometimes observe the *processo* of a given tone at the beginning and in the course of a composition, ending then in accordance with the difference of the plainsong, as you will understand from what follows.

Certain other tenors end on A *la mi re;* here you will need to consider and examine whether their *processo* is suited and rational to such an ending, for if a tenor ends irregularly in the first or second tone, not proceeding with its proper form, it may easily not belong to it, even though this step is one of its irregular finals and an ending of its Saeculorum or difference. As you will understand from what follows, this is because the third and fourth tones also use this step as a difference. For this reason, then, you will assign such a tenor to the first or second tone only when you find the proper form.[17]

Certain other compositions end on D *la sol re;* these are in my opinion to be assigned in the same way to the first and second tones, for it is clearly evident that from D *la sol re* to its diapason is the proper form of the first diapente and diatessaron, namely *re–la* and *re–sol.* When they ascend as far as the fifth or sixth step, and especially when they still further, they will be of the first tone.[18] But when they lack this extension to the upper limit of the diapente, proceeding rather in the lower register, they will be of the second tone and not of the first. This opinion of mine is supported by the venerable Father Zanetto, a musician of Venice.[19]

5. AN EXPLANATION OF THE THIRD AND FOURTH TONES

The few who fish these waters are in the habit of saying that every composition ending in the position E *la mi* is to be assigned to the fourth tone. They forget that this step is common also to the third, and in so doing seem to me to involve themselves in no little difficulty. Seeing that the difference often ends on this step in the fourth tone, many, thinking only of the ending of its Saeculorum, judge a composition to belong to it. Thus the greatest confusion may easily arise. It is accordingly necessary to consider at various times the final, the upward and downward range, the *processo*, the intonations, and the

16. For example, "Virgo celesti" by Loyset Compère, "D'ung aultre amer" and "De tous biens playne" by Hayne, "Ce n'est pas" by Pierre de La Rue, and "D'ung aultre amer" by Orto. [Au.]

17. As in "La plus de plus" by Josquin, which is of the first tone in view of the course of its diapente and its upward range, or in "Si mieulx" by Loyset Compère, which is of the second, as will be readily evident. [Au.]

18. Whether with a flat signature, as in "Pourtant si mon" by Antoine Busnois, "Gaude virgo," a motet by Costanzo Festa, "L'homme armé" *et sic de singulis* by Josquin, and "Hélas qu'il est à mon gré" by Japart; or without, as in "Fors seulement" by Pierre de La Rue, "Je déspite tous" by Brumel, and "Gaude Barbara" by Jean Mouton. [Au.]

19. For example, the mass *Hercules dux Ferrariae,* composed by Josquin, and many other works which I shall not enumerate, since you will readily understand them from their similarity to this one. [Au.] "Father Zanetto" is the music theorist and composer Giovanni del Lago; see Bonnie Blackburn, Edward Lowinsky, and Clement Miller, *A Correspondence of Renaissance Musicians* (Oxford: Clarendon Press, 1991), p. 129, n. 10.

differences, which, since they are of different sorts, end naturally in different ways.[20]

OPTIONAL ENDING FOR THE THIRD AND FOURTH TONES:

Certain other compositions ending in the position G *sol re ut* are said to be of the third tone, even though this is the step ordinary and regular to the seventh and eighth. You will need to give your most careful consideration to these and, above all, to their *processo,* for unless they have the form and order due and appropriate to the third tone, with this final they will never be assigned to it, but rather to the seventh or eighth. But where the natural form is found, they will always be assigned to the third tone, and not to the seventh or eighth, in view of their form and difference.[21] This opinion is likewise supported by the venerable Father Zanetto, Venetian musician.

You will also find certain other compositions ending on A *la mi re;* when these observe the appropriate *processo* they will be assigned to the third tone.[22] But when they have a flat signature, they are in my opinion to be assigned to the third tone the more readily, even though at the beginning and in their course they fail to proceed in the due and appropriate way, for it is evident that the regular structure of the tone[23] will prevail. But because of the inconvenience of their upward range, few such pieces will be found, unless written for equal voices or *voci mutate.*[24] So compositions of this sort are to be assigned to the third or fourth tone in view of their species and downward range, not because of their difference or *processo.* Thus it may be inferred that, in view of their extended downward range, they will in preference be assigned to the fourth tone.[25]

20. Thus, in the motet "Michael archangele" by Jacotin, the first part is in my opinion of the irregular third tone while the second ends in the regular third tone, not in the fourth; the same is true of "Malheur me bat" by Ockeghem, "Interveniat pro rege nostro" by Jacotin, and many other compositions, similar to these and having the regular final and the required *processo* and upward range. [Au.]
21. For example, "Nunca fué pena mayor," &c. [Au.]
22. For example, "Miserere mei Deus" by Josquin, "Laetatus sum" by Eustachio, "Benedic anima mea Dominum," in which the first part ends on the confinal, the second on the final, and the third on the difference, &c. [Au.]
23. Namely, *mi-mi* and *mi-la,* arising from the interval A *la mi re* to high E *la mi,* to which is added the upper diatessaron *mi-la.* [Au.]
24. That is, for a group of voices restricted to a similar, in this case high, compass. The more common term for such a group is *voci pari.*
25. For example, "O Maria rogamus te" in the *Motetti C* and many others which you will readily recognize on the same principle. [Au.]

6. AN EXPLANATION OF THE FIFTH AND SIXTH TONES

Spurred on by your affection and with my goal in sight, I turn to the question about which you may have been in doubt. Thus, in beginning this part of my explanation, I ask you to observe that compositions ending in the position F *fa ut* are to be assigned to the fifth or sixth tone. On this point I should like to remove any remaining uncertainty, for seeing that such compositions very often—indeed, almost always—have the flat signature and that the form of the tone is altered, it would be easy for you to believe the contrary, in view of certain opinions that I have expressed above.[26] Know, then, that in compositions such as these the older composers were more concerned with facility than with proper form and correct structure. For the fifth and sixth tones often require the help of the b-flat, although always to use it would be contrary to the tendencies of the mediations of these tones as laid down by the ancients. This opinion is likewise supported by the previously mentioned Venetian, Father Zanetto. For this reason, then, the older composers altered the third diapente, giving it the nature of the fourth, in order that the tritone which would otherwise occur in running through it might not cause inconvenience or harshness in their music.[27]

OPTIONAL ENDING FOR THE FIFTH AND SIXTH TONES:

And if certain other compositions, ending on A *la mi re*, are to be assigned to the fifth tone, know that at the beginning and in their course these must observe a *processo* suited to it; lacking this, the difference will have little force and, as previously explained, they may easily be of some other tone. Nevertheless, the composer may if he pleases observe this tone, but what is necessary

26. The reader, that is, having been told that in the D and F modes the flat signature does not effect a transformation (chap. 3), and having seen that the explanation of this given for the D modes (chap. 4) will not apply to the F, will have anticipated a difficulty at this point.

27. This is uniformly demonstrated in the following compositions of the fifth tone, compositions which cannot be otherwise assigned in view of their upward range and *processo:* "Stabat mater dolorosa" and "Alma redemptoris" by Josquin, "Hélas que pourra devenir" by Caron, "Quaeramus cum pastoribus" and "Illuminare illuminare Jerusalem" by Jean Mouton, and the Sanctus and Agnus Dei of the Mass of Our Lady by Pierre de La Rue. Those which do not have frequent *processo* in this high range, falling short of the diapente or hexachord, are to be assigned to the sixth tone as regularly ended, for example, "Brunette" by Stokhem, "Vostre bergeronette" by Compère, "Je ne demande" by Busnois, "Allez regretz" by Agricola, "A l'audience" by Hayne, "Sancta Trinitas unus Deus" and "Tempus meum est ut revertar ad eum" by Févin, "Celeste beneficium" by Jean Mouton, "'Egregie Christi" by Févin, &c. [Au.]

will be recognized more clearly in the psalms and the Magnificat. The sixth tone we do not concede on this step, for it has neither the form nor the difference.

Certain other compositions ending on B *fa* ♮ *mi* are said to be of the fifth tone, but we do not approve this in the absence of the flat signature (or figure) which on this step produces the proper structure both ascending and descending. Here, then, the final is rational, necessary, and governing, and in this way the proper form is recognized.[28]

Certain other compositions, ending on C *sol fa ut,* are said to be of the fifth tone, both with and without the flat signature;[29] this is solely in view of the difference which the plainsong sometimes exhibits here. The sixth tone is lacking on this step, even though it is the confinal of the fifth and sixth tones regularly ended, for the step can bear no form or difference appropriate to it.

7. An Explanation of the Seventh and Eighth Tones

Certain persons have held that the seventh and eighth tones may end regularly and irregularly on three steps, namely Gamma *ut,* C *fa ut,* and G *sol re ut,* and regarding these endings many advance many different opinions, especially regarding those on Gamma *ut* and C *fa ut.* Compositions ending on these steps they assign rather to the seventh tone than to the eighth, and this because such a composition seldom if ever descends as the plagal form requires. In view of this confusion I shall tell you that I cannot admit such opinions, for it is clear that these compositions continue to observe the natural requirements of the proper and regular tones. Those ending on Gamma *ut,* in view of their acquired form, peculiar to the seventh tone, I take to be of this tone and not of the eighth when they are without the flat signature, but of the first or second when they have it. But those ending on C *fa ut,* for the reason given above and also because they do not have the proper diatessaron, I assign to the eighth tone and not to the seventh.[30] This opinion is likewise held by the previously mentioned musician, Father Zanetto.

Certain other compositions end in the position G *sol re ut;* these are naturally and regularly to be assigned to the seventh tone or to the eighth in view of their proper final and natural form.[31]

28. As demonstrated in the chanson "La regretée," composed by Hayne, which is of the fifth tone in view of its species, cadences, and upward range; or in "O admirabile commercium" by Josquin, which is said to be of the sixth, as are certain others similar to it, although there are few of these. [Au.]

29. For example, "Si sumpsero" by Obrecht. [Au.]

30. As demonstrated in the following compositions: "Mon mari m'a diffamée" by Orto and the chanson called "E la la la"; following the same principle you will understand the rest. [Au.]

31. Thus the mass *Ut sol* by Jean Mouton and the Gloria of Our Lady by Pierre de La Rue are in our opinion to be assigned to the seventh tone in view of their species, their final, and their extended upward range; the same applies to "Multi sunt vocati pauci vero electi" by the venerable Father Zanetto of Venice and "Ascendens Christus in altum" by Hylaere. But "Si dedero" by Alexander Agricola and "C'est possible que l'homme peut" will be of the eighth tone in view

OPTIONAL ENDING FOR THE SEVENTH AND EIGHTH TONES:

Certain other compositions end in the position C *sol fa ut;* these are in my opinion to be assigned in the same way to the seventh tone or to the eighth in view of their difference and *processo,* the difference often ending on this step. Thus, if such a composition proceeds in the appropriate way it will most certainly be of the seventh tone or of the eighth in view of its final, still more reasonably so if it has the flat signature, for this will give it the proper structure, namely *ut–sol* and *re–sol,* the form peculiar to the seventh and eighth tones.[32]

Following these principles in your examinations and reflecting on the method set forth above, you will have a clear understanding of any other composition or tone suited and appropriate to figured music.

---

of their final and their *processo;* the same is true of "O venus bant" by Josquin, "Disant adieu-madame," "Je suis amie," "Myn morghem ghaf," "Hélas hélas" by Ninot, "E d'en revenez vous" by Compère, "Beata Dei genitrix," and many others which you will recognize on the same principle. [Au.]

32. Thus "Mes pensées" by Compère, "Madame hélas," "Comment peult" by Josquin, and "Mittit ad virginem" can be assigned only to the seventh tone, and also "Je cuide si ce temps"; and "Ne l'oserai je dire" will be of the eighth tone and not of the seventh, as its form and extended downward *processo* will show you. [Au.]

70 Heinrich Glarean

Heinrich Glarean (known as Glareanus), one of the great humanist-scholars of the sixteenth century, was born in the canton of Glarus in Switzerland in 1488 and died in Freiburg in 1563. A friend of Erasmus of Rotterdam, Glarean was a philosopher, theologian, philologist, historian, poet, and musical scholar. Already in 1512 he was crowned poet laureate by Emperor Maximilian I. Among his works of musical interest, the most important is the *Dodecachordon* (literally, the *Instrument of Twelve Strings*). Here he advocated a system of twelve modes, adding four new modes to the existing eight: Aeolian, Hypo-aeolian, Ionian, and Hypoionian. True to Glarean's humanist background, his discussion of the modes incorporates classical learning much more than Aaron's. Glarean rationalized his twelve-mode system by a scrupulous analysis, along ancient lines, of the pertinent octave species and their formation out of the conjunction of different species of fifth and fourth. He selected the names for his new modes after carefully scrutinizing ancient authorities and their varying terminologies. Nevertheless, his new modes, like Aaron's, had an empirical basis as well. This is clear from his use of Gregorian chant to exemplify the twelve-mode system (which also made a broader ideological point: Glarean was a staunch Catholic and resisted movements of Protestant reform). Glarean's empiricism is evident also in his presentation of numerous full compositions by composers of his time to exemplify his theory and in his observations that modern polyphonic practice tended to the frequent use of the octave species that we would call the major and natural minor modes.

Glarean's twelve-mode system was very influential. Zarlino embraced it in his *Istitutioni harmoniche* without mentioning Glarean and, later, went Glarean one better by renumbering his modes from the Ionian, beginning on C, rather than from the conventional starting-point, Dorian-D. In the present excerpt Glarean combines a paean to his favorite composer, Josquin Desprez, with an exemplification by means of Josquin's works of the mixture of authentic and plagal modal pairs.

FROM *Dodecachordon*
(1547)

BOOK 3

CHAPTER 24: EXAMPLES OF THE PAIRED COMBINATIONS OF THE MODES TOGETHER WITH AN ENCOMIUM OF JOSQUIN DESPREZ

So much for our examples of the twelve modes in that varied sort of music not (at least in our opinion) inappropriately called mensural, examples cited with all possible brevity from various authors in proof of those things that have seemed to us in need of proof. It now remains for us to give examples of these same modes in combination,[1] not commonplace examples, to be sure, but weighty ones elegantly illustrating the matter. And since in our preceding book[2] we have sufficiently discussed the actual nature of these combinations, we shall refrain from re-examining it here. All our examples will be in the order seen in our last book; thus, having begun with Dorian and Hypodorian, we shall then add examples of the other paired combinations, briefly expressing our opinion about these, partly to show others a better way of judging and, as it were, to open men's eyes, partly to make known the merits of the ingenious

TEXT: The original edition (Basle, 1547). Glarean gives the complete musical texts of the seven examples discussed in this chapter. These are omitted here. Translation by Oliver Strunk.

1. Examples, that is, in which the tenor or principal part has the combined plagal and authentic range.
2. 2.28–35.

in this art, merits which to certain sufficiently hostile judges seem commonplace, but which to us seem considerable and most worthy of admiration.

Now in this class of authors and in this great crowd of the ingenious there stands out as by far pre-eminent in temperament, conscientiousness, and industry (or I am mistaken in my feeling) Jodocus à Prato, whom people playfully (ὑποκοριστικῶς) call in his Belgian mother-tongue Josquin, as though they were to say "Little Jodocus." If this man, besides that native bent and strength of character by which he was distinguished, had had an understanding of the twelve modes and of the truth of musical theory, nature could have brought forth nothing more majestic and magnificent in this art; so versatile was his temperament in every respect, so armed with natural acumen and force, that there is nothing he could not have done in this profession. But moderation was wanting for the most part and, with learning, judgment; thus in certain places in his compositions he did not, as he should have, soberly repress the violent impulses of his unbridled temperament. Yet let this petty fault be condoned in view of the man's other incomparable gifts.

No one has more effectively expressed the passions of the soul in music than this symphonist, no one has more felicitously begun, no one has been able to compete in grace and facility on an equal footing with him, just as there is no Latin poet superior in the epic to Maro. For just as Maro, with his natural facility, was accustomed to adapt his poem to his subject so as to set weighty matters before the eyes of his readers with close-packed spondees, fleeting ones with unmixed dactyls, to use words suited to his every subject, in short, to undertake nothing inappropriately,[3] as Flaccus says of Homer, so our Josquin, where his matter requires it, now advances with impetuous and precipitate notes, now intones his subject in long-drawn tones, and, to sum up, has brought forth nothing that was not delightful to the ear and approved as ingenious by the learned, nothing, in short, that was not acceptable and pleasing, even when it seemed less erudite, to those who listened to it with judgment. In most of his works he is the magnificent virtuoso, as in the *Missa super voces musicales* and the *Missa ad fugam;* in some he is the mocker, as in the *Missa La sol fa re mi;* in some he extends himself in rivalry,[4] as in the *Missa de Beata Virgine;* although others have also frequently attempted all these things, they have not with the same felicity met with a corresponding success in their undertakings.

This was for us the reason why in this, the consummation of our work, we have by preference cited examples by this man. And although his talent is beyond description, more easily admired than properly explained, he still seems preferable to others, not only for his talent, but also for his diligence in emending his works. For those who have known him say that he brought his things forth with much hesitation and with corrections of all sorts, and that he

3. Maro is Virgil. Compare the similar remarks by Zarlino in no. 37 above, p. 295.
4. With Antoine Brumel; see below at n. 20.

gave no composition to the public unless he had kept it by him for several years, the opposite of what we said Jacob Obrecht is reported to have done. Hence some not inappropriately maintain that the one may justly be compared to Virgil, the other to Ovid. But if we admit this, to whom shall we more fittingly compare Pierre de La Rue, an astonishingly delightful composer, than to Horace, Isaac than perhaps to Lucan, Févin than to Claudianus, Brumel to Statius? Yet I should seem foolish, and rightly, if I were to speak with so little taste of these men, and perhaps I should deserve to hear that popular saying, "Shoemaker, stick to your last!" Hence I proceed to the explanation and judging of the examples.

Of the first combination, that of Dorian and Hypodorian, let our example be the melody "Victimae paschali laudes," on the Blessed Resurrection of Christ, as set by this same author Josquin, a melody that we have mentioned twice before and that we have further cited as an example of this combination in our second book.[5] In it, it will rightly be judged ingenious that the given theme is heard thus divided by intervals among the four voices, as is most fitting.[6] In its first part, the highest voice, borrowed from some well-known song,[7] presents the Hypodorian mode with an added ditone below. In the following part it is Dorian with an added diatessaron above. Here the ending is on the highest step of the diapason, whereas just the other way it ought to have been on the lowest; this part, however, is also borrowed,[8] and on this account he has not wished to alter it. The tenor is extended a ditone lower than the Hypodorian form requires, but the author does this with his usual license. The borrowed melodies he combines with other ancient ones, appropriately in the same mode, for melodies in other modes would not agree to this extent. At the same time, it was not difficult for this author to combine melodies belonging to different modes, even to do so gracefully, for he composed scarcely a single mass, be its mode what it may, without bringing in the Aeolian mode in the Nicene Creed,[9] something that others have attempted also, but not always with the same success. Each voice has something worthy of note, thus the tenor its stability, the bass its wonderful gravity, although I scarcely know whether it pleases everyone that he ascends as he does in the bass at the word "Galilaea." That this proceeds from the wantonness of his temperament we cannot deny; thus we must accept it gracefully as an addition. The cantus has an ancient flavor; the seventh note from the end is heard alone, with all the other voices pausing. Yet, in comparison with the genius of the man, all these things are wholly unimportant. Let us go on, then, to other examples.

5. 1.14 and 2.29.
6. Josquin treats the plainsong as a "wandering cantus firmus," giving stanza 1 to the tenor and, in stanza 2, l. 1 to the alto, l. 2 to the bass, l. 3 to the tenor, and so forth.
7. It is the superius of Ockeghem's chanson "D'ung aultre amer."
8. It is the superius of Hayne's chanson "De tous biens playne."
9. That is, without interpolating the Gregorian Credo, officially of Mode IV but assigned by Glarean (2.17) to the Aeolian mode.

Here, in the motet "De profundis," I wish everyone to observe closely what the beginning is like and with how much passion and how much majesty the composer has given us the opening words; instead of transposing the modes from their natural positions to the higher register (as is elsewhere the usual custom), he has combined the systems of the two; at the same time, with astonishing and carefully studied elegance, he has thrown the phrase into violent disorder, usurping now the leap of the Lydian, now that of the Ionian, until at length, by means of these most beautiful refinements, he glides, creeping unobserved and without offending the ear, from Dorian to Phrygian.[10] That this is difficult to do, especially in these two modes, the Dorian and Phrygian, we have already shown.[11] Thus, contrary to the nature of the modes, he has ended the combined systems of the Dorian and Hypodorian on E, the seat of the Phrygian. Yet there are other compositions in which he has done this also (nor is he alone in it), evidently from an immoderate love of novelty and an excessive eagerness to win a little glory for being unusual, a fault to which the more ingenious professors of the arts are in general so much given that, be it ever so peculiar to the symphonists, they still share it in common with many others. None the less the motet remains between A and d, respecting the limits of the Dorian and Hypodorian systems. And although by his unusual procedure he has sought nothing else, he has at least made it plain that, through the force of his temperament, he could bring it about that the charge customarily brought against the ancient musicians, namely, of progressing "From Dorian to Phrygian,"[12] would be brought in vain against him by whom it was so learnedly accomplished, without the slightest offense to the ear. But enough of this motet.[13]

The second combination is that of the Hypophrygian and Phrygian modes, extending from B to e. But the combination rarely descends in this way to B without descending also to A; thus it usually lies between C and e. Yet our Josquin, in setting the Genealogy of Christ Our Saviour according to the Evangelists Matthew and Luke for four voices in harmony in this combination, descends to A *re* and ascends to f, adding here a semitone and there a tone,

---

10. The word "phrase" *(phrasis)* has for Glarean the special meaning "melodic idiom"; the "phrase" of a given mode consists for him partly in its tendency to emphasize its natural arithmetic or harmonic division at the fourth or fifth, partly in its use of certain characteristic tone-successions taken over from plainsong. Compare 1.13, where the leaps characteristic of the eight modes of plainsong are discussed and illustrated; also 2.36. The leap characteristic of the Lydian mode is that from a to c; by Ionian leap Glarean must mean that from e to g.

11. 2.11, where the present example is also mentioned.

12. Ἀπὸ δορίου ἐπὶ φρύγιον. The proverb is also found in Gafori, *De harmonia musicorum instrumentorum opus* 4.2, and seems to harken back to Aristotle's story of Philoxenus attempting to compose a dithyramb in Dorian but being forced by the nature of the genre back to Phrygian; see *Politics* 1342b.

13. Despite the range of its tenor, by which Glarean has evidently been misled, Josquin's "De profundis" is clearly Hypophrygian, or combined Phrygian and Hypophrygian; cf. Zarlino, *Istitutioni harmoniche* 4.23.

and this with his usual license.[14] The first one, according to Matthew, he has arranged in accordance with the true final close of the mode, namely on E; we show it here. The second one, taken from Luke, he has forced to end on G, but without altering the phrase of the modes at the time, and this also with his usual license.[15] The motet has great majesty, and it is wonderful that from material so sterile, namely, from a bare catalogue of men, he has been able to fashion as many delights as though it had been some fertile narrative. Many other things might be said, but let some of these be left for others to discuss.

The third combination, that of Lydian and Hypolydian, is unusual in this our age, for, as we have often remarked in the foregoing, all compositions in these modes are forced into the Ionian.[16] But in our example, the Agnus Dei from the *Missa Fortuna desperata*, the reader may first admire the way in which a Lydian has been made from an Ionian, for the whole mass is sung in the Ionian mode. This is doubtless due to the bass, plunged into the lowest diapason. For in other compositions, as often as the tenor is Hypodorian, the bass is usually Dorian or Aeolian; again, just as a Phrygian tenor often has an Aeolian bass and cantus, here an Ionian bass has a Lydian tenor and alto.[17] But it is doubtful whether the author has done this by design or by accident. Aside from this, he talks nonsense with his canon, following the custom of the singers.[18] For who except Oedipus himself would understand such a riddle of the sphinx? He has humored the common singers, obeying the maxim, Ἀλωπεκίζειν πρὸς ἑτέραν ἀλώπεκα; that is, *Cum vulpe vulpinare tu quoque invicem*, as Master Erasmus has learnedly translated it, or, as the vulgar inelegantly put it, "Howl with the wolves, if you want to get along with them."[19]

The fourth combination is that of the Mixolydian and its plagal, the Hypomixolydian; in our age it is seldom used. Nevertheless, once the symphonists

14. *Werken, Motetten* (Amsterdam, 1926), vol. 1, pp. 59–69 (Matthew) and 70–81 (Luke). The tenor descends to A in the Luke genealogy only.

15. On this ending see 2.36, also no. 69 above (Aaron, chap. 5), p. 425.

16. No. 69 above (Aaron, chap. 6), p. 426.

17. See 3.13 on the "mysterious relationship" of the modes, where the present example is also mentioned. Here, as there, Glarean clearly has three distinct sorts of relationship in mind: 1) the natural relationship of any authentic mode to the plagal mode having the same final; 2) the special relationship of Phrygian to Aeolian, as a result of which a Phrygian composition may have marked Aeolian characteristics or an Aeolian composition a Phrygian final cadence; as an example of this relationship Glarean gives in 3.19 the motet "Tulerunt Dominum meum"; cf. Zarlino, *Istitutioni harmoniche* 4.30; 3) the peculiar relationship of D-Dorian to D-Aeolian (transposed Aeolian) and of F-Lydian to F-Ionian (transposed Ionian), of which the present example is an illustration.

18. In Agnus I the bass is to invert his part at an eleventh lower than written and multiply the durations by four (double augmentation). Petrucci's editions, followed by Glarean, hint at this in the following distich, which Glarean heads "the riddle of the sphinx": *In gradus undenos descendant multiplicantes / Consimilique modo crescant Antipodes uno* (Let them descend by eleven steps with multiplied measure; then once more in like manner increase, to antipodes changing).

19. See Desiderius Eramus, *Adagia* 1.2.28.

had perceived the magnificence of these modes from ancient examples of ecclesiastical melody, roused as it were with enthusiasm, they tried in a certain most praiseworthy rivalry to do their utmost with the melody "Et in terra pax" on the Most Blessed Virgin and Queen of Heaven, Mary, Mother of Jesus Christ, above all Antoine Brumel and our Josquin Desprez, at a time when both were verging toward extreme old age.[20] Brumel, in his setting, has spared no pains to show the singers his skill, nay, he has strained every fiber of his temperament to leave behind for later generations a specimen of his ingenuity. Yet, in my opinion at least, Josquin has by far surpassed him in natural force and ingenious penetration and has so borne himself in the contest that nature, mother of all, as though wishing to form from the four elements her most perfect creation, seems to me to have brought her utmost powers into play in order that it might be impossible to invent a better music. And thus the majority of the learned have not hesitated to award the first place to this composition, especially Joannes Vannius,[21] whom we have mentioned in connection with the Hypomixolydian mode and to whose judgment we gladly subscribe, both because he gave it before us and because he outdid us in this matter by far. At the beginning, the tenor descends once to the Hypomixolydian diatessaron, otherwise the entire melody is Mixolydian, not Hypomixolydian. To me, the greatest passion seems to have been expressed at the word "Primogenitus" in the first part of the setting; others prefer the second part. But there is no part whatever that does not contain something that you may greatly admire.

Of the fifth combination, that of Aeolian and Hypoaeolian, we should not again be giving the same example if we had been able to obtain or discover another one anywhere among the symphonists of our age. Although in our previous book[22] we also produced other examples of the combination, this one[23] was by far the most enlightening, as one by many treated yet by all perverted and transposed from its natural position, even mutilated or altered with respect to its two diatessarons above and below, namely by Brumel and Josquin in their two so celebrated masses of the Virgin Mary, Mother of God; for this reason we have earnestly entreated that excellent man, Master Gregor Meyer, the distinguished organist of the cathedral at Solothurn in Switzerland, to treat the theme worthily, with all the skill at his command, in its natural position and with the two diatessarons proper to and born with the body of the melody. In truth, we imagine this melody to be some splendid bird, whose body is the diapente *re–la* and whose two wings are the diatessarons *mi–la*. To sew to this body wings other than those with which it was born would be foolish, surely, unless like Aesop's crow it was to fly with strange plumage. We have

20. The Glorias of both Josquin's and Brumel's masses *De beata virgine* paraphrase Gloria IX, for the Mass on the Feast of the Blessed Virgin Mary; for the chant see *Gradual sacrosanctae romanae ecclesiae*, p. 30°.

21. This is Johannes Wannenmacher, Swiss choirmaster and composer.

22. 2.33

23. The Gregorian Kyrie "Cum jubilo" (*Gradual . . . romanae ecclesiae*, p. 29°).

prevailed upon him and, in all friendliness toward me and readiness to further liberal studies, he has sent us what we wanted; of this we now desire to make the reader a sharer. We do not at all hesitate to insert this composition among those of Josquin, such praise has been given to it; namely, the opinion of that learned man, Master John Alus, canon of the same cathedral and preacher of the Divine Word, who thinks that it would be no small ornament to the more serious studies, such as theology and sacred letters, if to these were added a knowledge of languages and of the mathematical disciplines, and that among these last it would most befit a priest of Holy Church if he knew music. Nor was the man mistaken in his opinion, for he had become versed in musical knowledge. We had his support in this work when he lived with us at Freiburg at the foot of the Black Forest and often refreshed us, now playing the organ, now joining to this the singing of things by Josquin. And so, since he has given the highest praise to this composition of our Gregor, he has easily won our approval and has been responsible for its coming into men's hands as worthy of the ears of the learned.

Of the sixth combination, that of Hyperaeolian and Hyperphrygian, we have deliberately omitted an example, for none is to be found anywhere and it would be foolish to invent one, especially with so great a choice of modes; the tenor, too, would have an outrageous ambitus, actually exceeding all the remaining combinations of the modes by an apotome. Aside from this, in our previous book we have given an invented example, less for imitation than for illustration, so that the matter might be understood, not so that something of the sort might be attempted by anyone, a thing we find that no one has attempted.[24]

Of the seventh and last combination, namely of Ionian and Hypoionian, our example, "Planxit autem David," is again by Josquin Desprez, the author of the examples of all the other combinations except the fifth. Of its beginning some will no doubt exclaim: "The mountain has labored and brought forth a mouse!" But they will not have considered that, throughout the motet, there is preserved what befits the mourner, who is wont at first to cry out frequently, then to murmur to himself, turning little by little to sorrowful complaints, thereupon to subside or sometimes, when passion breaks out anew, to raise his voice again, shouting out a cry. All these things we see most beautifully observed in this composition, as will be evident to the attentive reader. Nor is there in it anything unworthy of its author; by the gods, he has everywhere expressed the passion in a wonderful way, thus, at the very beginning of the tenor, at the word "Jonathan."

24. See 2.34.

71 Gioseffo Zarlino

FROM *Istitutioni harmoniche*
(1558)

BOOK THREE

26. WHAT IS SOUGHT IN EVERY COMPOSITION; AND FIRST, OF THE SUBJECT[1]

I shall come now to the discussion of counterpoint, but before I begin this discussion it must be understood that in every good counterpoint, or in every good composition, there are required many things, and one may say that it would be imperfect if one of them were lacking.

The first of these is the subject, without which one can do nothing. For just as the builder, in all his operations, looks always toward the end and founds his work upon some matter which he calls the subject, so the musician in his operations, looking toward the end which prompts him to work, discovers the matter or subject upon which he founds his composition. Thus he perfects his work in conformity with his chosen end. Or again, just as the poet, prompted by such an end to improve or to delight (as Horace shows so clearly in his *Art of Poetry,* when he says:

> Poets aim either to benefit, or to amuse,
> or to utter words at once both pleasing and helpful to life),[2]

takes as the subject of his poem some history or fable, discovered by himself or borrowed from others, which he adorns and polishes with various manners, as he may prefer, leaving out nothing that might be fit or worthy to delight the minds of his hearers, in such a way that he takes on something of the magnificent and marvelous; so the musician, apart from being prompted by the same end to improve or to delight the minds of his listeners with harmonious accents, takes the subject and founds upon it his composition, which he adorns with various modulations and various harmonies in such a way that he offers welcome pleasure to his hearers.

TEXT: The edition published as the first volume of the *Opere* (Venice, 1589), collated with the first and second editions (Venice, 1558 and 1562). The postils of the original and some of the additions of 1589 are given as author's notes. Translation by Oliver Strunk.

1. The first half of this chapter is literally translated by Pietro Cerone in his *El melopeo y maestro* (Naples, 1613), 12.1.
2. Ll. 333–34; trans. H. Rushton Fairclough, *Horace: Satires, Epistles and Ars Poetica* (Cambridge, Mass.: Harvard University Press, 1966), 479.

The second condition is that the composition should be principally composed of consonances; in addition, it should incidentally include many dissonances, suitably arranged in accordance with the rules which I propose to give later on.

The third is that the procedure of the parts should be good, that is, that the modulations[3] should proceed by true and legitimate intervals arising from the sonorous numbers,[4] so that through them may be acquired the usage of good harmonies.

The fourth condition to be sought is that the modulations and the concentus be varied, for harmony[5] has no other source than the diversity of the modulations and the diversity of the consonances variously combined.

The fifth is that the composition should be subjected to a prescribed and determined harmony, mode, or tone (call it as we will), and that it should not be disordered.

The sixth and last (aside from the others which might be added) is that the harmony it contains should be so adapted to the speech, that is, to the words, that in joyous matters the harmony will not be mournful, and vice versa, that in mournful ones the harmony will not be joyful.

3. "A movement made from one sound to another by means of various intervals" (2.14). Zarlino distinguishes two sorts of modulation: "improper," as in plainsong, and "proper," as in figured music. "Proper modulation" has these further divisions: first, sol-fa or solmization; second, the modulation of artificial instruments; third, modulation in which words are adapted to the musical figures.

4. "Sonorous number is number related to voices and to sounds" (1.19). For Zarlino, the sonorous (or harmonic) numbers are specifically the numbers 1 to 6, with their products and their squares. As he says in 1.15, the six-part number has its parts so proportioned that, when any two of them are taken, their relation gives us the ratio or form of one of the musical consonances, simple or composite. And these parts are so ordered that, if we take six strings stretched subject to the ratio of the numbers 1 to 6, when we strike them all together, our ear perceives no discrepancy and takes the highest pleasure in the harmony that arises; the opposite is the case if the order is changed in any respect. It should be noted that Zarlino does not say that the lengths of the strings correspond to the numbers 1 to 6; he says that they correspond to the ratios of these numbers. The relative lengths, as given in the *Dimostrationi armoniche* 3, *Definitione* 44, are 60, 30, 20, 15, 12, and 10; the resulting harmony will consist of unison, octave, twelfth, fifteenth, seventeenth, and nineteenth.

5. In 2.12 Zarlino defines harmony as having two varieties, "proper" and "improper." "Proper harmony" is a combination or mixture of low and high sounds, divided or not divided by intermediate sounds, which impresses the ear agreeably; it arises from the parts of a composition through the procedure which they make in accord with one another until they attain their end, and it has the power to dispose the soul to various passions. "Proper harmony" arises not only from consonances, but also from dissonances. It has two divisions: "perfect," as in the singing of many parts, and "imperfect," as in the singing of two parts only. "Improper harmony" arises when two sounds distant from one another with respect to the low and the high are heard divided by other intermediate sounds so that they give out an agreeable concentus, subject to several proportions. Musicians call such a combination a harmony. But, Zarlino says, it ought rather to be called a harmonious consonance, for it contains no modulation, and although its extremes are divided, it has no power to move the soul. "Improper harmony" has also two divisions: "simple," as in a combination of consonances arranged in harmonic proportion, and "by extension of meaning" (*ad un certo modo*), as in a combination otherwise arranged.

To assure a perfect understanding of the whole, I shall discuss these things separately as they become suited to my purpose and to my needs.

Beginning with the first, then, I say that, in every musical composition, what we call the subject is that part from which the composer derives the invention to make the other parts of the work, however many they may be. Such a subject may take many forms, as the composer may prefer and in accordance with the loftiness of his imagination: it may be his own invention, that is, it may be that he has discovered it of himself; again, it may be that he has borrowed it from the works of others, adapting it to his work and adorning it with various parts and various modulations. And such a subject may be of several kinds: it may be a tenor or some other part of any composition you please, whether of plainsong or of figured music; again, it may be two or more parts of which one follows another in consequence[6] or in some other way, for the various forms of such subjects are innumerable.

When the composer has discovered his subject, he will write the other parts in the way which we shall see later on. When this is done, our practical musicians call the manner of composing "making counterpoint."

But when the composer has not first discovered his subject, that part which he first puts into execution or with which he begins his work, whatever it may be or however it may begin, whether high, low, or intermediate, will always be the subject to which he will then adapt the other parts in consequence or in some other way, as he prefers, adapting the harmony to the words as the matter they contain demands. And when the composer goes on to derive the subject from the parts of the work, that is, when he derives one part from another and goes on to write the work all at once, as we shall see elsewhere, that small part which he derives without the others and upon which he then composes the parts of his composition will always be called the subject. This manner of composing practical musicians call "composing from fantasy," although it may also be called "counterpointing," or as they say, "making counterpoint."

27. THAT COMPOSITIONS SHOULD BE MADE UP PRIMARILY OF CONSONANCES, AND SECONDARILY AND INCIDENTALLY OF DISSONANCES

And although every composition, every counterpoint, and in a word every harmony is made up primarily and principally of consonances, dissonances are used secondarily and incidentally for the sake of greater beauty and elegance. Taken by themselves, these are not very acceptable to the ear; arranged as they

---

6. "Consequence we define as a certain repetition or return of a part or the whole of a modulation; it arises from an order and arrangement of many musical figures which the composer makes in one part of his composition and from which, after a certain and limited space of time, there follow one or more other parts, low, high, intermediate, or in the same sound, at the diapason, diapente, diatessaron, or unison, these proceeding one after another by the same intervals. Imitation we shall define as a repetition or return which does not proceed by the same intervals but by wholly different ones, only the movements made by the parts and the figures being similar" (3.54). Each has two varieties, strict and free, and may be either in direct or in contrary motion.

regularly should be and in accordance with the precepts which we shall give, the ear tolerates them to such an extent that, far from being offended, it receives from them great pleasure and delight.

From this, among many other advantages, the musician derives two of no little value: we have already stated the first, namely, that with their aid he may pass from one consonance to another;[7] the second is that a dissonance causes the consonance which immediately follows it to seem more acceptable. Thus it is perceived and recognized with greater pleasure by the ear, just as after darkness light is more acceptable and delightful to the eye, and after the bitter the sweet is more luscious and palatable. And from everyday experience with sounds we learn that if a dissonance offends the ear for a certain length of time, the consonance which follows is made more acceptable and more sweet.

Thus the ancient musicians judged that they should admit in composition not only the consonances which they called perfect and those which they called imperfect, but dissonances also, knowing that their compositions would thus attain to greater beauty and elegance than they would without them. For if they were made up entirely of consonances, although beautiful sounds and good effects would issue from them, they would still be somehow imperfect, both as sound and as composition, seeing that (the consonances not being blended with dissonances) they would lack the great elegance that dissonance affords.

And although I have said that the composer is to use consonances principally and dissonances incidentally, he is not to understand by this that he is to use them in his counterpoints or compositions as they come to hand, without any rule or any order, for this would lead to confusion; on the contrary, he must take care to use them in a regular and orderly manner so that the whole will be profitable. Above all (apart from other things) he must keep in mind the two considerations upon which (in my judgment) all the beauty, all the elegance, and all the excellence of music depend: the movements which the parts of the composition make in ascending or descending in similar or contrary motion, and the arrangement of the consonances in their proper places in the harmonies. Of these things I propose with God's help to speak as may suit my purpose, for this has always been my chief intention.

And to introduce this discussion I propose to explain certain rules laid down by the ancients, who recognized the importance of such matters; teaching by means of these the regular procedure to be followed in using the consonances and dissonances one after another in composition, they went on to give rules about the movements, which they did imperfectly. Thus I shall state and explain these rules in order, and from this explanation I shall go on to show with evident reason what is to be done and how the rules are to be understood, adding also certain further rules, not only useful but also most necessary to those who seek to train themselves in a regular and well-ordered way of composing music of any kind in a learned and elegant manner, with good reasons

7. 3. 17.

and good foundations. In this way everyone may know in what part to arrange the consonances and in what place to use the major and the minor in his compositions.

•   •   •   •   •

29. THAT TWO CONSONANCES SUBJECT TO THE SAME PROPORTION ARE NOT TO BE USED ONE AFTER ANOTHER, ASCENDING OR DESCENDING, WITHOUT A MEAN[8]

The ancient composers also avoided using one after another two perfect consonances of the same genus or species, their extremes subject to the same proportion, the modulations moving one step or more; thus they avoided using two or more unisons, two or more octaves, or two or more fifths, as seen in the following examples:

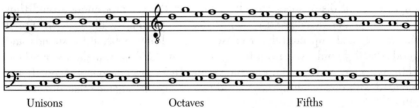

| Unisons | Octaves | Fifths |

For they knew very well that harmony can arise only from things that are among themselves diverse, discordant, and contrary, and not from things that are in complete agreement. Now if harmony arises from variety such as this, it is not sufficient that in music the parts of the composition be at a distance from one another with respect to the low and the high; the modulations must also be varied in their movements and must contain various consonances, subject to various proportions. And the more harmonious we judge a composition to be, the more we will find, between its several parts, different distances with respect to the low and the high, different movements, and different proportions. Perhaps the ancients saw that when consonances were not put together in the manner I have described, they were similar in their procedure and similar in the form of their proportions, although sometimes varied in their extremes with respect to the low and the high. Knowing, then, that such similarity can generate no variety in the concentus and judging (as was true) that perfect harmony consists in variety, not so much in the positions or distances of the parts of the composition as in the movements, the modulations, and the proportions, they held that in taking one after another two consonances similar in proportion, they were varying the position from low to high, or vice versa, without producing any good harmony, even though the extremes did vary one from another. Thus they did not wish that in composition two or more perfect consonances subject

8. Having concluded the discussion of his first and second requirements, Zarlino now skips over to the fourth, leaving the third for Chapters 30 and 31.

to the same proportion should be taken one after another, the parts ascending or descending together, without the mediation of another interval.

The unisons they especially avoided, for these sounds have no extremes and are neither different in position, nor at a distance from one another, nor productive of any variety in the procedure, but wholly similar in every respect. Nor in singing them does one find any difference with respect to the low and the high, for there is no interval between the one sound and the other, the sounds of the one part being in the same places as those of the other, as may be seen in the example above and in the definition given in Chapter 11, on the unison. Nor does one find any variety in the modulation, for the one part sings the very intervals by which the other proceeds.

The same might be said of two or more octaves, if it were not that their extremes differ from one another with respect to the low and the high; thus, being somewhat varied in its extremes, the octave affords the ear somewhat more pleasure than the unison.

And the same may be said of two or more fifths; since these progress by similar steps and proportions, some of the ancients were of the opinion that to a certain extent they gave rise rather to dissonance than to harmony or consonance.

Thus they held it as true that whenever one had arrived at perfect consonance one had attained the end and the perfection toward which music tends, and in order not to give the ear too much of this perfection they did not wish it repeated over and over again.

The truth and excellence of this admirable and useful admonition are confirmed by the operations of Nature, for in bringing into being the individuals of each species she makes them similar to one another in general, yet different in some particular, a difference or variety affording much pleasure to our senses. This admirable order the composer ought to imitate, for the more his operations resemble those of our great mother, the more he will be esteemed. And to this course the numbers and proportions invite him, for in their natural order one will not find two similar proportions following one another immediately, such as the progressions 1:1:1 or 2:2:2 or others like them, which would give the forms of two unisons, still less the progression 1:2:4:8, which is not harmonic but geometric and would give the forms of three consecutive octaves, and still less the progression 4:6:9, which would give the forms of two consecutive fifths. Thus he ought under no conditions to take one after another two unisons, or two octaves, or two fifths, since the natural cause of the consonances, which is the harmonic number, does not in its progression or natural order contain two similar proportions one after another without a mean, as may be seen in Chapter 15 of Part I. For although these consonances, taken in this manner, would obviously cause no dissonance between the parts, a certain heaviness would be heard which would displease.

For all these reasons, then, we ought under no conditions to offend against this rule, that is, we ought never to use the consonances one after another in the way described above; on the contrary, we should seek always to vary the sounds, the consonances, the movements, and the intervals, and in this way, from the variety of these things, we shall come to make a good and perfect harmony. Nor need it concern us that some have sought to do the opposite, rather (as we see from their compositions) from presumption and on their own authority than for any reason that they have had. For we ought not to imitate those who offend impertinently against the good manners and good rules of an art or science without giving any reason for doing so; we ought to imitate those who have conformed, conforming ourselves to them and embracing them as good masters, always avoiding the dreary and taking the good. And I say this for this reason: just as the sight of a picture is more delightful to the eye when it is painted with various colors than when it is painted with one color only, so the ear takes more pleasure and delight in the varied consonances which the more diligent composer puts into his compositions than in the simple and unvaried.

This the more diligent ancient musicians, to whom we are so much indebted, wished observed, and to it we add that, for the reasons already given, the composer ought not to use two or more imperfect consonances one after another, ascending or descending together, without a mean, such as two major or minor thirds, or two major or minor sixths, as seen in the example:

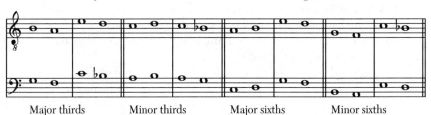

Major thirds   Minor thirds   Major sixths   Minor sixths

For not only do these offend against what I have said about the perfect consonances, but their procedure causes a certain bitterness to be heard, since there is altogether lacking in their modulations the interval of the major semitone, in which lies all the good in music and without which every modulation and every harmony is harsh, bitter, and as it were inconsonant. Another reason for this bitterness is that there is no harmonic relationship[9] between the parts or sounds of two major thirds or of two minor sixths, which makes these somewhat more dreary than the others, as we shall see later on. Thus in every progression or modulation which the parts make in singing together we ought to take special care that wherever possible at least one of them has or moves by the interval of the major semitone, so that the modulation and the harmony which arise from the movements which the parts of the composition make together may be more delightful and more sweet.[10] This is easily managed if the consonances

---

9. Non-harmonic relationship or, as we should call it, false relation is defined and discussed in Chapters 30 and 31.

10. "The semitone is indeed the salt (so to speak), the condiment, and the cause of every good modulation and every good harmony" (3.10, with reference to the role of the semitone in the

taken one after another are diverse in species, so that after the major third or sixth will follow the minor, or vice versa, or so that after the major third will follow the minor sixth, or after the latter the former, and after the minor third the major sixth, or in the same way after the major sixth the minor third.[11] Nor is there more reason for forbidding the use, one after another, of two perfect consonances than of two imperfect ones, for although the former are perfect consonances, each of the latter is found to be perfect in its proportion. And just as it may not be said with truth that one man is more man than another, so also it may not be said that a major or minor third or sixth taken below is greater or less than another taken above, or vice versa. Thus, since it is forbidden to use two perfect consonances of the same species one after another, we ought still less to use two imperfect ones of the same proportion, seeing that they are less consonant than the perfect.

But when two minor thirds, and similarly two major sixths, are used one after another, ascending or descending together by step, they may be tolerated, for although the major semitone is not heard in their modulations, and the thirds are naturally somewhat mournful and the sixths somewhat harsh, the slight difference that is heard in the movements of the parts gives a certain variety. For the lower part always ascends or descends by a minor tone and the upper by a major, or vice versa,[12] and this affords a certain satisfaction to the ear, the more so since the sounds of the parts stand in a harmonic relationship to one another. But when the parts move by leap we ought by no means to use two or more similar consonances one after another, ascending or descending, for apart from not observing the conditions touched on above, the sounds of the parts will not stand in a harmonic relationship to one another, as seen below:

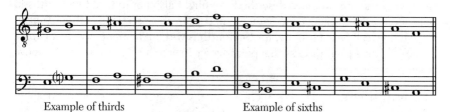

Example of thirds   Example of sixths

Thus, to avoid the errors that may occur when it becomes necessary to take two thirds or two sixths one after another, we shall take care to take first the

---

progressions major sixth to octave, major third to fifth, minor sixth to fifth, minor third to unison). "Guido places the semitone in the center of each of his hexachords, as though in the most worthy and most honored place, the seat of Virtue (as they say), for its excellence and nobility are such that without it every composition would be harsh and unbearable to hear, nor can one have any perfect harmony except by means of it" (3.19).

11. As in the first part of the musical example at the end of the present chapter.

12. In Zarlino's scale the minor tones are those from D to E and from G to A; all the others are major, including the tone b-flat to c.

major and then the minor, or vice versa, taking them in whatever manner we wish, with movements by step or by leap, for everything will now agree. And we ought also to take care that, in taking the third after the sixth or the sixth after the third, we make one of them major and the other minor, as we can when there is movement in each of the parts, above and below. But when there is no movement in one or other of them, this rule cannot be observed without departing from the rules which, for the well-being of the composition, we shall give later on. Thus after the major third we shall have to take the major sixth and after the minor third the minor sixth, or vice versa, as seen in the example below:

Example of everything that has been said

We shall add that, it being forbidden to take two perfect or imperfect consonances in the way we have described, we ought also not to take two fourths in any composition whatever, as some do in certain short sections of their *canzoni* which they call *falso bordone,* for the fourth is without a doubt a perfect consonance.[13] But I shall discuss this point when I show how to compose for more than two voices.

30. When the Parts of a Cantilena have between Them a Harmonic Relationship and How We May Use the Semidiapente and the Tritone in Composition

Before going on, I propose to explain what I have said above about the parts of the composition, namely, that sounds sometimes have and sometimes have not a harmonic relationship between them. It must first be understood that to say that the parts of a composition do not have between them a harmonic relationship is to say that between two consonances that two parts make one

---

13. "I am well aware that with many the authority of those who have taken this liberty will count more than the arguments I have put forward against it; let them do their worst by saying that what I hold in little esteem has been practised by many, for they are not capable of reason and do not wish to be." (3.61.).

after another in singing, ascending or descending together, or ascending and descending together, there comes to be heard the augmented diapason, or the semidiapente, or the tritone. This occurs in the crossing of the first figure or note of the upper part with the second figure or note of the lower, or of the first of the lower with the second of the upper. Such a relationship, then, can occur only when we have at least four figures or notes, namely, the two lower and the two upper figures or notes of two consonances, as seen here:[14]

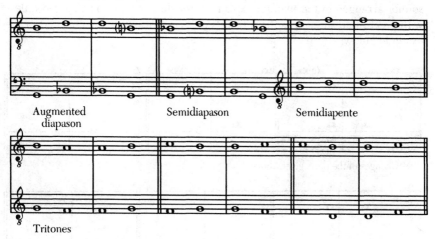

Augmented diapason   Semidiapason   Semidiapente

Tritones

Thus, in order that our compositions may be correct and purged of every error, we shall seek to avoid these relationships as much as we can, especially when we compose for two voices, since these give rise to a certain fastidiousness in discriminating ears. For intervals like these do not occur among the sonorous numbers and are not sung in any sort of composition, even though some have held a contrary opinion. But be this as it may, they are most difficult to sing and they make a dreary effect.

And I am much astonished by those who have not hesitated at all to require the singing or modulation of these intervals in the parts of their compositions, and I cannot imagine why they have done so. And although it is not so bad to find this in the relationship between two modulations as to find it in the modulation of a single part, the same evil that was heard in the single part is now heard divided between two, and it gives the same offense to the ear. For unless the evil is diminished, little or nothing relieves the offensive nature of a fault, even though it be more offensive from one than from many.

Thus, in a composition for several voices, those intervals that are not admit-

14. But when two parts ascend together and the one or the other makes a movement which involves the semitone, it seems that because of this movement they are tolerated by the ear, as are the first cases of the augmented diapason and the semidiapente in the first and third sections of the example. [Au.] (This sentence is not found in earlier editions of the *Istitutioni* and has accordingly been made a note.)

ted in modulation are to be so avoided that they will not be heard as relationships between the parts. This will have been done when the parts can be
interchanged by means of harmonically proportioned intervals of the diatonic
genus, that is, when we can ascend from the first sound of the lower part to
the following sound of the upper, or vice versa, by a legitimate and singable
interval. But this will not be the case when non-harmonic relationships are
heard between the parts of the composition, whatever it may be, among four
sounds arranged in the manner explained, for these cannot be changed unless
with great disadvantage, as the intervals of the last example are changed in the
example below:

Changes of the parts given above

Thus, whenever the parts of a composition or cantilena cannot be so interchanged that from this change there arises a procedure by true and legitimate
singable intervals, we ought to avoid it, especially if our compositions are to be
correct and purged of every error. But in compositions for more than two
voices it is often impossible to avoid such things and not to run into intricacies
of this kind. For it sometimes happens that the composer will write upon a
subject which repeatedly invites him to offend against this precept; thus, when
necessity compels him, he will ignore it, as when he sees that the parts of his
composition cannot be sung with comfort or when he wishes to adapt a consequent which may be sung with comfort, as we shall see elsewhere.[15] But when
necessity compels him to offend, he ought at least to take care that he does so
between diatonic steps and in steps which are natural and proper to the mode,
for these do not give rise to so dreary an effect as do those which are accidental,
being indicated within the composition by the signs ♮, ♯, and ♭.

Take note that I call those errors "natural" which arise in the way shown in
the first example above, and that I call those "accidental" which arise when,
between the true steps of the mode, there is inserted a step of another order,

15. 3.55, 63.

this step being the cause of the difficulty, as may happen in the Fifth Mode,[16] where the central step ♮ is often rejected in favor of the accidental ♭. Thus, between the ♭ and the ♮ preceding or following it, there will arise some one of the disorders in question, as seen in the first of the examples below. And this is the less agreeable since the ♮, which is the principal step of the mode, is absent from its proper place while the ♭, which is accidental, is present in its stead.

And although, for the reasons already given, we ought not to use these intervals in composition in this way, we may sometimes use the semidiapente as a single percussion if immediately after it we come to the ditone, for, as seen in the third of the examples below, the parts may be interchanged without disadvantage. This the better modern musicians observe, just as some of the more ancient observed it in the past.[17] And we are permitted to use not only the semidiapente, but in some cases the tritone also, as we shall see at the proper time. It will, however, be more advantageous to use the semidiapente than the tritone, for the consonances will then stand in their proper places, a thing which will not occur when the tritone is used. And we ought to take care that, in the parts involved, the semidiapente or tritone is immediately preceded by a consonance, no matter whether perfect or imperfect, for through the force of the preceding and following consonances the semidiapente comes to be tempered in such a way that, instead of making a dreary effect, it makes a good one, as experience proves and as is heard in the examples that follow.

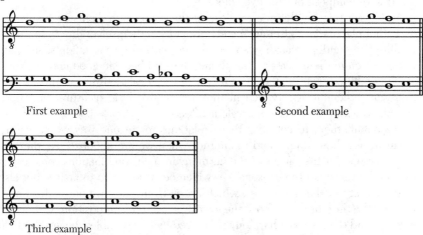

First example | Second example

Third example

16. The Third Mode of the ecclesiastical system (Glarean's Phrygian). Having adopted Glarean's twelve modes in the earlier editions of the *Istitutioni* (1558 and 1562), by 1571, when the *Dimostrationi* were first published, Zarlino had persuaded himself to renumber them, counting the authentic and plagal forms of the C mode as First and Second, and so forth. The various arguments for this renumbering are set forth in the *Dimostrationi* (5, Def. 8). The principal argument is that, in numbering the species of any interval, the point of departure ought to be the natural scale resulting from the harmonic numbers.

17. 3.61.

31. What Consideration is to be Paid to Related Intervals in Compositions for More than Two Voices

Aside from this, the composer should bear in mind that, when they occur in counterpoints without being combined with other intervals, such relationships as the tritone, the semidiapente, the semidiapason, and the others that are similar to them are counted among the things in music that can afford little pleasure. Thus we should oblige ourselves not to use them in simple compositions, which (as I have said) are those for two voices, or in other compositions when two parts sing alone, for the same effects will obviously be heard in these. This is because there will not in either case be present what we have called "perfect harmony," in which a body of consonances and harmonies is heard, the extreme sounds being divided by other mean sounds; on the contrary, there will be present only what we have called "imperfect harmony," in which only two parts are heard singing together, no other sound dividing.[18] And since the sense of hearing grasps two parts more fully than three or four, we ought to vary the harmony between the two as much as we can and to take care not to use these relationships, a thing which may be done without any difficulty.

But in compositions for more than two voices this consideration is not so necessary, both because we cannot always observe it without great inconvenience, and because variety now consists not only in the changing of consonances, but also in the changing of harmonies and positions, a thing which is not true of compositions for two voices.

And I say this for this reason: just as there are ingredients in medicines and other electuaries, bitter and even poisonous in themselves, but indubitably health-giving and less harsh when combined with other ingredients, so many things which in themselves are harsh and harmful become good and healthful when combined with others. Thus it is with these relationships in music. And there are other intervals which in themselves give little pleasure, but when combined with others make marvelous effects.

We ought, then, to consider these relationships in one way when we are about to use them simply and in another when we are about to use them in combination. For the variety of the harmony in such combinations consists not only in the variety of the consonances which occur between the parts, but also in the variety of the harmonies, which arises from the position of the sound forming the third or tenth above the lowest part of the composition. Either this is minor and the resulting harmony is ordered by or resembles the arithmetical proportion or mean, or it is major and the harmony is ordered by or resembles the harmonic.[19]

---

18. For "perfect" and "imperfect" harmony, Zarlino has "proper" and "improper," an obvious slip; cf. n. 5 above.
19. "Not with respect to the order of the proportions, which is actually arithmetic, but with respect to the proportions of the parts when the mean term has been interposed, for these are of the same quantity and proportion as are those produced by a harmonic mean term or divisor,

HARMONIC   ARITHMETIC

Ditone   Semiditone   Semiditone   Ditone

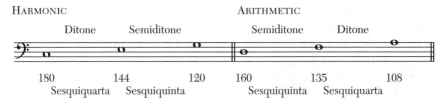

180   144   120   160   135   108
  Sesquiquarta   Sesquiquinta   Sesquiquinta   Sesquiquarta

On this variety depend the whole diversity and perfection of the harmonies. For (as I shall say elsewhere)[20] in the perfect composition the fifth and third, or their extensions, must always be actively present, seeing that apart from these two consonances the ear can desire no sound that falls between their extremes or beyond them and yet is wholly distinct and different from those that lie within the extremes of these two consonances combined. For in this combination occur all the different sounds that can form different harmonies. But since the extremes of the fifth are invariable and always placed subject to the same proportion, apart from certain cases in which the fifth is used imperfectly, the extremes of the thirds are given different positions. I do not say different in proportion; I say different in position, for (as I have said elsewhere[21]) when the major third is placed below, the harmony is made joyful and when it is placed above, the harmony is made mournful. Thus, from the different positions of the thirds which are placed in counterpoint between the extremes of the fifth or above the octave, the variety of harmony arises.

If, then, we wish to vary the harmony and to observe in so far as possible the rule laid down in Chapter 29 (although this is not so necessary in compositions for more than two voices as it is in those for two) we must take the different thirds in such a way that, after first taking the major third, which forms the harmonic mean, we then take the minor, which forms the arithmetical. This we would not be able to observe so easily if we were to take the non-harmonic relationships into consideration, for while we were seeking to avoid them, we would be continuing the concentus in one division for some time without the mediation of the other; thus to no purpose we would cause the composition to sound mournful to words that carry joyfulness with them or to sound joyful to words that treat of mournful matters. I do not go so far as to say that the composer may not take two arithmetical divisions one after another, but I do

---

although in the opposite order." (1.15.) The harmonic mean between two numbers (x and z) is a number (y) such that the difference between it and the smaller number $(y-x)$ is the same fraction of the smaller (x) as the difference between it and the larger number $(z-y)$ is of the larger (z). In Zarlino's example, 144 is the perfect harmonic mean between 120 and 180 because 24 (i.e., $144-120$) is one fifth of 120 and 36 (i.e., $180-144$) is one fifth of 180. The arithmetic mean between two numbers is larger than one by the same numerical amount as it is smaller than the other. Zarlino's 135 is only an approximate arithmetic mean between 108 and 160, as Zarlino recognizes at the end of his chapter. The exact arithmetic mean would be 134 (i.e., $160-134=134-108$). See also No. 2 (Plato, *Timaeus*,) pp. 19–23.

20. 3.59.

21. Chapter 10. [Au.]

say that he ought not to continue in this division for long, since to do so would make the concentus very melancholy. But to take two harmonic divisions one after another can never give offense, provided they be formed from natural steps, and with some judgment and purpose from accidental ones, for when its parts are thus arranged in order, harmony attains its ultimate end and makes its best effect.

But when two parts ascend or descend by one step or two steps we ought to use different divisions, especially when the tritone or semidiapente falls as a relationship between the two parts involved, that is, when in ascending or descending one step two major thirds are taken one after another, and when ascending or descending two steps two minor ones. But when the relationship is that of the semidiatessaron,[22] and it occurs between accidental signs, such as the ♯ and the ♭, or when only one of these signs is present, we need not avoid it at all, for the two divisions being harmonic it is obvious that they will make a good effect, even though they are not varied.

Nor need this astonish anyone, for if he will carefully examine the consonances arranged in the two orders, he will discover that the order which is arithmetical or resembles the arithmetical departs a little from the perfection of harmony, its parts being arranged out of their natural positions; on the other hand he will discover that the harmony which arises from or resembles the harmonic division is perfectly consonant, its parts being arranged and subject to the proper order of this proportion and according to the order which the sonorous numbers maintain in their natural succession, to be seen in Chapter 15 of Part I.

Let this be enough for the present; at another time, perhaps, I shall touch on this again in order that what I have said may be better understood.

•   •   •   •   •

40. The Procedure to be Followed in Writing Simple Counterpoints for Two Voices, Such as are Called Note Against Note

To come now to the application of the rules that I have given, I shall show the procedure to be followed in writing counterpoints, beginning with those which are written simply and for two voices, note against note. From these the

---

22. For *semidiatessaron* (diminished fourth) we ought probably to read *diapente superflua* (augmented fifth); diminished fourths, fifths, and octaves occur as false relations between minor consonances, augmented ones between major consonances. Zarlino has already shown how the diminished fourth and augmented fifth occur as false relations in the third musical example of Chap. 29.

Semidiatessaron   Augmented diapente

composer may go on to diminished counterpoints and to the usage of other compositions.[23] Wishing then to observe what has been observed by all good writers and compilers on every other subject, I shall with reason begin with simple things, both to make the reader more submissive and to avoid confusion.

First observing what was said above in Chapter 26, the composer will choose a tenor from any plainsong he pleases, and this will be the subject of his composition, that is, of his counterpoint. Then he will examine it carefully and will see in what mode it is composed, so that he may make the appropriate cadences in their proper places and may know from these the nature of his composition. For if inadvertently he were to make these inappropriately and out of their places, mixing those of one mode with those of another, the end of his composition would come to be dissonant with the beginning and the middle.

But assuming that the chosen subject is the plainsong tenor given below, which is subject to the Third Mode,[24] he will above all else observe what was said in Chapter 28 above about the procedure in beginning a composition. Thus we shall place the first figure or note of our counterpoint at such an interval from the first of the subject that they will have between them one of the perfect consonances. This done, we shall combine the second note of our counterpoint with the second of the subject in a consonance, either perfect or imperfect, but in any case different from the preceding one, so that we shall not be offending against what was said in Chapter 29, always having an eye to what was laid down in Chapter 38[25] and observing the teaching of Chapter 37,[26] taking care that the parts of the composition are as conjunct as possible and that they make no large leaps, so that the interval between them will not be too great. This done, we shall come to the third figure or note of our counterpoint and combine it with the third of the subject, varying not only the steps or positions but also the consonances, taking perfect consonance after imperfect, or vice versa, or taking one after another two perfect consonances or two imperfect ones different in species, according to the rules given in Chapter 33[27] and 34.[28] We shall do the same with the fourth note of our counterpoint and the fourth of the subject, and with the fifth, the sixth, and the others in order until we come to the end, where, following the rule given in the preceding chapter, we shall conclude our counterpoint with one of the perfect consonances.

But above all else we must take care that the contrapuntal part is not only varied in its different movements, touching different steps, now high, now low,

23. For simple and diminished counterpoint see no. 67 above (Tinctoris), p. 401.
24. The First Mode of the ecclesiastical system (Glarean's Dorian).
25. How we ought to proceed from one consonance to another.
26. That we ought to avoid as much as we can those movements that are made by leap, and in a similar way those distances that may occur between the parts of a composition.
27. When two or more perfect or imperfect consonances, subject to different forms and taken one immediately after another, are conceded.
28. That we do well to take imperfect consonance after perfect, or vice versa.

and now intermediate, but that it is varied also in its consonances with the subject. And we should see to it that the contrapuntal part sings well and proceeds in so far as possible by step, since there lies in this a part of the beauty of counterpoint. And added to the many other things that one may ask (as we shall see), this will bring it to its perfection.

Thus he who will first exercise himself in this simple manner of composing may afterwards go on easily and quickly to greater things. For seeking to write various counterpoints and compositions upon a single subject, now below and now above, he will make himself thoroughly familiar with the steps and with the intervals of each consonance; then, following the precepts which I am about to give, he will be able to go on to the diminution of the figures, that is, to diminished counterpoint, writing the contrapuntal parts sometimes in consequence with his subject and sometimes imitating them or writing them in other ways, as we shall see; and from this he will be able to go on to compositions for more voices, so that, aided by our directions and by his own talents, he will in a short time become a good composer. . . .

Thus the musician must also seek to vary his counterpoint upon the subject, and if he can invent many passages he will choose the one that is best, most suited to his purpose, and most capable of making his counterpoint sonorous and orderly; the others he will set aside. And when he has invented a passage such as might be appropriate for a cadence, if it is not at the moment to his purpose he will reserve it for some other more suitable place. This he will do if the clause or period in the words or speech has not come to an end, for he must always wait until each of these is finished; in a similar way he will take care that it is in the proper place and that the mode in which his composition stands requires it.

He who wishes to begin in the right way with the art of counterpoint must observe all these things. But above everything else he must industriously exercise himself in this sort of composition in order that he may thus arrive more easily at the practice of diminished counterpoint, in which, as we shall see later on, there are many other things that he may use. And in order that he may have some understanding of all that I have said, I shall give below some varied counterpoints, note against note, upon the subject already mentioned; once he has examined these, he will readily understand the things that I shall show later on[29] and will be able to work with greater ease.

Be advised, however, that to write counterpoint, note against note, appears to be and actually is somewhat more difficult than to write it diminished, for the one has not that liberty which the other has, seeing that in the one each note or figure may have one consonance only, while in the other it may have many of them, blended with dissonances according to the composer's pleasure and good judgment. Thus in the first sort the composer cannot at his pleasure arrange the parts so well that they will be without leaps, especially if he wishes

29. 3.42–44.

to write upon a single subject many counterpoints which will be different throughout. But this need not discourage him, for if the root tastes somewhat bitter, he will before long enjoy the fruits which spring from it, and these are sweet, luscious, and palatable. Thus virtue (as the wise affirm) has to do with the difficult and not with the easy.

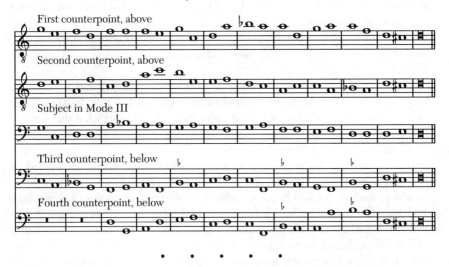

71. On the Benefit which Good Harmonies Derive from the Accidents Enumerated

And now, before going further, let us determine to what extent good and sonorous harmonies derive benefit from the accidents enumerated.[30] And adopting a somewhat lofty manner of speaking for the sake of greater clarity: if the true object of sensation is the body which moves it through the mediation of the sensory organ, it must be understood that, in so far as we consider such bodies according to the different reasons of their movements, we must necessarily postulate in sensation different powers. For considered in so far as it may be seen, an object is called visible and may not be perceived by any other sense than vision. These objects are in fact of two sorts, for they are either primary, as is the color which we see before anything else, or they are commensurate (or shall we say proportionate), and not color, and inherent in many things that are not colored, such as the fire, the moon, the sun, the stars, and other similar things. Indeed these objects have for this reason no proper name; they are simply called visible, and this includes all those things that are visible through light, such as all the luminous bodies, which are those that I have named above. In so far as an object may be heard, as are the voices and the sounds, it is called audible and may not be perceived by any other sense than hearing. The same

---

30. In 3.67–70, on mode, time, prolation, perfection, imperfection, and the various species and effects of the point or dot.

might also be said of the other kinds of objects. Such objects are called sensible particulars, since no one of them may be perceived by more than one of the senses which we have named.

To be sure, there are certain objects which are called common and which may be perceived by several senses; thus movement, rest, number, shape, and size may manifestly be seen, heard, and touched. Then there are certain other objects which are sensible by accident and which may not be perceived except through the mediation of something else; such are the sonorous bodies, which cannot be heard except through the mediation of the sound which is made in the air, as I have shown in Part II.[31]

The more pleasing and sweet these objects are to their particular sense, the more they are proportioned to it, and vice versa; thus the eye, looking at the sun, is offended, for this object is not proportioned to it. And what the philosophers say is true—that excess in the sensible object, if it does not corrupt the sense, at least corrupts the instrument.[32]

If, then, the particular sensible objects may not be perceived or judged by any other sense than that peculiar to them, as sound is by hearing, as color is by vision, and as the others are in order, let those who strive so hard and take such pains to introduce these intricacies into their compositions tell me (if they will) what and how much pleasure and benefit these may afford to the sense and whether these compositions of theirs are more beautiful and more sonorous than those that do not have such things, which are exclusively visible and fall under no other sense than vision and may not be heard in any way, since they are not common objects, perceptible to several senses, as were those mentioned above. If they have judgment, I know that they will reply that these things afford no benefit at all, for when they have been reduced to simple, ordinary notation and stripped of their ciphers, whatever and however great the harmony heard before, such and as great will be the harmony heard afterward. If, then, they are of no benefit at all in the formation of good harmonies, and if they afford no benefit at all to the sense, why to no purpose multiply the singer's duties and augment his vexations with things of this kind? For when he ought to be intent on singing cheerfully such compositions as are to the purpose, he must stand ready to consider chimeras of this sort, falling (according to the various accidents) under mode, time, and prolation, and he must allow nothing written to pass until he has examined it closely, seeing that if he does otherwise he will be thought (if I may say so) an awkward fellow and an ignoramus. And if these things afford no benefit, as they in truth do not, it seems to me sheer madness that anyone of lofty intelligence should have to end his studies and to waste his time and to vex himself about such irrelevant matters. Thus I counsel everyone to disregard these ciphers and to give his attention rather to those things that are productive of good harmonies and sweet ones.

31. Chapter 10. [Au.]
32. Aristotle, De anima [i.e., 424a, 435b]. [Au.]

Perhaps someone will say: "Is it not a fine thing to see a tenor well ordered under the signs of mode, time, and prolation, as contrived by the ancient musicians, who gave their attention to almost nothing else?"

It is indeed a fine thing, especially when it is written or painted, and miniatured too, by the hand of an outstanding scribe and miniaturist, using good inks, fine colors, and proportioned measures, and when (as I have seen) there is added to it a coat of arms, a miter, or a cardinal's hat, together with some other splendid object. But of what importance is this if a composition having a tenor written simply and without any intricacy is just as sonorous or as graceless as though it were full of such things?

Thus one may say with truth that this way of composing is simply an unnecessary multiplying of difficulty, and not a multiplying of harmony, and that it affords no benefit at all, since, as the philosophers hold, things are vainly multiplied when there is no purpose. For music, being the science which treats of the sounds and the voices, which are the particular objects of hearing, contemplates only the concord which arises from the strings and the voices (as Ammonius says[33]) and considers nothing else. Thus it seems to me that everything in music that is contemplative without being directed toward this end is vain and useless. For since music was indeed discovered to improve and to delight, as we have said at other times,[34] nothing in music has validity except the voices and the sounds which arise from the strings. These, as Aurelius Cassiodorus imagines, are so named because they move our hearts, a thing he shows most elegantly with the two Latin words *chordae* and *corda*.[35] Thus it is by this path that we perceive the improvement and delight that we derive from hearing harmonies and melodies.

From what has been said we may conclude, then, that this way of composing is not only useless but also harmful, as a loss of time, more precious than anything else, and that the points, lines, circles, semicircles, and other similar things depicted on the page are subject to the sense of vision and not to that of hearing, and that these are matters considered by the geometer, while the sounds and the voices (being in truth the particular objects of hearing) are matters primarily considered by the musician, although he incidentally considers many others.

Here, perhaps, someone will wish to reprehend and censure me, seeing that many learned and most celebrated ancient musicians, whose fame still lives among us, have practiced this way of composing and that I now wish to censure them.

To this I reply that if these critics will consider the matter, they will find that those compositions that are wrapped round with such restraints afford no greater benefit than they would if they were bare and plain, without any difficulty at all, and they will see that they complain with little reason, and they will

33. *In Praedicamentis.* [Au.]
34. 1.3. [Au.]
35. *Variae* 2.40 (Ad Boetium patricium). [Au.]

understand that they themselves are to be censured, as persons opposed to truth. For although the ancients followed this fashion, they were well aware that such accidents can afford no augmentation or diminution of the harmony. But they practiced such things to show that they were not ignorant of the speculations put forward by certain idle theorists of that day, seeing that the contemplative part of the science then consisted rather in the contemplation of accidents of this sort than in the contemplation of the sounds, the voices, and the other things discussed in Parts I and II of these my labors.

And of this we have the testimony of many books, written by various authors; these treat of nothing but circles and semicircles, with and without points, whole or divided not only once but two and three times, and in them one sees so many points, pauses, colors, ciphers, signs, numbers against numbers, and other strange things that they sometimes appear to be the books of a bewildered merchant. Nor does one read in these books anything that might lead to the understanding of anything subject to the judgment of the sense of hearing, as are the voices and sounds from which the harmonies and melodies arise; they treat only of the things that we have named. And although the fame of some of these musicians still lives honorably among us, they have acquired their reputation, not with such chimeras, but with the good harmonies, the harmonious concentus, and the beautiful inventions which are seen and heard in their works. And although they disordered these with their intricacies, they obliged themselves also, if not through speculation, at least with the aid of practice and their judgment, to reduce their harmonies to the ultimate perfection they could give them, even if the matter was misunderstood and abused by many others, as the many errors committed by the practical musicians in their works bear witness.

Then as to the rational, that is, speculative part, we see that there were few who kept to the good road, for apart from what Boethius wrote in Latin about our science, and this too we find imperfect, there has been no one (leaving Franchino[36] and Faber Stapulensis[37] to one side, for one may say that they were commentators on Boethius) who has gone further in speculating on things pertaining to music, discovering the true proportions of the musical intervals, except Lodovico Fogliano[38] of Modena,[39] who having perhaps considered what Ptolemy left written on the syntonic diatonic,[40] spared no pains in writing a

---

36. Zarlino refers here to Franchino Gafori's *Theoricum opus musice discipline* (Naples, 1480).

37. *Musica libris quatuor demonstrata* (Paris, 1496). The philosopher Faber is better known by the French version of his name, Jacques Lefèvre d'Étaples.

38. *Musica theorica* (Venice, 1529)

39. A note for the malicious. [Au.] (This note, which does not appear in the earlier editions of the *Istitutioni*, is aimed at Vincenzo Galilei, who in his *Dialogo della musica antica, et della moderna* [Florence, 1581], accuses Zarlino of appropriating Fogliano's ideas without giving him credit for them. Zarlino's defense may be seen in his *Sopplimenti* 3.2.)

40. In the syntonic diatonic of Ptolemy, the tetrachords of the Greater Perfect System are divided in the proportions 16:15, 9:8, 10:9. One of Zarlino's principal theses is that this division is the natural and inevitable one and the one actually used in the practical vocal music of his time.

Latin book on this branch of the science, showing as well as he could the true proportions of the intervals involved. The rest of the theoretical musicians, clinging to what Boethius wrote of these matters, did not wish or were not able to go further and gave themselves over to describing the things that we have named; these they made subject to the quantitative genus, as they called it, under which come mode, time, and prolation, as may be seen in the *Recaneto di musica*,[41] the *Toscanello*,[42] the *Scintille*,[43] and a thousand other similar books.

Besides this there are also conflicting opinions on these questions and long disputations, of which there is no end, then many tracts, invectives, and apologies, written by certain musicians against certain others, in which (although one reads them a thousand times), having read, reread, and examined them, one finds nothing but the innumerable villanies and slanders which they immodestly address to one another (O what shame!) and in the end so little good that one is dumbfounded.

But we may in truth excuse these writers. There were sophists in those days, just as there were sophists in the time of Socrates and Plato, and they were as much esteemed, and this quantitative genus of theirs (one may truly call it an *Arte sofistica* in music and its musicians sophists) was as much practiced in its time as was sophistry in the time of the philosophers in question. Thus we ought continually to praise God and to thank Him that little by little (I know not how) this thing is almost spent and extinct and that He has put us into an age concerned only with the multiplying of good concentus and good melodies, the true end toward which the musician ought to direct his every work.

$$\bullet \quad \bullet \quad \bullet \quad \bullet \quad \bullet$$

BOOK FOUR

32. How the Harmonies are Adapted to the Words Placed Beneath Them

Seeing that the time and place require it, it now remains to be determined how one ought to combine the harmonies with the words placed beneath them. I say "to combine the harmonies with the words" for this reason: although (following Plato's opinion) we have said in Part II[44] that melody is a combination of speech, harmony, and rhythm,[45] and although it seems that in such a combination no one of these things is prior to another, Plato gives speech the first place and makes the other two parts subservient to it, for after he has shown the whole by means of the parts, he says that harmony and rhythm ought to follow speech. And this is the obligation. For if in speech, whether by

41. The *Recanetum de musica aurea,* by Stefano Vanneo (Rome, 1533).
42. The *Toscanello in musica,* by Pietro Aaron (Venice, 1523).
43. The *Scintille di musica* by G. M. Lanfranco (Brescia, 1533).
44. Chapter 12.
45. *Republic* 3 [i.e. 398c]. [Au.]

way of narrative or of imitation (and these occur in speech), matters may be treated that are joyful or mournful, and grave or without gravity, and again modest or lascivious, we must also make a choice of a harmony and a rhythm similar to the nature of the matters contained in the speech in order that from the combination of these things, put together with proportion, may result a melody suited to the purpose.

We ought indeed to listen to what Horace says in his epistle on the *Art of Poetry:*

A theme for Comedy refuses to be set forth in verses of Tragedy;[46]

and to what Ovid says in this connection:

Achilles must not be told of in the numbers of Callimachus;
Cydippe suits not thy utterance, Homer.[47]

For if the poet is not permitted to write a comedy in tragic verse, the musician will also not be permitted to combine unsuitably these two things, namely, harmony and words.[48] Thus it will be inappropriate if in a joyful matter he uses a mournful harmony and a grave rhythm, neither where funereal and tearful matters are treated is he permitted to use a joyful harmony and a rhythm that is light or rapid, call it as we will. On the contrary, he must use joyful harmonies and rapid rhythms in joyful matters, and in mournful ones, mournful harmonies and grave rhythms, so that everything may be done with proportion.

He who has studied what I have written in Part III and has considered the nature of the mode in which he wishes to write his composition will, I think, know precisely how to do this. In so far as he can, he must take care to accompany each word in such a way that, if it denotes harshness, hardness, cruelty, bitterness, and other things of this sort, the harmony will be similar, that is, somewhat hard and harsh, but so that it does not offend. In the same way, if any word expresses complaint, grief, affliction, sighs, tears, and other things of this sort, the harmony will be full of sadness.[49]

Wishing to express effects of the first sort, he will do best to accustom himself to arrange the parts of his composition so that they proceed with such movements as are without the semitone, as are those of the tone and ditone, allowing the major sixth or thirteenth, which are naturally somewhat harsh, to be heard above the lowest tone of the concentus, and accompanying these with the syncope of the fourth or eleventh above this same tone, using rather slow movements; with these he may use the syncope of the seventh. But wishing to

---

46. L. 89. Trans. Fairclough, p. 459.

47. *Remediorum amoris*, 381–382. [Au.] Trans. J. H. Mozley in Ovid, *The Art of Love, and Other Poems* (London: Heinemann, 1929), p. 205.

48. The "Rules to be observed in dittying" given by Thomas Morley on pages 177 and 178 of his *Plaine and Easie Introduction* (London, 1597) are in effect an abridged translation of the remainder of this chapter.

49. Even though this be censured by some of our modern Aristarchs. [Au.] (Namely, Vincenzo Galilei, on pp. 88 and 89 of his *Dialogo della musica antica, et della moderna* [see no. 72 below, pp. 463–65]) But as to this, see Chapter II of Book VIII of our *Sopplimenti*. [Au.]

express effects of the second sort, he will use (always observing the rules that have been given) such movements as proceed by the semitone or semiditone or in some other similar way, often taking above the lowest tone of his composition the minor sixth or thirteenth, which are naturally soft and sweet, especially when they are combined in the right ways and with discretion and judgment.

Note, however, that the expression of these effects is to be attributed not only to the consonances that we have named, used as we have directed, but also to the movements that the parts make in singing, which are of two sorts—natural and accidental. The natural movements are those made between the natural steps of the music, where no sign or accidental step intervenes, and these have more virility than those made by means of the accidental steps, marked with the signs ♯ and ♭, which are indeed accidental and somewhat languid. In the same way there arises from the accidental movements a sort of interval called accidental, while from the natural movements arise the intervals called natural. We ought then to bear in mind that the natural movements make the music somewhat more sonorous and virile, while the accidental ones make it softer and somewhat more languid. Thus the natural movements may serve to express effects of our first sort, and the accidental ones may serve for the rest, so that combining with some judgment the intervals of the major and minor consonances and the natural and accidental movements, we will succeed in imitating the words with a thoroughly suitable harmony.

Then as to the observance of the rhythms, the primary consideration is the matter contained in the words: if this is joyful, we ought to proceed with swift and vigorous movements, that is, with figures carrying swiftness, such as the minim and semiminim; if it is mournful, we ought to proceed with slow and lingering movements.

Thus Adriano has taught us to express the one sort and the other in many compositions, among them "I vidi in terra angelici costumi," "Aspro core e selvaggio," and "Ove ch'i posi gli occhi," all written for six voices, "Quando fra l'altre donne" and "Giunto m'ha Amor" for five voices, and innumerable others.[50]

And although the ancients understood rhythms in another way than the moderns do, as is clear from many passages in Plato, we ought not only to keep this consideration in mind but also to take care that we adapt the words of the speech to the musical figures in such a way and with such rhythms that nothing barbarous is heard, not making short syllables long and long syllables short as is done every day in innumerable compositions, a truly shameful thing.[51] Nor do we find this vice only in figured music but, as is obvious to every man of

---

50. The works named here are all madrigals from Adriano Willaert's *Musica nova*. Zarlino was not the first writer to hold up this collection as exemplary of appropriate relations between music and words; see no. 48 above (Doni), pp. 333–35.

51. But as to this, what has been said in Chapter 13 of Book VIII of our *Sopplimenti* [On the three sorts of accents: grammatical, rhetorical, and musical] ought by all means to be carefully considered, so that all may go well and no error be committed. [Au.]

judgment, in plainsong also, for there are few chants that are not filled with
barbarous things of this kind. Thus over and over again we hear length given
to the penultimate syllables of such words as *Domínus, Angélus, Filíus, miracú-
lum, gloría,* and many others, syllables which are properly short and fleeting.
To correct this would be a most praiseworthy undertaking and an easy one, for
by changing it a very little, one would make the chant most suitable, nor would
this change its original form, since this consists solely of many figures or notes
in ligature, placed under the short syllables in question and inappropriately
making them long when a single figure would suffice.

In a similar way we ought to take care not to separate the parts of the speech
from one another with rests, so long as a clause, or any part of it, is incomplete
and the sense of the words imperfect, a thing done by some of little intelligence, and unless a period is complete and the sense of the words perfect we
ought not to make a cadence, especially one of the principal ones, or to use a
rest larger than that of the minim, nor should the rest of the minim be used
within the intermediate points. For this is in truth a vicious thing, and for all
that it is practiced by some little repentent practical musicians of our time,
anyone inclined to heed the matter may easily observe and understand it.

Thus, since the matter is of great importance, the composer ought to open
his eyes and not keep them closed so that he may not be thought ignorant of a
thing so necessary, and he ought to take care to use the rest of the minim or
semiminim (whichever suits his purpose) at the head of the intermediate points
of the speech, for these have the force of commas, while at the head of the
periods he may use whatever quantity of rest he chooses, for it seems to me
that when the rests are used in this manner one may best distinguish the members of the period from one another and without any difficulty hear the perfect
sense of the words.

33. The Procedure to be Followed in Placing the Musical Figures Under the Words[52]

Who will ever be able to recite, unless with great difficulty, the disorder and
the inelegance that many practical musicians support and have supported and
the confusion that they have caused in suitably adapting the musical figures to
the words of the speech? When I reflect that a science that has brought law
and good order to other things is in this respect so disorderly that it is barely
tolerable, I cannot help complaining, for some compositions are indeed dumb-
founding to hear and to see. It is not only that in the declamation of the words
one hears confused periods, incomplete clauses, unsuitable cadences, singing
without order, innumerable errors in applying the harmonies to the words,
little regard for mode, badly accommodated parts, passages without beauty,
rhythms without proportion, movements without purpose, figures badly numbered in time and prolation, and a thousand other disorders; one also finds the

---

52. Here as above Zarlino uses the word *figura* to mean "note."

musical figures so adapted to the words that the singer cannot determine or discover a suitable way of performing them. Now he sees two syllables under many figures, now under two figures many syllables. Now he hears the singer of another part who, at some point where the words require it, uses the apostrophe or elides the vowels; wishing to do the same in his part, he succeeds in missing the beautiful and elegant manner of singing and in putting a figure that carries length under a short syllable, or vice versa. Now he hears the singers of the other parts make a syllable long which in his must necessarily be short. Thus, hearing all this diversity, he does not know what to do and remains thoroughly bewildered and confused.

And since the whole consists in adapting the musical figures to the words beneath them, and since in composition it is required that the musical figures be used to mark and note the pitches so that the sounds and the voices may be properly performed in every modulation; and seeing that it is by means of such figures that we perform the rhythm, that is, the length and brevity of the syllables of the speech, and that over these syllables there are often put, not one, two, or three, but even more such figures, as may be required by the accents suitably arranged in the speech; therefore, in order that no confusion may arise in adapting the figures to the syllables and to the words, and wishing (if I can) to end all this disorder, to the many rules I have already given in various places in accordance with the requirements of my materials, I now add these, which will serve both the composer and the singer and will at the same time be to my purpose.

1. A suitable figure is to be placed below each long or short syllable so that nothing barbarous will be heard. For in figured music each musical figure that stands alone and is not in ligature (apart from the semiminim and all those that are smaller than the semiminim) carries its own syllable with it. This rule is observed in plainsong also, for to each square figure is adapted a syllable of its own, excepting for the middle notes, which are sometimes treated like minims or even semiminims, as may be seen in many chants, especially in the chant for the Nicene Creed, "Credo in unum Deum," which they call the Credo cardinale.[53]

2. Not more than one syllable, and that at the beginning, is to be adapted to each ligature of several notes or figures, whether in figured music or in plainsong.

3. No syllable is to be adapted to the dot placed after the figures of figured music, although this is sung.

4. It is not usual to place a syllable below a semiminim, or below those figures that are smaller than the semiminim, or below the figure immediately following.

5. It is not customary to place any syllable below the figures immediately following a dotted semibreve or dotted minim, when these following figures

---

53. Credo IV.

are valued at less than the dots, as are semiminims after a dotted semibreve or chromas after a dotted minim; the same is true of the figures that immediately follow these.

6. Should it be necessary to place a syllable below a semiminim, one may also place another syllable below the figure following.

7. At the beginning of a composition, or after any rest in the middle, the first figure, whatever it may be, must necessarily carry with it a syllable.

8. In plainsong no word or syllable is ever repeated, although one sometimes hears this done, a thing indeed to be censured; in figured music such repetitions are sometimes tolerated—not of a syllable or of a word, but of some part of the speech whose sense is complete. This may be done when there are figures in such quantity that words may be repeated conveniently. But to repeat a thing many times over does not, in my opinion, go over well, unless it be done to give greater emphasis to words that have in them some grave sense and are worthy of consideration.

9. When all the syllables of a period or of one part of the speech have been adapted to the musical figures and there remain only the penultimate syllable and the last, the penultimate syllable will have the privilege of bearing a number of small figures—two, three, or some other quantity—provided, however, that it be long and not short, for if it were short a barbarism would occur. Singing in this way, there arises what many call a *neuma*, which occurs when many figures are sung above a single syllable. But when figures are placed in this way, they offend against our first rule.

10. The final syllable of the speech will fall below the final figure of the composition, if our rules are observed.

Seeing that the reader will find innumerable examples of all these things if he will examine the learned works of Adriano and of those who have been and are his disciples and observers of the good rules, I shall go on without giving further examples to the discussion of the ligatures formed from certain of the musical figures, for these are useful in this connection.

72 Vincenzo Galilei

Vincenzo Galilei, father of the famous astronomer and natural philosopher Galileo Galilei, was born near Florence in the late 1520s. A fine lutenist, he enjoyed the patronage of the Florentine nobleman Giovanni de' Bardi and studied with Gioseffo Zarlino in Venice. He spent most of the 1560s in Pisa and returned to Florence in 1572. During that year he became acquainted with the researches into ancient Greek music that Girolamo Mei, a Florentine expatriate, was pursuing in Rome. The influence of Mei's views, especially regarding tuning systems, modes, and the means by which music moves the affections, led Galilei to question the contrapuntal practice of his day and brought him into open conflict with Zarlino. Galilei expressed his views in the *Dialogue on Ancient and Modern Music* (*Dialogo della musica antica, et della moderna*, 1581). Zarlino replied in his *Sopplimenti musicali* of 1588, and Galilei continued the exchange in his *Discorso intorno all'opere di Messer Gioseffo Zarlino* of 1589.

The excerpt below from the *Dialogo* is Galilei's famous chastisement of the expressive means associated especially, if not exclusively, with the contemporary madrigal. Its sentiments were inspired by letters Mei wrote to Galilei in the 1570s (especially no. 76 below, pp. 485–95) and shared by Galilei's patron Giovanni de' Bardi, who expressed similar concerns—if with greater urbanity—in a letter of ca. 1578 titled *Discorso sopra la musica, e'l cantar bene*. Both Galilei and Bardi thus aligned themselves with Renaissance traditions of solo song reaching back to Serafino Aquilano and beyond, and it is significant that Bardi's *Discorso* was addressed to Giulio Caccini, foremost exponent of solo song in the years around 1600.

FROM *Dialogue on Ancient and Modern Music*

(1581)

Bardi: Finally I come as I promised to the treatment of the most important and principal part of music, the imitation of the conceptions that are derived from the words. After disposing of this question I shall speak to you about the principles observed by the ancient musicians.

Our practical contrapuntists say, or rather hold to be certain, that they have expressed the conceptions of the mind in the proper manner and have imitated the words whenever, in setting to music a sonnet, *canzone, romanzo,* madrigal, or other poem in which there occurs a line saying, for example:

Bitter heart and savage, and cruel will,[1]

which is the first line of one of the sonnets of Petrarch, they have caused many sevenths, fourths, seconds, and major sixths to be sung between the parts and by means of these have made a rough, harsh, and unpleasant sound in the ears of the listeners.[2]

TEXT: The original edition (Venice, 1581). Some of the postils and one parenthesis of the original are given as author's notes. Translation by Oliver Strunk. The interlocutors of Galilei's dialogue are Giovanni de' Bardi and Piero Strozzi.

1. Petrarch, *Rime* 245, l. 1: *Aspro core et selvaggio et cruda voglia;* it will be recalled that Willaert's setting of this poem was cited by Zarlino in his *Istitutioni* 4.32 as a model of correct musical expression. See no. 71 above, p. 459.
2. Zarlino, *Istitutioni,* 3.66 and 4.32. [Au.] See no. 71 above (Zarlino), pp. 458–59.

The sound is indeed not unlike that given by the cithara of Orpheus in the hands of Neantius, the son of Pittacus, the tyrant of the Greek island of Lesbos, where flourished the greatest and most esteemed musicians of the world, in honor of whose greatness it had been deposited there, we read, after the death of the remarkable cithara player Pericletus, the glorious winner in the Carneian festival of the Lacedaemonians. When this Neantius played upon the cithara in question, it was revealed by his lack of skill that the strings were partly of wolf-gut and partly of lamb-gut, and because of this imperfection[3]—or because of the transgression he had committed in taking the sacred cithara from the temple by deceit, believing that the virtue of playing it well resided in it by magic, as in Bradamante's lance that of throwing to the ground whomsoever she touched with it[4]—he received, when he played it, condign punishment, being devoured by dogs. This was his only resemblance to the learned poet, sage priest, and unique musician who as you know was slain by the Bacchantes.

At another time they will say that they are imitating the words when among the conceptions of these there are any meaning "to flee" or "to fly"; these they will declaim with the greatest rapidity and the least grace imaginable. In connection with words meaning "to disappear," "to swoon," "to die," or actually "to be extinguished" they have made the parts break off so abruptly, that instead of inducing the passion corresponding to any of these, they have aroused laughter and at other times contempt in the listeners, who felt that they were being ridiculed. Then with words meaning "alone," "two," or "together" they have caused one lone part, or two, or all the parts together to sing with unheard-of elegance. Others, in the singing of this particular line from one of the sestinas of Petrarch:

And with the lame ox he will be pursuing Laura,[5]

have declaimed it to staggering, wavering, syncopated notes as though they had the hiccups. And when, as sometimes happens, the conceptions they have had in hand made mention of the rolling of the drum, or of the sound of the trumpet or any other such instrument, they have sought to represent its sound in their music, without minding at all that they were pronouncing these words in some unheard-of manner. Finding words denoting diversity of color, such as "dark" or "light" hair and similar expressions, they have put black or white notes beneath them to express this sort of conception craftily and gracefully, as they say, meanwhile making the sense of hearing subject to the accidents of color and shape, the particular objects of sight and, in solid bodies, of touch. Nor has there been any lack of those who, still more corrupt, have sought to portray with notes the words "azure" and "violet" according to their sound, just as the stringmakers nowadays color their gut strings. At another time, finding the line:

3. Fracastoro, *De sympathia et antipathia rerum*, i. [Au.]
4. Ariosto, *Orlando furioso* 8.17 and 30.15.
5. *Rime* 239 l. 36: *Et col bue zoppo andrem cacciando l'aura* (Galilei writes *andrà* and *Laura*).

> He descended into hell, into the lap of Pluto,

they have made one part of the composition descend in such a way that the singer has sounded more like someone groaning to frighten children and terrify them than like anyone singing sense. In the opposite way, finding this one:

> This one aspires to the stars,

in declaiming it they have ascended to a height that no one shrieking from excessive pain, internal or external, has ever reached. And coming, as sometimes happens, to words meaning "weep," "laugh," "sing," "shout," "shriek," or to "false deceits," "harsh chains," "hard bonds," "rugged mount," "unyielding rock," "cruel woman," and the like, to say nothing of their sighs, unusual forms, and so on, they have declaimed them, to color their absurd and vain designs, in manners more outlandish than those of any far-off barbarian.

Unhappy men, they do not perceive that if Isocrates or Corax or any of the other famous orators had ever, in an oration, uttered two of these words in such a fashion, they would have moved all their hearers to laughter and contempt and would besides this have been derided and despised by them as men foolish, abject, and worthless. And yet they wonder that the music of their times produces none of the notable effects that ancient music produced, when, quite the other way, they would have more cause for amazement if it were to produce any of them, seeing that their music is so remote from the ancient music and so unlike it as actually to be its contrary and its mortal enemy, as has been said and proved and will be proved still more, and seeing that it has no means enabling it even to think of producing such effects, let alone to obtain them. For its sole aim is to delight the ear, while that of ancient music is to induce in another the same passion that one feels oneself.[6] No person of judgment understands the expression of the conceptions of the mind by means of words in this ridiculous manner, but in another, far removed and very different.

Strozzi: I pray you, tell me how.

Bardi: In the same way that, among many others, those two famous orators that I mentioned a little while ago expressed them, and afterwards every musician of repute. And if they wish to understand the manner of it, I shall content myself with showing them how and from whom they can learn with little pain and trouble and with the greatest pleasure, and it will be thus: when they go for their amusement to the tragedies and comedies that the mummers act, let them a few times leave off their immoderate laughing, and instead be so good as to observe, when one quiet gentleman speaks with another, in what manner he speaks, how high or low his voice is pitched, with what volume of sound, with what sort of accents and gestures, and with what rapidity or slowness his words are uttered. Let them mark a little what difference obtains in all these things when one of them speaks with one of his servants, or one of these with another; let them observe the prince when he chances to be conversing with

---

6. Galilei borrows this important distinction from Girolamo Mei; see no. 76 below, p. 491.

one of his subjects and vassals; when with the petitioner who is entreating his favor; how the man infuriated or excited speaks; the married woman, the girl, the mere child, the clever harlot, the lover speaking to his mistress as he seeks to persuade her to grant his wishes, the man who laments, the one who cries out, the timid man, and the man exultant with joy. From these variations of circumstance, if they observe them attentively and examine them with care, they will be able to select the norm of what is fitting for the expression of any other conception whatever that can call for their handling.[7]

Every brute beast has the natural faculty of communicating its pleasure and its pain of body and mind, at least to those of its own species, nor was voice given to them by nature for any other purpose. And among rational animals there are some so stupid that, since they do not know, thanks to their worthlessness, how to make practical application of this faculty and how to profit by it on occasion, they believe that they are without it naturally.[8]

When the ancient musician sang any poem whatever, he first considered very diligently the character of the person speaking: his age, his sex, with whom he was speaking, and the effect he sought to produce by this means; and these conceptions, previously clothed by the poet in chosen words suited to such a need, the musician then expressed in the tone[9] and with the accents and gestures, the quantity and quality of sound, and the rhythm appropriate to that action and to such a person. For this reason we read of Timotheus, who in the opinion of Suidas was a player of the aulos and not of the cithara,[10] that when he roused the great Alexander with the difficult mode of Minerva to combat with the armies of his foes, not only did the circumstances mentioned reveal themselves in the rhythms, the words, and the conceptions of the entire song in conformity with his desire, but in my opinion at least, his habit, the aspect of his countenance, and each particular gesture and member must have shown

---

7. "*O bel discorso,* truly worthy of the great man he imagines himself to be! From it we may gather that what he actually wishes is to reduce music greatly in dignity and reputation, when, to learn imitation, he bids us go to hear the zanies in tragedies and comedies and to become out-and-out actors and buffoons. What has the musician to do with those who recite tragedies and comedies?" (Zarlino, *Sopplimenti* 8.11).

8. "Thus in his opinion it is a shameful thing to be more man than beast, or at least to be more the modest man than the buffoon, because at the right time and place the songs of the buffoon may move his listeners to laughter. It is not perceived that such imitations belong rather to the orator than to the musician and that when the singer uses such means, he ought rather to be called an actor or a buffoon, than a singer. Everyone knows that the orator who wishes to move the passions must study them and must imitate not only the actor but any other sort of person who might help him to this end. This the great orator Cicero did, practicing continually with the actor Roscius and the poet Architus. But in this case, what becomes the orator does not become the musician." (Zarlino, *Sopplimenti* 8.11).

9. Galilei is using the word "tone" *(tono)* in its technical sense, as a translation of the Greek *tonos* Mei had helped him to understand. See no. 76 below, pp. 491–92.

10. *Lexicon,* under Timotheus: "When on one occasion Timotheus the aulos-player played on the aulos the nome of Athena called Orthios, they say that Alexander was so moved that, as he listened, he sprang to arms and said that this should be the royal aulos-music." See also no. 45 above (Castiglione), pp. 326–27, n. 2.

on this occasion that he was burning with desire to fight, to overcome, and to conquer the enemy. For this reason Alexander was forced to cry out for his arms and to say that this should be the song of kings.[11] And rightly, for provided the impediments have been removed, if the musician has not the power to direct the minds of his listeners to their benefit, his science and knowledge are to be reputed null and vain, since the art of music was instituted and numbered among the liberal arts for no other purpose.

11. "So that this Timotheus of his ought, if not to be, at least to seem the most perfect of zanies and buffoons. But who ever heard finer or sweeter discourse than this, all stuff and nonsense? Thus, leaving the *zanni,* the *zannini,* and the *zannoli* to one side, we shall now explain how one ought to speak in an imitation made by means of music" (Zarlino, *Sopplimenti* 8.11). Zarlino goes on to a discussion of the references to music at the beginning of Aristotle's *Poetics.*

73 Joachim Burmeister

The idea of *musica poetica* was a distinctive contribution by German music theorists of the Renaissance. In the hands of Nicolaus Listenius, Heinrich Faber, Gallus Dressler, and other writers, it came, across the sixteenth century, to focus attention more and more on the compositional process and organizational techniques that resulted in a finished piece of music, as distinct from the more abstract procedures of melody and voice-leading that tended to preoccupy writers on counterpoint. The phrase *musica poetica* thus reflected the meaning of its Greek source—*poiein,* to make—rather than a concern with the rapprochement of music and poetry.

Joachim Burmeister's treatise *Musica poetica* of 1606 represents a culmination, of sorts, of this tradition. In it, as in two earlier treatises where he dealt with closely similar materials (*Hypomnematum musicae poeticae,* 1599, and *Musica autoschediastike,* 1601), he conceives the structure of a musical work by analogy to that of a classical oration. He divides the work into exordium, body, and peroration, and distinguishes the smaller affective periods that make up these sections. He studies the "ornaments" or musical gestures of the work as individual rhetorical figures, even borrowing names for them from the verbal figures of ancient and modern rhetoricians. And, near the end of the treatise, he presents a discussion from this perspective of the organization or *dispositio* of a complete motet by Orlando di Lasso. Burmeister's striking term for this treatment of large-scale rhetorical organization is "analysis." Burmeister's analysis emphasizes the division of a work into smaller constituent parts; in this it remains faithful to ancient rhetoricians' treatments of orations and reflects the original sense of his term, from the Greek *analyein,* to unloose, loosen, dissolve. Burmeister's approach certainly singles out techniques that are basic to various polyphonic styles of the late sixteenth century and no doubt captures as well widespread organizational practices. Many motets, madrigals, and chansons clearly show his three-section arrangement.

Burmeister's rhetorical orientation in such matters came to him naturally. Born at Lüneburg in 1564 and trained there by the rhetorician Lucas Lossius, cantor of two churches at Rostock from 1589, he earned his master's degree from the University of Rostock in 1593. From then until his death in 1629 he devoted himself to the teaching of Latin and Greek classics in the town school there.

FROM *Musica poetica*
(1606)

CHAPTER 15: THE ANALYSIS OR ARRANGEMENT[1] OF A MUSICAL PIECE

Musical analysis is the examination of a piece belonging to a certain mode and to a certain type of polyphony. The piece is to be divided into its affections or periods, so that the artfulness with which each period takes shape can be studied and adopted for imitation. There are five areas of analysis: (1) investigation of the mode; (2) investigation of the melodic genus; (3) investigation of the type of polyphony; (4) consideration of the quality; (5) sectioning of the piece into affections or periods.

Investigation of mode is the consideration of those aspects which are essential for understanding the constitution and identification of the mode, whether this be in pitch connections already made or still to be made.

Investigation of melodic genus is the examination of the interval of the fourth, whereby one studies how it is comprised of smaller intervals and used in a piece, and what character it bears.

Investigation of type of polyphony is the comparison of sounds in terms of duration or value.

Consideration of quality is the inquiry as to whether the melodic pitches display the *diezeugmenon* system, which is *cantus durus,* or the *synemmenon* system, which is *cantus mollis.*[2]

Sectioning of the piece into affections means its division into periods for the

TEXT: Joachim Burmeister, *Musica Poetica*, ed. Benito Rivera (New Haven: Yale University Press, 1993), pp. 201–7. Copyright 1993 by Yale University; reprinted by permission. Translation by Benito Rivera. I have adapted and abridged Rivera's annotations.

1. Arrangement or *dispositio* is the second in the traditional list of five functions in rhetoric: *inventio, dispositio, elocutio, memoria,* and *pronuntiatio.* See *Rhetorica ad Herennium* 1.2.3. "Dispositio is the suitable arrangement of the parts of the oration and of the arguments. It fulfills the function of bringing so much clarity to the speech that even if you have invented the best ideas, none of them will be worth anything when you do not proceed suitably or intelligently." Phillip Melanchthon, *Institutiones rhetoricae* (Strasbourg, 1523), fol. 22v. [Tr.]
2. That is, whether they display b-natural and hence use the "hard" hexachord starting from g (*cantus durus*) or b-flat and hence use the "soft" hexachord starting from f (*cantus mollis*). See no. 68 above (Ramis), p. 411, n. 12.

purpose of studying its artfulness and using it as a model for imitation. A piece has three parts: (1) the exordium, (2) the body of the piece, (3) the ending.[3]

The exordium is the first period or affection of the piece. It is often adorned by fugue, so that the ears and mind of the listener are rendered attentive to the song, and his good will is won over. The exordium extends up to the point where the fugal subject ends with the introduction of a true cadence or of a harmonic passage having the marks of a cadence. This is seen to happen where a new subject definitely different from the fugal subject is introduced. However, examples do not confirm that all musical pieces should always begin with the ornament of fugue. With this in mind, let the music student follow common practice and what it allows. Sometimes *noëma*[4] takes place in the exordium. When this happens, it should be for the sake of an aphoristic text[5] or for other purposes which common practice will show.

The body of the musical piece is the series of affections or periods between the exordium and the ending. In this section, textual passages similar to the various arguments of the *confirmatio* in rhetoric are instilled in the listener's mind in order that the proposition be more clearly grasped and considered.

The body should not be protracted too much, lest that which is overextended arouse the listener's displeasure. For everything that is excessive is odious and usually turns into a vice.

The ending is the principal cadence where either all the musical movement ceases or where one or two voices stop while the others continue with a brief passage called *supplementum*. By means of this, the forthcoming close in the music is more clearly impressed on the listeners' awareness.

EXAMPLE OF AN ANALYSIS OF ORLANDO'S FIVE-VOICE COMPOSITION *IN ME TRANSIERUNT*[6]

This elegant and splendid harmonic piece by Orlando di Lasso, *In me transierunt*, is delimited by the authentic Phrygian mode. For the ambitus of the whole combined system of all the voices is *B* to *ee*. The ambitus of the

---

3. Classical authors varied in their numbering of the parts of an oration. *Rhetorica ad Herennium* 1.3.4 lists six parts: *exordium, narratio, divisio, confirmatio, confutatio,* and *conclusio.* The broader threefold division was obviously inspired by Aristotle's injunction that a tragic drama or epic poem, to be a unified whole, must have a beginning *(arche),* middle *(meson),* and end *(teleute; Poetics* 7.3 and 23.1). Chapters 12–14 of Gallus Dressler, *Praecepta musicae poëticae* (Magdeburg, 1564), provide guidelines on the structuring of the *exordium, medium,* and *finis.* [Tr.]

4. In rhetorical theory *noëma* is a figure of brief, subtle speech, an aphorism, or a *sententia.* Burmeister's *noëma* is one of the sixteen harmonic, six melodic, and four mixed figures he defines in Chapter 12, "Musical Ornaments or Figures," from which the definitions in the following notes are derived (see Rivera, pp. 154–97). *Noëma* is homophony or note-against-note texture. Evidently Burmeister associated this texture with *sententiae* or aphorisms because of its ability to make the words stand out.

5. *Textus sententiosus.* According to Cicero the exordium of a speech ought to be "sententiosus" *(De inventione* 1.18.25). [Tr.]

6. Here Burmeister investigates in order all five "areas of analysis" he specified at the beginning of the chapter. For Lasso's motet, see Orlando di Lasso, *Sämtliche Werke,* ed. Franz Haberl and

individual voices are as follows. The discant is bounded by *e* and *ee*, the tenor by *E* and *e*, the bass by ♯*B* and ♯*b*, the alto by ♯*b* and ♯*bb*. The basis of temperament is authentic, because the diapente from *E* to ♮ or ♯*b* is clearly there.[7] Furthermore, the affinal cadence, which is fully formed as a *hexaphonal* cadence, is located where the diapente is divided into two equal parts.[8] The ambitus of the alto and bass is plagal, because their ambitus is mediated at the place which allows the diatessaron to be positioned in the lower part and the diapente in the higher. Fully formed cadences, especially *triphonal* ones, are located where through the long tradition of this mode they are wont to be found and encountered. The two semitones likewise appear in their proper places. For the place of the lower semitone is in the first, bottom interval of the authentic ambitus. The place of the upper semitone is analogously the same as that of the lower.[9] The harmony has its authentic and principal ending on *E*, which is, as is usually the case, the lowest note of the tenor's ambitus. The second point of consideration is that the piece pertains to the diatonic genus of melody, because its intervals are mostly formed by tone, tone, and semitone. Third, it belongs to the fractured type of polyphony. For the pitches are combined with one another in unequal values. Fourth, it pertains to the *diezeugmenon* quality. For throughout the piece a disjunction of tetrachords occurs at *a* and *b*.

This harmonic piece can be divided very appropriately into nine periods. The first comprises the exordium, which is adorned by two figures: *fuga realis* and *hypallage*.[10] Seven inner periods comprise the body of the piece, similar to the *confirmatio* of a speech (if one may thus compare one cognate art with another). The first of these is adorned with *hypotyposis, climax,* and *anadiplosis;*[11] the second is likewise, and to those figures may be added *anaph-*

Adolf Sandberger (21 vols., Leipzig: Breitkopf & Härtel, 1894–1926), vol. 9, pp. 49–52. For a discussion of Burmeister's analysis including a labeling of his figures in Lasso's score, see Claude V. Palisca, "*Ut Oratoria musica:* The Rhetorical Basis of Musical Mannerism," in Palisca, *Studies in the History of Italian Music and Music Theory* (Oxford: Clarendon Press, 1994), pp. 282–311; for the most part I have followed below Palisca's division of the motet.

7. In *Musica autoschediastike,* fols. L4r–v, Burmeister correctly identified A and ee, rather than ♯B and ee, as the boundary notes of the piece. Nevertheless he maintained that the diapente E–B was prominent. [Tr.]

8. That is, on G.

9. That is, in the first interval of the diatessaron, B–C.

10. "*Fuga realis* is that disposition of harmony wherein all the voices imitate, by using identical or similar intervals, a certain subject *[affectio]* drawn from one voice. . . ." Hypallage, in rhetorical theory various kinds of metonymic exchange, is in Burmeister's musical usage an imitation using an inversion of the original material. See mm. 1–20.

11. Mm. 20–26. Hypotyposis, in rhetorical theory a particularly vivid description, is for Burmeister an ornament vividly depicting the sense of the words or, more simply, a madrigalism. Climax, a gradual buildup through increasingly emphatic words or phrases, is melodic sequence. Anadiplosis, the repetition of a word at the end of one line to begin the next, is for Burmeister a technique whereby a largely homophonic passage (or *noëma*) involving one semichoir is restated twice more by other groupings of voices.

ora;[12] the third is adorned by *hypotyposis* and *mimesis;*[13] the fourth likewise, with the addition of *pathopoeia;*[14] the fifth by *fuga realis;*[15] the sixth by *anadiplosis* and *noëma;*[16] the seventh by *noëma* and *mimesis.*[17] The final, namely, the ninth, period is like the epilogue of a speech. This harmony displays a principal ending, otherwise called a *supplementum* of the final cadence, which very often includes the ornament of *auxesis;* here the principal ending is protracted through a series of concords built on pitches which establish the mode, and which the polyphonic piece as a whole is wont to articulate more often than the other pitches.[18]

12. Mm. 26–32. Anaphora, the use of the same word or phrase to begin several verses or sentences, is for Burmeister melodic imitation involving only some of the voices.
13. Mm. 32–41. Mimesis is similar to anadiplosis but involves only one restatement of the *noëma.*
14. Mm. 41–52. Pathopoeia, a general term for figures that arouse passion, is for Burmeister a musical arousing of emotions by the use of semitones not proper to the mode or melodic genus of the piece—i.e., chromaticism.
15. See mm. 52–67.
16. See mm. 67–73.
17. See mm. 73–77.
18. Mm. 78–87. Auxesis, an ordering of words or phrases so as to intensify meaning, is for Burmeister a mainly homophonic declamation of a word or words repeated two, three, or more times with "growing harmony," i.e., fuller and fuller scoring.

74 Pietro Pontio

Pietro Pontio, born at Parma in 1532, served as chapelmaster in cathedrals of Bergamo, Parma, and Milan for most of his career. He died at Parma in 1595. A prolific composer of Masses and other sacred works, Pontio is best remembered for his two dialogues on music theory and composition, the *Ragionamento di musica* (Discussion on Music) of 1588 and the *Dialogo . . . ove si tratta della theorica et prattica di musica* (Dialogue . . . That Treats the Theory and Practice of Music) of 1595. In both works Pontio reveals an approach to contrapuntal practice much indebted to Zarlino.

Particularly interesting is the final section of the *Ragionamento,* in which Pontio distinguishes different polyphonic genres according to the rhythms, textures, uses of preexistent materials, and expressive demeanors appropriate to them. Here Pontio displays the increasingly strict, even schematic sense of generic propriety that characterized many arts at the end of the Renaissance, including poetry, drama, and painting. He also reveals an attentiveness to large-scale compositional organization generally akin to Joachim Burmeister's (see no. 73 above, pp. 467–69), if with none of the German classicist's rhetorical orientation. Pontio's guidelines were widely disseminated, not only in his own *Ragionamento* but also in the sprawling treatise *El melopeo y maestro* of 1613 by Pietro Cerone, where they are repeated and elaborated.

FROM *Ragionamento di musica*
(1588)

BOOK 4

•   •   •   •   •

Paolo: You have heard so many things the contrapuntist or composer must consider regarding the manner of singing, the needs of the singer, and the propriety of the composition. Doubtless we can hardly talk about and enumerate all the things that must be considered in composing; but at least the ones discussed above will allow you to make a composition with many fewer errors than those circulating these days by various composers. It remains now to show you the manner or style (as we might say) to be employed in making a motet, a mass, and other compositions that originate, as I have said, in florid counterpoint. And with this may you content yourself.

Hettore: I am content with whatever pleases you, and I would very much welcome your showing me the manner of making a motet or other composition. Indeed I desire no more of you than this, since you have already instructed me in so many things pertinent to musical artifice. Please, therefore, speak.

Paolo: I do so willingly. The manner or style (as we wish to call it) for making a motet is grave and tranquil. The parts, especially the bass, move with gravity, and the composer should maintain such ordering of the parts from beginning to end. Likewise the individual subjects should be grave, even if nowadays some composers make motets and other sacred works in which this is not true. In these sometimes they put the parts together with quick, even very quick motion, using syncopated minims instead of syncopated semibreves and even semiminim and quaver rests, all of which are not suitable to the gravity of motets, so that their works almost seem madrigals or canzoni. If this happened once it would not be worth mention; but these composers proceed in this manner straight through to the end, so that in my judgment theirs is the style of madrigals, not motets, observing no gravity at all. One can see such gravity well observed by Jacquet,[1] Morales, Adriano,[2] Gombert, Palestrina, Phinot, and many other excellent composers whom I pass over for the sake of brevity. . . .

You may observe gravity and the grave style in this manner: When two parts sing together and there is in one a figure in breves, the other should move in a figure of minims or semiminims or semibreves on the upbeat, and not in quavers or semiquavers or even continuously in semiminims, which in their very

---

TEXT: The facsimile of the edition of 1588, ed. Suzanne Clercx (Kassel: Bärenreiter, 1959), pp. 153–61. Translation by Gary Tomlinson. For a translation of Cerone's reuse of this material see Oliver Strunk, *Source Readings in Music History* (New York: Norton, 1950), no. 28.

1. Jacquet of Mantua.
2. Willaert.

quick motion would rob the melody of all gravity. In making a motet for three voices, when in two parts there is a breve or two semibreves on the downbeat the third part should move in a figure in minims, semiminims, or semibreves on the upbeat, or in dotted minims likewise on the upbeat. In this way the composition will be grave and appropriate to the style of the motet. If the work is for four or five voices, when all are singing together two or three should always hold still while the others (or at least one of them) move in the manners just described, and not in quavers and semiquavers, which would make the style madrigalian. But since I cannot be as clear as I wish speaking only, I present here an example in which you may consider all these things:

Do you see how while the bass moves the soprano begins by imitating its breve motion? And how while the middle part holds still the other two move? If only one part were to move, that too would be fine and answer to the proper ordering and to gravity as well. But if all the parts held still at the same time, that would not be the motet style or serve the required ordering, as I have said.

Hettore: I find that I have understood all this; please proceed as you wish.

Paolo: The style or manner (as we might call it) of the mass is like that of the motet as far as the movement of the parts is concerned. But it differs in its ordering, since in the motet you may compose the beginning of the second part as you please, as long as it conforms to the mode; but in the mass the beginning of its first Kyrie must be similar to the beginnings of the Gloria, Credo, Sanctus, and first Agnus Dei. However, if indeed I say they must be similar I do not mean they should have the same consonances, as would happen, for instance, if at the beginning of the first Kyrie the tenor and then the soprano sang *ut mi fa sol sol la* and the same thing happened without any variety to begin the Gloria and the Credo. I do not mean this at all, but rather that you use the same subject in different manners, once beginning with the tenor, then with the soprano, then with the bass, so that there is variety in the parts if not in the subject. If I give you an example you will understand more easily what I mean:

From this small example you can see that the theme remains similar but not the consonances; and this is as it should be. Now if the first Kyrie uses a theme from the beginning of a motet or madrigal or some other piece, the Christe should borrow some other theme from the same piece. You may choose from it any theme that is appropriate to the mode. You may compose the beginning of the second Kyrie as you wish, but at its ending you should use the theme that ends the piece on which the mass is based. You can see this in the mass composed on *Salvum me fac Domine* by Vincenzo Ruffo, in the mass composed on *Si bona suscepimus* by Jacquet, in the mass Don Pietro Pontio composed on *Vestiva i colli* in his Third Book of Masses, and in works by others. Likewise the ends of the Gloria, Credo, Sanctus, and last Agnus must follow the same theme and ordering as the end of the Kyrie. This is the ordering one should follow.

If you wish to compose a mass on your own subject you should follow the same ordering as if you had composed it on a motet or canzone. And you should call this mass *Missa sine nomine* since it is not based on any other piece. You can see examples of this in the Second Book of Masses of Jacquet, the First Book of Vincenzo Ruffo, and also in the Second and Third Books à 5 of Pietro Pontio.

One can observe also that most composers make the parts go together, note against note, at the words *Iesu Christe,* out of reverence and because of the gravity of these words. The same thing usually happens at the words *Et incarnatus est de spiritu sancto ex Maria virgine et homo factus est,* as you can see in Josquin and other composers whom I pass over for the sake of brevity. Now you understand the ordering you should observe in composing a mass on some other piece or on a subject of your own. If you are satisfied with all this, I pass now to speak of psalms.

Hettore: I am indeed satisfied; continue as you wish.

Paolo: If you wish to compose psalms (leaving aside the canticle of the Virgin Mary, that is, the Magnificat, and the Benedictus and Nunc dimittis), you will not be able to compose brief verses if you imitate the psalm tone through all the parts. This will make long verses, inappropriate to psalms. But you may imitate with one part or two, provided the imitations carry the psalm tone. And even if you began all the parts together you would not be criticized. And so that the middle of the psalm verse is apparent you must also mark it with a cadence on the mediation of the psalm tone. Also you must make sure the words are enunciated and understood, pronouncing them almost simultaneously in the manner of one of those songs called *falsobordone.* You can see this done by Adriano, Jacquet, and others; it is done thus so that the listeners can understand the words. If it pleases you, you may set the last verse of the psalm[3] in a more learned style, with a canon à 5. Now you understand the manner or style (as we call it) for composing psalms. And if you put some imitation in the psalm verses it must be brief. This brevity may be achieved in two ways: first, the theme may be short, with few notes; second, the parts may follow one another a semibreve or breve apart, but not more. All this in order to make the verses brief and avoid falling into the motet style, and because such is required by psalms.

Now I will tell you how to compose the canticle of the Virgin Mary, that is, the Magnificat. Even though it is truly a psalm, nevertheless it is one of the most solemnly observed psalms, so if you wish to set it it requires a more learned style in which all the parts imitate the plainchant or some other theme. It does not matter if one part begins one, two, three, or even four breves after another, as long as the parts begin in imitation. It is necessary to mark the middle of the verse with its own cadence on the mediation of the psalm tone. Composers usually imitate the psalm tone either with all the parts or with two parts while the others have other melodies, as you can see in the Magnificat in the first mode of Morales, that is, *Anima mea dominum.* Don Pietro Pontio followed a similar ordering in the Magnificat *Anima mea dominum* in the third and fourth modes, and other composers have done likewise. You should also make sure the parts have some melodies that leave aside the psalm tone, as long as they are in the appropriate mode; but at the end one or two parts should carry the psalm tone. Sometimes you might arrange it so that one part sings the whole plainchant, a very praiseworthy approach that has been adopted by many excellent composers such as Morales, Carpentras, Giovanni Contino, Jacquet, and others. Other times you might arrange it so that one part sings the first half of the chant and the other part finishes it, and this arrange-

3. The *Gloria patri* or Lesser Doxology.

ment too is praised. Or you can make it so that, reaching the middle of the verse with no one carrying the chant, one or two parts then sing the end of the chant; or that one part sings the chant up to the middle of the verse and then the parts introduce new melodies without imitating the chant; or that one part sings the whole chant while the others sing other melodies around it, which is the most learned and ingenious manner of all. All these various methods are used in setting the Magnificat, Benedictus, and Nunc dimittis.

The chordal style, with all the parts moving together, is appropriate for setting readings for Holy Week,[4] as it is for the Gloria of the Magnificat and the *Incarnatus est* of the Mass. In such works the composer should employ dissonances to make the music plaintive, as the words require. So that you may better understand this I will show you an excerpt from such a composition:

You can see how at the end the parts all move together and how the dissonances make the composition plaintive. It is admissable at times for one or two parts to move on their own in order to vary the composition; but they must do so with gravity, using semibreves or dotted minims on the downbeat or upbeat, and also some undotted minims. This makes the composition grave and sad, as the words require. The composer must choose a mode that is naturally sad, such as the second, fourth, or sixth.[5] It is true that the practiced composer can make his music sad or happy as he wishes in any mode, using slow or quick rhythms. But in choosing sad modes to express the passions of the words of the kind of works we discuss here, the composer will be esteemed of sound judgment; while if he did differently he would be reputed a man of little judgment who poorly understood the sense of the words. Now you have understood all that pertains to this sort of composition, and I will tell you how to make a ricercar.

The style of a ricercar should show long melodies with the parts entering far

4. The *Lamentations of Jeremiah.*
5. That is, the octave species A–A with D final, B–B with E final, and C–C with F final, respectively; or, in the conventional ecclesiastical ordering of eight modes, the plagal modes hypodorian, hypophrygian, and hypolydian.

from one another so that in playing it the individual melodies can be easily heard. One part or another must always be moving, even if there are only two parts. It is not proper for the parts to stop together on a semibreve (as one could do in setting the readings for Holy Week). Neither is it proper to begin two parts together, except when they have different melodies. And since you may not understand my speaking about this as well as if I showed you, here is an example:

You may repeat the same subject in various ways two, three, four, or more times, as you can see in the ricercars of Jacques Buus, Annibale Padovano, Claudio da Correggio,[6] and Luzzasco. You may also make a subject from plainchant in semibreves, breves, longs, and maxims. It is also allowed to proceed from beginning to end with the same subject or, if that does not please, to invent a new subject and repeat it as many times as you wish in the varied manner I have described. This is the way you should make a ricercar. Now I will speak of the madrigal.

The subjects of the madrigal ought to be brief, not more than two or three semibreves long.

Hettore: Why is this so?

6. Claudio Merulo.

Paolo: the reason is that if they were longer they would be more appropriate to the motet or the mass than to the madrigal.

Hettore: I understand; continue.

Paolo: I say also that it is appropriate for the melodies of the madrigal to move in semibreves and syncopated minims. You should also know that often the parts may move together, but with the quick motions of semiminims or minims. You must make every effort to follow the words. When they treat of harsh and bitter things, you must find harsh and bitter music. When they concern running or combat the composer must speed up. When they speak of falling or rising up you will make the parts in your composition fall or rise either by step or by leap. Thus Orlando[7] made the upper parts and then the bass rise up at the words "A lofty subject for my lowly rhymes"[8] in *Già mi fu col desire* from his First Book for five voices. And thus Cipriano[9] made the parts descend by fifths in the first part of his canzone *A la dolce ombra* at the words "That was burning down on me from the third heaven."[10]

Now you have heard some of the features of the madrigal. And if I have not said everything about these various compositions, which would be impossible, you will excuse me. At least I have hinted at the manner each sort of composition should have, so that with study you may perfect each one. Your judgment, then, will supply all I have omitted, taking from me the willing desire I have of satisfying you.

7. Di Lasso.
8. "Alto soggetto alle mie basse rime."
9. De Rore.
10. "Che'n fin qua giù m'ardea dal terzo cielo"; see Petrarch, *Rime*, no. 142, 1.3. The poem is a *sestina*, not a canzone, though musicians' use of such poetic terminology was frequently loose.

75 Thomas Morley

Thomas Morley, one of the leading proponents of the vogue for Italian and Italianate music in late-Elizabethan England, was born in Norwich in 1557 or 1558. At some time in his youth he studied with William Byrd, and in 1588 he was awarded a bachelor's degree in music at Oxford. Subsequently he became organist at St. Paul's in London and in 1592 entered the Chapel Royal. He died during the first decade of the new century, probably in 1602.

Morley is particularly important as a composer, arranger, and editor of secular music. He was largely responsible for the dispersion of light Italian genres, the *canzonetta* and *balletto,* in England, and his own madrigals, canzonets, and ballets are remarkable for the grace and freshness of their melodic invention. Morley also left many English services, anthems, and psalms, a number of Latin motets, and instrumental works for consort and for keyboard. He is chiefly remembered, however, for his book, *A Plaine and Easie Introduction to Practi-call Musicke* (1597), one of the best organized and most useful of sixteenth-century musical handbooks. He dedicated it to his former teacher, Byrd.

Here Morley discusses the various secular vocal and instrumental genres that commanded so large a share of his creative energies.

FROM *A Plaine and Easie Introduction to Practicall Musicke*
(1597)

This much for motets, under which I comprehend all grave and sober music. The light music hath been of late more deeply dived into, so that there is no vanity which in it hath not been followed to the full, but the best kind of it is termed madrigal, a word for the etymology of which I can give no reason,[1] yet use showeth that it is a kind of music made upon songs and sonnets such as Petrarcha and many other poets of our time have excelled in.

This kind of music were not so much disallowable if the poets who compose the ditties would abstain from some obscenities which all honest ears abhor, and sometimes from blasphemies too such as this, "ch'altro di te iddio non voglio,"[2] which no man (at least who hath any hope of salvation) can sing without trembling. As for the music, it is next unto the motet the most artificial and to men of understanding most delightful. If therefore you will compose in this kind, you must possess yourself of an amorous humor (for in no composition shall you prove admirable except you put on and possess yourself wholly with that vein wherein you compose), so that you must in your music be wavering like the wind, sometimes wanton, sometimes drooping, sometimes grave and staid, otherwhile effeminate; you may maintain points[3] and revert them,[4] use triplas,[5] and show the very uttermost of your variety, and the more variety you show the better shall you please. In this kind our age excelleth, so that if you imitate any I would appoint you these for guides: Alfonso Ferrabosco for deep skill, Luca Marenzio for good air and fine invention, Horatio Vecchi, Stephàno

---

TEXT: The original edition (London, 1597), as reproduced in *Shakespeare Association Facsimiles* 14 (London, 1937), pp. 179–81.

1. The fourteenth-century etymology of the term remains uncertain to this day.
2. "Other than thee [my love] I'll have no god."
3. "We call that [a point or] a fugue when one part beginneth and the other singeth the same for some number of notes (which the first did sing)." (p. 76.)
4. "The reverting of a point (which also we term a revert) is when a point is made rising or falling and then turned to go the contrary way as many notes as it did at first." (p. 85.)
5. "Is that which diminisheth the value of the notes to one third part: for three breves are set for one, and three semibreves for one, and is known when two numbers are set before the song, whereof the one containeth the other thrice, thus: 3/1, 6/2, 9/3." (p. 29.)

Venturi, Ruggiero Giovanelli, and John Croce, with divers others who are very good, but not so generally good as these.

The second degree of gravity in this light music is given to canzonets, that is, little short songs, wherein little art can be showed, being made in strains,[6] the beginning of which is some point lightly touched, and every strain repeated except the middle, which is in composition of the music a counterfeit of the madrigal.

Of the nature of these are the Neapolitans, or *canzoni a la Napoletana*, different from them in nothing save in name, so that whosoever knoweth the nature of the one must needs know the other also, and if you think them worthy of your pains to compose them, you have a pattern of them in Luca Marenzio and John Ferretti, who as it should seem hath employed most of all his study that way.

The last degree of gravity (if they have any at all) is given to the *villanelle*, or country songs, which are made only for the ditty's sake, for, so they be aptly set to express the nature of the ditty, the composer (though he were never so excellent) will not stick to take many perfect chords of one kind together,[7] for in this kind they think it no fault (as being a kind of keeping decorum) to make a clownish music to a clownish matter, and though many times the ditty be fine enough, yet because it carrieth that name *villanella* they take those disallowances as being good enough for plow and cart.

There is also another kind more light than this which they term *balletti*, or dances, and are songs which being sung to a ditty may likewise be danced; these and all other kinds of light music saving the madrigal are by a general name called airs.[8] There be also another kind of ballets, commonly called fa las (the first set of that kind which I have seen was made by Gastoldi; if others have labored in the same field I know not), but a slight kind of music it is, and as I take it devised to be danced to voices.

The slightest kind of music (if they deserve the name of music) are the *vinate*, or drinking songs, for as I said before there is no kind of vanity whereunto they have not applied some music or other, as they have framed this to be sung in their drinking, but that vice being so rare among the Italians and Spaniards, I rather think that music to have been devised by or for the Germans (who in swarms do flock to the University of Italy) rather than for the Italians themselves.

There is likewise a kind of songs (which I had almost forgotten) called *Giustinianas* and are all written in the Bergamasca language. A wanton and rude

6. That is, in repeating sections, in the manner of dance music (see Morley's description below of the various dance movements).

7. That is, would not hesitate to use parallel fifths and octaves.

8. The distinction Morley alludes to here between the through-composed madrigal and all other, strophic genres, collectively known as airs (Italian *arie*) would remain in force through the first decades of the seventeenth century. For an earlier writer like Girolamo Mei (see no. 76 below, pp. 485–89) aria was a formally neutral term, connoting something close to our "melody" or "melodic style."

kind of music it is and like enough to carry the name of some notable courtesan of the city of Bergamo, for no man will deny that Giustiniana is the name of a woman.[9]

There be also many other kinds of songs which the Italians make, as *pastorellas* and *passamezos* with a ditty and such like, which it would be both tedious and superfluous to delate unto you in words. Therefore I will leave to speak any more of them and begin to declare unto you those kinds which they make without ditties.

The most principal and chiefest kind of music which is made without a ditty is the fantasy, that is, when a musician taketh a point at his pleasure and wresteth and turneth it as he list, making either much or little of it as shall seem best in his own conceit. In this may more art be shown than in any other music, because the composer is tied to nothing but that he may add, diminish, and alter at his pleasure. And this kind will bear any allowances whatsoever tolerable in other music, except changing the air and leaving the key, which in fantasy may never be suffered. Other things you may use at your pleasure, as bindings with discords, quick motions, slow motions, proportions, and what you list. Likewise this kind of music is with them who practise instruments of parts in greatest use, but for voices it is but seldom used.

The next in gravity and goodness unto this is called a pavan, a kind of staid music, ordained for grave dancing, and most commonly made of three strains, whereof every strain is played or sung twice. A strain they make to contain 8, 12, or 16 semibreves as they list, yet fewer than eight I have not seen in any pavan. In this you may not so much insist in following the point as in a fantasy, but it shall be enough to touch it once and so away to some close. Also in this you must cast your music by four, so that if you keep that rule it is no matter how many fours you put in your strain, for it will fall out well enough in the end, the art of dancing being come to that perfection that every reasonable dancer will make measure of no measure, so that it is no great matter of what number you make your strain.

After every pavan we usually set a galliard (that is, a kind of music made out of the other), causing it to go by a measure which the learned call *trochaicam rationem,* consisting of a long and a short stroke successively, for as the foot *trochaeus* consisteth of one syllable of two times and another of one time, so is the first of these two strokes double to the latter, the first being in time of a semibreve and the latter of a minim. This is a lighter and more stirring kind of dancing than the pavan, consisting of the same number of strains, and look how many fours of semibreves you put in the strain of your pavan, so many times six minims must you put in the strain of your galliard. The Italians make

9. Morley's naive definition is wholly misleading. The sixteenth-century *giustiniana* is a specifically Venetian form of the *villanella* that first appeared around 1560; the three singers, who invariably stutter, introduce themselves as old men in love; see Alfred Einstein, "The Greghesca and the Giustiniana of the Sixteenth Century," *Journal of Renaissance and Baroque Music* 1 (1946–47): 19–32.

their galliards (which they term *saltarelli*) plain, and frame ditties to them which in their mascarados they sing and dance, and many times without any instruments at all, but instead of instruments they have courtesans disguised in men's apparel who sing and dance to their own songs.

The alman is a more heavy dance than this (fitly representing the nature of the people whose name it carrieth), so that no extraordinary motions are used in dancing of it. It is made of strains, sometimes two, sometimes three, and every strain is made by four, but you must mark that the four of the pavan measure is in dupla proportion to the four of the alman measure, so that as the usual pavan containeth in a strain the time of sixteen semibreves, so the usual alman contains the time of eight, and most commonly in short notes.

Like unto this is the French *branle* (which they call *branle simple*), which goeth somewhat rounder in time than this, otherwise the measure is all one. The *branle de Poitou*, or *branle double*, is more quick in time (as being in a round tripla), but the strain is longer, containing most usually twelve whole strokes.

Like unto this (but more light) be the *voltes* and *courantes*, which being both of a measure are notwithstanding danced after sundry fashions, the *volte* rising and leaping, the *courante* trevising and running, in which measure also our country dance is made, though it be danced after another form than any of the former. All these be made in strains, either two or three, as shall seem best to the maker, but the *courante* has twice so much in a strain as the English country dance.

There be also many other kinds of dances (as hornpipes, jigs, and infinite more) which I cannot nominate unto you, but knowing these the rest cannot but be understood, as being one with some of these which I have already told you.

GLIMPSES OF OTHER MUSICAL WORLDS

76 Girolamo Mei

Girolamo Mei was born in Florence in 1519 and died in Rome in 1594. He received a thorough humanistic education from the Florentine philosopher Piero Vettori, whom he assisted in commentaries and editions of Aristotle and other authors. By 1551 Mei had begun the researches into ancient Greek music that would consume much of his energies in later life, but he seems not to have pursued these in earnest until after he settled permanently in Rome in 1559. There, from 1566 to 1573, he wrote his most important work, *De modis musicis antiquorum (On the Musical Modes of the Ancients);* it was not published.

In this treatise Mei revealed for the first time the fundamental differences between the ancient Greek keys, or *tonoi,* and the modern modes thought until then to correspond to them. He recognized that the *tonoi* were not octave species like the modes, but rather transpositional keys by which the whole system of ancient pitches was shifted up or down. (Modern scholars agree with Mei's view and believe these keys took on the regional-ethnic names—Dorian, Phrygian, etc.—of the particular octave species they shifted into a central ambitus or octave.) Mei argued also that ancient Greek music was monophonic and that the nature of modern polyphonic textures precluded them from achieving the emotional effects of ancient song.

Through the 1570s Mei explained his views in a lengthy correspondence with Vincenzo Galilei in Florence (see no. 72 above pp. 462–67). The following letter is an early and important summary of the issues involved. The first two thirds of it (here up through the discussion of the ancient *tonoi*) were published posthumously in the *Discorso sopra la musica antica e moderna di M. Girolamo Mei cittadino ed accademico fiorentino* (Venice, 1602).

Letter to Vincenzo Galilei

(1572)

Excellent and my most worthy Sir:

. . . Concerning your queries I shall reply under several headings as distinctly and expeditiously as I know how, in order to be understood, and as succinctly as I can, so as not to be tedious. I shall do this in whatever order turns out to be most convenient, without any regard for whether you asked them earlier or later, in the first or the second letter.

I told Mr. Pirro[1] by word of mouth, as he gave you to understand, that I considered it certain that the singing of the ancients was in every song a single

TEXT: Claude V. Palisca, *The Florentine Camerata: Documentary Studies and Translations* (New Haven: Yale University Press, 1989), pp. 56–75. Copyright 1989 by Yale University; reprinted by permission. Translation by Claude V. Palisca. I have adapted and shortened Palisca's annotations.

1. This may be Pirro del Bene, who was a member of the Alterati Academy in Florence, to which Mei belonged. [Tr.]

air, such as we hear today in church in the recitation of the psalmody of the Divine Office, and especially when it is celebrated solemnly; although among the ancients the chorus of those who sang was of many voices, as occurred in the tragedies, where by law the established number was fifteen, or in the ancient comedies, where it was likewise limited, but to twenty-four. As for the chorus of the satyr plays, dithyrambs, and other hymns, it was customary in that religion for a large number to sing them together, but I have not been able to ascertain how many.

I have spoken of the chorus only; concerning the actors onstage, whether of the tragedy, the comedy, or the satyr play, or concerning those who sang solo whatever kind of poem, whether to the lyre, the aulos, or other instrument, such reservations are not needed, because, there being only one voice, of necessity it could not sing more than one single air. As to whether the air of the voice was the same as the air of the instrument that accompanied, and whether the notes of the air that the voice sang were the same as those of the instrument with respect to high and low pitch, to the quickness or slowness of the duration or rhythm—about this we shall discourse in its place.

What chiefly persuaded me that the entire chorus sang one and the same air was observing that the music of the ancients was held to be a valuable medium for moving the affections, as witnessed by the many incidents related by the writers, and from noticing that our music instead is apt for anything else, to put it colloquially. Now all this naturally must arise from the opposite and contrary qualities that are intrinsically characteristic of these two kinds of music; the qualities of ancient music being suited and by nature apt for bringing about the effects that it produced; those of the moderns, on the contrary, for hindering them. And these foundations, qualities, and principles must be natural and stable, not man-made and variable.

Now, granted that music, insofar as pertains to song, revolves about qualities of the voice and especially with respect to whether it is high, intermediate, or low in pitch, the idea began to form in my mind that principally in these qualities must lie the basis for its power; and further, that since each of these qualities of the voice is not the same, it is not logical that they should have had the same capacity. Rather, since they were contrary among themselves and born of contrary movements, it was essential that each should have opposite properties, necessarily capable of producing contrary effects.

Now nature gave a voice to animals and especially to man for the expression of inner states. Therefore it is logical that, the various qualities of the voice being distinct, each should be appropriate for expressing the affection of certain determinate states, and each, furthermore, should express easily its own affection but not that of another. Thus the high-pitched voice could not suitably express the affections of the intermediate and far less those of the low, nor the intermediate any of those of the high or the low. Rather, the quality of one ought necessarily to impede the operation of the other, the two being opposites.

On the basis of these thoughts and foundations, I began to reason that if in their music the ancients had sung several airs mixed together in one and the same song, as our musicians do with their bass, tenor, contralto, and soprano, or with more or fewer parts than these at one and the same time, it would undoubtedly have been impossible for it ever to move vigorously the affections that it wished to move in the hearer, as may be read that it did at every turn in the accounts and testimonials of the great and noble writers. To appreciate the truth of this conclusion more clearly and as if before the eyes, we may take up again the real principles and foundations mentioned above and first see where they lead us when accompanied by the other conditions that must necessarily be present. Then we should verify this conclusion against the authority of what can be gathered from what we read in those authors who left some notice of this ancient music in their writings.

It is a certainty that the high and low pitch of the diastematic, or, to put it otherwise, intervallic, voice is the proper subject of music, for these qualities are born of diverse and altogether opposite causes, the first arising from the rapidity and the other from the sluggishness of the movement that produces them. These qualities are proper symbols and signs of diverse and altogether contrary affections of the living being, each of the qualities expressing naturally its own affection. At the same time it is clear that affections are moved in the souls of others by representing, as if before them, whether as objects or recollections, those affections that have been previously aroused by these images. Now this cannot be brought about by the voice except with its qualities of low, high, or intermediate pitch, which nature provided for this effect and which is a proper and natural sign of that affection which one wants to arouse in the listener.

It is likewise very well known that pitches intermediate between the extremely high and the extremely low are appropriate for showing a quiet and moderate disposition of the affections, while the very high are signs of a very excited and uplifted spirit, and the very low of abject and humble thoughts, in the same way that a tempo intermediate between rapid and slow reveals a poised spirit, while a rapid one manifests an excited spirit, and a slow tempo a sluggish and lazy one. It is clear that all these qualities both of pitch and of time have by their natures the capacity to move affections similar to their own. Therefore the excessively high and the extremely low tonoi were rejected by the Platonists in their republic,[2] the former for being plaintive and the latter lugubrious, only the intermediate ones being accepted. These same people dealt the same way with meters and rhythms. Moreover, all contrary qualities, whether natural or acquired, are weakened by mixing and confounding and somehow blunt each other's force, equally if their power and vigor are equal, proportionately if not. From this it arises that each one mixed with a diverse one operates in relation to that force either imperfectly or very little. For if you

2. Plato, *Republic* 3.398c. [Tr.]

mixed equal quantities of boiling and iced water, both equally removed from being temperate, one by excessive coldness, the other by excessive warmth, not only would each have no effect, but both would be reduced to a middling disposition, not able by its nature either to cool or to heat. Only if a subject were inclined to one or other excess would it perhaps be able to operate one way or the other.

Now, since all the things proposed are indubitably true, it is necessary that the forceful effect in stirring affections which one reads that the music of the ancients had arose solely from those properties that had the capacity of stirring those affections when nothing contrary was mixed in that might impede and weaken their operative force. It was consequently necessary that all the singers sang together, not only the same words, but the same tonos and the same air with the same quantity of duration and the same quality of meter and rhythm, all of which things together were able to produce the effect that the artist strove for and to which he aimed in his mind to lead. And this could not be anything but a united and plain song directed at a single end through its natural and rightful means.

Up to now our discussion has been based on the natural principles posited above. But that this was in fact the method of singing, in addition to other arguments that could be adduced, the following in particular should be sufficient proof. Among those very learned and searching ancient writers who wrote expressly and diligently about this art (of whom between the Greek and the Latin I have surely read fifteen),[3] in none is there found any term that corresponds to any of those parts that musicians from one hundred and fifty years ago—when the music of our day is believed to have had its origin—until now call bass, tenor, contralto, and soprano. I leave aside for the present Plato, Aristotle, Athenaeus,[4] Proclus,[5] Pollux,[6] Vitruvius,[7] and others who have spoken of this discipline incidentally, if at length and rather copiously, for it was not their purpose to relate every aspect of it, as someone might well think and say. As to whether before that time people sang several airs together, as became customary, it does not seem reasonable to believe that this ever happened.

Add to this the fact that in the ancient writers there is no recollection of those consonances which our musicians call imperfect, such as the semiditone and ditone, the minor or major hexachord, and all those others of which their songs are full. Whoever wishes to discuss this matter properly cannot, or rea-

---

3. At the end of this letter Mei provided Galilei with a list of sources he had read. It includes, among ancient Greek writers, Aristoxenus, Aristides Quintilianus, Nichomachus of Gerasa, pseudo-Plutarch, and Porphyry. For the complete list see Palisca, *The Florentine Camerata*, pp. 75–77.

4. Athenaeus, fl. 200 C.E., was the author of the *Deipnosophists*. [Tr.]

5. Proclus Diadochus, Neoplatonist philosopher, fifth century C.E., wrote a number of philosophical treatises; but Mei probably had in mind as relevant to music particularly *In primum Euclidis elementorum librum commentarii* and *In Platonis Timaeum commentaria*. [Tr.]

6. Julius Pollux, second century C.E., *Onomasticon*. [Tr..]

7. Vitruvius Pollio, *De architectura libri decem;* on music, 5.4. [Tr.]

sonably should, believe that this could have arisen from any other cause than that they did not use them and therefore did not know them in their practice, and that they did not consider them because of their imperfection. The reason why they did not use them was that they all sang together a single melody, for they aimed at a goal altogether different from that of moderns and therefore did not have that need for them that our musicians do.

·   ·   ·   ·   ·

It appears to be clear enough, then, for the reasons given, that the music of the ancients was a single melody and a single air, however many or few voices were singing. It should not seem strange if it had such lively effects in moving the affections of others, as we read, when it was composed—as we would say— by a good master and arranged by an artist who had good judgment in the art and performed by skilled persons and suitable voices. For everyone sang one and the same air in one simple tonos and in the best airs with a small number of steps in such a way that with its descents and ascents the voice did not go at all beyond the natural confines of the affection that the words wanted to express. They used at the same time a meter or rhythm, whether fast, slow, or moderate, according to the meaning of the idea that they aimed to express. In this way they could not help but achieve most of what they were expected to do.

Nor should it appear at all out of line (as they say) or strange that the music of our times does not work any of these miracles, since it conveys to the soul of the listener at one time diverse and contrary signs of affections as it mixes indistinctly together airs and tonoi that are completely dissimilar and of natures contrary to each other. Since each of these things has, naturally, its own quality and force, capable of stirring and moving through its resemblance appropriate affections, this music cannot generally by itself arouse any affection. Indeed, no one who considers the matter honestly will have cause to think of this as appearing in its nature otherwise.

·   ·   ·   ·   ·

To all the things that have been said concerning our music, add the taste for continuous delicacy of chords and consonances and a hundred other superflu- ous kinds of artifice that the moderns have pursued as if with a gun (as they say), seeking to ensnare our ears. It is a supreme hindrance in moving the soul to any affection to be chiefly preoccupied and almost bound by these straps of pleasure, all things different from, if not opposed to, what by nature is neces- sary to an affection, because affection and moral character tend to be some- thing natural, or at least they appear to be, and to have as their goal only to want to arouse the same effect in others. An example of this is when in a gathering some are weeping, others laughing, others conversing calmly, and others quarreling, while some dance drunkenly, and still others are doing other things, someone joins in who has no particular inclination to any of these affections; he will not be moved from his state except to be confused by the situation. If, on the other hand, someone joins a gathering in which everyone is lamenting or everyone is celebrating, only a great deal of preparation, both natural and spiritual, will prevent him from being moved and disposed in some way in keeping with these affections.

Consider further the supreme vanity of the use of many notes without any natural fittingness, whether considered in all its parts or together almost as a single corpus, or each by itself, something censured among the ancients by all men of judgment, among whom one does not hear perhaps any other complaint more frequently against the insolence and foolishness of the musicians of their times than that something is altogether unnatural, indeed, truly against every nature of affection. As anybody can hear, someone who laments never leaves the high pitches, and contrariwise someone who grieves does not leave the low pitches, unless a short distance, never crossing over into the intermediate pitches, which would not be suited to such a purpose. They would not trespass the limit, as we hear done in the airs of our musicians, which not only in the entire corpus of all their airs mixed together, but often in one only, whether soprano, tenor, or whatever it is, jumping now up, now down, through intermediate notes or directly, sometimes reach as much as an eleventh or twelfth.

Nor should we overlook the inestimable negligence of our musicians with respect to note values and rhythm in the various parts, whether each part is considered by itself or the entire corpus of them together. Extremely frequently, if not always, this is contrary to the nature of what would express the idea that the words signify, which arguably ought to be pursued beyond any other consideration. And this lacks any real distinction in each part; rather it differs haphazardly from one part to the other, since often the soprano hardly moves, while the tenor flies, and the bass goes strolling in slipper-socks, or, indeed, the other way around. How much imperfection this causes and how much it weakens the expression of the affections, through which the listener is moved to experience a similar feeling, does not require further explanation, for it is something that should be obvious to the little fishes, as they say, as well as to those who want to consider carefully the nature of each affection. For who is so dense as not easily to understand, if he looks around himself, that an infuriated person speaks hurriedly, and that the slowness of a suppliant's speech is different from the slowness of one who is calm? To this carelessness about tempo should be added their immoderate diminutions, starting from those notes called maxims and diminishing to those called sixteenth-notes, introduced without any reason or suitability to the natural movement of the voice.

On top of all these impediments nearly chief must be counted the disordered perturbation, mix-up, and mangling of the words. Thereby the power of the idea that may perchance be efficaciously expressed by them is not allowed to penetrate the intellect of the listener, as even the singers themselves can often recognize. The text, were it well understood, could by itself move and generate an affection in someone.

But what shall we say, besides, of that other unbecoming impertinence, that the soprano often sings the beginning of the words of a thought or repeats them, while the tenor is in the middle, the bass at the end, and the other parts elsewhere; or they are inconsistent among themselves in pronouncing the words? We cannot say, truly, other than that this too, along with the other conditions mentioned, drags behind the same standard—to distract the mind with diverse and, if necessary, contrary parts. This distraction means that all these points—as one may conceive them—strike helter-skelter and not on one center, not having thus sufficient value or force. Each one, being an impediment to the other, does not make an opening and does not penetrate, and thus does not stir an affection, the reverse of what the proverb tells us of the drop of water that, hitting the stone continually and unitedly in the same place, finally carves a hole in it.

· · · · · ·

As to the marvelous effects of the music of the ancients in moving the affections and not finding any trace of this in the modern, if we wish to look with a straight eye at the matters discussed above, it may happen that we shall marvel no more at the effects, because our music does not have the same goal. This may be because ours does not have any means of accomplishing this as the ancient did, since it has as its object the delectation of the sense of hearing, whereas the ancient had the object of leading someone else to the same affections as one's own.

The project that I have been pursuing for some time is to seek to discover what the ancients intended by tonos—that is, Dorian, Phrygian, and the like— and whether these were the same as those that the moderns call first, second, third, up to the eighth tone. It did not seem to me from what I had read that this was possible, and today I believe that it is very certain that they are not the same. Those that our musicians call tones do not have the same conditions that we know those ancient tonoi had. If Franchino,[8] Glarean, and the other great geniuses among the moderns wished to restore to our tones the names of the ancient, better to make us believe that they are the same and call the even-numbered or plagal—instead of *second, fourth, sixth,* and *eighth*—*Hypodorian, Hypophrygian, Hypolydian,* and *Hypomixolydian,* and the odd-numbered—instead of *first, third, fifth,* and *seventh*—*Dorian, Phrygian, Lydian,* and *Mixolydian,* nevertheless, what our musicians call *tones* are nothing but simple diverse species or forms of the diapason and octave,[9] differing in height of pitch one from another only according to how they are found collocated in the order of the system, constitution, or scale—as others call it—of the steps or musical pitches. Now among the ancients the Hypodorian and Hypophrygian tonoi, and so all the others, arose from mutations of locus[10] that were

8. That is, Gafori.
9. On the species of fifth and octave of the modes see no. 69 above (Aaron), chap. 1, pp. 418–19.
10. That is, transpositions. [Tr.]

applied to the entire constitutions of pitches, whether of the diapasons or octaves or of other systems and constitutions, whether perfect or imperfect, when in the mutation of locus they became higher or lower in pitch than they were naturally accustomed to be in the common constitution or system. This natural or common constitution or system unaltered with respect to locus they called the Dorian tonos.[11] Its proper diapason or octave was the middle one, contained within the two disjunct tetrachords—that is, between the step the ancients called *hypate meson,* our E la mi, and the step they called *nete diezeugmenon,* our e la mi, inclusively.

•   •   •   •   •

The songs of Olympus and Terpander, so far as pertains to singing, were without doubt, in my opinion, a plainchant accompanied by an instrument, the lyre or kithara, which may be taken as the same, in the case of Terpander, because he was a kitharode, or a pipe in the case of Olympus, since he was an aulete. Although these songs in their airs did not seek out in climbing or descending more than three strings each—so simple and natural were they— nevertheless they were so beautiful melodically and of such excellence that they were never equaled or improved upon by those musicians who followed, despite the many strings they put to use. And this is evidently what Plutarch's words mean when he says of them: "τρίχορδα γὰρ ὄντα καὶ ἁπλᾶ διαφέρει τῶν ποικιλων καὶ πολυχόρδων—With their three strings and their simplicity, they surpass so much those intricate compositions using many strings that none could imitate the style of Olympus, and all who compose melodies for many strings and in several modes are left far behind."[12] Although they were made from three strings and were simple, they nevertheless excelled and outshone the varied and polychordal compositions of others. Not that they sang with three notes, that is, in three airs at the same time, or played, as we in our times have heard done sometimes by certain great players who have ingeniously played on a viola with a bow three or four parts and airs at the same time. A sure sign that the words of that noble author should be understood in the way stated and not otherwise may be—besides the truth of what they signify—that in that place the author praises the simplicity of those who used few strings in comparison to those who used many. None—for example, Timotheus, Philoxenus, and an infinity of others, with all their multitude of strings—could equal the songs of Olympus. Timotheus expanded his lyre to eleven strings, whereas up to Terpander and others like him it did not go beyond seven. For this alteration he was exiled by the Spartans as a spoiler and destroyer of the ancient

11. Mei announces here for the first time his important discovery, elaborated in *De modis musicis antiquorum,* that the Greek tonoi were not modes in the medieval sense, but keys used to transpose the central octave or natural system, called Dorian, to higher or lower levels of pitch. [Tr.]

12. [Pseudo-] Plutarch *De musica* 1137b. [Tr.]

music.[13] It is altogether beyond the realm of possibility that Timotheus played together at one time ten or eleven parts or airs on the same lyre.

•   •   •   •   •

What the ancient musicians called *harmonia* in singing did not have anything in the world to do with consonances (as may be understood by whoever has some idea of the Greek language from the nature of the meaning of the word and its derivatives) but pertained to the composition of the air which was sung—that is, well adapted and suitably joined together according to the proper division and distinction of the intervals from one step to the other of a genus, which, whether used simply or mixed with others, was being sung or played.

The words or verse of Vergil: "Obloquitur numeris septem discrimina vocum"[14] do not mean, I believe, that Orpheus played seven parts on the lyre or was seconding or accompanying his singing of the chorus with consonances on the lyre, but that he with his lyre, which was made up of two conjoined tetrachords, which together contained only seven steps or pitches, as for example that of Terpander—and not like that of Timotheus or others which had a larger number—made it almost speak with his masterful and fitting accompaniment according to the melody, note values and rhythm of those who, in keeping with the habit of the choruses, danced as they sang. Here the poet's marvelous and deliberate care in this imitation should not be allowed idly to slip through one's hands. For, in order to make evident and to demonstrate that the playing of Orpheus had dignity, since it was customary to play the ancient rite πρόσ-χορδα,[15] that is, to play the same notes as those of the air that the chorus sang, he added: "Iam que eadem digitis iam pectina pulsa eburno."[16] In ancient times it was customary for the song of the chorus to be the principal part, while the instrument, almost like a servant, accompanied it, for human song was the real thing, whereas the accompaniment was its image. But then, under the pretext of carving a new path, musicians began to do the opposite—that is, to make the playing precede and the voice follow. We can read of many quarrels about this among the ancients, for with this mutation of custom they consented to having sensation become the principal and reason its subordinate. Because nothing else, in truth, would appear to have allowed the instrumental sound, invented to imitate the voice, to become the boss and to be obeyed by the voice in effecting the actions properly belonging to it, for nature gave the voice

---

13. Two sources for this story are Athenaeus *Deipnosophists* 636e and Pausanius *Descriptio graeciae* 3.13. [Tr.] Philoxenus (ca. 436–380 B.C.E.) was a composer of dithyrambs.

14. See no. 65 above (Gafori), p. 391, n. 7.

15. *Proschorda;* Pollux *Onomasticon* 4.63 defines this as the attuning of a melody to a stringed instrument—i.e., in unison. [Pseudo-] Plutarch *De musica* 1141b speaks of this method of accompaniment as ancient, before Crexus invented the method of accompanying with notes other than those of the vocal melody. [Tr.]

16. Virgil *Aeneid* 6.647: "striking them now with his fingers, now with his ivory quill" (trans. Fairclough). [Tr.]

expressly to man not so that he might with its pure sound, like animals which lack reason, express pleasure and pain, but so that, together with meaningful speech, he might suitably express the thoughts of his mind. Having reached this point, the corruption did not stop there. Almost content with this new status, it changed because of the march of time, and the manner of seconding the other became bastardized, to use this vulgar term. Whereas earlier one sang and played unitedly and always with the same durations and pitches, now the voice and instrument began not to correspond to each other πρόσχορδα—that is, with the same notes—but συμφώνως,[17] that is, with consonances and not with the same duration and measure, but with diminutions and *passaggi* and other such variations, all things imagined and thought up by the artists themselves in their ambition, all striving competitively to please most supremely the ears, without taking the intellect into account. This new allurement began to lead the soul astray from attention to the conceits and other imitations of the affections, almost enfeebling it with these excessive delicacies. Plato, in the seventh book of his *Laws*,[18] to counter these corruptions destructive of the rational parts and characteristic form of man, orders with great diligence and commands that his youth never be taught any style of music in which there is any diversity or variety of pitches or durations between the sound of the lyre and the song composed by the poet, which is as worthy as the poet-musician who composed the air, for in ancient times musician and poet were the same person.

These corruptions became every day greater, especially after the introduction of instruments with many strings, such as organs, spinets, harpsichords, lutes, and, in sum, all those that by means of many keys or many strings possess a large number of pitches. Whoever believed that out of this ultimately evolved this manner and custom of ours of singing together so many and diverse vocal airs would not have thought anything very far from the truth. For this, growing, as things pertaining to the arts do, whether useful or not, little by little grew so much in our times and became so extremely big, that this art, divorced from any care or law, has let itself become prey to the pure willfulness and power of its artists, without any more considered limitation or rule. Thus, through the ambition of each of them, the last not wishing to follow and approve the footsteps and works of those who came before them, so as not to appear to confess almost by tacit consensus that they were inferior in industry or genius, it easily came about that these musicians precipitated themselves at breakneck speed, as they say, to discover always new styles and new forms of song. Soon their vanity gave rise to such a paradox that they tolerated that the words of their songs were not understood or that the sentiment that actually appeared in the words could not be felt. Thus we could not claim—almost to our shame—to

17. *Symphonos;* the term *symphonia* meant consonance, but only fifths, fourths, and octaves were considered consonances. [Tr.]
18. 7.812d, where Plato criticized those musicians who accompanied in the *symphonos* style rather than *proschorda*. [Tr.]

have been born rational; it delights us more to be without intellect and entirely subject to any pleasure whatever than to be truly human beings. But this discussion is beside the point. . . .

Rome, May 8, 1572

77 Fray Toribio de Benavente, *called* Motolinia

Hernán Cortés and a ragtag group of Spanish soldiers first landed at the place on the Mexican mainland they called Veracruz on April 22, 1519. On the following November 8 they entered, dumbstruck with wonder, into Tenochtitlan, the great floating capital of the tributary state of the Aztecs (or, more properly, the Mexica). Less than two years later Cortés's capture and destruction of the city was complete.

The military conquest quickly set in motion extensive efforts to convert the indigenous Mexicans to Christianity. Among the earliest missionaries in the Valley of Mexico were twelve Franciscans, the so-called Mexican Apostles, who arrived in June 1524. Fray Toribio de Benavente (ca. 1495–ca. 1565) was one of them. He took the name by which he is remembered from the Mexica themselves, who are said to have remarked at his strict Franciscan habit "motolinia"—in Nahuatl, "he suffers" or "he is poor." Motolinia learned Nahuatl well and studied Mexican society, customs, and ritual extensively. He numbers with his fellow Franciscan Bernardino de Sahagún among the keenest European observers of indigenous Mexico. Of his two chief works, the *Historia de los indios de la Nueva España* (1541) and the closely related *Memoranda* (1530s?), the first emphasizes the progress of evangelization after the conquest while the second is richer in proto-ethnographic detail. Though both treatises influenced writers on Mexico of the following generations—the reading that follows, for example, was taken over almost verbatim by Fray Juan de Torquemada in his *Monarchia indiana* of 1615—neither was published for centuries after Motolinia's death. The *Historia* first emerged in 1858, the *Memoranda* only in 1903.

Book 2, Chapter 26 of the *Memoranda* comprises one of the lengthiest and most specific accounts of Mexican sung ritual that has come down to us. Motolinia's evident admiration for the grace, skill, precision, and careful preparation of the native performers is shared as well by other early European spectators. Across the later sixteenth century such admiration would turn increasingly to condemnation and repression, channeling indigenous energies into European music-making and Catholic public spectacles while driving native ritual underground, where it seems to have persisted for a time in secret ceremonies of song and dance.

FROM *Memoranda or Book of the Things of New Spain and of the Natives There*

(1530s?)

BOOK 2

CHAPTER 26: ON THE MANNER OF THE NATIVES' DANCING, ON THE GREAT SKILL AND CONFORMITY THEY OBSERVED IN DANCING AND SINGING, AND ON MANY OTHER THINGS OF THIS SORT; SO THAT THIS CHAPTER AND THOSE THAT FOLLOW ARE NO LESS NOTABLE THAN THE PRECEDING ONES.

Songs and dances were very important in all this land, both to celebrate the solemn festivals of the demons they honored as gods, whom they thought well served by such things, and for their own enjoyment and recreation. For this reason they gave two names to their dances, as is explained below.[1] And because in each town they put much stock in these things, each chieftain had a chapel in his house with his singers who composed the dances and songs; and these leaders sought out those who knew best how to compose songs in the meter and verses they practiced. They prized most *contrabajos*, because in the houses of the chiefs they frequently sang in a quiet voice.[2]

Most often they sang and danced in the principal festivals, which occurred every twenty days,[3] and in other less important festivals. The most important dances took place in the town plazas; other times they danced in the patio of the chieftain's house (for all the chieftains had large patios), or in the houses of lesser lords.

When they had won some battle, or when they elevated a new chieftain, or when a lord was married, or for some other novel event, the music masters

TEXT: *Memoriales de Fray Toribio de Motolinia,* ed. Luis García Pimentel (Mexico: Casa del Editor, 1903), pp. 339–43. Translation by Gary Tomlinson. Where possible I have retained Motolinia's fluctuation between present and past tenses.

1. 2.27, where Motolinia gives the indigenous names for dance for recreation (*nehtotiliztli*) and for solemn, penitential religious dance (*macehualiztli*). The same distinction, though without Nahuatl terminology, is made by the Dominican missionary Diego Duràn (1537–88) in his *Historia de las indias de Nueva-España e islas de tierra firme,* another important early source on Mexican song and dance; see Robert Stevenson, *Music in Aztec and Inca Territory* (Berkeley, University of California Press, 1968), p. 110.
2. Motolinia uses *contrabajo* to refer to a relatively high-pitched voice, not a low bass. The usage is confirmed by his discussion below of Mexican drums, where the higher-pitched *teponaztli* is said to serve as *contrabajo* to the lower *huehuetl.* See also Stevenson, *Music,* p. 98, n. 213.
3. That is, in each of the eighteen twenty-day months of the Mexican ritual calendar; to these 360 days were added five inauspicious or "barren" days, called *nemontemi,* filling out the solar year. Motolinia was one of the first Europeans to comprehend Mexican calendrical systems.

composed a new song, different from those celebrating the festivals of the demons or ancient exploits or past chieftains.

The singers decided some days before the festivals what they would sing. In the larger towns there were many singers, and if there were to be new songs and dances they gathered in advance so there would be no imperfections on the festival day. On the morning of that day they put a large mat in the middle of the plaza where they set up their drums. Then they gathered and dressed at the house of the chieftain; from there they came singing and dancing. Sometimes they began their dances in the morning, sometimes at the hour when we celebrate High Mass. At night they returned singing to the palace, there to end their song early in the night, or when the night was well advanced, or even at midnight.

There were two drums. One[4] was tall and round, fatter than a man, five hand-spans tall, of very good wood, well worked and hollowed out inside. On the outside it was painted, and on its mouth they stretched a well cured deerskin. From the edge to the middle it sounds pitches a fifth apart, and they tune its pitches higher or lower in order to match it to their songs. The other drum cannot be described without the aid of a picture;[5] this serves as *contrabajo.* Both drums have a good sound and can be heard a great distance away. When the dancers have taken their places they prepare to play the drums and two singers, the best, act as leaders in beginning the songs. The large, leather-covered drum is played with the hands, while the other is played with mallets, like Spanish drums (however differently it is made).

The chieftain, together with other lords and elders, goes before the drums, dancing. These men stand three or four fathoms deep around the mat, and around them come another growing multitude that fills out the circle. In the larger towns more than a thousand and even more than two thousand take part in this central place. Around them comes a procession of two lines of dancers, young men, expert dancers. The leaders are two men chosen from among the best dancers; they lead the dance. In these two lines, by means of certain turns and graceful postures, they face sometimes their companions in front of them and other times those behind them. A large number of dancers, sometimes as many as a thousand or more according to the town and the festival, participate in these two lines. Before wars, when they celebrated their festivals with great abandon in the large towns, three or four thousand or even more would gather to dance; but after the conquest, when their numbers were depleted and growing smaller, only half as many danced.[6]

4. The *huehuetl.*

5. This is the *teponaztli,* a drum fashioned from a hollowed log laid horizontal and cut with an H-shaped slit. The two resulting tongues, of different pitch, were played with rubber-tipped mallets.

6. The indigenous population of the central valley of Mexico, estimated at 10–25 million at the time of European contact, declined steadily thereafter, especially because of smallpox and other diseases brought by the Europeans. By the 1620s it reached its lowpoint, approximately 730,000. See Sherburne F. Cook and Woodrow Borah, *Essays in Population History* (3 vols., Berkeley: University of California Press, 1971–79).

When they are ready to start the dance three or four Indians blow very lively whistles. Then they play the drums quietly, growing louder little by little. Hearing that the drums have begun, the people all hear the song and begin to dance. The first songs are sung quietly and slowly, as if composed in the soft hexachord. The very first concerns the particular festival being celebrated. The two singing masters always begin the song, and then everyone in the whole circle proceeds to sing and dance together. The whole multitude coordinates the movements of their feet as well as the best dancers of Spain. What is more, their whole bodies—heads, arms, and hands—are so synchronized, measured, and ordered that they do not differ from one another by even half a beat; whatever one does with right foot or left, all the others do at the same time and on the same beat. When one lowers his left arm and raises his right, all the others do the same thing at the same time. In this way the drums, singing, and dancing are perfectly concerted. Everything is so synchronized that one does not differ a jot from another, and good Spanish dancers who see them are amazed and greatly esteem the native dances as well as the great accord and feeling they display.

The dancers in the outer ring make (as we might say) a small beat, that is, they place two beats in the time of one, moving quicker and putting more work into the dance; and all those in this circle move in time to one another. Those in the middle of the circle dance to the full beat and move both their feet and the rest of their bodies with much gravity. Some of them raise and lower their arms with much grace.

Each verse or couplet is repeated three or four times, and the song is so well tuned that the singing, drums, and dance all stay together. Having finished one song—though the first songs seem longer because they go slower, not one of them lasts a whole hour—having finished one, the pitch of the drum is changed. Everyone stops singing (though not dancing) for a few beats. Then the singing masters begin another song, a little higher and livelier than the one before it. Thus they raise the songs and change the pitches and the notes, moving from a low one to a high and from a dance to a quicker step.

Various boys and children also dance—sons of aristocrats, seven or eight years old, singing and dancing with their fathers. Since their voices have not yet broken, they add much grace to the song. Sometimes they play trumpets and some little flutes, not very well tuned; other times they play whistles and certain little bones that give a loud sound.[7] Others go disguised in dress and voice, impersonating peoples of foreign nations and speaking their languages. These are like clowns. They go along cutting capers, making a thousand faces

---

7. For a glossary of Mexica organology see Stevenson, *Music,* pp. 30–85. For the instruments Motolinia mentions here see especially the entries *atecocolli* and *tecciztli* (conch trumpets), *quiquiztli* (wooden trumpet), *tepuzquiquiztli* (copper trumpet), *chichtli* (whistle flute), *çoçoloctli* and *tlapitzalli* (flutes). For pictures and further discussion see Samuel Martí, *Instrumentos musicales precortesianos* (Mexico: Instituto Nacional de Antropología, 1955).

and cracking a thousand jokes that make whoever sees and hears them laugh. Some of them go as old women, others as fools.

From time to time some of the participants leave to rest and eat, and when they return others leave. Sometimes they bring bouquets of roses and garlands that they wear on their heads and on their dancing costumes, which are made of rich robes and feathers; and in their hands they carry small, pretty feathers. In these dances they also wear many emblems and insignias that tell who has been valiant in battle.

From the hour of vespers until nighttime the songs and dances get more and more lively and higher in pitch, and the playing more and more graceful. It almost seems that they sing the air of some festive hymn that they have among them. And the drums get higher and higher. And since there are many people they can be heard at a great distance, especially when the air carries their voices, and especially at night. Then they burn many great torches, which is really a sight to see.

The Spaniards call these dances *areito,* a word from the islands.[8]

8. That is, the West Indies. Specifically, the word comes from Hispaniola, where Columbus first landed, and is derived from Taino.

78 Bartolomé de Segovia?

In 1524 Spanish explorers off the western coast of South America intercepted a boat heading north that was laden with precious barter goods. It was the first unequivocal evidence the Europeans had seen of a prosperous civilization to the south, and it ensured that further explorations would soon lead to contact between the Spanish and Inca empires. In 1531 Francisco Pizarro embarked for Peru; in late 1532 he used treachery to capture the Inca Atahualpa at Cajamarca and imprisoned him. Pizarro executed Atahualpa the following August, installing his brother Manco Inca in his place as puppet ruler. In November 1533, the Spaniards entered unopposed into Cuzco.

In the next decade, the far-flung and loose-knit Inca political system dissolved quickly under a succession of conquistador-governors who conspired to murder one another as well as the native Peruvians who rose against them, under Manco Inca, in 1536. From this chaos there survived few notices of pre-Hispanic life and society—indeed Inca traces are startlingly sparse compared to the relative abundance of information we have from central Mexico. The account here, the most detailed description by a European of an Inca celebration in Cuzco, is then all the more valuable. The harvest celebration witnessed by our author was called Inti Raimi, or Festival of the Sun. Its long avenue of living and mummified nobility and its full day of song, timed to the waxing and waning of the sun, are richly suggestive of the careful spatio-cosmological orientations that were basic, as recent researches have shown, to Inca worship.

FROM *Relation of Many Occurrences in Peru: In Sum in Order to Convey in Writing How These Kingdoms Were Conquered and Colonized*

(1553)

These things happened in April 1535 when in the valley of Cuzco they harvested the maize and other crops. Each year after the harvest it was the custom of the rulers of Cuzco to make a great sacrifice to the sun and all the *huacas* or shrines of the city. This was done in them and through all the provinces and the whole kingdom. It was started by the Inca[1] and consisted of eight days of giving thanks to the sun for the harvest just completed and praying to the sun for bountiful future crops. . . .

They brought out onto a plain at the entrance to Cuzco where the sun rises all the figures from the shrines, and they put the more important of these under rich and well wrought feathered awnings, which were a splendid sight. From rows of these awnings they made an avenue, with one row of awnings facing the other more than thirty paces away. In this avenue gathered all the rulers and lords of Cuzco, but no people of lower station. These were *orejones*,[2] very richly dressed in cloaks and shirts of silver embroidery with bracelets and disks of fine shining gold on their heads. They formed two lines, each of more than three hundred lords. It was like a procession with one choir facing another, and they stood very quietly waiting for the sun to rise. When the sun was partly risen they began to intone a song with great order and harmony.

TEXT: *Relación de muchas cosas acaescidas en el Piru en suma para entender a la letra la manera que se tuvo en la conquista y poblazón de estos reinos*, in *Crónicas peruanas de interés indigena*, ed. Francisco Esteve Barba (Biblioteca de Autores Españoles, vol. 209, Madrid: Real Academia Española, 1968), pp. 81–82. Translation by Gary Tomlinson. For a discussion of the account, see Sabine MacCormack, *Religion in the Andes: Vision and Imagination in Early Colonial Peru* (Princeton: Princeton University Press, 1991), pp. 74–79. Arguments in favor of ascribing the *Relación* to the obscure cleric Bartolomé de Segovia and against its earlier ascription to Cristóbal de Molina are made by Raúl Porras Barrenechea, *Los cronistas del Perú (1528–1650) y otros ensayos* (Lima, Banco de Crédito del Perú, 1986), p. 317.

1. That is, the ruler; *inca* in Quechua signifies a male of royal blood.
2. Literally, "big ears," so called by the Spaniards because of the large gold ornaments they wore in their ear lobes.

While they sang each one tapped one of his feet, like our singers of polyphony, and as the sun rose they sang higher.

A little way from these rows the Inca had his tent in an enclosure with a chair and a very fine bench. And at the beginning of the singing he rose with great authority and put himself at the head of the lines and was the first to begin to sing; and as he did, so did the others. After he had stood for a little while he returned to his chair, where he remained conversing with those who came to him. On a few occasions, from time to time, he went and stood with his chorus for a while, and then he returned.

Thus they sang from sunrise until the sun had set completely. And since until midday the sun was rising, their voices grew, and from midday on they diminished, carefully following the progress of the sun. All this time they made many offerings. On one side, on an embankment where there was a tree, there were Indians who did nothing but throw meat into a great fire where it was burned and consumed in the flames. To another side the Inca threw many llamas that the common and poor Indians scrambled for; this was a source of great diversion. At eight o'clock more than two hundred young women came out of Cuzco carrying large, covered pitchers, each new and identical to the others, containing a great quantity of *chicha*.[3] They came five at a time, in great order and synchrony, each group awaiting its turn. They offered to the sun many baskets of an herb they eat, called in their language *coca*, which is a leaf rather like myrtle. And they observed many other ceremonies and offerings that would take long to recount.

Let it suffice to say that, when in the afternoon the sun began to set they showed great sadness on account of its absence in their song and their bearing, and they worked to diminish greatly their voices. And when the sun set completely and disappeared from their sight they showed great wonder and, joining hands, prayed to it with deepest humility. Then they removed all the apparatus of the festival and took down the awnings, and everyone went home. They returned those figures and awful relics to their houses and shrines. And thus in the same manner they celebrated for eight or nine days. And you should know that the figures of idols under those awnings were the past Incas who had ruled Cuzco.[4] Each one was served by a crowd of men who all day long shooed away flies with certain fans made of swan feathers with tiny mirrors on them and by its *mamacona*, who are like nuns; under each awning there were twelve or fifteen of them.[5]

---

3. A beer brewed from maize.
4. I.e. their mummified remains, fundamental to Inca worship, called *mallqui* in Quechua, *bultos* by the Spaniards. See MacCormack, *Religion*, pp. 68–71.
5. The *mamacona* were the leaders of corps of women chosen to serve the sun. See ibid., p. 458.

79 Filippo Pigafetta and Duarte Lopez

In the 1480s, the Portuguese sailor Diogo Cão, searching for trade routes to Asia that would not cross lands controlled by hostile Turks, first came across the estuary of the Congo (now the Zaire) River. Explorers, missionaries, and merchants soon followed, and by 1516 the Portuguese crown had established the Kingdom of the Congo as one of its protectorates along the African coast.

Almost a century after Cão, in 1578, Duarte Lopez sailed from Lisbon to Luanda, a newly fortified Portuguese settlement. He spent the next ten years in the Congo, mapping its inland reaches and residing at the court of its Christianized ruler, Alvaro I. In 1587 he left Africa, in the office of Congolese ambassador, to request increased missionary efforts from Philip II, King of Spain and Portugal, and Pope Sixtus V. After notable misadventures, including storms that blew him off course all the way to the West Indies, he reached Rome in 1588. There he met Filippo Pigafetta (1533–1604), soldier, writer, explorer, and agent for Pope Sixtus V through many parts of the Middle East and North Africa. From Lopez's testimony and other sources, Pigafetta compiled his *Relazione del Reame di Congo et delle circonvicine contrade (Relation on the Kingdom of the Congo and the Surrounding Regions)*, published at Rome in 1591. Though it saw only one Italian edition, the work was quickly dispersed across northern Europe. It was translated into Dutch, English, German, and Latin in the 1590s, the latter two translations serving as the first volume of Theodore de Bry's monumental collection of *Petits voyages*. The English translation was reprinted by Samuel Purchas in his own large compilation of travel narratives, *Purchas His Pilgrimes* (1617–25).

FROM *Relation on the Kingdom of the Congo and the Surrounding Regions*
(1591)

BOOK 2

CHAPTER 7: ON THE COURT OF THE KING OF THE CONGO AND ON THE CLOTHING OF THOSE PEOPLE BEFORE THEY BECAME CHRISTIANS; THEN ON THE ROYAL TABLE AND THE MANNERS OF THE COURT

• • • • •

The king of the Congo has a guard made up of Anzichi and men of other nations who stand around his palace armed in the manner I described before. When he wants to leave the palace they play the drums, which can be heard for five or six miles and let everyone know that he is coming forth. . . . The Mocicongos (as the inhabitants of the Congo call themselves in their tongue) . . . do not keep any histories of their ancient kings or memory of past ages, not knowing how to write. They measure time by the phases of the moon and do not know the hours of the day or night, speaking usually thus: At the time of such a moon, such a thing happened. They measure distances not in miles or any such units but in the days it takes a man, loaded down or not, to get there. For their gatherings and celebrations such as weddings they sing verses of love and play certain strangely formed lutes. These are in the rounded part of the body and in the neck somewhat similar to ours, but the flat part, where we carve the rosette, is covered with a very thin skin, like a bladder, instead of wood. The strings are made from strong, polished hairs from the tail of an elephant or from certain threads from the wood of the palm tree. They extend from the bottom of the instrument to the end of the neck and are tied to pegs of various sizes affixed to the neck. From the pegs they hang very thin plates of iron and silver, of different sizes depending on the size of the whole instrument. These jingle in various ways, giving out an intermittent sound, as the strings are played and the pegs from which they hang vibrate. The players pluck the strings in good proportion with their fingers and without the sort of plectrum we use to play the harp. They play masterfully and produce a melody or noise (I know not which to call it) that delights their senses. Moreover—and it is a wondrous thing—with this instrument they signify the concepts in their minds and make them understood so clearly that almost anything they can put across in speaking they can also express by touching this instrument with their

TEXT: Filippo Pigafetta, *Relazione del Reame di Congo et delle circonvicine contrade*, ed. Giorgio Raimondo Cardona (Milan: Bompiani, 1978), pp. 161–64. Translation by Gary Tomlinson.

hands. To the sound and rhythm of the music of this instrument they dance in good measure and clap their hands.[1] They also play flutes and pipes artfully at the king's court and dance to their sound in a grave and restrained fashion, almost in the manner of a *moresca*. The common people use small drums and flutes and other instruments, which they play in a less refined manner than the courtiers.

1. The lute with metal jingles Pigafetta describes survives today in various regions of West Africa; for pictures see *Musical Instruments of the World: An Illustrated Encyclopedia,* ed. the Diagram Group (Paddington Press Ltd., 1976), p. 178, and *The New Grove Dictionary of Musical Instruments,* ed. Stanley Sadie (3 vols., London: MacMillan, 1984), s.v. "Lute," fig. 1f; for description of a related Nigerian instrument see ibid., s.v. "Gurmi." Pigafetta's fascinating reference to speech-like performances on this lute might at first blush seem to confuse it with the famous West African "talking drums," alluded to, at any rate, at the beginning of the excerpt. But caution is needed here; ethnomusicologists have noted that African musicians reproduce the intonations of speech on various instruments other than drums (see Anthony King, "Talking drum," in *The New Grove Dictionary of Musical Instruments;* also, more tentatively, J. H. Kwabena Nketia, *The Music of Africa* [New York: Norton, 1974], p. 188).

80 Matteo Ricci

From the earliest years of their order, the Jesuits dreamed of Christianizing China. But their first efforts met with no success; Francis Xavier, founder of the Jesuit mission in India and the first Christian missionary to Japan, died in 1552 while awaiting permission to enter Canton.

In the same year, Matteo Ricci was born at Macerata, Italy. Taught at Jesuit schools first in his hometown and later in Florence and Rome, Ricci traveled to Portugal in 1577 and from there to Goa the following year. Four years later, now ordained a priest, he arrived in Macao. He would remain in China until his death in 1610. From Macao Ricci followed a slow northward trajectory, through Zhaoqing, Shaozhou, Nanchang, and Nanjing, toward his ultimate goal, Beijing. Only in May 1601, after two earlier unsuccessful attempts, did he win permission to live in the imperial capital, where he stayed for his last nine years.

In the 1590s Ricci gained an intimate knowledge of Chinese language, litera-ture, and philosophy, and in his missionary activity he pursued a method of accommodation to local customs and collaboration and debate with local intel-lectuals. This close contact belies the blank insensitivity to Chinese song and instrumental music evident in the excerpts that follow (contrast, for example, Motolinia's more positive tone in no. 77 above, pp. 495–99); perhaps such incomprehension reflects in part Ricci's general lack of musical training. In any case, the ultimate aims behind both Ricci's and Motolinia's accounts were the same: furthering Christian belief and identifying elements not reconcilable with it. Ricci reminds us of these aims in the final paragraphs excerpted here, describing how he turned the gift of a clavichord to the emperor Wanli into a means of proselytizing.

Ricci wrote his journals in Italian during his final years. The manuscript was translated into Latin and brought to Rome by Nicola Trigault, who published it there in 1615 as *De christiana expeditione apud Sinas suscepta ab Societate Jesu. Ex P. Matthaei Ricii . . . commentariis libri V* (*Five Books on the Christian Expedition to China Undertaken by the Society of Jesus. From the Commentaries of Father Matteo Ricci*). Ten further editions in Latin, French, German, Spanish, and Italian appeared in the next six years, and Samuel Purchas included excerpts in English in *Purchas His Pilgrimes*. The excerpts here are translated from Trigault's Latin, the version that was circulated widely in the seventeenth century. His sometimes free adaptation explains the wavering between Ricci's own voice and third-person references to him.

FROM *Five Books on the Christian Expedition to China*
(1615)

BOOK 1

CHAPTER 4: CONCERNING THE MECHANICAL ARTS AMONG THE CHINESE

•　　•　　•　　•　　•

Musical instruments are quite common and of many varieties, but the use of the organ and the clavichord is unknown, and the Chinese possess no instrument of the keyboard type. On all of their stringed instruments the strings are made of twisted cotton, and they seem to be ignorant of the fact that the guts of animals can be used for this purpose. Their practice agrees fairly well with ours in the use of instruments to be played in concert. The whole art of Chinese music seems to consist in producing a monotonous rhythmic beat as they know nothing of the variations and harmony that can be produced by combining different musical notes. However, they themselves are highly flattered by their own music which to the ear of a stranger represents nothing but a discordant jangle. Despite the fact that they claim the first rank in the field of harmonious concert music, they have expressed themselves pleased with organ music and with all our musical instruments which they have heard thus far. Perhaps they will judge in like manner of our vocal harmony and orchestration when

TEXT: *China in the Sixteenth Century* by Matthew Ricci, trans. Louis J. Gallagher, s.J., pp. 22–24, 335–36, 376–78. Copyright 1942 and renewed 1970 by Louis J. Gallagher. Reprinted by permission of Random House, Inc.

they have heard it. Up to the present they have not had this opportunity in our churches, as our modest beginnings here have not yet reached that stage of development. . . .

I believe this people is too much interested in dramatic representations and shows. At least they certainly surpass us in this respect. An exceedingly large number of the youth of the land is devoted to this activity. Some of them form traveling troupes which journey everywhere throughout the length and breadth of the country, while other groups reside permanently in the large centers and are in great demand for private as well as for public performances. Without question this is a curse in the empire, and so much so that it would be difficult to discover any other activity which is more prone to vice. Sometimes the leaders of the troupes of actors purchase young children and force them, almost from infancy, to take part in the choruses, to lead the dance, and to share in the acting and mimicry. Nearly all of their plays are of ancient origin, based upon history or fiction, and nowadays few new plays are being produced. These groups of actors are employed at all imposing banquets, and when they are called they come prepared to enact any of the ordinary plays. The host at the banquet is usually presented with a volume of plays and he selects the one or several he may like. The guests, between eating and drinking, follow the plays with so much satisfaction that the banquet at times may last for ten hours, and as one play leads to another the dramatic performance may last as long again as did the banquet. The text of these plays is generally sung, and it rarely happens that anything is enunciated in an ordinary tone of voice. . . .[1]

•　　•　　•　　•　　•

BOOK 4

CHAPTER 6: THE LEADERS AT NANKIN SOLICIT THE COMPANY OF FATHER RICCI

. . . Let us here insert a word about Chinese music, an art that is of considerable interest to Europeans. The leaders of the literary class observe a solemn day of sacrifice in honor of Confucius, if sacrifice is the proper word. The Chinese honor the great philosopher as a Master, and not as a deity, and they are accustomed to use the word sacrifice in a broad and indefinite sense. This particular celebration is attended with music, and on the previous day they invite the Chief of Magistrates to attend a rehearsal of the orchestra, to decide whether or not the music will be appropriate for the occasion. Father Ricci was

---

1. On the music drama of the late Ming dynasty see "China" in *The New Grove Dictionary of Music and Musicians,* section III.1 (Colin P. MacKerras) and Kuo-huang Han and Lindy Li Mark, "Evolution and Revolution in Chinese Music," in *Musics of Many Cultures,* ed. Elizabeth May (Berkeley: University of California Press, 1980), pp. 10–31, esp. p. 16. The opera Ricci describes was most likely *k'un-ch'ü,* a florid style, accompanied by flute *(ti-tzu)* or sometimes lute *(p'i-p'a),* that thrived among educated classes in the late sixteenth century.

invited to this rehearsal and as there was no question of attending a sacrifice, he accepted the invitation. This orchestral rehearsal was arranged by the priests of the literary class, called Tansu, and it was held in a hall or rather in the Royal Temple, built to honor the Lord of Heaven. Father Matthew was accompanied by the children of the High Magistrate. The priests who composed the orchestra were vested in sumptuous garments, as if they were to attend a sacrifice, and after paying their respects to the Magistrate, they set to playing their various instruments; bronze bells, basin shaped vessels, some made of stone, with skins over them like drums, stringed instruments like a lute,[2] bone flutes and organs played by blowing into them with the mouth rather than with bellows.[3] They had other instruments also shaped like animals, holding reeds in their teeth, through which air was forced from the empty interior. At this rehearsal these curious affairs were all sounded at once, with a result that can be readily imagined, as it was nothing other than a lack of concord, a discord of discords. The Chinese themselves are aware of this. One of their sages said on a certain occasion that the art of music known to their ancestors had evaporated with the centuries, and left only the instruments.

• • • • •

CHAPTER 12: FROM PRISON TO PEKIN BY THE KING'S COMMAND

. . . Later on, four of the eunuchs who played stringed instruments before the throne came, in the King's name, to see the Fathers. Playing on such instruments is considered to be an advanced art among the Chinese, and the palace musicians outrank the mathematicians. They conduct an elaborate school in the royal palace and they came to ask the Fathers to teach them to play on the clavichord, which was included in the royal presents. From being a casual student, Father Didaco had become very proficient on this instrument, and he went to the palace every day to give them a music lesson. It was at the suggestion of Father Ricci, made a long time before, that Father Didaco had taken lessons on the clavichord from Father Cattaneo, who was an accomplished musician, and in making the suggestion, he was looking forward to this very incident. The Chinese knew little or nothing about such an instrument, and Father Didaco had learned not only to play but to harmonize the various chords.

Contrary to the wishes of the Fathers, before beginning their lessons, the music pupils insisted upon going through the ceremonies, which are customary when a teacher meets new pupils, or rather when pupils select a new teacher. They asked Father Didaco to teach them with patience but with diligence, and not to become impatient if he found them slow to learn this art, hitherto unknown to them. Afterwards they went through the same ceremony with the clavichord, for an assurance of progress, as if it had been a living thing. Before

2. Probably the *p'i-p'a.*
3. The *sheng.*

long the Europeans were being entertained at meals and visited by some of the eunuchs in high position. Gradually they became known to the whole palace retinue with some of whom they formed permanent friendships. . . .

Each of the clavichord pupils was content with learning one piece. Two of the younger ones were apt enough at learning, but they waited for the others to complete the course, and so the time allotted for lessons was drawn out for more than a month. They were quite interested in having the pieces they were playing put to Chinese words, and Father Matthew took this occasion to compose eight pieces which he called "Songs for the Clavichord." These were lyrics, touching upon ethical subjects, teaching lessons of good morals and virtues, and aptly illustrated with quotations from Christian authors. These songs became so popular that numerous requests from the literati were received, asking for copies of them, and giving high praise to the lessons they taught. They said that these songs reminded the King that he should govern the realm with the virtues suggested in the songs, and in order to satisfy the demand for copies of them, the Fathers printed them, together with other pieces, as a musical booklet, written in European lettering and also in Chinese characters.[4]

4. On these songs and Ricci's use of music in his Christianizing effort see Jonathan D. Spence, *The Memory Palace of Matteo Ricci* (New York: Viking, 1984), pp. 197–200.

IV

THE BAROQUE ERA

Edited by MARGARET MURATA

INTRODUCTION

*T*he writing of music histories begins as a history of musical scores. The histories of Baroque music that were standard around 1950[1] relied on a number of important musical prints. The earliest of these—the elegant original publications of works by Peri, Caccini, Cavalieri, and Viadana—introduced a shorthand notation for basso continuo accompaniment and announced music that was new in harmony, rhythm, melody, and expression. To present the later phases of the Baroque, however, musicologists turned to the published "monuments" of music undertaken in the nineteenth century, such as Friedrich Chrysander's edition of Handel's works, published between 1858 and 1902; the Purcell Society's series, begun in 1878; the complete works of Corelli that Joseph Joachim and Chrysander edited between 1871 and 1891; Philip Spitta's edition of Schütz, begun in 1885; the Rameau edition begun by Camille Saint-Saëns in 1895; and of course, the original Bach Society collection of J. S. Bach's works, issued between 1851 and 1900. For the first edition of *Source Readings in Music History,* Oliver Strunk chose nineteen readings that dated from the years 1600 to 1725 to show the bases on which knowledge of such scores became part of a broader musical knowledge of the era in which opera and oratorio were invented, large-scale instrumental music evolved, and instruments and voices were indissolubly joined in public and private spaces.

Since the 1950s the repertory of music composed between 1600 and the mid-eighteenth century has been much expanded by the further exploration of musical sources, particularly for opera after 1640 and for keyboard music. These sources, mostly in manuscript, have become increasingly available in facsimile and in professional, recorded performances. The readings that Strunk offered are more meaningful today, when we can hear performances of Lully that give us a convincing idea of what it was that the nobleman Jean Laurent Le Cerf de la Viéville was defending when he championed French music over Italian, and when we can hear a continuo ensemble with the instruments that Agostino Agazzari described—citterns, Baroque harps, and a battery of lutes. We now also have performances of operas by Cesti and Purcell, of French lute and gamba suites, and of church cantatas by Buxtehude.

1. For example, Hugo Riemann, *Handbuch der Musikgeschichte,* vol. 2, *Das Generalbasszeitalter,* 2d ed. (Leipzig, 1922); Robert Haas, *Die Musik des Barocks* (Potsdam, 1928), Manfred Bukofzer, *Music in the Baroque Era* (New York, Norton, 1947). The second edition of the *Oxford History of Music* was begun in 1929.

The present collection of readings from what has traditionally been called the Baroque era reflects this increased accessibility to the repertory and includes more texts dating from the years 1650 to 1690 and 1723 to 1751. But the primary aim of this revised selection is not to provide a greater number of documents about a greater number of composers or musical genres and performances. Rather, it gives voice to the wide range of people who were intensely engaged in creating and thinking about music during a period of much change and controversy. The writing of music histories only begins with the study of scores and with accounts of people, places, and performances. The historian also seeks to find out how it came about that musicians did what they did and, if possible, why. The historian also wants to know what listeners of the past thought they were hearing and what it meant to them. The category "listeners," in this regard, always includes professional musicians with their expert ears, such as Pierfrancesco Tosi, a castrato who sang in London beginning in 1693, and Johann Mattheson, *Capellmeister* to a duke, two authors newly included here. But also to be counted as listeners are the gentleman viol player, the Sunday worshiper, the young princess at court eager to gain attention by her dancing, and the nobleman who held a box in a Venetian theater.

We can hear from such listeners because, during the seventeenth and eighteenth centuries, music became on the whole a more public affair and of greater social interest, more a subject for conversation and more likely to be written about, than it had been before. In fact, were the epithet "Baroque" not so common, several developments in musical life in these centuries could justify a label for the era that is less related to style, such as the historians' "early modern."[2] For not only were musical genres for public consumption established, such as opera and the concerto, but with them the foundations were laid for musical institutions such as the public concert and subscription opera theater that we now take for granted. Although many performers continued to serve noble patrons and religious establishments, the scope of the profession expanded considerably, as did its economic base. Several of the readings document these developments: a contract for an opera singer, the revised guild statutes for the instrumentalists of Paris, and a firsthand account of a concert series that began in London in the 1680s. The new public venues fostered the growth of music criticism, that is, writing about music by listeners, as opposed to the treatises by and for composers that had been more common earlier. *Amateurs* and critics are represented here by opera-goers such as François Raguenet, Joseph Addison, and the anonymous Italian "Truthful Reporter." We also hear from Grazioso Uberti, a jurist; Francesco Coli, a priest working for the Inquisition; society reporter Jean Loret; Roger North, once attorney general to the Queen of England; and Lady Mary Wortley Montagu, wife of an ambassador to the Ottoman Empire. Lady Mary excepted, none of these is a

---

2. For an assessment of what the word "Baroque" has come to mean in recent scholarship and a justification for its continued use, see Rosario Villari's introduction to his *Baroque Personae*, trans. L. G. Cochrane (Chicago: University of Chicago Press, 1995).

writer of recognized literary quality, yet each speaks for passionate listeners and for accomplished nonprofessionals and their private music-making at home.

Listeners have an important place in studies of Baroque music for several reasons. First of all, the ear was considered an important organ of learning, creativity, and judgment by the modernists of Monteverdi's generation. Controversies over the authority of the senses as against the authority of reason (which underlay the rules of musical composition) marked the opening of the era and persisted in diverse forms with different advocates well into the eighteenth century. Equally important was improvisation, which was called for in varying degrees in most Baroque genres, engaging performer and listener on a plane of immediacy. Furthermore, much that was considered modern in the first decades after 1600 arose from improvisational practice, as composers captured in score what had been enjoyed—or just tolerated—as transient or incidental in performance. The new scores, however, still left much unwritten. The twentieth-century's exploration of how to perform Baroque music exposed the range of what was not indicated in vocal scores or in the challenging array of music for many different kinds of instruments. The variability in what a Baroque score can suggest to performers (and to scholars) has delighted the ears of many and irritated those of others.

With the exception of music for unaccompanied solo instruments and for viol consorts, what we now call Baroque music has one element in common, the continuo bass line. Questions about the variety of instruments that played continuo and how harmonies were filled in by continuo players forced modern scholar-performers to seek answers outside of the scores. The search also led to information about tuning and temperament, bowing, rhythm and tempo, voice production, tonguing, and always, the which, how, how much, and when of improvising embellishments. With the information retrieved from the past, modern performers and instrument builders reconstructed and experimented with the same zeal for discovery that had inspired Italians of the early Baroque to try to recover the lost sounds of ancient Greek music. With all the many variables, music that might have been familiar to an audience in 1950 could easily have sounded less so in 1970 and different again in 1995.

Thus the core of any set of readings related to music of the "figured-bass era" and the starting point for any modern performer of its repertory must be the evidence for performance practices of the time. Tracing how this evidence has been transformed into performance over the last seventy years or so demonstrates how very little in the tutorial texts is prescriptive. The pursuit of information about performance practices is often regarded as a search for historical authenticity. Its intellectual value, however, has been in helping to analyze the indeterminate, creative relationship between performer and score—for the score of a Baroque composition is not a set of instructions from composer to performer. Following every rule and recommendation in historical tutors no more makes an accomplished performer of Baroque music than lead sheets and published instruction books on how to play jazz can produce a

player who can swing, improvise, and jam. And just as Louis Armstrong and
Miles Davis did not share exactly the same rhythmic, melodic, and harmonic
language, so suggestions for an ensemble in 1620 do not necessarily apply to
one in 1690. Section 4 of this collection, therefore, offers readings that sketch
general areas of performance that concern the Baroque repertory and that
exemplify some of the basic kinds of initiatives expected of performers. From
these the modern reader may gain a sense of the highly articulated and modulated shapes that seventeenth- and eighteenth-century listeners heard. What
the music historian Robert Haas had in his ear when he wrote about Monteverdi or Couperin in the 1920s was different from what we may hear on the
latest recordings, because modern performers have continually returned to and
reinterpreted the basic source readings on performance practices.

Given the multitude of handbooks and tutors that address idioms of performance by genre or national origin (many now available in facsimile and translation), Strunk's original selection of readings on performance practice has been
expanded only slightly. In cases where more modern, annotated translations
have appeared, for example, Caccini's instructions on singing in *Le nuove
musiche,* the reading given here may be shorter than Strunk's. The earliest
addition in this area is a set of excerpts from the anonymous treatise *The Choragus,* which came to light only in the 1980s. It is a comprehensive guide to
mounting works for the stage before the institution of the Venetian subscription theaters. The treatise covers all conceivable facets of production and gives
concrete demonstration of the high level of polish and elegant coordination
that the earliest producers of court opera expected to achieve. Gambist Christopher Simpson describes the elements of ensemble improvisation, revealing a
concern for the shape of the emerging composition that clearly takes its effect
on its listeners into account. Nothing in Lorenzo Penna's 1672 precepts for
continuo realization changed Agazzari's advice of sixty-five years earlier, but the
new contrapuntal and harmonic styles of the later seventeenth century
required additional instructions. To learn the "style, sweetness, ornaments, and
graces" of good singing, Penna charged students of voice to listen to good
singers. In fact, most of the musicians whose writings appear in this section
assumed that what they were explaining could be heard by their readers somewhere in live performance.

This was not the case with Georg Muffat's instructions. Like Schütz before
him and unlike the other writers on performance skills, Muffat's musical training was international. He provided his anthologies of suites for string ensembles (with continuo) with detailed instructions for their stylish execution in a
manner of playing that he knew was still foreign in the Germany of the 1690s.
His specific demonstrations of bowing indicate a highly articulated mode of
delivery that may also be foreign to students of the modern violin but that
helps us hear string compositions of his time in something like their varied
original voices. Knowing that the same rhythmic figure aims for a different
musical effect in Caccini than it does in Schubert or that a series of pitches can
be taken in six bow strokes rather than with one change of the bow alters one's

conception of the physical quality of the musical rhythm and phrasing. Such differences affect many aspects of performance, from the possible tempos for a composition to its dynamic shaping, and they influence the perceived expressive content of a score.

Arousing the passions through music was one of the aims of Baroque performers and composers alike. Pietro de' Bardi described how Jacopo Peri "sweetened" the "roughness and excessive antiquity" of the earliest examples of the new Florentine *stile rappresentativo* and in so doing "made it capable of moving the affections in a rare manner." In 1616 Claudio Monteverdi expressed little desire to compose music for a libretto that he felt did not bring him "in a natural progression to a conclusion that moved" him. Nearly a century later, Le Cerf de la Viéville spoke of the musician's "rekindling" the fire of feelings and of burning passions "with tones of quickening precision." For Tosi, writing in 1723, a pathetic aria rendered by a fine singer could cause "a human soul . . . to melt into tenderness and tears, from the violent motion of the affections." Though he criticized the succession of arias in the Italian operas he heard in 1697 as incoherent, the Frenchman François Raguenet acknowledged that they were declarations "of happy lovers, or complaints of the unfortunate; protestations of fidelity, or stings of jealousy; raptures of pleasure or pangs of sorrow, rage, and despair." Mattheson's statement in *The Complete Music Director* of 1739 that "the true goal of all melody can only be a type of diversion of the hearing through which the passions of the soul are stirred" would have been agreeable to almost all the writers represented here. For Rameau, even single chords and progressions of chords could express sadness, tenderness, gaiety, and surprise.

For some composers and listeners, music gained expressive force when it imitated speech. Rhythm and pitch, along with the emphases and phrasing produced by chord changes (and which are absent from speech), were considered resources for creating the oratorical delivery of a text. Their expressive effectiveness was tied to the aural cues specific to the language of the text and its literary genre. The readings by Peri and Le Cerf de la Viéville and a few comments by librettist Pier Jacopo Martello illustrate this theory, which exploits both the verbal efficacy of poetry and the musical power of its poetic rhythms and implied vocal intonations. The Frenchman avows that "the single secret is to apply such proportionate tones to the words [in an opera] that the verse is indistinguishable from and lives again in the music. This carries the feeling of all that the singer says right to the heart of the listener." In commenting on two lines from Lully's opera *Armide*, he exclaims, "What a passage! Each tone so fits each word that together they create an unmistakable impression on the soul of the listener."[3]

Other composers sought musical figures that could suggest or communicate a state of being by imitating aspects of human behavior other than vocal com-

---

3. In his letter to Monsieur de la °°° in the *Comparaison de la musique italienne et de la musique françoise* (Brussels, 1705), pp. 169, 173–74.

munication. Monteverdi's preface to his eighth book of madrigals of 1638 expresses his satisfaction at finding a musical equivalent of the *concitato,* or "excited," species of emotion by using rapidly repeating sixteenth notes in the instruments, which were accompanied by "words expressing anger and disdain." Modern listeners take the expressiveness of such kinesthetic imitation in music so much for granted that it is difficult to think of it as an accomplishment of the age, or to hear in Monteverdi a prefiguration of the improvisations for silent film by theater organists three centuries later. Instrumental music also came to portray feelings, as dance in the seventeenth century became increasingly imitative of character. A skilled dancer, wrote Abbé Michel de Pure in 1668, should be able "to give someone enraged an abrupt and fiery dance from which one can perceive the disorder of the character and his distraction." To portray a lover, the dancer would express "the various alterations that love, infirmity, chagrin, or joy can cause on the face or on other parts that seem the most affected by interior feelings." De Pure described how movements "pass through the body according to the disquiets and various agitations of the soul, which signify, against our own will, the interior feelings that we strive to hide and to keep secret."[4] The dancer then coordinates these movements to the concept of the dance and to the rhythm of the music. (For de Pure, this would have been music that Louis XIV's ensemble of "Twenty-Four Violins" played for the court ballets.) Resemblance or imitation, then, is the adaptation in art of those movements that proceed from feelings, which in France were identified as the passions and in Italy as the affections. These passions are within us—in the soul or the mind—and so can be detected or perceived only when they "move," causing the body to move.[5] A reciprocal mechanism occurs when an imitation or resemblance "arouses" the passions and causes the receiver to sense that excitation as a motion, or, in other words, as an emotion.

Modern science seeks these "motions" in electrochemical patterns of neurons firing in the brain. In the seventeenth century, the passions were associated with the four liquid humors of the body: phlegm, black bile, choler (also called yellow bile), and blood. These were held to correspond to four principal temperaments, or personalities: the phlegmatic, or slow and stolid person; the melancholy; the choleric, or hot-tempered; and the sanguine or cheerful. Yet though the sources of expression were fixed, their variety was not. Mattheson, for example, is able to characterize even "little, disesteemed dance melodies" with a happy assortment of moods: tender longing, dogged seriousness, pomp and conceit, agreeable joking, contentment and pleasantness, vacillation and instability, ardor and passion, and so forth. The different proportions, furthermore, of the four humors in each individual were considered to influence what motions would be perceived as pleasing or displeasing to a person. Athanasius Kircher illustrated some musical preferences, most of which, but not all, sound

4. The brief, localized ornaments of the French style perhaps behave as momentary betrayals of these "disquiets."

5. See also the discussion of imitation and expression by Wye Jamison Allanbrook in the introduction to "The Late Eighteenth Century," pp. 739–43.

utterly commonplace today. That "the melancholy love settings that are grave, dense, and mournful" remains a recognizable stereotype. Why "phlegmatics are affected by high women's voices, inasmuch as the high sound affects the phlegmatic humor favorably" is less obvious. The theory of the time, as Kircher expounded it, also extended from individuals to nations, as location and climate were thought to influence the balance of humors. The Germans, for example, being "born under a frozen sky . . . acquire a temperament that is serious, strong, constant, solid, and toilsome." Accordingly, they favor a musical style that is "serious, moderate, sober, and choral." Raguenet, ecstatic over what he heard as the boldness of Italian music in the late 1690s, attributed its style to the Italian national character, which, "being much more lively than the French," was capable of being moved to express passions in what was for him an extreme fashion.

> If a storm or rage is to be described in a symphony, their notes give us so natural an idea of it that our souls can hardly receive a stronger impression from the reality than they do from the description; everything is so brisk and piercing, so impetuous and affecting, that the imagination, the senses, the soul, and the body itself are all betrayed into a general transport. . . . A symphony of furies shakes the soul; it undermines and overthrows it, in spite of all; the violinist himself, whilst he is performing it, is seized with an unavoidable agony; he tortures his violin; he racks his body; he is no longer master of himself, but is agitated like one possessed with an irresistible motion.

Such reasoning extended to non-Western music as well. In a comparison between the music of Europe and that of the Ottoman court, the essayist Charles Fonton acknowledged that the Persian, Turkish, and Arabic music that he heard in Istanbul was passionate and moving. But, "adapted to the Asiatic genius, it is like the nation, soft and languorous, without energy and strength." Fonton asserted that "European ears require the strongest impressions, the most manly sounds and the most muscular, less of the melancholy and more of the gay. The people of the Orient are susceptible to the opposite sentiments."

Such general notions of how the era understood feelings to be expressions of character are essential for us to imagine their translation into music; for not to be found in this set of readings is any presentation of *Affektenlehre* as a musical "doctrine of the affections" more specific than the general beliefs about the perception of emotion. George Buelow convincingly demonstrated in 1983 that "this frequently misused word is apparently unknown in the musical literature of the Baroque."[6]

The seventeenth century faced many philosophical and moral issues with regard to representation and expression. Does an emotion generated by the operation of an imitation have a different status from one aroused by some other means? At the beginning of the seventeenth century, even language itself could be distrusted as a mode of representation. Philosophers and poets alike

6. George J. Buelow, "Johann Mattheson and the Invention of the *Affektenlehre*" in *New Mattheson Studies*, ed. George J. Buelow and Hans Joachim Marx (Cambridge: Cambridge University Press, 1983), pp. 393–407.

wrestled or played with the unreliability of language, treating it as a form of presentation not always congruent with reality.[7] Monteverdi's great critic Artusi believed that the senses were fallible. He disprized the new music for its appeal to and dependence on the senses and its attempt to be one, as it were, with poetic language. But the main fault of the new music, in his view, was its divergence from a rational system of harmony and counterpoint that was self-contained and not a representation of anything. If Renaissance counterpoint was correct, it was true.[8] The task that presented itself to the Baroque was to remove the uncertain status of representation, to turn it as closely as possible into "the real." Early science would do this by eventually converting perception into mathematical "proof." Raguenet wrote of a musical storm that made as much of an impression on the senses as a real storm, an impression that carried away "the imagination, the senses, the soul and even the body." In short time, *opera seria* would obviate any such betrayal of the senses, by offering such vivid musical portrayals within a higher ordering.[9] In *opera seria*, the representations of passions were collected and presented together in any opera as if each aria were a reference, an infinitely reproducible citation of a representation akin to a mathematical term, and not the thing itself. With this status, the arias could be safely acknowledged as "real," that is, as real portraits. Furthermore, the mechanism that was the libretto structure of the *opera seria*, based on the placement of arias within it, constituted its own discourse, free of any requirement to resemble "the real." When the librettist Martello described entrance, intermediate, and exit arias, his comment on the exit aria was "whether it is verisimilar is not material." Musical and, to an extent, narrative representation was thus subsumed in a methodical process that could lead no one astray. Moreover, after Rameau's proofs of their rational foundations, the procedures of tonal harmony restored the certainty of system to musical composition. Artusi's dilemma may be considered resolved in a statement such as

7. As expressed by Louis Marin: "Did not words, written or oral, interpose their own opacity between the reader and his visual experience of the world?" See his essay "Mimésis et description, ou de la curiosité à la méthode de l'âge de Montaigne à celui de Descartes" in *Documentary Culture: Florence and Rome from Grand-Duke Ferdinand I to Pope Alexander VII*, Villa Spelman Colloquia, vol. 3 (Bologna: Nuova Alfa Editoriale, 1992), pp. 23–47. In the first half of the century dissemblance and dissimulation are persistent topics. They are the weapons and defenses of the courtier, the illusions that keep human souls from God's grace. Many plays and operas turn on the unmasking of disguises or unknown identities. The importance of distrust was encapsulated in Descartes's first rule from his *Discourse on Method:* "The first rule was never to accept anything as true unless I recognized it to be evidently such."

8. See *Artusi, or the Imperfections of Modern Music* (Venice, 1600), especially p. 44; also Gary Tomlinson's introduction to "The Renaissance," pp. 285–87. For the seventeenth century, it took a Descartes to set aside the unreliability of both sense and reason and invent (or reinvent) the possibility of a nearly closed system of certainties.

9. The distinction between the reality of imitation and its intermediary status as representation is more marked in the language of Raguenet's translator, who renders "que souvent la réalité n'agit pas plus fortement sur l'ame" as "that our Souls can hardly receive a stronger Impression from the Reality than they do from the Description," and "que l'imagination, les sens, l'ame, & le corps même en sont entraînez d'un commun transport" as "that Imagination, . . . and the Body it self are all betray'd into a general Transport."

"Sweetness and tenderness are sometimes well enough expressed by prepared minor dissonances" from Rameau's *Treatise on Harmony.*

On its way from Artusi to Rameau, the Baroque was highly conscious of musical change and dealt with it in polemical exchanges, in the writing of music histories, and by the revival and maintenance of the music of its own past. The articulate and informative defenses of the moderns by Pietro della Valle and others that appeared in the 1640s[10] indicate that the most recent battle between the ancients and moderns in Italy had long since been won. In 1649 Marco Scacchi averred that "abandoning this modern style would be to destroy a large part of music, and indeed, it would be reduced to its first poverty."[11] Subsequent changes in musical style can be marked as each new cohort of moderns took hold. In the 1690s Muffat helped introduce the French ballet style of Lully to his German-speaking colleagues. In France itself, Le Cerf de la Viéville rose to defend Lully in 1704 against the proponents of contemporary Italian music. (The first French history of music appeared soon after, in 1715.)[12] By 1739, however, Mattheson is warning German composers that many of their French counterparts imitate the Italians too closely and that models of the newest *modern* style of melody, which was simple and natural, should be found by looking *back* to Lully.[13] Tosi in 1723 declared that the first composers "which pleased on the stage and in the chamber" were Piersimone Agostini (d. 1680) and Alessandro Stradella (d. 1682). These were Tosi's "ancients"; after them, he believed that his own generation had achieved a classic musical perfection against which he harshly criticized modern, contemporary singers and those who composed for them. Tosi in fact became a member of the first Academy of Ancient Music in London, whose first session indeed programmed a composition by Stradella, along with even more "ancient" works by Luca Marenzio.[14]

The treatment of differences in European music extended to the ways in which music of non-Europeans could be regarded. Fonton's essentialist explanation of why music of the East differed from the Europeans' has already been cited, but it is an "ancients versus moderns" perspective that underlay many comparative judgments between them. Both Fonton and Lady Mary Wortley Montagu heard and saw traces of pagan antiquity in Ottoman music. In Fonton's modernist view, the presence of these traces symptomized the slowness

---

10. Such as Della Valle's discourse arguing that "The music of our ages is not all inferior, but rather is better, than that of the past age," excerpted in No. 84 below, and the *Breve discorso sopra la musica moderna* by Marco Scacchi (Warsaw, 1649), translated by Tim Carter in *Polemics on the 'Musica Moderna'* (Cracow: Musica Jagellonica, 1993), pp. 31–69.

11. Scacchi, *Breve discorso*, ibid., p. 65.

12. The *Histoire de la musique et de ses effets depuis son origine jusqu'à present*, published by Jacques Bonnet from materials collected by Pierre Bourdelot and Pierre Bonnet-Bourdelot (Paris, 1715).

13. Mattheson, *Der vollkommene Capellmeister,* trans. Ernest Harriss (Ann Arbor: UMI Research Press, 1981), pt. 2, 5:60–63.

14. Marenzio died in 1599. For an account of the Academy see William Weber, *The Rise of Musical Classics in Eighteenth-Century England, A Study in Canon, Ritual, and Ideology* (Oxford: Clarendon Press, 1992), especially pp. 56–74.

of development in that region of the world. When Jean-Baptiste Du Halde related how the Chinese imperial court first encountered Western music notation, he could not hide his belief that notation is a practical invention of a creative civilization. In one aspect, however, he was forced to place China ahead of Europe on the wheel of progress. Because he considered the lack of counterpoint a defect in Chinese music, he speculated that its monophonic state could have resulted from the *degeneration* of Chinese music over the ages. For the Englishman Richard Ligon, the music of the African slaves that he heard on Barbados lacked melody. Though he was clearly taken by the drum ensembles, he nonetheless felt that he could have given the Africans "some hints of tune, which being understood, would have serv'd as a great addition to their harmony." Lady Mary's writing serves as an antidote to such views of cultural progress. We recognize what a quick ear she must have had, as she tells of joining in Greek dances as if participating in ancient rites, recognizes the spirituality of Sufi religious dancing, and compares the artful singing she heard in the chambers of Istanbul to the English air and Italian aria—not always to London's advantage. Writing in the form of letters, she was not obliged to edify her readers and offer descriptions intended to serve as exemplars. Nonetheless the vividness and sense of presentness in her accounts succeed in making her points of view seem to be the only ones possible for an enlightened and educated individual to hold. This gives Lady Mary no less a didactic responsibility than the authors in this collection who were teachers, proponents, and persuaders, whether ancient or modern.

• • •

The work of many scholars and scholar-performers has influenced this revision of *Source Readings* for the Baroque era. Among those who helped with translation and gave firm advice about particulars in the sources are Claude V. Palisca, Tim Carter, Giuseppina La Face, Luigi Rovighi, Eleanor Selfridge-Field, Beth Glixon, T. Frank Kennedy, Thomas J. Mathiesen, Dinko Fabris, John Hill, Rebecca Harris-Warrick, Ernest Harriss, Richard Charteris, Frederick Lau, Theodore N. Foss, and Judy Ho. Of those who helped with the search for the new contents, I wish also to acknowledge Laurence Dreyfus, who first undertook this project, Lowell Lindgren, Suzanne Cusick, Linda Austern, Robert Garfias, and Richard Crawford. Thanks for assistance are also due to the staffs of the William Andrews Clark Memorial Library at the University of California, Los Angeles, and the Interlibrary Loan Department and the Thesaurus Linguae Graecae at the University of California, Irvine.

I apologize to Hispanists for the continued absence of historical sources from Spain and its far-flung colonies. Other omissions and all errors are attributable to this editor's oversight or intransigence. For inspiration and encouragement I am in debt to Leo Treitler, the general editor of this series, and owe him a thousand thanks for his patience and unfailing acumen. The emphasis in this set of readings on music as an art of performance pays tribute to my late teacher but everpresent guide, Howard Mayer Brown.

ANCIENT MUSIC
AND MODERN

81 Pietro de' Bardi

In the 1570s, a circle of nobles, scholars, and musicians of Florence, Italy began to formulate a theoretical concept of expressive music through their study of the musical thought of the ancient Greeks and Romans, against which they measured the music of their own time and found it lacking. This group, or "camerata," met at the home of Giovanni de' Bardi, Count of Vernio (1534–1612), who became a promoter of reforms in singing, musical composition, and the staging of tragedy. Beginning in the 1580s, the group's theories of ancient music helped produce such new works as the monodies of Giulio Caccini and the first operas.

One of the earliest historians of this new music was the antiquarian and scholar Giovanni Battista Doni (1594–1647), who asked for a firsthand account of the Florentine Camerata from Bardi's son, Pietro. Born before 1570, son like father had been a member of an academy, the Alterati, with strong musical interests. As one of the founders of another academy, the Accademia della Crusca, he oversaw the first editions of the frequently revised and most authoritative dictionary of the Italian language. He continued his writing and other activities into the 1640s and died shortly after 1660. It should be noted that Bardi's reply to Doni recalls events that had occured almost half a century earlier.

Letter to Giovanni Battista Doni
(1634)

My Most Illustrious and Revered Patron, the most honored Giovan Battista Doni:

My father, Signor Giovanni, who took great delight in music and was in his day a composer of some reputation, always had about him the most celebrated men of the city, learned in this profession, and inviting them to his house, he formed a sort of delightful and continual academy from which vice and in particular every kind of gaming were absent. To this the noble youth of Florence were attracted with great profit to themselves, passing their time not only in pursuit of music, but also in discussing and receiving instruction in poetry, astrology, and other sciences which by turns lent value to this pleasant conversation.

Vincenzo Galilei, the father of the present famous astronomer and a man of certain repute in those days, was so taken with this distinguished assembly that, adding to practical music, in which he was highly regarded, the study of musical theory, he endeavored, with the help of these virtuosi and of his own frequent

TEXT: Angelo Solerti, *Le origini del melodramma* (Turin, 1903; repr. Bologna, 1969), pp. 143–47; translation by Oliver Strunk. Solerti also lists earlier editions. Doni made extensive use of this letter in chapter 9 of his *Treatise on Theatrical Music* (Florence, 1763, also in Solerti).

vigils, to extract the essence of the Greek, the Latin, and the more modern writers and by this means became a thorough master of the theory of every sort of music.

This great intellect recognized that, besides restoring ancient music insofar as so obscure a subject permitted, one of the chief aims of the academy was to improve modern music and to raise it in some degree from the wretched state to which it had been reduced, chiefly by the Goths, after the loss of the ancient music and the other liberal arts and sciences. Thus he was the first to let us hear singing in *stile rappresentativo,* in which arduous undertaking—then considered almost ridiculous—he was chiefly encouraged and assisted by my father, who toiled for entire nights and incurred great expense for the sake of this noble discovery, as the said Vincenzo gratefully acknowledges to my father in his learned book on ancient and modern music.[1] Accordingly he let us hear the lament of Count Ugolino, from Dante,[2] intelligibly sung by a good tenor and precisely accompanied by a consort of viols. This novelty, although it aroused considerable envy among the professional musicians, was pleasing to the true lovers of the art. Continuing with this undertaking, Galilei set to music a part of the Lamentations and Responds of Holy Week, and these were sung in devout company in the same manner.

Giulio Caccini, considered a rare singer and a man of taste, although very young, was at this time in my father's *camerata,* and feeling himself inclined toward this new music, he began, entirely under my father's instructions to sing ariettas, sonnets, and other poems suitable for being heard, to a single instrument and in a manner that astonished his hearers.

Also in Florence at this time was Jacopo Peri, who, as the first pupil of Cristofano Malvezzi, received high praise as a player of the organ and the keyboard instruments and as a composer of counterpoint, and he was rightly regarded as second to none of the singers in that city. This man, in competition with Giulio, brought the enterprise of the *stile rappresentativo* to light, and avoiding a certain roughness and excessive antiquity that had been felt in the compositions of Galilei, he, together with Giulio, sweetened this style and made it capable of moving the affections in a rare manner, as in the course of time was done by them both.

By so doing, these men acquired the title of the first singers and inventors of this manner of composing and singing. Peri had more science, and having found a way of imitating familiar speech by using few sounds,[3] and by meticulous exactness in other respects, he won great fame. Giulio's inventions had more elegance.

The first poem to be sung on the stage in *stile rappresentativo* was the *Story*

1. Vincenzo Galilei, *Dialogo della musica antica e della moderna* (Venice, 1581).

2. *Inferno,* canto 33, lines 4–75.

3. "Ricercar poche corde," which implies restriction to a narrow range of notes, can be understood as applying to the melodic range of the vocal line.

of Daphne by Signor Ottavio Rinuccini, set to music by Peri with a limited range of pitches, in short scenes, and recited and sung privately in a small room.[4] I was left speechless with amazement. It was sung to the accompaniment of a consort of instruments, an arrangement followed thereafter in the other comedies.[5] Caccini and Peri were under great obligation to Signor Ottavio but under still greater to Signor Jacopo Corsi,[6] who, becoming ardent and discontent with all but the superlative in this art, directed these composers with excellent ideas and marvelous doctrines, as befitted so noble an enterprise. These directions were carried out by Peri and Caccini in all their compositions of this sort and were combined by them in various manners.

After the *Dafne,* many stories were represented by Signor Ottavio himself, who, as good poet and good musician in one, was received with great applause, as was the affable Corsi, who supported the enterprise with a lavish hand. The most famous of these stories were the *Euridice* and the *Arianna;*[7] Besides these, many shorter ones were set to music by Caccini and Peri. Nor was there any want of men to imitate them, and in Florence, the first home of this sort of music, and in other cities of Italy, especially in Rome, these gave and are still giving a marvelous account of themselves on the dramatic stage. Among the foremost of these it seems fitting to place Monteverdi.

I fear that I have badly carried out Your Most Reverend Lordship's command, not only because I have been slow to obey Your Lordship, but also because I have far from satisfied myself, for there are few now living who remember the music of those times. Nonetheless I believe that as I serve You with heartfelt affection, so will the truth be confirmed of my small selection from the many things that might be said about this style of *musica rappresentativa,* which is in such esteem.

But I hope that I shall in some way be excused through the kindness of Your Most Excellent Lordship, to whom I wish a most happy Christmas and pray that God, father of all blessings, grant perfect felicity.

Florence, December 16, 1634
Your Very Illustrious and Reverend Lordship's most humble servant,
Pietro Bardi, Count of Vernio

4. For the involved history of this work, see Warren Kirkendale, *The Court Musicians in Florence during the Principate of the Medici* (Florence: L. S. Olschki, 1993), pp. 194–204. Peri himself sang the role of Apollo. Six excerpts from the score survive; see Kirkendale, p. 200.
5. "Comedy" was a general term during the period for any staged work with words, whether spoken or with music, whether serious, allegorical, humorous, etc.
6. See further reference to this influential patron and amateur by Peri in No. 107 below.
7. The separate settings of Rinuccini's *Euridice* by Peri and by Caccini, and Monteverdi's *Arianna* of 1608.

82 Giovanni Maria Artusi

Music theorists of the Renaissance traditionally wrote about the physics of sound, tuning, and musical composition in terms of pitch relations and drew upon examples of sacred polyphonic music for illustration. But at the end of the sixteenth century, new musical practices that were flourishing in polyphonic as well as in solo genres had gone beyond the foundations established by the Renaissance contrapuntists. In a set of dialogues published in 1600, Giovanni Maria Artusi (1546–1613), an Augustinian monk, attempted to point out the imperfections in the modern music he was hearing. The responses from the defenders of modern music forced him to issue a second part to his treatise, which he published in 1603. Artusi may also have been the "Antonio Braccino da Todi" who wrote two further critiques of the moderns. The first of these is lost; the second, published in 1608, addresses Giulio Cesare Monteverdi's defense of his brother Claudio's music (see No. 3 below) in response to Artusi's scrutiny in 1600 of Claudio's modernist "errors" in the five-voice madrigal "Cruda Amarilli."

In this part of the dialogue, the speaker Luca understands certain free, modern dissonances as examples of the kind of expressive graces that singers or instrumentalists often improvised in performance. The conservative Vario examines the voice leading in Monteverdi's madrigal and argues that no amount of looking for such musical figures as *accenti* or *portar la voce* can reveal any underlying contrapuntal structure that is regular and in conformance with good harmonic ratios. He accuses the moderns of relying on the ear alone, which, without intellect, may be fooled in its judgment. Although this is but one aspect of his extensive arguments, and though Luca's observations were written by Artusi, the examination of "Cruda Amarilli" reveals the profound difference in how the old and new practices regarded the nature of the musical object. In Artusi's view, much of modern music was defective, irrespective of its aims.

FROM *Artusi, or, Of the Imperfections of Modern Music*

(1600)

SECOND DISCOURSE

LUCA: Yesterday, sir, after I had left Your Lordship and was going toward the piazza, I was invited by some gentlemen to hear certain new madrigals.

TEXT: *L'Artusi overo Delle imperfettioni della moderna musica* (Venice, 1600; facs. Bologna, 1968), fols. 39–44. Translation by Oliver Strunk, revised by Margaret Murata.

Delighted by the amiability of my friends and by the newness of the compositions, I accompanied them to the house of Signor Antonio Goretti, a nobleman
of Ferrara, a young virtuoso and as great a lover of musicians as any man I
have ever known. I found there Signor Luzzasco and Signor Hippolito Fiorini,[1]
distinguished men, with whom had assembled many noble spirits, versed in
music. The madrigals were sung and repeated, but without giving the name of
the author. The texture *(tessitura)* was not unpleasing, even if, as Your Lordship
will see, it introduces new rules, new modes, and new turns of phrase. These
were, however, harsh and little pleasing to the ear, nor could they be otherwise;
for so long as they violate the good rules—in part founded upon experience,
the mother of all things, in part observed in nature, and in part proved by
demonstration—we must believe them deformations of the nature and propriety of true harmony, far removed from the musician's goal, which, as Your
Lordship said yesterday, is delectation.

But, in order that you may see the whole question and give me your opinion,
here are the passages, scattered here and there through the above-mentioned
madrigals, which I wrote out yesterday evening for my amusement.[2]

VARIO: Signor Luca, you bring me new things which astonish me not a little.
It pleases me, at my age, to see a new method of composing, though it would
please me much more if I saw that these passages were founded upon some
reason which could satisfy the intellect. But as castles in the air, chimeras
founded upon sand, these novelties do not please me; they deserve blame, not
praise. Let us see the passages, however.[3]

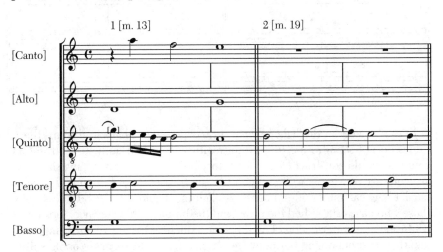

1. Goretti, Luzzaschi and Fiorini were, of course, real persons, prominent in the musical life of
   Ferrara. Luzzaschi, in particular, is cited by Monteverdi as one of those who "renewed" the
   "Second Practice." See No. 83 below. p. 540.
2. Luca put separate parts into score.
3. These musical examples are from "Cruda Amarilli," later published in 1603 in Claudio Monteverdi's *Fifth Book of Madrigals a 5.* Artusi's excerpts differ in a few minor points from the
   published version.

LUCA: Indeed, in the light of what little experience I have in this art, these things do not seem to me to be things with which their authors or inventors could or should construct even a four-story house, as they say, seeing that they are contrary to what is well and good in the institution of harmony. They are harsh to the ear, rather offending than delighting it; and to the good rules left by those who have established the order and the bounds of this science, they bring confusion and imperfection of no little consequence. Instead of enriching, augmenting, and ennobling harmony by various means, as so many noble spirits have done, they bring it to such estate that the beautiful and purified style is indistinguishable from the barbaric. And all the while they continue to excuse these things by various arguments in conformity with the style.

VARIO: You say well. But how can they excuse and defend these imperfections, which could not possibly be more absurd?

LUCA: Absurd? I do not know how you can defend that opinion of yours. They call absurd the things composed in another style and would have it that this is the true method of composition, declaring that this novelty and new order of composing is about to produce many effects which ordinary music, full of so many and such sweet harmonies, cannot and never will produce. And they will have it that the sense, hearing such asperities, will be moved and will do marvelous things.

VARIO: Are you in earnest or are you mocking me?

LUCA: Am I in earnest? It is rather they who mock those who hold otherwise.

VARIO: Since I see that you are not joking, I will tell you what I think, but take note that I shall not be so ready to yield to their opinion. And, for the first argument against them, I tell you that the high is a part of the low and arises from the low and, being a part of it, must continue to be related to it, as to its beginning or as the cloud to the spring from which it is derived. That this is true, the experiment of the monochord will show you. For if two strings of equal length and thickness are stretched over one and the same equal space and tuned perfectly in unison (which is regarded by the musician as a single sound, just as two surfaces which are throughout in contact with each other are regarded by Vitello[4] as a single surface), and if you cut off a part from one of these or bring out a high sound from it by placing a bridge under it, I say that beyond doubt the high will be a part of the low. And if you would know that a part produces the high sound, strike the whole and then the part which is high with respect to the whole, and it will necessarily be related to the low, as the part to the whole or as to its beginning. At the lowest note of the complete system, or of any composition, there may be represented an eye, sending forth various visible rays and regarding all the parts, observing in what proportion they correspond to their beginning and foundation. How then will the first, second, fourth, fifth and the other examples stand, if the higher part has no correspondence or harmonic proportion to the lower?

LUCA: They claim that they do observe harmonic relation, saying that the semiminim [A] in the first example, which is taken after the rest of the same value and which forms a sixteenth[5] with the lower part, would already be dissonant if the cantus were to sing as follows:

for then the tenor, singing the first semiminim an octave lower, would cause the second one, which forms the dissonance, to be heard with it above. Aside from this, they say, since the third of the four semiminims is consonant, what difference can it make if we cause a little more harshness to be heard by con-

4. Erasmus Vitello (Erazm Ciolek), Polish mathematician of the thirteenth century.
5. A major ninth.

verting two semiminims, one consonant, the other dissonant, into one minim wholly dissonant,[6] this is as though we were to sing four semiminims, alternately consonant and dissonant, following the rule for such figures. In this way they make all that they do more gross.

VARIO: Good! I follow you perfectly, and answer that the sense of hearing does not perceive what it does not hear and, not perceiving it, cannot present it to the intellect, there being nothing in the intellect that has not first been perceived by the senses. How absurd it is to say that the tenor sustains a note in one register while the soprano, immediately afterward in a higher register, produces the effect the tenor should have produced! Especially after the rest, how much more evident it is to the ear that the soprano sings a sixteenth and then a fourteenth![7] It is one thing that the ear should hear a dissonance in one part after a rest, another that, when several semiminims are successively taken by step, one after another, one is perceived to be consonant, another dissonant; one thing to hear two semiminims taken by step in the natural way, another to hear a minim, and that taken by leap, in place of the dissonant semiminim. This last offends the ear; the others do not, for the movement is by step.

LUCA: Well said. But they say that all this is called grace and is accented singing.[8]

VARIO: I do not remember having read in any author—and countless excellent ones have written of music—that there is such a thing as accented music. I shall welcome it if you will tell me what it is, according to the pretension of these modern composers.

LUCA: They say that the accents in compositions have a remarkable effect and that these accents occur only when a part ascends to a high note; for example, that when four notes ascend by step, the accent is made on the last note and not on the others, the voice beginning a third lower than the note on which the accent is to be produced and being carried gracefully to its level. But to produce good accord always, this demands the greatest discretion and judgment in the singer for its execution. Here is an example:[9]

6. F against G.

7. Sings a ninth and then a seventh.

8. For a discussion of this musical example in terms of the ornaments called *accenti*, see Claude V. Palisca, "The Artusi-Monteverdi Controversy," in *The New Monteverdi Companion* (London: Faber and Faber, 1985), pp. 130–32. See also the Glossary of Foreign Performance Terms, p. 731.

9. In Artusi's illustration of the *accento*, the ornament appears to "rob" time from the duration of the note to be accented, that is, it is "on the beat." In early seventeenth-century illustrations,

VARIO: I will tell you two things. First, that these words do not explain in clear terms the nature, the peculiarity, and the essence of this manner of accented singing, but seem to be a circumlocution calculated to show, not that they are disposed to regulate all things with rules founded on truth, but rather that they wish to confuse them. We must define what this accent is; then, we shall see whether the parts of our definition are mutually in accord, a thing which I do not know that any serious author has so far done. Second, this manner of singing that you call accented does not assume that the composers will employ barbarisms such as are seen in the examples you show me. It requires that the composers produce good accord (a point which you must note well and above all else) and that the singer use great discretion and judgment in "carrying the voice" *(nel portar la voce)* on such occasions.[10]

And if you tell me that the effect which the tenor produces in the seventh example tends to demonstrate this manner of accented singing, I will reply that since it does not make a good chord and therefore the singer does not know where he can "carry the voice" according to the opinion and will of the moderns, there must of necessity be an error in grammar. It would be better if, when they mean that the singer should, with judgment and discretion, "carry the voice," they were to introduce at that point some sign indicating their wish, in order that, perceiving the need, he might produce better accord and more pleasing harmony than he produces by singing along at his own will.

LUCA: Such an indication would not be unprofitable if one could reasonably discover a universal sign to indicate this manner of "carrying the voice" to the singer. But while these new inventors are exhausting themselves in new inventions to make this manifest, they go on scattering these passages through their compositions, which, when sung or sounded on different instruments by musicians accustomed to this kind of accented music, full of "suppositions,"[11] yield a not unpleasing harmony at which I marvel.

---

the *portar la voce* (see note 10 and the Glossary, p. 733) is also notated as a subdivision of the previous tone, that is, sounding "before the beat." The two effects are different but could be difficult to distinguish, depending on the tempo. Luca's fourth example [d] differs from his others, in that the new *accento* begins on the tone E, a step lower than the previous tone.

10. *Portar la voce*, literally "to carry the voice," is the name of the embellishment, which in other Italian treatises also involves rising pitches and unequal subdivision of a lower tone. Compare the French *port de voix*, and the example above. The Italian term does not seem to have entered the common vocabulary; it is not to be confused with the modern *portamento*. See the Glossary, p. 733.

11. *Suppositi* in Artusi refer to substitute notes. Compare *Artusi*, pt. 2 (1603), pp. 45–47: "But how many melodies have been written using sharps, flats, *fiori, fioretti, accenti,* and *suppositi,* and things against nature?" He rails against unnatural accidentals, intervals of sevenths in place

VARIO: This may result from two things. First, that the singers do not sing what is written, but go ahead "carrying the voice" and sustaining it in such a way that, when they perceive that it is about to produce some bad effect, they divert it elsewhere, taking it somewhere where it seems it will not offend the ear. The second thing is, that sensuous excess corrupts the sense, meaning simply that the ear is so taken up with the other parts that it does not fully perceive the offense committed against it (as it would if the composition were for two, three, or four voices), while reason, which knows and distinguishes the good from the bad, perceives right well that a deception is wrought on the sense, which receives the material only in a certain confused way, even though it border on truth. This manifestly is clearly seen when the organist adds to his other registers that of the twelfth; here it is reason and not the ear that discovers the many dissonances which occur among them.

LUCA: It is known that the ear is deceived, and to this these composers, or new inventors, apply themselves with enthusiasm. They seek only to satisfy the ear and with this aim toil night and day at their instruments to hear the effect which passages so made produce. The poor fellows do not perceive that what the instruments tell them is false and that it is one thing to search with voices and instruments for something pertaining to the harmonic faculty, another to arrive at the true and the exact by means of reason, seconded by the ear.

. . . But tell me if this science can be advanced by new modes of expression. Why is it that you are unwilling to augment it, or that augmenting it displeases you or does not seem good to you? The field is large; everyone is occupied with new things. Musicians too should expand their art, for making all compositions after one fashion sickens and disgusts the ear.

VARIO: I do not deny that discovering new things is not merely good but necessary. But tell me first why you wish to employ these dissonances as they employ them? If you do it in order to say, "I wish them to be plainly heard, but so that the ear may not be offended," why do you not use them in the ordinary way, conformable to reason, in accordance with what Adriano and Cipriano, Palestrina, Porta, Claudio, Gabrieli, Gastoldi, Nanino, Giovanelli,[12] and so many others in this academy have written? Have they perhaps failed to cause asperities to be heard? Look at Orlando Lasso, Filippo di Monte, Giaches Wert, and you will find full heaps of them. If you do not wish the ear to be so much offended by them, you will find the manner and order of their use in the same authors. Now, even if you wish dissonance to become consonant, it

---

of octaves, and certain harmonic relations that arise from figures created by *inganni,* that is, groups of tones that do not have the same pitch intervals but represent the same solmisation syllables. What he considers "true" as opposed to "false" *suppositi* appear to be substitutions that come under the practice of *musica ficta* (though he does not use the term), octave substitutions, and perhaps more diatonic forms of *inganni.*

12. Adrian Willaert, Cipriano de Rore, Giovanni Pierluigi da Palestrina, Costanzo Porta, Claudio Merulo, Giovanni or Andrea Gabrieli, Giovanni Gastoldi, Giovanni Maria or Giovanni Bernardino Nanino, Ruggiero Giovanelli.

remains necessary that it be contrary to consonance; by nature it is always dissonant and can hence become consonant only when consonance become dissonant. This brings us to impossibilities, although these new composers may perhaps so exert themselves that, in the course of time, they will discover a new method by which dissonance will become consonance, and consonance dissonance. And it is no great matter for lofty intelligences like these to be doing and inventing things of this kind exclusively.

LUCA: Their aim is precisely to temper to some degree the harshness of dissonance in another way than that used by their predecessors, and to this they devote their efforts.

VARIO: If the purpose can be attained by observing the precepts and good rules handed down by the theorists and followed by all the experts, what reason is there to go beyond the bounds to seek out new extravagances? Do you not know that all the arts and sciences have been brought under rules by scholars of the past and that the first elements, rules, and precepts on which they are founded have been handed down to us in order that, so long as there is no deviation from them, one person shall be able to understand what another says or does? And just as, to avoid confusion in the arts and sciences, it is not permitted to every schoolmaster to change the rules bequeathed by Guarino,[13] nor to every poet to put a long syllable in verse in place of a short one, nor to every arithmetician to corrupt the processes and proofs which are proper to that art, so it is not permitted to everyone who strings notes together to deprave and corrupt music, introducing new modes of composing with new principles founded on sand. Horace says:

> Est modus in rebus, sunt certi denique fines
> Quos ultra citraque nequit consistere rectum.[14]

LUCA: The truth is that all the arts and sciences have been brought under rules. But still, since dissonances are employed in harmonies as nonessentials, it seems that musicians are entitled to use them as they like. . . .

These musicians observe the rule that the part forming the dissonance with the lowest part has a harmonic correspondence with the tenor, so that it accords with every other part, while the lowest part also accords with every other part. Thus they make a mixture of their own.

VARIO: I see that this rule of theirs is observed in the first, fourth, fifth, sixth, and seventh examples. But in the sixth example, the eighth notes *(crome)* have no harmonic relation, either with the bass or with the tenor. With what sort of rule do you think they can save themselves?

LUCA: I do not know how they can help themselves here. I see the observance of no rule, although I believe that the eighths are the result of perceiving,

---

13. The grammatical *Regulae* of the humanist Guarino Veronese (1374–1460), a resident of Ferrara after 1429.
14. "There is a measure in all things. There are, in short, fixed bounds, beyond and short of which right can find no place," *Satires* 1.1. 106–7 (trans. Fairclough).

with instruments, that they do not greatly offend the ear because of their rapid movement.

VARIO: Are you not reminded of what Aristoxenus says of such men as these? Yesterday I gave you the substance of this thought; now I shall give you his very words. In the second book of his *Harmonics* he says: "It is therefore a very great and altogether disgraceful sin to refer the nature of a harmonic question to an instrument."[15] As regards the point that, because of their rapid movement they do not offend the ear, the intellect, recognizing the deception wrought upon the sense, declares that since these intervals are not consonant, but dissonant and placed at random, they can in no way be in a harmonic relation; that they can therefore cause no harmony pleasing to the ear; and that their rapidity, accompanied by so many parts making noise together, is nothing else than the sensuous excess which corrupts the sense.

LUCA: They think only of satisfying the sense, caring little that reason should enter here to judge their compositions.

VARIO: If such as these had read the ninth chapter of the first book of Boethius, and the first chapter of his fifth book,[16] and the first chapter of the first book of Ptolemy,[17] they would beyond doubt be of a different mind. . . . Through ignorance a man is unable to distinguish which activities are better and which worse, and as a result of this inability he commonly embraces many things from which he should flee and flees from many which he should follow and embrace. Of ignorance, then, are born compositions of this sort, which, like monstrosities, pass through the hands of this man and that, and these men do not know themselves what the real nature of these compositions is. For them it is enough to create a tumult of sounds, a confusion of absurdities, an assemblage of imperfections; and all springs from that ignorance with which they are beclouded. . . . Our ancients never taught that sevenths may be used absolutely and openly, as you see them used in the second, third, fourth, fifth, sixth, and seventh examples, for they do not give grace to the composition and, as I said a little while ago, the high part has no correspondence to its whole, beginning, or foundation.

LUCA: This is a new paradox.

VARIO: If this new paradox were reasonably founded on some reason, it would deserve much praise and would move onward to eternal life. But it is destined to have a short life, for demonstration can only show that truth is against it.

15. See Oliver Strunk, *Source Readings in Music History* (New York: Norton, 1950), p. 31. Artusi quotes Aristoxenus in the Latin translation of Antonio Gogava (Venice, 1562), much decried by sixteenth-century scholars of Greek.

16. From his *Fundamentals of Music* (1.9), "Not every judgment is to be pronounced by the senses, but reason is rather to be believed: wherein of the fallibility of the senses" and (5.1), "Of the nature of harmony, and what the means of judging it are, and whether the senses are always to be believed."

17. Claudius Ptolemaeus, *Of Harmonies,* chap. 1, "Of harmonic criteria."

83 Claudio and Giulio Cesare Monteverdi

By 1605 Claudio Monteverdi had served as musician to the Duke of Mantua for some fifteen years and had published sacred music, a volume of canzonets, and four books of polyphonic madrigals. In his fifth book of madrigals (1605), the first of his publications to indicate a *basso continuo,* he acknowledged Giovanni Maria Artusi's criticisms of his music with a brief announcement that he would produce a written explanation of the modern, or "second," practice. No such explanation was ever published and none is known to exist. But Giulio Cesare Monteverdi published a defense of his brother Claudio's new style in the form of an "explanation" of the 1605 announcement, which he issued in Claudio's *Scherzi musicali* of 1607. Giulio Cesare repeatedly takes great pains to demonstrate that recognized authorities such as Gioseffo Zarlino allowed for the existence of music composed in manners other than those treated in learned writings and that other sixteenth-century composers recognized as great had already anticipated many aspects of Claudio's madrigals that Artusi deemed faults. The Artusi-Monteverdi controversy centered on the combining of polyphonic lines. The key distinction that is often quoted from Monteverdi's defense is that harmony is said to control the contrapuntal lines in the older, "first" practice but obeys the words in the second practice. This did not mean, however, that in 1607, harmony should be subordinate to a single, dominating vocal line. Giulio Cesare adopted Plato's threefold definition of *melodia* as harmonic relation, rhythm, and text; that is, *melodia* signifies the totality of a composition (as it did for ancient music). He argues that these three components of music stand in different relationships to each other in different musical styles. The brothers also challenge Artusi to justify his opinions—not with words but with musical compositions of his own. Their challenge illustrates the esthetic belief of Baroque artists that the senses have a role in judging art, as Claudio himself wrote in 1605.

Giulio Cesare presented his defense in the form of annotations to Claudio's letter, which is reproduced first below.

Explanation of the Letter Printed in the Fifth Book of Madrigals

CLAUDIO MONTEVERDI'S LETTER
(1605)

Studious Readers,

Be not surprised that I am giving these madrigals to the press without first replying to the objections that Artusi made against some very minute portions of them. Being in the service of this Most Serene Highness of Mantua, I am not master of the time I would require. Nevertheless I wrote a reply to let it be known that I do not do things by chance, and as soon as it is rewritten it will see the light under the title *The Second Practice, or, the Perfection of Modern Music.* Some will wonder at this, not believing that there is any practice other than that taught by Zarlino. But let them be assured concerning consonances and dissonances that there is a different way of considering them from that already determined, one that defends the modern manner of composition with the assent of reason and of the senses. I wanted to say this both so that the expression "second practice" would not be appropriated by others and so that men of intellect might meanwhile consider other second thoughts concerning harmony. And have faith that the modern composer builds on foundations of truth.

Live happily.

GIULIO CESARE MONTEVERDI'S EXPLANATION OF THE LETTER
(1607)

Some months ago a letter of my brother Claudio Monteverdi was printed and given to the public. A certain person, under the fictitious name of Antonio Braccini da Todi,[1] has been at pains to make this seem to the world a chimera

---

TEXT: Claudio Monteverdi, *Il quinto libro de madrigali a cinque voci* (Venice, 1605), "Studiosi lettori," translated by Claude V. Palisca, "The Artusi-Monteverdi Controversy" in *The New Monteverdi Companion,* ed. Denis Arnold and Nigel Fortune (London: Faber and Faber, 1985), pp. 151–52, reprinted by permission; and Giulio Cesare Monteverdi, "Dichiaratione della lettera stampata nel quinto libro de' suoi madregali" in *Scherzi musicali a tre voci di Claudio Monteverde,* ed. Giulio Cesare Monteverdi (Venice, 1607), translation by Oliver Strunk. The Italian texts are available in Domenico de' Paoli, *Claudio Monteverdi: Lettere, dediche e prefazioni* (Rome, 1973), pp. 391–92 and 394–407. Giulio Cesare's annotations were originally interlined with Claudio's text, as they are below.

1. A first text by "Braccino" is unknown and may not have been published. Its author replied to Giulio Cesare Monteverdi in Antonio Braccino, *Discorso secondo musicale per la dichiaratione*

and a vanity. For this reason, impelled by the love I bear my brother and still more by the truth contained in his letter, and seeing that he pays attention to deeds and takes little notice of the words of others, and being unable to endure that his works should be so unjustly censured, I have determined to reply to the objections raised against them, declaring point for point in fuller detail what my brother, in his letter, compressed into little space, to the end that this person and whoever follows him may learn that the truth that it contains is very different from what he represents in his discussions. The letter says:

Be not surprised that I am giving these madrigals to the press without first replying to the objections that Artusi made

By "Artusi" is to be understood the book bearing the title, *L'Artusi, or, Of the Imperfections of Modern Music*, whose author, disregarding the civil precept of Horace, *Nec tua laudabis studia, haud aliena reprendes*[2] and without any cause given to him, and therefore unjustly, says the worst he can of certain musical compositions of my brother Claudio.

against some very minute portions of them.

These portions, called "passages" by Artusi, which are seen so lacerated by the said Artusi in his Second Discourse, are part of my brother's madrigal "Cruda Amarilli," and their harmony is part of the melody of which it is composed; for this reason, in respect of everything that constitutes "melody," he [Claudio] has called them portions and not "passages."

Being in the service of this Most Serene Highness of Mantua, I am not master of the time I would require.

This my brother said not only because of his responsibility for both church and chamber music, but also because of other extraordinary services; for, serving a great prince, he finds the greater part of his time taken up, now with tourneys, now with ballets, now with comedies and various concerts, and lastly in an ensemble of two *viole bastarde,* which responsibility and study are perhaps not so usual, as his adversary could have understood. And my brother has bided his time and continues to bide his time, not only for the reason and valid excuse set forth, but also because he knows that *properante omnia perverse agunt* [the hasty do all things badly], that excellence and speed are not companions in any undertaking whatsoever, and that perfect excellence requires the whole man, the more so in attempting to treat of a matter hardly touched upon by intelligent harmonic theorists, and not, like his opponent, of a matter *nota lippis atque tonsoribus* [familiar to the blear-eyed and to barbers].

Nevertheless I wrote a reply to let it be known that I do not do things by chance,

---

della lettera posta ne' Scherzi Musicali del Sig. Claudio Monteverdi (Venice, 1608; facs., Milan, 1924). It has been suggested that Braccino is Artusi himself.

2. *Epistles,* 1.18.39: "Praise not your own studies; blame not those of others."

My brother says that he does not compose his works by chance because, in this kind of music, it has been his intention to make the words the mistress of the harmony and not the servant, and because it is in this manner that his work is to be judged in the composition of the "melody." Of this Plato speaks *melodiam ex tribus constare oratione, harmonia, rithmo* [The "melody" is composed of three things: the words, the harmony, and the rhythm], and, a little further on, *Quin etiam consonum ipsum et dissonum eodem modo, quando-quidem rithmus et harmonia orationem sequitur non ipsa oratio rithmum et harmoniam sequitur.* [And so of the apt and the unapt, if the rhythm and the harmony follow the words, and not the words these.][3] Then, to give greater force to the words, he continues *quid vero loquendi modus ipsaque oratio non ne animi affectionem sequitur?* [Do not the manner of the diction and the words follow and conform to the disposition of the soul?] and then *orationen* [*sic*] *vero cetera quoq*[*ue*] *sequuntur* [indeed, all the rest follows and conforms to the words].

But in this case, Artusi takes certain portions, or, as he calls them, "passages," from my brother's madrigal "Cruda Amarilli," paying no attention to the words, but neglecting them as though they had nothing to do with the music, later showing the said "passages" deprived of their words, of all their harmony, and of their rhythm. But if, in the "passages" noted by him as false, he had shown the words that went with them, then the world would have known without fail where his judgment had gone astray, and he would not have said that they were chimeras and castles in the air for not entirely following the rules of the First Practice. But it would truly have been a beautiful demonstration if he had also done the same with Cipriano's madrigals "Dalle belle contrade," "Se ben il duol," "Et se pur mi mantieni, Amor," "Poiche m'invita amore," "Crudel acerba," "Un' altra volta,"[4] and, to conclude, with others whose harmony obeys their words exactly and which would indeed be left bodies without soul if they were left without this most important and principal part of music. By passing judgment on these "passages" without the words, his opponent implies that all excellence and beauty consist in the exact observance of the aforesaid rules of the First Practice, which make the harmony mistress of the words. This my brother will make apparent, knowing for certain that in a kind of composition such as this one of his, music turns on the perfection of the "melody," considered from which point of view the harmony, from being the mistress becomes the servant of the words, and the words the mistress of the harmony. This is the way of thinking to which the Second Practice, or modern usage, tends. On such a true basis, he promises to show, in refutation of his opponent, that the harmony of the madrigal "Cruda Amarilli" is not composed by chance, but with beautiful art and excellent study that is not understood by his adversary and unknown to him.

---

3. *Republic* 398d. Monteverdi quotes Plato in the Latin translation of Marsilio Ficino.

4. Madrigals from Rore's *Fifth Book of Madrigals a 5* (1566), *Fourth Book a 5* (1557), *Le vive fiamme* (1565), and *Second Book a 4* (1557).

And since my brother promises, in refutation of his opponent, to show in writing that with respect to the perfection of the "melody" the writings of his adversary are not based upon the truth of art, let his opponent, in refutation of my brother's madrigal, show the errors of others through the medium of the press with a comparable practical performance—with harmony observing the rules of the First Practice, that is, disregarding the perfection of the melody; considered from which point of view the harmony, from being servant, becomes mistress. For *purpura juxta purpuram dijudicanda* [purple ought to be judged with purple]. Using only words to oppose the deeds of another *nil agit exemplum litem quod lite resolvit* [offers the example that settling one dispute by another accomplishes nothing].[5]

Then let him allow the world to be the judge, and if he brings forward no deeds, but only words, deeds being what commend the master, my brother will again find himself meriting the praise, and not he. For as the sick man does not pronounce the physician intelligent from hearing him prate of Hippocrates and Galen, but does so when he recovers health by means of the diagnosis, so the world does not pronounce the musician intelligent from hearing him ply his tongue in telling of the honored theorists of harmony. For it was not in this way that Timotheus incited Alexander to war, but by singing. To such practical performance my brother invites his opponent, and not others, for he yields to them all, and honors and reveres them all. He invites his opponent once and for all, because he wishes to devote himself to music and not to writing, except as promised on this one occasion, and, following the divine Cipriano de Rore, the Prince of Venosa, Emilio del Cavaliere, Count Alfonso Fontanella, the Count of the Camerata, the Cavalier Turchi, Pecci, and other gentlemen of that heroic school, and wishes to pay no attention to nonsense and chimeras.[6]

and as soon as it is rewritten it will see the light under the title *Second Practice*

Because his opponent seeks to attack the modern music and to defend the old. These are indeed different from one another (in their manner of employing the consonances and dissonances, as my brother will make apparent). And since this difference is unknown to the opponent, let everyone understand what the one is and what the other, in order that the truth of the matter may be more clear. Both are honored, revered, and commended by my brother. To the old he has given the name of First Practice from its being the first practical usage, and the modern music he has called Second Practice from its being the second practical usage.

By First Practice he understands the one that turns on the perfection of the harmony, that is, the one that considers the harmony not commanded, but

5. Horace, *Satires* 2.3.103.
6. Venosa is Carlo del Gesualdo; also named are Giovanni de' Bardi, Giovanni del Turco, and Tomaso Pecci.

commanding, and not the servant, but the mistress of the words. This was begun by those first men who composed music in our notation for more than one voice, followed then and amplified by Ockeghem, Josquin Desprez, Pierre de la Rue, Jean Mouton, Crequillon, Clemens non Papa, Gombert, and others of those times, and was finally perfected by Messer Adriano [Willaert] in actual composition and by the most excellent Zarlino with most judicious rules.

By Second Practice—which was first renewed in our notation by Cipriano de Rore (as my brother will make apparent) and was followed and amplified not only by the gentlemen already mentioned, by Ingegneri, Marenzio, Giaches de Wert, Luzzasco, and likewise by Jacopo Peri, Giulio Caccini, and finally by loftier spirits with a better understanding of true art—he understands the one that turns on the perfection of the "melody," that is, the one that considers harmony commanded, not commanding and makes the words the mistress of the harmony. For such reasons, he has called it "second" and not "new," and he has called it "practice" and not "theory," because he understands its explanation to turn on the manner of employing the consonances and disso- nances in actual composition. He has not called it "Melodic Institutions" because he confesses that he is not one to undertake so great an enterprise, and he leaves the composition of such noble writings to the Cavalier Ercole Bottrigari and to the Reverend Zarlino. Zarlino used the title *Harmonic Institu- tions*[7] because he wished to teach the laws and rules of harmony; my brother has used the title "Second Practice," that is, second practical usage, because he wishes to make use of the considerations of that usage, that is, of melodic considerations and their explanations, employing only so many of them as con- cern his defense against his opponent.

or, the Perfections of Modern Music.

He will call it "Perfections of Modern Music" on the authority of Plato, who says, *Non ne et musica circa perfectionem melodiae versatur?*[8]

Some will wonder at this, not believing that there is any other practice than that taught by Zarlino.

He has said "some" and not "all," to indicate only the opponent and his followers. He has said "they will wonder" because he knows for certain that these men are wanting not only in understanding of the Second Practice, but (as he will make apparent) to a considerable extent, in that of the First also. They do not believe that there is any practice other than that of Messer Adri- ano, for the Reverend Zarlino did not intend to treat of any other practice, as he indeed declares, saying, "It never was nor is it my intention to treat of the usage of practice according to the manner of the ancients, either Greeks or Latins, even if at times I touch upon it. My intention is solely to describe the

7. Venice, 1558.
8. *Gorgias* 449d: "Does not music also turn on the perfection of the melody?"

method of those who have discovered our way of causing several parts to sound together with various modulations and various melodies, especially according to the way and manner observed by Messer Adriano."[9] Thus the Reverend Zarlino concedes that the practice taught by him is not the one and only truth. For this reason my brother intends to make use of the principles taught by Plato and practiced by the divine Cipriano and by modern usage, principles different from those taught and established by the Reverend Zarlino and practiced by Messer Adriano.

But let them be assured concerning consonances and dissonances

But let the opponent and his followers be assured that "with regard to the consonances and dissonances" [means] "with regard to the manner of employing the consonances and dissonances."

that there is a different way of considering them from that already determined,

By the "determined" way of considering the consonances and dissonances, which turns on the manner of their employment, my brother understands those rules of the Reverend Zarlino that are to be found in the third book of his *Institutions,* which tend to show the practical perfection of the harmony, not of the melody, as is clearly revealed by the musical examples he gives there. Showing in actual music the meaning of his precepts and laws, these [examples] are seen without regard for the words. Therefore they show the harmony to be the mistress and not the servant. For this reason, my brother will prove to the opponent and his followers that, when the harmony is the servant of the words, the manner of employing the consonances and dissonances is not determined in the abovementioned way. Therefore the one harmony differs from the other in this respect.

one that defends the modern manner of composition with the assent of reason and of the senses.

"With the assent of the reason" because he will take his stand upon the consonances and dissonances approved by mathematics (for he has said "with regard to the manner of employing them") and because he will likewise take his stand upon the command of the words, the chief mistress of the art considered from the point of view of the perfection of the melody, as Plato affirms in the third book of his *Republic*[10] (for he has said "Second Practice").

"With assent of the senses" because the combination of words commanding with rhythm and harmony obedient to them (and I say "obedient" because the combination in itself is not enough to perfect the melody) affects the disposition of mind. Here is what Plato says: *Sola enim melodia ab omnibus quotcunque distrahunt animum retrahens contrahit in se ipsum* [For only melody,

9. *Sopplimenti musicali,* bk. 1, chap. 1, p. 9.
10. *Republic* 398d p. 10.

turning the mind away from all things whatsoever that distract, reduces the mind to itself].[11]

And not harmony alone, be it ever so perfect, as the Reverend Zarlino concedes in these words, "If we take harmony absolutely, without adding to it anything else, it will have no power to produce any extrinsic effect." He adds a little further on, "In a certain way, it intrinsically prepares for and disposes to joy or sadness, but it does not on this account lead to the expression of any extrinsic effect."[12]

I wanted to say this both so that the expression "second practice" would not be appropriated by others

My brother has made known to the world that this expression is assuredly his, in order that it may be known and concluded that when his adversary said in the second part of *L'Artusi,*[13] p. 33: "This Second Practice, which may in all truth be said to be the dregs of the First . . . ," he spoke as he did to speak evil of my brother's works. This was in the year 1603, when my brother had first decided to begin writing his defense of himself against his opponent and when the expression "Second Practice" had barely passed his lips, a sure indication that his adversary was desirous of defaming in the same vein my brother's words and his music as well. And for what reason? Let him say it who knows; let him see it who can find it in writing! But why does the adversary show so much astonishment in that discourse of his, saying further, "You show yourself as jealous of that expression as though you feared that someone would rob you of it," as though he meant to say, in his language, "You should not fear such a theft, for you are not worth imitating, let alone robbing"? I inform him that, if the matter has to be considered in this light, my brother will have not a few arguments in his favor, in particular for the *canto alla francese* [melody in the French style] in this modern manner, which has been a matter of marvel for the three or four years since it was published and which he has applied now to motets, now to madrigals, now to canzonets and airs. Who before him brought it to Italy, until he returned from the baths of Spa[14] in the year 1599? Who before him began to apply it to Latin and Italian words in our tongue? Has he not then composed these *Scherzi?* There would be much to say of this to his advantage, and still more (if I wished) of other things, but I pass over them in silence since, as I have said, the matter does not need to be considered in this light. He will call it "Second Practice" with regard to the manner of its employment; with regard to its origin it might be called "First."

and so that man of intellect might meanwhile consider other second thoughts concerning harmony.

11. Marsilio Ficino, *Compendium in Timaeum,* chap. 30. Compare Plato, *Timaeus* 47d.
12. *Istituzioni armoniche,* pt. 2, chap. 7, p. 84.
13. Venice, 1603.
14. Belgian town southeast of Liège.

"Other thoughts," that is, not clinging obstinately to the belief that the whole requirement of art cannot be found elsewhere than in the rules of the First Practice on the ground that, in all varieties of composition, the harmony is always the same thing, being pre-determined and thus incapable of obeying the words perfectly. "Secondary thoughts," that is, concerning the Second Practice, or the perfection of the melody. "Concerning harmony," that is, concerning not merely the portions or "passages" of a composition, but its fruit. For if the opponent had considered the harmony of my brother's madrigal "O Mirtillo"[15] in this light, he would not, in that discourse of his, have uttered such extravagances with regard to its mode, although he appears to be speaking in general when he says this. *L'Artusi* has likewise explained and demonstrated the confusion introduced into composition by those who begin in one mode, follow this with another, and end with one wholly unrelated to the first and second ideas, which is like hearing the talk of a madman, who, as the saying goes, runs with the hare and hunts with the hounds. Poor fellow, he does not perceive that, while he is posing before the world as preceptor ordinary, he falls into the error of denying the mixed modes. If these did not exist, would not the Hymn of the Apostles,[16] which begins in the sixth mode and ends in the fourth, be running with the hare and hunting with the hounds? And likewise the Introit "Spiritus Domini replevit orbem terrarum" and especially the "Te Deum laudamus"? Would not Josquin be an ignoramus for having begun his mass on "Faisant regrets"[17] in the sixth mode and finished it in the second? The "Nasce la pena mia" of the excellent Striggio,[18] the harmony of which composition (from the point of view of the first practice) may well be called divine—would it not be a chimera, being built upon a mode consisting of the first, eight, eleventh, and fourth? The madrigal "Quando, signor, lasciaste" of the divine Cipriano de Rore[19] which begins in the eleventh mode, passes into the second and tenth in the middle, and ends in the first [mode], and the second part in the eighth—would not this thing of Cipriano's be a truly trifling vanity? And what would Messer Adriano be called for having begun in the first mode in "Ne projicias nos in tempore senectutis" (a motet for five voices to be found at the end of his first book),[20] making the middle in the second mode and the end in the fourth? But let the opponent read chapter 14 ["On the common or mixed modes"] of the fourth book of the Reverend Zarlino's *Institutions,* and he will learn.

And have faith that the modern composer builds on foundations of truth and you will fare well.

15. The madrigal from Monteverdi's *Madrigals,* Book 5 that follows "Cruda Amarilli."
16. "Exsultet coelum laudibus" from the Roman Antiphonary, *Hymni antiqui,* p. 33
17. His *Masses,* Book III (Venice, 1514).
18. Alessandro Striggio, *Madrigals* a 6 (1560).
19. His *Madrigals,* Book IV a 5 (1557).
20. Adrian Willaert, *Motecta* a 5, Book I (1539).

My brother has said this, finally, knowing that because of the command of the words, modern composition does not and cannot observe the rules of [the first] practice, and that only a method of composition that takes account of this command will be so accepted by the world that it may justly be called a usage. Therefore he cannot believe and never will believe—even if his own arguments are insufficient to sustain the truth of such a usage—that the world will be deceived, even if his opponent is. And farewell.

84 Pietro della Valle

The Roman nobleman Pietro della Valle (1586–1652) is best known for his travels—first throughout Italy, then on the sea fighting pirates—as a pilgrim to the Holy Land and as an observant sojourner in the Middle East, Persia, Turkey, and India. He left Rome before 1609 and returned in 1626 with his second wife, a Persian, and the remains of his first wife, a Georgian. He also brought back a memoir of his travels (published 1650–63), a grammar of the Turkish language, decipherments of cuneiform writing, notes on Eastern astrology, and a wealth of other exotica. He quickly reentered the world of the gentlemen's academies, which included musical performances at their meetings in his own palace. As a youth he had studied harpsichord, gamba, theorbo, counterpoint, and dancing, and had developed an ear that would prompt his studies of Neapolitan and Sicilian song, as well as music of the East. He wrote two librettos for music (in 1606 and 1629) and maintained an intense correspondence with the music antiquarian, Giovanni Battista Doni, proposing instruments that would execute all kinds of ancient and exotic modes. He and Doni had instruments built with multiple keyboards and fingerboards in order to play diatonic, chromatic, and enharmonic *genera* and transpositions of the modes. Della Valle composed four dialogues using these instruments, two of which received public performance at the oratory of San Marcello in 1641.

None of Della Valle's more uncommon interests diminished his appreciation of the public and private music that he heard around him, of which his 1640 discourse in favor of contemporary music bears vivid and concrete testimony. He begins with well-known arguments about compositional style itself—polyphony versus audibility of the text, and consistent imitative texture versus a variety of textures. He also provides a description of the newest musical genres, including the oratorio. But it is as a listener that Della Valle offers valuable comparisons of past and present performance and performers, describing the delight of improvised embellishment in sensitive ensemble playing, praising the greater variety of expressive devices used by modern singers, and extolling the abilities of the castrati and a new cohort of women singers.

FROM Of the Music of Our Time

Which Is Not At All Inferior but Rather Is Better than That of the Past Age

DISCOURSE TO LELIO GUIDICCIONI
(1640)

The other evening Your Lordship said that in the last fifty years music had lost much, and that today there weren't good men in this profession similar to those of the past age. I, who seemed in great measure to disagree, had many things to say to Your Lordship about this. But because we went on to other discussions, and then it came time to take leave of each other, I did not have the opportunity to offer Your Lordship my reasons, which I have decided to send to you written down, hoping that you would favor me by listening to them and would better consider them all together.

I say therefore, that in the first place we must distinguish things in order not to speak confusedly, because counterpoint is one thing, sound is another, melody another—all parts of music; and finally, music in an absolute sense is yet another. Music is a general name that comprises all the things mentioned above that are parts of it, and there are other parts besides. But let it suffice that we speak only of what I have named, to which the other things can easily be reduced. And speaking thus absolutely about music does not at all verify Your Lordship's proposition (pardon me for speaking freely, because it is allowed in differences of opinion and cannot be avoided) on the basis of what are, so to speak, the parts of it, which, I hope, will be proved to Your Lordship in full.

Counterpoint, that part of music most necessary to make good use of every other part, has for its aim not only the foundations of music, but perhaps even more, artifice and the most detailed subtleties of this art. These are fugues forwards and backwards, simple or double, imitations,[1] canons, and *perfidie*[2] and other elegances made like these, which, if used at the right time and place, adorn music marvelously. They are not however to be used continuously, neither always all of them nor always the same ones, but only those which are appropriate, whenever they are appropriate: now these, now those, and often

TEXT: "Della musica dell'età nostra, che non è punto inferiore, anzi è migliore di quella dell'età passata," in *De' trattati di musica di Gio. Batista Doni*, ed. Anton Francesco Gori, vol. 2 (Florence, 1763; facs. Bologna, 1974), pp. 249–64, repr. Angelo Solerti, *L'origine del melodramma* (Turin, 1903; facs. Bologna, [1969], pp. 148–79). Translation, by Margaret Murata, is from pp. 148–50, 156–57, 159–66. Guidiccioni (1582–1643), a classical scholar, poet, and literary critic, also wrote a "Discorso sopra la musica," which argues that music teaches virtue (ms. dated 1632).

1. Echoes or antiphonal effects.
2. Counterpoints built on ostinato basses. Zarlino called them *pertinacia*.

enough when they are not needed, none. And experience teaches us that the frequent use of these musical artifices is much more suited to instrumental music than to vocal, and especially when an instrument plays solo. From this I concede to Your Lordship that organs played with so much mastery by those good men that you named for me must have certainly carried people away. But in vocal music these refinements of artifice, although they work very well when made use of sparingly in suitable places (as one sees in many madrigals of the old masters and particularly in the famous "Vestiva i colli" by Palestrina), for the most part, nonetheless, they do not succeed, whether because in solo singing, which nowadays is much heard and is what pleases many people more, there is little place for them; whether, further, because in ensemble singing they create very bad effects, which composers of that time, begging Your Lordship's indulgence, hardly took into consideration, but effects which composers of today have known to anticipate with greater accuracy.[3]

·   ·   ·   ·   ·

Instrumental music should be considered differently according to the diverse ways in which it is used, because it is one thing to play alone, another to play in the company of other instruments, or of voices, or of voices and instruments together, and another to play in support of a choir.

In playing alone, more than in other forms, all the major artifices of counterpoint work well. But I remind Your Lordship that solo playing, no matter how well done, when it goes on for a long time becomes boring. It has often happened to different organists—and the best ones that, when overly enamored of their counterpoints, they made certain *ricercate*[4] too long, the little bell had to be rung to make them stop. Such a thing does not happen to those that sing; people are sorry when they finish and always want them to go on longer than they have. Under this subject of solo performance I also recognize as extremely great experts those that Your Lordship named, Claudio da Correggio in Parma, Luzzasco in Ferrara, Annibale Padovano, Andrea and Giovanni Gabrieli in Venice, Giovanni Macque in Naples, the Cavalier del Leuto[5] in Rome, and others like them, although they are known to me only by reputation. I am astonished, nonetheless, at what Your Lordship told me about Luzzasco: that

3. Della Valle continues by listing those "bad effects" of the contrapuntal style: the confusion of words and of fugal subjects, and the dominance of melodic and textural effects over what the words are saying.

4. To be understood here as "improvisations."

5. Claudio Merulo (1533–1604), organist at the cathedrals in Brescia, Venice, and then Parma, where he also served as organist to the Duke and the Company of the Steccata. Luzzasco Luzzaschi (d. 1607), organist to the Duke of Ferrara from 1564. Padovano (1527–1575), organist at San Marco, Venice and at the Austrian imperial court in Graz, where he became director of music. Andrea Gabrieli (1533–1585), organist at San Marco, Venice from 1566 until his death. His nephew Giovanni (1557–1612) succeeded him. Jean de Macque (d. 1614) lived in Rome from 1574, then served the viceregal chapel in Naples from 1599. The Cavaliere del Leuto (d. 1608) has not been identified; he was attached to the household of the Cardinal Montalto in Rome from before 1589 until his death.

he did not know how to make a trill, and that he would play the most refined details of his counterpoints so roughly, like a journeyman without any touch of gracefulness. I call this kind of performance bland, because it is just like a special dish, flavored with the best ingredients, but without any salt, or like statues that are roughed out with excellent design but are not finished or smooth or, like others of metal, which likewise of good design are only cast roughly and then neither touched up nor polished.

•   •   •   •   •

Playing in ensemble with other instruments does not demand so much the artifices of counterpoint as it does the art of embellishment; because if the player is good, he does not have to care so much about showing off his skills as a soloist as much as he must make adjustments to all the others. The same can be said of singers, since I don't consider a good singer one who, for example, having an excellent vocal ability always wants to be the one to do all the *passaggi*,[6] without giving time to the others to make some. Or if the others do execute them, he overpowers them with his own. Those that sing and play well in an ensemble must give time to each other; and they should play with the lightness of exchanges rather than with too many subtle contrapuntal artifices. They will demonstrate their skill in knowing how to restate well and promptly that which another has just done; in giving space to others and opportune occasions to restate that which they have done; and thus they will make their ability known to others with a different and not less skillful style, although not as difficult nor of such profound learning. Today not only the most excellent but also the ordinary instrumentalists do this, and they know far better than I think anyone that I heard from those past times could have done. When you play together with voices, the same holds true and more, as what I have said about instruments, because the instruments, serving the voices as the principals in the music, have no other aim than to accompany them well, a thing that I see the instrumentalists of today do with great judgment, so that I do not know how they could have ever done more in other times in this kind of playing. . . .

In singing, then, the only thing about which it is left to for us to speak, there are also several things to consider, because in addition to the differences in solo singing or in ensembles, one must further consider the goodness of the voices, the skill of the person singing, and finally the beauty of the works that are chosen to be sung. Solo singing demands either sweetness of voice or exquisite skill; but one or the other used with judgment, because otherwise you have nothing. Your Lordship praised Lodovico, a falsetto from the past known also to me (although when I was a boy),[7] saying that one long note well sung by him, as almost always he used to do, pleased you more than all the *passaggi* of the moderns. I answered you that Lodovico sang with judgment, because, since

6. A general term for ornamental, melismatic divisions of moderate to extensive duration; they were often improvised. See also the Glossary of Foreign Performance Terms (pp. 731–34).
7. Probably Lodovico Gualtero.

he had the sweet voice of the falsetto but did not have much technique, he
hardly ever used either *passaggi* or the other graces when he sang, except only
a good vocal placement and graceful finishes with those long notes of his, which
pleased very much because of the sweetness of his voice. At the same time,
however, or a little later, the tenor Giuseppino flourished,[8] who did exactly the
opposite for the same reason, recognizing his talent and availing himself of it.
Giuseppino's voice was not good, but he had very great agility. He did not have
the most artistry in the world, but his *passaggi* were natural. He sang moreover
with judgment as far as his self was concerned, because he made use of his
special talent. You hardly ever heard a long note from him without a trembling
trill; his singing was all *passaggi*. But with respect to others he did not sing with
judgment,[9] because most of the time he added *passaggi* where they should not
have gone. You never knew whether his singing was happy or sad, because it
was always of one kind. Or, to say it better, his singing was always happy in
every thing, whether that was appropriate or inappropriate, due to the
quickness of the notes that he continually spewed out, without his knowing, I
believe, what notes they were. I remember also from those times, but more
graciously, Melchior the bass,[10] who had my favor. And beyond his excellent
ability, he also had methods that after him remained for basses as standards in
elegant singing. I remember Giovanni Luca the falsetto, a great singer of
gorge[11] and *passaggi,* who sang as high as the stars; Orazietto, the best singer
in falsetto or in tenor; of Ottaviuccio and Del Verovio, famous tenors, and all
three of the last named sang in my *Carro.*[12] All these men, however, from their
trills and on to their *passaggi,* and with their good vocal placement, hardly had
other skills: of singing soft and loud, of increasing the voice little by little, of
diminishing it with grace, of expressing the affections, of following the words
and their meanings with judgment; of making the voice joyful or melancholy,
of making it plaintive or ardent when necessary, and similar other elegances
that singers of today do excellently well. In those times you heard no talk of
these nor, in Rome at least, did you ever know anything new, until in the last
years it was brought to us from the good school of Florence by Signor Emilio
de' Cavalieri who, above all, gave Rome a good taste in a little play in the

8. Giuseppino Cenci (d. 1616). Vincenzo Giustiniani considered him, along with Giulio Caccini,
   a major influence in establishing the monodic style (pp. 354–55).
9. When he sang with others.
10. Melchior Palentrotti (d. c. 1618), a Neapolitan bass who worked in Rome and Ferrara, and was
    associated with the Cardinal Montalto. He entered the Sistine Chapel choir in 1597 and sang
    the role of Pluto in the Florentine *Euridice* of Peri. For an aria with *passaggi* as he sang it, see
    Caccini's *Le nuove musiche* no. 13-b, "Muove sì dolce, e sì soave guerra."
11. A type of embellishment; see Glossary.
12. Most likely Giovanni Luca Conforti (ca. 1560–1608), author of a tutor for learning how to
    embellish vocal and instrumental music, as well as three volumes of embellished psalm settings;
    and Sistine Chapel singer Orazio Griffi. Ottavio Durante and Simone del Verovio were known
    as tenors and falsettists. The score to Della Valle's *Carro di fedeltà d'amore,* set to music by
    Paolo Quagliati, was published in 1611 (modern ed. by V. Gotwals and O. Keppler, Northamp-
    ton: 1957, Smith College Music Archives no. 13).

Oratorio of the Chiesa Nuova,[13] at which I was present when quite young. Since that time in which that good style was introduced also among us, a different, more refined manner than sung by their predecessors, we now hear the Nicolinis, the Bianchis, the Giovanninis, the Lorenzinis, the Marios and so many others[14] who equal these already, and without doubt do better than they, if not in other ways, at least in knowing how to sing with more judgment, whether in ensemble or alone. This aspect is the most important of all in our day: using judgment in an art that has become as perfected as I have described.

But leaving aside some other voices in order to say something about sopranos, who are the major ornament of music, Your Lordship wants to compare the falsettists of those times with the natural sopranos of the *castrati* that today we have in such abundance. Whoever in those days sang like a Guidobaldo, a Cavalier Loreto, a Gregorio, an Angeluccio, a Marc'Antonio[15] and so many others that I could name? The most that one could do then was to have a good boy [soprano]; but just when they began to understand a few things, they lost their voices. And while they had them, like persons who have no judgment because of their age, they also sang without taste and without style, exactly like things that are learned by rote, so that sometimes to hear them grated on my nerves unbearably. The sopranos of today, persons of judgment, of some age, with feelings, and of expertise in their exquisite art, sing with grace, with taste, with true refinement. Dressing themselves in the affections, they carry you away when you hear them. Of such sopranos in persons of judgment, the past age had only a Padre Soto and after that Padre Girolamo[16] who could more readily be included in our age than in the past one. We today have plenty of them in all the courts, all the chapels.

And beyond the castrati, where in the long gone days were so many of those women singers that today we have with singular excellence? In the days of our fathers, one Giulia—or Lulla, as we call her (whom even I came to know but not in her best years)—because she was pretty and could sort of improvise some villanella to a standard tune[17] at the harpsichord—or what do I know?—persuaded a duke to steal her, which resulted in great commotion. Vittoria,[18]

13. *La rappresentatione di anima, et di corpo* (Rome, 1600; repr. Farnborough, England, 1967).
14. Singers such as Sistine Chapel bass Bartolomeo Nicolini, tenor Francesco Bianchi, alto Lorenzo Sances, and soprano Mario Savioni.
15. Guidobaldo Boretti, Cavaliere Loreto Vittori, Gregorio Lazzarini, Angelo Ferrotti, and Marc'Antonio Pasqualini were all Sistine Chapel singers who also performed in the chamber and in operas.
16. Francisco Soto de Langa (d. 1619), Spanish soprano in the Sistine Chapel choir from 1562, priest of the Congregation of the Oratory, and composer of polyphonic *laude*. Girolamo Rosini (1581–1644), a virtuoso soprano much patronized by Cardinal Pietro Aldobrandini, had the distinction of being expelled from the Sistine Chapel choir; he later became prefect of music at the Chiesa Nuova from 1623 to his death.
17. "Cantava un poco ad aria," that is, sang strophes to a standard melodic formula.
18. Vittoria Archilei (1550–after 1620) known as "La Romanina," sang at the Medici court from 1588. Peri, Caccini, and Sigismondo d'India, among others, praised her subtle and virtuosic improvisatory style.

her friend, even though she wasn't pretty, was kept in the service of the Grand Dukes of Tuscany because she sang well with art and had a good voice, and was treated very well as long as she lived. But Hippolita[19] of Cardinal Montalto, more recent and who I believe is still living, won the battle at the wedding of Grand Duke Cosimo,[20] for in the concerts the best singers of all Italy competed together.

Today in Rome alone how many women do we have? how many did we have a few years ago? Who isn't beside himself when he hears Signora Leonora sing, with her archlute touched so freely and imaginatively? Who can pass sentence on who is the better of the two, Signora Leonora or Signora Caterina, her sister? Whoever has heard and seen Signora Adriana[21] their mother, as I have, in her more youthful years, and with that beauty that the world knows, on the sea in a galley boat at Posillipo with her gilt harp in hand, well needs to confess that in our times sirens are still to be found on those shores, but sirens who are benevolent and adorned as much with beauty as with *virtù*, not like those murderous evildoers of antiquity. And Signora Maddalena with her sister [Eleonora], whom we call the Lolli, and were the first that I heard sing well in Rome, after my return from the Levant. And Signora Sofonisba, whom an envious distance has stolen from us and to whom a few years ago Rome gave such grand accolades, more than were ever granted to any of the ancients in the Theater of Marcellus.[22] Who was there ever in the present age who could compare with her? Perhaps Camilluccia,[23] who with so many of her sisters and daughters made her house seem like a Mount Parnassus with all its Muses? But these have also been of our day, and similarly, the Signora Lucrezia Moretti, of Cardinal Borghese, today alive and well, and "la Laudomia" of the Muti family, who died recently. Also flourishing today more than ever are the Campanas, the Valerias,[24] and so many others famous for singing, among whom the contralto Signora Santa, whom I heard three or four years ago, was most refined. I could speak of one other also of great repute about whom I remain silent because to celebrate her only as a good singer, for her qualities, would seem to do her wrong. I remain silent similarly about the sister of Signora Adriana [Basile] whom I do not know, but understand she is in Germany where

19. Hippolita Recupito (d. 1650) and her husband Cesare Marotta (d.1630) both served Cardinal Montalto.
20. Cosimo II de' Medici (1590–1621) married Maria Maddalena, Archduchess of Austria in 1608. Recupito and Archilei performed together, along with the Caccini daughters, on several occasions during the wedding festivities.
21. Adriana Basile (ca. 1580–ca. 1641) and her daughters Caterina (1624–after 1670) and Leonora (1611–70) led celebrated lives as chamber musicians in Mantua, Rome and Naples. The women had as patrons the Gonzaga, the Barberini, the Rospigliosi, and Cardinal Mazarin.
22. The amphitheater by the Tiber completed in 13 B.C.E., dedicated to Marcellus, the nephew and son-in-law of Caesar Augustus.
23. Camilla Agazzari. Many of the women mentioned here have yet to be identified.
24. Anna di Valeria caught the French Ambassador's eye in 1635 in Rome. She appeared on the Venetian stage in the role of Poppea in the 1643 opera by Monteverdi.

she was called to serve the Emperor and does great honor to our age;[25] and thus also about Signora Francesca Caccini, young daughter of our [Giulio] Romano, who in Tuscany is called "la Cecchina," whom I also heard in Florence in my youth, and has been greatly admired for many years for her music, as much in singing as in composition, and for poetry, in Latin as well as in Tuscan. I remain silent because my intention here, as I have said, is to mention only those not only heard by me, but who have also flourished or are flourishing in Rome, since to search for all the others in the other cities and countries would be too much to do.

But where have I left the nuns, whom I should have named first, out of honor to them? La Verovia at Spirito Santo has stupefied the world for several years, nor have many years passed since that other nun and that lady, both students of hers I think, both sang with excellent charm in that same convent. Everyone knows how much fame the nun of Santa Lucia in Selce has.[26] Formerly people went out of wonderment to hear those of San Silvestro, now those of Monte Magnanapoli, those of Santa Chiara. The past era was never so rich, either in so many subjects, or such good ones at one time.

25. Margherita Basile (d. after 1636?) received an appointment at the imperial court in Vienna in 1631.
26. Anna Maria Cesi, who became a nun sometime between 1614, the year of her marriage to Prince Michele Peretti, and 1617, when a volume of spiritual monodies was dedicated to her.

85 Pierfrancesco Tosi

Pierfrancesco Tosi (1654–1732), a castrato, began his singing career in Italy and had moved by 1693 to London, where he sang public concerts and taught music. His volume on "ancient" and modern singers appeared in Italy just before he returned to London, having been on the road for twenty-three years as a political agent for the imperial court of the Hapsburgs. The treatise is often consulted for its explanations of appoggiaturas, trills, *passaggi*, the *messa di voce*, and other tools of the singer's trade, but all of Tosi's opinions are arguments against their abuse by younger singers and their teachers in contradistinction to the training and style that his generation represented. He decries the loss of lyric, *cantabile* singing to the virtuosity of modern, eighteenth-century pyrotechnics and the encroachments of the orchestra. Thus Tosi is an "ancient," trying to warn against what he hears as the excesses and imperfections of a new practice.

FROM *Observations on the Florid Song*
(1723)

Besides the errors in keeping time, there are other reasons, why a student should not imitate the modern gentlemen in singing arias, since it plainly appears that all their application now is to divide and subdivide in such a manner, that it is impossible to understand either words, thoughts, or modulation,[1] or to distinguish one aria from another, they singing them all so much alike, that, in hearing of one, you hear a thousand. —And must the *mode*[2] triumph? It was thought, not many years since, that in an opera, one rumbling aria full of divisions was sufficient for the most gurgling singer to spend his fire;[3] but the singers of the present time are not of that mind, but rather, as if they were not satisfied with transforming them all with a horrible metamorphosis into so many divisions, they, like racers, run full speed, with redoubled violence to their final cadences, to make reparation for the time they think they have lost during the course of the aria. . . .

I cannot positively tell, who that modern composer, or that ungrateful singer was, that had the heart to banish the delightful, soothing *pathetick*[4] from arias, as if no longer worthy of their commands, after having done them so long and pleasing service. Whoever he was, it is certain, he has deprived the profession of its most valuable excellence. Ask all the musicians in general, what their thoughts are of the *pathetick,* they all agree in the same opinion (a thing that seldom happens) and answer, that the *pathetick* is what is most delicious to the ear, what most sweetly affects the soul, and is the strongest basis of harmony. And must we be deprived of these charms, without knowing the reason why? Oh! I understand you: I ought not to ask the masters, but the audience, those capricious protectors of the *mode,* that cannot endure this; and herein lies my mistake. Alas! the mode and the multitude flow like torrents, which when at their height, having spent their violence, quickly disappear. The mischief is in the spring[5] itself; the fault is in the singers. They praise the *pathetick,* yet sing the *allegro.* He must want common sense who does not see through them. They know the first to be the most excellent, but they lay it aside, knowing it to be the most difficult.

TEXT: *Opinioni de' cantori antichi, e moderni o sieno osservazioni sopra il canto figurato* (Bologna, 1723; facs. ed. New York, 1968), from chap. 7, pp. 67–73, trans. [J. E.] Galliard, *Observations on the Florid Song; or, Sentiments on the Ancient and Modern Singers* (London, 1743; facs. Geneva, 1978), pp. 105–10; 112–17. Capitalization has been modernized. Some Italian words, such as *aria,* as well as some phrases that Galliard omitted, have been restored.

1. Nuances of phrasing and expression are more likely meant here, not "changes of key."
2. The word "mode" means "fashion" consistently, except at p. 46 below.
3. Those tremendous airs are called in Italian, *un' aria di bravura,* which cannot perhaps be better translated into English, than a *hectoring* song [Tr.].
4. Tosi's phrase is "l'amoroso patetico."
5. That is, the spring, or source of the water.

In former times divers arias were heard in the theatre in this delightful manner, preceded and accompanied with harmonious and well-modulated instruments, that ravished the senses of those who comprehended the contrivance and the melody; and if sung by one of those five or six eminent persons above-mentioned,[6] it was then impossible for a human soul not to melt into tenderness and tears from the violent motion of the affections. Oh! powerful proof to confound the idoliz'd *mode!* Are there in these times any, who are moved with tenderness, or sorrow? —No, (say all the auditors) no; for, the continual singing of the moderns in the *allegro* style, though when in perfection that deserves admiration, yet touches very slightly one that hath a delicate ear. The taste of those called the ancients was a mixture of the lively and the *cantabile,* the variety of which could not fail giving delight; but the moderns are so pre-possessed with taste in *mode,* that, rather than comply with the former, they are contented to lose the greatest part of its beauty. The study of the *pathetick* was the darling of the former; and application to the most difficult divisions is the only drift of the latter. Those perform'd with more judgment; and these execute with greater boldness. But since I have presum'd to compare the most celebrated singers in both styles, pardon me if I conclude with saying, that the moderns are arrived at the highest degree of perfection in singing to the ear; and that the ancients are inimitable in singing to the heart.

•   •   •   •   •

Gentlemen composers, (I do not speak to the eminent, but with all due respect) musick in my time has chang'd its style three times: the first which pleased on the stage, and in the chamber, was that of Pier. Simone, and of Stradella;[7] the second is of the best that are now living;[8] and I leave others to judge whether they be young and modern. But of your style, which is not quite established yet in Italy, and which has yet gained no credit at all beyond the Alps, those that come after us will soon give their opinion; for *modes* last not

6. Galliard, pp. 100–104, provides short biographical notices for Antonio Rivani, or Ciecolino; Francesco Pistocchi; "Sifacio," or Giovanni Francesco Grossi; Giovanni Buzzolini; Francesca Vanini, wife of bass Giuseppe Boschi; "La Santini," that is, Santa Stella, wife of composer Antonio Lotti; and the singer "Luigino," whose surname remains unknown.

7. Piersimone Agostini [d. 1680] lived about threescore years ago. Several cantatas of his composition are extant, some of them very difficult, not from the number of divisions in the vocal part, but from the expression, and the surprising incidents, and also the execution of the basses. He seems to be the first that put basses with so much vivacity; for Carissimi before him composed with more simplicity.[Tr.]

Alessandro Stradella [1644–1682] lived about Piersimone's time, or very little after. He was a most excellent composer, superior in all respects to the foregoing, and endowed with distinguishing personal qualifications. It is reported that his favourite instrument was the harp, with which he sometimes accompanied his voice, which was agreeable. To hear such a composer play on the harp must have been what we can have no notion of, by what we now hear. [Tr.]

8. When Tosi writ this, the composers in vogue were [Alessandro] Scarlatti, [Giovanni] Bononcini, [Francesco] Gasparini, [Luigi] Mancini, &c. The last and modern stile has pretty well spread itself all over Italy, and begins to have a great tendency to the fame beyond the Alps, as he calls it. [Tr.]

long. But if the profession is to continue, and end with the world, either you yourselves will see your mistake, or your successors will reform it. Would you know how? By banishing the abuses, and recalling the first, second, and third mode,[9] to relieve the fifth, sixth, and eighth, which are quite jaded. They will revive the fourth and seventh now dead to you, and buried in churches, for the final closes. To oblige the taste of the singers and the hearers, the *allegro* will now and then be mixed with the *pathetick*. The arias will not always be drowned with the indiscretion of the instruments, that hide the artful delicacy of the *piano,* and the soft voices, nay, even all voices which will not bawl. They will no longer bear being teased with unisons,[10] the invention of ignorance, to hide from the vulgar the insufficiency and inability of many men and women singers. They will recover the instrumental harmony now lost. They will compose more for the voice than the instruments. The part for the voice will no more have the mortification to resign its place to the violins. The soprano's and contr'alto's will no more sing the arias in the manner of the bass, in spight of a thousand octaves; and finally, their arias will be more affecting, and less alike, more natural and more lyric, more studied, and less painful to the singer; and so much the more grand, as they are remote from the vulgar. But, methinks, I hear it said, that the theatrical licence is great, and that the *mode* pleases, and that I grow too bold. And may I not reply, that the abuse is even greater, that the invention is pernicious, and that my opinion is not singular?

9. The *modes* here spoken of, our author has not well explained. The foundation he goes upon are the eight Church modes. But his meaning and complaint is, that commonly the compositions are in C, or in A, with their transpositions, and that the others are not used or known. [Tr.]. Galliard's original term for "mode" is the English "Mood." He correctly recognizes Tosi's complaint that modern music uses only the major and minor modes. Tosi suggests the revival of the Dorian and Phrygian.

10. The arias, sung in unison with the instruments, were invented in the Venetian operas to please the *barcaroles* [gondoliers], who are their watermen; and very often their applause supports an opera. The Roman School always distinguished itself and required compositions of study and care. How it is now at Rome is doubtful; but we do not hear that there are any Corellis. [Tr.] On the gondoliers, see the account of St. Didier in No. 91, p. 577.

THE PROFESSION AND ITS INSTITUTIONS

86 Heinrich Schütz

Heinrich Schütz (1585–1672) published three volumes of *Symphoniae sacrae* in 1629, 1647 and 1650. With the presentation of the last volume to his patron and employer of thirty-six years, Johann Georg I, Elector of Saxony, he also requested that he either be allowed to retire from his position as director of music or be given an assistant to help him in his duties. This request of early 1651 shows the conventional outline of Schütz's career, from chorister to service through the Thirty Years' War for the same ruling prince. It also documents the composer's atypical university education, his musical studies in Venice, Schütz's humanist view of his "profession and position," and finally, his desire to complete the publication of his musical works. His request to retire was not granted. Upon the death of the Elector in 1656 the direction of music at Dresden was divided among three masters of the chapel, Schütz, Giovanni Andrea Bontempi, and Vincenzo Albrici, portending the domination by professional Italians that was to come.

Memorandum to the Elector of Saxony
(1651)

Most Illustrious, Noble Elector, Most Gracious Lord,

With the present most humble offering of my little work,[1] which has just appeared under Your Electoral Highness's exalted name, I am at the same time moved to touch somewhat briefly on the course of my rather troubled life from youth to the present, begging in deep devotion that Your Electoral Highness receive it graciously and, if you are not opposed, to examine it at your leisure. Namely: that (after I was born into this world on St. Burkhard's Day, 1585) not very long thereafter but as early as my thirteenth year of age, I left my late parents' house in Weissenfels, and from that time on always lived abroad, and at first in fact I served as a choirboy for several years in the court ensemble of my lord the Landgrave Moritz in Cassel, but I both lived and was educated in school, and learned Latin and other languages in addition to music.

And as it was never my late parents' wish that I should now or ever make a profession of music, after I lost my soprano voice, on their advice I betook myself to the University of Marburg (in the company of my second brother, who thereafter became a Doctor of Law and who died a few years ago in

TEXT: Gina Spagnoli, *Letters and Documents of Heinrich Schütz, 1656–1672: An Annotated Translation* (Ann Arbor, 1990; reissued Rochester: University of Rochester Press, 1994), pp. 119–31, which gives the original German and this translation by Spagnoli, reprinted here by courtesy of the University of Rochester Press. The autograph manuscript (facs. Leipzig, 1972) is in the Dresden State Archives.

1. His *Symphoniae sacrae*, op. 12.

Leipzig as a member of the Supreme Court of the Judicature and in Your Electoral Highness's employ). There I intended to pursue the studies I had extensively undertaken elsewhere outside of music to choose a reliable profession and therein attain an honorable station. However, my plan was soon altered for me (undoubtedly by the will of God), namely in that my lord the Landgrave Moritz came to Marburg one day (who may perhaps have observed at the time when I was allowed to serve as a choirboy at his court that in some respects I was musically gifted by nature) and made me the following proposal: Because at that time a truly celebrated but quite old musician and composer was still living in Italy, I should not miss the opportunity to hear him and to learn something from him, and the aforementioned His noble Grace generously offered me at the time a stipend of 200 talers[2] yearly to carry out such a journey, which proposal I thereupon accepted most willingly with humble thanks (as a youth eager to see the world), and in 1609 departed for Venice, contrary, however, to my parents' wishes. Upon my arrival (after I had spent a little time with my master), I soon realized the importance and difficulty of the study of composition which I had undertaken and what an unfounded and poor beginning I had made in it so far, and therefore I regretted very much having turned away from those studies which were customary at German universities and in which I had already become rather advanced. I nonetheless patiently submitted and had to apply myself to that which had brought me there. So from that time on, all my previous studies laid aside, I began to deal only with the study of music with the greatest of all possible diligence to see how I would succeed. Then, with divine help, I progressed so far, without boasting, that after three years (and one year before I returned from Italy) I had published there my first little musical work in the Italian language,[3] with superior praise from the most distinguished musicians then in Venice, whence I sent it to my lord the Landgrave Moritz (to whom I dedicated it with humble acknowledgment). After the publication of my first little work, mentioned above, I was urged and encouraged not only by my teacher, Giovanni Gabrieli, but also by the Capellmeister and other distinguished musicians there that I should persist in the study of music and that I should anticipate every auspicious success therein.

And after I remained there another year (although at the expense of my parents) to learn yet something further from my studies, it happened that my aforementioned teacher died in Venice, whom I also accompanied to his final resting place. On his deathbed, he also bequeathed to me out of special affection, in his blessed memory, one of his rings he left behind which was

2. One Hessian *taler* was worth 32 *albus,* while the florin was worth 26 *albus.* In 1605 another young musician was given four taler by Moritz to go to the Frankfurt fair. In the first half of the century, organists in the region received salaries from about 30 to 60 florins annually (see Klaus Steinhaüser, *Die Musik an den Hessen-Darmstädtischen Lateinschulen im 16. und 17. Jahrhundert* [Giessen, 1936], p. 36). A cow could cost about ten florins.
3. His *Primo libro de Madrigali* (Venice, 1611).

presented and delivered after his death by his father confessor, an Augustinian monk (from the cloister where Dr. Luther once stayed). Thus the aforesaid premonition of my lord the Landgrave Moritz in Marburg proved true, that whoever wished to learn something from this certainly very highly talented man need remain absent no longer than I.

When I then returned to Germany from Italy for the first time in 1613, I indeed resolved to keep to myself my musical foundations, by now well established for some years, and to keep them hidden until I had developed them somewhat further and thereupon could distinguish myself with the publication of a worthy piece of work. And also at that time, I was not lacking advice and incentive from my parents and relatives, whose opinion was, in short, that I should make use of my other truly modest abilities and strive for advancement, and should treat music, however, as an avocation. As a result of their repeated unremitting admonition, I was finally persuaded and was about to seek out my books which I had previously laid aside when God Almighty (who no doubt had singled me out in the womb for the profession of music) ordained that in 1614 I be called to service in Dresden for the then impending royal christening of my lord the Duke August, now administrator of the archbishopric of Magdeburg (I do not know whether perhaps through the advice of Christoph von Loss, then privy councillor, or of Chamber Counselor Wolffersdorff, also designated commander of Weissenfels). After my arrival and passing an audition, the directorship of your music was soon thereafter graciously offered to me in Your Electoral Highness's name, from which then my parents and relatives as well as I obviously perceived the immutable will of God regarding my person, and hereby a goal was set for my vacillating plans, and I was persuaded not to refuse the honored position offered me, but to accept with humble thanks and to vow to fulfill it with my best efforts.

I hope Your Electoral Highness will to some extent remember my truly insignificant duties, indeed performed not without difficulty since the year 1615 (the year in which I personally assumed this post, and, as long as it pleases God and Your Electoral Highness, I shall hold in the future) until now, and thus over thirty-five years.

And if I may go so far as to praise the charity and favor granted to me by God (over such a long time), along with my private studies and the publication of various works, I have most humbly served Your Electoral Highness at many past diverse festivities which occured during this time, at imperial, royal, electoral, and princely gatherings, in this country and abroad, but particularly at each and every one of your own royal children's weddings, not less, too, at the receiving of their sacred christenings (except for my lady, now the Landgravine of Darmstadt, and my lord the Duke Johann Georg, the elector apparent). From the beginning of my directorship of Your Electoral Highness's court ensemble, I have also always endeavored to spread its fame above all others in Germany to the best of my ability, and, I hope, have always devoted myself to help uphold its praise and fame in some measure even up to the present.

Now I would indeed gladly and sincerely hope that the course of Your Electoral Highness's court ensemble which I have tended up until now could be directed by me in the future; however, not only due to my ceaseless study, travel, writing, and other constant work, which has been, without boasting, continuous since my youth (which my arduous profession and position unavoidably require, the smallest difficulties and hardships of which, then, in my opinion, even our own scholars themselves are in fact unable to judge, because at our German universities such studies are not pursued) but also due to my now advancing old age, diminishing eyesight, and spent vitality, I am now unable to serve it suitably any longer, nor uphold my good name, which I gained to some extent in my youth. I in no way dare continue, nor can I attempt, unless I want to endanger my health and collapse ere long, the constant studying, writing, and contemplation, [from which,] according to the physician's advice, I must henceforth refrain and forbear as much as possible. Therefore, Your Electoral Highness, I hereby submit this for your gracious consideration with due humility, and moreover in most humble devotion I respectfully entreat you, may it please Your Grace (not only because of the reasons I have already cited, but also in consideration of the fact that Your Electoral Highness's most beloved royal children are now all married) to remove me in future to a somewhat calmer situation, and (in order that I might again collect and complete my musical works, begun in my youth, and have them published in my memory) to free me from steady service, and to the extent that pleases Your Electoral Highness, to have me recognized and declared, as it were, a pensioner, in which case I must perhaps accept the situation if Your Electoral Highness were to modify somewhat my present wages, if it please Your Grace.

Nevertheless, I am as willing as I am indebted (in that Your Electoral Highness is unwilling to spare me from your chapel and to employ another Capellmeister at this time, but will continue to be satisfied with the poor service which I will be able to offer in my daily waning strength), yet to persevere in being of all possible aid and to devote myself further to serving the title of [Capellmeister] (of Your Electoral Highness's honored house) and I would hope finally to take [that title] with me to my grave, only if in future (especially since all those old musicians with whom I first began my directorship thirty-five years ago are now all dead and the very few remaining, owing to physical infirmity and old age, are not particularly suited to further service) another qualified person may be allied with me to relieve me in my work, who could daily manage the young people now thriving in the electoral ensemble, continuing the necessary rehearsals, frequently organize the music, and conduct.

Whereas with the imminent waning of my strength yet further (if God should allow me to live still longer) it is perhaps possible that I will experience (if Your Electoral Highness will graciously pardon me for bringing this up) what has happened to one not poorly qualified old cantor, who lives in a noteworthy place and whom I know well, who for some time has written to me and complained bitterly that his young town councillors are quite dissatisfied with his old-fashioned music and therefore would like very much to be rid of him, saying intentionally to his face in the town hall that a tailor of thirty years and a cantor of thirty years are of no use to anyone. And although I am certain that the fact that the young world soon becomes weary of the old customs and ways and changes them is not without its advantages, and though to be sure I anticipate none of this from my lords the sons of Your Electoral Highness (as my gracious lords have treated me kindly), I could encounter it from some other newly arrived young musicians who, with the rejection of the old, usually give preference to all of their new ways, although for poor reasons.

And since my lord the Duke Johann Georg the elector apparent's Italian eunuch, [Giovanni] Andrea Bontempi,[4] has many times made it known that especially since his youth he has been more devoted to composition than to singing and he has volunteered out of his own free will that at my request he would always willingly serve in my place and direct the ensemble, I therefore wish at the conclusion of this writing of mine to Your Electoral Highness to discover and moreover to learn your most gracious opinion in this matter: Namely, whether I may, with your most gracious consent, offer and employ the aforementioned Andrea Bontempi and allow him frequently to direct the ensemble in my place? This, in my modest judgment, Your Electoral Highness (indeed subject to correction) should allow immediately, and could observe and listen awhile for a trial period, so to speak, since he does not seek a salary increase or a change of title for his service, but is willing to be as content one way as the other with the support ordered by his most gracious lord the elector apparent. This young man is thus willing and very well qualified for such work. He has also acquired satisfactory recommendations in Venice (he remained there for eight years) where for several holiday celebrations he often took the Capellmeister's place in publicly directing the music in their churches. Therefore there is little to doubt regarding his qualifications; besides, he seems then to be, in his other transactions, a discreet, polite, good-natured, fine young man. Regarding Your Electoral Highness's most gracious will in this matter, I request a most gracious report, since without Your Electoral Highness's prior knowledge, it would not be proper for me to make constant use of the services of such a person.

Commending you hereupon to the powerful protection of the Almighty for prolonged [and] complete bodily health, long life, blissful reign, and your every other hope for the well-being of body and soul, while [commending] myself to the constant electoral grace most humbly and obediently. Dated Dresden on the fourteenth day of January. In the year of Christ our only Redeemer and Savior, 1651.

> Your Electoral Highness's most
> humble duty-bound old servant,
> Heinrich Schütz, Capellmeister
> In his own hand

4. Giovanni Andrea Bontempi (1625–1705), was a castrato singer from the area of Perugia. Trained in Italy, he began his service in Dresden in 1651.

87 Francesco Coli

Francesco Coli, a priest from Lucca and censor for the Venetian Inquisition, began a series of monthly publications in 1687 titled *Pallade veneta*, a "collection of flowery and novel gallantries from the gardens of the Adriatic." It reported military news, especially of the war with the Turks, but also included essays, poetry, and news of social events and affairs. Its first year included musical scores of arias from current operas. Coli addressed his reports to people outside of the Veneto in the form of letters. Those from 1687 chosen here were addressed to a young lady, Angela Caterina Lupori, of Lucca. They vividly describe musical performances by the poor or orphaned young women living in the Venetian institutions known as *ospedali,* in terms that attempt to conflate virtuosity and virtue and define morally acceptable vehicles of esthetic pleasure.

FROM *Pallade veneta*
(1687)

[MAY 1687]

Since it is not ever my intention to recount the separate details about these sacred choirs of chaste maidens,[1] lack of time not permitting it, I will only tell you that at sung Vespers on the solemn feast of Pentecost at the Mendicanti, which was a banquet of delights for the ear, one tasted, among other savory compositions, a solo *Laudate pueri* delivered by Signora Tonina, one of the singing girls of this learned choir, who is called this out of endearment. It was accompanied by an ensemble of instruments and by a basso continuo and was so well counterpointed and diverse, that Apollo himself in Parnassus neither enjoys a more pleasing voice among his Muses nor hears, moreover, any plectrum more sweet than did those who enjoyed the excellent music in that church. This *virtuosa* has a voice that is a gift from nature and is so unaffected, mellifluous, artful, and expressive of the *affetti,* adorned with so much grace, and of a bearing so elegant, that she has no equal. Her *passaggi* are so skillful,

TEXT: Eleanor Selfridge-Field, ed., *Pallade Veneta: Writings on Music in Venetian Society. 1650–1750* (Venice: Edizioni Fondazione Levi, 1985), nos. 27, 35, 45; pp. 171–72; 175–78; 183–85. Translation by Margaret Murata.

1. The four charity *ospedali* of Venice, those of the Mendicanti, the Derelitti, the Pietà, and the Incurabili, stressed musical education for their female charges to the extent of becoming famous as conservatories. The singers and instrumentalists performed regularly for liturgical services and in public concerts, typically hidden from public view.

she descends, rises, turns, and soars over the grille with such command over the scales, that the birds themselves, who are lighter and poised on wings, are not such absolute masters of the air as she, when she passes through the musical skies without fear. When we got to those words of the psalm, *Matrem filiorum laetantem,*[2] she opened the richest musical treasures, dispersed the most prized goods of her art, and created a majestic display of as much as could be shown in this plentiful gallery of song. Now I see that in describing the stylish manner of this lady, I have tried Your Ladyship's patience, and instead of bringing you delight, I may have put you in despair. Let's then break off this talk, and I'll hold off to another letter describing the lascivious siren, who takes fresh air in the evening by the sea that laps beneath our balconies and lets loose the voices of Paradise, even though they come from the mouth of hell, for she is an angel in her voice and a fury in her ways.

• • •

[JULY 1687]

In this seminary of melodious angels[3] are around forty girls who are trained for use in the choir, some of whom sing and play every kind of musical instrument with such sweetness that they have no equal among the laity. The Apollo of this Parnassus of virtuosos is the most excellent Dr. Domenico Partenio,[4] vice–chapel master of the ducal chapel of San Marco, whose compositions are so attractive that, coupled with the sweetness of those voices from Paradise, their concerts are like those of seraphim. They sang a solemn Mass in which each of the girls could show her own talents; and to not repeat so many times the well-deserved praises of Signora Tonina, who could never be sufficiently raised to heaven with honors, I will say that we heard a solo motet from Signora Maria Anna Ziani, with those sweet ornaments and pleasing *portamenti* that she can offer to test the art of music. Although she is a woman, she enjoys a naturally masculine voice, but a tender one, full, and of a timbre so suave that she sings baritone with such grace that it carries you away and carries with itself the souls of them who hear it. The whole audience rippled at the falling and rising of her *passaggi*. She comforted us with her gladness and just as she has the ability to sow content in one's breast by trilling or simulating joy, she has equally at hand the keys to open a prison of torments, should she encounter the flat keys, the sharp keys, the short rests.[5] Beyond the particular grace of her singing, this woman also plays the violin with such skill and melody that I dare to say that if Eurydice had possessed even only half as much high

2. "And gladdens her heart with children," the last line of Psalm 112, the fourth psalm for Sunday Vespers.
3. Coli heard the women at the Mendicanti on the feast day of Saint Mary Magdalene.
4. Partenio (before 1650–1701), a singer and composer, wrote his first opera *Genserico* for Venice in 1669. He became vice–chapel master at St. Mark's in 1685 and became its *maestro* in 1692.
5. A general term for all rests shorter than the minim (half note) was "sospiro," or "sigh."

virtù,[6] Orpheus would not have had to go down to free her from the jaws of Hell.

• • •

[AUGUST 1687]

My Lady, I have several times described to Your Ladyship the Mendicanti, the [Derelitti] of Santi Giovanni e Paolo, and the Incurabili;[7] but I do not remember, if due to my negligence, whether I have ever mentioned the Pietà, which is not inferior to those that I have named. Here also is nurtured a seminary for girls in the art of music and of playing every desirable instrument, and their students become such vivacious and stylish singers that they astound even their own teachers in the art; nor do I believe that there is any other place better in terms of having a team of instruments more practiced or more learned.

Here on the 28th, the feast of Saint Augustine, they sang an oratorio so much to the people's satisfaction that I imagine it will be necessary to repeat it several times, since one hears that the nobility and the populace want to satisfy their ears. The poetry was by Signor Bernardo Sandrinelli and the music by Signor Don Giacomo Spada, organist at St. Mark's, who has so lively a spirit in his works that he concedes nothing to Cavalli, to Frescobaldi, nor to any among the most original who have united voices with strings. The title of the piece was noted as *St. Mary of Egypt, Penitent*. The characters were these given below:

Santa Maria Egizziaca, portrayed by signora Lucretia
First Angel, by signora Prudenza
Second Angel, by signora Barbara
Penitence, by signora Paolina
The Narrator, by signora Lucietta
Zosima, by signora Francesca

This last one, beyond her ability in singing, possesses superhuman qualities in playing the theorbo, and plays the lute so nobly that, after the first part of the oratorio, she swept the entire audience into ecstasies of admiration with the stylish *ricercate*[8] that she executed on the lute. Their singing was so pleasing, so clean in enunciation, that there was nothing to do but ask for more. The acclaim for their virtuoso style of performance has been so noised about that all the people are awaiting the day it will be repeated. You can tell what kinds of virtuous entertainments these noble lords amuse themselves with, of which, as patrons of the virtuosos, the *literati* have sung the glories in every age.

6. Literally, "virtue," but in classically influenced culture, the word conflates moral character with superior merit and abilities, from which sense "virtuoso" descends.
7. See note 1 above.
8. Improvised music.

88 Johann Sebastian Bach

Johann Sebastian Bach (1685–1750) gained his appointment in 1723 as cantor of the St. Thomas School and director of music in Leipzig. His duties included teaching Latin (for which he hired a deputy), training the four choirs of school-boys, giving instrumental lessons to the most musical, and providing music for four of the city's churches and for its civic occasions. In a period of transition after the headmaster of the school died in 1729, the town council's accumulated complaints about Bach were aired, as were, in turn, Bach's dissatisfactions with the conditions of his position. After having met his obligations as composer, director, and teacher for seven years, Bach finally stated his requirements for performing contemporary concerted church music in a memorandum to the council, which was, characteristically, ignored.

Short but Most Necessary Draft for a Well-Appointed Church Music
With Certain Modest Reflections on the Decline of the Same
(1730)

A well-appointed church music requires vocalists and instrumentalists.

The vocalists in this place are made up of the pupils of the Thomas-Schule, being of four sorts, namely, sopranos [*Discantisten,*] altos, tenors, and basses.

In order that the choruses of church pieces may be performed as is fitting, the vocalists must in turn be divided into 2 sorts, namely, concertists and ripie-nists.

The concertists are ordinarily 4 in number, sometimes also 5, 6, 7, even 8, that is, if one wishes to perform music for two choirs [*per choros*].

The ripienists, too, must be at least 8, namely, two for each part.

The instrumentalists are also divided into various kinds, namely, violinists [*Violisten*][1] oboists, flutists, trumpeters, and drummers. N.B. The violinists include also those who play the violas, the violoncellos, and the *violones*.

The number of the *Alumni* [resident students] of the St. Thomas School is 55. These 55 are divided into 4 choirs, for the 4 churches in which they must partly perform concerted music with instruments [*musiciren*] partly sing motets, and partly sing chorales. In the 3 churches, St. Thomas's, St. Nicholas's,

---

TEXT: Hans T. David and Arthur Mendel, eds., *The New Bach Reader: A Life of Johann Sebastian Bach In Letters and Documents,* rev. and enl. by Christoph Wolff (New York: Norton, 1998).

1. That is, string players.

and the New Church, the pupils must all be musical. St. Peter's receives the residue [*Ausschuss*] namely, those who do not understand music and can only just barely sing a chorale.

Every musical choir should contain at least 3 sopranos, 3 altos, 3 tenors, and as many basses, so that even if one happens to fall ill (as very often happens, particularly at this time of year, as the prescriptions written by the school physician for the apothecary must show) at least a double-chorus motet may be sung. (N.B. Though it would be still better if the group were such that one could have 4 subjects on each voice and thus could provide every choir with 16 persons.) Hence, the number of those who must understand music comes to 36 persons.

The *instrumental music* consists of the following parts, namely:

2 or even 3 for the	*violin 1*
2 or 3 for the	*violin 2*
2 for the	*viola 1*
2 for the	*viola 2*
2 for the	*violoncello*
1 for the	*violon[e]*
2, or, if the piece requires, 3, for the	*oboe*
1, or even 2, for the	*bassoon*
3 for the	*trumpets*
1 for the	*kettledrums*

summa 18 persons at least, for the instrumental music

N.B. If it happens that the church piece is composed with flutes also (whether they are recorders [*à bec*] or transverse flutes, [*Traversieri*]), as very often happens for variety's sake, at least 2 more persons are needed, making altogether 20 instrumentalists.

The number of persons appointed to play church music is 8, namely, 4 town pipers [*Stadt Pfeifer*], 3 professional fiddlers [*Kunst Geiger*], and one apprentice. Modesty forbids me to speak at all truthfully of their qualities and musical knowledge. Nevertheless it must be remembered that they are partly *emeriti* and partly not at all in such practice [*exercitio*] as they should be.[2]

This is the plan for them:

Mr. Reiche	for the	1st *trumpet*
Mr. Genssmar	————	2nd *trumpet*
vacant	————	3rd *trumpet*
vacant	————	*kettledrums*
Mr. Rother	————	1st *violin*
Mr. Beyer	————	2nd *violin*
vacant	————	*viola*
vacant	————	*violoncello*
vacant	————	*violon[e]*

2. Two of the town musicians were past retirement age and were not in such good practice.

Mr. Gleditsch	————	1st *oboe*
Mr. Kornagel	————	2nd *oboe*
vacant	————	3rd *oboe* or *taille*
The Apprentice	————	*bassoon*

Thus there are lacking the following most necessary players, partly to reinforce certain voices, and partly to supply indispensable ones, namely:

2 *violinists* for the 1st *violin*
2 *violinists* for the 2nd *violin*
2 that play the *viola*
2 *violoncellists*
1 *violonist*
2 for the *flutes*

The lack that shows itself here has had to be supplied hitherto partly by the students [*studiosi*],[3] but mostly by the *alumni*.[4] Now, the *studiosi* have shown themselves willing to do this in the hope that one or the other would in time receive some kind of reward and perhaps be favored with a *stipendium* or *honorarium* (as was indeed formerly the custom). But since this has not occurred, but on the contrary, the few slight *beneficia* formerly devoted to the *chorus musicus* have been successively withdrawn, the willingness of the *studiosi*, too, has disappeared; for who will do work or perform services for nothing? Be it furthermore remembered that, since the 2nd *violin* usually, and the *viola*, *violoncello,* and *violone* always (in the absence of more capable subjects) have had to be played by students, it is easy to estimate how much the chorus has been deprived of in consequence. Thus far only the Sunday music has been touched upon. But if I should mention the music of the Holy Days (on which days I must supply both the principal churches with music), the deficiency of indispensable players will show even more clearly, particularly since I must give up to the other choir all those pupils who play one instrument or another and must get along altogether without their help.

Moreover, it cannot remain unmentioned that the fact that so many poorly equipped boys, and boys not at all talented for music, have been accepted[5] to date has necessarily caused the music to decline and deteriorate. For it is easy to see that a boy who knows nothing of music and who cannot indeed even form a second in his throat can have no natural musical talent, and *consequenter* can never be used for the musical service. And that those who do bring a few precepts with them when they come to school are not ready to be used immediately, as is required. For there is no time to instruct such pupils first for years until they are ready to be used, but on the contrary: as soon as they are accepted they are assigned to the various choirs and they must at least

---

3. Students of the University of Leipzig. [Tr.]
4. The younger resident pupils of the St. Thomas School.
5. Accepted into the school. [Tr.]

be sure of *measure,* and *pitch* in order to be of use in divine service. Now, if each year some of those who have accomplished something *in musicis* leave the school and their places are taken by others who either are not yet ready to be used or have no ability whatsoever, it is easy to understand that the *chorus musicus* must decline.

For it is notorious that my honored predecessors, Messrs. Schell[e] and Kuhnau, already had to rely on the help of the *studiosi* when they wished to produce a complete and well-sounding music which, indeed, they were enabled to this extent to do, that not only some vocalists, namely, a bass, a tenor, and even an alto, but also instrumentalists, especially two violinists, were favored with separate *stipendia* by A Most Noble and Most Wise Council and thus encouraged to reinforce the musical performances in the churches. Now, however, that the state of music is quite different from what it was, since our artistry has increased very much and the taste [*gusto*] has changed astonishingly, and accordingly the former style of music no longer seems to please our ears, considerable help is therefore all the more needed to choose and appoint such musicians as will satisfy the present musical taste, master the new kinds of music, and thus be in a position to do justice to the composer and his work. Now the few *beneficia,* which should have been increased rather than diminished, have been withdrawn entirely from the *chorus musicus.* It is, anyhow, somewhat strange that German musicians are expected to be capable of performing at once and *ex tempore* all kinds of music, whether it come from Italy or France, England or Poland, just as may be done, say, by those virtuosos for whom the music is written and who have studied it long beforehand, indeed, know it almost by heart, and who—it should be noted—receive good salaries besides, so that their work and industry is thus richly rewarded, while, on the other hand, these things are not taken into consideration, but they[6] are left to look out for their own wants, so that many a one, for worry about his bread, cannot think of improving—let alone distinguishing—himself. To illustrate this statement with an example one need only go to Dresden and see how the musicians there are paid by His Royal Majesty. It cannot fail, since the musicians are relieved of all concern for their living, free from *chagrin* and obliged each to master but a single instrument; it must be something choice and excellent to hear. The conclusion is accordingly easy to draw: that with the stopping of the *beneficia* the powers are taken from me to bring the music into a better state.

In conclusion I find it necessary to append the enumeration of the present *alumni,* to indicate the skill of each *in musicis* and thus to leave it to riper reflection whether in such circumstances the music can continue to be maintained, or whether its still greater decline is to be feared. It is, however, necessary to divide the whole group into three classes.

Accordingly those who are usable are as follows:

6. That is, German musicians. [Tr.]

(1) Pezold, Lange, Stoll, *Praefecti.* Frick, Krause, Kittler, Pohlreüter, Stein, Burckhard, Siegler, Nitzer, Reichhard, Krebs *major* and *minor,* Schönemann, Heder, and Dietel.

The names of the motet singers, who must first have further training in order to be used eventually for concerted music [*Figural Musik*], are as follows:

(2) Jänigke, Ludewig *major* and *minor,* Meissner, Neücke *major* and *minor,* Hillmeyer, Steidel, Hesse, Haupt, Suppius, Segnitz, Thieme, Keller, Röder, Ossan, Berger, Lösch, Hauptmann, and Sachse.

Those of the last sort are not *musici* at all, and their names are:

(3) Bauer, Gross, Eberhard, Braune, Seyman, Tietze, Hebenstreit, Wintzer, Össer, Leppert, Haussius, Feller, Crell, Zeymer, Guffer, Eichel, and Zwicker.

Total: 17 usable, 20 not yet usable, and 17 unfit.

Joh. Seb. Bach
Director Musices

Leipzig, August 23, 1730

89 Geronimo Lappoli and Anna Renzi

The institution of the Venetian opera house financed principally by subscribers made possible the new musical profession of the freelance opera singer. The Teatro Novissimo (The Newest Theater) was the first theater in Venice built to be devoted exclusively to opera. Geronimo Lappoli undertook four or five operatic seasons in the leased venue, defaulting on payments for the site in 1645. The Roman soprano Anna Renzi performed there in 1641 and 1642. The following year she sang in two operas at the Teatro Grimani (one role was that of Ottavia in Monteverdi's *Coronation of Poppea*) and returned to the Novissimo in 1644 and 1645. The contract between impresario and singer for Renzi to sing the title role in *Deidamia,* whose score is lost, reveals succinctly the legal expectations and perquisites on both sides. The opera opened less than a month after this contract was signed, on January 5, 1644.

Contract for the 1644 Season at the Teatro Novissimo

(1643)

Thursday, the seventeenth of the month of December 1643, at the residence of the below-mentioned Signora Anna near San Giovanni in Bragora.

The Most Illustrious Signor Geronimo Lappoli having requested the consent of the Most Illustrious Signora Anna Renzi to favor his theater called the Novissimo near SS. Giovanni et Paolo with her merit by performing in the operas, one or more, that will be given in said theater this coming carnival season, and, also due to the mediation of certain gentlemen, to which she has agreed, on the authority of the present instrument said Signora Anna for her part and said Signor Lappoli on the other do declare and agree upon the following, that is:

That said Signora Anna is obligated, as pledged, to perform in one or more operas that will be given in said Teatro Novissimo this coming Carnival, participating in every rehearsal of these very operas, only, however, those done in the theater or in the residence of Signora Anna herself.

Against this said Signor Geronimo promises to give to said Signora Anna 500 silver Venetian *scudi* cash[1] in this manner: that is, 100 *scudi* for all the present month of December, another 150 at the second performance, another 150 after half the performances, and at the next to last performance the remaining 100 *scudi*, without any opposition or delay.

And in case (God forbid) said Signora Anna should take ill after some of the performances have been done, in such case said Signora Anna may not claim other than one half of above-said 500 *scudi;* but if for any other cause or circumstance, nothing [else] excepted, Signor Lappoli should be prevented from presenting the show, he is held in such case to give her the 500 *scudi* in the manner above.

In addition, Signor Lappoli is held in any case to give and consign to her a box for her use for all of Carnival, and further [he must provide] all the costumes that must serve for the performances for said Signora Anna, completely at the expense of Signor Lappoli himself, which costumes will then remain with

---

TEXT: The text of the original document (Venice, Archivio di Stato, Archivio notarile, Acts of Fr. Beatian, *busta* 658, fols. 163v–164v) is given in Beth Glixon, "Private Lives of Public Women: *Prime donne* in Mid-Seventeenth-Century Venice," *Music and Letters* 76 (1995): 509–31, where portions are also given in English. The present translation is by Margaret Murata.

1. One Venetian silver *scudo* was worth 9 *lire* and 6 *soldi* in 1635 (with 20 *soldi* to a *lira*). The large sum of 500 silver *scudi* or 4,650 *lire* promised to Renzi may be compared with the 300 ducats (the equivalent of 1,920 Venetian *lire*) granted in 1643 as annual salary to Monteverdi's successor as chapel master at St. Mark's in Venice.

above-mentioned Signor Lappoli, all for which said Signor Geronimo pledges himself and his goods of all kinds, present and future.

As greater security for Signora Anna, present, with respect to the above-said matters, the excellent Signor Giosef Camis, Jewish physician, also present in person, does constitute himself and his heirs and successors guarantor, fidejussor,[2] and principal payor either for these 500 *scudi* or for that part which might be owed to said Signora Anna as stated above, as well as for every other obligation of said Signor Lappoli included in the present instrument, for which he pledges himself with his goods of all kinds, present and future.

Item, said Signor Geronimo promises to give to the Most Illustrious Signor Filiberto Laurenzi sixty silver *scudi* for which he is obligated to play in the rehearsals as well as in all the operas that will be given in above-said theater in the coming Carnival.

Item, to the same, another 25 *scudi* to teach the musicians, [and for] the prologue, and *intermedi*,[3] as said Signor Filiberto here present promises to perform in said capacities, as it has been agreed to above, etc.

Witnesses: The Most Illustrious Lord Francesco Michiel, son of the late
Most Illustrious Lord Antonio.
Lord Giorgio Giorgi [son of] the late Lord Antonio, Roman

2. In civil law, one who provides surety for another.
3. In other words, as a performer Laurenzi would participate in rehearsals and help prepare performers; as a composer he would provide the music for the prologue and *intermedi* (and earn a total of 85 *scudi*, or 790 *lire*, 10 *soldi*).

90 Evrard Titon du Tillet

In 1697 Evrard Titon du Tillet (1677–1762) purchased the office of first steward in the household of the twelve-year-old Duchess of Burgundy, newly married to the heir presumptive to the throne of his grandfather, the "Sun King" Louis XIV. The duchess became a constant delight of the monarch's last years. In 1708 Titon commissioned a colossal bronze sculpture that honored the great poets and musicians of the reign of the Sun King. A seven-and-one-half-foot model in bronze of the *Parnassus of France* was completed by 1718, though by then the duchess, her husband, and Louis XIV had all died. In hopes of gaining patrons to execute the sixty-foot monument, Titon published a description of the project in 1727 that gives invaluable biographical and bibliographic entries for the multitude of figures and ninety lesser ones to be portrayed in the sculpture. The musician with the highest place in this Parnassus was, of course, Jean-Baptiste Lully (1632–1687).

The final work was never cast, and Titon continued to expand the description of the *Parnassus of France* in book form. The 1732 edition offers 259 entries. His eulogies memorialized many writers and musicians that he knew of or had known personally. A supplementary essay to the 1743 edition, "The Famous Actors and Actresses of the Comedy and Opera, Whom Death Has Taken or Who Have Left the Theater," begins by recounting the life of Marie Le Rochois (c.1658–1728) a soprano whom he had heard perform in his youth. Titon's praise of Le Rochois conveys the expressive intensity he remembered in Lully's operas and indicates the high level of social esteem that a theatrical singer could achieve.

FROM THE First Supplement to
The Parnassus of France
(1743)

I will begin with the illustrious Mademoiselle Marie Rochois,[1] born of a good family of Caen, but little favored by the blessings of fortune, which thus obliged her, having come to Paris, to enter the Opéra in 1678, where Lully admitted her for the beauty of her voice. She began to distinguish herself in the role of Arethuse in the opera *Proserpine*[2] in 1680 and became in short time the greatest performer and the most perfect model for declamation who had appeared on stage. . . . She played heroines' roles and [Lully] often attributed to her the success of his operas. Indeed, beyond all the talents that she had for singing and for declamation, which she possessed in the highest degree, she had a great deal of the wit, knowledge and acuteness of any woman, and excellent and most unerring taste. If she surpassed herself in any one thing, it was, in my opinion, in her acting and in her expressive and striking *tableaux* in the roles she played, with which she delighted all her spectators. Even though she was fairly short, very dark, and looked very ordinary outside of the theater, with eyes close together which were, however, large, full of fire, and capable of expressing all the passions, she effaced all the most beautiful and more attractive actresses when she was on stage. She had the air of a queen and of a divinity, the head nobly placed, an admirable carriage, with all her movements beautiful, appropriate and natural. She understood marvelously well that which is called the *ritournelle*, which is played while the actress enters and presents herself to the audience, as in pantomime; in the silence, all the feelings and passions should be painted on the performer's face and be seen in her move-

TEXT: *Le Parnasse françois suivi des Remarques sur la poësie et la musique* (Geneva: Slatkine Reprints, 1971); facs. of eds. 1732–43, pp. 790–95. Translation by Margaret Murata.

1. In modern sources she is also called Marie Le Rochois and, erroneously, Marthe Le Rochois.
2. The ninth opera by Jean-Baptiste Lully; libretto by Philippe Quinault.

ments, something that great actors and actresses have not often understood. When she would become passionate and sing, one would notice only her on the stage. This struck me especially in the opera *Armide*,[3] in which she played the greatest and most powerful role in all our operas. She appeared in its first act between two of the most beautiful and imposing actresses ever seen on the stage, Mesdemoiselles Moreau and Desmatins,[4] who served her as confidantes and who sought to alleviate the sadness in which she appeared to be immersed. They sang to her these verses

> On a day of triumph, and in the midst of pleasure
> who could cause within you such melancholy gloom!
> All glory, greatness, and beauty with youthful bloom
>   now fulfill your desires beyond measure.
> . . . .
> In Hell you have come to extend your hand as law;
> defenseless against you is every valiant knight,
>   fallen before the force of your might, etc.[5]

At the moment in which Mademoiselle Rochois opened her arms and lifted her head with a majestic air, singing,

> Triumphed I have not o'er the most valorous of all,
> The invincible Renaud by my wrath has yet to fall.

these two confidantes were, in a manner of speaking, eclipsed. We saw only her on the stage and she alone seemed to fill it. And in what rapture we were in the fifth scene of the second act of the same opera, to see the dagger in her hand, ready to pierce the breast of Renaud, as he slept on his bed of grass! Fury animated her face, love seized her heart. Now one, now the other agitated her in turn; pity and tenderness succeeded them in the end, and love finished the victor. What beautiful and true bearing! What movements and different expressions in her eyes and on her face during this monologue of twenty-nine lines, which begins with these two

> Finally he is in my power,
> This mortal enemy, this haughty conqueror.[6]

One may say that this is the greatest piece in all our opera and the most difficult to deliver well, and it was one in which Mademoiselle Rochois shone the most, just as in the one at the end of the same opera where she sang

3. First performed in Paris in 1686, libretto by Quinault with music by Lully.
4. Fanchon Moreau (1668–after 1743); the Christian name of the soprano Desmatins (fl. 1682–c. 1708) is unknown.
5. These are the opening lines of the opera, act 1, scene 1, sung by Phenice, with a later speech sung by Sidonie. Titon's text varies from that in Robert Eitner's musical edition in *Publikation älterer praktischer und theoretischer Musikwerke*, vol. 14 (Leipzig: Breitkopf und Härtel, 1885). Titon's next quotation, of Armide's first words, immediately follows.
6. "Enfin il est en ma puissance," act 2, scene 5; a reprint of Eitner's edition of this scene is available in the *Norton Anthology of Music*, ed. by Claude V. Palisca, 3d ed. (New York, Norton, 1996), vol. 1, pp. 401–7.

The trait'rous Renaud flees from me,[7] etc.

It suffices to cite the opera *Armide* without enlarging upon the other operas of Lully in which she enchanted the spectators in the leading roles that she sang.

This great actress, sensing her voice and her powers diminishing due to the great efforts that she had made in 1697 when she had sung in the opera *Armide*, asked to retire in 1698, after having appeared in the first performance of the ballet *L'Europe galante* with music by Campra. The king granted her a pension of 1500 *livres*[8] from the Opéra, which, when added to a smaller one from the Duke of Sully, made it possible for her to live like a true *philosophe*, passing part of the year in a little country house that she had in Certrouville-sur-Seine, four leagues from Paris. Several great musicians, actors, and actresses, and other individuals of spirit and talent betook themselves to visit her with great pleasure during the time she was in Paris and profited from her amiable society, her knowledge and her good taste. She died there in a small apartment on the rue St. Honoré, near the Palais Royale,[9] on October 9, 1728, at about seventy years of age.

7. Act 5, scene 5, Armide's final soliloquy and the last scene of the opera.
8. In 1700, a standard unit (*voie*) of firewood for heating cost about 10.56 Parisian *livres;* in the year Le Rochois died, it had risen to 14 *livres.*
9. The Opéra was located here.

91 Alexandre-Toussaint Limojon, Sieur de Saint-Didier

The French nobleman Saint-Didier spent the years 1672–74 in Venice. Struck by the uniqueness of Venetian society and government, he began to write a thorough history of the republic and its people. However with the appearance in 1675 of the massive *History of the Government of Venice* by A.-N. Amelot de la Houssaie, a former secretary in the French embassy to Venice, Saint-Didier revised his project. He covered Venetian history and its government in parts 1 and 2, which he followed with observations on "the manner of living and customs of the Venetians." He wrote in his preface (in the language of the 1699 English translation), "I cannot think them less different from the other parts of Europe, than the Kingdom of China is from that part of France." In part 3, his preface continues, he aimed to describe "the conduct of the young nobility, with their particular customs. And the better to shew all the singularities of them, there is the manner of living of almost all the different degrees of people;

. . . [and] an exact description of all the publick diversions of Venice, to shew the mighty difference, between the relish of this people, and those of other nations." Those diversions included the Venetian public opera, which Saint-Didier duly compared with the court operas of Jean-Baptiste Lully.

FROM *The City and Republic of Venice*
(1680)

PART THREE: OF THE CUSTOMS AND MANNER OF LIVING OF THE VENETIAN GENTLEMEN AND LADIES, AS LIKEWISE OF OTHER SECULAR AND REGULAR PERSONS, WITH THE DESCRIPTION OF THE PUBLIC DIVERSIONS OF VENICE

OF THE OPERA

The invention of operas is due to the city of Venice. Although they were formerly particularly fine, yet Paris at present surpasses whatever can be seen here of this nature. It was not at first imagin'd that these compositions could agree with the genius of the French language, which is almost natural to the Italian; and in reality, if it had not been for that able master who first undertook it, who was no less familiar with all the beauties of the Italian musick, than with those delicacies of the French,[1] if it had not been, I say, for his great experience, in making those agreeable compositions which are sung in two such different ways, it may be believed, that this noble and magnificent diversion would not have been attended with that success which it has since had both at court and in town.

At Venice they act in several operas at a time.[2] The theaters are large and stately, the decorations [*décors*] noble and the alterations of them good. But they are very badly illuminated; the machines are sometimes passable and as often ridiculous; the number of actors is very great, they are all very well in clothes, but their actions are most commonly disagreeable.[3] These operas are long, yet they would divert the four hours which they last, if they were compos'd by better poets, that were a little more conversant with the rules of the

TEXT: *La Ville et la république de Venise* (Paris: C. Barbin, 1680), pt. 3, pp. 417–23; translation by F. Terne, *The City and Republick of Venice* (London: Char. Brome, 1699), pt. 3, pp. 60–65; capitalization and punctuation have been modernized. For the French text see H. Becker, ed., *Quellentexte zur Konzeption der europäischen Oper im 17. Jahrhundert* (Kassel: Bärenreiter, 1981), pp. 83–85.

1. Lully's name appears in the margin (it is not in the French edition). In 1675 Lully had presented four operas, by 1680, nine.
2. That is, several theaters were offering operas during the same weeks.
3. St. Didier refers to the theaters themselves, the stage sets and set changes, lighting, stage machines, costumes, and, probably, Italian stage gestures.

theater. For in this matter their present compositions are very deficient, inso-much they are frequently not worth the expence that is made upon them. The ballets or dancings between the acts are generally so pittiful, that they would be much better omitted; for one would imagine these dancers wore lead in their shoes. Yet the assembly bestow their applauses on them, which is meerly for want of having seen better.

The charms of their voices do make amends for all imperfections. These men without beards have delicate voices, besides which they are admirably suitable to the greatness of the theater.[4] They commonly have the best women singers of all Italy, for to get a famous girl from Rome or any other place, they do not scruple at giving four or five hundred pistoles,[5] with the charges of the journey, and yet their operas last no longer than the Carnival.[6] Their airs are languishing and touching; the whole composition is mingl'd with agreeable songs, that raise the attention. The symphony is mean,[7] inspiring rather melancholy than gaiety. It is compos'd of lutes, theorbos and harpsicords, yet they keep time to the voices, with the greatest exactness imaginable.

If the French have at first some difficulty to understand their words, the Italians and all other strangers have much more trouble in France, where they do not only sing lower,[8] but pronounce their words with much less distinction. The great chorus of musick that so often fills the French theater, of which one indeed can hardly distinguish the words, is very disagreeable to the Italians, who say that this is much more proper to the Church than the stage, as likewise that the great number of violins[9] spoils the symphony of the other musick, which they think can be only agreeable to the French, unless it is when they play alone in other occasions.[10] Although they allow the French to succeed very well in their dances, yet they are of the opinion, that there are too many of them in their operas, whose compositions are likewise too short for their fancies,[11] which they think are not sufficiently fill'd with intrigues. Their compositions are always concluded with the character of an old woman that gives good advice to the young, but falling in love herself without any probability of a return, she runs into the repetition of a great many pleasant fancies.

They that compose the musick of the opera endeavour to conclude the

---

4. The "voix argentines" or "silvered voices" of the castrati were able to fill the theaters with sound.

5. A term used for the French gold *louis*, which as of 1679 were in fact minted from Spanish coins in circulation. At this time its value wavered between ten and eleven Parisian *livres*, but it is unclear whether St. Didier is converting Venetian into French values in his report.

6. The Carnival season, which began sometime after Christmas and ended at Lent.

7. That is, the orchestra is small.

8. More softly.

9. This term includes all the strings.

10. The Italians complain of the French orchestra, except in purely instrumental music because, due to its size, its sound covers the voices.

11. "Compositions" here refers to the parts of the dramatic plot, not to musical numbers. The Italians preferred librettos in which multiple plots are intertwined.

scenes of the principal actors with airs that charm and elevate, that so they may acquire the applause of the audience, which succeeds so well to their intentions, that one hears nothing but a thousand "Benissimos" together. Yet nothing is so remarkable as the pleasant benedictions and the ridiculous wishes of the gondoliers in the pit to the women singers, who cry aloud to them, "Sia tu benedetta, benedetto el padre che te generò."[12] But these acclamations are not always within the bounds of modesty, for those impudent fellows say whatever they please, as being assur'd to make the assembly rather laugh than angry.

Some gentlemen have shewn themselves so transported and out of all bounds by the charming voices of these girls, as to bend themselves out of their boxes crying, "Ah cara! mi butto, mi butto,"[13] expressing after this manner the raptures of pleasure which these divine voices cause to them. I need not omit the priests in this place, for according to the example of Rome, they are no ways scrupulous of appearing upon the stage in all manner of parts, and by acquiring the character of a good actor they commonly get that of an honest man.[14] I remember once, that one of the spectators discerning a priest in the disguise of an old woman, cry'd aloud, "Ecco, Padre Pierro, che fa la vecchia."[15] Nevertheless all things pass with more decency at the opera than at the comedy,[16] as being most commonly frequented by the better sort of people. One pays four *livres* at the door, and two more for a chair in the pitt, which amounts to three shillings and sixpence English,[17] without reckoning the opera-book and the wax-candle every one buys; for without them even those of the country would hardly comprehend any thing of the history,[18] or the subject matter of the composition.

The *gentledonnas* frequent the opera much more than the comedy, by reason the diversions of that place are express'd with more civility than those of the other. As they are at this time allowed to dress with their jewels,[19] so they appear most splendidly by the means of the many lighted tapers which are in those boxes. Here their lovers are employed in the contemplation of their charms, and they on their side, shew by some signs that they are pleas'd with the assiduity of their services. Whenever a new girl appears to sing at the opera, the principal nobles esteem it a point of honour to be master of her, and if she sings well they spare nothing that may accomplish the design of getting her.

---

12. "Bless you, blessed be the father that conceived you!"
13. "O sweetheart! I'm going to jump, I'm going to jump."
14. Acquiring reputations as good actors gains them respect as men.
15. "Look, Father Peter's playing the old lady!"
16. Than in the spoken theater.
17. Forty-six French *sols,* which in terms of prices in Paris was the average price between 1670 and 1680 for about a hundred eggs.
18. The background events of the plot and the identification of the characters are often provided in librettos.
19. At various times Venetians were subject to sumptuary laws that affected the kinds of luxury items, or the materials of which they were made, that could be worn in public.

One of the Cornaros[20] was upon one of these occasions rival to the Duke of Mantua; they both endeavour'd to exceed each other in their presents, yet the charms of her voice were not accompanied with all those of beauty. The Venetian was successful and got the better of the Duke.

The owners of these admirable female singers print a great many songs[21] in praise of 'em, which are scatter'd up and down the pit and boxes, when any of 'em acquire the general applause of the audience.

20. The Venetian Cornaro (or Corner) family amassed immense wealth in the fourteenth century from their already considerable capital, by establishing sugar plantations on Cyprus, worked by slaves. They continued to hold the highest offices in Venetian government in the seventeenth and eighteenth centuries.

21. Sonnets; for a sampling see Lowell E. Lindgren and Carl B. Schmidt, "A Collection of 137 Broadsides Concerning Theatre in Late Seventeenth-Century Italy: An Annotated Catalogue," *Harvard Library Bulletin* 28 (1980):185–233.

92 "The Truthful Reporter"

The Roman Teatro delle Dame (Theater of the Ladies) opened in 1726 with the first performance in Rome of a libretto by Pietro Metastasio (to music by Leonardo Vinci). Another Roman opera house, the Teatro Argentina, was built in 1731 and is still in use today. In a series of letters, an opera lover who signed himself "Il relator sincero" left firsthand accounts of this flourishing time for new opera. They reveal what was important to a successful production, what strengths and weaknesses were noted in singers, how new music was assessed, and how vital it was to have good orchestral writing. His letters reveal the high expectations of the audience, especially in the Italians' love of complex plots and their demand for the dramatic integration of characterization, dancing, and musical style. In these two letters to an unknown and possibly fictitious "friend," the writer discusses operas by the Neapolitan Gaetano Latilla (1711–1788) and the Venetian Baldassare Galuppi (1706–1785). Then, as now, the opera season began after the Christmas holidays and ran through Carnival, with each theater usually mounting two works.

Two Letters on Opera in Rome

Rome, January 30, 1739

Dearest Friend,

Being obliged to satisfy your desire to know in detail the outcome, happy or unfortunate, of the operas in our theaters, I attended the staging of the second opera in the Teatro Alibert[1] entitled more truthfully, *Romolo,* or otherwise, *The Rape of the Sabine Women;* and telling you the title, I might as well speak of the libretto. It was damned by all. People say it is lacking in intrigue, which is what allows for surprise, and since it has in consequence no tumultuous actions, it cannot arouse the emotions of the people, which is the most necessary part of theater. The roles were not consistent at all; the versification most uneven in style and not lacking in many errors of language and diction.

The music of Signor Latilla[2] in the first act and part of the second is wondrously beautiful, both for its ideas and for the expression of feeling, and also for the impressive and novel harmony. On top of this, it appears competent, but without much flavor, and this, as far as people are saying, is not just because the libretto has become an oratorio and so is unsuitable to fire the inspiration of a composer, who can't extract manna from stones, but it is also because he himself wanted to vary his style and give a sample of himself to the canons of Santa Maria Maggiore where he is the designated maestro. He has written *a cappella,* whereupon begin the yawns in the audience, produced by the boredom that extended up till the chorus. It is said that the disaster of the second and third acts was partly due to the malice of the players; but this doesn't make sense. How could they not affect the opening sinfonia and the first act, but ruin the second and third? It has since revived a bit, since the drama has been fixed by shortening it a lot. On subsequent evenings, with everything in place, the public gave it general applause.

I won't speak to you of the Company. We will have to sigh for one eternally, as long as we are *amateurs* of such a fine art. Giorgi played the part of Tazio with a majesty, an expressiveness that I haven't words to convey to you. Annibali played Romolo with such gentle gravity that you would have believed that he intended to propose himself as our image of the Father of the great Roman Republic—if he weren't a castrato. Lorenzino, called the Bavarian, uttered a recitative in the third act with comic animation that delighted everyone. Porporino gave a demonstration quite different from the one he made in the first

TEXT: Fabrizio della Seta, "Il relator sincero (Cronache teatrali romane, 1739–1756)" in *Studi musicali* 9 (1980): 73–116, letters 1 and 3, pp. 86–88; 90–92. Sixteen of the original letters are in the Borghese Archives in the Vatican. Translation by Margaret Murata.

1. He calls the Teatro delle Dame by its name from 1717 to 1725, the Teatro Alibert.
2. Gaetano Latilla (1711–88) began his career writing comic operas for Naples; his first opera for Rome was a *dramma giocoso* staged in 1737 for the Teatro Tor di Nona; his first serious opera was a setting of Metastasio's *Demofoonte* for Venice in 1738. His collaborator on *Romolo* was Domingo Terradellas.

opera.[3] The *seconda donna* has much grace and has an action aria that was extremely well liked. The costumes of the men were first-rate, those of the women could not have been worse. The sets were mediocre, except for the last, which is a very beautiful creation. This is a sincere review; if you hear something different, it will be out of envy or flattery. Goodbye.

•   •   •

Rome, January 10, 1751

I am relieved, friend, from the regret that I had in sending you the day before yesterday the report about *Merope* at the Argentina,[4] and am feeling quite happy in having to describe to you the fortunate outcome last night of the opera at the Teatro delle Dame about the princess Antigona,[5] daughter of Oedipus and heir to the kingdom of Thebes, of which the author is Signor Gaetano Roccaforte, resident of the Lipari Islands, where instead of making lightning strikes, he has issued forth with his fiery spirit a drama in which he presents a mother who has never been a bride and expresses the feigned role of this princess with such tenderness, that it is necessary to weep at the power of his words.

Rome, dismayed by the unlucky event of the first opera, went to hear the second with suspended hopes, fearing to run into a similar disgrace. But quite soon it was clear that a celebrated *maestro di cappella* is useful to make even a bad actor look good; while in a company in which there is no star, you can still get pleasure and quite complete satisfaction.

This is all due to Signor Baldassare Galuppi, called il Buranello, who has made Rome hear what refined taste he has in musical composition. His great music was free of all exceptions and was applauded by all, because it was full of new ideas, of harmonious arias, of stupendous recitatives and strong scenes. The first act succeeded most beautifully. The second was a little tedious at the beginning, revived later, and finished with a marvelously wrought aria. The third held up because of the action scenes in it, and for a terzetto that is truly the soul of the work.

Lorenzino the Bavarian,[6] who, under the name of Antiope, priestess of a temple and interpreter of the oracles of Apollo, represented Antigona, sang with spirit and would have stood out more if he would rid himself of certain old-fashioned howls, when he wants to move into the high notes. The tenor Basteris,[7] as the figure of Creonte, tyrant and usurper of the Kingdom of Thebes that belonged to Princess Antigona, as much as he has a timbre similar to that of Vittorio Chiccheri and a pronunciation with the open E,[8] contributes nonethe-

3. Della Seta has identified these performers as Filippo Giorgi (fl. 1728–1749); alto castrato Domenico Annibali (c. 1705–1779 or later), who sang for Handel; Lorenzo Ghirardi (fl. 1738–44); and castrato soprano Antonio Uberti, known as "Porporino."
4. An earlier letter describes a performance of this score by Matteo Capranica.
5. This was the premier of *Antigona,* Galuppi's forty-sixth operatic score.
6. See note 3 above; for what little is known of the other singers named, see Della Seta, "Il relator sincero."
7. Gaetano Basteris.
8. This vowel sound is represented in the International Phonetic Alphabet as [ɛ].

less in his good way toward maintaining a great part of the reputation of the opera itself. Casimiro Venturini exacted great applause representing Euristeo, believed to be the widower of Antigona and destined by his father Creonte to be the husband of Ermione, since he sang with singular grace, making every effort to imitate the trills of Gizziello.[9] Much, however, is due to the orchestra, which made good for him, since with his thin voice he cannot lead them well in the finale. Giuseppe Belli, called Ermione, unknown daughter of Euristeo and of Antigona, did himself great honor and succeeded almost better than the *prima donna.* If the second tenor, in the person of the shepherd Alceste, believed to be the father of Ermione, had not moved like the marionettes on strings in the Vicolo dei Leutari,[10] he would have also got good marks, because he delivered with spirit. All the others are so well covered by the great sound of the orchestra and by the good music, that their defects do not appear.

The orchestra is memorable, and stands out from the beginning with a marvelous new *sinfonia* that is surprising.

The dances did not find favor, being too serious and long, and because people have seen those of Monsieur Sotter,[11] which have left a very refined taste.

The theater was completely lit up and was properly adorned. There were new costumes of splendid style, and old scenery out of storage, really ordinary and cheaply touched up by a famous painter who did the fireworks displays in Piazza Farnese.

At this unexpected success Rome has returned to nourish its good, old appetite and to declare the intention of taking itself to the Capranica and Valle[12] to amuse itself among the thespians. If, as I hope, this sincere witness of my well-owed attention pleases you, I will give myself the benefit of informing you at the right time about the second operas. Take care of yourself, and remember sometimes the person who doesn't forget You. Addio.

9. Castrato soprano Gioacchino Conti (1714–1761) created roles in Neapolitan operas of the 1730s and later sang for Handel in London and at the court in Lisbon to 1755.
10. "Alley of the lute-makers," a short street in Rome near the Palazzo Farnese.
11. François Sauveterre (d. 1775), who before this date had created ballets for theaters in Venice, Stuttgart, Florence, etc., including Rome in 1749.
12. Two other Roman theaters that presented operas.

93 Guillaume Dumanoir

Guillaume Dumanoir (1615–1697) headed the musicians' guild of France, known as the Confrérie de Saint-Julien-des-Ménétriers, (which maintained its own hospital and chapel). It had governed and protected freelance instrumentalists and dancing masters since 1321. As "King of the Violins" from November

1657, he oversaw the first major revision since 1407 of the articles governing the guild. The changes further institutionalized the profession and defined its jurisdictions clearly, especially with respect to "private" musicians such as those in the household of the King of France, whom Dumanoir also served. The 1658 statutes indicate the new prestige accorded instrumental musicians, though their hegemony was weakened when the dancing masters broke away in 1661 to take advantage of the even higher prestige that dance was gaining at the court of Louis XIV.

FROM Statutes of the Masters of Dance and Players of Instruments
(1658)

1. The masters in Paris and the other cities of this realm will be obliged to bind their apprentices for four full years, without being able to excuse them from said time, anticipate it, or discharge their brevets by more than one year,[1] on pain of a fine against these said masters of 150 *livres*,[2] a third to go to the King, a third to the confraternity of St. Julien,[3] and the other third to the king of the violins; and against said apprentices who wrongfully circumvent or gain said discharge for a longer time, [the penalty is] to be forever inadmissible to the mastership.

2. The above-said masters will be obliged, according to the accustomed manner, to present their apprentices at the time they accept them to the aforementioned king of the violins and have them register their brevets, both in his register and in that of the guild, for which registration said apprentice will pay to said king three *livres* and to the masters of the confraternity 30 *sols*.[4]

3. Said masters may not teach how to play instruments and other things except to those who are bound to them and currently dwell with them as apprentices, on pain of 50 *livres*, applicable as above.

4. When the said apprentices, after their terms of apprenticeship expire, present themselves to be admitted to the mastership, they will be obliged to demonstrate their skill before the said king, who may call twenty masters of his

TEXT: René Lespinasse, *Histoire générale de Paris: Les Métiers et corporations de la ville de Paris*, vol. 3 (Paris: Imprimerie National, 1897), pp. 587–89. The manuscript source from the Collection Lamoignon, tome 13, fol. 900, was first published in 1763. Translation by Margaret Murata.

1. For example, by buying out the contract of apprenticeship.
2. Examples of the value of a *livre*: in 1642 Dumanoir charged a nobleman ten *livres* a month for a period of eighteen months for daily dance lessons in the musician's home; wages for a lutenist of the king's chamber in 1658 were 600 *livres* a year.
3. The document mentions two separate, though overlapping social organizations, the *corporation* or guild and the *confrérie* of St. Julien of the Minstrels (here translated as "confraternity"), a musicians' benevolent society. The statutes are discussed in Catherine Massip, *La Vie des musiciens de Paris au temps de Mazarin (1643–1661)* (Paris: A. et J. Picard, 1976), pp. 70–86.
4. One *livre* = 20 *sols*. A *sol* would buy about nine eggs at this time.

choice for apprentices, and ten for sons of masters; and if he finds them able, he will deliver to them the patent of mastership.

5. Everyone who aspires to the mastership, whether they be apprentice or son of a master, will be obliged to receive the patents of said king, and will pay to the bursary of said guild for his right of reception and entry: if he is the son of a master, the sum of 25 *livres* only, and if he is an apprentice, the sum of 60 *livres*.

6. The husband of the daughter of a master, aspiring to the mastership, will enter as the son of a master, and will be received and treated in like manner.

7. The customs observed up to the present time with respect to the violins of the Chamber of His Majesty for the reception into the mastership will be continued, and they will be received on the basis of their brevet of retainership,[5] and upon payment by each for his right of reception the sum of 50 *livres* to the coffer of said corporation.

8. No person, royal subject or foreign, may conduct a school, teach dancing or the playing of high or low instruments privately, gather an ensemble night or day in order to give serenades or play said instruments in any weddings or assemblies public or private, nor anywhere else, nor in general do anything else concerning the exercise of said science, if he is not an admitted master or approved by said king or his lieutenants, upon pain of a fine of 100 *livres* for the first offense for each of the violations [and] seizure and sale of the instruments, all divisible a third to the confraternity of St. Julien and the remainder to above-said king of the violins or his lieutenants, and upon pain of corporal punishment for the second [offense].

9. The judgment of the Prefect of Paris of March 2, 1644, and the decree of Parliament of July 11, 1648, which confirmed it will be executed according to their form and terms, and in conformance with them, it is not permitted that masters or any other persons play instruments in cabarets and places of ill repute; and in case of violation, the instruments of the offenders will be broken and destroyed on the spot, without a formal trial, by the first commissioner or sergeant called upon by said king or one of the masters of the confraternity, and the offenders imprisoned for the payment of said fine, which cannot be waived or reduced for any reason, nor may the offenders be set free until the fines are paid.

10. The master of the fauxbourgs and of subordinate districts may not undertake any performing in the cities, neither make any oath nor mastership to the prejudice of said king, on pain of a fine of 100 *livres*, applicable as above.

11. The violins licensed to the Court may not gather any ensemble to play serenades nor play instruments, nor do any thing concerning said mastership, in the absence of His Majesty in this City of Paris.

12. Should any apprentice, during the time of his apprenticeship or after its expiration, go to play in cabarets or places of ill repute or other public places such as wedding halls, he may never aspire to the mastership; on the contrary he will be excluded forever.

---

5. That is, the terms of appointment to the royal household.

13. The masters may not encroach upon each other, nor present themselves before those [musicians] who would have need of them, nor take other than their companions to play with them; and when they are hired to someone for one or more days, neither the one who made the agreement nor the associates he chose [to play] with him, may excuse themselves for any cause from the service which they have promised, hiring other associates[6] in said time or contracting several jobs at the same time, upon pain of a fine of 30 *livres* for each offense, applicable as above.

14. No master may either associate or arrange to play in any place whatsoever with anyone who is licensed to the Court, or is an apprentice, or with anyone else who is not a master. And in case of a violation, any master who is found guilty will pay a sum of 10 *livres,* and anyone who is not a master, one half less.

15. Each of the said masters will be obliged to pay 30 *sols* a year as dues to the confraternity of St. Julien, and the revenues deriving from said dues and the fines applicable to said confraternity will be used to maintain the said chapel of St. Julien, and the dues to the coffer be used for the necessities of said corporation.

16. The masters of the confraternity who will be elected each year will be obliged to account for the proceeds of all said dues in the presence of said King of the Violins and the masters of the hall;[7] in the account he will give over the remainder, if there is any, into the hands of the one who takes his place.

•   •   •   •   •

20. The custom immemorial for admitting masters of the confraternity and masters of the hall will be continued, and in so doing, no one may be admitted as master of the confraternity who is not a master of the hall without the consent of said king and the other masters of the confraternity and of the hall, on any day other than that of St. Thomas. And for the admittance of a said master of the hall, each of those about to be admitted will pay to the coffer for the fees of entrance, 10 *livres.*

21. And because the king of the violins cannot be present in all the cities of this realm, he will be permitted to name lieutenants in each town, to have the present statutes and ordinances observed, to admit and approve masters; to which lieutenants all the necessary patents will be sent upon the nomination and presentation to said king and who will share in all instances half of the dues owed to abovesaid king in each admission of an apprentice and master.

Louis, by the grace of God, King of France and of Navarre . . . Given at Paris in the month of October, the year of grace 1658 and of our reign the sixteenth.

Registered in Paris, in Parliament, August 22, 1659; obtained and procured by Guillaume Dumanoir, king and master of all the master players of instruments and masters of dance, for all the realm of France.

6. Substitutes.
7. Dancing masters.

94 Roger North

Roger North (c. 1651–1734), the sixth son in a noble family from Cambridgeshire, England, grew up in a musical household (see No. 97 below). He trained in law and served the royal family in various legal offices but retired early from public life after the Glorious Revolution of 1688. He left copious writings on music, of which the latest appears to be his "Memoires of Musick, being some Historico-Critticall Collections of that Subject." His manuscript is dated 1728, but the work draws in part on his own earlier writing. The "Memoires" were first published in 1846 by Edward F. Rimbault for the Council of the Musical Antiquarian Society. In the extracts below, North reports on the lively concert life of late seventeenth-century London and on the first series of public instrumental concerts established there. Notices of the Banister concerts at White Friars that are mentioned by North appeared in the *London Gazette* between 1672 and 1678. Those held in York Buildings received notices until 1710. Later, occasional concerts were given there, such as a performance of Handel's *Esther* in 1732.

FROM *Memoirs of Music*
(1728)

THE RESTAURATION, AND THE STYLE OF BABTIST

But now to observe the stepps of the grand metamorforsis of musick, whereby it hath mounted into those altitudes of esteem it now enjoys: I must remember that upon the Restauration of King Charles,[1] the old way of consorts were layd aside at Court, and the King made an establishment, after a French model, of 24 violins, and the style of the musick was accordingly.[2] So that became the ordinary musick of the Court, Theaters, and such as courted the violin.

●   ●   ●   ●   ●

During the first years of Charles II all musick affected by the *beau-mond* run into the French way; and the rather, because at that time the master of the

TEXT: *Roger North on Music, Being a Selection of his Essays written during the years c. 1695–1728*, ed. John Wilson (London: Novello, 1959), pp. 349–53. Reproduced by permission of Novello and Co., Ltd. Further detailed annotations are in Mary Chan and Jamie C. Kassler, eds., *Roger North's* The Musicall Grammarian 1728 (Cambridge: Cambridge University Press, 1990), pp. 261–66.

1. Charles II returned from exile in France in 1660.
2. The 24 *violons* of Louis XIV were distributed six, four, four, four, and six instruments to five parts.

Court musick in France, whose name was Babtista (an Itallian frenchifyed)[3] had influenced the French style by infusing a great portion of the Italian harmony into it; whereby the Ayre was exceedingly improved. The manner was theatricall, and the setts of lessons composed, called *Branles* (as I take it) or Braules; that is, beginning with an Entry, and then *Courants,* &c. And the Entrys of Babtist ever were, and will be valued as most stately and compleat harmony; and all the compositions of the towne were strained to imitate Babtist's vein; and none came so neer it as the hon[ble] and worthy *vertuoso* M[r] Francis Roberts.[4] But the whole tendency of the ayre had more regard to the foot, than the ear, and no one could hear an *Entree* with its starts, and *saults,*[5] but must expect a dance to follow, so lively may human actions be pictured by musick.

•   •   •   •   •

This French manner of instrumentall musick did not gather so fast as to make a revolution all at once, but during the greatest part of that King's reigne, the old musick was used in the countrys, and in many meetings and societys in London; but the treble violl was discarded, and the violin took its place. In some familyes organs were used to accompany consorts, but the old masters would not allow the liberty of playing from a thro-base figured, as harpsicords of late have universally practised, but they formed the organ part express;[6] because the holding out the sound required exact concord, else the consort would suffer; or perhaps the organists had not then the skill as since, for now they desire onely figures. There were also divers societys of a politer sort, who were inquisitive after forrein consorts, and procured divers, as from Itally Cazzati and Vitali; and one from Sweeden by Becker[7] composed for from 2 to 6 parts, which was too good to be neglected and lost, as it is at present. And however England came to have the credit of musicall lovers, I know not, but am sure that there was a great flocking hither of forrein masters, as from Germany, Sheiffar, Vuoglesank, and others; and from France, Porter and Farinell, these latter for the violin. And they found here good encouragement, so that the nation (as I may terme it) of Musick was very well prepared for a revolution.

3. Jean-Baptiste Lully, dominant composer at the French court. North here describes as "sets of lessons" those varied movements that can make up an instrumental suite.
4. Or Robartes (d. 1718), a prominent lawyer and gentleman scientist and musician.
5. Leaps.
6. That is, they made their own short or reduced scores.
7. "Diverse" ensemble music ("consorts") from composers like Maurizio Cazzati (d. 1677), chapel master of the principal church in Bologna from 1657 to 1671, composer of vocal music as well as canzonas, trio and solo sonatas for violins and for trumpet; Giovanni Battista Vitali (1632–1692) of Bologna published twelve volumes of instrumental music, including the first Italian sonatas to include French dance movements; Dietrich Becker (1623–1679) was active in Hamburg from 1662 and influential in transforming the multipartite sonata into the suite.

THE PUBLICK MUSICK-MEETINGS

A great means of bringing that foreward was the humour[8] of following publick consorts, and it will not be out of the way to deduce them from the beginning. The first of those was in a lane behind Paul's,[9] where there was a chamber
organ that one Phillips played upon, and some shopkeepers and foremen came
weekly to sing in consort, and to hear, and injoy ale and tobacco; and after some
time the audience grew strong, and one Ben. Wallington got the reputation of
[a] notable base voice, who also set up for a composer, and hath some songs in
print, but of a very low sence; and their musick was cheifly out of Playford's
Catch Book. But this shewed an inclination of the citisens to follow musick.
And the same was confirmed by many litle enterteinements the masters voluntarily made for their scollars, for being knowne they were always crowded.

The next essay was of the elder Banister,[10] who had a good theatricall vein,
and in composition had a lively style peculiar to himself. He procured a large
room in Whitefryars, neer the Temple back gate,[11] and made a large raised box
for the musitians, whose modesty required curtaines. The room was rounded
with seats and small tables alehouse fashion. One s[hilling] was the price and
call for what you pleased. There was very good musick, for Banister found
means to procure the best hands in towne, and some voices to come and per-
forme there, and there wanted no variety of humour,[12] for Banister himself
(*inter alia*) did wonders upon a flageolett to a thro-base, and the severall masters had their solos. This continued full one winter, and more I remember not.

There was a society of Gentlemen of good esteem, whom I shall not name
for some of them as I hear are still living, that used to meet often for consort
after Babtist's manner; and falling into a weekly course, and performing
exceeding well, with bass violins (a course instrument[13] as it was then, which
they used to hire), their freinds and acquaintance were admitted, and by
degrees as the fame of their meeting spread, so many auditors came that their
room was crowded; and to prevent that inconvenience, they took a room in a
taverne in Fleet Street, and the taverner pretended to make formall seats, and
to take mony; and then the society disbanded.[14] But the taverner, finding the
sweet of vending wine and taking mony, hired masters to play, and made a

8. Inclination or tendency.
9. The cathedral of St. Paul in London.
10. John Banister (d. 1679), a royal violinist and composer.
11. East of the Inns of Court and formerly the site of a Carmelite foundation.
12. That is, variety of styles. The four liquid humors of ancient and medieval physiology—blood,
bile, phlegm, and choler—were thought to determine temperament. Music reflective of different moods, therefore, portrayed different "humors."
13. This "coarse" instrument is to be identified as the violoncello.
14. Castle Tavern in Fleet Street. Gentlemen, whether they performed for listeners or not, would
not have done so for gain. When the taverner elected to sell places at the concerts, thereby
turning it into a commercial enterprise, the original performers disbanded. They were replaced
by professionals.

pecuniary consort of it, to which for the reputation of the musick, numbers of people of good fashion and quallity repaired.

The Masters of Musick finding that mony was to be got this way, determined to take the buissness into their owne hands; and it proceeded so farr, that in York Buildings a fabrick[15] was reared and furnished on purpose for publik musick. And there was nothing of musick valued in towne, but was to be heard there. It was called the Musick Meeting; and all the Quallity and *beau mond* repaired to it. But the plan of this project was not so well layd as ought to have bin, for the time of their beginning was inconsistent with the park and the playhouses, which had a stronger attraction. And what was worse, the masters undertakers[16] were a rope of sand, not under the rule or order of any person, and every one foreward to advance his owne talents, and spightfull to each other, and out of emulation[17] substracting their skill in performing, all which together scandalized the company, and poysoned the enterteinement. Besides the whole was without designe or order; for one master brings a consort with fuges, anothers shews his guifts in a solo upon the violin, another sings, and then a famous lutinist comes foreward, and in this manner changes followed each other, with a full cessation of the musick between every one, and a gab-[b]le and bustle while they changed places; whereas all enterteinements of this kind ought to be projected as a drama, so as all the members shall uninterrupt-edly follow in order, and having a true connexion, set off each other. It is no wonder that the playhouses got ground, and as they ordered the matter, soon routed this musick meeting.

15. Building.
16. Entrepreneurs or agents.
17. Envy.

95 Roger North

In his 1695 autobiography *Notes of Me* (see also No. 98, below), North offered one of the earliest opinions regarding the order in which listeners experienced music, that is, the matter of programming, just discussed. The planning of esthetic experience—the manipulation of expectation and surprise on the part of the artist—was a major concern of the Baroque, whether in architecture, city planning, rhetoric, painting, or drama. The selection that follows not only describes an instrumental concert in more detail, but it also presents quite modern notions of a composition as a coherent development and of music as an art for listeners.

FROM *Notes of Me*
(c. 1695)

There is the same rule to be observed in all sorts of composed delights, formed for the regaling of mankind, whether it be fireworks, comedy, or musick. As for eating, I know not what rule to propose because all depends on appetite, which being sharp or cloyed, beginns and ends the matter, so let that pass. But to instance first in fireworks, the master must contrive that the beginning be moderate, for the least thing at first serves, and then other parts enter, with a noise and fire perpetually increasing, and the greatest fury must be the last, and then all expire at once. This draws the spectators from one degree of amazement to another, without any relapse or flagging, till it arives to the ackme, and then to cease; for the least pause, or abatement, nay non-progression, spoyles all. The like as to comedy, which is introduc't with slow, easy, and clear parts, and in the progress grows buisy, perplext, and at last dissolves in peace all at once—*Mercurio vindice*[1] Tragedy is the same; for that, in the way of sorrow and calamity, grows up gradually into a catastrofe of woe, ending as misery itself ends, in mortality.

So for a musicall enterteinement; if there be not a continuall procession of it, with increase of force, and intermixt with variety of measure and parts, to sett off and give lustre to each other, as light and darkness; but [instead] to stopp, and so the measure cease, and incoherent peices added, without designe, perhaps the severall parts and passages may be good in their kind, but the whole taken together cannot be a good enterteinement. As a comedy may have good scenes and be a very ill play. A song, a fuge, a solo, or any single peice (and so all the rest) may be very good in their severall kinds, but for want of a due coherence of the whole, the company not be pleased. And thus it is with the musick exhibited in London publiquely for 1/2 crownes.[2] A combination of masters agree to make a consort as they call it, but doe not submitt to the governement of any one, as should be done, to accomplish their designe. And in the performance, each takes his parts according as his opinion is of his owne excellence. The master violin must have its solo, then joyned with a lute, then a fuge, or sonnata, then a song, then the trumpet and haut-bois, and so other variety, as it happens. And upon every peice ended, the masters shift

---

TEXT: *Roger North on Music*, pp. 12–14. Reproduced by permission of Novello and Co., Ltd.

1. "With Mercury as deliverer."
2. A crown equalled five shillings. In 1675 three shillings would buy a pound of tobacco.

their places to make way for the next, the thro-base ceaseth, and the company know not whether all is ended, or any thing more to come, and what. Which pauses, and difforme[3] accidentall species of music presented one after the other, without judgment or designe, are so defective, as justly to be compared to a ballad singer, who having done one ballad, begins another to a pleasant new tune.

But this combination regulated, might exhibit very good musick; for the pert forewardness of some, or rather of all the masters, would be restrained, and they oblidged to take the parts designed and to stick to them, without perching forewards to shew their parts, and please themselves in being admired. And the thro-base should never cease but play continually, for that holds the audience in attention, and with the instruments (as some must be always) accompan[y]ing, will be no ill musick, wherein the master hath a latitude to bring in some caprice, or extravagance of measure or humour, conformeable to the musick past or next following. And then any single parts of voice, violin, lute, hautboys, trumpetts, or mixtures of them, may be introduc't, orderly and with coherence; so as the cessation of them before, was not a lacune or rupture, but a pause, as for breath; and when returned are a *denouement* of the enterteinement, so much prized in stage plays. And in short the whole is of a peice, and all the process of it considered and put together with skill and designe to give advantage to each part, and never lett the audience cease attention, but continually improve and raise it 'till the end, when the greatest force ceasing, speaks, there is no more. Such an enterteinement I never heard composed for an hour's passtime, which is enough, but my knowledge of the art tells me it should be so. But for smaller time it is common, as in the Itallian *sonnatas,* French *branles,* and English *fancys,* which well done are a specimen or model of what should be in greater designes. This is my apprehension, and censure,[4] touching these recreations, wherein the hearers are onely considered, and therefore fitt onely for great cittys full of idle people.

3. Not uniform, diverse.
4. "Understanding and criticism."

Domestic Music

96 Grazioso Uberti

A jurist from the Italian town of Cesena, Grazioso Uberti (c. 1574–1650) served as a lawyer to the Papal Curia in Rome. He published both juridical treatises and, as befitted a gentleman of letters at the time, Latin poetry. The *Contrasto musico* or "Musical Disagreement," subtitled "an amusing piece," offers a music lover's view of the major criticisms and defenses of the different kinds of music that could be encountered in Rome around 1630. The two speakers are Severo, who is irritated by the noisy school of music that his neighbor runs, and Giocondo, who has several musician friends. The book is divided into seven sections, each representing a different place in which music is made: the music school for boys, private homes, princes' palaces, churches, the Oratorio, the outdoors, and, finally, the houses of composers. Excerpted here from the section on music in private houses is a discussion of women and music. Uberti's use of ancient authors to lend authority to a point or opinion reveals the author's academic training.

FROM *The Musical Disagreement*
(1630)

GIOCONDO: . . . If you like, let us leave these private houses now.

SEVERO: Wait. There are still the ladies—the women singers, the spinsters who learn to sing, the ladies who entertain people in social gatherings with song.

GIOCONDO: If you think that this is not honest entertainment, let's just go.

SEVERO: Many say that nothing should be appreciated in women but honesty, that women should rather avoid dealing with men, than hold them in conversation and charm them with song.

GIOCONDO: The purpose of woman is to give birth to and to raise children, as Claudian said in *Against Eutropius*, Book 1:

> A woman is born to bear children and perpetuate the human race.[1]

Furthermore she should know how to manage a household and entertain herself with the distaff and needle, as Virgil said in the *Aeneid*, book 8:

> The housewife, her first task to sustain life
> by weaving and Minerva's humble arts,
> awakes the embers and the sleeping fires,
> as she adds on the night to her day's work

TEXT: *Il contrasto musico, opera dilettevole*, pt. 2 (Rome: L. Grignani, 1630). Repr. Lucca: Libreria Musicale Italiana, 1991), with an introduction by Giancarlo Rostirolla, pp. 67–73. Translation by Margaret Murata.

1. Loeb Classical Library, trans. M. Platnauer (Cambridge, Mass., 1922/1956), line 331; p. 163.

and keeps her housemaids toiling on at some
long chore by lamplight, that her husband's bed
be chaste, and that she raise her children well.[2]

And one shouldn't cause women to be seen, and gazed upon in case there should follow prejudice against their modesty, as Ovid says in book 1 of the *Art of Loving:*

They come to see, they come that they may be seen:
to chastity that place is fatal.[3]

This is all true. One shouldn't, however, keep women closed up as if in a dungeon to keep them from talking and being seen; because in this way you offend their wisdom, and you place their chastity in doubt. Those women are called wise who, being able to do something, do not do it. . . . The women are also chaste who guard themselves and have no need for a guardian husband, about which Ovid spoke well in the *Amores,* book 3, elegy 4:

Hard husband, by setting a keeper over your tender wife you nothing gain; 'tis her own nature must be each woman's guard. If she is pure when freed from every fear, then first is she pure; she who sins not because she may not—she sins! Grant you have guarded well the body, the mind is untrue; and no watch can be set o'er a woman's will. Nor can you guard her [mind], though you shut every door; with all shut out, a traitor will be within. She to whom erring is free, errs less; [the] very power makes less quick the seeds of sin.[4]

SEVERO: One should remove the opportunities to sin; and it seems that this music, this singing, invites a woman to social affairs; it exposes her to admiring gazes, to the desire of each person.

GIOCONDO: The opportunity for every evil is in leisure; about which Ovid says in book 1 of the *Remedies for Love:*

Toss your leisure away and you've broken the arrows of Cupid;
Toss your leisure away, his torch is extinguished and scorned.

• • • • •

Why did Aegisthus succumb to that adulterous passion?
That is no trouble at all—he had nothing to do.[5]

Therefore, one should ensure that women are not idle; when they are occupied in virtuous activities, there is no danger that they could be taken over by dishonest desires. In his *Dialogues,* the Greek author Lucian presents Venus screaming at her son Cupid, scolding him about why he had failed to wound Pallas, and has Cupid answer: because he never found her idle. If a woman be tired of sewing, of spinning, of household duties, what can she do for a little recreation? If she goes to the window to see who's passing by, she's a flirt. If she goes to the balcony

2. Uberti quotes lines 408–13; this trans. by A. Mandelbaum (New York, 1971), lines 533–42. Minerva was the Roman goddess of wisdom, of wool working, and of arts and crafts.
3. Loeb Classical Library, trans. J. H. Mozley (Cambridge, Mass., 1920/1962), lines 99–100; p. 19.
4. Loeb Classical Library, G. Showerman trans., rev. by G. P. Goold (Cambridge, Mass., 1977), lines 1–10.
5. Lines 139–40; 162–63 as trans. in *The Art of Love,* trans. R. Humphries (Indiana University Press, 1957), pp. 185–86.

to chat with her neighbor, she's a gossip; if she converse with men, she's a fuse near a fire; but if she sing and play, she is a *virtuosa* in no danger of stepping over any line. Father returns home burdened with household affairs: it quiets him a little. The mother, tired from caring for the family, nears her daughter at the instrument and sends forth her measured voice—oh what pleasure! oh what sweetness for the parents! On certain days the female relatives visit, the spinster friends, the neighbors; a young hand touches the harpsichord, imitating the garrulous bird with melodious voice—oh what sweetness, oh what melody! oh what gentle recreation for lady relatives, friends, neighbors!

SEVERO: Some think that singing is not appropriate to the female sex.

GIOCONDO: To these one can say that the Muses invented by the poets are not male, and that *music,* according to many, comes from the word "muse." One could also add that that concert which is born from music one calls *harmony,* a name which some say is derived from a woman named Harmony, who was the wife of Cadmus, who knew well how to play and sing; and to finish, I will cite Athenaeus on the ancient singers in book 1, chapter 7:

> Singers are to be honored, for the goddesses delight in the songs that the Muses have taught them.[6]

SEVERO: There remain certain others, who say that music from dishonest women should be condemned, because they should be avoided. With their singing and playing they mostly charm men just as bird hunters deceive birds by whistling.

GIOCONDO: It's true that one should shun wanton women. *Remove thy way from the evil woman and come not nigh the door of her house,* we are taught in Proverbs, chapter 5.[7] But it does not say that one ought to flee in order not to hear their singing, but rather in order not to desire their beauty and to not give in to their desires. Thus you read in the same Proverbs, chapter 6: *To keep thee from the prostitute, lust not after her beauty in thine heart; neither let her take thee with her eyelids.*[8] Or rather, music in regard to women like this is like an overcoat that covers every shame. Those women are named and praised for their music, for playing and singing, who are far from any trace of lascivious habits, which otherwise would render them odious and abominable. It seems to me that Isaiah said this in chapter 24 [i.e., 23]:

> Take a harp, go about the city, thou harlot that hast been forgotten; make sweet melody, sing many songs, that thou mayest be remembered.[9]

SEVERO: We have really swept these houses; let's go into the palaces in the courts.

GIOCONDO: I'm with you.

6. Uberti cites a Latin translation of *The Deipnosophists* by the late-classical Greek writer Athenaeus, bk. 1, chap. 24, lines 15–18 (Kaibel; Loeb I. 14c). The passage itself is a quotation from Homer's *Odyssey* (bk. 8, line 480), hence is about "ancient singers" of the archaic age.
7. Prov. 5:8.
8. Prov. 6:24–25.
9. Isa. 23:16.

97 Jean Loret

As a journalist, Jean Loret's distinction was to have disseminated the weekly news of Parisian society between 1650 and 1665 in verse, in what he termed a "gazette burlesque." The poems, appropriately written in doggerel meter and rhyme (reproduced here), were originally addressed to Marie d'Orléans, Mlle de Longueville. They were collected and published in three volumes in 1650, 1660, and 1665 under the title *La Muse historique*. After Loret's death in 1665, several writers continued the tradition to nearly the end of the century. Though each account may seem slight by itself, Loret took note of dance, domestic music making, and everyday performances in church—the kinds of occasions that typically pass without historical record.

FROM *The Historical Muse*

(1654)

I heard such melodies of sound
('twould make the gods to gather round)
from a guitar, and even more
the marvels were from a mandore:[1]
these gave my heart such cheer to see
in the home of Monsieur Sifrédy.[2]
And what's more, his charming niece
played for us many an excellent piece
on the viol and, more disarming,
upon her harpsichord so charming.
All that we've heard of Orpheus' glories
amounts to naught but fairy stories
compared to those celestial chords
a manner rare and fine affords
as we heard there the sound uncurl
from out the fingers of this girl:
the pretty airs she animated
left the listeners charmed and sated.

TEXT: In Yolande de Brossard, "La Vie musicale en France d'après Loret et ses continuateurs, 1650–1688," *Recherches sur la musique française classique* 10 (1970): 117–93; this poem for August 15, 1654, pp. 157–58. Translation by Margaret Murata.

1. A plucked string instrument with a rounded body, a cittern or cittern-like instrument.
2. The gentleman is unknown; a Sifrédy served as a steward in the queen's household, 1652–58, according to Brossard, "La Vie musicale en France," p. 192.

98 Roger North

Sometime after Roger North retired from the law (see No. 94 above) in 1688, he wrote his autobiography, the manuscript of which now rests in the British Library. His recollections of childhood on his grandfather's estate at Kirtling, Cambridgeshire, illustrate the transition from the Elizabethan traditions represented in old Lord North's household to the flourishing musical life in London at the end of the century. During Roger North's youth, regular music making was considered a domestic virtue that contributed to moral education. Occupation in musical performance prevented idleness, as noted by Grazioso Uberti (in No. 15), or less innocuous activities. In the later seventeenth century, the new professionalism in music encouraged music lovers to be passive auditors rather than performers. In North's view, the disappearance of amateur music making—which was due in part to the high level of musical difficulty to which listeners had become accustomed and in part to the attractions of London that had supplanted domestic performances—was a sign of the weakening culture of the landed families. North advises which instruments are best for boys and which for girls and is so sensitive about the moral value of musical instruction in the home that he warns fathers to choose their daughters' music teachers carefully.

FROM *Notes of Me*
(c. 1695)

As to musick, it was my fortune to be descended of a family where it was native. My Grandfather, Dudley the [3rd] Lord North, having travelled in Italy, where that muse is queen, took a liking to it. And when his vanitys, and attendant wants, had driven him into the country, his active spirit found imployment with many airey[1] enterteinements, as poetry, writing essays, building, making mottos and inscriptions. But his poetry call'd him to Musick, for he would have the masters sett his verses, and then his grand-children, my sisters, must sing them. And among others he used to be wonderfully pleas'd with these, being a corus of Diana's nymphs:

> She is chaste, and so are wee;
> Wee may chase, as well as she.

TEXT: From *Roger North on Music*, pp. 9–12 and 15–17 (see also Nos. 14 and 15, above). The dating of the manuscript is John Wilson's, as are all the words in square brackets. Reproduced by permission of Novello and Co., Ltd.

1. Imaginative.

And having a quarrell with an old gentleman, could not hold [from] goding him with poetry and the corus of a song run thus:

> A craven Cock, untry'd will look as brave,
> So will a Curr, a Buzzard, Jade, or knave.

This digression to shew how a retired old fantastik courtier could enterteine himself; . . .

He play'd on that antiquated instrument called the treble viol, now abrogated wholly by the use of the violin; and not onely his eldest son, my father, who for the most part resided with him, play'd, but *his* eldest son Charles, and yonger son [Francis] the Lord Keeper, most exquisitely and judiciously. And he kept an organist in the house, which was seldome without a profes't musick master. And the servants of parade, [such] as gentlemen ushers, and the steward, and clerck of the kitchen also play'd; which with the yong ladys my sisters singing, made a society of musick, such as was well esteemed in those times. And the course of the family was to have solemne musick 3 days in the week, and often every day, as masters supply'd noveltys for the enterteinement of the old lord. And on Sunday night, voices to the organ were a constant practise, and at other times symphonys intermixt with the instruments.

This good old lord took a fancy to a wood he had about a mile from his house, called Bansteads, scituate in a durty soyl, and of ill access. But he cut glades, and made arbours in it, and no name would fit the place but, *Tempe*.[2] Here he would convoque his musicall family, and songs were made and sett for celebrating the joys there, which were performed, and provisions carried up for more important regale of the company. The consorts were usually all viols to the organ or harpsicord.[3] The violin came in late, and imperfectly. When the hands were well supply'd, then a whole chest went to work, that is 6 violls, musick being formed for it; which would seem a strange sort of musick now, being an interwoven hum-drum, compared with the brisk *battuta*[4] derived from the French and Italian. But even that in its kind is well; and I must make a great difference when musick is to fill vacant time, which lyes on hand. Then, that which hath moderate buissness in it, and being harmonious, will lett one sleep or drouse in the hearing of it, without exciting the ball or dance, is well enough. But where heads are brisk and airey hunting of enterteinements, and brought to musick as the best, where it is expected to be accordingly, and the auditors have not leisure or patience to attend moderate things, but must be touched sensibly, brisk, and with *bon goust*;[5] then I confess this sort will not please; but it must come with all the advantages that can be, and even the best

---

2. A classical place name that signifies a pleasant rural setting.
3. The ensembles consisted of a chest, or family, of viols with a keyboard instrument playing either *basso continuo* or *basso seguente*.
4. Beat.
5. Good taste, here with the sense of a taste for the up-to-date.

and most *reliev*[6] harmony will scarce hold out any long time.[7]

And I may justly say, that the late improvements of Musick have bin the ruin, and almost banishment of it from the nation.[8] I shall speak more of this anon; now let me lament the disadvantage this age hath, and posterity will find, in the discontinuance of this enterteinement. And whether the now-reigning humour, of running to London, be more the cause it is discontinued, than the discontinuance of it be the cause (at least in some measure) of that, I will not determine; I am sure both are true *in quanto*.[9] The mischeif is plaine, that is, leaving the country, which I will not demonstrate here, but shew that want of country enterteinement must be a great cause of it. And that is done by observing that vice will start up to fill the vacancy. When wee know not how to pass the time, wee fall to drink. If company is not at home, wee goe out to marketts and meetings to find such as will joyne in debauchery, and the country is dull for want of plentifull and exquisite debauchery. There can scarce be a full family[10] kept, because this humour of drunkening lett in all manner of lewdness. Even father and daughters, with servants and children male and female, goe into promiscuousness. And it is scarce reasonable to expect better unless you can provide diversion, to fill the time of the less imploy'd part of a gentile[11] family, which [diversion] is, and when used heretofore was, of great use towards it. For yong spirits, put in any way, will be very buisy and imploy themselves, but not put into a way, pant after debauchery. Now when Musick was kept in an easy temperate air, practicable to moderate and imperfect hands, who for the most part are more earnest upon it than the most adept, it might be reteined in the country. But since it is arrived to such a pitch of perfection, that even masters, unless of the prime, cannot enterteine us, the plain way becomes contemptible and rediculous, therefore must needs be lay'd aside. By this you may judge what profit the publik hath from the improvement of Musick. I am almost of Plato's opinion, that the state ought to governe the use of it, but not for their reasons, but for the use it may be in diverting noble familys in a generous way of country living.

Nor is this improvement come to that height with us, that it should winn us so to it. I grant in Italy, and the Royall Chappell here, it hath bin extraordinary good. But look out among the celebrated enterteinements that have of late bin

6. Vivid or entertaining? Wilson suggests "clearly outlined," p. 11, note 5.
7. North recognizes here that the consort music performed in the 1650s was more "moderate," that is, has less contrast, in its harmony and rhythms and therefore bore sustained performance, unlike the French and Italian instrumental music of the 1690s that was more varied in harmony and derived from dance music, but passed quickly.
8. See No. 14 above; North is thinking of the advanced performance techniques and increased professionalism in music of the 1690s, as well as the establishment of public concerts in London, which he associates with the decline of music making in the home.
9. To a degree.
10. A household.
11. Genteel.

set up in this towne, and wee shall not find any that deserves the caracter of musicall enterteinement.

．　．　．　．　．

It is most certain that gentlemen are not oblidg'd to aime at that [same] perfection, as masters who are to earne their support by pleasing not themselves, for it is their day labour, but others. And therefore audiences are not so well when their owne enterteinement is the buissness,[12] because they indulge their owne defects, and are not distasted or discouraged by stopp, errors, and faults, which an audience would laugh att. But it is so unhappy that gentlemen, seeing and observing the performances of masters, are very desirous to doe the same; and finding the difficulty and the paines that is requisite to acquire it, are discouraged in the whole matter, and lay it aside; which is cheifly to be ascribed to this towne which is the bane of all industry, because many other pleasures stand with open armes to receive them. Whereas in the country, where there are not such variety of gay things to call yong folks away, it is incredible what application and industry will grow up in some active spirits. And this voluntarily, without being incited; as where there is an inlett to Musick, having time and a fancy to it, some will be wonderfully resigned to master a reasonable performance in it. And for want of this or some other vertuous, or at least harmless, imployment within doors, the youth of the country fall to sports, as doggs, horses, hauks and the like abroad, wherein they will become very exquisite artists; which I mention onely to shew how reasonable it is to have in a country family some subject of vertuous pastime, or arts more usefull if not gainefull professions, which may be as food to the industry of youth bred there; who will otherwise, as I noted, fall into sottishness and vice. And nothing, of the unprofitable kind, can be so good as Musick, who is a kind companion and admitts all to her graces, either men by themselves, or men and weomen together, or the latter single, with either instruments and voices, or either alone, as the capacitys are; and [these] fail not to enterteine themselves, and their parents and friends, with pleasures sensible to those that have found the sweets of them. And for this reason I would not have familys discouraged for want of perfection, which, to say truth, is not to be had out[side] of a trade, but to enter their youth, and give them good example, and they will be ambitious enough to improve; and if it be to be had, active spirits will find it. But after all, nothing of musick is so mean and ill performed, which is not comendable and extream usefull in a country family.

This letts me in to speak a litle of Teaching, on which much of this depends. For men the viol, violin, and the thro-base-instruments organ, harpsicord, and double base, are proper; for weomen the espinnett, or harpsicord, lute, and gittarr; for voices both. I cannot but comend the double base, or standing viol, for plaine bases, especially for accompan[y]ing voices, because of its softness

---

12. When they are performing for themselves, it is not so good for gentlemen to have an audience.

joyned with such a force as helps the voice very much. And the harpsicord for ladys, rather than the lute; one reason is, it keeps their body in a better posture than the other, which tends to make them crooked. The other instruments, and farther of these, I decline to critiscise, because I intend in a discourse apart to doe it fully.

But masters are first to be had, who can reasonably answer for what they undertake, and of those I recommend the elder, rather than the yonger, altho' the latter may be more aggreable for novelty and briskness, which is so in most things, especially Musick. My reason is, that the elder are better artists in teaching the principles of Musick, having more experience; and that is the main designe at first. Elegance of performance is the finishing, which will be look't after in time. First get a teacher who understands, and hath experience in teaching, which is a distinct art from playing, and few or scarce any yong men have it. When they teach it is meerly by imitation, and [they] know not the true reason of the excellencys they have, nor can obviate the devious errors of scollars,[13] nor so well judge of the beauty or deformity of habits, but will lett them run on till past cure. I might add other reasons, such as seducing yong people and betraying them to ruin, which they are too apt to doe; but of that I suppose parents are apt enough to take thought, for if not, their children, being fortunes especially daughters, are in much danger from such gamesters. But the ancienter men who have familys of their owne are safe and will be prudent. Their dullness, and perhaps humours, must be borne with, for they trade in air all together, which is a light buissness.

13. Pupils.

PRINCIPLES FOR PERFORMANCE

99 Giulio Caccini

Born in Rome, the tenor Giulio Caccini (1551–1618) performed and taught singing at the court of the grand duke of Tuscany in Florence for most of his professional life. Solo singing to instrumental accompaniment was by no means an exclusively Florentine practice in the last quarter of the sixteenth century, but in his personal style Caccini eschewed the extravagant improvisation prized at the time in both vocal and instrumental performance. Under the influence of scholars of the ancient Greek theater, he had participated in developing a new way of singing in staged dramas, a manner of "speaking in tones." This new manner influenced his chamber singing, in that he insisted that the invention and application of ornamental figures should serve to enhance the declamation and the expressive force of the text. Display of technical virtuosity was to disappear in favor of a musical representation of speech—but speech in the artfully simple, yet high literary manner of poets like Ottavio Rinuccini and Gabriele Chiabrera. This "speaking in tones" also required a flexible instrumental accompaniment, because word accents in Italian poetic lines do not make regular patterns of stress. The Florentine solution—in the form of the figured bass—was presented to the world in both of Caccini's landmark publications, the score to his opera *Euridice* and his collection of monodies called *Le nuove musiche* (*The New Music*). His bass lines, which prescribed more for the player than did guitar tablature, were still far from the complete scores given in lute or keyboard notation. Caccini's dedication to the opera briefly introduces both this new notation for the performers of the basso continuo and his new manner of singing.

Dedication to *Euridice*
(1600)

To the most illustrious lord, Signor Giovanni Bardi, Count of Vernio,[1] Lieutenant-General of both Companies of the Guard of Our Most Holy Father.

After composing the fable of Eurydice in music in *stile rappresentativo* and having it printed, I felt it to be part of my duty to dedicate it to Your Illustrious Lordship, whose especial servant I have always been and to whom I find myself under innumerable obligations. In it Your Lordship will recognize that style which, as Your Lordship knows, I used on other occasions, many years ago, in the eclogue of Sannazaro, "Itene all'ombra degli ameni faggi,"[2] and in other

---

TEXT: *L'Euridice composta in musica in stile rappresentativo* (Florence: Giorgio Marescotti, 1600; facs. Bologna, 1976), pp. [i–ii].; translation by Oliver Strunk. The Italian text is also available in A. Solerti, *Le origini del melodramma* (Turin, 1903; repr. Bologna [1969]), pp. 50–52 and in T. Carter and Z. Szweykowski, eds., *Composing Opera* (Cracow, 1994), also trans. into English.

1. For Bardi, see No. 1 above.
2. From the *Arcadia* of Jacopo Sannazaro. The line given is the beginning of the monologue of Montano in terza rima, following the "Prosa seconda." Caccini's music seems not to have been preserved.

madrigals of mine from that time. "Perfidissimo volto," "Vedrò il mio sol," "Dovrò dunque morire,"[3] and the like. This is likewise the manner which Your Lordship, in the years when Your Lordship's *camerata* was flourishing in Florence, discussing it in company with many other noble virtuosi, declared to be that used by the ancient Greeks when introducing song into the presentations of their tragedies and other fables.

Thus the harmony of the parts reciting in the present *Euridice* is supported above a *basso continuato*.[4] In this I have indicated the most necessary fourths, sixths, and sevenths, and major and minor thirds, for the rest leaving it to the judgment and art of the player to adapt the inner parts in their places. The notes of the bass I have sometimes tied in order that, in the passing of the many dissonances that occur, the note may not be struck again and the ear offended. In this manner of singing, I have used a certain *sprezzatura* which I deem to have an element of nobility, believing that with it I have approached that much nearer to ordinary speech. Further, when two sopranos are making *passaggi,* singing with the inner parts, I have not avoided the succession of two octaves or two fifths, thinking thereby, with their beauty and novelty, to cause a greater pleasure, especially since without these *passaggi,* all the parts are free from such faults.

I had thought on the present occasion to deliver a discourse to my readers upon the noble manner of singing, in my judgment the best one, so that others could practice it, along with some curious points relating to it, and with the new style of *passaggi* and *raddoppiate*[5] invented by me, which Vittoria Archilei, a singer of that excellence to which her resounding fame bears witness,[6] has long employed in singing my works. But since this has not at present seemed best to some of my friends (to whom I cannot and must not be disloyal), I have reserved this for another occasion,[7] enjoying, for the time being, this single satisfaction of having been the first to give songs of this kind and their style and manner to the press.[8] This manner appears throughout my other compositions, composed at various times going back more than fifteen years, as I have never used in them any art other than the imitation of the sentiments of the words, touching those notes more or less passionate that I judged most suitable for the grace which is required for good singing, which grace and which manner

---

3. *Le nuove muische,* nos. 6, 7, and 11. "Perfidissimo volto" appears in the *Norton Anthology of Music,* 3d ed., vol. 1, no. 54.
4. For examples of Caccini's *basso continuato,* see No. 20, pp. 103–8.
5. Literally, "redoublings;" but a precise meaning remains unclear; see the Glossary of Foreign Performance Terms.
6. Archilei, who had taken part in the Florentine *intermedi* of 1589, sang the role of Euridice at the first performance of the Peri-Caccini score; see also No. 4, note 18.
7. The promised discourse was subsequently published as the preface to *Le nuove musiche;* see No. 20.
8. Caccini evidently rushed into print in order to anticipate the publication of Peri's score. His claim is that he is the first to have printed songs in the new style. Peri's claim (see No. 27) is that his *Euridice* was performed before Caccini's was composed or printed.

of singing Your Most Illustrious Lordship has many times reported to me to be universally accepted in Rome as good.

Meanwhile I pray Your Lordship to receive with favor the expression of my good will, etc., and to continue to grant me Your Lordship's protection, under which shield I hope ever to be able to take refuge and be defended from the perils that commonly threaten things little used, knowing that Your Lordship will always be able to testify that my compositions are not unpleasing to a great prince who, having occasion to test all the good arts, can judge them supremely well. With which, kissing Your Illustrious Lordship's hand, I pray Our Lord to bestow happiness upon Your Lordship.

Florence, December 20, 1600

Your Illustrious Lordship's most affectionate and beholden servant,

Giulio Caccini

100 Giulio Caccini

Caccini's first publication of solo madrigals and arias included music from his entire active career. The preface addressed to the readers articulates the main principles upon which Caccini based the claim that his musical style was new. Among these were aspects of composition, such as the suppression of counterpoint, which freed the bass from the rhythms of the vocal line, and a free harmonic rhythm that followed the cadences of spoken Italian. Others were aspects of performance practice, such as his recommendation that ornamental figures should on the whole be of moderate duration and that expressive techniques be reserved for affective texts and be dependent, above all, on the meaning of the words. More particularly, Caccini explained his preferences regarding the special use of crescendos and decrescendos on the part of the singer, and he illustrated the *trillo* on one tone and the *gruppo,* the equivalent of the modern neighbor-note trill. With less comment he offered rhythmic variants of common figures and cadences, followed by examples in which all these devices are applied, including passages to be sung *senza misura,* that is, without strict adherence to the beats within the *tactus.*

FROM THE Preface to *Le nuove musiche*
(1602)

• • • • •

At the time that the most excellent *camerata* of the Most Illustrious Signor Giovanni Bardi, Count of Vernio, flourished in Florence, wherein not only a good number of the nobility met, but also the best musicians and clever men, poets, and philosophers of the city. I can truly say, since I attended as well, that I learned more from their learned discussions than I did in more than thirty years of studying counterpoint. This is because these discerning gentlemen always encouraged me and convinced me with the clearest arguments not to value that kind of music which does not allow the words to be understood well and which spoils the meaning and the poetic meter by now lengthening and now cutting the syllables short to fit the counterpoint, and thereby lacerating the poetry. And so I thought to follow that style so praised by Plato and the other philosophers who maintained music to be nothing other than rhythmic speech with pitch added (and not the reverse!), designed to enter into the minds of others and to create those wonderful effects that writers admire, which is something that cannot be achieved with the counterpoint of modern music. In solo singing, especially, with any stringed instrument, the quantity of *passaggi* sung on both long and short syllables meant that not a word could be understood; and in music of every kind, those who provided them would be exalted and praised as great singers by the mob. Seeing, as I am saying, that these kinds of music and musicians were offering no pleasure other than what harmony grants to the ear alone (since the mind cannot be moved by such music without understanding the words), it occurred to me to introduce a kind of music by which anyone could almost speak in music, using (as I have said elsewhere)[1] a certain noble *sprezzatura* in the melody, passing sometimes over some discords while sustaining the pitch of the bass note (except when I wanted to use it in a regular way) and with the middle lines played by the instrument to express some *affetto*,[2] as those lines are not of much other use.

At that time, furthermore, people were beginning to sing this kind of song for solo voice. I thought that they would have more power to delight and move than would several voices together, and so composed the madrigals "Perfidissimo volto," "Vedrò 'l mio sol," "Dovrò dunque morire," and similar pieces,

---

TEXT: *Le nuove musiche* (*The New Music;* Florence, 1602; facs. New York, 1973), pp. ii–x. Translation by Margaret Murata. Musical examples are here given in their original note values. For an extensively annotated translation of the complete preface into English, see H. Wiley Hitchcock, *Le nuove musiche* (Madison: A-R Editions, 1970), pp. 43–56. Hitchcock's example numbering is retained here.

1. See No. 19 above, p. 98.
2. The probable meaning here is of a brief ornament.

and especially an air on the eclogue by Sanazzaro,[3] "Itene a l'ombra de gli ameni faggi," in just that style that I used later for those plays that were staged and sung in Florence.

• • • • •

In madrigals as in arias I have always achieved the imitation of the ideas of the words, seeking out those notes that are more or less expressive, according to the sentiments of the words. So that they would have especial grace, I concealed as much of the art of counterpoint as I could. I have placed chords on the long syllables and passed over the short ones and also observed this same rule in making *passaggi*. For particular embellishments, however, I have sometimes used a few eighth notes (*crome*) up to the duration of a fourth of a *tactus*[4] or up to a half [of the *tactus*] at the most, largely on short syllables. These can be allowed, because these go by quickly and are not *passaggi* but just an extra graceful touch, and also because good judgment suffers some exception to every rule. But because earlier I have stated that those long turns of the voice are badly used, I must point out that singers do not make *passaggi* because they are necessary to a good singing style, but because, I believe, they titillate the ears of those who understand less well what it means to sing *con affetto*.[5] Because if they knew, then *passaggi* would be abhorred, since nothing is more contrary than they are to expressive singing (which is the reason I have been saying that those long runs are badly used). Therefore, I have introduced them in the kind of music that is less expressive, and used them on long, not short, syllables and in closing cadences.

I have no other technical points concerning vowels with respect to these long runs, except that the vowel "u" is better used in the soprano voice than in the tenor, and that the vowel "i" is better in the tenor than the vowel "u." The rest are all in common use, the open, rather than the closed vowels being much more sonorous,[6] as well as being the most suitable and the easiest with which to practice placement of the voice.

• • • • •

It remains to say now why the increasing and diminishing of the voice, exclamations, trills, *gruppi,* and the other above-mentioned effects are used indiscriminately, since one can call it indiscriminate use whenever others apply

3. Caccini cited the same four compositions in his preface to *Euridice;* see pp. 97–98 above, notes 2 and 3.
4. The *tactus* was the unit of measure. In duple meter it was usually a semibreve in common time, or a breve in "cut" time. Thus in these embellishments, the number of eighth notes did not last longer than a fourth or half of the prevailing *tactus.* In his edition, Hitchcock has observed (pp. 46–47) that ¢ (*tactus alla breve* or *tempus diminutim*) is the predominant mensuration sign in *Le nuove musiche.* This would allow an embellishment lasting four to eight eighth notes.
5. Expressively, moving the emotions.
6. As represented by the International Phonetic Alphabet, the Italian open vowels are [a], [ɛ], and [ɔ]; the closed vowels are [e], [i], [o] and [u].

these devices as much in canzonettas for dancing as in expressive music. This defect comes about (if I am not mistaken) when a singer does not at first have well in hand that which he wishes to sing. If he did, he would certainly not run into such errors as easily as do those who have been trained in a completely affective style (so to speak)—one that follows the general rule that the foundation of expression lies in the application of crescendos, decrescendos, and exclamations—and who then always make use of them in every kind of music without figuring out whether the words require it. There are [listeners] who well understand the ideas and sentiments of the words. They recognize our defects and know how to distinguish where more and where less of such expressiveness is wanted. In this respect we should strive most to please them and prize their praises more than the applause of any common ignoramus. This art does not suffer mediocrity, and the more exquisite refinements it has, the more effort and diligence we professors of this art ought to exert, with great study and love. This love has moved me (seeing that we obtain the light of every science and art from writings) to bequeath this little glimmer in the following notes and comments, by which I intend to show what befits him who professes to sing solo with chitarrone or other stringed instrument, even though he may already have been introduced to the theory of this music and play well enough. Not that this art cannot be acquired to some extent also by long practice, as one sees that many, both men and women have done—up to a certain point, however. The theoretical in what I write here will take one up to this mark.

In the profession of singer (on its own merits) not only are the details useful, but everything taken together makes it better. To proceed, then, in order, I will say that the first and most important foundations are the intonation of the voice on all pitches:[7] not only that nothing is amiss below or rise too much,[8] but also that one should begin in a stylish manner. Since there are more or less two of these [ways of beginning] in use, we shall see both one and the other, and with my comments below, we will demonstrate which one seems to me more suitable with the other effects, which follows later.

There are, then, some who sing the first note beginning a third lower [than notated] and others who sing this first note at its written tone, always with a crescendo, saying that this is the good way to offer the note with grace. As for the first way, it cannot always be used, because it does not always accord with the harmony; although whenever it is possible to do it, it has now become such a common device, that instead of adding grace, I would say that it is rather

7. Caccini uses the term "intonation" in two contemporary senses here, one referring to being in tune, the other indicating the opening of a musical composition, as in the intonation of a chant. He says little about the first.

8. This odd phrase refers to flatting and sharping. In Caccini's time normal tunings were unequally tempered, requiring a sensitive ear, although plucked string instruments like the lute and chitarrone have their frets placed at spacings that produce equal semitones. A later seventeenth-century translation into English published in John Playford's *Introduction to the Skill of Music* renders this phrase as "and not only that it be neither too high nor too low."

unpleasant to the ear (also because some remain at the lower third for too long a time, whereas it should barely be suggested). Beginners, especially, should use it rarely. Instead of this, I would choose the second way as more attractive, that of increasing the voice. But because I have never been content to stay within ordinary bounds and those observed by others, but have always rather gone in search of the most original possibilities (as long as novelty helps the musician achieve his goal, that is, to delight and move the affections of the soul), I found that a more expressive way to treat the note is to sing the tone in the opposite manner—that is, to sing the first note diminishing it, rather than as an exclamation, even though the exclamation is the principal means of moving the affections. An exclamation proper is nothing other than reinforcing the tone somewhat as you sustain it.[9] Such an increase of the note in a soprano part, especially in falsetto, often becomes harsh and insufferable to the ear, as I've heard on several occasions. Certainly, then, as an expressive device more suitable to move [the affections], diminishing the voice will make a better effect than will increasing it. Nevertheless in the above-mentioned first manner,[10] increasing the voice to make an exclamation, what usually happens is that in sustaining the note, it goes sharp, which is why I have said it appears forced and coarse. A completely opposite effect can be made by diminishing the note. Then while sustaining it, giving it a little extra spirit will always make it more expressive.[11] Beyond this, using sometimes now one, now the other, variety can be achieved, since variety is most necessary in this art, as long as it is directed to the abovesaid goal.

•   •   •   •   •

[Example A]

[*My heart, pray, do not languish.*]

What this manner of singing can be then—with greater or lesser grace—can be tried with the music provided with the words "Cor mio, deh, non languire"

9. "Et esclamazione propriamente altro non è, che nel lassare della voce rinforzarla alquanto."
10. Caccini means here the first of the present two alternatives: starting the first note either with a crescendo or with a decrescendo.
11. The main difference between the *esclamazione* and what Caccini is suggesting as an intonation, both of which soften the tone and then make it more intense, is the relative duration of the two changes. In the former, the *crescendo* is longer; in Caccini's intonation, it is the diminishing that is longer.

[see Ex. A],[12] by singing "Cor mio" on the first dotted minim [1], diminishing it little by little, and as the semiminim [2] falls, increasing the voice with a little more spirit. This will produce a very expressive exclamation also on the note that descends by step. But the word "deh" will appear even livelier due to the length of the note (which does not fall by step), and it will seem very smooth after the greater sixth that falls by leap [3]. I wanted to note this in order to show others not only what an exclamation is and whence it originates, but that, furthermore, there can be two kinds, one more expressive than the other, both in terms of the way in which they are notated or sung (in either of the two ways) and of the imitation of the word, when it has significance for the meaning. In addition, exclamations can be sung in all expressive music, according to the general rule of applying them on descending dotted minims and semiminims [𝅘𝅥. 𝅘𝅥.]. They will be very much more expressive as a result of the moving note that follows [the dotted] note, than [exclamations are] with semibreves alone [𝅝]. What will happen more with semibreves is the increasing and decreasing of the voice without making exclamations.[13] It follows that in tuneful music (*musiche ariose*) or dance songs, rather than these affective devices one should use only the liveliness of the song, which is usually conveyed by the melody itself. In these, although sometimes there may be places for a few exclamations, one should keep up the same liveliness and not apply any *affetto* that conveys a sense of languishing. Thus we come to recognize how much it is necessary for the singer to have a certain amount of judgment, which is accustomed to sometimes prevailing over art. We can also recognize from the above-written notes how much more graceful are the first four eighth notes on the second syllable of the word "languire," with the second dotted eighth held back, than are the last four equal ones, marked here "for example."

There are many things employed in a good style of singing, which, in order to find in them a greater elegance, are notated in one way but have a different effect, whence it is said that a person sings with more or less grace.[14] These things force me now to show, first, the way I describe the trill and the *gruppo* and the method I use to teach it to those of my household. Then later, in addition, I will demonstrate all the other more necessary effects, so that no refinement known to me remains without demonstration.

[Example B]

Trill, or plain shake   Gruppo, or double relish

12. The names for Caccini's figures are from the anonymous English translation in John Playford's *Introduction to the Skill of Music*, 4th–12th eds. (1664–94).
13. Hitchcock, *Le nuove musiche*, p. 50, note 29 also points out Caccini's distinction between smooth dynamic increase-and-decrease versus the "exclamation," differences which no doubt involved elements such as the attack on the initial consonant, as well differences in speed and range of dynamic change.
14. In other words, notation can be realized in different ways by different singers.

that you see written, the one and the other: that is, beginning with the first semiminim [♩] and restriking each note with the throat on the vowel "a" until the last breve, and similarly for the *gruppo* [Ex. B]. And how excellently well this trill and this *gruppo* were learned by my past wife using this model, I will leave to the judgment of whoever heard her sing in her time, just as I leave it to the judgment of others to hear with what refinement it is executed by my current wife. If it is true that experience is the mistress of all things, I can with some assurance state and say that there is no better means for teaching it, nor any better form in which notate it, than the way it has been expressed [here], both the one and the other. Because this trill and this *gruppo* are a necessary step to many things that are described here (which are effects of that grace that is most sought after in order to sing well, and, as was said above, depending on how they are written, can make the opposite effect from what is wanted), I will show not only how they can be used, but also, all those effects will be notated in two ways, on a note of the same duration. We will realize then, as repeated above several times, that all the refinements of this art can be learned from these writings, taken together with practical study.

[Example C]

15. Lucia Caccini, mother of musicians Francesca and Settimia, died in 1593. Within two years Giulio married Margherita Benevoli.

In the musical examples [Ex. C] we can see that of the two given, the second instance is more graceful than the first. And so that we can therefore gain better experience, some of them will be notated below with text and a bass line for the chitarrone, along with all the most affective gestures. By practicing these other examples, one will be able to exercise and acquire every greater perfection.

•   •   •   •   •

[Example F]

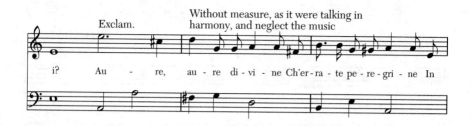

Since in the madrigal "Deh, dove son fuggiti" [see Ex. F] are contained all the best affective devices that could be used with respect to the nobility of this type of song, I wanted to notate it for you, as much to demonstrate where one should increase and diminish the voice—to make exclamations, trills and *gruppi*, and, in short, all the treasures of this art—as well as to not have to illustrate this again for all the compositions that follow. So this will serve as a model to recognize similar places in those pieces where they will be most necessary, according to the affections of the words. I have also come to call the style "noble" that, not subjecting itself to regular meter, often halves the duration of the notes, according to the meaning of the words. From this is born a line with "disregard" *(sprezzatura)*, as it is called.

To excel in this art, wherever there are many devices to be applied, it is necessary to have a good voice for them with regard to the breath, in order to be able to execute them in places where they are most necessary. In this regard, it is also advisable that a master of this art, when singing solo with a chitarrone or other stringed instrument and not being forced to adjust to any others, should choose a pitch level at which he can sing with a full, natural voice, in order to avoid going into falsetto.[16] To sing falsetto or at least forced tones, it is necessary to use the breath in order not to expose them much (since they typically offend the ear). And one needs breath in order to give greater animation to the increasing and diminishing of the voice, to exclamations, and to all the other effects we have demonstrated. Be careful not to run out of breath, then, where it is needed. The nobility of good singing, however, cannot come from falsetto; rather it will arise from a natural voice comfortable on all tones, which a person can adjust to his own ability, without relying on the breath for anything other than showing himself to be master of all the best expressive

---

16. The term "falsetto" appears to have come into use in English only in the late eighteenth century. Today it refers to an entire tessitura. Caccini's phrase in the plural, "le voci finte," refers to those tones on which a singer might or would need to use a "feigned" or "false" voice.

means that are required in this very noble style of singing. Fired in me by natural inclination and by virtue of so many years of study, my love of this way of singing, and of all music in general, will excuse me, if I have let myself get carried beyond what perhaps befits one who esteems not learning less than the communication of what has been learned, and the respect I bear to all masters of the art.

101 Lodovico Viadana

Born in Viadana near Mantua around 1560, Lodovico first appeared in print in 1588 with a set of vesper psalms. A Franciscan, he apparently taught plainsong to the clerics of the cathedral of Mantua before becoming its master of the chapel in the early 1590s. He held similar posts in the cities of Cremona, Reggio Emilia, Concordia (Portogruaro), and Fano. His itinerant life eventually led him back toward Viadana, and he died nearby in 1627 at the newly founded monastery of Sant' Andrea in Gualtieri.

Viadana published a number of volumes of sacred and secular polyphonic music, but his reputation rests chiefly upon the collection of *One Hundred Sacred Concertos,* all but two composed for one to four voices and organ, thought to have been written mostly in Rome around 1596 and published in Venice as op. 12 in 1602. It actually contains more than a hundred works; in addition to eleven solo concertos each for soprano, alto, tenor, and bass with basso continuo it offers twenty duets, seventeen trios, and sixteen concertos for four voices, as well as four psalms, two Magnificats, one instrumental canzona, and nine *falsibordoni.* It was reprinted immediately and repeatedly, appearing in a German edition in 1609 and achieving its eighth edition three years later. Although Viadana's vocal style belongs, not unexpectedly, to the sixteenth century, his practical reduction of the keyboard short score into a basso continuo part exerted a lasting influence on the rapid dissemination and development of sacred music for few voices. The general principles he set out in 1602 for realizing the bass remained valid in keyboard continuo performance long after musical style had changed.

Preface to *One Hundred Sacred Concertos, op. 12*

(1602)

Lodovico Viadana to his kind readers,

There have been many reasons (courteous readers) which have induced me to compose concertos of this kind, among which the following is one of the most important: I saw that singers wishing to sing to the organ, either with three voices, or two, or to a single one by itself, were sometimes forced by the lack of compositions suitable to their purpose to take one, two, or three parts from motets in five, six, seven, or even eight; these owing to the fact that they ought to be heard in conjuction with other parts, as being necessary for the imitations, closes, counterpoints, and other features of the composition as a whole, are full of long and repeated pauses; closes are missing, there is a lack of melody, and, in short, very little continuity or meaning, quite apart from the interruptions of the words, which are sometimes in part omitted and some-times separated by inconvenient breaks which render the style of performance either imperfect, or wearisome, or ugly, and far from pleasing to the listeners, not to mention the very great difficulty which the singers experience in perfor-mance.

Accordingly, having repeatedly given no little thought to these difficulties, I have tried very hard to find a way of remedying to some extent so notable a deficiency, and I believe, thank God, that I have at length found it, having to this end, composed some of these concertos of mine for a single voice (for sopranos, altos, tenors, or basses) and some others for the same parts in a variety of combinations, always making it my aim to give satisfaction thereby to singers of every description, combining the parts in every variety of ways, so that whoever wants a soprano with a tenor, a tenor with an alto, an alto with a cantus, a cantus with a bass, a bass with an alto, two sopranos, two altos, two tenors, or two basses, will find them all, perfectly adapted to his requirements; and whoever wants other combinations of the same parts will also find them in these concertos, now for three, and now for four voices, so that there will be no singer who will not be able to find among them plenty of pieces, perfectly suited to his requirements and in accordance with his taste, wherewith to do himself credit.

You will find some others which I have composed for instruments in various

TEXT: *Cento concerti ecclesiastici a una, a due, a tre, & a quattro voci con il basso continuo per sonar nell'organo* (Venice, 1602). A modern edition of the first part was edited by Claudio Gallico (Kassel: Bärenreiter, 1964), pp. 121–23. This translation, with emendations, from Franck Thomas Arnold, *The Art of Accompaniment from a Thorough-Bass* (London, 1931; repr. New York: Dover, 1965), pp. 2–4, 10–19 (with the Italian text); the last paragraph translated by Oliver Strunk.

ways, which makes the invention more complete and gives the concertos greater adaptability and variety.

Furthermore, I have taken particular care to avoid pauses in them, except so far as is necessitated by the character and form[1] of the melody.

I have, to the very best of my ability, endeavored to achieve an agreeable and graceful tunefulness in all the parts by making them singable and coherent.

I have not failed to introduce, where appropriate, certain figures and cadences, and other convenient opportunities for ornaments and passagework[2] and for giving other proofs of the aptitude and elegant style of the singers, although, for the most part, to facilitate matters, the stock *passaggi* have been used, such as nature itself provides, but more florid.

I have taken pains that the words should be so well disposed beneath the notes that, besides insuring their proper delivery all in complete and logical phrases, it should be possible for them to be clearly understood by the hearers, provided that they are delivered distinctly by the singers.

The other less important reason (in comparison with the one aforesaid) which has also made me hasten to publish this my invention is the following: seeing some of these *Concerti,* which I composed five or six years ago when in Rome (happening then to bethink myself of this new fashion), in such favor with many singers and musicians that they were not only found worthy to be sung again and again in many of the leading places of worship, but that some persons actually took occasion to imitate them very cleverly and to print some of these imitations[3] wherefore, both for the above reason and also to satisfy my friends, by whom I have frequently been most urgently requested and advised to publish my said concertos long before, I have at last made up my mind, after having completed the intended number, to print them, as I am now doing, being convinced that this work need not be altogether displeasing to discerning singers and musicians, and that even though it possess no other merit, a spirit ready and willing to see it done, at least, will not have been lacking, and since it provides, along with its novelty, more than ordinary food for thought, you cannot disdain to read the following instructions, which, in practice, will be of no slight assistance.

First. Concertos of this kind must be sung with refinement, discretion, and grace, using *accenti* with reason and *passaggi* with moderation and in their proper place: above all, not adding anything beyond what is printed in them, inasmuch as there are sometimes certain singers, who, because they are favored by nature with a certain agility of the throat, never sing the songs as they are written, not realizing that nowadays their like are not acceptable, but

1. "Il modo e la dispositione del canto." Pauses that Viadana aimed to avoid would occur when singers sang choral parts as solos or performed ensemble works with fewer lines sung than notated (with the organ covering all lines not sung).
2. "Accentuare e passeggiare," see the Glossary of Foreign Performance Terms for *accenti* and *passaggi.*
3. For example, the *Sacri concerti a due voci* of Gabriele Fattorini, published in Venice in 1600.

are, on the contrary, held in very low esteem indeed, particularly in Rome, where the true school of good singing flourishes.

Second. The organist is bound to play the organ part simply, and in particular with the left hand; if, however, he wants to execute some movement with the right hand, as by ornamenting the cadences, or by some appropriate embellishment, he must play in such a manner that the singer or singers are not covered or confused by too much movement.

Third. It will likewise be a good thing that the organist should first cast an eye over the concerto which is to be sung, since, by understanding the nature of the music, he will always execute the accompaniments better.

Fourth. Let the organist be warned always to make the cadences in their proper position: that is to say, if a concerto for one bass voice alone is being sung, to make a bass cadence; if it be for a tenor, to make a tenor cadence; if an alto or soprano, to make it in the places of the one or the other, since it would always have a bad effect if, while the soprano were making its cadence, the organ were to make it in the tenor, or if, while someone were singing the tenor cadence, the organ were to play it in the soprano.[4]

Fifth. When a concerto begins after the manner of a fugue, the organist begins also with a single note, and, on the entry of the several parts, it is at his discretion to accompany them as he pleases.

Sixth. No tablature has been made for these concertos, not in order to escape the trouble, but to make them easier for the organist to play, since as a matter of fact, not every one would play from a tablature at sight, and the majority would play from the *partitura* as being less trouble; organists, however, will be able to make the said tablature at their own convenience, which, to tell the truth, is much better.

Seventh. When passages in full harmony are played on the organ, they are to be played with hands and feet, but without the further addition of stops, because the character of these soft and delicate *concerti* does not bear the great noise of the full organ, besides which, in miniature *concerti*, it has something pedantic about it.

Eighth. Every care has been taken in assigning the accidentals where they occur, and the prudent organist will therefore see that he observes them.

Ninth. The organ part is never under any obligation to avoid two fifths or two octaves, but those parts which are sung by the voices are.

Tenth. If anyone should want to sing this kind of music without organ or

---

4. In the interpretation of this rule, which is a most important one, everything turns upon the exact sense to be attached to the words "in their proper place" (*à i lochi loro*). Do they simply refer to pitch, i.e., to the octave in which the "cadence" (tonic, leading note, tonic) is to be played, or the *part* of the harmony in which it is to appear? . . . [It] seems probable that Viadana's meaning was that, when a bass was singing, the "cadence" should be made in unison with the voice, and that, in the case of the other voices, it was to be in the *part of the harmony* corresponding to the voice in question. Generally speaking (except in the case of a high voice . . .), this would also imply identity of pitch. [Tr.]

clavichord[5] the effect will never be good; on the contrary, for the most part, dissonances will be heard.

Eleventh. In these concertos, falsettos will have a better effect than natural sopranos; because boys, for the most part, sing carelessly, and with little style[6] likewise because we have reckoned on distance to give greater charm; there is, however, no doubt that no money can pay a good natural soprano; but there are few of them.

Twelfth. When one wants to sing a concerto written in four equal voices,[7] the organist must never play up high, and, vice versa, when one wants to sing a concerto of high pitch, the organist must never play down low, unless it be in cadences in the octave, because it then gives charm.

Nor let anyone presume to tell me here that the said concertos are a little too difficult, for my intention has been to make them for those who understand and sing well, and not for those who abuse their craft. And be in good health.

5. "Manacordo"; the clavichord was a standard practice instrument for organists.

6. For the same judgment, see Pietro della Valle in No. 84, p. 549.

7. Strunk's emendation of Arnold's translation, which he explained: Viadana follows the usual practice of his time, which applies the expression *a voci pari* not only to music in a single register, high or low, but also to music in which the overall register is relatively restricted. Then in his "O sacrum convivium" *a voci pari* (Arnold, pp. 31–33) the four clefs are alto, tenor, tenor, and bass.

102 Agostino Agazzari

Agostino Agazzari (c. 1580–1642) and his father were ennobled by the Grand Duke of Tuscany in 1601, having probably resided in the Tuscan city of Siena for some time. Agostino served as organist at the cathedral in Siena from 1597 to 1602. He is best known for his activities during the next five years, which he spent in Rome as director of music at the German-Hungarian College and then at the Roman Seminary. He marked his return to Siena in 1607 with the publication of a little ten-page tutor on the performance of basso continuo lines which reflected his experience with the new styles of sacred and dramatic music in Rome. His precepts were anticipated in a letter of 1606 that was later published in Adriano Banchieri's *Conclusioni del suono dell'organo* (Bologna, 1609). Agazzari discusses the array of instruments that could play basso continuo and notes the distinctive contributions that each could make in an ensemble. What Agazzari does not stipulate are guidelines for choosing continuo instruments to play in different musical styles and genres, presumably because circumstance and taste allowed for a great amount of variety. He served as the master of the chapel at the cathedral of Siena for the rest of his life.

Of Playing upon a Bass with All Instruments and of Their Use in a Consort
(1607)

Having now to speak to you of musical instruments, I must first, for the sake of the order and brevity required in all discussions, classify them according to the needs of my subject and proposed material. I shall therefore divide them into classes, namely, into instruments like a foundation and instruments like ornaments. Like a foundation are those which guide and support the whole body of the voices and instruments of the consort; such are the organ, harpsichord, etc. Like ornaments are those which, in a playful and contrapuntal fashion, make the harmony more agreeable and sonorous, namely, the lute, theorbo, harp, *lirone, cetera,* spinet, *chitarrina,*[1] violin, pandora, and the like.

Further, some are stringed instruments, others wind instruments. Of those of this second group (excepting the organ) I shall say nothing, because they are not used in good and pleasing consorts, because of their insufficient union with the stringed instruments and because of the variation produced in them by the human breath, although they are mixed in great and noisy ones. Sometimes in a small consort, when there are *organetti* at the octave above, the trombone is used as a contrabass, but it must be well and softly played. All this I say in general, for in particular cases these instruments may be played so excellently by a master hand that they adorn and beautify the consort.

In the same way, among the stringed instruments, some have within them a perfect harmony of the parts, such as the organ [*sic*], harpsichord, lute, double harp, etc.; others have an imperfect one, such as the common cittern, *lirone, chitarrina,* etc.; others have little or none, such as the viol, violin, pandora,[2] etc. For this reason I shall speak in the first place of those instruments of the first class which are the foundation and have perfect harmony and in the second place of those which serve for ornament.

Having made this division and laid down these principles, let us come to the instructions for playing upon a bass. I say, then, that he who wishes to play well

TEXT: *Del sonare sopra 'l basso con tutti li stromenti, e dell'uso loro nel conserto* (Siena, 1607; facs. Milan, 1933; Bologna, 1969). Translation by Oliver Strunk, revised by Margaret Murata.

1. The *lirone* is a bass *lira da braccio,* a fretted, bowed instrument with nine to fourteen strings on the fingerboard and two to four drone strings. It typically played sustained chords, and in the seventeenth century was often the instrument of choice to accompany laments. The *cetera* or *cetra* is a six-course, wire-strung cittern, played with a plectrum. The *chitarrina* would be some sort of small guitar.
2. Agazzari appears to refer here to the range of chords or double-stops accessible on the instruments.

should understand three things. First he must know counterpoint (or at least sing with assurance, understand proportions and time,[3] and read in all the clefs) and must know how to resolve dissonances with consonances, how to distinguish the major and minor thirds and sixths, and other similar matters. Second, he must know how to play his instrument well, understanding its tablature or score, and must be very familiar with its keyboard or fingerboard in order not to have to search painfully for the consonances and beats during the music, knowing that his eye is busy watching the parts before him. Third, he must have a good ear in order to perceive the movements of the parts in their relation to one another. Of this I do not speak, for I could not say anything that would make anyone good who was poor in it by nature.

But to come to the point, I conclude that no definite rule can be laid down for playing works where there are no signs of any sort, it being necessary to be guided in these by the intention of the composer, who is free and can, if he sees fit, place on the first half of a note a fifth or sixth, or vice versa, and that a major or a minor one, as seems more suitable to him or as may be necessitated by the words. And even though some writers who treat of counterpoint have defined the order of progression from one consonance to another as though there were but one way, they are in the wrong. They will pardon me for saying this, for they show that they have not understood that the consonances and the harmony as a whole are subject and subordinate to the words, not vice versa, and this I shall defend, if need be, with all the reasons I can. While it is perfectly true that, absolutely and in general, it is possible to lay down definite rules of progression, when there are words they must be clothed with that suitable harmony which arouses or conveys some affect.

As no definite rule can be given, the player must necessarily rely upon his ear and follow the work and its movements. But if you would have an easy way of avoiding these obstacles and of playing the work exactly, take this one, indicating with figures above the notes of the bass[4] the consonances and dissonances placed there by the composer; for example, if on the first half of a note there is a fifth and then a sixth, or vice versa, or a fourth and then a third, as illustrated:

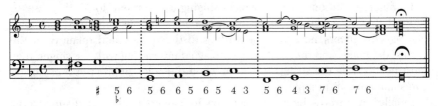

Further, you must know that all consonances are either natural or accidental to the mode. When they are natural, no accidental is written at all; for example,

3. Agazzari refers here to musical mensuration—how to perform metric notation and the proportional system of metric modulation.
4. Agazzari's figures have been moved below the continuo line, following modern convention.

when B is natural, the third above G (otherwise B-flat or B-natural) is naturally major. To make it minor, you must write a flat above the note G, in which case the third is accidentally minor. Conversely, when B is flat, to make the third major, you must write a sharp above the note B. I say the same of the sixths, reminding you that an accidental below or near a note refers to the note itself, while one above it refers to the consonance which must be realized, as in the following example:

All cadences, whether medial or final, require the major third, therefore some musicians do not indicate it; to be on the safe side, however, I advise writing the sign, especially in medial cadences.

The instruments being divided into two classes, it follows that they have different functions and are differently used. An instrument that serves as foundation must be played with great judgment and due regard for the size of the chorus; if there are many voices one should play with full harmonies, increasing the registers. While if there are few, one should use few consonances, decreasing the registers and playing the work as purely and exactly as possible, using few runs or divisions, occasionally supporting the voices with some contrabass notes and frequently avoiding the high ones which cover up the voices, especially the sopranos or falsettos. For this reason one should take the greatest possible care to avoid touching or diminishing with a division the note which the soprano sings, in order not to double it or obscure the excellence of the note itself or of the *passaggio* that the good singer improvises on it. For the same reason one does well to play within a rather small compass and in a low register.

I say the same of the lute, harp, theorbo, harpsichord, etc., when they serve as foundation with one or more voices singing above them, for in this case, to support the voice, they must maintain a solid, sonorous, sustained harmony, playing now *piano,* now *forte,* according to the quality and quantity of the voices, the place, and the work, while, to avoid interfering with the singer, they must not restrike the strings too often when the voice improvises a *passaggio* and some embellishment.

Finally, my purpose being to teach how to play upon a bass (not simply how to play, for this must be known beforehand), I take for granted a certain number of principles and terms; for example, that imperfect consonances progress to the nearest perfect ones; that cadences require the major third, as is for the most part true; that dissonances are resolved by the nearest consonance, the seventh by the sixth and the fourth by the third when the part containing the resolution lies above, the opposite when it lies below. But these matters I shall not discuss at length: he who does not know them must learn them. At present I shall teach the conduct of the hand on the organ.

The bass proceeds in many ways, namely, by step, by leap, by conjunct divisions,[5] or with disjunct notes of small value. When it ascends by step, the right hand must descend by step or leap [1]; conversely, when the left hand ascends or descends by a leap of a third, fourth, or fifth [2], the right hand must proceed by step, for it is not good for both to ascend or descend together. Not only is this ugly to see and to hear, but there is in it no variety at all, for it will be all octaves and fifths. When the bass ascends with a *tirata*, the right hand must remain stationary [3]. When the progression is disjunct, with notes of small value, each note must have its own accompaniment [4]. Here is an example of the whole:

*The parallel octaves are in the original example.

Having now spoken sufficiently of the instruments which serve as a foundation to enable a judicious man to obtain much light from this slender ray (for saying too much makes for confusion), I shall speak briefly of those which serve as ornaments.

These instruments, which are combined with the voices in various ways, are in my opinion so combined for no other purpose than to ornament and beautify, and indeed to season the consort. For this reason, these instruments should be used in a different way than those of the first class. While those maintained the tenor and a plain harmony, these must make the melody graceful and let it flower, each according to its quality, with a variety of beautiful counterpoints. But in this the one class differs from the other. While the instruments of the first class, playing the bass before them as it stands, require no great knowledge

---

5. Agazzari's term is "tirata continuata." A *tirata* is a figure of stepwise notes of equal value; see Glossary of Foreign Performance Terms.

of counterpoint in the player, those of the second class do require it, for the player must compose new parts above the bass and new and varied *passaggi* and counterpoints.

For this reason, the person who plays the lute (which is the noblest instrument of them all) must play it nobly, with much invention and variety, not as is done by those who, because they have a ready hand, do nothing but play runs and make divisions from beginning to end, especially when playing with other instruments which do the same, in all of which nothing is heard but mess and confusion, displeasing and disagreeable to the listener. Sometimes, therefore, the lutanist must use now gentle strokes and sweet restrikings; now broad *passaggi*, now rapid and repeated ones, sometimes something played on the bass strings, sometimes beautiful exchanges[6] and ostinatos, repeating and bringing out the same fugues at different pitches and in different places. He must, in short, so weave the voices together with long *groppi*, trills, and *accenti*,[7] each in its turn, that he gives grace to the ensemble and enjoyment and delight to the listeners, judiciously preventing these embellishments from conflicting with one another and allowing time to each, especially when instruments are similar, a thing to be avoided, in my opinion, unless they play at some distance from each other or are differently tuned and of different sizes.[8] And what I say of the lute as the principal instrument, I wish understood of the others in their kind, for it would take a long time to discuss them all separately.

But since each instrument has its own peculiar limitations, the player must take advantage of them and be guided by them to produce a good result. Bowed instruments, for example, have a different style than those plucked with a quill or with the finger. The player of the *lirone* must bow with long, clear, sonorous strokes, bringing out the inner parts well, with attention to the major and minor thirds and sixths, a matter difficult but important with that instrument. The violin requires beautiful *passaggi*, distinct and long, with playful figures and little echoes and imitations repeated in several places, expressive *accenti, arcate mute*,[9] *groppi*, trills, etc. The *violone*, as the low part, proceeds with gravity, supporting the harmony of the other parts with its sweet resonance, dwelling as much as possible on the heavier strings, frequently touching the lowest ones. The theorbo, with its full and gentle consonances, reinforces the melody greatly, restriking and lightly passing over its bourdon strings, its special excellence, with trills and *accenti muti* played with

6. "Belle gare," literally "contests."
7. These are all melodic ornaments. For *accenti*, see the Glossary of Foreign Performance Terms, p. 223.
8. Agazzari's comments reveal practical experience. Distance diminishes the roughness of unison or same-register playing that is not quite together or in tune. Plucked instruments in different tunings will naturally turn out figures around different pitches, as will instruments of different sizes, which have differences of register.
9. Literally, "mute bow strokes." The exact meaning of this phrase is unknown, but it may refer to playing tones on longer note values without the usual improvising of diminutions, and possibly, in analogy to the *accenti muti* of theorbo playing, some type of movement of the left hand that alters the pitch during a long-held tone. "Mute" may also imply a special kind of sound quality.

the left hand.[10] The double harp, which is everywhere useful, as much so in the soprano as in the bass, explores its entire range with gentle pizzicatos, echoes between the two hands, trills, etc.; in short, it aims at good counterpoint. The cittern, whether the common cittern or the *ceterone*[11] is used with other instruments in a playful way, making counterpoints upon the part. But all this must be done prudently. If the instruments are playing alone in concert, they must do everything and flavor the ensemble. If they play in company, each must regard the other, making space and not conflicting among themselves.[12] If there are many, they must each await their turn and not, chirping all at once like sparrows, try to shout one another down. Let these few remarks serve to give some light to him who seeks to learn. He who relies on his own efforts needs no instruction at all. I do not write for him—I esteem and honor him, but if perchance some wit desires to carry the discussion further, I am at his service.

Finally, one must know how to transpose music from one step to another that has all the consonances natural and proper to the given tone.[13] No other transposition is possible without a very disagreeable sound, for, as I have sometimes observed, in transposing a first or second tone, naturally pleasing because of its many B-flats, to some step whose tone requires B-natural, it will be difficult for the player to be cautious enough and avoid stumbling against some conflicting notes. Thus, with this crudity, the consort is spoiled and the listeners are offended, while the natural character of the given tone does not appear. Most natural and convenient of all is the transposition to the fourth or fifth, sometimes to a step lower or higher; in short, one must see which transposition is most appropriate and suitable to the given tone, not as is done by those who pretend to play every tone on every pitch. For if I could argue at length, I could show these their error and the impropriety of this.

Having treated thus far of playing upon a bass, it seems to me desirable to say something about the bass itself, for it has, I know, been censured by some, ignorant of its purpose or lacking the soul to play it. It is, then, for three reasons that this method has been introduced: first, because of the modern style of composing and singing recitative; second, because of its convenience; third, because of the number and variety of works which are necessary for concerted music.

As to the first reason, I shall say that, since the recent discovery of the true style of expressing the words, namely, the imitation of speech itself in the best possible manner, something which succeeds best with a single voice or with

10. "Accenti muti" are likely quick dissonances played on the fingerboard by the left hand alone after the string has been plucked.
11. A large cittern with one or more unstopped bass strings.
12. Agazzari's distinction here is between an ensemble in which all instruments are realizing a continuo bass line that has no composed melody line, which is common in the *sinfonia,* and an ensemble realizing a bass line to another composed part or parts.
13. Equal temperament was still a hundred years away, at least. In unequal temperaments, transposition could be made satisfactorily only to modes in which the sizes of the intervals relative to their scale steps were approximately those of the original mode. For a discussion of this problem see Arthur Mendel, "Pitch in the 16th and Early 17th Centuries," *Musical Quarterly* 34 (1948): 28–45, 199–221, 336–57, 575–93.

few voices, as in the modern airs of certain able men and as is now much practiced at Rome in concerted music, it is no longer necessary to make a score[14] or tablature, but, as we have said above, a bass with its signs suffices. And if anyone objects that a bass will not suffice to play ancient works, full of fugues and counterpoints, I shall reply that music of this kind is no longer in use, both because of the confusion and babel of the words, arising from the long and intricate imitations, and because it has no grace, for, with all the voices singing, one hears neither period nor sense, these being interfered with and covered up by imitations. Indeed, at every moment, each voice has different words, a thing displeasing to men of competence and judgment. And on this account music would have come very near to being banished from Holy Church by a sovereign pontiff had not Giovan Palestrina found the remedy, showing that the fault and error lay, not with music, but with the composers, and composing in confirmation of this the mass entitled *Missa Papae Marcelli.* For this reason, although such compositions are good according to the rules of counterpoint, they are at the same time faulty according to the law of music that is true and good, something which arises from disregarding the aim and function and good precepts of the latter, such composers wishing to stand solely on the observance of canonic treatment and imitation of the notes not on the affect and the resemblance to the words. Indeed, many of them wrote their music first and fitted words to it afterwards. For the moment, let this suffice, for it would not be to the purpose to discuss the matter at length in this place.

The second reason is the great convenience of the method, for with little labor the musician will have a large stock for his needs; apart from this, the learner is free from tablature, a matter difficult and burdensome to many and likewise very liable to error, the eye and mind being wholly occupied with following so many parts, especially when it is necessary to play concerted music on the spur of the moment.

The third and last reason, namely, the number of works which are necessary for concerted music, is alone sufficient ground, it seems to me, for introducing this so convenient method of playing. For if he were to put into tablature or score all the works which are sung in the course of a year in a single church in Rome, wherever the concert music is professional, the organist would need to have a larger library than a Doctor of Laws. There was then abundant reason for the introduction of this kind of bass, with the method described above, on the ground that there is no need for the player to play the parts as written, if he aims to accompany singing and not to play the work as written, a matter foreign to our subject. Accept what I have said in place of all I might have said, my desire being to satisfy in brief your courteous demands, so many times repeated, and not my natural bent, which is rather to learn from others than to teach them. Take it as it is, then, and let the shortness of the time be my excuse.

14. "Spartitura."

103 <u>Anonymous</u>

The unknown Italian author of the twenty-three chapters that make up *Il corago,* a manuscript treatise on the staging of dramatic works, certainly knew ancient and modern poetry and plays and had seen modern theatrical spectacles in Florence, Mantua, and Ferrara. The *choregos* was a wealthy producer in the ancient Greek theater and a kind of stage manager in the Roman whose Baroque-era counterpart could be considered an impresario. Writing sometime within the decade after 1628, the author needed neither to explain nor to justify modern spectacle but aimed, rather, to advise on all the aspects involved in producing and directing a well thought-out and polished court performance, an undertaking that required the supervision and coordination of "carpenters, tailors, builders, scene painters, singers, instrumentalists, dancers, actors, fencers, jousters, tourneymen, inventors of marvelous machines, and poets of the most sublime kind of poetry." Appropriately, the chapters focus on costumes, lighting, stage machines, and building temporary stages and sets, and he discusses practical alternatives for staging dramas, especially the new genre that would become known as opera. Chapters 11 and 12 even advise poets on how to write suitable verse for recitative and composers on how best to express the sense of poetry in their music. The next chapters illustrate considerations in choosing instrumental forces and where to place them, meter in recitative, stage placement and movement of the singers and chorus, theatrical dance, and stage combat. In the concreteness with which everything is discussed, this clearly experienced *corago* reveals a passion for the stage and standards for the ideal theatrical performance.

FROM *The Choragus, or, Some Observations for Staging Dramatic Works Well*

(c. 1630)

CHAPTER 13: WHETHER WINDS OR STRINGS ARE MORE SUITABLE TO ACCOMPANYING SUNG DRAMA

• • • • •

If you use string instruments, make sure that the sound goes upward and not to the near sides, because if the hall is big and it is necessary to play

TEXT: *Il corago, o vero alcune osservazioni per metter bene in scena le composizioni drammatiche,* Paolo Fabbri and Angelo Pompilio, eds. (Florence: L. S. Olschki, 1983), pp. 87–95. The manuscript

somewhat loudly, the important people in the audience who usually are near the stage will be deafened due to the overly robust sound, and they will not hear the singing well. For this reason it helps to make a well-enclosed partition of large boards between the instruments and the listener. String instruments should not be kept behind the scenes,[1] because since there are many of them they naturally block the passageways, bothering the singers. Second, because then the player and singer cannot see each other, and probably will not hear each other; for this reason some have placed the instruments above the houses of the stage between balustrades. But this orientation, aside from being an inconvenience to the sets, does not unite the instrumental sound very well with the voice of the actor. And what is worst is that the harpsichord player, who is used more than anyone, will not see the singer. And if the singer's voice is weak, the harpsichordist will not hear it, so that either someone will have to beat time or there will be the danger of disagreement. Others place said instruments at the threshold of the stage floor, raising a partition and a parapet between it and the listener, as far from the stage as is necessary in order to hold the instruments, but this method carries with it some inconveniences. First, that the players, being lower than the floor of the stage, if they are taller, will have their hair or heads seen, an enormous defect. They cannot see the actors well if they do not come downstage. Secondly, a parapet higher than the end of the stage ruins the borders of the set, and prevents one from seeing the feet and boots of the actors, with which the elegant individual who is fully seen brings about greater delight. Third, it takes the space from the best part of the hall that should belong to the listener and, with its extremely close sound, it offends the prominent people in the audience who might place themselves near the stage.

To escape these inconveniences, others place the players at the sides of the stage, beyond it, taking the place that belongs to the listener at the right and left of the sets, in little boxes at a height equal to the end of the stage. And these boxes, in order to obstruct the space and the view of the spectators less, have the shape of a triangle whose point is in the direction of the listener, that is, from the part farthest away from the set and next to the wall. This method seems most suitable because it leaves the stage free; it lets the principal player at least see and hear the singers, and it takes away less space belonging to the listener; nor will it offend the most important people in the audience, who usually sit in the middle.

---

source is Modena, Biblioteca Estense, MS. γ.F.6.11 (Campori collection). The editors speculate that the author could have been Pierfrancesco Rinuccini (1592–1657), son of Ottavio. A summary with some extended passages in English, including chapter 15 entire, is in R. Savage and M. Sansone, "Il corago and the Staging of Early Opera: Four Chapters from an Anonymous Treatise circa 1630," Early Music 17 (1989):494–511. Translation by Margaret Murata.

1. Some productions before this time placed the orchestra offstage. The long necks of archlutes easily get in the way, as do harps and harpsichords.

Last, you have to remember that if you want to use string instruments, it is necessary that from the musicians' platform there be a passage that goes backstage, so that any one of them can remove himself to tune his instrument, because that tuning is bothersome, especially if it goes on near the listeners for any length of time.

To remove the problem of the instruments' flatting little by little due to the extreme heat generated by the lights and breathing, it seems that no one before now has sufficiently anticipated keeping duplicate instruments that in due course can come and go. The least damage occurs when all the instruments go flat uniformly; then you do not have discords or notable ugliness. Placing two enclosed organs in these boxes, so that they overwhelm neither the voice of the singer nor the ear of the player so that he cannot hear the person reciting, seems to be the easiest way to hold the pitch, in order that the other instruments can come and tune, adjust, and stay in tune with perpetual diligence, which you cannot do with harpsichords.

CHAPTER 14: WHETHER THE RECITATIVE STYLE SHOULD BE SUNG WITH OR WITHOUT A BEAT

Some think that the recitative style must be used with a musical beat, for many reasons. First, for the greater sureness of the singer who, with the measure visible, is more certain not to err. Secondly, for greater security in keeping with the instrumentalist, who either cannot always see and hear the actor well who is singing or cannot give it much thought; this at least makes it easier for both sides. Thirdly, because in the long course of many works, it is inevitable that now and then passages will occur of very difficult music; also in terms of observing the time. Then it will be not only useful, but necessary, to have the beat.

Nonetheless, the common feeling and practice among those that sing on stage is not to use a beat. First, since the perfection of the recitative style taken to the stage lies in showing and imitating the natural manner of discourse, one must remove everything that demonstrates patent artifice as much as possible, if it is not absolutely necessary. The beat is not necessary; one knows often enough through experience.

Second, if it is necessary to conduct in such a way that the beat is seen by the player as well as the actor, it is inevitable that it will also be visible to the spectator, for whom it is extremely annoying to keep seeing that unseemly up and down for two or three hours.

Third, since the actor must stop to sigh at length as nature tells him and hold on to the same note more or less according to the affect, he should not be tied to any one else's measure, but should freely follow the impulse of feeling, which is of great importance in reciting well. . . .

In difficult passages with respect to rhythm or tempo, the instrumentalist should accommodate the actor, as long as the passage has been rehearsed beforehand several times and it has been determined that there is some aria or passage for many voices in madrigal style that will truly have need of conducting. Then it can be done; but this will happen rarely, and then you would beat for the entirety of that aria or madrigal for chorus, leaving the rest without beating.

CHAPTER 15: OF THE MANNER OF RECITING IN MUSIC

Two sorts of advice are useful to anyone who acts in singing in dramatic works. Some admonitions which are general and common to all actors and are fully part of this discussion, must be taken from what we will say further on about speaking on stage. Others, presupposing the common attributes of a good actor, are special to singers of *stil recitativo,* and these we must discuss briefly in giving the following reminders.

Because declaiming in song[2] goes more slowly than declaiming in speech, it is inevitable that making gestures will also be slower, so that the hand does not finish before the voice does. Therefore it will be necessary to move it very slowly right from the start, and the gesture ought to be broad. You should not sing continuously, even if there is no pause in the musical part; but at the end of each thought, the singer should stop a bit. Also the instrumentalist can sometimes stop, sometimes temporize on the same pitch, other times play special and different music, as long as they have rehearsed it well together beforehand.

If in ordinary acting one avoids walking while speaking, especially walking quickly, so much more should it be avoided during songs, which are noticeably altered and ruined by motion. It cannot be denied, however, that sometimes you will want to move while singing, when the affect and the narrative have been designed to show motion such as assault, flight, and other events, because then the song affected by movement will better express what is wanted. Walking about ought to be done from time to time in the midst of a song, during which there should be played either a ritornello made expressly, or other music, or at least arpeggios played gracefully on the same [bass] note. One could also improvise, because this variety can bring delight.[3] One should not always stop in the middle [of the stage] to sing, but now here, now there—naturally, however, and with a plan, especially if others are supposed to follow and move with you.

When the chorus performs roles, they will use both gestures and motions that are more natural and usual than when they imitate those who sing [solo]. And it will lend not a little grace, if persons who sing together with the same sentiment and feeling also have similar gestures, because in this manner we will see harmony in the gestures, too, which can look quite special. But how

2. "Recitar cantando."
3. That is, the instrumentalist may improvise a ritornello or interlude, if it is decided that the singer should move about during a song.

the chorus should conduct itself when they only sing, following the rhythm and harmony, will be treated below.[4]

. . . . . .

Above all, to be a good singing actor it would be necessary to be also a good speaking actor, as we have seen that some who have had special grace in acting have done marvels when they have known how to sing as well. . . . In the meantime, since the musician must cast the parts suitably and use everyone in the best way, he will try as much as possible to limit the singers who are excellent but bloodless and old to acting in roles that are not very active and that use stage devices, as in clouds and other machines in the air, where not much motion is required, nor the expressiveness of stage gestures.[5] . . . The musician must accompany his song with gesture according to the variety of affects, in the same way that the speaking actor does, as we will discuss next, observing, however, all that was said above of the differences that singing demands.

CHAPTER 16: OF THE MANNER OF SIMPLE DECLAMATION

The manner of reciting is of great importance, because something said by a person who knows how to deliver it well and accompany it with gesture will make a much greater impression on the spirits of the listeners and will more easily stir in them the affections of anger, of hatred, of passion, of happiness, and the like. This will not happen when it is simply narrated by someone without gesture or modulation of the voice. . . .

It falls to the choragus to impart what and how the gestures should be, according to the different aspect of the person that is being represented on stage, because sometimes a contrary gesture will serve well, [or] a discordant voice will please the listeners, when [for example] a servant is brought on stage who is pretending to be a prince, a woman, a lover, or the like, as we see every day.

. . . . .

Because the affections are different that one reveals with words, so must the gestures be with which they are accompanied. The act of praying goes well with the gesture made with both hands, which at the start are moved a little from within the arms; these, barely open, are then smoothly broadened outward. Nor would I be against inclining one's head a little to the side now and then at the same time. The act of praying or petitioning a god or deity, as happens in sacrifices, wants to be done with great submission and reverence. So it is useful at times to curve the chest and motion with a hand, or two, by bringing them up close to it, as it is also useful to kneel. This is always better

---

4. Chapter 17 is devoted to the chorus, chapter 18 to dances.
5. The next paragraph warns that stage machines that bear singers must also move slowly in order to avoid shaking and disturbing the singer.

done on one knee rather than two, taking care always to place on the ground that knee that is on the side of the spectators, in order to keep your face turned toward them as much as possible. In the act of anger, the gesture wants to be fierce and agitated, moving the hand with more or less fury according to the words. This gesture wants to be made for the most part by moving the hand towards the person and releasing it with force outward at the close of the sentences; furthermore it is better done with one hand, instead of two together.

The movements of grief want to be accompanied with a gesture made now with two hands, now with one. And it seems that this gesture is really a raising of the hand and leaving it—as if the words had become lost—not to say also to let that raised hand fall sometimes, striking lightly. But raising it upward is done very slowly and with great sensitivity. And because it is usual for a narration to occur here that tells the reason for the grief, let us see the gestures one should look for. Because a narration includes many and different actions, then so many and different ought to be the gestures that go with it. Sometimes one relates a duel or a battle, which should be indicated by gesturing now with both hands, now with one, now with the other separately, only in such a case will it be necessary to gesture with the left.[6] Sometimes one happens to narrate the death of some hero and the manner of the death itself, in which case it will be necessary to represent the gestures of the person whose death is being described. Another time it will be required to tell about something happy, which should be accompanied by a gesture of happiness. This is done by holding the arms a little arched, and from the middle where you should slowly approach, throwing them open with moderate quickness, turning your eyes now and then toward the sky and all around to signify your happiness, and pleading in a certain way with a movement of the head, as an invitation for all things to rejoice with you.

6. "If the person with whom you speak is on your right, you must not gesture with your left hand, which should always be avoided, because it is an ugly thing to see someone gesture with the left hand" (p. 94). In the same passage, we are told that the left hand is allowed to gesture, for example, when the right holds a spear.

104 Christopher Simpson

Christopher Simpson (c. 1605–1669), a well known performer on the viola da gamba, published two instructional books that were inspired by two of his noble students. His *Principles of Practical Musick* (1665/67) was designed for a ten-year-old Sir John St. Barbe to whom Simpson willed his music books. The more famous of the two books, *The Division-Violist* was first published in 1659. John, the son of Simpson's patron, Sir Robert Bolles, became an accomplished player under Simpson's tutelage. Dedicating the second edition to the younger Bolles, the author notes, not immodestly, "As it was made for You, so it has made You (by your ingenuity) not only the greatest Artist, but also the ablest Judge of it, that (I think) is this day in Europe; (I mean) of a Gentleman, and no Professor of the Science." The viol tutor offers elementary instruction in bowing, tuning, ornamenting, and recognizing intervals of pitch. The heart of the book is part 3, which treats of improvising florid counterpoint over a bass. The sections given here, however, demonstrate more than the art of melismatic invention. Simpson discusses ensemble improvisation and instructs players to consider variety, formal coherence, and bringing an improvisation to a satisfying close. These are all aspects that, in the end, determine a good composition, whether it is ever written down or not and whether it has been invented by a Christopher Simpson or a jazz improviser.

FROM *The Division-Viol, or, The Art of Playing* Ex Tempore *upon a Ground*
(1665)

PART III

§12. Concerning Ordering of Division

When you are to play division to a ground, I would have you, in the first place, to play over the ground itself, plainly and distinctly; for these reasons:

1. That others may hear what notes you divide upon.
2. That your self may be better possessed of the ayre[1] of the ground, in case you know it not before.
3. That he who plays the ground unto you may better perceive the measure of time.

The ground being played over, you may then break it into crochets and quavers;[2] or play some neat piece of slow descant to it, which you please. If your ground consist of two or three strains, you may do by the second or third, as you did by the first. This done, and your ground beginning over again, you may then break it into division of a quicker motion, driving on some point or points as hath been shewed. When you have prosecuted that manner of play so long as you think fitting, and shewed some command of hand; you may then fall off to slower descant or binding-notes,[3] as you see cause; playing also sometimes

TEXT: *The Division-Viol or The Art of Playing* Ex tempore *upon a Ground*, 2d ed. in Latin and English (London, 1665; facs. London, 1965), pp. 56–61. Capitalization has been modernized.

1. "Air" or melody.
2. Eighth and quarter notes.
3. Suspensions.

loud or soft, to express humour[4] and draw on attention. After this you may begin to play some skipping division; or points, or tripla's, or what your present fancy or invention shall prompt you to, changing still from one variety to another; for variety it is which chiefly pleaseth. The best division in the world, still continued, would become tedious to the hearer; and therefore you must so place and dispose your division, that the change of it from one kind to another may still beget a new attention. And this is generally to be observed, whether your ground consist of one or more strains, or be a continued ground; of which I must also speak a little.

§13. OF A CONTINUED GROUND

A continued ground used for playing or making division upon, is (commonly) the through-bass of some motet or madrigal, proposed or selected for that purpose. This, after you have played two or three semibreves of it plain, to let the organist know your measure; you may begin to divide, according to your fancy, or the former instructions, until you come near some cadence or close, where I would have you shew some agility of hand. There, if you please, you may rest a minim [♩], two or three, letting him that plays the ground go on: and then come in with some point: after which you may fall to descant, mixt division, tripla's, or what you please. In this manner, playing sometimes swift notes, sometimes slow; changing from this or that sort of division, as may best produce variety, you may carry on the rest of the ground; and if you have any thing more excellent than other, reserve it for the conclusion.

•   •   •

§ 15. OF TWO VIOLS PLAYING TOGETHER *EX TEMPORE* TO A GROUND

After this discourse of division for one viol,[5] I suppose it will not be unseasonable to speak something to two viols playing together upon a ground; in which kind of musick, I have had some experimental knowledge; and therefore will deliver it in such order and manner as I have known the practice of it; referring the improvement thereof to further experience.

First, let the ground be prick'd down in three several papers;[6] one for him who plays upon the organ or harpsichord: the other two for them that play upon the two viols: which, for order and brevity, we will distinguish by three letters *viz.* **A.** for organist, **B.** for the first Bass, and **C.** for the second. Each of these having the same ground before him, they may all three begin together; A. and B. playing the ground, and C. descanting to it, in slow notes, or such as may suit the beginning of the music. This done, let C. play the ground, and B.

---

4. Character or mood.
5. Section 14, "Of composing division for one viol to a ground," is omitted here.
6. Written out in parts for three instruments.

descant to it, as the other had done before, but with some little variation. If the ground consist of two strains, the like may be done in the second [strain]: one viol still playing the ground whilest the other descants or divides upon it.

The ground thus play'd over, C. may begin again and play a strain of quicker division; which ended, let B. answer the same with another something like it, but of a little more lofty ayre. For the better performance whereof, if there be any difference in the hands or inventions, I would have the better invention lead, but the more able hand still follow, that the music may not seem to flaccess[7] or lessen, but rather increase in the performance.

When the viols have thus (as it were) vied and revied one to the other, A. if he have ability of hand, may, upon a sign given him, put in his strain of division; the two viols playing one of them the ground, and the other slow descant to it. A. having finished his strain, a reply thereto may be made, first by one viol, and then by the other. Having answered one another in that same manner so long as they think fit, the two viols may divide a strain both together. In which doing, let B. break the ground, by moving into the octave upward or downward, and returning from thence either to his own note, or to meet the next note in the unison or octave. By this means, C., knowing B's motion, he knows also how to avoyd running into the same, and therefore will move into the third or fifth, (or sixth where it is required) meeting each succeeding note in some one of the said concords, until he come to the close; where he may (after he has divided the binding) meet the close note in the octave; which directions well observed, two viols may move in extemporary division a whole strain together, without any remarkable clashing in the consecution of fifths or eighths.

When they have proceeded thus far; C. may begin some point of division, of the length of a breve or semibreve, naming the said word, that B. may know his intentions: which ended, let B. answer the same upon the succeeding note or notes to the like quantity of time; taking it in that manner, one after another, so long as they please. This done, they may betake themselves to some other point of a different length, which will produce a new variety.

This contest in breves, semibreves, or minims being ended, they may give the sign to A., if (as I said) he have ability of hand, that he may begin his point as they had done one to another; which point may be answered by the viols, either singly or jointly. If jointly, it must be done according to the former instructions of dividing together; playing still slow notes and soft, whilst the organist divides; for the part which divides should always be heard loudest.

When this is done, both viols may play another strain together, either in quick or slow notes, which they please; and if the musick be not yet spun out to a sufficient length, they may begin to play triplas and proportions,[8] answering each other either in whole strains or parcels; and after that, join together in a thundering strain of quick division; with which they may conclude; or else

7. To become flaccid.
8. Sections in different meters with a common note value between them.

with a strain of slow and sweet notes, according as may best sute the circumstance of time and place.

I have known this kind of extemporary musick, sometimes (when it was performed by hands accustomed to play together) pass off with greater applause, than those divisions which had been most studiously composed.

105 Lorenzo Penna

Lorenzo Penna (1613–1693), a Carmelite monk and doctor of theology, held memberships in several academies and was among the founders of the Accademia Filarmonica of Bologna. He composed sacred music, but it was as a music pedagogue that he was most influential in the seventeenth century. He published a tutor for beginners in plainchant, the *Directory of Plainchant, from which to learn how to sing in choir* (1689), and a tutor called *Musical Daybreaks* (1672), which treats of *canto figurato,* that is, of singing countrapuntal music, and teaches the fundamentals of figured bass. The latter book descends from a line of elementary guides for musicians that begins in the Baroque era with the handbooks by church musicians such as Adriano Banchieri. Although their presentation of the elements of music remained fairly standard through the century (echoes of Agostino Agazzari and Lodovico Viadana may be heard in *Musical Daybreaks*), Penna also offers advice that goes beyond rules for reading musical notation and reveals his practical experience in training students of voice who will sing in ensembles and with continuo accompaniment. Above all, Penna tells his students to learn by listening to good performers.

FROM *Musical Daybreaks for Beginners in Measured Music*

(1684)

BOOK I

CHAPTER 21. SOME RULES TO FOLLOW AND SOME THINGS TO AVOID FOR BEGINNERS OF *CANTO FIGURATO*

1. When singing in an ensemble, no one voice should dominate any other; rather one should strive for equality, so that no one is either louder or softer than the others.

TEXT: *Li primi albori musicali per li principianti della musica figurata,* 4th ed. (Bologna, 1684; facs. Bologna, 1969), pp. 49–50; 183–87; 197–98. Translation by Margaret Murata.

2. You should not sing for yourself, being content just to read notes and get the rhythm right; and this is so that you won't sing out of tune.

3. Do not twist or distort your waist, your head, your eyes, your mouth, etc., because it is ugly to see.

4. Do not sing in your nose, or through your teeth, or in your throat.

5. Sing precisely with some mordents, *accenti,*[1] graces, etc., and if your voice has a natural trill or *gorga,* employ it in performance with great modesty, without using it on every note; and if you do not have it naturally, seek to develop one by artifice.

6. Give liveliness to the notes as well as to the words, making them clear and understandable.

7. If two parts have *gorghe* or trills, do them one after the other and not both together, one imitating the other in the exchange (*chiamate*).

8. In order for the five vowels to be sung with the proportionate opening of the mouth, you should know that

    for the A, you open the mouth at the maximum a little less than three fingers one above the other;

    for the E, at the maximum, a little less than two,

    for the I, of one finger,

    for the O, of three fingers,

    for the U, of one finger only.

9. Do not make *passaggi,* or *movimenti,*[2] on the vowels I and U.

10. Count the beats in your head, or at least softly, so as not to disturb your partner.

11. Follow the words, as discussed in chapter 18. That is, sing happily if the words are happy; if they are lively and spirited, sing with spirit and *vivace;* if they are about grief, pain, torment, etc., sing mournfully and slowly.

12. And lastly go as often as possible to concerts, especially where there are good singers, because you always learn something; and if nothing else, you will learn the style, the sweetness, the *accenti,* the graces, etc. of good singing. This much suffices for beginners in singing figured music.

---

1. Improvised escape tones on or before the beat; see the Glossary of Foreign Performance Terms, p. 223. Caccini's one-note trill was obsolete; the distinction between Penna's trill and the related *gorga* may have been one between trills beginning above the main note and on the main note. The complete text of Penna's chapter 19 "Of Melodic Accidentals" reads: "Because singing the notes and words in rhythm as they are written, without any embellishments would not give pleasure to the ear, one must learn to sing with some graces. Among the other things that give grace to singing are making some mordents and trills on the notes, emitting the voice now with smoothness, now with caprice, now with sweetness, etc., following as much as possible the sense of the words, pronouncing them distinctly to make them understood, etc. But because it is difficult to explain such things with written examples, and because the student is well informed by his maestro, not only about all that I have written here but about many other things that I will let go to avoid tedium, I will not put any more on paper. I only point out that in compositions where a "t" appears with a dot in this manner: **t.**, there a trill must be made."

2. *Movimenti* are illustrated in chapter 20 of book 1, as divisions between semibreves (pp. 46–49); see the Glossary of Foreign Performance Terms, p. 224.

BOOK III

Chapter 14. Of Accompanying Compositions for Solo Voice

In all compositions, whether in two, three, or four voices, etc., the organist must be accurate and ready of hand, eye, and ear, as well as of spirit, in order to accompany the singers' voices on the keyboard. But in compositions for solo voice, it is necessary to be very alert and ready to accompany the voice. And this is true as much in *ariette,* in quick pieces, etc., as well as in expressive and slow ones, etc.

Ordinarily in compositions for solo voice you see the singer's line in score, placed above the organist's line, scored up, although at times (but rarely) you will meet a part without it. In both cases you observe the following rules.

First rule

The organist should keep a quick, open eye not only on his part, but also on the singer's line, placed above, to accompany with the keys that correspond to the voice, for example, for a soprano, play in the soprano register [see Ex. A1]; if contralto, play in the alto register [Ex. A2], striving to be ready to touch the key to give the pitch to the singer.

[Example A1]   [Example A2]

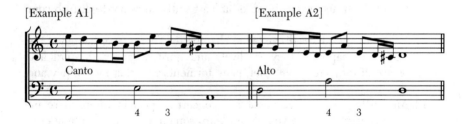

Canto   Alto

4   3   4   3

Second rule

When it is not possible to accompany all the notes sung, take only the consonances, or at least the first and last of the downbeat part of the *tactus,* and the first and last of the upbeat part,[3] letting the others go, as in the example, taken from the examples given above. All this holds true even in *ariette.* [Exx. B1 and B2]

---

3. "Levar di mano." In common time, the hand descended at the beginning of a semibreve *tactus,* or whole note, and rose on the second half. In modern terms, the "beat is in two." Penna is thus saying that the organist is to play on whatever begins the *tactus* and on the pickup to the second half of the *tactus;* similarly the continuo sounds the first and last notes of the second half of the *tactus.* If the *tactus* were a semibreve, chords would occur on each quarter-note. The implied falling and rising of the hand have been marked by the editor in the musical example.

[Example B1]   [Example B2]

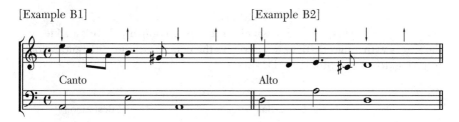

Canto   Alto

Third rule

In the ritornelli or during rests placed to relieve the singer, the organist should play something improvised, imitating the arietta or something spirited newly invented. This is clear without giving any examples.

Fourth rule

In the recitative style, where there are many expressive devices using dissonances, you must be ready to play them quickly, making the necessary harmony. The most frequent of the dissonant *affetti* are the following five:

• The first is based on the basso continuo which plays a tone of one or one-half measure, or longer, in the same place.
  • The second occurs when the basso continuo leaps down a fourth, or up a fifth.
  • The third, when it falls down a fifth or leaps up a fourth.
  • The fourth, when two successive notes descend by step, making a cadence.
  • The fifth, when the bass makes a suspension of a second, and resolves to a third, making a cadence.

The realizations of all five are in the following rules.

Fifth rule

If the bass remains on the same tone for one or one-half bar or for even more notes, the dissonances, or bad notes as we call them, must be played; which is to say the major 7ths, 9ths, 11ths, and minor 13ths, or their equivalents, all sounded together with the right hand, whether descending [Ex. C1] or ascending [Ex. C2]; and before resolving to the consonances, play the 10th or 12th, as it better.

[Example C1]   [Example C2]

Realization   Realization

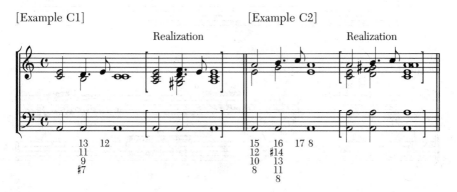

13   12   15   16   17 8
11   12 #14
9   10   13
#7   8   11
                                 8

Sixth rule

When the bass leaps a fourth down or a fifth up, accompany the dissonance of
the singer with a raised 4th or a raised 6th, the octave and the 10th, and before
resolving, touch the 9th. [Exx. D1–2]

[Example D1]   [Example D2]

Seventh rule

When the bass leaps a fifth down or a fourth up, make an accompaniment with
dissonances of a minor 7th [Ex. E1–2]. The accompaniment for the fourth and
fifth *affetti* are demonstrated in chapters 12 and 13 from the present third
book. You will find them there [Exx. E3–4].

[Example E1]   [Example E2]

[Example E3]
with the notes only   with the trill

[Example E4]
with the notes only   with the trills

BOOK III

CHAPTER 15. OF PLAYING FUGATO *A CAPPELLA*

In *a cappella* works (whether thin or thick), the fugue begins with one [vocal] line; then the second enters, and afterwards, the third, etc. Therefore the beginner should note that the fugue begins with one finger, playing the same note as the [voice] part that begins the fugue. . . .

BOOK III.

CHAPTER 20. SOME PRINCIPLES TO OBSERVE AND THINGS TO AVOID IN PLAYING ORGAN FROM A PART

1. As soon as you receive a part to play, try to understand its nature [in order] to realize it appropriately.
2. When the right hand rises, the fingers move one after the other, first the third, then the fourth, then the third, and so forth for as long as the line goes on and the fingers are not playing together. But on descending you change to third, second, third, etc. In the left hand you do the opposite. . . .
3. Both the left and right hands should not be held low with the fingers high, but the hands and the fingers should be extended to form a nice hand.

• • • • •

6. On a [bass] note that receives a 6th, this sixth can be alone without the octave; this will sound better.
7. It is good to play legato all the time, if it does not interfere with the singer's part.

• • • • •

9. All numbers [of a figured bass] which are above the octave must be played by the right hand, when playing in ensembles.
10. In performing with a soprano or contralto, you must not play above the part that sings, nor add diminutions.
11. With a tenor, you may play above and stay above [the singer's register], but do not play in octaves with the line he sings, nor [add] diminutions [to it].
12. With a bass, you can make a few *movimenti*,[4] but if the bass line has *passaggi*, it is not good to ornament at the same time.
13. When you accompany a solo voice, do not play more than three or (rarely) four notes at the same time;[5] it is not good to sound the octave above.

4. See above, note 2.
5. This is most applicable to the sustained sound of the organ.

14. With two parts, similarly, you should use few keys and avoid the octave.

15. In three and four parts you can fill out the sound a bit more, but rarely double the bass when it is on *mi* or ♯.[6]

16. In eight voices, in three or four choirs, etc., you fill and double even the doublings, the sharps, and whatever you want, because it will make a good effect with so much variety or sonority.

17. In accompanying instruments, it is good to avoid making *movimenti*, so that the listener can hear their ensemble, the imitations, the exchanges, the answers between them, etc.

18. Practice a lot, exercising yourself for speed, trills, as much with the right as with the left hand, because in this way you break in the hand and gain mastery over the keyboard.

19. Try to arpeggiate in order not to leave the instrument empty.

20. Go often to academies and concerts, noting well the techniques of those who play this instrument, to put them to use.

6. When it is on a note that would be solmized as "mi" or a note accidentally raised by a sharp. Such pitches are often secondary, applied leading tones.

106 Georg Muffat

Like the cosmopolitan Mozart, Georg Muffat (1653–1704) had firsthand opportunities to absorb the varied national styles of his day. Born in Savoy, he studied music in Paris from 1663 to 1669 while hardly out of childhood, then studied and served as a cathedral organist in Alsace, enrolled as a law student in Ingolstadt in 1674, worked in Vienna and Prague, and finally became organist and chamber musician to the Archbishop of Salzburg, all in his first twenty-five years. From 1680/81 to 1682 he was in the Rome of Arcangelo Corelli and Alessandro Scarlatti, and in 1690 he entered permanent employment in Germany with the Bishop of Passau. In addition to the Italianate concertos and French-influenced suites for instrumental ensemble for which he is best known, Muffat composed three operas for Salzburg, solo organ works, and a treatise on continuo practice.

Muffat published his suites and concertos only after he felt that the climate in Germany and Austria was open enough to their foreign-influenced styles. Even then, he provided prefaces in four languages to explain points of performance practice. These prefaces tell us much about violin playing in France and Italy and about what was not common practice in the German-speaking lands. He explained signs for sectional repetitions; the varied relationships between meter signs, tempo, and dance types; the practice of playing unequal notes that are notated with equal values; and differences among the French, Italians, and Germans in their ways of bowing. He touched briefly on his preferences for higher or lower pitches to serve as a reference pitch for tuning. And he illustrated standard melodic ornaments using an idiosyncratic system of signs that was neither French nor Italian and has therefore been avoided here. Muffat gives a view of string playing in the 1660s to 1690s and also heralds the absorption and integration of French and Italian idioms that mark the music of the next generation of German composers.

FROM Prefaces to *Florilegia*

PREFACE TO THE *FIRST FLORILEGIUM*
(1695)

Here you have my pieces, composed in Salzburg before I came to Passau and conforming in the main to the French ballet style, now submitted to you, gracious *amateur*,[1] for your entertainment and approval. Heard with pleasure by several princes and also praised by many of the higher nobility, they are published at the repeated entreaty of good friends and with the approbation of distinguished musicians, both Italian and German. To these requests I have given in the more gladly, observing that here in Germany the French style is gradually coming to the fore and flourishing. When this style was at its height under the celebrated J. Baptiste de Lully, I studied it diligently for the six years I was in Paris, beyond my other musical activities; and returning from France, I was perhaps the first to bring this manner, which is not displeasing to musicians of good taste, into Alsace; and driven from there by the last war, to Vienna in Austria and to Prague, and finally afterwards to Salzburg and Passau. Inasmuch as the ballet compositions of the said Lully, and other things in a similar style, entirely reject—for the sake of flowing and natural movement—all superfluous artifices, such as immoderate divisions as well as frequent and ill-sounding leaps, they had at first the misfortune in these countries to displease many of our musicians, who at that time were more intent on the variety of unusual conceits and artificialities than on grace. For this reason, when occasionally performed by those ignorant of the French manner or envious of foreign art, they came off badly, robbed of their proper tempo and usual ornaments. When, however, they were exhibited with greater perfection, first in Vienna by certain

---

TEXT: *Suavioris harmoniae instrumentalis hyporchematicae florilegium primum* (Augsburg: J. Koppmayr, 1695) and *Suavioris . . . florilegium secundum* (Passau, 1698). Modern edition in *Denkmäler der Tonkunst in Österreich*, Jg. 1, pt. 2, and Jg. 2, pt. 2, ed. Heinrich Rietsch (Vienna, 1894–95; repr. Graz, 1959). Muffat's prefaces in his Latin, German, Italian, and French versions are also available in Walter Kolneder, *Georg Muffat zur Aufführungspraxis* (Strasbourg: P. Heitz, 1970), pp. 30–37 and 44–98. Portions of the second preface are also in Carol MacClintock, *Readings in the History of Music in Performance* (Bloomington, 1979), pp. 297–303. Translation by Oliver Strunk, revised and expanded by Margaret Murata.

1. Music lover.

foreign violinists and soon after in Bavaria by His Electoral Serenity's excellent musicians, they were more favorably considered, and many began to form a better opinion of them and to accustom themselves to this style and grace, and even to study it, in order to conform to the genius of the princes and lords applauding such music. No doubt they discovered the truth of what an extremely discerning prince once said to me with regard to this style: namely, that what they had learned previously was more difficult than what, to charm the ear, they needed to have learned. Now that the ill-considered contempt for the aforesaid ballet style has gradually fallen off, it has seemed to me that I might the more confidently come forward with my admittedly insignificant pieces, which have as much need of the artistry and favor of our violinists as they appear simple. To give reasons for the names prefixed to each set seems needless, especially since these have been named only to distinguish one from another, either for some cause, or effect, or some event that happened to me, or for some state of mind in which I found myself.[2]

It still remains for me to remind and request such musicians as are as yet unfamiliar with the aforesaid style that, when notes are enclosed in such brackets as these ⌐‾‾‾‾‾⌐⌐‾‾‾‾⌐, after the first playing of those notes which precede the sign of repetition **.S.** ⫶‖⫶, in the second playing they are to omit them altogether, skipping instead straightway over to those notes which follow immediately after said repetition.[3] In addition, this sign **.S.**, whether placed at the very opening or after the sign of repetition ⫶‖⫶, marks the note from which the repetition should begin, omitting the preceding ones altogether.[4] This is also to be observed, following the most common practice, when it occurs near the middle of the second part or somewhat further from the end.[5] Although I find the practice not displeasing, of some who, having repeated the whole second part, retake this [petite] reprise a third time from said sign **.S.**, this is a matter to be settled by the musicians before the performance.

Beyond this, when the measure of two beats is marked **2** [or] ¢, it necessarily follows the common rule to go twice as fast as that which goes under the sign **C** divided into four.[6] This assumes that the measure **2** must be quite slow[7] in

---

2. The Latin titles of the seven suites making up the *Florilegium primum* might be translated: I. *Eusebia*—Piety; II. *Sperantis gaudia*—The Joys of the Hopeful; III. *Gratitudo*—Gratitude; IV. *Impatientia*—Impatience; V. *Sollicitudo*—Solicitude; VI. *Blanditiae*—Flatteries; VII. *Constantia*—Constancy.

3. This describes the notational practice of providing a repeated strain with first and second endings.

4. This explains the operation of the *dal segno* mark.

5. A "petite reprise."

6. The four prefaces use different idioms to mean the same thing: *dupplò citius* in Latin for "twice as fast," *noch einmal so geschwind* in German for "once again as fast"; and the Italian and French phrases—*a metà presto* and *la moitié plus vite*—which translate as "faster by half," all double the tempo when the duration of the note values is halved.

7. "Assai adagio o grave; Fort lente; Ziemlich langsam."

the overtures, preludes, and symphonies,[8] a little more gay for the ballets, and for the rest, in my opinion, almost always more moderately than under the ¢, which, however, goes less quickly in the gavottes than in the bourrées.[9] Further, when the measure **2** is performed very slowly and (as said above) in two, the notes have nearly the same value as they have with the Italian under the sign **C** played quickly in four under the additional word "Presto." The difference between the two is simply that in the latter case one must not, as in the former and better, give to successive eighth notes 𝄽 𝄽 ♪ ♪ a dotted rhythm 𝄾· 𝄿 ♪. ♪, but must, on the contrary, play them evenly. The *symphonie* of the fourth set, called *Impatientia,* provides an example of this.[10] As to the other signs, $\frac{3}{2}$ requires a very slow movement, $\frac{3}{4}$ a gayer one, yet uniformly somewhat slow in the sarabandes and airs; then more lively in the *rondeaux,* and finally the most lively but without haste in menuets, courantes and many other dances, as also in the fugues in the overtures. The remaining pieces, such as are called gigues and canaries, need to be played the fastest of all, no matter how the measure is marked.

Gracious *amateur,* may it please you to accept this my *Florilegium primum,* protecting it from the envious and grudging, and excusing such errors of mine and of the press as may have crept in. Await what is promised at the end of the work.[11] Farewell and favor him who would deserve your favor.

8. "Suonate."
9. For Muffat, then, the slowest tempo for an even meter is indicated by **C** in four, which occurs only once in the *First Florilegium,* in an Allemande with the cautionary word "Largo." Slow duple meters are given under the sign two, faster ones under ¢.

10. In Italian ("the latter") style, eighth notes are not subject to the French practice of performing equally notated subdivisions unequally.

An example of "the former" would be the passage from Muffat's overture to *Eusebia* in note 9, in which he indicated French unequal eighths by notating dotted eighths followed by sixteenths.
11. The afterword to the volume promises that further instructions for performance practice will appear in the second volume, which they did.

FROM PREFACE TO THE *SECOND FLORILEGIUM*
(1698)

FIRST OBSERVATIONS BY THE AUTHOR ON THE PERFORMANCE OF
BALLETS IN THE LULLIAN-FRENCH MANNER

The art of playing ballets on the violin in the manner of the most celebrated
Jean-Baptiste Lully (here understood in all its purity, admired and praised by
the world's most excellent masters) is so ingenious a study that one can scarcely
imagine anything more agreeable or more beautiful. To reveal to you, gracious
reader, its chief secrets, know that it has at one time two aims: namely, to
appeal to the ear in the most agreeable way and to indicate properly the measure of the dance, so that one may recognize at once to what variety each piece
belongs and may feel in one's affections and one's feet, as it were without noticing it at all, an inclination to dance. For this there are, in my opinion, five
considerations necessary.

First, one must, for purity of intonation, stop the strings accurately. Second,
the bow must be drawn in a uniform way by all the players. Third, one must
bear constantly in mind the time signature, or tempo and measure, proper to
each piece. Fourth, one must pay strict attention to the usual signs of repetition
introduced and also to the qualities of the style and of the art of dancing. Fifth,
one must use with discernment certain ornaments making the pieces much
more beautiful and agreeable, lighting them up, as it were, with sparkling precious stones. Of which the following distich:

> Contactus, plectrum, tempus, mos, atque venustas
> Efficient alacrem, dulcisonamque chelyn.[1]

I. CONTACTUS. ON PLAYING IN TUNE.

With regard to correct intonation, there is no difference among the best
masters, no matter what their nations be, whose precepts only weak pupils or
unprofessional ignoramuses fail to observe. Nothing serves better to avoid false
tones than instruction and correction by a good master, from whom one will
have learned the first principles of this art and of which I do not intend to treat
here. I will say only that after good instruction in how to acquire and maintain
a delicate ear, nothing is more helpful than frequent practice with players of
exquisite taste and to avoid playing with those who would corrupt more ears
and fingers than they would improve. Beyond this I have observed that the
defects of the majority who play falsely come from playing the two tones that
make the semitone (for example, *mi* and *fa;* E and F; A and B♭; B♮ and C; or

---

1. "Fingering, bowing, measure, practice, and ornamentation/Will to the viol bring liveliness and
   sweetness of tone." The distich reiterates the five topics Muffat will cover in the subsequent five
   sections.

F♯ and G; C♯ and D; G♯ and A, etc.). They never take the *mi*, or the sharp very high, nor that of the *fa* or the flat very low. They err greatly also against the true proportion of the pitches[2] and the course of the tones or modes, or against the harmonic relation with respect to that which went before or after, whenever they make trills or other embellishments with improper pitches. Finally they offend the ear even when playing in tune, when the strings are not played with enough force or attention; whence one hears a very unpleasant hiss, scrape, or squeaking.

II. PLECTRUM. HOW TO DRAW THE BOW.

Most Germans, in playing the high or middle parts, conform with the Lullistes in their manner of holding the bow, squeezing the hair with the thumb and resting the other fingers on top of it. The French hold it in the same way to play the "violoncino,"[3] The Italians differ with them in the soprano parts— since they do not touch the hair; so also the gambists, as well as others on the bass [part], who place the fingers between the hair and the stick.

Beyond this, although the best masters of all nations agree that inasmuch as a bow stroke is long, firm, equal, and sweet, so much is it to be valued. Nonetheless up to now, neither the Italians nor the Germans have always agreed on how much to draw it down or up; this is not the case with the French, except in rare and scattered cases. With all this it is evident that those who follow the manner of the late Lully, as do the French, the English, Dutch, and Flemings, and many others, all equally observe the same way of drawing the bow on the principal notes of the measure (even if there be a thousand playing together), especially with respect to those notes that begin the measure, those that finish the cadences, and those that most mark the movements of the dance. Since the kind of uniformity so helpful in expressing the rhythms of the dance has not been found in our German players (however expert), many nobles returning from those countries, noting such a great difference in ensemble, have often been amazed and complained of the alteration that the dances suffer. To avoid such inconveniences and the danger of some mix-ups in similar situations, I believed it would be of service to draw up here some of the principal rules of the French way of bowing: in the examples of which this sign **I**, placed above a note indicates a down-bow; and this other, *v*, an up-bow.

I.[4] The first note of each measure that begins without a quarter- or eighth-note rest, should always be a down-bow no matter what its value. This is the principal, general, and almost indispensable rule of the Lullistes, upon which

---

2. For example, in the era before equal temperament became widespread, semitones were of different sizes (in theory in the ratios of 8:9 and 9:10), and intervals of the perfect fifth and major and minor thirds were variously tempered.
3. The violoncello or bass instrument of the violin family.
4. When Muffat subdivides the five main topics marked I.–V., he again uses Roman numerals for the subdivisions.

nearly all the entire secret of bowing depends and the difference between them and the others, and which all other rules obey. But to know how the other notes are accommodated and played, it is necessary to observe the following rules.

II. In the common ordinary imperfect time of the theorists,[5] among the notes that divide the measure into equal parts, those that are odd are played with a down-bow and those that are even, with an up-bow. The odd are [beats] 1, 3, 5, 7, 9, 11, etc. and the even are 2, 4, 6, 8, 10, 12, etc. See Example A. This rule is also observed in triple meters and in other proportional meters with respect to notes equally subdivided. I am calling "subdivided" those that go more quickly than those that are denominated by the time signature. [Ex. B]. This manner of counting the equal notes remains in effect when quarter- or eighth-note rests take the place of notes. [Ex. C] For the rest, all the best players easily agree with this rule of the French.

III. Since, according to the first rule, the first note of the measure is a down-bow, of the three equal notes that make up a whole measure in triple time, the second is always an up-bow, and the third is again a down-bow, at least if the tempo is a little slow. This means that with the beginning of the second bar it

5. Duple measure indicated by the sign **C**.

is necessary to make two down-bows consecutively [Ex. D]. Most frequently, however, one plays the second as well as the third beats with an up-bow, dividing it distinctly in two (this is called *craquer*[6]), which is much easier, especially in tempos that are somewhat faster [Ex. E].

X. The "leftover" note before the beginning of a measure[7] [Ex. Y], or the quick note after a dot, or an eighth rest [Z], or any lesser note that follows a syncopation of greater value [AA], must always be an up-bow. Or if besides these cases an up-bow is required, it will be necessary to divide that up-bow in two, adding to it the succeeding one [Ex. BB].

Sometimes an exception is made of courantes because of the quickness of the notes that begin the second, fourth, sixth or similar even-numbered measures (thinking of them in triple time), which can sometimes be begun with an up-bow when it is more comfortable. Nonetheless those beats that mark the uneven measure and which most strongly mark the rhythm of the dance are always down-bow [CC]. Beside this, the first rule concerning the first note of the measure is rigorously observed. As far as the other beats that begin essential parts are concerned, or as for the rest of the measure, in gigues, canaries and other dances in compound time, it is often necessary to dispense with

6. To "crack" of "snap" implies a push, perhaps by flick of the hand off the wrist. The German text gives "hupfend," or "hopping." See the Glossary of Foreign Performance Terms, p. 224.
7. The "upbeat."

Rules 4, 8, and 10 because of the fast tempo[8] Example DD will show how to bow when there are frequent dotted rhythms mixed among the notes. Similarly because of the quickness of bourées and similar airs, one frequently breaks Rule 8, when (always keeping the validity of the first rule), the others are treated, as can be seen in Example EE. In these last three examples I have marked the licenses with an asterisk * under the notes. Finally, when two little notes, such as two sixteenths join just as a decoration of some other note, they are sometimes played each with its own bow stroke [FF] and at times for greater sweetness, one runs them into the previous note in one or two strokes [GG].

To do otherwise and play any downbeat with an up-bow is an obvious error

8. Rule 4 observes the **l v v** bowing for the three-note groups in meters of six, nine, and twelve beats. Rule 8: Of the three notes that make up the essential part of a measure in compound time, if the first is dotted, it should be played with a downbow [Ex. V].

in this style. This happens often with the Italians and Germans in triple meters, especially when the first note is of a lesser value than the second. From such contrariness of opinion and from the transgression against said first rule comes the very great difference that one finds in bowing, as much with regard to the first as to the others following that depend on it. To make it easier to understand this difference I wanted to mark the same succession of several notes played in the two different ways, that is, according to some Italians or Germans [HH], then in the French manner [II]. Furthermore this is contrary to the vivacity of the Lullistes and goes against Rule 7 (which runs the little note after a dot or an eighth rest to the following note in one bow stroke), as Example LL demonstrates. To play the French way, one must play according to Example MM, although the opposite is permitted whenever said little note is joined to the preceding one *en craquent* [NN].

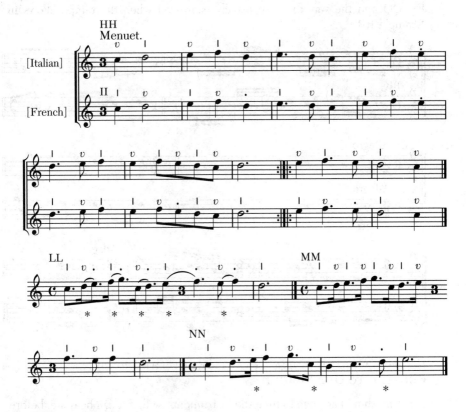

Behold the principal rules of the Lullian method of bowing, which is habitually observed as much for the violins as for the middle lines and even for the bass. The greatest dexterity of the true Lullistes consists of this, that among so many repeated down-bows one never hears anything disagreeable or coarse, but, on the contrary, one finds a marvelous joining of great speed and long bow strokes, an admirable evenness of beat with diversity of rhythm, and a tender sweetness with lively playing.

III. TEMPUS. ABOUT TIME.[9]

•   •   •   •   •

III. Subdivisions of the principal note value—which are sixteenths in common time, eighths in duple or *alla breve* time, those which are twice as fast as the main beats in moderately fast time, and compound meters—are not played equally as notated when given consecutively. They would sound sleepy, coarse, and dull. But these change in the French style by adding a dot to each of those that fall on an odd note, which by becoming longer makes the following one reciprocally shorter. See examples of the different kinds in various meters in Ex. QQ and the way they are usually expressed when the tempo allows in Example RR.

IV. *MOS.* CERTAIN OTHER PRACTICES OF THE LULLISTES RELATED TO OUR SUBJECT

I. One should arrange to tune the instruments well, if it can be done, before the arrival of the listeners, or it should be done at least as quickly and efficiently

9. In this section on meter and rhythm, Muffat refers the reader to his 1695 dances for point I (see above, pp. 138–39). For point II he notes six common rhythmic errors, such as rushing in subdivided passages and not giving the third beat in triple time its full value.

as will be possible.

II. One should refrain from making any commotion before playing and from so many confused preludes that at times, by filling the ear and the eye, make as great a nuisance before the overture as what comes after is a delight.

III. The tone to which the French tune [their instruments] is ordinarily one step lower and for operas a step and a half lower[10] than our German *Chor-Ton.* The so-called *Cornet-Ton* seems to them too high, too forced, and too screechy. If it were my choice, and as long as nothing else prevented it, I would always adopt the tone a step lower than what in Germany is called the *Chor-Ton,* with strings a little thicker; this does not lack vivacity along with its sweetness.

IV. One should distribute the parts and, according to the number of musicians, double them with such judgment that one can hear them all distinctly, aggreeably and with the usual ornaments. Nor should one put so many good violins only on the highest line that the middle parts and the bass are deprived of a sufficient number of capable musicians, which would hide one of the greatest ornaments of an ensemble. It displeases me to see this happen often on account of foolish obsessions with status that some have.

V. As for the instruments, the part the Italians call the "violetta" and the French "haute contre" will succeed better if played upon a medium-sized viola on the small side[11] than upon a violin. For the bass one wants what the Italians call a "violoncino" and the Germans a French bass,[12] which cannot be omitted without distorting the balance. One can double according to the number of musicians, which, if it is great and also mixed with a double bass, or the contrabass of the Italians (which is the *Violon* of the Germans), the ensemble will be so much the more majestic, even though up to now the French do not use them in *airs de ballets.*

---

10. The Paris opera orchestra tuned to an A^4 of c. 410 cycles per second in Lully's time, which seems to have risen to c. 422 cps by 1700. Muffat advocates the "high chamber-pitch" to which German harpsichords and strings tuned, as opposed to the "choir tone" set by the local organs.
11. "A little smaller than the *Taille.*"
12. "Une petite Basse à la françoise."

IMITATION AND EXPRESSION

107 Jacopo Peri

A singer, organist, and published composer by age 22, Jacopo Peri (1561–1633) played a central role in the formation of Baroque opera. As a singer-composer, he often wrote his own solos for collaborative theatrical projects and at times accompanied himself on the chitarrone. For example, he provided music for sections of the 1589 *intermedi* that were performed in Florence with the play *La pellegrina* and composed his own recitatives for the role of Clori in Marco da Gagliano's opera *La Flora,* staged in Florence in 1628. The most complete surviving theatrical score by Peri, his setting of Ottavio Rinuccini's libretto *Euridice,* was written for performance in Florence in 1600 and published within four months, along with a rival setting by Giulio Caccini. In the preface to his score, Peri explains how he had arrived at a new style of solo theatrical singing in 1597–98 for a staging of the Greek fable of Daphne and Apollo. Although as members of the Florentine Camerata he and Caccini had the same general aim of expressing poetic texts clearly and emotionally, Peri cites his models of verse recitation and describes more precisely how music becomes the elocution of the text. The musical representation of the sound of speech would continue to be a critical issue in vocal music throughout the Baroque era, for example, in the differences over operatic music between Jean Laurent Le Cerf de la Viéville and François Raguenet at the beginning of the next century.

Preface to *The Music for Euridice*
(1601)

Before I offer you (kind readers) this my music, I have judged it appropriate to make known to you what induced me to discover this new manner of song, since reason should be the beginning and fount of all human operations, and he who cannot offer reasons easily gives one to believe that he has acted by chance. Although Signor Emilio Cavaliere, before any other, so far as I know, enabled us with marvelous invention to hear our music on the stage, nonetheless it pleased the Signori Jacopo Corsi and Ottavio Rinuccini (as early as 1594) that I, employing it in another guise, should set to music the tale of Daphne, written by Signor Ottavio, to make a simple trial of what the song of our age could do. Whence, seeing that it was a question of dramatic poetry and that, therefore, one should imitate in song a person speaking (and without a doubt, no one ever spoke singing), I judged that the ancient Greeks and

TEXT: *Le musiche sopra L'Euridice* (Florence, 1600 [i.e., 1601]; facs. New York: Broude Brothers, 1973 and Bologna: Forni Editore, 1973), pp. iii–iv; translation by Tim Carter. The Italian text of this and the front matter to other opera scores, translated into English, also appears in T. Carter and Z. Szweykowski, *Composing Opera: From* Dafne *to* Ulisse Errante (Cracow: Musica Iagellonica, 1994).

Romans (who, according to the opinion of many, sang their tragedies throughout on the stage) used a harmony which, going beyond that of ordinary speech,
fell so short of the melody of song that it assumed an intermediate form. And
this is the reason why we see in their poetry that the iamb had a place which
is not elevated like the hexameter,[1] but yet is said to proceed beyond the confines of everyday speech. And therefore, rejecting every other type of song
heard up to now, I set myself to discovering the imitation that is due to these
poems. And I considered that that type of voice assigned to singing by the
ancients which they called "diastematic" (as it were, sustained and suspended)
could at times speed up and take an intermediate path between the suspended
and slow movements of song and the fluent, rapid ones of speech, and thus
suit my intention (just as they, too, accommodated it in reading their poetry and
heroic verse,)[2] approaching the other [species] of speech, which they called
"continuous," and which our moderns (although perhaps for another end) have
also done in their music. I realized, similarly, that in our speech some words
are intoned in such a manner that harmony can be founded upon them, and
that while speaking one passes through many other [words] which are not
intoned, until one returns to another that can move to a new consonance. And
taking note of these manners and those accents that serve us in grief, joy, and
in similar states, I made the bass move in time to these, now faster, now slower,
according to the emotions; and I held it firm through the dissonances and
consonances until the voice of the speaker, passing though various notes,
arrived at that which, being intoned in ordinary speech, opens the way to a
new harmony. And [I did] this not only so that the flow of the speech would
not offend the ear (as if stumbling in encountering the repeated notes of the
more frequent consonances), or so that it might not seem in a way to dance to
the movement of the bass—particularly in sad or serious subjects, since happier subjects require by their nature more frequent movements—but also
because the use of dissonances would either diminish or mask the advantage
thereby gained because of the necessity of intoning every note,[3] which the
ancient musics had perhaps less need of doing. And so (even though I would
not be so bold as to claim that this was the type of song used in Greek and
Roman plays) I have thus believed it to be the only type that our music can

1. Dactylic hexameters were the poetic meter of ancient epic poetry; iambs were common in
   ancient drama, especially in dialogue.
2. Renaissance musical theorists inherited from Greek and Latin writers the distinction between
   the continuous species of voice—the speaking or reading voice—and the diastematic or intervallic one, which was suitable for musical melody. Aristides Quintilianus furthermore recognized
   an intermediate species—that of poetic recitation, to which Peri's intermediate manner is analogous. See Claude V. Palisca, *Humanism in Renaissance Thought* (New Haven: Yale University
   Press, 1985), pp. 408–33, esp. pp. 428–30 (see also p. 49 above).
3. Peri is here describing the irregularity of his harmonic rhythm, compared to the regular coordination of chord change and meter in the systematic contrapuntal style. When many vocal tones,
   which had to be sung, were treated in the new style as passing consonances and dissonances,
   harmonic change served instead to emphasize the irregular stresses of Italian verse. The problem of harmonization did not apply to Greek and Roman music.

give us to suit our speech. Whence, having had my opinion heard by these gentlemen, I demonstrated to them this new manner of singing, and it gave the greatest pleasure, not only to Signor Jacopo,[4] who had already composed some most beautiful airs for this tale, but also to Signor Piero Strozzi, to Signor Francesco Cini, and to other most learned gentlemen (for music flourishes today among the nobility) and also to that celebrated lady whom one may call the Euterpe of our age, Signora Vettoria Archilei,[5] who has always made my music worthy of her song, adorning it not only with those *gruppi*[6] and with those long roulades both simple and double which, by the liveliness of her wit, are encountered at every moment—more to obey the practice of our times than because she judges that in them consist the beauty and force of our singing—but also those sorts of delights and graces which cannot be written, and if written cannot be learned from the notation. Messer Giovan Battista Jacomelli[7] heard and commended it,[8] who, most excellent in all the parts of music, has as it were changed his surname to "Violino," on which [instument] he is marvelous. And for three successive years, when it was performed in Carnival, it was heard with greatest delight and received with universal applause by whomever found himself there. But the present *Euridice* had better fortune, not because those lords and other worthy men that I have mentioned heard it, and also Signor Count Alfonso Fontanella and Signor Orazio Vecchi, most noble witnesses to my thought, but because it was performed before so great a queen[9] and so many famous princes of Italy and France, and was sung by most excellent musicians of our time. Among whom, Signor Francesco Rasi, a nobleman from Arezzo, played Aminta; Signor Antonio Brandi, Arcetro; and Signor Melchior Palantrotti, Pluto. And from behind the stage performed gentlemen distinguished for the nobility of their blood and for the excellence of their music: Signor Jacopo Corsi, whom I have mentioned so often, played the harpsichord, and Signor Don Grazia Montalvo a chitarrone, Messer Giovanbattista dal Violino[10] a large *lira,* and Messer Giovanni Lapi a large lute. And although until then I had done it in the precise way in which it now appears, nonetheless Giulio Caccini (called "Romano"), whose great merit is known to the world, wrote the arias of Euridice and some of those for the shepherd and nymph of the chorus, and the choruses "Al canto, al ballo," "Sospirate," and "Poi che gli eterni imperi"; and this [was done] because they were to be sung by persons dependent upon him, the which arias can be seen in his [score], which was

---

4. Jacopo Corsi (1561–1602), Florentine patron of music from the 1580s. He composed some preliminary music for the opera *Dafne,* which was performed in 1598 with music by Peri.
5. See No. 4 above, p. 41, note 18, and No. 19, page 98, note 6.
6. Trills; see Caccini, No. 20 above.
7. Active in Rome from 1574 to 1583 and a musician of Ferdinando I de' Medici, Jacomelli sang tenor in the Sistine Chapel choir (before being expelled in 1585), and played violin, viola, keyboard, and harp. He went to Florence in 1587, where he died in 1608.
8. The opera *Dafne.*
9. Maria de' Medici, Queen of France and Navarre.
10. That is, Giacomelli, mentioned above.

composed and printed, however, after mine was performed before Her Most Christian Majesty.[11]

So receive it kindly, courteous Readers, and although I may not have arrived by this means where it seemed I could reach (since concern about novelty has acted as a brake on my course), welcome it nevertheless, and perhaps it will happen that on another occasion I may show you something more perfect than this. Meanwhile, it will seem to me that I have done enough, having opened up the path to the skills of others to progress in my footsteps to glory, where it was not given me to be able to arrive. And I hope that the use of the dissonances, played and sung without fear, with discretion, and accurately (having pleased so many and such worthy men) will not cause you annoyance, especially in the more sad and serious airs of Orfeo, Arcetro, and Dafne, who was played with much grace by Jacopo Giusti, a little boy from Lucca.

And live happily.

Notice

Above the bass part, the sharp next to a 6 indicates a major sixth, and the minor [sixth] is without the sharp, which when it is alone is a sign of the major third or tenth, and the flat the minor third or tenth. And do not ever use it except for that note alone where it is indicated, even though there may be several [notes] on one and the same pitch.

11. Maria de' Medici.

108 Claudio Monteverdi

Although he had become *maestro di cappella* at St. Mark's in Venice in 1613, Claudio Monteverdi did not dissolve his ties with his former ducal patrons, the Gonzagas of Mantua, especially since they offered him continued opportunities to compose theatrical music. In late 1616 plans were begun for a maritime spectacle with music to celebrate the wedding of Ferdinando Gonzaga, the new duke, and Caterina de' Medici, sister of the Grand Duke of Tuscany. Monteverdi received the proposal from Alessandro Striggio (who had written the libretto for Monteverdi's 1607 opera *Orfeo*) with due obsequiousness, but he protested its lack of opportunities to express strong human feelings. The proposed *Marriage of Tethys,* to a libretto by Scipione Agnelli, appears to have been like a set of old-fashioned *intermedio* tableaux, and it was eventually abandoned even though Monteverdi had nearly completed the score.

Letter to Alessandro Striggio
(1616)

My Most Illustrious Lord and most esteemed patron,

I was very happy to receive from Signor Carlo de' Torri the letter from Your Most Illustrious Lordship and the *librettino* containing the *favola marittima* of the *Marriage of Tethys*.[1] Your Most Illustrious Lordship writes that you send it to me so that I should look at it carefully and later tell you what I think of it, since it is to be set to music for the forthcoming wedding of His Most Serene Highness.[2] I, my Most Illustrious Lord, who desire nothing other than to be worthy to serve His Most Serene Highness in something, will say nothing at first other than that I offer myself readily to all that which His Most Serene Highness shall ever deign to command me, and without objection, will always honor and revere all that His Most Serene Highness should command. Thus, if His Most Serene Highness has approved this [story], this would be, then, both very fine and much to my taste. But since you add that I should speak, I am ready to obey Your Most Illustrious Lordship's orders with all respect and promptness, understanding that what I say is trivial, coming from a person who is worth little *in toto* and a person who always honors every *virtuoso,* in particular the present gentleman poet, whose name I do not know, and so much more so since this profession of poetry is not mine.

I shall speak, therefore, with all respect, in obedience to you, since you so command. I shall speak and say first that, in general, music wants to be mistress of the air and not only of the water: I mean, in my language, that the ensembles[3] described in this story are all low and near the earth—a very great defect in making beautiful harmonies, since the harmonies will be given to the largest wind instruments in the stage area, [making the harmonies] difficult to be heard by everyone and coordinated [with the instruments] offstage (and I leave this matter to the judgment of your most refined and intelligent taste), so that with this defect, instead of one chitarrone you will want three of them, in place of one harp three will be needed, and so on; and instead of a delicate singer's voice you will want a forced one. Besides this, the correct imitation of speech would need, in my judgment, to be dependent on wind instruments rather than on delicate strings, since the harmonies of the tritons and other marine gods, I would think, should be with trombones and *cornetti* and not with cetras or harpsichords and harps, because, since this production is to be on water, it has to be outside the city[4] Plato teaches that "you should have kitharas in the town

TEXT: Claudio Monteverdi, *Lettere,* ed. Éva Lax (Florence, 1994), pp. 48–51; translation by Margaret Murata.

1. In Greek mythology, Tethys is a Titanness, daughter of Uranus and Gaia and wife of Oceanus; thus the tale is "maritime."
2. Ferdinando Gonzaga, Duke of Mantua.
3. "Concerti."

and tibias in the fields;"[5] so either the delicate instruments are inappropriate or the appropriate ones are not delicate.

Besides this, I noticed that the interlocutors are winds, cupids, zephyrs, and sirens, and so there will be need of many sopranos; and on top of this, the winds are supposed to sing, that is, the west and the north winds! And how, dear Sir, will I be able to imitate the speech of the winds, if winds don't speak?! How will I be able to move the affections with them? Arianna[6] moved us because she was a woman, and likewise Orfeo moved us because he was a man and not a wind. Harmonies can imitate themselves—and without words;[7] the noise of the winds, the bleating of sheep, the neighing of horses and so forth, but they do not imitate the speech of winds that does not exist!

Next, the dances in the course of this story are few, and they don't have the feet of dances.[8]

Next, the whole story, at least to my not inconsiderable ignorance, does not move me at all, and what is more, it is with difficulty that I understand it; nor do I feel that I am led in a natural progression to a conclusion that moves me: [the story of] Arianna leads me to a proper lament and Orfeo to a perfect prayer; but this story—I don't know to what end. Given this, what does Your Most Illustrious Lordship want the music to do here? Nonetheless, I will always accept everything with all respect and honor, whenever His Most Serene Highness should so command and please, since he is my patron without any question.

And whenever His Most Serene Highness should order that this be set to music, seeing that in it more deities than others speak, whom I like to hear singing in a refined style,[9] I would say that the sirens could be sung by the three sisters, that is Andriana [sic] and the others,[10] who could also write their own parts (likewise Signor Rasi his part, also Signor Don Francesco[11] and so forth for the other men) and here [we would] be copying Signor Cardinal Montalto who presented a comedy[12] in which each person who sang in it wrote his or her own part. For, if it were the case that this story progressed to a single conclusion, like Arianna and Orfeo, then you would also want a single hand,

---

4. The city of Mantua is bordered on the north by three lakes.
5. *Republic* 399d (*SR* 1).
6. The abandonment of Ariadne by Theseus was the subject of Monteverdi's opera *Arianna*, written for Mantua in 1608. His 1607 opera about Orpheus and Eurydice was also commissioned for Mantua.
7. Sounds can imitate other nonverbal sounds.
8. The poetic meters of dance songs.
9. "Di garbo."
10. Adriana, Margherita, and Vittoria Basile; see No. 4 above, p. 42, note 21.
11. Francesco Rasi (1574–1621), a tenor, had sung in Peri's *Euridice* and in Caccini's *Rapimento di Cefalo*, most likely the title role in the 1607 *Orfeo* and probably the part of Theseus in the 1608 *Arianna*, among other productions. He completed an opera *Cibele e Ati* (not performed), for the same Gonzaga wedding for which *Teti* was planned. Francesco Dognazzi, also a tenor, was awarded an annual pension by the Gonzaga in 1616.
12. *L'Amor pudico* (Rome, 1614).

that is, one that was inclined to speak while singing and not, as in this case, sing while speaking.[13] Also in this regard, I consider the speeches in each part too long from the sirens on, and in certain other short exchanges.

Excuse me, dear Sir, if I have said too much, [it was] not to belittle any thing, but in my desire to obey your orders, so that if I should be so ordered to have to set it in music, Your Most Illustrious Lordship may take my thoughts into consideration. Regard me, I beg you with all affection, a most devoted and most humble servant of His Most Serene Highness, to whom I bow most humbly; and I kiss the hands of Your Most Illustrious Lordship with every affection and pray that God grant you every happiness.

From Venice, December 9, 1616

13. "Al parlar cantando e non . . . al cantar parlando." Monteverdi paraphrases the Florentines' expression for the new monodic style, *recitar cantando.*

109 Claudio Monteverdi

Monteverdi's search for expressive means in music was tantalizingly articulated in 1638, when he published his first serious collection in several years: the *Madrigali guerrieri, et amorosi* (*Madrigals Warlike and Amorous*). The volume, his eighth book of madrigals, also included some small theatrical works; one, the famed *Combat of Tancred and Clorinda,* dated back to 1624. In his preface to the reader, Monteverdi explains how he had discovered new musical styles by searching for *similitudine del affetto,* that is, the "resemblance of emotion."

Preface to *Madrigali guerrieri, et amorosi*
(1638)

I have reflected that the principal passions or affections of our mind are three, namely, anger, moderation, and humility or supplication; so the best philosophers declare, and the very nature of our voice indicates this in having high, low, and middle registers. The art of music also points clearly to these

TEXT: *Madrigali guerrieri, et amorosi . . . Libro ottavo* (Venice, 1638); facs. and an Eng. trans. of preface (New York: Dover, 1991), p. xv. This translation by Oliver Strunk, revised by Margaret Murata.

three in its terms "agitated," "soft," and "moderate."[1] In all the works of former composers I have indeed found examples of the "soft" and the "moderate," but never of the "agitated," a genus nevertheless described by Plato in the third book of his *Rhetoric* in these words: "Take that harmony that would fittingly imitate the utterances and the accents of a brave man who is engaged in warfare."[2] And since I was aware that it is contraries which greatly move our mind, and that this is the purpose which all good music should have—as Boethius asserts, saying, "Music is related to us, and either ennobles or corrupts the character"[3]—for this reason I have applied myself with no small diligence and toil to rediscover this genus.

After reflecting that in the pyrrhic measure the tempo is fast and, according to all the best philosophers, used warlike, agitated leaps, and in the spondaic, the tempo slow and the opposite,[4] I began, therefore, to consider the semibreve [○, which, sounded once, I proposed should correspond to one stroke of a spondaic measure; when this was divided into sixteen *semicrome* [♪] and restruck one after the other and combined with words expressing anger and disdain, I recognized in this brief sample a resemblance to the affect I sought, although the words did not follow in their meter the rapidity of the instrument.

To obtain a better proof, I took the divine Tasso, as a poet who expresses with the greatest propriety and naturalness the qualities which he wishes to describe, and selected his description of the combat of Tancred and Clorinda[5] which gave me two contrary passions to set in song, war—that is, supplication, and death. In the year 1624 it was heard by the best citizens of the noble city of Venice in a noble room of my own patron and special protector Signor Girolamo Mocenigo, a prominent cavalier and among the first commanders of the Most Serene Republic; it was received with much applause and praise.

After the apparent success of my first attempt to depict anger, I proceeded with greater zeal to make a fuller investigation, and composed other works in that kind, both ecclesiastical[6] and for chamber performance. Further, this genus found such favor with the composers of music that they not only praised it by word of mouth, but, to my great pleasure and honor, they showed this by written work in imitation of mine. For this reason I have thought it best to make known that the investigation and the first essay in this genus, so necessary to the art of music, came from me. It may be said with reason that until the present, music has been imperfect, having had only the two *genera*—"soft" and "moderate."

It seemed at first to the musicians, especially to those who were called on to

1. "Concitato, molle" and "temprato."
2. *Republic* 399a (*SR* 1).
3. *De institutione musica*, I, i.
4. Plato, *Laws* 816c.
5. *La Gerusalemme liberata*, 12, lines 52–68 by Torquato Tasso (1544–1595), Italian epic poet.
6. An example is Monteverdi's motet "Laudate Dominum in sanctis ejus," published in his *Selva morale et spirituale* (Venice, 1640).

play the basso continuo, more ridiculous than praiseworthy to drum on a single string sixteen times in one *tactus,* and so they reduced this multiplicity to one stroke per *tactus,* sounding the spondaic instead of the pyrrhic foot and destroying the resemblance to agitated speech. Take notice, therefore, that the basso continuo must be played, along with its accompanying parts, in the form and manner of its genus as written. Similarly, you will find all the other directions necessary for performance of the other compositions in the other genus. For the manners of performance must take account of three things: text, harmony, and rhythm.[7]

My discovery of this warlike genus has given me occasion to write certain madrigals which I have called *guerrieri.* And since the music played before great princes at their courts to please their delicate taste is of three kinds, according to the method of performance—theater music, chamber music, and dance music—I have indicated these in my present work with the titles *guerriera, amorosa,* and *rappresentativa.*[8]

I know that this work will be imperfect, for I have but little skill, particularly in the genus *guerriero,* because it is new and *omne principium est debile.*[9] I therefore pray the benevolent reader to accept my good will, which will await from his learned pen a greater perfection in the said genus, because *inventis facile est addere.*[10] Farewell.

7. Plato, *Republic* 398d (p. 10).
8. This seems to say, but cannot mean, that there is a correspondence between Monteverdi's three methods of performance and his three varieties of madrigal. Among the *Madrigali guerrieri,* for example, some are *teatrali,* some *da camera,* some *da ballo.* To put it differently, *guerriero* and *amoroso* corresponds to kinds of music—*concitato* and *molle*—while *rappresentativo* corresponds to *teatrale,* a method of performance. [Tr.]
9. "Every beginning is feeble."
10. "It is easy to add to inventions."

110 Michel de Pure

The Abbé Michel de Pure (1620–1680) is best known for a work of fiction, *La Prétieuse, or Mystery Down the Lane* (published in four parts, 1656–58). It is, however, neither a novel nor a mystery but an extended dialogue on love, literature, and beauty modeled on the conversations of the consciously cultured salons of Paris, which de Pure knew firsthand. The manners, language, and preoccupations of this intellectual world of women and worldly men gave us the word "preciosity," which suggests their excessive refinement. The death of prime minister Cardinal Jules Mazarin in 1661 reduced de Pure's political standing at court, so he returned to scholarship. Between 1663 and 1666 he published translations into French of Quintilian, histories of the East and West Indies, and of Africa, followed in 1668 by an original work about theatrical and outdoor spectacles, *Aspects of Ancient and Modern Spectacles.* The book describes contemporary jousts, military exercises, and, above all, dance, "one of the principal external ornaments" of a gentleman and "a certain testament of praiseworthy and careful breeding." By placing these activities in the light of Greek and Roman culture, de Pure must have hoped to flatter the King's love of ballet and ingratiate himself back into court circles. Although he thought of the *bourrée* and *menuet* as newfangled inventions of the dancing masters, de Pure clearly regarded dance with its music as a form that at its best revealed the inner passions, apart from any songs, narrative, or poetry that might be included in a ballet. Dance, with its music, was "a mute representation, in which gestures and movements signify what could be expressed in words."

FROM *Aspects of Ancient and Modern Spectacles*

(1668)

CHAPTER 9: OF BALLET

SECTION VIII. DANCING IN BALLET

• • • • •

Dancing in ballet does not consist simply of subtle movements of the feet or of various turns of the body. It is composed of both and includes all that a nimble and well-instructed body can accomplish in gesture or action in order to express something without speaking. Nevertheless, even though it must be bolder and more vigorous than the common dancing one does at balls and in ordinary and domestic dances, which women as well as men pride themselves on performing well—even though, as I was saying, it must have a quality more lively and gay, it nonetheless has its own rules or laws that render it perfect or defective, according to whether one follows them or ignores them.

The principal and most important rule is to make the dancing expressive, so that the head, the shoulders, the arms, the hands communicate what the dancer does not speak. At the time of Nero, a barbarian king preferred a mime over all the other presents he could hope for from the Emperor, because of the fine talent he had of speaking with his hands while dancing and of representing with his gestures all that he could have stated by means of words. It is

TEXT: *Idée des spectacles anciens et nouveaux* (Paris, 1668; repr. Geneva: Minkoff, 1972). pp. 248–51; 260–65. Carol MacClintock, *Readings in the History of Music in Performance* (Bloomington and London: Indiana University Press, [1979]), offers two additional excerpts from de Pure, pp. 205–8. Translation by Margaret Murata.

easy to see by this that his dancing did not consist solely in the dexterity of his feet, nor in the rightness of his rhythm (for he even wanted to do without all the instruments that were used in those times), but in a certain deliberate manner, modelled on natural movements that pass through the body according to the disquiets and various agitations of the soul, and which signify, against our own will, the interior feelings that we strive to hide and to keep secret. Therein lies the ability of a master dancer: to accord this movement of the dancing with his concept [and] with the rhythm of the music, and to do it so that he does not contradict either the one or the other, [for example,] to give to an enraged character an abrupt and fiery dance from which one can perceive the disorder of the character and his distraction by means of special *temps* or broken *coupés*.[1] Likewise in a lover, in a sick person, in a sad person or in a playful one, he must try to be expressive and to paint well the various alterations that love, infirmity, chagrin, or joy can cause on the face or on other parts that seem the most affected by interior feelings and which by a natural and imperceptible relation become totally charged with them, and despite all our resolve and all our discretion, produce them outwardly. Without this, ballet dancing is nothing but a convulsion of the master[2] and of the dancer, a *bizzarerie* without spirit and without design and, in short, nothing but a defective dance and acrobatic leaping that signify nothing and have no more sense than the one who has done them and made them up.

SECTION X. BALLET MUSIC

•　　•　　•　　•　　•

The first and most essential beauty of music for ballet is its seemliness; that is to say, the just relation that the air[3] must have with the thing represented. In an oration one seeks the argument and the conclusion; one criticizes incongruities and digressions. Conversation requires that one speak appropriately: and ballet demands airs that are suitable to its subject. If one is to represent a woman who weeps over the loss of her husband or of her children, one should resort to lugubrious sounds with heavy accents and slow motions. Anyone who then would use a joyous, lively, subtle air would create an incongruity and a discrepancy not only disagreeable but also embarrassing for the spectator and for the subject. For who does not know that grief is the enemy of happy tunes, and who would not be misled to hear a joyous air with sad steps and with drooping gestures?

•　　•　　•　　•　　•

This first rule does not, however, exclude several others which are very important and of great beauty. For example, the constraint placed upon the musician in terms of the subject and its individuality does not at all excuse him

---

1. The *temps* and *pas coupé* were fundamental steps in court dancing, with many variants.
2. The choreographer.
3. "Air" refers to more than the melody; it includes the entire musical composition as performed, which should have the character of its subject.

from making beautiful tunes, maintaining the melody, and caring about the ears of those who listen to it. To succeed in this, one must have more than precepts: only nature may fully inspire his beautiful and happy ideas that charm everyone. For the talent to please is a gift of heaven and the stars, rather than of rules and practice.

•   •   •   •   •

There is, however, generally speaking a certain movement that one is obliged to observe in all the airs for the ballet and in all those of all kinds of dances, and especially French ones. I say French, because I have noted among foreigners movements considerably slower and more lyric. The Italians, who do not ordinarily dance except to guitars, and the Spanish, who use nothing but harps, are astounded by the quickness of our violins and of their melodies, and of their *tirades*[4] at each half-bar or at each semibreve. And far from easily catching on to the rhythms of our dancing, they sweat blood and tears even while singing, in order to give this joyous and sudden movement to their melodies and to execute one of our rhythms. But we will speak of this elsewhere and more amply. It suffices at this point and on this subject to emphasize that music for ballet should be neither held back nor be as languishing as one could make it, if it were just a matter of singing. It is necessary to go yet a little further than with vocal decorations; the ornaments should have a strongly expressed passion or an individual vivacity. The music must always have something of the lofty and bright. It is necessary above all that the air be shorter rather than longer, whether for the convenience of the dancer or whether to liven things up for the sake of the coming break, with the *capriole*[5] or other leap that could be made at the cadence. As far as the length of the two parts of the air are concerned, it makes no difference whether they are equal or not; the musician can do as he likes.

4. Ornamental scale passages; compare the Italian *tirata.* See the Glossary of Foreign Performance Terms, p. 734.
5. A quick beating of the straight legs in a spring.

111 François Raguenet

As French and Italian music developed along separate lines in the seventeenth century, several French visitors to Italy became strong partisans of Italian music, especially of music for the theater. The Abbé François Raguenet (c. 1660–1722), priest, physician, and historian, had heard the operas of Jean-Baptiste Lully sung in Paris by actresses such as Marie Le Rochois. Visiting the Cardinal de Bouillon in Rome from 1697, Raguenet heard the new works of Arcangelo Corelli and Giovanni Bononcini. He published his enthusiastic opinions of this newest Italian music in a *Paralele des Italiens et des François en ce qui regarde la musique et les opéra*. In this comparison he praised the poetic design, lyricism, costumes, dancing, and bass roles of the Lullian stage but found it all pale next to the sound of the Roman orchestra and the vocal abilities of the castrati. Raguenet, in short, was willing to accept less refinement in poetry, plot, dramaturgy, and instrumental sound in exchange for the Italians' vivid musical means of communicating emotions. His opinions met with some agreement in France, but they also provoked immediate defenders of French music, among them Jean Laurent Le Cerf de la Viéville, whose counter-comparison of the two styles provoked Raguenet to publish a *Défense* in 1705 of his own *Parallele*. The polemic continued back and forth and remained alive in reprints and translations as late as 1759, although the arguments over expressiveness in music persisted even as European musical style changed. Raguenet's strong initial reaction to Italian opera heralds the force of the late Baroque style, with its use of melodic motives for representation, its strongly modulating and tonal harmony, and its more contrapuntal textures. His praise of Italian music also offers rare testimony to a high degree of close listening to those formal aspects of music that indeed contribute to its expressiveness.

FROM *A Comparison between the French and Italian Music and Operas*
(1702)

There are so many things wherein the French musick has the advantage over the Italian, and as many more wherein the Italian is superior to the French, that, without a particular examination into the one, and the other, I think it impossible to draw a just parallel between 'em, or entertain a right judgment of either.

The operas are the compositions that admit of the greatest variety and extent; and they are common both to the Italians and French. 'Tis in these the masters of both nations endeavour, more particularly, to exert themselves, and make their genius shine: and 'tis on these therefore I intend to build my present comparison. But in this there are many things that require a particular distinction, such as the Italian language and the French, of which one may be more favorable than the other for music; the composition of the play that the

TEXT: *Paralele des italiens et des françois, en ce qui regarde la musique et les opéra* (Paris, 1702; facs. ed. Geneva, 1976), pp. 1–60; anonymous English translation as *A Comparison Between the French and Italian Musick and Opera's* (London, 1709; facsim. Farnborough, 1968), pp. 1–29. Only a very few of the original translator's notes are retained here; capitalization has been modernized and minor emendations in light of the French text have been inserted. See also the edition by Oliver Strunk of the London version in the *Musical Quarterly* 32 (1946):411–36.

musicians set to music, the qualifications of the actors; those of the performers; the different sorts of voices; the recitative, the airs, the symphonies, the choruses, the dances, the machines, the decorations, and whatever else is essential to an opera, or serves to make the entertainment compleat and perfect. And these things ought to be particularly inquired into, before we can pretend to determine in favour either of the Italian or French.

Our opera's are writ much better than the Italian; they are regular, coherent designs; and, if repeated without the music,[1] they are as entertaining as any of our other pieces that are purely dramatick. Nothing can be more natural and lively, than their dialogues; the gods are made to speak with a dignity suitable to their character; kings with all the majesty their rank requires; and the nymphs and shepherds with a softness and innocent mirth, peculiar to the plains. Love, jealousie, anger, and the rest of the passions, are touch'd with the greatest art and nicety; and there are few of our tragedies, or comedies, that appear more beautiful than Quinault's opera's.[2]

On the other hand, the Italian opera's are poor, incoherent rapsodies, without any connexion or design; all their pieces, properly speaking, are patched up with thin, insipid scraps; their scenes consist of some trivial dialogues, or soliloquy, at the end of which they foist in one of their best airs, which concludes the scene. These airs are seldom of a piece with the rest of the opera, being usually written by other poets, either occasionally, or in the body of some other work. When the undertaker of an opera has fix'd himself in a town, and got his company together, he makes choice of the subject he likes best, such as Camilla, Themistocles, Xerxes, &c.[3] But this piece, as I just now observ'd, is no better than a patchwork, larded with the best airs his performers are acquainted with, which airs are like saddles, fit for all horses alike; they are declarations of love made on one side, and embraced or rejected on the other; transports of happy lovers, or complaints of the unfortunate; protestations of fidelity, or stings of jealousie; raptures of pleasure, or pangs of sorrow, rage, and despair. And one of these airs you are sure to find at the end of every scene. Now certainly such an opera made of fragments cobbled together and stitched-up patches can never be set in competition with our opera's, which are wrought up with great exactness and marvelous conduct.

Besides, our opera's have a farther advantage over the Italian, in respect of

1. That is, if they are spoken or read.
2. Philippe Quinault (1635–1688), playwright and the principal librettist for Jean-Baptiste Lully, with whom he collaborated on fourteen stage premieres between 1668 and 1686. The two invented the five-act *tragédie en musique*.
3. These are characters in two operas given at the Teatro Capranica that Raguenet attended in Rome in 1698 and to which he refers later: *Rinnovata Camilla, Regina de' Volsci* (libretto by S. Stampiglia, music by Giovanni Bononcini) and *Temistocle in bando* (libretto by A. Morselli, originally for Venice, 1683; music for each act respectively by Giovanni Lulier, M. A. Ziani, and G. Bononcini). Both were designed and produced by Filippo Acciaiuoli.

the voice, and that is the bass,[4] which is so frequent among us, and so rarely to be met with in Italy. For every man, that has an ear, will witness with me, that nothing can be more charming than a good bass; the simple sound of these basses, which sometimes seems to sink into a profound abyss, has something wonderfully charming in it. The air receives a stronger concussion from these deep voices, than it doth from those that are higher, and is consequently fill'd with a more agreeable and extensive harmony. When the persons of gods or kings, a Jupiter, Neptune, Priam or Agamemnon, are brought on the stage, our actors, with their deep voices, give 'em an air of majesty, quite different from that of the falsettists or the feign'd basses among the Italians, which have neither depth nor strength. Besides, the blending of the basses with the upper parts forms an agreeable contrast, and makes us perceive the beauties of the one from the opposition they meet with from the other, a pleasure to which the Italians are perfect strangers, the voices of their singers, who are, for the most part, castrati, being perfectly like those of their women.

Besides the advantages we claim from the beauty of our designs, and the variety of voices, we receive still more from our choruses, dances, and other *divertissements,* in which we infinitely excell the Italians. They, instead of these choruses and *divertissements,* which furnish our opera's with an agreeable variety, and give 'em a peculiar air of grandure and magnificence, have usually nothing but some burlesque scenes of a buffoon; some old woman that's to be in love with a young footman; or a conjurer that shall turn a cat into a bird, a fiddler into an owl, and play a few other tricks of legerdemain, that are only fit to divert the mob. And for their dancers, they are the poorest creatures in the world; they are all of a lump, without arms, legs, a shape or air.

As to the instruments, our masters touch the violin much finer, and with a greater nicety than they do in Italy. All the Italians' bow strokes sound harsh, when they detach them from each other, and when they want to connect the tones, they fiddle in a most disagreeable manner. Moreover, besides all the instruments that are common to us, as well as the Italians, we have the hautbois, which, by their sounds, equally mellow and piercing, have infinitely the advantage of the violins, in all brisk, lively airs; and the flutes, which so many of our great artists[5] have taught to groan after so moving a manner, in our moanful airs, and sigh so amorously in those that are tender.

Finally, we have the advantage of 'em in dress. Our habits[6] infinitely excell

---

4. "Basses-contres." The translator adds: "I can't think the base-voice more proper for a king, a hero, or any other distinguish'd person, than the counter-tenor, since the difference of the voice in man is meerly accidental. And as the abilities of a man's mind are not measur'd by his stature, so certainly we are not to judge a heroe by his voice. For this reason I can't see why the part of Caesar or Alexander may not properly enough be perform'd by a counter-tenor or tenor, or any other voice, provided the performer, in acting as well as singing, is able to maintain the dignity of the character he represents" (p. 6, note 5).

5. Phil[i]bert, Philidor, Descoteaux, & the Hotteterres. [Au.]

6. Costumes.

all we see abroad, both in costliness and fancy. The Italians themselves will own, that no dancers in Europe are equal to ours; the Combatants and Cyclops in *Perseus,* the Tremblers and Smiths in *Isis,* the Unlucky Dreams in *Atys,* and our other ballet *entrées,* are originals in their kind, as well in respect of the airs, compos'd by Lully, as of the steps which Beauchamp has adapted to those airs.[7] The theatre produced nothing like it 'till those two great men appear'd; 'tis an entertainment of which they are the sole inventors, and they have carried it to so high a degree of perfection, that as no person either in Italy or else-where, has hitherto rival'd 'em, so, I fear, the world will never produce their equal. No theatre can represent a fight more lively, than we see it sometimes express'd in our dances; and, in a word, ev'ry thing is performed with an unex-ceptionable nicety; the conduct and economy, through the whole, is so admira-ble, that no man, of common understanding, will deny, but that the French opera's form a more lively representation than the Italian, and that a meer spectator must be much better pleas'd in France than Italy. This is the sum of what can be offer'd to our advantage, in behalf of our musick and opera's; let us now examine wherein the Italians have the advantage over us in these two points.

The Italian language is much more naturally adapted to musick than ours; their vowels are all sonorous, whereas above half of ours are mute, or at best bear a very small part in pronunciation; so that, in the first place, no cadence, or beautiful passage, can be form'd upon the syllables that consist of those vowels, and, in second place, one cannot hear but half the words, so that we are left to guess at what the French are singing, whereas the Italian is perfectly understood. Besides, though all the Italian vowels are full and open, yet the composers choose out of them such as they judge most proper for their finest divisions. They generally make choice of the vowel *a,* which, being clearer and more distinct than any of the rest, expresses the beauty of the cadences, and divisions, to a better advantage. Whereas we make use of all the vowels indif-ferently, those that are mute, as well as those that are sonorous; nay, very often we pitch upon a diphthong, as in the words *chaîne* and *gloire,* etc., which syllables, consisting of two vowels join'd together, create a confus'd sound, and want that clearness and beauty that we find in the simple vowels. But this is not the most material part to be consider'd in musick; let us now examine into its essence, and form, that is, the structure of the airs, either distinctly consid-er'd, or in relation to the different parts, of which the whole composition con-sists.

The Italians are more bold and hardy in their airs, than the French; they carry their point[8] farther, both in their tender songs and those that are more lively, as well as in their other compositions; nay, they often unite styles, which the French think incompatible. The French, in those compositions that consist

7. Raguenet cites three operas by Quinault and Lully. Pierre Beauchamps (1631–1705) provided the choreography for *Isis* (1677) and *Atys* (1676).
8. "Le caractère."

of many parts, seldom regard more than that which is principal, whereas the Italians usually study to make all the parts equally shining, and beautiful. In short, the invention of the one is inexhaustible, but the genius of the other is narrow and constrain'd; this the reader will fully understand when we descend to particulars.

It is not to be wonder'd that the Italians think our musick dull and stupifying, that, according to their taste, it appears flat and insipid, if we consider the nature of the French airs compar'd to those of the Italian. The French in their airs aim at the soft, the easie, the flowing, and coherent; the whole air is of the same tone, or if sometimes they venture to vary it, they do it with so many preparations, they so qualifie it, that still the air seems to be as natural and consistent as if they had attempted no change at all; there is nothing bold and adventurous in it; it's all equal and of a piece. But the Italians pass boldly, and in an instant from sharps to flats and from flats to sharps;[9] they venture the boldest cadences, and the most irregular dissonances; and their airs are so out of the way that they resemble the compositions of no other nation in the world.

The French would think themselves undone, if they offended in the least against the rules; they flatter, tickle, and court the ear, and are still doubtful of success, tho' ev'ry thing be done with an exact regularity. The more daring Italian changes the tone and the mode without any awe or hesitation; he makes double or treble cadences[10] of seven or eight bars together, upon tones we should think incapable of the least division. He'll make a swelling[11] of so prodigious a length, that they who are unacquainted with it can't chuse but be offended at first to see him so adventurous; but before he has done, they'll think they can't sufficiently admire him. He'll have passages of such an extent, as will perfectly confound his auditors at first, and upon such irregular tones as shall instill a terror as well as surprize into the listener, who will immediately conclude, that the whole concert is degenerating into a dreadful dissonance; and betraying 'em by that means into a concern for the musick, which seems to be upon the brink of ruin, he immediately reconciles 'em by such regular cadences that everyone is surpriz'd to see harmony rising again in a manner out of discord itself, and owing its greatest beauties to those irregularities which seem'd to threaten it with destruction. The Italians venture at ev'ry thing that is harsh, and out of the way, but then they do it like people that have a right to venture, and are sure of success. Under a notion of being the greatest and most absolute masters of musick in the world, like despotic soveraigns,

---

9. That is, from major to minor and from minor to major. Le Cerf de la Viéville (see No. 112 below) challenged this point by saying, "Can you still find these changes affective, when they are so frequent?" (*Comparison between Italian and French Music*, pt. 1, 2d. ed. [1705], pp. 27–28).

10. "Cadences doublées & redoublées"; see "raddoppiate" in the Glossary of Foreign Performance Terms, p. 733.

11. By the Italians call'd *messe di voce*. [Tr.] The French word here is "tenuës."

they dispense with its rules in hardy but fortunate sallies; they exert themselves above the art, but like masters of that art, whose laws they follow, or transgress at pleasure, they insult the niceness of the ear which others court; they defie and compel it; they master and conquer it with charms, which owe their irresistible force to the boldness of the adventurous composer.

Sometimes we meet with a swelling, to which the first notes of the thorough bass jarr so harshly, as the ear is highly offended with it; but the bass, continuing to play on, returns at last to the swelling with such beautiful intervals, that we quickly discover the composer's design in the choice of those discords, was to give the hearer a more true and perfect relish of the ravishing notes that on a sudden restore the whole harmony.

Let a Frenchman be set to sing one of these dissonances, and he'll want courage enough to support it with that resolution wherewith it must be sustain'd to make it succeed; his ear, being accustom'd to the most soft and natural intervals, is startled at such an irregularity; he trembles and is in a sweat whilst he attempts to sing it; whereas the Italians, who are inur'd from their youth to these dissonances, sing the most irregular notes with the same assurance they would the most beautiful, and perform ev'ry thing with a confidence that secures 'em of success.[12]

Musick is become exceeding common in Italy; the Italians sing from their cradles, they sing at all times and places; a natural uniform song is too vulgar for their ears. Such airs are to them like things tasteless, and decay'd. If you would hit their palate, you must regale it with variety, and be continually passing from one key to another, though you venture at the most uncommon, and unnatural passages. Without this you'll be unable to keep 'em awake, or excite their attention. But let us continue this comparison, and bring forth the different characters of their airs.

As the Italians are naturally much more lively than the French, so are they more sensible of the passions, and consequently express 'em more lively in all their productions. If a storm, or rage, is to be describ'd in a symphony, their notes give us so natural an idea of it, that our souls can hardly receive a stronger impression from the reality than they do from the description; every thing is so brisk and piercing, so impetuous and affecting, that the imagination, the senses, the soul, and the body itself are all betray'd into a general transport; 'tis impossible not to be borne down with the rapidity of these movements. A symphony of furies shakes the soul; it undermines and overthrows it in spite of all; the violinist himself, whilst he is performing it, is seiz'd with an unavoidable agony; he tortures his violin; he racks his body; he is no longer master of himself, but is agitated like one possessed with an irresistible motion.

12. Le Cerf de la Viéville responded to this description (*Comparison,* pt. 1, pp. 37–38): "But these kinds of adornments should not be so extravagant, and in making them so, the Italians break the rules at every moment. . . . The first time one hears them in the works of Italian composers, they are enchanting; the second time, they are painful; the third, offensive; the fourth time, revolting. They do everything to excess."

If, on the other side, the symphony is to express a calm and tranquility, which requires a quite different style, they however execute it with an equal success. Here the notes descend so low, that the soul is swallow'd with 'em in the profound abyss. There are bow strokes of an infinite length, ling'ring on a dying sound, which decays gradually 'till at last it absolutely expires. Their symphonies of sleep insensibly steal the soul from the body, and so suspend its faculties, and operations, that being bound up, as it were, in the harmony, that entirely possesses and enchants it, it's as dead to every thing else, as if all its powers were captivated by a real sleep.

In short, as for the conformity of the air with the sense of the words, I never heard any symphony comparable to that which was performed at Rome in the Oratory of St. Jerome of Charity, on St. Martin's Day in the year 1697, upon these two words—"Mille saette," a thousand arrows.[13] The air consisted of disjointed notes,[14] like those in a jigg, which gave the soul a lively impression of an arrow; and that wrought so effectually upon the imagination, that every violin appear'd to be a bow, and their bows were like so many flying arrows, darting their pointed heads upon every part of the symphony. Nothing can be more masterly, or more happily express'd. So that be their airs either of a sprightly or gentle style, let 'em be impetuous or languishing, in all these the Italians are equally preferable to the French. But there is one thing beyond all this, which neither the French, nor any other nation, besides themselves, in the world, ever attempted; for they will sometimes unite in a most surprizing manner, the tender with the sprightly, as may be instanced in that celebrated air, "Mai non si vidde ancor più bella fedeltà," &c.,[15] which is the softest and most tender of any in the world, and yet its symphony is as lively, and piercing as ever was composed. These different characters are they able to unite so artfully, that, far from destroying a contrary by its contrary, they make the one serve to embellish the other.

But if we now proceed from the simple airs to a consideration of those pieces that consist of several parts, we there shall find the mighty advantages the Italians have over the French. I never met with a master in France, but what agreed, that the Italians knew much better how to turn, and vary a trio than the French. Among us the first upper part is generally beautiful enough; but then the second usually descends too low to deserve our attention. In Italy the upper parts are generally three or four notes higher than in France; so that their seconds are high enough to have as much beauty as the very first with us.[16] Besides, all their

13. San Girolamo della Carità was a meeting place of the first Oratorians under St. Philip Neri beginning in 1552. It was a venue for musical performances open to the public through the seventeenth century.
14. "Notes pointées," or staccato.
15. From the opera *Camilla* by Giovanni Bononcini; see No. 111, p. 672, n. 3.
16. Le Cerf replied to this objection of Raguenet in his Second Dialogue (*Comparison*, pt. 1, pp. 64–65): "The first upper parts of the Italians squeak because they are too high; their second upper parts have the fault of being too close to the first and too far from the bass, which is the third part."

three parts are so equally good, that it is often difficult to find which is the subject. Lully has composed some after this manner, but they are few in number, whereas we hardly meet with any in Italy that are otherwise.

But of compositions consisting of more parts than three, the advantages of the Italian masters will still appear greater.[17] In France, it's sufficient if the subject be beautiful, we rarely find that the parts which accompany it are so much as coherent. We have some thorough-basses, indeed, which are good grounds; and which, for that reason, are highly extoll'd by us. But where this happens the upper parts grow very poor; they give way to the bass, which then becomes the subject. As for the accompaniments of the violin, they are for the most part nothing but single strokes of the bow, heard by intervals, without any uniform coherent musick, serving only to express, from time to time, a few accords. Whereas in Italy, the first and second upper part, the thorough-bass, and all the other parts that concur to the composition of the fullest pieces, are equally finish'd. The parts for the violins are usually as beautiful as the air it self. So that after we have been entertain'd with something very charming in the air, we are insensibly captivated by the parts that accompany it, which are equally engaging and make us quit the subject to listen to them. Everything is so exactly beautiful that it's difficult to find out the principal part. Sometimes the thorough-bass lays so fast hold of our ear, that in list'ning to it we forget the subject; at other times the subject is so insinuating, that we no longer regard the bass, when all on a sudden the violins become so ravishing, that we mind neither the bass, nor the subject. 'Tis too much for one soul to taste the several beauties of so many parts. She must multiply herself before she can relish and digest three or four delights at once, which are all beautiful alike; 'tis transport, inchantment, and ectasie of pleasure; her faculties are upon so great a stretch, she's forced to ease her self by exclamations; she waits impatiently for the end of the air that she may have a breathing room; she sometimes finds it impossible to wait so long, and then the musick is interrupted by an universal applause. These are the daily effects of the Italian compositions, which everyone who has been in Italy can abundantly testifie; we meet with the like in no other nation whatsoever. They are beauties improv'd to such a degree of excellence, as not to be reach'd by the imagination, 'till master'd by the understanding; and when they are understood our imaginations can form nothing beyond 'em.

17. Compare Le Cerf (*Comparison,* pt. 1, pp. 70–71): " 'Is it in the choruses that the advantage of the Italians is supposed to lie? . . . Everyone knows that choruses are out of use in Italy, indeed beyond the means of the ordinary Italian opera house. . . . How many singers do you suppose an Italian company has?'

'Say twenty or twenty-five, Monsieur, as in our own.'

'Nothing of the sort, Madame; usually six or seven or eight. Those marvelous opera companies in Venice, Naples, and Rome consist of seven or eight voices. . . . When the composer of an opera aspires to the glory of having included a chorus in his work, as a rarity, it is these seven or eight persons as a group who form it, all singing together—the king, the clown, the queen, and the old woman.' "

112 Jean Laurent Le Cerf de la Viéville

Lord of Freneuse and Keeper of the Seals for the parliament of Normandy, Jean Laurent Le Cerf de la Viéville (1674–1707) quickly rose to defend French music in his *Comparison between Italian and French Music,* published in 1704 explicitly as a refutation of François Raguenet's pro-Italian comparison of 1702. In the face of reviews and Raguenet's subsequently published defense of his opinions, Le Cerf quickly brought out a second edition of his *Comparison* with new sections, including a "Treatise on Good Taste" (Brussels, 1705). An additional volume published in 1706 compared French and Italian sacred music and also included a response to Raguenet's *Defense of the Parallel.* Le Cerf began his criticism by attacking Raguenet's spelling of musical terms and ended with a detailed examination of cantatas by Giovanni Bononcini, which he judged only on the basis of a printed score, having had no opportunity to hear them performed.

Le Cerf characterized French music in general as "sage, unie & naturelle," that is, as orderly, even, and natural, as opposed to the "forced, disjointed, incoherent and unnatural taste" of the Italians. Italian music was fine in small portions, but for extended works like operas, French music was to be preferred, as white meat was preferable to ragouts. His standard for good taste in music required that music be natural, expressive, and harmonious. For Le Cerf an expressive air was one in which "the notes are perfectly suited to the words," as he states in dialogue 6 from the *Comparison* (p. 302). This primacy of the text, including its vocables, it intonation, its own rhythm, and its grammar, as well as its meaning and significance, meant that for him music would always be judged as an imitation of language and not as those sonorous forms inspired by language over which Raguenet had rhapsodized. When Jacopo Peri had advocated a close adherence of music to its text a hundred years earlier, he had helped transform musical style. Le Cerf's similar position was now a conservative one. His view of what is expressive in music and what music expresses was stated most clearly in his "Letter to Monsieur de la ***" from part 1 of the *Comparison.*

FROM *Comparison between Italian and French Music*

(1704)

LETTER TO MONSIEUR DE LA °°°

What do reason and the good authors[1] tell us about what is beauty in painting, the art of the painter? To represent things perfectly, as they are. It is to paint grapes so well, like Zeuxis, that birds come and peck at them; it is to paint a curtain so well, as did Parrasius, that Zeuxis himself stretches out a hand to lift it. What is the beauty of poetry? It is doing with words what a painter does with colors. *Ut pictura poesis erit.*[2]

And you know that Aristotle in his *Poetics*[3] speaks only of imitating, which is to say, painting. All the genres of poetry, according to him, are just different *imitations* of different pictures. Perfection in poetry consists of describing the things of which it speaks with terms so appropriate and exact that the reader can imagine that he sees them. Thus when Virgil describes a serpent that a passerby happened upon unawares, *Improvisum aspris*, etc.,[4] I have fear and I am ready to flee like the passerby. When the feelings of the heart are painted so vividly, the reader, struck by what another has felt or knows, can feel them himself and share all the passions that the poet grants his heroes. Thus when Virgil portrays for me Dido agitated by a growing love that she fights in vain, I am disturbed, I am anxious, and I hope along with her. She becomes alarmed, then furious at the departure of her lover, she despairs, she stabs herself: I cannot blame Aeneas, because he is forced to leave her by the gods, but I almost hate him at that moment, and I feel pity, and I weep at Dido's pyre, as did St. Augustine, who did not control his tears when reading such touching poetry.

What, at the present time, is the beauty of the music of opera? It lies in rendering the verse of these operas into a painting that actually speaks. It is, so to speak, giving the finishing touches by applying the final colors.[5] Now how

TEXT: *Comparaison de la musique italienne, et de la musique françoise*, part 1, 2d ed. (Brussels: Fr. Foppens, 1705; repr. Geneva: Minkoff, 1972), pp. 151–83; this excerpt, pp. 167–73. Translation by Margaret Murata.

1. The ancient writers.
2. Horace, *The Art of Poetry* [Au.], line 361: "Poetry is like painting."
3. Πᾶσαι τυγχάνουσιν οὖσαι μιμήσεις τὸ σύνολον. Omnes sunt imitatio in universam. Aristotle, *Poetics* 6.1 [Au.]: "They are all in their general essence, modes of imitation" (1447a, lines 15–16).
4. *Aeneid* 1.2 [Au.]: "A rude surprise."
5. Traditional painting in oils built up forms and figures in precise stages that had been practiced since the Renaissance. Design and modeling were executed in monochrome or with a limited palette before colors were employed. The basic procedures are articulated in Giorgio Vasari's

does music *re-paint* the poetry, how do they mutually serve each other, unless they are exactly matched and blended together in the most perfect agreement? The single secret is to apply such proportionate tones to the words that the verse is indistinguishable from and lives again in the music. This carries the feeling of all that the singer says right to the heart of the listener. *Voilà*, this is what we call expression.

Expression is the common goal of painting and of poetry retouched by music. On this footing, if a musician adds a musical idea to some verse that does not suit it at all, it will not matter whether this idea is new and learned or whether the basso continuo resolves the dissonances elegantly. If the poetry and music are badly joined, they will separate from each other, and my attention will wander at this division, and the pleasure which my ears could have from the harmonies will be unknown by my heart—and from that moment, be completely cold. Painting differently is not painting more, which is why it is bad. When the musician plays and fools around on unimportant or serious words by adding runs and roulades, I know at once that the sense does not require these niceties at all. This is not a harmonious representation, and so it is worthless. If, however, the musician sets the words vividly and exactly, the object is doubly represented by the poetry and by the music. Only when they are equal can I be happy with this arrangement.[6] This is painting and it is good. When there are feelings, burning passions, and the musician maintains them, or rather, when he once more rekindles their fire with tones of quickening precision, my heart will feel them, whether it has them or not. This is marvelous painting and it is excellent.

But, you say to me, here we have only common harmonies. So be it. Provided that these harmonies are not at all defective and do not disfigure the beauty of the expression, the listener could want no more. An accompaniment that is wrong or too dull does not necessarily commit a perceptible offense on the subject, as happens when one impermissibly uses a poor word to express the happiest thought. But also as soon as my thought pleases on its own, makes an impression and conveys a feeling, I have no need at all to go on searching for an elegant phrase. It is sufficient that the words do convey the sense. It follows that expression, which must be the goal of the musician, is therefore the most important thing in music, because of all the things in the world, it is this that succeeds in achieving its aim. To express well is to paint well. This is the masterpiece, this the highest peak, *voilà*, everything. Though it can cost the musician to achieve this by the appearance of sterility, of learning disregarded, he will always gain enough. If he does not succeed, learning and productiveness, no matter how sustained, will not take the place of that value in the mind of a

---

Lives of the Painters (1550, 1568); see in *Vasari on Technique,* trans. L. S. Maclehose (London, 1907; repr. New York: Dover, 1960), "Of Painting," ch. 7: "Of painting in oil or on panel or canvas."

6. "Cette convenance," as in a marriage of convenience, or arranged marriage.

reasonable listener. If it is absent, they will not excuse it. Your hero is dying of love and from grief, he says, and what he sings says nothing, isn't expressive at all: I will not be the least interested in his pain, which is what was wanted. . . . But should the accompaniment cleave the rocks. . . . pleasant recompense! Is it the orchestra who is the hero? . . . No, it is the singer . . . Well then, if the singer himself moves me, if a tender and expressive song portrays that he is suffering and if it spares no pains to move me on his behalf, as to the orchestra, it is only there on forgiveness and by accident.

> Si vis me flere, dolendum est
> Primum ipsi tibi.[7]

If the orchestra unites with the singer in order to touch me and to move me, so much the better, for then there are two means of expression instead of one. But the first and the most essential is that of the singer. Reason and experience lead us to find it so essential that once again, nothing compares with it. The power of something beautifully expressed diffuses into an entire scene, and its effect is as general as it is fixed. It is enjoyed by the ignorant, by the connoisseur, by men and by women. It is imprinted on the minds of the audience, who leave thinking about it. That is why, upon leaving our operas, everyone sings something that he has remembered. Certain airs travel from mouth to mouth; they become familiar to those at court, in the city, and in the provinces. Who will not know it? In contrast, one hardly ever remembers an Italian instrumental work, even if it has been heard ten times. Our ears that receive the airs of Lully so quickly and easily do not accept those of the Italian masters the same way without study and trouble. Why is this? It is, one would say, because we are French, not Italians. . . . And you boast that more than half the musicians in France have become Italian by inclination, and that a thousand folk know Italian. Thus neither the country nor the language matters much. But rather it is that the great beauties, beautiful things drawn from nature's breast, the really truthful expressions make themselves felt by all men, and that false beauties are far from having this privilege.

•   •   •   •   •

7. Horace, *The Art of Poetry* [Au.], lines 102–3: "To make me weep, you must first yourself feel grief."

113 Joseph Addison

Joseph Addison (1672–1719), the great English essayist and man of letters, was the leading contributor to the periodicals *The Tatler, The Spectator,* and *The Guardian,* published by his friend Richard Steele from 1709 to 1713. Particularly important are Addison's contributions to *The Spectator,* a paper that stood for reason and moderation in an age of bitter party strife. In his essays, Addison showed himself an able painter of life and manners. His witty, distinguished writings exerted an important influence on criticism, not only in England but also in France and Germany.

In the present essay he demonstrates that agreed-upon artifices are essential to representation in the theater by showing that "shadows and realities ought not be mixed together." His own opera *Rosamond,* set to music by Thomas Clayton in 1707, has been forgotten by history. More memorable are his reactions to a landmark Italian opera by Handel, who had arrived in London at the end of 1710.

FROM *The Spectator*

(1711)

Spectatum admissi risum teneatis?—Hor[ace][1]

An opera may be allowed to be extravagantly lavish in its decorations, as its only design is to gratify the senses, and keep up an indolent attention in the audience. Common sense, however, requires, that there should be nothing in the scenes and machines which may appear childish and absurd. How would the wits of King Charles's time have laughed to have seen Nicolini[2] exposed to a tempest in robes of ermine, and sailing in an open boat upon a sea of pasteboard! What a field of raillery would they have been let into, had they been entertained with painted dragons spitting wildfire, enchanted chariots drawn by Flanders mares, and real cascades in artificial landscapes![3] A little skill in

TEXT: From *The Spectator* for Tuesday, March 6, 1711, as edited by G. Gregory Smith for Everyman's Library (London, 1907), vol. 1, pp. 20–23. Especially useful are the annotations in the edition by Donald F. Bond (Oxford: Clarendon Press, 1965), vol. 1, pp. 22–31.

1. "If you were admitted to see this, could you hold back your laughter?" The quotation is from line 5 of *The Art of Poetry* by Horace. Addison expected his readers to remember its context: a painting of a human head on a horse's neck, with feathers on randomly affixed limbs and the upper torso of an attractive woman whose body ends in that of a black fish.
2. Nicolò Grimaldi (1673–1732), known as Nicolini, who sang in London at the Theatre in the Haymarket during the seasons of 1708 to 1712 and 1715 to 1717, created the principal castrato roles in Handel's operas *Rinaldo* (1711) and *Amadigi* (1715).
3. These references are without exception to the stage machinery of Handel's *Rinaldo.*

criticism would inform us, that shadows and realities ought not to be mixed together in the same piece; and that the scenes which are designed as the representations of nature, should be filled with resemblances, and not with the things themselves. If one would represent a wide champaign country[4] filled with herds and flocks, it would be ridiculous to draw the country only upon the scenes, and to crowd several parts of the stage with sheep and oxen. This is joining together inconsistencies, and making the decoration partly real and partly imaginary. I would recommend what I have here said to the directors, as well as to the admirers, of our modern opera.

As I was walking in the streets about a fortnight ago, I saw an ordinary fellow carrying a cage full of little birds upon his shoulder; and, as I was wondering with myself what use he would put them to, he was met very luckily by an acquaintance, who had the same curiosity. Upon his asking him what he had upon his shoulder, he told him, that he had been buying sparrows for the opera. Sparrows for the opera! says his friend, licking his lips; what, are they to be roasted? No, no, says the other; they are to enter towards the end of the first act, and to fly about the stage.

This strange dialogue awakened my curiosity so far, that I immediately bought the opera,[5] by which means I perceived the sparrows were to act the part of singing birds in a delightful grove; though, upon a nearer inquiry, I found the sparrows put the same trick upon the audience, that Sir Martin Mar-all practised upon his mistress;[6] for, though they flew in sight, the music proceeded from a consort of flagelets and bird-calls[7] which were planted behind the scenes. At the same time I made this discovery, I found, by the discourse of the actors, that there were great designs on foot for the improvement of the opera; that it had been proposed to break down a part of the wall, and to surprise the audience with a party of an hundred horse; and that there was actually a project of bringing the New River into the house, to be employed in jetteaus[8] and water-works. This project, as I have since heard, is postponed till the summer season; when it is thought the coolness that proceeds from fountains and cascades will be more acceptable and refreshing to people of quality. In the meantime, to find out a more agreeable entertainment for the winter season, the opera of *Rinaldo* is filled with thunder and lightning, illuminations and fireworks; which the audience may look upon without catching cold, and indeed without much danger of being burnt; for there are several engines filled with water, and ready to play at a minute's warning, in case any

4. A plain.
5. Its libretto.
6. A character in John Dryden's comedy of the same name. In act 5, Sir Martin acts out the singing of a serenade to the lute, while the actual singing and playing is done in an adjoining room by his man. The scheme miscarries.
7. Almirena's cavatina "Augelletti che cantate" ("Little birds who sing," *Rinaldo* act 1, scene 6) has an accompaniment for flauto piccolo (or "flageolett" as Handel calls it in his autograph score), two flutes, and strings.
8. "Jetto," English for *jet d'eaux,* or fountain.

such accident should happen. However, as I have a very great friendship for the owner of this theatre, I hope that he has been wise enough to insure his house before he would let this opera be acted in it.

It is no wonder that those scenes should be very surprising, which were contrived by two poets of different nations,[9] and raised by two magicians of different sexes. Armida (as we are told in the argument) was an Amazonian enchantress, and poor signor Cassani (as we learn from the persons represented) a Christian conjuror (Mago Christiano).[10] I must confess I am very much puzzled to find how an Amazon should be versed in the black art; or how a good Christian (for such is the part of the magician) should deal with the devil.

To consider the poets after the conjurors, I shall give you a taste of the Italian from the first lines of his preface: *Eccoti, benigno lettore, un parto di poche sere, che se ben nato di notte, non è però aborto di tenebre, mà si farà conoscere figliolo d'Apollo con qualche raggio di Parnasso.* "Behold, gentle reader, the birth of a few evenings, which, though it be the offspring of the night, is not the abortive of darkness, but will make itself known to be the son of Apollo, with a certain ray of Parnassus." He afterwards proceeds to call Mynheer Hendel the Orpheus of our age, and to acquaint us, in the same sublimity of style, that he composed this opera in a fortnight. Such are the wits to whose tastes we so ambitiously conform ourselves. The truth of it is, the finest writers among the modern Italians express themselves in such a florid form of words, and such tedious circumlocutions, as are used by none but pedants in our own country; and at the same time fill their writings with such poor imaginations and conceits, as our youths are ashamed of before they have been two years at the university. Some may be apt to think that it is the difference of genius which produces this difference in the works of the two nations; but to show there is nothing in this, if we look into the writings of the old Italians, such as Cicero and Virgil, we shall find that the English writers, in their way of thinking and expressing themselves, resemble those authors much more than the modern Italians pretend to do. And as for the poet himself,[11] from whom the dreams of this opera are taken, I must entirely agree with Monsieur Boileau, that one verse in Virgil is worth all the clinquant or tinsel of Tasso.[12]

But to return to the sparrows; there have been so many flights of them let loose in this opera, that it is feared the house will never get rid of them; and that in other plays they make their entrance in very wrong and improper scenes, so as to be seen flying in a lady's bed-chamber, or perching upon a

---

9. Aaron Hill and Giacomo Rossi.
10. Giuseppe Cassani (fl. 1700–1728), an alto castrato.
11. Torquato Tasso (1544–1595), from whose epic poem *Gerusalemme liberata* the story of Rinaldo is drawn.
12. Nicholas Boileau (1636–1711), *Satire* 9, lines 173–76: "Tous les jours à la Cour un Sot de qualité / Peut juger de travers avec impunité: / À Malherbe, à Racan, préferer Theophile, / Et le clinquant du Tasse, à tout l'or de Virgile."

king's throne; besides the inconveniences which the heads of the audience may sometimes suffer from them. I am credibly informed, that there was once a design of casting into an opera the story of Whittington and his cat, and that in order to do it, there had been got together a great quantity of mice; but Mr. Rich, the proprietor of the playhouse,[13] very prudently considered, that it would be impossible for the cat to kill them all, and that consequently the princes of the stage might be as much infested with mice, as the prince of the island was before the cat's arrival upon it; for which reason he would not permit it to be acted in his house. And indeed I cannot blame him: for, as he said very well upon that occasion, I do not hear that any of the performers in our opera pretend to equal the famous pied piper, who made all the mice of a great town in Germany follow his music, and by that means cleared the place of those little noxious animals.

Before I dismiss this paper, I must inform my reader, that I hear there is a treaty on foot with London and Wise (who will be appointed gardeners of the playhouse) to furnish the opera of Rinaldo and Armida with an orange-grove; and that the next time it is acted, the singing birds will be impersonated by tom-tits: the undertakers[14] being resolved to spare neither pains nor money for the gratification of the audience.

13. Christopher Rich, the former proprietor of the Drury Lane Theatre.
14. Producers.

114 Pier Jacopo Martello

The earliest writings of Pier Jacopo Martello (1665–1727) were occasional poems, pastorals, tragedies, and at least three operas. Much of this work was published in collected editions of 1709 *(Teatro)* and 1710 *(Versi e prose)*. Both volumes were issued in Rome, when Martello was serving as the Bolognese representative to the Vatican. He spent most of 1713 as a member of a papal legation in Paris. There, in the literary circle around Antonio Conti, he partici-pated in the arguments over the relative merits of French and Italian theater. These encounters prompted Martello to write a dialogue on ancient and modern tragedy, which was seen into print by Conti in 1714, after Martello had returned to Rome. The spirit of Aristotle (in the guise of an old traveler) and the classiciz-ing tendencies of the new Arcadian reformers of literature and theater inform the discursive text—hardly a conversation between opposing views, as "Aris-totle" appears as an authority on both the ancients and the moderns. Martello soon brought out an Italian edition (1715), whose fifth section, or "session," concerns contemporary opera. He demonstrates the extent to which opera is a nonliterary genre and asserts that it should therefore not be criticized in the same way as drama. With a somewhat sardonic tone, "Aristotle" nevertheless proceeds to describe the construction of a turn-of-the century libretto—from the meters of the verse to the placement of arias in the acts. These elements are considered only in terms of general formal effectiveness, because Martello first lays down the premise that music is by nature expressive and pleasurable purely as sound. Beyond the beauty of sound, the conventions of opera admit and order musical variety: "whether it is verisimilar is not material." Jean Laurent Le Cerf de la Viéville thought of music as colors added to poetry. For Martello, "the musical composition is the very substance of operas, and all the other parts are incidental, poetry among them."

FROM *On Ancient and Modern Tragedy*
(1715)

I shall inquire then, whether, in order to delight, opera must have the help of words and poetry: and I will frankly declare it does not. When, at night, I listen to one or several nightingales singing and almost conversing in song, I find that this drama of unseen birds delights me and draws me away from all troubling thoughts, so that I will sit long and listen to them; yet Nature limits their warbling to but a few strains, which are much the same if not identical. A serenade of instruments, too, can make a man appear on the balcony and spend several hours there, unconsciously, while the music lasts; and his delight is greater, since the players with their various instruments can produce symphonies as diverse as those of the nightingales were similar. And just as we find it more pleasant to listen to the chirping of birds or the play of instruments within a green wood or in sight of a lovely garden, so are we more refreshed by human voices when we hear them in enchanting surroundings, and even more delighted when the songs alternate amid a wondrous variety of scenes. Consider, further, how much more delightful that songbird will be if it is also beautiful and (O joy!) covered with variegated feathers. Similarly, how much more satisfying is that lute or flute if, having a good sound, it is also handsomely made, inlaid with mother-of-pearl and ivory that add richness to musical perfection. Thus shall we be better pleased by a voice emerging from a shapely mouth, assisted by a pretty complexion and a face of goodly proportions, the whole supported upon a prettily outstretched neck—and even more if it issues

TEXT: *Della tragedia antica e moderna* (Rome: F. Gonzaga, 1715; facs. Bologna, 1978), pp. 18–21, 28–29, 35–44; mod. ed. in his *Scritti critici e satirici*, ed. Hannibal S. Noce (Bari: G. Laterza e figli, 1963), Sessione quinta, pp. 270–96, trans. by Piero Weiss in "Pier Jacopo Martello on Opera (1715): An Annotated Translation," in the *Musical Quarterly* 66 (1980): 378–403, which translates all of Session 5. Reprinted by permission of Oxford University Press.

from a woman whose bosom, heaving to fetch the breath that is to form the song, prefigures it, so to speak, her breasts all atremble. And we shall enjoy ourselves better to see that lovely body clothed in rich, charming, whimsical garments; these shall be her feathers, her precious inlays.

Behold, then, our entertainment, delightful enough in itself, enhanced by scenery, personal beauty, and costumes. But see how insatiable we are, especially when wallowing in pleasure! Knowing that birds can whistle and instruments sound but that man alone can reason, we insist that to the sweetness of human song be added the sweetness of words to tell us of the inner motions of the soul; so that here is one more delight come to assist our entertainment, and here, finally, is Poetry. But poor Poetry cuts quite another figure here than she does in tragedy and comedy. In those she has the principal place, in opera the lowest; there she commands as mistress, here she attends as servant. But let us not abase Poetry by lending her name to such slavish verses.

. . . . .

But if (said I) under a Prince's patronage a Poet may write *melodrammi* not entirely to the distaste of the literati, let me have some norms at least for these, for it is not impossible that, for reasons of convenience or out of obligation, I should find it necessary to write such a work. Let me add that in my city the operas, though commercial, are sometimes subsidized by the nobility, who put sufficient restraints upon the Impresario's greed to prevent it from wholly swallowing up those elements which please honest people and the literati, of whom Bologna is the fatherland. And so I await a system from you, be it what it may, by which a skillful Poet may trace a drama that can be read as well as listened to.

Then Aristotle said: Since you ask me to present you with some rules for a type of composition which, in order to be pleasing, should be devoid of rules, I will mention some to you, and they shall be based on observation and experience rather than reason; and to satisfy you I will endeavor to combine the tasks of choragus, composer of the music, singer, and poet, almost forgetting that I am a philosopher.

. . . . .

Before you cut the cloth of the acts into scenes, I exhort you to show it all to the composer and ask him which voice, in his judgment, you should place at the beginning, middle, and end of each act. You must, however, stipulate (he will not object) that each act shall contain one *scena di forza,* so called because of some violent or unusual opposition of contrary passions, or some untoward event unexpected by the audience. Thus laid out, the opera, I warrant, will be successful; and now you will have nothing left to do but to cast your drama into verse.

It must be entirely made up of recitative and ariettas, or canzonettas, as they are also called. Every scene must contain either recitative, or an arietta, or (the usual case) both one and the other. Anything in the way or narration or unimpassioned expression should be expressed in recitative verse. But whatever is motivated by passion or somehow reflects greater vehemence tends toward the canzonetta. The recitative we prefer to have short enough so that it will not put us to sleep with its tediousness, and long enough so that we will understand what is happening. Its sentences and construction must be easy, and compact, rather than extended; this will make it more useful for the composer of the music, the singer, and the listener: for the composer, because he will then be able to enliven the recitative (a dead thing in itself) with a variety of cadences; for the singer, since he will thus be able to catch his breath when he sings it and renew his vocal powers at the rests; and for the listener (unaccustomed to the transformation wrought by music in the ordinary sound of words), because he will have to strain less than if the meaning had to be wrested from a tangle of inverted phrases. The recitative must be contained in verses of seven and eleven syllables, alternated and mixed as seems best; and if the cadences, at least, are rhymed, it will enhance the charm of the music. What I have said regarding the brevity of recitatives must suffer some qualification in the scenes I have termed *scene di forza:* for there the recitative must predominate at the expense of the ariettas, since it is better able to convey the pulse of the action and place it in the foreground. And here the Poet may vent himself somewhat and offer a modest sample of his talent; a prudent musical composer will allow it; nor will the singers, themselves expert at staging, refuse him; and the Impresario will be obliged to like it.

Canzonettas are either simple or compound. We shall call them simple when they are sung by one voice only, compound when sung by two or more voices. Those sung by two voices we will call duets; those sung by more may be termed choruses. Of the simple arias, we shall call some entrances, others exits, and others intermediate. From these expressions their use can be deduced. Entrances are used when a character enters upon the stage, and these tend to be acceptable in soliloquies; and the apostrophizing figure[1] is of their very essence. But of these you shall make sparing use. The same caution is advisable for the intermediate [arias]; for they have a chilling effect when, in mid-scene, mute actors are obliged to stand about and listen while another actor sings away at his leisure. Here, therefore, we should have some concomitant action, so that the others may at least be given something to do and not stand idle; in that case these [arias] will produce an excellent effect. [Intermediate arias] are the only type in which the questioning mode may occasionally be tolerated; this is odious in all other types, since it gives no occasion for variety in the music. Exit arias must close every scene, and no singer may exit without first warbling a canzonetta. Whether 'tis verisimilar is not material. It is much too pleasant to hear a scene end with spirit and vivacity. Mind, however, that when you end a scene with an exit aria you do not begin the very next one with an

---

1. Addresses to persons or entities not present.

entrance aria. That would rob the music of its chiaroscuro. The instrumental *ricercate* would tumble over each other and instead of helping would hinder the effect.[2] Hence it is that entrance arias usually make their best effect at the beginning of an act.

Duets are heard with pleasure in mid-scene because they afford action to more than one actor; but I should also like to see a duet at the end of the second act. Choruses at the end of the last act are inescapable, since the public enjoys hearing the combination of all the voices which it applauded singly in the course of the opera; and the noise made by singers and instruments causes everyone to rise and leave feeling replete and elated with the music they have heard, and wishing to come back for more.

These ariettas, or canzonettas, must be so distributed that the singers with the highest standing receive an equal number, for the singers' professional jealousy is inflexible and punctilious; and for that matter it is useful to the production of the drama that the best voices should be displayed equally to the audience.

These ariettas are composed in different meters,[3] as you Italians put it. Let the eight-syllable verse, which is the most sonorous, have pride of place above the others; namely,

> Innamora amor le belle.
> [Love loves beautiful women.]

Be sure to keep in mind that every aria must have its refrain *(intercalare)*. Refrain is what the professionals call the first part of an aria which is later repeated by the singer; for since it is here that the composer displays the full glitter of his musical artifice, he takes pleasure in its repetition. The singers take pleasure in it, too, as does the public. . . . But oh, the disjointed meters your versifiers have invented, meters incapable of good harmony which I do not advise you to use. But these will succeed better if you will adapt them to the passions that are best expressed by their means. Rage is best, nay almost exclusively conveyed in its full horror by the ten-syllable verse.[4] . . . The six-syllable line with the accent on the antepenult portrays very well the enfeebled state of a soul given over to amorous languor.[5] . . .

We must still treat of the style best suited to opera. I believe this type of composition, such as it is, calls for moderation and charm rather than gravity and magnificence; music, an art invented to delight and lift the spirits, needs to be buttressed by words and sentiments clothed in the spirit of delightfulness.

2. If each aria has its own ritornello music, then the closing ritornello of an exit aria would go right into the opening ritornello of an ensuing aria.
3. That is, the texts of the arias have differing poetic meters.
4. His example is: Sibillanti dell'orride Eumenidi / veggio in campo rizzarsi le vipere, / minacciando di mordermi il sen (Hissing vipers of the horrid Furies I see arise upon the field, threatening to bite my breast).
5. His example, with the antepenultimate syllables indicated: Le luci ténere / della mia Vénere / mi fan languir (The tender eyes of my Venus make me languish).

This is not to say that from time to time you may not introduce magnificence, if only to set off the charming element: for a bit of sour mixed with the sweet adds a piquancy that is most welcome to the palate; but if the sourness is overwhelming, pleasure turns to disgust, and delicate damsels will spit it out. Let me repeat, therefore, that your constructions must be easy, your sentences clear and not long, the words plain and attractive, the rhymes not insipid, the verses fluent and tenderly sonorous. In the arias I advise you to use similes involving little butterflies, little ships, a little bird, a little brook: these things all lead the imagination to I know not what pleasant realms of thought and so refresh it; and just as those objects are charming, so too are the words that conjure them up and portray them to our fancy; and the musical composer always soars in them with his loveliest notes; and you will have noticed that even in the worst operas, singers win particular applause in these arias, to which the diminutives (so hateful to the French language and temperament) add much grace. Fix it in your mind, too, that the more general the sentiments in an aria, the more pleasing they will be to the public; for, finding them verisimilar or true, they store them up to make honest use of with their ladies and to sing them as daily occasion arises between lovers for jealousy, indignation, mutual promises, absences, and the like; and this will also be most convenient for you, since Poets find it much easier to treat in generalities, and can fill their poetic wardrobes with them while out walking, and later use them to dress up the recitatives of operas. But in the action arias, you must avoid generalities and concentrate entirely on the particulars, for if the action is not to cool off, then the words must lend it life and be perfectly suited to it and to none other.

115 Jean-Philippe Rameau

When his epoch-making *Treatise on Harmony* appeared in 1722, Jean-Philippe Rameau (1683–1764) had a resumé of changing employment as an organist and teacher but few credentials as a composer. It would be another ten years before he would settle in Paris and write *Hippolyte et Aricie,* the first of his thirty operas. His great first treatise was succeeded by five more major theoretical volumes, most immediately the *New System for Music Theory* (1726) and the *Generation of Harmony* (1737). Together these books examined, explored, and codified the harmonic principles of European music, with a focus on chords rather than counterpoint. Although musicians had been performing from figured bass lines for over a hundred years, it was Rameau who conceptualized the fundamental bass—that is, a theoretical bass made up of the "roots" of chords— and the tonal grammar of late Baroque harmony.

In the two chapters offered here, Rameau recognizes the purely melodic nature of the music of the ancient Greeks and Romans, affirms the primacy of harmony in the generation of melody, reminds his readers that music is a language learned "by ear," and ends by discussing some expressive properties of consonance and dissonance.

FROM *Treatise on Harmony*
(1722)

BOOK TWO

CHAPTER NINETEEN. CONTINUATION OF THE PRECEDING CHAPTER, IN WHICH IT APPEARS THAT MELODY ARISES FROM HARMONY

It would seem at first that harmony arises from melody, since the melodies produced by each voice come together to form the harmony. It is first necessary, however, to find a course for each voice which will permit them all to harmonize well together. No matter what melodic progression is used for each individual part, the voices will join together to form a good harmony only with great difficulty, if indeed at all, unless the progressions are dictated by the rules of harmony. Nonetheless, in order to make this harmonic whole more intelligible, one generally begins by teaching how to write a melodic line. No matter what progress may have been made, however, the ideas developed will disappear as soon as another part has to be added. We are then no longer the master of the melodic line. In looking for the direction a part should take with respect to another part, we often lose sight of the original direction, or at least are obliged to change it. Otherwise, the constraining influence of this first part will not always permit us to give the other parts melodic lines as perfect as we might wish. It is harmony then that guides us, and not melody. Certainly a knowledgeable musician can compose a beautiful melodic line suitable to the harmony, but from where does this happy ability come? May nature be responsible? Doubtless. But if, on the contrary, she has refused her gift, how can he succeed? Only by means of the rules. But from where are these rules derived? This is what we must investigate.

Does the first division of the string offer two sounds from which a melody may be formed? Certainly not, for the man who sings only octaves will not form a very good melodic line. The second and the third divisions of the string, from which harmony is derived, provide us with sounds which are no more

TEXT: *Traité de l'harmonie reduite à ses principes naturels* (Paris, 1722), bk. 2, chaps. 19–20, pp. 138–43; trans. by Philip Gossett (New York: Dover, 1971), pp. 152–56; reprinted with permission. Both chapters are also translated into English in E. Fubini, *Music and Culture in Eighteenth-Century Europe*, ed. Bonnie J. Blackburn (Chicago: University of Chicago Press, 1994), pp. 136–40.

suitable to melody, since a melodic line composed only of thirds, fourths, fifths, sixths, and octaves will still not be perfect. Harmony then is generated first, and it is from harmony that the rules of melody must be derived; indeed this is what we do by taking separately the aforementioned harmonic intervals, and forming from them a fundamental progression which is still not a melody. But when these intervals are put together above one of their component sounds, they naturally follow a diatonic course. This course is determined by the progression they follow, when each serves as a foundation for the others. We then derive from these consonant and diatonic progressions all the melody needed. Thus, we have to be acquainted with harmonic intervals before melodic ones, and the only melodic line we can teach a beginner is one consisting of consonant intervals, if indeed these can be called melodic. We shall see furthermore in chapter 21 that the ancients derived their modulation from melody alone, whereas it really arises from harmony.

Once this consonant progression is grasped, it is as simple to add three sounds above the sound used as bass as it is to add only one. We explain this as follows: It is possible, and sometimes compulsory, to place a third, a fifth, or an octave above the bass. Now, in order to use any one of them, we must understand them all. When we understand them all, however, it is no more difficult to use them together than separately. Thus, the part which has formed the third will form the fifth when the bass descends a third; this can be explained in no other way. But when in these different progressions of a bass we find the third here, the octave there, and the fifth in a third place, then we must always know how each interval should proceed according to the different progressions of the bass. Thus, without being aware of it, we teach four-part composition while explaining only two-part composition. Since each of the consonances is met alternately, the progression of each individual consonance with respect to the different progressions of the bass should be known. It is thus no more difficult to use them together than separately. It is all the better, for if we cannot distinguish them when they are all together, we need only consider them individually. Thus, by one device or another we can find the means of composing a perfect harmony in four parts from which we can draw all the knowledge necessary to reach perfection. In addition, the explanation which we add keeps us from being misled. We may cite the experience several people have had; knowing no more at first than the value of the notes, after reading our rules twice, they were able to compose a harmony as perfect as could be desired. If the composer gives himself the satisfaction of hearing what he has written, his ear will become formed little by little.[1] Once he becomes sensitive to perfect harmony, to which these introductory studies lead, he may be certain of a success which depends completely on these first principles.

There can be no further doubt that once four parts are familiar to us, we can reduce them to three and to two. Composition in two parts can give us no

1. It is partly for this reason that we give rules of accompaniment. [Au.]

knowledge, however, for even if we understood it perfectly, which is almost impossible, there is no fundamental to guide us. Everything that may be taught in this manner is always sterile, whether because our memory is insufficient or because the subject may be covered only with great difficulty. At the end, we are obliged to add the words: *Caetera docebit usus.*[2] If we wish to pass from two to three or to four parts, we find that what has been said is of such little substance that genius and taste as fully developed as that of these great masters would be necessary in order to understand what they wish to teach us. Zarlino says that composition in four parts can hardly be taught on paper, and he leaves four-part writing to the discretion of those composers who can achieve this on the basis of his preceding rules concerning two and three parts.[3] Our opinion is quite the opposite, for as we have said harmony may be taught only in four parts. Everything in harmony may then be found in just two chords (as we have indicated everywhere) and it is very simple to reduce these four parts to three or to two. Zarlino, on the other hand, does not even give a clear definition of these two or three parts, and he claims that he is unable to define four parts. He says this even though he is convinced that a perfect harmony consists of four parts, which he compares to the four elements.[4] In conclusion, we affirm that though it has been impossible to understand fully the rules given until now concerning harmony, the source we have proposed will certainly lead to an understanding which is all-embracing.

CHAPTER TWENTY. ON THE PROPERTIES OF CHORDS

Harmony may unquestionably excite different passions in us depending on the chords that are used. There are chords which are sad, languishing, tender, pleasant, gay, and surprising. There are also certain progressions of chords which express the same passions. Although this is beyond my scope, I shall explain it as fully as my experience enables me to do.

Consonant chords can be found everywhere, but they should predominate in cheerful and pompous music. As it is impossible to avoid using dissonant chords there, these chords must arise naturally. The dissonance must be prepared whenever possible, and the most exposed parts, i.e., the treble and bass, should always be consonant with one another.

Sweetness and tenderness are sometimes expressed well by prepared minor dissonances.

Tender lamentations sometimes demand dissonances by borrowing and by supposition, minor rather than major. Any major dissonances present should occur in middle parts rather than in the extremes.

---

2. "Experience will teach the rest."

3. [Zarlino, *Istitutioni harmoniche,*] pt. 3, chap. 65, p. 320 [Au.]: "Necessary observations on compositions for four and more voices."

4. [Zarlino,] chap. 58, p. 281 [Au.]: "The method to be followed in composing music for more than two voices and the names of the parts."

Languor and suffering may be expressed well with dissonances by borrowing and especially with chromaticism, of which we shall speak in the following book.

Despair and all passions which lead to fury or strike violently demand all types of unprepared dissonances, with the major dissonances particularly occurring in the treble. In certain expressions of this nature, it is even effective to pass from one key to another by means of an unprepared major dissonance, as long as the ear is not too greatly offended by an overly large disproportion between the two keys. Hence, this must be done discerningly, just like everything else, for to pile up dissonance upon dissonance every time that a dissonance might occur would be a defect infinitely greater than to use only consonances. Dissonance should be employed only with great discretion. Sometimes we should even avoid its use in chords from which it should ordinarily not be separated, suppressing it skillfully when its harshness is unsuited to the expression, and distributing those consonances which form the rest of the chord through all the parts. We should remember that the seventh, from which all dissonances arise, is only a sound added to the perfect chord, that it consequently does not destroy the fundamental of this chord, and that it may always be suppressed when this is judged appropriate.

Melody has no less expressive force than harmony, but giving definite rules for its use is almost impossible, since good taste plays a greater part in this than anything else. We shall leave to privileged geniuses the pleasure of distinguishing themselves in this domain on which depends almost all the strength of sentiment. We hope that those able men to whom we have said nothing new will not bear us ill-will for having revealed secrets of which they wished perhaps to be the sole trustees. Our little knowledge does not permit us to argue with them about this last degree of perfection, without which the most beautiful harmony may become insipid. In this manner they are always in a position to surpass others. This does not mean that when we know how to arrange appropriately a succession of chords we are unable to derive from it a melody suitable to our subject, as we shall see later; but good taste is always the prime mover here.[5]

In the use of melody, it seems that the Ancients surpassed us, if we may believe what they say. Of this one it is claimed that his melody made Ulysses weep; that one obliged Alexander to take up arms; another made a furious youth soft and human. On all sides, we see the astounding effects of their music. Zarlino comments very sensibly, saying first that the word harmony often signifies only a simple melody to them, and that all these effects arise more from an energetic discourse, whose force is increased by the manner in which they declaim the text while singing, [rather] than from melody alone; for their melody could certainly not have profited from all the diversity which the perfect harmony unknown to them procures for us today. Their harmony, Zarlino says further,[6] consisted of a perfect chord above which they sang their

5. In French this expression is "le premier moteur," an interesting metaphysical metaphor. [Tr.]
6. [Zarlino, *Istitutioni*], pt. 3, chap. 79, p. 356 [Au.]: "Of the things which contribute to the composition of the genera."

different sorts of airs (as with our bagpipes or hurdy-gurdies); Zarlino called this *Sinfonia.*[7]

A good musician should surrender himself to all the characters he wishes to portray. Like a skillful actor he should take the place of the speaker, believe himself to be at the locations where the different events he wishes to depict occur, and participate in these events as do those most involved in them. He must declaim the text well, at least to himself, and must feel when and to what degree the voice should rise or fall, so that he may shape his melody, harmony, modulation, and movement accordingly.

7. "Musettes," "vielles," and "hurdy-gurdy." All these instruments involve drones above which the singer moves with greater freedom. Rameau could be referring either to the instruments or to the characteristic pieces styled on them. [Tr.]

116 Johann Mattheson

In the many conflicts between "ancients" and "moderns" that characterize the Baroque era, Johann Mattheson (1681–1764) took a modernist side against those Lutheran conservatives who deplored both the new Italianate music associated with the theater and the French *galant* style of instrumental music. In their view, both were destroying the rational and well-established foundations of German composition. Mattheson's musical experiences—as opera singer, organist, music director at the Hamburg cathedral for thirteen years (1715–28), composer of operas, oratorios, and chamber music, polemicist, and pedagogue—all contributed to his massive treatise of 1739, *Der vollkommene Capellmeister* (*The Complete Music Director*), which is subtitled *Basic Information about All Those Things That Anyone Who Wants to Direct a Chapel Honorably and Successfully Must Understand, Be Able to Do, and Bring to Perfection.* The volume was not modeled on traditional theoretical treatises and is peppered throughout with Mattheson's rejection of precepts derived from classical writers, his refutations of some newer ideas (such as those of Rameau on harmony), and his practical sense. His aim was not to educate an ordinary professional but to help invent a modern one. That a knowledge of instrumental music was deemed essential for the new musician is shown by the extent to which Mattheson discusses it. The excerpts here from part 2 describe and try to explain affect in instrumental music by means of specific references to tempo and intervals, and also by an examination of phrasing and motivic recurrences.

FROM *The Complete Music Director*

(1739)

PART TWO

CHAPTER 12: THE DIFFERENCE BETWEEN VOCAL AND INSTRUMENTAL MELODIES

All music making is either vocal or instrumental, and the latter is made on certain tools suited for it which are usually called instruments. The human voice likewise has its own natural tools, though these are different from the artificial. The latter are made while the former are inborn. From this it follows that essentially there must be two different classes of melodies, which are called vocal and instrumental. For one must deal differently with things that are made through artifice than with the natural and inborn.

* * * * *

The first of seventeen differences between a vocal and instrumental melody is that the former is, in a manner of speaking, the mother, but the latter is her daughter. Such a comparison shows not only the degree difference but also the type of relationship. For just as a mother must necessarily be older than her natural daughter, so also vocal melody no doubt existed earlier in this nether-world than did instrumental music. Hence the former not only has rank and privilege, but also directs the daughter to conform to her motherly precepts as best as possible, in order to make everything beautifully graceful and flowing, so that one might hear whose child she is.

Through such observation we can easily perceive which instrumental melodies are true daughters and which are produced as if out of wedlock, according to how they take after the mother, or deviate from her type. On the other hand, just as the motherly quality requires much modesty and reservation, the childlike is more lively and youthful. From this it can be seen how improper it would be if the mother were to deck herself out with the attire of the daughter; and if the latter were to select the attire of the matron. It is best to have each in its proper place.

The second difference between singing and playing follows automatically from this principle. That is, the former precedes, and the latter follows. As natural as this rule seems to be, indeed, as reasonable as it is, things are almost always done in the opposite manner. For who, when he sets out to instruct others in the art of composition begins with a vocal melody? Does not everyone

TEXT: *Der vollkommene Capellmeister* (Hamburg, 1739; rpt. Kassel, 1954), pt. 2, pp. 203–4, 207–10, 223–24, 227–28, 230–31, and 233–34. Translation by Ernest C. Harriss for this edition. For a translation of the complete treatise, see his *Johann Mattheson's* Der vollkommene Capellmeister, *a Revised Translation with Critical Commentary* (Ann Arbor, 1981).

first reach for all sorts of instrumental pieces, sonatas, overtures, etc., before he knows how to sing and write down a single chorale correctly, much less to elaborate on one artistically?

•   •   •   •   •

The twelfth and most familiar difference between our vocal and instrumental melodies is this: that instrumentalists do not have to deal with words, as do singers. But here there is something quite unknown, or at least unobserved. Namely, that instrumental melodies can do without the words themselves, but not without the affections. I do not know how most of our present-day concertizers and fathers of notes will respond on this point. They would deny the basic principles of music and would rather displace its true purpose rather than yield in this, which they can indeed do in *practice* yet never in *theoretice*.

So since the true goal of all melody can only be a type of diversion of the hearing through which the passions of the soul are stirred, no one will accomplish this goal who is not intent upon it, who is not himself moved, and who scarcely thinks of a passion at all, unless it were of the sort that emerges involuntarily. But if he is moved in a nobler manner and also desires to move others with harmony, then he must know how to express sincerely all of the emotions of the heart merely through the selected sounds themselves and their skillful combination, without words, in a way that the auditor might fully grasp and clearly comprehend the impetus, the sense, the meaning, and the expression, as well as all the pertaining divisions and caesuras, as if it were an actual narration. Then what a joy it is! Much more art and a more powerful imagination is required if one wants to achieve this without, rather than with, words.[1]

Now one would scarcely believe that the affections would have to be as greatly differentiated even in little, disesteemed dance melodies, as light and shadow can be. I give only one illustration of this; e.g., the affect is a good bit more sublime and stately in a chaconne than in a passacaglia. The affection of a courante is directed toward a tender longing. I am not speaking of an Italian violin corrente. A dogged seriousness is the only thing encountered in a sarabande. The purpose is pomp and conceit in an *entrée,* and pleasant joking in a rigadoun. The aim is contentment and pleasantness in a bourée, liveliness in a rondeau, vacillation and instability in a passepied, ardor and passion in a gigue, exulting or unrestrained joy in a gavotte, temperate diversion in a minuet, etc.

As regards the jubilant joy of dancing, it occurs to me that the wise Spartans would sometimes have very drunk slaves dance and rejoice[2] in front of their children in order to teach them to abhor immoderation. This is a use[3] of the

---

1. Harmony can express, personify, and articulate everything, even without the help of words. [J. B. Louis Gresset], *Discours sur l'harmonie* (Paris, 1737) p. 76. One can see from this that the wise French are also of my opinion in this respect: as if we had come to agreement about it. [Au.]

2. As a strong man rejoices who comes from drinking. Psalm 78:66. [Au.]

3. In short, the dance itself, which at first glance seems to be nothing but pleasure, also conceals useful lessons, [Gresset], *Disc[ours]sur l'harm[onie]*, p. 79. Though anger, rage, despair, weakness, sensual pleasure, and voluptuousness are also represented by dance. [Au.]

art of dancing and its melodies which is well worth paying special attention to, since some ugly passions and depravities are thereby made despicable, while other praiseworthy affections and virtues are awakened.

This uncommon diversity in the expression of the affections as well as the observation of all caesuras of musical rhetoric can even more clearly be perceived when examining larger and more imposing instrumental pieces, if the composers are of the right kind, e.g., where an *Adagio* indicates distress, a *Lamento* lamentation, a *Lento* relief, an *Andante* hope, an *Affetuoso* love, an *Allegro* comfort, a *Presto* eagerness,[4] etc. This can happen whether a composer has thought about it or not, if his genius functions properly, which can often occur without our knowledge and assistance.

When listening to the first part of a good overture, I feel a special elevation of the spirit. The second part on the other hand expands minds with great joy; and if a serious ending follows, then everything is brought together to a normal restful conclusion.[5] It seems to me that this is a pleasantly alternating movement that an orator could scarcely surpass. Anyone who is paying attention can see in the face of an attentive listener what he perceives in his heart.

If I hear a solemn *sinfonia* in the church, a prayerful trembling comes over me. If a powerful instrumental choir is also worked in, this causes great admiration within me. If the organ begins to roar and thunder, I am seized with the fear of God. Then if a joyous hallelujah brings everything to a close, my heart leaps in my breast. This occurs even if, on account of the distance or for some other reason, I were to understand neither the meaning of this word nor understand anything else, indeed, even if words were not used, but merely the instruments and expressive sounds.

Now if one cannot really say that a composer measures or counts his phrases and cadences, nor that he always considers in advance whether he should use a musical comma here or a *colon*[6] there, etc., which nevertheless are indispensable for clarity and for stirring the affections, still it is certain that skilled and successful masters always do this, with great diligence in graceful expression or writing, as it should be done without thinking about it. However, one enlightens a student in no small measure when, as here, occasion is given to note such things for him in their artistic form, and to provide, though in an unforced manner, a clear conception of the essential nature of such components, related matters, and differences in melodies.

There will be more opportunity to deal with this in the next chapter, with the presentation of the categories and types of all or at least of most melodies. And thus I mention this only briefly here, for, as we have seen, instrumental melody differs from vocal mainly in the fact that the former, without the aid of

4. It is known that these adjectives that indicate the particular feelings in melodies are often used to differentiate the movements as if they were true nouns. [Au.]

5. Mattheson refers here to the sections in contrasting tempos of the typical French overture.

6. A Latin term for a member of a period: a division of a compound or complex sentence, of which the first part consists of two or more clauses separable by semicolons.

words and voices, attempts to express just as much as the latter does with words. So much for the twelfth difference.

•   •   •   •   •

If we discussed the essential sensitivity and expression of the affections in instrumental melodies above, then it is easy to perceive that the theory on *emphasis* also belongs here,[7] only with the difference that vocal melody derives its emphasis from the words, while instrumental melody derives its emphasis from the sound. And that is the fifteenth difference. This seems to be quite a state of affairs. Yet anyone who will not disdain selecting certain prominent passages from good French instrumental pieces will soon find how the knot would be undone, and how he could make his sounds also speak with good emphasis. Commonly this sounding emphasis is prominent in the ascending half step. E.g.:

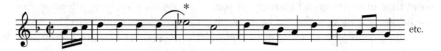

It is rather striking that the small intervals generally and much more often must serve for such matters of emphasis than do the larger ones, just about as we have seen above with the seemingly insignificant conjunctions. It is also to be observed here that not every melodic accent contains emphasis; but that the latter so to speak would contain a doubled accent. In the musical example quoted, eight [notes] are accented,[8] and yet only one has true emphasis, where the asterisk stands.

•   •   •   •   •

Chapter 13: The Categories of Melodies and their Special Characteristics

•   •   •   •   •

As has already been pointed out above, everything has to be said about instrumental pieces which the art of composition requires of vocal melodies,[9] indeed, often more. This will be reinforced as we move on to instrumental melodies and their types. For here one turns first to the affections, which are expressed with sounds alone, without words; then to the caesuras in the musical rhetoric, where the words cannot show us the way because they are not used; third to stress, to emphasis; fourth to the geometric;[10] and fifth to the arithme-

---

7. Mattheson discusses the creation of musical emphasis or stress in vocal melodies through pitch and rhythm in part 2, chapter 8.
8. The tones on the duple divisions of the measure.
9. This section follows 78 paragraphs on vocal music.
10. By geometric, Mattheson means the proportional metric relation of phrases, or *numerum sectionalem*.

tic relationship.[11] Even if one were to examine the smallest melody, this will be found to be true.

· · · · ·

Something fresh and brisk might, in its turn, follow these serious melodies, namely VII.[12] the *Gigue* with its types, which are: the common one, the *Loure,* the *Canarie,* the *Giga.* The common or English gigues are characterized by an ardent and fleeting zeal, a rage that soon subsides. On the other hand, the loures or the slow and dotted ones reveal a proud, arrogant nature. For this reason they are very beloved by the Spanish. Canaries must contain great eagerness and swiftness; but still sound a little simple. Finally, the Italian *gige* [*sic*], which are not used for dancing, but for fiddling (from which their name might also derive),[13] constrain themselves to extreme speed or volatility; though for the most part in a flowing and uninterrupted manner, like the smoothly flowing current of a brook.

All of these new observations are not so much directed toward the full understanding merely of dances as toward the discovery of the riches concealed therein and the skilled application of these, with the multitude of other and seemingly more important things: especially with beautiful vocal pieces and the expression of passions of all sorts; wherein innumerable and indeed unbelievable inventions come forth from these modest sources. One should reflect well on this suggestion.

Here there are, as with some of the other categories of melodies, also ariettas *a tempo di Giga* for singing; principally the *Loures,* which have a not unpleasant effect. Merely with the gigue style I can express four principal affects: passion or zeal; pride; foolish ambition; and the volatile spirit. The simplicity of the Canarie gigues is particularly expressed through the fact that all four sections and repetitions always conclude in the tonic key, and in no other.

· · · · ·

Everyone probably knows that there is a category in instrumental, dancing, and vocal melodies with the name XIII. the *Courante,* or *Corrente.* There are those for dancing, for the keyboard, lute etc., for the violin, and for singing. If the courante is used for dancing, there is an absolutely irrevocable rule to which the composer must precisely attend . . . No other meter but three-two, $\frac{3}{2}$, can be used.

But if the melody is for the keyboard, then it is permitted more freedom. It has almost no bounds on the violin (not excluding the viola da gamba), but seeks fully to justify its name through continuous running, yet so that it is

11. "Arithmetic" refers here to rhythm. When rhythmic motives recur, Mattheson observes their "arithmetic uniformity."
12. Omitted are Mattheson's discussion of sixteen types of vocal melody and the first six types of instrumental melody. He discusses the gigue seventh; the courante is thirteenth, and the sonata, the nineteenth type.
13. In the International Phonetic Alphabet, the pronunciation of *Geige,* the German word for violin, is [gaigə], which Mattheson relates to the Italian *giga* [dʒiga].

pleasant and charming. Vocal courantes come the closest to those for dancing, though they actually only use the *tempo di corrente,* the movement, and not its whole structure.

The lutanists' masterpiece, especially in France, is usually the courante, to which one applies his toil and art to advantage. The passion or affection that should be presented in a courante is that of sweet hopefulness. For there is something of the courageous, something of longing, and something of the cheerful in this melody. Only those things of which hope is composed.

Perhaps because nobody might have said this before or scarcely have thought it, many will think that I seek something in these things that is not to be found there, but that originated in my own mind. Yet I can make it almost palpably obvious to everyone that the above three conditions, and consequently the affection arising from them, are to be encountered and must be in a good courante. Let us select an old, very familiar melody for this, for the modern ones not only go off the beaten path, but one might also object that I had composed it and arranged it according to my conception only to support the above statement on hopefulness. I am quite certain that if the connoisseurs of the lute examine their courantes, they will find it just as true as with the following one.

Up to the middle of the third measure, where the † stands, there is something of the courageous in this melody, especially right in the very first measure. No one can deny that. From there to the middle of the eighth measure, where the same sign of the cross is found, a longing is expressed; above all in the last three and one-half measures, and by means of the repeating cadence in the fifth downwards. Finally, a little joy arises toward the end, especially in the ninth measure.

I have examined a considerable number of courantes in this way, many of which are better and have a more proper geometric relationship. But all are by true and proven composers who have done this from natural instinct, *par instinct,* without plan or intent. And the truth of what I say here on the affection is consistently demonstrated. I could very easily produce and analyze similar examples from all of the other genres; however, then we would far exceed the limitations set for us.

$$\bullet \quad \bullet \quad \bullet \quad \bullet \quad \bullet$$

A much more important piece among the categories of instrumental melodies is occupied by XIX. the *Sonata*, with several violins or on one specific instrument alone, e.g., on the transverse flute, etc. Its aim is primarily towards complaisance or kindness, since a certain *complaisance* must predominate in sonatas that is accommodating to everyone, and with which every listener is served. A melancholy person will find something pitiful and compassionate, a sensuous person something pretty, an angry person something violent, and so on, in the sundry diversities in sonatas.[14] The composer must make such a purpose clear with his *adagio, andante, presto,* etc., then his work will succeed.

For some years rudimentary sonatas for the keyboard have been composed with good success. They do not yet have the right form and tend to be more animated than animating, i.e., they aim more towards the movement of the fingers than of the heart. Yet amazement over uncommon dexterity is also a type of affection that often gives rise to envy, though it is said that its true mother is ignorance. The French are becoming pure Italians, both in this sonata business as well as in their recent cantatas. The result is mainly a patchwork of nothing but pieced-together little phrases, and is not natural.

14. For a further exposition of the human temperaments and music, see Kircher in No. 117 below.

DIFFERENCES
NOTED

117 Athanasius Kircher

Born in 1601 or 1602 near Fulda in Germany, Athanasius Kircher received a Jesuit education and became a priest and a teacher of mathematics, Greek, Hebrew, and Syriac at various Jesuit colleges. In 1631, when the Protestant Swedish army besieged Würzburg, Kircher transferred from his university post there and followed an itinerary that led him from Germany to Avignon and on to Rome, in 1635. He remained there as a professor of mathematics, physics, and Oriental languages at the Collegio Romano until his death in 1680.

His Latin treatise *Musurgia universalis* could be called a compendium of harmonic relations in fields as diverse as chemistry, ethics, politics, and the heavenly orders. It speaks as authoritatively about mathematical proportions, acoustics, and the physiology of hearing as it does about the notation of birdsong, the composition of music, and the construction of musical instruments. Topics are presented in the hierarchical format traditional for learned exposition. Kircher's arguments, however, are more essays than they are demonstrations of scientific proof. With 1,500 copies printed, the *Musurgia* must have been known to all later serious writers on music.

In the first part of book 7, the perpetual question of whether ancient or modern music was superior led Kircher to posit general explanations of difference based on what today we call "nature and nurture." According to Kircher, listeners, whether ancient or modern, acquire musical taste according to their essential natures. These are determined by the proportions of the four humors in the body, which differ according to geographical location. Kircher fully believed, furthermore, that the nature, or original inclinations, of individuals and cultures could be altered or modified by exposure to and familiarization with the new or foreign. This was the belief that underlay the strategy of adaptation that enabled the Jesuit order to establish footholds in most of the non-European regions of the world. In the course of discussing the reasons for difference, Kircher listed characterizations of national styles in European music that reappear in many later musical commentaries.

FROM *Musurgia universalis, or, The Great Art of Consonances and Dissonances*

(1650)

VOLUME 1, BOOK 7

INQUIRY V: WHETHER THE EXAMINED MUSIC OF THE ANCIENTS WAS MORE PERFECT AND SUPERIOR THAN THE MUSIC OF THE MODERNS

My first proposition is that the customary style of music in any one place follows from the natural temperament[1] of its people and their constitution, which is particular to any one region. Inasmuch as this is true, nothing further is necessary for proof except some examples themselves. Just as the Phrygians certainly differed from the Dorians in musical style, and the Dorians from the Lydians, so did the latter differ from the Phrygians, as the Dorian, Phrygian, Lydian and Ionian compositions clearly demonstrate, in which indeed each of these nations so firmly kept to its own style. The Dorians thought that allowing anything other than Dorian was impermissible, the Phrygians other than Phrygian, the Lydians other than Lydian. For instance, since the Dorians, who were benevolent and mild by instinct, bore themselves in religious rites with remarkable piety, they cultivated melody consistent with this inclination in everything that was Dorian. The Phrygians, a more lustful kind of people, chose a Phrygian style given to enjoyment and dancing, as being in conformance with their character. And experience teaches us what in modern times is the case in the most civilized nations of the whole world, in all parts of Europe. The Italians have a melodic style different from the Germans; these differ from the Italians and the French. The French and Italians differ from the Spanish, and the English have I know not what sort of strangeness, for each natural temperament there is an appropriate style according to the customs of the nation. The Italians hate the dour seriousness in the German style more than is just. They disdain in the French those frequent graces in their pieces and in the Spanish, a certain gravity both pompous and studied. The French, Germans, and Spanish find fault with the Italians, more than is just, on account of their unchecked

---

TEXT: *Musurgia universalis sive Ars magna consoni et dissoni*, 2 vols. (Rome, 1650; facs. ed. Hildesheim, 1970), tome 1, bk. 7, pp. 542–45. Translation by Margaret Murata.

1. The Latin word here is *complexio*. The English equivalent, "complexion," has changed its meaning since the seventeenth century when it indicated the combination in each person of the four humors of the body. The balance among them was held to determine the temperament of the individual: choleric, sanguine, phlegmatic, or melancholy.

chains of notes, which they call trills and *groppi*,[2] which they think of as unpleasant and tiresome repetitions whose indiscreet application decreases the charm of all their music rather than increasing it. Furthermore, as they say, there are the rustic and confused excesses of goat-like voices which, they also say, move us more to laughter than to feeling. As the old saying goes, "The Italians bleat, the Spanish bark, the Germans bellow, the French warble."[3]

This very difference in musical style of the different nations does not come from anywhere else except either from the spirit of the place and natural tendency, or from custom maintained by long-standing habit,[4] finally becoming nature. The Germans for the most part are born under a frozen sky and acquire a temperament that is serious, strong, constant, solid, and toilsome, to which qualities their music conforms. And just as these qualities are consistent with lower voices, compared to people of the south, the Germans rise to higher pitches with difficulty. Thus from natural propensity they choose that in which they can succeed best, namely, a style that is serious, moderate, sober, and choral. The French on the contrary are more changeable, having been allotted a temperament that is cheerful, lively, and innocent of restraint. They love a style that is similar to this temperament: whence they give themselves for the most part to the hyporchematic style,[5] that is, to ensemble dancing, leaps, and similar very suitable dances (which they present to airs such as galliards, passamezzos, and courantes).[6] The Spanish not only do not stand out so much as

2. For *groppi*, see Caccini in No. 99, p. 612. The criticism of the florid Italian style may refer to the earlier Roman art of vocal embellishment, especially in sacred solo music, as taught in the manuals of Giovanni Conforti and Francesco Severi. See also Pietro della Valle in No. 84, pp. 547–48.

3. This "old saying" was repeated and modified by the later Jesuit writer Claude-François Ménestrier in his *Des Représentations en musique anciennes et modernes* (Paris, 1681; facs. Geneva, 1972), p. 107: "The French warble, the Spanish bark or screech, the Italians bleat like goats and the Germans bellow. . . . One can add that the English whistle and the Turks howl." Ménestrier adds that the German "bellowing" is amplified by their use of serpents and sackbuts in ensembles (p. 108); compare Lady Montagu's observation in No. 119, p. 716. An early characterization of this sort is that by John the Deacon, ninth-century biographer of St. Gregory the Great, in his explanation of the inability of the Germans and Gauls to maintain the "suavity" of Roman chant: "For Alpine bodies, which make an incredible din with the thundering of their voices, do not properly echo the elegance of the received melody" (p. 179 above).

4. Ménestrier repeats Kircher, p. 107: "Each nation has its character in terms of song and music, as for the most part in other things that depend on the differences of the spirit of the place, usage, and customs."

5. From the Greek for a "choral hymn." In the seventeenth century, the term came to indicate music for dancing. The hyporchematic is Kircher's third category of theatrical music (vol. 1, p. 310); it includes "other species such as canzonas, allemandes, galliards, passamezzos, duplas, and sarabandes, most in use by the French and Germans."

6. These national characterizations are passed from writer to writer. In the *Critische Musicus* (rev. ed., Leipzig, 1745) of Johann Adolph Scheibe, for September 17, 1737 one reads: "The French style, or rather the French musical style is completely lively and cheerful. It is brief and very natural. . . . The rhythm and meter are clearly heard all the time (p. 146)," and "One sees that . . . German music is serious, highly worked and artful (*ernsthaft, arbeitsam und künstlich*)," (p. 150).

cultivators of music but they also have very little worthy of comparison with others, if one excepts two men, one in theory, Salinas,[7] and the other in practical music, Christopher Morales,[8] as praiseworthy as any in music. Finally, Italy justly appointed to itself the first place in music from the beginning, for there has not been a single age when all the principal composers did not produce music out of Italy, to the continual wonderment of all, with the most precious works. Composers who met with this most temperate clime thus also arrived at a style completely perfect and temperate that corresponded to their natures, neither a lascivious style with too much hyporchematic dancing nor a vulgar one that uses a hypatodic style.[9] They used all styles appropriately and with the best judgment, and were truly born for music.[10] . . .

As for the fact that the style of the Italians and French pleases the Germans very little, and that of the Germans hardly pleases the Italians or French, I think this happens for a variety of reasons. Firstly, out of patriotism and inordinate affection to both nation and country, each nation always prefers its own above others. Secondly, according to the opposing styles of their innate character and then because of custom maintained by long-standing habit, each nation enjoys only its own music that it has been used to since its earliest age. Hence we see that upon first hearing, the music of the Italians, albeit charming, pleases the French and Germans very little, as being to their suffering ears an unusual style, contrary to themselves and of a particular impetuosity. Or even more plain to see, how the peoples of the East—Greeks, Syrians, Egyptians, Africans sojourning in Rome—could hardly endure the refined music of the Romans. They preferred their confused and discordant voices (you would more truly call it the howling and shrieking of animals) to said music from many parasangs away.[11] All this proceeds, as I have said, due to custom acquired from long use: for if said nations had finally become accustomed to the music of the Romans, they would not only have preferred it to other music, but they would also have desired it avidly and seemed to love it.

7. Francisco de Salinas (1513–1590), organist in the viceregal chapel in Naples, chair of music at the University of Salamanca, and author of a theoretical treatise on music (1577).

8. Cristóbal de Morales (1500–1553), composer of mostly liturgical music who worked at the cathedrals in Ávila, Toledo, and Málaga as well as in the private chapels of the pope and the Duke of Arcos.

9. Probably music of low sounds. G. B. Doni defines a "hypatodia organica" as the *basso continuo* in his *Progymnastica musicae*, bk. 1 (1763), p. 231.

10. Ménestrier, *Des Représentations*, pp. 138–39, condenses Kircher's description relating climate to style: "Each people has its different customs and usages which are naturally subject to the same movements of the soul and to the same passions. Thus, although nature is the same everywhere, the different climates vary so strongly, that customs are not the same in every country . . . A Frenchman will be angered by something else than will a Spaniard, and just as one is almost always excited to violent motions, the other attempts to maintain a false gravity, because he is accustomed to this studied dignity; the other instead is freer and naturally accustomed to not restraining and deceiving himself."

11. A "parasang" is a Persian measure of length, between three and three and one half miles. Being distant many parasangs was a common figurative expression found even in English of the time.

And however different are the styles of different nations, despite the famous competition between them and their contesting for primacy of place, the particular style of each should not therefore be despised; for each nation has its own taste in writing songs. The Germans love the choral style for several voices in their compositions, as they love a variety astonishing in manner. What they cultivate as their most favored are choruses formed ingeniously with suspensions and fugues, with voices artfully following upon each other in the motet style. The French titillate the ears marvelously with clever songs and pieces put together in a variety of ways, embracing the hyporchematic style. The Italians, as I said, make use of every style: the motet, the church style, the madrigalian, the hyporchematic. They do not affect just the ears with this variety, but they also draw out both the torments and the passions of the soul, arousing them in every possible way with great power.

My second proposition is that just as the different nations each enjoy a different musical style, so in each nation people of diverse temperament are affected by diverse styles, each principally in conformance with their natural propensities. Hence all do not equally enjoy the same compositions, just as not everything edible is eaten with equal pleasure. The melancholy find pleasure in settings that are grave, dense, and mournful. The sanguine, because their spirits are easily agitated and titillated, are indiscriminately affected by the hyporchematic style. The choleric, because of the force of their bubbling bile, have an appetite for similar musical motion. Hence the military man, accustomed to trumpets and drums, seems to dislike all music that is more refined. Phlegmatics are affected by high women's voices in chorus, inasmuch as the high sound affects the phlegmatic humor favorably, whence its pleasure and charm. Here again certain airs will have rather great power over one person, and none over another. One person will be affected by this mode, another by that one, since all things depend on the different make up of the temperaments, as will be demonstrated later more amply. What indeed is the case is not only that different people enjoy different music but, rather, different intervals. There are those whom thirds please; several are delighted by sixths. Not absent also are those who would be attached to the harsh and discordant, all of which depends on the character of the nation, its propensities, particular temperament, and the customs it maintains.

•　•　•　•　•

118 Richard Ligon

Although Richard Ligon's history of Barbados has served as a primary source for studying the colonial history of the West Indies and their plantation slave economies, the author remains a shadowy figure. He played theorbo and served as executor for the estate of his friend, the composer John Coprario (c.1575–1626). He apparently had connections with London theater musicians, who came upon hard times when the theaters were closed down in 1642. He left England for the New World in 1647 in unexplained dire straits, only to return in 1650 to England and be thrown in debtor's prison, where he wrote the record of his voyage and sojourn. He first published these observations of life on the island of Barbados in 1657. On his voyage, an old expatriate English musician surprised him by his plain style of playing without ornaments, and once on the island, he had many opportunities to hear the music making of the Africans enslaved there.

FROM *A True & Exact History of the Island of Barbados*
(1673)

. . . Upon the sixteenth day of June, 1647, we embark'd in the Downs on the good ship called the *Achilles,* a vessel of 350 tunns, the Master Thomas Crowder of London. And no sooner were we all aboard, but we presently weighed anchor and put to sea in so cold weather as at that time of the year, I have not felt the like. . . . But before we came to St. Iago,[1] we were to have visited a small island called Soll, by the intreaty of a Portugal[2] we carried with us. . . . But when we came within sight of it, it appeared to us full of high and steep rocks (the highest of which were mere stone, without any soil at all) and they of so great a height, as we seldom saw the tops, whilst we lay before it; . . . and on the brow of the hill towards the right hand, a very high and steep precipice of a rock, in which stood the house of the Padre Vagado, fixt on the top of the rock. A house fit enough for such a master; for though he were the chief commander of the island, yet by his port and house he kept, he was more

---

TEXT: *A True & Exact History of the Island of Barbadoes* (2d ed., London, 1673; facs. London, 1970), pp. 1, 7–9, 12, 43, 46–52, 106–7. Punctuation and orthography have been modernized. All ellipses are editorial. See further Christopher D. S. Field, "Musical Observations from Barbados, 1647–50," *Musical Times* 115 (1974): 565–67.

1. One of the ten Cape Verde Islands.
2. A Portuguese named Bernardo Mendes de Sousa.

like a hermit than a governor. His family consisting of a mulatto of his own getting,[3] three negroes, a fiddler, and a wench. . . .

Dinner being nearly half done (the Padre, Bernardo, and the other black attendants waiting on us) in comes an old fellow, whose complexion was raised out of the red sack;[4] for near that colour it was: his head and beard milk white, his countenance bold and cheerful, a lute in his hand, and play'd for us a novelty, the *passeme sares galiard,* a tune in great esteem in Harry the fourth's days.[5] For when Sir John Falstaff makes his *amours* to Mistress Doll Tear-Sheet, Sneake and his Company the admired fiddlers of that age, playes this tune, which put a thought into my head, that if Time and Tune be the composites[6] of musick, what a long time this tune had in sayling from England to this place. But we being sufficiently satisfied with this kind of harmony, desired a song, which he performed in as antique a manner; both savouring much of antiquity: no graces, double relishes, trillos, groppos, or piano forte's, but plain as a packstaff. His lute, too, was but of ten strings, and that was in fashion in King David's days, so that the rarity of this antique piece pleas'd me beyond measure.

Dinner being ended, and the padre well near weary of his waiting, we rose, and made room for better company. For now the padre and his black mistress were to take their turns—a negro of the greatest beauty and majesty together that ever I saw in one woman.

·   ·   ·   ·   ·

The island [of Barbados] is divided into three sorts of men, *viz.,* masters, servants, and slaves. The slaves and their posterity, being subject to their masters for ever, are kept and preserv'd with greater care than the servants, who are theirs but for five years, according to the law of the Island. . . . It has been accounted a strange thing that the negroes, being more than double the numbers of the Christians that are there, . . . should not commit some horrid massacre upon the Christians, thereby to enfranchise themselves and become masters of the island. But there are three reasons that take away this wonder; the one is, they are not suffered to touch or handle any weapons; the other, that they are held in such awe and slavery, as they are fearful to appear in any daring act. . . . Besides these, there is a third reason, which stops all designs of that kind, and that is, they are fetch'd from several parts of Africa, who speak several languages, and by that means, one of them understands not another: for some of them are fetch'd from Guinny and Binny, some from Cutchew, some from Angola, and some from the River of Gambia.[7] . . .

3. Though a priest, Padre Vagado was the father.
4. Red wine.
5. Ligon attributes this galliard on the chord pattern called the *passamezzo* to the early fifteenth century, because he associates it with Shakespeare's play *Henry IV,* part 2, in which "Sneak and his company" appear.
6. Components.
7. Guinea, Benin, Cacheu (Guinea-Bissau), and the other places are all on the west coast of the African continent.

We had an excellent negro in the plantation, whose name was Macow and was our chief musician, a very valiant man and was keeper of our plantain grove. . . . On Sunday [the slaves] rest and have the whole day at their pleasure, and most of them use it as a day of rest and pleasure. But some of them who will make benefit of that day's liberty, go where the mangrove trees grow and gather the bark, of which they make ropes, which they truck away for other commodities, as shirts and drawers.

In the afternoons on Sundays, they have their musick, which is of kettle drums, and those of several sizes. Upon the smallest the best musician plays, and the other come in as choruses. The drum, all men know, has but one tone; and therefore variety of tunes have little to do in this musick, and yet so strangely they vary their time, as 'tis a pleasure to the most curious ears, and it was to me one of the strangest noises that ever I heard made of one tone. And if they had the variety of tune, which gives the greater scope in music, as they have of time, they would do wonders in that art. And if I had not fallen sick before my coming away, at least seven months in one sickness, I had given them some hints of tunes, which being understood, would have serv'd as a great addition to their harmony; for time without tune is not an eighth part of the science of music.

I found Macow very apt for it of himself, and one day coming into the house (which none of the negroes use to do, unless an officer, as he was), he found me playing on a theorbo, and singing to it, which he hearkened very attentively to. And when I had done, he took the theorbo in his hand and strook[8] one string, stopping it by degrees upon every fret, and finding the notes to varie, till it came to the body of the instrument; and that the nearer the body of the instrument he stopped, the smaller or higher the sound was, which he found was by the shortening of the string. [He] considered with himself how he might make some tryal of this experiment upon such an instrument as he could come by, having no hope ever to have any instrument of this kind to practice on. In a day or two after, walking in the plantain grove to refresh me in that cool shade and to delight myself with the sight of those plants, which are so beautiful, . . . I found this negro (whose office it was to attend there) being the keeper of that grove, sitting on the ground, and before him a piece of large timber, upon which he had laid cross, six billets, and having a handsaw and a hatchet by him, would cut the billets by little and little, till he had brought them to the tunes[9] he would fit them to. For the shorter they were, the higher the notes, which he tryed by knocking upon the ends of them with a stick which he had in his hand. When I found him at it, I took the stick out of his hand and tried the sound, finding the six billets to have six distinct notes, one above another, which put me in a wonder, how he of himself should, without teaching, do so much.[10] I then shewed him the difference between flats and sharps, which he presently

8. Stroked.
9. Pitches.
10. Macow had constructed an instrument recognizable as the African xylophone known as the *balafo*.

apprehended, as between *Fa* and *Mi*: and he would have cut two more billets to those tunes, but I had then no time to see it done and so left him to his own enquiries. I say thus much to let you see that some of these people are capable of learning arts.

. . . On Sundayes in the afternoon, their musick playes and to dancing they go, the men by themselves and the women by themselves, no mixt dancing. Their motions are rather what they aim at, than what they do; and by that means, transgress the less upon the Sunday, their hands having more of motion than their feet, and their heads more than their hands. They may dance a whole day and ne'r heat themselves; yet, now and then, one of the activest amongst them will leap bolt upright and fall in his place again, but without cutting a caper. When they have danc'd an hour or two, the men fall to wrestle (the musick playing all the while). . . .

When any of them dye, they dig a grave, and at evening they bury him, clapping and wringing their hands, and making a doleful sound with their voices. . . . Some of them, who have been bred up amongst the Portugals, have some extraordinary qualities, which the others have not; as singing and fencing. . . . For their singing, I cannot much commend that, having heard so good in Europe; but for their voices, I have heard many of them very loud and sweet.

·   ·   ·   ·   ·

Some other kinds of pleasures they have in England, which are not so fully enjoyed in the Barbadoes, as smooth champion[11] to walk or ride on, with variety of landscapes at several distances; . . . As for musick and such sounds as please the ear, they [the colonists] wish some supplies may come from England, both for instruments and voices, to delight the sense, that sometimes when they are tir'd out with their labor, they may have some refreshment by their ears; and to that end, they had a purpose to send for the Musick that were wont to play at the Black-Fryars,[12] and to allow them a competent salary to make them live as happily there as they had done in England. And had not extream weakness by a miserable long sickness made me uncapable of any undertaking, they had employed me in the business, as the likeliest to prevail with those men, whose persons and qualities were well known to me in England. And though I found at Barbadoes some who had musical minds, yet, I found others whose souls were so fixt upon and so riveted to the earth and the profits that arise out of it, as their souls were lifted no higher. And those men think and have been heard to say that three whip-sawes, going all at once in a frame or pit, is the best and sweetest musick that can enter their ears; and to hear a cow of their own, or an assinigo[13] bray, no sound can please them better. But these men's souls were never lifted up so high as to hear the musick of the spheres, nor to be judges of that science as 'tis practised here on earth; and therefore we will leave them to their own earthly delights.

11. Grassy lawn.
12. Musicians who played at the Blackfriars Theatre in London, demolished in 1655.
13. A little ass.

119 Lady Mary Wortley Montagu

Mary Pierrepont (1689–1762), whose father was the fifth earl and first Duke of Kensington, taught herself Latin as a girl, eloped with Edward Wortley Montagu at the age of twenty-three, and four years later accompanied her husband to Turkey, where he served as ambassador to the Sublime Porte. Some of her writing appeared anonymously or in pirated editions during her lifetime, but it was the posthumous publication of her Turkish Embassy letters in 1763 that established her reputation as a fine writer and as a sympathetic and straightforward observer of her own and others' ways. Further volumes of her letters soon appeared, and a collected edition of her letters and works was issued in 1837. The present extracts describe musical performances and her thoughts about them as taken from letters written from abroad in 1717 and 1718. One relates privileged visits to the wives of the grand vizier and of the *kâhya* (the second in command of the Ottoman Empire). Her correspondents here are her sister, Lady Frances, Countess of Mar; Lady Elizabeth, Countess of Bristol; and the poet Alexander Pope.

FROM Letters of 1717–1718

To Lady————. Vienna, Jan. 1, 1717

... You may tell all the world in my name that they are never so well inform'd of my affairs as I am myself, and that I am very positive I am at this time at Vienna, where the carnival is begun and all sort of diversions in perpetual practise except that of masqueing, which is never permitted during a war with the Turks. The balls are in public places, where the men pay a gold ducat at entrance, but the ladies nothing.[1] I am told that these houses get sometimes a 1,000 ducats on a night. They are very magnificently furnish'd, and the music good if they had not that detestable custom of mixing hunting horns with it that almost deafen the company, but that noise is so agreeable here they never make a consort without 'em.[2] The ball always concludes with English country dances to the number of 30 or 40 couple, and so ill danc'd that there is very little pleasure in 'em. They know but half a dozen, and they have danc'd them

TEXT: Lady Mary's Turkish letters have appeared many times in print and reprints. Robert Halsband's edition returned to manuscript sources in the Harrowby Manuscript Trust, Stafford, in *The Complete Letters of Lady Mary Wortley Montagu*, 3 vols. (Oxford, 1965), in which the Turkish letters appear in volume 1 with extensive annotations. In the present text most spelling and capitalization have been modernized. Ellipses are all editorial.

1. The ducat at this time was worth four florins. When Antonio Caldara was appointed to the Imperial court in 1716 his annual salary was 1,600 florins; Johann Joseph Fux, the director of music at court received a salary of 3,100 florins from 1715.
2. See No. 117, p. 709, note 3.

over and over this 50 year. I would fain have taught them some new ones, but I found it would be some months labor to make them comprehend 'em.

Last night there was an Italian comedy acted at Court. The scenes were pretty, but the comedy itself such intolerable low farce without either wit or humor, that I was surpriz'd how all the Court could sit there attentively for 4 hours together. No women are suffer'd to act on the stage, and the men dress'd like 'em were such awkward figures they very much added to the ridicule of the spectacle. What completed the diversion was the excessive cold, which was so great I thought I should have died there. It is now the very extremity of the winter here.

• • •

To Alexander Pope, Adrianople, April 1 [1717]

... The summer is already far advanced in this part of the world and for some miles round Adrianople the whole ground is laid out in gardens and the banks of the river set with rows of fruit trees, under which all the most considerable Turks divert themselves every evening, ... drinking their coffee and generally attended by some slave with a fine voice, or that plays on some instrument. ... I have often seen them and their children sitting on the banks of the river and playing on a rural instrument, perfectly answering the description of the ancient fistula;[3] being composed of unequal reeds with a simple but agreeable softness in the sound. Mr. Addison[4] might here make the experiment he speaks of in his travels, there not being one instrument of music among the Greek or Roman statues that is not to be found in the hands of the people of this country.

... I read over your Homer[5] here with an infinite pleasure, and find several little passages explain'd that I did not before entirely comprehend the beauty of, many of the customs and much of the dress then in fashion being yet retain'd; and I don't wonder to find more remains here of an age so distant than it is to be found in any other country. ... Their manner of dancing is certainly the same that Diana is sung [sic] to have danced by [the] Eurotas.[6] The great Lady still leads the dance and is follow'd by a troop of young girls who imitate her steps, and, if she sings, make up the chorus. The tunes are extremely gay and lively, yet with something in 'em wonderful soft. The steps are varied according to the pleasure of her that leads the dance, but always in exact time and infinitely more agreeable than any of our dances, at least in my opinion. I sometimes make one in the train, but am not skilful enough to lead. These are Grecian dances, the Turkish being very different.

3. Normally *fistula* refers to a pipe; Lady Mary's description fits a syrinx or panpipes.
4. Joseph Addison; see No. 113.
5. Pope's translation of Homer's *Iliad* into English. In this part of her letter Lady Mary finds continuity between Homer's Greeks and the customs and dress she sees around her. Charles Fonton, in the next reading, also believed that remnants of ancient music were preserved in the music of the peoples of the Turkish Empire.
6. A river in the Greek Peleponnese.

• • •

To Lady Mar, Adrianople, April 18 [1717]

. . . To confess the truth my head is so full of my entertainment yesterday that 'tis absolutely necessary for my own repose to give it some vent. Without farther preface I will then begin my story.

I was invited to dine with the Grand Vizier's Lady[7] and 'twas with a great deal of pleasure I prepar'd myself for an entertainment which was never given before to any Christian. . . . She entertain'd me with all kind of civility till dinner came in. . . . The treat concluded with coffee and perfumes, which is a high mark of respect. Two slaves kneeling cens'd my hair, clothes, and handkerchief. After this ceremony she commanded her slaves to play and dance, which they did with their guitars in their hands, and she excus'd to me their want of skill, saying she took no care to accomplish them in that art. I return'd her thanks and soon after took my leave.

I was conducted back in the same manner I enter'd, and would have gone straight to my own house, but the Greek lady with me earnestly solicited me to visit the Kahya's Lady, saying he was the 2nd Officer in the Empire. . . . I had found so little diversion in this harem that I had no mind to go into another, but her importunity prevail'd with me, and I am extreme glad that I was so complaisant. All things here were with quite another air than at the Grand Vizier's, and the very house confess'd the difference between an old devote[8] and a young beauty. It was nicely clean and magnificent. I was met at the door by 2 black eunuchs who led me through a long gallery between 2 ranks of beautiful young girls with their hair finely plaited almost hanging to their feet, all dress'd in fine light damasks brocaded with silver. . . .

[Fatima's] fair maids were ranged below the sofa to the number of 20, and put me in mind of the pictures of the ancient nymphs. I did not think all nature could have furnish'd such a scene of beauty. She made them a sign to play and dance. Four of them immediately begun to play some soft airs on instruments between a lute and a guitar, which they accompanied with their voices while the others danc'd by turns. The dance was very different from what I had seen before. Nothing could be more artful or more proper to raise certain ideas, the tunes so soft, the motions so languishing, accompanied with pauses and dying eyes, half falling back and then recovering themselves in so artful a manner that I am very positive the coldest and most rigid prude upon earth could not have look'd upon them without thinking of something not to be spoke of. I suppose you may have read that the Turks have no music but what is shocking to the ears, but this account is from those who never heard any but what is play'd in the streets, and is just as reasonable as if a foreigner should take his

---

7. The wife of Arnavut Hacı Halil paşa.
8. The grand vizier's wife had told Lady Mary that "her whole expense was in charity and her employment praying to God."

ideas of the English music from the bladder and string, and marrow bones and cleavers. I can assure you that the music is extremely pathetic. 'Tis true I am enclin'd to prefer the Italian, but perhaps I am partial. I am acquainted with a Greek lady who sings better than Mrs Robinson,[9] and is very well skill'd in both, who gives the preference to the Turkish. 'Tis certain they have very fine natural voices; these were very agreeable.

When the dance was over 4 fair slaves came into the room with silver censers in their hands and perfum'd the air with amber, aloes wood and other rich scents. After this they serv'd me coffee upon their knees in the finest Japan china with soûcoupes of silver gilt.

•   •   •

To Alexander Pope, Belgrade Village, June 17 [1717]

... I have already let you know that I am still alive, but to say truth I look upon my present circumstances to be exactly the same with those of departed spirits. The heats of Constantinople have driven me to this place which perfectly answers the description of the Elysian fields. I am in the middle of a wood consisting chiefly of fruit trees, water'd by a vast number of fountains ... within view of the Black Sea, from whence we perpetually enjoy the refreshment of cool breezes that makes us insensible of the heat of the summer. The village is wholly inhabited by the richest amongst the Christians, who meet every night at a fountain 40 paces from my house to sing and dance, the beauty and dress of the women exactly resembling the ideas of the ancient nymphs as they are given us by the representations of the poets and painters. ... To say truth, I am sometimes very weary of this singing and dancing and sunshine, and wish for the smoke and impertinencies in which you toil, though I endeavor to persuade my self that I live in a more agreeable variety than you do, and that Monday setting of partridges, Tuesday reading English, Wednesday studying the Turkish language (in which, by the way, I am already very learned), Thursday classical authors. Friday spent in writing, Saturday at my needle, and Sunday admitting of visits and hearing music, is a better way of disposing the week than Monday at the Drawing Room,[10] Tuesday Lady Mohun's,[11] Wednesday the Opera, Thursday the Play, Friday Mrs. Chetwynd's,[12] etc.: a perpetual round of hearing the same scandal and seeing the same follies acted over and over, which here affect me no more than they do other dead people. I can now hear of displeasing things with pity and without indignation.

•   •   •

9. Anastasia Robinson (1692–1755), soprano, then contralto of the London stage. She sang leading roles in operas by Handel, Alessandro Scarlatti, and Giovanni Bononcini between 1714 and 1724, retiring from the stage upon her marriage to the Earl of Peterborough.
10. At St. James's Palace, the residence of the English royal family.
11. Elizabeth Lawrence (d. 1725), widow of the fourth Baron Mohun, mother of Lady Rich.
12. Mary Berkeley (d. 1741).

To Lady Bristol, [Constantinople, 10 April 1718]

... I had the curiosity to visit one of [the monasteries] and observe the devotions of the dervishes, which are as whimsical as any in Rome. These fellows have permission to marry, but are confin'd to an odd habit,[13] which is only a piece of coarse white cloth wrapp'd about 'em, with their legs and arms naked. Their order has few other rules, except that of performing their fantastic rites every Tuesday and Friday, which is in this manner. They meet together in a large hall, where they all stand with the eyes fix'd on the ground and their arms across, while the imam or preacher reads part of the Alcoran,[14] from a pulpit plac'd in the midst; and when he has done, 8 or 10 of them make a melancholy consort with their pipes, which are no unmusical instruments.[15] Then he reads again and makes a short exposition on what he has read, after which they sing and play till their superior (the only one of them dress'd in green) rises and begins a sort of solemn dance. They all stand about him in a regular figure; and while some play, the others tie their robe (which is very wide), fast round their waists and begin to turn round with an amazing swiftness and yet with great regard to the music, moving slower or faster as the tune is played. This lasts above an hour without any of them shewing the least appearance of giddiness, which is not to be wonder'd at when it is consider'd they are all us'd to it from infancy, most of them being devoted to this way of life from their birth, and sons of dervishes. There turn'd amongst them some little dervishes of 6 or 7 years old who seem'd no more disorder'd by that exercise than the others. At the end of their ceremony they shout out: "There is no other God but God, and Mahomet is his prophet;" after which they kiss the Superior's hand and retire. The whole is perform'd with the most solemn gravity. Nothing can be more austere than the form of these people. They never raise their eyes and seem devoted to contemplation, and as ridiculous as this is in description, there is something touching in the air of submission and mortification they assume.

•   •   •   •   •   •

13. Type of clothing.
14. The Koran.
15. The Turkish *ney*.

120 Charles Fonton

Next to nothing is known about the Frenchman Charles Fonton, except that he had studied "Oriental" languages and was clearly interested in the music and the musical instruments he encountered in Constantinople in the mid-eighteenth century. Recognizing that all peoples have their own customs and preferences, he hoped to dispel some of the ignorance and "universal prejudgment" with which "Oriental"—that is Persian, Arabic, or Turkish music—was heard by Europeans. His views survive in a manuscript dated 1751 whose full title reads: "Essay on Oriental Music as Compared with European Music, which attempts to give a general idea of the music of the peoples of the East, of their specific tastes, and of their rules of melody and combining tones, with a summary of their principal instruments." For the latter he provided pen and ink illustrations annotated in Turkish. The nineteenth-century critic and historian François-Joseph Fétis noted in his biographical dictionary of 1835–44 that he thought Fonton's information fairly useless; the essay, however, articulates some notable views clearly. In his introduction Fonton asks whether "most things are not relative and arbitrary, as far as what is true and beautiful." In the second section, given in full here, he nonetheless goes on to judge difference on grounds other than those of truth and beauty. He states that a present practice that has undergone little change must come from a less developed stage of culture, even if in this case it originates from the "ancients," and he equates Eastern music with his perception of Turkish culture as "effeminate," according to his notions of masculine and feminine traits.

FROM *Essay on Oriental Music Compared to the European*
(1751)

ARTICLE II. OF THE MUSIC OF THE ORIENTALS AND OF THEIR PARTICULAR TASTE

Since all peoples in general, however different their customs and character, nevertheless agree about the victorious charm of music and are responsive to it, it follows necessarily that each separate people should have a kind of music that is its own and is capable of moving them. Indeed, the tender and passionate Italian sighs in his airs and paints his passions. The lively and joyful Frenchman, is pleased by the agreeable sounds of a music that is playful and gay. The

TEXT: "Essay sur la musique orientale comparée a la musique européenne," in Bibliothèque national, Fonds fr. nouv. acq. 4023, pp. 37–45. Translation by Margaret Murata. A translation into Turkish by Cem Behar was published in 1987 (Istanbul: Pan Yayancalak).

spirited and hot-headed Englishman lends himself only to harmonies fitting his character. Any others than these would hardly touch him. The dour and heavy German, satisfied by sounds less sweet and affected, does not get excited by great delicacy in harmony. In a word, each country has, down to the least things, some trait that characterizes it and makes it different from the others. The Orientals also make a separate picture. Distant from our manners and customs in everything, they do not come close to us any the more in their music, which bears no relation to that of any European peoples. We also do not need to know the music of the ancients well to be able to assess that it is absolutely the same case with it. But at least there is room to believe that if some vestige of it remains, it must be among the Orientals, among whom the most part of their arts has been preserved much as it was since their beginnings, almost without any development or improvement.

Several prejudgments seem to authorize this opinion. The simplicity and naturalness that reign in Oriental music; the same taste universally widespread among the different peoples of the Orient; certain airs and certain dances which are spoken of in well-known ancient authors and up to the present by people of this land. All this forms the presumption that one can regard this, if not as proof of, then at least as traits of resemblance between the music of the ancients and modern Oriental music.

However the case may be, it is an established fact that this music is hardly so much to be rejected as one imagines, nor is it so disagreeable that one could not comprehend it. In the judgment of connoisseurs, it has the beauty of its species. But it is difficult to give a just and precise idea of it, because music is the kind of thing of which one feels the effect and does not express it. Everything that one can say in general, and in spite of its critics, is that it is passionate and moving.[1] It inspires feeling (le sentiment) and gives birth to pleasure. Adapted to the Asiatic genius, it is like the nation, soft and languorous, without energy and strength, and has neither the vivacity nor the spirit of ours. The great defect of which it can be accused is that of being too uniform. It is unaware of the admirable variety in art that imitates nature and that knows how to rouse and present all the passions without confusing one with another. As different in the tender and the graceful as in the grand and sublime, the impressions that music makes should not be the same. The soul changes situation and object according to the different movements that harmonies produce in it and which it obeys without coercion. It is this successive passing from one feeling to another, this undergoing of different transformations, that keeps it in a continual agitation, constantly providing the intelligence (l'esprit) with new perceptions and perpetuating the intoxication and enchantment of our senses.

It is rare to find in Oriental music this effect of variety which originates in the diversity of our sensations. The uniformity and monotony that reigns in it poses an obstacle. There is only, so to speak, one part of ourselves that is sus-

---

1. Fonton's phrase is "pathetique et touchante."

ceptible, because there is only one of our faculties that operates. The soul is moved, but not in all its capacity. It is true that this music excels in the chromatic genus, of which it is fond. I can swear that it does move and penetrate and make one feel tender, perhaps more than does any other music. It is a pleasure that one experiences, but it is one of a thousand that one could experience. Even this pleasure ceases, on account of its continuousness, and it often degenerates into a languidness and inevitable ennui.

Indeed, if a music is monotonous, admirable as it may be otherwise, it will inevitably cause drowsiness and sleep. Reiteration of the same impressions on the fibers of the organ of hearing slow down the movement of the animal spirits by suspending activity and action, not allowing any other change and, by natural consequence, promoting sleep. What contributes further to this deadening in relation to us, is the effeminacy of most Oriental airs,[2] so contrary to our inclinations. Our attention does not know how to be captivated for long, if it is not wakened at times by something lively and animated. European ears require the strongest impressions, the most manly sounds and the most muscular, less of the melancholy and more of the gay. The people of the Orient are susceptible to the opposite sentiments. The same difference that nature has placed in our tendencies and our characters, she has also placed in the object of our likes and desires. All things provide us daily with new proofs. Since we are divided in everything else, we would be pretending in vain to be united by the usual charms that music exerts. This would be allying two incompatible things and putting some badly assorted figures in the same picture. Oriental music is compared by its partisans to a peaceful, tranquil stream, whose sweet and soothing murmuring enchains the soul and puts it to sleep in the bosom of pleasure. If I may be permitted to express myself exactly, I would say, following this comparison, that European music is a great and majestic river that sends forth its waters judiciously, measures its course by the needs of the lands that it waters, and carries with itself everywhere riches and abundance. I leave it to the connoisseurs to decide the justness of the parallel.

2. Fonton's phrase is "la moleste effeminee" or literally "effeminate molestation." Traits that he considers "feminine" are apparent throughout the essay.

121 Jean Baptiste Du Halde

A moment of intersection between European and Chinese music occurred under the reign of the Manchurian Emperor Kangxi (1662–1722), whose court produced—among various monumental collections of Chinese scholarly knowledge—*The True Meaning of Tones,* a treatise published in 1723 in a compendium along with other calendrical and acoustic subjects. The emperor's interest in music was spurred by his musical encounters with Jesuit missionaries, especially Tomas Pereira (1645–1708), who arrived in Beijing in 1673 and who eventually lived at the palace and wore the emblem of the Imperial dragon, and Teodorico Pedrini (1670–1746), who arrived in Beijing in 1711 and taught music to the children at court.

Jean Baptiste Du Halde (1674–1743), the Jesuit who served in Paris as secretary for correspondence from missionaries abroad, compiled an encyclopedic four-volume treatise on China and Chinese history and civilization. Published in 1735, the book appeared in English as early as 1736, in German from 1747 to 1756, and in Russian in 1770. It was based on the extensive missionary reports Du Halde had received, and it testifies to the Jesuit presence at the imperial court at a time of high scholarly activity. Kangxi appears prominently with regard to music, which Du Halde treats as it had been handled in his sources: anecdotally in association with the emperors of China (whose reigns are described in chronological order) and as documentary history in a section of transcriptions compiled on Kangxi's orders and preserved with the emperor's comments. One example of such an ancient declaration is given here. The longest treatment of music occurs as part of a section on the "other sciences," where the discussion of music follows sections on logic and rhetoric.

FROM *Geographical, Historical, Chronological, Political, and Physical Description of the Empire of China and of Chinese Tartary*

(1735)

THE KNOWLEDGE OF THE CHINESE IN THE OTHER SCIENCES

As one takes a look at the great numbers of libraries that are found in China, all magnificently built, equally decorated, and enriched by a prodigious quantity of books; when one considers the astonishing multitude of their doctors, and colleges established in all the cities of the empire, their observatories and the attentiveness with which they make observations; when, in addition, one reflects on the fact that study is the unique way to achieve rank and that one is raised only in proportion to one's abilities; that for more than four thousand years, there has not been, according to the laws of the empire, any but men of letters who govern the cities and provinces and who are appointed in all the posts of tribunals and of the court, then one will be tempted to believe that of nearly all the nations in the world, the Chinese nation is the most spiritual and learned.

Meanwhile in the short time one visits there, one is soon disillusioned. It is true, and one cannot forbear from acknowledging that the Chinese have much intellect: but is it with this intellect that one invents, analyzes, excavates, and investigates? They have made discoveries in all the sciences, and yet they have not perfected any of those that we call speculative and which demand some subtlety and analysis. Nevertheless, I do not wish to speak ill of the essence of their intellect nor, even less, to assert that they lack the intelligence and that cleverness that understands different subjects, seeing that they succeed in other areas which demand as much genius and understanding as our speculative sciences. But two principal obstacles oppose the progress that could have been made in these kinds of knowledge. That is, first, that there is nothing within or without the empire to stimulate and support competition; and in second place, that those who could gain distinction have no reward awaiting them. . . .

TEXT: *Description géographique, historique, chronologique, politique, et physique de l'empire de la Chine et de la Tartarie chinoise*, 4 vols. (Paris, 1735), 2: 405; 3: 264–68. Translation by Margaret Murata. Excerpts from the English translation of London, 1738–41, are in Frank Ll. Harrison, *Time, Place and Music: An Anthology of Ethnomusicological Observation, ca. 1550 to ca. 1800* (Amsterdam, 1973), pp. 161–66.

OF THEIR MUSIC

If you will believe the Chinese, they are the first inventors of music, and they boast of having formerly brought it to the highest perfection. But if what they say be true, it must have strangely degenerated, for it is at present so imperfect that it scarcely deserves the name, as may be judged by some of their airs, which I have notated to give some idea of them [see Example].

Chinese airs

Indeed in former times, music was in great esteem, and Confucius, their greatest sage, undertook to introduce its rules into every province[1] whose government he was entrusted with. The Chinese themselves of today greatly bewail the loss of these ancient books which dealt with music.

At present music is seldom used but at plays, certain holidays, weddings, and on such like occasions. The *bonzes*[2] employ it at funerals, but when they sing, they never raise and lower their voices a semitone, but only a third, a fifth, or an octave, and this harmony is very charming to the ears of the Chinese. In like manner the beauty of the concerts does not consist at all in variety of tones or of differences between parts. They all sing the same air, as is the practice throughout Asia. European music does not displease them, provided there be only one voice singing, accompanied by some instruments. But what is most marvelous in this music—I mean the contrast of different voices, of low and high sounds, sharps, fugues, and suspensions (*syncopes*)—is not at all to their taste, and seems to them a disagreeable confusion.

1. Confucius lived in the late sixth century B.C.E. Du Halde calls "the provinces" those regions that were generally separate kingdoms before the Han dynasty, c. 200 B.C.E.
2. Although the term *bonze* generally refers to the Buddhist priesthood, Du Halde probably did not intend any sectarian designation.

Unlike us they have no musical notation, nor any signs that mark the difference of pitches, the rising or falling of the voice, and all the other variations that constitute harmony; they have, however, certain characters[3] that allow one to recognize the different tones. The airs that they sing or play upon their instruments are only learned by practice after hearing them sung. Nevertheless, they make new ones from time to time, and the late Emperor Kangxi composed some himself. These airs, well played upon their instruments or sung by a good voice, have something in them that will please even a European ear.

The ease with which we are able to retain an air at only one hearing by means of notation surprised the late Emperor Kangxi extremely. In the year 1679, he called Father Grimaldi and Father Pereira[4] to the palace to play upon the organ and the harpsichord that they had formerly given him. He enjoyed our European airs and seemed to take great pleasure in them. Then he ordered his musicians to play a Chinese air upon one of their instruments and played it himself with much grace. Father Pereira took his notebooks and wrote down all the melody while the musicians were performing; and when they had finished, the Father repeated it without missing a note, as if he had practiced it a long time. The Emperor had such difficulty believing it, he seemed surprised. He bestowed great praise on the justness, beauty, and fluency of European music. He admired above all the fact that this Father had in so short a time learned an air which had given him and his musicians no small trouble; and that by help of certain signs, he was made so perceptive of it that it was impossible for him to forget it.

To be the more sure of this, he made several further trials. He sang many different airs, which the Father wrote down and repeated immediately after with the greatest exactness. "It must be owned," cried the Emperor, "that European music is incomparable, and this Father," speaking of Father Pereira, "has not his equal in all the empire." This ruler afterwards established an Academy for Music, composed of all those[5] who were most skilled in this area and committed it to the care of his third son,[6] a man of letters who had read a great deal. They began by examining all the authors that had written on this subject, causing all sorts of instruments to be made after the ancient manner and according to settled dimensions. The faults of these instruments emerged and were corrected by more modern rules.

After this they compiled a book in four volumes with the title *The True Doctrine of the Lü Lü, Written by the Emperor's Order.* To these they added

---

3. Ideograms.
4. Filippo Maria Grimaldi and Tomas Pereira, both Jesuits.
5. The other Chinese scholars were He Guozong (d. 1766), Zhang Zhao (1691–1745), Yin Reng (1674–1725), Yin Lu (1695–1767), Yin Zhi (1677–1732), Mei Gucheng (d. 1763), Chen Menglei (1651–?), Zhang Ying (1638–1708), Fang Bao (1668–1749), and Li Guangdi (1642–1718); see Gerlinde Gild-Bohne, *Das Lü Lü Zheng Yi Xubian* (Göttingen, 1991).
6. Yin Zhi, a member of the Academy of Music; see note 5 above.

a fifth, containing all the elements of European music, written by Father Pereira.[7]

The Chinese have invented eight sorts of musical instrument which they think are the closest to the human voice.[8] Some are of metal like our bells; others are made of stone, and one among the rest has some resemblance to our trumpets. There are others of skins like our drums, of which there are several kinds, and some so heavy, that to fit them for beating on they must be propped with a piece of wood. They have huge instruments with strings, but the strings are generally of silk, seldom of gut. Their fiddles (*vielles*), like those played by blind people, are as their violins: both have but three strings which one plays with a bow. But there is one instrument with seven strings, very much esteemed and not disagreeable when played upon by a skillful hand. There are others also, but they are made wholly of wood, being pretty large tablets which they clap against each other. The *bonzes* use a little board, which they touch with much art, and in good time. In short, they do have wind music. Such are their flutes, which are of two or three sorts, and an instrument composed of several pipes, which has some resemblance to our organ and on the whole an agreeable sound, but is very little, being carried in the hand.

• • •

DECLARATION OF THE EMPEROR AI DI FOR REFORMING MUSIC[9]

At present, three great abuses prevail among us: prodigality in eating and dress, etc., the search for thousands of vain ornaments, and a passion for the tender, effeminate music of Zheng and Wei.[10] From prodigality follows the ruin of families; they fall in the third generation, and the whole empire becomes poorer. The desire for vain ornaments occasions multitudes of people to attend only very useless arts and to neglect agriculture. Finally effeminate tender music inspires licentiousness. To pretend, while these subsist, to intro-

---

7. The title given here is a translation of Du Halde's translation of *Lülü zhengyi*, which he called "La Vraye Doctrine du Ly lu." The sense of the Chinese title is "rectifying the meaning of the tones." The fifth, supplementary volume that describes elementary European music theory is the *Houbian* allegedly begun by Pereira and continued by Pedrini. It translates Western terms into Chinese. A modern translation of the supplement into German appears in Gild-Bohne, note 5 above.

8. The "eight sorts of musical instruments" is a conceptual category in Chinese music, that of *bayin* or "eight sounds." The eight are metal, stone, skin, silk, bamboo, wood, gourd, and earth. The "tablets" are the large wooden clappers called *paiban*. The small "pipe organ" mentioned by Du Halde is the *sheng*. The large silk-strung instruments may be the *zheng;* the seven-string instrument is probably the *qin*, whose invention is attributed to Fu Xi, the first emperor of China (see Du Halde, vol. 1, p. 273).

9. Du Halde drew upon the *Imperial Collection Containing Edicts, Declarations, Ordinances and Instructions of the Emperors of Different Dynasties* that Emperor Kangxi had had his scholars assemble. Although Du Halde's immediate source representing this collection is not known, among the documents was an edict on music over 1,700 years old, which he presented with Kangxi's remarks. Du Halde's words are in italics. Ai Di, a Han emperor, reigned 7–1 B.C.E.

10. These are the names of a country, formerly two petty kingdoms. [Tr.]

duce plenty and innocence into a state is to pretend that a muddy spring makes a pure and limpid stream. Confucius was quite right to say that the music of Zheng should be avoided, because it inspired looseness of manners.

By these presents, we discharge our musical establishment and all the officials who were in charge of it. As for the usual music for the ceremony of Tiao,[11] we do not plan to affect them nor the instruments of war. These are things approved in our [jing][12] but no officials are appointed for these purposes. It is our wish that there be an inquiry ascertaining to which of the other officials it will be proper to commit the management of these matters.

• • •

The Emperor Kangxi, who loved music and involved himself in it, made the following remarks about this declaration: Music has the virtue to calm the heart, and it is for this that the wise man loves it. Also, while amusing himself, he may take exercise in governing well by a very correct and ready application of government to music.[13] But with regard to wanton music, that admits of no comparison. To what good end is so much expense? Ai Di was right to fire them.[14] *A gloss says that he saved in this regard the appointments and maintenance of 440 persons.*

11. Frederick Lau, whose help with this text has been invaluable, has suggested that, as opposed to *Gong Diao* or "court music," the "ceremony of *Tiao*" is the *jiaosi,* a rite performed only by the emperor. The term implies an offering to nature or to spirits of nature.

12. Ancient books of rules [Tr.]. Du Halde uses the word "King" here; without seeing the Chinese character it is difficult to know what Chinese word was meant in his source. The word "jing," which means "classic," could refer, according to F. Lau (see note 11 above), to the ancient *Lüshi Chunqiu,* which includes sections on the use of music in various ceremonies.

13. Kang Xi is comparing the knowledge and discipline required for musical performance to the just application of laws by a ruler.

14. That is, the officials in charge of the musical establishment.

GLOSSARY OF FOREIGN
PERFORMANCE TERMS

accento (It., pl. *accenti;* Lat. *superjectio, accentus*)   A short, local ornament. Vocal illustrations from Zacconi (1592) to Bismantova (1677) suggest
they are usually escape tones added to descending passing figures that
emphasize the tone to which they move, or anticipations of the next tone in
rising stepwise motion. Various writers describe subtle changes of volume
and tempo that are part of its execution. Muffat (1698, his Example YY)
recognizes six types of single-note accents. The upper accent, the lower
accent (Lat. *subsumptio*), and the salterello (in French *sursaut*) come before
the second tone (beginning the new bow stroke). He gives the superficial, or
common accent; the *calamento* (Fr. *relâchement*), and *dispersione* as subdivisions of the first tone, taken with the same bow. These accent the second
tone by leaping to it.

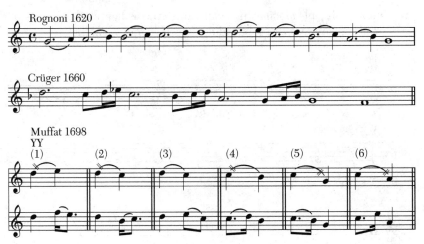

Rognoni 1620

Crüger 1660

Muffat 1698
YY
(1)   (2)   (3)   (4)   (5)   (6)

Artusi's examples of *accenti* in the *Imperfections of Modern Music* (1600)
resemble more the *portar la voce*. Muffat classes the *port de voix* as a a type
of "accentuation." See also PORTAR LA VOCE.

affetto (It., pl. *affetti*)   A general term for short, local ornaments. Apart from
its use in music, "affetto" may also refer to an affection, or passion. Both
senses come together in a description by Caccini (1614): "Affect, for whoever sings, is nothing other than the expression of the words chosen to be

sung and their ideas, by means of the power of different notes and their varied stresses, tempered by softness and loudness, a power capable of moving the affection of the listener."

craquer (Fr.)   In string playing, to take two or more detached notes in a single bow stroke, usually an up-bow.

esclamazione (It., pl. *esclamazioni*)   As defined first by Caccini in *Le nuove musiche* (1602), a technique for singing longer tones, in which the voice "relaxes" a bit after the first attack and then intensifies for the duration of the note. This intensification is usually translated in modern terms as a gradual *crescendo*. Dotted values appear in many illustrations, with the voice relaxing again for the smaller note or notes that follow the longer one.

gorgia or **gorga** (It., pl. *gorghe*)   A general name for vocal embellishments; related to the verb "gorgheggiare," to warble. In Zacconi (1592, bk. 1, chap. 66), they apply to note values of eighths and sixteenths (*crome, semicrome*).

groppo, gruppo (It., pl. *groppi, gruppi*)   In the earlier seventeenth century, the name for a neighbor-note trill. In most illustrations, it is notated with equally subdivided note values and closes with a turning figure. Whether they are "simple" or "double" seems to depend on their duration.

movimento (It., pl. *movimenti*)   Simple, stepwise figures that fill in pitch intervals of various sizes, subdividing tones of various lengths.

passaggi (It., sing. *passaggio;* Fr. *passages;* Eng. divisions, diminutions; Lat. *variatio, transitus*)   Embellishments created by ornamental subdivisions, often extremely rapid, of melodic tones, usually continuing for a measure or more. Although they originated in the sixteenth century as improvised

diminutions, in the early seventeenth century, a number of composers published "motetti passeggiati" and "arie passeggiate" (J. Kapsberger, 1612),
"psalmi passeggiati" (F. Severi, 1615), etc. See Francesco Rognoni's *Selva de
varii passaggi secondo l'uso moderno* (1620).

portar la voce (It., Fr. *port de voix*)   A re-articulated "accento." The re-
articulation of the first tone of the pair can be a subdivision of it, or it can
be on the beat of the second tone, delaying and robbing it of a little time. In
his *Imperfections of Modern Music,* Artusi illustrates the latter as an example
of *accento.* Depending on the affect desired, time and loudness, and perhaps
pitch (e.g., in the application of a tremolo or microtonal changes) were
adjusted to intensify its effect. Muffat (1698, his Example ZZ) equates *port
de voix* with the Italian term "appoggiatura," that is, an *accento* with the re-
articulation of the first tone of a pair occurring on the new bow stroke.

raddoppiate (It., sing. *raddoppiata*)   Probably meaning doubled figures or
notes in a melismatic embellishment, in two senses: (1) doubling by repetition of the figure itself (which lengthens the embellishment; examples identified in Crüger 1660 are melodic sequences); or (2) mixing subdivisions of
differing note values in the same melisma, which increases its speed. The
latter sense is implied by the seventeenth-century phrases "double relish" or
in French, *double cadence.*

ricercata (It., usually pl. *ricercate*)   A general term for free improvisations on
keyboard or plucked string instrument that does not exclude fugal textures;
a prelude. This sense is still given in the 1708 *Dictionaire de musique* of
S. Brossard. Roger North (1728) called it "a this-way-that-way manner, like
searching."

sprezzatura (It.)   In general, ease of manner, with the inborn bearing of good
breeding. As used by the Florentine monodists, its achievement in singing

depended on several musical techniques that imparted flexibility, graciousness, and spontaneity in performance. As described by Giulio Caccini (1614), "*Sprezzatura* is that elegance given to a melody by several incorrect eighths or sixteenths on different tones, incorrect with respect to their rhythm *(tempo)*, thus freeing the melody from a certain narrow limitation and dryness and making it pleasant, free, and airy, just as in common speech, eloquence and invention make affable and sweet the matters being spoken of."

tenuë (Fr., pl. *tenuës*)   A tone held for the length of a measure or more.

tirata (It., *tirate;* Fr. *tirade,* pl. *tirades)*   A stepwise succession of notes of the same rhythmic value. Toward the end of the seventeenth century, they were often of eighth or sixteenth notes, beginning after a rest on the beat.

vaghezza (It., usually pl. *vaghezze)*   A term for ornaments in general.

References

Lodovico Zacconi, *Prattica di musica* (Venice, 1592; repr. 1967, 1982).

Giovanni Maria Artusi, *L'Artusi, overo Delle imperfettioni della moderna musica* (Venice, 1600; repr. 1968).

Giulio Caccini, *Le nuove musiche* (Florence, 1602); mod. ed. by H. Wiley Hitchcock (Madison, 1970).

Giulio Caccini, *Nuove musiche e nuove maniera di scriverle* (Florence, 1614); mod. ed. by H. Wiley Hitchcock (Madison, 1978).

Francesco Rognoni, *Selva di varii passaggi secondo l'uso moderno* (Milan, 1620; repr. 1970).

Johannes Crüger, *Musicae practicae praecepta brevia* (Berlin, 1660).

Lorenzo Penna, *Li primi albori musicali* (Bologna 1672; repr. of 4th, 1684 ed. Bologna, 1969).

Bartolome. Bismantova, "Compendio musicale," MS dated Ferrara, 1677–79 (facs. ed. Florence, 1978).

Georg Muffat, *Suavioris harmoniae instrumentalis hyporchematicae florilegium secundum* (Passau, 1698), preface; mod. ed. by W. Kolneder (Strasbourg, 1970).

Sébastien de Brossard, *Dictionaire de musique* (Amsterdam, n.d.; repr. Geneva, 1992).

Roger North, "The Musical Grammarian," in *Roger North's The Musical Grammarian 1728,* ed. by M. Chan and J. C. Kassler (Cambridge, 1990).

V

THE LATE EIGHTEENTH CENTURY

Edited by WYE JAMISON ALLANBROOK

INTRODUCTION

*W*hen the first edition of *Source Readings in Music History* was reissued in 1965 in five separate volumes devoted to the five canonical periods of music history, the documents from the latter half of the eighteenth century were collected under the customary heading "The Classic Era." In the years since, however, there has been a growing recognition that period labels are vexed, each in its own way, and perhaps none more than this one. Like most period labels in music history ("Romantic" being a notable exception), "Classic" or "Classical" is a designation applied only in retrospect; it is not to be found anywhere in the pages of the method books and essays from which these selections are drawn. Such designations nevertheless offer a taxonomic power and convenience of reference that are considered by the user to outweigh the dangers of the procrustean bed they provide for the time period in question. In this particular case, however, the label bespeaks an act of appropriation that long posed a serious barrier to our coming to understand late eighteenth-century music as an independent phenomenon. In at least two of the word's accepted senses—"model of excellence" and "that which is distinguished from Romantic"—"Classic" is a designation given by writers whose gaze is turned back to the past, in a spirit either of self-congratulation or of conservative dismay: they think to find there the source of what is best in the writer's present, or to divine a benchmark against which to measure modern decline. Behind either search lies a tacit confidence about continuity between the present and its recent past: if one claims a work or a style as a model, there is a presumption that one knows how to use it, and hence what it is. The process of appropriation began in the early nineteenth century when E. T. A. Hoffmann declared the music of the preceding decades truly romantic—of a piece with his musical present. In an 1813 article titled "Beethoven's Instrumental Music,"[1] Hoffmann pronounced instrumental music to be the "only genuinely romantic art," because "its sole subject is the infinite." Beethoven, of course, he judged to be the most profound practitioner of this new and transcendent music, in which "the lyre of Orpheus opened the portals of Orcus" to "disclose . . . an unknown realm." But he also swept Mozart and Haydn into the charmed circle, styling them as the originators of the Romantic spirit, and in so doing he fixed them firmly on this side of the boundary between the musical past and present. Although a later generation reclassified

1. See No. 160, pp. 1193–98.

these first two Romantics as Classic prototypes for the Romantic canon, they never lost their claim to kinship, but were treated as familial and hence familiar—as composers whose stylistic premises were transparent, presenting no obscurity to the critical eye.

This assumption endured with remarkable persistence in one form or another for almost 150 years. Since in the late 1940s, when the original version of this anthology was being assembled, the music of the late eighteenth century was still considered continuous with "our music," there seemed to be little point in seriously examining the premises of its composition. The great pedagogical treatises of the mid-eighteenth century—of Leopold Mozart and Carl Philipp Emanuel Bach, for example—were just beginning to appear in English editions as Oliver Strunk was preparing translations from them for the first edition of *Source Readings*. The notion of instrumental music's "transcendence" and the formalist attitudes that it implied were common currency. The vocabulary of analysis was still that imposed by nineteenth-century theorists of "sonata form." Standard teaching editions of Mozart piano sonatas still came with a critical apparatus at the top of the page identifying Exposition, Development, Recapitulation, and Principal and Secondary Theme; these instructions seemed as indisputable as the directions for rendering ornaments which appeared at the foot of the page. It is not surprising that the only real intellectual matter of the period seemed to reside in quasi-literary issues such as the "Querelle des bouffons" (the "Quarrel of the Comedians," the Parisian pamphlet war over the merits of French and Italian music that raged in the early 1750s), the virtues of "reform" (Gluckian) opera, and, in performance practice, the correct rendering of the trill.

Only recently have musicologists, in part through investigations of some of the texts newly included in this volume, begun to realize that this utterly familiar music was nonetheless written under premises more remote from us than could previously have been conceived. The late eighteenth century was an era of practical pedagogues in the Capellmeister tradition, "compleat" musicians trained to competence in every aspect of composition and performance, sacred and secular, in a court's music "chapel," and prepared to instruct their successors in similar skills. They wrote composition method books much as they did instrument tutors—in the conviction that composition is a craft (rather than an unconscious creative act), and thus teachable to the pliant student. They started their musical apprentices off with small pieces, teaching them rules of thumb that led seamlessly to the composition of larger works. Joseph Riepel's *praeceptor* states with playful clarity twice in nine pages, in graphic outsize fonts, a principle that will have its final working-out in the *Versuch einer Anleitung zur Composition,* the composition treatise of Heinrich Christoph Koch: A MINUET IS NOTHING OTHER THAN A CONCERTO, AN ARIA, OR A SYMPHONY. "Minuet" in this sentence translates into the minimal version of what today is often called "rounded binary form"—a sixteen-measure piece organized in units of four measures (subdividable into two-measure units) that makes a full circuit harmonically, and achieves rhetorical completeness through an increasingly emphatic degree of punctuation at the ends of its articulating cuts or phrase lengths. Symphony and sonata movements, as both Riepel and Koch go on to show, are simply expanded versions of the basic minuet syntax; *galant* dance rhetoric provides the skeleton for composition.

Dice games for composing minuets were a parlor commonplace, and a spirit of gamesmanship suffuses these expansions, which are achieved by paraphrase and parody, by combination and permutation, in short, by an understanding of "the mechanical rules of melody," in Koch's own formulation. The teaching of classical rhetoric that was crucial for Riepel and Koch—and to the music of their contemporaries—was not the doctrine of figures or local embellishments, but the more basic one of prosodic lengths. Essentially Koch's "mechanical rules" show the composer how to invent articulated segments that are intrinsically musical, yet have the conviction of good verbal rhetoric—the equivalent in music of ancient rhetoric's *kommata* ("coins" or "chips"), *kola* ("members"), and *periodoi* ("circuits" or "cycles")—commas, colons, and periods.[2] Koch calls them incises *(Einschnitte)*, phrases *(Sätze)*, and periods *(Perioden)*. These names were originally coined to refer to the lengths themselves, not to the signs that designate the ends of the lengths; the marks of punctuation took their names from the cuts they punctuate. Koch's teachings of "melodic punctuation" (again his own formulation) are not in fact rules but the enunciation of syntactical paths with subsidiary options. The thrust of the Ciceronian period lies behind them: expansion is not symmetrical (architectonic) but linear or dynamic. More and greater lengths are required toward the end of a section or movement, where persuasion naturally concentrates its efforts. An architecture that was "frozen music," as Goethe famously declared, would have resulted in startlingly misshapen buildings.

Rather than a prefabricated vessel filled with striking musical ideas (a description more appropriate to Romantic sonata form), a movement of a musical work was to these teachers a canny manipulation of these musical lengths or phrases, conceived in rhetoric, as it were, and generated in dance. Koch's definition of the composition of movements and works as "the connection of melodic sections into periods of greater length" is not the same as "form"; the emphasis is on process—construction—rather than structure, the fluid over the frozen. Later in the *Versuch,* Koch extends a simple eight-measure bourrée tune to thirty-two measures to become a section of a sonata movement by means of his expansion techniques. As commas and colons are joined in periods, periods are joined to make the larger whole, and these shapes find differentiation according to medium and occasion—symphony, quartet, concerto. The essential shape for the larger works, like that of the smaller ones, is binary: one massive period with "appendices," closing on the key of the fifth degree,

---

2. See, for example, Johann Mattheson, *Der vollkommene Capellmeister,* trans. Ernest C. Harriss (Ann Arbor, Michigan: UMI Press, 1981), pt. II, chap. 9.

comprises the first part, while the second is divided into two, with anticipatory and recapitulatory functions. Like Koch, Francesco Galeazzi and Jérôme-Joseph de Momigny see a movement as essentially created of periods; they take a step beyond Koch, however, in classifying periods by affect and function. Galeazzi articulates the frequent habit of the cantabile period, which he calls the *passo caratteristico* or "characteristic passage," and Momigny in 1806 differentiates periods even more narrowly, inventing an analytical vocabulary—"opening," "spirited," and "connective" periods, for example—that reflects their functions as dynamic rather than architectonic entities. Discussions of instrumental genres by Johann Joachim Quantz in the 1750s and Koch in the 1790s provide a gauge of instrumental music's gradual advance toward independence and individuation. For Quantz a symphony is still a *sinfonia*—an opera prelude (he complains that it is chronically unsuitable to the ensuing action). Koch, on the other hand, is describing fully independent symphony, quartet, and concerto movements, and has obviously been moved by the newly achieved grandeur of these genres. He compares the concerto to a Greek tragedy in its passionate dialogue between actors and chorus.

In this comparison of Koch's, as well as in the preceding discussion of instrumental music, speech and voice are fundamental reference points. The word *melody—Melodie, chant, cantilena*—has a remarkable prominence in most of the texts included here, in discussions of compositional techniques as well as in those of expression. This focus on the leading line in preference to the supporting harmony—either that of contrapuntal parts or of the *basse fondamentale*—is a significant compositional premise, which had been urged previously by Johann Mattheson in the earlier part of the century.[3] The operative metaphor is not the Romantic "song without words," but a precise and articulate melos. Jean-Jacques Rousseau, in his *Essay on the Origin of Language*, considers melody to be the equivalent of design or line in painting, and in his *Letter on French Music* he stresses the importance of the "unity of melody," that is, music in which all parts function as support for the cantilena. Galeazzi defines and discusses a movement as a "well-conducted melody." It is in this understanding of melody that the mechanical and the expressive meet. "After all," writes Vincenzo Manfredini, "music is only singing," or, in other commonplaces of the day, a melody that must "speak to the heart" (again Rousseau) through a "language of feelings" (Daniel Gottlob Türk).[4] The human voice implies expressive intent, and the cantilena leads the listener through a movement. One can learn to deploy the instrumental cantilena as mechanical figures, but once in place it is expressive as the human voice is expressive—a leading edge that controls the design with a projection of one or another pas-

3. Mattheson, pt. II, chaps. 1–41.
4. Hester Piozzi draws an analogy between melody and harmony, innocence and virtue, and comes down on the side of virtue (that is, complexity—"worked-outness"). But it was precisely the quality of "innocence"—a simple directness that "moves the heart"—that the composers of the late 1700s set as their goal.

sion. Hoffmann had speculated that Beethoven was less successful in writing vocal music because that medium "excludes the character of indefinite longing"; since words must always signify, vocal music is too precise. That very precision of reference was the virtue that had moved eighteenth-century writers to hold up the vocal as their paradigm: reference to a shared world of human experience was the means by which music moved its auditors. Momigny reflects this idea when he supplies the cantilena of the first movement of Mozart's String Quartet in D Minor, K. 421, with an imagined text that conveys the affect of noble pathos embodied in the music by personifying it in the figure of *Didone abbandonata*. Here the instrumental is not the ineffable, as it later becomes; explanation of its nonsemantic reference takes the form of translating its commas, colons, and periods into the signifying lengths of speech. Momigny's dramatic text is a "program," perhaps, but an analytical one, reflecting his confidence that one can articulate the "precise" (his word) intentions of the composer.

Momigny's immediate predecessors, however, did not need to illustrate the dominant expression of a piece by crafting a parallel poem. Expression could still be objectified into affects or stances, and the means of its communication—for both composer and performer—were a matter of instruction. What makes this possible is the connection of expression with gesture; oft quoted is Cicero's statement in *De oratore:* "Every motion of the soul has by nature its own look and sound and gesture; one's whole frame and countenance and all the sounds one utters resound like strings in a lyre as they are struck by a motion of the soul."[5] Each affect has a characteristic motion, which can be given musical shape to a great extent—as Johann Philipp Kirnberger points out—by the proper choice of meter. Kirnberger urges the performer to internalize these gestures by assiduous practice in the rhythms of social dance music. All pedagogues worth their salt include a discussion that resembles Kirnberger's anatomy of meters, though not as tirelessly complete. Although Kirnberger was considered old-fashioned because of his focus on the music of J. S. Bach, Türk echoes many of Kirnberger's prescriptions at the end of the century, turning them into finely detailed instructions to the amateur keyboard player for the performance of music expressing various affects. Türk also includes the ubiquitous discussion on the taxonomy of style—high, middle, low; church, chamber, theater; French, German, Italian; strict, free:[6] shared human venues as well as shared human passions dictate the shape and texture

5. See, for example, Charles Batteux, *The Fine Arts Reduced to a Single Principle* (Paris, 1747), trans. Edward A. Lippman, in *Musical Aesthetics: A Historical Reader, Volume I: Antiquity to the Eighteenth Century* (New York: Pendragon Press, 1986), p. 266; Daniel Webb, *Observations on the Correspondence between Poetry and Music* (London, 1769), in Lippman, vol. 1, p. 202; Johann Nikolaus Forkel, *Allgemeine Geschichte der Musik* (Leipzig, 1788), p. 282, n. 5.

6. See, for example, Mattheson, pt. 1, chap. 10; Johann Adolf Scheibe, *Der critische Musikus* (Leipzig, 1745), vol. 1, chaps 13–15, 23–24; Koch, *Musikalisches Lexikon* (Frankfurt, 1802), "Styl, Schreibart." Hester Lynch Piozzi's account of various countries' predilections in music, heavily colored with *sensibilité*, is an idiosyncratic version of the taxonomy of national styles.

of a work. On the other hand, personal style—that most remarked on and remarkable characteristic of Romantic composers—merits only a passing mention in Türk's discussion, just as Koch cites Mozart and Haydn not as world-historical figures but as composers who excelled in meeting the requirements of a particular genre. Only Johann Friedrich Reichardt's whimsical imagining that Haydn, Mozart, and Beethoven built themselves distinctive styles as snails construct their shells—a summerhouse, a palace, and a cathedral respectively—foreshadows later attitudes, both in its stress on individual stylistic differences and in its choice of the architectural metaphor.

Among those who wrote more generally about style and expression there is little disagreement yet—with the possible exception of Michel-Paul-Guy de Chabanon—about the existence of a codifiable relation between expression and gesture, or expression and motion. Some balk at the use of the traditional word "imitation" to describe music's depiction of the motions of the soul, preferring to limit the term's significance to the representation of natural phenomena and calling any other use "expression." But they all take for granted an external referent for the act: it is not "self-expression." Often, taking their cue from Cicero, they elaborate an actual physiology for the relation—a theory of sympathetic vibrations in which the impression of the passion is communicated to the soul via the effect of the tones on the nerves. Johann Jakob Engel is impressed by the phenomenon of the musical glasses, an instrument whose eerie tones were said to be capable of sending the average person into a deep melancholy: "man is only an instrument," writes Chabanon. This doctrine leads Engel to a psychophysiological theory of music as an imitation that "paints" not an external object, but the impression the object makes on the soul. Because its objects are human passions, which can be represented by certain codifiable note patterns, Engel's remains a theory of affect, but one that by internalizing expression confirms with a new certainty that mere natural phenomena are not a proper object of imitation. Chabanon, on the other hand, is a maverick who takes a strong stand against imitation, preferring to think of music as direct, unmediated sensation, with no capacity for reference. But even in his writings the prevailing teachings are deep-seated: he still assumes a natural connection between the motion of tones and states of the soul. He is, perhaps unwittingly, one of the few writers to articulate and give grudging approval to the kind of mediated or topical imitation that was so central to the expressive vocabulary of late eighteenth-century compositions. In his formulation, imitation is plausible when the composer "gives one melody the character of another," that is, when serious music imitates occasional music, and the common coin of popular song and dance becomes the expressive vocabulary of symphonies and sonatas. Mozart stands somewhere between Engel and Chabanon, taking what could be characterized as a more "composerly" view. To him music both is and is not the things it imitates: it can paint a throbbing heart, but it also has forms and syntactical properties that are irreducibly its own, and not to be exceeded. Two currents seem to flow together in his opinion—an assumption that music is not entirely a mimetic art, because at some level its materials are distinguished as well by a purely internal consistency of relation, and a conviction reflecting the widespread notion that the more violent and base passions are not appropriate subjects for music: the art should edify, not introduce degraded motions into the soul. As music comes to be considered at once more private and more transcendental, such seemingly conservative opinions will become a staple of the new aesthetic.

Vocal music being the eighteenth century's dominant paradigm, opera may seem to come late to this essay, but with good reason. While *opera buffa* was the operatic genre that exerted the most pressure on the development of late eighteenth-century style, as a popular form it had developed no real critical or pedagogical texts of its own. Opera was, of course, at the forefront of critical debate throughout the century. A prodigious amount of ink was expended in discussions of the relative merits of French and Italian opera in the three famous literary duels of the eighteenth century: the first revolved around the opera of Lully, a second—the notorious "Querelle des bouffons"—was sparked by the 1752 appearance in Paris of a troupe of Italian *buffi,* or comedians, and the third pitted the operas of Christoph Willibald Gluck against those of the Italian Niccolò Piccinni. In addition to the question of music and national character, there were several other axes to this famous debate, only roughly coincident: old versus new-fangled, words versus music, serious versus comic, and reform versus unreconstructed, or "whatever will sell." Mozart and Francesco Algarotti could be seen as staking out opposing extremes in the words and music debate: Algarotti (seconded by the reform-minded Gluck) described the composer as a tyrannical sovereign, while Mozart, in a letter to his father, playfully compared the poet to a trumpet player, a mere purveyor of professional tricks. Although not an essay on musical comedy *per se,* Rousseau's famous *Letter on French Music* was occasioned by comic opera, in the form of Giovanni Battista Pergolesi's intermezzo *La serva padrona* (in his lamentably short life, this Neapolitan composer managed to create two cultural icons—this intermezzo and his *Stabat mater,* the most frequently published work in the latter half of the century). Rousseau's bellicose declaration that "the French have no music and cannot have any; or . . . if they ever have, it will be so much the worse for them" was quoted persistently in essays throughout the rest of the century, and *buffa* arias were praised for their simplicity and clarity of motive, the propulsive power and expressive flexibility of their rhythms, and the aptness of their language for musical setting; the Chevalier Chastellux credited the Italians with having invented the musical period (drawing his paradigm not from *opera buffa* but from *opera seria*—his idol was the poet Pietro Metastasio).[7] The reverence that Charles Burney expressed upon entering the

7. F-J. de Chastellux, *Essai sur l'union de la poésie et de la musique* (Paris, 1765), p. 17.

city of Naples, "impressed with the highest of ideas of the perfect state in which I should find practical music," is a tribute to the extraordinary influence that city had had in Europe as the birthplace of *opera buffa*.

While all the programs of earnest reformers could not make the operas of Gluck any more than a memorable cul-de-sac in operatic history, *buffa* not only defined three of the greatest operas that hold the stage today—*Le nozze di Figaro, Don Giovanni,* and *Così fan tutte*—but also played a significant role in the shaping of late eighteenth-century style, one that even today is incompletely articulated. In addition to the considerable impact of its simplicity and popular spirit, *buffa* made a critical contribution to the development of contrast as a compositional premise through the witty economy of comic representation that enabled characteristic styles or *topoi* to bump up against one another while remaining recognizable entities. Yet *buffa* had no Tosi, no Mancini.[8] Scrambling to get the next new work on the boards, its composers did not take the time to frame statements of intent in the form of dedicatory epistles, and the art was too much of a popular form to encourage systematizers. Praise of *buffa's* power came from some unlikely quarters: Algarotti admired its direct expressiveness, which he claimed occurred *faute de mieux,* as a result of the limited abilities of its singers, and Mancini expressed admiration for its actors, the like of which were unfortunately no longer to be found on the *seria* stage. But Vincenzo Manfredini's rather chaotic polemic—an attempt to define an eighteenth-century *seconda prattica*—is as close as we come to a description of the aria styles of Mozart and his colleagues, and it does not offer much in the way of definition.

There is, however, an extraordinary and baffling work of the imagination that enacts *buffa's* power in an unforgettable but unsettling way: Denis Diderot's *Rameau's Nephew*. Left unpublished until 1804, it could be said to a point a way—a *via negativa*—to the aesthetic conversion that occurred at the beginning of the nineteenth century. Halfway through the dialogue, the Nephew, that brilliantly abject changeling and court jester, delivers a pedantic lecture on the Rousseauian view of melody as an imitation of the cry of passion, in which he compares *buffa's* Parisian triumph to an act of religious subversion (the bloodless *coup d'état* of the foreign god). Then he is off into a manic display—a performance of a performance, affecting all the styles, playing all the parts, working himself into an inspired frenzy. But this time when the lyre of Orpheus opens the portals of Orcus, all that happens is that gibbering ghosts fly forth, brushing past the faces of the astonished spectators. In the hands of this imitator, the kaleidoscopic *buffa* style—the style of styles—suddenly seems morally bankrupt. Lacking a moral self, the Nephew is caught in an infinite

---

8. Pier Francesco Tosi (c. 1653–1732) and Giambattista Mancini (1714–1800), both eminent castrati who were also singing teachers, wrote the definitive texts on vocal practice in *opera seria* for the early and later halves of the eighteenth century. For Tosi's treatise see pp. 551–54; for Mancini's see pp. 865–75.

regress, standing ever outside of the things he imitates with such devilish clarity. One thinks of Don Giovanni and Leporello expressing exaggerated comic pity at the antics of the fulminating Elvira. Until now we have been tacitly viewing the imitator as a benevolent deity, arranging his representations on the magic-lantern screen for our pleasure and edification. In this account he becomes a fractured soul, a madman, a demon perhaps. Perhaps the escape from this dark side of comedy lies in E. T. A. Hoffmann's "music of indefinite longing"—a longing for a lost innocence. Germaine de Staël gives a positive face to this nostalgia in her brief essay on Rousseau. The metaphysics of sensibility transforms the characteristic style—in this case the Swiss herdsman's song, the *ranz des vaches*—from a representation among representations into a Proustian object that provides a window into a lost past, where women are young again and men are moral. Wrenched from the context of the variegated mimetic discourse shaped by *buffa,* the musical *topos* has become a signifier of our separation from Arcadia, and a stimulus to the state of yearning melancholy that seems to offer to lead us back. There would be no recrossing this deep aesthetic divide.

·   ·   ·

It is in the very nature of this project that the following list of acknowledgments is long. It was clear from the start that a satisfactory completion would depend on extensive consultation with my colleagues in the field. Consult I did, and was overwhelmed by the volume and generosity of the replies. An extraordinary number of people took time away from their work to reflect on what texts they would like to see represented in an anthology of this sort. If there are significant omissions in this selection—and there certainly are—my consultants bear no blame for my idiosyncrasies. But from them I derived a rich list of suggestions and, more important, a valuable perspective against which to make my final choices. I owe particular thanks in this regard to Katherine Bergeron, Bruce Alan Brown, Scott Burnham, Floyd K. Grave, Deborah Hayes, Eugene Helm, Jan LaRue, Janet M. Levy, Justin London, Frederick Neumann, William S. Newman, Ruth Halle Rowen, Susan Snook-Luther, Jane R. Stevens, Cynthia Verba, and Neal Zaslaw. Special gratitude is due to Leonard G. Ratner, who consulted with me at length; to Mary Hunter, whose guidance was critical in the selection of new texts concerning opera; to Stefan Eckert and Ingeborg Ratner for their help on the Riepel translation; and to Curtis Price and his colleagues Robert Hume and Judith Milhous, who generously ˙prepared a selection from the diaries of Susanna Burney that they are just now bringing to light. I am grateful to all those who allowed me to reprint their translations, and especially to Nancy K. Baker, Bathia Churgin, and Raymond Haggh, who worked closely with me in preparing the final selection from their work. Jeanne Pang Goyal of Stanford University, Wallace Plourde at the St. John's College Library, and Judy Tsou at the UC Berkeley Music Library tracked down elusive texts. Consultations with my Strunk coworkers Ruth Solie and Margaret Murata were informative and consoling, Michael Ochs was forbearing beyond my deserts in the final stages of the process, and Leo Treitler has been the consummate editor, whose intelligence and tact have made a pleasure out of hard work.

THE PRACTICE OF COMPOSITION: MEASURE AND PHRASE

122 Joseph Riepel

Joseph Riepel was born in Austria in 1709 and schooled in Linz and Graz, where he studied philosophy and music. After some years of study in Dresden with a pupil of Johann Joseph Fux, he moved to Regensburg in 1751, where he pursued a career as a composer, violinist, and theorist in the chapel of the Count of Thurn and Taxis until his death in 1782.

Riepel's major theoretical work was *Anfangsgründe zur musicalischen Setz-kunst (Fundamentals of Musical Composition)* a work published in five chapters over a period of sixteen years, from 1752 till 1768. It is cast as a dialogue between a pupil and a teacher, probably in imitation of the *Gradus ad Parnassum* of Fux, to whom Riepel pays tribute in his first chapter. In the same section he seeks to regularize the study of melody, a concern relatively new to eighteenth-century theory and probably activated by the growing popularity of the *galant* style, with its emphasis on short phrases organized into clear and symmetrical periods. The first book of its kind to appear, Riepel's treatise may not have the lucidity of organization attained by his successor, Heinrich Christoph Koch, but his influence on Koch was considerable. Koch praises Riepel as one who "shed the first rays of light" over "matters that were then still completely hidden in darkness."

FROM *Fundamentals of Musical Composition*

(1752)

CHAPTER ONE. DE RHYTHMOPOEÏA, OR ABOUT RHYTHMIC ORDERING[1]

Pupil. My honorable schoolmaster in Monsberg sends friendly greetings to your honor, and asks whether you might teach me a little something in composition.

Master. I am glad the schoolmaster has so much confidence in me.

Pupil. He thinks very highly of your honor, that much I know.

TEXT: The original edition (Frankfurt and Leipzig, 1752), pp. 1–9. Translation by Wye J. Allanbrook.

1. *De metro.* Although often, even among the most trustworthy writers, foot, meter, and rhythm are absolutely the same. So says Vossius, *De poematum cantu et viribus rhythmi,* p. 11. [Au.] Isaac Vossius was a Netherlands scholar whose treatise *On the Song of Poetry and the Powers of Rhythm,* delivered as lectures at Oxford in 1673, concerned the expressive powers of meter and rhythm.

Master. I am obliged to him. But excessive ceremony could possibly just get in our way. Never in my life have I been able to tolerate these titles. If it's all right with you, let us say *du* to one another.

Pupil. With the greatest of pleasure; this way I know that we are dealing with each other sincerely. As you can see, my teacher has supplied me with a few sheets of paper, so that you can write down the fundamental rules for me.

Master. Given the inexhaustible sea of music, it is less feasible to contain all the rules of composition on a few sheets of paper than it is to squeeze the Danube through a narrow fountain.[2]

Pupil. But my master says that I should try to be finished with you soon. He himself wants to take me under his wing afterwards, and make a complete man out of me.

Master. I believe that. I know many schoolmasters who are always ready to give advice to any would-be Capellmeister. I hope your master is not the worst of them. But I will say this to you—We won't be finished with our writing in two or three days, especially since I at any rate do not have the time to be brief as well as clear. So I'll be direct at some times, circuitous at others, and I'll write down only a little something about all these rules. But it's better to write extensively about this little something than nothing at all. In short: in fourteen days you should learn from me what it took me more than fourteen years to learn from others. But *nota bene:* only in so far as you grasp everything well. Now tell me if you have good notions and thoughts in your head to put on paper.

Pupil. Oh yes, if I can only compose the bass for them.

Master. That you should learn from me in a single day. But first I want to know whether you have an adequate knowledge of the proper arrangement of the melody. For he who wishes to build houses must have the proper materials.

Pupil. Then I'll quickly compose some French dances, or so-called minuets, to prove my capability.

Master. It is certainly no great glory to compose minuets, but on the other hand it is very exacting. For a *minuet,* as far as its working-out is concerned, is *nothing other than a concerto, an aria, or a symphony.* You'll see this clearly in a few days. So we'll tend to begin in a wholly small and insignificant fashion, but with the aim of achieving from that something greater and more praiseworthy.

Pupil. In my opinion there is nothing in the world easier to compose than a minuet. I've actually ventured to write down a whole dozen quickly, one after another. Just look, for example, at one in C. (I just want to see what fault will be found with it.)

---

2. *Verum gutta cavat lapidem* [But a drop will hollow out a stone]. And I make this remark just as a pastime; I'm not willingly idle when I can have something to make sport with. [Au.].

I have written in numbers above the measures so that if, contrary to all expectation, there should be any error you can point it out more clearly. I certainly don't mean to boast.

Master. Good heavens! You don't yet know one note from another. I will extract from this minuet—if I must call it that—some singing or cantabile measures. Otherwise, please whom it will, I myself wouldn't give you good pipe tobacco for it.

Pupil. I couldn't have dreamt this. What's the reason?

Master. No. 1. I say that *an even number of measures is pleasing to the ear in all compositions,* and is especially required in a minuet. But in the second part you composed an uneven number of measures, namely thirteen.

No. 2. Each part generally should contain no more than eight measures. It's true you haven't made this error in the first part, but you have in the second; probably because you don't yet know how to distinguish among a *Zweyer,* a *Dreyer,* and a *Vierer.*[3] Therefore you have

No. 3. not really separated off the opening, or *theme,* and articulated it fully with distinct *Zweyer* or *Vierer.*

No. 4. I see some measures that are without motion, and some where the notes run too much by step. But until the cadence a minuet requires notes that move either perfectly or imperfectly.[4]

No. 5. I don't see a single measure in the second part that resembles one in the first. But one must take particular care with that, since a minuet *must be as coherent as a concerto, an aria, or a symphony,* etc. Consequently I could make at least a half dozen minuets out of yours, because it contains so many different kinds of notes and measures.

No. 6. An experienced natural scientist once confided in me that a minuet

---

3. By *Zweyer, Dreyer,* and *Vierer* Riepel means "two-measure unit," "three-measure unit," and "four-measure unit." Since there is no satisfactory English equivalent, the terms and their plurals (identical to the singulars) have been left untranslated in the text.

4. By "perfect" motion Riepel means at least quarter-note motion on every beat in a measure; by "imperfect" motion he means a motion of a half note and a quarter note. The third alternative—a dotted half note—he calls "dead." See p. 757, where he explains the term.

will succeed without much effort, and advance with unfailing propriety, if it rises in the first part and falls back again in the second. But I see just the opposite in yours.

No. 7. Keen connoisseurs of minuets require the fourth and fifth measures to be clearly distinguished, especially in the first part. That is, if the fourth measure has notes that move perfectly, then the fifth should consist of notes that move imperfectly; or the opposite.

Pupil. This is dreadful! If I just knew right now what a *Zweyer* and a *Dreyer* were, or a moving or running note, I would begin to make changes immediately.

Master. A *Zweyer*[5] consists of two measures that are generally similar in motion to the two measures following them:

But in these neighboring *Zweyer* the notes shouldn't all move exactly alike. You can also do the following:

or

Now a *Dreyer*[6] consists of three such measures:

or

5. *Binarius.* [Au.]
6. *Ternarius.* [Au.]

Pupil. I understand that very well now, for you can see it and hear it. But which ones are better for a minuet—the *Zweyer* or the *Dreyer?*

Master. The *Zweyer;* the *Dreyer* aren't of any use here. But I'll tell you today when and where these can be put to good use.

Pupil. Then you can make a *Dreyer* out of a *Zweyer,* and vice versa, by cutting a measure off, for example, or adding one.

Master. Absolutely. Now a *Vierer*[7] consists of four measures:

This kind of *Vierer* can always have a seat and a vote in a minuet.

Pupil. I can see that, because it is not very different from two *Zweyer:*

Master. If a *Vierer* doesn't follow, then in a pinch I wouldn't finally dispute your opinion. But the *Zweyer* look clearer in the following version than in yours:

Pupil. This is true, but how does it happen?

Master. Because here the second *Zweyer* ends a tone higher. Your *Zweyer,* on the other hand, both end on the tone F.

Pupil. Now I see that too. But tell me which ones are better, the *Zweyer* or the *Vierer?*

Master. I don't know of any difference between the two.

Pupil. But I am surprised my teacher never said anything to me about such useful and necessary things. Perhaps he doesn't even know what a *Zweyer,* a *Dreyer,* and a *Vierer* are.

Master. Hush! That would be astonishing. Then how could he pass himself off as a composer? For that means having perfect mastery of *rhythmic ordering,* which among other things is *a major part of the composition of all works of music;* and fugues are not completely excluded from this. How this is we will see further on.[8]

---

7. *Quaternarius.* [Au.]

8. One or another old-fashioned quibbler may certainly be very surprised about this, especially one who does not want to understand what is newfangled. But we are talking here about people like me, since I have very often had to hear the word *newfangled* [*neugebacken*]. [Au.] Riepel

Pupil. Then we'll let it go in the meantime. First I'll improve my minuet with regard to No. 1, and just cut out the third measure ✠ in the second part to make a *Zweyer* out of a *Dreyer:*

Menuet

This way the second part contains exactly twelve measures.

And this correction was made according to precept No. 1.

Now just tell me quickly, what are notes that run stepwise?

Master. This sort of thing, for example:

They precede or follow one another without jumping a line or a space.[9] On the other hand the following are notes that move disjunctly:

For some jump from line to line, and some from space to space.

Pupil. Excellent! You mentioned in No. 2 that in each section there should only be eight measures. So I'll omit the extra stepwise notes, namely measures 5 through 8 in the second part:

---

seems to be saying that composers who persist in writing in the old-fashioned fugal style, of whom the pupil's first teacher must be one, will be surprised to discover that fugues should also be governed by modern metrical practices. He sees himself here as a man of reason and moderation caught between pedants and facile innovators—a familiar modern dilemma.

9. *Intervallum.* [Au.]

and make quarter notes out of the ninth and tenth measures, which are now measures 5 ✠ 6:

Menuet

In all there are just sixteen measures.

And this correction was made according to precept No. 2.

But why are notes running stepwise not desirable?

Master. Oh, they are perfectly desirable, and certainly in an *Allegro assai* or a *Tempo presto* and *prestissimo* of a symphony, a concerto or solo, and so forth, they are the best notes of all, because they are flowing and light, and don't hinder the quick strokes of the bow. Moreover, singers like them as well as instrumentalists do, although *they prefer ascending to descending ones:*

as being *easier* than the following:

Pupil. And probably also easier for flutes, oboes, horns, and trumpets?

Master. Absolutely; particularly for them.

Pupil. I must make a note of this *wonder of nature.* I think that hundreds of compositional decisions rest on this point.

Master. But a minuet always requires notes that move perfectly, namely quarter notes:

They can also be varied or altered:

But in a minuet I can't tolerate the following variation, where the full quarter note stands last:

Pupil. Then it probably wouldn't be desirable in the following version, would it?

Master. Finally, a single such ✠ measure can slip through. Now I would also prefer to let the last four measures of your minuet stay as they are:

Pupil. And why these precisely?

Master. Because the minuet strains to make its cadence or rest just as a hungry man wants supper after work, or—You shouldn't laugh; for *a beginner* in particular *must conceive of this and a thousand other similes if he doesn't want to fill his compositions with* empty, silly, and *pedantic notes.*

Pupil. Now don't take me wrong, but on account of precept No. 3 I would rather lay out the entire minuet with clear *Zweyer* and *Vierer:*

And that was according to precept No. 3.

Master. Before you turn to No. 4, I must tell you that a motionless note should never be used in the middle of such a short or dance-style minuet except at the end of the first and second parts. But you can bring this kind of motionless or dead note to life in the following way:

These measures move imperfectly:

Now two measures of this type are quite useless in a minuet. You should always precede or follow one of them with a measure of perfect motion:

Pupil. Fine. Now I'll alter the minuet again, and also make the fifth measure ✠ of the first part a little more alive:

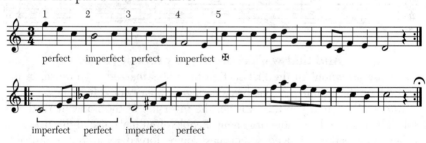

And that was according to precept No. 4.

Now I know that I can use measures with perfect motion throughout (with the exception of the last notes of both sections):

Master. This one is more lively; the previous one, on the other hand, was more *singing*, and that *cantabile* is produced by measures with imperfect motion.

Pupil. I already know that. I just need to ask whether I can also use dotted notes:

Master. No. I don't think these are at all desirable in a minuet—unless the dancing-master has gone lame. I like the following type about two-thirds better:

Pupil. Fine. I'll be guided accordingly. And concerning No. 5, I think that in the minuet that I corrected before there is enough similarity. I will set out the minuet once again and indicate the similarity with the sign ✠:

And that was according to precept No. 5.

Pay close attention! In the first section the notes marked ✠ go down, in the second, up. So I think that one hears enough similarity or coherence.

Master. Who told you this? Listen, the inversion of the notes marked ✠ is taken by many to be a mere ornament. People often make use of this device in other compositions; indeed sometimes you're forced to it. But I probably wouldn't have noticed it immediately in your minuet if I hadn't seen the explanatory sign ✠ by it.

Pupil. Then I certainly could have done it this way:

or this way:

or with a double correspondence:

If I had time, I would want to bring out still more correspondences. But I would rather ask you concerning No. 6, what rising and falling are?

Master. Isn't this very easy to understand?

rising   falling

Pupil. Good. I'll make my minuet rise and fall too:

And that was according to precept No. 6.

Master. Wait a minute! You're climbing too high. Let me put it this way: in this version the minuet is too youthful, since its melody loses its *seriousness and maturity.*

Pupil. I could certainly just begin lower:

Master. That's very good. But you don't need to rise or fall in every *Zweyer.* Even the cadences are not completely bound to this rule. Hence the cadence of the second part can often by itself express the fall, just as in the first part a single note (marked ✠) can express the rise:

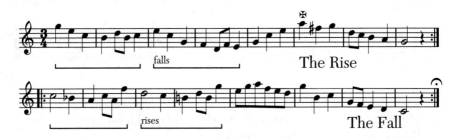

Pupil. Excuse me, but it still doesn't please me nearly as well as an orderly rise and fall. I hope to do better.

Master. As for No. 7, in the fourth and fifth measures I'll mark with larger numbers both the imperfect and the perfect motion:

or the opposite:

Pupil. What does the second part say to that?

Master. It could also behave this way if it wanted to. But it is often so undisciplined that it will not follow any rule. Moreover, the first part can captivate the amateur listener so quickly that he won't fret much about the second part, especially since it is only considered to be a close for the first part.

Pupil. I will compose yet another one, and introduce the same movements into the second part also:

or the opposite:

And finally that was according to No. 7.

So now can I boast that I know how to compose an orderly minuet?

Master. You must never boast.[10] Also, the rules by themselves do not amount to so much. For someone else might compose a minuet whose arrangement was not so orderly as yours, but whose melody[11] was more lively. And that minuet would probably find much more approval among the dilettantes than yours would, after all the rules and measurements we have researched together.

Pupil. Well do I know that one must always and above all look for a good melody.

---

10. *Propria laus olfacit male* [Self-praise has a bad smell]: we are speaking Latin. But a touch of self-love and a desire for honor are certainly as little harmful to the student as they are to all honorable men in the world. [Au.]

11. *Il cantabile.* [Au.]

123 Johann Philipp Kirnberger

Johann Philipp Kirnberger (1721–1783) was a member of a distinguished group of musical pedagogues in Berlin in the latter half of the eighteenth century, along with Friedrich Wilhelm Marpurg, Carl Philipp Emanuel Bach, Johann Joachim Quantz, Johann Georg Sulzer, and Johann Abraham Peter Schulz. It is likely that Kirnberger studied with Johann Sebastian Bach in Leipzig sometime in 1741. He revered Bach as a composer and teacher, and saw himself as propagating Bach's teaching methods in his principal treatise, *Die Kunst des reinen Satzes in der Musik* (*The Art of Strict Musical Composition*). This work, along with most of Kirnberger's other writings and compositions, was written in the service of Princess Anna Amalia of Prussia; he held this position from 1758 until his death.

Kirnberger's reverence for Bach has caused him to be considered conservative for his time, but he is actually more a transitional figure. He composed in the *galant* as well as the strict style, and urged social dance pieces as models for the study of meter and rhythm in performance. *Die Kunst des reinen Satzes in der Musik* is known principally for its harmonic teachings: it synthesizes the principles of Rameau with figured-bass practice, and the study of counterpoint with a harmonic orientation. The section on tempo and meter also reflects a time of transition: the connection Kirnberger makes between musical movement and the passions was still operative at the time, and while he discusses some time signatures that were no longer in use, their vestiges survived in the more limited spectrum of meters used by *galant* composers.

FROM *The Art of Strict Musical Composition*

(1776)

VOLUME 2, PART 1, CHAPTER 4
TEMPO, METER, AND RHYTHM

A succession of notes that mean nothing by themselves and are differentiated from one another only by pitch can be transformed into a real melody—one that has a definite character and depicts a passion or a particular sentiment—by means of tempo, meter, and rhythm, which give the melody its character and expression. It is immediately apparent to everyone that the most moving melody would be completely stripped of all its power and expression if

TEXT: As translated by David Beach and Jurgen Thym in J. P. Kirnberger, *The Art of Strict Musical Composition* (New Haven: Yale University Press, 1982), pp. 375–77; 380–82; 384–88; 390–92; 394–98; 399–400. The music examples have been renumbered.

one note after another were performed without precise regulation of speed, without accents, and without rest points, even if performed with the strictest observance of pitch. Even common speech would become partly incomprehensible and completely disagreeable if a proper measure of speed were not observed in the delivery, if the words were not separated from one another by the accents associated with the length and brevity of the syllables, and finally if the phrases and sentences were not differentiated by rest points. Such a lifeless delivery would make the most beautiful speech sound no better than the letter-by-letter reading of children.

Thus tempo, meter, and rhythm give melody its life and power. *Tempo* defines the rate of speed, which by itself is already important since it designates a lively or quiet character. *Meter* determines the accents in addition to the length and brevity of the notes and the lighter or more emphatic delivery; and it shapes the notes into words, so to speak. But *rhythm* establishes for the ear the individual phrases formed by the words and the periods composed of several phrases. Melody is transformed into a comprehensible and stimulating speech by the proper combination of these three things.

But it must be kept in mind that none of these elements is sufficient by itself to give the melody a precise character; the true expression of the melody is determined only by their synthesis and their interaction. Two compositions may have the same rate of *allegro* or *largo,* yet still have an entirely different effect; according to the type of meter, the motion is more hurried or emphatic, lighter or heavier, even while the speed remains the same. From this it is clear that tempo and meter must combine their forces. The same is also true of rhythm: the components from which a melody is formed can assume an entirely different expression depending on meter and tempo.

Thus, whoever wants to write a melody must pay attention to the combined effect of tempo, meter, and rhythm and must consider none of these without regard to the other two. Nevertheless, it is unavoidable for me to discuss each of them separately here and to tell the aspiring composer what he needs to know about each individual point.

I. Tempo

The composer must never forget that every melody is supposed to be a natural and faithful illustration or portrayal of a mood or sentiment, insofar as it can be represented by a succession of notes. The term *Gemüthsbewegung,* which we Germans give to passions or affections, already indicates their analogy to tempo.[1] In fact, every passion and every sentiment—in its intrinsic effect as well as in the words by which it is expressed—has its faster or slower, more violent or more passive tempo. This tempo must be correctly captured by the composer to conform with the type of sentiment he has to express.

---

1. The German words used by Kirnberger for tempo are *Bewegung* and *Taktbewegung.* The former also has a more general meaning that has been translated throughout as "motion." [Tr.]

Thus I must admonish the aspiring composer above all that he study diligently the nature of every passion and sentiment with regard to tempo, so that he does not make the terrible mistake of giving the melody a slow tempo where it should be fast, or a fast tempo where it should be slow. However, this is a field that is not limited to music, and that the composer has in common with the orator and poet.

Furthermore, he must have acquired a correct feeling for the natural tempo of every meter, or for what is called *tempo giusto*. This is attained by diligent study of all kinds of dance pieces. Every dance piece has its definite tempo, determined by the meter and the note values that are employed in it. Regarding meter, those having larger values, like alla breve, $\frac{3}{2}$, and $\frac{6}{4}$ meter, have a heavier and slower tempo than those of smaller values, like $\frac{2}{4}$, $\frac{3}{4}$, and $\frac{6}{8}$ meter, and these in turn are less lively than $\frac{3}{8}$ or $\frac{6}{16}$ meter. Thus, for example, a loure in $\frac{3}{2}$ meter has a slower tempo than a minuet in $\frac{3}{4}$ meter, and the latter is in turn slower than a passepied in $\frac{3}{8}$. Regarding note values, dance pieces involving sixteenth and thirty-second notes have a slower tempo than those that tolerate only eighth and at most sixteenth notes as the fastest note values in the same meter. Thus, for example, a sarabande in $\frac{3}{4}$ meter has a slower tempo than a minuet, even though both are written in the same meter.

Thus the *tempo giusto* is determined by the meter and by the longer and shorter note values of a composition. Once the young composer has a feeling for this, he will soon understand to what degree the adjectives *largo, adagio, andante, allegro, presto,* and their modifications *larghetto, andantino, allegretto,* and *prestissimo* add to or take away from the fast or slow motion of the natural tempo. He will soon be able not only to write in every type of tempo, but also in such a way that this tempo is captured quickly and correctly by the performers.

However, tempo in music is not limited just to the different degrees of slow and fast motion. There are passions "in which the images flow monotonously like a gentle brook; others where they flow faster with a moderate stir, but without delay; some in which the succession of images is similar to wild brooks swollen by heavy rains, which rush violently along and sweep with them everything that stands in their way; and again others in which the images are similar to the wild sea, which violently beats against the shore and then recedes to crash again with new force."[2] Similarly, tempo in melody can also be violent or tender, skipping or monotonous, fiery or bland even when the degree of fast or slow motion is the same, depending upon the type of note values chosen for the melody.

•   •   •   •   •

Thus the composer, in constructing a piece, has to consider two things regarding tempo: (1) the slow or fast pace of the tempo; and (2) the characteris-

---

2. See the article "Ausdruck" in Sulzer's [*Allgemeine*] *Theorie der schönen Künste* [Leipzig, 1771–74]. [Au.].

tic motion of the parts of the measure, or the type of rhythmic changes. Lively sentiments generally require a fast tempo; but the expression can become playful, or flirtatious, or happy, or tender, or pathetic by means of the type of characteristic motion of the parts of the measure, or the rhythmic steps. Likewise, a slower tempo generally is appropriate to the expression of sad sentiments, but through the second type of motion the expression can become more or less agitated, tender or violent, gentle or painful. Of course, it is not the motion alone that has this effect; the remaining good qualities of an expressive melody must be united with it, but then it contributes most forcefully to the expression.

This may be sufficient to draw the prospective composer's attention to the effect of motion in general. In the following two sections of this chapter we will have the opportunity to discuss in greater detail the particular effects of metric and rhythmic motion. Therefore, it may suffice here to add a couple of remarks for the young composer regarding motion in general.

He must be careful in writing a piece not to make it hurry or drag. Although these words are common only in the theory of performance, they can also be applied to composition. It can easily happen that a composer, without noticing it, rushes the tempo in writing a fiery Allegro, or lets it drag in a sad Largo; or, out of fondness for a phrase, he may unwittingly become lax about the tempo, so that the phrase becomes vague because of its fast rate of rhythmic motion or dull because of its slowness. The composer suffers in the performance of such pieces, but through his own fault.

He must not overstep the limits of fast or slow tempo. What is too fast cannot be performed clearly, and what is too slow cannot be comprehended. This applies mainly to pieces where the composer himself indicates the tempo.

Because of the long period of vibration of low notes, all short note values must be avoided in the low register; but in the high register they are more effective than long sustained notes. The progression of the bass generally relates to that of the highest part like the walk of a mature man to that of a young girl. Where she takes two or three steps, he takes only one, yet both cover the same distance. Not that a young girl could not go slowly and a mature man quickly, but it is not as natural. Similarly, the voices in the middle registers can be considered as gaits of boys and young adults by analogy to the shorter or longer note values of their rhythmic steps.

Finally, the composer must not neglect to designate the tempo of his piece as precisely as possible whenever it cannot be determined from the features given above. He must use the terms *allegro assai, allegro moderato, poco allegro,* etc., wherever the word *allegro* would indicate a tempo that is too fast or not fast enough. The same is true of slow pieces. The words that refer to characteristic motion, such as *maestoso, scherzando, vivo, mesto,* etc., are often of the greatest significance in expressive pieces, and not meaningless for those who want to perform a piece well. Hasse is so precise in the designation of his tempi that he often makes lengthy descriptions of how the piece is to be performed: *Andantino grazioso, ma non patetico, non languente; Allegro vivo, e con spirito,* or *allegro vivo, che arrivi quasi all'allegro intiero; un poco lento, e maestoso, ma che non languisca, e abbia il dovuto suo moto.*[3]

II. METER

If one imagines a melody in which all the notes are presented with the same intensity or stress, and in which they have the same length or duration (as if, for example, the melody were to consist only of whole notes), it would be comparable to a monotonously flowing stream. What distinguishes one melody from another is the faster or slower current: one is comparable to a thundering stream, another to a gentle, somewhat faster or slower flowing river, and a third to a gently rippling brook. If a more or less full and consonant harmony is imagined along with such a melody, one has everything that could distinguish one melody from another.

The entire power or expression of such a melody would consist only of a gentle and light or a lively and strong current, which would lull us to sleep or wake us up. If melody is to become similar to speech and adapted to the expression of various emotions and sentiments, individual notes must be turned into meaningful words and several words into comprehensible phrases. This transformation of a mere stream of notes into a melody resembling speech is accomplished in part by accents that are given to a few notes, and partly by the difference in their durations. It is just the same as with common speech, where we distinguish words and sentences only by means of the accents and durations of syllables.

Meter actually consists of the precise uniformity of accents that are given to a few notes and of the completely regular distribution of long and short syllables. That is, when these heavier or lighter accents recur at regular intervals, the melody acquires a meter or a measure. If these accents were not distributed regularly, so that no precise periodic recurrence occurred, the melody would be similar only to common prosaic speech; but with this periodic return it is comparable to poetic speech, which has its precise meter.

This matter can also be conceived by picturing a simple motion. A melody that just flows along without accents resembles a continuous motion, like that created when a body falls or is thrown through the air; but an accented melody is similar to a motion divided into steps or to walking. Just as walking receives its particular character from the type as well as the speed of the steps, melody receives its character and expression in quite a similar way.

A regular walk has steps of equal length, each of which represents a measure of the melody. However, the steps can consist of more or fewer little movements or *beats,* and these movements or beats, all of which are of the same

3. "A little Andante that is graceful, but not pathetic or languishing; an Allegro that is lively and spirited; a lively Allegro that is almost a full Allegro; rather slow and majestic, but without languishing, and with its own proper motion."

duration, can have smaller divisions or parts; they can also be distinguished by other modifications—by gradations of heavy and light, flowing or leaping, etc. If a precise uniformity is observed in the steps and small movements, this results in the measured walk which we call dance, and this is precisely analogous to measured melody. In just the same way as dance expresses or portrays various sentiments merely by motion, melody does it merely by notes.

Whoever considers this closely will easily understand how much the character of a melody depends on tempo and meter. The clearest examples of this can be found in the various dance melodies. However, it is not possible to give definite rules that would specify the most suitable tempo and meter for every type of sentiment. For the most part, it depends on a refined and accurate sensitivity.

Everything that can be said to a composer about this subject beyond what I have already stated about tempo is contained in the following main topics: (1) that all types of meters invented and in use up to now be described to him, each according to its true structure and its precise execution; (2) that the spirit or character of each meter be defined as precisely as possible; (3) finally, for the situation where the melody is to be written to a given text, that directions be given how the best or at least a suitable type of meter is to be chosen for it. I will have to discuss these three points here.

* * * * *

The measure consists of two, three, or four equal beats; besides these, there is no other natural type of measure.

To all appearances, only three time signatures would be required to indicate these meters, namely, one that indicates a measure of two, another that indicates a measure of three, and a third that indicates a measure of four beats. However, from what we have stated already in the preceding section of this chapter about *tempo giusto* and the natural motion of longer and shorter note values, it becomes clear, for example, that a measure of two quarter notes and another of two half notes, and likewise a measure of three quarter notes and another of three eighth notes, indicate a different tempo, even though they have the same number of beats. In addition, longer note values are always performed with more weight and emphasis than shorter ones; consequently a composition that is to be performed with weight and emphasis can only be notated with long note values, and another that is to be performed in a light and playful manner can only be notated with short note values.

From this the necessity of different meters with the same number of beats becomes apparent, which we shall now consider in greater detail. In general, meters are divided into even and odd; *even* are those of two and four beats; and *odd,* those of three beats, which are also called triple meters. Furthermore, a distinction is made between simple and compound meters: *simple* meters are constituted in such a way that each measure amounts to only one foot, which cannot be divided in the middle; however, *compound* meters can be divided in the middle of each measure, since they are composed of two simple meters, as will be shown in greater detail below.

Before we list the meters in order, it must still be noted that it is just as easy to divide each beat of a meter into three parts or to triple it as it is to perceive triple meter; this is already obvious from the existence of triplets. This gives rise to meters of *triple beats,* where three pulses fall on one beat. We shall indicate these now, along with the meters from which they are derived, and shall note what is necessary regarding their true structure, their usefulness or unusefulness, and their exact execution. [See Table 1.[4]]

TABLE 1

SIMPLE EVEN METERS OF TWO BEATS

1. $\frac{2}{1}$ meter or $\boldsymbol{\phi}$:   tripled—$\frac{6}{2}$ meter.
2. $\frac{2}{2}$ meter or $\boldsymbol{\mathfrak{C}}$:   tripled—$\frac{6}{4}$ meter.
3. $\frac{2}{4}$ meter: tripled—$\frac{6}{8}$ meter.
4. $\frac{2}{8}$ meter: tripled—$\frac{6}{16}$ meter.

SIMPLE EVEN METERS OF FOUR BEATS

1. $\frac{4}{2}$ meter or $\mathbf{O}$:   tripled—$\frac{12}{4}$ meter.
2. $\frac{4}{4}$ meter or $\mathbf{C}$:   tripled—$\frac{12}{8}$ meter.
3. $\frac{4}{8}$ meter: tripled—$\frac{12}{16}$ meter.

SIMPLE ODD METERS OF THREE BEATS

1. $\frac{3}{1}$ meter or 3:   tripled—$\frac{9}{2}$ meter.
2. $\frac{3}{2}$ meter: tripled—$\frac{9}{4}$ meter.
3. $\frac{3}{4}$ meter: tripled—$\frac{9}{8}$ meter.
4. $\frac{3}{8}$ meter: tripled—$\frac{9}{16}$ meter.
5. $\frac{3}{16}$ meter: tripled—$\frac{9}{32}$ meter.

4. It is clear from this table that Kirnberger's conception of the distinction between simple and compound meter is not consistent with the commonly accepted definition of these terms. The meters listed in the right column, those that are derived from the simple meters in the left column by multiples of three, are normally considered as compound meters; Kirnberger, however, considers them among the simple meters. According to Kirnberger, compound meters, the most useful of which are listed in Table 4.2, are derived from simple meters by multiples of two. This definition leads to certain inconsistencies; no meter of nine (three triple beats), for example, can be considered as compound, since it cannot be divided in the middle. Other meters, like $\frac{6}{8}$, can be simple (derived from $\frac{3}{4}$) or compound (derived from $\frac{3}{8}$); but in both cases, the measure is divided into two triple beats. [Tr.]

OBSERVATIONS ABOUT SIMPLE EVEN METERS OF TWO BEATS

(A) $\frac{2}{1}$ meter, which is also called *large alla breve* by some, consists of two whole notes or semibreves per measure. However, as is the case with the $\frac{6}{2}$ meter of two triple beats that is derived from it, it is no longer used because of the confusion caused by the rests, since the same rest has a value of half a measure at one time and a whole measure at another. In place of these, it is better to use $\frac{2}{2}$ and $\frac{6}{4}$ with the adjective *grave* to indicate the emphatic and weighty performance required by these meters. I know of only one Credo by the elder Bach in the large alla breve meter of two beats, which he designated, however, with **C** to show that the rests have the same value as in ordinary alla breve time.[5] Telemann, however, has even written church pieces in $\frac{6}{1}$ and other similar meters; one can easily see that these are only eccentricities.

(B) $\frac{2}{2}$ meter, or rather *alla breve*, which is always designated by ¢ or ₵, is most often used in church pieces, fugues, and elaborate choruses. It is to be noted about this meter that it is very serious and emphatic, yet is performed twice as fast as its note values indicate, unless a slower tempo is specified by the adjectives *grave, adagio*, etc. The same is true of the $\frac{6}{4}$ meter of two triple beats that is derived from $\frac{2}{2}$ meter, but the *tempo giusto* of this meter is somewhat more moderate. Both meters tolerate no shorter notes values than eighths.

(C) $\frac{2}{4}$ meter has the same tempo as alla breve but is performed much more lightly. The difference in performance between the two meters is too noticeable for anyone to believe that it makes no difference whether a piece is written in **C** or in $\frac{2}{4}$. Consider, for example, the following melodic phrase in both meters:

Example 1

(A) Tempo giusto

(B) Tempo giusto

If this phrase is performed correctly, everyone will notice that it is much more serious and emphatic in *alla breve* (A) than in $\frac{2}{4}$ (B) meter, where it comes close to being playful. This is the difference between meters having the same number of beats, as was noted above.

$\frac{2}{4}$ meter as well as the $\frac{6}{8}$ meter that is derived from it are most often used in chamber and theater pieces. In their natural tempi, sixteenth notes and a few thirty-second notes in succession are their shortest note values. But if the tempo is modified by the adjectives *andante, largo, allegro*, etc., more or none of these note values can be used, depending on the rate of speed.

5. The work to which Kirnberger refers is the Credo from the *Mass in B Minor* (BWV 232). [Tr.]

(D) $\frac{2}{8}$ meter would be appropriate only for short amusing dance pieces because of its fast tempo and its all too great lightness of execution. However, it is not in use, and we would not have mentioned it if $\frac{6}{16}$ meter—which is derived from it and in which many pieces have been written—did not have to be listed. It differs greatly from $\frac{6}{8}$ meter in the hurried nature of its tempo and the lightness of its execution. J. S. Bach and Couperin[6] have written some of their pieces in $\frac{6}{16}$ meter, not without good reason. Who does not know the Bach fugue at (A) in Example 2?[7]

Example 2

(A)

(B)

If this theme is rewritten as at (B), the tempo is no longer the same, the gait is much more ponderous, and the notes, particularly the passing notes, are emphasized too much; in short, the expression of the piece as a whole suffers and is no longer the one given to it by Bach. If this fugue is to be performed correctly on the keyboard, the notes must be played lightly and without the least pressure in a fast tempo; this is what $\frac{6}{16}$ meter requires. On the violin, pieces in this and other similarly light meters are to be played just with the point of the bow; however, weightier meters require a longer stroke and more bow pressure. The fact that these and several other meters that we shall list are considered superfluous and obsolete today indicates either that good and correct execution has been lost or that an aspect of expression which is easy to obtain only in these meters is entirely unknown to us. Both of these conclusions do little credit to the art, which supposedly has reached its peak in our time.

•   •   •   •   •

OBSERVATIONS ABOUT SIMPLE EVEN METERS OF FOUR BEATS

(A) $\frac{4}{2}$ meter, or **O**, like $\frac{2}{1}$ time, is no longer in use; it also is objectionable because of the confusion caused by its rests, as is the $\frac{12}{3}$ meter of four triple beats derived from it. They are mentioned here only because one now and then comes across old pieces in these meters. Instead of these, it is better to use $\frac{4}{4}$ and $\frac{12}{8}$ meter with the adjective *grave* to designate the weighty tempo and emphatic performance appropriate to the former meters. If young composers should come across church pieces in *alla breve* time where there are four half

6. Former court organist in Paris. He has published many pieces engraved in copper under the title *Pièces de Clavecin*, which in all respects are models of good keyboard pieces. [Au.]
7. Fugue in F major (BWV 880) from *Das wohltemperierte Klavier*, Part 2. [Tr.]

notes between two barlines, they must not let themselves be misled and conclude that the meter is $\frac{4}{2}$. This occurs only as a convenience for the composer to avoid an excess of barlines and ties, and he is free to do so. But this does not change the nature of the ¢ measure, which always has the same stress every other half note; and the upbeat and downbeat of the measure is fixed even when four, six, and more measures are joined without barline, as Handel, among others, has frequently done in his oratorios. Furthermore, this does not cause confusion regarding the rests, whose value always remains the same in such situations.

(B) $\frac{4}{4}$ meter, which is designated by **C**, is of two types: either it is used with the adjective *grave* in place of the $\frac{4}{2}$ meter just mentioned, in which case it is called large $\frac{4}{4}$ time; or it is the so-called common even meter, which is also called small $\frac{4}{4}$ time.

Large $\frac{4}{4}$ time is of extremely weighty tempo and execution and, because of its emphatic nature, is suited primarily to church pieces, choruses, and fugues. Eighth and a few sixteenth notes in succession are its fastest note values. To distinguish it from small $\frac{4}{4}$ time, it should be designated by $\frac{4}{4}$ instead of **C**. The two meters have nothing in common except for their signatures.

Small $\frac{4}{4}$ time has a more lively tempo and a far lighter execution. It tolerates all note values up to sixteenth notes and is used very often in all styles.

The same is true of $\frac{12}{8}$ meter of four triple beats that is derived from $\frac{4}{4}$ meter. A few older composers who were very sensitive about the manner in which their pieces were performed often designated pieces consisting only of sixteenth notes by $\frac{24}{16}$ instead of $\frac{12}{8}$ to indicate that the sixteenth notes should be performed lightly, quickly, and without the slightest pressure on the first note of each beat. Composers and performers today seem to know so little about these subtleties that they believe, on the contrary, that such meter designations were only an eccentricity of the older composers.

(C) $\frac{4}{8}$ is the lightest of the quadruple meters in execution and tempo. It is distinguished from $\frac{2}{4}$ meter by the weight of its beats, all of which are equally stressed; but in $\frac{2}{4}$ meter the first and third beats are emphasized.

Example 3

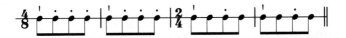

Therefore, it has a somewhat slower tempo than $\frac{2}{4}$ meter. Yet, since the liveliness of the tempo makes the stress of the beats less noticeable in both meters, the two are not as different from one another as are $\frac{4}{4}$ meter and *alla breve*. Furthermore, today's composers no longer designate pieces with $\frac{4}{8}$, but always with $\frac{2}{4}$ instead.

Although $\frac{12}{16}$ meter of four triple beats, which is derived from $\frac{4}{8}$ meter, is presently neglected and $\frac{12}{8}$ meter is always written instead, it is completely different from the latter in its greater lightness of execution. The elder Bach has certainly not written the fugue at (A) in Example 4 in $\frac{12}{8}$ and the other at (B) in $\frac{12}{16}$ without good reason.[8]

Example 4

Everyone will easily perceive the distinction between the two meters in these examples. The one at (A) designates a slower tempo and a more emphatic performance; furthermore, many sixteenth notes can be used in this meter. However, no shorter note values can be used in the one at (B), and the six-teenth notes are performed quickly and plainly, without any emphasis. Handel, Bach, and Couperin have written many pieces in $\frac{12}{16}$ meter.

In quadruple meter, the first and third beats are accented, but the second and fourth unaccented. The former are also called strong and the latter weak beats. Of the accented beats, the first is in turn stressed more than the third, as can be seen from Example 5, where ‾ means accented, and ˘ unaccented.

Example 5

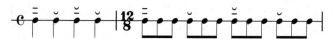

Therefore the principal notes of the melody must always fall on the first beat; the other notes receive more or less weight depending on the intrinsic stress of the other beats. In these meters, the closing note always falls on the first beat and must last four beats, except in pieces where the phrase begins on the upbeat, because the cadence is felt only up to the point where a new phrase can begin.

•   •   •   •   •

OBSERVATIONS ABOUT ODD METERS OF THREE BEATS

(A) $\frac{3}{1}$ meter, which consists of three whole notes per measure, and the $\frac{9}{2}$ meter of three triple beats that is derived from it are of no use whatsoever. The weighty and emphatic performance that would be specified by both is achieved by means of the two following meters, particularly if the adjective *grave* is added; furthermore, in the latter the eye is not exhausted by the many large

8. The first is the subject of the Fughetta in C minor (BWV 961); the second is the subject of the Fugue in C-sharp Minor (BWV 873) from *Das wohltemperierte Klavier*, Part 2. [Tr.]

notes and rests that cause only ambiguity and confusion in the former meters.

(B) $\frac{3}{2}$ meter is used very often, especially in church pieces, because of the ponderous and slow performance indicated by its note values. In this style, quarter and, at most, eighth notes are its fastest note values. In the chamber style, sixteenth notes can also be used in $\frac{3}{2}$ meter; C. P. E. Bach has even begun a symphony in this meter with many thirty-second notes in a row.[9] With such note values, the three beats of this meter must be indicated most clearly in the other voices; otherwise the melody would remain fuzzy and incomprehensible to the listener.

Because of the different weights of their beats, $\frac{3}{2}$ meter has no other similarity with $\frac{6}{4}$ meter except that both contain six quarter notes. Yet it is to be noted as something special that good composers of old have treated the courante, which is generally written in $\frac{3}{2}$, in such a way that both meters were often combined in it. Consider, for example, the first part of a courante for keyboard by Couperin in Example 6.[10]

Example 6

9. Wotquenne lists a symphony in E-flat for two horns, two oboes, two violins, viola, and bass (1757) that begins with continuous sixteenth-note (but not thirty-second-note) motion in $\frac{3}{2}$ meter. See Alfred Wotquenne, *C. Ph. Em. Bach: Thematisches Verzeichnis seiner Werke* (Leipzig, 1905), no. 179 (p. 61). [Tr.]
10. François Couperin, *Pièces de Clavecin*, Book I (Paris, 1713), first order, first courante. [Tr.]

The second and sixth measures and the bass melody of the seventh measure of this courante are in $\frac{3}{2}$ meter, but the other measures are written in $\frac{6}{4}$. In the works of J. S. Bach there are a number of courantes treated in this same way.

The $\frac{9}{4}$ meter of [three] triple beats that is derived from $\frac{3}{2}$ occurs rarely, since $\frac{9}{8}$ is used instead. But it is easily understood that the two meters are very different with respect to the performance and tempo that they specify. In the church style, where a ponderous and emphatic execution is generally combined with a subdued and slow tempo, $\frac{9}{4}$ meter is preferable by far to $\frac{9}{8}$, since a melody that assumes a serious expression in the former meter can easily appear playful in the latter:

Example 7

(C) Because of its lighter execution, $\frac{3}{4}$ meter is not as common in the church style as $\frac{3}{2}$; but it is used very often in the chamber and theatrical styles.

Its natural tempo is that of a minuet, and in this tempo it does not tolerate many sixteenth notes, even less thirty-second notes, in succession. However, since it assumes all degrees of tempo from the adjectives *adagio, allegro,* etc., all note values that fit this tempo can be used, depending on the rate of speed.

The $\frac{9}{8}$ meter of three triple beats that is derived from $\frac{3}{4}$ has the same tempo as $\frac{3}{4}$, but the eighth notes are performed more lightly than in $\frac{3}{4}$.

It is a mistake to consider this meter as a $\frac{3}{4}$ meter whose beats consist of triplets. He who has only a moderate command of performance knows that triplets in $\frac{3}{4}$ meter are played differently from eighths in $\frac{9}{8}$ meter. The former are played very lightly and without the slightest pressure on the last note, but the latter heavier and with some weight on the last note. The former never or only rarely permit a harmony to be sounded with the last note, but the latter do very often. The former do not permit any arpeggiations in sixteenth notes, but the latter do very easily. If the two meters were not distinguished by special qualities, all gigues in $\frac{6}{8}$ could also be written in $\frac{2}{4}$; $\frac{12}{8}$ would be a $\mathbf{C}$ meter, and $\frac{6}{8}$ a $\frac{2}{4}$ meter. How senseless this is can easily be discovered by anyone who rewrites, for example, a gigue in $\frac{12}{8}$ or $\frac{6}{8}$ meter in $\mathbf{C}$ or $\frac{2}{4}$ meter.

$\frac{3}{4}$ and $\frac{9}{8}$ meter gave the older composers the opportunity to use an $\frac{18}{16}$ meter of three sextuplet beats when they wanted to indicate that the piece should be performed lightly, swiftly, and without the slightest pressure on the first note of each beat:

Example 8

However, since such subtleties of performance have been lost to such a degree that even many who are called virtuosos perform six beamed sixteenths like two compounded triplets, $\frac{18}{16}$ meter belongs among the meters that are lost and highly dispensable today.

(D) $\frac{3}{8}$ meter has the lively tempo of a passepied; it is performed in a light but not an entirely playful manner and is widely used in chamber and theatrical music.

$\frac{9}{16}$ meter of three triple beats that is derived from $\frac{3}{8}$ was used in many ways by the older composers for gigue-like pieces that are to be performed extremely quickly and lightly. But it no longer occurs in contemporary music; $\frac{9}{8}$ meter appears in its place.

(E) $\frac{3}{16}$ meter, which indicates the truly light performance of hasty pieces and dances that are commonly written in $\frac{3}{8}$, where only one beat can be heard for each measure because of the very fast tempo, has been used rarely. In Handel's keyboard suites there is a gigue in $\frac{3}{16}$ meter that begins as shown in Example 9.

Example 9

That this is nothing other than $\frac{3}{16}$ meter—even though the signature is $\frac{12}{8}$ instead of $\frac{3}{16}$ in the edition by John Walsh[11]—is evident from the concluding note, which falls on the downbeat and lasts for just three sixteenths. This is not possible in $\frac{12}{16}$ meter but is possible in compound $\frac{6}{16}$ meter, as will be shown in greater detail when we discuss compound meters.

$\frac{9}{32}$ meter of three triple beats that is derived from $\frac{3}{16}$ is of no use at all and, furthermore, has never been used.

These triple meters have the common element that, in each, three beats are felt per measure, the first of which is always accented, the third unaccented. The second can be accented or unaccented, depending on the nature of the piece. That is, it is usually accented in ponderous meters and in serious pieces, as in chaconnes and many sarabandes; but in light meters this second beat is weak. This two-fold treatment of the second beat in triple meter is clarified by Example 10.

11. In the Walsh edition of the second volume of these suites (London, 1736?), the meter signature is given as $\frac{12}{8}$ but the piece is notated in $\frac{12}{16}$. Kirnberger, however, insists that the meter is really $\frac{3}{16}$ but notated in $\frac{12}{16}$ to avoid writing so many barlines. [Tr.]

Example 10

In the first example, a nonessential dissonance, which can only appear on a strong beat, falls on the second quarter. In the second, the cadence falls on the same beat; consequently it is also accented here. But in the third example it is weak.

What I have stated previously about the treatment of even meters with regard to the different weights of the beats can easily be applied to triple meter as well. Suspensions or nonessential dissonances, principal notes, and cadences can fall only on accented beats. However, cadences on the second strong beat of the triple measure are less common than those on the first, or downbeat. Many English and, particularly, Scottish dances deviate from this rule and conclude on the upbeat; but in this way they acquire a somewhat strange flavor, which is noticeable even to an untrained ear.

When eighth notes occur in $\frac{3}{4}$ meter and sixteenths in $\frac{3}{8}$, the first of these eighths or sixteenths is accented.

•   •   •   •   •

Let this now suffice concerning knowledge of the mechanical nature of all common meters. . . . I now have to consider:

2. the spirit of actual character of each of these meters from the standpoint of their power to express sentiments and passions.

Here it is not so much the even or odd number of beats in a measure that matters as the slower or faster tempo and the heavier or lighter gait of the measure. One meter can be used for contrasting passions, depending upon the tempo and other factors. However, since each meter has a treatment that is most suitable and natural to it, or, if one wants, most common, then it also has to this extent a special character that can, of course, be taken away from it by a strange and unusual treatment.

Thus, what I have to say here concerns the special ease with which this or that meter can assume a certain character.

It is to be noted in general that, among the meters which have the same number of beats, the one that has larger or longer beats is naturally a bit more serious than the one of shorter beats. Thus $\frac{4}{4}$ meter is less lively than $\frac{4}{8}$ meter; $\frac{3}{2}$ meter is more ponderous than $\frac{3}{4}$, and the latter is not as lively as $\frac{3}{8}$.

For solemn and pathetic pieces, *alla breve* is especially appropriate and is therefore used in motets and other solemn church pieces. Large $\frac{4}{4}$ meter has a very emphatic and serious motion and is suited to stately choruses, to fugues in church pieces, and generally to pieces where pomp and gravity is required. $\frac{3}{2}$ meter is emphatic and very serious as long as not too many short notes are used. $\frac{4}{4}$ meter is best suited for a lively and exhilarating expression that is still somewhat emphatic. $\frac{2}{4}$ is also lively but certainly combined with more lightness and, for that reason, can be used well to express playfulness. $\frac{4}{8}$ meter is definitely totally fleeting, and its liveliness no longer contains any of the emphasis of $\frac{4}{4}$ meter. The character of $\frac{3}{4}$ appears to be gentle and noble, particularly when it consists only, or at least mostly, of quarter notes. But $\frac{3}{8}$ meter has a liveliness that is somewhat frolicsome.

These general characters are defined even more specifically by the particular note value that prevails and by rules that determine progression by larger or smaller intervals. The character of $\frac{3}{4}$ meter is entirely different when quarter notes are used almost exclusively throughout than when many eighths and even smaller notes occur, and when it progresses mostly by small intervals than when leaps occur more often. Since many dances receive their peculiar character from such special determining features within the same meter, and since I plan to discuss this matter in a special chapter, I will have the opportunity to speak there about the character of such pieces that are bound to specific rules.

From the few remarks that I have made here about the different characters of the meters, it is evident that this difference of meters is very well suited to express particular nuances of the passions.

Each passion has its own degrees of strength and, if I may say so, its own deeper or shallower character. Joy, for example, can be solemn and almost exalted; it can be overwhelming, but also leaping and frolicsome. Joy can have these and even more levels and nuances, and such is the case with the other passions as well. Above all, the composer must have a definite impression of the particular passion that he has to portray and then choose a more ponderous or lighter meter depending upon whether the affect in its particular nuance requires one or the other.

124 Heinrich Christoph Koch

Heinrich Christoph Koch was born in 1749 into a family of musicians who worked at the court of Rudolstadt, a provincial town in eastern Germany. Except for a brief period spent studying in Berlin, Dresden, and Weimar in 1773, he remained in Rudolstadt as a court violinist and composer until his death in 1816 (his compositions, unpublished except in his own treatise, were largely ceremonial cantatas and miscellaneous instrumental music). In 1792 he withdrew from the post of *Kapellmeister* to the more modest rank of *Konzertmeister* in order to concentrate on his work as a teacher. From this position of quiet seclusion he wrote two of the most important pedagogical works of the later eighteenth century: *Versuch einer Anleitung zur Composition* (*Introductory Essay on Composition;* 1782–93) and the *Musikalisches Lexikon* (*Music Lexicon;* 1802). The *Versuch* is a systematic treatise on composition for the beginner. Although it includes discussions of all the elements of music, Koch was fully aware of the central role played by melody in the *galant* aesthetic of "stirring the feelings," and placed his primary emphasis on the study of its "mechanical rules." These rules are the new teachings of melodic syntax, of the period, and of the period's extension into the full-fledged instrumental forms of the symphony and the concerto. As examples Koch cites the music of his day, of Carl Heinrich Graun, Franz Benda, and Haydn; in the third volume of the *Versuch* he praises Mozart's six quartets dedicated to Haydn.

FROM *Introductory Essay on Composition*

(1782–93)

[VOLUME 2 (1787)]

PART 2. ON THE MECHANICAL RULES OF MELODY: ON THE WAY IN WHICH MELODY IS CONNECTED WITH RESPECT TO THE MECHANICAL RULES

SECTION 3. ON THE NATURE OF MELODIC SECTIONS

§77. Certain more or less noticeable resting points for the mind are generally necessary in speech and thus also in the products of those fine arts which attain their goal through speech, namely poetry and rhetoric, if the subject that they present is to be comprehensible. Such resting points for the mind are just as necessary in melody if it is to affect our feelings. This is a fact which has never yet been called into question and therefore requires no further proof.

By means of these more or less noticeable resting points, the products of these fine arts can be broken up into larger and smaller sections. Speech, for example, breaks down into various periods or sentences through the most noticeable of these resting points; through the less noticeable the sentence, in turn, breaks down into separate phrases and parts of speech. Just as in speech, the melody of a composition can be broken up into periods by means of analogous resting points, and these, again, into single phrases and melodic segments.

In this section, we shall necessarily first become acquainted with the material nature of the sections which form the periods of melody. Then we can profitably study their formal nature, that is, the way in which the smaller melodic sections are connected into a principal section of the whole, or the construction of melodic periods.

§78. If we consider the various sections in musical works which compose

TEXT: As translated by Nancy Kovaleff Baker in *Heinrich Christoph Koch: Introductory Essay on Composition* (New Haven: Yale University Press, 1983), pp. 1–3, 6–9, 11, 13–16, 41–43, 45–46, 65–66, 85–86, 95–96, with minor alterations. The music examples have been renumbered.

their periods, then two main characteristics are found through which they distinguish themselves as divisions of the whole. The first is the type of their endings, or that which characterizes the resting points in the material aspect of the art. The second is the length of these sections, together with a certain proportion or relation between them which can be found in the number of their measures once they are reduced to their essential components.

The endings of these sections are certain formulas, which let us clearly recognize the more or less noticeable resting points. We have as yet no generally accepted technical term which would appropriately express not only the variety of these formulas in general, but also the particular order in which the different kinds and types can follow one another in the construction of melodic periods.[1] For lack of a completely suitable term and on account of its similarity to the labelling of the larger and smaller resting points in speech, we shall call this *melodic punctuation.*[2]

The length of these melodic sections, on the other hand, and the proportion or relationship which they have amongst themselves with regard to the number of measures will be called *rhythm.*

§79. Now the divisions of melody formed through resting points for the mind are of such a nature that one alone may or may not be understood as a section of a period; that is, these divisions may contain either complete or incomplete thoughts. If such a melodic section contains only an incomplete idea, another one must be added if it is to be understood or felt as a complete section; this will be called an *incise.*[3] However, if the thought is considered complete as a section, then something more may still be required to express the idea or feeling of the entire period. In other words, the complete thought is of such a kind that the period either cannot or can be closed with it. In the first case it will be called a *phrase of partial close,* and in the second case, because of its character-

---

1. The term "ordering of tones" can express neither the different kinds and types of ending formulas of melodic sections nor the manner of their connection into periods. For according to its components it can do no more than either show the propriety in the sequence of tones, which in the first section I called "melodic progression," or indicate an aspect of modulation, namely, the order in which the different subsidiary keys of a main key of a composition can be made to be heard. [Au.]

2. Even this term is not completely suitable, for the resting points are something essential not only in speech but also in melody. In the first, the distinguishing marks in their visible presentation are nothing more than an aid to discover more quickly the more or less noticeable resting points (which even without punctuation marks would still be there). In melody there is no need of this aid, because its resting points affect our feeling enough that there is no need to use special signs to indicate them. Nevertheless, these subjects have a great deal of similarity; for example, a dot ends the periods of speech in the same way as the cadence closes the periods of melody; the phrase of partial close and the incise differentiate the melodic sections of the period just as do the semicolon and comma the smaller sections of the periods in speech. It is this similarity in particular which induced me to use the term "punctuation" in connection with the differentiation of melodic sections. [Au.] "Phrase of partial close" and "incise" translate the German terms *Absatz* and *Einschnitt,* which Koch uses along with *Schlußsatz,* or "closing phrase," to designate the three types of melodic sections according to the finality of their punctuation; see §79.

3. From the Latin *incisio,* or "clause."

istic cadence formula, we shall call it a *closing phrase,* in order to distinguish it from the phrase of partial close.

From this division there result three different types of melodic sections, namely incises, phrases of partial close, and closing phrases. According to the introduction in the preceding section [§78], what is important for all of these divisions is the formula through which they become noticeable as resting points, or, to use our chosen term, their punctuation mark and also the length or number of their measures.

•   •   •   •   •

§80. Completeness in melodic phrases manifests itself in different ways. (1) A phrase may contain only as much as is absolutely necessary for it to be understood and felt as an independent section of the whole; such a phrase I shall call a *basic phrase.* Or, (2) it may also contain a clarification, a more complete definition of the feeling, and in this case the phrase is an *extended phrase.* Or, (3) two or more phrases, complete in themselves, are combined so that externally they appear in the form of a single phrase; such a phrase we wish to call a *compound phrase.*

CHAPTER 1. ON BASIC PHRASES AND THE INCISES CONTAINED IN THEM

•   •   •   •   •

§82. A basic phrase is complete when it can be understood or felt as a self-sufficient section of the whole, without a preceding or succeeding incomplete segment fortuitously connected with it. The following phrases in Examples 1 through 4, for instance, are of this type.

Example 1

Example 2

Example 3

Example 4

Allegretto

The dissimilarity among these basic, complete phrases referred to in §79 shows itself when we compare them with one another. Some are of such a nature that we necessarily expect still one or more sections to follow in the whole to which they are joined because (usually) they cannot close the whole themselves. Both phrases in Examples 1 and 2 are of this type and are called phrases of partial close because they are unable to conclude the whole. The phrases in Examples 3 and 4, on the other hand, can close the whole after other preceding sections, and because of their characteristic ending formula we call them closing phrases.

Furthermore, the essential difference between a phrase of partial close and a closing phrase depends on nothing more than the essential difference of ending formulas. Hence phrases of partial close can be transformed into closing phrases through alteration of their ending formula, and vice versa. Thus, for example, the phrases of partial close found above in Examples 1 and 2 are changed into closing phrases in Examples 5 and 6, and, conversely, the closing phrases in Examples 3 and 4 are changed into phrases of partial close in Examples 7 and 8.

Example 5

Example 6

Example 7

Example 8

§83. In complete phrases the melody may cohere so closely that no notice-able resting points can be discovered by which these complete phrases may be broken up into incomplete segments. Or the melody of these phrases may contain noticeable resting points, so that the phrases can be broken up into incomplete segments. Examples of the first category of these complete phrases are presented in the previous section [§82]; examples of the second category will be more closely examined forthwith.

§84. When we sing or play the following phrases in Examples 9 through 11, our feeling persuades us that (1) the resting points which cut up the phrase into incomplete segments are felt at the places marked Δ and that (2) when we sing or play these phrases only up to the sign Δ, they still need something more to be complete. They do not impress us as complete phrases unless we connect the segment immediately following Δ.

Example 9

Example 10

Example 11

These resting points in the complete phrases, or these still incomplete seg-ments of a phrase, are called incises.[4] They may not be revealed through any-

---

4. Henceforth Koch uses the sign △ to indicate incises and the sign □ to indicate complete phrases or phrases of partial close.

thing external, as in the quoted examples, or they may contain an outward sign
of a short rest, as in Examples 12 through 14.

Example 12

Example 13

Example 14

• • • • •

1. On the length of basic phrases and the incises contained in them

§86. Complete phrases need less or more length depending on whether they
are basic or somewhat extended phrases. Because in this chapter we shall first
consider the nature of basic phrases so that we can later understand more
clearly how and through what means they can be extended, we now deal only
with the length of basic phrases.

§87. Most common, and also, on the whole, most useful and most pleasing
for our feelings are those basic phrases which are completed in the fourth
measure of simple meters. For that reason they are called *four-measure
phrases*. They may actually appear as four measures in simple meters or in
compound meters in the form of only two measures. All of the preceding examples in the chapter are of this nature.

• • • • •

§88. When four-measure phrases are broken down into smaller segments
through resting points, they contain, according to §83, either complete or
incomplete incises.[5] The most common incises of four-measure units are those

---

5. Koch defines a complete incise as one that "takes two or more measures of a simple meter,"
   while an incomplete incise "fills only a single measure" (§85). Simple meters are those in which

complete incises which consist of two measures and thus divide the phrase into two segments of equal length. . . . Very unusual, on the other hand, is a complete incise of three measures *in a four-measure unit,* as in Example 15.

Example 15

If the four-measure phrase contains incomplete incises, however, then usually two incomplete incises follow one another and form a complete incise of two measures, as in Example 16. . . .

Example 16

More unusual are basic phrases of four measures in which one incomplete incise is not followed immediately by another similar one, but is closely connected with the next segment of the phrase, as in Example 17.

Example 17

§89. Not all basic phrases are complete in the fourth measure; often such a phrase becomes complete only in the fifth or sixth, occasionally not until the seventh measure. These basic phrases of more than four measures should not be confused with extended phrases of the same number of measures, because the former require a different treatment from the latter in the joining of phrases in a period.

If a phrase is complete in the fifth measure of a simple meter then it is called a *five-measure phrase.* Such a phrase can arise in three ways:

It can arise (1) from a four-measure phrase, by means of the extension of two metrical units to two measures. When, for example, the metrical units of

---

the measure has only one downbeat, or strong part ($\frac{2}{2}$, $\frac{2}{4}$, $\frac{3}{4}$, and $\frac{3}{8}$), while compound meters consist of a pair of these measures with the barline omitted ($\frac{4}{4}$, $\frac{6}{4}$, and $\frac{6}{8}$).

the first measure in the phrases of Examples 18–20 are extended to complete measures and thereby made more emphatic, this results in the five-measure phrases in Examples 21–23.[6]

Example 18

Example 19

Example 20

Example 21

Example 22

Graun

Example 23

Graun

When a four-measure unit which is to be extended to a five-measure unit contains a complete incise of two measures, as does, for instance, the phrase in Example 20, then not only the first segment can contain the extension as in Example 23, but also the second, as in Example 24.

6. Examples 22 and 23 are taken from Carl Heinrich Graun's opera *Catone in Utica*. [Tr.]

Example 24

But in practice, the extension of the first segment occurs far more often than the extension of the second one.

The five-measure unit can also arise (2) from the joining of two unequal segments, of which each is incomplete in itself and in which there is no extension. In this case, the first segment of the phrase, or the incise, is longer than the second segment, as in Example 25.

Example 25

More unusual is the case in which the second segment of a five-measure phrase not arising through extension is the longer one, as in Example 26.[7]

Example 26

CHAPTER 2. ON EXTENDED PHRASES

§105. A phrase is extended when it contains more than is absolutely necessary for its completeness. The extension of a phrase through which the feeling it contains is defined more precisely can be brought about by various means. The first of these means is the repetition of a segment of a phrase, and this can occur either in the same key which underlies the passage to be repeated or in another key.[8]

If the repetition of a segment of a phrase occurs in the same key, then either the repetition has the same underlying harmony, or it occurs on degrees of the scale which require a different harmony.

7. Koch discusses means of composing six- and seven-measure phrases in §90 and §91.

8. In periods often entire complete phrases are repeated, sometimes in the same key, sometimes also in another key. The discussion of such repetitions does not belong in this part, which is concerned only with the nature of melodic sections, but in the following one, where the connection of these divisions is treated. [Au.] Koch refers here to Section 4, "On the Connection of Melodic Sections, or the Construction of Periods," parts of which are excerpted on pp. 790–95 and 807–19.

The repetition is made with a segment of the phrase which either does or does not contain the ending formula of the complete phrase. In the first instance, when the punctuation figure of the phrase must also be repeated, the repetition (especially when it is varied) has the appearance of an appendix. This instance will be separately treated later, after consideration of the repetition of those segments in which the punctuation formula of the complete phrase is not repeated.

§106. When a basic phrase is extended through the repetition of only a single measure, then this repetition always occurs in the same key. The measure which is reiterated can be the first or one of the middle measures of the phrase, for instance Examples 27 and 28.

Example 27

Example 28

Composers usually tend to have this single repeated measure performed more softly or more loudly and, moreover, the repetition itself can be varied in different ways without damage, as in Examples 29 and 30.

Example 29

Example 30

In this case, the repetition of a measure is not only on the same harmonic basis, but also on the same degrees of the scale. *Such a five-measure phrase arising through the repetition of a measure retains the value of a four-measure phrase under all circumstances relating to the connection of several melodic*

sections. It is considered as a four-measure unit with regard to the rhythmic relation of phrases.

A single measure of the phrase may be repeated so that the repetition does occur on the same underlying harmony, but the upper voice is inverted with the middle voice, whether actually present or only presumed, as in Example 31.

Example 31

The perceptibility of the repetition is often lost through this inversion of voices. Such a four-measure phrase, changed into a five-measure one in which the repetition of a measure is not noticeable enough because of the inversion of the upper voices, is usually treated as a five-measure unit in the construction of periods.

§107. In practice, far more common than the repetition of a single measure is the extension of a basic phrase through the repetition of two measures which form an incise; for instance, Example 32. Both these repeated measures can be varied in all possible ways, for instance as in Example 33.

Example 32

Example 33

When in the repetition of two measures the upper voices are inverted as in Example 34, then feeling never fails to recognize this repetition.

Example 34

Thus such a four-measure phrase, which has been extended to six measures by the repetition of two, is always considered as a four-measure unit with respect to the rhythmic relations of phrases.

•   •   •   •   •

§110. The second means through which a phrase can be extended and the content of it more closely defined is the addition of an explanation, an appendix, which further clarifies the phrase. This appendix can be a section of the phrase itself, whose repetition makes the content of the phrase more emphatic, as in Examples 35 and 36, or it may be an incomplete segment which is not yet present in the phrase but which is able to define its content more closely, as in Examples 37 and 38.

Example 35

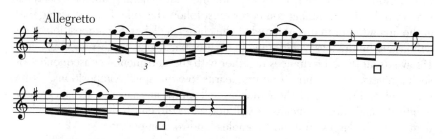

Example 36

Example 37

Example 38

•   •   •   •   •

[VOLUME 3 (1793)]

SECTION 4. ON THE CONNECTION OF MELODIC SECTIONS, OR THE
CONSTRUCTION OF PERIODS

•   •   •   •   •

§7. It is recognized as a general rule that with every skill to be acquired, one must proceed gradually from the easier to the more difficult, from the simpler to the more complicated. Likewise with the skill of joining melodic sections into a whole, the beginning composer must follow this rule. For supposing that at the first attempt to invent a melody he chose an elaborate composition, then a thousand hindrances would stand in his way, partly real, partly only imaginary. He avoids all these hindrances together with the detrimental consequences of such a reversed procedure if he first learns to write small compositions.[9] If he is then given instruction in how such a small composition can be given a greater length through various means, it will not seem difficult to him to proceed by degrees to the largest and most complex kinds of compositions.

To give the beginner opportunity for this gradual progress, I am dividing the various ways of connecting melodic sections into different chapters. Thus the second chapter is to treat the diverse ways of connecting melodic sections in short compositions.

In the third, I shall attempt to show how these small compositions can be enlarged by different means.

The subject of the following chapters, however, will be the ways of connecting several melodic sections, or the arrangement of larger compositions.[10]

In this way I hope to be able to make comprehensible to the beginner the various methods of connecting melodic sections. Moreover, this gives me the best opportunity to show without long-windedness the most essential matters concerning the arrangement of each particular composition, which I promised to do in the introduction to the first volume.

Remark

I have further divided the chapters which concern this subject into special exercises, partly in order not to weary the beginner through the quick succession of the several ways of connecting phrases, but especially in order to give him more opportunity to exercise his power of invention through imitating all particular methods of connection. Nothing will be troublesome about these exercises if he is sufficiently practiced in counterpoint and has studied the contents of the second part of the second volume with the necessary attention.

9. Here and afterwards in this section, by "composition" I understand not the joining of several individual movements, for example an Allegro, Andante, and Presto, into a symphony or sonata, but I mean each of these individual movements separately. I will not use the customary expression "section" because I have applied it already too precisely to the parts of a whole. [Au.] Unlike the English word "section," the German word *Satz* is readily used to designate an entire movement as well as a portion of a movement. Because *Satz* is so important to Koch as "phrase," he wants to reserve it for that use exclusively.

10. Portions of this chapter are included on pp. 807–19.

But is not genius too greatly limited or indeed even suppressed through such imitations in which a certain form is determined? The reason for this objection is well known. From time immemorial there have been people who wished to shake off all imagined constraints of art, who chose to concede everything to genius, but nothing at all to craft. If young composers who wish to use these pages for instruction should be taken in by this prejudice, I can say nothing further here than to reassure them that their genius neither will nor can as yet show itself to its total extent, and that no other way can probably be devised to lead their genius in the right direction. If one has once used the proper ways of connecting melodic sections through imitation of the correct forms, then these fetters fall off by themselves.

·   ·   ·   ·   ·

CHAPTER 2: ON THE CONNECTION OF MELODIC SECTIONS INTO PERIODS OF SHORT LENGTH, OR THE ARRANGEMENT OF SHORT COMPOSITIONS

·   ·   ·   ·   ·

Exercise 1, in which four melodic sections are connected,
of which two contain a cadence in the main key

§24. In this case the two sections which contain the cadence are usually the second and fourth phrase; that is, they divide the whole into two small periods or sections, which are either repeated as a reprise or performed without repetition. Now with regard to both those melodic sections which close not with cadences, but merely with phrase-endings, four different situations or punctuation forms are possible here. For with our accepted condition that the second and fourth section make a cadence in the main key, either (1) the first melodic section can close with a phrase-ending on the triad of the main key, that is as a I-phrase, the third section with a phrase-ending on the triad of the fifth, that is as a V-phrase.[11] Example 39 is such a case.[12]

Example 39

11. In §93–§104 Koch discusses the "ending formulas" of melodic sections (a matter already touched on in §82). There are essentially two types, each involving closure on the strong beat of a measure on a note (often embellished) of the triad that is the goal of that particular section. If the triad is on the keynote of the composition, the phrase is called a I-phrase [*Grundabsatz*], if on the fifth degree, then a *V-phrase* [*Quintabsatz*]. In §25 Koch lists the other three possibilities for the endings of melodic sections 1 and 3 when 2 and 4 end in the main key: V and I, V and V, and I and I.

12. This minuet by Haydn is the third movement of a divertimento for two violins, flute, oboe, violoncello, and bass composed before 1766, Hoboken II:1. [Tr.]

Remark 1

In connection with the example, the opportunity immediately arises to make a remark which had occurred to me in §22.[13]

This short composition has the most perfect unity. It consists of four melodic sections and contains only a single main idea, which, however, is modified in various ways. This is the first four-measure phrase, which initially appears as a I-phrase, but immediately afterwards has been repeated and changed into a closing phrase. In the second section, the phrase which is a V-phrase and with its repetition is the closing phrase is essentially the very same phrase; it has merely been given a different turn. The phrase has been played in contrary motion and through a passing modulation has been given more variety.

From this it is apparent that a single phrase can indeed be sufficient for such a short composition if the composer knows how to give it a different direction and connection so that the whole, despite its unity, obtains nevertheless the necessary variety.

But one must not believe that in such short compositions of four phrases the three last phrases always have to arise through modification of the first. No! In most such compositions two truly different melodic sections are connected; the remaining two then arise partly through alteration and partly also through repetition of the preceding sections, as in Example 40.

Example 40

13. In §22 Koch enunciates the important late eighteenth-century principle of unity tempered by variety, explaining that using four different melodic sections in one short composition would result in too much variety, destroying the coherence of the whole.

Compositions of this kind are found in which even three different melodic sections have been connected, without the piece being deprived of all unity. But in this case the fourth phrase necessarily must be a clear repetition of the first or second phrase, otherwise the piece would lose its unity. When the second section of the preceding minuet is composed in the manner of Example 41, it is a short piece of sixteen measures which contains three different phrases.

Example 41

In most cases, however, the composition is better when the connected phrases are more similar to each other, as in Examples 39 and 40.

.   .   .   .   .

Exercise 2, in which four melodic sections are connected,
of which one contains a cadence in a secondary key

§30. Here, too, the first cadence, which closes in a secondary key, is usually made by means of the second phrase, and the whole is divided into two periods of equal size.

When the major mode is used, this secondary key in which the second phrase closes is the major key of the fifth; but when the minor mode is used, it can be either the minor key of the fifth or the major key of the third.

§31. In the major mode, when the second phrase closes with a cadence in the fifth, again four different punctuation forms arise with regard to the first and third phrases. (1) The first melodic section can be a I-phrase, the third a V-phrase. This is the most usual form for four melodic sections of which the second closes with a cadence in the fifth (Example 42).[14]

Example 42

14. In order not to give examples only in the meter and tempo of the minuet, I choose for this exercise the type of short composition described in §20, and I leave it to the beginner to practice these forms also on the minuet or other dance melodies. [Au.] Koch classifies short compositions into three types: dance melodies, melodies for songs and odes, and "short pieces of no defined character, whose meter, tempo, and arrangement of rhythm and punctuation depend entirely upon the imagination of the composer." This last is the type of composition described in §20.

(2) Both the first and the third melodic section can be a V-phrase. When the first phrase of the Allegretto of Example 42 is altered, the punctuation form shown is obtained (Example 43).[15]

Example 43

etc.

15. Koch goes on to give examples of the other two possibilities for the endings of melodic sections 1 and 3 (V and I, I and I), and closes §31 with a lengthy discussion of the various ways in which melodic section 3 can lead back into the closing section.

THE PRACTICE OF COMPOSITION: MOVEMENT AND WORK

125 Johann Joachim Quantz

An outstanding flute player and composer for the flute, Johann Joachim Quantz began his career as an oboist in the Dresden town band in 1716. He was born in 1697 and received his first training in counterpoint under J. D. Zelenka, a pupil of Fux, in Vienna. In 1724 he set out on a series of extended journeys. He visited Italy, where he studied in Rome with Francesco Gasparini. In 1726 he went to Paris, where he stayed seven months and published several instrumental works, and in 1727 to London, where he stayed three months. In 1728 Quantz entered into relations with Frederick the Great, who became a great admirer of his art and engaged him in 1741 as a flutist and composer to his court. He retained this position until his death in 1773.

Quantz was an extremely prolific composer: for the King alone he wrote three hundred concertos and two hundred other compositions. His best-known work, however, and the one that best testifies to the solidity of his musicianship, is his method for the flute, *Versuch einer Anweisung die Flöte traversière zu spielen* (*Essay on a Method for Playing the Transverse Flute;* 1752). The book does not confine itself to flute playing but discusses questions of general importance for the musical practice and musical aesthetics of the time.

FROM *Essay on a Method for Playing the Transverse Flute*

(1752)

CHAPTER 18. HOW A PERFORMER AND A PIECE OF MUSIC OUGHT TO BE JUDGED

28. To judge an instrumental composition properly, we must have an exact knowledge, not only of the characteristics of each type of piece which may occur, but also, as already observed, of the instruments themselves. In itself, a piece may conform both to good taste and to the rules of composition, and hence be well written, but still run counter to the instrument. On the other hand, a piece may conform to the instrument, but be in itself useless. Vocal music has certain advantages which instrumental music must do without. The words and the human voice work to the composer's greatest advantage, with regard both to invention and to characterization. Experience clearly shows this when, in the absence of voices, arias are played on an instrument. Without words and without the human voice, instrumental music, quite as much as vocal music, should express certain passions and transport the listeners from one to another. But if this is to be properly managed, to compensate for the

TEXT: The original edition (Berlin, 1752), pp. 293–305. Translation by Oliver Strunk, with minor alterations.

absence of words and of the human voice, neither the composer nor the performer may have a soul of wood.

29. The principal types of instrumental composition in which voices take no part are: the concerto, the overture, the sinfonia, the quartet, the trio, and the solo. In each of the following there are two varieties: the concerto, the trio, and the solo. We have *concerti grossi* and *concerti da camera*. The trios are, as the phrase goes, either elaborate or *galant*. With the solos the case is the same.

30. The concertos were originated by the Italians. Torelli is said to have written the first ones. A *concerto grosso* consists of a mixture of various concerted instruments wherein, as an invariable rule, two or more parts—the number may sometimes run as high as eight or even higher—concert with one another. In the *concerto da camera*, however, there is only a single concerted instrument.

31. The qualities of a *concerto grosso* require, in each of its movements: (1) a majestic ritornello at the beginning, which should be more harmonic than melodic, more serious than humorous, and relieved by unisons; (2) a skillful mixture of the imitations in the concerted parts, in order that the ear may be unexpectedly surprised, now by this instrument, now by that; (3) these imitations must be made up of short and pleasing ideas; (4) there must be a constant alternation of the brilliant and the ingratiating; (5) the inner tutti sections must be kept short; (6) the alternations of the concerted instruments must be so distributed that one is not heard too much and another too little; (7) now and then, after a trio, there must be woven in a short solo for one instrument or another; (8) before the end the solo instruments must briefly repeat what they had at the beginning; and (9) the final tutti must conclude with the loftiest and most majestic ideas of the first ritornello. Such a concerto requires numerous accompanying players, a large place, a serious performance, and a moderate tempo.

32. Of concertos with a single concerted instrument, the so-called *concerti da camera*, there are likewise two varieties. Some, like the *concerto grosso*, require many accompanying players, others a few. Unless this is observed, neither the one nor the other has its proper effect. From the first ritornello one can gather to which variety a concerto belongs. If it is serious, majestic, more harmonic than melodic, and relieved by many unisons, the harmony changing, not with eighth or quarter measures, but with half or full measures, many players must accompany. If, on the other hand, it consists in a fleeting, humorous, gay, or singing melody, the harmony changing rapidly, it will have a better effect with a few players accompanying than with many.

33. A serious concerto, that is, a simple one written for many players, requires the following in the first movement: (1) There should be a majestic ritornello, with all the parts well elaborated. (2) There should be a pleasing and intelligible melody. (3) There should be regular imitations. (4) The best ideas of the ritornello may be broken up and used for relief within or between the solos. (5) The thoroughbass should sound well and be suitable for use as a bass.

(6) The composer should write no more inner parts than the principal part permits, for it is often more effective to double the principal melody than to introduce forced inner parts. (7) The progressions of the thoroughbass and of the inner parts may neither impede the principal part in its liveliness nor drown out or stifle it. (8) A proportional length must be observed in the ritornello. It should consist of at least two main sections. The second of these, since it is to be repeated at the end of the movement as a conclusion, must be clothed with the finest and most majestic ideas. (9) Insofar as the opening idea of the ritornello is neither singing nor wholly suitable for solo use, the composer must introduce a new idea, directly contrasted with the first, but so joined to it that it is not evident whether it is introduced from necessity or after due deliberation. (10) The solo sections must be in part singing, while the ingratiating quality should be in part relieved by brilliant, melodious, harmonious passages, always suited to the instrument, and also, to maintain the fire to the end, by short, lively, majestic tutti sections. (11) The concerted or solo sections may not be too short or the inner tuttis too long. (12) The accompaniment to the solo must contain no progressions which might obscure the concerted part; on the contrary, it must be made up alternately of many parts and few, in order that the principal part may now and then have room to come to the fore with greater freedom. In general, light and shade must be maintained throughout. When the solo passages permit it, or when the composer knows how to invent such as will, it is most effective that the accompanying parts beneath them should introduce something familiar from the ritornello. (13) The modulation must always be correct and natural, not touching on any key so remote that it might offend the ear. (14) The laws of meter, to which the composer has at all times to pay strict attention, must here, too, be exactly observed. The caesuras, or divisions of the melody, may not fall on the second or fourth quarter in common duple time, or on the third or fifth beat in triple. The composer must endeavor to maintain the meter with which he begins, whether it be by whole or half measures or, in triple time, by two-, four-, or eight-measure phrases; otherwise the most artful composition becomes defective. In triple time, in an arioso, if the melody permits frequent divisions, successive caesuras after three- and two-measure phrases are permitted. (15) The composer may not follow up the solo passages with uniform transpositions *ad nauseam;* on the contrary, he must imperceptibly interrupt and shorten them at the right time. (16) The ending may not be hurried unduly or bitten off too short; on the contrary, the composer should endeavor to make it thoroughly solid. Nor may he conclude with wholly new ideas; on the contrary, the last solo section must repeat the most pleasing of those ideas that have been heard before. (17) The last tutti, finally, must conclude the Allegro, as briefly as possible, with the second section of the first ritornello.

34. Not every variety of measure is suitable for the first movement of a majestic concerto. If the movement is to be lively, the composer may employ common duple time, in which the smallest note is the sixteenth, permitting the

caesura to fall on the second half of the measure. If it is also to be majestic, he should choose a broader meter, one in which the caesura regularly occupies the full measure and falls only on the down beat. If, however, it is to be both serious and majestic, he may choose for it, in common duple time, a moderate tempo in which the smallest note is the thirty-second, the caesura falling on the second half of the measure. The dotted sixteenths will in this case contribute much to the majesty of the ritornello. The movement may be defined by the word *allegretto*. Notes of this kind can also be written in the moderate alla breve time. It is only necessary to change the eighths to quarters, the sixteenths to eighths, and the thirty-seconds to sixteenths. In this case, however, the caesura may always fall on the beginning of the measure. The ordinary alla breve time, in which the smallest note is the eighth, is to be regarded as the equivalent of two-four time and is more suited to the last movement than to the first, for, unless one writes continually in the strict style, using all the voices, it is more expressive of the pleasing than of the majestic. In general, triple time is little used for the first movement, unless in the form of three-four time with occasional sixteenths and a movement in eighths in the inner and lowest parts, the harmony changing, as a rule, only with full measures.

35. The Adagio must be distinguished from the first Allegro in every respect—in its musical rhyme-structure, its meter, and its key. If the Allegro is in one of the major keys, for example in C major, the Adagio may, as one prefers, be in C minor, E minor, A minor, F major, G major, or even G minor. If, on the other hand, the first Allegro is in one of the minor keys, for example in C minor, the Adagio may be in E-flat major, F minor, G minor, or A-flat major. These successions of keys are the most natural. The ear is never offended by them, and the same relationships apply to all keys, whatever they may be called. He who wishes to surprise the listener in a painful and disagreeable way is at liberty to choose, beyond these keys, such as may give pleasure to him alone. To say the least, considerable caution is necessary in this regard.

36. For the arousing and subsequent stilling of the passions the Adagio offers greater opportunity than the Allegro. In former times it was for the most part written in a plain dry style, more harmonic than melodic. The composers left to the performers what had been expected of themselves, namely, to make the melody singable, but this could not be well accomplished without considerable addition of embellishments. In other words, in those days it was much easier to write an Adagio than to play one. Now, as it may be readily imagined that such an Adagio did not always have the good fortune to fall into skillful hands, and since the performance was seldom as successful as the author might have wished, there has come of this evil some good, namely, that composers have for some time past begun to make their Adagios more singing. By this means the composer has more honor and the performer less of a puzzle; moreover, the Adagio itself can no longer be distorted or mutilated in such a variety of ways as was formerly often the case.

37. But since the Adagio does not usually find as many admirers as the Allegro among the musically uninstructed, the composer must endeavor in every possible way to make it pleasing even to those listeners without musical experience. To this end, he should above all strictly observe the following rules. (1) He must aim studiously at the greatest possible brevity, both in the ritornellos and in the solo sections. (2) The ritornello must be melodious, harmonious, and expressive. (3) The principal part must have a melody which, though it permits some addition of embellishments, may still please without them. (4) The melody of the principal part must alternate with the tutti sections used between for relief. (5) This melody must be just as touching and expressive as though there were words below it. (6) From time to time something from the ritornello must be introduced. (7) The composer may not wander off into too many keys, for this is the greatest impediment to brevity. (8) The accompaniment beneath the solo must be rather more plain than figured, in order that the principal part may not be prevented from making ornaments and may retain complete freedom to introduce, judiciously and reasonably, many or few embellishments. (9) The composer, finally, must endeavor to characterize the Adagio with some epithet clearly expressing the passion contained therein, in order that the required tempo may be readily determined.

38. The final Allegro of a concerto must be very different from the first movement, not only in its style and nature, but also in its meter. The last Allegro must be just as humorous and sprightly as the first is serious. To this end, the following meters will prove useful: $\frac{2}{4}$, $\frac{3}{4}$, $\frac{3}{8}$, $\frac{6}{8}$, $\frac{9}{8}$, and $\frac{12}{8}$. In no case should all three movements of a concerto be written in the same meter. But if the first movement is in duple time and the second in triple, the last may be written either in triple or in two-four time. In no case, however, may it stand in common duple time, for this would be too serious and hence as little suited to the last movement as two-four or a rapid triple time to the first. Similarly, all three movements may not begin on the same step, but, if the upper part begins on the keynote in the first movement, it may begin on the third in the second movement and on the fifth in the third. And although the last movement is in the key of the first, the composer, to avoid similarity in the modulations, must still be careful not to pass through the same succession of keys in the last movement as he did in the first.

39. Generally speaking, in the last movement (1) The ritornello must be short, lively, fiery, but at the same time somewhat playful. (2) The principal part must have a simple melody, pleasing and fleeting. (3) The solo passages should be easy, in order that the rapidity of the movement may not be impeded. They must, furthermore, bear no similarity to those in the first movement. For example, if the solos in the first movement are made up of broken notes and arpeggios, those in the last movement may proceed by step or by turn figures. Or if there are triplets in the first movement, the passages in the last movement may be made up of even notes, or vice versa. (4) The laws of

meter must be observed with the utmost severity. For the shorter and more rapid the variety of measure, the more painful it is if these laws are violated. In $\frac{2}{4}$ and in rapid $\frac{3}{4}$, $\frac{3}{8}$, and $\frac{6}{8}$ time, the caesura, then, must always fall on the beginning of every second measure, the principal divisions on the fourth and eighth measures. (5) The accompaniment may not employ too many voices or be overcrowded; on the contrary, it must be made up of such notes as the accompanying parts can produce without undue movement or effort, for the last movement is as a rule played very rapidly.

40. To insure a proportional length, even in a concerto, consult a timepiece. If the first movement takes five minutes, the Adagio five to six, and the last movement three to four, the whole is of the proper length. And it is in general more advantageous if the listeners find a piece rather too short than too long.

41. He who now understands how to make a concerto of this sort will also have no difficulty in contriving a humorous little *concerto da camera* of the playful kind. It will, then, be unnecessary to discuss this separately.

42. An overture, played before an opera, requires a majestic beginning, full of gravity, a brilliant, well-elaborated principal section, and a good combination of different instruments, such as flutes, oboes, or horns. Its origin is due to the French. Lully has provided excellent models. Some German composers, however, among them Handel and Telemann, have far surpassed him in this. Indeed, the French fare with their overtures very much as do the Italians with their concertos. Still, in view of their excellent effect, it is a pity that the overtures are not more usual in Germany.

43. The Italian sinfonias, having the same purpose as the overtures, naturally require precisely the same qualities for their majestic display. But since most of them are contrived by composers such as have exercised their genius more in vocal than in instrumental music, we have thus far only a very few sinfonias that are perfect in all respects, and thus can serve as a good model. Sometimes it seems as though the composers of opera, in contriving their sinfonias, went about it as do those painters who, in finishing a portrait, use the leftover colors to fill in the sky or the costume. In the meantime it stands to reason, as previously mentioned, that a sinfonia should have some connection with the content of its opera or at least with the first scene of it and not, as frequently occurs, conclude invariably with a gay minuet. I have no wish to propose a model in this regard, for it is impossible to bring under a single head all the circumstances that may occur at the beginning of an opera. At the same time, I believe that it should be very easy to find a mean. It is admittedly quite unnecessary that the sinfonia before an opera consist always of three movements; could the composer not conclude, perhaps, with the first or second? For example, if the first scene involved heroic or other fiery passions, he might end his sinfonia with the first movement. If mournful or amorous passions occurred in it, he might stop after the second movement. But if the first scene involved no specific passions at all, these appearing only in the course of the opera or at the end, he might close with the third movement. By so doing, he would have an opportunity to arrange

each movement in a way suitable to the matter at hand. The sinfonia, moreover, would still retain its usefulness for other purposes.

44. A quartet, that is, a sonata for three concerted instruments and a thoroughbass, is the real touchstone of the true contrapuntist, as it is also an affair wherein many a one not properly grounded in his art may come to grief. Its use has never become really common; as a result, it may not even be known to everyone. Indeed, it is to be feared that in the end this kind of music will have to suffer the fate of the lost arts. A good quartet implies: (1) pure four-part writing; (2) a good harmonious melody; (3) short, regular imitations; (4) a judicious combination of the concerted instruments; (5) a proper thoroughbass suited for use as a bass; (6) ideas of the sort that are mutually invertible, so that one may build either above or below them, the inner parts maintaining an at least tolerable and not displeasing melodic line; (7) that it must not be obvious whether this part or that one has the advantage; (8) that each part, after a rest, must reenter, not as inner part, but as principal part and with a pleasing melody (this, however, is to be understood as applying, not to the thoroughbass, but only to the three concerted parts); (9) that if there is a fugue, it must be carried out in a masterly and at the same time tasteful fashion in all four parts, observing all the rules. A certain set of six quartets for various instruments, chiefly flute, oboe, and violin, composed quite some time ago by Herr Telemann, may serve as particularly beautiful models of this kind of music.

45. A trio, while it is a task less tedious for the composer than a quartet, nevertheless requires on his part almost the same degree of artistry, if it is in its way to be of the proper sort. Yet it has the advantage that the ideas introduced may be more *galant* and pleasing than in the quartet, for there is one concerted part the less. In a trio, then, the composer must follow these rules: (1) He must invent a melody which will tolerate a singing counterpoint. (2) The subjects proposed at the beginning of each movement may not be too long, especially in the Adagio, for in the imitations which the second part makes at the fifth, fourth, and unison, an overlong subject can easily become wearisome. (3) No part may propose any subject that the other cannot answer. (4) The imitations must be brief and the passages brilliant. (5) In the repetition of the most pleasing ideas a good order must be maintained. (6) The two principal parts must be so written that the thoroughbass below may be natural and sound well. (7) If a fugue is introduced, it must be, as in the quartet, carried out in all the parts, not only correctly, observing all the rules of composition, but also tastefully. The episodes, whether they consist of passages or of other imitations, must be pleasing and brilliant. (8) While progressions of the two principal parts in parallel thirds and sixths are an ornament of the trio, they must not be overdone or run into the ground, but rather interrupted by passages or other imitations. (9) The trio, finally, must be so contrived that one can scarcely guess which of the two parts is the first.

46. To write a solo is today no longer regarded as an art. Almost every instrumentalist occupies himself in this way. If he has no ideas, he helps himself with

borrowed ones. If he is lacking in knowledge of the rules of composition, he lets someone else write the bass for him. As a result, our time brings forth, instead of good models, many monstrosities.

47. As a matter of fact, it is by no means so easy to write a good solo. There are composers who understand composition perfectly and are successful in works for many voices, but who write poor solos. On the other hand, there are composers for whom solos turn out better than pieces for many voices. He who succeeds in both is fortunate. Little need as there is to have mastered all the innermost secrets of composition in order to write a good solo, there is as little chance of accomplishing anything reasonable of this kind without having some understanding of harmony.

48. If a solo is to reflect credit on the composer and the performer, then (1) its Adagio must be in itself singing and expressive; (2) the performer must have opportunities to show his judgment, invention, and insight; (3) the delicate must be relieved from time to time by something ingenious; (4) the thoroughbass must be a natural one, above which one can build easily; (5) no idea may be too often repeated, either in the same key or in a transposition, for not only can this make difficulties for the player, but it can also become tiresome for the listeners; (6) the natural melody must be interrupted occasionally by dissonances, to arouse the passions of the listeners in a suitable manner; (7) the Adagio must not be too long.

49. The first Allegro requires: (1) a flowing, coherent, and somewhat serious melody; (2) well-connected ideas; (3) brilliant passages, well unified melodically; (4) a good order in the repetition of the ideas; (5) choice and beautiful progressions at the end of the first part, so arranged that, in a transposition, they may conclude the second part also; (6) that the first part be somewhat shorter than the second; (7) that the most brilliant passages be reserved for the second part; (8) that the thoroughbass be natural, causing such progressions as will maintain a continuous liveliness.

50. The second Allegro may be either very lively and rapid, or moderate and aria-like. In this, the composer must be guided by the first movement. If it is serious, the last movement may be lively. But if it is lively and rapid, the last movement may be moderate and aria-like. With regard to variety of meter, what was said of the concertos must also be observed here, lest one movement be like the other. In general, if a solo is to please everyone, it must be so contrived that it affords nourishment to each listener's temperamental inclinations. It must be neither purely cantabile nor purely spirited from beginning to end. And just as each movement must be very different from any other, the individual movements must be in themselves good mixtures of pleasing and brilliant ideas. For the most beautiful melody will in the end prove a soporific if it is never relieved, and continuous liveliness and unmitigated difficulty arouse astonishment but do not particularly move. Indeed, such mixtures of contrasted ideas should be the aim, not merely in the solo, but in all kinds of music. If a composer knows how to hit this off properly and thereby to set in motion the passions of his listeners, one may truly say of him that he has

attained a high degree of good taste and found, so to speak, the musical philosopher's stone.[1]

1. Compare Charles Burney's characterization of John Christian Bach (*A General History of Music*, vol. 4, p. 483): "Bach seems to have been the first composer who observed the law of *contrast* as a *principle*. Before his time, contrast there frequently was, in the works of others; but it seems to have been accidental. Bach in his symphonies and other instrumental pieces, as well as his songs, seldom failed, after a rapid and noisy passage to introduce one that was slow and soothing."

126 Heinrich Christoph Koch

FROM *Introductory Essay on Composition*
(1782–93)

[VOLUME 3 (1793)]

PART 2. ON THE MECHANICAL RULES OF MELODY:
ON THE WAY IN WHICH MELODY IS CONNECTED WITH
RESPECT TO THE MECHANICAL RULES

SECTION 4. ON THE CONNECTION OF MELODIC SECTIONS, OR THE
CONSTRUCTION OF PERIODS

CHAPTER 4. ON THE CONNECTION OF MELODIC SECTIONS INTO
PERIODS OF GREATER LENGTH, OR THE ARRANGEMENT OF LARGER
COMPOSITIONS

1. *On the Nature and Arrangement of the Most Common Compositions*

V. *On the symphony*

§100. The symphony is an instrumental piece of many parts, of which the four main ones, namely the first and second violin, viola, and bass, are strongly reinforced. It is used not only for the introduction of a play and a cantata, but also for the opening of chamber music or concerts. In the first case, it often consists of only a single Allegro; but in the latter case, it usually contains three movements of different character. For the most part, the character of magnifi-

TEXT: *Versuch einer Anleitung zur Composition* as translated by Nancy Kovaleff Baker in *Heinrich Christoph Koch: Introductory Essay on Composition* (New Haven: Yale University Press, 1983), pp. 197–204, 207–13, with minor alterations.

cence and grandeur belongs to the first Allegro, the character of pleasantness to the Andante, and of gaiety to the last Allegro.

Because the symphony is one of the most important compositions for those composers who wish to occupy themselves only with instrumental pieces, a closer description of its characteristics is not out of place here. Thus I shall insert an extract concerning the aesthetic nature of this composition from Sulzer's *Allgemeine Theorie der schönen Künste*.[1]

> One can compare the symphony with an instrumental chorus just as the sonata with an instrumental cantata. In the latter, the melody of the main part, which is only set simply, can be composed so that it bears and often even requires decoration. In the symphony, on the other hand, where every voice is set more simply, the melody must already contain the maximum force in the notes written out, and no voice can bear the least decoration or coloratura. Because it is not an exercise like the sonata but must be sightread, there must be no difficulties which cannot be confronted and clearly played at once by many.
>
> The symphony is particularly suited for the expression of greatness, solemnity, and grandeur. Its goal is to prepare the listener for important music or, in a chamber concert, to summon all the magnificence of instrumental music. If it is to satisfy this goal completely and be an integral part of the opera or church music which it precedes, then, besides expressing greatness and solemnity, it must put the listener into the frame of mind which the following piece requires. It must distinguish itself by the distinct style proper for either church or theater.
>
> The chamber symphony, which is an independent whole, aiming at no following music, attains its purpose only through a sonorous, brilliant, and fiery style. The Allegros of the best chamber symphonies contain great and bold ideas—powerful bass melodies and unisons; concerting middle parts; free imitations; often a fugally treated theme; sudden transitions and digressions from one key to another, which are more striking the weaker the connection is; and considerable gradations of loud and soft, especially the crescendo, which is of the greatest effect when it is used together with an ascending melody which increases in expression. . . .
>
> The Andante or Largo between the first and last Allegro has, to be sure, no such closely defined character, but often is of pleasant, or somber, or melancholy expression; yet it must have a style which is in keeping with the dignity of the symphony. . . .
>
> Opera symphonies are like the chamber symphony more or less, but adapted to the character of the opera to be presented. Yet it seems that they tolerate less extravagance and need not be so elaborate, because the listener is more attentive to what follows than to the symphony itself. . . .

§101. The first Allegro of the symphony, to which the description above particularly applies, has two sections which may be performed with or without repetition. The first of these consists only of a single main period and contains

---

1. Johann Georg Sulzer, ed., *Allgemeine Theorie der schönen Künste* (*A General Theory of the Fine Arts*) (Leipzig, 1771–74), "Symphonie." Sulzer's was the earliest comprehensive German encyclopedia of the arts. The article on the symphony was written by Johann Abraham Peter Schulz, a German conductor and composer who was a pupil of Johann Philipp Kirnberger. Sulzer had originally assigned the articles on music to Kirnberger, who was the sole author from the start of the alphabet through "Modulation." Because of ill health, Kirnberger then enlisted Schulz's aid, and later entrusted to him the composition of the remaining articles, starting with the letter *s*. Koch made considerable use of the work, quoting it extensively both here and in his *Musikalisches Lexikon*. The ellipsis marks in the extract indicate Koch's own ellipses.

the plan of the symphony; that is, the main melodic phrases are presented in their original order and afterwards a few of them are fragmented. Following the cadence a clarifying period is often appended that continues and closes in the same key in which the preceding one also had closed. Thus it is nothing else than an appendix to the first period and both united may quite properly be considered a single main period.

The construction of this period, as also of the other periods of the symphony, differs from that of the sonata and the concerto not through modulations to other keys, nor through a specific succession or alternation of I- or V-phrases. Rather it differs in that (1) its melodic sections tend to be more extended already with their first presentation than in other compositions, and especially (2) these melodic sections usually are more attached to each other and flow more forcefully than in the periods of other pieces, that is, they are linked so that their phrase-endings are less perceptible. For the most part, a melodic section is directly connected with the caesura tone of the preceding phrase-ending. Very often no formal phrase-ending is written until the rushing and sonorous phrases are exchanged for a more singing phrase, usually to be played with less force. Thus many such periods are found in which a formal phrase-ending is not heard until there has been a modulation into the most closely related key. For the main melodic sections are all presented in the main key just as infrequently in the symphony as in other compositions. Rather, after the theme has been heard with another main phrase, the third such phrase usually modulates to the key of the fifth—in the minor mode also towards the third—in which the remaining sections are presented, because the second and larger half of this first period is devoted particularly to this key.

In the newer symphonies, the first Allegro tends to be preceded by a brief introductory passage which is slow and serious. This introduction differs from the so-called Grave of the overture in that it requires neither characteristic figures nor a special meter. Rather it can appear in all meters and use all figures which have an earnest character. Discounting passing modulations, this passage remains in the main key, in which it closes either with a V-phrase-ending or with a cadence. Often a seventh with a fermata is added to the triad ending the V-phrase, or the cadence runs over into the following Allegro; that is, the caesura tone of the cadence is at the same time the first note of the Allegro.

§102. The second section of the first Allegro consists of two main periods, of which the first tends to have greatly diverse types of construction. Nevertheless, if one discounts the smaller variations, they may be reduced to the following two main types of treatment.

The first and most usual construction of the first period of the second section begins in the key of the fifth[2] with the theme, occasionally also with another main melodic idea, either note for note, in inversion, or also with other more

2. If the composition is in a minor key and the first period has ended in the major key of the third, then it is the minor key of the fifth. But if in a minor key the first period closes in the minor key of its fifth, then there is a modulation to the major key of its third in this second period. [Au.]

or less considerable alterations. After that it either modulates back into the main key by means of another melodic idea, and from this to the minor key of the sixth, or also to the minor key of the second or third. Or it may not first return to the main key; rather the phrase that goes from the fifth into one of the keys mentioned may be led there by means of a sequence or another type of extension, with which generally one or several passing modulations are used. Then a few of those melodic sections that are best suited for presentation in one of these keys[3] are repeated or dissected in another form or combination than they had in the first period, whereupon the period ends in this key.

Usually a short phrase is connected with this second main period of the symphony, which consists of a segment of a main melodic idea drawn out in a sequential way. By this means the modulation is carried back to the main key, in which the last main period begins.

The other method of building this period frequently used in modern symphonies is to continue, dissect, or transpose a phrase contained in the first section—often only a segment of it—that is especially suitable for such treatment. This is done either in the upper part alone or also alternately in other parts. There may be passing modulations in several keys, some closely and some distantly related, before the modulation into that key in which the period is to end. Either this happens only until the ending of the V-phrase in this key, or the phrase is continued in a similar manner until the close of the entire period. An example of this latter type of treatment will be given later, when we consider the connection of periods in particular. However, if the fragmentation of such a phrase is carried only to the end of the V-phrase in that key in which this period will close, then after this V-phrase a few melodic ideas of the first period, usually changed somewhat, are presented in that closing key before the cadence arrives. Examples of this may be found in many Haydn and nearly all Dittersdorf symphonies.

In this case too the period usually acquires the appendix mentioned before, which modulates back to the main key for the beginning of the last period.

By the way, modern symphonies do not always start this second period in the key of the fifth; often it begins in an entirely unexpected key, either without any preparation or by means of only a few introductory tones that follow the cadence in the fifth.

§103. The last period of our first Allegro, which is devoted above all to the main key, most frequently begins again with the theme in this key, but occasionally may also start with another main melodic idea. The most prominent phrases are now compressed, as it were, during which the melody usually shifts to the key of the fourth, but, without making a cadence in it, soon again returns to the main key. Finally the second half of the first period, or those melodic

---

3. It should not be forgotten, however, that this matter is considered here not aesthetically, but only technically. [Au.]

ideas of the first period which followed the V-phrase in the fifth, is repeated in the main key and with this the Allegro ends.

§104. The Andante or Adagio of the symphony is found in three different forms. In the first of these, already used in the older symphonies, the Andante has two main sections, which are presented with or without repetition. The first section always consists of only one main period, as in the Allegro; when based in a major key, it modulates to the key of the fifth, but, based in a minor key, it modulates either to the major key of the third or to the minor key of the fifth, and closes therein.

With the second section, the question is whether or not the Andante is to be greatly extended. If the movement is to be very long, then it tends to have two main periods, which in their external structure are very similar to both those periods of the second section of the Allegro described above in §102. The most important external difference is that in the Andante the melodic ideas are less extended and not so often compounded; thus more formal phrase-endings are used than in the Allegro. This accords with the nature of the feelings which tend to be expressed in slow movements. . . .[4]

On the other hand, if the Andante is not to be very long, then these two periods are contracted into a single one. This happens if the working-out of the melodic ideas in the minor key of the sixth or second and the cadence in this key are omitted. After the theme has been presented in the fifth and there has been a modulation back to the main key, the minor key of the sixth, second, or third is touched either not at all or only in passing. Then the theme is repeated again or, without that repetition, those phrases which followed the V-phrase in the first period are presented again in the main key. Examples of this sort are not hard to find, for nearly every short, complete Andante or Allegretto shows the use of this form.

§105. The second form which the Andante of the symphony takes is the rondo. Nothing else important remains to be said of this here, because it already has been described above in connection with the aria.[5]

§106. The third design or form of the Andante shows the use of variations on a short *andante* or *adagio* passage. This usually consists of two sections of eight to ten measures each and often has an appendix, which is presented between every variation as a ritornello. The variations of the principal melody are performed either by the first violin alone, or in alternation with other parts. Examples of this form are found in very many symphonies by Haydn, who not only was the first one to make use of it in an Andante movement but also has produced first-rate masterpieces in it.

4. Koch here cites the Andantino e cantabile of Haydn's Symphony No. 42 as an example of an Andante in which the second section contains two periods.

5. In §85 and §86 Koch describes the form familiar to us today, where a simple theme (the *Rondosatz,* consisting of a V-phrase repeated to end as a I-phrase) alternates with two couplets, the first in the dominant and the second in a closely related key.

§107. According to the character which it assumes, the last Allegro of the symphony appears either in the form of the first Allegro or as a rondo. Sometimes it also contains variations on a typical dance melody or on a short *allegro* passage; these variations are, however, usually mixed with brief episodes in closely related keys, after the manner of the rondo.

Remark
Many composers like to add to the symphony a minuet with a so-called trio, which comes sometimes before, but mostly after the Andante. Because such a minuet is not intended for the dance, not only can its length be arbitrary, but it can also contain sections of an uneven number of measures.

VI. *On the sonata*

§108. The sonata, with its various species—the duet, trio, and quartet—has no definite character, but its main sections, namely its Adagio and both Allegros, can assume every character, every expression which music is capable of describing. "In a sonata," says Sulzer, "the composer can aim at expressing either a monologue in tones of sadness, lamentation, or affection, pleasure, and cheerfulness; or he can try to sustain purely in sentiment-laden tones a dialogue among similar or contrasting characters; or he may merely depict passionate, violent, contradictory, or mild and placid emotions, pleasantly flowing on."[6]

Because in the composition of sonatas the main parts are only set simply, the melody of the sonata must stand in relation to the melody of the symphony just as the melody of the aria does to the melody of the chorus. That is, because it depicts the feelings of single people, the melody of a sonata must be extremely developed and must present the finest nuances of feelings, whereas the melody of the symphony must distinguish itself not through such refinement of expression, but through force and energy. In short, the feelings must be presented and modified differently in the sonata and symphony.

§109. The *two-voice sonata* or the *solo,* because it expresses the individual feelings of a single person, necessarily requires the greatest refinement of expression and of the modifications of the feelings to be portrayed. Thus the melody must be most highly developed. Because every instrument is capable of different refinements of expression which it alone can produce, the composition of a sonata requires the most exact knowledge of that instrument for which such a piece is to be composed. Thus good sonatas can only be expected from those composers who also are virtuosi on the instrument for which they write such pieces.

Among the Germans, *C. P. E. Bach* has distinguished himself particularly in this type of composition through his clavier sonatas. Only his highly developed, personal style of playing, combined with the most profound knowledge of composition, could bring about what he has achieved in this line.

---

6. Sulzer, ed., *Allgemeine Theorie,* "Sonate" [Tr.]

For the violin and flute *Franz Benda* and *Quantz* have composed sonatas of which many completely correspond to the ideal one inevitably forms of a good sonata. It is only unfortunate that the path broken by these men was subsequently followed by far too few. Much too often a more refined and cultivated expression was replaced by empty noises with many difficulties, which left the heart the more unstirred the more the fingers moved.

Noisy, overcomplicated sonatas are, to be sure, a necessity for those soloists who wish to display mere technical skill on the instrument, and not expression of feelings. But more thought should be given to the general usefulness of sonatas designed for the public. For not only amateurs but also most artists are concerned more about expressive pieces than about difficult works of this kind. Proof of this is given by the clavier sonatas of *Türk*, which are generally loved because along with the suitable presentation of pleasant feelings they do not frighten off the amateur by too many difficulties. Moreover, they are written in a style which is very affecting for any feeling not yet overindulged—all qualities which can rightly be required of compositions of this kind which are intended for the public.

§110. The external arrangement of the sonata, namely, the different forms of both its Allegros and its Adagio, need not be examined in particular here, for the sonata assumes all the forms which already have been described before in connection with the symphony. Thus, for example, the first Allegro has two sections which are usually repeated. The first of these sections contains one main period, the second section has two, and all follow the same course of modulation as the main periods of the symphony. The last Allegro also can have either the form just indicated, or the form of the rondo, or also variations on a short passage such as has been described in §20.[7]

But as similar to one another as the forms of the sonata and the symphony may be in the number of periods and the course of modulation, as different, conversely, is the inner nature of the melody in the two. This difference, however, can be better felt than described; only the following external distinction can generally be observed: in the sonata the melodic sections are not connected as continuously as in the symphony, but more often are separated through formal phrase-endings. They are not usually extended through the continuation of a segment of this or that melodic section or through sequences, but more often by clarifying additions, defining the feeling most accurately.

·   ·   ·   ·   ·

IX. *On the quartet*

§118. The quartet, currently the favorite piece of small musical societies, is cultivated very assiduously by the more modern composers.

If it really is to consist of four obbligato voices of which none has priority over the others, then it must be treated according to fugal method.

7. See p. 794, n. 14.

But because the modern quartets are composed in the *galant* style, there are four main voices which alternately predominate and sometimes this one, sometimes that one forms the customary bass.

While one of these parts concerns itself with the delivery of the main melody, the other two melodic voices must proceed in connected melodies which promote the expression without obscuring the main melody. From this it is evident that the quartet is one of the most difficult of all kinds of compositions, which only the composer completely trained and experienced through much practice may attempt.

Among the more modern composers, *Haydn, Pleyel,* and *Hoffmeister* have enriched the public the most with this type of sonata. The late *Mozart* also had engravings made in Vienna of six quartets for two violins, viola, and violoncello with a dedication to Haydn.[8] Among all modern four-part sonatas these most closely correspond to the concept of a true quartet and are unique on account of their special mixture of the strict and free styles and the treatment of harmony.

X. *On the concerto*

§119. The *concerto,* an instrumental piece in which a main part is accompanied by an entire orchestra, also has no definite nature. But its three main sections, namely its two allegros and its adagio, can assume every mood which music is capable of expressing.

It is that piece with which the virtuosos usually may be heard on their instrument; thus there are concertos for all of the standard instruments of an orchestra.

For reasons shown in connection with the solo, the composer can, however, write a good concerto only for that instrument which he himself plays with a certain degree of skill. Not only did many a concerto player formerly lack a sufficient number of such pieces, but also he often could not use those which were obtainable because of the special way of playing which they required. Thus nothing else remained for many concerto players, especially those who played an instrument for which not many concertos had yet been composed or become known, than to compose their concerto parts and their accompaniment themselves, as best they could, or to let them be composed by others. Nowadays, since various instrumentalists of all kinds concern themselves with composition, this product of music is so assiduously cultivated that there is no reason to complain about the lack of concertos for any instrument. Nevertheless, the procedure referred to before remains the story of many a concerto which now appears in public. Moreover, there are musicians who make a commercial business of adapting concertos by once popular masters for every instrument through transpositions in other keys and through alteration of passages without compunction. Indeed it is certain that composers even write

---

8. Koch is referring to Mozart's "Haydn" Quartets, K. 387, 421, 428, 458, 464, and 465, which were published in 1785. [Tr.]

concertos in advance for a possible commission without yet knowing for which instrument the passages still lacking should be suited. But these are only special cases. The concerto is subject to a far more detrimental abuse, however, in that the expression "to play in company" all too often is understood as nothing more than to demonstrate skill in a clean and plain execution of the melodic figures and in overcoming well-chosen difficulties. Instead the skill attained should be used only to present the expression of certain feelings through a most highly refined performance appropriate to them.

If concertos were composed and performed more generally according to a better model, then many men of taste would be more satisfied with this type of composition. *Sulzer*, for example, whose judgments concerning the other kinds of compositions we so readily defer to, says of the concerto that it is basically nothing but an exercise for composer and player and an entirely indeterminate pleasure for the ear, aiming at nothing more.[9]

But is this verdict perhaps too harsh? Should not this judgment be directed towards only such concertos as are condemned by discerning concerto players themselves?

If one disregards the abuses of the concerto, shown before, which do not yet generally prevail, why should the concerto alone be merely exercise for composer and player? Why should this composition alone be a mere pleasure for the ear, aiming at nothing further?

Sulzer concedes that in the sonata music can show its ability to portray feelings without words. Why should music have this ability less in the concerto, since the composer possesses in its richer accompaniment more means to increase the expression of the main part than he does in the sonata? What is particularly offensive to *Sulzer* seems to be the form of the concerto, for he says in the article "Sonata": "The form of a concerto appears to be intended more to give a skillful player the opportunity to be heard accompanied by many instruments than to render the passions."[10]

If one discounts the ritornellos in a concerto, which after all can be as little detrimental to the expression of feelings in this composition as they are in the aria, what difference remains then between the form of the sonata and that of the concerto which promotes the expression of feelings in the sonata but could be detrimental to it in the concerto? Perhaps *Sulzer* understands here by the form of the concerto merely that usage by which long passages are composed in certain places in the periods of a concerto which are nothing more than an exercise for the player, because in most cases they have so little in common with the expression of a definite feeling that they may be transferred to any concertos? This seems to be the most probable. But the presence of these passages is anything but essential in the form of the concerto.

It appears to me that the concerto must be judged from an entirely different

9. Sulzer, ed., *Allgemeine Theorie*, "Concert." [Tr.]
10. Ibid., "Sonate." [Tr.]

point of view than the solo. The expression of feeling by the solo player is like a monologue in passionate tones, in which the solo player is, as it were, communing with himself; nothing external has the slightest influence on the expression of his feeling. But consider a well-worked-out concerto in which, during the solo, the accompanying voices are not merely there to sound this or that missing interval of the chords between the soprano and bass. There is a passionate dialogue between the concerto player and the accompanying orchestra. He expresses his feelings to the orchestra, and through short interspersed phrases it signals to him sometimes approval, sometimes acceptance of his expression, as it were. Now in the Allegro it tries to stimulate his noble feelings still more; now it commiserates with him, now comforts him in the Adagio. In short, by a concerto I imagine something similar to the tragedy of the ancients, where the actor expressed his feelings not towards the pit, but to the chorus. The chorus was involved most closely with the action and was at the same time justified in participating in the expression of feelings. Then the listener, without losing anything, is just the third person, who can take part in the passionate performance of the concerto player and the accompanying orchestra. Ponder these ideas further, listen to most of C. P. E. Bach's concertos, which so completely correspond to this ideal, or better, from which this ideal is derived, and then judge whether the concerto is no more than mere exercise for composer and player, no more than mere pleasure for the ear, aiming at nothing else.[11]

§120. The first Allegro of the concerto contains three main periods performed by the soloist, which are enclosed by four subsidiary periods performed by the orchestra as ritornellos.

In modern concertos, the first ritornello is generally worked out at length. It consists of the principal melodic sections of the plan of the Allegro, which are brought into a different connection and extended through other means than in the solo of the concerto part.[12] With these sections a few suitable subsidiary ideas are connected in the ritornello which again lead to a main idea.

At present this ritornello takes three different forms. It either (1) makes up only one period, in which the melody stays in the main key throughout the entire passage (with the exception of short passing modulations); or (2) consists of two periods connected with one another. In this case, when it is based in a major key, there is a modulation to the key of the fifth,[13] after the V-phrase of this key a cantabile phrase from the solo is played, and then the first period of

---

11. Because the composition of concertos tends to be the *ne plus ultra* of most beginning composers, it is hoped one will not find this digression on the worth of this composition and the abuses to which it is subjected entirely useless and unnecessary. [Au.]

12. As has already been shown . . . the first main period of the solo part is worked out before the ritornello is arranged as the introduction to the solo part. [Au.] Koch refers here to a discussion earlier in the *Versuch* where, following Sulzer, he divides the compositional process into three phases—*plan, realization,* and *elaboration* (vol. 2, pt. 1). In the concerto, the first main period of the solo contains the plan of the work and is composed first. The opening ritornello is part of the second phase, or realization, and is composed after the first period of the solo.

13. The application to the minor mode has already been mentioned several times in discussions of the preceding types of compositions. [Au.]

the ritornello is closed with a formal cadence in this key. With the caesura note of this cadence, a phrase begins which leads the melody back into the main key in one of those ways described in §31.[14] After the return to the main key, a melodic section of the first period is usually repeated, in order to give the entire ritornello a certain kind of completion and to maintain the unity of this passage before the close follows with the principal cadence in the main key. However the first ritornello is also formed so that (3) there is indeed a formal modulation into the key of the fifth, and after the V-phrase in it a principal melodic section is played in this key. But immediately afterwards, without a formal close in this key, there is a modulation back to the main key and the ritornello concludes. This last form is the most usual in more modern concertos.

§121. Lately a short introductory passage of slow tempo and earnest character has preceded the first Allegro of a concerto.[15] It is used in modern symphonies and has already been described above in connection with the symphony. In the concerto also, this passage usually closes with the so-called half cadence, after which the ritornello of the first Allegro begins without interruption.

§122. With the entry of the first main period, or the first solo part, the cadence of the ritornello generally comes to rest completely before the solo begins. That is, the solo does not enter with the caesura note, but first begins its period after a fully completed close of the ritornello. On the other hand, the second solo and also the entrance of the [second] ritornello do not leave the cadence completely at rest but enter with its caesura tone.

§123. Nothing remains to be noted in connection with the three main periods of the solo part, for they have the same external arrangement and the same course of modulation as the three main periods in the first Allegro of the symphony. The type of melody, on the other hand, is very similar to that of the sonata. It is just as developed as in the sonata, but usually is more protracted through the means of extension already known to us, and the melodic sections are better connected through the omission of the ending formulas of phrases. At the caesura-note of phrases or incises, the melody of the main part is sometimes interrupted by the orchestra with short passages, which consist either of repeated segments of the principal melody or of phrases which occurred only in the ritornello.

In well-composed concertos, every single part of the accompanying orchestra makes its contribution to the main part, according to the ideal described before. As a segment of the whole, it is involved in the passionate dialogue and has the right to show its feelings concerning the main part through short phrases. To this end, these voices do not always wait for the conclusion of the

14. See p. 795, n. 15.
15. C. P. E. Bach did compose slow introductions to two of his harpsichord concertos, W. 41 (1769) and W. 43, no. 5 (1772), and Anton Rosetti (c. 1750–1792), Bohemian composer, conductor, and double-bass player, wrote a Grave introduction to his Grand Concerto in F Major for two horns (c. 1785). This practice, however, was certainly not the norm. [Tr.]

incise or phrase in the principal part, but throughout its performance may be heard alternately in brief imitations; yet they must be placed and arranged so that they do not obscure the performance of the main part.

The beginning composer can get to know the treatment of the accompaniment to the concerto just described nowhere better than in the clavier concertos of *C. P. E. Bach*. In addition to the skill of forming the melody so that it permits such imitations in the accompaniment, much practical experience and artistic feeling are required not to overdo the effect and harm the main voice.

§124. At the caesura-tone of the first main period, which, as has been mentioned already, closes in the key of the fifth, the second ritornello begins again with the main phrase. It repeats a few melodic sections which already were contained in the first ritornello and closes likewise with a formal cadence in the key of the fifth. With the caesura-tone of this cadence, the second solo part begins in this key again. In fact, the second solo usually starts with a melodic section which was not contained in the first period, but is a powerful, conspicuous, yet suitable subsidiary idea, which again leads very appropriately to a main idea.

This period is treated like the second main period of the first Allegro of the symphony; therefore it is closed in the minor key of the sixth, at times also in the minor key of the second or third. With its caesura-note, a short ritornello begins which forms the subsidiary period already described in connection with the symphony. By means of a melodic section that is extended through sequence or the continuation of a metrical formula, the ritornello modulates back into the main key, in which it closes with a V-phrase; thus the third solo of the principal part can again begin in the main key.

§125. In its form the third solo part in the concerto again resembles the third main period of the first Allegro of the symphony. At the caesura-tone of this period, the ripieno parts usually introduce, by means of a few measures, a fermata on the six-four chord of the keynote. The soloist sustains this longer than the other instruments and connects with it either a free fantasy or a capriccio, which is mistakenly called a cadenza because it is made at the close of the composition. With the caesura-tone of this so-called cadenza, which always ends with a formal cadence, the last ritornello begins. This generally consists of the last melodic sections of the initial ritornello, with which the entire first Allegro concludes.

§126. The Adagio of the concerto usually takes the form already described in §84 in connection with the aria.[16] In the more modern concertos, however, instead of the customary Adagio, often a so-called romance is composed. This

---

16. In §84 Koch essentially describes the *da capo* and its modifications. In its most common form, the aria "has two main periods in the first section. . . . A short instrumental interlude separates [the first section] from the second section, which in this case is only a single period, and after the second section the first is repeated either entirely or only in part" (Baker, p. 169). The other forms of aria that Koch discusses are the Rondo (§85–§86), and one he styles a more modern form (§87), which has a section in slow tempo followed by a quicker second section.

has a definite character, which one can best get to know from Sulzer's description of the romance in poetry.

"Nowadays," says Sulzer, "the name romance is given to short narrative songs in the extremely simple and somewhat antiquated tone of the old rhymed romances. Their content may be a passionate, tragic, amorous, or even merely entertaining narrative.[17] . . . Ideas and expression must be of the utmost simplicity and very naive."[18]

This composition usually takes the form of the rondo, which already has been described at length.[19]

§127. The last section of the concerto is either an Allegro or a Presto. It may take the form of the first Allegro, or of an ordinary rondo with very amplified episodes, or of variations on a short melody consisting of two sections. The essentials of the variation form have also been mentioned in connection with the last Allegro of the symphony.

---

17. In music this last type of romance is not used, because now it is composed only in a slow tempo. [Au.]
18. Sulzer, ed., *Allgemeine Theorie*, "Romanze." [Tr.]
19. See above, §105 and p. 812, n. 6.

127 Francesco Galeazzi

Francesco Galeazzi's career as violinist, composer, and teacher took him from Turin, the city of his birth in 1758, to Rome where he practiced his art as music director of the Teatro Valle, and finally to Ascoli, where he resided until his death in Rome in 1819. His *Elementi teorico-pratici di musica* (*Theoretical-Practical Elements of Music*) resembles Quantz's *Versuch* in that it is no mere instrument tutor, but a comprehensive work. While it includes the expected violin tutor and a brief history of music, the fourth part is a treatise on composition that covers a wide range of topics, from harmony, counterpoint, and rhythm to the affects of keys and the invention of melodic figures through combination and permutation. Galeazzi's discussion of writing large-scale compositions occurs in the second section of the volume, headed "Melodia," in which he describes a movement of a composition as a "well-conducted melody." With remarkable clarity and detail he spells out the periods of this spun-out cantilena with their various functions, including the "Characteristic Passage," which has sometimes been interpreted as an early version of the "second theme" of nineteenth-century sonata-form theorists.

FROM *Theoretical-Practical Elements of Music*

(1796)

ARTICLE III. OF MELODY IN PARTICULAR, AND OF ITS PARTS, MEMBERS, AND RULES

23. To find a motive or to continue it even for a few measures is indeed the work of a beginner, but not that of the perfect composer. In the larger pieces of music, such as arias, or other pieces of theatrical or church music, and in instrumental music, such as symphonies, trios, quartets, concertos, etc., when the motive has been written, nothing has yet been accomplished. This much is certainly true, that the best composers do not make any distinction among motives; each one is equally good to them. But let us not anticipate something we must discuss shortly. The art, then, of the perfect composer does not consist in the discovery of *galant* motives or agreeable passages, but consists in the exact conduct of an entire piece of music. It is principally here that one recognizes the ability and knowledge of a great master, since any very mediocre motive can, if well developed, make an excellent composition.

24. Therefore, since we have to discuss here the most interesting aspect of modern music, that is, the conduct one must follow in laying out the melodies, we shall advise our reader first to learn from compositions by others how to discern and distinguish well parts and members, which we shall here enumerate and explain in all detail. Every well-conducted melody is divided into two parts, either connected, or separated in the middle by a repeat sign. The first part is usually composed of the following members: 1. Introduction, 2. Principal Motive, 3. Second Motive, 4. Departure to the most closely related keys, 5. Characteristic Passage or Intermediate Passage, 6. Cadential Period, and 7. Coda. The second part is then composed of these members: 1. Motive, 2. Modulation, 3. Reprise, 4. Repetition of the Characteristic Passage, 5. Repetition of the Cadential Period, and 6. Repetition of the Coda.

25. Now let us analyze all these members, one by one, and demonstrate their arrangement and order in the very simple little melody that we give [Example 1]. The periods and the conduct of this short melody shall serve as a model for

Example 1

[Principal Motive]

TEXT: Vol. 2, pp. 253–60, translated by Bathia Churgin, *Journal of the American Musicological Society* 21 (1968), 189–99, with minor alterations.

all the others in any other style, either vocal or mixed, and this by necessity, in order not to increase by too much the already abundant number of examples in this volume.

26. The Introduction is nothing but a preparation for the true Motive of a composition. It is not always used, and it is the composer's choice to introduce it. In the example given by us this member is lacking, but it will be observed that Example 2 is the introduction of a trio from one of my works. It is therefore sometimes possible, instead of beginning with the true motive, first to present a section of cantilena in preparation for it. If this section is suitable, and connected in a natural way to the motive, it makes an excellent effect, provided that it makes a cadence, either formal or implied, at the moment when the motive begins. It is good practice that the Introduction (if there is one) be sometimes recalled in the course of the melody, so that it should not seem to be a section that has been detached, and entirely separated from the rest. For the fundamental rule for the conduct of the composition consists in the *unity of ideas*.

Example 2

27. The Motive, then, is nothing but the principal idea of the melody—the subject or theme, one might say, of the musical discourse—and the whole composition must revolve around it. The Introduction may begin on any note, and even outside the key, but the Motive must infallibly begin with the notes constituting the key, that is, with its first, third, or fifth degree. In addition, it must be well rounded and lucid, for, being the theme of the discourse, if it is not well understood, the discourse that follows will not be understood either. The Motive should always terminate with a cadence either in the principal key, or on its fifth or fourth. In duets, terzets, and quartets, vocal as well as instrumental, the period is often repeated twice in different voices. The Motive in our example extends from measure 1 to measure 9. The Motive, then, is a most essential member of every melody. It is characteristic of beginners to rack their brains to select a beautiful Motive for their compositions without reflecting that every good composition must always grow in effect from the beginning to the end. Now, if one selects a wonderful Motive, it will be very difficult for the composition to keep growing in interest; on the contrary, indeed, it will considerably decline. This will totally discredit the composition in spite of a most beautiful Motive. If, on the contrary, one uses a mediocre Motive, well conducted according to the precepts we will now give, the composition will keep increasing its effect, which will make it more interesting and agreeable to the audience at every moment, and earn it more than the usual applause. It is precisely this that we see to be the practice of the most classical writers. Hence ordinarily an excellent Motive is in most cases the mark of a poor composition, for the merit of a composition consists, as has already been said, in the conduct and not in the Motive.

28. I call the *second Motive* what is named the countersubject in the fugue: that is, an idea which is either derived from the first motive or is entirely new, but which, well connected with the first, immediately follows the period of the Motive, and also sometimes serves to lead out of the key, terminating in the fifth of the key, or in the minor third for keys of the minor third. In most cases, if the Motive has ended its period in the fifth of the key, the Second Motive will begin in this same key; but if the Motive has cadenced in the principal key, then the Second Motive will begin in this key, leading then, as has been said, to the fifth or the fourth, etc. This period only occurs in very long pieces; in short pieces it is omitted, so that it is not essential. In the given example [Ex.

1] the Second Motive is tightly connected in measure 10 to the following period, which serves to depart from the key and go to the fifth, which is usually the first modulation to be heard.

29. The *Departure from the Key* follows either immediately after the Second Motive or with it, if there is one, or else immediately after the true Motive. In pieces of some length it is not good to leave the key too soon, in order to give the ear time to master fully the idea of the principal key; while if one leaves the key too soon, people will no longer know what key the composition is in. Then the first modulation is made to the most closely related keys, namely to the fifth or to the fourth in keys with a major third, and also to the minor third in keys of the minor third, as was stated above. This period must not be dragged on too long, but should end in the fifth of the key in which it is actually set, so that the following period may emerge with more prominence and individuality. In the example in front of us, what we have discussed here extends through measure 16, where we see the cadence in D, the fifth of the key of G, to which the modulation or Departure from the Key was made. Such a period is always necessary, and it often becomes mingled with that of the Second Motive, as happens in our example.

30. The *Characteristic Passage* or *Intermediate Passage* is a new idea, which is introduced toward the middle of the first part for the sake of greater beauty. This must be gentle, expressive, and tender in almost all kinds of compositions, and must be presented in the same key as the one to which the modulation was made. Often such a period is repeated, but only in more extended compositions; in short compositions it is very often omitted entirely. The period may be seen from measure 17 to measure 20.

31. The Cadential Period then follows. This is a new idea, but it is always dependent on previous ideas, especially on the principal Motive or the Second Motive, and in it the melody is made ready and prepared for the cadence. If the voice or instrument has shown off its gentleness and expression in the Characteristic Passage, it will display animation and skill, with agility of voice or hand, in the period we are now discussing. Consequently, this period in vocal music is a good place for figuration and brilliant passagework, and in instrumental music for the most difficult passages, which then close with a final cadence. Such a period is seen in the example from measure 21 to measure 24, where the final cadence takes place. In instrumental music very often this period is repeated twice, arranged in two different parts in order that each performer may exhibit his particular ability. In short pieces it is presented only once, and it is an essential period, since it is one that concludes the composition.

32. After making the final cadence, which concludes the last cadential period, it is not unusual that instead of ending the first part here, a new period, called a Coda, is elegantly added. It is an addition to or prolonging of the cadence, and therefore not an essential period, but it serves very well to link the ideas which end the first part with those which have begun it, or with those

with which the second part begins, as we intend to point out. And this is its principal function. It can be seen from measure 24 until the end of the first part.

33. It is well to know here that in all pieces of music, of whatever kind or style, whether divided in the middle by a repeat sign or continuous, the first part always closes in the fifth of the principal key, rarely in the fourth, and often in the minor third of keys with a minor third.

34. The second part then also begins with its Motive, which can be done in four different ways: 1. Beginning it with an Introduction, either analogous to the first part, if there is one, and transposed to the fifth of the key, or modulating in various ways. This method, however, is tedious and little practiced by good composers. 2. Beginning the second part with the same Motive as the first, transposed to the fifth of the key. This method is also in disuse, like the former, since it does not introduce any variety into the compositions, which is always the purpose of all the skills of genius. But the following two are the most commendable methods: 3. One can begin the second part with some passage freely taken from the first, and especially from the Coda (if there was one), but in the same key in which the first part ends; and this is precisely the practice in our example, from measure 29 to measure 34, where the beginning of the first part is developed out of the outline of the last two measures of the Coda. 4. Finally, the last method is to begin the second part with an idea that is quite new and foreign. In such a case, however, it is not good to present it in the key in which the first part ends, but rather, for greatest surprise, it should be in some related key, but separated and unexpected. This period is always essential.

35. Then follows the *Modulation,* which is always made using passages and ideas linked with the first or second motive, or with the motive of the second part. So it is as regards the melody, but concerning the methods and rules to follow in modulation and long modulatory progression,[1] this subject of greatest importance merits a separate article, which will follow.

36. The *Reprise* succeeds the Modulation. However remote the Modulation is from the main key of the composition, it must draw closer little by little, until the Reprise, that is, the first Motive of Part I in the proper natural key in which it was originally written, falls in quite naturally and regularly. If the piece is a long one, the true Motive in the principal key is taken up again as has been said, but if one does not want to make the composition too long, then it will be enough to repeat instead the Characteristic Passage transposed to the same fundamental key. In our example the Modulation may been seen to continue through measure 41, at which point the principal Motive is then resumed in its proper key. In such a case, the motive itself has to be conducted gradually to the fourth of the key, as can be seen here in measure 48, and it then makes a cadence on the fifth as is done in measure 52. Or if the second

---

1. Galeazzi explains this term (*circolazione*) in his article on modulation (vol. 2, pp. 264–65). [Tr.]

method has been used—that is, the reprise of the Characteristic Passage—
then the Modulation ends on the fifth of the key, in order to start the Characteristic Passage next in the main key; and also in this case it is good practice
for the harmony somewhere to touch, although in passing, on the fourth of the
key.

37. The repetition of the last three periods of the first part is made by
transposing them to the principal key and writing them one after another, in
the same order they had in the first part. The Characteristic Passage must be
the same as that of the first part (the key alone being changed), but the cadential period may be varied if one wishes, provided that it maintains a certain
analogy with that of the first part. The Coda can even be omitted or completely
changed if one does not wish to repeat it just as it was in the first part, as is
done in our example. A most beautiful device is often practiced here, which is
to recapitulate in the Coda the motive of the first part, or the Introduction, if
there was one, or some other passage that is both remarkable and well suited
to end with; this produces a wonderful effect, reviving the idea of the Theme
of the composition and bringing together its parts. In this example the repetition of the Characteristic Passage can be seen from measure 53 to measure 55
[56], that of the Cadential period from measure 56 [57] to measure 59, and
finally the repetition of the Coda until the end of the piece.

38. Such is, more or less, the structure and conduct of the melody generally
speaking, as is the fashion according to the present style. Since, however, each
kind of musical composition has its proper character, and therefore a somewhat
different conduct from the others, we shall speak of this separately in the following articles.

128 Jérôme-Joseph de Momigny

Born in Belgium in 1762, Jérôme-Joseph de Momigny received his early training
as an organist. He lived in Lyons during the French Revolution, and moved to
Paris in 1800 to open a publishing house. A theorist of universalist ambitions,
he intended to formulate a music theory based on natural principles that would
replace all others, and to publish texts that would do the same. This grandiose
plan failed, and he was driven into bankruptcy in 1828. His final years were
marked by pronounced mental deterioration; he died in the lunatic asylum at
Charenton in 1842.

The title of Momigny's 1806 treatise—*Cours complet d'harmonie et de composition* (*A Complete Course of Harmony and Composition*)—announces his
fundamentalist goals, and its dedication leaves no room for doubt: his work is

"based on incontestable principles drawn from nature, which are in accord with all good practical works, ancient and modern, and which because of their clarity are within the reach of all." Although Momigny's messianic certainty may strike us as naive, he was an original and independent thinker and his treatise is is a mine of interesting theories. He endeavored to expand current notions of tonality, beginning with a Rameau-like system based on the chord of nature. He also developed a detailed account of phrase structure, which he put into practice in extended musical analyses of Haydn's Symphony No. 103 and of Mozart's D-minor Quartet, K. 421, which follows here. These analyses, which wander from narrow discussions of melodic detail to the broadest considerations of the poetics of expression, consistently reveal Momigny's wide-ranging musical intelligence.

FROM *A Complete Course of Harmony and Composition*

(1806)

CHAPTER XXX. ON COMPOSITION, STRICT OR FREE, IN FOUR PARTS

ANALYSIS OF A QUARTET BY MOZART. ABOUT THE MUSICAL STYLE OF THIS PIECE.

The style of this *Allegro Moderato* is noble and pathetic. I decided that the best way to have my readers recognize its true expression was to add words to it.[1] But since these verses, if one can call them that, were improvised, as it were, they ought not to be judged in any other regard than that of their agreement with the sense of the music.

I thought I perceived that the feelings expressed by the composer were those of a lover who is on the point of being abandoned by the hero she adores: *Dido,* who had had a similar misfortune to complain of, came immediately to mind. Her noble rank, the intensity of her love, the renown of her misfortune—all this convinced me to make her the heroine of this piece. She should be made to speak in a manner worthy of herself, but this is the task of a great lyric poet. It is sufficient to my task that the feelings of this unhappy queen be recounted and carefully set to music that renders them faithfully.

•   •   •   •   •

TEXT: The original edition (Paris, 1806), vol. 1, p. 371; vol. 2, pp. 388–98, 401–403. Translation by Wye J. Allanbrook. The music example is transcribed from vol. 2 of the plates that accompany the edition; a piano reduction of the music has been omitted.

1. Momigny's text and a translation may be found on pp. 847–48.

CHAPTER XXXI

ANALYSIS OF THE SECOND REPRISE OF THE ALLEGRO MODERATO OF THE MOZART QUARTET

It is particularly in the first part of the second reprise of a great piece that a good composer makes himself known. It is there, above all, that genius needs to rely on skill. It is there that one must develop all the riches of harmony, all the depth of counterpoint—in short all the unexpected and delightful devices that the magic art of transitions has to offer.

But it is also in the second reprise of a great piece that anyone who has not studied music well is forced in spite of himself to reveal his poverty and impotence. He can still deceive the ignorant many with a chaotic din, or with forced transitions. But the true connoisseur can no more be duped by this charlatanism, by this empty noise, by this false science, than by the bad Latin that *Molière* most wittily placed in the mouth of Sganarelle.[2]

When one wishes to form an opinion about a piece of music, one must first see if the author has depicted there what he should depict, and at what point he has seized the truth of the expression, or to what point he could carry it, using the means that his art affords. Then one must see if the style of the piece is pure and correct, if each verse has a good rhythm, if each period is well rounded, if each voice or part remains within its proper range. Finally one must see if the ensemble makes the full impression that the subject requires; and to assign to a composer the place that he deserves to occupy in public opinion, one must in addition consider what degree of natural and of acquired talent the piece supposes, in accordance with which one judges it.

Imbued with these ideas, let us go on to analyze the second reprise of the quartet [see music example, pp. 101–13].

The beginning of this second reprise is for two measures the same as that of the first, except that instead of $D\ d,\ d\ d,\ c\sharp\ d,\ d\ d$, it is $E\flat\ e\flat,\ e\flat\ e\flat,\ d\ e\flat,\ e\flat\ e\flat$.[3]

Although on the keyboard the key of D minor is next to the key of $E\flat$ major, they are nonetheless quite distant from one another in the feeling that they stir. Moreover, this perfect major chord $E\flat\ g\ b\flat\ e\flat$ is not that of a tonic but of a dominant. Note that the $b\flat$ of the preceding measure is a $c\flat$, and that this $c\flat$ that *Mozart* has nevertheless written $b\natural$, in order to cause more surprise, is announced as the sixth note of the key of $E\flat$ minor, taken in the diminished seventh chord of the leading-tone $d\ f\ a\flat\ c\flat$. But as this chord is not followed by the perfect minor chord $e\flat\ g\flat\ b\flat$, but by the perfect major chord $e\flat\ g\ b\flat$, that $d\ f\ a\flat\ c\flat$ that we took first as a diminished seventh chord of the leading tone of the key of $E\flat$ minor is incontestably the chord of the chromatic fourth of the

---

2. Sganarelle, the protagonist of Molière's farce *Le Médecin malgré lui,* spouts nonsense Latin to convince his patients that he is a doctor.

3. The commas in these renderings represent not barlines but motivic articulations.

key of $A\flat$.[4] But are we in $A\flat$ major or $A\flat$ minor? We don't know yet, since the dominant chord is the same in minor as it is in major. But we quickly find out what to hold on to, since when the $c\flat$ appears,[5] it indicates that we are in $A\flat$ minor. But this does not last long; I see in the second part of the third measure a $g\flat$ in the cello that seems to want to lead us into $B\flat$ minor. But the $e\flat$ of the dominant seventh chord of the key of $b\flat$, $f\ a\ c\ e\flat$, which changes suddenly into a $d\sharp$, leads us into a minor rather than directing us into $B\flat$ minor.

By means of this $d\sharp$, substituted for $e\flat$, the dominant seventh chord $f\ a\ c\ e\flat$ is transformed into that of the diminished seventh and diminished third on the chromatically raised fourth degree of the key of A minor, which is $d\sharp\ f\ a\ c$. It appears here under the form of the augmented sixth attached to a perfect major chord, $f\ a\ c\ d\sharp$. Thus the f of the cello becomes the sixth of the key of A minor, instead of remaining the dominant of the key of $B\flat$.[6]

The movement from $e\flat$ to $d\sharp$, thereby changing the key, is an *enharmonic* transition.

Although we talk a great deal about the enharmonic genre, there is still not, properly speaking, a genre of this nature in music: there are only *enharmonic* transitions. And although J. J. *Rousseau* affirms, perhaps according to serious composers, but certainly according to poor musicians, *that the enharmonic genre is the first that had been used among the Greeks,*[7] one ought to take care not to believe it. *For it is as if he were maintaining that the first objects that struck the eyes of the Athenians were those that one can only perceive with the help of a microscope,* which is to misunderstand the nature of our constitution. In short, *enharmonics* are for our ear just about what *microscopic* objects are for sight.

One could also compare enharmonics to homonyms. We know that a homonym is a word whose sound, and sometimes whose spelling, represents several different objects. For example the word *son* denotes equally the ringing of a bell or the sound of any stringed instrument, the bran one extracts from *wheat,* and the masculine possessive pronoun *son,* as in this phrase: le *son* de *son* violon ne vaut pas le *son* de ma farine.[8] Likewise on the piano the $e\flat$ and $d\sharp$ are represented by the same key. There is no transition when this key or any other is only taken under one single aspect. But when the two aspects are used consecutively, and by means of this device one changes key, this is a enhar-

---

4. Momigny makes heavy weather out of the brief inflection of the minor mode in the diminished-seventh chord that precedes the V^7 of $E\flat$ in the second ending to the first reprise (see example, p. 101, m. 1). Calling the $E\flat$ major chord a dominant needlessly complicates the analysis of an already complex passage.

5. In the second measure of the second reprise.

6. The $d\sharp$ combines with the f to form an augmented sixth, which expands to the dominant octave on e.

7. In the *Dictionnaire de musique* (Paris, 1768) Rousseau says only that the enharmonic genre was "according to some, the first of the three to be discovered" ("Enharmonique," p. 192).

8. "The *sound* of *his* violin is not worth the *bran* from my meal." The equivalent homonyms are, of course, not available in English.

monic transition whether one passes from $d\sharp$ to $e\flat$, or from $e\flat$ to $d\sharp$, and likewise successively with regard to all the other keys.

Why, one may ask, did *Mozart* not write a $d\sharp$ in the place of $e\flat$, just as you yourself have indicated by writing $d\sharp$ over the $e\flat$ that precedes the $e\natural$ (see example, p. 102, m. 5). It is so that the performer will rest on the $e\flat$, and not go looking for a $d\sharp$ that would seem to be a dissonance and that would torment the ear rather than agreeably surprising it.

This proves to us that we should feel some regret for those pianos with quarter tones that were so complicated and difficult to make and to play. It refutes what many theorists have put forward in that regard.

Since the enharmonic is only, if I can express myself thus, a kind of marvelous flying bridge by means of which one passes, almost magically, from one climate into another far distant, this is reason enough for us to be very reserved in the use that one can make of it. *To abuse it is to proclaim the pretensions of a novice rather than to demonstrate the skill of a great master.* But let us go on.

Mozart, who composed almost all his first reprise in the free style, begins to make use of a subject here, after the first two measures of the second reprise.

This subject is furnished by the second measure of the beginning: $E\flat$ d $e\flat$ $e\flat$ $e\flat$.

After the first violin has played the subject twice, the cello takes hold of it, sounding it three times in its turn, but in A minor. The viola becomes the echo of the cello at the distance of a half-measure, repeating the same motive in *broken imitation* at the octave. It continues with the same subject, but shortens it and climbs diatonically, $f\sharp$ e $f\sharp f\sharp$, $g\sharp f\sharp$ $g\sharp$ $g\sharp$.

Over this cello and viola, which present only a subordinate subject, the second violin plays no. 1, the principal motive, a $g\sharp$ c b e, imitated at the second and *alla stretta,* that is to say, in rhythmic compression, by the first violin: no. 2, $b\natural$ a d c f. This is true skill. For all its merit, it is not coldly calculated, but has a somber and genuine expression that penetrates to the depths of the soul. This should be attributed equally to the rhythm, the movement, and the intonations of the passage.

With the words *voilà le prix de tant d'amour!* ["this is my reward for such a love!"] Mozart resumes the free style exclusively until the fifth verse.

How the anger of the queen of Carthage bursts out in the music of the third musical verse! and how the last syllable of the word *amour* is felicitously placed on the $b\flat$, in order to express the grief that Dido feels at having rashly abandoned herself to this passion for a perjurer! The second time she repeats this word she cannot finish it, because she is choked by the grief that overwhelms her. It is here that the viola part, which represents her sister or confidante, takes up the word to address to the Trojan the reproaches that *Dido* no longer has the strength to make herself.

Did *Mozart* invent a new subject for this? He refrains from displaying that barren abundance so contrary to *unity*, that reveals a student. On the contrary, as a great contrapuntalist, he brings back his first motive here—not simply and as it has already been heard, for that would only be babble, but elaborated anew, and in a manner that produces a great effect.

In the first period of this second reprise he had taken for subject only one of the measures of his first motive—the second of these two measures. Here he takes two of them, the first and the second. *A A, a a, g♯a, a a.*

After the first measure, an imitation in stretto at the second with this same subject is heard in the second violin. The cello enters one eighth note afterward, and plays a subordinate motive as accompaniment. This cello motive is an imitation, as regards rhythm, of the accompaniment that is found in the viola and in the second violin in the first measures of the second reprise.

In the three first measures of the reprise *Mozart* could have put half notes in the second violin and viola just as he did in the cello. Probably he preferred to use an eighth-note rest and three eighth notes to keep the passage from becoming languid.

Dido, throwing an angry look at *Aeneas,* says to him: *Fuis, malheureux!* ["Fly away, you wretch!"] It is a shortened imitation of the passage in the second violin, at the second above, and *alla stretta.*

The cello, which during this time has kept to the subordinate motive, in its turn lays hold of the principal subject, and says: *D D, d d, c♯d, d d.*

The subordinate motive in the cello then passes to the viola. The imitation in stretto at the second, or rather at the ninth above the principal subject in the cello, is reproduced in the second violin—*e♭ e♭, e♭ e♭, d e♭, e♭ e♭*—and then in the first violin one measure after—*f♯f♯, f♯ g.*

Note the gradual rise of the subject of the fifth verse. This subject is successively carried on six consecutive degrees of the musical scale, moving from *a* up to *f♯* inclusively. The viola begins on *a,* the second violin on *b♭,* the first violin on *c♯,* the cello on *D,* the second violin on *e♭,* and the first on *f♯.*

A student would have put all these imitations of the same subject in the same part. Then we would no longer have heard anything but a kind of scale in place of this dialogue that is so compressed, so pressing, and so admirable. At the moment when *Mozart* abandons this subject, the viola catches hold of the imitation of a motive that has already been heard, both toward the end of the first reprise and in the *link* that joins this reprise with the second—*d g b♭ b♭ b♭.* This subordinate theme is immediately imitated by the second violin, while the first violin plays that other most expressive subject, that transport of the soul, *D, c b♭ a, g f e.*

In this place *Dido,* seeing that her disdain does not have a powerful enough effect on the heart of *Aeneas,* again has recourse to supplication, saying to him: *Non! reste encore.* ["No! stay here."] Easily deceived, she adds (in an aside): *Il paraît s'attendrir!* ["He seems to be moved!"]

In order to fit the words to this passage in a suitable manner, it was necessary to think the aside out carefully. Since the preceding subject has no connection with the one to which these words are set, it could have seemed to be a shortcoming, whereas it is a genuine beauty.

Mozart, who is always careful not to multiply subjects unnecessarily, uses the same subordinate theme here that he had just put in the viola and second violin. So this latter imitates the principal subject at the fifth below with these notes: *G, f e d c b♭ a*. Then *Dido* says a second time, but one degree lower than the first: *Non! reste encore* (eighth verse).

Again the second violin imitates the melody at the fifth below, with these notes: *F, e d c b♭ a g*.

Here Mozart avoids a third repetition, which would be an error, known as *Rosalie*, or a third *révérence*.[9] Without abandoning the subordinate motive in the viola, he compresses the principal subject in the two violins, which gives this passage more movement and passion.

The large intervals that the first violin covers also add much to the effect of this verse, and paint in a very sensitive manner the confusion that reigns in *Dido*'s soul.

In the ninth verse *Dido*, eyes full of tears of love, addresses this prayer to *Aeneas*: *À l'objet qui t'adore, rends la vie et le bonheur* ["Return life and happiness to this creature who worships you"]. She breaks off suddenly in the middle of the last word, as if struck by a sudden but fatal light, which illuminates the feelings and intentions of *Anchises'* son. Then she says to him, *Non, déchire mon coeur, ingrat!* ["No, tear my heart to pieces, thankless wretch!"]

In the music of the ninth verse the harmonic cadences are compressed to the point that toward the end they are composed only of two eighth notes each. This verse itself ends with melodic cadences in sixteenth notes, which gives the style of this period an astonishing passion that transports and ravishes the soul.

The motive that *Mozart* uses in the tenth verse is the same as that which has just been heard as a subordinate motive in the course of the third period.

Note that from the seventh to the tenth verse the cello *has been controlled by a motive* composed of a quarter note and a dotted eighth—*b♭ g, b♭ c, e c, e f, a f, a b♭, d b♭, d e.* This bass line contains two voices in one: one part could do *b♭ g, b♭ c* and the other *e c, e f*, etc. But having already arranged the three upper parts, *Mozart* saw that he had to make the cello take by itself what could have been played by the viola and cello in turn.

At the notes *g d, g c♯* the harmonic cadences contract, lasting no more

9. Alluding to the three reverences habitual, at least in earlier times, when one arrived at a formal gathering. [Au.] *Rosalie* (or *Rosalia*, from the title of an Italian popular song, *Rosalia, mia cara*) is a pejorative term usually applied to excessive use of sequences in exact transposition up or down a whole step. The transposition here is not exact, and Momigny's concern seems to be instead with excessive repetition. His remarks in this paragraph apply ahead to the ninth verse of his text.

than a half-measure each. In the tenth verse the cello is no longer under constraint.

In the viola and above the held note in the cello is the subordinate harmonic motive $c\sharp$ *e a a a*. This motive is successively imitated by the two violins—*a c$\sharp$ e, e e e: c$\sharp$ e a, a a a a*. In this cadence the principal motive is *a b$\flat$*, in the following one *b$\flat$ c$\sharp$*, and then *c$\sharp$ d*. Consequently the first violin takes the subordinate motive immediately before the principal subject, doing the job of two parts.

The first part of the second reprise finishes with the complement of the fourth period, for the fifth is only a short connective period, that is, a link that joins the first part of this reprise to the second.

Second Part of the Second Reprise

The second part of the *second reprise* of this movement is the exact repetition of the beginning of the first reprise up to the chord of the false fifth and major sixth *c$\sharp$ e g b$\flat$*, on the *e* of the cello that ends the eighth period. The material from here to the end of the movement is only the remainder of the first reprise transposed from F major to D minor, but with the modifications necessitated by this change of mode, and with some other trivial differences dictated by taste or sensibility.

So just as one divides a building into three parts—the dome and two wings—and a sermon into three points, so also does a substantial movement in music fall into three *parts*. These parts subdivide into *periods*, these periods into *verses*, these verses into *phrases*, these phrases into *propositions*, and these propositions or cadences into *members*.

To speak more precisely, I will divide the periods into *principal periods* and *lesser periods*. I will allow four kinds of principal periods: *opening* periods, *spirited* periods, *melodic* periods, and *flashes*.

There are three sorts of lesser periods: *intermediary*, *complementary*, and connective or *linking* periods.

Opening periods are those with which one begins a movement. Ordinarily this period also begins the third part of the musical discourse.

The *spirited* period is one that ordinarily is placed after the opening period and a gentle intermediary period. This spirited period is full of vigor, and quite often closes the first large portion of the first reprise.

Melodic periods are those that are preeminently cantabile.

The periods I call *flashes* are those that serve to demonstrate the skill and competence of the performer.

Intermediary periods are all those that are placed between the principal ones, and are neither complementary nor conjunctional.

Complementary periods are those that one uses to make a meaning more complete.

The complementary period thus serves as a kind of cornice or border for the period that precedes it.

Connective periods are large *links* that serve to bind together two periods that usually could not be immediately placed one after the other without shocking the ear, or at least leaving it unsatisfied.

· ● ● ● ●

THE PERIODS OF THE SECOND REPRISE

The period that begins the second reprise is not a simple opening period in which the composer abandons himself to his genius, but one of those in which genius is controlled by a *theme*. This period, which we would expect to finish with the first verse, is augmented by a *supplement* that contains the entire second verse and a complement that only finishes when the fifth verse begins. As a result, the period is very well balanced.

The second period is of the intermediary type. But it has such skilled counterpoint that it deserves a place in the rank of the finest principal periods.

The third period has even more exaltation, yet no less depth. This intermediary period, like the preceding one, belongs in the number of those that one would search for in vain in most composers. Keep in mind that most of these composers have only a very weak tincture of the profound art of counterpoint, and seem completely alien to the inspired power that great knowledge nourishes.

The complement of this period is itself a little period, which serves as the frame to the preceding one, although not in the manner of frames of paintings, which draw their name from their squared shape[10] and surround a picture on all sides. A frame of the sort that I call a complementary period touches the period it completes only on one side, comprising what the Italians have called a *coda* (tail)—one or two periods that are added to close a movement more completely.[11]

The fifth period is connective, since it attaches the first part of the second reprise to the second.

The first reprise and the second part of the second reprise are in some way like the two wings of a building. The first part of the second reprise lies between the two other parts like a dome between two lateral pavilions. The part of this opening period to which are set the words *Ingrat! je veux me plaindre, et non pas t'attendrir* ["Thankless wretch! I want to protest, and not to relent"] seems to me sublime.[12]

10. *Cadre*, the French word for "frame," comes from the Latin *quadratum*, "four-sided thing" or "square."
11. Momigny seems to have left out a number here, labeling as the complement of the fourth period what is actually the complement of the third, and continuing in the error by calling the next period the fifth.
12. "The opening period . . . is divided into two full-scale verses, attached by a semi-harmonic link" (Momigny, *Cours complet,* vol. 2, p. 398).

There are many definitions of the sublime; it is in my view a *bon mot* of the soul. The intellect alone can in no way produce the sublime. Further, one does not say of a remark, however intelligent it may be, that it is sublime, although one says that it is acute, pointed, ingenious. In general the sublime is the expression of what a noble soul experiences in a extraordinary situation.

In a serious situation, but one that it wants to expose to humor, the intellect gives birth to an epigram. In a situation of the greatest moment, a great soul portrays itself by a sublime remark.

The seventh period responds to the second period of the first reprise,[13] but I have separated its complement here: it forms the eighth period.

The ninth period responds to the third period of the first reprise.[14] I have also separated its complement to form the tenth period.

The fourth period of the first reprise is the counterpart of the eleventh period of this one.[15]

13. "The second period is of the class of *intermediaries*. It is attached to the first period by a melodic link, *a f d a*. It is also divided into two verses [the third and fourth], attached to one another by the *melodic link a g♯ a g♯ a g♯ a*. The fifth, sixth, seventh, and eighth verses, included in this period, nevertheless form a separate little period, called a complementary period" (Momigny, vol. 2, 398–99).

14. "The third period . . . is another intermediary period. It closes with the tenth verse [the twenty-fourth in the second reprise]; the eleventh and twelfth [the twenty-fifth and twenty-sixth, or the tenth period] form a period complementary to this one" (Momigny, vol. 2, p. 399).

15. The . . . fourth period is not precisely a spirited period because it does not make enough racket. But it can still be considered as one, whether because of its imitations in stretto, because of the fervor with which the parts answer one another, or finally because of the abandon that prevails in the melody of the fourteenth [thirtieth] verse" (Momigny, vol. 2, p. 399).

Example [from Mozart, String Quartet, K. 421]

1st period

Hé - las! mes lar - mes, mes ap-pas, ne te touch-ent pas.

1st verse

No. 2.

Tu veux me don-ner ___ le tré - pas. Mons -

No. 1.

2nd verse

- tre in - di - gne du jour, voi-là le prix de tant d'a-

3rd verse

mour! oui, voi-là le prix de tant d'a-mour!

4th verse   *5th verse*

Fuis, mal - heu-reux!   Fuis, mal - heu-

6th verse

3rd period   *aside, hopefully*

reux! Non! reste en - co - re. (Il pa-rait s'at-ten-drir!)

7th verse

8th verse

9th verse

10th verse   11th verse

fais mon dé-plai-sir, in - grat! ___ je veux me plain-dre et non pas t'at - ten-drir.

Ah! quand tu fais mon dé-plai-sir, in - grat! _ je veux me plain - dre, me

16th verse

7th period

plain-dre et non pas _ t'at-ten-drir. Quoi! tu peux me quit-ter _ sans rou-gir?

17th verse

18th verse

8th period

Quoi! tu peux me quit - ter__ sans rou - gir? Quoi! rien ne peux te re - te -

19th verse

9th period

nir? Fuis! non, reste, ou je vais mou -

20th verse *21st verse* *22nd verse* *23rd verse*

rir__ reste, ou je vais mou - rir__ reste,_ ou je vais mou -

24th verse

12th period

31st verse

rir. Ah, si ja-mais pour toi ___ j'eûs quel - ques char-

mes, ___ viens, ___ ta - rir, viens, ta - rir ___ mes

pleurs. Ah! ___ si ja-mais Di - don ___ eût ₋ pour ₋ toi ___ quel - ques

cresc.

32nd verse

char-mes, ne _ vois _ pas _ sans pi - tié, _ ne vois pas _ sans pi-tié cou - ler mes _

pleurs. Sois sen - sible à mes mal-

33rd verse *34th verse*

heurs, _ sois sen - sible _ à ___ mes mal - heurs. Sois sen - sible à mes mal -

35th verse

heurs, sois ____ sen - sible _ à ___mes   mal - heurs.

36th verse

15th period

Quoi! tu ne ré-ponds rien?

p

37th verse

16th period

Quoi! tu ne ré-ponds rien?   Quoi! tu ne ré-ponds rien?

38th verse   *39th verse*

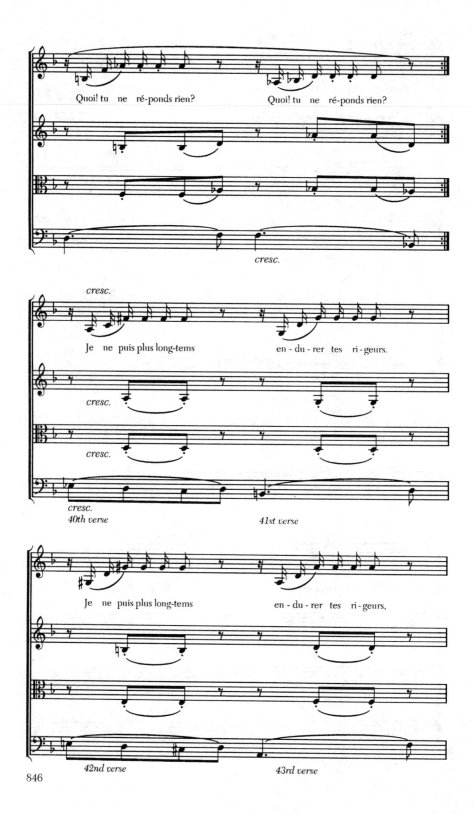

TEXT: DIDO'S LAMENT

Reprise II, Part I

Hélas! mes larmes, mes appas,	Alas! my tears, my charms,
Ne te touchent pas.	don't touch you.
Tu veux me donner le trépas.	You want me to die.
Monstre indigne du jour,	O monster unworthy of the light,
Voilà le prix de tant d'amour!	this is my reward for such a love!
Fuis, malheureux! Non! reste encore.	Fly away, you wretch! No! stay here.
(*à part, avec espoir*) Il paraît s'atten-	(*Aside, hopefully*) He seems to be
drir!	moved!

À l'objet qui t'adore
Rends la vie et le bonheur.
Non, déchire mon coeur,
Ingrat!

To this creature who worships you,
return life and happiness.
No, tear my heart to pieces,
Thankless wretch!

Reprise II, Part II

Ah! quand tu fais mon déplaisir,
Ingrat, je veux me plaindre
Et non pas t'attendrir.
Quoi! tu peux me quitter sans
    rougir?
Quoi! rien ne peut te retenir?
Fuis! non, reste, ou je vais mourir.
Arrête, arrête, ou je vais mourir.
Je t'enprie! je t'enprie!
Si je te perds, je vais mourir.
Ah, si jamais pour toi j'eûs quelques
    charmes,
Viens, tarir mes pleurs.
Ah! si jamais Didon eût pour toi quel-
    ques charmes,
Ne vois pas sans pitié couler mes
    pleurs.
Sois sensible à mes malheurs.
Quoi! tu ne réponds rien?
Je ne puis plus longtemps endurer tes
    rigueurs.
Je le sens; je meurs.

Ah! when you cause me grief,
thankless wretch, I want to protest,
and not to relent.
What! can you leave me without
    blushing with shame?
What! can nothing restrain you?
Fly away! No, stay, or I shall die.
Stop, stop, or I shall die.
I beg you! I beg you!
If I lose you, I shall die.
Ah, if I ever had any charms for
    you,
come and dry my tears.
Ah, if Dido ever had any charms
    for you,
do not watch my tears flow without
    pity.
Be moved by my misery
What! you do not respond?
I cannot endure your cruelty any
    longer.
I feel it; I am dying.

$\mathcal{P}$ERFORMANCE
PRACTICES

129 Carl Philipp Emanuel Bach

Johann Sebastian's second son, sometimes called the "Berlin" or "Hamburg" Bach, Carl Philipp Emanuel Bach was born in 1714 at Weimar. In 1738 he moved to Berlin and in 1740 became harpsichordist to Frederick the Great. In 1767 Bach gave up this position to become Telemann's successor as director of church music at Hamburg. He died there in 1788.

As a composer, Bach wrote works for clavichord and pianoforte as well as for harpsichord, and preferred the latter two instruments for the practice of improvisation. While his keyboard sonatas established him as the primary representation of the *galant* in Germany, many of them borrow features from the improvisatory mode—declamation, abrupt changes of mood, sudden modulations to remote keys—to create a powerfully emotive rhetoric often called the "sensitive" (*empfindsam*) style. He was also known for his virtuoso harpsichord concertos, chamber music, and symphonies, and he composed much sacred music during his tenure in Hamburg.

His theoretical work, the *Versuch über die wahre Art, das Clavier zu spielen* (*Essay on the Proper Manner of Playing a Keyboard Instrument;* in two parts, 1753–62) has remained to the present day a source of primary importance for the musical practice of the time.

FROM *Essay on the Proper Manner of Playing a Keyboard Instrument*

(1753)

CHAPTER 2. ABOUT EMBELLISHMENTS IN GENERAL

1. No one, perhaps, has ever questioned the necessity of embellishments. We may perceive this from our meeting them everywhere in great abundance. Indeed, when we consider the good they do, they are indispensable. They tie the notes together; they enliven them; they give them, when necessary, a special emphasis and weight; they make them pleasing and hence arouse a special attention; they help to clarify their content; whatever its nature, whether sad, gay, or of any other sort we please, they invariably contribute their share; they provide the correct manner of delivery with a considerable part of its occasion and material; a mediocre composition may be assisted by them, while without them the finest melody must seem empty and monotonous, the clearest content at all times unclear.

TEXT: As edited by Walter Niemann from the second (1759) edition of the original (5th ed., Leipzig, 1925), pp. 24–31. Translation by Oliver Strunk, with minor alterations.

2. For all the good embellishments may thus do, they may do equal harm if we choose bad ones or apply them in an unskillful way, apart from their proper place and in excess of their due number.

3. For this reason, those who in their pieces clearly indicate the embellishments that belong to them have always followed a safer procedure than if they had left their works to the discretion of unskilled performers.

4. Also in this respect we must do justice to the French for being unusually careful in the marking of their pieces. In Germany, the greatest masters of our instrument have done the same, and who knows but what the reasonable choice and number of their embellishments may have given the occasion to the French today of no longer burdening, as formerly, almost every note with such an ornament, thereby concealing the necessary clarity and noble simplicity of the melody.

5. From this we see that we must learn to distinguish good embellishments from bad, to perform the good ones correctly, and to apply them in their proper place and in due number.

6. The embellishments lend themselves readily to a division into two classes. To the first I assign those customarily indicated either by certain accepted signs or by a few small notes; to the second may be assigned the rest, which have no signs and are made up of many small notes.

7. Since this second class of embellishments depends especially on musical taste and is hence all too subject to change, since in works for the clavier it is for the most part found written out, and since we can in any case do without it, in view of the sufficient number of the others, I shall treat it only briefly at the end in connection with fermatas.[1] Otherwise I shall concern myself only with embellishments of the first class, inasmuch as they have for the most part belonged for some time past to the very nature, as it were, of clavier playing, and will no doubt always remain the fashion. To these familiar embellishments I shall add a few new ones; I shall explain them and, as far as possible, determine their position; I shall, for convenience's sake, give at the same time their fingering and, where it is noteworthy, the manner of their delivery; I shall illustrate with examples what cannot always be said with sufficient clarity; I shall say what needs to be said about certain incorrect or at least ambiguous signs, so that one may learn to distinguish them from the correct ones, likewise about embellishments to be rejected; finally I shall refer my readers to the sample pieces,[2] and shall hope, by all these means, to clear away more or less the false notion of the necessity of redundant fancy notes in clavier playing which here and there has taken root.

---

1. Bach follows this general introduction with sections on the appoggiatura, trill, turn, mordent, compound appoggiatura, slide, and snap, closing the chapter with a section on the elaboration of fermatas.

2. Originally bound with the musical examples of the *Versuch* were *Achtzehn Probestücke in sechs Sonaten* (*Eighteen Sample Pieces in Six Sonatas*). They are available printed separately in modern editions.

8. Regardless of this, anyone who has the skill is at liberty to introduce embellishments more lavish than ours. He need only take care, in so doing, that this occurs seldom, in the right place, and without doing violence to the affect of the piece. Of himself he will understand that, for example, the depiction of innocence or sadness will tolerate less ornamenting than the other passions. He who in this heeds what is needed may be allowed to have his way, for he skillfully combines with the singing style of playing his instrument the elements of surprise and fire in which the instruments have the advantage of the voice and, as a result, knows how to awaken and maintain by means of constant change a high degree of attention in his listeners. This difference between instrument and voice may be preserved unhesitatingly. He who bestows on these embellishments the care they need may be otherwise unconcerned as to whether what he plays can or cannot be sung.

9. At the same time, an overlavish treatment, even of our sort of embellishments, is to be avoided above all things. Let them be regarded as decorations which can overload the finest building, as spices which can spoil the finest food. Many notes, being of no consequence, must be spared them; many notes, sparkling enough in themselves, will likewise not tolerate them, for embellishments should only intensify the weightiness and simplicity of such notes, distinguishing them from others. Failing this, I should commit the same error as the speaker who places an emphatic stress on every word; everything sounds the same and is in consequence unclear.

10. We shall see in what follows that some situations permit more than one sort of embellishment; in such cases, let us take advantage of variation; let us apply, here an ingratiating embellishment, here a sparkling one, and sometimes, for variety's sake, let us use a wholly plain delivery if the notes permit it, without embellishment but in accordance both with the rules of good delivery, to be treated in the next part, and with the true affect.

11. It is difficult to determine the position of each embellishment with absolute precision, for each composer, provided he does no violence to good taste, is at liberty in his inventions to prescribe in most places any embellishment he pleases. In this we are content to instruct our readers by a few well-established rules and examples and by pointing out, in any case, the impossibility of applying a particular embellishment. In those pieces which indicate all embellishments there is no need for concern, while in those which indicate little or nothing the embellishments are customarily supplied in the regular way.

12. Since to this day I can name no one who has anticipated me in this difficult matter and who might have cleared for me this treacherous path, I trust that no one will blame me for believing that, even within certain well-established situations, there may perhaps be still a possibility of exception.

13. And since, to make a reasonable use of this material, he must attend to many small details, the reader should exercise his ear as much as possible by diligent listening to good performances and, the better to understand many things, must have mastered above all the art of thoroughbass. Experience has

shown that he who has no thorough understanding of harmony is, in applying the embellishments, always fumbling in the dark, and that he has to thank mere chance, and never his insight, for a fortunate outcome. To this end, where necessary, I shall always add the bass of the examples.

14. Although the singers and the players of instruments other than ours, if they wish to play their pieces well, can no more do without most of our embellishments than we can ourselves, we players of the clavier have followed the more orderly procedure by giving certain signs to the embellishments, clearly indicating the manner of playing our pieces.

15. Since the others did not observe this praiseworthy precaution, and sought, on the contrary, to indicate everything by a few signs, not only has the teaching of embellishments become more painful to them than to players of the clavier, but we have also seen the rise of many ambiguous, indeed false signs which sometimes, even today, cause many pieces to be performed unsuitably. For example, the mordent is in music a necessary and familiar embellishment, yet there are few, apart from players of the clavier, who know its sign. I know of a piece in which, as a result of this, a particular passage has often been ruined. This passage, if it is not to sound untasteful, must be played with a long mordent, something which no one would hit upon without an indication. The necessity of using as its indication a sign known only to players of the clavier, there being no other, has resulted in its being confused with the sign of a trill. We shall see in what follows how disagreeable an effect has arisen from the great difference between these two embellishments.

16. Since the French are careful in placing the signs of their embellishments, it follows that, in hitherto departing altogether, as we have, unfortunately, from their pieces and from their way of playing the clavier, we have at the same time also deviated from the precise indication of our embellishments to such an extent that today these once so familiar signs are already becoming unfamiliar, even to players of the clavier.

17. The notes comprised in the embellishments take their accidentals from the key signature. Nevertheless, we shall see in what follows that there are frequent exceptions to this rule, readily discovered by a practiced ear, caused sometimes by the preceding notes, sometimes by the following ones, and in general by the modulations of a melody into another key.

18. But in order that the reader may also overcome those difficulties that arise on this account, I have found it necessary to retain that practice according to which the accidentals are indicated along with the embellishments in all cases. One will find them in the sample pieces wherever necessary, now singly, now in pairs.

19. All embellishments must stand in a proportioned relation to the value of their note, to the tempo, and to the content of the piece. Especially in those cases where various sorts of embellishments occur and where the affect is not too restricting, it should be remarked that the more notes an embellishment comprises, the longer the note to which it is applied must be, no matter

whether this length arises from the value of the note or from the tempo of the piece. The player must avoid detracting from the brilliance that an embellishment is intended to produce by allowing too much of the value of its note to remain left over; at the same time, he must also avoid occasioning a lack of clarity by performing certain embellishments too quickly, something which occurs mainly when he applies many embellishments or embellishments of many notes to notes of small value.

20. Although we shall see in what follows that the player may sometimes intentionally apply to a long note an embellishment that does not wholly fill out its value, he may not release the last note of such an embellishment until the following note is due, for the chief aim of all embellishments should be to tie the notes together.

21. We see, then, that embellishments are used more in slow and moderate tempi than in rapid ones, more in connection with long notes than with short ones.

22. Whatever needs to be observed regarding the value of the notes, the signs, and the small notes, I shall always include as a part of my explanations. The reader will also find the small notes with their actual values printed in the sample pieces.

23. All embellishments indicated by small notes belong to the note that follows; the preceding note, in consequence, never diminishes in value, while the following note loses as much as is made up by the small notes taken together. This observation is the more necessary in that it is commonly disregarded and in that I have been unable to avoid sometimes detaching certain small notes from their main note in the sample pieces, the space being so crowded with signs for fingering, embellishments, and delivery.

24. In accordance with this rule, then, these small notes are struck in place of the main note that follows, together with the bass or with the other parts. Through them the player slides into the note following; this too is very often disregarded in that he pounces roughly upon the main note after having, in addition, unskillfully applied or produced the embellishments associated with the small notes.

25. Our present taste being what it is and the good Italian way of singing having made considerable contribution to it, the player cannot manage with the French embellishments alone; for this reason, I have had to compile my embellishments from more than one nation. To these I have added a few new ones. Apart from this, I believe that the best way of playing the clavier or any other instrument is that which succeeds in skillfully combining what is neat and brilliant in the French taste with what is ingratiating in the Italian way of singing. For this union the Germans are particularly well adapted as long as they remain unprejudiced.

26. At the same time, it is possible that a few will not be wholly satisfied with my choice of embellishments, having perhaps embraced one taste alone; I believe, however, that no one can be a thorough judge of anything in music

unless he has heard all kinds and knows how to find what is best in each. What is more, I agree with a certain great man who declared that, while one taste has more good in it than another, there is none the less in every taste some particular thing that is good, no taste being as yet so perfect that it will not still tolerate further additions. By means of such additions and refinements we have reached the point at which we are and shall continue to go on and on. This, however, cannot possibly happen if we work at and, as it were, worship one sort of taste alone; on the contrary, we must know how to profit by whatever is good, wherever it may be found.

27. Therefore, since the embellishments together with the manner of their employment make a considerable contribution to fine taste, the player should be neither so changeable that without further inquiry he accepts at every moment each new embellishment, regardless of its sponsor, nor yet so prejudiced in favor of himself and his own taste that out of vanity he refuses to accept anything new whatsoever. He should of course put the new thing to a rigorous test before he adopts it, and it is possible that in time the introduction of unnatural novelties will make good taste as rare as art. At the same time, to keep pace with the fashion, the player should be, if not the first, then not the last to take up new embellishments. Let him not oppose them if they do not always appeal to him at first. New things, attractive as they are occasionally, sometimes seem to us perverse. And this is often evidence of the worth of a thing which will in the long run last longer than others that are overly pleasing in the beginning. These last are as a rule so run into the ground that they soon become repellent.

28. While most of my examples of embellishments are for the right hand, I by no means deny these graces to the left; on the contrary, I urge every player to exercise each hand alone in all of them, for this brings with it a dexterity and lightness in the production of other notes. We shall see in what follows that certain embellishments also often occur in the bass. Moreover, the player is obliged to reproduce all imitations to the last detail. In short, the left hand must have exercise in this to manage it skillfully; failing this, it will be better to omit the embellishments, which lose their charm if we perform them badly.

130 Leopold Mozart

Leopold Mozart, the father of Wolfgang Amadeus and himself an excellent violinist and a respectable composer, was born at Augsburg in 1719. He entered the service of the Prince-Bishop of Salzburg, served as a composer and assistant *maestro di cappella* to the episcopal court, and died at Salzburg in 1787.

Leopold Mozart was a prolific composer and wrote a large quantity of works

in varied forms of sacred and secular music: masses, motets, symphonies, serenades, concertos, oratorios, operas, etc. His best-known work, however, is
probably his method for the violin, *Versuch einer gründlichen Violinschule*
(*Essay on the Fundamental Principles of Violin Playing*) published in the year of
Wolfgang's birth (1756), one of the oldest and most solid books of its kind. It is,
with Johann Joachim Quantz's method for the flute and C. P. E. Bach's method
for keyboard instruments, an important source for the study of musical practice
in the mid-eighteenth century.

FROM *Essay on the Fundamental Principles of Violin Playing*
(1756)

CHAPTER TWELVE: ON READING MUSIC CORRECTLY AND ON GOOD DELIVERY IN GENERAL

1. Everything turns on good performance: everyday experience confirms this
rule. Many a half-composer is pleased and delighted when he hears his musical
Galimathias performed by good players who know how to apply the passion,
which he has not even thought about, in its proper place, how to make the
greatest possible distinction in the characters, which has never occurred to
him, and consequently how, by means of a good delivery, to render the whole
wretched scribble tolerable to the ears of the listeners. But on the other hand,
who does not know that the best composition is often so miserably performed
that the composer himself has difficulty enough in recognizing his own work?

2. The good delivery of a composition in the present taste is not as simple as
those people believe who think they are doing very well if, following their own
ideas, they ornament and contort a piece in a truly idiotic fashion and who have
no conception whatever of the passion that is supposed to be expressed in it.
But who are these people? In the main they are those who, since they can
scarcely play in time, even tolerably, begin at once with concertos and solos in
order (as they stupidly imagine) to establish themselves as quickly as possible
in the company of the virtuosi. Some actually reach such a point that, in a few
concertos or solos that they have practiced thoroughly, they play off the most
difficult passages with uncommon facility. These they know by heart. But if
they are to perform even a few minuets in the cantabile style directed by the
composer, they are in no position to do so—indeed one sees this already in the
concertos they have studied. For as long as they play an Allegro, things still go
well, but as soon as they come to an Adagio, they betray their gross ignorance
and their poor judgment in every single measure of the piece. They play without order and without expression; they fail to distinguish the loud and the soft;

TEXT: The facsimile reprint of the original edition of 1756 (Vienna, 1922), pp. 252–64. Translation
by Oliver Strunk.

the embellishments are applied in the wrong places, too thickly crowded and for the most part confused; sometimes, just the other way, the notes are too expressionless and one sees that the player does not know what to do. In such players one can seldom hope any longer for improvement, for of all people they are the most prepossessed in their own favor, and he would incur their highest displeasure who sought, out of the goodness of his heart, to persuade them of their mistakes.

3. To read correctly, as directed, the musical compositions of the good masters and to play each piece in accordance with the passion prevailing in it calls for far more art than to study the most difficult concertos and solos. To do the latter does not require much intelligence. And if the player is adroit enough to figure out the fingering he can learn the most difficult passages by himself, provided he practices them diligently. But to do the former is not as easy as this. For the player has not only to attend closely to every annotation and direction and to play the work as it is set down and not otherwise; he has also to enter into the passion that is to be expressed and to apply and to execute all the runs, the legatos and staccatos, the fortes and pianos, in a word, everything that bears in any way on the tasteful delivery of a piece, observing in this a certain good style that can be learned only by sound judgment through long experience.

4. Let the reader now decide for himself whether, among violinists, the good orchestral player ought not to be prized far more highly than the mere soloist. The soloist can play everything as he pleases and adjust its delivery to his own ideas, even to his own hand; the orchestral player must have the ability to grasp at once and to deliver properly the taste, the ideas, and the expression of different composers. The soloist, to bring things out cleanly, has only to practice at home—others must adapt themselves to him; the orchestral player must read everything at sight—often, indeed, passages such as run counter to the natural arrangement of the measure;[1] he must adapt himself to others. The soloist, if only he has a clean delivery, can in general play his concertos acceptably, even with distinction; the orchestral player, on the other hand, must have a considerable grasp of music in general, of the art of composition, and of differences in characters, nay, he must have a peculiarly versatile talent if he is to fill his office creditably, especially if he is ever to act as the leader of an orchestra. Are there some who believe that, among violinists, one finds more good orchestral players than soloists? They are mistaken. Poor accompanists are admittedly numerous enough, but there are very few good ones, for today everyone wants to be the soloist. But as to what an orchestra consisting entirely of soloists is like, I leave

---

1. *Contra metrum musicum.* Of this I have already given notice in Chapter 1, Section 2, §4, note *d*. And I do not know what I am to think when I see an aria, by one of those Italian composers who are so celebrated just now, which runs so counter to the musical meter that one would suppose it made by a pupil. [Au.] In the note *d* to which Mozart refers, it is pointed out that common time ordinarily has two divisions only and that infractions of this rule are excused only in peasant dances or other unusual melodies.

this to those gentlemen composers who have performed their works under such conditions. Few soloists read well, for it is their habit to be continually introducing details of their own invention and to regard themselves alone, paying little regard to others.[2]

5. Thus, until the player can accompany quite well, he must play no solos. He must first know exactly how to execute all the various strokes of the bow; he must understand how to apply the fortes and pianos in the proper place and to the proper degree; he must learn how to distinguish the characters of pieces and how to deliver each passage according to its required and peculiar taste; in a word, before he begins to play solos and concertos, he must be able to read the works of many gifted persons correctly and elegantly. From a painting, one sees at once whether he who has painted it is a master of drawing; in the same way, many a musician would play his solo more intelligently if he had ever learned to deliver a symphony or trio in accordance with the good taste it required or to accompany an aria with the proper passion and in accordance with the character peculiar to it. I shall endeavor to set down some brief rules which the player can make profitable use of in the performance of a piece of music.

6. The player must of course tune his instrument carefully and exactly to those of his fellows; this he already knows and my mentioning the matter may seem somewhat superfluous. But since even those who wish to pass for first violinists often fail to tune their instruments exactly together, I find it absolutely necessary to mention the matter here, the more so since it is to the first violinist that the rest are supposed to tune. In playing with the organ or harpsichord, these determine the pitch; if neither one is present, the pitch is taken from the wind instruments. Some tune the A-string first, others the D. Both do well, if only they tune carefully and exactly. I would mention only one other point; in a warm room the pitch of the stringed instruments gradually falls, in a cold one it gradually rises.

7. Before beginning to play a piece, the player must thoroughly examine and consider it. He must discover the character, the tempo, and the sort of movement that it requires and must carefully determine whether there is not concealed in it some passage, seemingly unimportant at first sight, which will nonetheless be far from easy to play, demanding a special style of delivery and expression. Then, during the performance itself, he must spare no pains to discover and deliver correctly the passion that the composer has sought to apply and, since the mournful and the merry often alternate, he must be intent on delivering each of these in its own style. In a word, he must play everything in such a way that he will himself be moved by it.[3]

---

2. But what I say does not at all apply to those great virtuosi who, in addition to being extraordinarily gifted as players of concertos, are also good orchestral players. Such people are really deserving of the highest esteem. [Au.]

3. It is bad enough that many a player never gives a thought to what he is doing and simply plays off his music as though in a dream or as though he were actually playing for himself alone. If

8. From this it follows that the player must pay the strictest attention to the prescribed pianos and fortes and not always be scraping away on one level. Nay, without direction and, as a rule, of himself, he must know how to relieve the soft with the loud and how to apply each of these in its proper place, for, following the familiar expression in painting, this is called light and shade. Notes that are raised by a sharp or natural he ought always to attack somewhat more vigorously, reducing his tone again for the continuation of the melody:

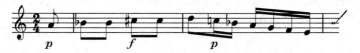

In the same way he should differentiate in intensity a note that is momentarily lowered by a flat or natural:

With half notes that occur among shorter values, the invariable custom is to attack them vigorously and then to diminish the tone again:

Indeed, quarters are sometimes also played in just this way:

And this is the expression actually called for by the composer when he marks a note with an *f* or *p*, that is, with a forte or piano. But after the player has vigorously attacked the note, he must not let his bow leave the strings, as some clumsy players do; the stroke must be continued and consequently the tone still heard, though it will gently taper off.[4]

---

such a player, at the beginning of a piece, gets a few beats ahead of the tempo, he does not notice it, and I will wager that he would finish the piece several measures before his fellows if his neighbor or the leader himself did not call his attention to it. [Au.]

4. Let the reader look up what I have said about this on p. 44, note *k*. [Au.] In this note (chap. 1, sec. 3, §18), Mozart complains of those who cannot play a half note or even a quarter without dividing it into two parts.

9. The accent,[5] expression, or intensity of the tone will fall as a rule on the strong or initial note that the Italians call the *nota buona*. But there are distinct varieties of these initial or "good" notes. The particularly strong notes are the following: in every measure, the note beginning the first quarter; in the half measure, the first note, or, in $\frac{4}{4}$ time, the first note of the third quarter; in $\frac{6}{4}$ and $\frac{6}{8}$ time, the first notes of the first and fourth quarters; in $\frac{12}{8}$ time, the first notes of the first, fourth, seventh, and tenth quarters. These, then, are the initial notes on which the maximum intensity of the tone will fall, wherever the composer has indicated no other expression. In the ordinary accompaniments for an aria or concerto, in which as a rule only eighth and sixteenth notes occur, they are usually written nowadays as separate notes or are at least marked for a few measures at the beginning with a little stroke:

$f \quad p \qquad f \quad p \qquad f \quad p \qquad f \quad p$

The player must accordingly continue in this way to attack the first note vigorously until a change occurs.

10. The other "good" notes are those which are always distinguished from the rest by a slightly increased intensity, but to which this increased intensity must be very moderately applied. They are: in alla breve time, the quarters and eighth notes, and, in the so-called half triple time, the quarters; further, in common time and in $\frac{2}{4}$ and $\frac{3}{4}$ time, the eighth and sixteenth notes; finally, in $\frac{3}{8}$ and $\frac{6}{8}$ time, the sixteenth notes; and so forth. When several notes of this sort follow one after another, slurred two and two, the accent will fall on the first of each two, and this first note will not only be attacked somewhat more vigorously but will also be sustained somewhat longer while the second note will be bound to it quite gently and quietly, and somewhat retarded.[6] It often happens, however, that three, four, and even more such notes are bound together by a slur of this sort. In such a case, the player must attack the first of them somewhat more vigorously and sustain it longer and must bind the rest to it in the same bow, without the slightest stress, by reducing the intensity more and more.[7]

5. By the word "accent" I understand here, not the French *port de voix*, which Rousseau tries to explain in his *Méthode pour apprendre à chanter*, p. 56, but a pressure (*expression*) or stress, an emphasis, from the Greek ἐν (*in*) and φάσις (*apparitio, dictio*). [Au.]

6. Let the reader look at the illustration of this in Chapter 7, Section 1, §3, and in particular let him read §5 in Chapter 7, Section 2, and look at the musical examples. [Au.] Chapter 7, "On the many different sorts of bowing," deals in Section 1 with notes of equal value and in Section 2 with figures consisting of notes of unequal value.

7. Let the reader call Chapter 7 to mind from time to time, especially what was said there in Section 1, §20. [Au.] The concluding paragraph (§20) of Section 1 explains that after mastering the various ways of bowing the examples that have been given, the student must learn to play them with taste and so that their variety is immediately perceptible.

11. From Chapters 6[8] and 7 the reader has seen how much the melody may be differentiated by the legatos and staccatos. The player, then, must not only pay the strictest attention to such legatos as are written out and indicated, but since in many a composition nothing is indicated at all, he must know how to apply the legato and staccato himself in a tasteful manner and in the proper place. The chapter on the many varieties of bowing, particularly in its second section, will serve to show the player how to go about making such alteration in this as he thinks proper, provided always that it is in keeping with the character of the piece.

12. Today, in certain passages, one finds the skillful composer applying the expression in a quite special, unusual, and unexpected way which would puzzle many if it were not indicated.

For the expression and the intensity of the tone fall here on the last quarter of the measure, and the first quarter of the measure following is to be bound to it very quietly, without being stressed. The player, then, is by no means to distinguish these two notes by a pressure from the bow, but is to play them as though they formed a single half note.[9]

13. In cheerful pieces, to make the delivery really lively, the accent is usually applied to the highest note. This leads to the stress falling on the last note of the second and fourth quarters in common time and on the end of the second quarter in $\frac{2}{4}$ time, especially when the piece begins with an upbeat.

But in pieces that are slow and sad, this may not be done, for here the upbeat must be not detached but sustained, and delivered in a singing style.

14. In $\frac{3}{4}$ and $\frac{3}{8}$ time the accent may also fall on the second quarter.

---

8. Chapter 6 is titled "On the so-called triplets."

9. Here too let the reader call to mind §18 and note *k* in Chapter 1, Section 3. [Au.] The paragraph in question deals in greater detail with the correct performance of syncopations like those just described; for Mozart's "Note *k*," see p. 860, n. 4.

15. The player will notice that, in the example last given, the dotted quarter (d) in the first measure is slurred to the eighth note (c) that follows. Accordingly, at the dot he must not bear down with his bow, but, as in all other situations of this kind, he must attack the quarter with a moderate intensity, hold out the time of the dot without stress, and very quietly bind the following eighth note to it.[10]

16. In the same way, such notes as these, which would otherwise be divided off according to the measure, must never be divided, nor may their division be indicated by a stress; on the contrary, the player must simply attack them and sustain them quietly, exactly as though they stood at the beginning of the quarter.[11] This manner of delivery gives rise to a sort of broken tempo which makes a very strange and agreeable impression, since either the inner voice or the bass seems to separate itself from the upper voice; it has the further effect that in certain passages the fifths do not sound together, but are heard alternately, one after the other. Here, for example, are three voices.

17. Not only in the situation just discussed, but wherever a forte is prescribed, the player must moderate the intensity, not foolishly sawing away, above all in accompanying a concerto. Some people either do not do a thing at all or, in doing it, are certain to exaggerate it. The player must be guided by the passion. Sometimes a note requires a rather vigorous attack, at other times a moderate one, at still other times one that is barely perceptible. The first usually occurs in connection with a sudden expression that all the instruments make together; as a rule, this is indicated by the direction *fp*.

fp

The second occurs in connection with those especially prominent notes that were discussed in §9 of this chapter. The third occurs in connection with all the remaining notes first enumerated in §10; to these the player must apply a barely perceptible stress. For even though he sees many fortes written into the accompaniment of a concerto, he must apply the intensity in moderation and

10. I have already drawn attention to this in Chapter 1, Section 3, §9. [Au.]
11. Let the reader just look at §§21, 22, and 23 in Chapter 4, where he will also find examples enough. Here belongs also what was said at the end of Chapter 1, Section 3, §18, by no means forgetting note *k*. [Au.] The several paragraphs in Chapter 4 deal with various ways of bowing such rhythms as eighth, quarter, eighth, or sixteenth, eighth, sixteenth; for Mozart's references to Chapter 1, see p. 860, n. 4 and p. 862, n. 9

not so exaggerate it that he drowns out the soloist. Quite the other way, such intensity, sparingly and briefly applied, must set off the solo part, give spirit to the melody, help out the soloist, and make easier for him the task of properly characterizing the piece.

18. The player, just as he must pay the strictest attention to the legatos, staccatos, fortes, and pianos required by the expression, must also avoid playing away continually with a dragging heavy bow and must be guided by the passion predominating in each passage. Lively and playful passages must be distinguished by light short strokes and played off joyously and rapidly, just as pieces that are slow and sad must be delivered with long-drawn strokes, richly and tenderly.

19. As a rule, in accompanying a concerto the player must not sustain the notes but must play them off quickly, and in $\frac{6}{8}$ and $\frac{12}{8}$ time, to avoid making the delivery drowsy, must cut off the quarters almost as though they were eighth notes. But let him see to it that the tempo remains steady and that the quarters are more audible than the eighth notes.

20. Many who have no notion of taste are never willing to maintain a steady tempo in accompanying a concerto, but are constantly at pains to yield to the soloist. These are accompanists for bunglers and not for masters. If the player has before him some Italian prima donna who cannot even carry off in the proper tempo what she has learned by heart, or any other fancied virtuoso of this sort, he must admittedly skip over whole half-measures if he is to prevent a public disgrace. But when he accompanies a true virtuoso, one who is worthy of this title, he must not allow himself to be seduced into hesitating or hurrying by the prolongations and anticipations of the notes that the soloist knows how to bring in so skillfully and touchingly, but must at all times continue to play in the same steady tempo. Otherwise what the soloist has sought to build up will be torn down again by his accompanying.[12]

21. Furthermore, if the performance is to be good, the players must pay strict attention to one another and especially to their leader in order that they may not only begin together but may also play throughout in the same tempo and with the same expression. There are certain passages in playing which one

12. The skillful accompanist, then, must be able to judge his soloist. To a respectable virtuoso he must by no means yield, for to do so would ruin the soloist's *tempo rubato*. But what this "stolen time" is may be more easily demonstrated than described. Has he to do, on the contrary, with a fancied virtuoso? Then, in an Adagio cantabile, he may often sustain an eighth note for half a measure until the soloist comes to himself, as it were, after his paroxysm, and nothing goes in time, for the soloist plays in the style of a recitative. [Au.]

easily falls to hurrying.[13] Aside from this, the players must take care to play off the chords quickly and together, the short notes following a dot or a rest of small value somewhat after the beat and rapidly.[14] If several notes are to be played as an upbeat or after a short rest, the usual thing is to take them in a down-bow, including the first note of the following quarter in the same stroke. Here the players must pay special attention to one another and not begin too early. This is an example with chords and rests of small value.

22. All that I have set down in this last chapter bears in particular on reading music correctly and in general on the clean and sensible delivery of a well-written piece of music. And all the pains that I have taken in the writing of this book have been directed toward one end: to set the beginner on the right path and to prepare him for the recognition and perception of a good musical taste. So I shall stop here, although I have still many things to say to the musical fraternity. Who knows? I may make bold to enrich the musical world with another book if I see that this my desire to serve the beginner has not been altogether useless.

13. Let the reader just call to mind §38 in Chapter 4. And in Chapters 6 and 7 I have stressed the importance of a steady tempo more than once. [Au.] Paragraph 38 of Chapter 4 deals with the bowing and correct performance of continuous sixteenths; for Chapters 6 and 7, see p. 861, n. 6 and p. 862, n. 8.
14. Let the reader look up what I have written in §§2 and 3 of Chapter 7, Section 2, and also the musical examples given in this connection. [Au.] These two paragraphs deal more explicitly with the correct performance of the short note or notes following a dot.

131 Giambattista Mancini

The first edition of Giambattista Mancini's *Riflessioni pratiche sul canto figurato* (*Practical Reflections on Singing*) was published in Vienna in 1774. Charles Burney, who called the treatise "admirable" and "useful," saw it as a supplement to Pier Francesco Tosi's *Thoughts on Ancient and Modern Singers* (1723); the two works were the preeminent practical treatises on singing written in the eighteenth century. Born in 1714, Mancini studied voice in Naples and Bologna, as well as counterpoint and composition with Padre Giovanni Battista Martini. Mancini, a castrato, had an operatic career in Italy and Germany but gained his primary reputation as a teacher. In 1757 the Empress Maria Theresa invited him to Vienna to teach her daughters singing. He remained there until his death in 1800.

The second Italian edition of Mancini's treatise (entitled as above, a slight variation on the original title) was issued in controversy. Published in 1777, with the encouragement of his friend Padre Martini, it contained long interpolations in several chapters responding to attacks by Vincenzo Manfredini on his teaching techniques. The differences between Mancini and Manfredini were those of practical musician versus theorist, conservative versus progressive, and apostle of agility versus proponent of simple, direct expression (Mancini was particularly stung by Manfredini's attack on his veneration of the trill). In his remarks about declamation and recitative Mancini urged the expressive claims of reform opera, rendering extravagant praise to the genius of Gluck.

FROM *Practical Reflections on Singing*
(1777)

ARTICLE XIII: ABOUT THE ATTAINMENTS NECESSARY TO RECITE WELL IN THE THEATER

As I have already said, it is not the beauty and agility of the voice alone that single out an artist. In addition a fine style of reciting should yield one a proper success, and with it approbation and greater profit.

An actor recites well when, entering thoroughly into the character of the person he represents, he unfolds that character naturally, using action, the voice, and the proper affects, and when he brings that character so clearly to life that the spectator says, for example, that man is *Caesar,* or this man is *Alexander.*

Now, an actor will never be able to express those affects naturally, nor make the spectators recognize their effects clearly, if he does not understand the force of the words; if he does not know the true character of the person he represents; if he does not speak a good Tuscan; and if above all he does not project an exact, clear, and complete pronunciation of the words, although without exaggeration.

I have heard reports of the diligence and serious study that the famous *Pistocchi*[1] put into teaching his students in order to make their pronunciation perfect. As a result the audience would be able to hear all the words, to the

TEXT: The third edition (Milan, 1777), pp. 218–47. Translation by Wye J. Allanbrook.

1. Francesco Antonio Pistocchi (1659–1726) was a castrato who later in his career established a preeminent singing school in Bologna. He taught Mancini's teacher, Antonio Bernacchi, and Mancini praises him highly in Article 2 of this treatise.

point of distinguishing, when they were uttered, certain doubled letters like *tt,* *rr, ss,* and so on.

In order to acquire these different attainments, an actor needs to undertake three different courses of study—*grammar, history,* and the *Italian* language.

The force and power of a word do not always emerge from its nature alone; very often the manner with which it is uttered diminishes or increases its power. One learns this style of utterance from the study of grammar. In fact one should speak as one writes. For without commas and periods a person reading would not be able to understand the true sense of a text, or at least would easily be deceived in making it out. In the same way a person who is listening to someone speak at length and never hears him pause or change the tone of his voice will never be able to understand him well.

One learns this ordered mode of writing, reading, and speaking from grammar.

Just listen to the speech of a good orator, and hear how many rests, what variety of tones, how many different emphases he uses to express its meanings. Now he raises his voice, now he lowers it; now he hurries a bit, now he grows harsh and now gentle, according to the various passions that he wishes to stir in the listener. But since grammatical rules are only theoretical, you must learn the practice by reading Tuscan books and listening to Italian orators.

When you happen to be alone in your room it would be useful to read aloud some good book, especially of poetry. This is the most useful training, and an easy way of coming to speak with the necessary pauses and tonal inflections. As a consequence you will also speak well in public.

The study of grammar should be followed by the study of *sacred, secular,* and *mythological* history.

You will find professors who certainly do not spend the whole day in leisure, and are not unlearned in any literature. They read about the origin of nations, their vicissitudes, the overthrow of authority, wars, truces, the consequent peace, and the like. This knowledge can certainly serve them as pleasure and ornament, but it cannot be said to be a necessary attainment for an actor. A virtuoso in music must be a traveller, but it is fully sufficient that he know about the predominant merits and passions of one nation. He should know the most common manner of speaking there, habits of dress, and, in short, the kinds of things that usually distinguish one nation from another of the ones in which he may chance to be. But *sacred, secular,* and *mythological* history is an indispensable necessity for an actor.

For example, suppose you want an actor to play *Julius Caesar* in the scene when he was betrayed and assaulted in the Senate by the conspirators. Would it not be ridiculous if he did not know how to vest himself with the powerful spirit of such a hero; if instead of having Caesar suffer an unexpected attack with a firm brow and brave spirit, he represented the man with acts of fear, retreat, and cowardice?

Would it not be ridiculous if in a mythological drama, Mercury appearing on stage from one side, Neptune from the other, the actor performed the part of the young god with the actions, habits, and manners of an old man, and the part of the old god, on the other hand, with agility, vivacity, and spirit?

Would it not be ridiculous if in a sacred drama representing the famous sacrifice of Abraham the actor showed us the knife trembling in the hands of that most obedient patriarch, and resistance and tears in the religious resignation of Isaac? But all this could happen if that actor had not at least tasted the first pages of history.

It remains to say something about those two languages *Latin* and *Italian*. Of the first I will not speak, since every professor sees how necessary it is for vocal music in church, in order at least to know how to distinguish the longs and the shorts. Furthermore, I have limited the scope of these articles of mine strictly to vocal music in the theater.

So let us speak of Italian. All nations are constrained to confess, whether they want to or not, that this language of all others is the most harmonious, the sweetest, and the easiest to adapt to good music. Read the *Lettre sur la musique française* of Monsieur *Rousseau*,[2] and you will see if I speak the truth; yet he is a French writer. By the Italian language he means the language when it is most purified and unblemished—as the saying goes, the *Florentine* tongue on the lips of a *Sienese,* with the grace of a *Pistoian.*

All the other languages, Italian though they may be, have defects for use in the theater. They lack that melody and sweetness that, thanks to a good accent, the purified language possesses. On the contrary, the further their open vowels are from having a complete, precise, and finished sound, the more those vowels are incompatible with good music. For they are a species of diphthong, or compound of two different sounds. And this is precisely the reason why the French language is so little suited to music.

Now not all those who choose the profession of singing can be Tuscan; that choice is not equally free to all the states and provinces that make up fair Italy. But Bolognese, Modenese, Milanese, Venetians, and distinguished Neapolitans learn the true language from their teachers, and learn it almost better sometimes than those very Florentines. For it is difficult for them to rid themselves of a bad habit of the throat that is native to them, commonly called *gorgia.*[3]

A far easier and more effective approach for a young man who is already devoted to this profession is to live for some years in Tuscany. Many have done this—even I myself. For young people converse easily and take in the language unthinkingly, as a baby does milk—without school, without study, and without art. In these circumstances nature and age are the perfect teachers. But since for various reasons this approach is not open to everyone, I suggest another one, namely reading books and conversing with men who speak with a pure pronunciation and good diction.

2. See pp. 161–74.
3. *La gorgia toscana* is the Tuscan habit of adding an 'h' sound to 'c' before 'a,' 'o,' and 'u.'

Here, succinctly set down, are the three most effective methods for correcting a bad pronunciation and a bad accent. How necessary for a singer are a perfect pronunciation, a perfect accent, and a perfect delivery of the words has been demonstrated by the example of all those excellent professors I mentioned in the second chapter.[4]

Even though these men were mostly Neapolitans, Bolognese, Lombards, and who knows what else, no matter in what theater of any nation or country they performed they were taken by all to be true Tuscans.

The divine *Demosthenes* was also aware of this excellence in an actor; he knew how prejudicial defective pronunciation was to anyone who must orate and declaim in public. Therefore this great man, although he was acclaimed as the first orator of Greece and knew in fact that he was such, feared that the shortcomings in his speech could easily cause him to lose both his name and his reputation, and the universal esteem of his and other nations. So with infinite discomfort he declaimed aloud in isolated places, holding little pebbles in his mouth in order to loosen the native constrictions of his tongue. With this useful example he showed us how important it is to remove the defects of our tongue, no matter what the cost.

I hope that the examples I have set down have persuaded my young lovers of vocal music to spare no labor or toil in becoming skilled in this arena. I value it highly, since it seems to me to be the cause of all that is perfect, graceful, and attractive in every melody.

ARTICLE XIV: ABOUT RECITATIVE AND DELIVERY

Once the student has completed the studies necessary for good declamation as I have described them—the study of the *Latin and Italian* languages, and of history—and has acquitted himself in them with profit, he can without hesitation take up the study of the dramatic art.

This notable art, through what fate I know not, in our times counts few good students in its numbers, having declined from that high degree of splendor and excellence it inhabited forty years ago.

Many of our actors believe that they have sufficiently discharged their duty in the theater when they sing the solo arias perfectly, even though their articulation of the recitative has nothing genuine in it, and is not accompanied by a suitable delivery.

Others are certainly aware of the necessity for good declamation and for good delivery, but justify themselves with false excuses. They indict modern writers, saying that it is impossible to declaim the recitatives that are written these days because they interrupt and upset the true sense of the words by constant motions and sudden modulations in the bass, and so on.

So they sigh, affecting to envy the fortunate lot of those actors who could perform the operas written by an Alessandro *Scarlatti, Bononcino, Gasparini,*

4. Article 2 contains an extensive discussion of Italian singers of the previous hundred years.

Francesco *Mancini,* Domenico *Sarro,* Federico *Hendel,* Francesco *Durante,* and other famous men of this sort.[5]

But to convince our actors of their error and affectation, and to make them recognize that most of the time the blame for bad declamation is theirs, one need only remind them of operas written by *Porpora,* Leonardo *Vinci,* Leonardo *Leo,* Francesco *Feo,* or *Pergolese.*[6] Let them take a look, and then say if they find in these recitatives the kind of interruption and confusion they claim is caused by the music.

Let them take into consideration the operas of a Giovanni *Hasse,* Baldassare *Galuppi (Buranello),* Niccolò *Jommelli,* Gaetano *Latilla,* Pasquale *Cafaro,* Davide *Perez,* Gennaro *Manna,* Tommaso *Trajetta,* Niccola *Piccinni,* Antonio *Sacchini, Reichart,* J. C. *Bach,* Antonio *Mazzoni* Bolognese, Pietro *Guglielmi,* Amadeo *Naumann Misliweózek,* Pasquale *Anfossi,* Giovanni *Paisiello,* Carlo *Monza, Tozzi, Borroni, Bertoni,* Giambattista *Borghi,* Tommaso *Giordano,* and Floriano *Gassmann,* most recently deceased.[7] In addition to his commendable service in this Imperial Court, Gassmann has left us notable operas and even more notable students; among them Antonio *Salieri,* the chamber virtuoso of the Imperial Court, clearly stands out.

Let them consider those operas of Giuseppe *Bonno,*[8] successor to *Gassmann* in the imperial service and a name very well known to the republic of music.

Let them consider the other operas of the Cavaliere Christophe *Gluck,* also in the service of the Imperial Court. The vast and penetrating creative genius

5. This list and the two that follow it enumerate well-known composers of vocal music throughout the eighteenth century. This first group flourished around the turn of the century, and includes names that would have been canonical to Mancini's readers. Four of them—Durante, Mancini, Sarro, and Scarlatti—are associated with the Neapolitan school.

6. This second group, all of them Neapolitan in origin and training, were of a slightly later generation, flourishing in the second quarter of the century. Leo was Mancini's teacher in Naples when the author was fourteen.

7. With this group, Mancini moves to the generation of composers who flourished in the second half of the century, most of whom were alive and productive at the time he was writing. The list in the first edition included only Galuppi, Gluck, Jommelli, Cafaro, and Hasse, and was enormously expanded for this edition of 1777.

8. The noble Signora Marianna *Martinez* of Vienna bears witness most genuinely to the praises owed this celebrated master. This incomparable damsel, gifted with a superior talent for music, received both rudiments and refinement from the esteemed Signor *Bonno.* Her progress in these was so rapid that in a short time she became the object of the admiration of all the most famous masters of music. Her compositions have been in great demand, receiving acclaim in Naples, Bologna, and many of the most renowned cities of Italy.

I myself heard her sing in her earliest years, playing the cembalo with a surprising mastery to accompany her own vocal compositions. She sang and expressed them with such power of musical measure that Signore Abbate *Metastasio* himself experienced in them that emotion he knew so well how to stir in the human heart with his inimitable dramatic poems. Thus among the other unanimous acclamations, the celebrated Padre Martini begged the honor of numbering in our Accademia Filarmonica of Bologna this woman who, although a dilettante, could justly be called a great mistress and rare genius of music. [Au.]

This note was added in the 1777 edition. For Burney's equally glowing account of Signora Martinez, see *Dr. Burney's Musical Tours in Europe,* P. Scholes, ed. (Oxford: Oxford University Press, 1959), II, 106–7, 109, 117, 119–20, 122.

of this man has not only made him possessor of the most profound secrets and hidden insights of philosophy and other sciences, but has unfolded from the breast of that immense talent all things rare, noble, interesting, and sublime that music was concealing. I speak particularly of French music, of which he was the reformer, or, better, the dictator. What can I say of such merit? What luster can my weak voice add to the glory and fame of a man who is immortalized and venerated as the tutelary deity of music not only in his country, but in all the corners of Europe? What can one say further, having remembered that the French nation, oversolicitous of the glory of its own sons and harsh in scrutinizing that of foreigners, gave high praise to the composer of *Orfeo,* of *Ifigenia,* of *Alceste,* and of *Paride e Elena,* and erected a bust of him halfway through the eighteenth century?[9]

If the theatrical art is in decline, as it surely is, this ought not to be blamed on the *maestri di cappella,* but without a doubt on the actors alone. They are the ones who beat and batter the recitatives because they will not take the trouble to learn the rules of perfect declamation.

. . . . .

How have the *opere buffe* and dances that at one time served only as intermezzos in *opere serie* both come to stand on their own, and to become principal spectacles instead of accessories, if not by means of the dramatic art? The actors and comics with their gesticulation and the dancers with their pantomime are today effectively the only ones who still use and appreciate good acting, and are consequently also the only ones who receive the good effects of applause and esteem.

I hope by this to have succinctly but sufficiently proved that to be a good actor it is not enough just to sing well: one must also have good declamation and acting skills. It remains for me to speak my mind about how recitative ought to be declaimed, and with what sort of delivery.

It is a given that we have two kinds of recitative: the one has come to be called *simple,* and we term the other *instrumental.* We call *simple* the type that is accompanied by bass alone. This recitative was invented by Giacomo *Peri* about 1600, in order not to allow the dialogue that occurs in plays among the arias, duets, terzets, and choruses to languish completely. When spoken recitative has been written by a learned and knowledgeable master, it is extremely natural. For not only are the simple notes that constitute it placed in the natural range of each voice, but they are articulated and shaped in such a way that they perfectly imitate a natural discourse. Hence all the periods can be distinguished throughout, and question marks, exclamation marks, and full stops can

---

9. I will not go on to mention many others who would clearly deserve it, both so as not to diverge too far from my path, and because they are well enough known. For who does not know the worth of a *Wagenseil,* lost to the Imperial Court on March 1, 1777? Or of Giuseppe *Steffan,* also in the imperial service, who is, without challenge, the best harpsichord performer in Europe? [Au.] The paragraph in praise of Gluck and this footnote were added in the 1777 edition.

be apprehended. All this is expressed in the vocal line, which varies with the motion and diversity of tones. And the tones vary precisely as the sentiments of the words are diverse, and according to the various emotions that the words are intended to arouse in the souls of the audience.

The other recitative is called *instrumental* because it requires the accompaniment of the orchestra. Its vocal line is not at all different from that of the *simple*. The methods of the two are always the same, except that in the *instrumental* orchestral accompaniment is added so that the orchestra can act when the actor is constrained to a dumb show. Thus the orchestra always follows the actor, even when he is speaking, in order to give greater prominence and embellishment to what he says. Customarily the voice and orchestra are required to perform strictly in tempo in order not to intrude on the feeling and power of the expression. This type of recitative was invented for no other end than to give prominence to the sort of primary and interesting scene that closes with some kind of stirring aria of rage or tenderness, distinguishing it from the others. When such recitatives are written well and well performed they cause universal satisfaction, and are sometimes the mainstay of an entire opera.

Now the vocal line of these various recitatives, although sung, ought always to have a looseness of style that resembles a perfect and simple spoken declamation. Thus it would be a failing if instead of declaiming the recitative loosely an actor wanted to sing it with a constant legato style, without ever thinking to distinguish the periods and the various meanings of the words by restraining and reinforcing, detaching and smoothing his tone, as an educated man does when he speaks or reads. This is the appropriate time to mention that recitative stands or falls entirely on the knowledge of the placement of appoggiaturas, or the musical accent, as it is commonly called. This priceless accent, which constitutes all that is agreeable in a fine vocal line, consists, to be brief, of a note one tone higher than what is written. It is customarily performed only on the occasion when a few syllables making up a word are found on notes of the same pitch. For greater clarity here is an example:

Example 5.111

On - de mai   tu   ve - des - ti...

I ought to inform you now that we have two accents. The one is called "restrained," as in the exclamation, *O Dio!*, and the second "relaxed."[10] This latter can be languid, or hasty, or serious and sustained, depending on the various affects it expresses. The virtue of teacher and student consists in knowing how to recognize these accents and use them well.

10. *Trattenuto* and *sciolto*.

Since I already discussed in the preceding chapter what kind of study the student needs in order to understand the importance of these vocal inflections, it is not necessary for me to repeat it here. I shall say only that I advise the student to undertake this study while he is still under the direction of a good teacher, who can show him the right way to take advantage of it.

I know that at one time the opinion was current among our professors that the recitatives for the chamber should be delivered differently than those for the theater, and likewise those for the concert hall or the church. As much as I have thought about this, I have not found any convincing reason why this difference should exist. I think that no matter whether they are intended for church, theater, or chamber, recitatives ought always to be delivered in the same fashion. By this I mean with a clear and natural voice, which gives each word the full force due it, and that articulates the commas and periods so that the spectators can understand the meaning of the poetry. So I have concluded that if there exists any difference among these recitatives relative to place, it consists in the quantity of the voice alone, so that the singer, whatever his powers, ought always to adapt to the place in which he sings.

But above all, even if the recitative is uttered with the necessary vocal inflections, pauses, and periods, it will still always be languid and slack if it is not accompanied by a suitable delivery. This is what gives power, expression, and liveliness to the discourse. Gesture is the thing that miraculously expresses the nature of the character one wishes to represent. In the last analysis it is delivery that makes a true actor; so Cicero himself said that all the nobility and excellence of an actor consists in delivery: *actio, actio, actio.*[11]

But do not deceive yourself that this is a pure gift of nature. Learning it requires art and study. Granted, by nature one person more than another has a good disposition for performance, but the disposition for learning something does not in itself cause that thing to be already learned. What comes from nature flawed and crude must be polished and refined with art and study. People say—and it is very true—that one's delivery should be natural rather than studied, and never, above all, too affected, which is a defect that still prevails among many. This does not mean, however, that one should not study the true style of acting, but only that one should not make delivery affected, adapting and conforming it to the words being spoken and the character being represented. This power to adapt and conform is what we call naturalness, which is precisely what is to be learned from study. The good that nature can provide for an actor is restricted to a fine physique and perhaps to some elegance in the movements of the arm.

It is true that the study of delivery does not have sure and precise rules from which a diligent student can learn exactly what posture he ought to assume on any particular occasion. But it does have general rules that will suffice to mold

---

11. Delivery—*actio* (*hypocrisis* in the Greek)—was the all-important fifth and last division of classical rhetoric; see Cicero, *De oratore* 3.56–61.

a good actor. The particular rules that teach one what gestures to make in a given situation are all practical, and should be either spelled out by someone with mature judgment, or learned from attentive observation of the movements of fine actors in those situations. The general rules are also theoretical, and can thus be learned both from teachers and from books.

Principal among these is that of making an entrance gracefully, and of knowing how to walk the boards with a natural decorum. All this can be nowhere learned better than in a dancing school, where one finds out how to move the feet with grace, to control the arms, to turn the head, and to move the whole body with refinement. Schools of fencing and horseback riding are also of some benefit, especially in situations where the actor must perform one of these actions. In addition, all of them make the body robust, agile, and relaxed.

The power to make easy and pliant changes of countenance—or, as they say, knowing how to "work in mask"—is also a necessity for an actor. Knowing how to change expression, to appear first proud, or gentle, or tender and passionate, then angry and scornful, according to the affects and to the impression that is to be aroused or received, is the finest part of delivery that the actor can use. It all depends on these inflections happening naturally and at the right time. Hence an actor is guilty of a great failing when, while listening to his companion on stage tell a story of disgrace or good fortune, he remains indifferent and in his original mood during the whole time of the narrative, and only shows signs of wonder or pleasure or pain at the end of it—and all at once. These signs, to be expressed naturally, should be manifested little by little, starting at the moment when one can understand from the story something of the whole deed, and growing as the grief or agitation to be elicited by the story naturally ought to grow. Hence an actor must always be attentive and collected not only when he himself is speaking but also when he is being spoken to. When he speaks and is distracted, it is very likely not only that he will fail in delivery, but also that he will sing out of tune. In addition to offending the ears of the listeners, this error is likely to disconcert his companion and place him in real danger of failing, for he will have to start again. If an actor does not pay attention to the one who is speaking, he cannot engage in byplay with that person nor display the internal agitations that the other's speech ought to arouse in him. Nevertheless one sees too many actors who, instead of paying attention to what they are saying and to what has just been said to them, amuse themselves by admiring the scenery, looking in the boxes, or greeting friends, all actions that reflect badly not just on the part they are playing, but also on the wisdom of a knowledgeable singer, and on one's sense of duty.

For his delivery to succeed perfectly the actor must also have accurately in his memory both the words and the music of his part. If he goes on stage without knowing them perfectly, founding all his hopes of success on the help of the prompter and the motives in the orchestra, he will not be able to accompany everything he says with a suitable natural delivery. For since in that situation he has to think about the words and the music, he cannot at the same time pay attention to and reflect on his delivery; being completely occupied in what he should say and at what point, he cannot prepare himself for what comes next.

Finally, so that the delivery be well adapted to the words and to the character, the actor ought thoroughly to understand what he is saying and the particular character he is representing, or else he may make embarrassing mistakes.

I certainly do not consider it useless to repeat my concerns to diligent students, so that they will not neglect this very necessary study of delivery.

This science is more difficult than can be imagined, but still we have sure ways and means for learning the true rules, and for acting with power. The general rules are spelled out by teachers; the particular rules are learned practically, from observation of the most convincing actors and from the instruction of expert practitioners, who should be consulted about the precise cases in which a particular action or gesture takes place.

There are many of these experts; in fact all refined cities abound in them, especially in Italy, where noblemen, men of letters, and statesmen recite plays for their own private pleasure. Insofar as they are fine actors themselves, they will willingly instruct whoever asks them. For example, the Marchese *Teodoli* in Rome, the Marchese *di Liveri*, the lawyer Giuseppe *Santoro* in Naples,[12] and many, many others had excellent students, including in our own times our celebrated *Metastasio* in Vienna. His students Signora Teresa *de Reutter*[13] and Angelo Maria *Monticelli*,[14] who learned so well following his instructions, demonstrate clearly how capable he was in this art.

If an actor fails in dramatic action, he has only himself to blame; he cannot excuse himself by saying that he had no means by which to learn the art of the theater.

12. These particular amateur actors have not been identified.
13. According to Mancini, Reutter was a singer in the Imperial Court at Vienna.
14. Italian castrato soprano (c.1712–1758) who had a considerable career in Italy, London, and Dresden. His acting skills were praised by Charles Burney and others.

132 Daniel Gottlob Türk

Daniel Gottlob Türk was a German pedagogue and composer of great intellect, energy, and education. Born in Saxony in 1750, he studied music from childhood; the teacher of his formative years was Johann Adam Hiller in Leipzig, where he studied from 1772 to 1774. Under Hiller's guidance, Türk gained experience in music of all types, including opera and choral music; he also studied keyboard using C. P. E. Bach's *Versuch*. In 1774, he moved to Halle to take a teaching position, and he became a mainstay of that city's musical life, living there until his death in 1813. Although early efforts at composition included symphonies and cantatas, he made keyboard music his principal pre-occupation, publishing fifteen volumes of keyboard sonatas during his years in Halle. He was a serious scholar, known for his extensive library.

Türk wrote his *Klavierschule (School of Clavier Playing)* after he retired from general teaching to a position as organist and music director of a church in Halle. It is the last of the great eighteenth-century keyboard manuals and has the broadest range of them all. Reaching a larger and less well-educated audience than did earlier manuals, it provided its users with a context for taste and style that they could no longer be assumed to possess of themselves.

FROM *School of Clavier Playing*
(1789)

CHAPTER SIX: CONCERNING EXECUTION

PART ONE: CONCERNING EXECUTION IN GENERAL AND ITS GENERAL REQUIREMENTS

1. I have already taken the opportunity to touch upon one thing or another required for good execution, but in order that the student can comfortably survey the entire subject, I have arranged the various components of good execution in sequence in the present chapter, and now and then have added some observations which are perhaps not generally known.

2. Whoever performs a composition so that its intrinsic affect (character, etc.), even in every single passage, is most faithfully expressed (made perceptible) and that the tones become, so to speak, a language of feelings, of this person it is said that he is a good executant. Good execution, therefore, is the most important, but at the same time, the most difficult task of making music.

3. One knows from experience that a composition leaves a very different impression depending on whether it is more or less effectively executed. Mediocre works can be uncommonly improved by a good and expressive execution, and on the contrary, the most moving Adagio, poorly executed, loses almost all of its effect, or even provokes unpleasant feelings. In the latter instance it can scarcely be believed that one is hearing the same composition which during a good performance evoked so much delight.

> Composers are to be pitied because they must so often surrender their works to players who have no feeling and sense, for in such cases their aims are either not at all or only half achieved. Other artists are more certain of well-deserved applause for they perform their own works themselves most of the time.

TEXT: Translation by Raymond H. Haggh in *School of Clavier Playing* (Lincoln: University of Nebraska Press, 1982), pp. 321–22, 337–42, 347–53, 358–60, 363–64, 397–400, with minor alterations.

4. It becomes sufficiently clear from these few words that execution must be of the utmost importance for the musician. For even with all his facility in reading notes and in playing,[1] he will never attain his main purpose, which is to move the heart of his listener, without good execution. Whoever possesses both extraordinarily facility and good execution has attributes which are not only praiseworthy but also rare.

5. In my opinion, the following characteristics are particularly typical of good execution: (1) in general, an already achieved facility in playing and note reading, security in rhythm, and knowledge of thoroughbass as well as of the composition to be performed; but in particular (2) clarity of execution, (3) expression of the predominant character, (4) appropriate use of ornaments and other devices of the same sort, and (5) genuine feeling for all the emotions and passions which are expressed in music.

* * * * *

PART THREE: CONCERNING THE EXPRESSION OF THE
PREVAILING CHARACTER

26. If everything that has been taught in the last two parts is followed in the most meticulous way, it is still not possible to have good execution because the most essential part is missing, namely the expression of the prevailing character, without which no listener can be moved to any great degree. This effect, which is the highest goal of music, can only be induced when the artist has the capacity to become infused with the predominant affect and to communicate his feelings to others through the eloquence of music. Expression is therefore that part of a good execution in which the true master, full of genuine feeling for his art, distinguishes himself noticeably from the average musician. Mechanical skill can ultimately be learned by much practice; only expression presupposes—other than mechanical facility—a broad range of knowledge, and above all things, a sensitive soul. It certainly would be a futile endeavor, therefore, if one were to attempt to enumerate in order everything that is required for expression and to specify all of this through rules, because expression depends so much on that which no rule can teach, namely on the individual feelings themselves. Nevertheless, there are some means which can more or less contribute to the strengthening of expression and which to some extent can be put down in the form of written instruction, although it is even in this regard incomparably better to listen to singers and players of great sensitivity. For as has been said, certain subtleties of expression cannot really be described; they must be *heard*.

27. The words "Will he come soon? " can merely through the tone of the speaker receive a quite different meaning. Through them a yearning desire, a vehement impatience, a tender plea, a defiant command, irony, etc., can be

---

1. It is possible to read notes with skill, that is, to be able to perceive several at one glance, and in spite of this not to be able to achieve particular dexterity in playing. [Au.]

expressed. The single word "God!" can denote an exclamation of joy, of pain, of despair, the greatest anxiety, pity, astonishment, etc., in various degrees. In the same way tones by changes in the execution can produce a very different effect. It is therefore extremely necessary to study the expression of feelings and passions in the most careful way, make them one's own, and learn to apply them correctly.

28. Outside of those requirements mentioned in the two previous paragraphs that are indispensable for expression, I also include (1) the suitable degree of loudness and softness of tone, (2) the detaching, sustaining, and slurring of tones, and (3) the correct tempo.

29. Even with the most painstaking marking, it is not possible to specify every degree of loudness and softness of tone. As many words as we have for this purpose, they are by far not sufficient for the indication of all possible gradations. The player must himself feel and learn to judge what degree of loudness and softness of tone is required by the character of the music to be expressed in any given case. The adding of *forte* and *piano* specifies the expression only approximately and in general; to what an excess would these words have to be added if every note which required a special shading would be so indicated.

30. Concerning the intensity of tone required in any given case, I content myself in remarking that generally, compositions of a spirited, happy, lively, sublime, magnificent, proud, daring, courageous, serious, fiery, wild, and furious character[2] all require a certain degree of loudness. This degree must even be increased or decreased according to whether the feeling or passion is represented in a more vehement or more moderate manner. What a number of degrees of loudness are thus required for all this! And now let us consider that in each composition various gradations are again necessary which must all be in a proper relation to the whole. A *forte* in an Allegro furioso must therefore be a great deal louder than in an Allegro in which only a moderate degree of joy prevails, etc.

Compositions of a gentle, innocent, naive, pleading, tender, moving, sad, melancholy, and the like character all require a softer execution. The degree of loudness, however, must exactly correspond to each sentiment being expressed and as a result is different in most of the cases just mentioned. As with compositions which are to be played forcefully, other than the strength already due to them,[3] a still even greater degree for a *fortissimo* must be possible, and in the same manner, a *piano* and *pianissimo* should be possible in compositions that are to be played softly.

2. I indicate here and further below a few character types one at a time which border closely on each other and which must almost be treated in the same way, in order that the student generally knows whether by this or that title of a composition, loudness or softness must be applied. I gladly admit that the above-mentioned gradations are not always possible to a perceptible degree of loudness on the clavichord. [Au.]

3. That is, what is marked in the music. [Tr.]

Note 1. The composer often specifies the main degree of loudness or softness by the words *sempre forte* or *sempre piano* which are placed at the beginning of the composition. The *sempre*, however, should not be taken too literally, for the composer is only saying that the execution should be generally loud or soft. Certain musical thoughts, in spite of this, must be suitably modified according to the affect (played stronger or weaker).

Note 2. In the application of *forte* and *fortissimo*[4] I must warn against a very common mistake. Many players strike the keys with such force or press them down so violently in order to maintain the sounding of the tone that (particularly in one-part passages) the pitch becomes too high and consequently impure. It is probably for this reason, among others, that some persons, of whom I myself know a few, do not value the clavichord as much as they should, or even might have an antipathy toward it, because they believe that playing expressively and impurely are inseparable. However, the overemphasis of the tone is for the most part the player's fault or comes from a too weak stringing of the instrument.[5] Even played with the greatest possible degree of strength, the tone must not go higher in pitch; it is simply a matter of the way in which the key is struck or pressed down. That it is possible, however, to play with expression and not to commit this mistake is proved by all really good clavichord players.

31. To specify whether a specific passage must be played somewhat louder or softer than the preceding and following is utterly impossible; nevertheless, one can generally assume that the livelier parts of a composition can be played louder and the tenderly singing, etc., parts can be played softer, even if in the first case no *forte,* and in the second, no *piano* has been indicated. When a musical thought is repeated, then it is customary to play it softly the second time, provided it has been played loudly the first. On the other hand, a repeated passage may also be played louder, especially when the composer has made it livelier through elaborations. In general, one must even play single tones of importance with more emphasis than the others.

32. Good taste has made it a rule that dissonances or dissonant chords must generally be struck with more force than consonant ones, for the reason that the passions should be especially aroused by dissonances.[6] If one considers this rule particularly with relation to the degree of the dissonance, it then follows that the sharper the dissonance or the more dissonances contained in a chord, the louder must the harmony be played. Yet this rule cannot and should not always be strictly followed, because otherwise too much variety is likely to result.

4. Also for tones which are slurred, or when *tenuto* is written over a note. [Au.]
5. A clavichord which is properly strung and yet does not tolerate a full and emphatic stroke is a poor instrument and therefore does not come into consideration. [Au.]
6. Since the passions are not of a single kind and since certain passions can also be aroused without dissonances, etc., then when viewed from this position, this principle, which has become a rule, is probably not so generally valid. At least it would not follow that dissonances be struck in all cases with more force than consonant chords. There are other reasons, however, which appear to be more convincing to me and which illuminate the necessity of the rule given above. A continuing pleasant sensation will gradually become weaker, or if it continues longer, will cease to be pleasant if it is not interrupted at times. If this interruption is of an unpleasant nature, one finds the ensuing pleasure so much the more stimulating. Since through dissonances a kind of unpleasant sensation, or at least a hoping and expectation, a desire for repose and the like, is

Here are some harmonies which are strongly dissonant and must therefore be played with emphasis.

Example 1a

The following chords are less dissonant. Therefore they require a more moderate degree of loudness.

Example 1b

and so on.

That chords which are more or less consonant should be played with varying degrees of loudness is probably too great a subtlety and only a matter for the very skilled player.

33. The harmonies by means of which a modulation into a somewhat distant key is suddenly made or through which the modulation takes an unexpected turn are also played relatively loudly and emphatically in order that they surprise even more in a manner that accords with their purpose. For example:

Example 2

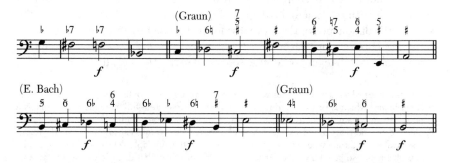

awakened, it follows that dissonant chords among others must for this reason be played with force, so that the consonant chords will then effect an even more pleasant sensation and an even more reassuring resolution, etc. Moreover, dissonances make the particular contribution that the spirit is not so quickly fatigued as it would be from a sequence of nothing but consonances, and that as a result, a composition, if I may say so, becomes appetizing. Therefore dissonances, as it were, are for music just what spices are for food. [Au.]

34. The so-called deceptive cadences (*cadenze d'inganno*) also require a greater or lesser degree of loudness according to whether they are more or less unexpected, and whether they lead to a more distant or more closely related key. For example:

Example 3

After the second d in the bass, g should actually follow; since this does not occur and the expected does not materialize, then the unexpected harmony must be played with force in order that it surprise more. When similar deceptions (deceptive cadences) occur only in the melody, the unexpected tone is played more loudly. For example:

Example 4

• • • • •

43. The particular ways in which a heavy or light execution can be brought about have been described in §36 to §42. For a *heavy* execution every tone must be played firmly (with emphasis) and held out until the very end of the prescribed duration of the note. *Light* execution is that in which every tone is played with less firmness (emphasis), and the finger lifted from the key somewhat sooner than the actually prescribed duration. In order to avoid a misunderstanding I must also remark that the terms heavy and light in general refer more to the sustaining or detaching of a tone than to the softness or loudness

of the same. For in certain cases, for example in an Allegro vivo, scherzando, Vivace con allegrezza, etc., the execution must be rather light (short) but at the same time more or less loud, whereas pieces of a melancholy character, for example an Adagio mesto, con afflizione, etc., although played slurred and consequently with a certain heaviness, must nevertheless not be executed too loudly. In most cases, however, heavy and loud are indeed to be combined.

Whether the execution is to be heavy or light may be determined (1) from the character and the purpose of a composition (§45); (2) from the designated tempo; (3) from the meter; (4) from the note values used; and (5) from the manner in which the notes progress, etc. In addition, national taste, the style of the composer, and the instrument for which the composition is written must be taken into consideration.

44. Compositions of an exalted, serious, solemn, pathetic, and similar character must be given a heavy execution with fullness and force, strongly accented and the like. To these types of compositions belong those which are headed *grave, pomposo, patetico, maestoso, sostenuto,* and the like. A somewhat lighter and markedly softer execution is required by compositions of a pleasant, gentle, agreeable character, consequently those which are customarily marked *compiacevole, con dolcezza, glissicato, lusingando, pastorale, piacevole,* and the like. Compositions in which lively, humorous, and joyous feelings are predominant, for example, *Allegro scherzando, burlesco, giocoso, con allegrezza, risvegliato,* etc., must be played quite lightly whereas melancholy and similar affects particularly call for the slurring of tones and portato. Compositions of the latter type are designated by the words *con afflizione, con amarezza, doloroso, lagrimoso, languido,* and *mesto* among others.

> It is understood that in all of the aforementioned cases various degrees of heavy or light execution must be applied.

45. Compositions which have a more serious purpose, such as fugues, well-composed sonatas, religious odes and songs, etc.,[7] call for a heavier execution than, for example, certain playful divertimentos, humorous songs, lively dances, and the like.

46. Whether a heavy or light execution is to be chosen may also be determined from the tempo. A Presto must be played more lightly than an Allegro; this in turn must be played more lightly than an Andante, etc. In general, the heaviest execution is called for by compositions in slow tempos.

47. That meter has very marked influence on heavy or light execution, or certainly should have, has already been mentioned in passing.[8] The following

---

7. If I were not writing primarily for the clavichord player, then I would include everything written for the church in this category. [Au.]

8. Türk refers here to a brief discussion of strong and weak beats in Chap. 1, §55, n. 3. The simple duration of a note is called its "external value," its emphasis in the measure its "internal value." Strong beats—usually downbeats—are "internally long," non-thetic beats "internally short." "Long" and "short," however, seem to imply greater emphasis rather than an actual change in duration.

should be noted in this connection. The larger the values of the main beats of a measure, the heavier must be the execution. Therefore, a composition in $\frac{3}{2}$ (Ex. 5a), for example, is played more heavily than it would be if it were in $\frac{3}{4}$ (Ex. 5b)[9] or even in $\frac{3}{8}$ (Ex. 5c). Thus Graun wanted to specify a heavier execution by the meter in Example 5d[10] in combination with a faster tempo.

Example 5

For this reason all tones in Examples 5a and 5d must be played with emphasis and held down for their full value. In 5b and 5e the execution must already be lighter and in 5c and 5f it must be very light. Even if *Adagio* were written over Examples 5c and 5f, a good player would not play these tones with as much emphasis as in the *alla breve* in 5a and 5d. Moreover, it follows from what has been said that the meters $\frac{2}{8}$, $\frac{4}{8}$, $\frac{3}{16}$, $\frac{6}{16}$, and the like require the lightest execution.

> Incidentally, I should like to note that compositions in triple meters with short note values can be given a sort of comically hopping motion if the player accents the first note too strongly.

48. Various species of notes require, without regarding the kind of meter, a more or less heavy execution. For example, if in a composition there occur mostly larger note values, namely whole, half, and quarter notes, then the execution must be generally heavier than if many eighth and sixteenth notes, etc., were intermingled. Dotted notes especially—in addition to the attention which

9. For reasons of space I had to omit the bass and the middle voices. [Au.]
10. Carl Heinrich Graun, "Christus hat uns ein Vorbild gelassen [Christ has left us a model]," *Der Tod Jesu*, fourteenth movement. [Tr.]

must be given to the proper arrangement of note values as well as to heavy or light execution—require a very varied treatment according to the context in which they occur. It is customary, for the most part,[11] to dwell on dotted notes longer (and therefore to play the following shorter notes even more quickly) than the notation indicates. For example:

Examples 6a–d

The realization of dotted notes as shown in Example 6b is generally chosen when the character of the composition is serious, solemn, exalted, etc.; so it is not only for an actual Grave but also for overtures or compositions which are marked *sostenuto*, and the like. The dotted notes are executed in this case with emphasis, consequently they are prolonged. For the expression of livelier or more joyous feelings, the playing must be somewhat lighter, approximately as in 6c. The execution shown in Example 6d is particularly chosen for compositions which are to be played in a vehement or defiant manner or those which are marked *staccato*.[12] The keys are to be struck firmly, but the fingers should be raised sooner than they would be for places which are to be played with a certain solemn dignity. For agreeable and lyric thoughts and the like, dotted notes are prolonged a little as shown below in 6e—even though not too perceptibly; in any case they will be played more gently (less accented). Especially in such cases the short notes after the dot are to be played softly and should be slurred. If a second voice occurs with the voice containing the dotted notes, as in 6f, then the prescribed values are to be retained.

11. All possible cases cannot be specified; nevertheless, one can accept as a rule for this that the value of the dot not be prolonged when the note following it has the full value of a metric unit, or in slower tempo, the value of a beat division. However, even this rule is probably not without its exceptions and for the beginner cannot be of too much value. How necessary it would be, therefore, for dotted notes to be notated more exactly. Since at present the meaning of two dots placed after a note is known by almost everyone, then their usage or another more painstaking notation would cause all doubts to be removed in most cases. [Au.]

12. But this kind of execution is extremely poor and quite contrary to the required expression for—as an example—the closing chorus from Graun's *Tod Jesu:* "Hier liegen wir gerührte Sünder" [Here we lie, awe-struck sinners]; nevertheless, it is not seldom that this splendid chorus is heard performed in such a defiant way. [Au.]

Examples 6e–f

Now and then when several voices are involved, the dotted notes are pro-longed in only one voice and the short notes in both voices are played at the same time in order that the whole be more uniform.

Example 7

The short rests which take the place of dots are also often prolonged in compositions of a lively character and the like, as here in Example 8b.

Example 8

Figures in which the first note is short and the second is dotted are slurred without exception and played for the most part in a caressing manner. The first (short) note, of course, is to be accented but the emphasis should be only a very gentle one.

Example 9

The first note should not be rushed, especially in a slow tempo, because the melody can easily degenerate into flippancy, or lose its essential roundness if the first tone is played too short, and, moreover, if the dot is transformed into an incorrect rest, as in Example 9b.

Formerly, for similar figures the first note was given a very short duration. Even Agricola still writes: "When the short note comes first and a dot is placed after the second note, then the first note is played as quickly as possible and the remainder is given to the note which is dotted."[13] Bach, on the other hand, says on page 113: "The first note should not be done away with too quickly if the tempo is moderate or slow."[14]

49. Even with regard to harmony and the progression of some intervals, a heavy or light execution is required. A composition with many dissonances must therefore be executed more heavily than another in which for the most part light, consonant harmonies are employed. Compositions with much passage work in general require a lighter execution than those in which many singable sections are found. In particular, skipping passages are played more lightly than those which move by step, etc.

50. In consideration of national taste, the style of the composer, and the instrument for which a composition has been written, the following should be noted in illustration of §43.

A composition which has been written in the Italian national taste requires in general[15] a medium (between heavy and light) execution. The performance of a French composition must be lighter. On the contrary, the works of German composers for the most part demand a heavier and more robust execution.

In the same way the style of a composer also presumes an individual mode of treatment. A composition of Handel, Sebastian Bach, etc., must be given a more emphatic execution than, for example, a modern concerto of Mozart or Kozeluch, among others.

Sonatas for the harpsichord do not require the heavy execution which is taken for granted for those composed for the clavichord by C. P. E. Bach.

Heavy or light execution, however, must not only correspond to the whole but also to every single part of a composition. In a composition of animated character which is to be executed lightly there can appear passages which notwithstanding the general character of the composition are more dignified and require a heavier execution. If I might express myself in the terminology of painting, then I would say that certain parts must be given light and others shadow. Therefore in fugues, for example, or compositions in strict style, the theme (subject) in particular, as well as the imitative parts must be executed with emphasis, in order that they be more conspicuous. A majestic *all'unisono* also requires a heavy and forceful execution, unless the composer has specified the opposite for certain reasons.

13. Johann Friedrich Agricola's *Anleitung zu Singkunst* (*Introduction to the Art of Singing*, Berlin, 1757) is a translation with running commentary of Pier Francesco Tosi's *Opinioni de' cantori antichi e moderni* ((*Opinions of Ancient and Modern Singers*, Bologna, 1723). See p. 744, n. 8.
14. Carl Philipp Emanuel Bach, *Versuch über die wahre Art das Clavier zu spielen* (Berlin, 1753). Türk owned the second, 1759 edition of Bach's *Versuch*. The quotation he cites is on p. 128, §24, of the 1753 edition. See *Essay on the True Art of Playing Keyboard Instruments, by Carl Philipp Emanuel Bach,* trans. and ed. William J. Mitchell (New York: W. W. Norton 1949), 158.
15. Of course, there are many exceptions to this. [Au.]

51. Besides what has been mentioned in this part, correct tempo contributes to expression to a very large degree. In order to be convinced of this, one ought to play a well-known composition in its proper tempo and then too slowly or too fast immediately afterward. If the tempo is taken too slowly then even the most excellent composition will become feeble or dull; if the tempo is taken too fast, the clarity and at the same time the intended effect are either completely lost or at least partly forfeited. I have especially noted that compositions which are marked *Vivace* are usually played too fast. Presumably this term, which particularly specifies the kind of execution, is incorrectly applied only to the tempo. This must then be the reason that, for example, Graun's aria "So stehet ein Berg Gottes,"[16] etc., is often played much too fast. This is also frequently the case with compositions marked *Grave, maestoso, Marcia,* etc.

· · · · ·

PART FIVE: CONCERNING THE NEED FOR PERSONAL AND GENUINE FEELING FOR ALL THE EMOTIONS AND PASSIONS WHICH CAN BE EXPRESSED IN MUSIC

63. Even when the composer has indicated the proper manner of expression as well as he can—in general and for specific parts—and the player has appropriately made use of all the means discussed in the preceding sections, there still remain special cases for which the expression can be heightened by *extraordinary* means. Among these I include particularly the following: (1) playing without keeping steady time; (2) quickening and hesitating; (3) the so-called *tempo rubato.* These three resources *when used sparingly and at the right time* can be of great effect.

64. In addition to free fantasies, cadenzas, fermatas, and the like, those passages marked *Recitativo* must be played more according to feeling than to meter. Some passages of this sort are found now and then in sonatas, concertos, and the like, for example in the Andante of the first sonata by C. P. E. Bach dedicated to the King of Prussia. Such passages would have a poor effect if they were played strictly according to the specified values of the notes (measured). The more important notes must therefore be played slower and louder, and the less important notes more quickly and softer, approximately the way a sensitive singer would sing these notes or a good orator would declaim the words thereto.

65. It is difficult to specify all of the places where quickening and hesitating can take place; nevertheless, I will seek to make at least some of them known. I am assuming, however, that the means which I am about to describe will only be used when one is playing alone or with a very attentive accompanist.

---

16. "So stands a mountain of God," *Der Tod Jesu,* thirteenth movement.

That this intentional quickening or hesitating should not be mistaken for the faulty hurrying, etc., mentioned in the Introduction, is obvious.

66. In compositions whose character is vehemence, anger, rage, fury, and the like, the most forceful passages can be played with a somewhat hastened (*accelerando*) motion. Also, certain thoughts which are repeated in a more intensified manner (generally higher) require that the speed be increased to some extent. Sometimes, when gentle feelings are interrupted by a lively passage, the latter can be played somewhat more rapidly.[17] A hastening of the tempo may also take place in a passage where a vehement affect is unexpectedly to be aroused.

67. For extraordinarily tender, longing, or melancholy passages, in which the emotion, as it were, is concentrated in one point, the effect can be very much intensified by an increasing hesitation (*Anhalten, tardando*). The tempo is also taken gradually slower for tones before certain fermatas as if their powers were gradually being exhausted. The passages toward the end of a composition (or part of a composition) which are marked *diminuendo, diluendo, smorzando,* and the like can also be played in a somewhat more lingering manner.

68. A tenderly moving passage between two lively and fiery thoughts (as in the first part of my easy clavichord sonatas, pages 10, 11, 25ff.) can be executed in a somewhat hesitating manner; but in this case, the tempo is not taken gradually slower, but *immediately* a little slower (however, only a *little*). Compositions in which two characters of opposite types are represented especially provide a suitable opportunity for a gradual slowing of the tempo. Thus Bach has written a most excellent sonata "which as it were constitutes a conversation between *Melancholicus* and *Sanguineus.*"[18] In a similar manner, E. W. Wolf, in his six little sonatas from the year 1779, page 10ff., describes an estranged married couple of the common folk. In general, the gradual slowing of tempo can take place most appropriately in slow tempos.

·   ·   ·   ·   ·

72. The so-called *tempo rubato* or *robato* (actually *stolen* time) I have specified in §63 as the third resource whose application should be left to the sensitivity and insight of the player. This term appears with more than one meaning. Commonly it is understood as a kind of shortening or lengthening of notes, or the displacement (dislocation) of these. There is something taken away (stolen) from the duration of a note and for this, another note is given that much more, as in the following Examples 10b and c.

17. There are some passages of this type in the first sonata of the second collection of my longer sonatas. [Au.]

18. Sulzer's words in the article *Sonate*. [Au.] The work is a trio sonata by C. P. E. Bach for two violins and bass (W. 161, no. 1) published in 1751. Bach prefaces the sonata, the first of two, with a detailed description of the conversation between the two characters, *Melancholicus* and *Sanguineus*.

Example 10a–c

Example 10a shows the basic notes; in 10b *tempo rubato* is put to use by means of the *anticipation* (*anticipatio*) and in 10c by means of the *retardation* (*retardatio*). From this it can be seen that through this kind of execution, the tempo, or even more, the meter as a whole is not displaced. Consequently, the customary but somewhat ambiguous German term *verrücktes Zeitmaß* ["displaced tempo"] is not very fitting, for the bass voice goes its way according to the meter (without displacement), and only the notes of the melody are moved out of place, as it were. For this reason the expression *Versetzen* (or *Verziehen*) ["changing the place of" or "dragging out"] the *notes* or the *beat divisions* would be more correct. Even when more notes are added to the melody, as in Examples 10e and 10f, both voices must nevertheless correctly coincide each time at the beginning of the measure. In this case then there results no actual displacement of the tempo.

Example 10d–f

This dragging out of notes, as it is otherwise called, must be applied with great care, because errors in the harmony could result. The anticipating in Example 10f would only be bearable in rather slow tempo.

•   •   •   •   •   •

SUPPLEMENT, PART FIVE: CONCERNING STYLE, MANNER, COUNTERPOINT, AND INVERSION

54. By *style* (manner of writing) is meant a certain individual character of composition, or the way in which each person composes. Diversity of style, therefore, also requires diversity of execution (see pt. 6, §50). Style is particularly varied in consideration of the locality and the nation. With regard to the locality, one namely differentiates between church, theater, and chamber style, and with regard to nations, chiefly between the Italian, French, and German styles (taste).

55. The *church style* requires a serious character united with dignity, solem-

nity, magnificence, sublime greatness, powerful harmonies, and the strict following of the rules, etc. The strict style[19] is particularly put to use.

> Compositions written in the church style are oratorios, passions, sacred cantatas, masses, hymns, and such special church compositions as psalms, motets, and the like.

The *theater style* is to a certain degree less reliant upon strict observance of the rules,[20] and in contrast, the expression must be fiery, brilliant, and characteristic to a high degree. This kind of expression often borders on the picturesque. In short, the theater style seeks to represent the feelings and passions in their totality and, in order to achieve this purpose, makes use of means that are not allowed in the church style.

> Serious operas, comic operettas, the pastorale, serenades, and the like are written in theater style.

The *chamber style* holds, as it were, a middle ground between church and theater style and unites things found only occasionally in the aforementioned styles of writing. Artful harmony, striking turns of expression, boldness, fire, expression of feelings, magnificence, beautiful sound, in short everything that does not run contrary to the rules of composition and strict setting is here in its proper place. Composers in this style of writing take special note of the facility of the player or singer and seek to use every instrument as much as possible.

> Pieces in chamber style are some cantatas, vocal pieces, and songs; besides these, there are symphonies, sonatas, duos, trios, quartets, and the like, concertos, solos, divertimenti, partitas, certain dances, etc.

56. The *Italian style* is pleasing, singing, full (often overladen), brilliant, diverse, and expressive. At least it was so characterized formerly. At present, there is to be sure also much that is aimless, often heard, insignificant, shallow, and the like in the works of various Italian composers; nevertheless, for the most part it must be conceded to their merit that their melodies have a certain (captivating) suppleness.

The *French style* is supposed to be, according to Rousseau's judgment, stale, dull or hard, poorly cadenced, and monotonous,[21] a judgment which is certainly too harsh and testifies to the exclusive preference which the author had for Italian music.[22] For outside of the fact that French composers do at times write in a somewhat dry and empty manner, or neglect the harmonic aspect a

19. Concerning this there is more to say in §57. [Au.]
20. I would like to say that the theater style needs to be less according to academic precepts; nevertheless, mistakes against the rules of harmony and the like are not excused. [Au.]
21. See the *Dictionnaire de musique* under the article *Style*. [Au.]
22. Even Germans give a more favorable judgment of French music. Walther, for example, writing before Rousseau, says that the French style is natural, flowing, tender, etc. In Scheibe's *Der critische Musicus* on page 146 (2d ed.) it is said: "The manner of writing of the French is concise and very natural, far removed from all exotic and bombastic excesses." Even Quantz does not degrade the French style to such a degree as Rousseau. [Au.]

little, in spite of this, at present their taste must be more justly acknowledged. Among composers for keyboard instruments they have already long achieved an imposing position and it is beyond all doubt that in this regard they deserve to be much preferred over the Italian composers.

Rousseau also did not view the *German style* of writing from an advantageous position. He says that it is hopping (*sautillant*), mincing (*coupé*), but harmonic for all that. Although this may have been formerly somewhat the case in pieces for the keyboard (with regard to "hopping" and "mincing"), it is certainly no longer true at present. I think that our style manifests itself much more by its effort, solidity, and powerful harmonies. Moreover, we have taken some things from the Italians and the French, and probably not always the most inferior. We are also able to set many really great masters in composition and on instruments, yes, even in singing, over against the foreigners. Be that as it may, we could have left many things to the Italians, for it seems to be that our excellent and powerful style has in recent times begun to degenerate into facile trifling, etc.

> Until now there has still been no individual style attributed to the English. It is remarkable, of course, that a large number of their important composers were Germans, for example, Handel, C. Bach, Fischer, Abel, and Schröter among others.
>
> In earlier writings can be found diverse stylistic divisions which are in part superfluous and in part even ridiculous. Thus, for example, Walther, among others, also mentions a fawning and a base style.

57. Besides the classification of styles which has been given, it is also customary to distinguish between the strict style and the free. A strict (contrapuntal) style is the one in which the composer follows all the rules of harmony and modulation in the strictest manner, mixing in artful imitations and many tied notes, working out the theme carefully, and the like, in short, allowing more art to be heard than euphony. In the free (*galant*) manner of composition, the composer is not so slavishly bound to the rules of harmony, modulation, and the like. He often permits bold changes, which could even be contrary to the generally accepted rules of modulation, assuming that the composer in doing this proceeds with proper insight and judgment, and with it is able to attain a certain goal. In general, the free style of writing has expression and euphony rather than art as its chief purpose.

58. When speaking of the special way in which a composer, without taking into consideration national taste, differs from others with regard to design and execution, one means his manner of composition. Therefore, one speaks of the Bach manner, the Benda manner, the Gluck manner, the Haydn manner, and so on. Since almost every composer has his own manner of composition, the one more or less different from the other, the player must adjust his execution accordingly (pt. 6, §50).

CRITICAL VIEWS
OF FRENCH AND
ITALIAN OPERA

133 Jean-Jacques Rousseau

Jean-Jacques Rousseau was born at Geneva in 1712 and died in 1778 near Paris. With his battle cry, "Retournons à la nature," Rousseau exerted a deep and lasting influence on the music of his time. He was not technically trained as a musician, but this did not prevent him from taking a passionate interest in things musical. In the "Querelle des Bouffons" Rousseau fought on the side of the partisans of the Italian *opera buffa*. His most important writing in this field is his *Lettre sur la musique française* (*Letter on French Music,* 1753); a reference to its sweeping indictment of French music is almost *de rigueur* in later writings of the period.

Rousseau even tried his hand as composer of a comic opera on a French text in which he attempted to follow the principles of the *opera buffa*. The work—*Le Devin du village* (*The Village Soothsayer,* 1752)—was extremely successful and played an important role in forming the style of French *opéra comique*. Rousseau was also the author of a valuable *Dictionnaire de musique* (1768).

FROM *Letter on French Music*
(1753)

To The Reader:

Since the quarrel which arose last year at the Opéra[1] produced nothing but abuse, bestowed by the one party with much wit and by the other with much animosity, I was unwilling to take any part in it, for that kind of contest was wholly unsuited to me and I was well aware that it was not a time to speak only reason. Now that the buffoons are dismissed, or the next thing to it, and there is no more question of cabals, I think I may venture my opinion, and shall state it with my customary frankness, without fear of offending anyone by so doing. It even seems to me that in a subject of this kind, any reserve would be an affront to my readers, for I admit that I should have a poor opinion of a people who attached a ridiculous importance to their songs, who made more of their musicians than of their philosophers, and among whom one needed to speak more circumspectly of music than of the gravest questions of morality.

Do you remember, sir, the story, told by M. de Fontenelle,[2] of the Silesian infant who was born with a golden tooth? Immediately all the doctors of Germany exhausted themselves in learned disquisitions on how it was possible to be born with a golden tooth; the last thing that anyone thought of was to verify

---

TEXT: The original edition (Paris, 1753). Translation by William Strunk, Jr., and Oliver Strunk. Except for notes 1, 12, 19, and 20, the editorial notes in this selection are by Harvey Olnick.

1. See p. 9.
2. Bernard Le Bovier de Fontenelle (1657–1757), *littérateur,* perpetual secretary of the Académie des Beaux-Arts, and author of the famous remark, "Sonate, que me veux-tu?"

the fact; and it was found that the tooth was not golden. To avoid a similar embarrassment, it would be well, before speaking of the excellence of our music, to make sure of its existence, and to examine first, not whether it is made of gold, but whether we have one.

The Germans, the Spaniards, and the English have long claimed to possess a music peculiar to their own language; they had, in fact, national operas which they admired in perfect good faith, and they were firmly persuaded that their glory would be at stake if they allowed those masterpieces, insupportable to any ears but their own, to be abolished. Pleasure has at last prevailed over vanity with them, or, at least, they have found a pleasure more easily understood in sacrificing to taste and to reason the prejudices which often make nations ridiculous by the very honor which they attach to them.

We still have in France the same feeling about our music that they had then about theirs, but who will give us the assurance that because we have been more stubborn, our obstinacy has been better grounded? Would it not then be fitting, in order to form a proper judgment of French music, that we should for once try to test it in the crucible of reason and see if it can endure the ordeal?

It is not my intention to delve deeply into this subject; that is not the business of a letter; perhaps it is not mine. I wish only to try to establish certain principles by which, until better have been found, the masters of the art, or rather the philosophers, may direct their researches; for, as a sage once said, it is the office of the poet to write poetry and that of the musician to compose music, but it is the province only of the philosopher to discuss the one and the other well.[3]

·   ·   ·   ·   ·

The Italians pretend that our melody is flat and devoid of tune, and all the neutral nations[4] unanimously confirm their judgment on this point. On our side we accuse their music of being bizarre and baroque.[5] I had rather believe that both are mistaken than be reduced to saying that in countries where the sciences and the arts have arrived at so high a degree of perfection, music has still to be born.

The least partial among us[6] content themselves with saying that Italian music

3. Omitted here is an extended section in which Rousseau seeks to prove that the Italian language is best suited for musical setting.
4. There was a time, says Milord Shaftesbury, when the practice of speaking French had made French music fashionable among us. But Italian music, by giving us a nearer view of nature, soon gave us a distaste for the other and made us see it as dull, as flat, and as doleful as it really is. [Au.]
5. It seems to me that people no longer dare make this reproach so frequently since it has been heard in our country. Thus this admirable music has only to show itself as it is in order to clear itself of all the faults of which it is accused. [Au.]
6. Many condemn the total exclusion of French music unhesitatingly pronounced by the amateurs of music; these conciliatory moderates would have no exclusive tastes, as if the love of what is good ought to compel a love of what is bad. [Au.]

and French music are both good, each in its kind, each for its own language; but besides the refusal of other nations to agree to this parity, there still remains the question, which of the two languages is by its nature adapted to the best kind of music. This is a question much agitated in France, but which will never be agitated elsewhere, a question which can be decided only by an ear perfectly impartial, and which consequently becomes every day more difficult to resolve in the only country in which it is a problem. Here are some experiments on this subject which everyone is free to verify, and which, it seems to me, can serve to give the answer, at least so far as regards melody, to which alone almost the whole dispute is reducible.

I took, in the two kinds of music, airs equally esteemed each in its own kind, and divesting them, the one of its *ports-de-voix*[7] and its perpetual *cadences* the other of the implied notes which the composer does not trouble to write, but leaves to the discretion of the singer;[8] I sol-fa'd them exactly by note, without any ornament and without adding anything of my own to the sense or connection of the phrases. I will not tell you what effect this comparison produced upon my mind, because I have the right to offer my reasons but not to impose my authority. I merely report to you the means which I adopted to form my own opinion, in order that you, in turn, may employ them yourself if you find them good. I must warn you only that this experiment requires more precautions than one would think. The first and most difficult of all is that one must maintain good faith and be equally fair in choosing and in judging. The second is that, in order to attempt this examination, one must necessarily be equally acquainted with both styles; otherwise the one which happened to be the more familiar would constantly present itself to the prejudice of the other. And this second condition is hardly easier than the first, for of all those who are well acquainted with both kinds of music, no one hesitates in his choice, and one can tell from the absurdly confused arguments of those who have undertaken to attack Italian music, how much they know of it and of the art in general.

I must add that it is essential to proceed in exact time, but I foresee that this warning, superfluous in any other country, will be quite useless in France, and this sole omission necessarily involves incompetence in judgment.

With all these precautions taken, the character of each kind of music is not slow in declaring itself, and then it is quite hard not to clothe the phrases with

7. The *port-de-voix* is a specifically French *agrément,* an upward resolving appoggiatura executed by means of a mordent. *Cadence* is the French word for trill. See musical illustrations in Rousseau's *Dictionnaire de musique* (Paris, 1768), Plate B, Figure 13.

8. This procedure gives all the advantages to the French music, for the implied notes in Italian music are no less of the essence of the melody than those which are written out. It is less a question of what is written than of what should be sung, and this manner of writing notes ought simply to pass as a sort of abbreviation; whereas the *cadences* and *ports-de-voix* of French music are indeed, if you will, demanded by the style, but are not essential to the melody; they are a kind of make-up which covers its ugliness without removing it and which only makes it the more ridiculous to sensitive ears. [Au.]

the ideas which are suited to them and not to add to them, at least mentally, the turns and ornaments which one is able to refuse them in singing; nor must one rest the matter on a single trial, for one air may give more pleasure than another without determining which kind of music has the preference, and a rational judgment can be formed only after a great number of trials. Besides, by foregoing a knowledge of the words, one remains ignorant of the most important element in the melody, namely the expression, and all that can be determined in this way is whether the modulation is good and whether the tune is natural and beautiful. All this shows us how hard it is to take enough precautions against prejudice and what great need we have of reasoning to put us in a condition to form a sane judgment in matters of taste.

I made another experiment which requires fewer precautions and which may perhaps seem more decisive. I gave to Italians the most beautiful airs of Lully to sing, and to French musicians some airs of Leo and of Pergolesi,[9] and I observed that while the French singers were very far from apprehending the true taste of these pieces, they were still sensible of their melody and drew from them in their own fashion melodious, agreeable, and well-cadenced musical phrases. But the Italians, while they sol-fa'd our most pathetic airs with the greatest exactness, could never recognize in them either the phrasing or the time; for them it was not a kind of music which made sense, but only a series of notes set down without choice and as it were at random; they sang them precisely as you would read Arabic words written in French characters.[10]

Third experiment. I saw at Venice and an Armenian, a man of intelligence, who had never heard any music, and in whose presence were performed, in the same concert, a French monologue which began with these words:

Temple sacré, séjour tranquille,[11]

and an air of Galuppi, which began with these:

Voi che languite
Senza speranza.[12]

9. Jean-Baptiste Lully (1632–1687) was the creator of the essential form of French opera, the *tragédie lyrique*. Born in Florence as Giovanni Battista Lulli (a form of his name he consistently avoided), he left Italy at the age of eleven to become a servant in a noble French household. Leonardo Leo (1694–1744) was an opera composer of the Neapolitan school and the teacher of Jommelli, who is mentioned below. Giovanni Battista Pergolesi (1710–1736) is best known for his setting of the *Stabat mater* and the comic intermezzo *La serva padrona* (1733), which became the rallying point for the Italian faction in the "Querelle des bouffons" after it was performed in 1752 by an Italian troupe on the stage of the Paris Opéra.

10. Our musicians profess to derive a great advantage from this difference. "We can perform Italian music," they say, with their customary pride, "and the Italians cannot perform ours; therefore our music is better than theirs." They fail to see that they ought to draw a quite contrary conclusion and say, "therefore the Italians have melody and we have none."[Au.]

11. From Jean Philippe Rameau's *Hippolyte et Aricis* (text by Simon Joseph Pelegrin) performed in 1733: Act I, Scene I (*Oeuvres completes*, vol. 6, p. 53).

12. A pasticcio of the opera *Arsace* performed in Venice in 1743 contains an aria set to this text by Baldassare Galuppi.

Both were sung, the French piece indifferently and the Italian badly, by a man familiar only with French music and at that time a great enthusiast for that of M. Rameau. I observed that during the French song the Armenian showed more surprise than pleasure, but everybody observed that from the first bars of the Italian air his face and his eyes grew soft; he was enchanted; he surrendered his soul to the impressions of the music; and though he understood little of the language, the mere sounds visibly enraptured him. From that moment he could not be induced to listen to any French air.

But without seeking examples elsewhere, have we not even among us many persons who, knowing no opera but our own, believe in good faith that they have no taste for singing and are disabused only by the Italian intermezzi? It is precisely because they like only the true music that they think they do not like music.

I allow that the great number of its faults has made me doubt the existence of our melody and has made me suspect that it might well be only a sort of modulated plainsong which has nothing agreeable in itself and which pleases only with the aid of certain arbitrary ornaments, and then only such persons as have agreed to consider them beautiful. Thus our music is hardly endurable to our own ears when it is performed by mediocre voices lacking the art to make it effective. It takes a Fel or a Jélyotte[13] to sing French music, but any voice is good in Italian music, because the beauties of Italian singing are in the music itself, whereas those of French singing, if there are any, are all in the art of the singer.[14]

Three things seem to me to unite in contributing to the perfection of Italian melody. The first is the softness of the language, which makes all the inflections easy and leaves the taste of the musician free to make a more exquisite choice among them, to give a greater variety to his combinations, and to provide each singer with a particular style of singing, so that each man has the character and tone which are proper to him and distinguish him from other men.

The second is the boldness of the modulations, which, although less servilely prepared than our own, are much more pleasing from being made more perceptible, and without imparting any harshness to the song, add a lively energy

---

13. Marie Fel (1713–1794) and Pierre Jélyotte (1713–1797), the two leading singers of the French lyric stage, are best known for their performances in traditional French opera. Although they sang in Rousseau's *Le Devin du village*, they avoided taking sides in the aesthetic battle of the time.

14. Besides, it is a mistake to believe that the Italian singers generally have less voice than the French. On the contrary they must have a stronger and more harmonious resonance to make themselves heard in the immense theaters of Italy without ceasing to keep the sound under the control which Italian music requires. French singing demands all the power of the lungs, the whole extent of the voice. "Louder," say our singing masters; "more volume; open your mouth; use all your voice." "Softer," say the Italian masters; "don't force it; sing at your ease; make your notes soft, flexible, and flowing; save the outbursts for those rare, brief moments when you must astonish and overwhelm." Now it seems to me that when it is necessary to make oneself heard, the man who can do so without screaming must have the stronger voice. [Au.]

to the expression. It is by this means that the musician, passing abruptly from one key or mode to another, and suppressing, when necessary, the intermediate and pedantic transitions, is able to express the reticences, the interruptions, the falterings, which are the language of impetuous passion so often employed by the ardent Metastasio, which a Porpora, a Galuppi, a Cocchi, a Jommelli, a Perez, a Terradellas have so often successfully reproduced,[15] and of which our lyric poets know as little as do our musicians.

The third advantage, the one which gives to melody its greatest effect, is the extreme exactness of time which is felt in the slowest as well as in the liveliest movements, an exactness which makes the singing animated and interesting, the accompaniments lively and rhythmical; which really multiplies the tunes by making as many different melodies out of a single combination of sounds as there are ways of scanning them; which conveys every sentiment to the heart and every picture to the mind; which enables the musician to express in his air all the imaginable characters of words, many of which we have no idea of;[16] and which renders all the movements proper to express all the characters,[17] or at the will of the composer renders a single movement proper to contrast and change the character.

These, in my opinion, are the sources from which Italian music derives its charms and its energy, to which may be added a new and strong proof of the advantage of its melody, in that it does not require so often as ours those frequent inversions of harmony which give to the thoroughbass a melody worthy of a soprano. Those who find such great beauties in French melody might very well tell us to which of these things it owes them or show us the advantages it has to take their place.

On first acquaintance with Italian melody, one finds in it only graces and believes it suited only to express agreeable sentiments, but with the least study of its pathetic and tragic character, one is soon surprised by the force imparted to it by the art of the composer in their great pieces of music. It is by the aid of these scientific modulations, of this simple and pure harmony, of these lively and brilliant accompaniments that their divine performances harrow or enrap-

15. With the exception of the *buffa* composer Galuppi, this list names the more prominent opera composers associated with the Neapolitan school. Galuppi was performed by the Italian troupe, but few of the works of the others appeared on the Paris stage, their operas gaining standing by performances of isolated arias and by the accounts of those who had heard them elsewhere.

16. Not to depart from the comic style, the only one known to Paris, consider the airs, "Quando sciolto avrò il contratto," "Io ho un vespaio," "O questo o quello t'hai a risolvere," "Ha un gusto da stordire," "Stizzoso mio, stizzoso," "Io sono una donzella," "Quanti maestri, quanti dottori," "I sbirri già lo aspettano," "Ma dunque il testamento," "Senti me, se brami stare, o che risa! che piacere!" all characters of airs of which French music has not the first elements and of which it is incapable of expressing a single word. [Au.]

17. I shall content myself with citing a single example, but a very striking one: the air, "Se pur d'un infelice," in *The Intriguing Chambermaid* [*La Finta cameriera*], a very pathetic air with a very lively movement, which lacks only a voice to sing it, an orchestra to accompany it, ears to hear it, and the second part, which should not be suppressed. [Au.]

ture the soul, carry away the spectator, and force from him, in his transports, the cries with which our placid operas were never honored.

How does the musician succeed in producing these grand effects? Is it by contrasting the movements, by multiplying the harmonies, the notes, the parts? Is it by heaping design upon design, instrument upon instrument? Any such jumble, which is only a bad substitute where genius is lacking, would stifle the music instead of enlivening it and would destroy the interest by dividing the attention. Whatever harmony several parts, each perfectly melodious, may be capable of producing together, the effect of these beautiful melodies disappears as soon as they are heard simultaneously, and there is heard only a chord succession, which one may say is always lifeless when not animated by melody; so that the more one heaps up inappropriate melodies, the less the music is pleasing and melodious, because it is impossible for the ear to follow several melodies at once, and as one effaces the impression of another, the sum total is only noise and confusion. For a piece of music to become interesting, for it to convey to the soul the sentiments which it is intended to arouse, all the parts must concur in reinforcing the impression of the subject: the harmony must serve only to make it more energetic; the accompaniment must embellish it without covering it up or disfiguring it; the bass, by a uniform and simple progression, must somehow guide the singer and the listener without either's perceiving it; in a word, the entire ensemble must at one time convey only one melody to the ear and only one idea to the mind.

This unity of melody seems to me to be an indispensable rule, no less important in music than the unity of action in tragedy, for it is based on the same principle and directed toward the same object. Thus all the good Italian composers conform to it with a care which sometimes degenerates into affectation, and with the least reflection one soon perceives that from it their music derives its principal effect. It is in this great rule that one must seek the cause of the frequent accompaniments in unison which are observed in Italian music and which, reinforcing the idea of the melody, at the same time render its notes more soft and mellow and less tiring for the voice. These unisons are not practicable in our music, unless it be in some types of airs chosen for the purpose and adapted to it. A pathetic French air would never be tolerable if accompanied in this manner, because, as vocal and instrumental music with us have different characters, we cannot employ in the one the same devices which suit the other without offending against the melody and the style; leaving out of account that as the time is always vague and undetermined, especially in slow airs, the instruments and the voice would never be in agreement and would not keep step well enough to produce a pleasing effect together. A further beauty resulting from these unisons is to give a more sensible expression to the vocal melody, now by letting it unexpectedly reinforce the instruments in a passage, now by letting it make them more tender, now by letting it give them some striking, energetic phrase of the melody of which it is itself incapable, but for which the listener, skillfully deceived, never fails to give it credit when the orchestra knows how to bring it to the fore at the right moment. From this arises also that perfect correspondence between the ritornelli and the melody, as the result of which all the strokes which we admire in the one are only the development of the other, so that the source of all the beauties of the accompaniment is always to be sought in the vocal part; this accompaniment is so wholly of a piece with the singing and corresponds so exactly to the words that it often seems to determine the action and to dictate to the actor the gesture which he is to make,[18] and an actor who would be incapable of playing the part with the words alone might play it very correctly with the music, because the music performs so well its function of interpreter.

Besides this, the Italian accompaniments are very far from always being in unison with the voice. There are two very frequent cases in which the music separates them. One is when the voice, lightly singing a passage over a series of harmonies, so holds the attention that the accompaniment cannot share it; yet even then this accompaniment is made so simple that the ear, affected only by agreeable harmonies, does not perceive in them any harmony which could distract it.

The other case demands a little more effort to be comprehended. "When the musician understands his art," says the author of the *Letter on the Deaf and Dumb*,[19] "the parts of the accompaniment concur either in reinforcing the expression of the vocal part, or in adding new ideas demanded by the subject and beyond the capacity of the vocal part to express." This passage seems to me to contain a very useful precept, and this is how I think it should be understood.

If the vocal part is of such a nature as to require some additions, or as our old musicians used to say, some divisions, which add to the expression or to the agreeableness without thereby destroying the unity of the melody, so that the ear, which would perhaps blame them if made by the voice, approves of them in the accompaniment and allows itself to be gently affected without being made less attentive to the vocal part, then the skillful musician, by managing them properly and disposing them with taste, will embellish his subject and give it more expression without impairing its unity; and although the accompaniment will not be exactly like the vocal part, the two will nevertheless constitute only a single air and a single melody. For if the sense of the words connotes some accessory idea, the musician will superimpose this during the pauses of the voice or while it sustains some note, and will thus be able to present it to the hearer without distracting him from the idea expressed by the voice. The

---

18. Numerous examples may be found in the intermezzi which have been performed for us this year, among others in the air "Ha un gusto di stordire" in *The Music Master* [*Il Maestro di musica*]; in that of "Son padrone" in *The Vain Woman* [*La Donna superba*]; in that of "Vi stò ben" in [*Livietta e*] *Tracollo;* in that of "Tu non pensi" in *The Bohemian* [*La Zingara*]; and in nearly all of those which require acting. [Au.]

19. Denis Diderot's *Lettre sur les sourds et muets* (Paris, 1751), an essay that takes as a central theme the relation between language and gesture. Its assertion that the French language in its logical clarity is unsuited to poetry gave additional support to Rousseau's position.

advantage will be still greater if this accessory idea can be expressed by a restrained and continuous accompaniment, producing a slight murmur rather than a real melody, like the sound of a river or the twittering of birds, for then the composer can completely separate the vocal part from the accompaniment, and assigning to the latter only the expression of the accessory idea, he will dispose his vocal part in such a way as to give frequent openings to the orchestra, taking care to insure that the instrumental part is always dominated by the vocal, a matter depending more upon the art of the composer than on the execution of the instruments; but this demands a consummate experience, in order to avoid a double melody.

This is all that the rule of unity can concede to the taste of the musician in order to ornament the singing or to make it more expressive, whether by embellishing the principal subject or by adding to this another which remains subordinate. But to make the violins play by themselves on one side, the flutes on another, the bassoons on a third, each with a special motive and almost without any mutual relation, and to call all this chaos music is to insult alike the ear and the judgment of the hearers.[20]

・ ・ ・ ・ ・

If I may be allowed to state my frank opinion, I find that the further our music advances toward apparent perfection, the more it is actually deteriorating.

It was perhaps necessary that it should reach its present state, in order that our ears might insensibly become accustomed to reject the prejudices of habit and to enjoy airs other than those with which our nurses sang us to sleep; but I foresee that to bring it to the very mediocre degree of merit of which it is capable, we shall sooner or later have to begin by once more descending (or reascending) to the state to which Lully brought it. Let us agree that the harmony of that famous musician is purer and less inverted; that his basses are more natural and proceed more directly; that his melody is more flowing; that his accompaniments, less burdened, spring more truly from the subject and depart from it less; that his recitative is much less mannered than ours, and consequently much better. This is confirmed by the style of the execution, for the old recitative was sung by the actors of that time in a way wholly different from that of today. It was livelier and less dragging; it was sung less and declaimed more.[21] In our recitative the *cadences* and *ports-de-voix* have been multiplied; it has become still more languid and has hardly anything left to distinguish it from what we call "air."

20. Omitted here is a section in which Rousseau praises Italian accompaniments for the sparseness of their harmonic doublings; in comparison, French accompaniments, as he states at the end of the *Lettre,* suggest the "padding of a pupil."
21. This is proved by the time of the representation of Lully's operas, much longer now than in his day by the unanimous report of those who have seen them long ago. Thus, whenever these operas are revived, they call for considerable cutting. [Au.]

Now that airs and recitatives have been mentioned, you will permit me, sir, to conclude this letter with some observations on the one and the other which will perhaps throw some helpful light on the solution of the problem involved.

One may judge of the idea our musicians have of the nature of an opera by the singularity of their nomenclature. Those grand pieces of Italian music which ravish the soul, those masterpieces of genius which draw tears, which offer the most striking pictures, which paint the liveliest situations and fill the soul with all the passions they express, the French call "ariettes." They give the name of "airs" to those insipid little ditties which they interpolate in the scenes of their operas, and reserve that of "monologues" particularly to those long-drawn-out and tedious lamentations which if only sung in tune and without screams would put everybody to sleep.

In the Italian opera all the airs grow out of the situation and form a part of the scene. Now a despairing father imagines he sees the ghost of a son whom he has unjustly put to death upbraid him with his cruelty; now an easygoing prince, compelled to give an example of severity, entreats the gods to deprive him of his rule or to give him a less susceptible heart. Here a tender mother weeps to recover her son whom she thought dead; there we hear the language of love, not filled with that insipid rigmarole of "flames" and "chains,"[22] but tragic, animated, ardent, and faltering, and befitting impetuous passion. Upon such words it is appropriate to lavish all the wealth of a music full of force and expression and to enhance the energy of the poetry by that of harmony and melody.

The words of our ariettes, on the contrary, always detached from the subject, are only a wretched medley of honeyed phrases which one is only too glad not to understand. They are a random assemblage of the small number of sonorous words that our language can furnish, turned and twisted in every manner except the one that might give them some meaning. It is upon such impertinent nonsense that our musicians exhaust their taste and knowledge and our actors waste their gestures and lungs; it is over these extravagant pieces that our women go into ecstasies of admiration. And the most striking proof that French music is incapable of either description or expression is that it cannot display the few beauties at its command except upon words which have no meaning.

Meanwhile, to hear the French talk of music, one would imagine that in their operas it depicts great scenes and great passions, and that only ariettes are found in Italian operas, to which the very word "ariette" and the ridiculous thing it signifies are equally unknown. We must not be surprised by the grossness of these prejudices: Italian music has no enemies, even among ourselves, but those who know nothing about it, and all Frenchmen who have tried to

---

22. The special attention given to the musical setting of such words in the *tragédie-lyrique* grew out of classical French declamation. Compare Diderot, who has the same complaint (see pp. 924–27, 930–32).

study it with the sole aim of criticizing it understandingly have soon become its most zealous admirers.[23]

After the "ariettes," which constitute the triumph of modern taste in Paris, come the famous monologues which are admired in our old operas. In this connection it is to be noted that our most beautiful airs are always in the monologues and never in the scenes, for, as our actors have no art of pantomime and the music does not indicate any gesture or depict any situation, the one who remains silent has no notion what to do with himself while the other is singing.

The drawling nature of our language, the little flexibility of our voices, and the doleful tone which perpetually reigns in our opera, give a slow tempo to nearly all our French monologues, and as the time or beat is not made perceptible either in the melody or in the bass or in the accompaniment, nothing drags so much or is so relaxed, so languid, as these beautiful monologues, which everybody admires while he yawns; they aim to be sad and are only tiresome; they aim to touch the heart and only distress the ear.

The Italians are more adroit in their Adagios, for when the time is so slow that there is any danger of weakening the sense of the rhythm, they make their bass proceed by notes of equal value which mark the movement, while the accompaniment also marks it by subdivisions of the beats, which, keeping the voice and the ear in time, make the melody more pleasing and above all more energetic by this exactness. But the nature of French music forbids our composers this resource, for if the actor were compelled to keep time, he would immediately be prevented from displaying his voice and his action, from dwelling on his notes, from swelling and prolonging them, and from screaming at the top of his lungs, and in consequence he would no longer be applauded.

But what still more effectively prevents monotony and boredom in the Italian tragedies is the advantage of being able to express all the passions and depict all the characters in whatever measure and time the composer pleases. Our melody, which in itself expresses nothing, derives all its expression from the tempo one gives to it. It is of necessity sad in a slow tempo, furious or gay in a lively one, serious in a moderate one; the melody itself counts for almost nothing in this; the tempo alone, or, to put it more accurately, the degree of rapidity alone determines the character. But Italian melody finds in every tempo expressions for all characters, pictures for all objects. When the musician so chooses, it is sad in a slow tempo, and, as I have already said, it changes character in the same movement at the pleasure of the composer. Contrasts are thereby made easy, without depending for this on the poet and without the risk of conflicts with the sense.

Here is the source of that prodigious variety which the great masters of Italy were able to display in their operas without ever departing from nature, a

23. A presupposition little favorable to French music appears in this: those who despise it most are precisely those who know it best, for it is as ridiculous when examined as it is intolerable when heard. [Au.]

variety which prevents monotony, languor, and ennui, and which French musicians cannot imitate because their tempi are prescribed by the sense of the words and they are forced to adhere to them unless they are willing to fall into ridiculous inconsistencies.

With regard to the recitative, of which it remains for me to speak, it seems to me that to judge it properly we must begin by knowing exactly what it is, for of all those who have discussed it I am so far unaware of any one who has thought of defining it. I do not know, sir, what idea you may have of that word; as for myself, I call recitative a harmonious declamation, that is, a declamation of which all the inflections are formed by harmonious intervals. It therefore follows that as each language has its own peculiar declamation, each language ought also to have its own peculiar recitative. This does not preclude one from very properly comparing one recitative with another to discover which of the two is the better, that is, the better adapted to its purpose.

Recitative is necessary in lyric drama, first, to connect the action and preserve the unity; second, to set off the airs, of which a continuous succession would be insupportable; third, to express a number of things which cannot be expressed by lyric, cadenced music. Mere declamation cannot be suitable for all that in a lyric work, because the transition from speech to song and especially that from song to speech has an abruptness which the ear does not readily accept, and presents a shocking contrast which destroys all the illusion and in consequence the interest.[24] For there is a kind of probability which must be preserved even at the Opéra, by making the language so homogeneous that the whole may at least be taken for a hypothetical language. Add to this that the aid of the harmonies augments the energy of musical declamation and compensates advantageously for what is less natural in its intonations.

It is evident, according to these notions, that the best recitative, in any language whatever, if this language fulfills the necessary conditions, is that which comes the nearest to speaking; if there were one which came so near to it as to deceive the ear or the mind while still preserving the required harmony, one might boldly pronounce that it had attained to the highest perfection of which any recitative is capable.

Let us now examine by this rule what in France is called "recitative." I pray you, tell me what relation you find between that recitative and our declamation. How can you ever conceive that the French language, of which the accent is so uniform, so simple, so modest, so unlike that of song, can be properly rendered by the shrill and noisy intonations of that recitative, and that there should be any relation whatever between the soft inflection of speech and these prolonged and exaggerated sounds, or rather these perpetual shrieks which form the tissue of that part of our music even more than that of the airs? For instance, let anyone who knows how to read recite the first four lines of the

24. Rousseau refers to the Opéra-Comique, which was then giving performances of mixed song and declamation (*comédies mêlées d'ariettes*) at the fairs of St. Germain and St. Laurent.

famous recognition scene of Iphigénie; you will barely detect a few slight inequalities, a few feeble inflections of the voice, in a tranquil recital which has
nothing lively or impassioned, nothing which compels the speaker to raise or
lower the voice. Then have one of our actresses deliver the same lines as set to
music by the composer, and try, if you can, to endure that extravagant shrieking
which shifts at each moment from low to high and from high to low, traverses
without a subject the whole vocal register, and interrupts the recital in the
wrong place to string some beautiful notes upon syllables without meaning,
which correspond to no pause in the sense. Add to this the *fredons*,[25] *cadences*,
and *ports-de-voix* which recur at every moment, and tell me what analogy there
can be between speech and this pretended recitative, or at least show me some
ground on which one may find reason to vaunt this wonderful French recitative
whose invention is Lully's title to glory.

It is very amusing to see the partisans of French music take refuge in the
character of the language and attribute to it the faults of which they do not
dare to accuse their idol, whereas it is evident on all grounds that the recitative
most suitable to the French language must be almost the opposite of that which
is in use; that it must range within very small intervals, without much raising
or lowering of the voice; with few prolonged notes, no sudden outbursts, still
fewer shrieks; especially, nothing which resembles melody; little inequality in
the duration or value of the notes or in their intensity either. In a word, the
true French recitative, if one is possible, will be found only by a path directly
opposite to that taken by Lully and his successors, by some new path which
assuredly the French composers, so proud of their false learning and consequently so far from feeling and loving what is true, will not soon be willing to
seek and which they will probably never find.

Here would be the place to show you, by the example of Italian recitative,
that all the conditions which I have postulated in a good recitative can actually
be found there; that it can have at the same time all the vivacity and all the
energy of harmony; that it can proceed as rapidly as speech and be as melodious as veritable song; that it can indicate all the inflections with which the most
vehement passions animate discourse, without straining the voice of the singer
or deafening the ears of the listeners. I could show you how, with the aid of a
particular basic progression, one may multiply the modulations of the recitative
in a way suitable to it and which contributes to distinguishing it from the airs
when, in order to preserve the graces of the melody, the key must be less
frequently changed; how, especially, when one wishes to give passion the time
to display all its movements, it is possible, by means of a skillfully managed
interlude, to make the orchestra express by varied and pathetic phrases what
the actor can only relate—a master stroke of the musician's art, by which, in an
accompanied recitative,[26] he may combine the most affecting melody with all

25. Literally a short roulade, here implying excessive ornamentation.
26. I had hoped that Signor Caffarelli would give us, in the concert of sacred music, some example
of grand recitative and of pathetic melody, in order to let the pretended connoisseurs hear for

the vehemence of declamation without ever confusing the one with the other. I could unfold to you all the numberless beauties of that admirable recitative of which in France so many absurd tales are told, as absurd as the judgments which people presume to pass on them, as if one could judge of a recitative without a thorough knowledge of the language to which it belongs. But to enter into these details it would be necessary, so to speak, to create a new dictionary, to coin terms every moment in order to present to French readers ideas unknown among them, and to address them in language which would seem meaningless to them. In a word, one would be obliged, in order to make one-self clear, to speak a language they understood, and consequently to speak of any science or art whatever except music alone. Therefore I shall not go into this subject with an affected detail which would do nothing to instruct my readers and concerning which they might presume that I owed the apparent force of my arguments only to their ignorance in this matter.

· · · · ·

I think that I have shown that there is neither measure nor melody in French music, because the language is not capable of them; that French singing is a continual squalling, insupportable to an unprejudiced ear; that its harmony is crude and devoid of expression and suggests only the padding of a pupil; that French "airs" are not airs; that French recitative is not recitative. From this I conclude that the French have no music and cannot have any;[27] or that if they ever have, it will be so much the worse for them.

I am, etc.

---

once what they have so long been passing judgment on, but I found, from his reasons for doing nothing of the kind, that he knew better than I the capacity of his hearers. [Au.]

Gaetano Majorano, called Caffarelli after his earliest protector (1703–1783), one of the leading Italian castrati. Louis XV engaged him to entertain the Dauphine, according to the *Mémoires du duc de Luynes* (vol. 12, p. 471 and vol. 13, p. 10), and while in Paris he was also heard at the Concert Spirituel on November 5, 1753—an event Rousseau presumably attended.

27. I do not call it having a music to import that of another language and try to apply it to one's own, and I had rather we kept our wretched and absurd singing than that we should still more absurdly unite Italian melody with the French language. This distasteful combination, which will perhaps from now on constitute the study of our musicians, is too monstrous to be accepted, and the character of our language will never lend itself to it. At most, some comic pieces will succeed in passing by reason of their orchestral part, but I boldly predict that the tragic style will never be attempted. At the Opéra-Comique this winter the public applauded the work of a man of talent who seems to have listened with good ears, and who has translated the style into French as closely as is possible; his accompaniments are well imitated without being copied; and if he has written no melody, it is because it is impossible to write any. Young musicians who feel that you have talent, continue in public to despise Italian music; I am well aware that your present interest requires it; but in private make haste to study that language and that music if you wish to be able some day to turn against your comrades the disdain which today you affect for your masters. [Au.]

134 Francesco Algarotti

Born at Venice in 1712 and educated in Rome and Bologna, Francesco Algarotti was a cosmopolitan savant who was welcomed into educated circles in London and Paris, where he lived for a time with Voltaire. In 1740 he went to Berlin at the invitation of Frederick the Great, and remained there for nine years in close touch with the King, assisting him in the translation of opera librettos. He returned to Italy in 1753 because of ill health, and died in Pisa in 1764.

Algarotti's *Saggio sopra l'opera in musica* (*An Essay on the Opera,* 1755) became the principal text of reform opera. Comparing the singer-driven opera of Italy to the better integrated operatic productions he had seen in the north, he advocated subsuming all elements of the spectacle under a unifying poetic idea, calling for a return to the austerities of Greek tragedy. In the service of this neoclassical program, he argued the appropriateness of subjects like the story of Iphigenia or of Virgil's Dido. His influence can be seen clearly in later reform documents such as Gluck's Preface to *Alceste.*

FROM *An Essay on the Opera*
(1755)

CHAPTER I. OF THE POEM, ARGUMENT, OR BUSINESS OF AN OPERA

As soon as the desired regulation shall have been introduced on the theatre it will then be incumbent to proceed to the various constituent parts of an opera in order that those amendments should be made in each whereof they severally now appear the most deficient. The leading object to be maturely considered is the nature of the subject to be chosen, an article of much more consequence than is commonly imagined; for the success or failure of the drama depends, in a great measure, on a good or bad choice of the subject. It is here of no less consequence than, in architecture, the plan is to an edifice, or the canvas, in painting, is to a picture; because thereon the poet draws the outlines of his intended representation, and its coloring is the task of the musical composer. It is therefore the poet's duty, as chief engineer of the undertaking, to give directions to the dancers, the machinists, the painters; nay, down even to those who are entrusted with the care of the wardrobe and dressing the performers. The poet is to carry in his mind a comprehensive view of the *whole* of the drama; because those parts which are not the productions of his pen ought to flow from the dictates of his actuating judgment, which is to give being and movement to the whole.

TEXT: The original edition of the anonymous English translation of 1767, pp. 10–49.

At the first institution of operas, the poets imagined the heathen mythology to be the best source from which they could derive subjects for their dramas. Hence Daphne, Eurydice, Ariadne, were made choice of by Ottavio Rinuccini and are looked upon as the eldest musical dramas, having been exhibited about the beginning of the last century. There was, besides, Poliziano's *Orpheus,*[1] which also had been represented with instrumental accompaniments, as well as another performance that was no more than a medley of dancing and music, contrived by Bergonzo Botta for the entertainment of a Duke of Milan in the city of Tortona.[2] A particular species of drama was exhibited at Venice for the amusement of Henry the Third; it had been set to music by the famous Zarlino.[3] Add to these some other performances, which ought only to be considered as so many rough sketches and preludes to a complete opera.

The intent of our poets was to revive the Greek tragedy in all its lustre and to introduce Melpomene on our stage, attended by music, dancing, and all that imperial pomp with which, at the brilliant period of a Sophocles and Euripides, she was wont to be escorted. And that such splendid pageantry might appear to be the genuine right of tragedy, the poets had recourse for their subjects to the heroic ages and heathen mythology. From that fountain, the bard, according to his inventive pleasure, introduced on the theatre all the deities of paganism; now shifting his scene to Olympus, now fixing it in the Elysian shades, now plunging it down to Tartarus, with as much ease as if to Argos or to Thebes. And thus, by the intervention of superior beings, he gave an air of probability to most surprising and wonderful events. Every circumstance being thus elevated above the sphere of mortal existence, it necessarily followed that the singing of actors in an opera appeared a true imitation of the language made use of by the deities they represented.

This then was the original cause why, in the first dramas that had been exhibited in the courts of sovereigns or the palaces of princes in order to celebrate their nuptials, such expensive machinery was employed; not an article was omitted that could excite an idea of what is most wonderful to be seen either on earth or in the heavens. To superadd a greater diversity and thereby give a new animation to the whole, crowded choruses of singers were admitted, as well as dances of various contrivance, with a special attention that the execution of the ballet should coincide and be combined with the choral song; all which pleasing effects were made to spring naturally from the subject of the drama.

No doubt then can remain of the exquisite delight that such magic representations must have given to an enraptured assembly; for although it consisted but of a single subject, it nevertheless displayed an almost infinite variety of entertainment. There is even now frequent opportunity of seeing, on the

---

1. Performed at Mantua, probably in the Carnival season of 1480.
2. The medley referred to was a festal play with music to celebrate the wedding of Gian Galeazzo Sforza and Isabella of Aragon. The performance of this unnamed work took place in 1488.
3. A reference to Cornelio Frangipane's *Tragedia* of 1574, the music not by Zarlino but by Claudio Merulo.

French musical theatre, a spirited likeness to what is here advanced; because the opera was first introduced in Paris by Cardinal Mazarin, whither it carried the same magnificent apparatus with which it had made its appearance at his time in Italy.

These representations must, however, have afterwards suffered not a little by the intermixture of buffoon characters, which are such ill-suited companions of the dignity of heroes and of gods; for by making the spectators laugh out of season, they disconcert the solemnity of the piece. Some traces of this theatric impropriety are even now observable in the eldest of the French musical dramas.[4]

The opera did not long remain confined in the courts of sovereigns and palaces of princes, but, emancipating itself from such thralldom, displayed its charms on public theatres, to which the curious of all ranks were admitted for pay. But in this situation, as must obviously occur to whoever reflects, it was impossible that the pomp and splendor which was attendant on this entertainment from its origin could be continued. The falling off, in that article, was occasioned principally by the exorbitant salaries the singers insisted on, which had been but inconsiderable at the first outset of the musical drama; as for instance, a certain female singer was called *La Centoventi,* "The Hundred-and-Twenty,"[5] for having received so many crowns for her performance during a single carnival, a sum which hath been amazingly exceeded since, almost beyond all bounds.

Hence arose the necessity for opera directors to change their measures and to be as frugally economical on the one hand as they found themselves unavoidably profuse on the other. Through such saving, the opera may be said to have fallen from heaven upon the earth and, being divorced from an intercourse with gods, to have humbly resigned itself to that of mortals.

Thenceforward prevailed a general renunciation of all subjects to be found in the fabulous accounts of the heathen deities, and none were made choice of but those derived from the histories of humble mankind, because less magnificent in their nature, and therefore less liable to large disbursements for their exhibition.

The directors, obliged to circumspection for their own safety, were induced to imagine they might supply the place of all that costly pomp and splendid variety of decoration, to which the dazzled spectators had been accustomed so long, by introducing a chaster regularity into their drama, seconded by the auxiliary charms of a more poetical diction as well as by the concurring powers of a more exquisite musical composition. This project gained ground the faster from the public's observing that one of these arts was entirely employed in modeling itself on our ancient authors, and the other solely intent on enriching itself with new ornaments; which made operas to be looked upon by many as

---

4. Comic characters appear in the first three operas of Lully (*Cadmus,* 1673; *Alceste,* 1674; *Thésée,* 1675) but not in the later works.
5. This singer has not been further identified.

having nearly reached the pinnacle of perfection. However, that these representations might not appear too naked and uniform, interludes and ballets, to amuse the audience, were introduced between the acts; and thus, by degrees, the opera took that form which is now practised on our theatres.

It is an incontrovertible fact that subjects for an operatical drama, whether taken from pagan mythology or historians, have inevitable inconveniences annexed to them. The fabulous subjects, on account of the great number of machines and magnificent apparatus which they require, often distress the poet into limits too narrow for him to carry on and unravel his plot with propriety; because he is not allowed either sufficient time or space to display the passions of each character, so absolutely necessary to the completing of an opera, which, in the main, is nothing more than a tragic poem recited to musical sounds. And from the inconvenience alluded to here, it has happened that a great number of the French operas, as well as the first of the Italian, are nothing better than entertainments for the eyes, having more the appearance of a masquerade than of a regular dramatic performance; because therein the principal action is whelmed, as it were, under a heap of accessories, and, the poetical part being so flimsy and wretched, it was with just reason called a string of madrigals.

On the other hand, the subjects taken from history are liable to the objection of their not being so well adapted to music, which seems to exclude them from all plea of probability. This impleaded error may be observed every day upon the Italian stage. For who can be brought to think that the trillings of an air flow so justifiably from the mouth of a Julius Caesar or a Cato as from the lips of Venus or Apollo? Moreover, historical subjects do not furnish so striking a variety as those that are fabulous; they are apt to be too austere and monotonous. The stage, in such representations, would forever exhibit an almost solitary scene unless we are willing to number, among the ranks of actors, the mob of attendants that crowd after sovereigns, even into their closets. Besides, it is no easy matter to contrive ballets or interludes suitable to subjects taken from history; because all such entertainments ought to form a kind of social union and become, as it were, constituent parts of the whole. Such, for example, on the French stage, is the "Ballet of the Shepherds," that celebrates the marriage of Medoro with Angelica and makes Orlando acquainted with his accumulated wretchedness.[6] But this is far from being the effect of entertainments obtruded into the Italian operas, in which, although the subject be Roman and the ballet consist of dancers dressed like Roman soldiers, yet so unconnected is it with the business of the drama that the scozzese or furlana might as well be danced. And this is the reason why subjects chosen from history are for the most part necessitated to appear naked or to make use of such alien accoutrements as neither belong, nor are by any means suitable to them.

In order to obviate such inconveniences, the only means left to the poet is to exert all his judgement and taste in choosing the subject of his drama, that thereby he may attain his end, which is to delight the eyes and the ears, to

6. In Jean Baptiste Lully's *Roland* (1685), act 2, scene 5.

rouse up and to affect the hearts of an audience, without the risk of sinning against reason or common sense. Wherefore the most prudent method he can adopt will be to make choice of an event that has happened either in very remote times, or in countries very distant from us and quite estranged from our usages, which may afford various incidents of the marvellous, notwithstanding that the subject, at the same time, be extremely simple and not unknown, two desirable requisites.

The great distance of place where the action is fixed will prevent the recital of it to musical sounds from appearing quite so improbable to us. The marvellousness of the theme will furnish the author with an opportunity of interweaving therewith dances, choruses, and a variety of scenical decorations. The simplicity and notoriety of it will exempt his muse from the perplexing trouble and tedious preparations necessary to make the personages of a drama known, that, suitable to his notification, may be displayed their passions, the main spring and actuating spirit of the stage.

The two operas of *Didone* and *Achille in Sciro,* written by the celebrated Metastasio, come very near to the mark proposed here.[7] The subjects of these dramatic poems are simple and taken from very remote antiquity, but without being too far-fetched. In the midst of their most impassioned scenes, there is an opportunity of introducing splendid banquets, magnificent embassies, embarkations, choruses, battles, conflagrations, &c, so as to give a farther extension to the sovereignty of the musical drama, and make its rightfulness be more ascertained than has been hitherto allowed.

The same doctrine may be advanced in regard to an opera on the subject of Montezuma, as much on account of the greatness, as of the novelty of such an action as that emperor's catastrophe must afford. A display of the Mexican and Spanish customs, seen for the first time together, must form a most beautiful contrast; and the barbaric magnificence of America would receive various heightenings by being opposed in different views to that of Europe.[8]

Several subjects may likewise be taken from Ariosto and Tasso, equally fitting as Montezuma for the opera theatre; for besides these being so universally known, they would furnish not only a fine field for exercising the passions, but also for introducing all the surprising illusions of the magic art.

An opera of Aeneas in Troy, or of Iphigenia in Aulis, would answer the same purpose;[9] and to the great variety for scenes and machinery, still greater height-

---

7. Metastasio's *Didone abbandonata* was first set to music by Domenico Sarro in 1724; the first setting of his *Achille in Sciro* (1736) was by Antonio Caldara.
8. Montezuma has been chosen for the subject of an opera, performed with the greatest magnificence at the Theatre Royal of Berlin. [Au.] Carl Heinrich Graun's *Montezuma*, a setting of G. P. Tagliazucchi's Italian version of a French libretto by Frederick the Great, was first performed on January 6, 1755, in Berlin. Algarotti signed the dedication of his *Saggio* on October 6, 1754. Yet this reference to the subject of Montezuma was surely written with the forthcoming performance in mind; Frederick had written to Algarotti about his plans for the opera as early as October 1753.
9. Algarotti outlines an opera on the first of these subjects at the end of his *Saggio* and after this prints his own libretto on the second.

enings might be derived from the enchanting *poetry* of Virgil and Euripides.

There are many other subjects to the full as applicable to the stage and that may be found equally fraught with marvellous incidents. Let then a poet who is judicious enough make a prudent collection of the subjects truly dramatic that are to be found in tracing the fabulous accounts of the heathen gods, and do the same also in regard to more modern times. Such a proceeding relative to the opera would not be unlike to what is oft-times found necessary in states, which it is impossible to preserve from decay and in the unimpaired enjoyment of their constitutional vigor without making them revert from time to time to their original principles.

CHAPTER II. ON THE MUSICAL COMPOSITION FOR OPERAS

No art now appears to stand so much in need of having the conclusive maxim of the preceding chapter put in practice as that of music; so greatly has it degenerated from its former dignity. For by laying aside every regard to decorum, and by scorning to keep within the bounds prescribed, it has suffered itself to be led far, very far astray in a bewildering pursuit of new-fangled whimsies and capricious conceits. Wherefore it would now be very seasonable to revive the decree made by the Lacedaemonians against that man who, through a distempered passion for novelty, had so sophisticated their music with his crotchety innovations that, from noble and manly, he rendered it effeminate and disgusting.

Mankind in general, it must be owned, are actuated by a love of novelty; and it is as true that, without it, music, like every other art, could not have received the great improvements it has. What we here implead is not a chaste passion for novelty, but a too great fondness for it; because it was that which reduced music to the declining state so much lamented by all true connoisseurs. While arts are in their infancy the love of novelty is no doubt essential, as it is to that they owe their being, and after, by its kindly influence, are improved, matured, and brought to perfection; but that point being once attained, the indulging this passion too far will, from benign and vivifying, become noxious and fatal. The arts have experienced this vicissitude in almost every nation where they have appeared, as, among the Italians, hath music at this time in a more remarkable manner.

On its revival in Italy, though in very barbarous times, this elegant art soon made its power be known throughout Europe; nay more, it was cultivated to such a degree by the tramontane nations that it may without exaggeration be asserted, the Italians themselves were, for a certain period of time, glad to receive instructions from them.

On the return of music to Venice, Rome, Bologna, and Naples, as to its native place, such considerable improvements were made there in the musical art, during the two last centuries, that foreigners, in their turn, repaired thither for instruction; and such would be now the case were they not deterred from so doing by the raging frenzy after novelty that prevails in all the Italian schools. For, as if music were yet unrudimented and in its infancy, the mistaken professors spare no pains to trick out their art with every species of grotesque imagination and fantastical combination which they think can be executed by sounds. The public too, as if they were likewise in a state of childhood, change almost every moment their notions of, and fondness for things, rejecting today with scorn what yesterday was so passionately admired. The taste in singing, which, some years ago, enraptured audiences hung upon with wonder and delight, is now received with a supercilious disapprobation; not because it is sunk in real merit, but for the very groundless reason of its being old and not in frequent use. And thus we see that in compositions instituted for the representation of nature, whose mode is ever one, there is the same desire of changing as in the fluctuating fashions of the dresses we wear.

Another principal reason that can be assigned for the present degeneracy of music is the authority, power, and supreme command usurped in its name; because the composer, in consequence, acts like a despotic sovereign, contracting all the views of pleasing to his department alone. It is almost impossible to persuade him that he ought to be in a subordinate station, that music derives its greatest merit from being no more than an auxiliary, the handmaid to poetry. His chief business then is to predispose the minds of the audience for receiving the impression to be excited by the poet's verse, to infuse such a general tendency in their affections as to make them analogous with those particular ideas which the poet means to inspire. In fine, its genuine office is to communicate a more animating energy to the language of the muses.

That old and just charge, enforced by critics against operatical performances, of making their heroes and heroines die *singing*, can be ascribed to no other cause but the defect of a proper harmony between the words and the music. Were all ridiculous quavering omitted when the serious passions are to speak, and were the musical composition judiciously adapted to them, then it would not appear more improbable that a person should die singing, than reciting, verses.

It is an undeniable fact that, in the earliest ages, the poets were all musical proficients; the vocal part, then, ranked as it should, which was to render the thoughts of the mind and affections of the heart with more forcible, more lively, and more kindling expression. But now that the twin sisters, poetry and music, go no longer hand in hand, it is not at all surprising, if the business of the one is to add coloring to what the other has designated, that the coloring, separately considered, appear beautiful; yet, upon a nice examination of the whole, the contours offend by not being properly rounded and by the absence of a social blending of the parts throughout. Nor can a remedy be applied to so great an evil otherwise but by the modest discretion of a composer who will not think it beneath him to receive from the poet's mouth the purport of his meaning and intention; who will also make himself a competent master of the author's sense before he writes a note of music and will ever afterwards confer with him concerning the music he shall have composed; and, by thus proceeding, keep up such a dependence and friendly intercourse as subsisted between Lully and Quinault, Vinci and Metastasio, which indeed the true regulation of an operatical theatre requires.

Among the errors observable in the present system of music, the most obvious, and that which first strikes the ears at the very opening of an opera, is the hackneyed manner of composing overtures, which are always made to consist of two allegros with one grave and to be as noisy as possible. Thus are they void of variation, and so jog on much alike. Yet what a wide difference ought to be perceived between that, for example, which precedes the death of Dido and that which is prefixed to the nuptials of Demetrius and Cleonice. The main drift of an overture should be to announce, in a certain manner, the business of the drama, and consequently prepare the audience to receive those affecting impressions that are to result from the whole of the performance, so that from hence a leading view and presaging notions of it may be conceived, as is of an oration from the exordium. But our present composers look upon an overture as an article quite detached and absolutely different from the poet's drama. They use it as an opportunity of playing off a tempestuous music to stun the ears of an audience. If some, however, employ it as an exordium, it is of a kindred complection to those of certain writers, who with big and pompous words repeatedly display before us the loftiness of the subject and the lowness of their genius; which preluding would suit any other subject as well and might as judiciously be prefixed for an exordium to one oration as another.[10]

After the overture, the next article that presents itself to our consideration is the recitative; and as it is wont to be the most noisy part of an opera, so is it the least attended to and the most neglected. It seems as if our musical composers were of opinion that the recitative is not of consequence enough to deserve their attention, they deeming it incapable of exciting any great delight. But the ancient masters thought in a quite different manner. There needs no stronger proof than to read what Jacopo Peri, who may be justly called the inventor of the recitative, wrote in his dedication to *Euridice*.[11] When he had applied himself to an investigation of that species of musical imitation which would the readiest lend itself to theatric exhibitions, he directed his tasteful researches to discover the manner which had been employed by the ancient Greeks on similar occasions. He carefully observed the Italian words which are capable of intonation or consonance and those which are not. He was very exact in minuting down our several modes of pronunciation, as well as the different accents of grief, of joy, and of all the other affections incident to the human frame, and that in order to make the bass move a timing attendance to them, now with more energy, now with less, according to the nature of each. So

10. Compare the criticism of Johann Joachim Quantz (pp. 70–71 above).
11. See pp. 605–7 above.

nicely scrupulous was he in his course of vocal experiments that he scrutinized intimately the very nature of the Italian language; on which account, in order to be more accurate, he frequently consulted with several gentlemen not less remarkable for the delicacy of their ears, than for their being uncommonly skilled both in the arts of music and poetry.

The final conclusion of his ingenious inquiry was that the groundwork of all such imitation should be an harmony chastely following nature step by step; a something between common speaking and melody; a well-combined system between that kind of performance which the ancients called the *diastematica*,[12] as if held in and suspended, and the other, called the *continuata*.[13] Such were the studies of the musical composers in former times. They proceeded in the improvement of their art with the utmost care and attention; and the effect proved that they did not lose their time in the pursuit of unprofitable subtleties.

The recitative in their time was made to vary with the subject and assume a complection suitable to the spirit of the words. It sometimes moved with a rapidity equal to that of the text and at others with an attendant slowness; but never failed to mark, in a conspicuous manner, those inflections and sallies which the violence of our passions can transfuse into the expression of them. All musical compositions finished in so masterly a manner were heard with delight. Numbers now living must remember how certain passages of simple recitative have affected the minds of an audience to a degree that no modern air is able to produce.

However, the recitative, all disregarded as it may be, has been known to excite emotions in an audience when it was of the *obbligato* kind, as the artists term it, that is, when strictly accompanied with instruments.[14] Perhaps it would not be improper to employ it oftener than is now the custom. What a kindling warmth might be communicated to the recitative if, where a passion exerts itself, it were to be enforced by the united orchestra! By so doing, the heart and mind at once would be stormed, as it were, by all the powers of music. A more evincing instance of such an effect cannot be quoted than the greater part of the last act of *Didone,* set to music by Vinci,[15] which is executed in the taste recommended here; and no doubt but Virgil's self would be pleased to hear a composition so animating and so terrible.

Another good purpose which must be derived from such a practice is that then would not appear to us so enormous the great variety and disproportion

---

12. Diastematica implies, according to the sense of the ancients, a simple interval, in opposition to a compound one, by them called a system. [Note from translator's glossary.]

13. Continuata, in vocal music, means to continue or hold on a sound with an equal strength or manner, or to continue a movement in an equal degree of time all the way. [Note from translator's glossary.]

14. For Metastasio's views on the subject, see his letter to Johann Adolph Hasse, published by Charles Burney in his *Memoirs of the Life and Writings of the Abate Metastasio* (London, 1796), vol. 1, pp. 315–30.

15. The *Didone abbandonata* of the Neapolitan composer Leonardo Vinci, set to Metastasio's libretto, was first performed in Rome in January, 1726.

now observable in the *andamento* of the recitative and that of the airs; but, on the contrary, a more friendly agreement among the several parts of an opera would be the result. The connoisseurs have often been displeased with those sudden transitions where, from a recitative in the *andantissimo* and gentlest movement, the performers are made to skip off and bound away into *ariettas* of the briskest execution, which is to the full as absurd as if a person, when soberly walking, should all on the sudden set to leaping and capering.

The surest method to bring about a better understanding among the several constituent parts of an opera would be not to crowd so much art into the airs and to curb the instrumental part more than is now the custom. In every period of the opera these two formed the most brilliant parts of it; and, in proportion as the musical composition has been more and more refined, so have they received still greater heightenings. They were naked formerly in comparison of what we see them now and were in as absolute a state of simplicity as they had been at their origin, insomuch that, either in point of melody or accompaniments, they did not rise above recitative.

Old Scarlatti was the first who infused life, movement, and spirit in them. It was he who clothed their nakedness with the splendid attire of noble accompaniments, but they were dealt out by him in a sober and judicious manner. They were by no means intricate or obscure, but open and obvious; highly finished, yet free from all the minuteness of affectation; and that not so much on account of the vastness of the theatres, by means of which many of the minor excellencies in musical performances may be lost, as in regard to the voices, to which alone they should be made subservient.

But unwarrantable changes have happened, since that great master's time down to ours, in which all the bounds of discretion are wantonly overleapt. The airs now are whelmed under and disfigured by crowded ornaments with which unnatural method the rage of novelty labors to embellish them. How tediously prolix are those *ritornelli* that precede them; nay, and are often superfluous! For can anything be more improbable than that, in an air expressive of wrath, an actor should calmly wait with his hand stuck in his sword-belt until the *ritornello* be over to give vent to a passion that is supposed to be boiling in his breast? And after the *ritornello* then comes on the part to be sung, but the multitude of fiddles, etc., that accompany it in general produce no better an effect than to astonish the faculty of hearing and to drown the voice of a singer? Why is there not more use made of the basses, and why not increase the number of bass viols, which are the shades of music? Where is the necessity for so many fiddles, with which our orchestras are now thronged? Fewer would do, for they prove in this case like too many hands on board of a ship which, instead of being assistant, are a great impediment to its navigation. Why are not lutes and harps allowed a place? With their light and piercing notes they would give a sprightliness to the *ripienos*. Why is the *violetta* excluded from our orchestras, since from its institution it was intended to act a middle part between the fiddles and the basses in order that harmony might thence ensue?

But one of the most favorite practices now, and which indeed makes our theatres to resound with peals of applause, is, in an *air,* to form a contest between the voice and a hautboy or between the voice and a trumpet so as to exhibit, as it were, a kind of musical tilting-match with the utmost exertion on either side. But such a skirmishing of voices and instruments is very displeasing to the judicious part of the audience, who, on the contrary, would receive the greatest delight from the airs being accompanied by instruments differently qualified from the present in use, and perhaps even by the organ, as hath been formerly practiced.[16] The consequence then would be that the respective qualities of instruments would be properly adapted to the nature of the words which they are intended to accompany, and that they would aptly glide into those parts where a due expression of the passion should stand most in need of them. Then the accompaniment would be of service to the singer's voice by enforcing the pathetic affections of the song, and would prove not unlike to the numbers of elegant and harmonious prose, which, according to the maxim of a learned sage, ought to be like the beating on an anvil by smiths, at once both musical and skilfully labored.

These faults, however considerable, are not the greatest that have been introduced in the composition of airs; we must go farther back to investigate the first source of this evil, which, in the judgment of the most able professors, is to be found in the misconduct of choosing the subject of an air, because rarely any attention is paid to the *andamento* of the melody being natural and corresponding to the sense of the words it is to convey; besides, the extravagant varieties which it is now made to shift and turn about after cannot be managed to tend to one common center or point of unity. For the chief view of our present musical composers is to court, flatter, and surprise the ears, but not at all either to affect the heart or kindle the imagination of those who hear them; wherefore, to accomplish their favorite end, they frequently bound over all rules. To be prodigal of shining passages, to repeat words without end, and musically to interweave or entangle them as they please are the three principal methods by which they carry on their operations.

The first of these expedients is indeed big with danger when we attend to the good effect that is to be expected from melody, because through its middle situation it possesses more of the *virtù*. Moreover, music delights to make an use of acute notes in her compositions similar to that which painting does with striking lights in her performances.

In regard to brilliant passages, common sense forbids the introduction of them excepting where the words are expressive of passion or movement; otherwise they deserve no milder an appellation than being so many impertinent interruptions of the musical sense.

The repeating of words and these chiming rencounters that are made for the

16. In the orchestra of the theatre in the famous villa of Cataio an organ is now to be seen. [Au.]
   The villa Cataio, near Padua, was erected in 1570 by Pio Enea degli Obizzi, a Paduan nobleman with a strong interest in the theater.

sake of sound merely and are devoid of meaning prove intolerable to a judicious ear. Words are to be treated in no other manner but according as the passion dictates; and, when the sense of an air is finished, the first part of it ought never to be sung over again; which is one of our modern innovations and quite repugnant to the natural process of our speech and passions, that are not accustomed to thus turn about and recoil upon themselves.

Most people who frequent our Italian theatres must have observed that, even when the sense of an air breathes a roused and furious tendency, yet, if the words "father" or "son" be in the text, the composer never fails to slacken his notes, to give them all the softness he can, and to stop in a moment the impetuosity of the tune. Moreover he flatters himself, on such an occasion, that, besides having clothed the words with sentimental sounds suitable to them, he hath also given to them an additional seasoning of variety.

But in our sense he hath entirely spoiled all with such a dissonance of expression that will ever be objected to by all who have the least pretensions to judgment and taste. The duty of a composer is to express the sense, not of this or that particular word, but the comprehensive meaning of all the words in the air. It is also his duty to make variety flow from the several modifications the subject in itself is capable of, and not from adjuncts that adventitiously fasten themselves thereon and are foreign from, preposterous, or repugnant to the poet's intention.

It seems that our composers take the same mistaken pains which some writers do, who, regardless of connection and order in a discourse, bend all their thoughts to collect and string together a number of finely sounding words. But, notwithstanding such words are ever so harmonious, a discourse so written would prove an useless, vain, and contemptible performance. The same may be said of every musical composition which is not calculated either to express some sentiment or awaken the idea of some imagery of the mind.[17] Like what we have compared it to, it must turn out but an useless and a vain production, which, should it be received with a temporary and slight applause, must soon be consigned to perpetual silence and oblivion, notwithstanding all the art that might have been employed in choosing the musical combinations. On the contrary, those airs alone remain forever engraven on the memory of the public that paint images to the mind or express the passions, and are for that reason called the speaking airs because more congenial to nature; which can never be justly imitated but by a beautiful simplicity, which will always bear away the palm from the most labored refinements of art.

Although poetry and music be so near akin to each other, yet they have pursued different views here in Italy. The muse presiding over harmony was

17. "All music that paints nothing is only noise, and, were it not for custom that unnatures everything, it would excite no more pleasure than a sequel of harmonious and finely sounding words without any order or connection."—Preface of the *Encyclopédie*. [Au.] Algarotti's quotation is from the "Discours preliminaire" of Jean le Rond d'Alembert.

too chaste in the last century to give in to those affectations and languishing airs which she is at present so fond of indulging. She then knew the way to the human heart and how to stamp permanent impressions thereon; she possessed the secret of incorporating herself, as it were, with the meaning of the words, and, that the probability might seem the greater, she was to the last degree simple, yet affecting, though at the same time the poetic muse had run away from all semblance of truth to make a parade of hyperbolical, far-fetched, fantastical whimsies. Since that time, by a strange vicissitude, as soon as poetry was made to return into the right path, music ran astray.

Such excellent masters as a Cesti and a Carissimi had the hard fate of composing music for words in the style of the Achillino,[18] men who were equal to the noble task of conveying in musical numbers the sighs and love-breathings of a Petrarch. But now, alas, the elegant, the terse, the graceful poems of Metastasio are degraded into music by wretched composers. It must not, however, be hence concluded that no vestige of true music is to be perceived among us, because, as a proof against such an opinion, and that no small one, may be produced our intermezzi and comic operas, wherein the first of all musical requisites, that of expression, takes the lead more than in any other of our compositions; which is owing perhaps to the impossibility the masters found of indulging their own fancy in a wanton display of all the secrets of their art and the manifold treasures of musical knowledge, from which ostentatious prodigality they were luckily prevented by the very limited abilities of their singers. Wherefore, in their own despite, they found themselves obliged to cultivate simplicity and follow nature. Whatever may have been the cause, this style soon obtained the vogue and triumphed over every other although called plebeian. Why did it succeed? Because it was fraught with truth, that in all arts and sciences must ultimately prevail.

To this kind of performance we owe the extending of our musical fame on the other side of the Alps among the French, who had been at all times our rivals in every polite art. The emulous contention which had so long subsisted between them and us for a pre-eminence in music is universally known. No means could be hit on by our artists to make their execution agreeable to Gallic ears, and the Italian melody was abhorred by them as much as had been, in former times, an Italian regency.

But no sooner was heard upon the theatre of Paris the natural yet elegant style of the *Serva padrona,* rich with airs so expressive and duets so pleasing, than the far greater part of the French became not only proselytes to, but even zealous advocates in behalf of the Italian music. A revolution so sudden was caused by an intermezzo and two comic actors.[19] The like had been attempted in vain in the most elaborate pieces of eminent composers through a long series

---

18. G. F. Achillini (1466–1538), prolific author of pedantic verse.
19. For the "Querelle des bouffons," see pp. 743–45, 895–908, and 922–32.

of years, although bedizened over with so many brilliant passages, surprising shakes, etc. Nor did the repeated efforts of our most celebrated performers, vocal or instrumental, fare better.

Nevertheless, all the good musical composition modern Italy can boast of is not absolutely confined to the intermezzi and comic operas; for it must be confessed that in some of our late serious pieces there are parts not unworthy of the best masters and the most applauded era of music. Several instances are to be found in the works of Pergolesi and Vinci, whom death too soon snatched from us, as well as in those of Galuppi, Jommelli, "Il Sassone,"[20] that are deserving to be for ever in esteem.

Through the energy of the composition of these masters, music makes an audience feel sometimes from the stage the very same effects that were formerly felt in the chapels under the direction of Palestrina and Rodio.[21] We have likewise proofs of the like powerful influence in the skilful productions of Benedetto Marcello, a man second in merit to none among the ancients and certainly the first among the moderns. Who ever was more animated with a divine flame in conceiving and more judicious in conducting his works than Marcello? In the cantatas of Timotheus and Cassandra and in the celebrated collection of psalms[22] he hath expressed in a wonderful manner not only all the different passions of the heart, but even the most delicate sentiments of the mind. He has, moreover, the art of representing to our fancy things even inanimate. He found out the secret of associating with all the gracefulness and charms of the modern the chaste correctness of ancient music, which in him appears like the attractive graces of a beloved and respected matron.

20. Johann Adolf Hasse.
21. Rocco Rodio, a Neapolitan composer of the sixteenth century and the author of a treatise, *Regole di musica*, published in 1609.
22. Benedetto Marcello's *Timoteo* (1726) has the subtitle *Gli effetti della musica;* the four volumes of his *Estro poetico-armonico*, collected settings of fifty paraphrases from the Psalms, were first published in Venice from 1724 to 1727.

135 Denis Diderot

Denis Diderot, *philosophe* and principal editor of the *Encyclopédie,* playwright and art critic, scattered discussions of musical issues throughout his writings, often in an important thematic way. Such is the case with this extraordinary dialogue, *Le neveu de Rameau (Rameau's Nephew),* a work written in the 1760s or 1770s that remained unpublished in Diderot's lifetime (it first appeared in 1805, in a German translation by Goethe). The dialogue takes place between a Diderot-like figure and a certain nephew of Jean-Philippe Rameau who was a music teacher and professional parasite. Apparently in life as in fiction, the

Nephew was extravagantly changeable—a strange mixture of utter baseness and nobility. Their encounter occurs in a Parisian café frequented by chess players. Although Diderot at first pretends mere amusement at his old friend's antics, he is clearly transfixed by the man's strange blend of nihilism and innocent candor. The Nephew turns up in Hegel's *Phenomenology of Spirit* as the exemplar of "alienated consciousness."

Near the end of the dialogue, a conversation about music arises after the Nephew, having related with cheerful detachment the tale of a despicable extortion by a fabled renegade, asks for a chorus of praise in honor of his own degradation. He proceeds to render it himself in mime, and the conversation turns on this peculiar pivot to a critique of French opera in the vein of Rousseau. Although it could stand alone as a straightforward entry in the "Querelle des bouffons," embedded in this dialogue the musical discussion raises serious questions about the relation of seeming to being and art to morality. In the words of the Nephew, "Can the style of an evil man have any unity?"

FROM *Rameau's Nephew*

(?1760s–70s)

I: I don't know which strikes me as more horrible, the villainy of your renegade or the tone in which you talk about it.

He: That's just what I was saying to you. The enormity of the deed carries you beyond mere contempt, and that is the explanation of my candor. I wanted you to know how I excelled in my art, I wanted to force you to admit that at least I was unique in my degradation, and classify me in your mind with the great blackguards, and then exclaim: *Vivat Mascarillus, fourbum imperator!*[1] Come on, join in, Mr. Philosopher, chorus: *Vivat Mascarillus, fourbum imperator!*

(Thereupon he began to execute a quite extraordinary fugue. At one moment the theme was solemn and full of majesty and at the next light and frolicsome, at one moment he was imitating the bass and at the next one of the upper parts. With outstretched arms and neck he indicated the held notes, and both performed and composed a song of triumph in which you could see he was better versed in good music than in good conduct.

As for me, I didn't know whether to stay or run away, laugh or be furious. I stayed, with the object of turning the conversation on to some other subject which would dispel the horror that filled my soul. I was beginning to find irksome the presence of a man who discussed a horrible act, an execrable

---

TEXT: As translated by Leonard Tancock, *Diderot: Rameau's Nephew, D'Alembert's Dream* (New York: Penguin Books, 1966), pp. 96–108, with minor alterations. Reproduced by permission of Penguin Books Ltd.

1. "Long live Mascarille, king of the rogues!" In Molière's *L'Étourdi* (act 2, scene 8) the conniving valet Mascarille, at a moment when his projects are going particularly well, fantasizes a portrait of himself painted as a hero, with this legend in gold letters at the base.

crime, like a connoisseur of painting or poetry examining the beauties of a work of art, or a moralist or historian picking out and illuminating the circumstances of a heroic deed. I became preoccupied in spite of myself. He noticed it and said:)

He: What's the matter? Do you feel ill?

I: A bit, but it will pass off.

He: You have that worried look of a man hag-ridden by some disturbing thought.

I: That's so.

(After a moment of silence on his part and mine, during which he walked up and down whistling and singing, I tried to get him back to his own talent by saying:) What are you doing just now?

He: Nothing.

I: Very tiring.

He: I was silly enough as it was; I have been to hear this music by Duni[2] and our other youngsters, and that has finished me off.

I: So you approve of this style of music?

He: Of course.

I: And you find beauty in these modern tunes?

He: Do I find beauty? Good Lord, you bet I do! How well it is suited to the words! What realism! What expressiveness!

I: Every imitative art has its model in nature. What is the musician's model when he writes a tune?

He: Why not go back to the beginning? What is a tune?

I: I confess the question is beyond me. That's what we are all like: in our memories we have nothing but words, and we think we understand them through the frequent use and even correct application we make of them, but in our minds we have only vague notions. When I pronounce the word "tune" I have no clearer idea than you and most of your kind when you say "reputation, blame, honor, vice, virtue, modesty, decency, shame, ridicule."

He: A tune is an imitation, by means of the sounds of a scale (invented by art or inspired by nature, as you please), either by the voice or by an instrument, of the physical sounds or accents of passion. And you see that by changing the variables the same definition would apply exactly to painting, rhetoric, sculpture, or poetry. Now to come to your question: what is the model for a musician or a tune? Declamation, if the model is alive and thinking; noise, if the model is inanimate. Declamation should be thought of as a line, and the tune as another line that snakes its way over the first. The more vigorous and true the declamation, which is the basis of the tune, and the more closely the tune fits it and the more points of contact it has with it, the truer that tune will be and

---

2. Egidio Romoaldo Duni (1709–1775; Diderot gives his name the French spelling *Douni*), Italian composer who successfully adapted French declamation to the musical style of *opera buffa*. With Pierre Alexandre Monsigny and François-André Danican Philidor, Duni is regarded as having defined the shape and style of the *opéra comique*.

the more beautiful. And that is what our younger musicians have seen so clearly. When you hear *Je suis un pauvre diable* you think you can tell it is a miser's plaint, for even if he didn't sing he would address the earth in the same tone when hiding his gold therein: *O terre, reçois mon trésor.*[3] And that young girl, for example, who feels her heart beating, who blushes and in confusion begs his lordship to let her go—how else could she express herself?[4] There are all kinds of characters in these works, and an infinite variety of modes of declamation. Sublime, I tell you! Go and listen to the piece when the young man, feeling himself on the point of death, cries: *Mon coeur s'en va.*[5] Listen to the air, listen to the instrumental setting, and then try and tell me the difference there is between the real behavior of a dying man and the turn of this air. You will see whether the line of the melody doesn't coincide exactly with that of the declamation. I am not going into time, which is another condition of song; I am sticking to expression, and nothing is more obvious than the following passage which I have read somewhere: *Musices seminarium accentus.*[6] Accent is the nursery-bed of melody. Hence you can tell how difficult the technique of recitative is, and how important. There is no good tune from which you cannot make a fine recitative, and no recitative from which a skilled person cannot make a fine tune. I would not like to guarantee that a good speaker will sing well, but I should be surprised if a good singer could not speak well. Believe all I say on this score, for it is the truth.

I: I should be only too willing to believe you if I were not prevented by one little difficulty.

He: What difficulty?

I: Just this: if this kind of music is sublime, then that of the divine Lully, Campra, Destouches, and Mouret, and even, between ourselves, of your dear uncle,[7] must be a bit dull.

He (whispering into my ear): I don't want to be overheard, and there are lots of people here who know me, but it *is* dull. It's not that I care twopence about dear uncle, if "dear" he be. He is made of stone. He would see my

3. "I am a poor devil"; "Oh earth, receive my treasure"—words from airs sung by the crazy miser Sordide in Duni's *L'Isle des fous* (*The Isle of Madmen*, 1760).

4. The young girl is Nicette, another character in Duni's *L'Isle des fous*.

5. "My heart is failing"—from *Le Maréchal-ferrant* (*The Blacksmith*, 1761), by François-André Danican Philidor (1726–1795), the most famous member of a family prominent in French musical life for over a century. He was also a master chess player, who frequented the café where this dialogue takes place. "The French are much indebted to M. Philidor, for being among the first to betray them into a toleration of Italian music, by adopting French words to it, and afterwards by imitating the Italian style in several comic operas, which have had great success, particularly, *Le Marechal Ferrant*" (Charles Burney, *The Present State of Music in France and Italy* [London, 1771], pp. 26–27).

6. A phrase Diderot quotes several times in his writings, always without attribution. It is found in the works of Martianus Capella, a fifth-century writer on the liberal arts. Rousseau also quotes it, in the article "Accent" in his *Dictionnaire*, but attributes it to Dionysius of Halicarnassus.

7. Composers favored by the partisans of French opera in the "Querelle des bouffons." For the "Querelle des bouffons," see pp. 743–45, 895–908, and 921–22.

tongue hanging out a foot and never so much as give me a glass of water, but for all his making the hell of a hullabaloo at the octave or the seventh—la-la-la, dee-dee-dee, tum-te-tum—people who are beginning to get the hang of things and no longer take a din for music will never be content with that. There should be a police order forbidding all and sundry to have the *Stabat* of Pergolesi[8] sung. That *Stabat* ought to have been burned by the public hangman. Lord! these confounded Bouffons, with their *Serva Padrone,* their *Tracollo,*[9] have given us a real kick in the backside. In the old days a thing like *Tancrède, Issé, L'Europe galante, Les Indes* and *Castor, Les Talents lyriques* ran for four, five, or six months.[10] The performances of *Armide*[11] went on for ever. But nowadays they all fall down one after the other, like houses of cards. And Rebel and Francoeur breathe fire and slaughter and declare that all is lost and they are ruined, and that, if these circus performers are going to be put up with much longer, national music will go to the devil and the royal academy in the cul-de-sac will have to shut up shop.[12] And there is some truth in it, too. The old wigs who have been going there every Friday for the past thirty or forty years are getting bored and beginning to yawn, for some reason or other, instead of having a good time as they used to. And they wonder why, and can't find the answer. Why don't they ask me? Duni's prophecy will come true, and the way things are going I'll be damned if, four or five years after *Le Peintre amoureux de son modèle,*[13] there will be as much as a cat left to skin in the celebrated Impasse.[14] The good people have given up their own symphonies to play Italian ones, thinking they would accustom their ears to these without detriment to their vocal music, just as though orchestral music did not bear the same relationship to singing (allowances being made for the greater freedom

8. Giovanni Battista Pergolesi's setting of the *Stabat mater* (1736), for two solo voices and strings, was first published in London in 1749. Almost universally admired, it was the most frequently printed work in the eighteenth century. It entered the regular repertoire of the Concert Spirituel in Paris after its first performance there in 1753. See pp. 743, 928, n. 22, and 979.

9. Operas by Pergolesi: *La serva padrona* (Naples, 1733; first performed in Paris in 1746), the comic intermezzo that touched off the "Querelle des bouffons," and *Livietta e Tracollo* (Naples, 1734; see p. 898, n. 9, and p. 902, n. 18).

10. *Tancrède* (1702) and *L'Europe galante* (1697) are by André Campra, *Issé* (1697) by André Cardinal Destouches, *Les Indes galantes* (1735), *Castor et Pollux* (1737), and *Les Talents lyriques* (1739) by Rameau.

11. *Armide* (1686), an opera by Jean-Baptiste Lully to a libretto by Philippe Quinault, was revived at the Opéra as late as 1766.

12. The composers François Rebel (1701–1775) and François Francoeur (1698–1787) were co-directors of the Paris Opéra (the Académie Royale de Musique) from 1741 to 1767, with a brief intermission from 1753 to 1757. Because at that time the Académie was located at the end of a cul-de-sac or *impasse,* it was nicknamed the "Royal Academy of the cul-de-sac"—the Dead-End Academy. The Nephew surely had this in mind a few lines earlier when he rather rudely referred to the triumph of the *bouffons* as "a real kick in the *cul*" (politely, "backside").

13. *The Painter Who Fell in Love with his Model* (1757), *opéra comique* by the Italian composer Egidio Duni. See n. 2 above. By "Duni's prophecy" the Nephew probably meant this opera, which was enormously popular and was considered by some to have been the work that set the French taste for Italian music.

14. See n. 12.

due to range of instrument and nimbleness of finger) as singing to normal declamation. As though the violin were not the ape of the singer, who in his turn will become the ape of the violin one of these days, when technical difficulty replaces beauty. The first person to play Locatelli was the apostle of modern music.[15] What nonsense! We shall become inured to the imitation of the accents of passion and of the phenomena of nature by melody or voice or instrument, for that is the whole extent and object of music; and shall we keep our taste for rapine, lances, glories, triumphs, and victories?[16] *Va-t-en voir s'ils viennent, Jean.*[17] They supposed they could weep or laugh at scenes from tragedy or comedy set to music, that the tones of madness, hatred, jealousy, the genuine pathos of love, the ironies and jokes of the Italian or French stage could be presented to their ears and that nevertheless they could still admire *Ragonde* and *Platée.*[18] You can bet your boots that even if they saw over and over again with what ease, flexibility, and gentleness the harmony, prosody, ellipses, and inversions of the Italian language suited the art, movement, expressiveness and turns of music, and relative length of sounds, they would still fail to realize how stiff, dead, heavy, clumsy, pedantic, and monotonous their own language is. Well, there it is. They have persuaded themselves that after having mingled their tears with those of a mother mourning the death of her son, or trembled at the decree of a tyrant ordering a murder, they won't get bored with their fairy-tales, their insipid mythology, their sugary little madrigals which show up the bad taste of the poet as clearly as they do the poverty of the art which uses them. Simple souls! It is not so, and cannot be. Truth, goodness, and beauty have their claims. You may contest them, but in the end you will admire. Anything not bearing their stamp is admired for a time, but in the end you yawn. Yawn, then gentlemen, yawn your fill, don't you worry! The reign of nature is quietly coming in, and that of my trinity, against which the gates of hell shall not prevail: truth, which is the father, begets goodness, which is the son, whence proceeds the beautiful, which is the holy ghost. The foreign god takes his place unobtrusively beside the idol of the country, but little by little he strengthens his position, and one fine day he gives his comrade a shove with his elbow and wallop! down goes the idol. That, they say, is how the Jesuits planted Christianity in China and the Indies. And the Jansenists can say what they like, this kind of politics which moves noiselessly, bloodlessly, towards its goal, with no martyrs and not a single tuft of hair pulled out, seems the best to me.

15. When the French began to play the music of Pietro Antonio Locatelli (1695–1764), considered an innovator in Italian instrumental music, they were unknowingly accustoming themselves to Italian vocal music as well, or to the "modern" style.

16. This list is a paraphrase of one that Diderot the interlocutor uses at the beginning of the dialogue, when introducing the Nephew, to characterize the subject matter of the operas of Rameau.

17. "Go see if they're coming, John"—the refrain of a popular song that came to be a proverbial expression of disbelief.

18. *Le mariage di Ragonde* (1714), opera by Jean-Joseph Mouret, and *Platée* (1745), *comédie lyrique* by Rameau.

I: There is a certain amount of sense in everything you have been saying.

He: Sense! It's as well, for devil take me if I have been trying. It just comes, easy as wink. I am like those musicians in the Impasse, when my uncle arrived; if I hit the mark, well and good. A coal-heaver will always talk better about his own job than a whole Academy and all the Duhamels[19] in the world . . .

(And off he went, walking up and down and humming some of the tunes from *L'Isle des fous, Le Peintre amoureux de son modèle, Le Maréchal-ferrant,* and *La Plaideuse,*[20]) and now and again he raised his hands and eyes to heaven and exclaimed: "Isn't that beautiful! God, isn't it beautiful! How can anyone wear a pair of ears on his head and question it?" He began to warm up and sang, at first softly; then as he grew more impassioned, he raised his voice and there followed gestures, grimaces, and bodily contortions, and I said: "Here we go, he's getting carried away and some new scene is working up." And indeed off he went with a shout: *Je suis un pauvre misérable. . . . Monseigneur, Monseigneur, laissez-moi partir. . . . O terre, reçois mon or, conserve bien mon trésor. . . . Mon âme, mon âme, ma vie! O terre!. . . . Le violà le petit ami, le voilà le petit ami!. . . Aspettare e non venire. . . . A Zerbina penserete. . . . Sempre in contrasti con te si sta. . . .*[21] He sang thirty tunes on top of each other and all mixed up: Italian, French, tragic, comic, of all sorts and descriptions, sometimes in a bass voice going down to the infernal regions, and sometimes bursting himself in a falsetto voice he would split the heavens asunder, taking off the walk, deportment, and gestures of the different singing parts: in turn raging, pacified, imperious, scornful. Here we have a young girl weeping, and he mimes all her simpering ways; there a priest, king, tyrant, threatening, commanding, flying into a rage, or a slave obeying. He relents, wails, complains, laughs, never losing sight of tone, rhythm, the meaning of the words, and the character of the music. All the chess players had left their boards and gathered round him. Outside, the café windows were thronged with passers-by who had stopped because of the noise. There were bursts of laughter fit to split the ceiling open. He noticed nothing, but went on, possessed by such a frenzy, an enthusiasm so near to madness that it was uncertain whether he would ever get over it, whether he should not be packed off in a cab straight to Bedlam. Singing a part of the Jommelli *Lamentations*[22] he rendered the finest bits of

---

19. Henri-Louis Duhamel du Monceaux (1700–82), a French savant, engineer, and agriculturalist, who wrote a vast number of treatises on botanical subjects. Diderot used several of them in writing technical articles for the *Encyclopédie.*

20. For the first three works, see nn. 3, 13, and 5. *Le procès, ou La plaideuse (The Lawsuit, or The Maid-Litigant), opéra comique* by Duni (1762).

21. Ariettes from *l'Isle des fous:* "I am a poor wretch . . . O Milord, Milord, let me leave. . . . O earth, receive my gold, preserve my treasure. . . . My soul, my soul, my life! O earth! . . . There's my little friend, my little friend!" Arias from *La serva padrona:* "To wait and have no one come. . . . Think about Zerbina. . . . With you it's always strife. . . ."

22. Like Pergolesi's *Stabat mater,* Niccolò Jommelli's *Lamentations of Jeremiah* (1751) had been performed at the Concert Spirituel.

each piece with incredible accuracy, truth, and emotion, and the fine accompanied recitative in which the prophet depicts the desolation of Jerusalem was mingled with a flood of tears which forced all eyes to weep. Everything was there: the delicacy of the air and expressive power as well as grief. He laid stress upon the places where the composer had specially shown his great mastery, sometimes leaving the vocal line to take up the instrumental parts, which he would suddenly abandon to return to the voice part, intertwining them so as to preserve the connecting links and the unity of the whole, captivating our souls and holding them in the most singular state of suspense I have ever experienced. Did I admire? Yes, I did. Was I touched with pity? Yes, I was. But a tinge of ridicule ran through these sentiments and discolored them.

But you would have gone off into roars of laughter at the way he mimicked the various instruments. With cheeks puffed out and a hoarse, dark tone he did the horns and bassoons, a bright, nasal tone for the oboes, quickening his voice with incredible agility for the stringed instruments to which he tried to get the closest approximation; he whistled the recorders and cooed the flutes, shouting, singing, and throwing himself about like a mad thing: a one-man show featuring dancers male and female, singers of both sexes, a whole orchestra, a complete opera house, dividing himself into twenty different stage parts, tearing up and down, stopping, like one possessed, with flashing eyes and foaming mouth. The weather was terribly hot, and the sweat running down the furrows of his brow and cheeks mingled with the powder from his hair and ran in streaks down the top of his coat. What didn't he do? He wept, laughed, sighed, his gaze was tender, soft, or furious: a woman swooning with grief, a poor wretch abandoned in the depth of his despair, a temple rising into view, birds falling silent at eventide, waters murmuring in a cool, solitary place or tumbling in torrents down the mountainside, a thunderstorm, a hurricane, the shrieks of the dying mingled with the howling of the tempest and the crash of thunder; night with its shadows, darkness, and silence, for even silence itself can be depicted in sound. By now he was quite beside himself. Knocked out with fatigue, like a man coming out of a deep sleep or long trance, he stood there motionless, dazed, astonished, looking about him and trying to recognize his surroundings. Waiting for his strength and memory to come back, he mechanically wiped his face. Like a person waking up to see a large number of people gathered round his bed and totally oblivious or profoundly ignorant of what he had been doing, his first impulse was to cry out "Well, gentlemen, what's up? What are you laughing at? Why are you so surprised? What's up?" Then he went on: "Now that's what you call music and a musician. And yet, gentlemen, you mustn't look down on some of the things in Lully. I defy anyone to better the scene *Ah, j'attendrai*,[23] without altering the words. You mustn't look down on some parts of Campra, or my uncle's violin airs and

23. "Ah! I shall await . . ." The first words of the monologue of Roland in Lully's *Roland* (1685).

his gavottes, his entries for soldiers, priests, sacrificers . . . *Pâles flambeaux, nuit plus affreuse que les ténèbres . . . Dieu du Tartare, Dieu de l'oubli. . . .*"[24] At this point he raised his voice, held on to the notes, and neighbors came to their windows while we stuck our fingers in our ears. "This," he went on, "is where you need lung-power, a powerful organ, plenty of wind. But soon it will be good-bye to Assumption; Lent and Epiphany have already come and gone. They don't yet know what to set to music, nor, therefore, what a musician wants. Lyric poetry has yet to be born. But they will come to it through hearing Pergolesi, the Saxon,[25] Terradellas, Traetta, and the rest; through reading Metastasio they will have to come to it.")

I: You mean to say that Quinault, La Motte, Fontenelle[26] didn't know anything about it?

He: Not for the modern style. There aren't six lines together in all their charming poems that you can set to music. Ingenious aphorisms, light, tender, delicate madrigals, but if you want to see how lacking all this is in material for our art, which is the most forceful of all, not even excepting that of Demosthenes, get someone to recite these pieces, and how cold, tired, and monotonous they will sound! There is nothing in them that can serve as a basis for song. I would just as soon have to set the *Maximes* of La Rochefoucauld or the *Pensées* of Pascal to music. It is the animal cry of passion that should dictate the melodic line, and these moments should tumble out quickly one after the other, phrases must be short and the meaning self-contained, so that the musician can utilize the whole and each part, omitting one word or repeating it, adding a missing word, turning it inside out like a polyp,[27] without destroying it. All this makes lyric poetry in French a much more difficult problem than in languages with inversions, which have these natural advantages.[28] . . . *Barbare, cruel, plonge ton poignard dans mon sein. Me voilà prête à recevoir le coup fatal. Frappe. Ose. . . . Ah! je languis, je meurs. . . . Un feu secret s'allume dans mes sens. . . . Cruel amour, que veux-tu de moi? . . . Laisse-moi la douce paix*

24. "Pale torches, night more frightful than the shadows . . . God of Tartarus, God of the forgotten man." The first is an air of Telaire in Rameau's *Castor et Pollux* (1737), the second the air of Envie in Rameau's *Le Temple de la gloire* (1745).
25. Johann Adolf Hasse.
26. All three wrote opera libretti for French tragic opera and *opéra ballet,* Philippe Quinault (1635–88) for Lully, Antoine Houdar La Motte (1672–1731) for Campra and Destouches among others, and Bernard le Bovier de Fontenelle (1687–1757) for Lully.
27. In 1740 the naturalist Abraham Trembley observed that the tiny creature known as the freshwater polyp was capable of regeneration: when it was cut into any number of parts, each part would become a complete animal. He also performed experiments showing that the polyp could live and function when turned inside out. The discovery became a subject of intense controversy not only among naturalists, but also among philosophers.
28. A reference to a contemporaneous debate about the relation of word order to expression in French and Classical languages. Against a popular claim that French word order was the most natural order for a language, Charles Batteux had recently argued that in fact its rigid rules of word succession prevented inversion, which more heavily inflected languages like Greek and Latin allow, and which Batteux saw as more "natural" (*Letters on the French Phrase as Compared to the Latin Phrase* [1747–48]).

dont j'ai joui. . . . Rends-moi la raison. . . .[29] The passions must be strong and the sensibility of composer and poet must be very great. The aria is almost always the peroration of a scene. What we want is exclamations, interjections, suspensions, interruptions, affirmations, negations; we call out, invoke, shout, groan, weep, or have a good laugh. No witticisms, epigrams, none of your well-turned thoughts—all that is far too removed from unvarnished nature. And don't imagine that the technique of stage actors and their declamation can serve as a model. Pooh! we want something more energetic, less stilted, truer to life. The simple language and normal expression of emotion are all the more essential because our language is more monotonous and less highly stressed. The cry of animal instinct or that of a man under stress of emotion will supply them.

(While he was saying all this the crowds round us had melted away, either because they understood nothing he was saying or found it uninteresting, for generally speaking a child like a man and a man like a child would rather be amused than instructed; everybody was back at his game and we were left alone in our corner. Slumped on a seat with his head against the wall, arms hanging limp and eyes half shut, he said: 'I don't know what's the matter with me; when I came here I was fresh and full of life and now I am knocked out and exhausted, as though I had walked thirty miles. It has come over me all of a sudden."

I: Would you like a drink?

He: I don't mind if I do. I feel hoarse. I've no go left in me and I've a bit of a pain in my chest. I get it like this nearly every day, I don't know why.

I: What will you have?

He: Whatever you like. I'm not fussy. Poverty has taught me to make do with anything.

(Beer and lemonade are brought. He fills and empties a big glass two or three times straight off. Then, like a man restored, he coughs hard, has a good stretch, and goes on:)

But don't you think, my lord Philosopher, that it is a very odd thing that a foreigner, an Italian, a Duni should come and teach us how to put the stress into our own music, and adapt our vocal music to every tempo, measure, interval, and kind of declamation without upsetting prosody? And yet it wouldn't have taken all that doing. Anyone who had ever heard a beggar asking for alms in the street, a man in a towering rage, a woman mad with jealousy, a despairing lover, a flatterer—yes, a flatterer lowering his voice and dwelling on each syllable in honeyed tones—in short a passion, any passion, so long as it was strong enough to act as a model for a musician, should have noticed two things: one, that syllables, whether long or short, have no fixed duration nor even a settled

---

29. "Barbarous one, cruel one, plunge your dagger into my breast. I am here, ready to receive the fatal blow. Strike. Dare. . . . Ah! I languish, I die. . . . A secret fire is kindled in my senses. . . . Cruel love, what do you want of me? . . . Leave me the sweet peace that I have enjoyed. . . . Give me back my reason."

connection between their durations, and the other, that passion does almost what it likes with prosody; it jumps over the widest intervals, so that a man crying out from the depths of his grief: "*Ah, malheureux que je suis!*"[30] goes up in pitch on the exclamatory syllable to his highest and shrillest tone, and down on the others to his deepest and most solemn, spreading over an octave or even greater interval and giving each sound the quantity required by the turn of the melody without offending the ear, although the long and short syllables are not kept to the length or brevity of normal speech. What a way we have come since we used to cite the parenthesis in *Armide: Le vainqueur de Renaud (si quel- qu'un le peut être)*, or: *Obéissons sans balancer* from *Les Indes galantes*[31] as miracles of musical declamation! Now these miracles make me shrug my shoulders with pity. The way the art is advancing I don't know where it will end! Meanwhile let's have a drink.

(And he had two or three without realizing what he was doing. He would have drowned himself, just as he had exhausted himself, without noticing, had I not moved away the bottle he was absentmindedly feeling for. Then I said:)

I: How is it that with a discrimination as delicate as yours and your remark- able sensitiveness for the beauties of the musical art, you are so blind to the fine things of morality, so insensitive to the charms of virtue?

He: Apparently because some things need a sense I don't possess, a fiber that hasn't been vouchsafed me, or a slack one that you can tweak as much as you like but it won't vibrate; or again it may be that I have always lived with good musicians and bad people. Hence it has come about that my ear has become very sharp and my heart very deaf.

30. "Ah, how unhappy I am!"
31. See nn. 11 and 10.

136 Christoph Willibald Gluck

Born in 1714 near the German-Bohemian border, Christoph Willibald Gluck is the master who liberated the opera from the conventions of contemporary Ital- ian *opera seria* and created a new operatic style based on truly dramatic expres- sion. After studying for four years with Sammartini in Milan and visiting London and various cities on the Continent, Gluck settled in Vienna in 1750.

The opera *Orfeo ed Euridice*, written in 1762, marks a turning point in Gluck's career. Here he applied for the first time his new ideas, supported by his able and original librettist, Ranieri de' Calzabigi. Gluck gives an explanation of his aims in the prefaces to the printed scores of his operas *Alceste* (1768) and *Paride ed Elena* (1770). In 1772, Gluck found a new and congenial collaborator in F. L. G. le Bland Du Roullet, who had adapted Racine's *Iphigénie* as an opera libretto. The new score—*Iphigénie en Aulide*—was accepted by the Paris Opéra, and Gluck himself went to Paris to direct the rehearsals. After reinforcing his position with *Armide* (1777) and *Iphigénie en Tauride* (1779), Gluck returned, crowned with fresh laurels, to Vienna, where he died in 1787.

Dedication for *Alceste*

(1769)

YOUR ROYAL HIGHNESS:

When I undertook to write the music for *Alceste*, I resolved to divest it entirely of all those abuses, introduced into it either by the mistaken vanity of singers or by the too great complaisance of composers, which have so long disfigured Italian opera and made of the most splendid and most beautiful of spectacles the most ridiculous and wearisome. I have striven to restrict music to its true office of serving poetry by means of expression and by following the situations of the story, without interrupting the action or stifling it with a useless superfluity of ornaments; and I believed that it should do this in the same way as telling colors affect a correct and well-ordered drawing, by a well-assorted contrast of light and shade, which serves to animate the figures without altering their contours. Thus I did not wish to arrest an actor in the greatest heat of dialogue in order to wait for a tiresome *ritornello,* nor to hold him up in the middle of a word on a vowel favorable to his voice, nor to make display of the agility of his fine voice in some long-drawn passage, nor to wait while the orchestra gives him time to recover his breath for a cadenza. I did not think it my duty to pass quickly over the second section[1] of an aria of which the words are perhaps the most impassioned and important, in order to repeat regularly four times over those of the first part, and to finish the aria where its sense may perhaps not end for the convenience of the singer who wishes to show that he can capriciously vary a passage in a number of guises; in short, I have sought to abolish all the abuses against which good sense and reason have long cried out in vain.

I have felt that the overture ought to apprise the spectators of the nature of the action that is to be represented and to form, so to speak, its argument; that the concerted instruments should be introduced in proportion to the interest and the intensity of the words, and not leave that sharp contrast between the

TEXT: As translated by Eric Blom in Alfred Einstein, *Gluck* (London: J. M. Dent & Sons, 1936), pp. 98–100.

1. By "second section" Gluck means the central or contrasting section of the da capo aria. The first section of such an aria regularly presented its full text twice and had then to be repeated after the central or contrasting section, hence Gluck's reference to repeating the words of the first part "four times over." Frederick the Great says much the same thing in a letter of May 4, 1754, quoted in *Denkmäler der Tonkunst in Österreich*, vol. 15 (1904), p. ix.

aria and the recitative in the dialogue, so as not to break a period unreasonably nor wantonly disturb the force and heat of the action.

Furthermore, I believed that my greatest labor should be devoted to seeking a beautiful simplicity, and I have avoided making displays of difficulty at the expense of clearness; nor did I judge it desirable to discover novelties if it was not naturally suggested by the situation and the expression; and there is no rule which I have not thought it right to set aside willingly for the sake of an intended effect.

Such are my principles. By good fortune my designs were wonderfully furthered by the libretto, in which the celebrated author, devising a new dramatic scheme, for florid descriptions, unnatural paragons, and sententious, cold morality, had substituted heartfelt language, strong passions, interesting situations and an endlessly varied spectacle. The success of the work justified my maxims, and the universal approbation of so enlightened a city has made it clearly evident that simplicity, truth, and naturalness are the great principles of beauty in all artistic manifestations. For all that, in spite of repeated urgings on the part of some most eminent persons to decide upon the publication of this opera of mine in print, I was well aware of all the risk run in combating such firmly and profoundly rooted prejudices, and I thus felt the necessity of fortifying myself with the most powerful patronage of YOUR ROYAL HIGHNESS, whose August Name I beg you may have the grace to prefix to this my opera, a name which with so much justice enjoys the suffrages of an enlightened Europe. The great protector of the fine arts, who reigns over a nation that had the glory of making them arise again from universal oppression and which itself has produced the greatest models, in a city that was always the first to shake off the yoke of vulgar prejudices in order to clear a path for perfection, may alone undertake the reform of that noble spectacle in which all the fine arts take so great a share. If this should succeed, the glory of having moved the first stone will remain for me, and in this public testimonial of Your Highness's furtherance of the same, I have the honor to subscribe myself, with the most humble respect,

Your Royal Highness's

Most humble, most devoted, and most obliged servant,

CHRISTOFORO GLUCK

137 Vincenzo Manfredini

Born in Pistoia in 1737, Vincenzo Manfredini spent the middle years of his life in Bologna writing and teaching. In his twenties, however, he had served as *maestro di cappella* in the court at St. Petersburg until he was replaced by Baldassare Galuppi in 1769, and he returned to that city just before his death in 1799.

Whether nature or circumstance made Manfredini a polemicist is not entirely clear, but both his major publications involved him in public disputes. His quarrel with Giambattista Mancini he seems to have initiated, at least in print, in his *Rules of Harmony* (1775), to which Mancini responded in a new edition of his treatise on singing. After Manfredini reviewed the first volume of Stefano Arteaga's history of opera in a Bologna journal in 1785, Arteaga, a Spanish musician who had been a student of Padre Giovanni Battista Martini in Bologna, printed extracts from the review in the third volume of his history, accompanying them with acid commentary. Manfredini retaliated in kind in his *Difesa della musica moderna, e de' suoi celebri esecutori (A Defense of Modern Music and its Distinguished Practitioners)*, yet another entry in the continuing dialogue between *musica antica* and *musica moderna*. As one of the few music pedagogues to go on record against the "Hellenicizing," antiquarian tendencies of reform opera, Manfredini defended the expressive directness of the new aria styles against those who put ancient music forward as a model for simplicity and expressiveness. His style, however, is flatfooted and bombastic, achieving none of the virtues of the music he praises.

FROM *A Defense of Modern Music and Its Distinguished Practitioners*
(1788)

CONCLUSION

Now I have finished my *responses*,[1] and consequently the occasion to extend any further my defense of modern music and its excellent practitioners, whether professors or dilettantes. But the cause is so good and just that it in no way required a wordy discourse to sustain it. Nevertheless, anyone who thinks that Signor Arteaga was the only person to believe that modern music was not the equal of ancient would be very much mistaken. On the contrary,

TEXT: The original edition (Bologna, 1788), pp. 189–207. Translation by Wye J. Allanbrook.

1. The "responses" referred to are Manfredini's section-by-section critique of Arteaga's commentary on Manfredini's review of Arteaga's history of opera; see the introduction.

he has only been following in the footsteps of certain scholars and learned composers, who have gone so far as to suppose that something is a defect when it is actually a virtue.[2] Unfortunately prejudices, fierce enemies of the truth, are adopted sometimes even by preeminent men. This comes about, in my opinion, from a principle common to all the arts, but one that ought not to be a consideration in music and all other creative arts. Without innovation, as I said earlier, all the arts would still be in their infancy. Yet innovation has always been a theme that artists have raised their voices to denounce, especially those artists who are already developed and with reputations. This may be because they have too much veneration for tradition, or because they are not capable of doing otherwise. But certainly if there is any art in which one ought to strive for innovation, for a means of making the art more pleasing and expressive, that art ought properly to be music. For as was said, it has been the last to be revived, and only in these recent times has it been carried, if not to the summit, at least to the nearest degree of perfection. Thanks for this are due precisely to certain sublime geniuses and creators who knew how to conquer and over-throw the barriers of prejudice by means of innovation. These individuals have brought about a more pleasing, more expressive, and truer music, a music that is not at all that of the ancients, which had too many *voices, fugues, points of imitation, ligatures, countersubjects,* and in sum was more harmonic than melodic. There is general agreement about instrumental music, therefore, that it is in a lofty position now, and that ancient music did not achieve so much.

But what else does this kind of music contain, if not vocal lines or melodies that are more spirited, more pleasing, and more meaningful than the ancient ones? They are melodies almost all of which derive from vocal music, whose follower and companion instrumental music has been and always will be. It is simply true that instrumental music is for the most part a copy and imitation of the vocal. When it doesn't sing, it doesn't express—that is, it says nothing and it is worth nothing at all. So while instrumental music has greatly improved, it first had to be made into vocal music, and whoever denies this can deny anything. But to convince oneself that modern music, whether instrumental or vocal, is absolutely better than ancient music, it is enough to compare good

2. In the music of our day (says the aforesaid Padre Martini) they look only for variety in ideas; a choice of intervals most apt to stimulate the senses; the most delicate and tender affects; a combination of those movements, those figures, and those instruments that produce the most surprise, and stir up the most racket; and in the singers and instrumentalists they seek only something that is on the lips of every professor, which they call *good taste.* (See *History of Music,* vol. 2, p. 281). All this that Padre Martini said with an air of contempt is in my opinion the finest praise that can be given to modern music. God willing, the assertions of Padre Martini would turn out to be true, that is, composers would always seek out tender and delicate affects when circumstances require it, and singers and instrumentalists would always look for *good taste,* without which no music will ever be able to be perfect. [Au.]

Padre Martini was the mentor of both Giambattista Mancini and Stefano Arteaga; he himself wrote a comic intermezzo, *Il maestro di musica* (1746), in which he contrasted the old and the new—expressive and virtuoso—styles of singing.

modern compositions with ancient ones. It is enough to observe the change that occurs between musical works written at various periods by the same fine modern masters, who managed by means of repeated experience to alleviate some improbabilities, inconsistencies, and prejudices. For since the art of music was new, the time had to be right for it to be brought to a degree of excellence it had not yet attained. This happy transaction was reserved for our century, which was destined if not to perfect completely certain arts and sciences, at least to clarify and improve them in great part, and among these arts one should certainly number music. In fact does there not exist a great difference between music written seventy, forty, twenty years ago, and that of the present? Then to believe that such a difference arises because music does not have a fixed style, and because now it is generally in decline—both of these opinions seem to me to be false. They have been advanced too easily by a person who, since he is not acquainted with this art nor has he practiced it, as is required, cannot form of it a reasonable judgment.

It is natural that all the arts and sciences that have not yet reached their total perfection must undergo alteration. Since music (as I have said many times, and it is indisputable) has recently been reborn, cultivated, and improved, the changes it has had to undergo are not few. Some writers have believed these changes to be imperfections, when it is completely the contrary.

One must remember that since music is a very rich art, like poetry, painting and so on, it has many manners and styles, and even more fashions. Hence one must be acquainted with them all and have a solid knowledge of what music is in order to make a sound decision about whether a certain manner or style is good or bad; or whether a particular fashion that differs from another is good or bad, or if they are both good. I think further that among the fine works in every class, by the same fine authors and different ones, comparisons to the benefit or disadvantage of one or the other should not be so easily proposed. For any one of those works can be excellent, one because of one merit, another because of another. Anyone who would assert, for example, that the St. Cecilia of Raphael is a better and more beautiful work than the St. Peter of Guido,[3] or *Orlando furioso* better than *Gerusalemme liberata*,[4] or the Pergolesi *Stabat* better than the Jommelli *Miserere*, etc., or would assert the contrary, would be making a bad argument. For each of these very beautiful works has its particular merit, as do their respective creators, who themselves ought to be admired and not compared. The same can be said of many other things, provided they are good, for each has its own worth, and can be most perfect in its class. But let us look separately at the stronger reasons that cause some of the proponents of ancient music to think that the music of our *opera seria* is in decline (for no

3. Guido Reni, Italian painter who flourished in the first half of the seventeenth century.
4. The two great Italian epics were published in the sixteenth century, *Orlando furioso* by Lodovico Ariosto in 1516 (with subsequent editions in 1521 and 1532) and *Gerusalemme liberata* by Torquato Tasso in 1581.

one would be so untutored as to try to maintain of the music of *opera buffa* that it has not made incredible progress from the time when Buranello[5] flourished up until now.) People say, "You no longer hear a truly cantabile aria. Now they only compose *rondòs*, noisy arias, bravura arias . . . and all this because musicians no longer know how to sing . . . it is the orchestra that sings," and so on. These finicky gentlemen know that the term *rondò*, taken from the French, is often badly applied, since not all those arias that partly resemble *rondòs* are true *rondòs*. On the contrary, they are grand and sublime arias that contain two *themes* or subjects, one slow and the other spirited, repeated only two times. These arias are certainly better than the so-called *arie cantabili* of old, because they are more natural, more genuine, and more expressive.[6]

In the first place, many *arie cantabili* of thirty or forty years ago contained so much passagework or brilliant figuration (almost always quite remote from the sentiment of the words and the character of the aria), put there expressly in order that the singer should demonstrate his learning in varying them. These passages did great harm to the expression, to the authenticity, to the power of the action, and so on.

Second, many things about these arias were badly conceived and consequently harmful to reason and verisimilitude, for example: the habit of repeating the words of the first part of an aria four times and the words of the second only once; having two and sometimes four cadenzas; being condemned to death and going off calmly, without fury; saying good-bye but never leaving; vocalizing on words before their end, and so on. These things even occur sometimes in the arias of well-known composers, who have written them either to indulge the singer or through habit. Are our arias not much more natural and more pleasing, especially those with two themes and two perceptibly different tempos? If they contain one such bit of passagework that is nothing compared to the many that would have been used in times past. Moreover, arias like these lack the aforesaid inconveniences of the *da capo*, the cadenza, and so on. They finish convincingly, with the expression that the situation requires and in the tempo in which they are being executed. Now not all arias written some years ago that have a cadenza or a *da capo*, and so on, are defective; there are some excellent ones, written by fine composers. That came about precisely because, as I said, music is rich in fashions and styles. Hence the most important study for a composer consists in knowing how to discover those styles that will always be attractive, especially when they have been adapted to the situation and the circumstances. Besides, it is simply true that the aforementioned arias in two tempos are not true *rondòs*, although they bear some resemblance to them. Instead they are magnificent and truly heroic arias, which the masters who

5. Baldassare Galuppi (1706–1785), often known as Buranello, after his birthplace.
6. Manfredini is referring here to the fashionable new two-tempo rondò, with a slow first section and a faster, more showy second section, frequent in operas of the 1760s and after, such as those of Galuppi, Niccolò Piccinni, Giovanni Paisiello, and Mozart. Fiordiligi's rondò "Per pietà, ben mio," in Mozart's *Così fan tutte*, is a good example of a rondò.

composed them very rarely—perhaps never—had distinguished with the term *rondò*. They did not even distinguish true *rondòs* with this term, but called them instead cavatinas, or "little arias," such as "Che farò senza Euridice" by Gluck, "Idol mio, che fiero istante" by Buranello, "Idol mio se più non vivi" by Sacchini, and many others of this type.[7]

As for the arias written in past years called *arie di bravura*, without taking merit from those that possess it, many of them contain so much passagework or brilliant figuration that they come off rather badly. Ours also contain some of these passages, but they have more relation to the sentiment of the words, and they are more tasteful, because more varied. In short, because they are adapted more to the themes and characters of the arias, they are not tiresome, boring, and out of place, but highly interesting, pleasing, and agreeable. So I conclude by saying that if for the aforesaid reasons modern arias are more perfect than ancient ones, it is certain too that our musicians know how to sing with more expression and more naturalness than did ancient musicians. And if the orchestra also sings, so much the better, because music is only singing. It is enough that the orchestra sings well, that is, that the instruments moderate their unisons with the voice part in order not to cover it, so that the words can be heard clearly; that when the vocal line is proceeding, the instruments wait on it, so to speak, by playing few notes, and *piano*. But when the poetry and the situation require more significant instrumental accompaniments, consisting of a kind of melody that is more eloquent and richer, it ought to be composed in such a way that the principal melody, which should always be that of the vocal line, stands out clearly, and is not destroyed. Now in all this our fine composers certainly do not fail, nor do our good orchestras fail nor our fine instrumentalists, nor are we lacking in the finest singers.[8] So let Signor Arteaga repeat that most composers do not write music as one ought, that most singers do not sing from the heart, that most players do not perform with clarity and expression. These objections (as I hope I have already demonstrated to him)

7. For example, unlike the new-fangled two-tempoed Italian *rondò* that Manfredini had previously praised, Gluck's well-known "Che farò senza Euridice" from *Orfeo ed Euridice* (Vienna, 1762) displays the features usually characteristic of rondo construction. The aria consists of a closed musical couplet on a single text performed three times, and framing two "episodes" of freer, more declamatory material.

8. Take note that I speak here, as always throughout this defense, of skilled professionals only. For I too willingly agree with Signor Arteaga, and with anyone who has asserted it before him, that there are many mediocre and unfortunate practitioners who were probably intended for something else than the pursuit of music. I also agree that many masters very often destroy the melody, covering and mixing the voice part with a hodge-podge of unsuitable and poorly conceived accompaniments. They make use of certain extravagant innovations, jeopardizing the most reasonable laws of modulation, of spontaneity, and of verisimilitude. They may do this to support the talent of a person who lacks training when they ought to do just the contrary, for praise from the unskilled is not genuine praise. Again I candidly confess that in churches they introduce inappropriately, and against the spirit of devotion, a theater style of the most brazen sort. But I will never agree that all masters fall into such errors, and through them have caused music to decline. For on the contrary, music owes a great debt to the fine modern composers who are bringing it to a degree of perfection unattained in the past. [Au.]

are frivolous, and an insufficient basis for deducing the decline of music. For the general run of practitioners in all the arts and sciences will always be less skilled and less perfectly accomplished.

I cannot better close this defense of modern music than by reproducing for the public the genuine and impartial eulogy for one of its better creators, Maestro Sacchini, who died in Paris last year.[9] Because this eulogy was composed in the capital of France, in a language different from ours, it will perhaps not be known to all Italians. So I set it forth here with great pleasure, because while it is written with great musical learning that can instruct young composers, it also serves as a eulogy, so to speak, for the celebrated Maestro Piccinni himself, the author, one of the solid supporters and creators of modern music—that is to say, of the best music. Yes, of the best without doubt; since it is obvious that good modern music surpasses not only the most ancient music, but in general also that of fifty and sixty years ago. It does this in many regards, but especially in that of melody, which is the most essential part of all music. Rousseau wrote, in the letter on French music already cited,[10] that Corelli, Bononcini, Vinci, and Pergolesi are the first men who made music. He meant by this that the music of masters previous to those men cannot be called music, since it was too little melodic, too artificial, and full of counterpoint. To these four masters, however, one ought to add the two Scarlattis (Alessandro and Domenico), Porpora, Marcello, Handel, Clari, and so on. Yet our good music assuredly surpasses that of these great masters mentioned above (except for Pergolesi, some of whose compositions were invented and perfected in an instant, as it were, by that sublime genius). It surpasses their music, as I have already said, in its most essential part, which is without a doubt good melody, and this consists in a pleasing and varied singing line. If you examine the music of those composers—Pergolesi always excepted—you will find much counterpoint there, and great exertion, but melody is rare, and hence there is little spontaneity and variety. The style of their pieces is for the most part a fugato or point of imitation that is drawn out too long. That is to say that since they lacked invention, they thought that a few thoughts or scraps of melody would suffice to constitute an entire and lengthy composition. How monotonous and boring such music must turn out to be, I leave to the consideration of anyone who has just a simple idea of good taste. How much more to be preferred is the music of the fine modern masters (into whose number, however, I do admit, besides Pergolesi, also Leo, Durante, Hasse, Galuppi, Jommelli, Traetta, and various others, who contributed greatly to its improvement and left monuments that will always be sound and lovely, even though written many years ago). Because these masters adapt and unite harmony to melody, the *imitative* style to the ideal and varied style, art to nature, etc., their music does not appear so uni-

---

9. The eulogy is omitted here.

10. Manfredini cites the *Lettre sur la musique française* in his last "response," p. 185, note, where he praises Rousseau as a man "who could speak of music because he understood it deeply." The excerpt from Rousseau's *Letter* on pp. 895–908 of this volume omits this passage.

form and tedious; it pleases connoisseurs and amateurs alike.

Is it not the same with modern *fugues?* Since they are divided up and inter-woven with new thoughts that are not derived from those of the same *fugues,* are they not very much more pleasing and more perfect than the ancient ones? We agree, and openly avow that ancient music was never so animated, ordered, and expressive as is the modern. Well I know that Algarotti, Sulzer, Brown, Padre Martini, and so many others whom Signor Arteaga has supported in many matters did not think this way. But not all the music he thought to be imperfect was truly so, and so much the less is ours. I wonder if those well-known men had heard and carefully considered all this fine music, truly expres-sive and eloquent, and composed by so many fine modern masters who are still alive, would they have dared to denounce it? Or again, after having heard so much of Hasse, Buranello, Jommelli, Perez, Gluck, and so on, how could they ever ignore its superiority over ancient music, and the progress that it has always been making? Did they perhaps contend that music was all fine and irreproachable, and, like the goddess Minerva, born in an instant, completely formed and perfect? And why attribute to the music the great abuses to which operas are often subjected? For they derive from worse abuses, like those of bad direction at the hand of almost any impresario, without subordination to the poet or the composer, and so on. But in spite of such excesses fine compos-ers have always made every effort to sustain and improve music. They have been encouraged in that effort not by the enormity of the rewards nor by the justice rendered to them (for these things happen rarely), but by the particular character of their art, which like all the arts depends on talent and inspiration. One does not attain excellence in it simply by means of wealth, rank, and study but by an wholly natural inclination, and after the means of success have been rendered easier by the repeated labors of our predecessors.

EXPRESSION AND SENSIBILITY

138 Jean-Jacques Rousseau

FROM *Essay on the Origin of Languages, Which Treats of Melody and Musical Imitation*

(c. 1760)

CHAPTER TWELVE: THE ORIGIN OF MUSIC
AND ITS RELATIONS

With the first voices came the first articulations or sounds formed according to the respective passions that dictated them. Anger produces menacing cries articulated by the tongue and the palate. But the voice of tenderness is softer: its medium is the glottis. And such an utterance becomes a sound. It may occur with ordinary or unusual tones, it may be more or less sharply accented, according to the feeling to which it is joined. Thus rhythm and sounds are born with syllables: all voices speak under the influence of passion, which adorns them with all their éclat. Thus verse, singing, and speech have a common origin. Around the fountains of which I spoke,[1] the first discourses were the first songs. The periodic recurrences and measures of rhythm, the melodious modulations of accent, gave birth to poetry and music along with language. Or, rather that was the only language in those happy climes and happy times, when the only pressing needs that required the agreement of others were those to which the heart gave birth.

The first tales, the first speeches, the first laws, were in verse. Poetry was devised before prose. That was bound to be, since feelings speak before reason. And so it was bound to be the same with music. At first, there was no music but melody and no other melody than the varied sounds of speech. Accents constituted singing, quantity constituted measure, and one spoke as much by natural sounds and rhythm as by articulations and words. To speak and to sing were formerly one, says Strabo,[2] which shows that in his opinion poetry is the source of eloquence.[3] It should be said that both had the same source, not that they were initially the same thing. Considering the way in which the earliest

---

TEXT: *Essay on the Origin of Languages, Which Treats of Melody and Musical Imitation.* Translation by John H. Moran (Chicago: University of Chicago Press, 1966), pp. 50–65. Original title: *Essai sur l'origine des langues où il est parlé de la mélodie et de l'imitation musicale.*

1. "There at last was the true cradle of nations: From the pure crystal of the fountains flow the first fires of love." (Chapter 9, "Formation of the Southern Languages.")
2. Greek geographer and historian (63 B.C.E.–24 C.E.) known for his seventeen-volume geography, which provides information about the Mediterranean countries in the early common era.
3. *Geography*, Bk. I. [Au.]

societies were bound together, is it surprising that the first stories were in verse and the first laws were sung? Is it surprising that the first grammarians subordinated their art to music and were professors of both?[4]

A tongue which has only articulations and words has only half its riches. True, it expresses ideas; but for the expression of feelings and images it still needs rhythm and sounds, which is to say melody, something the Greek tongue has and ours lacks.

We are always astonished by the prodigious effects of eloquence, poetry, and music among the Greeks. These effects are incomprehensible to our minds because we do not try to do such things any more. All that we can manage is to appear to believe them out of kindness toward our scholars.[5] Burette,[6] having translated certain Greek musical pieces as well as could be, into our musical notation, was simple enough to have them played at the Academy of Belles-Lettres; and the academicians were patient enough to listen to them. Such an experiment is admirable, in a country whose music all other nations find indescribable. Ask any foreign musician to perform a French operatic monologue and I defy you to recognize any part of it. Yet these are the same Frenchmen who purport to determine the melody of an ode of Pindar set to music two thousand years ago!

I have read that the Indians in America, having seen the amazing results of firearms, would gather musket balls from the ground; they would throw them by hand, making a loud noise with the mouth. They were quite surprised that

4. "*Archytas atque Aristoxenes etiam subjectam grammaticen musicae putaverunt, et eosdem utriusque rei praeceptores fuisse.... Tum Eupolis, apud quem Prodamus et musicen et litteras docet. Et Maricas, qui est Hyperbolus, nihil se ex musicis scire nisi litteras confitetur.*" Quintillian, Bk. I, ch. 10. [Au.] "Archytas and Aristoxenes also considered grammar to be included under music, and the same masters taught both.... Then too, Eupolis has Prodamus teaching both music and letters. And Maricas, who is Hyperbolus, admits that he knows nothing of music except letters." [Tr.]

5. No doubt allowance must be made for Greek exaggeration in all such matters; but one concedes too much to modern prejudice if one pushes it discounting to the point where all differences vanish. "When Greek music in the time of Amphion and Orpheus had reached the level it has attained today in the remotest provincial cities," says Abbé Terrasson, "it would interrupt the course of rivers, attract oak trees, and move cliffs. Today, having reached a very high degree of perfection, it is very much loved, it is just as pervasively beautiful, but it leaves everything in place. Thus, for example, it includes the verses of Homer, a poet born in the infancy of the human spirit, compared to those who followed. We are enraptured by these verses, but today we are content simply to enjoy and esteem those good poets." Undoubtedly the Abbé Terrasson has had some acquaintance with philosophy, but he does not show it in this passage. [Au.]

   The Abbé Jean Terrasson (1670–1750), professor of Greek and Latin at the Collège de France, is best known for his romance *Sethos,* the tale of an Egyptian prince's initiation into the mysteries, which is considered a source for the libretto of Mozart's *Die Zauberflöte.* In the ongoing discussions about the competing virtues of the ancients and the moderns, Terrasson took the part of the moderns. In his *Critical Dissertation on Homer's "Iliad"* he enumerated the faults in Homer and called for a poetics "founded on reason."

6. Pierre-Jean Burette (1665–1747), Parisian musician and scholar of great erudition who gave himself to the study of ancient music. His essays on the subject are cited frequently by his contemporaries.

they did not kill anyone. Our orators, our musicians, and our scholars are like these Indians. It is not remarkable that we do not do as much with our music as the Greeks did with theirs. On the contrary, it would be remarkable if one produced the same results with such different instruments.

CHAPTER THIRTEEN: ON MELODY

No one doubts that man is changed by his feelings. But instead of distinguishing the changes, we confuse them with their causes. We attach far too little importance to sensations. We do not see that frequently they have no effect on us merely as sensations, but as signs or images, and also that their moral effects have moral causes. Just as the feelings that a painting excites in us are not at all due to colors, the power of music over our souls is not at all the work of sounds. Beautiful, subtly shaded colors are a pleasing sight; but this is purely a pleasure of the sense. It is the drawing, the representation, which gives life and spirit to these colors. The passions they express are what stir ours; the objects they represent are what affect us. Colors entail no interest or feeling at all. The strokes of a touching picture affect us even in a print. Without these strokes in the picture, the colors would do nothing more.

The role of melody in music is precisely that of drawing in a painting. This is what constitutes the strokes and figures, of which the harmony and the sounds are merely the colors. But, it is said, melody is merely a succession of sounds. No doubt. And drawing is only an arrangement of colors. An orator uses ink to write out his compositions: does that mean ink is a very eloquent liquid?

Imagine a country in which no one has any idea of drawing, but where many people who spend their lives combining and mixing various shades of color are considered to excel at painting. Those people would regard our painting precisely as we consider Greek music. If they heard of the emotions aroused in us by beautiful paintings, the spell of a pathetic scene, their scholars would rush into a ponderous investigation of the material, comparing their colors to ours, determining whether our green is more delicate or our red more brilliant. They would try to find out which color combinations drew tears, which could arouse anger. The Burettes of that country would examine just a few tattered scraps of our paintings. Then they would ask with surprise what is so remarkable about such coloring.

And if a start were made in a neighboring country toward the development of line and stroke, an incipient drawing, some still imperfect figure, it would all be treated as merely capricious, baroque daubing. And, for the sake of taste, one would cling to this simple style, which really expresses nothing, but brilliantly produces beautiful nuances, big slabs of color, long series of gradually shaded hues, without a hint of drawing.

Finally, the power of progress would lead to experiments with the prism. And immediately some famous artist would base a beautiful system on it. Gentlemen, he will tell you, true philosophy requires that things be traced to physical causes. Behold the analysis of light; behold the primary colors; observe their relations, their proportions. These are the true principles of the pleasure that painting gives you. All this mysterious talk of drawing, representation, figure, is just the charlatanry of French painters who think that by their imitations they can produce I know not what stirrings of the spirit, while it is known that nothing is involved but sensation. You hear of the marvels of their pictures; but look at my colors.

French painters, he would continue, may have seen a rainbow. Nature may have given them some taste for nuance, some sense of color. But I have revealed to you the great and true principles of art. I say of art! of all the arts, gentlemen, and of all the sciences. The analysis of colors, the calculation of prismatic refractions, give you the only exact relations in nature, the rule of all relations. And everything in the universe is nothing but relations. Thus one knows everything when one knows how to paint; one knows everything when one knows how to match colors.

What are we to say of a painter sufficiently devoid of feeling and taste to think like that, stupidly restricting the pleasurable character of his art to its mere mechanics? What shall we say of a musician, similarly quite prejudiced, who considers harmony the sole source of the great effects of music. Let us consign the first to housepainting and condemn the other to doing French opera.[7]

Music is no more the art of combining sounds to please the ear than painting is the art of combining colors to please the eye. If there were no more to it than that, they would both be natural sciences rather than fine arts. Imitation alone raises them to this level. But what makes painting an imitative art? Drawing. What makes music another? Melody.

CHAPTER FOURTEEN: ON HARMONY

The beauty of sounds is natural. Their effect is purely physical. It is due to the coincidence of various particles of air set in motion by the sonorous body and all their aliquots, perhaps to infinity: the total effect is pleasing. Everyone in the world takes pleasure in hearing beautiful sounds. But if the pleasure is not enlivened by melodious inflections that are familiar to them, it will not be at all delightful, will not become at all voluptuous. The songs most beautiful to us will only moderately move those to whom they are quite unfamiliar. It is a tongue for which one needs a dictionary.

Harmony, properly speaking, is a still more difficult matter. Being only conventionally beautiful, it does not in any way please the completely unpracticed ear. Development of sensitivity and taste for it requires long exposure. To the

---

7. In this paragraph and in Chapter 14 Rousseau is attacking Jean-Philippe Rameau, who considered music a science of which the universal principle was harmony. Rousseau also attacks Rameau in his *Lettre sur la musique française* (see pp. 161–74).

uncultured ear, our consonances are merely noise. It is not surprising that when natural proportions are impaired, the corresponding natural pleasure is destroyed.

A sound is accompanied by all its concomitant harmonic sounds so related in terms of power and interval as to harmonize most perfectly with that sound. Join to it the third or fifth or some other consonance; you do not join anything to it, you redouble it. You retain the relation of interval while changing that of force. By intensifying one consonance and not the others, you break up the proportion. In trying to do better than nature, you do worse. Your ear and your taste are impaired by a poor understanding of the art. Naturally, the only harmony is unison.

M. Rameau proposes that, by a certain unity, each treble naturally suggests its bass and that an untrained person with a true ear will naturally begin to sing that bass. That is the prejudice of a musician, against all experience. Not only will those who have no idea of either bass or harmony fail to find it, but even if they could be made to understand it, they would be displeased by it, preferring simple unison.

Even if one spent a thousand years calculating the relations of sounds and the laws of harmony, how would one ever make of that art an imitative art? Where is the principle of this supposed imitation? Of what harmony is it the sign? And what do chords have in common with our passions?

When the same question is applied to melody, the reply is the same: it is in the mind of the reader beforehand. By imitating the inflections of the voice, melody expresses pity, cries of sorrow and joy, threats and groans. All the vocal signs of passion are within its domain. It imitates the tones of languages, and the twists produced in every idiom by certain psychic acts.[8] Not only does it imitate, it bespeaks. And its language, though inarticulate, is lively, ardent, passionate; and it has a hundred times the vigor of speech itself. This is what gives music its power of representation and song its power over sensitive hearts. In certain systems, harmony can bring about unification through binding the succession of sounds according to laws of modulation; rendering intonation more appropriate and offering some definite aural evidence of this aptness; fixing and reconciling consonant intervals, and coordinating imperceptible inflections. But in the process it also shackles melody, draining it of energy and expressiveness. It wipes out passionate accent, replacing it with the harmonic interval. It is restricted to only two types of songs, within which its possibilities are determined by the number of oral tones. It eliminates many sounds or intervals which do not fit into its system. Thus in brief, it separates singing from speech, setting these two languages against each other to their mutual deprivation of all authenticity, so that it is absurd for them to occur together in a pathetic subject. That is why the expression of strong and serious passion in song always seems ridiculous, for it is known that in our languages the passions

---

8. *Mouvemens de l'âme.* [Tr.]

have no musical inflection at all, and that northern peoples do not die singing any more than swans do.[9]

By itself, harmony is insufficient even for those expressions that seem to depend uniquely on it. Thunder, murmuring waters, winds, tempests, are but poorly rendered by simple harmonies. Whatever one does, noise alone does not speak to the spirit at all. The objects of which one speaks must be understood. In all imitation, some form of discourse must substitute for the voice of nature. The musician who would represent noise by noise deceives himself. He knows nothing of either the weakness or the strength of his art, concerning which his judgment is tasteless and unenlightened.

Let him realize that he will have to render noise in song; that to produce the croaking of frogs, he will have to have them sing. For it is not enough to imitate them; he must do so touchingly and pleasantly. Otherwise, his tedious imitation is nothing, and will neither interest nor impress anyone.

CHAPTER FIFTEEN: THAT OUR MOST LIVELY SENSATIONS FREQUENTLY ARE PRODUCED BY MORAL IMPRESSIONS

As much as one might want to consider sounds only in terms of the shock that they excite in our nerves, this would not touch the true principle of music, nor its power over men's hearts. The sounds of a melody do not affect us merely as sounds, but as signs of our affections, of our feelings. It is thus that they excite in us the emotions which they express, whose image we recognize in them. Something of this moral effect is perceivable even in animals. The barking of one dog will attract another. When my cat hears me imitate a mewing, I see it become immediately attentive, alert, agitated. When it discovers that I am just counterfeiting the voice of its species, it relaxes and resumes its rest. Since there is nothing at all different in the stimulation of the sense organ, and the cat had initially been deceived, what accounts for the difference?

Unless the influence of sensations upon us is due mainly to moral causes, why are we so sensitive to impressions that mean nothing to the uncivilized? Why is our most touching music only a pointless noise to the ear of a West Indian? Are his nerves of a different nature from ours? Why are they not excited in the same way? Or, why should the same stimulus excite some people very much and others so little?

The healing of tarantula bites is cited in proof of the physical power of sounds. But in fact this evidence proves quite the opposite. What is needed for curing those bitten by this insect are neither isolated sounds, nor even simply tunes. Rather, each needs tunes with familiar melodies and understandable lyrics. Italian tunes are needed for Italians; for Turks, Turkish tunes. Each is

---

9. "In southern climes, where nature is bountiful, needs are born of passion. In cold countries, where she is miserly, passions are born of need, and the languages, sad daughters of necessity, reflect their austere origin" (Chapter 10, "Formation of the Languages of the North").

affected only by accents familiar to him. His nerves yield only to what his spirit predisposes them. One must speak to him in a language he understands, if he is to be moved by what he is told. The cantatas of Bernier[10] are said to have cured the fever of a French musician. They would have given one to a musician of any other nation.

The same differences can be observed relative to the other senses, even the crudest. Suppose a man has his hand placed and his eyes fixed upon the same object, while he alternately believes it to be alive and not alive: the effect on his senses would be the same, but what a different impression! Roundness, whiteness, firmness, pleasant warmth, springy resistance, and successive rising would give him only a pleasant but insipid feeling if he did not believe he felt a heart full of life beating under it all.

I know of only one affective sense in which there is no moral element: that is taste. And, accordingly, gluttony is the main vice only of those who have no sense of taste.

If those who philosophize about the power of sensations would begin by distinguishing pure sense impressions from the intellectual and moral impressions received through the senses, but of which the senses are only the occasional causes, they would avoid the error of attributing to sense objects a power they do not have, or that they have only in relation to affections of the soul which they represent to us. Colors and sounds can do much, as representatives and signs, very little simply as objects of sense. Series of sounds or of chords will perhaps amuse me for a moment; but to charm me and soften me, these series must offer something that is neither sound nor chord, and moves me in spite of myself. Even songs that are merely pleasant but say nothing, are tiresome. For the ear does not so much convey pleasure to the heart as the heart conveys it to the ear. I believe that through developing these ideas, we shall be spared stupid arguments about ancient music. But in this century when all the operations of the soul have to be materialized, and deprived of all morality and human feeling, I am deluded if the new philosophy does not become as destructive of good taste as of virtue.

CHAPTER SIXTEEN: FALSE ANALOGY BETWEEN COLORS AND SOUNDS

There is no kind of absurdity that has not been given a place in the treatment of fine arts by physical observation. The same relations have been discovered in the analysis of sound as in the analysis of light. This analogy has been seized upon immediately and eagerly, with no concern for reason or experience. The systematizing spirit has confused everything, and presumes, out of ignorance, to paint for the ears and sing for the eyes. I have seen the famous clavichord

---

10. Nicolas Bernier (1665–1734), French composer and teacher, *sous-maître* of the king's chapel from 1723 to his death, who in addition to sacred vocal motets composed a number of secular cantatas.

on which music is supposedly made with colors. It would be a complete misunderstanding of the workings of nature not to see that the effect of colors is in their stability and that that of sounds is in their succession.

All the riches of color display themselves at a given moment. Everything is taken in at first glance. But the more one looks, the more one is enchanted; one need only admire and contemplate, endlessly.

This is not true of sound. Nature does not analyze sounds or isolate harmonics. On the contrary, it hides such distinctions under the appearance of unison. Or, if it does sometimes separate them, as in the modulated singing of man and the warbling of some birds, it is in succession, one after the other. Nature inspires songs, not accords; she speaks of melody, not harmony. Colors are the clothing of inanimate objects. All matter is colored. But sounds manifest movement. A voice bespeaks a sensitive being. Only living bodies sing. It is not an automatic flute player that plays the flute; it is the engineer who measured the wind and made the fingers move.

Thus each sense has its proper domain. The domain of music is time; that of painting is space. To multiply the sounds heard at a given time, or to present colors in sequence, is to alter their economy, putting the eye in the place of the ear, and the ear in the place of the eye.

You say: Just as color is determined by the angle of refraction of the ray it emits, each sound is determined by the number of vibrations of a sounding object in a given time period. But the relations of these angles and of these numbers will be the same. The analogy is evident. Agreed. Yet this analogy is rational, not experiential. So this is not an issue. The angle of refraction is primarily experiential and measurable, while the number of vibrations is not. Sounding bodies, subject to air currents, incessantly change in volume and tone. Colors are durable, sounds vanish. And one is never sure that later sounds will be the same as those that preceded. Further, each color is absolute and independent while each sound is, for us, only relative, distinguished only by comparison. A sound, considered in itself, has no absolute character by which it is recognizable. It is hard or soft, has an acute or grave accent in relation to another. In itself, none of this applies to it. Even in the harmonic system, no sound is anything by nature. It is neither tonic, nor dominant, nor harmonic nor fundamental, because all these properties are only relational; and because the whole system could vary from grave to acute, each sound changing its rank and position in the system according to the extent to which the system itself changes. But the properties of colors are not at all relational. Yellow is yellow, independently of red and of blue. Everywhere it is sensate and recognizable. As soon as its angle of refraction is determined, one can be certain that one has the same yellow at all times.

The locus of colors is not in colored bodies, but in light. For an object to be visible, it must be illuminated. Sounds also need a mover, and in order for them to exist, a sonorous body must be struck. This is another advantage of sight, for the perpetual emanation of the stars is its natural stimulus, while nature alone engenders little sound. And, unless one believes in the harmony of the celestial spheres, it must be produced by living beings.

From this it is evident that painting is closer to nature and that music is more dependent on human art. It is evident also that the one is more interesting than the other precisely because it does more to relate man to man, and always gives us some idea of our kind. Painting is often dead and inanimate. It can carry you to the depths of the desert; but as soon as vocal signs strike your ear, they announce to you a being like yourself. They are, so to speak, the voice of the soul. If you hear them in the wilderness, they tell you you are not there alone. Birds whistle; man alone sings. And one cannot hear either singing or a symphony without immediately acknowledging the presence of another intelligent being.

It is one of the great advantages of the musician that he can represent things that cannot be heard, while it is impossible to represent in painting things which cannot be seen. And the greatest marvel, for an art whose only medium is motion, is to represent repose. Sleep, the calm of night, even silence, enter into musical pictures. It is known that noise can produce the effect of silence, and silence the effect of noise, as when one falls asleep at a dull monotonous lecture and wakes up as soon as it ends. But music affects us more deeply, arousing through one sense feelings similar to those aroused through another. But, since its result must be perceptible, and its impression weak, painting lacks this power: it cannot imitate music as music can imitate it. Even if the whole of nature were asleep, those who contemplate it would not be. And the musician's art consists of substituting for an imperceptible image of the object the movements which its presence excites in the heart of the contemplator. Not only will it agitate the sea, fan flames, and engorge a stream, but it will depict the horrors of a frightening wilderness, darken the walls of a dungeon, calm a tempest, subdue the winds, and the orchestra will lavish new freshness upon the forest. It does not represent these things directly, but excites in the soul the same feelings one experiences in seeing them.

CHAPTER SEVENTEEN: AN ERROR OF MUSICIANS HARMFUL TO THEIR ART

See how everything continually takes us back to the moral effects of which I spoke, and how far from understanding the power of their art are those many musicians who think of the potency of sounds only in terms of air pressure and string vibrations. The more they assimilate it to purely physical impressions, the farther they get from its source and the more they deprive it of its primitive energy. In dropping its oral tone and sticking exclusively to the establishment of harmonics, music becomes noisier to the ear and less pleasing to the heart. As soon as its stops singing, it stops speaking. And then, with all its accord and all its harmony it will have no more effect upon us.

139 Johann Jakob Engel

As a student of philosophy and theology in Leipzig, Johann Jakob Engel (1741–1802) grew interested in musical theater, and wrote a libretto based on Carlo Goldoni's *Lo speziale* that was later set to music by Christian Gottlob Neefe (*Der Apotheker*, 1771). Appointed professor of philosophy and liberal arts in Berlin in 1775, he continued writing for the theater, publishing a collection of comedies in 1785. He became an important figure in Berlin intellectual life and in 1788 was appointed director of the newly established National Theater of Berlin. His writings went through several editions and were translated into French and Italian.

Über die musikalische Malerey (*On Painting in Music*) is primarily concerned with representation in music. Music must "paint," Engel writes, but it is least effective when it tries to paint external objects: it should depict instead the impression an object makes on the soul. Thus representation becomes internalized, its proper subject the expression of the passions. Expression does not, however, translate into *self*-expression; the passions are affects common to all, and music's means to depict them can to some extent be codified. Engel's concept of mediated representation has been connected by modern writers such as Adolf Sandberger with Beethoven's famous characterization of the "Pastorale" Symphony as "mehr Ausdruck der Empfindung als Mahlerey" ("more an expression of feeling than painting").

FROM *On Painting in Music*
(1780)

To the Royal Capellmeister Herr Reichardt[1]

Dearest Friend!

As I see it, the investigation you have assigned me amounts to the following four questions:

First: What does "painting" mean?
Second: What means does music have for painting?
Third: What is it in a position to paint by these means?
Fourth: What should it paint, and what should it refrain from painting?

If one wanted to give an exhaustive answer to these questions, it would lead hither and yon, in a very rarefied, almost hairsplitting investigation. I will avoid

---

Text: *Schriften* (Berlin, 1844), vol. 4, pp. 136–56. Translation by Wye J. Allanbrook.

1. Johann Friedrich Reichardt became Capellmeister at the court of Frederick the Great in the same year that Engel took up residence in Berlin; see pp. 1029–41.

these subtleties, introducing only the premises that seem to me absolutely necessary and hurrying on to practical matters.

Painting does not mean bringing an object to the understanding by means of signs that have been agreed upon in a merely arbitrary fashion, but bringing that object before the perception of the senses by means of natural signs. The word "lion" merely stimulates a representation in my understanding; the picture of a lion actually places the visible phenomenon before my eyes. The word "roar" already has a sort of pictorial content; Benda's expression of it in *Ariadne* is an even more complete painting of a roar.

Certainly in poetry the word is used in a somewhat different fashion. A poet is considered all the more a painter:

First: the more he goes into the particular and individual in his representations; the more he gives them sensuousness and animation through more precise specification. Language usually furnishes him only with general notions for the understanding, which the listener or reader must first change into images for the imagination. Through a more precise specification of these notions the poet comes to the aid of the imagination, and stimulates it to think of images from a specific viewpoint, with a superior power and clarity.

Second: the more he brings the mechanical—the sound of the words and the cadence of the meter—into agreement with the inner meaning of the discourse. In other words, the more he introduces a resemblance with the represented object itself into the perception of the signs that signify these objects. Or in other words still, the more he makes his merely arbitrary signs approximate the natural ones.

In music this first understanding of the word "painting" does not apply, leaving only the second. Musical tones are not arbitrary signs, since there is no agreement about what they are supposed to make one think. They make their effect not by something signified through them, but by themselves alone, as particular kinds of impressions on our hearing. The composer has nothing general to individualize; he has no notions of the understanding to beautify by making them specific. But by means of his tones as by means of natural signs, he can stimulate representations of other related objects. He can suggest these objects to us by means of tones just as the painter tries to suggest his through colors. And then he must do what the poet does as painter in the second sense: he must make his tones as imitative as possible, and lend them as much similarity to the objects as possible.

Now this painting is either *complete* or *incomplete*. The one type brings the entire phenomenon before our perception, while the other presents only its separate parts or *properties*.

Complete painting obviously takes place only when the object itself is audible, and compatible with regular tones and measured rhythm.

As regards incomplete painting:

First: the object can be a phenomenon compounded of the impressions of different senses, where the audible is mixed with the visible and so forth. By imitating the audible the composer arouses in the imagination the representation of the whole. This is the way to paint a battle, a storm, or a hurricane, for example.

Second: the object may contain absolutely nothing audible, but still share with audible tones certain general properties, which provide the imagination with an easy passage from one to the other.

That is, there are similarities not merely between objects of a single sense, but also between those of different senses. Slowness and quickness, for example, occur just as much in a sequence of tones as they do in a sequence of visual impressions. I will call all such similarities *transcendental* similarities.

Now the composer ferrets out such transcendental similarities, and manages at least an incomplete painting of the quick dash of an *Atalanta*—which of course only mime can imitate completely—by means of the quick sequence of his tones. If he can put it together with the imitation of painting, then he has depicted at the same time the audible part of the phenomenon: his painting is twofold.

This possibility multiplies the objects that the composer can paint. Many objects of the other senses, especially of sight—the external sense most fertile in concepts—are susceptible to musical imitation by means of their transcendental similarities with tones.

At the same time, however, it becomes clear, at least in part, why musical imitation remains generally so indefinite—why it is so difficult, without the help of words, to understand the painting composer. Imitation is almost always only incomplete, only partial, only with respect to general properties, whether an externally sensed object or an inner feeling is imitated. For the feeling is also imitated only in a general way; it can be individualized only through a particular representation of the object arousing it. More about this is soon to follow.

To list all the transcendental similarities that serve this imitation would be as superfluous as it would be impossible. Nature goes into such fine detail on this that the most detailed investigation could hardly follow her. But those who have investigated the origins of language, among others a well-known sect of ancient philosophers,[2] have already provided some ideas that are also useful for this theory.

These ancient philosophers remind me that for our incomplete painting there is still another powerful means at hand. That is, the composer still paints:

Third: when he imitates not a part or a property of the object itself, but the impression that this object tends to make on the soul. Imitation in music obtains its broadest range by this means. For now we no longer require in the object itself those qualities I called transcendental similarities. Even color is paintable. For the impression of a delicate color bears some resemblance to the impression of a gentle tone on the soul.

2. The Stoics. See Tiedemann's *System of Stoic Philosophy,* vol. 1, p. 147ff. [Au.] Dietrich Tiedemann was a German philosopher whose *Geist der spekulativen Philosophie* (6 vols., Marburg, 1791–97) was the first modern history of philosophy.

In order to understand how these impressions, or indeed all inner feelings of the soul, can be painted, and why such painting succeeds best in music, and further, why even such painting must still always remain incomplete, we must answer the second question we posed above: What means has music for painting?

I put down here what I know, and as well as I know it. It is the task of a master in the art to amend any incorrect ideas I may have, and to supplement any deficient ones.

The means for musical painting are, to my knowledge:

First: The choice of *mode*—major and minor.

Second: The choice of the *tone* from which the piece should proceed. Each of the twelve major and minor scales differs from the others through its own different intervals, and receives from that its own character. *C major* and *A major* diverge in character most of all because the progressions of their scales are the least similar; and a characteristic instrumental piece transposed out of *C major* into *A major* will be almost unrecognizable. The same holds for the minor modes.

Third: Melody. It is of great importance whether the tones progress in either small or large intervals, in light or heavy ones, whether in uniformly long or short notes, or in mixed ones. Also whether this mixing comes about according to a manifest order or with apparent irregularity, whether the embellishments are simple, or manifold and rich, etc. I doubt that everything that comes under consideration here can be listed.

Fourth: Movement. Under this head are included measures that are duple or triple, long or short; quick or slow, simple or varied and manifold movement in different voices; parallel, non-parallel, or even contrary motion, and so on.

Fifth: Rhythm. The periods and their sections are either long or short, equal or unequal.

Sixth: Harmony, the combining of simultaneously sounding tones in direct or indirect consonances. In consideration here are: the way to combine simpler or more complex, lighter or heavier proportions; the way these compounded proportions progress, which can occur in an endless number of shifts; the slowness or rapidity of the shifts; the fullness or emptiness, clarity or obscurity, purity or impurity, of the harmony (an impurity that is often only apparent), and so on.

Seventh: The choice of *voices.* Deep, high, medium voices, a particular mixture of the voices—each has a different effect.

Eighth: The choice of *instruments,* according to their own very different characters, and the way in which they are mixed.

Ninth: Loudness and softness, their shading in its different degrees, and the manner of the shading.

How by using these devices to their fullest extent the composer can paint the inner feelings and movements of the soul will become clear in the following observations.

First: All representations of the passions in the soul are inseparably bound up with certain corresponding movements in the nervous system, and are maintained and strengthened by the perception of these movements. But it is not just that these corresponding natural vibrations arise in the body when the representations of the passions have already been stimulated in the soul; these representations also arise in the soul if the related vibrations are already produced in the body. The action is reciprocal: the same path that runs from the soul into the body runs back from the body into the soul. By nothing else, however, are these vibrations so certainly, so powerfully, so variously produced, as by tones. Thus nature herself makes use chiefly of tones in order to stir up the instinctive sympathy that exists among beasts of the same species. The howls of a beast in pain set the nerves of a beast that is not in pain into a similar vibration, and that similar vibration arouses a similar feeling in the latter beast's soul. Hence this feeling takes the name of com-passion, or shared pain. The same goes for con-celebration, or shared joy.[3]

Second: The various kinds of representations of the passions differ in the fullness and wealth of the several representations united in each; in the greater variety of the multiplicity that is united in each; in the greater or lesser accord within this variety, which poses a greater or lesser obstacle to comprehending the whole representation and thinking it through; in the slower or quicker succession of representations; in the smaller or larger steps according as more or fewer intermediate representations are skipped over; in the greater or lesser uniformity of the progression, since some are slow and others quick in their progression while others, extremely irregular, are sometimes halting in their course and sometimes move more quickly, and so on.

I will give just a few examples. Representations of the exalted have a very weighty content, so their movement is slow. Representations of joy have a content that is easily grasped, so their movement is sprightly, the leaps not large. Fear works more quickly, but in a broken style, with a handful of discordant ideas. Melancholy steals off in slow and lingering steps, using closely related ideas.

Have I made it clear in these remarks:

First: how music can paint or imitate the inner feelings of the soul? It chooses tones that have a certain effect on the nerves, which is similar to the impression of a given feeling. To this end it also chooses particular instruments and higher or lower tones. If the tones of a Franklin harmonica[4] fling a man of only somewhat sensitive nerves irresistibly into melancholy, then on the other hand the blare of the trumpet and the roll of the drums move him just as

---

3. There is no precise English equivalent for the German word pair *Mitleiden* and *Mitfreude*—feelings of sympathy for another's pain and for another's joy.

4. The "armonica," Benjamin Franklin's mechanized version of the musical glasses, proved very popular in Europe; Mozart wrote his Quintet K. 617 for armonica, flute, oboe, viola, and cello for the blind virtuoso Marianne Kirchgessner. The instrument was reputed to have an unsettling effect on the nerves of the player.

irresistibly to transports of joy and exaltation. And while the higher tones are more appropriate to all the sprightly, happy feelings and the middle tones to all the soft, gentle ones, so are the lower tones most suited for all the sad, gruesome, mournful ones. Thus in the first three words of the line

Sacri orrori, ombre felici![5]

Hasse sank ever further into the depths; but the last word he suddenly set on high.

But music paints the feelings infinitely better still when in the representation of these corresponding nerve vibrations, and especially in their succession, it brings out all the analogies with the feelings noted above by means of a wise choice of pitch, of key, of harmony, melody, meter, and tempo. It accomplishes this by giving the harmony more or less richness or poverty, lightness or heaviness, by letting the melody proceed in closer or more distant intervals, by making the tempo faster or slower, more or less uniform, and so on.

Second: Have I made it clear why music succeeds best when painting the feelings? For it takes effect here with all its powers assembled; here it applies all its devices as one; here it concentrates all its effects. This will very rarely be the case if it only paints the objects that give rise to feelings. These objects it can usually signify only by single, weak, and distant similarities, while the feelings it can signify by a multitude of very particular similarities.

Third: Have I made it clear why nevertheless even this kind of painting still remains incomplete? As has already been remarked above, a feeling cannot be individualized except by a particular representation of the object arousing it. In this respect music must always be far behind. All it can do, with the concentrated power of all its devices, is indicate classes or types of feelings, even if they consist of low-level, more specific types of feelings. The more special and individual aspects—whatever must be first apprehended from the particular nature and context of the object—remains consistently unspecified, precisely because music cannot also indicate that special nature and context.

From these two last remarks, which I believe to be clear and evident, two rules follow directly:

The *first* rule is that the composer should always paint feelings rather than objects of feelings; always the state into which the soul and with it the body are conveyed through contemplation of a certain matter and event, rather than this matter and event itself. For one should prefer to execute with every art whatever it allows one to execute best—most perfectly. So in the kind of storm symphony that appears in various operas, it is always better to paint the inner movements of the soul in a storm than the storm that occasions these movements. Even though there is much in that phenomenon that would be audible, the former method is always more successful than the latter. On this basis alone

---

5. "Sacred terrors, fortunate shades!" Engel drew this and two other examples in this essay from arias in Johann Adolf Hasse's oratorio *Sant'Elena al Calvario* (Dresden, 1746; rev. Vienna, 1753, 1772).

Hiller's storm symphony in *Der Jagd* is undoubtedly superior to *Philidor's*.[6]

But there is still another and, as it seems to me, more powerful ground for this rule. For since music is essentially created for the feelings, since everything in it works toward this goal, the composer cannot fail, even if he is merely painting an object, to express certain feelings that the soul enters into and wants to pursue. But it almost always turns out that, despite the effort of the composer to imitate a particular thing or event, the soul is driven unpleasantly from feeling to feeling, and is led astray in the entire sequence of its representations.

The *second* rule is that the composer must not try to paint a sequence of feelings that, because it is dependent on some other sequence of occasions or considerations, will have an incomprehensible or nonsensical effect if one does not have in mind simultaneously that other sequence on which this one depends. Let me explain further.

Suppose that the most beautiful accompanied recitative of a *Hasse* were performed without the voices, or, even better perhaps, that a duodrama of *Benda's* were performed by the orchestra alone, without the characters.[7] What would you think you heard in the best work, one composed with the finest taste and the most correct judgment? Nothing other than the wild fantasy of a person delirious with fever. But why? Clearly because the sequence of ideas or events, which is what makes the sequence of feelings comprehensible, has been removed from the whole. And will it not be the same thing when a composer makes up his mind, as has actually happened, to put in the overture to an opera the whole sequence of feelings that is to be aroused in the spectators during the course of the action? In my opinion at least, the overture with which *Monsigny* opens his *Deserteur*—it has many admirers—as well as the one with which he opens his *Bel Arsène*, have always just seemed very tasteless.[8]

If a symphony or a sonata—any musical work not supported by speech or the art of gesture—is intended to be more than just an agreeable noise, a pleasing buzz of tones, it must contain the realization of a single passion, although certainly that realization can take the form of a variety of feelings. It must contain the sort of sequence of feelings that would evolve by itself in a soul completely immersed in a passion, unhindered by externals, and uninterrupted in the free flow of its ideas. If I may be permitted to assume a theory

---

6. The comparison is apt, since Johann Adam Hiller (1728–1804) turned to French models for *The Hunt* (Weimar, 1770) and other of his operas written in the 1760s and '70s.

7. Georg Benda wrote three stage works consisting of a spoken text with musical accompaniment— *Ariadne auf Naxos* and *Medea* in 1775 and *Pygmalion*, to Rousseau's text, in 1780 (see p. 981, n. 2). Called generically "melodramas," they were also often termed "duodramas" or "monodramas" after the number of participating characters; they were generally short pieces involving only a soloist or a duo.

8. *The Deserter* (1769) and *The Fair Arsene* (1775), by Pierre Alexandre Monsigny (1729–1817), a native French composer of meager musical training but who, with François-André Danican Philidor and Egidio Duni, is ranked among the founders of the *opéra comique*. He was known for the richness of his writing for instruments.

of the various sequences of ideas and their principles that has not yet become well-known, I would say that this sequence of ideas must not be other than the *lyric*.

I am coming to what you most expect from me—the specification of rules for vocal composition. Before all else I must distinguish between the voices and the accompaniment. I will take up the former first.

Everything I have to say here is based on the distinction between *painting* and *expression*. This distinction has existed for a long time, but nevertheless, I fear, has not been given proper attention.

A pure idea of the understanding that has no reference to our desire, the pure, passionless representation of a thing as it is, without associated representations concerning whether it is good or bad, whether it compliments or counters our natural inclinations—this is not an aesthetic notion suited to the fine arts. It is not the sort of thing that the true poet will write, and least of all that he will write to be set to music. In every true poetic notion, and still more in every musico-poetic notion, we must be able to distinguish two things—the representation of the object, and the representation of the relation this object has to our desires. For we will esteem or despise it, love or hate it, be angry at it, frightened by it, or delight in it, stand in awe of it or pine for it, and so on.

In short, in any such notion two things must be distinguishable—the *objective* and the *subjective*.

In order to anticipate any confusion or misinterpretation, let me remind you that something that originally was subjective can become objective. That is, the representation of a feeling, whether someone else's or our own, can become the source of a new feeling, and sometimes even of a different, a contrary feeling. Someone else's joy can stir me to anger; I can be saddened to see myself take pleasure in something that my reason does not accept. In these examples the joy and pleasure are objective, the anger and sadness subjective.

In vocal music now, *painting* means the depiction of the *objective*, while the depiction of the *subjective* is no longer considered painting, but *expression*.

Fundamentally, of course, both are contained in our previous understanding of painting. Expression one could explain as the painting of the subjective—the painting of feeling. But I would prefer not to use the word feeling because a feeling is not always subjective, that is, the feeling prevailing in the soul right now. The subjective, as I said before, can become the objective; in the same way, I now say, can expression become painting. For example, if feeling is the object of a feeling, and the musician expresses the former feeling that is the object and not the latter, then he is painting. Or perhaps an object usually causes a certain feeling, but in the present case causes a different feeling, possibly one that is completely the opposite. If the composer takes the former for the latter, he has not expressed, but painted.

I hope by the above to have thoroughly specified and clarified the rule we so often repeat to the composer of vocal music, that it should express, and not paint.

This rule hardly needs proof. For:

First: If the objective is not in itself subjective, if it is an external matter or event, then according to one of the previous remarks, the vocal composer who would rather paint than express would be working for the very effect he can least obtain. And even if the objective is originally subjective, then it would still be quite absurd to prefer to paint the feeling that is not at the moment the ruling one rather than the one that now should engage the singer's entire soul.

Second: What else should song be but the most lively, sensuous, passionate speech? And what above all does a man in a passion want to use his speech for? What to him is the most important thing? Certainly not to describe the nature of the object that puts him in the passion, but to pour out and communicate the passion itself. Everything in him works toward this end—the tone of the voice, the facial muscles, the hands and feet.

Thus only expression attains the goal of song; painting destroys it.

But what if painting and expression sometimes coincide? That is, what if the painting of the objective sometimes serves as the expression of the subjective? Indeed if the expression of the subjective sometimes cannot occur without the painting of the objective?

This is in fact so often the case that I would like people to understand the previous rule differently. Instead of saying "The vocal composer should not paint, but express," we should rather say, "The vocal composer should take care not to paint against the expression." That he has painted is not in itself an error, for he can and should paint. It is only an error when he has painted the wrong thing or in the wrong place.

This insight is based on a distinction in our feelings to which we still probably pay too little attention. On the spur of the moment the following is the best way I know to state it. In the one kind of feeling the subjective fuses with— loses itself in—the objective. The passion can only satisfy itself by embracing the object as much as possible, the entire soul by imitating the object as much as possible. In the other kind of feeling the subjective and objective are in clear contrast with one another, and the passion satisfies itself by putting the soul in a setting that is completely opposed to the nature of the object. Since this distinction subdivides the feelings differently than do any of the well-known classifications, I suggest a new designation, in order to be able to express myself more succinctly. The former kind of feeling I will call *homogeneous*, the latter *heterogeneous*.

Examples will make everything clearer. Admiration of a great or noble object is a homogeneous feeling. The contemplating subject assumes as much as possible the nature and quality of the contemplated object. When one thinks on great objects, says *Home*,[9] the voice becomes full, and the breast expands. People who are thinking exalted thoughts raise their heads and lift their voices

9. Henry Home, Lord Kames (1696–1782), a Scottish judge whose *Elements of Criticism* (1762), praised by Samuel Johnson, was a systematic attempt to look beyond the conventional rules of literary composition to investigate the metaphysical principles of the fine arts.

and hands. The subject seeks in every way to imitate the object.

The case is already different with respect to adoration. Here the subject is in contrast with the object. He feels his own weakness, baseness, insignificance, and imperfection in relation to this object: the head is bowed; voice and hands sink down.

This is even more the case with fear. The greatness and strength that are perceived in the object are directed against the subject. The grander and stronger the one, the baser and weaker is the other. The fuller, more exalted, and more splendid the painting, the weaker, more diminished, and subdued is the expression.

From this the following rule directly emerges: in homogeneous feelings painting is expression; with heterogeneous ones painting destroys expression.

Nonetheless even when painting is actually justifiable, the composer should not paint recklessly. I will record here the cautions that are to be noted with this rule. But I will not bring proof, because I think that they are demonstrated by the previous remarks.

First: In the object to be painted there may be several attributes that music is capable of painting. The composer must take care to include only the ones in the prevailing sequence of ideas to which the soul attends. In the concept *sea,* for example, one should probably take into consideration in the actual association of ideas only its dangers, its depths, its broad expanse. It would be the most obvious sin against expression in this case to paint the gentle washing of the waves. If I remember correctly after so many years, *Hasse* did not avoid this error in the aria mentioned above, from the *Sant'Elena.* In the lines:

> Questo è il suol, per cui passai
> Tanti regni e tanto mar,[10]

he gave the last word an extension in the Italian manner expressing a gentle undulation, which must have been far from the mind of St. Helen as she sang. Generally this idea is certainly not suitable to be painted. But it is astonishing to what extent the Italian singsong has destroyed expression, even in the work of our most talented composers.

Second: If in the whole concept there is no precise, musically paintable attribute in the actual sequence of ideas that particularly attracts the attention, then the composer must refrain from descriptive painting altogether, and use simple declamation.

Third: He must judge the importance of each member of the whole sequence of representations—how long, with what degree of attention, the soul would linger on it. And then, if painting should turn out to become expression, he must decide how deeply he should venture to engage in painting. If instead of the main concept on which the soul is concentrating its full attention and around which all the others build and unite, he seizes on one of the secondary

---

10. "This is the hallowed ground [the tomb of Christ] for the sake of which I have travelled so far on land and sea."

concepts as the focus of his painting, he has committed the very same blunder as if he had set a misplaced stress. It is actually one that is even more unpleasant, because a passage of painting does not slip by as quickly as a tone.

Fourth: The severest offences against expression would be for the composer to paint not the idea but the word, to develop a representation that the words deny and negate, or to hold to the mere picture—to the metaphor—rather than to the things themselves. But we need not give warnings against errors of this sort; all warning is wasted on a person who could actually commit them.

I will still add a couple of remarks, however, in order to anticipate possible objections you might make.

First: Sometimes even in heterogeneous feelings painting accidentally becomes expression. For example, the object of veneration may be the humility, gentleness, and submissiveness of a holy man, or the object of fear may be the uncertainty of the surrounding darkness and a deep, distant, intermittent roar heard in this darkness. In this case the composer can choose almost no other expression than the one with which he would also paint the object.

Second: Occasionally the painting of a secondary detail, which, strictly speaking, should not be considered in the sequence of ideas, turns out either to aid the expression, or at least not to hinder it. *Hasse* in the aria:

> Del Calvario già sorger le cime
> Veggo altere di tempio sublime,
> E i gran Duci del Rè delle sfere
> Pellegrini la tomba adorar![11]

from the oratorio mentioned several times earlier, has introduced the sort of painting of a secondary detail that does not offend my sensibilities at any rate. He paints the arrival of the great commanders-in-chief with a magnificent phrase in march style, which seems remarkably well suited to the joyously exalted feeling that should dominate the whole of the aria. Genius commits those apparent transgressions of the rules in all the arts, and the critic is wrong to find fault with them. But it is equally wrong to allow genius to set itself above all the rules on this account. As long as genius is really genius it remains within the rules, and seems to be violating them only because the rules are still not sufficiently defined and modified. In fact the relation that prevails between theory and practice in most of the arts is still the following: theory is far less useful for perfecting works than are works useful for correcting theory.

As to the instrumental accompaniment, this is primarily what I have to say: far more painting is allowed there than in the voice. Hence in the accompaniments of their arias, and especially in their recitatives, even the best, most expressive composers have not limited themselves to carrying on the expression of the feeling, but have often tried as well to support and enhance that feeling by depicting the object that gave rise to it. *Graun* in the well-known aria:

11. "Already from Calvary I see the proud spires of the lofty temple rising, and the grand Dukes of the King of the heavens coming as pilgrims to worship at the tomb!"

Wenn ich am Rande dieses Lebens
Abgründe sehe . . . [12]

introduced a splendid painting of the dreadful judge into the accompaniment, and this was no error. In the voice, on the other hand, it would be an obvious error.

Nevertheless even in the accompaniment the painting must depict only essential attributes of the object that have a connection with the feeling, and the painting must not be so heterogeneous to the expression that it destroys the feeling instead of maintaining it. This would be the case, for example, if a serious sequence of thoughts were interrupted by a bit of comic painting. This error has been made often by one recent composer—or rather, a composer only lately become well-known, who is otherwise excellent. It makes the most adverse impression in the world when in a thoroughly serious and uplifting piece the beating of the heart is accompanied with *pizzicato,* or the hissing of the serpent is imitated by the violins.

If it were not unsuitable in a letter to you, I would also apply the rules I have established to declamation and mime. For in truth these rules hold for all the kinetic arts. But you can apply them automatically as soon as you have just the slightest notion of those arts and the means by which they operate.

I am with the greatest esteem, etc.

12. "When I see the abysses at the brink of this life . . . " This text is the second section of a da capo aria from Carl Heinrich Graun's Passion cantata *Der Tod Jesu* (1755). It continues: "When I hear the Judge approach with his scales and thunderbolts, and the globe quakes at his step, who then will be my protector?" Engel must be referring to the disjunct dotted figures in the accompaniment that alternate with its pulsing bass line.

140 Wolfgang Amadeus Mozart

We have few substantive statements from Mozart about the nature of the musical art and the process of composition. Fortunately, however, he was in lively correspondence with his father from Vienna while he was composing *Idomeneo,* in 1780–81, and *Die Entführung aus dem Serail,* in the fall of 1781. In the case of *Idomeneo,* Leopold Mozart was the intermediary between his son and the librettist, the Jesuit-trained Giovanni Battista Varesco, a chaplain to the Archbishop of Salzburg. Hence son and father had long exchanges about issues of dramatic effectiveness—where best to place an aria, for example, how to make the action seem natural, or how long a section should last. Mozart was anxious to keep the speech of the subterranean voice tellingly brief, remarking that the Ghost's speech in *Hamlet* (which he had most probably seen in a Salzburg adaptation) would be far more effective if it were not so long. In composing *Die Entführung,* Mozart again worked closely with a compliant librettist,

Gottlieb Stephanie, the director of the National-Singspiel in Vienna. In the following two letters to his father about this collaboration, Mozart touched on a wide range of subjects—characterization in music and the nature of musical expression, the relation of words to music, the success of the Italian comic style, and the problems attendant on meeting the demands of performers and audience.

Letters to His Father

Vienna, September 26, 1781

Mon Trés Cher Pére!

Forgive me for having made you pay an extra heavy postage fee the other day. But I happened to have no necessary business to report and thought that it would afford you pleasure if I gave you some idea of my opera. As the original text began with a monologue,[1] I asked Herr Stephanie to make a little arietta out of it—and then to put in a duet instead of making the two chatter together after Osmin's short song.[2] As we have given the part of Osmin to Herr Fischer,[3] who certainly has an excellent bass voice (in spite of the fact that the Archbishop[4] told me that he sang too low for a bass and that I assured him that he would sing higher next time), we must take advantage of it, particularly as he has the whole Viennese public on his side. But in the original libretto Osmin has only this short song and nothing else to sing, except in the trio and the finale; so he has been given an aria in Act 1, and he is to have another in Act 2. I have explained to Stephanie the words I require for this aria—indeed I had finished composing most of the music for it before Stephanie knew anything whatever about it. I am enclosing only the beginning and the end, which is bound to have a good effect. Osmin's rage is turned into the comic mode by bringing in Turkish music. In working out the aria I have (in spite of our Salzburg Midas)[5] allowed Fischer's beautiful deep notes to glow. The passage "Drum beim Barte des Propheten"[6] is indeed in the same tempo, but with rapid notes; and as Osmin's rage gradually increases—just as one thinks the aria is at an end—the Allegro assai, in a totally different tempo and in a different key, is bound to make the very best effect. For a person who finds himself

TEXT: Translation by Emily Anderson, *The Letters of Mozart and His Family* (2 vols.; London: St. Martin's Press, 1966), vol. 2, pp. 768–70, 772–73, with minor alterations. Used by permission of The Macmillan Press Ltd.

1. The original text, *Belmonte und Konstanze* (1780), was the work of Christoph Friedrich Bretzner (1748–1807), a Leipzig merchant who had written several popular light-opera libretti.
2. It is worthy of note that the part of Osmin, which in Bretzner's libretto is negligible, was transformed by Mozart in collaboration with Stephanie into a towering figure in *Die Entführung*. Possibly Mozart was encouraged to do this as he was composing for a magnificent singer. [Tr.]
3. Ludwig Fischer (1745–1825), a preeminent German bass, worked in Vienna from 1780 to 1783.
4. Hieronymus, Count Colloredo, Archbishop of Salzburg since 1772, was Mozart's patron.
5. That is, the Archbishop. [Tr.]
6. "Thus by the beard of the prophets . . . " (Act 1, no. 3).

in such a towering rage oversteps all bounds of order, proportion, and purpose—he does not recognize himself; so the music, too, must no longer recognize itself. But since the passions, whether violent or not, must never be expressed to the point of exciting disgust, and music, even in the most terrible situations, must still give pleasure and never offend the ear, that is, must always remain *music,* so I have not chosen a key remote from F (in which the aria is written) but one related to it—not the nearest, D minor, but the more remote A minor. Let me now turn to Belmonte's aria in A major, "O wie ängstlich, o wie feurig."[7] Would you like to know how I have expressed it—and even indicated his throbbing heart? By the two violins playing octaves. This is the favorite aria of all those who have heard it, and it is mine also. I wrote it expressly to suit Adamberger's voice.[8] You feel the trembling—the faltering—you see how his throbbing breast begins to swell; this I have expressed by a crescendo. You hear the whispering and the sighing—which I have indicated by the first violins with mutes and a flute playing in unison.

The Janissary chorus is, as such, all that can be desired, that is, short, lively, and written to please the Viennese. I have sacrificed Constanze's aria a little to the flexible throat of Mlle Cavalieri,[9] "Trennung war mein banges Los and nun schwimmt mein Aug' in Tränen."[10] I have tried to express her feelings, as far as an Italian bravura aria will allow it. I have changed the "Hui" to "schnell," so it now runs thus—"Doch wie schnell schwand meine Freude."[11] I really don't know what our German poets are thinking of. Even if they do not understand the theater, or at all events operas, yet they should not make their characters talk as if they were addressing a herd of swine. Hui, sow!

Now for the trio at the close of Act I. Pedrillo has passed off his master as an architect—to give him an opportunity of meeting his Constanze in the garden. Bassa Selim has taken him into his service. Osmin, the steward, knows nothing of this, and being a rude churl and a sworn foe to all strangers, is impertinent and refuses to let them into the garden. It opens quite abruptly—and because the words lend themselves to it, I have made it a fairly respectable piece of three-part writing. Then the major key begins at once *pianissimo*—it must go very quickly—and wind up with a great deal of noise, which is always appropriate at the end of an act. The more noise the better, and the shorter the better, so that the audience may not have time to cool down with their applause.

I have sent you only fourteen bars of the overture, which is very short with

7. "O how fearfully, O how passionately [beats my loving heart]" (Act 1, no. 4).
8. Josef Valentin Adamberger (1743–1804) was a German tenor based in Vienna during the 1780s who was particularly known for his performance of expressive arias in moderate tempos.
9. Caterina Cavalieri, an Austrian soprano, was known for her imposing upper range and impressive flexibility. She also appeared as Donna Elvira in the first Vienna production of Mozart's *Don Giovanni.*
10. "Parting was my dreadful fate, and now my eyes swim with tears" ("Ah ich liebte," Act 1, no. 6).
11. "But how quickly my joy vanished."

alternate *fortes* and *pianos*, the Turkish music always coming in at the *fortes*. The overture modulates through different keys; and I doubt whether anyone, even if his previous night has been a sleepless one, could go to sleep over it. Now comes the rub! The first act was finished more than three weeks ago, as was also one aria in Act II and the drunken duet[12] (*per i signori viennesi*) which consists entirely of *my Turkish tattoo*. But I cannot compose any more, because the whole story is being altered—and, to tell the truth, at my own request. At the beginning of Act 3 there is a charming quintet or rather finale, but I should prefer to have it at the end of Act 2.[13] In order to make this practicable, great changes must be made, in fact an entirely new plot must be introduced—and Stephanie is up to the eyes in other work. So we must have a little patience. Everyone abuses Stephanie. It may be that in my case he is only very friendly to my face. But after all he is arranging the libretto for me—and, what is more, as I want it—exactly—and, by Heaven, I do not ask anything more of him. Well, how I have been chattering to you about my opera! But I cannot help it. Please send me the march[14] that I mentioned the other day.[15] Gilowsky says that Daubrawaick[16] will soon be here. Fräulein Auernhammer[17] and I are longing to have the two double concertos.[18] I hope we shall not wait as vainly as the Jews for their Messiah. Well, adieu. Farewell. I kiss your hands a thousand times and embrace with all my heart my dear sister, whose health, I hope, is improving, and am ever your most obedient son

W: A: MOZART

Vienna, October 13, 1781

Mon Trés Cher Pére!

•   •   •   •   •

Now as to the libretto of the opera. You are quite right so far as Stephanie's work is concerned. Still, the poetry is perfectly in keeping with the character of stupid, surly, malicious Osmin. I am well aware that the verse is not of the best, but it fitted in and it agreed so well with the musical ideas which already were buzzing in my head, that it could not fail to please me; and I would like

---

12. The duet between Pedrillo and Osmin, "Vivat Bacchus, Bacchus lebe." [Tr.]
13. This is the quartet at the end of Act 2. [Tr.]
14. Probably K. 249, written in 1776 for the wedding of Elizabeth Haffner to F. X. Späth, for which Mozart also composed K. 250 [248b], the Haffner serenade. [Tr.]
15. The letter in which Mozart made this request has unfortunately been lost. [Tr.]
16. Franz Wenzel Gilowsky von Urazowa (1757–1816) was a young surgeon in Vienna and had been best man at Mozart's wedding. Daubrawaick was possibly a son of Johann Anton Daubrawa von Daubrawaick, Court Councillor in Salzburg, who was to bring Mozart music from Salzburg. [Tr.]
17. Fräulein Josepha Auernhammer (1758–1820) became Mozart's pupil on the clavier, and he wrote for her his sonata for two pianos, K. 448 [375a]. [Tr.]
18. K. 365 [316a], composed in 1779, and K. 242, a concerto for three claviers, composed in 1776, which Mozart himself had arranged for two. [Tr.]

to wager that when it is performed, no deficiencies will be found. As for the poetry which was there originally, I really have nothing to say against it. Belmonte's aria "O wie ängstlich" could hardly be better written for music. Except for "Hui" and "Kummer ruht in meinem Schoss"[19] (for sorrow—cannot rest), the aria too is not bad, particularly the first part. Besides, I should say that in an opera the poetry must be altogether the obedient daughter of the music. Why do Italian comic operas please everywhere—in spite of their miserable libretti—even in Paris, where I myself witnessed their success? Just because there the music reigns supreme and when one listens to it all else is forgotten. Why, an opera is sure of success when the plot is well worked out, the words written solely for the music and not shoved in here and there to suit some miserable rhyme (which, God knows, never enhances the value of any theatrical performance, be it what it may, but rather detracts from it)—I mean, words or even entire verses which ruin the composer's whole idea. Verses are indeed the most indispensable element for music—but rhymes—solely for the sake of rhyming—the most detrimental. Those high and mighty people who set to work in this pedantic fashion will always come to grief, both they and their music. The best thing of all is when a good composer, who understands the stage and is talented enough to make sound suggestions, meets an able poet, that true phoenix; in that case no fears need be entertained as to the applause even of the ignorant. Poets almost remind me of trumpeters with their professional tricks! If we composers were always to stick so faithfully to our rules (which were very good at a time when no one knew better), we should be concocting music as unpalatable as their libretti.

Well, I think I have chattered enough nonsense to you; so I must now enquire about what interests me most of all, and that is, your health, my most beloved father! In my last letter I suggested two remedies for giddiness, which, if you do not know them, you will probably not think any good. But I have been assured that they would certainly have a splendid effect; and the pleasure of thinking that you might recover made me believe this assurance so entirely that I could not refrain from suggesting them with my heart's wishes and with the sincere desire that you may not need them—but that if you do use them, you will recover completely. I trust that my sister is improving daily. I kiss her with all my heart and, my dearest, most beloved father, I kiss your hands a thousand times and am ever your most obedient son.

W. A. MOZART

[P. S.:] As soon as I receive the watch, I shall return yours. Adieu.

19. "Sorrow rests in my bosom."

141 Michel-Paul-Guy de Chabanon

Michel-Paul-Guy de Chabanon was a well-educated man of broad interests: in addition to musical pursuits, he wrote translations and commentaries of ancient Greek texts. Born in the West Indies in 1729 or 1730, he was educated in Paris, where he lived until his death in 1792. He was a violinist of considerable reputation and a composer of instrumental works as well as a youthful opera and several librettos. Although Jean-Philippe Rameau was his mentor and friend (he published a eulogy for the composer after his death in 1764), and he remained faithful to the conviction that the French did indeed have a music, nonetheless his notions about the primacy of melody in music were closer to those of Rousseau. With this independence of mind, and perhaps also because of his involvement with instrumental music, he was able to stand outside the wrangles of the "Querelle des bouffons" and its successors.

In his essay *De la musique considérée en elle-même et dans ses rapports avec la parole, les langues, la poésie, et le théâtre* (*On Music Considered in Itself and in Its Relations with Speech, Languages, Poetry, and the Theater*) he became one of the first writers to argue for the autonomy of music, for its independence from the strictures of imitation. Music to him was most appropriately nonrepresentational, and imitation an unnatural conjuring trick. He did not, however, take the position to the conclusions that would be reached by some nineteenth-century aestheticians. His proposal—that music can offer to the ear only voluptuous sensation—showed a willingness to accept disappointing limits for the art in return for the gift of autonomy.

FROM *On Music Considered in Itself and in Its Relations with Speech, Languages, Poetry, and the Theater*

(1785)

CHAPTER III. CONTINUATION OF THE SAME INVESTIGATION

Let us extend the principle I have just established[1] as far as it can go; let us carry it to the point of exaggeration. None of the steps we take beyond the truth will be wasted in our investigations; to go beyond our limits in this way is to explore the approaches to the place in which we are trying to make ourselves unassailable.

To take the words in their strict sense, song can only imitate that which sings. What am I saying? Its power does not always extend as far as that. The warbling of birds could never be well rendered by our music. For music is subject to laws, to harmonic relationships, while the birds, inaccurate melodists that they are, connect their tones according to an order that harmony does not approve. Also since the time when the lyric poets called the birds to the aid of the art that they favored, this art, ineffectual in its means of imitation, has not gained one step toward the object that people have so often prescribed that it imitate. A strange art of imitation, that renders the things most analogous to it in such a way that the copy never resembles the model!

I should not suppress the response that M. l'Abbé Morellet makes to this difficulty, which he himself proposed; the more ingenious it is, the more it is our duty to cite it.[2]

> All the arts make a kind of contract with the soul and the senses they affect: this contract consists in demanding liberties, and promising pleasures that they would not give without these happy liberties .... Music takes such liberties: it demands that its movement be rhythmic and its periods rounded off, that the voice be supported and strengthened by the accompaniment, *which is certainly not in nature.*

TEXT: The original edition (Paris, 1785; Slatkin Reprints: Geneva, 1969), pp. 46–63, 104–113. Translation by Wye J. Allanbrook.

1. In Chapter 2 Chabanon states that the essence of music is song, or melody, and that only through singing can music please. Music in its primitive state is only song, and we should look to this primitive state to know its essence.
2. The brief essay in which M. l'Abbé Morellet discusses musical expression is full of shrewd and accurate opinions: I doubt that anything better has been written on music. [Au.] In his short essay *On Expression in Music and Imitation in the Arts* (1771), André Morellet argued that music, like the other arts, is imitative, and that proper imitation is a selective activity—the embellishment of nature rather than its slavish simulation.

Without a doubt this alters the truth of the imitation, but increases its beauty at the same time, and gives the copy a charm that nature refused to the original.

Nothing resembles the song of the nightingale so much as the sounds of that little pipe that children fill with water, and set to chirping with their breath. What pleasure does this imitation give us? None. But if we hear a flexible voice and a pleasing symphony expressing (less clearly, to be sure) the song of the same nightingale, the ear and the soul are in rapture. For the arts are something more than a precise imitation of nature.

I understand everything that is ingenious and true in this response. But may I be permitted to ask M. l'Abbé Morellet why poetry, painting, and sculpture are obliged to give us faithful, precise images that resemble the objects they imitate, and why music is exempt? Isn't it because this art is less than the others an art of imitation? The children's pipe that we take for the nightingale itself gives us no pleasure, and the light symphony, which resembles the bird song almost not at all, pleases and charms us. Do not these two facts demonstrate that imitation has very little place in the pleasure that music gives us, and that that pleasure depends almost entirely on the charm of melody?

Man's instinct is prodigiously imitative; he demonstrates this from infancy. But if I am not deceived, imitation only amuses him in so far as he understands its difficulty and its success astonishes him: if a child with his mouth alone were to mimic the nightingale as perfectly as he did with the pipe, we would hear him with more pleasure and interest than we did the pipe. Thus it is certainly wrong that, in the theory of the arts, we pretend to count as nothing a difficulty conquered; it ought to be of great account in the pleasure that the arts provide. The noble impression of the sublime arises partly from the surprise that a conception that is very remote from us causes in us. What we discover easily we enjoy only slightly.

But, you may say, if music is not the imitation of nature, then what is it? What a strange need of the human mind to torment itself with difficulties that it conjures up gratuitously, and that it cannot resolve because they are meaningless! Music is for the hearing what the objects that affect them agreeably are for each of our senses. Why then do you not want the ear to have its immediate pleasures, its voluptuous sensations, just as do sight and smell? And in music are they other than those pleasures that result from tones harmoniously combined? Is it because it pleased you to call music an art that you mean to subject it to all things characteristic of the arts? Come now! Do you know to what extent this term *art* is suited to music? We will examine that eventually; first let us finish demonstrating that music pleases independently of all imitation.

CHAPTER IV. MUSIC PLEASES INDEPENDENTLY OF ALL IMITATION

Animals are susceptible to music. Thus music need not imitate in order to please, for the most perfect imitation is nothing to an animal. If you show one its image drawn on canvas, it will be neither moved nor surprised by the sight. We only enjoy imitation to the extent that we understand its difficulty, but this understanding exceeds the intelligence of animals.

The baby who delights in the songs of his nurse does not seek in them anything that is imitative; he enjoys them like the milk that nourishes him.

The savage, the black, the sailor, the common man—they repeat the songs that amuse them without at the same time requiring the character of the songs to accord with the actual disposition of their souls.

A skilled hand preluding on the harp or harpsichord engages the most knowledgeable listeners. Imitation counts for nothing in the formation of a prelude.

Music has soothed, even cured, sick people: this fact is attested by the Academy of Sciences, and I have seen proof of it. A young person bled six times for an acute pain in the eye forgot his sufferings for two hours while hearing someone play the harpsichord. Is it by virtue of the imitation that such a spell is brought about? Is a mind seized by suffering in a state to enjoy a pleasure that requires reflection?

Thus music acts immediately on our senses. But the human mind, that quick, active, curious, reflective intelligence, interferes with the pleasure of the senses; it cannot be an idle and indifferent spectator. What part can it take in sounds, which because they have in themselves no determinate meaning never offer clear and distinct ideas? It searches for relationships there, for analogies with various objects and with various natural effects. And what happens? Among the nations where intelligence has been brought to perfection, music, anxious to obtain in some way the approval of the intellect, strives to present to it the kinds of relationships or analogies that will please it. Music imitates to the extent that it can, and at the express command of the intellect, which, enticing the art further than its end directs, proposes imitation to it as a secondary goal. But the intellect, which for its own part appreciates the weakness of the means that music uses in order to succeed in imitation, makes few difficulties on this point. The slightest analogies, the most flimsy relationships suffice for it. It calls this art *imitative,* when it scarcely imitates. It bears in mind the efforts that music makes to please it, and is content with the part that has been assigned it in pleasures that would seem to have been designed uniquely for the ear.

No one who has not been completely blinded by the systematic spirit, which one should not want to impose either on oneself or on others, should silence objections that are contrary to the opinion one holds. Here is an objection that at first intimidated me in my opinion: If the pleasure of music is for the ear what a handsome face is for our eyes, why is it more necessary to make one of these sensations imitative than it is the other? Aristotle, in his *Problems,*[3] pro-

---

3. The *Problemata,* attributed to Aristotle and assembled around 100 C.E., were collections of materials compiled by his successors.

poses to himself almost the same difficulty, in different terms. This is how he answers it:

> No sensation produced by an object without movement can be imitative; it cannot have any conformity with our actions, our customs, or our characters. If you have the ear hear only one tone, and you continue its duration, this lifeless and inactive sensation will not represent anything to the intellect. On the other hand, if several tones succeed one another, as in music, their progression, be it slow or rapid, uniform or varied, will give them a character, and make them capable of being likened to other objects.

Thus a handsome face, presenting just the same sight and same object, is at the most capable of being compared only to another handsome object itself. But for want of variation and difference, it does not lead the intellect to make it the symbol of disparate actions and effects.

I want to note that it is only proper for music to link to one another the successive sensations it causes in us, so that they relate to and modify one another. Let us try to make that clearer. If you affect the senses of sight, smell, or touch successively by the presence of various objects that replace one another, these sensations will not be bound to one another, and the one that is ceasing will have no effect on the one that supplants it.[4] But in music the tone you no longer hear is bound by memory to those that follow it. Together they are a body; they are parts of the same whole. To distort the phrase you are hearing, sometimes all that is needed is to detach it from the one that came before.

CHAPTER V. IN WHAT MANNER MUSIC PRODUCES ITS IMITATIONS.[5]

See how quickly we have moved away from the paradox that we seemed at first to want to maintain, that music lacks the proper means for imitation. In the process of pruning from that assertion what was exaggerated in it, we are brought to the examination of the means by which music imitates. Music likens (as much as it can) its sounds to other sounds, its movements to other movements, and the sensations that it produces to affections that are analogous to them. This last means of imitating will be the subject of another chapter.

Musical imitation is perceptibly genuine only when it has songs for its object. In music one truthfully imitates military fanfares, hunting airs, rustic songs, etc. It is only a question of giving one melody the character of another melody. In that case, art suffers no violence. When it moves beyond that, however, imitation grows weak, because of the insufficiency of means that music may employ.

---

4. In *Observations on Music* (1779), an earlier version of this essay, Chabanon adds by way of example that if you smell a rose after having smelled another flower, the rose's perfume will not be modified.

5. This chapter is one of those where our ideas happen to be in agreement with those of M. l'Abbé Morellet. [Au.]

Is it a question of representing a brook? The continual slight fluctuation of two notes that are neighbors to each other makes the music ripple rather like the water that flows along. This relationship, which presents itself first to the intellect, is the only one of which the art has availed itself up to now, and I doubt we will ever discover another one more striking. The desire to depict a brook thus necessarily unites all the musicians who have it and who will have it with a melodic configuration that is common knowledge and almost worn out. The disposition of the notes is as it were foreseen and given in advance. Melody, the slave of this constraint, will have less grace and novelty. According to this calculation, the ear loses by that representation almost everything that the intellect gains from it.

Now add to the depiction of the brooks the twittering of the birds. In this case the imitative musician makes the voice and instruments sustain long cadences; he mixes in roulades, although there has never been a bird that used roulades in its song. This imitation has the double inconvenience of being quite imperfect on the one hand, and on the other, of constraining musician to forms that have been often used. M. l'Abbé Morellet is lavish in his praise of the Italian air whose words are *If the nightingale loses* [*its mate*]. Although I do not recall that air precisely, I would venture to guarantee that the part of it that is the most agreeable is not that part that strives to imitate the song of the nightingale.

Given a skillful composer forced by the text to depict the brook that murmurs and the bird that twitters, would we dare to blame him if he reasoned as follows? "My art cannot render with truth the effects that my poet expects of it: in striving to achieve them, I run the risk of resembling all those who have attempted the same picture. The depiction of the water, of the flowers, of the zephyrs, of the greenery, is considered so lyrical only because the view of a cheerful and pastoral site produces a gentle impression on our senses, and disposes our souls to a blissful calm. If then, refraining from imitating what I cannot render, I were to imagine only a suave and tranquil melody, the sort one would like to hear when resting in the cool shade, in sight of the most beautiful countryside, would I be failing my poet and my art?" As long as this reasoning artist was a man of talent, so that he could execute such a plan, I know no way in which the partisans of imitation could reproach him.

The sky is overcast, the winds whistle, the thunder prolongs its long reverberations from one end of the horizon to the other. . . . How ineffective music is in depicting such effects, especially if the musician strives to detail them, and introduces the expectation of a painted likeness! Here a volley of ascending or descending notes will express either the lightning, or the force of the wind, or the thunderclap. For he has a choice among all these effects; the same vivid trait belongs to them all, and suits them equally. Instead, do away with all these busy pictures that depict nothing, and paint in broad strokes! Let the fracas, the tumult, the disorder of the symphony depict the disorder and the noise of the storm, and above all let the melody be such that no one can say: *All this is mere noise, without expression or character.*

One day I was present at an evening concert on the boulevard; the orchestra was numerous and quite loud. They were performing the overture from *Pygmalion.*[6] It looked as though it was going to storm. At the *fortissimo* of the reprise we heard a thunder clap. We all felt an extraordinary relation between the symphony and the meteor that rumbled in the sky. Rameau turned out in that moment to have made a picture with an intention and a resemblance that neither he nor anyone else would have suspected. Musical artists, you who reflect on your art, does this example teach you anything?

There is one effect in nature that music renders rather truthfully—the moaning of the angry waves. Many basses playing in unison, and making the melody roll like waves that rise and fall, create a tumult similar to that of an agitated sea. We all once heard a symphony in which the author had used this unison, without pictorial intent. The imitative effect of it was so generally felt that this symphony was called *The Tempest*, although there was nothing else there that could justify this designation. Given such facts, would one not be right to call music *the art of painting without suspecting it?*

Let us speak of another imitation, the kind that depicts to one of our senses what is subject to another, as when sound imitates light.

Everyone knows the story of the blind man who was given a picture in which one could see men, trees, and herds. The incredulous blind man carefully ran his hand over all the parts of the canvas, and finding there only a plane surface, could not imagine that so many different objects were represented on it. This example proves that one sense is not the judge of something that another sense experiences. Also, it is not properly for the ear that we depict in music what strikes the eyes: it is for the intellect, which, situated between the two senses, combines and compares their sensations.

If you tell a musician to depict the light taken abstractly, he will confess the impotence of his art. But tell him to paint the dawn, and he will feel that the contrast of clear and piercing sounds, put into opposition with mute and veiled sounds, can resemble the contrast between light and darkness. From this point of comparison he knows how to imitate. But what is he actually depicting? Not day and night, but only a contrast, and a contrast of any kind. The first one that comes into your mind will be expressed just as well by the same music as that of light and darkness.

Let us not fear to repeat this for the instruction of artists: the musician who produces such pictures does nothing if he does not produce them with felicitous melodies. To paint is only the second of his duties; to sing is the first. If he does not satisfy that, what is he worth? Because of the weakness in his art he paints imperfectly; because of the weakness in his own talent, he fails in the principal functions of his art.

---

6. An *acte de ballet* composed by Jean-Philippe Rameau and first performed in 1748.

How can music paint what strikes the eyes, while painting makes no attempt to render what is in the province of hearing? Painting is bound by its essence to imitate, and that faithfully; if painting does not imitate, it is no longer anything. Speaking only to the eyes, it can only imitate what strikes the sight. Music, on the contrary, pleases without imitation, by the sensations that it brings about. Since its pictures are always imperfect, consisting often of a simple and slender analogy with the object it wishes to paint, such relationships multiply easily. In short, painting imitates only what is proper to it, because it must imitate rigorously. Music can paint everything, because it paints it all imperfectly.

•　　•　　•　　•　　•

CHAPTER X. OF THE MUSICAL SENSATIONS APPLICABLE TO OUR VARIOUS AFFECTIONS, AND OF THE NATURAL MEANS OF EXPRESSION PROPER TO MUSIC

A particular song pleases you—you love to hear it. That can only be because it produces in you an impression of some kind. Study this impression; examine its nature and character. It is impossible that you would not recognize whether it is bitter or sweet, lively or tranquil; the movement alone should indicate this to you. Is it sweet or tender? Adapt to it words of the same sort, and you will render expressive a piece of music that earlier you wouldn't have suspected of being so. From a sensation that is all but vague and indeterminate, you shape a sentiment of which you can give an account.

I beg the reader to master his imagination, and not to let it go faster than this discussion allows. A little further on he will find the developments and clarifications that he has a right to expect from us.

The air that we would call *tender* does not perhaps dispose us precisely in the same circumstance of body and mind as we would experience if we were actually moved to pity by a wife, a father, or a friend. But between these two situations, the one actual, the other musical (if I may be allowed this manner of speaking), the analogy is such that the mind agrees to accept the one for the other.

Why, it will be said, do you want the effect of such music to be only a sensation, and not a distinct sentiment? — Reader, I wish it for this reason: because in questioning you about an air without words that may have given you pleasure, if I ask you what distinct sentiment it arouses in you, you would not know how to tell me. I suggest a tender air, and I ask you if it is the tenderness of a happy or an unhappy lover that the air inspires in you; if it is that of a lover for his mistress, or of a son for his father, etc., etc., etc. If all these different feelings equally suit the air of which we are speaking, am I wrong if I would sooner call its effect a rather vague sensation than a determinate sentiment? Moreover—I repeat this once more—let us not go any faster than necessary. What we are advancing here in a general and superficial manner will be determined elsewhere with more precision.

What are the natural means that give melody a character of sadness or of gaiety, of gentleness or of resolution? In undertaking to resolve such questions, I advance, so to speak, into the shadows with which nature cloaks and surrounds all first causes. I will go wherever the torch of experience leads me. And the more obscure the subject is, the more I will make it my duty only to lay down incontestable assertions.

It is the nature of sustained tones to impart a character of sadness. Don't think that this is a fact of convention. No; men have not made a contract among themselves to find the cry of the turtle-dove plaintive and the song of the blackbird joyful. If the nightingale mingles several tones with one another and sounds them together, you will associate with this musical language a notion less sad than if the solitary bird had made a sound in the night that he drew out for several beats. Is it not recognized that a uniform sound, like that of a voice that reads on the same tone, induces us to sleep? If the sound has this direct an effect on us, why should we deny other effects that are no more astonishing?

In general the minor mode produces an impression that is gentler, softer, and more sensitive than that of the major mode. Don't ask the reason for it; no one is in a position to tell you. But a move from one of these modes to the other makes this different impression perceptible to every musical ear. The sixth note of the scale in the minor mode is more sensitive than all the others; each time it appears, even in the most joyful Allegro, it requires from the performer a softer and more expressive inflection. The fourth note of the scale has this quality in the major mode. It is the note that by means of its intrinsic quality summons the performer to a pathetic expression even when the rest of the melody is directing him to a different sensation. High-pitched tones have a certain clarity and brilliance that seem to invite the soul to joy. Compare the high strings of the harp to the low strings of the same instrument, and you will feel how the latter dispose the soul more easily to tenderness. Who knows if these broad undulations of strings that are long and less taut do not communicate similar vibrations to our nerves, and if this disposition of our body is not what gives us affective sentiments? Believe me, man is only an instrument; his fibers respond to the strings of the lyrical instruments, which assail these fibers and interrogate them. Each tone, each instrument has its own qualities, from which melody profits handily, but which she also controls at her pleasure; for the most sensitive instrument can successfully articulate joyful songs.

Tender music uses movements without rapidity. It binds the sounds, rather than contrasting them or making them collide with one another. In music of this character the staccato breve does not imperiously control the dotted long that is joined to it, and the performer tempers his tones with broad vibrato. Those whom taste inclines to sadness draw out the sounds (following the observation that we have already made), and their bow fears to leave the string; their voice gives the song a certain indolent idleness. Joyful music dots the notes and makes the tones leap; the bow is always in the air, and the voice imitates it.

These are pretty much the natural means that music has at its disposal, and with the aid of which it produces sensations in us. The composer, man of genius that he is, who has experienced all these effects and applies them appropriately to words and situations, is an expressive musician. It will be obvious to the reader that all the means of expression are in the province of melody, not of harmony.

An essential observation, and one that stands at the very foundation of our doctrine, is that in the most expressive air, almost always—I would even say necessarily—there are ideas and passages contradictory to the character of the expression that ought to dominate it. Let us cite an example. In the first verset of the *Stabat*,[7] I see no verse or word that does not require the same nuance of sadness.

> Stabat mater dolorosa,
> Juxta crucem lacrimosa,
> Dum pendebat Filius.[8]

At the beginning of the work music makes use of all its expressive means. The tempo is slow, the sounds weak and veiled; they progress slowly, and legato. The expression is well established here. In the tenth measure, however, everything changes: a *fortissimo* succeeds a *piano,* and the sounds that cringed darkling in the bass of the *octave* suddenly rise up, reinforced to excess, and combat with and contradict those that preceded them with their proud *détaché.* Where does this incongruity come from? From the fact that music, in its essence, is not an imitative art. It lends itself to imitation as much as it can, but this act of complaisance cannot distract it from the functions that its actual nature imposes on it. One of these necessary functions is to vary its modifications from moment to moment, combining in the same piece the *gentle* and the *strong,* the *legato* and the *détaché,* the proud articulation and the tender one. This art, so considered, is of an ungovernable inconstancy; all its charm depends on its rapid transformations. I know that it often comes back to the same things in each piece, but without lingering on them. Now across all these fleeting and fugitive forms how do you expect the imitation to be unified, and to progress with an even step? On limping foot it follows this playful and changeable thing that is music, overtaking it sometimes, and sometimes letting it go its way alone. If the proof I advance for this is found in the first couplet of the *Stabat*—so beautiful, so expressive, so short, and composed of only two ideas—in what Italian air will this proof not manifest itself with even more clarity?

Reader, no matter how little of a musician you may be, you are now in a position to judge the dramatic system of M. Gluck. Now you understand how, being devoted to expression, which he rightly regards as the foundation of all theatrical illusion, he only permits himself an entire air when the situation itself

---

7. Most probably the setting of the *Stabat mater* by Pergolesi; see pp. 743 and 926, n. 8.
8. "There stood the grieving mother / Weeping beside the cross, / While her son was crucified."

permits music those digressions, those indeterminate wanderings in which melody delights. Whenever a periodic and coherent song would make the action languish, and would transform the actor into a singer at his music stand, M. Gluck quickly cuts off this melody that has just begun, and by another movement, or a simple recitative, he restores the singing to the continuity of the action, and makes them flow together. It is inconceivable that a system so true could have been disapproved of in a country where the art of the theater is so well known. It is even more inconceivable that among its critics there could have been men who in their position and their wisdom ought to have defended the rights of the stage against the rights of music. In Italy men of letters have said that theater music was no longer for the enjoyment of intellectuals. Here the intellectuals, not being real musicians, have maintained that the operas of M. Gluck were made more for the intellect than for the ear. But while they were entertaining this judgment, the most delicate and trained ears were nourishing themselves with delights from M. Gluck's music. I do not think that there have ever been judgments more calculated to astonish.

142 Germaine de Staël

Germaine de Staël (1766–1817) was a fresh young intelligence shaped in the salons of pre-Revolutionary Paris. She was the daughter of a middle-class Swiss banker, Jacques Necker, who as the finance minister for Louis XVI managed to keep the loyalty both of the monarch and the people, at least in the Revolution's early days. She became a literary critic and novelist as well as a passionate student of politics who spoke out against the monarchy in a manner uncharacteristic of any private citizen, much less a woman.

De Staël's first published work was her *Lettres sur Rosseau* (*Letters on Rousseau*) of 1788. Rousseau was clearly a formative influence in her early years, and in fact she understood him well, in both his innocence and his monstrousness, as she makes clear in an essay on his character included in that collection. She also understood and shared his feeling about the relation of sensibility to the intellect; in her preface she remarks that she has found pleasure in recalling to memory—retracing—the sensation of her enthusiasm for him. Her interest in music here, like her interest in botany, is an interest in its objects as profound mnemonic devices, capable of summoning one to reflections about the best and the deepest in the natural state of humankind. Rousseau, composer and theorist, evinced the same Romantic sensibility.

FROM *Letters on Rousseau*
(1788)

ON ROUSSEAU'S TASTE FOR MUSIC AND BOTANY

Rousseau wrote several works on music; he loved this art with passion all his life. *The Village Soothsayer*[1] even shows some talent for composition. He tried to make melodramas adopted in France, using *Pygmalion* as an example, and perhaps this genre should not have been rejected.[2] When words and music follow each other, both effects are increased; sometimes they are improved by not being harnessed together. Music expresses situations; words develop them. Music can take on the portrayal of impulses beyond words; words can portray feelings that are too nuanced for music. Pygmalion's monologue is so eloquent that it seems perfectly likely for the statue to come to life at the sound of his voice, and we are tempted to believe that the gods played no part in this miracle.

Rousseau composed simple, touching airs for a number of romances, the kind of melody that blends in with the situation of one's soul, the kind one can still sing when one is unhappy. A few of them seem national to me; as I heard them I felt myself transported to our mountain peaks, when the sound of the shepherd's flute is slowly prolonged in the distance by a succession of repeated echoes. These airs remind me of the kind of music, calm rather than somber, that lends itself to the listener's sentiments and becomes for him the expression of his own feelings. Where is the sensitive man who has never been touched by music? An unfortunate person who can listen to it is given the sweet satisfaction of shedding tears, and his despair is replaced by melancholy; while one listens, one's sensations are enough for both mind and heart, leaving no emptiness in either. Some melodies put one in ecstasy for a moment; a choir of angels always heralds rapture into heaven. How powerfully memories are retraced by music! how inseparable it becomes from them! What man in the midst of life's passions could be unmoved by hearing the tune that enlivened the dances and games of his peaceful childhood! What woman whose beauty has been withered by time could keep from tears at the sound of the romance her lover once sang for her! The tune of this romance, even more than its words, renews in

---

TEXT: *Major Writings of Germaine de Staël,* trans. Vivian Folkenflik (New York: Columbia University Press, 1987), pp. 50–52.

1. *Le Devin du village,* words and music by Rousseau.
2. Rousseau's *Pygmalion* was composed in 1762 and first performed in Lyons in 1770, with music by Horace Coignet (except for an overture and Andante that Rousseau himself may have composed). This work is generally considered to be the first in which a spoken text alternated with music that reflects the changing affects of the words. Although the genre did not take root in France, it spread to Austria and Germany, where it was taken up enthusiastically. See p. 960 and n. 7.

her heart the emotions of youth. No accessory circumstance such as the sight of places or things that once surrounded us is connected to the events of our lives the way music is. The memories which come to us through music are not accompanied by any regrets; for a moment music gives us back the pleasures it retraces, and we feel them again rather than recollect them. Rousseau loved only melancholy airs; that is the kind of music one wants in the country. All nature seems to accompany the plaintive sounds of a touching voice. To feel such pleasures, one needs a pure and gentle soul. A man disturbed by the remembrance of his errors would not be able to bear the reverie into which we are thrown by touching music. A man tormented by heartrending remorse would be afraid to get that close to himself, to make all his feelings alive again, to feel them all slowly, one at a time. I am inclined to trust anyone who is enraptured by music, flowers, and the country. Ah! a penchant for vice must surely be born within man's heart, because all the sensations he receives from the objects surrounding him draw him away from it. I don't know—but often at the end of a lovely day, in a country retreat, at the sight of a starry sky, it has seemed to me that the spectacle of nature was speaking to the soul of virtue, hope, and goodness.

For a while Rousseau turned his attention to botany; this is one way of taking a detailed interest in the countryside. He had adopted a system which may show the extent of his belief that man's own memory is what spoils the pleasure aroused by his contemplation of nature. Rousseau distinguished plants by their forms, rather than by their properties; he thought it degrading to relate them to the use man could make of them. I must admit I am not in favor of adopting this opinion; to consider the works of the Creator destined to a final cause is no desecration, and the world looks more imposing and majestic to someone who sees in it only a single thought. But Rousseau's poetic, savage imagination could not bear to link the image of a shrub or flower, ornaments of nature, to the memory of men's sicknesses and infirmities. In his *Confessions* he paints an enchanting picture of his rapture at seeing periwinkle again.[3] The sight of it had the same effect on him as that tune it is forbidden to play to the Swiss army when they are out of their country, for fear they will desert.[4] This peri-

---

3. In the *Confessions*, Book 6, Rousseau gives an account of sighting, while botanizing in 1764, some periwinkle, a creeping plant with a modest blue flower. Madeleine-like, the discovery of the plant instantaneously evokes in him vividly precise memories of the happiest days of his life, nearly fifty years earlier, with his patroness in Les Charmettes, their isolated country retreat.

4. Of the *ranz des vaches*, the Swiss mountain melody that herdsmen play on an alphorn to summon the cows, Rousseau writes the following in his *Dictionnaire* ([Paris, 1768], "Musique"): "This air [is] so dear to the Swiss that playing it among their troops was banned on pain of death, since it made those who heard it melt with tears, desert, or die, so much did it stir in them the passionate desire to see their country again. It would be vain to search in this tune for the powerful accents capable of producing such astonishing effects. These effects . . . only come from habit, from memories, from the thousand circumstances which, retraced by this tune for those who hear it, and recalling for them their country, their early pleasures, their youth, their way of life, stir in them a bitter grief at having lost all that. Thus the *music* does not act precisely like *music*, but like a commemorative sign."

winkle could inspire in Rousseau a passion to return to the Vaud country; this single circumstance made all his memories present to him. His mistress, his country, his youth, his loves—he found and felt every one of them again, and all at one time.

143 Hester Lynch Piozzi

Hester Lynch Piozzi (1741–1821) is best known as the confidante of Dr. Samuel Johnson. Johnson was drawn to her for her intelligence and wit, and for her lively open manner in company; their friendship seems to have been a deep one. Her marriage to Henry Thrale, a wealthy brewer, while supported by little beyond an affection born of habit, persisted through twelve pregnancies (four daughters surviving into adulthood) until Thrale's death in 1781. Fortunately, Thrale was a cultivated man who enjoyed intelligent company. Dr. Johnson attached himself to the pair, often living at their country house and depending on "his dear Master and Mistress" for conversation and consolation. Charles Burney and his daughter Fanny, the actor David Garrick, Sir Joshua Reynolds, and Edmund Burke were also regular visitors. After Thrale's death, Hester Lynch fell passionately in love with Gabriel Piozzi, an Italian singer and teacher. Their marriage brought rejection by her daughters and many of her friends—Johnson and Fanny Burney foremost among them—who were shocked at this unsuitable attachment to a foreigner. Stubbornly enjoying her newfound happiness, she spent several years on the continent with Piozzi, and then returned to London and a thriving social life with a new circle of friends.

Hester Piozzi was a tireless diarist, who committed most of her writing before her second marriage to this form. After Johnson's death, however, she published collections of his letters and of Johnsonian anecdotes. On her return to England Piozzi brought out this book of synonyms, aimed at helping foreigners sort out the subtleties of English usage while offering her opportunities for expansive flights of associative fancy.

FROM *British Synonymy; or, An Attempt at Regulating the Choice of Words in Familiar Conversation*

(1794)

MELODY, HARMONY, MUSICK

These terms are used as synonymes only by people who revert not to their derivation; when the last is soon discovered to contain the other two, while the first means merely the air—or, as Italians better express it, *la cantilena*—because our very word MELODY implies *honey-sweet singing, mellifluous* succession of simple sounds, so as to produce agreeable and sometimes almost enchanting effect. Meanwhile both co-operation and combination are understood to meet in the term HARMONY; which, like every other science, is the result of knowledge operating on genius, and adds in the audience a degree of astonishment to approbation, enriching all our sensations of delight, and clustering them into a maturity of perfection.

MELODY is to HARMONY what innocence is to virtue; the last could not exist without the former, on which they are founded; but we esteem him who enlarges simplicity into excellence, and prize the opening chorus of *Acis and Galatea*[1] beyond the "Voi Amanti" of Giardini,[2] although this last-named composition is elegant, and the other vulgar. Where the original thought, however, like Corregio's Magdalen in the Dresden Gallery set round with jewels, is lost in the blaze of accompaniment, our loss is the less if *that* thought should be somewhat coarse or indelicate; but MUSICK of this kind pleases an Italian ear far less than do Sacchini's sweetly soothing MELODIES, never overlaid by that fulness of HARMONY with which German composers sometimes perplex instead of informing their hearers. *His* choruses in *Erifile*,[3] though nothing deficient either in richness or radiance, are ever transparent; while the charming subject (not an instant lost to view) reminds one of some fine shell coloured by Nature's hand, but seen to most advantage through the clear waves that wash the coast of Coromandel when mild monsoons are blowing. With regard to MUSICK, Plato said long ago, that if any considerable alteration took place in the MUSICK of a country, he should, from that single circumstance, predict innovation in the laws, a change of customs, and subversion of the govern-

---

TEXT: The original edition (London: G. G. and J. Robinson, 1794), vol. 2, pp. 21–29.

1. Oratorio by Handel, first performed in England in 1718, and in 1732 with added airs.
2. Felice Giardini was an Italian violinist who spent most of his career in London, as director of the King's Theatre opera orchestra and sometime impresario. He wrote several operas, most of which are lost, and arias for pasticcios. He was an intimate of Charles Burney, who called him "the greatest performer in Europe." Later, they parted in bitterness. See also pp. 990 and 1002.
3. Antonio Sacchini was an Italian opera composer who lived in London for nearly ten years, from 1772 to 1781. His *Erifile* was performed in London in 1778.

ment.[4] Rousseau, in imitation of this sentiment, which he had probably read *translated* as well as myself, actually foretold it of the French, without acknowledging whence his idea sprung; and truly did he foretell it. "The French," says he, "have no MUSICK now—nor can have, because their language is not capable of musical expression; but if ever they *do* get into a better style—(which they certainly soon did, changing Lulli and Rameau for Gluck, and for Piccinni)—*tant pis pour eux.*"[5]

Rousseau had indeed the fate of Cassandra, little less mad than himself; and Burney justly observed, that it was strange a nation so frequently accused of volatility and caprice, should have invariably manifested a steady perseverance and constancy to one particular taste in this art, which the strongest ridicule and contempt of other countries could never vanquish or turn out of its course. He has however lived to see them change their mode of receiving pleasure from this very science; has seen them accomplish the predictions of Rousseau, and confirm the opinions of Plato; seen them murder their own monarch, set fire to their own cities, and blaze themselves away—a wonder to fools, a beacon to wise men. This example has at least served to shew the use of those three words which occasioned so long a speculation. MELODY is chiefly used speaking of vocal MUSICK, and HARMONY means many parts combining to form composition. Shall I digress in saying that this latter seems the genuine taste of the English, who love plenty and opulence in all things? Our MELODIES are commonly vulgar, but we like to see them richly drest; and the late silly humour of listening to tunes made upon three notes only, is a mere whim of the moment, as it was to dote upon old ballads about twenty or thirty years ago; it will die away in a twelvemonth—for simplicity cannot please without elegance: nor does it really please a British ear, even when exquisitely sweet and delicate. We buy Blair's Works,[6] but would rather study Warburton's;[7] we talk of tender Venetian airs, but our hearts acknowledge Handel. Meantime 'tis unjust to say that German MUSICK is not expressive; when the Italians say so they mean it is not *amorous:* but other affections inhabit other souls; and surely the last-named immortal composer has no rival in the power of expressing and exciting sublime devotion and rapturous sentiment. See his grand chorus, *Unto us a Son is born,* &c. Pleyel's Quartettos[8] too, which have all somewhat of a drum and fife in them, express what Germans ever have excelled in—regularity, order, discipline, arms, in a word, war. When such MUSICK is playing, it reminds one of Rowe's verses which say so very truly, that

4. See, for example, Plato, *Laws* 3. 700a–701d.
5. "So much the worse for them." See p. 908.
6. Hugh Blair (1718–1800), a native of Edinburgh, and author of an essay on rhetoric, *Lectures on Rhetoric and Belles Lettres* (1783), whom the Piozzis had met when traveling in Scotland in 1789.
7. William Warburton (1698–1779), Anglican bishop and literary critic who was a friend of Alexander Pope. Piozzi met Warburton once in her youth.
8. The Parisian music publisher Ignace Pleyel (1757–1831), who was born in Austria and studied with Haydn in the early 1770s, was a prolific composer whose works were enormously popular in the late eighteenth century.

> The sound of arms shall wake our martial ardour,
> And cure the amorous sickness of a soul
> Begun by sloth and nursed with too much ease.
> The idle god of love supinely dreams
> Amidst inglorious shades and purling streams;
> In rosy fetters and fantastic chains
> He binds deluded maids and simple swains;
> With soft enjoyment wooes them to forget
> The hardy toils and labours of the great:
> But if the warlike trumpet's loud alarms
> To virtuous acts excite, and manly arms,
> The coward boy avows his abject fear,
> Sublime on silken wings he cuts the air,
> Scar'd at the noble noise and thunder of the war.[9]

What then do those critics look for, who lament that German MUSICK is not *expressive?* They look for plaintive sounds meant to raise tender emotions in the breast; and this is the peculiar province of MELODY—which, like Anacreon's lyre, vibrates to amorous touches only, and resounds with nothing but love. Of this sovereign power,

> To take the 'prison'd soul, and lap it in Elysium,[10]

Italy has long remained in full possession: the Syren's coast is still the residence of melting softness and of sweet seduction. The MUSICK of a nation naturally represents that nation's favourite energies, pervading every thought and every action; while even the devotion of that warm soil is tenderness, not sublimity;—and either the natives impress their gentle souls with the contemplation of a Saviour newly laid, in innocence and infant sweetness, upon the spotless bosom of more than female beauty—or else rack their soft hearts with the afflicting passions; and with eyes fixed upon a bleeding crucifix, weep their Redeemer's human sufferings, as though he were never to re-assume divinity. Meantime the piety of Lutherans soars a sublimer flight; and when they set before the eyes of their glowing imagination Messiah ever blessed, they kindle into rapture, and break out with pious transport.

> Hallelujah! for the Lord God Omnipotent reigneth, &c.

They think of him that sitteth high above the heavens, begotten before all worlds!

> *Effulgence of the Father! Son beloved!*[11]

With such impressions, such energies, such inspiration—Milton wrote poetry, and Handel composed MUSICK.

---

9. Nicholas Rowe (1674–1718), a dramatist in the sentimental style who succeeded Nahum Tate as poet laureate of England. He also compiled the first critical edition of Shakespeare.
10. John Milton, *Comus* ll. 253–57: "The Sirens three, . . . Who as they sung, would take the prison'd soul, / And lap it in *Elysium.*"
11. John Milton, *Paradise Lost*, bk. 6, l. 680. God speaks: "Effulgence of my Glorie, Son beloved."

DIARISTS AND HISTORIANS

144 Charles Burney

In 1744 Charles Burney, son of a Shrewsbury dancing master, left the country for London to become apprenticed to the composer Thomas Arne. After a period of varied employment as a practical musician both in London and out, he took up permanent residence in London in 1760 as a society music teacher. His real ambition, however, was to make a comprehensive study of the history of music. By 1769 he had taken his doctorate at Oxford and begun to amass a sizable music library. He rapidly gathered distinction as a scholar, in correspondence with Diderot and Rousseau in France, and joined a distinguished London circle that included Dr. Johnson, Joshua Reynolds, and the actor David Garrick. Burney died in 1814.

Burney made extensive journeys to the Continent to assemble the materials for his story—to France and Italy in 1770 and to the Low Countries, Germany, and Austria in 1772. The impressions gathered in the course of these tours he set down in two travel diaries: *The Present State of Music in France and Italy* (1771), and *The Present State of Music in Germany, the Netherlands and United Provinces* (1773). The first volume of his *General History of Music* appeared in 1776, and the fourth and final volume in 1789. Other writings include a biography of Pietro Metastasio and fragments for a set of memoirs (heavily expurgated, unfortunately, by his daughter, the novelist Fanny Burney). Burney's works are of inestimable importance to scholars for their voluminous information and lively opinions about late eighteenth-century musical life.

FROM *The Present State of Music in France and Italy*

(1771)

NAPLES

I entered this city, impressed with the highest ideas of the perfect state in which I should find practical music. It was at Naples only that I expected to have my ears gratified with every musical luxury and refinement which Italy could afford. My visits to other places were in the way of *business,* for the performance of a *task* I had assigned myself;[1] but I came hither animated by the hope of pleasure. And what lover of music could be in the place which had produced the two Scarlattis, Vinci, Leo, Pergolesi, Porpora, Farinelli, Jommelli, Piccinni, and innumerable others of the first eminence among composers and performers, both vocal and instrumental, without the most sanguine expecta-

TEXT: The original edition (London, 1771), pp. 291–93, 298–04, 305–07, 316–19, 324–30, 335–40, 352–58.

1. The collection of materials for his *General History of Music.*

tions. How far these expectations were gratified, the reader will find in the course of my narrative, which is constantly a faithful transcript of my feelings at the time I entered them in my journal, immediately after hearing and seeing, with a mind not conscious of any prejudice or partiality.

I arrived here about five o'clock in the evening, on Tuesday, October 16,[2] and at night went to the Teatro de' Fiorentini to hear the comic opera of *Gelosia per gelosia*, set to music by Signor Piccinni. This theatre is as small as Mr. Foote's in London,[3] but higher, as there are five rows of boxes in it. Notwithstanding the court was at Portici, and a great number of families at their *villeggiature*, or country houses, so great is the reputation of Signor Piccinni, that every part of the house was crowded. Indeed this opera had nothing else but the merit and reputation of the composer to support it, as both the drama and singing were bad. There was, however, a comic character performed by Signor Casaccia, a man of infinite humor; the whole house was in a roar the instant he appeared; and the pleasantry of this actor did not consist in buffoonery, nor was it local, which in Italy, and, indeed, elsewhere, is often the case; but was of that original and general sort as would excite laughter at all times and in all places.

The airs of this burletta are full of pretty passages, and, in general, most ingeniously accompanied: there was no dancing, so that the acts, of which there were three, seemed rather long.

•   •   •   •   •

Thursday 18. I was very happy to find, upon my arrival at Naples, that though many persons to whom I had letters were in the country, yet Signor Jommelli and Signor Piccinni were in town. Jommelli was preparing a serious opera for the great theatre of San Carlo, and Piccinni had just brought the burletta on the stage which I have mentioned before.

This morning I visited Signor Piccinni, and had the pleasure of a long conversation with him. He seems to live in a reputable way, has a good house, and many servants and attendants about him. He is not more than four or five and forty; looks well, has a very animated countenance, and is a polite and agreeable little man, though rather grave in his manner for a Neapolitan possessed of so much fire and genius. His family is rather numerous; one of his sons is a student in the University of Padua. After reading a letter which Mr. Giardini[4] was so obliging as to give me to him, he told me he should be extremely glad if he could be of any use either to me or my work. My first enquiries were concerning the Neapolitan Conservatorios; for he having been brought up in one of them himself, his information was likely to be authentic and satisfactory. In my first visit I confined my questions chiefly to the four following subjects:

2. Burney had left Rome for Naples on Sunday, October 14, 1770.
3. The "New" Theatre in the Haymarket, opened in 1767.
4. Felice de Giardini (1716–96), an Italian composer and violinist resident in London. See pp. 984, n. 2, and 1002.

1. The antiquity of these establishments.
2. Their names.
3. The number of masters and scholars.
4. The time for admission, and for quitting these schools.

To my first demand he answered that the Conservatorios were of ancient standing, as might be seen by the ruinous condition of one of the buildings, which was ready to tumble down.[5]

To my second, that their names were *San Onofrio, La Pietà,* and *Santa Maria di Loreto.*

To my third question he answered that the number of scholars in the first Conservatorio is about ninety, in the second a hundred and twenty, and in the other, two hundred.

That each of them has two principal *maestri di cappella,* the first of whom superintends and corrects the compositions of the students; the second the singing and gives lessons. That there are assistant masters, who are called *maestri secolari;* one for the violin, one for the violoncello, one for the harpsichord, one for the hautbois, one for the French horn, and so for other instruments.

To my fourth inquiry he answered that boys are admitted from eight or ten to twenty years of age; that when they are taken in young they are bound for eight years; but, when more advanced, their admission is difficult, except they have made a considerable progress in the study and practice of music. That after boys have been in a Conservatorio for some years, if no genius is discovered, they are dismissed to make way for others. That some are taken in as pensioners, who pay for their teaching; and others, after having served their time out, are retained to teach the rest; but that in both these cases they are allowed to go out of the Conservatorio at pleasure.

I inquired throughout Italy at what place boys were chiefly qualified for singing by castration, but could get no certain intelligence. I was told at Milan that it was at Venice; at Venice that it was at Bologna; but at Bologna the fact was denied, and I was referred to Florence; from Florence to Rome, and from Rome I was sent to Naples. The operation most certainly is against law in all these places, as well as against nature; and all the Italians are so much ashamed of it that in every province they transfer it to some other.

> Ask where's the North? at York, 'tis on the Tweed;
> In Scotland, at the Orcades; and there,
> At Greenland, Zembla, or the Lord knows where.
> —Pope, *Essay on Man.*

However, with respect to the Conservatorios at Naples, Mr. Gemineau, the British consul, who has so long resided there and who has made very particular inquiries, assured me, and his account was confirmed by Dr. Cirillo, an eminent

---

5. I afterwards obtained, from good authority, the exact date of each of these foundations; their fixed and stated rules, amounting to thirty-one; and the orders given to the rectors for regulating the conduct and studies of the boys, every month in the year. [Au.]

and learned Neapolitan physician, that this practice is absolutely forbidden in the Conservatorios, and that the young *castrati* come from Leccia in Apuglia; but, before the operation is performed, they are brought to a Conservatorio to be tried as to the probability of voice, and then are taken home by their parents for this barbarous purpose. It is, however, death by the laws to all those who perform the operation, and excommunication to everyone concerned in it, unless it be done, as is often pretended, upon account of some disorders which may be supposed to require it, and with the consent of the boy. And there are instances of its being done even at the request of the boy himself, as was the case of the Grassetto at Rome.[6] But as to these previous trials of the voice, it is my opinion that the cruel operation is but too frequently performed without trial, or at least without sufficient proofs of an improvable voice; otherwise such numbers could never be found in every great town throughout Italy, without any voice at all, or at least without one sufficient to compensate such a loss. Indeed all the *musici*[7] in the churches at present are made up of the refuse of the opera houses, and it is very rare to meet with a tolerable voice upon the establishment in any church throughout Italy. The virtuosi who sing there occasionally, upon great festivals only, are usually strangers, and paid by the time.

From hence I went directly to the comic opera, which, tonight,[8] was at the *Teatro Nuovo*. This house is not only less than the *Fiorentini,* but is older and more dirty. The way to it, for carriages, is through streets very narrow, and extremely inconvenient. This burletta was called the *Trame per Amore,* and set by Signor Giovanni Paesiello, *Maestro di Cappella Napolitano.* The singing was but indifferent; there were nine characters in the piece, and yet not one good voice among them; however, the music pleased me very much; it was full of fire and fancy, the ritornels abounding in new passages, and the vocal parts in elegant and simple melodies, such as might be remembered and carried away after the first hearing, or be performed in private by a small band, or even without any other instrument than a harpsichord.[9] The overture, of one movement only, was quite comic, and contained a perpetual succession of pleasant passages. There was no dancing, which made it necessary to spin the acts out

6. "*Il Grassetto,* a boy who submitted to mutilation by his own choice and against the advice of his friends for the preservation of his voice, which is indeed a very good one." (Burney, *France and Italy,* p. 259 [Rome, Sept 22].)
7. The word *musico,* in Italy, seems now wholly appropriated to a singer with a soprano or contralto voice, which has been preserved by art. [Au.]
8. The date is still October 18.
9. This is seldom the case in modern opera songs, so crowded is the score and the orchestra. Indeed Piccinni is accused of employing instruments to such excess, that in Italy no copyist will transcribe one of his operas without being paid a zechin more than for one by any other composer. But in burlettas he has generally bad voices to write for, and is obliged to produce all his effects with instruments; and, indeed, this kind of drama usually abounds with brawls and *squabbles,* which it is necessary to enforce with the orchestra. [Au.]

to rather a tiresome length. The airs were much applauded, though it was the fourteenth representation of the opera. The author was engaged to compose for Turin, at the next carnival, for which place he set out while I was at Naples. The performance began about a quarter before eight, and continued till past eleven o'clock.

• • • • •

Friday 26. This morning I first had the pleasure of seeing and conversing with Signor Jommelli, who arrived at Naples from the country but the night before. He is extremely corpulent, and, in the face, not unlike what I remember Handel to have been, yet far more polite and soft in his manner. I found him in his night-gown, at an instrument, writing. He received me very politely, and made many apologies for not having called on me, in consequence of a card I had left at his house; but apologies were indeed unnecessary, as he was but just come to town, and at the point of bringing out a new opera that must have occupied both his time and thoughts sufficiently. He had heard of me from Mr. Hamilton.[10] I gave him Padre Martini's letter, and after he had read it we went to business directly. I told him my errand to Italy, and showed him my plan, for I knew his time was precious. He read it with great attention, and conversed very openly and rationally; said the part I had undertaken was much neglected at present in Italy; that the Conservatorios, of which, I told him, I wished for information, were now at a low ebb, though formerly so fruitful in great men. He mentioned to me a person of great learning who had been translating David's Psalms into excellent Italian verse; in the course of which work he had found it necessary to write a dissertation on the music of the ancients, which he had communicated to him. He said this writer was a fine and subtle critic; had differed in several points from Padre Martini; had been in correspondence with Metastasio, and had received a long letter from him on the subject of lyric poetry and music; all of which he thought necessary for me to see. He promised to procure me the book, and to make me acquainted with the author.[11] He spoke very much in praise of Alessandro Scarlatti, as to his church music, such as motets, masses, and oratorios; promised to procure me information concerning the Conservatorios, and whatever else was to my purpose, and in his power. He took down my direction, and assured me that the instant he had got his opera[12] on the stage he should be entirely at my service. Upon my telling him that my time for remaining at Naples was very short, that I should even then have been on the road on my way home but for his opera, which I so much wished to hear; that besides urgent business in

10. The British Minister to the Court of Naples.
11. Saverio Mattei, whose biography of Metastasio was published in 1785. For Metastasio's letters to him see Burney's *Memoirs of the Life and Writings of the Abate Metastasio* (London, 1796), vol. 2, pp. 378–420 and vol. 3, pp. 115–53.
12. His *Demofoonte*. Actually, this was an old work; first performed in Padua on June 16, 1743, it had already been heard in London, Milan, and Stuttgart.

England, there was great probability of a war, which would keep me a prisoner on the continent: he, in answer to that, and with great appearance of sincerity, said, if after I returned to England anything of importance to my plan occurred, he would not fail of sending it to me. In short, I went away in high good humor with this truly great composer, who is indisputably one of the first of his profession now alive in the universe; for were I to name the living composers of Italy for the stage, according to my idea of their merit, it would be in the following order: Jommelli, Galuppi, Piccinni, and Sacchini. It is, however, difficult to decide which of the two composers first mentioned has merited most from the public; Jommelli's works are full of great and noble ideas, treated with taste and learning; Galuppi's abound in fancy, fire, and feeling; Piccinni has far surpassed all his contemporaries in the comic style; and Sacchini seems the most promising composer in the serious.

•   •   •   •   •

Wednesday, October 31. This morning I went with young Oliver[13] to his conservatorio of S. Onofrio, and visited all the rooms where the boys practise, sleep, and eat. On the first flight of stairs was a trumpeter, screaming upon his instrument till he was ready to burst; on the second was a French horn, bellowing in the same manner. In the common practising room there was a *Dutch concert,* consisting of seven or eight harpsichords, more than as many violins, and several voices, all performing different things, and in different keys: other boys were writing in the same room; but it being holiday time, many were absent who usually study and practise in this room. The jumbling them all together in this manner may be convenient for the house, and may teach the boys to attend to their own parts with firmness, whatever else may be going forward at the same time; it may likewise give them force, by obliging them to play loud in order to hear themselves; but in the midst of such jargon, and continued dissonance, it is wholly impossible to give any kind of polish or finishing to their performance; hence the slovenly coarseness so remarkable in their public exhibitions; and the total want of taste, neatness, and expression in all these young musicians, till they have acquired them elsewhere.

The beds, which are in the same room, serve for seats to the harpsichords and other instruments. Out of thirty or forty boys who were practising, I could discover but two that were playing the same piece; some of those who were practising on the violin seemed to have a great deal of hand. The violoncellos practise in another room; and the flutes, oboes, and other wind instruments in a third, except the trumpets and horns, which are obliged to fag, either on the stairs, or on the top of the house.

There are in this college sixteen young *castrati,* and these lie upstairs, by themselves, in warmer apartments than the other boys, for fear of colds, which

13. "A young Englishman who has been four years in the Conservatorio of S. Onofrio." (Burney, *France and Italy,* p. 324 [Naples, Oct. 27].)

might not only render their delicate voices unfit for exercise at present, but hazard the entire loss of them forever.

The only vacation in these schools in the whole year is in autumn, and that for a few days only: during the winter, the boys rise two hours before it is light, from which time they continue their exercise, an hour and a half at dinner excepted, till eight o'clock at night; and this constant perseverance, for a number of years, with genius and good teaching, must produce great musicians.

After dinner I went to the theatre of San Carlo, to hear Jommelli's new opera rehearsed. There were only two acts finished, but these pleased me much, except the overture, which was short, and rather disappointed me, as I expected more would have been made of the first movement; but as to the songs and accompanied recitatives, there was merit of some kind or other in them all, as I hardly remember one that was so indifferent as not to seize the attention. The subject of the opera was Demophontes; the names of the singers I knew not then, except Aprile, the first man, and Bianchi, the first woman. Aprile has rather a weak and uneven voice, but is constantly steady as to intonation. He has a good person, a good shake, and much taste and expression. La Bianchi has a sweet and elegant toned voice, always perfectly in tune, with an admirable portamento; I never heard anyone sing with more ease; or in a manner so totally free from affectation. The rest of the vocal performers were all above mediocrity: a tenor with both voice and judgment sufficient to engage attention; a very fine contralto; a young man with a soprano voice, whose singing was full of feeling and expression; and a second woman, whose performance was far from despicable. Such performers as these were necessary for the music, which is in a difficult style, more full of instrumental effects than vocal. Sometimes it may be thought rather labored, but it is admirable in the *tout ensemble,* masterly in modulation, and in melody full of new passages.[14] This was the first rehearsal, and the instruments were rough and unsteady, not being as yet certain of the exact time or expression of the movements; but, as far as I was then able to judge, the composition was perfectly suited to the talents of the performers, who, though all good, yet not being of the very first and most exquisite class, were more in want of the assistance of instruments to mark the images, and enforce the passion, which the poetry points out.

The public expectation from this production of Jommelli, if a judgement may be formed from the number of persons who attended this first rehearsal, was very great; for the pit was crowded, and many of the boxes were filled with the families of persons of condition.

The theatre of San Carlo is a noble and elegant structure: the form is oval, or rather the section of an egg, the end next the stage being cut. There are seven ranges of boxes, sufficient in size to contain ten or twelve persons in each, who sit in chairs, in the same manner as in a private house. In every

---

14. Jommelli is now said to write more for the *learned few,* than for the *feeling many.* [Au.]

range there are thirty boxes, except the three lowest ranges, which, by the King's box being taken out of them, are reduced to twenty-nine. In the pit there are fourteen or fifteen rows of seats, which are very roomy and commodious, with leather cushions and stuffed backs, each separated from the other by a broad rest for the elbow: in the middle of the pit there are thirty of these seats in a row.

•   •   •   •   •

Sunday 4. At night I went to the first public representation of Signor Jommelli's opera of *Demofoonte,* in the grand theatre of San Carlo, where I was honored with a place in Mr. Hamilton's box. It is not easy to imagine or describe the grandeur and magnificence of this spectacle. It being the great festival of St. Charles and the King of Spain's name-day, the court was in grand gala, and the house was not only doubly illuminated, but amazingly crowded with well-dressed company.[15] In the front of each box there is a mirror, three or four feet long by two or three wide, before which are two large wax tapers; these, by reflection, being multiplied, and added to the lights of the stage and to those within the boxes, make the splendor too much for the aching sight. The King and Queen were present. Their majesties have a large box in the front of the house, which contains in height and breadth the space of four other boxes. The stage is of an immense size, and the scenes, dresses, and decorations were extremely magnificent; and I think this theatre superior, in these particulars, as well as in the music, to that of the great French opera at Paris.

But M. de la Lande, after allowing that "the opera in Italy is very well as to music and words," concludes with saying "that it is not, in his opinion, quite so in other respects, and for the following reasons:

1. There is scarce any machinery in the operas of Italy.[16]
2. There is not such a multitude of rich and superb dresses as at Paris.
3. The number and variety of the actors are less.[17]
4. The choruses are fewer and less labored. And
5. The union of song and dance is neglected."[18]

To all which objections, a real lover of music would perhaps say, *so much the better.*

M. de la Lande, however, allows that the hands employed in the orchestra are more numerous and various, but complains that the fine voices in an Italian opera are not only too few, but are too much occupied by the music and its embellishments to attend to declamation and gesture.

15. The fourth of November is likewise celebrated as the name-day of the Queen of Naples and the Prince of Asturias. [Au.]
16. The Italians have long given up those puerile representations of flying gods and goddesses, of which the French are still so fond and so vain. [Au.]
17. If the characters are fewer, the dresses must be so, of course. [Au.]
18. [Joseph Jerome Lalande], *Voyage d'un François* [*en Italie* (1765–66)], vol. 6. [Au.]

With regard to this last charge, it is by no means a just one; for whoever remembers Pertici and Laschi, in the burlettas of London, about twenty years ago, or has seen the *Buona figliuola*[19] there lately, when Signora Guadagni, Signor Lovatini, and Signor Morigi were in it; or in the serious operas of past times remembers Monticelli, Elisi, Mingotti, Colomba Mattei, Mansoli, or, above all, in the present operas has seen Signor Guadagni, must allow that many of the Italians not only recite well, but are *excellent actors*.

Give to a lover of music an opera in a noble theatre, at least twice as large as that of the French capital, in which the poetry and music are good and the vocal and instrumental parts well performed, and he will deny himself the rest without murmuring; though his ear should be less stunned with choruses, and his eye less dazzled with machinery, dresses, and dances than at Paris.

But to return to the theatre of San Carlo, which, as a spectacle, surpasses all that poetry or romance have painted: yet with all this, it must be owned that the magnitude of the building and noise of the audience are such, that neither the voices or instruments can be heard distinctly. I was told, however, that on account of the King and Queen being present, the people were much less noisy than on common nights. There was not a hand moved by way of applause during the whole representation, though the audience in general seemed pleased with the music: but, to say the truth, it did not afford me the same delight as at the rehearsal; nor did the singers, though they exerted themselves more, appear to equal advantage: not one of the present voices is sufficiently powerful for such a theatre, when so crowded and so noisy. Signora Bianchi, the first woman, whose sweet voice and simple manner of singing gave me and others so much pleasure at the rehearsal, did not satisfy the Neapolitans, who have been accustomed to the force and brilliancy of a Gabrieli, a Taiber, and a De Amici. There is too much simplicity in her manner for the depraved appetites of these *enfants gâtés*, who are never pleased but when astonished. As to the music, much of the *claire obscure* was lost, and nothing could be heard distinctly but those noisy and furious parts which were meant merely to give *relief* to the rest; the mezzotints and background were generally lost, and indeed little was left but the bold and coarse strokes of the composer's pencil.[20]

•　　•　　•　　•　　•

Wednesday 7. Today I was favored at dinner with the company of Signor Fabio, the first violin of the opera of San Carlo; he was so obliging and so humble as to bring with him his violin. It is very common in the great cities of Italy to see performers of the first eminence carry their own instruments through the streets. This seems a trivial circumstance to mention, yet it strongly marks the difference of manners and characters in two countries not very

19. By Niccolò Piccinni.
20. Leopold Mozart, in a letter written in Milan on December 22, 1770, says that the opera "failed so miserably that people are even wanting to substitute another" (*The Letters of Mozart & His Family,* trans. Emily Anderson [London, 1938], vol. 1, p. 258).

remote from each other. In Italy, the leader of the first opera in the world carries the instrument of his fame and fortune about him, with as much pride as a soldier does his sword or musket; while, in England, the indignities he would receive from the populace would soon impress his mind with shame for himself and fear for his instrument.

I obtained from Signor Fabio an exact account of the number of hands employed in the great opera orchestra: there are 18 first and 18 second violins, 5 double basses, and but 2 violoncellos; which I think has a bad effect, the double bass being played so coarsely throughout Italy that it produces a sound no more musical than the stroke of a hammer. This performer, who is a fat, good-natured man, by being long accustomed to lead so great a number of hands, has acquired a style of playing which is somewhat rough and inelegant, and consequently more fit for an orchestra than a chamber. He sang, however, several buffo songs very well and accompanied himself on the violin in so masterly a manner as to produce most of the effects of a numerous band. After dinner, he had a second to accompany him in one of Giardini's solos, and in several other things.

I spent this whole evening with Barbella,[21] who now delivered to me all the materials which he had been able to recollect, relative to a history of the Neapolitan conservatorios, as well as anecdotes of the old composers and performers of that school: besides these, I wrote down all the verbal information I could extract from his memory, concerning musical persons and things. During my visit, I heard one of his best scholars play a solo of Giardini's composition very well; he was the most brilliant performer on the violin that I met with at Naples.

And now, having given the reader an account of the musical entertainment I received at Naples, I hope I shall be indulged with the liberty of making a few reflections before I quit this city; which has so long been regarded as the center of harmony, and the fountain from which genius, taste, and learning have flowed to every other part of Europe that even those who have an opportunity of judging for themselves take upon trust the truth of the fact, and give the Neapolitans credit for more than they deserve at present, however they may have been entitled to this celebrity in times past.

M. de la Lande's account of music at Naples is so far from exact, that it would incline his reader to suppose one of two things, either that he did not attend to it, or that he had not a very distinguishing ear.

> Music [says this author] is in a particular manner the triumph of the Neapolitans; it seems as if the tympanum in this country was more braced, more harmonical, and more sonorous, than in the rest of Europe; the whole nation is vocal, every gesture and inflection of voice of the inhabitants, and even their prosody of syllables in conversation, breathe harmony and music. Hence Naples is the principal source of Italian music, of great composers, and of excellent operas.[22]

21. Emanuele Barbella, an Italian composer and violinist, at one time resident in London.
22. *Voyage d'un François*, vol. 6. The inaccuracy with which M. de la L. speaks about music and musicians runs through his work. He places Corelli and Galuppi among the Neapolitan com-

I am ready to grant that the Neapolitans have a natural disposition to music; but can by no means allow that they have voices more flexible and a language more harmonious than the inhabitants of the other parts of Italy, as the direct contrary seems true. The singing in the streets is far less pleasing, though more original than elsewhere; and the Neapolitan language is generally said to be the most barbarous jargon among all the different dialects of Italy.[23]

But though the rising generation of Neapolitan musicians cannot be said to possess either taste, delicacy, or expression, yet their compositions, it must be allowed, are excellent with respect to counterpoint and invention, and in their manner of executing them, there is an energy and fire not to be met with perhaps in the whole universe: it is so ardent as to border upon fury; and from this impetuosity of genius, it is common for a Neapolitan composer, in a movement which begins in a mild and sober manner, to set the orchestra in flames before it is finished. Dr. Johnson says that Shakespeare, in tragedy, is always struggling after some occasion to be comic; and the Neapolitans, like high bred horses, are impatient of the rein, and eagerly accelerate their motion to the utmost of their speed. The pathetic and the graceful are seldom attempted in the Conservatorios; and those refined and studied graces, which not only change, but improve passages, and which so few are able to find, are less sought after by the generality of performers at Naples, than in any other part of Italy.

---

posers; whereas it is well known that Corelli was of the Roman school, and he himself says in another place (vol. 5) that Galuppi was of the Venetian. [Au.]

23. A sufficient proof of the Neapolitan language being only a *patois* or provincial dialect, is that it remains merely oral, the natives themselves, who are well educated, never daring to write in it. [Au.]

145 Susannah Burney

Susannah Elizabeth Burney (1755–1800) was the daughter of the music historian Dr. Charles Burney. Although overshadowed by her sister Fanny, the celebrated novelist, Susan (as she was known to her family) was also a gifted writer, especially about music. From 1779 to 1780 she wrote a series of long letters from London to her sister, who was in the country working on a novel. The letters give a vivid account of the famous musicians Susan met and the Italian operas she attended. She was much more concerned than her father about dramatic aspects of opera, and she was more knowledgeable about musical style and technique than Fanny. In the following excerpts from the letter-diary, Susan describes a rehearsal of the pasticcio *Alessandro nell'Indie* in November 1779 and the bumpy reception accorded to Antonio Sacchini's *Rinaldo* later in the same season.

FROM Letter-Journal
(1779–80)

20 November 1779. Yesterday Morning Mr. Burney[1] and my sister came. I went to the Opera House a little *entremblant;* however, upon naming my father, we were very civilly allowed to pass. The opera was begun. We had lost the overture and a song or two I believe; Manzoletto[2] was then singing. We went into the pit, where there were two or three people. But two boxes were occupied—one by Lady Mary Duncan, the other by two ladies I did not know. I believe the rehearsal was intended to be quite private. . . . The opera is a pasticcio, and has been got together in such a hurry that though advertised to be under the *direction of Bertoni*[3] I fancy he can have composed nothing purposely for it, and indeed that there are but few songs of his introduced. This I supposed by observing that he did not stand forwards as *direttore* to above three or four throughout the opera; all the singers acted as *maestro* during their own songs. As I had read the opera [libretto] previous to the rehearsal I found that the scene which contains Porus's first song, "Vedrai con tuo periglio," was over, which I regretted infinitely. However I afterwards found it was omitted. But Pacchierotti[4] in a beautiful cavatina "Se mai più sarò geloso" which is placed about the middle of the first act charmed me indeed more than anything that followed in his part, or in course in that of any body else, throughout the whole opera. It is elegant, charming music, and admits of all those refinements and graces in which Pacchierotti so peculiarly excells. And he *did* sing it like a very angel. To *you* [her sister Fanny] it will give little trouble to conceive the pleasure I felt at hearing his most sweet voice, and that in such sweet music; but I would not answer for the *conception.* . . . As an opera, I confess I have heard few that seemed to me possessed of a smaller number of fine, or even of *pleasing* airs than the present *Alessandro;* and I am sorry to say that, except the cavatina I have already mentioned, I am far from being charmed with anything even in Pacchierotti's part. Madame Le Brun[5] sings a

TEXT: British Library Egerton MS 3691, edited by Curtis Price, Judith Milhous, and Robert D. Hume. The notes are by these editors and Wye J. Allanbrook.

1. Susan's cousin and brother-in-law, Charles Rousseau, a well-known pianist.
2. The stage name of Angiolo Monanni (fl. 1779–82), a well-respected castrato of the second rank.
3. Ferdinando Bertoni (1725–1813), a celebrated composer of *opera seria* who was a friend of the castrato Pacchierotti (see n. 4), and accompanied him to England. He later (1785) was appointed maestro di capella of San Marco in Venice.
4. Gasparo Pacchierotti (1740–1821), generally regarded as one of the greatest castratos of the eighteenth century.
5. The soprano Franziska Lebrun, née Danzi (1756–1791), a singer of great skill and clarity, but of whom Charles Burney complains that having lived so long with an oboist her voice had taken on a "cold and instrumental" quality. She also turned her hand to composition, writing some ballet music and sonatas for keyboard and violin.

great deal in it, in *her* style very well—her voice being generally clear and her intonation extremely good, but her singing seems to me in almost every particular exactly the reverse of Pacchierotti's. Hers seems a bad imitation of an instrument; his what no instrumental performer on earth can equal: all softness, feeling, expression, while she is ever *trilling*, and diminishing instead of adding to the merit of her songs by the graces she introduces.

Madame Le Brun's songs, except two, I cannot I confess recollect anything of, but I believe their style was unmasked, for she cannot sing a cantabile, which prevents there being much variety in her airs; but one of the two I remember was a *chicherichi*[6] song in the second act—a bravura composed purposely for her which goes *up to the high*, and a very unpleasing one I think. Her husband,[7] who looks a conceited fop, gave the time etc. when she sung, and the *composition* for ought I know might be his. I should suspect her rondeau in the last act at least to be his, as it is very French. Tessier[8] in his advertisement of this opera, says that in it *many songs of Handel* will be introduced; the *many* however consist in *two*, one of which, being sung by Manzoletto, may be fairly said to be *too many*. Such an impertinent imitation it is of Paccheriotti as makes one sick. His other songs I don't remember nor anything of Trebbi's[9] part, except that it was very heavy, and that he sang very much out of tune. Micheli[10] has a song, the instrumental parts of which are interesting. Pozzi[11] has a minuet in the first act, the music of which is vile; in the second a bravura by Bertoni which is *pretty enuff!* But in the third she has, perhaps, the best song in the opera, at least that which, excepting "Se mai più sarò geloso," seemed to *me* much the best. It is a bravura, and a very difficult one, yet full of elegant and pleasing passages, very much in Sacchini's[12] style. They led it so fast, that before she came to the end of it, she *non poteva più*,[13] and was obliged to stop for breath lery for merry.[14] Cramer[15] then with his accustomed good humour began it again slower, which I was very glad of, as we had an opportunity of hearing this charming song again, and to more advantage, as Pozzi being then more at her ease, executed it infinitely better.

Pacchierotti sings in the first act only "Se mai più sarò geloso" and the duet

6. Italian for "cock-a-doodle-do."

7. The oboist Ludwig August Lebrun (1752–1790).

8. Antoine Le Texier (c. 1737–1814), the manager of the opera company.

9. Giuseppi Trebbi (fl. 1775–82), a buffo singer, whom Charles Burney also criticizes.

10. Leopoldo De Michele (fl. 1761–91), a regular singer of the second rank, mentioned several times by Charles Burney.

11. Anna Pozzi (fl. 1776–88), a young Italian soprano who had greater success later in Italy than in her three London seasons.

12. See p. 266, n. 3. For Charles Burney's opinion of Sacchini, see p. 994.

13. "She could do no more," that is, she ran out of steam.

14. Helter-skelter.

15. Wilhelm Cramer (1745–1799), a German violinist, born in Mannheim, who after a stint in the famous Mannheim orchestra came to London, where he took up permanent residence. One of England's foremost violinists, he was concertmaster not only of the opera house orchestra, but also of several concert orchestras.

which I cannot like, though it is Piccinni's;[16] but great men are not always equal, and human genius has a period at which it seldom fails to decline. This it seems is Piccinni's last[17] work. It is in the beginning old fashioned and in the end incoherent, difficult, and unpleasing—*selon moi*,[18] and indeed *selon* every body but one I have heard mention it. But he[19] is a legion! In the second act Pacchierotti sings a song of Handel's, "Return oh God of Hosts," from *Samson*. It is, in its solemn and antique style a fine song. Pacchierotti expressed it like an angel, but, keeping himself I trust in reserve for the time of public perfor-mance, was *too* chaste and too *retenue*,[20] a fault of which he is indeed not often guilty. It is adapted to Italian words. After this he sings a bravura by Piccinni which is *extremely* difficult, but which did not seem to me either pleasing or calculated to shew his talents to any advantage. However, he sung so much *a sotto voce* that it was not very easy to form a judgement concerning him in it. He has a pretty rondeau in the last act, which he likewise whispered, owing I believe to the presence of that oaf the Duke of C[umberlan]d, for after he appeared, which was during the second act, Pacchierotti seemed displeased, out of spirits, and exerted himself in nothing. I believe you were at home when Giardini[21] gave us an account of his behavior to poor Pacchierotti when Lady Mary Duncan introduced him to his Royal Highness at Windsor. *Wretched doings! Nothing could be more shabby!* At first we had seated ourselves in a very obscure part of the pit, but when Pacchierotti began his cavatina, he sung, though divinely, so *piano*, that we moved nearer the orchestra. By this means Mr. Burney was soon espied by many who know him in the band. Cramer bowed in the most respectful polite manner that could be to us all. He is a *charming Creachur*, so mild, so gentlemanlike in his manner of speaking to the band, at the same time that it is evident he quite suffers when anything goes wrong. The wind instruments were all out of tune, and though I pitied poor Cramer 'twas impossible not to laugh. After repeatedly desiring the French horn players to make their instruments sharper, at last he called out in a voice which proved that he with difficulty could repress a degree of indignation and with his foreign accent, "Gentelmen [*sic*] . . . You are not in tune at all?" "It's a very sharp morning, sir," said one of them. "We shall do better another time." Another said that the crook he used was right, but Cramer desired he would try the other. He did so. "Why that is *better*," said Cramer, as indeed it clearly was. "Very well sir," said the stupid, earless wretch, "I'll be sure to use it." Presently after, in another passage the bassoon player was dreadfully and ridic-ulously out of tune. Cramer stopped again, and Clementi,[22] to point out in the

16. For Charles Burney's opinion of Piccinni, see pp. 990–91 and 994.
17. Most recent.
18. "According to me."
19. Pacchierotti.
20. "Restrained."
21. See pp. 984, n. 2, and 990.
22. Muzio Clementi (1752–1832), composer and piano virtuoso, at the beginning of his distin-guished career.

most forcible manner possible why he did so, played over the passage with natural notes in the treble and flat in the bass. I don't know whether you can understand what I mean, but it had the most dissonant and comical effect and produced the best imitation of their accompaniment that can be conceived. Pacchierotti, whose song was playing, then went and whispered something to Cramer, who in consequence of it, called to the bassoon player by his name, and desired he would omit playing that passage. "Yes, sir, to be sure I will," cried the dolt whose stupid, shameless insensibility made everybody laugh, and spite of his evident vexation Cramer [too] at last, till he seemed almost choaked by it. Tessier did not appear till the rehearsal was nearly over, and did not know us as we sat in a dark place. Indeed, I believe, had we been in any other, I was the only one he would have known. I was not very miserable at this, especially as the only person I saw by whom I at all wished myself noticed was not long without observing me: this was, need I say, Pacchierotti. We had approached the orchestra very gently during his cavatina; presently after it the weather was so cold that he gave two or three jumps to warm himself. During this performance, he caught our eyes, and almost while he was yet *en l'air* took off his hat, laughing and bowing. "Il fait bien froid," said he, to excuse his exhibition I suppose; "très froid en verité."[23] As soon as the duet which ends the act was over, which is, by the way, preceded by some delightful recitative, I missed Pacchierotti on the stage, and presently heard his voice behind me. "How does Miss Burney do?" said he, "and Mr. Burney and Mrs. Burney? . . . All well I hope?" "Very happy to see and hear him again," I told him. He expressed much good natured concern at hearing my mother was yet confined and said, "I wished much to wait upon you this morning, but there was the rehearsal— tomorrow again . . . but Sunday, in the evening . . . I will try." I told him we should be most happy to see him. "And when," said he, "do you expect your sister?" "I hope next week." "Oh yes . . . when the Parliament makes its meeting." Mr. Burney then began cutting up[24] the duet, in doing which I found, as indeed he might have foreseen, he was in the wrong box. Had Pacchierotti disliked it, certainly in a pasticcio where there could be no obligation to do it, he would not have sung it. He said it was Piccinni's last composition. "Une musique qui n'a pas été entendue encore, et *belle en verité*,"[25] and attributed Mr. Burney's not liking it to its having been ill executed, but hoped Tuesday night it would go better. Because Mr. Burney talks such good French and Italian he would not speak English to poor Pacchierotti as *I* did and, I believe, bothered him to death. He asked me if I had heard the cavatina. I said it was beautiful, and begged to know the composer, but the noise of the instruments was so great I could not hear his answer. However, he said of the music, "Elle est charmante, il est vrai."[26] I then asked if he had not another song before it.

---

23. "It's very cold, truly very cold."
24. Criticizing.
25. "Music that has not been heard yet, and truly beautiful."
26. "It is charming, it is true."

"No, dans le premier acte rien que ce morceau et le duo," but seeing me look *malcontente,* "Mai j'ai bien assez," added he, "vous verrez, dans le second acte j'ai deux airs, et puis un rondeau dans le troisième. J'ai un beaucoup à fatiguer en verité."[27] The *Sultano Generoso*[28] was in his head I dare say. Micheli was singing: "à present il faut écouter les Instrumens," said I. "Il est vrai,"[29] said he, laughing. The next air was Pozzi's which he *brava*'d away like anything. He told me 'twas Bertoni's song. In this pretty manner did he set with us till recalled on the stage to sing, and indeed the time he spent with us was more agreeably passed by me than any other during which he was *not* singing.

I came home extremely well pleased with my entertainment, though not totally so with the opera in general. There will be another rehearsal Monday, but though we may go to it free gratis, for nothing at all, our dear fastidious sister thinks it not worth while to come to it.

•   •   •   •   •

I had a nice conclusion of my confab with Pacchierotti. I asked him whose was the cavatina he sung in the first act of *Alessandro.* "Piccinni's," he told me, as was the duet. He had particularly wished Madame Le Brun likewise to sing an air of Piccinni's to these words: "Se mai turbo il tuo riposo," and indeed for a very good reason. I don't know whether you are acquainted with the opera, but Porus, whose jealousy occasions the great distress of the piece, having received the strongest proofs of his mistress's attachments sings "Se mai più sarò geloso, mi punirca i sacre nume che dell'India e domator" [*sic*].[30] She in her turn sings "Se mai turbo il tuo riposo, se m'accende pace mai non abbia il cor."[31] Soon after Porus's jealousy being again awakened, they insult each other with their former protestations. This is the subject of the duet. Porus begins it with the words of Cleofida, "Se mai turbo" etc., and she then repeats his "Se mai più sarò geloso" etc. Now, you will readily conceive that the two airs and the duet ought to be the composition of the same master. Piccinni made the subject of the latter the same with that of the two airs, which added much to its effect. "Et quand je l'ai chanté avec la De Amicis,"[32] said Pacchierotti, "dans ces Paroles *Se mai più sarò geloso,* elle a imité ma manière de chanter la cavatina, et moi aussi à mon tour j'a che [*sic*] d'exprimer *Se mai turbo il tuo riposo* de la façon qu'elle l'avait faite. Ce qui a fait un effet je vous assure que je ne puis vous dire. J'avais expliqué à Madame Le Brun comme j'ai l'honneur de vous de faire à vous, et comme j'ai beaucoup d'estime et pour son caractère et

27. "No, in the first act there is nothing but this piece and the duo. But I have plenty; you will see, in the second act I have two arias, and then a rondeau in the third. I have enough to tire me, truly."
28. Actually *Il soldano generoso,* a pasticcio arranged by Bertoni and given later in the season, on December 14, 1779.
29. "Now it's necessary to listen to the instruments." "It is true."
30. "If I am ever jealous again, may the gods who conquered India punish me."
31. "If I ever trouble your repose, may my heart have no peace."
32. Anna Lucia De Amicis (c. 1733–1816), Italian soprano who had a distinguished career, primarily in Italy.

pour son mérite je desirais et véritablement que nous nous entendions bien sur ce sujet aussi bien pour son interêt que pour la mienne. Et bien nous nous etions convenus de tout ici et en avions même parlé de nouveau je passé au soir. Eh bien, le matin arrive et, à la répétition, sans me dire un seul mot, je suis tout surpris de l'entendre chanter un autre air, au quel vous avez peut être remarquée que M. Le Brun a donné le ton."[33] How injudiciously and wantonly ill bred and impertinent! Pacchierotti repeated several times that he knew he had no title to expect her to sing an air disagreeable to her, had she objected to it when they were together. But to accept and then change it without deigning to give a reason or make an apology was a want of politeness and consideration which he did not expect. He attributed it however to her husband, I found, who is I believe an insolent, disagreeable man. I mentioned with admiration the sweet recitative before the duet. "Eh le duo aussi est beau je vous assure mademoiselle," said Pacchierotti, "s'il est chanté comme il faut. J'espère une autre fois qu'il vous plaira."[34]

Speaking of the *désagrément* attending his situation, owing to the jealousy, caprice, or caballing spirits of those he had to deal with he said, "Si dieu me fait la grace jamais de me tirer du théâtre je m'estimerai bien heureux je vous assure!"[35] My father promised to send him any English books he could wish for when he should be gone. "Mais sans la conversation," said he, "j'ai peur que j'oublierai tout." "Il faut donc rester," said I. "Ah mademoiselle! Vous voyez, apres cette année je n'aurai plus rien à faire. Et de rester me sera impossible!"[36]

· · · · ·

Wednesday morning, 19 April 1780. Etty[37] came and accompanied me to the Opera House. When we went in a dance was rehearsing by Mademoiselle Bacelli and Signor Guiardele.[38] I was however in a relief at hearing from Cramer who was behind the scenes that it would soon be over, and the

33. "And when I sang with De Amicis, at those words *Se mai più sarò geloso* she imitated the way in which I sang the cavatina, and I also in my turn conveyed *Se mai turbo il tuo riposo* in the way that she had done it. I assure you, this had an effect that I cannot describe. I had explained to Madame Le Brun as I have had the honor of explaining to you, and as I had much admiration both for her character and for her talent I would truly desire that we understand one another well on this subject, as well for her interest as for mine. And we certainly were agreed about it all here, and we had even spoken of it again before I left for the evening. Well, the morning came and, at the rehearsal, without saying a single word to me, I was completely surprised to hear her sing another air, to which you perhaps would have observed that M. Le Brun gave the tone."

34. "Ah, I assure you, Mademoiselle, the duo is also fine, if it is sung as it ought to be. I hope that it will please you some other time."

35. "If God did me the favor of taking me away from the theater, I would think myself very happy, I assure you!"

36. But without conversation I'm afraid that I will forget everything." "Then you must stay here." "Ah mademoiselle! You see, after this year I won't have anything more to do. And it will be impossible for me to stay."

37. Susan's elder sister, Hester (1749–1832).

38. Favre Guiardele (fl. 1775–1802), a protégé of the choreographer Jean-George Noverre.

opera[39] was then to be rehearsed. I saw Lady Clarges and Miss Bulls in an opposite box, which made me not ambitious of figuring in the pit. However, as the woman to whom we applied for a box was not kind, we even made the best of our way to the above mentioned place. Here in a minute we were followed and joined by Cramer, to whom my sister and I both paid our compliments concerning his great benefit.[40] "But," said he, "had you not better be in a box Ma'am to day?" We said we could not get one. "Oh dear," said he, "I will get one for you in a minute if you will give me leave. It's very cold here indeed." We made proper speeches, but Cramer with the utmost good humour and readiness opened a side box for us where we sat very comfortably, though at too great a distance from the stage to see well, or be at all discoverable to those upon it, which I was sorry for as by this means Pacchierotti could not see that we had made use of his intelligence concerning the rehearsal. Lady Clarges and Miss Bulls had some other engagement and went away before the end of the second act. Lady Mary Duncan, Lady [Mount] Edgcumbe, the Harris's, and Brudenells, Duke of Dorset, Jack Parsons, Mr. Southwell, Rauzzini, Vachon, and a few others we distinguished in the boxes and on the stage.

There was no *maestro*! Poor Sacchini confined wholly to his bed with the gout, and Mattei says fretting himself to death, that this opera like *Enea e Lavinea*[41] must come out without his being able to act as director, or know whether things go well or ill. Indeed, though Cramer took great pains this morning, nothing seemed to go so well as at the rehearsal in the room[42] of last week, owing to carelessness in some of the performers and forgetfulness in others. Scarce anything was repeated; all hurried over, and Madame Le Brun's great song in the second act and a great deal of recitative not even rehearsed, nor was the rondeau tried, though I heard by Mattei it was quite finished some days before, and though there will be but one more rehearsal of this opera. 'Tis indeed very hard on Sacchini, and may well fret him.

As I gave you so full an account of *Rinaldo* before, I shall have the less to mention concerning it this time. Zampieri, or Lampieri, as some call him,[43] rehearsed a song in the first act, a mezzo bravura not so pretty as his two other songs, and as a singer I like him even less than before. He was insufferably out of tune. Pozzi's bravura in the second act I like far less than that she had in the first act of *Enea e Lavinia*. It does not hang together so well as Sacchini's songs generally do, but her other two airs are indeed beautiful. Madame Le Brun's first song too is full of delightful passages, and must be listened to with pleasure notwithstanding she sings it. This and Trebbi's second song, which is a bravura

39. Sacchini's *Rinaldo* (London, King's Theatre, April 1780) was a revival of his *Armida*, first performed in Milan in 1772.
40. A concert for which all the receipts, less the rental of the room and payment of the other artists, went to the star performer, in this case Cramer.
41. Sacchini's *Enea e Lavina* was first performed at King's Theatre, London, in March 1779.
42. The coffee room at the King's Theatre, which doubled as a rehearsal hall.
43. Nicola(?) Sampieri (fl. 1780–1800?).

abounding in new and charming accompaniments, pleased me yet more than at the first rehearsal. Pacchierotti's part I could not be more enchanted with than I was on the first hearing. He sung divinely, and made *sans y pense*[44] a delightful cadence to his first song.

When all was over my sister and I in coming away saw Bertoni with whom we stopped to speak a little while Pacchierotti in the midst of a very animated conversation bowed to me at a distance, but seemed to me to be engaged in a dispute with an Italian who held a letter open in his hand. . . .

Dr. Johnson has just called—but for a minute. He had a coach waiting for him and would not even set down, though he was very smiling and good humoured. He came to tell us he accepted an invitation which was sent him this morning to dine with us next Sunday. Mrs. Williams will likewise come. *I wiss to my art* you were at home!

Friday evening, 21 April 1780. Ah, ma chère Fanni! I have been to another and the last rehearsal of *Rinaldo* this morning; I am returned more distractedly in love with it than ever yet had many little things to abate my pleasure too. My mother, Charlotte,[45] and I went, and were immediately shown to a box, which was rather a wonder, as I never before saw so crowded a rehearsal. Not only the pit and stage were full, and the stage boxes, but much the greater number of the second range of side boxes were occupied. Lady Clarges and Miss Bulls were in a stage box opposite us but could not distinguish us; nor could anybody else indeed, as we were so far back as to be totally in the dark. However, my mother made herself known to Mr. Harris[46] who sat in the box next us, and was very polite and charming, as was Miss Louisa, who came in afterwards, and compared notes with me during all the opera. Lady Mary Duncan, Lady [Mount] Edgcumbe, his honour and Mrs. Brudenell, Jack Parsons, Lady Caermarthen, Lady Lucan, Mr. Southwell, Mr. Price, the Duke of Queensbury, Lady Hales and Miss Coussmaker etc. were there. Cramer found us out in passing from the stage into the pit, and came between every act to speak to us and lament with me that the dances were rehearsed, which were so long and so very tiresome they fatigued us all abominably. I could dwell on the merits of every part of the opera for ages, but think it would be making too free with your time and patience, so shall hold back. However, I must say that even in the most inferior pieces of *Rinaldo* charming passages and infinite entertainment must be met with but all Trebbi's part. Madame Le Brun's, the recitatives throughout, overture, duet, trio, quintetto, Pozzi's first and last song, and Paccheriotti's part are divine indeed. And from what I can remember of the latter, even were *he* not to sing it I am sure it would still yet be charming. Yet most certain it is that he adds infinite grace and beauty to everything he

44. "Without thinking about it."
45. A younger sister of Susan and Fanny.
46. Perhaps James Harris (1709–1780), author of the influential essay *Three Treatises: The First Concerning Art: The Second Concerning Music, Painting and Poetry: The Third Concerning Happiness* (1744), who was a friend of the Burney family.

performs, and can give merit even when it is wholly wanting. His rondo was rehearsed to day, and I have it by heart. It is different from every other I remember, and full of grace and elegance. It ends allegro. 'Tis a most sweet thing!

In the beginning of the last act the Harris's finding one of the stage boxes had been evacuated, and wishing as I did to be nearer the performers, left their box and went into the other. We then moved into their box, but presently Mr. Harris returned to us and stayed during the last act with us, and my dear father joined us at the end.

Soon after this removal we were spied out by Pacchierotti who had before not known us. He bowed smiling to me, and presently, passed by some ladies in the stage boxes to speak to me. "I wished Ma'am," said he, "to have waited upon you this week, but I have been *so* busy I could not. I have been very sorry indeed." I told him we knew how much he must be hurried and scarce had hoped to see him. And then, fearing to inconvenience the ladies in the next box, whom he stood before[,] he retired again, but I just told him I had been charmed with his rondo. He looked very pale indeed, and told my father who spoke to him in coming in he was far from well, and this rehearsal (owing to *three dances* besides those interwoven in the piece being rehearsed) was enough to kill him.

•　　•　　•　　•　　•

Monday Morning, 24 April 1780. Mr. Barry[47] was here Saturday evening but left us as did Miss Young who was much fatigued by her journey, before my father returned from the opera. There was a great house, and the opera went off he says with uncommon éclat, though poor Pacchierotti was ill and frightened and sung more flat than he has done before this season. The torches too of some of the furies in the last act went out, which set many fools laughing and so disturbed Pacchierotti that he could scarce sing a note, and this vexatious circumstance ruined the effect of the recitative and air with which I was so struck at the rehearsals. However, I hope this will not happen again, for had I been there I should have been ready to say with disappointment and vexation, as nothing in the opera at the rehearsals affected me so greatly as the composition and performance of this scene. My father could not get behind the scenes to speak to Pacchierotti. His cantabile was encored.

•　　•　　•　　•　　•

This morning I was upstairs preparing to go out when a carriage stopped at our door, which on looking out of the window I discovered to be Pacchierotti's. I made all possible haste downstairs and saw Pacchierotti dressed for the day, and looking much better than on Friday, notwithstanding that his face appeared to me not to be quite clean, which was afterwards accounted for. "I intended ma'am," said he, "to come here last night, but I was prevented, and as I have

47. The painter James Barry.

engagements for every night this week, I was determined to wait upon you in the morning." I told him he was very good, and my mother said we had the more obligation to him because he had already seen my father that morning. "Yes ma'am, and I hope," said he laughing, "he will bring you my respects, as I did desire him to do." I enquired after Bertoni. He had just met him he said in Oxford Road and that he was *si enjoué*[48] and looked so gay he was delighted at it! "Were you at the opera ma'am," said he, "Saturday?" I was obliged to answer in the negative. "But you heard that there was some mischief happened?" "Yes. My father told me the furies disturbed you . . ." "Oh! I was so angry, ma'am. My best scene in the last act it was quite spoiled." "And how was it," asked my mother? "Oh! I assure you I never was so *wexed* . . . Indeed! Four *Disgraziate furie!*—ungraceful furies, they came out, and by their bad actions and ridiculous manner they made all the people laugh, and indeed I could not tell how to go on; and all the time they kept beating me like a martyr. You see ma'am my face how it is bruised." I then found that a large discolored spot on his chin which I had taken for dirt, was the effect of a blow given him by these careless and awkward beasts! You'll exclaim as I did, especially when he went on and told us that he had had another blow on his head, which yet pained him extremely, and *several* on his shoulders and back. "Yet," said he, "I spoke to them in every language I knew and bid them stop: 'it is enough'; 'basta'; 'c'est assez.' Indeed, when I found they would not desist, I had a great will to strike them myself, I felt such . . . *rabbia*—rage. Indeed, and then in the newspaper the next day they put it in that I was embarrassed, and sung too much at the private concerts. Now on a first night I never exert myself so much. I never felt more *impegno . . . premura*[49] . . . more desire to succeed, but these *dirty scrubs* . . . indeed they quite made me mad." After compassionating him and railing with all my heart at the *dirty scrubs,* I told him I hoped there would be another rehearsal before Saturday, that these wretches might be better instructed. "Oh," said he, "if this had been properly rehearsed before the time of performance, nothing of this sort could have happened. But the dancing master,[50] he is so *fool* and so *pride*"—"so foolish and so proud," said I. "Yes, ma'am, that he will not do anything he is requested, but all his own way. But we must rehearse the dances on Friday and tomorrow too then will be a rehearsal of the *Olimpiade,* for the sake of Madame Le Brun."

• • • • •

Saturday, 29 April 1780. Sacchini appeared at the harpsichord tonight, which he could not do last Saturday. He was much applauded the moment he appeared but looked indeed *à faire compassion!*[51] Very, *very* ill. I hope however he was satisfied with the manner in which his charming opera was per-

48. "So playful."
49. "Zeal . . . eagerness."
50. Guiardele.
51. "Pitiful."

formed and received. I do not now regret I did not go the first night, because though it was greatly applauded, many things failed, and nothing was so correct as at this second performance. 'Tis a very dramatic opera, and I find not Badini's[52] but merely sewn together by him. The scenery is very good and machinery not bad. I like all but some monsters who in the first scene are supposed to terrify Ubaldo from pursuing his way to Armida's enchanted palace, but who appear so very *tame,* that one longs to pat their heads and caress them like a good natured Pomeranian dog. The scene of the furies went off extremely well. There were twelve of them, and they kept a respectful distance from Pacchierotti, and seemed only inclined to guard the myrtle, not to beat him again like a martyr. The music is so fine, and the opera went off so well that though I was in pain from my head to my foot before it began, I felt no complaints during the whole opera. I was in Elysium and will insist upon it that there are medicinal powers in music.

The overture, Trebbi's recitative and first air charmed me as much as ever, and Pozzi's sweet song. Even Sampiere I could bear as there are such pretty passages in his songs, though they are of a second or perhaps third rate. Madame Le Brun's first song is full of charming *pensieri,* and indeed I never liked her better. She acts in Armida really extraordinarily well. But how was I delighted when Rinaldo appeared, surrounded by dancing nymphs, with the sweetest accompanied recitative imaginable, that he *so sings!* 'Tis really worth while to get his part by heart that one may not lose a word. Indeed, every passion, every line of the opera is beautifully set, and with infinite expression and feeling by Sacchini, and Pacchierotti not only in his airs, but in every word of the recitative delights me: so much *sense;* so much *sensibility;* such judicious, such energetic, such affecting expression does he give to everything! His first sweet song "Resta ingrata, io parto, addio," he sung most charmingly. And the duet. But I must not dwell again upon *every thing.* In the second act he sung his fine cantabile very finely, and very *chastely,* but it was not encored. He made the finest cadences I almost ever heard, very recherché, yet simple and in the style of the song. There were some beasts in the house (Tenducci[53] I saw and firmly believe to have been one of them) who blew their noses, coughed, spit, and did everything possible but *hiss* during every one of his songs, in a shameful manner. They meant to disturb him and make him sing ill and out of tune, to prevent people from hearing him, and to persuade him and everyone that the public wished not to listen to him. I am *certain* it was the effect of malice not accident, because the house was stiller during Zampieri's and even Micheli's songs than during Pacchierotti's. Is it not enough to make one sick that there should be such envy and such worthlessness in the world?

52. Carlo Francesco Badini (fl. 1770–1793), house poet at the King's Theatre.
53. Giusto Ferdinando Tenducci (c. 1735–1790), a rival castrato.

These wretches produced in part the effect they desired in his first song, when he was two or three times disturbed I am certain by the noise. The cantabile however could not be better sung, but the rumor of these creatures I am certain prevented it from being *felt* as it ought to be, and consequently from being encored. Pozzi's furious song, which I like less than most in the opera, though it describes a storm and expresses it indeed vastly well, was vehemently applauded by all whose hands had not moved to Pacchierotti, not from admiration of her but to mortify *him!* After this follows a most divine scene of accompanied recitative by Pacchierotti, and one of the sweetest rondeau's in the world; and this was encored, but opposed by the snakes who were *semés ça et la*[54] in the galleries. However, the encore was so strong and so well kept up that he returned, and repeated it better than ever.

A fine scene of accompanied recitative followed by Madame Le Brun, a pretty cavatina, more accompanied recitative and the scene ends with a furious song, of the *chicherichi* sort, but very animated and clever; and then some snakes immediately encored this, though there is not an Italian that can bear Madame Le Brun's singing. During the encore and opposition to the rondo, I observed that Piozzi[55] was totally neutral, and indeed he never stirred his hands to Pacchierotti throughout the opera, but how, though he condemns and hates Madame Le Brun's singing, he encored her with violence. "Mais est-ce-que vous dites encore pour vous moquer d'elle," said I, laughing. "Eh pourquoi voulez vous pas que je dise encore mademoiselle," said he, *fiercement.* "C'est trop juste, pourquoi ne faut il pas qu'elle repète son air *aussi?*"[56] Don't you admire this sort of reasoning? So, because Pacchierotti sung like a divinity and enchanted all that had ears and were not devoured by envy and malice it was *trop juste* that Madame Le Brun should likewise be encored. The trio was strongly encored but two songs having been repeated in the same act the encore was not carried. In the last act I was delighted by Trebbi's sweet song, by the finest recitative in the world of Pacchierotti, by Pozzi's syrenish song, who appears at the head of a number of fair nymphs in defence of the myrtle; by Madame Le Brun's slow song which she sung uncommonly well and acted better, and finally and most strongly was I affected by the recitative of Pacchierotti and air which he sings surrounded by the furies. Yet to say the truth these same furies, the thunder, lightning, scenery etc. add nothing to the effect of the music, but rather I think serve to disturb and interrupt one's attention, in so much that I dare say every one who *heard with ears* at the rehearsals of *Rinaldo* were more touched by this scene than at the public representation. It reminded me of the witches in *Macbeth,* whose speeches when they are *read*

54. "Sown here and there."
55. Gabriele Mario Piozzi, tenor and singing teacher, later married to Hester Lynch Piozzi (see p. 983).
56. "But are you saying encore to make fun of her?" "Eh, why do you not want me to say encore, mademoiselle? It's too just, why isn't it necessary for her to repeat her air *also?*"

freeze one with horror, but when repeated on the stage lose all their effect and become even ludicrous by the absurd appearance of gestures of the actors. However, the scene in question yet holds its ground with me, and seems to me the *plus beau morceau de l'opéra.*[57] It ends delightful by the sweet quintetto. Sacchini continued after the curtain was let down to be applauded till he had left the orchestra. Indeed he merited every mark of approbation the opera could receive. There was such a house as only Cramer's [benefit] could exceed. Indeed except on the stage it could not well be fuller. We came away before the last dance.

57. "The finest piece of the opera."

146 Johann Nikolaus Forkel

In his twentieth year Johann Nikolaus Forkel (1749–1818) matriculated at the University of Göttingen, and he remained there until his death, having been appointed music director in 1779. Although he was a practicing musician, his real talents lay in music history and bibliography. He surrounded himself with an extensive library and he conceived of and brought nearly to completion a universal history of music: beginning with the Egyptians, it breaks off in the sixteenth century. What distinguishes Forkel's history from its predecessors is not the breadth of its coverage, however, but its systematizing "introduction," an essay of sixty-eight pages divided into 135 titled sections. The principles outlined in the essay, a taxonomy of music into five essential branches and three evolutionary stages, provide a theoretical framework for the history that follows. The *Allgemeine Geschichte der Musik* (*A General History of Music*) is further supported by a massive annotated bibliography, *Allgemeine Litteratur der Musik* (*General Bibliography of Writings on Music,* 1792), consisting of some three thousand citations from antiquity to the late eighteenth century. This systematizing bent and diligent scholarship earned Forkel his reputation as the founder of modern musicology.

The notion of musical progress outlined in the *Geschichte* was critical to Forkel's thought; music for him had reached its zenith in the works of J. S. Bach and in his own time had fallen into a period of decadence, from which it might be rescued by an accurate extraction of compositional rules from all of music history. In this spirit Forkel wrote the first biography of Bach—a work that, true to his love of system, was to take its place as the culmination of the history he never completed.

FROM *A General History of Music*
(1788–1801)

INTRODUCTION

§1. [THE BENEFITS OF AN ACCURATE PRESENTATION OF THE RANGE
OF MUSIC, AND HOW IT HAS GRADUALLY ATTAINED SUCH A GREAT
RANGE.][1]

The different configurations in which music appears in the narrative of its
fortunes over the millennia, among both ancient and modern peoples, cannot
be correctly surveyed and evaluated without a precise conception of its gradual
development, from the first elements to the highest and most perfect union of
all individual parts in the whole. In the first epochs, among the first of earth's
peoples, music appears in its infancy, as it were; only the first and simplest
parts of the whole can be observed. In the periods immediately following,
nations that are somewhat more cultivated augment those few parts and first
elements with some new ones, but without coming noticeably closer to the
perfection of the whole. Finally, while among still later and more developed
peoples this increase in the number of the individual parts can be more or less
apparent, still perhaps no single people may gather all the individual parts of
the whole into one and thereby offer a model of the art in its highest perfection.
How is it possible today to make a correct evaluation of all these variations,
which arise not only from the lesser and greater quantities of individual parts,
but also from the influence of different climates, social conditions, the way of
life, moral values, and other cultural habits of the nations? Only if one knows
how the art has necessarily been constituted as regards its inner nature, in its
infancy as well as step by step in each epoch of its development; only if there
exists a standard by which, at least to some extent, the condition in which it
endured among various peoples can be determined. Such a standard must be
the correct conception of music in its entire extent.

Like all products of nature, the arts and sciences grow to perfection only
gradually. The interval between their first beginning and their highest perfection is filled with such a variety of intermediate creations that not only is the
stepwise progression from the simple to the complex, the small to the large,
everywhere apparent, but also each individual degree in this gradation can be
examined itself as a whole. Thus the sciences and arts resemble polyps, whose

TEXT: The original edition, vol. 1 (Leipzig, 1788), pp. 1–6, 31–35, 91–93. Translation by Wye J.
Allanbrook.

1. The headings following the numbered sections are not included in the text but are supplied
   from Forkel's table of contents.

hundred limbs, if cut up, each live on their own—seemingly perfect polyps, but in miniature.[2]

Thus a picture that represents the stepwise development of music from its first beginnings to its highest perfection—one that genuinely manifests the course taken by the human intellect in the development of its capabilities generally, but in particular in our art—seems to be the best means to enable the reader to evaluate more certainly all the possible variations in which this art appears in all the nations that have become known to us, and at least not to be without a basis for determining where and when it had or could have had true inner worth. The drawing of such a picture entails many difficulties, for several reasons. First of all, its individual features are scattered about in the whole of nature, and can be gathered together only with great effort. Second, these features, even if they have been successfully gathered together, can be united in a whole only with great difficulty. And finally, in the third place, it is not sufficient to ascertain from ancient and modern historians what these individual features were and are: one must in addition be a theorist, critic, and even a moralist, in order to be able to demonstrate what they would have had to be. This last requirement compels the painter of such a picture to proceed like Apelles, who in order to paint a perfect Venus united the most beautiful features of several beautiful women into a whole. In music, as in all her works, nature has only scattered about individual things of beauty; it is the task of human beings to search them out, and to produce by means of their appropriate arrangement new creations—creations more perfect than those of nature herself.

§2. [THIS ACCURATE PRESENTATION CAN BE MOST EASILY ACHIEVED BY THE COMPARISON OF MUSIC WITH LANGUAGE.]

The similarity that obtains between the language of human beings and their music—a similarity that extends not only to their origin but also to their full development, from its first beginning to its highest perfection—can furnish the surest guide in these matters. In its genesis music, like language, is nothing other than the expression of a feeling through the passions of the tones. The two of them arise from a common source—sensation. When subsequently they separated, each on its own path became what it was capable of becoming—the one, the language of the intellect, and the other, the language of the heart. Yet there remained to them both so many signs of their common origin that even at their furthest remove they still speak to the understanding and the heart in similar ways. The derivation and multiplication of their expressions from the first utterances of the feelings, the construction and composition of those expressions with a view not only to awakening feelings or concepts, but also to awakening and communicating them precisely and without ambiguity: in brief,

2. For the important biological discovery of the 1740s that suggested this comparison to Forkel, see p. 930, n. 27.

all the qualities that make the one into the consummate language of the understanding make the other similarly into the consummate language of the heart.
Thus whoever knows the nature of the one can be easily brought to a correct
and full understanding of the other by observation of the similarity prevailing
between them. What can be said here only provisionally about the similarity of
the construction of the language of our feelings and the language of our ideas[3]
will best be confirmed if in the course of this introduction that similarity is kept
in mind at all times, and the ground and cause of the relation always pointed
out at appropriate moments. .

THE FIRST PERIOD OF THE ART

§3. [IT CONSISTS MERELY OF DISCONNECTED TONES AND NOISE.]

Although tone—or rather, as it must be called at this juncture, sound—is
only the means by which music is made perceptible, in primitive, uncultivated
nations it is generally taken for the thing itself. Indeed they consider every
individual sound to be music. Consider pure sound in its various modifications:
loud, soft, sharp and rough, gentle, dark, muffled, thick, thin, and so on. Furthermore, consider how in these various modifications sound is capable of
affecting the hearing, and therefore the feelings, of human beings.[4] Then there
is little reason to be surprised that the pleasure sound can already stimulate in
itself may come to be considered a pleasure that arises from actual music. In

3. In *Dell'origine e delle regole della musica* [*On the Origin and Principles of Music,* 1774], Antonio
   Eximeno has undertaken a similar comparison, but in a wholly different fashion from that undertaken here, as the following will make clear. He does agree that music is a true language, but he
   looks for this similarity not in the like derivation and construction of its means of expression—
   in a word, not in the inner qualities of the art—but only in its externals, namely in prosody. Thus
   in his comparison he does not go beyond the first exclamatory utterances, believing that music
   originated and was developed out of these utterances alone, in gradual combination with prosody. Now this is certainly very superficial; but a man like Eximeno, who at the time of the
   publication of his works had previously studied music for only four years, could scarcely penetrate more deeply into the true nature of the art.
       The Spaniard Francisco Salinas understood this relationship far better. In the preface to his
   treatise *De musica* [in seven books; 1577] he includes the following passage: "They (grammar
   and music), however, are from their very beginnings so similar that they were thought to be not
   merely sisters, but almost twins. For grammar takes its beginning from letters, from which it
   receives its name; then using syllables, which arise from a combination of letters, and words,
   which are constituted from a union of syllables, it strives to arrive at the completion of a complete utterance. Similarly music, named for the Muses, to whom antiquity attributed every
   manner of skill in performing, completes and composes a melody or song from tones, from
   intervals made by a combination of tones, and from consonances, which arise from a union of
   intervals." Salinas was professor of music at Salamanca; his treatise appeared in 1577. [Au.]
4. The natural cause of the pleasure and displeasure arising from the tones of both animate and
   inanimate beings in nature lies in the relationship of these tones to the auditory nerves. The
   tones or voices of living beings are expressions of their various emotional states, and consequently generate another cause of pleasure and displeasure through sympathy. See Dietrich
   Tiedemann's "Aphorisms on the Feelings," in *Das deutsche Museum* (December 1777). [Au.]
   For Tiedemann, see also p. 956, n. 2.

his primal condition man is a passive creature; his soul has not yet been put into action. Sense impressions are thus still the only impressions that he can receive; he is not yet capable of other impressions, in which his intellect first must make a comparison, and derive from the observation of a proportion or a symmetry a feeling of pleasure. These sense impressions must be all the more intense and stirring the less the intellect is cultivated, and capable itself of being engaged.

This explains why we find in all wild and uncivilized nations such great pleasure taken in the clamor of noisy instruments—in drums, for example, and rattles, in blaring trumpets, and extremely loud, ferocious shrieks. Nature has established a wholly unmediated union between the heart and the hearing of human beings; all passions are communicated through their own proper tones, which stir in the heart of the hearer the very passional sensation from which they resulted.[5] This relation of unmediated perception between tone, hearing, and the heart is the same in all peoples, the most savage as well as the most civilized, with this one difference: the more savage a people, the more it remains merely sensuous and poor in mental representations, the more powerful are its sensations and its organs of sense. Thus in this primal state the pure tone, taken for itself alone as an expression of the passions, must be crude and vigorous, and entirely in keeping with the power of these sense organs.

§4. [MAN IN HIS EARLIEST STATE STILL CANNOT CONNECT REPRESENTATIONS AND CONCEPTS WITH FEELINGS.]

It is a generally understood premise that all our knowledge originally proceeds from perception. But it was necessary, in addition, that representations and concepts be gradually united with this perceptual knowledge. A perception in itself is nothing more than the consciousness of an impression on the external or internal senses. In order for it to become a representation, the soul must try to observe in that impression something by which to distinguish it, and must generally strive to bring this consciousness, which previously was only obscure, to full clarity. Only then does the perception turn into a representation, and a person now is able not only to perceive a loud and strong tone, but also to determine whether this loud and strong tone is harsh or tender. If the soul's observational power increases further, so that it can distinguish the entire multiplicity that can be observed in a tone, then the representation attains an even higher degree of clarity, and if the perception's mode of being is grasped along with its cause, it can become a concept in the true sense. Now the person no longer only discerns whether a strong tone is harsh or tender, but also why it is so.

5. See Johann Georg Sulzer's *Allgemeine Theorie der schönen Künste* [Leipzig, 1771–74], article "Musik," and Cicero, *De oratore*, 3.216: "Every motion of the soul has by nature its own look and sound and gesture; one's whole frame and countenance and all the sounds one utters resound like strings in a lyre as they are struck by a motion of the soul." [Au.] See p. 741 and n. 5.

§5. [MAN LEARNS TO DO THIS VERY LATE, AND THUS CANNOT
OBSERVE ANY DISTINCTION AMONG THE TONES.]

But before a people reaches this point—before, in other words, it learns to
connect representations and concepts with its perceptions of tones—it must
first have spent centuries only perceiving. And even when it does begin to
connect representations and concepts with perceptions, these representations
are long so imperfect and limited that their influence on development of any
kind remains unnoticed for just that long a time. Extensive experience and
practice are required in order to make the connection between perception and
representation as it occurs among cultivated peoples. This can best be observed
in all those unfamiliar phemenona that appear to us for the first time. It is
thus undeniable—and history attests it—that entire peoples can have loved
and practiced music for hundreds of years without coming to an awareness of
the primary distinctions discernable in tones. If a man first advances in representations and concepts under civil government, if his body first loses its
coarseness and raw force as his intellect gains in ideas, then we must not only
be able to conceive of this person in civil circumstances, but we must have
conceived of him there for a considerable time before we can presume that
the gently fluting tone of a nightingale might please him more—might leave a
more pleasant impression on his hearing—than the loud bellowing or
screeching sounds from his own throat, or from those of his equally crude
brethren. Thus the very first music of rough and uncultivated nations was nothing more than a noisy clamoring without regard to any of the endless modifications that music allows.

§6. [RHYTHM WAS THE SINGLE EXPEDIENT MAN HAD TO MAKE HIS
SIMPLE TONES ENTERTAINING.]

One may well ask, however, how this sort of racket could please entire peoples for hundreds of years. If nothing were added to this racket by which it
could be more entertaining, and even pleasing for its duration, then it would
surely be incomprehensible, and an unbearable monotony even for the rough-
est and most uncivilized men. In his first stage of development, however, a man
soon notices that a certain regular kind of repetition makes all simple things
more entertaining. This regular repetition of simple things that in themselves
are not susceptible of any diversity we term in music *beat,* or, using the original
word, *rhythm.* Tone is in itself the expression of a sensation. Sensation follows
the laws of motion, because it is itself a motion. Consequently, the sensation
aroused by a simple tone, if it is to be entertaining, must be renewed from
time to time by the motion or repetition of the simple tone according to a
certain order. The extent of the diversion that can be provided by such a rhythmic repetition of simple tones, whose monotony would otherwise grow wearisome, can be ascertained from the use that in modern times we still make of
our drums. These mere variations of rhythmic beats not only facilitate the

motion of walking and determine the pace of the step, but also may awaken some feeling of bravery and courage in the hearts of those men for whom this warlike, purely rhythmic music is chiefly intended. There is an excellent discussion of the causes of these rhythmic effects in the article "Rhythm" in Sulzer's *Encyclopedia,* to which I refer the reader in order to avoid prolixity here.[6] Hence not only can we accept this effect of rhythm as certain and undeniable, but we can also be satisfied that all half-wild, half-civilized peoples made their first music—that is, their simple sounds and noises—varied and entertaining by this means alone, and not by modifications in the tones themselves. Abundant proof of this is provided by their instruments—their drums, rattles, clappers, and so on: without additional rhythmic motion and variety these instruments would be capable of generating even for the crudest of peoples only a wearisome and hence intolerable monotony.

§7. [WHAT IS COMPREHENDED UNDER A MUSIC CONSISTING OF SINGLE TONES.]

In order not to cause misunderstanding, however, and to make this first stage of music as clear as possible for the reader, let me suggest that the monotony or simplicity of sound in question here must not be conceived as though it had arisen from a single tone in the most literal sense. It is called monotonous only insofar as the few tones of such a music had no coherence with one another. I will explain further. Music can be called "many-toned" only when a succession of tones, however brief, is arranged in such a way as to bring into being a certain kind of melody—namely, a complete melodic statement, whose various members have various significations. In language this is a sentence, which not only signifies a thing in itself, but also a quality of that thing, joining the two together. For example, I may not only say *tree,* but *tall tree,* or *the tree is tall,* and so on. Now in its language an uncultivated people only very slowly achieves this kind of signifying, through which not only are things signified, but also their difference from other similar things. Likewise it was undoubtedly only very late, probably later still than in the case of speech,[7] that a succession of tones came to be arranged so as to generate for the senses a melody similar to a sentence in speech. And as long as a music lacks this coherence in its tones, as long as a minimum of two or three tones are not so combined that in their connection they achieve a different significance, as long as each tone must be considered for itself alone without any further relationships, connections, and

6. See p. 808, n. 1.

7. The laws that the soul observes in thinking were certainly discovered earlier than those for the feelings. The soul is more conscious of its operations in thinking than it is in feeling. Thus in the latter case the soul must first reassemble by means of recollection the scattered fragments of its state of feeling, examine them in others, and out of these collected observations gradually construct a theory. See Johann August Eberhard's *Allgemeine Theorie des Denkens und Empfindens* [*General Theory of Thinking and Feeling,* 1786], p. 98. [Au.]. Johann August Eberhard (1739–1809) was a philosopher and lexicographer who wrote extensively on esthetics and ethics.

associations, then no matter how many distinct and single, deep or high sounds this music consists of, it cannot be called anything but "single-toned." That no savage and uncultivated nation has had—and still has—such a tone series is proven for us by the musical compositions of such peoples that are known to us; they are merely rhythmic, and have so little coherence in the truly musical sense that they can be compared with sentences in speech that consist only of nouns. Indeed, with their lack of melodic coherence the tones of these pieces are so peculiar that travellers among those peoples who actually heard them could scarcely comprehend them and render them in European notation.

§8. [THIS FIRST STAGE OF MUSIC LASTED FOR A VERY LONG TIME, AND STILL ENDURES AMONG MANY PEOPLES. FOR DESPITE ITS INFERIOR NATURE, UNCULTIVATED PEOPLES STILL FIND IT VERY ENTERTAINING.]

How long a people can tolerate this first crude state of music cannot be precisely determined. We do still find it today, however, among many Asiatic, African, and American peoples, whom we also know to have made no progress for millennia in other branches of culture.

Moreover, as inferior as this crude, barbaric music is in itself, it still serves uncultivated peoples as pleasure and amusement in several ways. They combine it with dance, and use it not only for domestic and social diversion, but also in religious ceremonies and in their wars. But in all these different usages it is always the same deafening and concussive noise, which they love all the more the less their intellect is engaged or capable of engagement.

THE SECOND PERIOD OF THE ART

§9. [THE SIMILARITY BETWEEN THE UTTERANCES OF FEELINGS AND THOUGHTS.]

The similarity that can be observed in more than one respect between feelings and thoughts must necessarily have prompted man, with the growth of his intellect, partly just to increase the expressions not only of thoughts but also of feelings, but partly also gradually to adapt these expressions more precisely to the characteristic and manifold manner in which feelings and thoughts are customarily uttered. Hitherto his speech-sounds had been nothing but interjections and simple words, with which he designated the external objects most closely surrounding him. With increasing observation of these objects, however, he gradually discovered ever new aspects—new characteristics—of the objects, by which to distinguish them from other objects of a similar kind, for the designation of which simple words were no longer sufficient. The speech-sounds of his feelings were just as simple—mere sounds without connection. The more often the same feeling was reawakened, the more intimately did the feeling man grow acquainted with it. He had necessarily to notice that there were differentiations among feelings as well as among physical objects and thoughts—that there were primary and secondary feelings, more or less pleasant and unpleasant feelings, happy and sad ones, and so forth—and that for the expression, representation, or imitation of these feelings the individual high or low sounds hitherto in use were just as insufficient as were the single tones of speech for the designation of external objects with their variations and special characteristics.

§10. [THE SIMILARITY BETWEEN SCALES AND PARTS OF SPEECH ARISING FROM THIS SIMILARITY BETWEEN THOUGHTS AND FEELINGS.]

In language this observation of the different qualities and relations of external objects and thoughts gradually gave rise to the discovery of the parts of speech, as we call them, as well as to inflections and diverse alterations of the original sounds of speech. In music, or the language of the feelings, it led to a combination of tones that in their mutual relations consisted of primary and secondary tones, or (to borrow grammatical terminology) of noun-, adjective-, and conjunction-tones. Through these first efforts—these first steps in the development of a true language of tones or feelings—the groundwork was laid for the regular and coherent successions of tones we now call scales. The final development of these scales, however, cost the human intellect so much strain and effort that it could be fully accomplished only after several millennia.

·   ·   ·   ·   ·

REFLECTIONS ON MUSICAL NOTATION

§58. III.

The third place among the auxiliary sciences belonging to musical grammar[8] is taken by the art of writing down music, which is also called the art of notation, or is designated by its technical name *semiography* (the doctrine of signs).

Writing presupposes thought, because it is the visible sign of a thought, used when someone wants either to share that thought with another person or to recall it privately. The case is the same with musical notation, which comprises the visible signs of audible interconnected tones, which by its means can either be shared with others or recalled to one's own mind.

§59. [NOTATION CAN HAVE BEEN INVENTED ONLY AFTER MUSIC WAS RATHER MORE DEVELOPED.]

It is not my intention here to investigate the many ways in which such visible signs of tones could have been or actually have been devised. Not only do we not have enough information about the subject, but also this kind of investiga-

8. Forkel assigns the first two places to physical and mathematical acoustics (§52–§57).

tion belongs to the history of the doctrine of signs, which will appear in the sequel to this work. I shall only say as a preliminary that the musical art had already to have attained a considerable scope and degree of development before any appropriate signs at all could have been discovered for the tones—signs, that is, that not only could be adapted perfectly to the music of the time, but could also follow it through all the steps of its development and refinement. We know that the first language writing was nothing but a crude picturing of visible objects. In this period what was not visually perceived could also not be visibly expressed. Like air, a tone is a body, but an invisible one; man must thus have devised signs for it at least as late as he devised signs for invisible thoughts. If we now know that in language writing thoughts were initially given signs only according to certain relations and similarities that they had with external visible objects—namely, pictorially, then we ought not to be surprised that as long as tones are still left unconnected, no similarity with external visible objects can be observed, and hence not even this type of inferior pictographic writing can occur. Therefore history also, insofar as it has left us accounts about this matter, confirms that no people could arrive at any method at all for translating its melodies into signs before the invention of alphabetical writing.

§60. [HOW IT HAPPENS THAT NO PEOPLE COULD WRITE DOWN A MELODY BEFORE THE INVENTION OF ALPHABETICAL WRITING.]

This was in all likelihood because a people that was about to devise an alphabetical script already had to be extremely enlightened. It already had to be capable of transferring every external visible or audible perception into the soul as a picture, and of turning it into thoughts or abstract ideas. In other words, perceptions would already have had to be changed into representations and concepts. With this capacity to abstract, a relationship could also gradually be observed among tones, and be put into signs at least to some extent by the very means used to designate the sounds of speech. It is most regrettable that the path by which the human intellect gradually arrived at the discovery of its written characters of all kinds lies so obscure before us—so obscure that we can scarcely make out its least trace. In language writing there are still at least some traces visible, although very slight, by which we can conjecture to some extent how human beings passed step by step from pictographs to syllabic and alphabetical script. In music notation, however, we are completely cast adrift, and apparently must give up even the slightest hope of making discoveries in a matter at once so interesting and so important to human understanding.

§61. [THE INCONVENIENCE AND IMPERFECTION OF THE FIRST MUSIC NOTATION.]

It is well known that letters of the alphabet were used for the designation of tones by all ancient peoples, and still for a good while through the Middle Ages; for the most part, with the exception of a few small alterations, our modern names for tones are written as they were then. But this system of signs, when it was not meant to serve as mere nomenclature as it does with us, had the inconvenience that it must signify with different signs not only each tone but also all the different relations of a tone, necessitating an astonishing multiplicity of signs even if the melody that was to be designated was only of limited range. This condition of the notational art is proof that people had not thoroughly investigated the countless ways in which tones are differentiated, in order to observe how many of these features are essential to the tone and how many are merely accidental. In short, they were still not capable of dividing the whole gamut of tones into classes according to their similarities and differences, or of resolving them into their principal varieties, and consequently could not even designate the tones that were similar to each other with similar signs, or the genuinely different ones with dissimilar signs. A similar situation obtains in syllabic writing, which also had need of an astonishing quantity of signs as long as the words and syllables were not resolved into their simplest sounds. Hence syllabic writing was so inconvenient that with the multiplication of concepts and the ever-increasing need for writing, people necessarily had to abolish it and seek out better means. Language and writing always proceeded at an equal pace in their development; therefore music and notation can be presumed to have done the same. Thus we can safely conclude that a people who used this kind of notation must have had an extremely imperfect, extremely unordered music.

§62. [INITIALLY NO ONE CAME UP WITH A PICTORIAL REPRESENTATION OF SCALES.]

Since at first man arrived at all knowledge through pictorial representations, it is surprising that in music he missed this path, which could have led him most securely and swiftly to his goal. Certainly a single tone cannot be conceived of by way of an image. But once a succession of interconnected tones is present, when one hears it or sees it struck on an instrument there arises an image of an ascent and descent, or a ladder, and what would be easier and more natural in this case than to have a single arbitrary sign of a tone ascending and descending stepwise? We have no evidence whether the Greeks named their tones series merely "systems" (a term found in most Greek writers), or also named them after this image, as happened in the Middle Ages. For what the Romans long after them called *scala* was to the Greeks a rhetorical figure named *climax*, and it had no actual relationship to their music.[9] But no matter whether they had such a nomenclature, it is still certain that, like other ancient peoples whose notation we know something about, they wrote their notes or musical

9. *Climax* (Greek, "ladder") is the term for a rhetorical figure in which there is a gradual ascent in intensity in parallel word forms ("I came, I saw, I conquered"). The word does, however, become a musical term when the Latin *climacus* is used in neumatic notation to denote a neume of three notes descending. Forkel seems to have some awareness here of the medieval neumes as iconic representations of ascending and descending figures.

letters horizontally, completely contrary to the image of a tone series.[10] Thus what man hit on first in language writing—that is, a sign imitating the picture of an object—he hit upon last in musical notation.

§63. [EVEN AFTER ACHIEVING A PICTORIAL REPRESENTATION, FOR A LONG TIME THEY STILL CONFUSED THE TONES AND WORDS OF A SONG WITH ONE ANOTHER.]

Our modern notation is really a sequence of such pictorial representations, but only very slowly has it become what it now is. The habit the ancients had of writing their tone signs horizontally over the text of a melody had been widely propagated in the Middle Ages, but with the already considerable difference that in place of the great variety of Greek letters they used a small

10. The Arabs call their music *ilm el edwar*, or "the science of the circle," and even write their melodies in circles, in which as many lines are drawn on top of one another as the melody contains intervals. These lines, which are drawn inside a circle, all have different colors in addition. Thus if, for example, they are to designate seven tones—which the Arabs call *alif, be, gim, dal, hé, waw, zal'n*, corresponding to our A, B, C, D, E, F, G—they must be of seven different colors. The line that signifies the lowest tones, namely the *Alif* or our A, is green, the second rose-colored, the third a kind of blue, the fourth violet, the fifth brown, the sixth black, and the seventh light blue. The following is an illustration of this kind of Arab notation:

Tone of all tones.				
			7	G
	Note.		6	F
	Quick fall downward.		5	E
First note.			4	D
Fall. Quick note.	Note.		3	C
	Fall. Upward. Note. End.		2	B
			1	A

Circle of the mode Zirafkend.

number of Latin ones. Although they now began to sense the ascending and descending motion of the melody, this feeling still appears to have been so obscure that in pictorial representations they confused melody and text with one another, and let words rise and fall between the drawn lines in the place of tones. It was still thus in the time of Hucbald, who lived in the tenth century, as can be seen from the *Musica enchiriadis,* printed in Martin Gerbert, *Scriptores ecclesiastici di musica sacra* [1784] vol. 1, pp. 152ff.[11]

●   ●   ●   ●   ●

CHAPTER II. THE HISTORY OF MUSIC IN EGYPT

§ 30. [REFLECTIONS ON BRUCE'S LETTER[12] AND A DEDUCTION ABOUT THE INTRINSIC CHARACTER OF ANCIENT EGYPTIAN MUSIC.]

From these reports, which are in part very valuable, as well as from the number of musical instruments previously described that according to the testi-

---

To interpret this kind of notation, in German it would mean something like the following:
1) Take the tone D.
2) From here drop down to C.
3) Move from there to F.
4) And drop again to B, through all the tones lying in between.
5) Make a pause here.
6) Climb up again to C and
7) end on B.
Arab notation also has its abbreviations, which, however, are altogether proof of its deficiency. These abbreviations always have the same color as the line on which they stand. *Makhadz* signifies the first note, *sooud,* the rise of the voice, *tertib,* the continuation by one degree, *sooud lilefra,* the quick rise of the voice, *houbouth,* a fall, *houbouth bil tertib,* a gradual fall, *serian,* quickly, *houbouth bil efrâ,* a quick fall, *thafr,* a leap, *afk,* a quick motion, *rikz,* the last note of the piece. Thus the Arabs have no actual notational signs, but only such signs as can suggest the course of a melody only to a certain extent, by very difficult means. Thus Arab musicians know all their melodies by heart, and the one who knows them best is the most honored person among them. Since the Arabs were after all a learned people, and were always great friends of music, as the surviving manuscripts of Avicenna [Ibn Sina], Alpharabius [Al-Farabi], Abdulcadir ['Abd al-Qadir], Alschalahi, and others can testify, and still their notation could not attain even a mediocre degree of perfection, this is fresh proof that finding the true path to the true notation has cost uncommonly great toil and struggle. One finds traces of a notation among the Persians, the Chinese, and several other non-European peoples, ancient as well as modern, but they have all come no further—and not even as far as—the Arabs. [Au.]
This lengthy note on Arab music consists of kernels of truth distorted by a good deal of misinformation. What Forkel's source or sources for the note were is not known. The notational elements he mentions did exist in Arab music: musical modes were thought of as cyclical, as in Forkel's circle (one of the most famous books on Arab music is the *Kitab al-adwar,* or *Book on the Cyclic Forms of Musical Modes*), and colors were used as representations of chords. But Forkel's combination of these elements makes little sense; his source may well have been a person who knew some Arabic but little about Arab music.
11. The treatise *Musica enchiriadis* (c. 900) was incorrectly attributed to Hucbald by Gerbert. Hucbald's treatise *De harmonica institutione* (c. 880) is printed in the same volume. See the excerpt from *Musica enchiriadis, SR* 2.
12. The previous section (§29) consists of Forkel's translation of a letter to Charles Burney from James Bruce, the famous explorer of the sources of the Nile (*Travels to Discover the Source of the Nile* [London, 1790]) concerning Egyptian musical instruments. Burney published the let-

mony of earlier historians were in use among the Egyptians, we can now conclude with certainty that music was practiced and beloved in Egypt from the earliest times. But how this Egyptian music was constituted cannot easily be determined: did it attain a considerable degree of development or, as is probably to be concluded from most of their instruments, the Theban harp described by Bruce included, did it remain a crude beginning for the art, a matter unworthy of the consideration of posterity? The determination of this question would require accounts of a completely different sort than those that remain to us. Beyond instruments there are still so many requirements even for a moderate degree of perfection in this art, which were altogether overlooked by the historians of Egyptian arts and sciences; without them a truly considerable development can be imagined as little in music as in the other arts and sciences. Thus we are obliged either to give up the determination of this question entirely or to risk conjectures and inferences that indeed, if they are deduced from things whose true character is more precisely known, can be brought to a higher degree of plausibility, but never to full certainty. Nevertheless I will dare a few such deductions.

§31. [WHETHER THE EGYPTIANS HAD A MUSIC NOTATION.]

The art of notation—or the science of writing down musical thoughts—is as important to music as the art of writing is to scholarship. If we had not invented signs for the various utterances of a language by means of which these utterances could be made visible and permanent, so to speak, they might have developed much later, or more probably might never have attained the perfection in which we now see them. The situation is the same with the language of music: its utterances vanish just as quickly as do the utterances of the spoken language, and it is an undeniable truth that all peoples who do not know how to write down their melodies continue to have an extremely insignificant music. The entire music of such peoples consists of songs of such a small range that everyone is able to remember them easily by heart; there is no use thinking of anything that even begins to resemble a coherent musical discourse. Language and writing, music and notation—the elements of both these pairs stand in such a natural and necessary relation with each other that they can only attain perfection at an equal pace, and neither can thrive without the other.

§32. [GENERAL REFLECTIONS ON THE WRITING OF EARLY PEOPLES.]

At present most writers unanimously consider the Phoenicians[13] to have been the first people in the ancient world to possess writing and the

---

ter in his *General History of Music* (vol. 1, pp. 177–83), along with Bruce's sketch of a "Theban harp" (plate 1, vol. 1, p. 391).

13. "If rumor is to be believed, it was the Phoenicians who first dared to capture an utterance by marking it down with crude figures." Lucan. [Au.] This remark—actually two dactyllic-hexameter verses from the Roman poet Lucan's *Bellum civile* (*Pharsalia*), an epic account of the civil

Egyptians the second; but it is recognized just as unanimously that this early writing was still extremely deficient. Naturally the first attempts were simply intended to preserve the memory of events and discoveries that these people believed would be of consequence to posterity. There is sufficient proof that in the first millennia the means to attain these ends were not only columns, altars, and other devices of a similar sort, but also—indeed primarily—songs and regular festivals. The most common of these devices were songs, which were introduced by all peoples in the most remote past, and in more modern times as well as in the ancient world. The Egyptians,[14] Phoenicians,[15] Arabs,[16] Chinese,[17] Gauls,[18] Greeks,[19] Mexicans,[20] Peruvians,[21] and even the ancient inhabitants of the North, of Brazil,[22]

---

wars between Caesar and Pompey—seems to have served eighteenth-century writers as a *locus classicus* for the account of the Phoenicians' invention of writing. See Charles Burney, *A General History of Music,* vol. 1, 220.

14. Clemens of Alexandria, *Stromata libri VIII* [*Tapestries, Eight Volumes*], I.6. p. 757. [Au.]

15. Sanchoniathon in Eusebius, [*De evangelica praeparatione (Preparation for the Gospel)*], Bk. 1, p. 38. [Au.] Sanchoniathon was a Phoenician writer of great antiquity (conjectures range from the thirteenth to the sixth century B.C.E.) whose writings about Phoenician mythology and religion were translated by Philo of Biblos around 100 C.E. The fourth-century Christian bishop and church historian Eusebius of Caesarea included extracts from this translation in his essay on the Gospels.

16. The Book of Job, chap. 36, v. 24. [Au.]

17. *Lettres edifiantes* [*et curieuses, écrites des missions étrangères, par quelques missionaires de la Compagnie de Jesus*] (*Curious and Edifying Letters Written from Foreign Missions, by some Jesuit Missionaries*), (Paris, 1729), vol. 19, p. 477, [Au.] A letter from a Jesuit in China describes the ancient ethical books of the Chinese, one type of which contains songs describing paradigmatic deeds of Chinese heroes.

18. Tacitus, *De moribus Germanorum,* chap. 2, cited in *Bibliothéque universelle,* vol. 6, p. 299. [Au.] In this passage Tacitus states that ancient songs were the only source of historical tradition among the German tribes.

19. *Mémoires* [*de Littérature tirés des Registers*] *de l'Académie des Inscriptions* [*et belles lettres*] (43 vols.; Paris, 1728–86)], vol. 6, p. 165. Tacitus, *Annales,* lib. 4. chap. 43. [Au.] In this passage from the *Annals* Tacitus tells of a dispute between the Spartans and their neighbors the Messenians over the possession of a temple, in which both sides cited the songs of ancient poets as evidence for their case. The Tacitus passage is cited in the *Mémoires* by a certain M. Freret in an essay on the validity of the evidence in the works of ancient historians.

20. Theodore de Bry, *Historia Americae* [1590–1634], vol. 2, p. 4.; p. 123. [Au.] The fourteen lavish volumes about travels in the Americas published by de Bry and his family were the first such series to contain accurate illustrations of life in the New World.

21. *Histoire des Incas, rois du Perou,* [trans. Thomas François Dalibard from the Spanish of Garcilaso de la Vega; 2 vols. (Paris, 1744)], vol. 1, p. 321; vol. 2, p. 56, 57, 145. It is said that the Peruvians still sing an ode from their earliest times that contains the history of the world according to their ancient theology. [Au.] Vega, the illegitimate son of a Spanish knight and an Inca princess who was raised in Peru, wrote histories of the Indians of South America and of the expeditions of the Spanish conquistadors.

22. *Voyages de* [*François*] *Coreal* [*aux Indes Occidentales,* 1666–97, trans. from the Spanish; 2 vols. (Paris, Noel Pissot, 1722)], vol. 1, pp. 199, 203. J[ean] de Léry, *Histoire d'un voyage faict en la terre du Brésil* [1578], p. 248. [Au.] Coreal in these passages mentions songs of Brazilian savages containing a flood narrative much like the story of Noah, a description of a paradise resembling the Elysian Fields, and tales of the cannibal prowess of their valiant ances-

Iceland,[23] Greenland,[24] Virginia,[25] Santo Domingo,[26] and Canada[27] had them, and some peoples continued to use them even after the invention of alphabetical writing, as can be seen from the Song of Moses upon the miraculous crossing of the Red Sea.

§33. [CONTINUATION.]

From these first attempts to transmit the memory of events the way to further perfection was taken with slow steps. The picturing of physical objects, which was common among the ancient Egyptians, and which in more recent times has been found among the Mexicans,[28] persisted for a long time before it could be extended to a still imperfect hieroglyphic writing. But since people soon sensed that even these hieroglyphics were not capable of any great perfection, and could not accomplish what was expected of them, given the gradual extension of concepts and the growth of language, they had to make a radical departure from the original path, and seek out another way to attain their goal. At this point they first invented signs for whole words and syllables, and then moved gradually from this word- and syllable-based writing to an alphabetical writing, which is now in general use among the most cultivated of earth's peoples. How much time and effort these grand and important inventions must have cost the human spirit can easily be imagined by anyone who has the least notion of the construction of languages, and realizes that there is no necessary connection between the sound of the words and their arbitrary signs that could have led people easily from one to the other.

That the invention of music notation must have cost the human spirit no less effort and toil can be most easily attested by the millenia required for its

---

tors. A fourth edition of the Léry (Geneva, 1600) recounts songs dealing with the same subjects (p. 315).

23. *Bibliothèque ancienne et moderne* [29 vols. (Amsterdam, 1714–27)], vol. 2, p. 241. [Au.] Reviewed in this publication is a history of Iceland by Arius, translated into Latin by Torfe (*Historia rerum Norvegicarum,* 4 v. [Copenhagen, 1711]). The review mentions an Icelandic *edde* or ode by one Semund that chronicles deeds of past history.

24. [John Anderson], *Histoire naturelle de l'Islande,* [*du Groenland, du detroit de Davis, et d'autres pays situés sous le Nord (A Natural History of Iceland, Greenland, the Davis Straits, and Other Countries Situated in the North),* 2 vols.; trans. from the German by Gottfried Sellius (Paris, S. Jorry, 1750)], vol. 2, p. 232. [Au.] Anderson describes a ceremony in which songs about a tribe's past exploits in hunting, fishing, and so on are sung to the beat of a drum.

25. *Journal des sçavans,* March 1681, p. 46. [Au.] This reference has not been identified.

26. [Abbé Prévost, ed.], *Histoire generale des voyages* [64 vols.; Paris: Didot, 1746–89], vol. 12, p. 219. [Au.] The explorer Jean Diaz de Solis tells of Santo Domingan natives whose songs, taking the place of books, "serve as their annals," preserving all their historical knowledge.

27. [Joseph-François Lafitau], *Moeurs des sauvages [ameriquains, comparées aux moeurs des premiers temps,* 2 vols. (Paris, 1724)], vol. 1. p. 519. [Au.] Description of song festivals among Canadian tribes in which the first songs performed chronicle the ancient exploits of the tribe.

28. See *Allgemeine Historie der Reisen zu Wasser und Lande* [21 vols.; 1757], in the description of the conquest of Mexico, where it is alleged that the inhabitants gave Montezuma the news of the landing of Cortez by means of a drawing. [Au.]

development, of which we now avail ourselves. A more detailed history of the matter in the sequel to this work will make it clearer and more vivid.

§34. [WE FIND NO EVIDENCE THAT THE EGYPTIANS HAD A MUSIC NOTATION.]

Now as certain as it is that one can draw conclusions about the cultivation of a people from the quality of its language and writing, it is equally certain that a similar conclusion can be drawn concerning music and notation. But writers of antiquity do not tell us whether the Egyptians had a notation of any kind. If there is not even the smallest suggestion of it, we must be willing to consider what Dionysus[29] says in his treatise on the art of interpretation—that the Egyptians designated the tones of their music by the vowels of their alphabet. But since this is merely a matter of nomenclature, nothing can actually be proven by it.

§35. [THEY MAY HAVE HAD ONE THAT WAS SIMILAR TO THE NOTATION OF THE CHINESE.]

The similarity between the Egyptians and the Chinese in physical form, manners, taste, customary attachments, and so on, and de Guignes's opinion that 1122 years before Christ a colony of Egyptians travelled to China[30] could perhaps suggest some conjectures on this obscure subject. The Chinese actually have a musical notation, although compared to ours it is extremely undeveloped, as is their music in general. Like many peoples, they make use of the letters of their language script for that purpose, and even write them in the same way as in their language, in vertical columns begun on the righthand side.[31] Since not only the letters of the Egyptians but also the way they are written have many similarities with the Chinese method, it could perhaps be conjectured from this correspondence that the Egyptians could also have had a similar notation. But even if they actually did have such a thing, it would not permit us to reach the most favorable conclusions about the perfection of their music, but would rather be proof that among them this art had never emerged from a true state of childhood. With all the praise that has been bestowed on the music of the Chinese, the greatest admirers of Chinese arts and sciences still cannot help but grant that their notation has great inconveniences, and would be of use to no other music but that of the Chinese. If these admirers think that the acknowledged uselessness of Chinese notation for other than

---

29. Dionysius of Halicarnassus [fl. c. 20 B.C.] was a Greek historian and teacher of rhetoric. His *De compositione verborum* (*On the Arrangement of Words*) is one of the few treatises of antiquity to treat word order and euphony.

30. Joseph de Guignes (1721–1800), *Mémoire dans lequel on prouve, que les chinois sont une colonie egyptienne* (*Memoir in Which It Is Proved that the Chinese Are an Egyptian Colony*), Paris, 1759.

31. A demonstration of this Chinese notation can be found in the *Essai sur la musique ancienne et moderne* by [Jean-Benjamin de] La Borde [4 vols. (Paris, 1780)], vol. 1, p. 144. [Au.]

Chinese styles of music does the music of this country no dishonor, and is, moreover, perfectly consonant with its perfection and intrinsic worth, then they only show that they have not yet received sufficient instruction in these matters. Poverty in signs presupposes poverty in words and concepts, just as too great a variety of the same presupposes disorder and confusion. The Chinese are manifestly in the latter condition regarding the signs of their language, which number 80,000 and are altogether so copious that learning them constitutes the single, lifelong occupation of a scholar among them. Everything we know about their music shows that concerning their notation the former condition prevails.

§36. [BUT THIS IS MERELY AN INSUBSTANTIAL CONJECTURE.]

Nonetheless, the observation of this similarity that obtains between the ancient Egyptians and the Chinese in customs, habits, taste, and other matters justifies only a weak conjecture with regard to the notation of the former people, one that cannot be supported by a single proof. Since the example of countless other nations shows that it is possible to have some sort of music for many centuries without being able to write it down, we may be least liable to error if we make the general assumption that the Egyptians were in no way acquainted with the formidable art of writing music. Not only the erudition of this people, but also its other arts (insofar as their nature is known to us) provide more than one reason to come to such a conclusion, and to accept it as a positive truth, at least as long as no one happens upon the holy book of Mercury, in which the hymns to the Egyptian gods were written down, and by deciphering them convinces us of the contrary view.

147 Johann Friedrich Reichardt

Born at Königsberg in 1752, Johann Friedrich Reichardt began as a student of philosophy and music. He spent the years 1771–74 traveling in Germany and published his impressions in three volumes. In 1775 he became Capellmeister at the court of Frederick the Great, but left this position in 1785 to go to London and Paris; his sympathetic view of the French Revolution undoubtedly had something to do with this. After Frederick's death he returned to Berlin, but was forced to leave again. He died at Halle in 1814.

Reichardt's literary production is a considerable one. He was a man of broad culture who handled his pen with great skill. The books in which he collected his impressions of Germany (1774–76), Paris (1804–5), and Vienna (1810) are valued not only for the information they contain, but also for their pleasant style.

FROM *Personal Letters Written on a Trip to Vienna*
(1810)

ELEVENTH LETTER

[November 30, 1808] I have been anxiously awaiting a wholly free and quiet moment to describe faithfully for you a touching scene which I had with old Haydn. Fräulein von Kurzbeck, whom he loves like a father,[1] and Frau von Pereira, full of admiration for him, as for everything great and beautiful, were my guides. As a fitting overture to the scene, Fraülein von Kurzbeck played for me beforehand on her fortepiano a big and difficult sonata by our late Prince Louis Ferdinand. A pupil of Clementi's, she played it in quite masterly fashion, with delicate expression and equally perfect execution which left nothing whatever to be desired in point of purity and clarity.

In one of the outlying suburbs we had to drive nearly an hour into the remotest alleys and corners. Here, in the small but quite attractive garden house which belongs to him, we found the splendid old man, seated at a table covered with a green cloth. Fully dressed in a simple but neat gray-cloth suit with white buttons and an elegantly groomed and powdered curly wig, he sat there quite stiffly, almost rigid, drawn up close to the table, both hands resting on top of it, not unlike a lifelike wax figure. Fräulein Kurzbeck first explained to him that she would like to introduce me; I was almost afraid he would not know my name, or would perhaps not recall it in this state of apathy, and I was really taken aback and (I may honestly say) ashamed when the old hero opened his eyes wider—they still have an animated sparkle—and said: "Reichardt? A——man! Where is he?" I had just come in, and with outstretched arms he

TEXT: *Vertraute Briefe geschrieben auf einer Reise nach Wien und den österreichischen Staaten zu Ende 1808 und zu Anfang 1809* (Amsterdam, 1810), vol. 1, pp. 161–68, 204–10, 218–22, 231–32, 254–58, 450–54; vol. 2, pp. 138–39, 143–44, 146–50. Translation by Oliver Strunk, with additions by Wye J. Allanbrook.

1. Magdalene von Kurzböck, to whom Haydn dedicated his piano trio in E-flat minor and the Viennese edition of his piano sonata in E-flat (No. 52). Reichardt, who had already met Fräulein von Kurzböck at Baron von Arnsteiner's, has this to say of her (vol. 1, p. 145): "One of the most interesting acquaintances I made was Fräulein von Kurzböck, who was presented to me as the greatest pianist among the ladies of the local musical world, and that is saying a good deal. For a long time I had been hearing about her great talent, and I had just heard about it again in Dresden and Prague; I had thus been looking forward particularly to making her acquaintance. She received me as well and as graciously as if she had been looking forward in the same way to meeting me."

called to me from across the table: "Dearest Reichardt, do come! I must embrace you!" With that he kissed me, pressing my hand tightly and convulsively, then ran his thin hand three or four times over my cheeks, saying to the others: "What pleases me is that the——artist also has such a good honest face." I sat down beside him and retained his hand in mine. He looked at me for a time, deeply affected, then added: "Still so fresh! Alas, I have put too great a strain on my powers—already I am altogether a child"—and wept bitter tears. The ladies were about to interrupt in order to spare him. "No, let me go on, children," the dear old man exclaimed; "this does me good; these are in reality tears of joy over the man beside me; he will fare better." I was seldom able to bring forth a friendly word of gratitude and could only fervently kiss his hand.

Frau von Pereira, whom he had at first not recognized with his feeble memory, reminded him in a childlike, playful way of various jokes, and he presently joined her in this style, of which he is said to have always been very fond. With this the ladies thought we ought to leave the weak old man, lest in the end he be too much affected, and we took our farewell. Scarcely had we gotten out the door, however, when he called us back, exclaiming: "After all, I must show Reichardt my treasures too!" At that a servant girl brought in all sorts of beautiful things, some of them quite valuable. The most interesting among them was a rather large flat box which Princess Esterhazy, the wife of the now reigning prince[2]—the son of the prince who was for the greater part of Haydn's life his master—had had made for him after her own express design. It was of black ebony, heavily mounted in gold and ornamented with a gold bas-relief.[3] On the lid had been painted the beautiful affecting scene in the Akademiesaal, which, on the occasion of the last great performance of Haydn's *Schöpfung*, proved a veritable apotheosis for the composer.[4] (Collin recently recited to me a really beautiful descriptive poem on this scene.[5]) In the box lay a magnificent big autograph album, likewise black and gold, signed on the cover by the Princess, most cordially inscribed within by the whole princely family. I should be the first artist to inscribe myself, the old man said, and he would have the book sent to me. The whole box, incidentally, was filled on either side with the most dainty writing things and with all sorts of pleasant and useful instruments of gold and fine English steelwork.

2. Marie von Lichtenstein, Princess Esterhazy, wife of Prince Nicholas II.
3. For the later history of this box, see Pohl-Botstiber, *Joseph Haydn,* vol. 3 (Leipzig, 1927), pp. 258–59.
4. This miniature, by Balthasar Wigand, is reproduced in many modern sources. The performance in question had taken place on March 27, 1808, some months before Reichardt's arrival in Vienna.
5. Heinrich Josef von Collin (1771–1811), Viennese poet and dramatist and author of the tragedy *Coriolan* for which Beethoven wrote his famous overture. A translation of Collin's encomium to Haydn can be found in *Haydn: Two Contemporary Portraits,* trans. and ed. Vernon Gotwals (Madison: Univ. of Wisconsin Press, 1968), pp. 178–79.

Then he showed me further a great number of gold medals—from the musical society in St. Petersburg, from the Paris concerts, for which he wrote several symphonies expressly, and from many others—also a perfectly magnificent ring from the Russian Czar, a diploma from the National Institute in Paris, another from Vienna, conferring honorary citizenship on him, and many other things of this sort. In them the kind old man seems to live again quite happily.

When after a full hour we took leave in earnest, he detained me alone, holding my hand firmly, and told me, while kissing me repeatedly, that I should visit him at least once a week as long as I remained here. I shall not soil this recital with the little anxious touches of avarice he betrayed, in the midst of treasures he could no longer even use—but they went straight to my heart.

The excellent Beethoven I have also called on, having found him out at last. People here take so little interest in him that no one was able to tell me his address,[6] and it really cost me considerable trouble to locate him. I found him finally in a great deserted and lonely house. At first he looked almost as gloomy as his surroundings, but presently he grew more cheerful and appeared to take quite as much pleasure in seeing me again as I in seeing him, commenting also, openly and cordially, on many things about which I needed information. His is a powerful nature, outwardly Cyclops-like, but in reality sincere, friendly, and kind. He lives much of the time with a Hungarian Countess Erdödy, who occupies the front part of the great house,[7] but he has broken off completely with Prince Lichnowsky, who lives upstairs and with whom for several years he spent all his time. I wanted also to call on the Prince, who is an old acquaintance, and on his wife, a daughter of the excellent Countess von Thun, to whom I owe the greater part of the amenities of my previous stay in Vienna,[8] but I found neither one at home and soon afterwards learned that the Princess lives in virtually complete retirement.

Salieri, who occupies a fine-looking house of his own, I found sitting with a cloth greatcoat over his clothes and frock coat among the music and musical instruments which quite fill his big room, for he never heats it; he wanted me to put on again my own greatcoat, which I had left in the anteroom, but at the moment I was not so chilled, although I cannot ordinarily be as tough as this coarse Italian nature. He has aged, to be sure, since I last saw him, but for all that is still, as he always was, the quite extraordinarily elegant and adroit Italian gentleman in his physiognomy and manner. He too spoke to me in a friendly and confidential way about many things and characterized for me the singers and orchestras of the various theaters with equal frankness and precision. I took leave of him with a sense of pleasure and gratitude.

•　　•　　•　　•　　•

6. Krugerstrasse, 1704.
7. To Countess Erdödy, Beethoven dedicated the piano trios, Op. 70, on one of which he was still working at the time of Reichardt's call, also the two sonatas, Op. 102, for cello and piano.
8. During his travels between 1771 and 1774.

THIRTEENTH LETTER

[December 10, 1808] Today I must speak to you about a very fine quartet series that Herr Schuppanzigh, an excellent violinist in the service of Prince von Rasumovsky, the former Russian envoy to the imperial court, has opened by subscription for the winter. The concerts will take place in a private house every Thursday from twelve to two. Last Thursday we heard the first one; there was as yet no great company in attendance, but what there was consisted entirely of ardent and attentive friends of music, precisely the proper public for this most elegant and most congenial of all musical combinations. Had Haydn given us only the quartet, inspiring other genial artists to follow his example, it would already have been enough to make him a great benefactor of the whole world of music. Difficult as it is to bring this sort of music to perfection in performance—for the whole and each of its single parts are heard in their entirety and satisfy only in the most perfect intonation, ensemble, and blending—it is the first variety to be provided wherever good friends of music meet to play together. And since it is charitably rooted in the human makeup that expectation and capacity as a rule keep more or less in step and go hand in hand, each one takes at least some degree of pleasure in the performance, once he has brought to it all that he can offer it individually or through his immediate background. On this account the exacting connoisseur and critic not infrequently finds such groups working away with great enthusiasm, perfectly at home, when he himself, spurred by his overtrained artistic nature, would like to run away.

Here, however, such was not the case. The quartet is on the whole well balanced, although some say that last year, when Herr Kraft[9] played with them, the balance was better. Herr Schuppanzigh himself has an original, piquant style most appropriate to the humorous quartets of Haydn, Mozart, and Beethoven—or, perhaps more accurately, a product of the capricious manner of performance suited to these masterpieces. He plays the most difficult passages clearly, although not always quite in tune, a consideration to which the local virtuosi seem in general to be superior; he also accents very correctly and significantly, and his cantabile, too, is often quite singing and affecting. He is likewise a good leader for his carefully chosen colleagues, who enter admirably into the spirit of the composer, though he disturbed me often with his accursed fashion, generally introduced here, of beating time with his foot, even when there was no need for it, sometimes out of habit alone, at other times only to reinforce the *forte*. Generally speaking, one seldom hears a *forte* here—let alone a *fortissimo*—without the leader's joining in with his foot. For me this ruins the pure free enjoyment, and every such beat interrupts for me the coordinated and perfected performance which it is supposed to help bring about

9. The cellist Anton Kraft. Reichardt will have heard the quartet with Joseph Linke as cellist. Kraft subsequently formed a quartet of his own; Reichardt heard their first concert early in 1809 (vol. 1, p. 368).

and which I had expected from this public production. At rehearsal, where one must continue practicing and assist oneself by all possible means of direction until the piece goes together perfectly, there one may beat time and even shout as much as one pleases. At the performance itself, repose in all things is the chief requirement; all preliminary scaffolding must now disappear altogether, and it is far better to let a mistake pass without censure, whether actually committed or only feared, than to try to help matters by using strong measures. Not to mention that the inexperienced and uninformed listener will probably not notice the mistake in any case, while the more competent will notice it no less and be doubly offended. Furthermore, an attentive and conscientious colleague ought never to be disconcerted by such shameful public prompting—it can only disturb his repose and control, on which above all the perfection of the performance depends; an inattentive and sluggish colleague ought not to count on so ordinary a means of assistance and stimulation. Each one must help with all his senses and his entire attention; he who is incapable of this cannot be trained to it by beating time.

At this first quartet morning there was performed—besides a very naïve and charming quartet by Haydn, full of good humor and innocence, and a more powerful, more elaborate one by Mozart—Beethoven's clear and beautiful Sextet with wind instruments, which made a fine vigorous effect.[10] In this a horn player from the orchestra of the Theater an der Wien gave me quite special pleasure, reminding me, with his beautiful tone and accurate, positive intonation of the half tones, of our late excellent Türschmidt.

I shall certainly not willingly neglect this agreeable quartet series, to which Herr Schuppanzigh has given me a ticket.

A few days later, Beethoven gave me the pleasure of inviting this same pleasing quartet to Countess von Erdödy's in order that I might hear something of his new works. He played himself in a brand new trio of considerable force and originality for fortepiano, violin, and violoncello, altogether excellent and resolute.[11]

The quartet played further several of his older and extremely difficult quartets. Herr Schuppanzigh revealed a quite special skill and dexterity in the performance of these difficult Beethoven compositions, in which the violin frequently competes with the piano in the execution of the most difficult keyboard figures, the piano with the violin in singing tone.[12]

The dear Countess, a touchingly cheerful invalid, with a friend of hers, a Hungarian lady also, took such keen and enthusiastic pleasure in each beautiful bold stroke, in each fine well-turned inflection, that the sight of her did me almost as much good as Beethoven's masterly conceptions and performance. Fortunate artist, who can count on such a listener!

10. Op. 81b, an early work not published until 1810.
11. Probably the Trio in D Major, Op. 70, No. 1, the first of the pair to be completed.
12. The works referred to must be Beethoven's early piano quartets, WoO 36, in E-flat major, D major, and C major (composed in 1785 but not published until 1828).

．　．　．　．　．

The Liebhaberkonzerte[13] have begun here for the winter, and the one I have just attended was nearly the death of me, for all that the company was very agreeable. In three rather small rooms, the like of which I have scarcely seen here before, a great crowd of listeners of all classes and an almost equally great one of musicians were so crammed together that I lost both my breath and my hearing. Fortunately, however, I did not also lose my sight, for a part of the company consisted of very attractive fine ladies, some of whom also sang very nicely. But even excellent things by Beethoven, Romberg, Paër, and others could have no effect, since in the narrow space one was quite deafened by the noise of the trumpets, kettledrums, and wind instruments of all sorts. At the same time I was offered something quite perfect to listen to—something that was also thoroughly appropriate here and for this reason did me the more good. It was a Neapolitan guitarist, who played so well that he recalled to me the good old days of the real lute playing; never have I heard anything so perfect from so imperfect an instrument. Two Italians, with agreeable tenor and bass voices, then sang with him a little French romance, "La Sentinelle": facing the enemy in the moonlight, a soldier stands on guard, confiding to the winds for his sweetheart that he watches, lives, fights, and dies for her alone. The elegant Italian, into the bargain a quite handsome young man, a regular Antinoüs, had very cleverly arranged for the guitar a wholly delightful marchlike melody, enriching it with lively interludes. This was perfectly suited to the room and to the company, which was likewise enchanted by it and appeared not to notice that the whole agreeable impression was destroyed again by Beethoven's gigantic and overpowering overture to Collin's *Coriolanus*. In the narrow rooms, my head and heart were nearly burst with the vigorous blows and crack-ings which each one strained himself to the utmost in augmenting, for the composer himself was present. It gave me great pleasure to see the excellent Beethoven not only on hand but much made of, the more so since he has in mind and heart the fatal hypochondriac delusion that everyone here persecutes and despises him. To be sure, his stubborn outward manner may frighten off some of the jolly good-natured Viennese, and many of those who acknowledge his great talent and merits may perhaps not employ sufficient humanity and delicacy to so offer the sensitive, irritable, distrustful artist the means of enjoying life that he may accept them gladly and also take satisfaction in them as an artist. It often pains me to the quick when I see this altogether excellent and splendid man gloomy and unhappy, although I am at the same time per-suaded that it is only in his willful mood of deep discontent that his best and most original works can be produced. Those who are capable of appreciating these works ought never to lose sight of this or to take offense at any of his

---

13. The orchestra of the Liebhaberkonzerte was made up of amateurs, with a few professional players for the wind instruments.

outward peculiarities or rough corners. Only then are they true, genuine admirers of his.

FOURTEENTH LETTER

[December 16, 1808.] On Sunday[14] I heard that fine quartet again. Three works were played, one by Haydn, then one by Mozart, and finally one by Beethoven; this last was particularly good. It was very interesting to me to observe in this succession how the three true humorists, each according to his individual nature, have further developed the genre. Haydn created it out of the pure, luminous fountain of his charming, original nature. In artlessness and cheerful humor he forever remains unique. Mozart's more robust nature and richer imagination gained further ground, and expressed in many a piece the heights and depths of his inner being. He was himself also more of a virtuoso in performance, and thus expected far more of the performers. In addition, he placed more importance in an artfully developed work, and thus built out of Haydn's charmingly imagined summerhouse his own palace. Beethoven settled down in this palace very early, and thus in order for him too to express his own nature in its own forms, he was left no choice but to build a bold and defiant tower on top of which no one could easily place anything more without breaking his neck. Repeatedly there has occurred to me in this context Michelangelo's proud and daring notion of placing the magnificent Pantheon on his St. Peter's as a dome.

•   •   •   •   •

SEVENTEENTH LETTER

[December 25, 1808] The past week, during which the theaters were closed, the evenings filled with public concerts and musical performances, caused me no little embarrassment in my ardent resolve to hear everything. This applies particularly to the twenty-second, when the local musicians gave the first of this season's great performances at the Burgtheater for their deserving widows' fund, while on the same day Beethoven also gave at the great suburban theater a concert for his benefit, at which only his own works were played. This last I could not conceivably miss; that morning, accordingly, I accepted with many thanks the kind invitation of Prince von Lobkowitz to join him in his box. There we sat, in the most bitter cold, from half past six until half past ten, and confirmed for ourselves the maxim that one may easily have too much of a good thing, still more of a powerful one. Nevertheless—though many a mishap in performance tried our patience to the limit—I was no more willing to leave before the final conclusion of the concert than was the extremely polite and good-natured prince, whose box was in the first balcony, quite near the stage, so that the orchestra, with Beethoven conducting in the midst of it, was almost

14. December 15.

on top of us. Poor Beethoven, who had from this concert his first and only ready profit of the whole year, found considerable hostility and only feeble support in the arrangements and performance. The singers and orchestra were made up of very heterogeneous elements, and it had not even been possible to arrange one full rehearsal of all the pieces on the program, every one of which was filled with the greatest difficulties. How much of the output of this fruitful genius and tireless worker was none the less performed during the four hours will astonish you.

To begin with, a pastoral symphony, or recollections of country life. First movement: Agreeable impressions awakening in man on arrival in the country. Second movement: Scene by the brook. Third movement: Joyous amusements of the country folk. Fourth movement: Thunder and storm. Fifth movement: Benevolent feelings after the storm, joined with thanks to the Divinity. Each number was a very long and fully worked-out movement, filled with the liveliest images and the most brilliant ideas and figures; as a result, this one pastoral symphony alone lasted longer than an entire court concert is allowed to last with us.

Then followed, as the sixth piece, a long Italian scena,[15] sung by Mlle. Killizky, the beautiful Bohemian with the beautiful voice.[16] That today this pretty child rather shivered than sang could not be taken amiss, in view of the bitter cold; in our box near by, we too were shivering, wrapped in our furs and greatcoats.

Seventh piece: A Gloria, with choruses and solos, whose performance, unfortunately, miscarried altogether.[17]

Eighth piece: A new concerto for fortepiano, terribly difficult, which Beethoven played astonishingly well in the fastest possible tempos.[18] The Adagio, a masterpiece of beautiful sustained melody, he actually sang on his instrument with a deep melancholy feeling which awakened its response in me.

Ninth piece: A great symphony,[19] very elaborate and too long. A cavalier sitting near us reported having observed at the rehearsal that the violoncello part, busily occupied, amounted alone to thirty-four sheets. But the copyists here are quite as expert in spreading things out as are at home our lawyer's clerks and court recorders.

Tenth piece: A Sanctus, again with choruses and solos,[20] unfortunately—like the Gloria—a complete failure in performance.

Eleventh piece: A long fantasy, in which Beethoven revealed his full mastery. And finally, by way of conclusion, another fantasy, in which the orchestra

---

15. "Ah, perfido!" Op. 65.
16. Mlle. Killizky (Josephine Killitschgy), Ignaz Schuppanzigh's sister-in-law, was a last-minute substitute.
17. From the Mass in C, Op. 86.
18. The Fourth Piano Concerto, Op. 58.
19. The Fifth Symphony, Op. 67.
20. Again from the Mass in C.

presently came in and was actually followed at the end by the chorus.[21] This strange idea met with disaster in performance as the result of an orchestral confusion so complete that Beethoven, with the inspired ardor of the artist, thinking no longer of his public or of his surroundings, shouted out that one should stop and begin over again. You can imagine how I and all his other friends suffered at this. In that moment, indeed, I wished that I had had the courage to leave earlier after all.[22]

·   ·   ·   ·   ·

TWENTY-SEVENTH LETTER

[February 25, 1809] Dear father Haydn I am still unable to see again; as often as we send out word to him, asking after his health and for an appointment agreeable to him, we receive from his people the invariable answer that he is very weak and can see no one. Clementi too is most desirous of seeing him again; since his arrival, he has still to succeed in doing so.[23] I fear that his noble spirit will soon depart from us. Although strictly speaking he has for some years been as good as morally dead for the world,[24] one still fears always the final extinguishing of the divine flame which, throughout a half century, has so magnificently lighted the way for us.

Not without being deeply touched can I recall how one of his first "cassations," as he called his cheery, youthful quartets, gave me my earliest artistic joy and was at the same time the chief display piece of my boyish virtuosity;[25] how his quartets, constantly increasing in inner content and character, offered me the best of nourishment and training as well as the most delightful enjoyment; how, on my many visits to England, and especially in France, his superb symphonies were almost everywhere the greatest and the most beautiful that I heard played; how later on his larger choral works for the church and concert hall brought me the keenest and most varied pleasure; and how, after all this, because of a combination of circumstances, I was never able to meet this hero—this patriarch of music—never able to imprint upon his lips or fatherly hand my ardent thanks for all this instruction and enjoyment—until the utmost weakness of mind and body made this for him, as for me, almost a torture.

21. The Choral Fantasy, Op. 80, a work subjected to further revision before its publication in 1811.
22. The announcement of this concert in the *Wiener Zeitung* for December 17 describes the program as consisting entirely of new works, not previously heard in public. With the exception of the scena "Ah, perfido!" and the movements from the Mass in C, which had already been heard in performances away from Vienna, this seems to have been strictly true.
23. Clementi had been in Vienna since the latter part of 1808.
24. In a letter to Breitkopf & Härtel written on June 12, 1799, Haydn himself refers to a falling-off of his mental powers; his last significant work was the "Harmoniemesse," completed during the summer of 1802; his death occurred on May 31, 1809, only a few months after the date of this entry in Reichardt's journal.
25. The Quartet in B-flat, Op. 1, No. 1. In his biography, *Johann Friedrich Reichardt* (Augsburg, 1865; vol. 1, p. 61), H. M. Schletterer reports that Reichardt spoke of this quartet as his boyhood "show piece."

Nearly and deeply affected, I wrote soon after this into his handsome album a choral setting of these magnificent lines from Goethe's "Euphrosyne":[26]

Cliffs stand firmly based; the water eternally plunges;
    Down from its cloudy cleft foaming and roaring it falls.
Ever the pines are green, and even in winter the copses
    Foster on leafless twigs buds that are hid from the eye.
Each thing arises and passes by law; a wavering fortune
    Governs the life of man, treasure of priceless worth.
Not at the brink of the grave does the father, departing contented,
    Nod farewell to his son, blooming and splendid heir;
Nor is the old man's eye closed always by hand of the younger,
    Willingly parting from light, weak giving place to the strong.
Ah, more often does fate perversely order man's life-days:
    Helpless an old man mourns children and grandsons in vain,
Standing, a desolate tree, round which all shattered the branches
    Lie upon every side, ravaged by tempest of hail.

To this I added, from the bottom of my heart: "Also to see the shell of the spirit that will live on among us forever and that created for us a new life, rich in joys and destined—so long as harmony shall remain the highest expression of the endless—to outlive all posterity; also to see the shell so soon demolished filled my innermost being with that deep melancholy which sprang from the heart of the poet and which, in memory of a solemn, never-to-be-forgotten hour, I dared to set to music. For I regard myself as fortunate in having gazed deeply into the soul-filled eye—in having pressed passionately to my heart and to my lips the loving, consecrating hand."

THIRTY-SEVENTH LETTER

[April? 1809] For everyone, surely, who can enjoy the good things of life, especially for the artist, perhaps quite especially for the musical artist, Vienna is the richest, happiest, and most agreeable residence in Europe. Vienna has everything that marks a great capital in a quite unusually high degree. It has a great, wealthy, cultivated, art-loving, hospitable, well-mannered, elegant nobility; it has a wealthy, sociable, hospitable middle class and bourgeoisie, as little lacking in cultivated and well-informed gentlemen and gracious families; it has a well-to-do, good-natured, jovial populace. All classes love amusement and good living, and things are so arranged that all classes may find well provided and may enjoy in all convenience and security every amusement that modern society knows and loves.

•   •   •   •   •

In the city and in the suburbs five theaters of the most varied sort give performances all the year round. At the two court theaters in the city itself,

26. This is now published in the third number of my *Goethe's Lieder, Oden, Balladen und Romanzen* (Leipzig, 1809). [Au.]

one sees everything outstanding in the way of grand and comic opera, comedy, and tragedy that Germany produces—and, in some measure, Italy and France as well; the same is true of the great suburban Theater an der Wien, where in addition the great romantic magic operas are given with unusual magnificence. At all three theaters, great pantomimic ballets, heroic and comic, are often given also. Two smaller theaters in the Leopoldstadt and Josephstadt play popular dramas of the jolliest kind. On days when no play is scheduled, all these theaters give great concerts and performances of the most important ancient and modern music for church and concert hall. Aside from this, all winter long there are frequent public concerts, by local and visiting musicians, and excellent quartet and amateur concerts by subscription.

For dancing, Vienna makes the greatest and most varied provisions that any city in the world can boast of. The large and small Redoutensaal, the Apollo-saal, the Mehlgrube, the Neue Welt, and countless others are dance halls which offer to all classes the gayest, most elegant, and most convenient resorts. The dance music is everywhere outstanding, the service with everything in the way of food and drink is perfect. And with all these amusements, there prevails the best and most jovial spirit, with never a trace of oppressing distinctions.

•   •   •   •   •

Viennese society is, moreover, so rich and so agreeable that, as regards hospitality, good living, freedom, and general merriment, Vienna has no equal in all Europe. He who enjoys the good fortune, in Vienna, of coming to know the societies of the various classes, from the higher nobility down to the petite bourgeoisie, enjoys in the highest degree and in the freest and most agreeable way everything charming, delightful, and satisfying that Europe has to offer. At the same time to have everywhere before one's eyes ladies who are beautiful, cheerful, and merry, who are neither affected nor yet impudently forward, is a pleasure one experiences nowhere in the world to the extent one does in Vienna.

To these countless and inexhaustible attractions of Vienna is further to be reckoned that thousands of strangers from all parts and countries of Europe have residences here and travel constantly back and forth, while some have established themselves with taste and not infrequently on a grand scale and live here in great splendor and hospitality. This applies especially to Russians and Poles, who bring the good sociable spirit with them and amalgamate themselves with the Viennese the more easily. Aside from them, the great Bohemian, Moravian, and Hungarian families, like the Austrians, live regularly all winter long in Vienna, giving it the brilliance and magnificence that make it the great splendid imperial city, for the court itself prefers a retired family life to external pomp and show. Yet the court appears also with great dignity and no little brilliance at the few public festivities which it still maintains. The greatest brilliance consists, however, in the rich background provided by the higher nobility of the crown lands.

In the mild and imperceptible gradations from the higher princely nobility, with an annual income of a million, a half million, or a quarter of a million gulden, to the lesser courtly nobility, with an income of a hundred thousand gulden or over; from thence to the petty new nobility, who not infrequently have and spend as much, if not still more—the bankers and great landowners and manufacturers are included here; and so on through the bourgeoisie proper down to the well-to-do petite bourgeoisie; in the way that all the great public diversions and amusements are enjoyed by all classes without any abrupt divisions or offending distinctions—in these respects, Vienna is again quite alone among the great cities of Europe. If, with respect to the first part of this observation, London shows certain similarities, with respect to the second, it is after all very different. In London, an ordinary citizen does not venture into the parterre of the great Italian opera—the drama of the nobility and the great rich world—without having at least marked himself as an elegant and wealthy gentleman by some outward sign—a fine, expensive ring, or something of the sort—and he can in no way obtain admission to a concert or any other sort of entertainment offered by subscription to the nobility—the Concerts of Ancient Musick, for example—unless he is at least related to the great noble families.

Through the utter banishment of all splendor and affectation in everyday costume, even in the greatest houses and circles, Viennese society has gained still more, and I do not know what one could wish added to it to make it perfectly agreeable.

Thus I had the good fortune to spend in Vienna a whole winter, richer in amusements and pleasures of every kind than any winter I have ever before experienced, for all my good fortune in my many earlier travels. If I have one regret it is that the winter continued severe too long to permit my again enjoying to my heart's content the great public art treasures, which, with the utmost liberality, stand free and open to everyone winter and summer and from which, on my first visit to Vienna, I derived so much pleasure and profit. My own work and the hope of being able to remain in Vienna undisturbed throughout the lovely spring season, so endlessly rich in pleasures here, caused me to put off many things, the more so since the extraordinary hospitality of the highest and most noble as well as greatest and most agreeable houses and families offered me daily so rich a social life.

VI

THE NINETEENTH CENTURY

Edited by RUTH A. SOLIE

INTRODUCTION

*W*hen the original edition of *Source Readings in Music History* appeared in 1950, the nineteenth-century portion of its contents focused exclusively on Romantic phenomena; when the later paper edition of this fascicle appeared, it was quite appropriately titled *The Romantic Era*. Music scholarship in Oliver Strunk's generation habitually treated "Romanticism" as synonymous with the century as a whole (when indeed it dealt with the nineteenth century at all).[1] By now, however, most musicologists would argue that a more nuanced view is necessary. It is not that we have devised a finer grid for discriminating musical style periods within the century: on the contrary, even the latest studies agree—whether with conviction or resignation—that musical style remained "romantic" until something "modernist," or perhaps "impressionist," arrived on the scene.[2]

But there is more to the history of music than the history of compositional styles. Subsuming a whole century under one label fails us in at least two dimensions. Culturally, it speaks only to the preoccupations of the composer/artist circle and not very accurately to the interests or beliefs of the era as a whole—a kind of historical representation that Jacques Barzun once described as "all butter and no bread."[3] It is the genius who is the principal denizen of the Romantic world, and we are not even sure, in most cases, to what extent the audience shared the beliefs and enthusiasms of that personage. More significantly, the label "Romantic" ignores the enormous social and intellectual changes that occurred during the course of the century, such as the emergence of middle-class cultural dominance, the development of positivism and histori-

1. Only a few years later, during his presidency of the American Musicological Society, Strunk identified the nineteenth century, along with the Middle Ages, as the two periods most in need of study by musicologists. ("The Prospect Before Us," a talk delivered in observance of the Society's twenty-fifth anniversary; twenty-fifth annual meetings of the AMS, Chicago, December 27, 1959.)

2. Carl Dahlhaus calls this attribution a "bad blunder" but acknowledges its ubiquity and suggests no real alternative (*Nineteenth-Century Music*, trans. J. Bradford Robinson [Berkeley: University of California Press, 1989], p. 16). See also Rey M. Longyear, *Nineteenth-Century Romanticism in Music* (Englewood Cliffs, N.J.: Prentice-Hall, 1969) and Leon Plantinga, *Romantic Music: A History of Musical Style in Nineteenth-Century Europe* (New York: W. W. Norton, 1984). In literary scholarship, of course, Romanticism is understood as a phenomenon of some three or four decades, in part actually preceding the nineteenth century.

3. "The highbrow's culture is too likely to be a very thin slice of life—all butter and no bread—and as such incapable of standing by itself." Jacques Barzun, "Cultural History as a Synthesis," in *The Varieties of History: From Voltaire to the Present*, ed. Fritz Stern (New York, 1972), p. 393.

cism as the primary modes of intellectual inquiry, and the upending of Romantic idealism in Marxist (and other) materialist philosophies. Such events, together with the great cultural impact of the global empires that European nations had acquired by the end of the century, affected how music was produced and understood. Friedrich Blume argued that "Romanticism is no definable style but a spiritual attitude,"[4] and that attitude neither permeated all levels of culture nor lasted out the century.

None of this is to say that the Romantic literary and musical movement is no longer of interest as such. Its principal hallmark as a cultural-historical development was the rejection of Enlightenment rationalism and classical authority in favor of imagination, feeling, and transcendence. This predilection has permanently affected Western attitudes toward aesthetic experience and no doubt helped give rise to the gulf between the "two cultures" of the twentieth century. Wilhelm Heinrich Wackenroder describes his fictional young genius, Joseph Berglinger, as aspiring to something higher than "ordinary earthly tasks" such as, in particular, the "secret enervating poison" of the scientific and medical study practiced by Berglinger's father. This dichotomy, though transformed almost beyond recognition, can still be glimpsed in Hermann Helmholtz's commitment, on the one hand, to the scientific exploration of musical phenomena and his relief, on the other hand, that explaining their mysterious aesthetic power is not his task.

For the Romantics, of course, aesthetic experience was at the same time a spiritual, even religious, matter. "An art work," Wagner tells us, "is religion brought to life." Our pluralist sensibilities may be surprised by the intense association of Romanticism with Christianity—on the grounds that Christian faith merges us with the infinite. We may even find slightly shocking Jean Paul's assertion that, because of this association, Venus may be beautiful but the Madonna can be romantic. He juxtaposes Greek and Christian cultures directly, to the detriment of the former, in rejecting the classical models beloved of eighteenth-century art. Mazzini invokes the Gothic cathedral to exemplify the kind of cultural-religious expression that the music of the future might become. Margaret Fuller, in pondering what we can learn from the lives of great musicians, calls them "high-priests of sound" with a special connection to the higher realms.

Nor was Romanticism a democratic or *laissez-faire* aesthetic, despite its occasional rhetoric of egalitarianism.[5] In an argument that sounds remarkably up-to-date, Fuller laments the characteristic American resistance to the "love of greatness," dismissing the interest of some in reading the "simple annals of

---

4. Friedrich Blume, *Classic and Romantic Music: A Comprehensive Survey*, trans. M. D. Herter Norton (New York: W. W. Norton, 1970), p. 103.

5. That is, the claim that the social origins of the genius are irrelevant was characteristic of Romanticism, but the notion that Everyman could write music as valuable as the genius's was emphatically not. See Part III of Leonard B. Meyer, *Style and Music: Theory, History, and Ideology* (Philadelphia: University of Pennsylvania Press, 1989).

the poor" with the argument that genius is our only profitable object of study because it reveals to us what we might at our best become. Philistinism was regarded as a major cultural problem, with John Sullivan Dwight battling it in the pages of his *Journal* every bit as fervently as Schumann and his League of David. Dwight not only champions music education to combat philistine attitudes, he insists that, since the "simple masses" respond to "high-spiced advertisement" that finer instincts deplore, concert programming must be planned to edify the "truly musical" rather than entertain "the unmusical many."

Even so, the Romantic musical world was not a seamless garment, as Raphael Georg Kiesewetter observed in characterizing the period as the era of Beethoven and Rossini. The persistent debate over the respective merits of "playing North and singing South"—and contemporary participants were interested as much in the contrast of attitudes as of musical styles—surfaces again and again in texts about music. Jean Paul attributes the difference to climate and relative distance from Greece. With gentle irony and stylistic acumen, George Eliot puts the pro-North polemic into the mouth of her fictional musician, Klesmer, at the same time permitting one of her quintessential propertied philistines to complain of Klesmer's own music that it sounds "like a jar of leeches," without clear formal demarcations. With less subtlety but compensating heights of passion, the political activist Giuseppe Mazzini calls for a Hegelian synthesis, not only of German and Italian musical styles, but of their entire essences as oppositional cultures and philosophies. For Mazzini the classic "contest" between melody and harmony betokens another sort of rift that must be healed—that between individual and society. It is particularly interesting that both Mazzini and Wagner envision a future in which such racial and national differences—although seen to be absolute and of ancient standing— would be transcended in a universal humanist sensibility.

To a considerable extent, the North-South argument was fueled by the Romantic view of music as a matter of personal expression: innate differences could be expected to surface. The ideas, feelings, attitudes, and narratives that are suggested as falling within music's expressive purview—or thought to be useful in helping listeners understand music—are the feature of Romanticism that may be most alien to late twentieth-century academic sensibilities. Writers made widely differing claims about the relation of music to its composer, to its listener, and to objects in the world, and argued their positions energetically. At the same time, the variety of audiences and of purposes for which they wrote assured a spectrum of rhetorical styles that were often difficult to interpret and compare. Schumann, for instance, maintained that the familiar characters of *Don Giovanni* seem to exist and act unproblematically in Chopin's variations on Mozart's theme, winking at us from among the notes. E. T. A. Hoffmann urges that music not be concerned with the representation of definite emotions and events, but proceeds to read both narratives and dramatic scenarios freely, distinguishing the symphonies of Haydn, Mozart, and Beethoven according to the scenes they bring before the imagination. Even Berlioz, who devotes more space than most of his contemporaries to compositional shoptalk, does not balk at words like "depicts" in his discussion of Rossini's overture, and commends Beethoven for a symphonic movement in which an "illusion is complete." We see here quite normal ways of describing music before Eduard Hanslick made his fateful attempt to confine aesthetic discourse to philosophically appropriate channels. Hanslick's efforts, it must be said, were more efficacious in the long term than in his own era: the disputatious assortment of metaphoric, visual, and ascriptive languages remained the norm for most of the century.

Gender metaphors, whether celebrating sexual difference or (more often) anxious about its abrogation, simply abound from one end of the nineteenth century to the other, seeming sometimes to be the foundational trope for the culture as a whole. Such metaphoric systems are, of course, notorious for the mutability of their specific meanings and referents—Romantic gender is not the same as Victorian. But one of the most fascinating and characteristic aspects of their nineteenth-century manifestation is the almost ubiquitous association of music itself with the female or the feminine. Wagner is well known for the sensational mating, described in *Opera and Drama*,[6] of female music with male poetry. A more prim scenario is scripted in Mazzini's call for the rescue of both music and womanhood from prostitution, and as well in Dwight's related insistence that honor and modesty are "two qualities as inseparable in the artistic character as they are in woman." Most strikingly, in Wackenroder's story it is Joseph Berglinger, not any of his five *lumpen* sisters, who is "like a maiden" in the delicacy and musical sensibility of his inner life—which may serve as a reminder that gender stereotypes, where common enough to saturate a culture, have a life of their own independent of mere biology.

In pondering the almost obsessive concern with the "music of the future" that developed around mid-century, we become aware that other intellectual realms and movements beyond Romanticism affected what must otherwise seem a remarkably rarefied discourse. The anxiety of composers about their rightful place in the onflowing "mainstream" of music, which persisted nearly to our own generation, seems to emerge from the confluence of two strains: the overwhelming sense of history that marked nineteenth-century culture generally, and scientific theorizing about evolution as a mechanism for that very history. The promiscuous application of ideas about evolution to a wide variety of social, moral, and cultural processes was the common coin of intellectual life.[7] In such an atmosphere, it is scarcely surprising that Wagner struggled

6. See many passages throughout, but especially pt. 1, sec. 7 (*"Die Musik ist ein Weib"*), and pt. 3, sec. 4. In *The Artwork of the Future* Wagner uses an older trope, the Sister Arts, and thus treats dance, poetry, and music as female.

7. Many theorists of evolution—from Jean-Baptiste de Lamarck, Erasmus Darwin, and George-Louis Leclerc de Buffon in the eighteenth century to Charles Lyell and many others in the nineteenth—had offered their ideas to the scientific community and in many cases the public,

so mightily to prove that his innovations in music drama were part of a "neces-sary" evolutionary path that music must take; that Adolf Bernhard Marx assures us that music has completed all the "essential tasks" assigned to it in human history now that Beethoven has made "the last unquestionable progress" in the art; or that Mazzini simply assumes that the continued spiritual and political maturation of human societies will necessarily yield up post-Romantic music of a higher sort, ready to undertake a new and more solemn mission. Every-thing evolved, and most people (if not most scientists) understood evolution as a process that always operated for the better.

The same serene confidence prevailed as European and American scholars, musicians, and audiences increasingly confronted the alien musics of faraway parts of the world. In the later years of the century, groups of non-Western musicians were frequently brought in to perform at international expositions—indeed, whole "native" villages were sometimes set up for viewing, as though in a zoo.[8] By all accounts, Europeans and Americans alike were fascinated by these spectacles, but the intellectual framework that held the new ethno-graphic information was relentlessly evolutionary: each cultural type could be assigned a rung on the developmental ladder, leading inexorably to the advanced near-perfection of Western music, often exemplified by Wagner or Beethoven. Richard Wallaschek likens "savages" to children in the "mistakes and peculiarities" of their attempts at cultural production. His simile differs strikingly from Margaret Fuller's Romantic one, in which it is artists who are "the young children of our sickly manhood" in their uncalculating innocence and perfectibility.

Scientific thought also inflects the nationalism so characteristic of the era. While its emergence in music and in other cultural venues was intimately bound up with political developments in Europe that encouraged expressions of national identity and consciousness, it is also true that notions of characteris-tic national and racial difference were supported by contemporary anthropol-ogy, ethnology, and the variety of far-flung geographical explorations that accompanied empire. After all, composers did not simply mine their own cul-tural heritages for folk references in obviously patriotic gestures, they also explored innumerable exotic musical traditions, whether in hopes of experienc-ing something of the essence of those cultures or merely for novelty value. Such references occur at all levels of musical culture, proliferating in increasing variety as the century goes on.

The era's own understanding of such essences is captured well in Dwight's description of the National Peace Jubilee of 1869 as a successful expression of

---

well before Charles Darwin's publications appeared. Although it is Herbert Spencer's name that is principally associated with "social Darwinism," his ideas too had frequently been anticipated in efforts to explain or prescribe cultural change and to buttress the belief in progress that was the principal industry of the Victorian era.

8. One riveting account is offered by Stewart Culin in "Retrospect of the Folk-Lore of the Colum-bian Exposition," *Journal of American Folklore* 7 (1894): 51–59.

"the genius of a great, free People," whose planners had been determined "that it should be American in some sense which they could be proud of." American culture, already understood as uniquely heterogeneous even before the great waves of immigration, presented a puzzle to a society so committed to national essences. By the 1890s, when Dvořák visited the United States, certain anomalies were impossible to ignore. His European experience had taught him that "the music of the people, sooner or later, will . . . creep into the books of composers," but who *were* the American people? All races, Dvořák thought, have their distinctive musics, which they will recognize spontaneously "even if they have never heard them before," whence his confused but earnest suggestion that composers in the United States might exploit the music of Black people and American Indians as sources of a "truly American" musical language—never mind the characteristic confusion of race and nation. Here the essential ideal has become a desideratum rather than an expectation, an irresistible imperative to forge a homogeneity from a diverse population.

The music of African-Americans, emancipated from slavery only after mid-century, was commonly seen as an expression of the essential nature of a relatively unevolved—and therefore innocent and childlike—people apparently acquiescent in their enslavement. A dash of cold water is offered by Frederick Douglass's explanation of slave songs as noisy "tracers" required by overseers, or perhaps as coded communications about escape plans. Douglass himself is less interested in speculation about racial character than in the commonalities he heard between slave songs and the songs of the Irish during the famine of 1845 as expressions of human misery.

Early developments in scientific psychology also went a long way toward undermining essential tenets of Romantic faith by investigating the very powers of the soul that Romantics had deemed ineffable. "Emotion" for Edmund Gurney is a far cry from what it was for E. T. A. Hoffmann—just as far as Helmholtz's "nature" is from Wackenroder's. Or we might more properly say that under the sway of Romanticism, emotion was the preeminent aesthetic value and the guarantor of authenticity and individuality (we must demand, says Liszt, "emotional content in the formal container") while under positivism emotion itself became an object of study. Gurney is interested in *why* human beings are able to have emotional responses to patterns of notes, "by what alchemy abstract forms of sound . . . are capable of transformation into phenomena charged with feeling"—a question, incidentally, that also interested Hanslick. The answer, Gurney believes, is that evolution favors the exercise of musical skills, although peoples at different developmental "stages" are moved by music of strikingly different levels of quality. He guesses, for example, that the ancient Greeks were "spellbound by performances for the like of which we should probably tell a street-performer to pass on," as though emotional fastidiousness itself were an evolving genetic trait.

Similarly, Richard Wallaschek argues in his pioneering ethnomusicological study—in contradiction to other theorists who held that the aesthetic realm lay outside the scope of natural selection—that human societies develop musical abilities "as practical life-preserving and life-continuing activities." In other words, he maintains, as Gurney does, that musical activity has an evolutionary advantage. Although Wallaschek is no popularizer of simplistic views of evolution—his argument is for nurture over nature, for the view that individual talent is determined by the state of the culture into which a child is born rather than an innate, racially-determined ability—his Darwinian commitment can be seen in his insistence that primitive societies form a developmental "bridge," emotionally and psychologically as well as physically, between animal and human worlds.

•　　•　　•

Many of our authors, from E. T. A. Hoffman to Margaret Fuller to Richard Wallaschek, characterize the nineteenth century as preeminently *the* era of music. The claim is richly confirmed by the frequency with which music became a subject of study by newly developing sciences and was made a testing ground for theories, like evolution, that were at the center of discourse. For this reason an extraordinary number of nineteenth-century documents could claim our attention as students of the "living record" of music history that Strunk sought to compile. Many colleagues helped with the nearly impossible task of selection: I wish to thank Raphael Atlas, William Austin, Peter Bloom, Philip Bohlman, Reinhold Brinkmann, Malcolm Hamrick Brown, Scott Burnham, Marcis Citron, Jon Finson, Bea Friedland, Joseph Horowitz, Lawrence Kramer, Richard Kramer, Ralph Locke, Rena Mueller, Roger Parker, Harold Powers, Lee Rothfarb, Margaret Sarkissian, Maynard Solomon, R. Larry Todd, James Webster, and Elizabeth Wood, all of whom generously contributed suggestions, citations, offers of assistance, and even photocopies. My coworkers on the Strunk project, especially Wye Allanbrook, Robert Morgan, Gary Tomlinson, and Leo Treitler, were also invaluably and unflaggingly helpful. No volume however gargantuan could have contained so many generous offerings; in any event, my own education has been immensely enriched by them.

THE ROMANTIC ARTIST

148 Jean Paul

"The highest criticism is that which leaves an impression identical with the one called forth by the thing criticized. In this sense Jean Paul, with a poetic companion-piece, can perhaps contribute more to the understanding of a symphony or fantasy by Beethoven, without even speaking of the music, than a dozen of those little critics of the arts who lean their ladders against the Colossus and take its exact measurements."

Strange to say, this observation of Schumann's is not altogether wide of the mark. A self-taught amateur whose piano playing did not go beyond the improvisation of extravagant rhapsodies, Jean Paul responded almost as a clairvoyant to the poetic side of musical composition; a musical writer who never wrote on music, he exerted a compelling influence on the music and musical criticism of his time. By 1800, thanks to the musical episodes and allusions in his early novels, his name had become so closely identified with music in the minds of his readers that a sentimental ode by Andreas Kretschmer could win immediate and widespread popularity simply by being printed under the title "Jean Paul's Favorite Song." Two well-known writers on music sought him out and recorded their impressions of his personality—Johann Friedrich Reichardt, who spent an evening with him in 1796, and Ludwig Rellstab, who called on him in 1822 with a letter from Ludwig Tieck. For many of his contemporaries he was the literary counterpart of Beethoven. August Lewald, who knew them both, found that they had much in common and reports that the resemblance extended even to physical characteristics. "Beethoven was somewhat smaller," he wrote in 1836, "but one noticed at once the same powerful nature, the same indifference to external appearance, the same kindliness, the same simplicity and cordiality. If we look at their works we find the same profundity, the same sharp characterization, the same painting of details; quiet states of temperament are described and sudden outbursts of extreme passion; ideas that might have been drawn from the most commonplace reality alternate with the highest flights into the sublime. I am confident that I can rediscover in Beethoven's symphonies the Swedish country parson's Sunday (*Flegeljahre,*) the unfortunate's dream (*Herbst-Blumine,*) Natalia Aquilana's letter (*Siebenkäs,*) and the most magnificent episodes of the *Titan.* Only in Jean Paul's improvisation, however, did his kinship with Beethoven become truly evident."

The son of a musician whose father had been a musician before him, Jean Paul (properly Johann Paul Friedrich Richter) was born at Wunsiedel in the Bavarian Fichtelgebirge on March 21, 1763. After attending the university in Leipzig he lived for a time in Hof and later in Weimar; in 1804 he settled in Bayreuth, where he continued a resident until his death on November 14, 1825. Two of Jean Paul's shorter writings, *Quintus Fixlein* and *Des Feldpredigers Schmelzle Reise nach Flätz,* were translated into English by Carlyle.

FROM *Elementary Course in Aesthetics*
(2d ed., 1813)

22. THE NATURE OF ROMANTIC POETRY

THE SOUTHERN AND THE NORTHERN DISTINGUISHED

"The origin and character of all recent poetry is so readily derived from Christianity that one could quite as well call this poetry Christian as romantic." With this assertion the author of the present paragraphs opened fire some years ago;[1] refuted and instructed, however, by more than one worthy critic of the arts, he has felt called upon to alter some details, removing them as one might remove a suburb to protect a fortification or a city as a whole. The first question is: Wherein does the romantic style[2] differ from the Greek? Greek images, stimuli, motives, sensations, characters, even technical restrictions are easily transplanted into a romantic poem without the latter's surrendering on this account its universal spirit; in the other direction, however, the transplanted romantic stimulus finds no congenial place in the Greek art work, unless it be a stimulus of the exalted sort, and then only because the exalted, like a borderline divinity, links the romantic with the antique. Even the so-called modern irregularity, for example that of the Italian opera or the Spanish comedy, may—since mere technique has not the power to divide the spiritual sphere of poetry into an old world and an American new one—be pervaded and animated with the spirit of Antiquity; this is nicely supported by the observation of Bouterwek,[3] who says that Italian poetry, for all its lack of ideas, through its clarity, simplicity, and grace follows and approaches the Greek model more nearly than any other modern sort, and this though the Italian forms have traveled further from the Greek than either the German or the English. And with this correct observation Bouterwek refutes that other one of his,[4] according to which romanticism is precisely to be found in an un-Greek community of the serious, indeed tragic, and the comic. For this is as little a necessary characteristic of the romantic, where it is often absent, as its opposite is of the antique, where it is frequently present, for example, in Aristophanes, who sternly and crassly blends the exaltation of the choruses with the humiliation of the gods them-

TEXT: *Vorschule der Aesthetik. Sämtliche Werke*, pt. 1, vol. 11 (Weimar, 1935), 75–81. Translation by Oliver Strunk, using the notes of Eduard Berend, the editor of this volume of Jean Paul's collected works.

1. The first edition of the *Vorschule* was published in 1804.
2. Schiller calls it the *modern,* as though everything written since Grecian times were modern and new, irrespective of whether one or two thousand years old; likewise the *sentimental,* an epithet which the romanticists Ariosto and Cervantes would not have taken over-seriously. [Au] In Schiller's "Über naive und sentimentalische Dichtung," first published in *Die Horen* for 1795 and 1796.
3. *Geschichte der Poesie und Beredsamkeit* (Göttingen, 1801–19), vol. 2, p. 544
4. In his review of the *Vorschule.*

selves, as though blending an intensification of an emotion with its comic relaxation.

Rather let us ask feeling why, for example, it calls even a countryside romantic. A statue, through its sharp, closed outlines, excludes everything romantic; painting begins to approach it more closely through its groups of human figures and, without them, attains it in landscapes, for example in those of Claude.[5] A Dutch garden seems only to deny everything romantic, but an English one, reaching out into the indefinite landscape, can surround us with a romantic countryside, that is, with a background of imagination set free amid the beautiful. What is it, further, that confers on the following poetic examples their romantic stamp? In the tragedy *Numantia* of Cervantes, the citizens, in order not to fall victims to hunger and the Romans, dedicate themselves in a body to a common death. When they have carried this out and the empty city is strewn with corpses and funeral pyres, Fame appears on the walls and proclaims to the enemy the suicide of the city and the future brilliance of Spain. Again, in the midst of Homer, the romantic passage in which Jupiter surveys from Mount Olympus, at one time and under one sun, the warlike upwrought Trojan plain and the far Arcadian meadows, filled with men of peace.[6] Or, although it sparkles less brightly, the passage in Schiller's *Tell* in which the eye of the poet sweeps down from the towering chain of mountain peaks to the long, laughing wheatfields of the German lowlands.[7] In all these examples, the decisive element is not that of *exaltation,* which, as we have said, readily flows over into the romantic, but that of *expanse.*[8] Romanticism is beauty without bounds— the beautiful infinite, just as there is an exalted infinite. Thus Homer, in the example we have given, is romantic, while in the passage in which Ajax prays to the gods from the darkened battlefield, asking only for light,[9] he is merely exalted. It is more than a simile to call romanticism the wavelike ringing of a string or bell, in which the tone-wave fades into ever further distances, finally losing itself in us so that, while already silent without, it still resounds within. In the same way, the moonlight is at once a romantic image and a romantic example. To the Greeks, who defined things sharply, the half-light of the

5. Claude Lorrain (Claude Gellée), French landscape painter of the seventeenth century.
6. *Iliad*, 13.1.
7. *Wilhelm Tell*, act 3, sc. 3.
8. For musical illustrations of the application of this thoroughly romantic principle, see Liszt's *Ce qu'on entend sur la montagne* (after Victor Hugo), or the closing moments of Wagner's *Tristan und Isolde:*

In dem wogendem Schwall,	In the surging swell,
in dem tönendem Schall,	in the ocean of sound,
in des Welt-Atems	in the world-breath's
wehendem All—	drifting All,
ertrinken,	to drown,
versinken—	engulfed,
unbewußt	without thought—
höchste Lust!	highest bliss!

9. *Iliad*, 17.645.

romantic was so remote and foreign that even Plato, so much the poet and so close to the Christian upheaval, in treating a genuinely romantic-infinite subject—the relation of our petty finite world to the resplendent hall and starry roof of the infinite—expresses it only through the confined and angular allegory of a cave, from out which we chain-bound ones see passing in procession the shadows of the true beings who move behind us.[10]

If poetry is prophecy, then romanticism is being aware of a larger future than there is room for here below; romantic blossoms float about us, just as wholly unfamiliar sorts of seeds drifted through the all-connecting sea from the New World, even before it had been discovered, to the Norwegian shore.

Who is the author of this romanticism? Not in every land and century the Christian religion, to be sure; to this divine mother, however, all its others are somehow related. Two un-Christian varieties of romanticism, historically and climatically independent of one another, are those of India and the Edda. Old Norse romanticism, bordering more nearly on the exalted, finds for the ghostly Orcus in the shadowy realm of its climatically darkened and awe-inspiring natural environment, in its nights and on its mountains, a boundless spirit world in which the narrow sensual world dissolves and sinks from sight; here Ossian[11] belongs, with his evening and night pieces in which the heavenly nebulous stars of the past stand twinkling above the thick nocturnal mist of the present; only in the past does he find future and eternity.

Everything in his poem is music, but it is a distant and hence a doubled music, grown faint in endless space like an echo that enchants, not through its crudely faithful reproduction of a sound, but through its attenuating mitigation of it.

Hindu romanticism has as its element an all-enlivening religion which, through animism, has broken away the confines from the sensual world; this world has become as expansive as the spirit world itself, yet it is filled, not with mischievous spirits, but with cajoling ones, and earth and sky reach out toward one another as they do at sea. To the Hindu a flower is more alive than to the Norseman a man. To this, add the climate, that voluptuous bridal night of nature, and the Hindu himself, who, like the bee reposing in the honey-filled calix of the tulip, is swung to and fro by tepid west winds and takes his rest in a delightful rocking. Precisely for this reason, Hindu romanticism had inevitably to lose itself more and more in the magic of the senses, and if the moonlight and the echo are characteristics and images of other romantic kinds, the Hindu kind may be characterized by its dark perfume, the more so since this so frequently pervades its poetry and its life.

10. *Republic,* 7.514–521B.

11. Great as are the advantages of Ahlwardt's translation, thanks to the discovery of the purer text, it seems to me nonetheless that far too little of the praise that is its due has been accorded to the lightness, the fidelity, and the euphonies of the translation by Jung.[Au.] James Macpherson's pretended translations from "Ossian" had been translated into German by F. W. Jung in 1808 and by C. W. Ahlwardt in 1811.

Through its predilection for the exalted and the lyric, through its incapacity for drama and characterization—above all, through its Oriental mode of thought and feeling—Oriental poetry is related less to the Greek than to the romantic. This mode of thought and feeling—namely, the sense of the mortal futility of our night's shadows (shadows cast, not by a sun, but as though by moon and stars—shadows that the meager light itself resembles); the sense that we live our day of life under a total eclipse filled with horror and the flying things of night (like those eclipses in which the moon quite swallows up the sun and stands alone before it with a radiant ring)—this mode of thought and feeling, which Herder, the great delineator of the East, has so exactly painted for the North,[12] could but approach romantic poetry by the path by which a kindred Christianity quite reached and formed it.

We come at length to Christian romanticism, respecting which we must first show why in the South (particularly in Italy and Spain) it took on and created other forms than in the North, where, as was shown above, the very soil made of the heathen outer court a romantically Christian holy of holies. In its natural environment, and then because of manifold historic connections, the South presents an aspect so very different from the North that such reflections as derive romanticism from sources wholly distinct from Christian ones must be considered or corrected.

For the southerly and earliest variety, Bouterwek names these sources:[13] first, the heightened respect for womankind, brought in by the ancient Goths, then, the more spiritualized form of love.

But it was the Christian temple that gave shelter to romantic love, not the prehistoric German forest, and a Petrarch who is not a Christian is unthinkable. The one and only Mary ennobles every woman; hence, while a Venus can only be beautiful, a Madonna can be romantic. This higher form of love was or is precisely a blossoming and blooming from out Christianity, which, with its consuming hatred of the earthly, transformed the beautiful body into the beautiful soul that one might love the other—beauty, then, in the infinite. The name "Platonic love" is borrowed, notoriously, from another sort of love, from that pure unsullied friendship between youths in itself so innocent that the Greek lawgivers counted it a duty, so fanatical that the lover was punished for the errors of the loved one; here, then, simply directed toward another sex, we have again as with the ancient Goths the same deifying love, held—to prevent its profanation—as far as possible from nature, not the love that sanctifies through Christianity and clothes the loved one with the luster of romance.

The spirit of chivalry—which, apart from this, embroidered side by side upon its banners love and religion, *dame* and *Notre Dame*—and the Crusades, named sires of romanticism as second choices, these are children of the Christian spirit. . . . To enter the promised land, which two religions at once and the

12. Above all in his *Älteste Urkunde* (Riga, 1774), p. 95, and *Zerstreute Blätter,* Vol. 4 (Gotha, 1792), p. 131.
13. *Geschichte der Poesie und Beredsamkeit,* vol. 1, p. 22.

greatest being on earth had elevated for the imagination to a twilight realm of holy anticipation and to an isthmus between the first world and the second, to enter this land was to glorify oneself romantically and with two strengths, with valor and with faith, to make oneself master, literally and poetically, of one's baser earthly nature. What comparable result could the heroic ages and the voyages of the Argonauts bring forth?

As servants and silent creatures of romanticism we reckon further the ascending centuries which, allying all peoples more and more closely with one another, round off their sharp corners from without, while from within, through the rising sunlight of abstraction, like a form of Christianity, they break up more and more the solid material world. All this emboldens one to prophesy that, as time goes on, the writing of poetry will become more and more romantic, freer from rules or richer in them, that its separation from Greece will become wider and wider, and that the wings of its winged steed will so multiply that, precisely with the crowd, it will experience greater and greater difficulty in maintaining a steady course, unless, like Ezekiel's seraphim, it uses certain wings merely to cover its face.[14] But as for that, what concern have aestheticians and their prolegomena with time and eternity? Is only creeping philosophy to make progress, and soaring poetry lamely to gather rust? After three or four thousand years and their millions of *horae* is there to be no other division of poetry than Schiller's dull division of it into the *horae*[15] of the sentimental and the naïve? One might maintain that every century is romantic in a different way, just as one might, in jest or in earnest, place a different sort of poetry in every planet. Poetry, like all that is divine in man, is fettered to its time and place; at one time it must become Carpenter's Son and Jew, yet at another its state of abasement may begin on Mount Tabor and its transfiguration take place on a sun and blind us.[16]

Aside from this, it follows of itself that Christianity, although the common father of all romantic children, must in the South beget one sort of child, in the North another. The romanticism of the South—in Italy, climatically related to Greece—must blow more gently in an Ariosto, flying and fleeing less from the antique form, than that of the North in a Shakespeare, just as in turn the same southern variety takes on a different and orientally bolder form in torrid Spain. The poetry and the romanticism of the North is an aeolian harp through which the tempest of reality sweeps in melodies, its howlings resolved in tones, yet melancholy trembles on these strings—at times indeed a grief rends its way in.

14. Ezekiel, 1:11; Isaiah, 6:2.
15. Jean Paul is using the word *horae* (*Horen*) both in its literal sense and in reference to the periodical *Die Horen*, edited by Schiller and published monthly from 1795 to 1797. See note 2 above.
16. An ancient tradition makes Mount Tabor the scene of the Transfiguration. Matt. 17:1–9; Mark 9:2–10; Luke 9:28–36.

149 Wilhelm Wackenroder

Born in Berlin in 1773, Wilhelm Heinrich Wackenroder was one of the first of the German romanticists. He was a fellow student of Ludwig Tieck's at Erlangen and Göttingen and inspired his friend with his own enthusiasm for the art of the Middle Ages. Wackenroder sought with romantic fervor to penetrate the mystery of music and emphasized in his writings the close relationship between religious feeling and artistic creation. This is the main theme of his *Herzensergiessungen eines kunstliebenden Klosterbruders* (1797). Wackenroder's premature death at the age of twenty-five was a great blow to Tieck, who completed and published his friend's posthumous *Phantasien über die Kunst für Freunde der Kunst* (1799).

The Remarkable Musical Life of the Musician Joseph Berglinger
(1797)

PART ONE

I have often looked backward and gathered in for my enjoyment the art-historical treasures of past centuries; but now my inclination impels me to tarry for once with the present time and to try my hand at the story of an artist whom I knew from his early youth and who was my most intimate friend. Alas, to my regret you soon departed this world, my Joseph, and not easily shall I find your like again! But I shall console myself by retracing in my thoughts the story of your genius, from the beginning, and by retelling it for those to whom it may give pleasure—just as, in happy hours, you often spoke of it to me at length, and just as I myself came inwardly to know you.

•　•　•

Joseph Berglinger was born in a little town in the south of Germany. His mother was taken from the world as she brought him into it; his father, already a somewhat elderly man, was a doctor of medical science in straitened circumstances. Fortune had turned her back on him, and it was only by dint of much perspiration that he got along in life with his six children (for Joseph had five sisters), the more so since he was now without a capable housekeeper.

TEXT: "Das merkwürdige musikalische Leben des Tonkünstlers Joseph Berglinger," from his *Herzensergiessungen eines kunstliebenden Klosterbruders* (Confessions of an Art-Loving Friar). *Kunstanschauung der Frühromantik.* ed. Andreas Müller (Leipzig, 1931), 89–105. Translation by Oliver Strunk.

The father had formerly been a tender and very kindhearted man who liked nothing better than to give such help, counsel, and alms as he could afford; after a good deed, he slept better than usual; deeply moved and grateful to God, he could long thrive on the good works of his heart; he nourished his spirit in preference with affecting sentiments. Indeed, one cannot but give way to a profoundly melancholy admiration when one contemplates the enviable simplicity of these souls who discover in the ordinary manifestations of a kindly heart a source of grandeur so inexhaustible that it becomes the whole heaven on earth that reconciles them to the world at large and preserves them in constant and comfortable contentment. When he considered his father, Joseph was entirely of this mind; but Heaven had once and for all so constituted him that he aspired steadily to something higher; he was not content with mere spiritual health or satisfied that his soul should carry out its ordinary earthly tasks—to work and to do good; he wanted it to dance as well in exuberant high spirits—to shout to Heaven, as to its source, for joy.

His father's temperament, however, comprised still other elements. He was a hardworking and conscientious doctor and had known no other diversion, his whole life long, than the curious knowledge of things hidden in the human body and the vast science of all the wretched ills and ailments of mankind. As often happens, this intensive study became a secret enervating poison which penetrated his very arteries and gnawed, in his breast, through many a responsive cord. To this was added his discontent with his wretched poverty, and finally his age. All these things served to undermine his former kindliness, for, where the soul is not strong, whatever a man comes into contact with is absorbed into his blood and alters his inner nature without his knowing it.

The children of the old doctor grew up under his care like weeds in a deserted garden. Joseph's sisters were some of them sickly, some of them feebleminded, and, in their dark little room, they led a pitiable and lonely life.

In such a family no one could have been more out of place than Joseph, whose whole life was a beautiful fantasy and a heavenly dream. His soul was like a delicate young tree whose seed a bird has dropped into a ruined wall, where, among the rough stones, it springs up like a maiden. He was always by himself, alone and quiet, feeding only on his inner fantasies; on this account, his father considered him too a little foolish and unbalanced. He was sincerely fond of his father and his sisters, but most of all he prized his inner life, keeping it secret and hidden from others. Thus one secretes a jewel casket, to which one gives no one the key.

Music had from the first been his chief joy. Occasionally he heard someone play the piano and could even play a little himself. In time, by means of this often-repeated pleasure, he developed himself in a way so peculiarly his own that his being became thoroughly musical and his temperament, lured on by the art, wandered about continually among the shady bypaths of poetic feeling.

An outstanding chapter in his life was a visit to the episcopal residence, whither a well-to-do relation, who lived there and had taken a fancy to him, carried him off for a few weeks. Here he was really in his element; his spirit was fascinated by beautiful music, thousand-sided, and, not unlike a butterfly, it fluttered about in the congenial breeze.

Above all he visited the churches to hear the sacred oratorios, cantilenas, and choruses resounding in the full blast of trumpet and trombone beneath the vaulted roofs; from inner piety, he often listened humbly on his knees. Before the music began, as he stood there in the tightly packed and faintly murmuring congestion of the crowd, it seemed to him as though he heard buzzing about him, unmelodiously confused, as at a great fair, the common-place and ordinary life of man; his brain was paralyzed with empty earthly trivialities. Full of expectation, he awaited the first sound of the instruments; as this now broke forth from out the muffled silence, long drawn and mighty as the sigh of a wind from heaven, and as the full force of the sound swept by above his head, it seemed to him as though his soul had all at once unfurled great wings: he felt himself raised up above the barren heath, the dark cloud-curtain shutting out the mortal eye was drawn, and he soared up into the radi-ant sky. Then he held his body still and motionless, fixing his gaze steadfastly on the floor. The present sank away before him; his being was cleansed of all the pettiness of this world—veritable dust on the soul's luster; the music set his nerves tingling with a gentle thrill, calling up changing images before him with its changes. Thus, listening to certain joyous and soul-stirring songs in praise of God, he seemed quite plainly to see David in his royal mantle, a crown upon his head, dancing toward him and shouting psalms before the Ark of the Covenant; he saw all his enthusiasm, all his movements, and his heart leapt in his breast. A thousand sensations latent within him were liberated and marvelously interwoven. Indeed, at certain passages in the music, finally, an isolated ray of light fell on his soul; at this, it seemed to him as though he all at once grew wiser and was looking down, with clearer sight and a certain inspired and placid melancholy, on all the busy world below.

This much is certain: When the music was over and he left the church, he thought himself made purer and more noble. His entire being still glowed with the spiritual wine that had intoxicated him, and he saw all passersby with differ-ent eyes. Now when he chanced to see a group of people standing together on the pavement and laughing or exchanging gossip, it made a quite peculiarly disagreeable impression on him. As long as you live, he thought, you must hold fast, unwavering, to this beautiful poetic ecstasy, and your whole life must be a piece of music. When he went to lunch at his relation's and had thoroughly enjoyed his meal in a company not more than usually hearty and jovial, it dis-pleased him that he had let himself be drawn again so soon into the prosaic life and that his rapture had vanished like a gleaming cloud.

His whole life long he was tormented by this bitter dissension between his inborn lofty enthusiasm and our common mortal lot, which breaks in daily on our reveries, forcibly bringing us down to earth.

When Joseph was at a great concert he seated himself in a corner, without so much as glancing at the brilliant assembly of listeners, and listened with precisely the same reverence as if he had been in church—just as still and motionless, his eyes cast down to the floor in the same way. Not the slightest sound escaped him, and his keen attention left him in the end quite limp and exhausted. His soul, eternally in motion, was wholly a play of sounds; it was as though, liberated from his body, it fluttered about the more freely, or even as though his body too had become a part of his soul. Thus freely and easily was his entire being wound round with the lovely harmonies, and the music's foldings and windings left their impress on his responsive soul. At the lighthearted and delightful symphonies for full orchestra of which he was particularly fond, it seemed to him quite often as though he saw a merry chorus of youths and maidens dancing on a sunny meadow, skipping forward and backward, single couples speaking to each other in pantomime from time to time, then losing themselves again amid the joyous crowd. Certain passages in this music were for him so clear and forceful that the sounds seemed words. At other times again, the music called forth a wondrous blend of gladness and sadness in his heart, so that he was equally inclined to smile and weep—a mood we meet so often on our way through life, for whose expression there is no fitter art than music. And with what delight and astonishment he listened to that sort of music which, beginning like a brook with some cheery, sunny melody, turns imperceptibly and wonderfully, as it goes on, into increasingly troubled windings, to break at last into a loud and violent sob, or to rush by, as though through a wild chasm, with an alarming roar! These many-sided moods now all of them impressed upon his soul new thoughts and visual images, invariably corresponding—a wondrous gift of music, the art of which it may be said in general that the more dark and mysterious its language, the greater its power to affect us, the more general the uproar into which it throws all forces of our being.

The happy days that Joseph had spent in the episcopal residence came to an end at last, and he returned again to his birthplace and to his father's house. How sad was this return, how doleful and depressed he felt at being once more in a household whose entire life and strife turned only on the bare satisfying of the most essential physical needs and with a father who so little approved of his inclinations, who despised and detested all the arts as servants of extravagant desires and passions and as flatterers of the elegant world! From the very first it had displeased him that his Joseph had so fastened his heart on music; now that this inclination in the boy was growing by leaps and bounds, he made a determined and serious effort to convert him, from a harmful propensity for an art whose practice was little better than idleness and which catered merely to sensual excess, to medicine, as the most beneficent science and as the one most generally useful to the human race. He took great pains to instruct his son himself in its elementary principles and gave him books to read.

This was a truly distressing and painful situation for poor Joseph. Secretly he buried his enthusiasm deep in his breast, not to offend his father, and sought to compel himself, if possible, to master a useful science on the side. Yet in his soul there was a constant struggle. In his textbooks he could read one page ten times over without grasping what he read; unceasingly within, his soul sang its melodious fantasies on and on. His father was much distressed about him.

In secret his passionate love of music came to dominate him more and more. If for several weeks he heard no music, he became actually sick at heart; he noted that his feelings dried up, an emptiness arose within him, and he experienced a downright longing to be again inspired. Then even ordinary players, on church festival and consecration days, could with their wind instruments move him to feelings which they themselves had never felt. And as often as a great concert was to be heard in a neighboring town, he rushed out, ardent and eager, into the most violent snow, storm, or rain.

Scarcely a day went by without his calling sadly to mind those wonderful weeks in the episcopal residence, without his soul's reviewing the priceless things that he had heard there. Often he repeated to himself from memory the lovely and touching words of the sacred oratorio which had been the first that he had heard and which had made a particularly deep impression on him:

Stabat mater dolorosa	The sorrowful mother stood
Juxta crucem lacrymosa,	In tears beside the cross
Dum pendebat Filius	From which hung her Son.
Cujus animam gementem,	Her soul—lamenting,
Contristantem et dolentem,	Saddened and suffering—
Pertransivit gladius.	Was pierced by a sword.
O quam tristis et afflicta	O, how sad and dejected
Fuit illa benedicta	Was that blessed
Mater Unigeniti!	Mother of the Only-begotten!
Quae moerebat, et dolebat,	How she grieved, sorrowed,
Et tremebat, cum videbat	And trembled when she saw
Nati poenas inclyti.[1]	Her Son's punishment.

And so forth.

But alas for those enchanted hours, in which he lived as in an ethereal dream or had just come quite intoxicated from the enjoyment of a splendid piece of music; when they were interrupted for him—by his sisters, quarreling over a new dress, by his father, unable to give the eldest daughter enough money for her housekeeping or telling the story of a thoroughly wretched and pitiable invalid, or by some old beggar-woman, all bent over, coming to the door, unable to shield herself in her rags from the wintry frost—alas, there is in all the world no feeling so intensely bitter and heartrending as that with which Joseph was then torn. Dear God, he thought, is this the world as it is—and is it Thy will that I should plunge into the turmoil of the crowd and share the general misery? So it seems, and, as my father constantly preaches, it is the destiny and

1. *Stabat mater* is a sequence, assigned in the Roman liturgy to the Feast of the Seven Sorrows (September 15); its later polyphonic settings are also frequently used during Lent. Wackenroder is probably thinking of the setting by Pergolesi.

duty of man to share it, to give advice and alms, to bind up loathesome wounds, to heal odious diseases. And yet again an inner voice calls out to me quite clearly: "No! No! You have been born to a higher, nobler end!" With thoughts like these he often tormented himself for hours at a time, finding no way out; before he knew it, however, there vanished from his soul those unpleasant pictures which seemed to pull him by force into the mire of this life, and his spirit floated once more unruffled on the breeze.

In time he became thoroughly convinced that God had sent him into the world to become a really distinguished artist, and it may sometimes have occurred to him that, in view of the gloomy and confining poverty of his youth, Providence might be going to reward him all the more brilliantly. Many will consider it a novelesque and unnatural invention, but it is none the less strictly true that in his loneliness, from an ardent impulse of his heart, he often fell on his knees and prayed God to so guide him that he might some day become an altogether splendid artist in the sight of God and man. At this time, his pulse often violently agitated by the pressure of ideas directed steadily toward one point, he wrote down a number of shorter poems, setting forth his state of mind or the praise of music, and these, without knowing the rules, he set joyously to music after his childish heartfelt fashion. A sample of these songs is the following, a prayer which he addressed to music's sainted patron:

> See me comfortless and weeping,
> Solitary vigil keeping,
>   Saint Cecilia, blessed maid;
> See me all the world forsaking,
> On my knees entreaty making;
>   Oh, I pray thee, grant me aid.
>
> Let the hearts of men be captured,
> By my music's tones enraptured,
>   Till my power has no bound,
> And the world be penetrated,
> Fantasy-intoxicated,
>   By the sympathetic sound.

Perhaps for more than a year poor Joseph tormented himself, brooding alone over the step he wished to take. An irresistible force drew his spirit back to that splendid city which he regarded as his paradise, for he was consumed by the desire to learn his art there from the ground up. But it was his relations with his father that weighed particularly on his heart. Having no doubt observed that Joseph was no longer at all willing to apply himself seriously and industriously to his scientific studies, his father had indeed already half given him up, withdrawing himself into his displeasure which, with his advancing age, increased by leaps and bounds. He no longer paid much attention to the boy. Joseph, meanwhile, did not on this account give up his childlike feeling; he struggled continually against his inclination and still had not the heart to breathe, in his father's presence, a word of what he had to reveal. For whole days at a time he tortured himself by weighing one course against another, but he simply could not extricate himself from the horrible abyss of doubt; his ardent prayers were all to no avail—this almost broke his heart. To the utterly gloomy and distressed state of mind in which he was at this time, these lines, which I found among his papers, bear witness:

> Ah, what are these forces that surround me
> And in their embrace have tightly bound me,
> Calling me away—shall I obey them?
> Urging me from home—can I gainsay them?
> I must bear, though guiltless of transgression,
> Torture and temptation and oppression.
>
> That Thou'lt deign to save me, I implore Thee
> Bury me in earth, call me before Thee;
> Otherwise I cannot long withstand it,
> Must live at the will (if it demand it)
> Of that unknown force whose awful power
> Governs me more fully every hour.

From day to day his distress grew more and more acute, the temptation to escape to the splendid city stronger and stronger. But, he thought, will not Providence come to my aid—will it give me no sign at all? His suffering finally reached its highest peak when his father, in connection with some family disagreement, addressed him sharply in a tone quite different from his usual one, afterwards consistently repulsing him. Now the die was cast; from now on he turned his back on all doubts and scruples; he would now consider the matter no further. The Easter holiday was at hand; this he would celebrate with the others at home; but as soon as it was over—out into the wide world.

It was over. He awaited the first fine morning, for the bright sunshine seemed to lure him on as though by magic; then, early in the morning, he ran out of the house and away—one was used to this in him—but this time he did not come back. With delight and with a pounding heart he hastened through the narrow alleys of the little town; hurrying past everything he saw about him, he could scarcely keep from leaping into the open air. On one corner he met an old relation. "Why in such a hurry, cousin?" she asked. "Are you fetching vegetables for the table from the market again?" Yes, yes, called Joseph to himself, and, trembling with joy, he ran out through the gates.

But when he had gone a little distance into the country, he looked about and burst into tears. Shall I turn back, he thought. But he ran on, as though his heels were on fire, and wept continually, so that it looked as though he were running away from his tears. His way led now through many an unfamiliar village and past many an unfamiliar face; the sight of the unfamiliar world revived his courage, he felt strong and free—he came nearer and nearer—and at last—Heavens, what delight!—at last he saw lying before him the towers of the splendid city.

PART TWO

I return to my Joseph a number of years after we left him; he has become Capellmeister in the episcopal residence and lives in great splendor. His relation, having received him very cordially, has been the author of his good fortune, has seen to it that he was given the most thorough training in music, and has also more or less reconciled Joseph's father, little by little, to the step his son had taken. By exceptional application Joseph has worked his way up, to attain at length the highest rung of success that he could possibly wish.

Yet the things of this world change before our very eyes. On one occasion, after he had been Capellmeister for several years, he wrote me the following letter:

Dear Padre:

It is a miserable life I lead—the more you seek to comfort me, the more keenly I am aware of it.

When I recall the dreams of my youth—how blissfully happy I was in those dreams! I thought I wanted to give my fancy free rein continuously and to let out my full heart in works of art. But how strange and austere even my first years of study seemed to me—how I felt when I stepped behind the curtain! To think that all melodies (although they had aroused the most heterogeneous and often the most wondrous emotions in me) were based on a single inevitable mathematical law— that, instead of trying my wings, I had first to learn to climb around in the unwieldy framework and cage of artistic grammar! How I had to torture myself to produce a thing faultlessly correct with the machinelike reason of ordinary science before I could think of making my feelings a subject for music! It was a tiresome mechanical task. But even so, I still had buoyant youthful energy and confidence in the magnificent future. And now? The magnificent future has become the lamentable present.

What happy hours I spent as a boy in the great concert hall, sitting quietly and unnoticed in a corner, enchanted by all the splendor and magnificence, and wishing ever so ardently that these listeners might some day gather to hear my works, to surrender their feelings to me! Now I sit often enough in this same hall, even perform my works there, but in a very different frame of mind indeed. To think I could have imagined that these listeners, parading in gold and silk, had gathered to enjoy a work of art, to warm their hearts, to offer their feelings to the artist! If, even in the majestic cathedral, on the most sacred holiday, when everything great and beautiful that art and religion possess violently forces itself on them, these souls are not so much as warmed, is one to expect it in the concert hall? Feeling and understanding for art have gone out of fashion and become unseemly; to feel, in the presence of an artwork, is considered quite as odd and laughable as suddenly to speak in verse and rhyme in company, when one otherwise gets through one's life with sensible prose, intelligible to all. Yet for these souls I wear out my spirit and work myself up to do things in such a way that they may arouse feeling! This is the high calling to which I had believed myself born.

And when on occasion someone who has a sort of halfway feeling seeks to praise me and to commend me critically and to propound critical questions for me to answer, I am always tempted to beg him not to be at such pains to learn about feeling from books. Heaven knows, when I have enjoyed a piece of music—or any other delightful work of art—and my whole being is full of it, I should paint my feeling on the canvas with a single stroke, if only a single color could express it. I cannot bestow false praise, and I can bring forth nothing clever.

To be sure, there is a little consolation in the thought that perhaps—in some obscure corner of Germany to which this or that work of mine may penetrate some day, even though long after my death—there may be someone whom Heaven has made so sympathetic to my soul that he will feel on hearing my melodies precisely what I felt in writing them—precisely what I sought to put in them. A lovely idea, with which, no doubt, one may pleasantly deceive oneself for a time!

Most horrible of all, however, are those other circumstances with which the artist is hemmed in. To speak of all the loathsome envy and spiteful conduct, of all the untoward petty customs and usages, of all the subordination of art to the will of a court—to speak a word of this is repugnant to me; it is all so undignified, so humiliating to man's soul, that I cannot bring a syllable of it past my lips. A threefold misfortune for music that the mere existence of a work requires such a number of hands! I collect myself and lift up my entire soul to produce a great work—and a hundred unfeeling empty-headed fellows put in their word and demand this and that.

In my youth I thought to avoid the misery of earthly life; now, more than ever, I have sunk into the mire. This much seems certain, sad to say—for all our exertion of our spiritual wings we cannot escape this earth; it pulls us back by force, and we fall again into the common human herd.

They are pitiable artists, those I see about me, even the noblest ones so petty that, for conceit, they do not know what to do once a work of theirs has become a general favorite. Dear God, is not one half our merit due to art's divinity, to nature's eternal harmony, the other half to the gracious Creator who gave us the power to make use of this treasure? Those charming melodies which can call forth in us the most varied emotions thousandfold, have they not sprung, all of them, from the unique and wondrous triad, founded an eternity since by nature? Those melancholy feelings, half soothing, half painful, which music inspires in us, we know not how, what are they after all but the mysterious effect of alternating major and minor? Ought we not to thank our Maker if he now grants us just the skill to combine these sounds, in sympathy from the first with the human soul, so that they move the heart? Art, surely, is what we should worship, not the artist—he is but a feeble instrument.

You see that my ardor and my love for music are no less strong than formerly. And this is just the reason why I am so miserable in this . . . but I shall drop the subject and not annoy you further by describing all the loathsome reality about me. Enough—I live in a very impure atmosphere. How far more ideally I lived in those days when I still merely enjoyed art, in youthful innocence and peaceful solitude, than I do now that I practice it, in the dazzling glare of the world, surrounded only by silks, stars and crosses of honor, and people of culture and taste! What should I like? I should like to leave all this culture high and dry and run away to the simple shepherd in the Swiss mountains to play with him those Alpine songs which make him homesick wherever he hears them.

From this fragmentarily written letter one can realize in part the situation in which Joseph found himself. He felt neglected and alone amid the buzzing of the many unharmonious souls about him; his art was deeply degraded in his eyes in that, so far as he knew, there was no one on whom it made a lively impression, for it seemed to him created only to move the human heart. In many a dark hour he was in utter despair, thinking: How strange and singular is art! Is then its mysterious power for me alone—is it to all other men mere sensual pleasure and agreeable amusement? What is it really and in fact, if it is nothing to all men and something to me alone? Is it not a most absurd idea to make this art one's whole aim and chief business and to imagine a thousand wonderful things about its great effects on human temperament—about an art which, in everyday reality, plays much the same role as card-playing or any other pastime?

When such thoughts occurred to him, it seemed to him that he had been the greatest of visionaries to have striven so hard to make a practical artist of himself for the world. He hit on the idea that the artist should be artist for himself alone, to his own heart's exaltation, and for the one or two who understand him. And I cannot call this idea wholly incorrect.

But I must sum up briefly the remainder of my Joseph's life, for my memories of it are beginning to depress me.

For a number of years he continued to live on in this way as Capellmeister, and, as time went on, his discouragement increased, as did his uneasy realization that, for all his deep feeling and intimate understanding of art, he was of no use to the world, less influential than a common tradesman. Often and regretfully he recalled the pure ideal enthusiasm of his boyhood and with it how his father had tried to make a doctor of him so that he might lessen man's misery, heal the unfortunate, and thus make himself useful in the world. This had perhaps been better, he thought more than once.

His father, meanwhile, had at his age grown very weak. Joseph wrote regularly to his eldest sister and sent her something toward his father's support. He could not bring himself to pay him an actual visit and felt that this would be beyond him. He became more despondent; his life was far spent.

On one occasion he had performed in the concert hall a new and beautiful piece of music of his own composition; it seemed the first time that he had made any impression on the hearts of his listeners. The general astonishment, the silent approval, so much more welcome than noisy applause, made him happy in the thought that this time he had perhaps been worthy of his art; once more he was encouraged to begin work anew. But when he went out on to the street, a girl, dressed very miserably, crept up and sought to speak to him. Heavens, he cried; it was his youngest sister and she was in a wretched state. She had run on foot from her home to bring him the news that his father was about to die and had insistently demanded to speak with him before the end. At that, the music in his breast broke off; in a heavy stupor he made his preparations and set off in haste for his birthplace.

The scenes which took place at his father's bedside I shall not describe. But let the reader not believe that there were any melancholy long-drawn-out debates; without wasting many words they understood each other fully—in this respect, indeed, it seems that nature mocks us generally, men never understanding one another properly until these critical last moments. At the same time, he was smitten to the heart by all that he saw. His sisters were in the most deplorable circumstances; two of them had fallen from grace and run away; the eldest, to whom he regularly sent money, had wasted most of it, letting his father starve; in the end his father died miserably before his eyes; alas, it was horrible, the way his poor heart was wounded through and through and torn to bits. He did what he could for his sisters and went home, for his affairs recalled him.

For the impending Easter festival he was to write a new Passion music; his envious rivals were eagerly awaiting it. Yet, as often as he sat down to work, he burst into a flood of tears; his tortured heart would not let him recover himself. He lay deeply depressed, buried among the leavings of this world. At length, by an effort, he tore himself free, stretching out his arms to heaven in an impassioned prayer; he filled his soul with the most sublime poetry, with a full and exultant hymn, and, in a marvelous inspiration, but still violently shaken emotionally, he set down a Passion music which, with its deeply affecting melodies, embodying all the pains of suffering, will forever remain a masterpiece. His soul was like that of the invalid who, in a strange paroxysm, exhibits greater strength than the healthy man.

But after he had performed the oratorio in the cathedral on Easter Sunday, straining himself to the utmost in feverish agitation, he felt faint and exhausted. Like an unhealthy dew, a nervous weakness attacked all his fibers; he was ill for a time and died not long afterwards, in the bloom of his years.

Many a tear have I offered to his memory, and a strange feeling comes over me when I review his life. Why did Heaven ordain that the struggle between his lofty enthusiasm and the common misery of this earth should make him unhappy his whole life long and in the end tear quite apart the twofold nature of his mind and body?

The ways of Providence are hidden from us. But let us marvel once again at the diversity of those inspired beings whom Heaven sends into the world to serve the arts.

A Raphael brought forth in all innocence and artlessness works of the utmost ingenuity in which we see revealed the whole of Heaven; a Guido Reni, leading a wild gambler's life, created the gentlest and most sacred paintings; an Albrecht Dürer, a simple citizen of Nuremberg, in that same cell in which his wicked wife abused him daily, produced with the antlike industry of the mechanic artworks highly spiritual in content; yet Joseph, in whose harmonious music lies such mysterious beauty, differed from them all.

Alas, his lofty fantasy was what destroyed him. Shall I say that he was perhaps created rather to enjoy art than to practice it? Those in whom art works silently and secretly, like an inner genius, not hindering their doings upon earth—are they perhaps more fortunately constituted? And must the ceaselessly inspired one, if he would be true artist, perhaps not weave his lofty fantasies, like a stout strand, boldly and firmly into this earthly life? Indeed, is not perhaps this incomprehensible creative power something altogether different and—as it now seems to me—something still more marvelous and godlike than the power of fantasy?

The spirit of art is and remains for man eternally a mystery, and he grows dizzy when he seeks to plumb its depths; at the same time, it is eternally an object for his highest admiration, as must be said of all the great things in this world.

• • •

But after these recollections of my Joseph I can write no more. I conclude my book—in the hope that it may have served to awaken good ideas in some one or other of my readers.

150 Margaret Fuller

Sarah Margaret Fuller Ossoli, born in Massachusetts in 1810, was a critic, teacher, and feminist. She was an intellectual prodigy as a child and became especially well known for the brilliance of her conversation. For five years in Boston she conducted "conversations" for women, to encourage their participation in cultural and intellectual life. A member of the American transcendentalist movement, she edited *The Dial,* the transcendentalists' magazine, from 1840 to 1842 and published in its pages many pieces of her own writing.

In 1844 Fuller moved to New York, where she became the literature and arts critic of Horace Greeley's *New York Tribune.* She continued as a foreign correspondent for that newspaper after moving to Italy a few years later, remaining there when revolution broke out in Rome. Her manuscript history of that revolution was lost in the 1850 shipwreck off Fire Island, New York, that also claimed Fuller's life.

Fuller's essay is an extended meditation on the lives of artistic geniuses and the lessons those lives may hold for us. While not a book review, the argument focuses on five actual composer biographies and uses extended quotations from them to illustrate her points. Fuller does not give complete citations for the books she discusses, but they may be identified as follows: Friedrich Schlichtegroll's *Mozarts Leben* (1794) in a French translation by Bombet (a pseudonym of Marie-Henri Beyle, who also used the pseudonym Stendhal); Johann Nikolaus Forkel's *Über Johann Sebastian Bachs Leben, Kunst und Kunstwerke* (1802), in an English translation (1820); Bombet's *Vies de Haydn, de Mozart et de Métastase* (1814); Anton Schindler's *Biographie von Ludwig van Beethoven* (1840); and an unidentified life of Handel, which may have been John Mainwaring's *Memoirs of the Life of the Late George Frederick Handel* (1760) since she characterizes it as being "in the style of the days of Addison and Steele." Only the introduction and conclusion of the long essay are given here.

FROM Lives of the Great Composers, Haydn, Mozart, Handel, Bach, Beethoven
(1841)

The lives of the musicians are imperfectly written for this obvious reason. The soul of the great musician can only be expressed in music. This language is so much more ready, flexible, full, and rapid than any other, that we can never expect the minds of those accustomed to its use to be expressed by act or word, with even that degree of adequacy, which we find in those of other men. They are accustomed to a higher stimulus, a more fluent existence. We must read them in their works; this, true of artists in every department, is especially so of the high-priests of sound.

Yet the eye, which has followed with rapture the flight of the bird till it is quite vanished in the blue serene, reverts with pleasure to the nest which it finds of materials and architecture, that, if wisely examined, correspond entirely with all previously imagined of the songster's history and habits. The biography of the artist is a scanty gloss upon the grand text of his works, but we examine it with a deliberate tenderness, and could not spare those half-effaced pencil marks of daily life.

In vain the healthy reactions of nature have so boldly in our own day challenged the love of greatness, and bid us turn from Boswellism[1] to read the record of the village clerk. These obscure men, you say, have hearts also, busy lives, expanding souls. Study the simple annals of the poor, and you find there, only restricted and stifled by accident, Milton, Calderon, or Michel Angelo. Precisely for that, precisely because we might be such as these, if temperament and position had seconded the soul's behest, must we seek with eagerness this spectacle of the occasional manifestation of that degree of development which we call hero, poet, artist, martyr. A sense of the depths of love and pity in our obscure and private breasts bids us demand to see their sources burst up somewhere through the lava of circumstance, and Peter Bell has no sooner felt his first throb of penitence and piety, than he prepares to read the lives of the saints.

Of all those forms of life which in their greater achievement shadow forth what the accomplishment of our life in the ages must be, the artist's life is the fairest in this, that it weaves its web most soft and full, because of the material most at command. Like the hero, the statesman, the martyr, the artist differs from other men only in this, that the voice of the demon within the breast

TEXT: *The Dial: A Magazine for Literature, Philosophy, and Religion* 2, no. 2 (October 1841): 148–151, 202–3. I am grateful to Ora Frishberg Saloman for assistance in identifying the five composer biographies listed above.

1. James Boswell (1740–1795) is best known as the biographer of Samuel Johnson.

speaks louder, or is more early and steadily obeyed than by men in general. But colors, and marble, and paper scores are more easily found to use, and more under command, than the occasions of life or the wills of other men, so that we see in the poet's work, if not a higher sentiment, or a deeper meaning, a more frequent and more perfect fulfilment than in him who builds his temple from the world day by day, or makes a nation his canvass and his pallette.

It is also easier to us to get the scope of the artist's design and its growth as the area where we see it does not stretch vision beyond its power. The Sybil of Michel Angelo indeed shares the growth of centuries, as much as Luther's Reformation, but the first apparition of the one strikes both the senses and the soul, the other only the latter, so we look most easily and with liveliest impression at the Sybil.

Add the benefits of rehearsal and repetition. The grand Napoleon drama could be acted but once, but Mozart's Don Giovanni presents to us the same thought seven times a week, if we wish to yield to it so many.

The artists too are the young children of our sickly manhood, or wearied out old age. On us life has pressed till the form is marred and bowed down, but their youth is immortal, invincible, to us the inexhaustible prophecy of a second birth. From the naive lispings of their uncalculating lives are heard anew the tones of that mystic song we call Perfectibility, Perfection.

Artist biographies, scanty as they are, are always beautiful. The tedious cavil of the Teuton cannot degrade, nor the sultry superlatives of the Italian wither them. If any fidelity be preserved in the record, it always casts new light on their works. The exuberance of Italian praise is the better extreme of the two, for the heart, with all its blunders, tells truth more easily than the head. The records before us of the great composers are by the patient and reverent Germans, the sensible, never to be duped Englishman, or the sprightly Frenchman; but a Vasari[2] was needed also to cast a broader sunlight on the scene. All artist lives are interesting. And those of the musicians, peculiarly so to-day, when Music is *the* living, growing art. Sculpture, Painting, Architecture are indeed not dead, but the life they exhibit is as the putting forth of young scions from an old root. The manifestation is hopeful rather than commanding. But music, after all the wonderful exploits of the last century, grows and towers yet. Beethoven, towering far above our heads, still with colossal gesture points above. Music is pausing now to explain, arrange, or explore the treasures so rapidly accumulated; but how great the genius thus employed, how vast the promise for the next revelation! Beethoven seems to have chronicled all the sobs, the heart-heavings, and god-like Promethean thefts of the Earth-spirit. Mozart has called to the sister stars, as Handel and Haydn have told to other spheres what has been actually performed in this; surely they will answer through the next magician.

2. Giorgio Vasari (1511–1574), Italian painter and architect, and author of *Lives of the Most Eminent Italian Architects, Painters and Sculptors* (1550).

The thought of the law that supersedes all thoughts, which pierces us the moment we have gone far in any department of knowledge or creative genius, seizes and lifts us from the ground in Music. "Were but this known all would be accomplished" is sung to us ever in the triumphs of Harmony. What the other arts indicate and Philosophy infers, this all-enfolding language declares, nay publishes, and we lose all care for to-morrow or modern life in the truth averred of old, that all truth is comprised in music and mathematics.

> By one pervading spirit
> Of tones and numbers all things are controlled,
> As sages taught where *faith* was found to merit
> Initiation in that mystery old.
> —Wordsworth, "Stanzas on the power of sounds"

A very slight knowledge of music makes it the best means of interpretation. We meet our friend in a melody as in a glance of the eye, far beyond where words have strength to climb; we explain by the corresponding tone in an instrument that trait in our admired picture, for which no sufficiently subtle analogy had yet been found. Botany had never touched our true knowledge of our favorite flower, but a symphony displays the same attitude and hues; the philosophic historian had failed to explain the motive of our favorite hero, but every bugle calls and every trumpet proclaims him. He that hath ears to hear, let him hear!

Of course we claim for music only a greater rapidity, fulness, and, above all, delicacy of utterance. All is in each and each in all, so that the most barbarous stammering of the Hottentot indicates the secret of man, as clearly as the rudest zoophyte the perfection of organized being, or the first stop on the reed the harmonies of heaven. But music, by the ready medium, the stimulus and the upbearing elasticity it offers for the inspirations of thought, alone seems to present a living form rather than a dead monument to the desires of Genius.

•   •   •   •   •

In three respects these artists, all true artists, resemble one another. Clear decision. The intuitive faculty speaks clear in those devoted to the worship of Beauty. They are not subject to mental conflict, they ask not counsel of experience. They take what they want as simply as the bird goes in search of its proper food, so soon as its wings are grown.

Like nature they love the work for its own sake. The philosopher is ever seeking the thought through the symbol, but the artist is happy at the implication of the thought in his work. He does not reason about "religion or thorough bass." His answer in Haydn's, "I thought it best so." From each achievement grows up a still higher ideal, and when his work is finished, it is nothing to the artist who has made of it the step by which he ascended, but while he was engaged in it, it was all to him, and filled his soul with a parental joy.

They do not criticise, but affirm. They have no need to deny aught, much less one another. All excellence to them was genial; imperfection only left room for new creative power to display itself. An everlasting yes breathes from the life, from the work of the artist. Nature echoes it, and leaves to society the work of saying no, if it will. But it will not, except for the moment. It weans itself for the moment, and turns pettishly away from genius, but soon stumbling, groping, and lonely, cries aloud for its nurse. The age cries *now*, and what an answer is prophesied by such harbinger stars as these at which we have been gazing. We will engrave their names on the breastplate, and wear them as a talisman of hope.

151 George Eliot

The novels of Mary Ann Evans (1819–1880), who used the pen name George Eliot, are particularly celebrated for their intellectual and historical depth, their moral sensibility, and the acuteness of their social descriptions. *Daniel Deronda,* her last novel, is no exception. Its principal historical material is the Zionist movement and the social situation of Jews in England; its moral themes are responsibility and kinship. Music plays an important role, as it frequently does in Eliot's work, as an index of character. In the two excerpts given here, two very different young women sing for the distinguished musician Julius Klesmer and encounter two very different responses.

The scenes reveal Eliot's keen understanding of the musical mores and debates of the day: the famed philistinism of the English, the entrapment of young women like Gwendolen Harleth in meaningless musical study for largely decorative purposes, the battle between German Wagnerian music and Italian music and the ideology underlying that dispute. There is also, Eliot makes clear, the persistent tinge of anti-Semitism; nearly all of the characters in the novel who are represented as genuine, natural musicians are Jewish, and Klesmer's very name means "musician" in Yiddish. The model for the composer / pianist Klesmer may have been Anton Rubinstein, whom Eliot met in Weimar during a visit to Liszt, or may, indeed, have been Liszt himself.

FROM *Daniel Deronda*

(1878)

"Ah, here comes Herr Klesmer," said Mrs. Arrowpoint, rising; and presently bringing him to Gwendolen, she left them to a dialogue which was agreeable

TEXT: Cabinet edition (Edinburgh and London: Blackwood, 1878), portions of chaps. 5 and 39.

on both sides, Herr Klesmer being a felicitous combination of the German, the Sclave, and the Semite, with grand features, brown hair floating in artistic fashion, and brown eyes in spectacles. His English had little foreignness except its fluency; and his alarming cleverness was made less formidable just then by a certain softening air of silliness which will sometimes befall even Genius in the desire of being agreeable to Beauty.

Music was soon begun. Miss Arrowpoint and Herr Klesmer played a four-handed piece on two pianos which convinced the company in general that it was long, and Gwendolen in particular that the neutral, placid-faced Miss Arrowpoint had a mastery of the instrument which put her own execution out of the question—though she was not discouraged as to her often-praised touch and style. After this every one became anxious to hear Gwendolen sing; especially Mr. Arrowpoint; as was natural in a host and a perfect gentleman, of whom no one had anything to say but that he had married Miss Cuttler, and imported the best cigars; and he led her to the piano with easy politeness. Herr Klesmer closed the instrument in readiness for her, and smiled with pleasure at her approach; then placed himself at the distance of a few feet so that he could see her as she sang.

Gwendolen was not nervous: what she undertook to do she did without trembling, and singing was an enjoyment to her. Her voice was a moderately powerful soprano (someone had told her it was like Jenny Lind's), her ear good, and she was able to keep in tune, so that her singing gave pleasure to ordinary hearers, and she had been used to unmingled applause. She had the rare advantage of looking almost prettier when she was singing than at other times, and that Herr Klesmer was in front of her seemed not disagreeable. Her song, determined on beforehand, was a favourite aria of Bellini's, in which she felt quite sure of herself.

"Charming!" said Mr. Arrowpoint, who had remained near, and the word was echoed around without more insincerity than we recognise in a brotherly way as human. But Herr Klesmer stood like a statue—if a statue can be imagined in spectacles; at least, he was as mute as a statue. Gwendolen was pressed to keep her seat and double the general pleasure, and she did not wish to refuse; but before resolving to do so, she moved a little towards Herr Klesmer, saying, with a look of smiling appeal, "It would be too cruel to a great musician. You cannot like to hear poor amateur singing."

"No, truly; but that makes nothing," said Herr Klesmer, suddenly speaking in an odious German fashion with staccato endings, quite unobservable in him before, and apparently depending on a change of mood, as Irishmen resume their strongest brogue when they are fervid or quarrelsome. "That makes nothing. It is always acceptable to see you sing."

Was there ever so unexpected an assertion of superiority? at least before the late Teutonic conquests? Gwendolen coloured deeply, but, with her usual presence of mind, did not show an ungraceful resentment by moving away immediately; and Miss Arrowpoint, who had been near enough to overhear (and also to observe that Herr Klesmer's mode of looking at Gwendolen was more conspicuously admiring than was quite consistent with good taste), now with the utmost tact and kindness came close to her and said—

"Imagine what I have to go through with this professor! He can hardly tolerate anything we English do in music. We can only put up with his severity, and make use of it to find out the worst that can be said of us. It is a little comfort to know that; and one can bear it when everyone else is admiring."

"I should be very much obliged to him for telling me the worst," said Gwendolen, recovering herself. "I daresay I have been extremely ill taught, in addition to having no talent—only liking for music." This was very well expressed considering that it had never entered her mind before.

"Yes, it is true; you have not been well taught," said Herr Klesmer, quietly. Woman was dear to him, but music was dearer. "Still, you are not quite without gifts. You sing in tune, and you have a pretty fair organ. But you produce your notes badly; and that music which you sing is beneath you. It is a form of melody which expresses a puerile state of culture—a dangling, canting, see-saw kind of stuff—the passion and thought of people without any breadth of horizon. There is a sort of self-satisfied folly about every phrase of such melody: no cries of deep, mysterious passion—no conflict—no sense of the universal. It makes men small as they listen to it. Sing now something larger. And I shall see."

"Oh, not now—by-and-by," said Gwendolen, with a sinking of heart at the sudden width of horizon opened round her small musical performance. For a young lady desiring to lead, this first encounter in her campaign was startling. But she was bent on not behaving foolishly, and Miss Arrowpoint helped her by saying—

"Yes, by-and-by. I always require half an hour to get up my courage after being criticised by Herr Klesmer. We will ask him to play to us now: he is bound to show us what is good music."

To be quite safe on this point Herr Klesmer played a composition of his own, a fantasia called *Freudvoll, Leidvoll, Gedankenvoll*[1]—an extensive commentary on some melodic ideas not too grossly evident; and he certainly fetched as much variety and depth of passion out of the piano as that moderately responsive instrument lends itself to, having an imperious magic in his fingers that seemed to send a nerve-thrill through ivory key and wooden hammer, and compel the strings to make a quivering lingering speech for him. Gwendolen, in spite of her wounded egoism, had fulness of nature enough to feel the power of this playing, and it gradually turned her inward sob of mortification into an excitement which lifted her for the moment into a desperate indifference about her own doings, or at least a determination to get a superiority over them by laughing at them as if they belonged to somebody else. Her eyes had become brighter, her cheeks slightly flushed, and her tongue ready for any mischievous remarks.

---

1. "Joyful, Sorrowful, Thoughtful."

"I wish you would sing to us again, Miss Harleth," said young Clintock, the archdeacon's classical son, who had been so fortunate as to take her to dinner, and came up to renew conversation as soon as Herr Klesmer's performance was ended. "That is the style of music for me. I never can make anything of this tip-top playing. It is like a jar of leeches, where you can never tell either beginnings or endings. I could listen to your singing all day."

"Yes, we should be glad of something popular now—another song from you would be a relaxation," said Mrs. Arrowpoint, who had also come near with polite intentions.

"That must be because you are in a puerile state of culture, and have no breadth of horizon. I have just learned that. I have been taught how bad my taste is, and am feeling growing pains. They are never pleasant," said Gwendolen, not taking any notice of Mrs. Arrowpoint, and looking up with a bright smile at young Clintock.

Mrs. Arrowpoint was not insensible to this rudeness, but merely said, "Well, we will not press anything disagreeably:" and as there was a perceptible outrush of imprisoned conversation just then, and a movement of guests seeking each other, she remained seated where she was, and looked round her with the relief of the hostess at finding she is not needed.

· · · · ·

About four o'clock wheels paused before the door, and there came one of those knocks with an accompanying ring which serve to magnify the sense of social existence in a region where the most enlivening signals are usually those of the muffin-man. All the girls were at home, and the two rooms were thrown together to make space for Kate's drawing, as well as a great length of embroidery which had taken the place of the satin cushions—a sort of *pièce de résistance* in the courses of needlework, taken up by any clever fingers that happened to be at liberty. It stretched across the front room picturesquely enough, Mrs. Meyrick bending over it at one corner, Mab in the middle, and Amy at the other end. Mirah, whose performances in point of sewing were on the makeshift level of the tailor-bird's, her education in that branch having been much neglected, was acting as reader to the party, seated on a camp-stool; in which position she also served Kate as model for a title-page vignette, symbolising a fair public absorbed in the successive volumes of the Family Teatable. She was giving forth with charming distinctness the delightful Essay of Elia, *The Praise of Chimney-Sweeps*, and all were smiling over the "innocent blacknesses," when the imposing knock and ring called their thoughts to loftier spheres, and they looked up in wonderment.

"Dear me!" said Mrs. Meyrick; "can it be Lady Mallinger? Is there a grand carriage, Amy?"

"No—only a hansom cab. It must be a gentleman."

"The Prime Minister, I should think," said Kate, drily. "Hans says the greatest man in London may get into a hansom cab."

"Oh, oh, oh!" cried Mab. "Suppose it should be Lord Russell!"

The five bright faces were all looking amused when the old maid-servant bringing in a card distractedly left the parlour-door open, and there was seen bowing towards Mrs. Meyrick a figure quite unlike that of the respected Premier—tall and physically impressive even in his kid and kerseymere, with massive face, flamboyant hair, and gold spectacles: in fact, as Mrs Meyrick saw from the card, *Julius Klesmer.*

Even embarrassment could hardly have made the "little mother" awkward, but quick in her perceptions she was at once aware of the situation, and felt well satisfied that the great personage had come to Mirah instead of requiring her to come to him; taking it as a sign of active interest. But when he entered, the rooms shrank into closets, the cottage piano, Mab thought, seemed a ridiculous toy, and the entire family existence as petty and private as an establishment of mice in the Tuileries. Klesmer's personality, especially his way of glancing round him, immediately suggested vast areas and a multitudinous audience, and probably they made the usual scenery of his consciousness, for we all of us carry on our thinking in some habitual *locus* where there is a presence of other souls, and those who take in a larger sweep than their neighbours are apt to seem mightily vain and affected. Klesmer was vain, but not more so than many contemporaries of heavy aspect, whose vanity leaps out and startles one like a spear out of a walking-stick; as to his carriage and gestures, these were as natural to him as the length of his fingers; and the rankest affectation he could have shown would have been to look diffident and demure. While his grandiose air was making Mab feel herself a ridiculous toy to match the cottage piano, he was taking in the details around him with a keen and thoroughly kind sensibility. He remembered a home no larger than this on the outskirts of Bohemia; and in the figurative Bohemia too he had had large acquaintance with the variety and romance which belong to small incomes. He addressed Mrs. Meyrick with the utmost deference.

"I hope I have not taken too great a freedom. Being in the neighbourhood, I ventured to save time by calling. Our friend Mr. Deronda mentioned to me an understanding that I was to have the honour of becoming acquainted with a young lady here—Miss Lapidoth."

Klesmer had really discerned Mirah in the first moment of entering, but with subtle politeness he looked round bowingly at the three sisters as if he were uncertain which was the young lady in question.

"Those are my daughters: this is Miss Lapidoth," said Mrs. Meyrick, waving her hand towards Mirah.

"Ah," said Klesmer, in a tone of gratified expectation, turning a radiant smile and deep bow to Mirah, who, instead of being in the least taken by surprise, had a calm pleasure in her face. She liked the look of Klesmer, feeling sure that he would scold her, like a great musician and a kind man.

"You will not object to beginning our acquaintance by singing to me," he added, aware that they would all be relieved by getting rid of preliminaries.

"I shall be very glad. It is good of you to be willing to listen to me," said Mirah, moving to the piano. "Shall I accompany myself?"

"By all means," said Klesmer, seating himself, at Mrs. Meyrick's invitation, where he could have a good view of the singer. The acute little mother would not have acknowledged the weakness, but she really said to herself, "He will like her singing better if he sees her."

All the feminine hearts except Mirah's were beating fast with anxiety, thinking Klesmer terrific as he sat with his listening frown on, and only daring to look at him furtively. If he did say anything severe it would be so hard for them all. They could only comfort themselves with thinking that Prince Camaralzaman,[2] who had heard the finest things, preferred Mirah's singing to any other:—also she appeared to be doing her very best, as if she were more instead of less at ease than usual.

The song she had chosen was a fine setting of some words selected from Leopardi's grand Ode to Italy:—

> *O patria mia, vedo le mura e gli archi*
> *E le colonne e i simulacri e l'erme*
> *Torri degli avi nostri—*

This was recitative: then followed—

> *Ma la gloria non vedo—*

a mournful melody, a rhythmic plaint. After this came a climax of devout triumph—passing from the subdued adoration of a happy Andante in the words—

> *Beatissimi voi,*
> *Che offriste il petto alle nemiche lance*
> *Per amor di costei che al sol vi diede—*

to the joyous outburst of an exultant Allegro in—

> *Oh viva, oh viva:*
> *Beatissimi voi*
> *Mentre nel mondo si favelli o scriva.*[3]

2. Qamar-al-Zaman, a character in *The Arabian Nights;* the Meyrick girls' nickname for Daniel Deronda.

3.   O my country, I see the walls and arches,
                   The columns and statues and the
                   Towers of our forefathers . . .

                   But I do not see glory . . .

                   Blessed are you
                   Who offered your breast to enemy lances
                   For love of those who gave you life . . .

                   Hail to you,
                   Most blessed
                   As long as men shall speak or write.
                   (Giacomo Leopardi, "All'Italia" (1818), *Canti*, vol. 1.)

When she had ended, Klesmer said after a moment—

"That is Joseph Leo's[4] music."

"Yes, he was my last master—at Vienna: so fierce and so good," said Mirah, with a melancholy smile. "He prophesied that my voice would not do for the stage. And he was right."

"*Con*tinue, if you please," said Klesmer, putting out his lips and shaking his long fingers, while he went on with a smothered articulation quite unintelligible to the audience.

The three girls detested him unanimously for not saying one word of praise. Mrs. Meyrick was a little alarmed.

Mirah, simply bent on doing what Klesmer desired, and imagining that he would now like to hear her sing some German, went through Prince Radzivill's[5] music to Gretchen's songs in the Faust, one after the other, without any interrogatory pause. When she had finished he rose and walked to the extremity of the small space at command, then walked back to the piano, where Mirah had risen from her seat and stood looking towards him with her little hands crossed before her, meekly awaiting judgment; then with a sudden unknitting of his brow and with beaming eyes, he put out his hand and said abruptly, "Let us shake hands: you are a musician."

4. Leo is, like Klesmer himself, an invention of Eliot's.
5. Anton Heinrich Radziwill (1775–1833), composer and patron of music; his *Goethes Faust* was composed in 1819.

THE MUSIC OF
THE FUTURE

152 Giuseppe Mazzini

An Italian patriot and revolutionary who was continually under sentence for conspiring to overthrow absolutist governments, Giuseppe Mazzini (1805–1872) spent much of his life abroad in exile, living sometimes in France, sometimes in Switzerland, and for a considerable time in England. His mind was seldom far from Italy, however, and he was a prolific essayist and propagandist for the unification of the Italian states and their liberation from foreign domination.

Mazzini's writings in the early nineteenth century look beyond Romanticism to a time when the energies of art and of culture as a whole would be turned toward the cause of political liberation and human moral development. In this process, he argued, national styles must fall away, leaving behind a genuinely European art. His *Filosofia della musica*, first published in a Parisian journal, presents an agenda for composers of the future along these lines, urging a synthesis of the best aspects of both warring musical factions, North and South.

In a later note to this text (1867), Mazzini celebrated the major operas of Giacomo Meyerbeer, proclaiming that here was discovered the prophet and precursor (though not yet the fulfillment) of the music of the future.

FROM *Philosophy of Music*
(1836)

Let us return to music, taking consolation for the terrible condition of current taste in the hopes emanating from this divine art, despite the depths to which it has currently sunk. Music, like woman, is so holy with anticipation and purification, that even when men sully it with prostitution, they cannot totally obliterate the aura of promise that crowns it. Even in the midst of that music which today we condemn, there is still a ferment of life that foretells new destinies, a new development, a new and more solemn mission. The image of beauty and of eternal harmony appears in it in fragments, but still it does appear. You might say that an angel, out of the abyss into which he has been thrown, still manages to address us as if from paradise. Perhaps in the future it will fall to woman and to music to carry a broader responsibility for resurrection than has so far been anticipated. Perhaps to music first, because music, speaking to all humanity in a single voice, will have the responsibility of initiating an idea which in turn will be interpreted and developed by the other arts. Music is the faith of a world whose poetry is one and the same as its philosophy. And great eras begin with faith. In any case, the initiative for the new musical

TEXT: *Filosofia della musica, e Estetica musicale del primo Ottocento, testi scelti . . .* , ed. Marcello de Angelis (Florence: Guaraldi, 1977), pp. 48–61, 76–77. Translation by Yvonne Freccero, with Giovanna Bellesia and John Sessions.

synthesis will come, unless I am mistaken, from Italy. The only possible contender would be Germany. But Germany, intent these days on applied knowledge, and weary from a long stretch of centuries spent in the strictly theoretical sphere of abstraction, has been forced inevitably into a reaction all the more violent for its late arrival, against the tendency toward mysticism that has dominated it totally until now. And the power to initiate an era in an art that is more spiritual than any other is forbidden to those who make common cause with materialism and even actively embrace it. Among us, these days, movement can only go in the opposite direction, and therefore we are in the very best condition for creation. Because whatever one may say—and although the Italians, a great many at least, even now deny it—surely all or almost all the origins of great things must arise from Italy.

Let us suppose that there is a rebirth of faith, that materialism is at an end, and that analysis, which is in sole control these days, has been confined to the role it was meant to fulfill, which is the verification and step-by-step application of a synthesis. Let us suppose that tastes evolve from the exhausted mission of the eighteenth century toward the ultimate future of the nineteenth. Let us suppose a holy enthusiasm, and a public ready for the artist—a condition without which there is nothing to be hoped for—which path should genius choose? For which problem should it seek the solution? And what will be these tendencies of the musical era that awaits initiation?—in other words, where are we? What limits have we reached? Only the knowledge of current tendencies, of limits reached, of the philosophical terms that define art, can reveal for us what is to be done, the secret of future art.

Inclinations are about as infinite as the talents that surround us, but a closer look reveals that they are all secondary and confined to questions of *form*, interesting in a superficial way, rather than focussing on the intimate life, the substance, the idea that is the soul of music. As far as the latter is concerned we find that all tendencies are reduced to two; all things are organized, properly speaking, into two primary groups, centering around two sovereign elements.

These are the two eternal elements of all things, the two principles constantly in operation, and one or the other of them is foremost in all the problems that have wearied the human mind for thousands of years; the two terms that in all matters end up in conflict, and whose continuing development in two converging lines, from century to century, define the subject matter of history: man and humanity, individual thought and social thought.

Hovering between these two principles, today as always, are science or systematic thought and Art which is its manifestation. Of the two tendencies produced by these terms, one makes the individual its center and revolves around him, while the other forgets the individual and obliterates him in the vast reaches of a concept of universal unity. One is nourished on analysis, the other on synthesis—both are exclusive and self-contained, and they have perpetuated to this day a controversy that divides human forces and impedes progress, since one, denying a common purpose to individual actions, is dragged into ruin through analysis of a materialist sort and the other, having lost itself in the paths of an unapplied synthesis, evaporates into vagueness, into the indefinite, into a sphere of mysticism unconducive to real achievements. Whoever settles this argument, bringing the two tendencies together in one purpose without repudiating either of the original terms, will have solved the problem. Eclecticism, which in recent times has misled the best minds, has done nothing but delineate the problem.

Demonstration of these two tendencies—in philosophy, in history, in literature, in the physical sciences, in all branches of intellectual development—is not within the scope of this work. Readers may do it for themselves, because it has never been more evident than today.

But in music, where, as I have said, the action of this general law has never been noticed, neither observed nor suspected, these tendencies are nevertheless even more noticeable than elsewhere. *Melody* and *harmony* are the two generative elements. The first represents individuality, the other social thought. In the perfect accord of these two basic terms of all music—and then in the consecration of this accord to a sublime purpose or a holy mission—lies the secret of Art, the concept of a European music which, consciously or unconsciously, we all invoke.

These days, corresponding to the two tendencies that hinge on one or the other of these elements, are two schools, two camps, you might say two distinct zones: the North and the South, German and Italian music. I know of no other music that exists by itself, independent in its essential concept from these two, nor do I believe that anyone else, even allowing for the delusions of patriotic pride, can find one.

Italian music is *melodic*[1] in the highest degree. Since the time when Palestrina translated Christianity into tones, and initiated the Italian school with his melodies, it has assumed and maintained this characteristic. The spirit of the Middle Ages breathes in it and inspires it. *Individuality*, meanwhile, as a theme that finds in Italy a more deeply felt and more vigorous expression than anywhere else, has generally speaking inspired our music, and dominates it entirely. The ego reigns, despotic and alone. It indulges itself; it obeys every whim of a will that brooks no opposition; it goes where it will and is spurred on by desire. Rational and consistent standards, a life that moves in a single

---

1. I am speaking of *predominant* characteristics in this rapid sketch of Italian and German music. Neither school could concentrate on one element so that the other were excluded, remaining subdued and almost supplementary. In Italian music, and particularly in the time of living masters, *harmony* often invades the work and outstrips its rival, just as in German music, particularly in Beethoven, *melody* often rises in divine expression above the characteristic harmony of the school. But these usurpations are only apparent; being brief, they interrupt but do not eliminate the domination of the other.

It is useless to point out the misunderstanding of someone who confuses *melody* with human intonation, and *harmony* with instrumentation. Obviously, even instrumentation can be *melodic*, and indeed it is most of the time in Rossini. [Au.]

direction, thoughtfully directed toward a purpose, these do not exist. What do exist are the powerful sensation, the rapid and violent outburst.

Italian music surrounds itself with concrete objects, receives the sensations that come from them, then sends them back embellished, made divine. Lyrical to the point of frenzy, passionate to the point of intoxication, volcanic like the land where it was born, brilliant as the sun that shines on that land, it darts about rapidly, paying little or no attention to whys and wherefores or to transitions, bounding from one thing to another, from sentiment to sentiment, from thought to thought, from ecstatic joy to disconsolate grief, from laughter to tears, from anger to love, from heaven to hell—and always with power and emotion, always stirred up in some way, a life with twice the intensity of other lives, a heart that beats feverishly. To it belongs inspiration: boundless inspiration, an inspiration that is eminently *artistic* rather than religious. Sometimes it prays––and when it glimpses a ray of light from heaven, from the soul, when it feels a breath of the great universe and prostrates itself in adoration, it is sublime. Its prayer is that of a saint, of someone in rapture, but briefly, and you feel that if it bows its head, the very next moment it may lift it in an attitude of freedom and independence; you feel that it has bent under the force of a passing enthusiasm, not the habit of an ingrained religious sentiment.

Religious beliefs live on a faith in something that exists beyond the visible world, on a longing for the infinite, and on a purpose and a mission that invade all of life and are apparent in the least little act. But Italian music has faith only in itself, has no purpose other than itself. *Art for Art* is the supreme rubric of Italian music. Hence the lack of unity, hence its fragmented, disconnected, and spasmodic progress. It hoards secrets of power that, if honed toward an end, would stir up all creation to achieve it. But where is this end? The lever is lacking the fulcrum, there is no bond to link the thousands of sensations represented by its melodies. Like Faust, it can say: I have traversed the entire universe in my flight; but in bits and pieces, analyzing one thing after another— but the soul, and the God of the universe, where are they?

For such music, as for every period, or people, or discipline that in the course of development represents and idolizes *individuality*, there necessarily had to appear a man who would sum up everything within himself, becoming its symbol and bringing it to completion.

And along came Rossini.

Rossini is a Titan, a powerful and daring Titan. Rossini is the Napoleon of a musical era. Careful examination reveals that Rossini has accomplished in music what romanticism accomplished in literature. He has decreed the independence of music. He has disavowed the principle of authority which the inept masses want to impose on the creative artist, and he has proclaimed the omnipotence of genius. When he came along the old rules weighed heavily on the head of the *artist,* just as theories of imitation and the stale Aristotelian unities of classicism stayed the hand of anyone who tried to write dramas or poems. And he became the champion of all those who groaned but did not dare to free themselves from that tyranny. He called for revolt, and he dared. That is supreme praise; perhaps if he had not dared—if when the graybeards croaked, *don't do it,* he had not had the courage to reply, *I will do it*—there would now be no hope for the rebirth of music out of the torpor that threatened to overtake it and make it sterile. Gathering inspiration from the fine effort of Mayer,[2] and from the genius that was stirring in his soul, Rossini broke the spell and ended the long slumber: music was saved. Because of him, we can talk today of a European musical initiative. Because of him we can, without presuming, have faith that this initiative will come from Italy and nowhere else.

It is no use, however, to exaggerate or misunderstand Rossini's role in the progress of the art; the mission he undertook does not escape the confines of the era which we declare extinct, or nearly so. It is a mission for a genius who *summarizes* but does not *initiate.* He did not change or destroy the long-standing characteristics of the Italian school: he reconsecrated them. He did not introduce a new element that abolished or dramatically changed the old one, he raised its dominant element to the highest possible level of development; he pushed it to its ultimate consequence; he reduced it to a formula and once more placed it on the throne from which the pedants had driven it, without considering that whoever destroys something has the responsibility to replace it with something better. And all those who still look on Rossini as the creator of a school or era of music, as the leader of a radical revolution in taste and in the destiny of art, are mistaken. They forget the condition music was in just before Rossini; they make the same mistake that was made about literary romanticism by those who wanted to find in it a faith, an organic theory, a new literary synthesis: what is worse, they perpetuate the past while proclaiming the future.

Rossini did not create, he restored. He rebelled, not against the generative element, not against the fundamental concept of Italian music, but rather on behalf of that concept, fallen into oblivion as it was through its loss of vitality; he rebelled against the dictates of the scholars and the servility of their disciples, and against the vacuum both groups conspired to create. He innovated, but more in *form* than in *substance,* more in his method of development and use of material than in underlying principle. He found new manifestations of the thought of the era; he translated it in a thousand different ways; he crowned it with such detailed work, with such fertile additions, with such decorative art, that while a few may be his peers none could outdo him. He exemplified and developed this thought and goaded it this way and that until it was exhausted. He did not surpass it.[3] More powerful in fantasy than in profound thought or

2. Apparently Johann Simon Mayr (1763–1845), whose operas were influential on Rossini's.

3. Yet he did surpass it occasionally: he exceeded it perhaps in *Moses* [i.e., *Mosè in Egitto*]; he went beyond, certainly, in the third act of *Otello,* that divine work, which belongs entirely to the new era, because of its height of dramatic expression, the aura of destiny that breathes through it, its amazing unity of inspiration. But I am speaking of a genre, of a predominant concept, not of one scene or one act, but of the entire work of Rossini. Certainly he anticipated the social music,

feeling, a genius of freedom rather than of synthesis, he may have glimpsed but did not embrace the future. Perhaps also he lacked that single-mindedness and high purpose that keeps its gaze on the generations to come rather than on its contemporaries; he sought fame, not glory; he sacrificed the god to the idol; he worshipped the effect, not the intent, not the mission. He was left with the ability to form a sect, but not to found a faith.

Where is the new element in Rossini, where the foundation of a new school? Where is there a single concept that dominates his artistic life, that unites his series of compositions into an epic? We must look for it in every scene, or rather in every piece, in every *motive* in his music; not in the system, not in his works, not in his entire output. The edifice he has erected, like that of Nimrod,[4] rends the sky; but there is within it, as in Nimrod's, a confusion of languages. *Individuality* is seated at the summit: free, unrestrained, fantastic, represented by a brilliant *melody,* palpable, unambiguous, like the sensation that suggested it.

Everything in Rossini is conspicuous, defined, prominent; the indefinite, the delicately shaded, the ethereal, which would seem to belong more particularly to the nature of music, have given way, almost taken flight, before the invasion of an impulsive style—sharp, assertive, provocative, tangible. You might say that Rossini's melodies were carved in bas-relief. You might say they had all been poured out from the artist's imagination under a Neapolitan summer sky, at noon, when the sun floods everything, when it beats down vertically and eliminates the body's shadow. It is a music without shade, without mysteries, without dusk. It gives expression to decisive passions decisively felt—anger, grief, love, vengeance, jubilation, despair—and all are set forth so that the soul of the listener is entirely passive: subjugated, spellbound, immobilized. There are few if any gradations of feeling, there is no breath of the invisible world around us. The instrumentation often hints at an echo of this world and appears to look at infinity; but almost always it retreats, *it is individualized,* and it too becomes melody. Rossini and the Italian school whose various explorations and systems he brought together and fused into one, together represent man without God, individual powers not harmonized by a supreme law, not ordered by a single purpose, not consecrated to an eternal faith.

German music proceeds along a different road. There you have God without man, his image on earth, an active and progressive creature called on to expound the thought whose symbol is the earthly universe. There you find temple, religion, altar, and incense; but the faith lacks its worshiper and its

---

the musical drama of the future. Where is there a genius who, coming at the end of an era, is not on occasion illuminated by the rays of the era about to come, who does not anticipate its thought for a few moments? But between the presentiment and the feeling, between instinctively intuiting an era and initiating it, is as great a difference as that which separates reality from uncertain hope. [Au.]

4. Nimrod (Genesis 10:8–12), "the first potentate on earth," whose empire included the city of Babel.

priest. *Harmonic* in the highest degree, it represents *social* thought, the general concept, the *idea,* but without the *individuality* that translates thought into action, that develops the idea in its various applications, that sets forth and symbolizes the idea. The ego is lost. The soul lives, but a life not of this world. As in a life of dreams, when the senses are silent and the spirit looks into another world, where everything is lighter, and the pace more rapid, and all the images float in the infinite, German music lulls our instincts and material powers and lifts up the soul, through vast lands, unknown but vaguely remembered—faint, revealed to you as if you had glimpsed them in your first infant visions, between maternal caresses, so that the tumult and the joys and sorrows of the earth vanish.

This music is supremely elegiac: a music of remembered desires, of melancholy hopes and of a sadness that cannot be comforted by human lips; a music of angels who have wandered from their heavenly dwelling. Its home is infinity, for which it longs. Like Northern poetry, where it is not led astray by the influence of a foreign school and preserves its primitive nature, German music passes lightly over earthly fields, skims over the material world, but keeps its eyes turned to heaven. You might say it only places a foot on the ground in order to leap. You might say it is like a young girl born for smiles who has not found an answering smile, one full of the spirit of love who has not found anything mortal that merits being loved, and who dreams of another heaven, another universe, in which there would be the form of a being who would answer her love, who would respond to her virgin smile, and whom she would adore without coming to know.

And this form, this type of immortal beauty, appears and reappears every so often in German music, but imaginary, vague, lightly outlined. Its melody is brief, hesitant, fleetingly drawn; and while Italian melody defines, integrates, and forces an emotion upon you, in this music it appears veiled, mysterious, barely enough to leave you with a memory and the need to recreate it, to recompose the image for yourself. The one drags you forcefully to the ultimate limits of passion, the other points the way and then leaves you. German music is a music of preparation, a deeply religious music, although of a religion that has no creed and so no active faith to be translated into deeds; no martyrdom, no victory. It stretches around you a chain of tone-gradations, masterfully linked; it embraces you with a musical wave of chords that soothe you, comfort you, awaken the heart. It rouses the imagination, rouses whatever faculties you possess: to what end?—the music ends and you sink back into the real world and the prosaic life that teems around you, bringing with you the awareness of a different world, seen from a distance but indeterminate—the sense of having touched the primal mysteries of a great initiation, never begun so no longer strong in will, no longer firm against the assaults of fortune. Italian music lacks the sanctifying concept of all efforts: the moral thought that stimulates the forces of the mind, the blessing of a mission. German music lacks the energy to carry it out, the actual instrument of the conquest; it lacks, not the sentiment, but the concrete form of the mission. Italian music is rendered barren by materialism; German music is uselessly consumed in mysticism.

Thus the two schools proceed as distinct and jealous rivals, and they remain, the one school preferred in the North, the other in the South. And the music we propose, European music, will not exist until the two are fused into one and take on a social purpose—until united in the awareness of unity, the two elements that today form two worlds join together to inspire one. The sanctity of the faith that distinguishes the German school will bless the power of action that vibrates in the Italian school, and musical expression will combine the two basic terms: individuality and the thought of the universe—God and man.

Is this a utopia?

Even Rossini's music was a utopia in the days of Guglielmi and Piccinni.[5] Even the hugely synthesizing poetry of Alighieri[6] was utopian, at a time when the art was confined to the ballads of the Provençal troubadours and the clumsy works of Guittone.[7] Who in those days would have predicted that a poet would arise who would join heaven and earth in his poems, whose language, form, and power would all burst forth out of nothing, thanks to his genius; who would concentrate in his verses the whole soul of the Middle Ages as well as the idea of the era to come; who would make of one poem a national and religious monument, visible to the most distant generations, a poet who, five centuries before its first indications and tentative developments, would impart to his works and incarnate in his life the principle of the Italian mission in Europe? Would the prediction have found believers or mockers in Italy? Yet Dante did appear and did lay the foundations; and from his works today are drawn the norms that regulate our reborn literature, and later, when Dante's works have readers more worthy of them, there will emerge the origin of entirely other concepts and omens of Italian destiny.

And when I pause at sunset, my soul weary of the present and disconsolate about the future, when I stand before one of those churches to which traditional ignorance has given the name Gothic, and contemplate the soul of Christianity pouring out of the building, and prayer arching up, winding around the spires of the columns, hurling itself over the pinnacles into the sky, and the blood of martyrs mixed with the colors of hope displayed to God like a pledge of faith through the long glazed windows, and the believer's spirit wandering in its longing for the infinite, under the deep and mysterious vaults of the cathedral, and the spirit of Christ descending from the immense dome to the sanctuary, spreading around the vast walls and embracing the entire church with his love and benediction, peopling it with his apostles, his saints and confessors to tell the faithful about the Christian tradition, the persecutions

5. Pier Alessandro Guglielmi (1728–1804) and Niccolò Piccinni (1728–1800), Italian opera composers.
6. That is, Dante Alighieri (1265–1321): medieval poet, author of *The Divine Comedy*.
7. Probably Guittone d'Arezzo (c. 1230–1294), whose obscure style of writing was characteristic of Italian poetry before the *dolce stil nuovo* and Dante.

endured, the examples of virtue, resignation, and sacrifice, and from time to time thundering out his laws upon the organ—well, then—and no matter how vast a mission the era will impose—I do not despair of art, neither of its power nor of the miracles that genius will draw forth from it.

What? A synthesis, an era, a religion is sculptured in stone: architecture has been able to summarize the dominant thought of eighteen centuries in a cathedral—can music not do as much? If the idea of a social art or literature is not rejected, why hesitate at the idea of a social music? The synthesis of an era is expressed in all its art forms, and its spirit dominates them all, especially synthetic and religious music which surpasses all the others by its very nature. Music begins where poetry leaves off, and proceeds directly according to general formulae while its sister arts must move from specific cases and subjects to reach that point. Will music, which is the algebra of the immanent soul of humanity, alone remain inaccessible to the European synthesis, a stranger in its own time, a lone flower plucked out of the crown that the universe weaves for its creator? And in the land of Porpora and Pergolesi, in the land that gave Martini to *harmony* and Rossini to *melody,* can we doubt that a genius will arise who will unite two schools and purify them by interpreting in notes the thought of which the nineteenth century is the initiator?

That genius will appear. When the time is ripe and there are believers to venerate creative works, he will most certainly appear. It is not for me to say how or by what path he will reach his goal. The ways of genius are hidden, like those of God who inspires him. Criticism can and should anticipate his birth— in general terms—and it should declare what the urgent needs of the time are, and how great. It should prepare the people and clear the way for him—nothing more; nor do I intend to overstep these limits.

Today I urge emancipation from Rossini and the musical era he represents. I urge us to believe that he did not begin a school but ended one—that a school has ended when, driven to its ultimate consequences, it has exhausted all of the vitality that has carried it to that point, and that whoever persists in the footsteps of Rossini is condemned to be no more than a satellite—more or less splendid, but forever a satellite. I urge us to believe that to be renewed music must become *spiritualized,* that to resurrect its strength it must be reconsecrated to a mission. For music not to be ruined by the useless or the strange it needs to connect, to unite this mission with the general mission of the arts of the era, and seek its character in the era itself. In other words, music must become social and identify with the progressive movement of the universe. And I urge you to believe that today it is not a question of perpetuating or restoring an *Italian school* but of deriving *from Italy* the foundations of a *European school of music.*

●　　●　　●　　●　　●

But . . . musical reform will be accomplished. When a school or a trend or an era is exhausted, when a course has been run and nothing remains but to retrace it, reform is imminent, inevitable, and certain, because human ability cannot retreat. Young artists should prepare themselves, like devotees of religious mysteries, for the initiation of a new school of music. We are at a *vigil of arms,* as soldiers used to assemble in silence and solitude, meditating on what they must undertake, on the breadth of the mission to which they must dedicate themselves the next day, and in the generous and fervent hope of a new dawn.

Young artists must exalt themselves with the study of national songs, of patriotic stories and the mysteries of poetry and of nature, to a broader horizon than that offered by the rule books and the ancient canons of art. Music is the fragrance of the universe, and to deal with it properly the artist must be immersed in love, in faith, in the study of the harmonies that float on earth and in the heavens, in the thought of the universe. He must become familiar with the music of the great, not just the great of one country, or one school, or one time, but with the great of all countries, all schools, and all times. Not to analyze and dissect them with the cold and ancient doctrines of the music professors, but to gather into himself the creative and unifying spirit that moves through these works; not to imitate them narrowly and slavishly, but to emulate them freely, linking each new work to theirs.

Young artists should sanctify their souls with enthusiasm, with the breath of that eternal poetry that materialism has hidden but not banished from our land, worshipping art as something holy, a link between man and heaven. They should adore art, establishing for it a high social purpose, dedicating it to moral regeneration, cherishing it in their breasts and in their life, bright, pure, uncontaminated by commerce, or frivolity, or by the many excrescences that spoil the beautiful world of creation. Inspiration will descend on them like an angel of life and harmony, and their tombs will be emblazoned with the blessings of the grateful generations who have benefited, something that is worth more than a thousand honors, more than anything, just as virtue outweighs fortune's riches, and self-regard is greater than praise, and love greater than all earthly power.

153 Richard Wagner

The Artwork of the Future belongs to the most critical period in Richard Wagner's life, the first years of his exile and of his residence in Zurich, the years between the end of his work on *Lohengrin* (1847) and the beginning of his work on the *Ring* (1853). During this lull in his artistic productivity, Wagner endeavored to come to terms with the problem of the opera and with himself;

the results of this soul-searching are his three capital essays—*Art and Revolution* (1849), *The Artwork of the Future* (1850), and *Opera and Drama* (1852)—and in a larger sense, the great music dramas of his maturity and old age. Three times, later on, he attempted to summarize the contents of these essays—first in *A Communication to My Friends* (1852), then in *"Music of the Future"* (1860), finally in *On the Destiny of Opera* (1869); in 1879, near the end of his life, he returned to the problem once more in a series of three further essays—*On the Writing of Poetry and Music, On the Writing of Operatic Poetry and Music in Particular,* and *On the Application of Music to the Drama.*

It is well known that the three major essays of Wagner's earlier years in Zurich were written under the immediate influence of the philosopher Ludwig Feuerbach (1804–1872), author of *The Essence of Christianity* (1841), whose repeated attacks upon orthodox theology had attracted the interest of Karl Marx and Friedrich Engels and had made him, somewhat to his astonishment, the idol of the "Young German" intellectuals sympathetic to the uprisings of 1849. In his autobiography, Wagner tells us himself that his acquaintance with Feuerbach's reputation dates from his last years in Dresden; traces of Feuerbach's influence have even been detected in Wagner's *Jesus of Nazareth,* a dramatic synopsis sketched at just this time. As to *The Artwork of the Future,* this essay owes its very title to Feuerbach's *Principles of the Philosophy of the Future* (1843), and in its original edition as a separate monograph it was introduced by a letter from Wagner to Feuerbach, beginning: "To no one but you, my dear sir, can I dedicate this work, for with it I give you back your own property."

In later life, after his conversion to Arthur Schopenhauer and to a more prudent political philosophy, Wagner did what he could to play down the revolutionary character of his earlier writings and to represent his youthful enthusiasm for Feuerbach as an unimportant passing phase. This is already evident to some extent in the summary incorporated in his *"Music of the Future."* It became still more evident with the publication of the third and fourth volumes of his *Collected Writings* in 1872; here the dedication to Feuerbach is silently suppressed, while the foreword to the third volume contains this apologia: "From my reading of several of the works of Ludwig Feuerbach, which held a lively interest for me at the time, I had taken over various designations for concepts which I then applied to artistic ideas to which they could not always clearly correspond. Herein I surrendered myself without critical reflection to a brilliant author who appealed to my mood of the moment, particularly in that he bade farewell to philosophy (in which he believed himself to have discovered nothing but disguised theology) and addressed himself instead to a view of human nature in which I was persuaded that I could recognize again the artistic man I had had in mind. Thus there arose a certain reckless confusion, which revealed itself in a hastiness and lack of clarity in the use of philosophical schemes." Wagner then goes on to criticize his earlier use of Feuerbach's terminology, particularly of the expressions "willfulness" *(Willkür)* and "instinct" *(Unwillkür),* for which he now suggests the substitution, by the reader, of Schopenhauer's "will" *(Wille)* and "conscious will" *(Verstandeswille).* Still more exaggerated is Wagner's account of his relation to Feuerbach in his posthumously published autobiography: "Before long," he says, "it had already become impossible for me to return to his writings, and I recall that his book *On the Essence of Religion,* which appeared soon after this, so repelled me by the monotony of its title that when Herwegh opened it for me I clapped it shut before his eyes." How far from the truth this is, can be gathered from Wagner's letter of June 8, 1853, addressed to the imprisoned Röckel, his fellow revolutionary, and accompanied by a copy of the book in question: "Feuerbach's book is to a certain extent a résumé of all that he has hitherto done in the field of philosophy. It is not one of his really celebrated works, such as *The Essence of Christianity* or *Thoughts upon Death and Immortality,* but it is a shortcut to a complete knowledge of his mental development and of the latest results of his speculations. I should be glad to think of you as strengthened and encouraged by contact with this clear, vigorous mind."

In *A Communication to My Friends,* speaking of the contradictions between his new theories and his earlier scores, Wagner has this to say: "The contradictions to which I refer will not even exist for the man who has accustomed himself to look at phenomena from the point of view of their development in time. The man who, in judging a phenomenon, takes this developmental factor into consideration will meet with contradictions only when the phenomenon in question is an unnatural, unreasonable one, set apart from space and time; to disregard the developmental factor altogether, to combine its various and clearly distinguishable phases, belonging to different times, into one indistinguishable mass, this is in itself an unnatural, unreasonable way of looking at things, one that can be adopted by our monumental-historical criticism, but not by the healthy criticism of a sympathetic and sensitive heart. . . . Critics who make a pretence of judging my artistic activity as a whole have sometimes proceeded in this uncritical, inattentive, and insensitive way; taking as relevant to their judgment views on the nature of art which I had made known from a standpoint arrived at only after a gradual and deliberate development, they have applied these views to the very artworks in which the natural developmental process that led me to the standpoint in question began. . . . It does not occur to them at all, when they compare the newly acquired standpoint with the older one left behind, that these are in fact two essentially different points of view, each one of them logically developed in itself, and that it would have been much better to have explained the new standpoint in the light of the old one than it was to judge the one abandoned in the light of the one adopted."

Wagner's objection is well taken. Yet later on, as we have seen, he was himself guilty of an uncritical procedure very similar to the one complained of here. Wagner too endeavored to combine two clearly distinguishable phases of his development, the middle and the late, into one indistinguishable mass. But whereas his critics had sought, as he puts it, "to kill two flies at one blow," Wagner seeks to prove the essential identity of two points of view that are essentially opposed.

Friedrich Wilhelm Nietzsche, in his *Genealogy of Morals* (1887), sums up Wagner's dilemma with telling irony: "Think of the enthusiasm with which Wagner formerly followed in the footsteps of the philosopher Feuerbach: Feuerbach's expression 'healthy sensuality'—to Wagner, as to many Germans ('Young Germans,' they called themselves), this sounded in the thirties and forties like the word of redemption. Did he finally *learn* a different view? For it seems at least that at the end he wished to *teach* a different one."

FROM *The Artwork of the Future*
(1850)

MAN AND ART IN GENERAL

NATURE, MAN, AND ART

As man is to nature, so art is to man.

When nature had of itself developed to that state which encompassed the conditions for man's existence, then man arose of himself; once human life engenders of itself the conditions for the appearance of the artwork, the artwork comes into being of itself.

Nature begets and shapes aimlessly and instinctively, according to need, hence of necessity; this same necessity is the begetting and shaping force in human life; only what is aimless and instinctive arises from genuine need, and only in need lies the cause of life.

Natural necessity man recognizes only in the continuity of natural phenomena; until he grasps this continuity, he thinks nature willful.

From that moment in which man became sensible of his divergence from nature and thereby took the first step of all in his development as man, freeing himself from the unconsciousness of natural animal life to pass over into conscious life—when he thus placed himself in opposition to nature and when, as an immediate result of this, his sense of his dependence on nature led to the development in him of thought—from that moment, as the first assertion of consciousness, error began. But error is the father of knowledge, and the history of the begetting of knowledge from error is the history of the human race from the myth of primeval time to the present day.

Man erred from the time when he placed the cause of natural phenomena outside the state of nature itself, assumed for material phenomena an ideal origin, namely a willful origin of his own conceiving, and took the infinite continuity of nature's unconscious and purposeless activity for the purposeful behavior of will's noncontinuous, finite manifestations. Knowledge consists in the correction of this error, this correction in the perception of necessity in those phenomena for which we had assumed a willful origin.

Through this knowledge nature becomes conscious of self—to be precise, in man, who arrived at his knowledge of nature only through his distinction between self and nature, which he thus made an object. But this distinction disappears again at the moment when man recognizes nature's state as identical with his own; recognizes the same necessity in all that genuinely exists and

TEXT: *Das Kunstwerk der Zukunft. Sämtliche Schriften und Dichtungen,* 6th ed., Leipzig, 1912–14. Wagner divides the essay into five chapters; the present abridged translation includes chapter 1, sections 1 and 6; chapter 2, section 4 abbreviated; chapter 4, abbreviated. Translation by Oliver Strunk.

lives, hence in human existence no less than in natural existence; and recognizes not only the connection of the natural phenomena with one another, but also his own connection with them.

If, through its connection with man, nature attains now to consciousness, and if the activity of this consciousness is to be human life itself—as though a representation, a picture, of nature—then human life itself attains to understanding through science, which makes of human life in turn an object of experience. But the activity of the consciousness won through science, the representation of the life made known through this activity, the copy of its necessity and truth is *art*.[1]

Man will not be that which he can and should be until his life is a faithful mirror of nature, a conscious pursuit of the only real necessity, *inner natural necessity*, not a subordination to an *outer* imagined *force*, imitating imagination, and hence not necessary but *willful*. Then man will really be man; thus far he has always merely existed by virtue of some predicate derived from religion, nationality, or state. In the same way, art too will not be that which it can and should be until it is or can be a faithful, manifestly conscious copy of genuine man and of the genuine, naturally necessary life of man, in other words, until it need no longer borrow from the errors, perversities, and unnatural distortions of our modern life the conditions of its being.

Genuine man, therefore, will not come into being until his life is shaped and ordered by true human nature and not by the willful law of state; genuine art will not live until its shapings need be subject only to the law of nature and not to the despotic caprice of fashion. For just as man becomes free only when he becomes joyously conscious of his connection with nature, so art becomes free only when it has no longer to be ashamed of its connection with life. Only in joyous consciousness of his connection with nature does man overcome his dependence on it; art overcomes its dependence on life only in its connection with the life of genuine, free men.

*   •   •   •   •   •*

A STANDARD FOR THE ARTWORK OF THE FUTURE

It is not the individual mind, striving through art for fulfillment in nature, that has the power to create the art work of the future; only the collective mind, satisfied in life, has this power. But the individual can form an idea of it, and it is precisely the character of his striving—his striving for *nature*—which prevents this idea from being a mere fancy. He who longs to return to nature and who is hence unsatisfied in the modern present, finds not only in the totality of nature, but above all in *man's nature*, as it presents itself to him historically, those images which, when he beholds them, enable him to reconcile himself to life in general. In this nature he recognizes an image of all future things, already formed on a small scale; to imagine this scale expanded to its

---

1. Art in general, that is, or the art of the future in particular. [Au.]

furthest compass lies within the conceptual limits of the impulse of his need for nature.

History plainly presents two principal currents in the development of mankind—the *racial-national* and the *unnational-universal*. If we now look forward to the completion of this second developmental process in the future, we have plainly before our eyes the completed course of the first one in the past. To what heights man has been able to develop, subjected to this first, almost directly formative influence—insofar as racial origin, linguistic affiliation, similarity of climate, and the natural character of a common native land permitted him to yield unconsciously to nature's influence—we have every reason to take the keenest pleasure in acknowledging. In the natural morality of all peoples, insofar as they include the normal human being—even those cried down as rawest—we learn for the first time to recognize the truth of human nature in its full nobility, its genuine beauty. Not *one* genuine virtue has been adopted by any religion whatever as a divine command which had not been included of itself in this natural morality; not *one* genuinely human concept of right has been developed by the later civilized state—and then, unfortunately, to the point of complete distortion!—which had not already been given positive expression in this natural morality; not *one* discovery genuinely useful to the community has been appropriated by later culture—with arrogant ingratitude!—which had not been derived from the operation of the native intelligence of the guardians of this natural morality.

That *art* is not an *artificial* product—that the need of art is not one willfully induced, but rather one native to the natural, genuine, unspoiled human being—who demonstrates this more strikingly than precisely these peoples? Indeed, from what circumstance could our mind deduce the demonstration of art's necessity, if not from the perception of this artistic impulse and its splendid fruits among these naturally developed peoples, among the people in general? Before what phenomenon do we stand with a more humiliating sense of the impotence of our frivolous culture than before the art of the *Hellenes?* To this, to this art of all-loving Mother Nature's favored children, those most beautiful human beings whose proud mother holds them up to us, even in these nebulous and hoary days of our present fashionable culture, as an undeniable and triumphant proof of what she can do—to the splendid art of the Greeks we look, to learn from intimate understanding of it how the artwork of the future must be constituted! Mother Nature has done all she could—she has borne the Hellenes, nourished them at her breasts, formed them through her maternal wisdom; now she sets them before us with maternal pride and out of maternal love calls to us all: "This I have done for you; now, out of love for yourselves, do what you can!"

Thus it is our task to make of *Hellenic* art the altogether *human* art; to remove from it the conditions under which it was precisely a *Hellenic*, and not an altogether *human* art; to widen the *garb of religion*, in which alone it was a communal Hellenic art, and after removing which, as an egoistic individual art species, it could no longer fill the need of the community, but only that of luxury—however beautiful!—to widen this garb of the specifically *Hellenic religion* to the bond of the religion of the future—that of *universality*—in order to form for ourselves even now a just conception of the artwork of the future. Yet, unfortunate as we are, it is precisely the power to close this bond, this *religion of the future,* that we lack, for after all, no matter how many of us may feel this urge to the artwork of the future, we are *singular* and *individual.* An artwork is religion brought to life; religions, however, are created, not by the artist, but by the *folk.*

Let us, then, be content that for the present—without egoistic vanity, without wishing to seek satisfaction in any selfish illusion whatsoever, but with sincere and affectionate resignation to the hope for the artwork of the future—we test first of all the nature of the art varieties which today, in their dismembered condition, make up the present general state of art; that we brace ourselves for this test by a glance at the art of the Hellenes; and that we then boldly and confidently draw our conclusions as to the *great universal artwork of the future!*

· · · · ·

THE ART OF TONE

The sea divides and connects the continents; thus the art of tone divides and connects the two extreme antitheses of human art, the arts of dancing and of poetry.

It is man's *heart;* the blood, circulating from this center, gives to the flesh, turned outward, its warm, lively color—at the same time it nourishes the brain nerves, tending inward, with waves of resilient energy. Without the activity of the heart, the activity of the brain would remain a mere mechanical performance, the activity of the body's external organs equally mechanical and unfeeling. Through the heart, the intellect is made sensible of its relation to the body as a whole—the mere man of the senses attains to intellectual activity.

But the organ of the heart is *tone,* and its artistically conscious speech is the *art of tone.* This is the full, flowing heart-love that ennobles sensual pleasure and humanizes spiritual thought. Through the art of tone, the arts of poetry and dancing understand each other; in the one there blend in affectionate fusion the laws governing the manifestations natural to the others—in the one the will of the others becomes instinctive will, the measure of poetry and the beat of dancing become the inevitable rhythm of the heartthrob.

If music receives from its sister arts the conditions of its manifestation, it gives these back to them, made infinitely beautiful, as the conditions of their manifestation; if dancing supplies music with its law of motion, music returns it in the form of rhythm, spiritually and sensually embodied as a measure for ennobled and intelligible movement; if poetry supplies music with its meaningful series of clear-cut words, intelligibly united through meaning and measure as material bodies, rich in idea, for the consolidation of its infinitely fluid tonal element, music returns this ordered series of quasi-intellectual, unfulfilled speech-sounds—indirectly representative, concentrated as image but not yet as immediate, inevitably true expression—in the form of *melody,* directly addressed to feeling, unerringly vindicated and fulfilled.

In musically animated *rhythm* and *melody,* dancing and poetry regain their own being, sensually objectified and made infinitely beautiful and capable; they recognize and love each other. But rhythm and melody are the *arms* with which Music encircles her sisters in affectionate entwinement; they are the *shores* by means of which she, the *sea,* unites two continents. Should the sea recede from the shores, should the abysmal waste spread out between it and them, no jaunty sailing ship will any longer range from the one continent to the other; they will forever remain divided—unless mechanical inventions, perhaps railroads, succeed in making the waste passable; then, doubtless, one will also pass clean across the sea in steamships; the breath of the all-animating breeze will give place to the puff of the machine; what difference need it make that the wind naturally blows eastward?—the machine clatters westward, precisely where we wish to go; thus the ballet maker sends across the steam-conquered sea of music to the poetry continent for the program of his new pantomime, while the stage piece fabricator fetches from the dancing continent as much leg seasoning as he happens to need to liven up a stale situation. Let us see what has happened to Sister Music since the death of all-loving Father *Drama!*

Not yet may we give up our figure of the *sea* as music's being. If *rhythm* and *melody* are the shores at which the tonal art meets with and makes fruitful the two continents of the arts primevally related to it, then tone itself is the primeval fluid element, and the immeasurable expanse of this fluid is the sea of *harmony.* Our eye is aware only of its surface; its depth only our heart's depth comprehends. Up from its bottom, dark as night, it spreads out to its mirroring surface, bright as the sun; from the one shore radiate on it the rings of rhythm, drawn wider and wider—from the shadowy valleys of the other shore rises the longing breeze which agitates the placid surface in waves of melody, gracefully rising and falling.

Into this sea man dives to yield himself again, radiant and refreshed, to the light of day; he feels his heart expand with wonder when he looks down into these depths, capable of unimaginable possibilities, whose bottom his eye is never to fathom, whose fathomlessness fills him accordingly with astonishment and forebodings of the infinite. This is the depth and infinity of nature itself, which veils from man's searching eye the impenetrable mystery of its budding, begetting, and longing, precisely because the eye can comprehend only what has become visible—the budded, the begotten, the longed for. This nature is in turn none other than the *nature of the human heart itself,* which encompasses the feelings of love and longing in their most infinite being, which is itself love and longing, and which—since in its insatiable longing it desires itself alone—grasps and comprehends itself alone.

*   *   *   *   *

But in nature everything immeasurable seeks its measure, everything limitless draws limits for itself, the elements concentrate themselves at last as
definite phenomena; thus also the boundless sea of Christian longing found the
new coastland against which it might break its impatience. There on the far
horizon, where we had fondly imagined the entrance into the limitless heaven-
space, always sought but never found, there at last the boldest of all navigators
discovered land—inhabited by peoples—actual, blissful land. Through his discovery the wide ocean was not only measured, but also made for mankind an
inland sea about which the coasts spread themselves out only in inconceivably
wider circles. But if Columbus taught us to sail the ocean and thus to connect
all the earth's continents; if through his discovery the shortsighted national man
has, from the point of view of world history, become the all-seeing universal
man—has become man altogether; so through the hero who sailed the wide
shoreless sea of absolute music to its limits were won the new undreamed-of
coasts which now no longer divide this sea from the old primevally human
continents, but *connect* them for the newborn fortunate artistic humanity of
the future. This hero is none other than—*Beethoven.*[2]

When Music freed herself from the round of her sisters—just as her frivolous sister, Dancing, had taken from her the rhythmic measure—she took with
her from her brooding sister, Poetry, as an indispensable, immediate life condition, the *word;* not by any means, however, the human creative, ideally poetic
word, but only the materially indispensable word, the concentrated tone. If she
had relinquished the rhythmic beat to her parting sister, Dancing, to use as she
pleased, she now built herself up solely through the word, the word of Christian faith, that fluid, spineless, evanescent thing which soon, gladly and unre-
sistingly, placed itself altogether in her power. The more the word took refuge
in the mere stammering of humility, the mere lisping of implicit, childlike love,
the more inevitable was Music's recognition of her need to shape herself from
the inexhaustible depths of her own fluid being. The struggle for such a shaping
is the building up of *harmony.*

Harmony grows from the bottom up as a true column of related tonal materials, fitted together and arranged in strata laid one above another. The ceaseless changing of such columns, constantly rising up anew, each one adjoining
another, constitutes the sole possibility of absolute harmonic movement on a
horizontal plane. The perception of the need to care for the beauty of this
movement on a horizontal plane is foreign to the nature of absolute harmony;
harmony knows only the beauty of the changing play of the colors of its columns, not the charm of their orderly arrangement as perceived in time—for
this is the work of rhythm. The inexhaustible many-sidedness of this changing

---

2. See *Oper und Drama,* chap. 1, sec. 5 (or, as translated by William Ashton Ellis [*Richard
Wagner's Prose Works* (London, 1893)], Part I, pp. 70–71) where Wagner returns to this comparison of Beethoven to Columbus and develops it further.

play of colors is, on the other hand, the eternally productive source from whence harmony, in boundless self-satisfaction, derives the power to present itself unceasingly as new; the breath of life, moving and animating this restless change—which, in its turn is willfully self-conditioning—is the nature of tone itself, the breath of the impenetrable, all-powerful longing of the heart. The realm of harmony, then, knows no beginning or end; is like the objectless and self-consuming fervor of the temperament which, ignorant of its source, remains itself alone; is desiring, longing, raging, languishing—*perishing,* that is, dying without having satisfied itself in an object—dying, in other words, without dying; and hence, again and again, returns to self.

As long as the word was in power, it ruled beginning and end; when it sank to the fathomless bottom of harmony, when it remained only a "groaning and sighing of the soul"—as at the fervent height of Catholic church music—then, at the topmost stratum of those harmonic columns, the stratum of unrhythmic melody, the word was willfully tossed as though from wave to wave, and harmony, with its infinite possibilities, had now to lay down for itself self-derived laws for its finite manifestation. The nature of harmony corresponds to no other capacity of man as artist; it sees itself reflected, neither in the physically determined movements of the body, nor in the logical progression of thought; it can conceive its just measure, neither, as thought does, in the recognized necessity of the world of material phenomena, nor, as bodily movement does, in the presentation, as perceived in time, of its instinctive, richly conditioned character; it is like a natural force, apprehended, but not comprehended, by man. From out its own fathomless depths, from an outer—not inner—necessity to limit itself for positive finite manifestation, harmony must shape for itself the laws it will obey. These laws of harmonic succession, based on relationship, just as the harmonic columns, or harmonies, were themselves formed from the relationship of tonal materials, combine now as a just measure, which sets a beneficial limit to the monstrous range of willful possibilities. They permit the widest possible selection from out the sphere of harmonic families, expand to the point of free choice the possibility of connections through elective relationship with members of distant families, demand above all, however, a strict conformity to the house rules of the family momentarily chosen and an implicit acceptance of them for the sake of a salutary end. To postulate or to define this end—in other words, the just measure of the expansion of the musical composition in time—lies beyond the power of the innumerable rules of harmonic decorum; these, as that part of music which can be scientifically taught or learned, while they can separate the fluid tonal mass of harmony, dividing it into bounded smaller masses, cannot determine the just measure of these bounded masses in time.

If music, grown to harmony, could not possibly go on to derive from itself its law of expansion in time, once the limiting power of speech had been swallowed up, it was obliged to turn to those remnants of the rhythmic beat that dancing had left behind for it; rhythmic figures had to enliven the harmony;

their alternation, their return, their division and union had to affect the fluid expanse of harmony as the word had originally affected tone, concentrating it and bringing it to a definitely timed conclusion. This rhythmic enlivening, however, was not based on any inner necessity, crying out for purely human presentation; its motive power was not the man of feeling, thought, and will as he reveals himself in speech and bodily movement, but an *outer* necessity which harmony, demanding an egoistic conclusion, had made its own. This rhythmic alternation and shaping, not motivated by an inner necessity, could therefore be enlivened only according to willful laws and discoveries. These laws and discoveries are those of *counterpoint*.

Counterpoint, in its various progeny, normal and abnormal, is the artificial play of art with art, the mathematics of feeling, the mechanical rhythm of egoistic harmony. With its discovery abstract music was so pleased that it gave itself out as the one and only absolute and self-sufficient art—as the art owing its existence, not to any human need whatever, but simply to *itself*, to its divine and absolute nature. Quite naturally, the willful man considers himself the one man absolutely justified. Music, to be sure, owed to its arbitrary will alone only its seeming independence, for these tone-mechanical, contrapuntal pieces of art handiwork were altogether incapable of filling a *spiritual need*. In its pride, then, music had become its own direct antithesis; from a concern of the *heart* it had become a concern of the *mind*, from an expression of the boundless spiritual longing of the Christian it had become a balance sheet of the modern money market.

The living breath of the human voice, eternally beautiful and instinctively noble as it burst forth from the breast of the living folk, always young and fresh, blew this contrapuntal house of cards to the four winds. The *folk tune*, still true to self in undistorted grace—the *song* with positive limits, intimately entwined and one with poetry—lifted itself up on its elastic pinions into the regions of the scientifically musical world, with its need for beauty, and announced a joyous redemption. This world wished once more to set forth *men*, to cause men—not reeds—to sing; to this end it took possession of the folk tune and constructed from it the *operatic aria*. Just as the art of dancing had taken possession of the folk dance, to refresh itself, as it required, at this source and to employ it, as fashion dictated, in artistic combination, so also the elegant art of opera dealt with the folk tune; it now grasped, not the *whole* man, to indulge him artistically to the full according to his natural need, but only the *singing* man—and in the tune he sang, not the folk poem with its innate creative power, but only the melodious tune, abstracted from the poem, to which it now adapted as it pleased fashionably conventional, intentionally meaningless literary phrases; it was not the throbbing heart of the nightingale, but only its throbbing throat, that it understood and sought to imitate. Just as the art dancer trained his legs in the most varied and yet most uniform bends, twists, and whirls to vary the folk dance, which he could not of himself develop further, so the art singer trained his throat in endless ornaments and scrollwork of all sorts to paraphrase and change the tune taken from the lips of the folk, which he could from its nature never create anew; thus the place which contrapuntal cleverness had vacated was taken only by a mechanical dexterity of another kind. Here we need not characterize at greater length the repulsive, indescribably disgusting perversion and distortion of the folk tune as manifested in the modern operatic aria—for it is in point of fact only a mutilated folk tune, not by any means an original invention—as, in derision of all nature, of all human feeling, it frees itself from any linguistically poetic basis and, as a lifeless, soulless toy of fashion, tickles the ear of the idiotic world of the opera house; we need only admit with sorrowful sincerity that our modern public actually takes it for the whole of music.

But remote from this public and the makers and sellers of fashionable wares who serve it, the innermost being of music was to soar up from its bottomless depths, with all the undiminished abundance of its untried capacity, to a redemption in the radiance of the universal, *single* art of the future, and was to take this flight from that bottom which is the bottom of all purely human art—that of *plastic bodily movement*, represented in musical *rhythm*.

If, in the lisping of the stereotyped Christian word, eternally and eternally repeated to the point of utter thoughtlessness, the *human voice* had at length completely taken refuge in a merely sensual and fluid tone device by means of which alone the art of music, wholly withdrawn from poetry, continued to present itself, the tone devices, mechanically transmitted at its side as voluptuous accompaniments of the art of dancing, had developed an increasingly heightened capacity for expression. To these devices, the bearers of the dance tune, *rhythmic melody* had been assigned as an exclusive possession, and since, in their combined effect, these readily absorbed the element of Christian harmony, all responsibility for music's further development *from within itself* devolved on them. The *harmonized dance* is the basis of the richest artwork of the modern *symphony*. This dance made in its turn an appetizing morsel for the counterpoint machine, which freed it from its obedient devotion to its mistress, the corporeal art of dancing, and caused it now to leap and turn at *its* command. Yet the warm life breath of the natural folk tune had only to inspire the leather harness of this dance, trained up in counterpoint, and it became at once the living flesh of the humanly beautiful artwork. This artwork, in its highest perfection, is the *symphony of Haydn, Mozart, and Beethoven*.

In the symphony of *Haydn*, the rhythmic dance melody moves with all the fresh serenity of youth; its interweavings, dissolvings, and recombinings, though carried out with the utmost contrapuntal skill, reveal themselves scarcely any longer as products of a thus skillful process, but rather as proper to the character of a dance governed by highly imaginative rules, so warmly are they permeated by the breath of genuinely and joyously human life. The middle movement of the symphony, in a more moderate tempo, we see assigned by Haydn to the swelling breadth of the simply melodious folk tune; following the rules of melos peculiar to singing, he expands this, intensifying it in higher flights and enlivening it in repetitions many-sided in their expression. The melody thus conditioned was elemental to the symphony of *Mozart,* with his wealth of song and delight in singing. He inspired his instruments with the ardent breath of the *human voice,* to which his genius was overwhelmingly inclined. The rich, indomitable tide of harmony he brought to bear on melody's heart, as though restlessly anxious to give synthetically to the purely instrumental melody that depth of feeling and fervor which, in the innermost heart, makes of the natural human voice an inexhaustible source of expression. As to all those things in his symphonies which lay more or less remote from the satisfying of this, his primary aim, if Mozart to a certain extent merely dispatched them with uncommonly skillful contrapuntal treatment according to the traditional usage, becoming stable even in him, he intensified the capacity of the purely instrumental for singing expression to such a point that it could encompass, not only serenity and placid easy intimacy, as had been the case with Haydn, but also the whole depth of the heart's infinite longing.

The immeasurable capacity of instrumental music for the expression of impulses and desires of elemental intensity was opened up by *Beethoven.* He it was who released to unrestricted freedom the innermost being of Christian harmony, that fathomless sea so boundlessly vast, so restlessly mobile. Borne by instruments alone, the *harmonic melody*—for thus we must call the melody isolated from the spoken line, to distinguish it from the rhythmic dance melody—was capable of the most unlimited expression and of the widest possible treatment. In long connected sequences and in larger, smaller, indeed smallest fragments, it became, under the poetic hands of the master, the sounds, syllables, words, and phrases of a language which could express the unheard, the unsaid, the unuttered.

•   •   •   •   •

What inimitable art Beethoven employed in his C-minor Symphony to guide his ship out of the ocean of endless longing into the harbor of fulfillment! He succeeded in intensifying the expression of his music almost to the point of moral resolve, yet was unable to proclaim this resolve itself. Without moral support, after each exertion of will, we are alarmed at the prospect that we may quite as well be headed, not for victory, but for relapse into suffering; indeed, such a relapse must seem to us rather more necessary than the morally unmotivated triumph, which—not a necessary achievement, but a willful gift of grace—can hence not lift us up or satisfy us *morally,* after the longing of the heart, as we require.

Who was less satisfied by this victory than Beethoven himself, may we presume? Was he tempted to another of this kind? The thoughtless army of his imitators, no doubt, who, having survived the tribulation of minor, concoct continual triumphs for themselves out of the glorious jubilation of major—but not the chosen master who was in his works to write the *world history of music.*

With reverent awe he refrained from plunging himself again into that sea of boundless and insatiable longing, bending his steps rather toward those light-hearted, vigorous beings whom he saw jesting, dancing, and wooing in the green meadows at the edge of the fragrant woods, spread out under sunny skies. There, in the shadow of the trees, to the rustling of the foliage and the familiar rippling of the brook, he made a salutary covenant with nature; there he felt himself a man, his longing driven back into his breast before the power of the sweet inspiring *prospect*. In gratitude to this prospect, in faith and all humility, he named the single movements of the composition thus inspired for the scenes from life whose aspect had summoned them forth; the whole he called *Recollections of Country Life*.

And yet they were in truth no more than recollections—images, not immediate and concrete reality. Toward this reality, however, he was impelled with all the force of necessary artist's longing. To give his tonal forms that concentration, that immediately perceptible, sure, and concrete solidity, which, to his joy and comfort, he had observed in natural phenomena—this was the generous spirit of that joyous urge that created for us the incomparably magnificent A-major Symphony. All violence, all longing and storming of the heart, have turned here to the rapturous exuberance of joy which carries us along in bacchanalian insistence through all the realms of nature, through all the streams and seas of life, self-confidently exultant everywhere we tread to the bold measure of this human dance of the spheres. This symphony is the very *apotheosis of the dance;* it is the highest being of the dance, the most blissful act of bodily movement, ideally embodied, as it were, in tone. Melody and harmony fill out together the bony frame of rhythm with firm human figures, slender and voluptuous, which almost before our eyes, here with supple giant limbs, there with delicate elastic flexibility, join the round to which the immortal melody sounds on and on, now charming, now bold, now serious,[3] now boisterous, now thoughtful, now exultant, until, in the last whirling of desire, a jubilant kiss brings to an end the last embrace.

And yet these blissful dancers were but tonally represented, tonally imitated beings! Like another Prometheus, forming men from *clay (Thon)*, Beethoven had sought to form men from *tone (Ton)*. Neither from clay nor tone, however, but from both substances at once must man, the likeness of life-giving Zeus, be created. If the creatures of Prometheus were present to the *eye* alone, Beethoven's were so only to the *ear. But only there where eye and ear mutually assure each other of his presence do we have the whole artistic man.*

Where indeed should Beethoven have found those beings to whom he might

3. To the rhythm of the second movement, solemnly striding along, a secondary theme lifts up its longing plaint; about that rhythm, whose steady step is heard unceasingly throughout the whole, this yearning melody entwines itself, as does about the oak the ivy, which, but for its encircling of the powerful trunk, would curl and wind chaotically along the ground, luxuriantly forlorn, but which now, as a rich ornament of the rough oak's bark, gains sure and substantial form from the solidity of the tree itself. With what want of discernment this deeply significant discovery of Beethoven's has been exploited by our modern composers of instrumental music, with their eternal "secondary theme-making." [Au.]

have offered his hand across the element of his music? Those beings with hearts so open that he might have let the all-powerful stream of his harmonious tones flood into them? With forms so vigorously beautiful that his melodious rhythms might have *borne* them, not *tread* them underfoot? Alas, no brotherly Prometheus, who might have shown such beings to him, came to his help from any side! He had himself to begin by discovering the *land of the man of the future*.

From the shores of dancing he plunged again into that endless sea from out whose depths he had once saved himself on these same shores, into the sea of insatiable heart's longing. But on this stormy voyage he set out aboard a strong-built ship, firmly joined as though by giant hands; with a sure grasp he bent the powerful tiller; he *knew* his journey's goal and was resolved to reach it. What he sought was not the preparation of imaginary triumphs for himself, not to sail back idly into the home port after boldly surmounted hardships; he sought to bound the limits of the ocean, to find the land which needs must lie beyond the watery wastes.

Thus the master forced his way through the most unheard-of possibilities of absolute tonal language—not by hurriedly stealing past them, but by proclaiming them completely, to their last sound, from his heart's fullest depths—until he reached that point at which the navigator begins to sound the sea's depths with his lead; at which he touches solid bottom at ever increasing heights as the strands of the new continent reach toward him from afar; at which he must decide whether to turn about into the fathomless ocean or whether to drop anchor in the new banks. But it was no rude hankering for the sea that had urged the master on to this long voyage; he wished and had to land in the new world, for it was to this end that the voyage had been undertaken. Resolutely he threw out his anchor, and this anchor was the *word*. This word, however, was not that willful, meaningless word which the fashionable singer chews over and over as the mere gristle of the vocal tone; it was the necessary, all-powerful, all-uniting word in which the whole stream of full heartfelt emotion is poured out; the safe harbor for the restless wanderer; the light lighting the night of endless longing; the word redeemed humanity proclaims from out the fullness of the world's heart; the word which Beethoven set as a crown upon the summit of his creations in tone. This word was—"*Joy!*" And with this word he called to all mankind: "*Be embraced, ye countless millions! And to all the world this kiss!*" And *this* word will become the language of the *artwork of the future*.

This *last symphony* of Beethoven's is the redemption of music out of its own element as a *universal art*. It is the *human* gospel of the art of the future. Beyond it there can be no *progress*, for there can follow on it immediately only the completed artwork of the future, *the universal drama*, to which Beethoven has forged for us the artistic key.

Thus from within itself music accomplished what no one of the other arts was capable of in isolation. Each of these arts, in its barren independence, helped itself only by taking and egoistic borrowing; not one was capable of being *itself* and of weaving from within itself the all-uniting bond. The art of tone, by being wholly *itself* and by moving from within its own primeval element, attained strength for the most tremendous and most generous of all self-sacrifices—that of self-control, indeed of self-denial—thus to offer to its sister arts a redeeming hand. Music has proved itself the *heart*, connecting head and limbs, and, what is not without significance, it is precisely music which, in the modern present, has spread to so unusual an extent through every branch of public life.

To form a clear conception of the *thoroughly inconsistent* spirit of this public life, we must consider, first of all, *that it was by no means a collective effort of the artists, as a body, and the public—indeed not even a collective effort of the musical artists themselves*—which brought to completion that tremendous process which we have just seen take place; *quite the other way, it was purely a superabundant artist individual* who individually absorbed the spirit of that collectivity wanting in the public, who actually began, indeed, by producing this collectivity in himself, out of the abundance of his own being, joined to the abundance of musical possibility, as something he himself longed for as an artist. We see that this wondrous creative process, as it is present in the symphonies of Beethoven as an increasingly determining, living force, was not only achieved by the master in the most complete isolation, but actually was not *understood* at all—or rather, was *misunderstood* in the most shameful way—by the company of artists. The forms in which the master proclaimed his artistic, world-historical struggle remained for the composers of his and the succeeding age mere *formulas*, passing through mannerism into fashion, and although no composer of instrumental music was so much as able to reveal the slightest originality, even in these forms, there was not one who lacked the courage to keep on writing symphonies and similar pieces, not one who even suspected that the *last* symphony had already been *written*.[4] Thus too, we have had to stand by while Beethoven's great voyage of world discovery—that unique, altogether inimitable feat which we saw accomplished in his "Symphony of Joy" as the final and boldest venture of his genius—was after the event reundertaken, with the most idiotic naïveté, and, without hardship, suc-

4. He who specifically undertakes to write the history of instrumental music since Beethoven will no doubt have within this period to report on isolated phenomena, capable, assuredly, of arousing a particular and interested attention. But he who considers the history of the arts from a point of view as broad as is here necessary has to restrict himself to its chief moments alone; whatever departs from or derives from these moments he must leave out of account. And the more unmistakably such isolated phenomena reveal great talent, the more strikingly do precisely these phenomena prove—in view of the general sterility of the whole artistic impulse behind them—that, once there has been expressed in their particular art variety what Beethoven expressed in music, whatever is left to be discovered has to do with technical procedures, perhaps, but not with the living spirit. In the great universal artwork of the future it will be possible to keep on making new discoveries forever—but not in the individual art variety which, after having been conducted into universality as music was by Beethoven, perseveres in its isolated development. [Au.]

cessfully weathered. A new genre, a "symphony with choruses"—this was all one saw in it. Why should not this or that composer also write his Symphony with Choruses? Why should not "God the Lord" be resoundingly praised at the end, after He has helped to conduct the three preliminary instrumental movements to the most facile of possible conclusions?[5] Thus Columbus discovered America only for the fulsome petty profiteering of our time.

*   *   *   *   *

You exert yourselves to no purpose when, to still your own childishly egoistic longing for productivity, you seek to deny the destructive, world-historical, musical significance of Beethoven's last symphony; not even the stupidity which enables you actually to misunderstand the work can save you! Do as you please; take no notice of Beethoven whatever, grope after Mozart, gird yourselves with Bach, write symphonies with or without voices, write masses, oratorios—those sexless operatic embryos!—make songs without words, operas without texts; you produce nothing that has real life in it. For behold—you do not have the *faith!*—the great faith in the necessity of what you do! You have only the faith of the foolish—the superstitious faith in the possibility of the necessity of your egoistic willfulness!

Surveying the busy desolation of our musical art world; becoming aware of the absolute impotence of this art substance, for all its eternal ogling of itself; viewing this shapeless mess, of which the dregs are the dried-up impertinence of pedantry, from which, for all its profoundly reflecting, ever-so-musical, self-arrogated mastery, can finally rise to the broad daylight of modern public life, as an artificially distilled stench, only emotionally dissolute Italian opera arias or impudent French cancan dance tunes; appraising, in short, this complete creative incapacity, we look about us fearlessly for the great destructive stroke of destiny which will put an end to all this immoderately inflated musical rubbish to make room for the artwork of the future, in which genuine music will in truth assume no insignificant role, to which in this soil, however, air and room to breathe are peremptorily denied.[6]

*   *   *   *   *

5. An allusion to Mendelssohn's *Lobgesang.*
6. Lengthily though I have spoken here about the nature of music, in comparison with the other art varieties (a procedure fully justified, I may add, by the peculiar character of music and by the peculiar and truly productive developmental process resulting from this character), I am well aware of the many-sided incompleteness of my discussion; not one book, however, but many books would be needed to lay bare exhaustively the immorality, the weakness, the meanness of the ties connecting our modern music and our modern life; to explore the unfortunate overemotional side of music, which makes it subject to the speculation of our education maniacs, our "improvers of the people," who seek to mix the honey of music with the vinegar-sourish sweat of the mistreated factory worker as the one possible mitigation of his sufferings (somewhat as our sages of the state and bourse are at pains to stuff the servile rags of religion into the gaping holes in the policeman's care of society); and finally to explain the saddening psychological

FUNDAMENTALS OF THE ARTWORK OF THE FUTURE

If we consider the situation of modern art—insofar as it is actually *art*—in relation to public life, we recognize first of all its complete inability to influence this public life in accordance with its high purpose. This is because, as a mere cultural product, it has not grown out of life, and because, as a hothouse plant, it cannot possibly take root in the natural soil and natural climate of the present. Art has become the exclusive property of an artist class; it gives pleasure only to those who *understand* it, requiring for its understanding a special study, remote from real life, the study of *art connoisseurship*. This study and the understanding it affords are thought today to be within the reach of everyone who has the money to pay for the art pleasures offered for sale; yet if we ask the artist whether the great multitude of our art amateurs are capable of understanding him in his highest flights, he can answer only with a deep sigh. And if he now reflects on the infinitely greater multitude of those who must remain cut off, as a result of the influence of our social conditions, unfavorable from every point of view, not only from the understanding, but even from the enjoyment of modern art, the artist of today cannot but become conscious that his whole artistic activity is, strictly speaking, only an egoistic self-complacent activity for activity's sake and that, in its relation to public life, his art is mere luxury, superfluity, and selfish pastime. The disparity, daily observed and bitterly deplored, between so-called culture and the lack of it is so monstrous, a mean between them so unthinkable, their reconciliation so impossible, that, granted a minimum of honesty, the modern art based on this unnatural culture would have to admit, to its deepest shame, that it owed its existence to a life element which in turn could base *its* existence only on the utter lack of culture in the real mass of humanity. The one thing that, in this, its allotted situation, modern art should be able to do—and, where there is honesty, does endeavor to do—namely, *to further the diffusion of culture*—it cannot do, for the simple reason that art, to have any influence on life, must be itself the flowering of a *natural* culture—that is, of one that has grown up from below—and can never be in a position to rain down culture from above. At best, then, our cultured art resembles the speaker who seeks to communicate with a people in a language which it does not understand—all that he says, his most ingenious sayings above all, can lead only to the most laughable confusions and misunderstandings.

Let us first make apparent how modern art is to proceed if it would attain *theoretically* to the redemption of its uncomprehended self from out of its isolated situation and to the widest possible understanding of the public; how this redemption can become possible only through the *practical* mediation of the public will then be readily apparent of itself.

---

phenomenon that a man may be not only cowardly and base, but also *stupid*, without these qualities preventing him from being a perfectly respectable musician. [Au.]

•   •   •   •   •

Man as artist can be fully satisfied only in the union of all the art varieties in the *collective* artwork; in every *individualization* of his artistic capacities he is *unfree*, not wholly that which he can be; in the collective artwork he is *free*, wholly that which he can be.

The *true* aim of art is accordingly *all-embracing*; everyone animated by the true artistic impulse seeks to attain, through the full development of his particular capacity, not the glorification of *this particular capacity*, but the glorification *in art of mankind in general*.

The highest collective artwork is the *drama*; it is present in its *ultimate completeness* only when *each art variety, in its ultimate completeness*, is present in it.

True drama can be conceived only as resulting from the *collective impulse of all the arts* to communicate in the most immediate way with a *collective public*; each individual art variety can reveal itself as *fully understandable* to this collective public only through collective communication, together with the other art varieties, in the drama, for the aim of each individual art variety is fully attained only in the mutually understanding and understandable cooperation of all the art varieties.

154 Adolf Bernhard Marx

Adolf Bernhard Marx (1795?–1866) was well regarded as a music critic and pedagogue, although in the twentieth century he is remembered chiefly as a music theorist. In addition to his critical writing for the *Berliner allgemeine musikalische Zeitung,* which he founded, and his critical and biographical work on Beethoven, Marx devoted much of his career to the preparation of books intended for his students at the University of Berlin or for popular musical education: most notably, his four-volume *Lehre von der musikalischen Komposition* (1837–47) and the briefer, simplified *Allgemeine Musiklehre* (1839).

A. B. Marx is remembered particularly as the coiner of the term *Sonatenform* and for his detailed discussions of compositional procedures used in such movements (see no. 164, pp. 1223–31). He was one of the earliest writers to expound on notions of musical form, and his treatment of the subject became a model for later theorists. In particular, Marx saw the basis of form in the shaping of thematic statements and their alternation with transitional sections; as a result he insisted upon a three-part conceptualization of sonata form, as opposed to the customary two-part model based on harmonic process.

Marx's more philosophical or abstract book, *Die Musik des neunzehnten Jahrhunderts und ihre Pflege,* is also profoundly concerned with music pedagogy. Here, rather than technical matters, he explores the ethical, moral, and historical imperatives of proper teaching.

FROM *The Music of the Nineteenth Century*
(1854)

THE FUTURE

Where do we stand? Whither are we going in our art? May we expect of it new revelations, a new circle of ideas, and a new phase of development; or what destiny awaits it in the further existence of nations?

To these questions we have been led by the contemplation of the present state of music.

But it may be asked: Are we, short-sighted mortals, able to penetrate the future? May not those apparitions which we persuade ourselves to be signs of the future turn out mere idle dreams, possibly to be convicted of their fallacy by the very next day, and laughed to scorn, with all their cares and hopes and preparations, by the bright splendour of to-morrow's rising sun?

I ask, in reply: Can we evade this question of the future? Is it possible for us, even if we had the wish, to confine our thoughts to that moment of time which we term the present; and which, whilst we are naming it, disappears already in the stream of the past; leaving us to the next moment of time, which just now belonged to the future, but has become present, until it shall have passed away as swiftly as the former? To him who labours, the future is an inseparable continuation of the present: his work of yesterday was intended for to-day, and continues to live, together with him and the work which this day has brought forth. To the contemplating mind also, the present and future appear as an uninterrupted current of causes and consequences, and the knowledge of the past and present serves it as a light into the future. In this point of view it is, that the history of the different arts, as well as of the nations, is a truly divine revelation of the eternal guide, Reason: inasmuch as it discloses to us that unalterable law of causes and consequences, that inexorable decree of necessity, according to which all that has come into being and all that has happened, continue to operate upon the times and acts that follow. This alone constitutes the spiritual connexion, the significancy and value of our existence.

TEXT: *The Music of the Nineteenth Century, and Its Culture: Method of Musical Instruction,* trans. of *Die Musik des neunzehnten Jahrhunderts und ihre Pflege,* by August Heinrich Wehrhan (London, 1855), pp. 80–86.

The life of every individual being, as well as that of the nations, the life of the human mind, in all its forms of belief, of art and of science, is subject to and obeys the eternal call "onwards!" Imbecility and hypocrisy alone are reactionary; these alone dare to command "stillstand" (which would be living death), or preach "retrogression," or hope for and try to bring about the restoration of that which has passed away. Yesterday never returns, for it is the preceding condition of to-day; and whether you blame or acquiesce in to-day, it will be followed in unalterable sequence by to-morrow, in which it will continue to live and operate in all its plenitude. It is thus with the life of individuals and nations, it is the same in the state, in the family, and in the arts.

In order to convince every one of the necessity of progress in art, it is sufficient to refer to a simple practical observation, which proves the utter impossibility of remaining stationary, or successfully imitating the productions of a previous period of art, even if they should have remained ever so interesting and dear to us. What musician or amateur is not, even to this day, enchanted with Haydn's symphonies, so full of youthful freshness and unsurpassed in their charming innocence and playful sprightliness? In vain have teachers and critics from time to time urged that other composers should attempt the same style of music. The thing is simply impossible. To original and honest minds the request itself is objectionable, whilst those willing to imitate or repeat—these Pleyels, Wanhalls, and others of the same stamp[1]—have served up nothing but coarse and tasteless fare. We observe and are delighted at the careless ease and playfulness with which 'father' Haydn makes his bassoon and flute dance along, or perform what else he wishes them to do; and yet not one of our instrumentalists has attempted the same thing without becoming vulgar or baroque. So also has Mozart been imitated by hundreds of opera composers (his Magic Flute has led to "magic bells," "magic fiddles," and "magic bassoons;" his Papageno to *Larifaris*), but by no one more faithfully than by the burgomaster Wolfram, of Teplitz, who, some thirty years ago, was even greeted as a "second" Mozart. Who knows anything about Wolfram nowadays? We must go forwards, because we cannot recede.

To go forwards is a matter of necessity; how, and whither, are questions which could be solved with equal certainty, if we were fully acquainted with all the preceding circumstances, causes, and connexions. Proportionate to the knowledge and circumspection with which we approach the boundary between the present and the future, will be the clearness of our view beyond it, unless narrow prejudices or paltry timidity obscure our sight. But we never can close our eyes to that enigma. The onward pressure of life itself constrains us to put that question, and to answer it as well as we are able. Those ardent disciples of our art who prophecy of a "music of the future" may err, more or less, in certain

---

1. Ignace Joseph Pleyel (1757–1831), composer and piano maker; Johann Baptist Vanhal (1739–1813), composer and music teacher.

things; but they cannot be mistaken in the presentiment that the mind must move onwards. They burn with the thirst of life, and they feel the impulse and courage to obey the true command of life—"march on!" They see before them a hopeful future, full of new enjoyments and new revelations, not knowing whether much or little of it shall fall within the circle of their life. The future beyond, is their own by faith; as it was to those champions of liberty, who, with the ever true and glorious shout, *"L'avenir est à nous,"* marched on to victory— or death.

For there is another alternative, also, which we must look boldly in the face. Immortality does not belong to any individual being: neither does immortality belong to any individual art, but only to the spirit which calls it forth out of itself, now in this form of manifestation, and now in another, as its necessary expression and the characteristic element of its life. This we observe everywhere. Nations have gone down, together with their arts and sciences; so ancient Egypt, India, Assyria, all Asia, once so crowded with nations and highly adorned with works of art. Perished is that unparalleled national drama of Æschylus, and every attempt to restore it to life (like those made formerly by Caccini and his associates, and of late by Mendelssohn) has proved a mockery, a caricature devoid of all those elements—the cosmology, religion, traditions, and manners of the Greek nation, and even the sublime site of representation by the side of the steep cliff of the Acropolis, and under the serene and luminous sky of Hellas—which imparted life and reality to the original. The epos has died away with the ancient traditions; the plastic art of Greece has disappeared with the gods that peopled Olympus and the youthful, joyous, and beautiful race of the Hellenes. It was not the want of creative power that made the Buonarottis and Thorwaldsens[2] inferior to the Ancients; but it was the difference of soil and clime; the want of that serenity and mildness of the atmosphere which makes existence a pleasure; of that youthful innocence and freshness, and that pure sensuous susceptibility which roused the Greeks to delight in the mutual contemplation of the beauty of their well-formed limbs; of that perfection of bodily form exhibited in their martial games, their dances and religious processions; of that fulness of existence which had not yet ascetically divided itself into an abstract mind and a contaminated and shame-deserving body, but which in godlike images idealized itself, and, thus idealized, became its own admirer.

And yet we do not look back with sorrow or childish regret. That rich existence had lived its time; and terminated after it had fully satisfied the youthful spirit of mankind, filling even to overflow the temples and market places, the streets and groves, until the "marble population" left living beings scarcely room to walk. To that people, existing so entirely in and for the

---

2. Buonarotti: Michelangelo Buonarroti (1475–1564); Bertel Thorvaldsen (ca. 1770–1844), Danish sculptor active in Rome, a prominent Neoclassicist.

sunny outer world, music was merely a means of making language more sonorous, just as the acoustic vases in their theatres served to increase the resonance of sound. But when the spirit retired from the outer to the mystic inner world of the soul, then musical art became its place of abode and its proper organ.

And should we tremble, if, having groped its way and lived through this region of twilight and deeply hidden mysteries, our satiated spirit—now or at some future time—should seek for new gratification and a new existence in some other sphere? What those Hellenes created still exists and will exist for ever in the spirit of mankind; it does not cease to elevate and adorn also our existence, as long as we find sense and room for it. More it cannot be to us, for we have lived and grown beyond the deification of the bodily man, beyond the legends and traditions of little Hellas, and the fated *future* of the ancients, veiled in awe and mystery. And so, also, all that the sweet strains of sound have ever whispered and sung to us will live and move for ever in the soul of mankind, even though the human spirit should find another form of revelation than that which we call music. And if, now or hereafter, the spirit should in fresh youth proceed to reveal itself in new forms, even then those flattering strains will still remain the echoes of the soft confessions of the heart, a balm and comfort after the heat and toil of the day; they will adorn, as now, our public festivals, and wing the foot for dance or battle. No more will be required of them, if such a time arrive, nor any more accepted.

And here my sympathizing heart—for I feel with them—turns to the faithful band of those who, even in the face of this momentous "if," are drawn with irresistible force towards the altar of our art, and feel constrained to cling to it, although it be deserted by the people—not from choice, but of necessity, and in obedience to the spirit's call that draws them onwards to some other sphere. It was not love of gain, or thirst for fame—the spurious artist's idols—which brought you to the altar; nor is it indolence, or ostentatious pride in what you have acquired and learnt, or a stubborn refusal to open your eyes to the dawning light of the new day, which keeps you there. It was the disposition of your mind—you do not know who tuned its strings—which led you there; and there creative love has kindled in your bosom, there is the focus of your thoughts and visions, and there one of those eternal melodies has vibrated through your heart. You could not and cannot help prophesying those visions which grew up flaming in your spirit; and having once begun, you must persist, although the wave of time is rolling past your sanctuary. You cannot "limp after strange gods," in whom you have no faith, and whom you do not love; neither can you make "concessions," and fancy that by falsely putting Yes and No together, and sacrificing at two different altars, you will be able surreptitiously to serve the cause of truth. You must proclaim what dwells within your soul, *or* cease to speak. To the world you are "foolishness and an offence;" but the poet has sung of you:

Sagt es Niemand, nur den Weisen,
Weil die Menge gleich verhöhnet,
Das Lebend'ge, will ich preisen,
Das nach Flammentod sich sehnet.[3]

Your love and faithfulness alone remain your consolation and reward. The chattering multitude passes by, heedless of you; except, perhaps, that here and there a contemplative wanderer will look with transitory emotion upon that fidelity which will not leave even the grave of its devotion and affection; as, in the times of youthful and victorious Christianity, the last small bands of unbelievers, though chased from place to place, clung to the broken altars of their gods. You are the witnesses of sunken glory; your works remain to testify of your sincerity and of the immortality of that idea by which you were inspired. Then dedicate those works, as Æschylus did of old, to "time," to a discerning future; convinced that, if you sink into the grave to be forgotten for a period, like Sebastian Bach, that last evangelist, the following century will recognise you in your real being and truthfulness. But still your faithful service must not and cannot stop the Dionysian march of the spirit through the mountain passes and deep gorges of existence. "Onwards!" the call resounds, and resounds without intermission.

• • •

Does it sound for our art also? And, if so, does it point to the present time or to the nearest future? Or shall a longer period elapse before our art shall be awakened to new achievements, and to a new phase of existence?

Let us, first of all, endeavour to determine more precisely the real significance of this question, and the moment when it will certainly press more imperatively for solution.

The art of sound will certainly never cease to delight sensuous man, and to call forth emotions in the feeling heart. For it is inborn to man, and constitutes a part of his nature; the man without music is an incomplete being. We may also rest assured that this art will always continue to find talents and followers in the repetition of favorite forms, and the application of such forms to subjects of a kindred nature. But this does not touch the real question as to the future of our art. The essence of art is CREATION, the realization of the ideal, and a consequent progress from that which already exists to that which remains still to be accomplished. It counts its epochs of existence by the successive revelation of these ideals: those who raise such heavenly forms from the undulating and life-breathing motion of general art have been inspired with creative power; to them alone pertains the epithet Divine—the name of Genius, so often lavished in vain. It is they alone in whom and through whom all progress is effected, in whom the future becomes reality, whilst it is the mission of *talent* /

3. Tell it no one but the wise; / For the multitude would sneer—/ The Living Being will I prize / That yearns for death in flames. (Goethe, "Selige Sehnsucht," *West-Östlicher Divan*).

to spread those creations of genius over the breadth of life, to refresh and fructify every thing around them, and prepare it for the next creative epoch. So the waters of Egypt's one living stream are conducted over the whole country by means of canals, ditches, trenches, and water-wheels. A similar distribution is to be observed in the life of art.

The question of the future, therefore, relates to *new creations* produced by the power of genius. It starts from the last that have been revealed.

The last unquestionable progress in musical art is associated with the name of Beethoven; it is the spiritualization of instrumental music, by raising it to the sphere of definite conceptions and ideas. The question, taken strictly, is, whether another real progress has been effected since his time, or whether any further progress is still to be expected. To undertake to answer such a question must appear an act of great temerity, and yet an answer to it can be no longer refused. Every thinking man puts this question to himself, although he may not have the courage or feel called upon to answer it aloud.

One leading idea, which will assist us in the execution of this task, has already been established by the foregoing inquiries. It is this—that the different epochs of progress in art effected by the power of genius do not occur accidentally and irregularly, but appear to be regulated according to the strictest laws of reason and consistency. Art, like every other organism, develops itself according to the conditions and exigencies of its existence, and its creations are always in keeping with the actual condition and the wants of the human mind. It was impossible for Bach to treat his parts as individual and characteristic exponents, both of word and sentiment, until those parts had been made pliant and singable by the contrapuntists of the middle ages. Haydn had first to finish his childlike blissful play with the orchestra, before Beethoven was enabled to unlock the spiritual depths of this region of fairy life. Nowhere but in the sacerdotal service of the Catholic Church could Palestrina find his place, for therein lived his people and his Lord. Nothing, on the other hand, but the people's own song (Volkslied) could sound in opposition to it in our dear, liberated Germany, so long as the Reformation continued to be the work of the people, and formed an element of its existence; until that people turned away from its haughty rulers imbued with French manners, and clung for support and consolation to the "Word of God" alone, which Bach was sent to expound in its true power and fulness. The artist only gives form and expression to that which, although still void of shape and form, is already in existence amongst the people.

There is another point which must be kept well in sight, in order that the lines of demarcation between the past and future may not be obliterated. This is the remarkable phenomenon, that art—like life itself—appears periodically to return to certain ideas and forms; and yet progresses with these forms until they appear satisfactory and perfect, when it proceeds to others of a decidedly different nature. This phenomenon may be observed in individual artists, as well as in different nations and times. Thus, e. g. the simplest form of vocal music, the song, has been repeated by singers of all times and nations. Thus, also, the form of the musical drama may be traced far beyond the Greeks to the most ancient nations of Eastern Asia; it makes its appearance again in the 13th century (if not sooner), and once more in the 16th century, when its further cultivation is taken up by France, Italy, and Germany. Thus, also—to mention a special case—Bach's Chromatic Fantasia, and Beethoven's Fantasia with Orchestra and Chorus, as also his Ninth Symphony, are based upon the same idea. But in these cases there is only an apparent repetition, easily and clearly distinguishable, to a more searching eye, from the non-progressive or even retrogressive reproduction of previous forms. For, in the latter, we perceive as clearly the naked "repeat" (*Noch-Einmal*) of something that had before been, and has seen its day, and therefore is now void of life and truth, as we behold, in the former mode of revival, that unconscious dialectic power of the artistic mind which turns and works the same idea until it has brought it to full maturity and truth.

•　•　•

If we examine the past development of musical art from this point of view, we obtain at once a distinct perception of the different stages through which it has passed, and the tasks which remain still to be accomplished.

Looking at this development as a whole, and not in its details, it appears that music has completed all its essential tasks. After all that has been said in the preceding chapters, we can now pronounce the essential and ultimate object of every art to be this: that it shall reveal in its productions the spirit of man, and the essence of his life; and that all its forms shall be filled with this spirit. Thus the life of musical art must first manifest itself in a sensuous form, as a delightful sensuous exercise. This consciousness of sensuous delight must next raise itself to the higher, but still dim and uncertain, sphere of emotion. After this, the spoken word, the definite expression of the mind, had not only to be joined externally to the tune, but so entirely incorporated with it as to become music itself; whilst music, on the other hand, acquired a definite expression by the help of language. This new tongue of word and tone united was the condition and commencement of the musical drama, the opera. Finally, music had to endeavour, by itself alone, to seize and reveal so much of man's spiritual life as comes within its sphere. Further it cannot go; the near approach to the ultimate boundary is everywhere perceptible; music is no longer an isolated art, and people already begin to inquire and dispute about its power and right to receive and interpret, by itself alone, those revelations of the spirit.

Music
CRITICISM

155 François-Joseph Fétis

Frédéric Chopin, at the time completely unknown in Paris, gave his first concert there on February 26, 1832, in the piano-maker Camille Pleyel's showrooms, then located at 9, rue Cadet. The concert was a grand success and led to his immediate celebrity in the French capital.

The varied offerings of the concert that are discussed here are typical of the period and remind us of the importance of the soirée as a musical institution. Reviews at the time rarely identify programs with precision, of course, and François-Joseph Fétis's is no exception. Though it is unsigned, the authoritative tone, the historical perspective (far more informative than Schumann's famous review of Chopin's Op. 2 [see pp. 102–3]), and the vocabulary—including the use of such a characteristic phrase as "autant d'étonnement que de plaisir," which he elsewhere applied to Berlioz—suggest that the author of the column is indeed the editor of the *Revue Musicale*.

In addition to the intrinsic interest both of the information offered here and of Fétis's recognition of Chopin's talent, students of the cultural history of music will also be struck by this very early positing of a spiritual opposition between Chopin and Beethoven that became a commonplace later in the century. Chopin himself would have been bemused by the cliché; he told Eugène Delacroix that Beethoven's music is obscure because "he turns his back on eternal principles" (*The Journal of Eugène Delacroix*, trans. Walter Pach [New York, 1948], p. 195; diary entry for 7 April 1849).

The Concert of Monsieur Chopin from Warsaw
(1832)

These days, to say of a pianist that he is highly talented, or even, if you wish, that he is *supremely talented,* is simply to say that he is the rival or the enemy of a few other artists of the first rank whose names come immediately to mind. To add that his compositions are very good is merely to suggest that they fall into a category analogous to that of the works of Hummel, for example, and of a small number of other celebrated composers. But with such praises it is difficult to give an idea of novelty or of originality because, except for a few nuances of style and niceties of structure, music by pianists is generally written in certain conventional forms that one may consider fundamental, forms that have been used again and again for more than thirty years. This is the great shortcoming of piano music, and even our most accomplished artists have been unable to eliminate it from their works.

TEXT: *Revue Musicale* (March 3, 1832): 38–39, translated by Peter Bloom, who also provided most of the introduction and the information in the notes.

But here we have a young man who, giving himself over to his natural inclinations and following no models whatsoever, has effected, if not a total resuscitation of piano music, at least a part of what we have so long been searching for in vain—that is, a plethora of original ideas of a sort nowhere else to be found. This is not by any means to say that M. Chopin is gifted with the powerful spirit of a Beethoven, nor that there is in Chopin's music anything of the majestic force that one finds in the music of that great man: Beethoven wrote music *for piano,* but here I am speaking of music *for pianists*—and it is in this realm that I find in M. Chopin's inspirations the sign of a formal renaissance that could eventually exercise enormous influence upon this branch of art.

At the concert he gave on the 26th of this [*recte* last] month in the salons of MM. Pleyel and Company, M. Chopin played a concerto that surprised listeners as much as it pleased them both because of the novelty of its melodic ideas and because of its virtuoso passages, its modulations, and its larger structural organization.[1] There is vitality in his melody, fantasy in his passage-work, and originality in everything. Too many colorful modulations, so much confusion in linking phrases that it sometimes seems as though one is hearing an improvisation rather than a written composition—these are the imperfections that are found intermingled with the virtues I have just mentioned. But they are the imperfections of the youthful artist, and they will disappear as he gains greater experience. Indeed, if M. Chopin's subsequent works fulfill the promise of his debut, we can be sure that he will enjoy a brilliant and well-deserved reputation.

As a performer, this young artist also merits great praise. His playing is elegant, relaxed, and graceful; it is marked by both brilliance and clarity. He draws little sound from the instrument and resembles in this respect the majority of the German pianists. But the study of this aspect of his art, which he has undertaken with M. Kalkbrenner, cannot fail to provide him with that important quality upon which the confidence to perform depends, and without which one cannot shape the natural sounds of the instrument.

Apart from the concerto I have just spoken about, two further, quite remarkable works were heard on the same evening. One was a string quintet, performed with the emotional energy and kaleidoscopic inspiration that distinguish the playing of M. Baillot. The other was a piece for six pianos written by M. Kalkbrenner and performed by the composer along with MM. Chopin, Stammati, Hiller, Osborne, and Sowinski.[2] This piece, in which the instruments are deployed with great artifice and whose style is eminently graceful and elegant, had already been heard several years ago, and with great success, in the

1. The E-Minor Concerto, the future Op. 11 (dedicated to Kalkbrenner). [Tr.]
2. The string quintet was Beethoven's in C Major, Op. 29 (Fétis, following contemporary usage, refers to the work as "un quintetto pour le violon"). The work for six pianos, originally scored for two, plus two violins, viola, cello, and double bass *ad libitum,* was an arrangement of Kalkbrenner's *Grande Polonaise, précédée d'une Introduction et d'une marche,* Op. 92. [Tr.]

salons of MM. Pleyel and Company. It gave no less pleasure this second time around.

A solo for oboe, performed by M. Brod with the aplomb for which he is justly renowned, and several works sung by M. Boulanger and Mlles Isambert and Toméoni, completed this musical soirée, one of the most agreeable that we have heard this year.[3]

3. Chopin also played his Variations on Mozart's *Là ci darem la mano,* Op. 2, with quintet or second-piano accompaniment, and, solo, selected Mazurkas and Nocturnes. Among the artists who contributed to the concert were the members of the Baillot Quintet (Pierre Baillot and Jean-Joseph Vidal, violin, Chrétien Urhan and Théophile Tilmant, viola, and Louis Norblin, cello), the oboist Henri Brod, and the pianists Friedrich Kalkbrenner, Ferdinand Hiller, George Osborne, Camille Stamaty, and Albert Sowinski, as well as the singers Ernest Boulanger (Nadia's and Lili's father) and Mesdemoiselles Toméoni and Isambert (whose first names are not recorded in the literature). For further information, see Jean-Jacques Eigeldinger, "Les Premiers Concerts de Chopin à Paris," in *Music in Paris in the Eighteen-Thirties,* ed. Peter Bloom (Stuyvesant, NY: Pendragon Press, 1987), pp. 251–97; and Joel-Marie Fauquet, *Les Sociétés de musique de chambre à Paris de la Restauration à 1870* (Paris: Aux Amateurs de livres, 1986). [Tr.]

156 Hector Berlioz

In 1856, on Hector Berlioz's election to the Institute, his friends were outraged and his enemies consoled by a malicious bon mot put into circulation by the music critic of the *Revue des deux mondes:* "Instead of a musician, the Institute has chosen a journalist." Yet a casual reader of the Parisian press of those days might almost have believed this true. Since 1823, Berlioz had been a regular contributor to one musical or literary review after another; by 1863, when he gave up his long-standing association with the *Journal des débats,* he had published more than 900 separate pieces—leading articles, letters from abroad, humorous sketches, fictitious anecdotes, imaginary conversations, *causeries* and *feuilletons* of every sort and description. Only a small part of this enormous production is assembled in his three volumes of collected writings—*Les soirées de l'orchestre* (1852), *Les grotesques de la musique* (1859), and *A travers chants* (1862); other pieces were salvaged in his *Voyage musical* (1844) and in the two volumes of his memoirs, printed in 1865 but not published until after his death.

"Music is not made for everyone, nor everyone for music"—this is perhaps the central article of Berlioz's critical creed, and in the essay translated below it recurs again and again with the persistence of an *idée fixe.* But in writing on *William Tell,* Berlioz also reveals many of the other facets of his critical personality—his preoccupation with the poetic and the picturesque, his capacity for enthusiasm and for indignation, his horror of the mediocre and his impatience with all that fails to measure up to the very highest standards, his contempt for everything academic, his intense dissatisfaction with the commercial and official aspects of musical life. Above all, he reveals his sense of justice and his readiness to acknowledge merit, even in the camp of the enemy. From the first, Berlioz had taken his stand with the opponents of Gioachino Rossini and "the party of the dilettanti." But he has undertaken to review *William Tell* and he does so without *parti pris* and without hypocrisy.

Rossini's *William Tell*
(1834)

[PART 1]

Tired of hearing perpetual criticism of his works from the point of view of dramatic expression, still more tired, perhaps, of the blind admiration of his fanatical adherents, Rossini has found a very simple means of silencing the one and getting rid of the others. This has been to write a score—one seriously thought out, considered at leisure, and conscientiously executed from beginning to end in accordance with the requirements imposed upon all time by taste and good sense. He has written *William Tell*. This splendid work is thus to be regarded as an application of the author's new theories, as a sign of those greater and nobler capacities whose development the requirements of the sensual people for whom he has written until now have necessarily made impossible. It is from this point of view that we shall examine—without favor, but also without the least bias—Rossini's latest score.

If we consider only the testimonials that it has earned, the applause that it has called forth, and the conversions that it has made, *William Tell* has unquestionably had an immense success—a success that has taken the form of spontaneous admiration with some and of reflection and analysis with many others. And yet one is obliged to admit that to this glory it has not been able to add that other glory of which directors, and sometimes even authors, are more appreciative than of any other—popular success, that is, box-office success. The party of the dilettanti is hostile to *William Tell* and finds it cold and tiresome. The reasons for such a difference of opinion will become clear, we hope, in the course of the examination of this important production which we invite the reader to make with us. Let us follow the author step by step as he hurries along the new path that he has chosen, one that he would have reached the end of more rapidly and with a steadier pace if the force of deeply rooted habit had not caused him to cast an occasional glance behind him. These rare deviations once again bear out the old proverb: "In the arts one must take sides; there is no middle ground."

TEXT: "Guillaume-Tell, de Rossini." *Gazette musicale de Paris*, vol. 1 (1834), pp. 326–27, 336–39, 341–43, 349–51. Berlioz's essay was not written until five years after the first performance of the opera, which took place in Paris on August 3, 1829. Translation by Oliver Strunk.

For the first time Rossini has sought to compose an overture meeting the dramatic requirements recognized by every nation in Europe, Italy alone excepted. In making his debut in this style of instrumental music, entirely new to him, he has enlarged the form, so that his overture has in fact become a symphony in four distinct movements instead of the piece in two movements usually thought to be sufficient.

The first movement depicts most successfully, in our opinion, the calm of profound solitude, the solemn silence of nature when the elements and the human passions are at rest. It is a poetic beginning to which the animated scenes that are to follow form a most striking contrast—a contrast in expression, even a contrast in instrumentation, this first part being written for five solo violoncellos, accompanied by the rest of the cellos and contrabasses, while the entire orchestra is brought into play in the next movement, "The Storm."

In this, it seems to us, our author would have done well to abandon the square-cut rhythms, the symmetrical phrase structures, and the periodically returning cadences that he uses so effectively at all other times: "often a beautiful disorder is an effect of art," as an author says whose classical reserve is beyond question.[1] Beethoven proves this in the prodigious cataclysm of his pastoral symphony; at the same time he attains the end which the Italian composer lets us expect but does not give us. Several of the harmonic devices are remarkable and ingeniously brought in; among others, the chord of the minor ninth gives rise to effects that are indeed singular. But it is disappointing to rediscover in the storm scene of *William Tell* those staccato notes of the wind instruments which the amateurs call "drops of rain"; Rossini has already used this device in the little storm in the *Barber of Seville* and perhaps in other operas. In compensation he manages to draw from the bass drum without the cymbals picturesque noises in which the imagination readily rediscovers the reechoing of distant thunder among the anfractuosities of the mountains. The inevitable decrescendo of the storm is handled with unusual skill. In short, it is not arresting or overpowering like Beethoven's storm, a musical tableau which will perhaps remain forever unequalled, and it lacks that sombre, desolate character which we admire so much in the introduction to *Iphigenia in Tauris,* but it is beautiful and full of majesty. Unfortunately the musician is always in evidence; we never lose sight of him in his combinations, even in those which seem the most eccentric. Beethoven on the other hand has known how to reveal himself wholly to the attentive listener: it is no longer an orchestra that one hears, it is no longer music, but rather the tumultuous voice of the heavenly torrents blended with the uproar of the earthly ones, with the furious claps of thunder, with the crashing of uprooted trees, with the gusts of an exterminating wind, with the frightened cries of men and the lowing of the herds. This is terrifying, it makes one shudder, the illusion is complete. The emotion that Rossini arouses in the same situation falls far short of attaining the same degree of— But let us continue.

---

1. Boileau, *L' Art poétique,* Canto 2, line 72.

The storm is followed by a pastoral scene, refreshing in the extreme; the melody of the English horn in the style of the *ranz des vaches*[2] is delicious, and the gamboling of the flute above this peaceful song is ravishing in its freshness and gaiety. We note in passing that the triangle, periodically sounding its tiny pianissimo strokes, is in its right place here; it represents the little bell sounded by the flocks as they saunter quietly along while the shepherds call and answer with their joyful songs. "So you find dramatic meaning in this use of the triangle," someone asks us; "in that case, pray be good enough to tell us what is represented by the violins, violas, basses, clarinets, and so forth." To this I should reply that these are musical instruments, essential to the existence of the art, while the triangle, being only a piece of iron whose sound does not belong to the class of sounds with definite pitch, ought not to be heard in the course of a sweet and tranquil movement unless its presence there is perfectly motivated, failing which it will seem only bizarre and ridiculous.

With the last note of the English horn, which sings the pastoral melody, the trumpets enter with a rapid incisive fanfare on B, the major third in the key of G, established in the previous movement, and in two measures this B becomes the dominant in E major, thus determining in a manner as simple as it is unexpected the tonality of the Allegro that follows. This last part of the overture is treated with a *brio* and a verve that invariably excite the transports of the house. Yet it is built upon a rhythm that has by now become hackneyed, and its theme is almost exactly the same as that of the Overture to *Fernand Cortez*. The staccato figuration of the first violins, bounding from C-sharp minor to G-sharp minor, is a particularly grateful episode, ingeniously interpolated into the midst of this warlike instrumentation; it also provides a means of returning to the principal theme and gives to this return an irresistible impetuosity which the author has known how to make the most of. The peroration of the saucy Allegro has genuine warmth. In short, despite its lack of originality in theme and rhythm, and despite its somewhat vulgar use of the bass drum, most disagreeable at certain moments, constantly pounding away on the strong beats as in a *pas redoublé* or the music of a country dance, one has to admit that the piece as a whole is treated with undeniable mastery and with an élan more captivating, perhaps, than any that Rossini has shown before, and that the overture to *William Tell* is the work of an enormous talent, so much like genius that it might easily be mistaken for it.

[PART 2]

Act 1 opens with a chorus that has a beautiful and noble simplicity. Placid joy is the feeling that the composer was to paint, and it is difficult to imagine anything better, more truthful, and at the same time more delicate than the melody he has given to these lines:

---

2. A traditional Swiss melody, played on the alphorn, to gather cows.

How clear a day the skies foretell!
Come bid it welcome with a song!

The vocal harmonies, supported by an accompaniment in the style of the *ranz des vaches,* breathe happiness and peace. Towards the end of the piece, the modulation from G to E-flat becomes original because of the way in which it is presented and makes an excellent effect.

The *romance* that follows ("Hasten aboard my boat") does not seem to us to be on the same level. Its melody is not always as naive as it should be for the song of a fisherman of Unterwald; many phrases are soiled by that affected style that the singers with their banal embellishments have unfortunately put into circulation. Besides, one scarcely knows why a Swiss should be accompanied by two harps.

Tell, who has been silent throughout the introduction and the fisherman's first stanza, comes forward with a measured monologue full of character; it sets before us the concentrated indignation of a lover of liberty, deeply proud of soul. Its instrumentation is perfect, likewise its modulations, although in the vocal part there are some intervals whose intonation is quite difficult.

At this point the general defect of the work as a whole begins to make itself felt. The scene is too long, and since the three pieces of which it consists are not very different in their coloring, the result is a tiring monotony which is further accentuated by the silence of the orchestra during the *romance.* In general, unless the stage is animated by a powerful dramatic interest, it is seldom that this kind of instrumental inactivity does not cause a fatal indifference, at least at the Opéra. Aside from this, the house is so enormous that a single voice, singing way at the back of the stage, reaches the listener deprived of that warm vibrancy that is the life of music and without which a melody can seldom stand out clearly and make its full effect.

After the intoning of a *ranz des vaches* with its echoes, in which four horns in G and E represent the Alpine trumpet, an Allegro vivace revives the attention. This is a chorus, full of impassioned verve, and it would be admirable if the meaning of the text were just the opposite of what it actually is. The key is E minor and the melody is so full of alarm and agitation that at the first performance, not hearing the words, as usually happens in large theatres, I expected the news of some catastrophe—at the very least, the assassination of Father Melchthal. Yet, far from it, the chorus sings:

From the mountains a summons
To repose sounds a call;
A festival shall lighten
Our labors in the field.

It is the first time that Rossini has been guilty of this particular kind of incongruity.

After this chorus, which is the second in this scene, there follows an accompanied recitative and then a third chorus, *maestoso,* chiefly remarkable for the rare felicity of the scale from the B in the middle register to the high B which the soprano spreads obliquely against the harmonic background. But the action does not progress, and this defect is made still more glaring by a fourth chorus, rather more violent than joyous in character, sung throughout in full voice, scored throughout for full orchestra, and accompanied by great strokes of the bass drum on the first beat of each measure. Wholly superfluous from the dramatic point of view, the piece has little musical interest. Ruthless cuts have been made in the present score, yet great care has been taken to delete nothing here; this would have been too reasonable. Those who make cuts know only how to cut out the good things; in castrating, it is precisely the noblest parts that are removed. By actual count, then, there are four fully developed choruses here, to do honor to "the clear day" and "the rustic festival," to celebrate "labor and love," and to speak of "the horns that reecho close by the roaring torrents." This is an awkward blunder, especially at the beginning, this monotony in the choice of means, wholly unjustified by the requirements of the drama, whose progress it aimlessly brings to a standstill. It appears that the work has been dominated at many points by the same unfortunate influence which led the composer astray at this one. I say "the composer," for a man like Rossini always gets what he wants from his poet, and it is well known that for *William Tell* he insisted on a thousand changes which M. Jouy did not refuse him.

Lack of variety even affects the melodic style: the vocal part is full of repeated dominants, and the composer turns about the fifth step of the scale with tiresome persistence, as though it held for him an almost irresistible attraction. Here are some examples from Act 1. During the fanfare of the four horns in E-flat, Arnold sings:

> Have a care! Have a care!
> The approach of the Austrian tyrant
> Is announced by the horns from the mountain.

All these words are on a single note—B-flat. In the duet that follows, Arnold again resorts to this B-flat, the dominant in E-flat, for the recitation of two whole lines:

> Under the yoke of such oppression
> What great heart would not be cast down?

Further on, after the modulation to D minor, Tell and Arnold sing alternately on A, the dominant of the new key:

TELL: Let's be men and we shall win!
ARNOLD: What revenge can end these affronts?
TELL: Ev'ry evil rule is unstable.

Against this obstinate droning of the dominant, the five syllables on D, F, and C-sharp at the ends of the phrases can barely be made out. The key changes to F, and the dominant, C, appears again immediately:

ARNOLD: Think of all you may lose!
TELL: No matter!
ARNOLD: What acclaim can we hope from defeat?

And later on:

ARNOLD: Your expectation?
TELL: To be victorious,
         And yours as well; I must know what you hope.

Nor is this all; the dominants continue:

> When the signal sounds for the combat,
> My friend, I shall be there.

The E-flat fanfare of the horns begins again and Tell exclaims:

> The signal! Gessler comes.
> Even now as he taunts us,
> Willing slave of his whim, are you waiting
> To entreat the disdain of a favoring glance?

These four lines are entirely on the dominant, B-flat. True to his favorite note, Tell again returns to it in order to say, near the end of the movement:

> The music calls; I hear the wedding chorus;
> Oh, trouble not the shepherds at their feast
> Nor spoil their pleasures with your sad lament!

A defect as serious as this does immense harm to the general effect of the fine duet. I say "fine," for despite this chiming of dominants, it is really admirable in all other respects: the instrumentation is treated with unusual care and delicacy; the modulations are varied; Arnold's melody ("Oh Mathilda, my soul's precious idol") is suave in the extreme; many of Tell's phrases are full of dramatic accents; and except for the music of the line "But at virtue's call I obey," the whole has great nobility.

The pieces that follow are all of them more or less noteworthy. We cite in preference the A minor chorus:

> Goddess Hymen,
> Thy bright feast day
> Dawns for us.

This would have a novel, piquant effect if it were sung as one has the right to demand that all choruses should be at the Royal Academy of Music. The pantomimic Allegro of the archers also has great energy, and several *airs de danse* are distinguished by their fresh melodies and the exceptional finish of their orchestration.

The grand finale which crowns the act seems to us much less satisfactory. The beginning brings in the voices and orchestra a return of the dominant pedal-points which have been absent for some time. After a few exclamations by the chorus of Swiss, one hears Gessler's soldiers:

> The hour of justice now is striking.
> The murd'rer be accursed!
> No quarter!

All this is recited on B, the dominant in E minor, which has already been used as a pedal by the basses of the orchestra during the first nineteen measures of the introduction. Confronted by this persistent tendency of the composer's to fall back on the most familiar and monotonous of musical formulas, one can only suppose it to be due to sheer laziness. It is very practical indeed to write a phrase for orchestra whose harmony turns about the two fundamental chords of the key and then, when one has a leftover bit of text to add to it, to set this to the dominant, the note common to the two chords—this saves the composer much time and trouble. After this introductory movement there follows a chorus ("Virgin, adored by ev'ry Christian"); the tempo is slow—I might say, almost dragging—and the piece is accompanied in a very ordinary fashion, so that its effect is to hold up the action and the musical interest most inappropriately. Little is added by the syllabic asides of the soldiers' chorus during the singing of the women:

> How they tremble with fright!
> Do as we bid!
> Your own lives are at stake!

The music for these words is neither menacing nor ironic: it is simply a succession of notes, mere padding to fill out the harmonies, expressing neither contempt nor anger. At length, when the women have finished their long prayer, Rudolf—Gessler's most ardent satellite—breaks out in a violent rage. The orchestra takes a tumultuous headlong plunge, the trombones bellow, the violins utter shrill cries, the instruments vie with one another in elaborating "the horrors of plundering and pillage" with which the Swiss are threatened; unfortunately, the whole is a copy of the finale of *La Vestale*. The figuration of the basses and violas, the strident chords of the brass, the incisive scales of the first violins, the syllabic accompaniment of the second chorus beneath the broad melody of the soprano—Spontini has them all. Let us add, however, that the *stretta* of this chorus contains a magnificent effect due wholly to Rossini. It is the syncopated descending scale for the whole chorus, singing in octaves, while trebles, flutes, and first violins forcefully sustain the major third E to G-sharp; against this interval the notes D-sharp, A, and F-sharp of the lower voices collide in violent agitation. This idea alone, in its grandeur and force, completely effaces all previous sections of the finale. These are now wholly forgotten. At the beginning one was indifferent—in the end one is moved; the author seemed to lack invention—he has redeemed himself and astonished us with an unexpected stroke. Rossini is full of such contrast.

[PART 3]

The curtain rises on Act 2. We are witnesses of a hunt; horses cross the stage at a gallop. The fanfare which we heard two or three times during the preced-

ing act resounds again; it is differently scored, to be sure, and linked to a characteristic chorus, but it is a misfortune that so undistinguished a theme should
be heard so frequently. The development of the drama imposed it, the musician will tell us. Nevertheless, as we have said before, Rossini might have
obtained from his librettist a different arrangement of the scenes and thus have
avoided these numerous chances for monotony. He failed to do so and, now
that it is too late, he regrets it. Let us go on. Halfway through the chorus just
mentioned there is a diatonic passage played in unison by the horns and the
four bassoons that has an energy all its own, and the piece as a whole would be
captivating were it not for the torture inflicted upon the listener who is at all
sensitive by the innumerable strokes of the bass drum on the strong beats,
whose effect is the more unfortunate since they again call attention to rhythmic
constructions that are completely lacking in originality.

To all this I am sure that Rossini will reply: "Those constructions which seem
to you so contemptible are precisely the ones that the public understands the
most readily." "Granted," I should answer; "but if you profess so great a respect
for the propensities of the vulgar, you ought also to limit yourself to the most
commonplace things in melody, harmony, and instrumentation. This is just
what you have taken care not to do. Why, then, do you condemn rhythm alone
to vulgarity? Besides, in the arts, criticism cannot and should not take account
of considerations of this kind. Am I on the same footing as an amateur who
hears an opera once every three or four months, I who have occupied myself
exclusively with music for so many years? Haven't my ears become more delicate than those of the student whose hobby it is to play flute duets on Sundays?
Am I as ignorant as the shopkeeper on the Rue Saint-Denis? In a word, do
you not admit that there is progress in music, and in criticism a quality that
distinguishes it from blind instinct, namely taste and judgment? Of course you
do. This being the case, the ease or difficulty with which the public understands
new departures counts for little; this has to do with material results, with business, while it is art that concerns us. Besides, the public—especially in Paris—
is not as stupid as some would like to think; it does not reject innovations if
they are presented with the right sort of candor. The people who are hostile to
innovations are—need I name them?—the *demi-savans*. No, frankly; excuses
of this kind are unacceptable. You have written a commonplace rhythm, not
because the public would have rejected another, but because it was easier and
above all quicker to repeat what had already been used over and over again
than to search for more novel and more distinguished combinations."

The distant "Bell Chorus," a contrast in style to the chorus that preceded it,
seems to bear out this opinion of ours. Here the whole is full of charm—pure,
fresh, and novel. The end of the piece even presents a chord succession whose
effect is delightful, although the harmonies succeed one another in an order
prohibited by every rule adopted since the schools began. I refer to the diatonic
succession of triads in parallel motion which occurs in connection with the
fourfold repetition of the line, "The night has come." A Master of Musical
Science would call this kind of part-writing most incorrect: the basses and first

sopranos are continually at the octave, the basses and second sopranos continually at the fifth. After the C major triad come those in B major and A minor and finally that in G major, the prevailing tonic. The agreeable effect resulting from these four consecutive fifths and octaves is due, in the first place, to the short pause that separates the chords, a pause sufficient to isolate the harmonies one from another and to give to each fundamental the aspect of a new tonic; in the second place, to the naïve coloring of the piece, which not only authorizes this infraction of a time-honored rule, but makes it highly picturesque. Beethoven has already written a similar succession of triads in the first movement of his heroic symphony; everyone knows the majestic nobility of this passage. Believe then, if you must, in absolute rules!

Hardly has this evening hymn died away like a graceful sunset when we are greeted with another return of the horn fanfare with its inevitable pedal point on the dominant:

> There sounds a call, the horn of Gessler.
> It bids us return; we obey it.

The chief huntsman and the chorus recite these two lines in their entirety on B-flat. Our earlier observations have here a more direct and a more particular application.

With the following number the composer begins a higher flight; this is quite another style. Mathilda's entrance is preceded by a long ritornello doubly interesting as harmony and as dramatic expression. There is real passion in this, and that feverish agitation that animates the heart of a young woman obliged to conceal her love. Then comes a recitative, perfect in its diction and admirably commented upon by the orchestra, which reproduces fragments of the ritornello. After this introduction follows the well-known *romance,* "Somber forests."

Rossini has, in our opinion, written few pieces as elegant, as fresh, as distinguished in their melody, and as ingenious in their modulations as this one: aside from the immense merit of the vocal part and the harmony, it involves a style of accompaniment for the violas and first violins that is full of melancholy, also—at the beginning of each stanza—a pianissimo effect for the kettledrum that rouses the listener's attention in a lively manner. One seems to hear one of those natural sounds whose cause remains unknown, one of those strange noises which attract our attention on a clear day in the deep forest and which redouble in us the feeling of silence and isolation. This is poetry, this is music, this is art—beautiful, noble, and pure, just as its votaries would have it always.

This style is sustained until the end of the act, and from henceforth marvel follows marvel. In the duet between Arnold and Mathilda, so full of chivalrous passion, we mention as a blemish the long pedal of the horns and trumpets on G, alternately tonic and dominant, the effect of which is at certain moments atrocious. Then too we shall reproach the composer for having blindly followed the example of the older French composers, who would have thought themselves disgraced if they had failed to bring in the trumpets at once whenever the words made any mention of glory or victory. In this respect Rossini treats us like the dilettanti of 1803, like the admirers of Sédaine and Monsigny.[3]

> Ah, return to war and to glory,
> Take wing and make me proud once more!
> One gains a name if one's a victor;
> The world will then approve my choice.

"Out with the obbligato fanfare," Rossini will have said on reading this in his libretto; "I am writing for France." Finally, it seems to us that this duet, which is developed at considerable length, would gain if there were no repetition of the motive which the two singers have together, "The one who adores you." Since the tempo of this passage is slower than the rest, the repetition necessarily brings with it two interruptions which break up the general pace and detract from the animated effect of the scene by prolonging it uselessly.

But from this point until the final chord of the second act, this defect does not recur. Walter and Tell enter unexpectedly; Mathilda takes flight, Arnold remains to listen to bitter reproaches on his love for the daughter of the Helvetian tyrant. Nothing could be more beautiful, more expressive, more noble than this recitative, both in the vocal parts and in the orchestra. Two phrases are particularly striking in the verity of their expression. One is Walter's counsel:

> Perhaps, though, you should alter
> And take the pains to know us better.

The other is Tell's apostrophe:

> Do you know what it is to feel love for one's country?

At length, the tragic ritornello of the trio is unfolded. Here we confess that, despite our role as critic and the obligations that it brings with it, it is impossible for us to apply the cold blade of the scalpel to the heart of this sublime creation. What should we analyze? The passion, the despair, the tears, the lamentations of a son horrified by the news of his father's murder? God forbid! Or should we make frivolous observations about details, quibble with the author over a *gruppetto* or a solo passage for the flute or an obscure moment in the second violin part? Not I! If others have the courage for it, let them attempt it. As for me, I have none at all—I can only join the crowd in shouting: "Beautiful! Superb! Admirable! Ravishing!"

But I shall have to be sparing of my enthusiastic adjectives, for I am going to need them for the rest of the act, which remains almost continuously on this same high level. The arrival of the three cantons affords the composer an opportunity to write three pieces in three wholly different styles. The first

3. The year in which Berlioz was born. Michel-Jean Sedaine (1719–1797), librettist, and Pierre-Alexandre Monsigny (1729–1817), composer, sustained a highly successful operatic collaboration during the 1760s and '70s.

chorus is in a strong, robust style which paints for us a working people with calloused hands and arms that never tire. In the second chorus and the chaste sweetness of its melody we recognize the timid shepherds; the expression of their fears is ravishing in its grace and naïveté. The fishermen from the canton of Uri arrive by boat from the lake while the orchestra imitates as faithfully as music can the movements and the cadenced efforts of a crew of oarsmen. Hardly have these latecomers disembarked when the three choruses unite in a syllabic ensemble, rapidly recited in half voice and accompanied by the pizzicati of the strings and an occasional muffled chord from the wind instruments:

> Before you, Tell, you see
> Three peoples as one band,
> Our rights our only arms
> Against a vile oppressor.

First recited by the chorus of fishermen and then taken up by the two other choruses, who mingle with it their exclamations and their laconic asides, this phrase is dramatically most realistic. Here is a crowd in which each individual, moved by hope and fear, can scarcely hold back the sentiments that agitate him, a crowd in which all wish to speak and each man interrupts his neighbor. Be it said in passing that the execution of this *coro parlato* is extremely difficult, a fact that may in part excuse the choristers of the Opéra, who usually recite it very badly indeed.

But Tell is about to speak and all grow silent—*arrectis auribus adstant.*[4] He stirs them, he inflames them, he apprises them of Melchthal's cruel death, he promises them arms; finally he asks them directly:

TELL: Do you agree to help?
CHORUS: We one and all agree.
TELL: You will join us?
CHORUS: We will.
TELL: Even in death?
CHORUS: We will.

Then, uniting their voices, they swear a grave and solemn oath to "the God of kings and of shepherds" to free themselves from slavery and to exterminate their tyrants. Their gravity under these circumstances, which would be absurd if they were Frenchmen or Italians, is admirable for a cold-blooded people like the Swiss, whose decisions, if less precipitate, are not lacking in steadfastness or in assurance of attainment. The movement becomes animated only at the end, when Arnold catches sight of the first rays of the rising sun:

ARNOLD: The time has come.
WALTER: For us this is a time of danger.
TELL: Nay, of vict'ry!
WALTER: What answer shall we give him?
ARNOLD: To arms!

4. "They stand by with attentive ears." Vergil, *Aeneid* 1. 152. [Fairclough, trans.].

ARNOLD ⎫
TELL   ⎬ To arms!
WALTER ⎭

Then the whole chorus, the soloists, the orchestra, and the percussion instruments, which have not been heard since the beginning of the act, one and all take up the cry: "To arms!" And at this last and most terrible war cry which bursts forth from all these breasts, shivering in the dawn of the first day of liberty, the entire instrumental mass hurls itself like an avalanche into an impetuous Allegro!

Ah, it is sublime! Let us take breath.

[PART 4]

We left Arnold in despair, thinking only of war and vengeance. His father's death, imposing new obligations upon him, has torn him abruptly from the attraction that had lured him little by little towards the ranks of his country's enemies. Filled with gloomy thoughts, his words to Mathilda at the beginning of Act 3 reveal his fierce and somber pre-occupation:

ARNOLD: I tarry to avenge my father.
MATHILDA: What is your hope?
ARNOLD: It is blood that I hope for;
   I renounce Fortune's favors all,
   I renounce all love and all friendship,
   Even glory, even marriage.
MATHILDA: And I, Melchthal?
ARNOLD: My father's dead.

The expression of these agitated sentiments dominates the whole of the long ritornello which precedes and prepares the entrance of the two lovers. After a short but energetic recitative, in which Arnold sings another five-measure phrase on a single note, an E, the great agitato aria of Mathilda begins.

At the outset, this piece is not as happy in its choice of melody and in its dramatic expression as we find it at the end. The composer seems to have begun it in cold blood and to have come to life by degrees as he penetrated his subject. The first phrase is what we might call "a phrase in compartments" (*une phrase à compartimens*); it belongs to that vast family of melodies consisting of eight measures, four of them on the tonic and as many on the dominant, examples of which occur at the beginning of nearly every concerto of Viotti, Rode, Kreutzer, and their imitators. This is a style in which each development can be foreseen well in advance; in composing this, his latest and perhaps his most important work, it would seem to us that Rossini ought to have abandoned it once and for all. Aside from this, the two lines that follow cry out for an expressive musical setting:

> In my heart solitude unending!
> Shall you never be at my side?

Rossini has failed to give it to them. What he has written is cold and common-place, despite an instrumentation that might have been less tortured in its superabundant luxuriousness. As though to efface the memory of this some-what scholastic beginning, the peroration is admirable in its originality, its grace, and its sentiment. The liveliest imagination could not have asked the composer for a style of declamation more truthful or more noble than that in which he has caused Mathilda to exclaim, with melancholy abandon:

> To the land of the stranger
> Whose shore you seek, I may not follow
> To offer you my tender care,
> And yet all my heart shall be with you,
> To all your woes it shall be true.

We are not as satisfied with the ensemble for the two voices which closes the scene. As the farewell of two lovers who separate, never to see each other again, it should have been heartbreaking; apart from Mathilda's chromatic vocalization on the word "Melchthal," it is only brilliant and overscored for the wind instruments, without contrasts or oppositions.

At the same time, it is greatly to be regretted—even if only because of the fine flashes of inspiration which we have mentioned—that the scene is entirely suppressed in the performances being given today. At present the act begins with the chorus of Gessler's soldiers, who are engaged in a brutal and arrogant celebration of the hundredth anniversary of the conquest of Switzerland and its addition to the German Empire.

After this there is dancing, of course; at the Opéra, an excuse for a ballet would be found, even in a representation of the Last Judgment. What difference does it make?—the *airs de danse,* all of them saturated with the Swiss melodic idiom, have rare elegance and are written with care (I except only the Allegro in G called the "Pas de soldats"). It is in the midst of this ballet that we meet the celebrated Tyrolienne, so popular nowadays, remarkable for its modulations and for the vocal rhythm which serves as its accompaniment. Before Rossini, no one writing for the stage had thought of using an immediate succession of chords having the character of contrasted tonic harmonies, such as the one that occurs in the thirty-third measure, where the melody outlines an arpeggio within the major triad on B, only to fall back at once into the one on G, the true tonic. This little piece, doubtless written one morning at the breakfast table, has had a truly incredible success, while beauties of an incom-parably higher order have won only very limited approval, although this approval is, to be sure, of quite another sort than that which has welcomed the pretty Tyrolienne so graciously. With some composers, the applause of the crowd is useful but scarcely flattering—for these artists, only the opinion of the discriminating has real value. With others it is just the opposite: only quantity has value, while quality is almost worthless. Until their more frequent dealings with Europeans taught them the value of money, the American Indians pre-ferred a hundred sous to a single gold piece.

After the dances comes the famous scene of the apple. Its style is in general nervous and dramatic. One of Tell's phrases in his dialogue with Gessler seems to us to have real character:

GESSLER: My captive shall he be.
TELL: Let us hope he may be your last.

On the other hand, a movement that seems to us absolutely false in sentiment and expression is that in which Tell, concerned for his son, takes him aside, embraces him, and orders him to leave:

> My heart's dearest treasure,
> Receive my embraces,
> Then depart from me.

Instead of this, it would have been enough to have made him a sign and to have uttered quickly these two words: "Save thyself!" To elaborate upon this idea in an Andante would perhaps have done no harm in an Italian opera, a really Italian one, but in a work like *William Tell*, where reason has been admitted to full civic rights, where not everything is directed towards permitting the singers to shine, such a piece is more than an incongruity—it is an outright nonsense.

The recitative that follows exactly meets the requirements that we have just laid down:

> Rejoin your mother! These my orders:
> That the flame on the mountains now be lighted
> To give to our allies the command to rebel.

This precipitate utterance throws an even more glaring light on the faulty expression that shocked us when this idea was presented before. In compensation, the composer offers us Tell's touching instructions to his little son:

> Move not a muscle, be calm and fearless,
> In prayer bend a suppliant knee!

How admirably the accompaniment of the violoncellos weeps beneath the voice of this father whose heart is breaking as he embraces his boy! The orchestra, almost silent, is heard only in pizzicato chords, each group followed by a rest of half a measure. The bassoons, pianissimo, sustain long plaintive notes. How filled all this is with emotion and anguish—how expressive of the anticipated great event about to be accomplished!

> My son, my son, think of thy mother!
> Patiently she waits for us both.

These last phrases of the melody are irresistibly lifelike; they go straight to the heart.

Let the partisans of popular opinion say what they please. If this sublime inspiration arouses only polite and infrequent applause, there is something about it that is nobler, higher, worthier for a man to take pride in having created, than there is in a graceful Tyrolienne, even though it be applauded by a hundred thousand and sung by the women and children of all Europe. There is a difference between the pretty and the beautiful. To pretend to side with the majority, and to value prettiness at the expense of that which addresses itself to the heart's most intimate sentiments, this is the part of the shrewd businessman, but not that of the artist conscious of his dignity and independence.

The finale of this act includes, in its first section, an admirably energetic passage which is invariably annihilated at the Opéra by the inadequacy of the singer; this is the sudden outburst of the timid Mathilda:

> I claim him as my ward in the name of the sov'reign.
> In indignation a people is watching,
> Take care, take care, he is safe in my arms.

This general indignation is skillfully portrayed, both in the vocal part and in the orchestra; it is as lifelike as Gluck and Spontini. As an accompaniment to the ingeniously modulated melody of the sopranos, the syllabic theme of the men's chorus ("When their pride has misled them") makes an excellent effect. On the other hand, the *stretta* of this chorus consists only of furious cries; to be sure, they are motivated by the text, but they arouse no emotion in the listener, whose ears are needlessly outraged. Here again, it would perhaps have been better to change the wording of the libretto, for it would be difficult if not impossible to set the line, "Cursèd be Gessler's name," except as a savage vociferation having neither melody nor rhythm and paralyzing by its violence all feeling for harmony.

Act 4 reestablishes the individual passions and affords a needed relaxation after the uproar of the preceding scenes. Arnold revisits his father's deserted cottage; his heart filled with a hopeless love and with projects of vengeance, all his senses stirred by the recollections of bloody carnage always before his mind's eye, he breaks down, overcome by the enormity of the affecting contrast. All is calm and silent. Here is peace—and the tomb. And yet an infinity separates him from that breast upon which, at a moment like this, he would so gladly pour out his tears of filial piety, from that heart close to which his own would beat less sadly. Mathilda shall never be his. The situation is poetic, even poignantly melancholy, and it has inspired the musician to write an air which we do not hesitate to pronounce the most beautiful of the entire score. Here the young Melchthal pours out all the sufferings of his soul; here his mournful recollections of the past are painted in the most ravishing of melodies; harmony and modulation are employed only to reinforce the melodic expression, never out of purely musical caprice.

The Allegro with choruses, which follows, is full of spirit and makes a worthy crown for an equally fine scene. At the same time, the piece has only a very indifferent effect upon the public, to judge from the applause with which it is received. For the many it is too refined; delicate shadings like these nearly always escape their attention. Alas, if one could only reduce the public to an assembly of fifty sensible and intelligent persons, how blissful it would be to be an artist!

Since the first performance, the trio accompanied only by the wind instruments has been suppressed, also the piece immediately following it, the prayer sung during the storm. The cut is most inopportune, particularly in view of the prayer, a masterpiece in the picturesque style, whose musical conception is novel enough to have warranted some allowance being made in its favor. Aside from the mise-en-scène, considerations having to do with the decor or the stage machinery were no doubt responsible for the suppression of this interesting part of the score. The thing was accordingly done without hesitation—everyone knows that at the Opéra the directors *support* the music.

From this moment until the final chorus, we shall find nothing but padding. The outbursts of the orchestra while Tell struggles on the lake with the storm, the fragments of recitative interrupted by the chorus—these are things that the musician writes with confidence that no one will listen to them.

The final chorus is another story:

> About us all changes and grows.
> Fresh the air!

This is a beautiful harmonic broadening-out. The *ranz des vaches* floats gracefully above these massive chords and the hymn of Swiss liberty soars upward to heaven, calm and imposing, like the prayer of a just man.

157 Robert Schumann

In contrast to Hector Berlioz, the professional man of letters, Robert Schumann brings to his critical writing romantic idealism and a high purpose. As he tells us himself in his introductory essay, the founding of the *Neue Zeitschrift* in 1834 was a direct outgrowth of his dissatisfaction with the existing state of music and of his desire to bring about a rehabilitation of the poetic principle, "the very thing," as he said later on, "by which we should like to have these pages distinguished from others." The editorial position of the new journal is perhaps most forcefully summed up in Schumann's "speech from the throne" for 1839: "A stern attitude towards foreign trash, benevolence towards aspiring younger artists, enthusiasm for everything masterly that the past has bequeathed." On the whole, these aims are not so very different from those implicit in Berlioz; it is simply that Schumann has less self-interest and less worldly wisdom and that he goes about his task in a more serious way, more humbly and more charitably, if also with greater chauvinism.

"The present is characterized by its parties," Schumann writes in another connection (1836). "Like the political present, one can divide the musical into liberals, middlemen, and reactionaries, or into romanticists, moderns, and classicists. On the right sit the elderly—the contrapuntists, the anti-chromaticists; on the left the youthful—the revolutionaries in their Phrygian caps, the anti-formalists, the genially impudent, among whom the Beethovenians stand out as a special class; in the *Juste Milieu* young and old mingle irresolutely—here are included most of the creations of the day, the offspring which the moment brings forth and then destroys."

In his day, Schumann stood at the very center of the Romantic movement in German music, yet he makes little effort to define its aims and aspirations for us. To him, clearly, these were self-evident: "It is scarcely credible that a distinct romantic school could be formed in music, which is in itself romantic." But in his review of Stephen Heller's Opus 7 (1837) Schumann comes as close as he ever does to a definition and in so doing defines for us also his own personal style. "I am heartily sick of the word 'romanticist,' " he says; "I have not pronounced it ten times in my whole life; and yet—if I wished to confer a brief designation upon our young seer, I should call him one, and what a one! Of that vague, nihilistic disorder behind which some search for romanticism, and of that crass, scribbling materialism which the French neo-romanticists affect, our composer—thank Heaven!—knows nothing; on the contrary, he perceives things naturally, for the most part, and expresses himself clearly and judiciously. Yet on taking up his compositions one senses that there is something more than this lurking in the background—an attractive, individual half-light, more like dawn than dusk, which causes one to see his otherwise clear-cut configurations under an unaccustomed glow. . . . And do not let me overlook the dedication— the coincidence is astonishing. You recall, Eusebius, that we once dedicated something to the Wina of the *Flegeljahre* [by Jean Paul]; the dedication of these impromptus also names one of Jean Paul's constellations—Liane von Froulay [in Jean Paul's *Titan*]. We have in general much in common, an admission that no one should misinterpret—it is too obvious."

FROM *Davidsbündlerblätter*

INTRODUCTORY
(1854)

Near the end of the year 1833 there met in Leipzig, every evening and as though by chance, a number of musicians, chiefly younger men, primarily for social companionship, not less, however, for an exchange of ideas about the art which was for them the meat and drink of life—music. It cannot be said that

TEXT: *Gesammelte Schriften über Musik und Musiker* (Leipzig, 1854); for the essay "New Paths," *Neue Zeitschrift für Musik* 33 (1853): 185–86. Translation by Oliver Strunk. The title "Pages from the League of David" refers to warriors against the Philistines (2 Samuel 5).

musical conditions in Germany were particularly encouraging at the time. On the stage Rossini still ruled, at the piano, with few rivals, Herz and Hünten. And yet only a few years had elapsed since Beethoven, Weber, and Schubert had lived among us. Mendelssohn's star was in the ascendant, to be sure, and marvelous reports were heard of a Pole, one Chopin—but it was not until later that these exerted lasting influence. Then one day an idea flashed across the minds of these young hotheads: Let us not sit idly by; let us attack, that things may become better; let us attack, that the poetic in art may again be held in honor! In this way the first pages of a "New Journal for Music" came into being. But the joy of the solid unanimity of this union of young talents did not continue long. In one of the most cherished comrades, Ludwig Schunke,[1] death claimed a sacrifice. As to the others,[2] some removed from Leipzig altogether for a time. The undertaking was on the point of dissolution. Then one of their number, precisely the musical visionary of the company, one who had until now dreamed away his life more at the piano than among books, decided to take the editing of the publication in hand;[3] he continued to guide it for nearly ten years, to the year 1844. So there arose a series of essays, from which this volume offers a selection. The greater part of the views therein expressed are still his today. What he set down, in hope and fear, about many an artistic phenomenon has in the course of time been substantiated.

Here ought also to be mentioned another league, a more than secret one in that it existed only in the head of its founder—the "Davidsbündler." In order to represent various points of view within the view of art as a whole, it seemed not inappropriate to invent contrasted types of artist, among which Florestan and Eusebius were the most significant, between whom Master Raro stood as intermediary. Like a red thread, this "Davidsbündler" company wound itself through the journal, humorously blending "Wahrheit und Dichtung."[4] Later on, these comrades, not unwelcome to the readers of that time, disappeared entirely from the paper, and from the time when a Peri enticed them into distant climes, nothing further has been heard of their literary efforts.

Should these collected pages, while reflecting a highly agitated time, likewise contribute to divert the attention of those now living to artistic phenomena already nearly submerged by the stream of the present, the aim of their publication will have been fulfilled.

•　　•　　•　　•　　•

1. Talented composer and pianist, friend of Schumann's, coeditor of the *Zeitschrift* during its first year, Schunke died on December 7, 1834, shortly before his twenty-fourth birthday.
2. In addition to Schunke, Schumann's chief collaborators during the first year were Friedrich Wieck and Julius Knorr.
3. During its first year, the *Zeitschrift* described itself as "published by a society of artists and friends of art"; with the first number of the second volume this is changed to read "published under the direction of R. Schumann in association with a number of artists and friends of art."
4. An allusion to the title of Goethe's autobiography, *Aus meinem Leben: Dichtung und Wahrheit.*

AN OPUS TWO[5]
(1831)

Not long ago Eusebius stole quietly in through the door. You know the ironic smile on his pale face with which he seeks to arouse our expectations. I was sitting at the piano with Florestan, who, as you know, is one of those rare men of music who foresee, as it were, all coming, novel, or extraordinary things. None the less there was a surprise in store for him today. With the words "Hats off, gentlemen, a genius!" Eusebius placed a piece of music on the stand. We were not allowed to see the title. I leafed about absentmindedly among the pages; this veiled, silent enjoyment of music has something magical about it. Furthermore, as it seems to me, every composer has his own special way of arranging notes for the eye: Beethoven looks different on paper from Mozart, very much as Jean Paul's prose looks different from Goethe's. In this case, however, it was as though unfamiliar eyes were everywhere gazing out at me strangely—flower-eyes, basilisk-eyes, peacock-eyes, maiden-eyes; here and there things grew clearer—I thought I saw Mozart's "Là ci darem la mano" woven about with a hundred harmonies; Leporello seemed to be actually winking at me, and Don Giovanni flew past me in a white cloak. "Now play it!" Florestan suggested. Eusebius obeyed; huddled in a window alcove, we listened. As though inspired, Eusebius played on, leading past us countless figures from the realest of lives; it was as though the inspiration of the moment lifted his fingers above the usual measure of their capabilities. Florestan's entire approval, except for a blissful smile, consisted, to be sure, in nothing but the remark that the variations might perhaps be by Beethoven or Schubert, had either of them been piano virtuosi—but when he turned to the title page, read nothing more than:

> Là ci darem la mano
> varié pour le pianoforte par
> Frédéric Chopin
> Oeuvre 2

and both of us called out in amazement "An opus two!"—and when every face flowed somewhat with more than usual astonishment and, aside from a few exclamations, little was to be distinguished but: "At last, here's something sensible again—Chopin—the name is new to me—who is he?—in any case a genius—isn't that Zerlina laughing there or perhaps even Leporello?"—then, indeed, arose a scene which I prefer not to describe. Excited with wine, Chopin, and talking back and forth, we went off to Master Raro, who laughed a great deal and showed little curiosity about our Opus 2—"for I know you and your newfangled enthusiasm too well—just bring your Chopin here to me some time." We promised it for the next day. Presently Eusebius bid us an

---

5. This essay was published as early as 1831 in the *Allgemeine musikalische Zeitung*. As the one in which the Davidsbündler make their first appearance, it is given a place here also. [Au.]

indifferent good night; I remained for a while with Master Raro; Florestan, who for some time had had no lodgings, fled through the moonlit alley to my house. I found him in my room at midnight, lying on the sofa, his eyes closed.

"Chopin's variations," he began, as though in a dream, "they are still going around in my head. Surely the whole is dramatic and sufficiently Chopinesque; the introduction, self-contained though it is—can you recall Leporello's leaping thirds?—seems to me to belong least of all to the rest; but the theme—why does he write it in B-flat?—the variations, the final movement, and the Adagio—these are really something—here genius crops up in every measure. Of course, dear Julius, the speaking parts are Don Giovanni, Zerlina, Leporello, and Masetto. In the theme, Zerlina's reply is drawn amorously enough. The first variation might perhaps be called somewhat elegant and coquettish—in it, the Spanish grandee toys aimiably with the peasant maid. This becomes self-evident in the second, which is already much more intimate, comic, and quarrelsome, exactly as though two lovers were chasing each other and laughing more than usual. But in the third—how everything is changed! This is pure moonshine and fairy spell—Masetto watches from afar and curses rather audibly, to be sure, but Don Giovanni is little disturbed. And now the fourth—what is your idea of it? Eusebius played it quite clearly—doesn't it jump about saucily and impudently as it approaches the man, although the Adagio (it seems natural to me that Chopin repeats the first part) is in B-flat minor, than which nothing could be more fitting, for it reproaches the Don, as though moralizing, with his misdeeds. It is bold, surely, and beautiful that Leporello listens, laughs, and mocks from behind the shrubbery, that the oboes and clarinets pour out seductive magic, and that the B-flat major, in full blossom, marks well the moment of the first kiss. Yet all of this is as nothing in comparison with the final movement—is there more wine, Julius?—this is Mozart's whole finale—popping corks and clinking bottles everywhere, in the midst of things Leporello's voice, then the grasping evil spirits in pursuit, the fleeing Don Giovanni—and finally the end, so beautifully soothing, so truly conclusive." Only in Switzerland, Florestan added, had he experienced anything similar to this ending; there, on a fine day, when the evening sun climbs higher and higher to the topmost peak where finally its last beam vanishes, there comes a moment in which one seems to see the white Alp-giants close their eyes. One feels only that one has seen a heavenly vision. "Now Julius, wake up, you too, to new dreams—and go to sleep!"

"Florestan of my heart," I answered, "these private feelings are perhaps praiseworthy, if somewhat subjective; but little as Chopin needs to think of listening to his genius, I still shall also bow my head before such genius, such aspiration, such mastery."

With that we fell asleep.

Julius[6]

6. This essay was Schumann's first published writing.

FLORESTAN'S SHROVE TUESDAY ADDRESS DELIVERED AFTER A PERFORMANCE OF BEETHOVEN'S LAST SYMPHONY
(1835)

Florestan climbed on to the piano and spoke as follows:

Assembled Davidsbündler, that is, youths and men who are to slay the Philistines, musical and otherwise, especially the tallest ones (see the last numbers of the *Comet*[7] for 1833).

I am never overenthusiastic, best of friends! The truth is, I know the symphony better than I know myself. I shall not waste a word on it. After it, anything I could say would be as dull as ditch water, Davidsbündler. I have celebrated regular Ovidian Tristia, have heard anthropological lectures. One can scarcely be fanatical about some things, scarcely paint some satires with one's facial expression, scarcely—as Jean Paul's Giannozzo[8] did—sit low enough in the balloon for men not to believe that one concerns oneself about them, so far, far below do these two-legged creatures, which one calls men, file through the narrow pass, which one may in any case call life. To be sure, I was not at all annoyed by what little I heard. In the main I laughed at Eusebius. A regular clown, he flew impertinently at a fat neighbor who inquired confidentially during the Adagio: "Sir, did not Beethoven also write a battle symphony?" "Yes, that's the 'Pastoral' Symphony," our Euseb replied indifferently. "Quite right, so it is," the fat one expanded, resuming his meditations.

Men must deserve noses, otherwise God would not have provided them. They tolerate much, these audiences, and of this I could cite you magnificent examples; for instance, rascal, when at a concert you were turning the pages of one of Field's nocturnes for me. Unluckily, on one of the most broken-down rattle-boxes that was ever inflicted upon a company of listeners, instead of the pedal I stumbled on the Janissary stop[9]—piano enough, fortunately, so that I could yield to the impulse of the moment and, repeating the stroke softly from time to time, could let the audience believe some sort of march was being played in the distance. Of course Eusebius did his part by spreading the story; the audience, however, outdid themselves in applause.

Any number of similar anecdotes had occurred to me during the Adagio—when the first chord of the Finale broke in. "What is it, Cantor," I said to a trembling fellow next to me, "but a triad with a suspended fifth, somewhat whimsically laid out, in that one does not know which to accept as the bass—

---

7. An "Unterhaltungsblatt" published in Altenburg from 1830 to 1836. In its issue for August 27, 1832, it had printed Schumann's "Reminiscences from Clara Wieck's Last Concerts in Leipzig."
8. Principal character in Jean Paul's "Des Luftschiffers Giannozzo Seebuch," one of the humorous supplements to the second volume of his *Titan* (1801).
9. A pedal producing the effect of bass drum and cymbals or triangle, much favored during the vogue of "Turkish music."

the A of the kettledrum or the F of the bassoons? Just have a look at Türk, Section 19, page 7!"[10] "Sir, you speak very loud and are surely joking." With a small and terrifying voice I whispered in his ear: "Cantor, watch out for storms! The lightning sends ahead no liveried lackeys before it strikes; at the most there is first a storm and after it a thunderbolt. That's just its way." "All the same, such dissonances ought to be prepared." Just at that moment came the second one. "Cantor, the fine trumpet seventh shall excuse you." I was quite exhausted with my restraint—I should have soothed him with a sound blow.

Now you gave me a memorable moment, conductor, when you hit the tempo of the low theme in the basses so squarely on the line that I forgot much of my annoyance at the first movement, in which, despite the modest pretense of the direction "Un poco maestoso," there speaks the full, deliberate stride of godlike majesty.

"What do you suppose Beethoven meant by those basses?" "Sir," I replied gravely enough, "a genius often jests; it seems to be a sort of night watchman's song." Gone was the exquisite moment, once again Satan was set loose. Then I remarked the Beethoven devotees—the way they stood there goggle-eyed, saying: "That's by our Beethoven. That's a German work. In the last movement there's a double fugue. Some reproach him for not excelling in this department, but how he has done it—yes, this is *our* Beethoven." Another choir chimed in with: "It seems as though all forms of poetry are combined in the work: in the first movement the epic, in the second the humorous, in the third the lyric, in the fourth—the blend of them all—the drama." Still another choir really applied itself to praising: "It's a gigantic work, colossal, comparable to the pyramids of Egypt." Still another went in for description: "The symphony tells the story of man's creation: first chaos, then the divine command 'Let there be light,' then the sun rising on the first man, who is delighted with such splendor—in short, it is the whole first chapter of the Pentateuch."

I became more frantic and more quiet. And while they were eagerly following the text and finally applauding, I seized Eusebius by the arm and pulled him down the brightly lighted stairs, smiling faces on either hand.

Below, in the darkness of the street lamps, Eusebius said, as though to himself: "Beethoven—what depths there are in the word, even the deep sonority of the syllables resounding as into an eternity! For this name, it is as though there could be no other characters." "Eusebius," I said with genuine calm, "do you too condescend to praise Beethoven? Like a lion, he would have raised himself up before you and have asked: 'Who, then, are you who presume this?' I do not address myself to you, Eusebius; you mean well—but must a great man then always have a thousand dwarfs in his train? They believe they understand him—who so aspired, who struggled against countless attacks—as they

10. Daniel Gottlob Türk, *Kurze Anweisung zum Generalbaßspielen* (Halle, 1791).

smile and clap their hands. Do those who are not accountable to me for the simplest musical rule have the effrontery to evaluate a master as a whole? Do these, all of whom I put to flight if I drop merely the word 'counterpoint'—do these who perhaps appreciate this and that at second hand and at once call out: 'Oh, this fits our corpus perfectly!'—do these who wish to talk of exceptions to rules they do not know—do these who prize in him, not the measure of his gigantic powers, but precisely the excess—shallow men of the world—wandering sorrows of Werther—overgrown, bragging boys—do these presume to love him, even praise him?"

Davidsbündler, at the moment I can think of no one so entitled but the provincial Silesian nobleman who recently wrote to a music dealer in this fashion:

> Dear sir:
>   At last I have my music cabinet nearly in order. You ought to see how splendid it is. Alabaster columns on the inside, a mirror with silk curtains, busts of composers—in short, magnificent! In order, however, to give it a final touch of real elegance I ask you to send me, further, the complete works of Beethoven, *for I like this composer very much.*

What more there is that I should say, I should, in my opinion, scarcely know.

ENTHUSIASTIC LETTERS[11]
(1835)

I. EUSEBIUS TO CHIARA

After each of our musical feasts for the soul there always reappears an angelic face which, down to the roguish line about the chin, more than resembles that of a certain Clara.[12] Why are you not with us, and how may you have thought last night of us Firlenzer, from the "Calm Sea"[13] to the resplendent ending of the Symphony in B-flat major?[14]

Except for a concert itself, I know of nothing finer than the hour before one, during which one hums ethereal melodies to oneself, the finger on the lips, walks up and down discreetly on one's toes, performs whole overtures on the windowpanes. . . . Just then it struck a quarter of. And now, with Florestan, I mounted the polished stairs.

---

11. These letters might also have been called "Wahrheit und Dichtung." They have to do with the first Gewandhaus concerts held under Mendelssohn's direction in October, 1835. [Au.]
    The concerts in question were the first four in the subscription series; their dates were October 4, 11, 22, and 29. They are also covered in more conventional reviews published in the *Allgemeine musikalische Zeitung* for October 14 and 21 and for December 16, with the help of which it is possible to supply certain details passed over in Schumann's account.
12. Quoted from an earlier letter to Clara (*Jugendbriefe* [Leipzig, 1885], p. 266). At the time of the writing of these letters, Clara Wieck was just sixteen.
13. Mendelssohn's overture.
14. Beethoven's Fourth Symphony.

"Seb," said he, "I look forward tonight to many things: first to the whole program itself, for which one thirsts after the dry summer; then to F. Meritis,[15] who for the first time marches into battle with his orchestra; then to the singer Maria,[16] with her vestal voice; finally to the public as a whole, expecting miracles—that public to which, as you know, I usually attach only too little importance." At the word "public" we stood before the old chatelain with his Commendatore face, who had much to do and finally let us in with an expression of annoyance, for as usual Florestan had forgotten his ticket. As I entered the brightly lighted golden hall I may, to judge from my face, have delivered perhaps the following address:

"With gentle tread I make my entrance, for I seem to see welling up here and there the faces of those unique ones to whom is given the fine art of uplifting and delighting hundreds in a single moment. There I see Mozart, stamping his feet to the symphony until a shoe-buckle flies off; there Hummel, the old master, improvising at the piano; there Catalani, pulling off her shawl, for the sound-absorbing carpet has been forgotten; there Weber; there Spohr; and many another. And there I thought also of you, my pure bright Chiara— of how at other times you spied down from your box with the lorgnette that so well becomes you." This train of thought was interrupted by the angry eye of Florestan, who stood, rooted to the spot, in his old corner by the door, and in his angry eye stood something like this:

"Think, Public, of my having you together again at last and of my being able to set you one against another. . . . Long ago, overt ones, I wanted to establish concerts for deaf-mutes which might serve you as a pattern of how to behave at concerts, especially at the finest. . . . Like Tsing-Sing,[17] you were to have been turned to a stone pagoda, had you dared to repeat anything of what you saw in music's magic realm," and so forth. The sudden deathlike silence of the public broke in on my reflections. F. Meritis came forward. A hundred hearts went out to him in that first moment.

Do you remember how, leaving Padua one evening, we went down the Brenta; how the tropical Italian night closed the eyes of one after another? And how, in the morning, a voice suddenly called out: "Ecco, ecco, signori— Venezia!"—and the sea lay spread out before us, calm and stupendous; how on the furthest horizon there sounded up and down a delicate tinkle, as though the little waves were speaking to one another in a dream? Behold—such is the wafting and weaving of the "Calm Sea";[18] one actually grows drowsy from it and is rather thought than thinking. The Beethovenian chorus after Goethe[19] and the accentuated word sound almost raw in contrast to the spider's-web

15. Mendelssohn.
16. Henriette Grabau.
17. A character in Auber's opera *Le Cheval de bronze* (1835).
18. The overture by Mendelssohn.
19. Beethoven's Opus 112.

tone of the violins. Toward the end there occurs a single detached harmony—here perhaps a Nereid fixes the poet with her seductive glance, seeking to draw him under—then for the first time a wave beats higher, the sea grows by degrees more talkative, the sails flutter, the pennant leaps with joy, and now holloa, away, away, away. . . . Which overture of F. Meritis did I prefer, some artless person asked me; at once the tonalities E minor, B minor, and D major[20] entwined themselves as in a triad of the Graces and I could think of no answer better than the best—"Each one!" F. Meritis conducted as though he had composed the overture himself, and though the orchestra played accordingly, I was struck by Florestan's remarking that he himself had played rather in this style when he came from the provinces to Master Raro as an apprentice. "My most fatal crisis," he continued, "was this intermediate state between nature and art; always ardent as was my grasp, I had now to take everything slowly and precisely, for my technique was everywhere found wanting; presently there arose such a stumbling and stiffness that I began to doubt my talent; the crisis, fortunately, did not last long." I for my part was disturbed, in the overture as in the symphony, by the baton,[21] and I agreed with Florestan when he held that, in the symphony, the orchestra should stand there as a republic, acknowledging no superior. At the same time it was a joy to see F. Meritis and the way in which his eye anticipated every nuance in the music's intellectual windings, from the most delicate to the most powerful, and in which, as the most blissful one, he swam ahead of the rest, so different from those conductors on whom one sometimes chances, who threaten with their scepter to beat score, orchestra, and public all in one.

You know how little patience I have with quarrels over tempi and how for me the movement's inner measure is the sole determinant. Thus the relatively fast Allegro that is cold sounds always more sluggish than the relatively slow one that is sanguine. In the orchestra it is also a question of quality—where this is relatively coarse and dense the orchestra can give to the detail and to the whole more emphasis and import; where this is relatively small and fine, as with our Firlenzer, one must help out the lack of resonance with driving tempi. In a word, the Scherzo of the symphony seemed to me too slow; one noticed this quite clearly also in the restlessness with which the orchestra sought to be at rest. Still, what is this to you in Milan—and, strictly speaking, how little it is to me, for I can after all imagine the Scherzo just as I want it whenever I please.

You asked whether Maria would find Firlenz as cordial as it used to be. How can you doubt it? Only she chose an aria which brought her more honor as an artist than applause as a virtuosa.[22] Then a Westphalian music director[23] played

20. A Midsummer Night's Dream, Fingal's Cave, Calm Sea and Happy Voyage.
21. Before Mendelssohn, in the days when Matthai was in charge, the orchestral works were performed without a conductor beating time.
22. Weber's inserted aria (1818) "Was sag ich? Schaudern macht mich der Gedanke!" for Cherubini's Lodoiska (1791).
23. Otto Gerke.

a violin concerto by Spohr[24]—good enough, but too lean and colorless.

In the choice of pieces, everyone professed to see a change in policy; if formerly, from the very beginning of the Firlenzer concerts, Italian butterflies fluttered about the German oaks, this time these last stood quite alone, as powerful as they were somber. One party sought to read in this a reaction; I take it rather for chance than for intention. All of us know how necessary it is to protect Germany from an invasion by your favorites; let this be done with foresight, however, and more by encouraging the youthful spirits in the Fatherland than by a needless defense against a force which, like a fashion, comes in and goes out.

Just at midnight Florestan came in with Jonathan, a new Davidsbündler, the two of them fencing furiously with one another over the aristocracy of mind and the republic of opinion. At last Florestan has found an opponent who gives him diamonds to crack. Of this mighty one you will hear more later on.

Enough for today. Do not forget to look in the calendar sometimes for August 13, where an Aurora links your name with mine.

Eusebius.

2. TO CHIARA

The letter carrier coming toward me blossomed out into a flower when I saw the shimmering red "Milano" on your letter. With delight I too recall my first visit to the Scala, just when Rubini was singing there with Méric-Lalande. For Italian music one must listen to in Italian company; German music one can enjoy under any sky.

I was quite right in not reading into the program of the last concert a reactionary intention, for the very next ones brought something Hesperidian. Whereat it was Florestan who amused me most; he finds this actually tiresome, and—out of mere irritation with those Handelians and other fanatics who talk as though they had themselves composed the *Samson* in their nightshirts—does not exactly attack the Hesperidian music, but compares it vaguely with "fruit salad," with "Titian flesh without spirit," and so forth, yet in so comical a tone that you could laugh out loud, did not his eagle eye bear down on you. "As a matter of fact," he said on one occasion, "to be annoyed with Italian things is long since out of fashion, and, in any case, why beat about with a club in this flowery fragrance which flies in and flies out? I should not know which world to choose—one full of nothing but refractory Beethovens or one full of dancing swans of Pesaro. Only two things puzzle me: our fair singers, who after all never know what to sing (excepting everything or nothing)—why do they never chance on something small, say, on a song by Weber, Schubert, Wiedebein; and then our German composers of vocal music, who complain that so little of their work reaches the concert hall—why do they never think of concert pieces, concert arias, concert scenas, and write something of this kind?"

24. No. 11 in G major, Opus 70.

The singer[25] (not Maria), who sang something from *Torvaldo*,[26] began her "Dove son? Chi m'aita?" in such a tremble that I responded inwardly: "In Firlenz, deary; aide-toi et le ciel t'aidera!" Presently, however, she showed her brighter side, the public its well-meant approval. "If only our German song-birds," Florestan interposed, "would not look on themselves as children who think one does not see them when they close their eyes; as it is, they usually hide themselves so stealthily behind their music that one pays the more atten-tion to their faces and thus notices the difference between them and those Italian girls whom I saw singing at one another in the Academy at Milan with eyes rolling so wildly that I feared their artificial passion might burst into flames; this last I exaggerate—still, I should like to read in German eyes some-thing of the dramatic situation, something of the music's joy and grief; beautiful singing from a face of marble makes one doubtful of inner advantage; I mean this in a sort of general way."

Then you ought to have seen Meritis playing the Mendelssohn Concerto in G Minor! Seating himself at the piano as innocently as a child, he now took captive one heart after another, drawing them along behind him in swarms, and, when he set you free, you knew only that you had flown past Grecian isles of the gods and had been set down again in the Firlenzer hall, safe and sound. "You are a very happy master in your art," said Florestan to Meritis when it was over, and both of them were right. Though my Florestan had spoken not a word to me about the concert, I caught him very neatly yesterday. To be pre-cise, I saw him turning over the leaves of a book and noting something down. When he had gone, opposite this passage in his diary—"About some things in this world there is nothing to be said at all—for example, about Mozart's C Major Symphony with the fugue, about many things in Shakespeare, about some things in Beethoven"—I read, written in the margin: "And about Meritis, when he plays the concerto by M."

We were highly delighted with an energetic overture of Weber's,[27] the mother of so many of those little fellows who tag along behind her, ditto with a violin concerto played by young ———,[28] for it does one good to be able to prophesy with conviction of a hard worker that his path will lead to mastery. With things repeated year in and year out—symphonies excepted—I shall not detain you. Your earlier comment on Onslow's Symphony in A[29]—that, having heard it twice, you knew it by heart, bar for bar—is also mine, although I do not know the real reason for this rapid commission to memory. On the one hand I see that the instruments still cling to one another too much and are piled on one another too heterogeneously; on the other hand the melodic

25. Fräulein Weinhold, from Amsterdam.
26. Rossini's *Torvaldo e Dorliska.*
27. Either the Overture to the *Beherrscher der Geister,* played at the third concert on October 22, or that to *Euryanthe,* played at the fourth concert on October 29, probably the former.
28. Wilhelm Uhlrich, who played a concerto by L. W. Maurer.
29. No. 1, Op. 41, played at the fourth concert, on October 29.

threads—the principal and subsidiary ideas—come through so decidedly that, in view of the thick instrumental combination, their very prominence seems to me most strange. The principle ruling here is a mystery to me, and I cannot express it clearly. Perhaps it will stir you to reflection. I feel most at home in the elegant ballroom turmoil of the Minuet, where everything sparkles with pearls and diamonds; in the Trio I see a scene in an adjoining sitting room, into which, through the frequently opened ballroom doors, there penetrates the sound of violins, drowning out words of love. What do you think?

This brings me very conveniently indeed to the A Major Symphony of Beethoven[30] which we heard not long ago. Moderately delighted, we went, late in the evening as it was, to Master Raro. You know Florestan—the way he sits at the piano and, while improvising, speaks, laughs, weeps, gets up, sits down again, and so forth, as though in his sleep. Zilia[31] sat in the bay window, other Davidsbündler here and there in various groups. There was much discussion. "I had to laugh"—thus Florestan began, beginning at the same time the beginning of the symphony—"to laugh at a dried-up notary who discovered in it a battle of Titans, with their effectual destruction in the last movement, but who stole quietly past the Allegretto because it did not fit in with his idea; to laugh in general at those who talk endlessly of the innocence and absolute beauty of music in itself—of course art should conceal, and not repeat, the unfortunate octaves and fifths of life—of course I find, often in certain saintly arias (for example, Marschner's), beauty without truth and, sometimes in Beethoven (but seldom), the latter without the former. But most of all my fingers itch to get at those who maintain that Beethoven, in his symphonies, surrendered always to the grandest sentiments, the sublimest reflections, on God, immortality, and the cosmos, for if that gifted man does point toward heaven with the branches of his flowering crown, he none the less spreads out his roots in his beloved earth. To come to the symphony, the idea that follows is not mine at all, but rather someone's in an old number of the *Cäcilia*[32] (the scene there changed—out of a perhaps exaggerated delicacy toward Beethoven which might well have been spared—to the elegant hall of a count or some such place).

"It is the merriest of weddings, the bride a heavenly child with a rose in her hair—but with one only. I am mistaken if the guests do not gather in the introduction, do not greet one another profusely with inverted commas—very much mistaken if merry flutes do not remind us that the whole village, with its maypoles and their many-colored ribbons, takes joy in Rosa, the bride—very much mistaken if the trembling glance of her pale mother does not seem to ask: 'Dost not know that we must part?' and if Rosa, quite overcome, does not throw herself into her mother's arms, drawing the bridegroom after her with one hand. Now it grows very quiet in the village outside (here Florestan

30. Played at the third concert, on October 22.
31. Clara Wieck.
32. A musical journal published in Mainz by Schott, beginning in 1824.

entered the Allegretto, breaking off pieces here and there); only from time to time a butterfly floats by or a cherry blossom falls. The organ begins, the sun stands at its height, occasional long diagonal beams play through the church with bits of dust, the bells ring diligently, churchgoers gradually take their places, pews are opened and shut, some peasants look closely at their hymn-books, others up into the choir loft, the procession draws nearer—at its head choirboys with lighted tapers and censers, then friends—often turning around to stare at the couple accompanied by the priest—then the parents and friends of the bride, with the assembled youth of the village bringing up the rear. How everything arranges itself, how the priest ascends to the altar, how he addresses, now the bride and now the fortunate one, how he speaks to them of the duties of the bond and of its purposes and of how they may find happi-ness in harmony and love of one another, how he then asks for her 'I do,' which assumes so much forever and forever, and how she pronounces it, firm and sustained—all this prevents my painting the picture further—do as you please with the finale"—thus Florestan broke off, tearing into the end of the Alle-gretto, and it sounded as though the sexton had so slammed the doors shut that the whole church echoed.

Enough. In me, too, Florestan's interpretation has stirred up something, and my alphabet begins to run together. There is much more for me to tell you, but the outdoors calls. Wait out the interval until my next letter with faith in a better beginning.

Eusebius.

DANCE LITERATURE
(1836)

J. C. Kessler:[33] Three Polonaises, Op. 25
Sigismund Thalberg:[34] Twelve Waltzes, Op. 4
Clara Wieck: *Valses romantiques*, Op. 4
Leopold, Edler von Meyer:[35] Salon (Six Waltzes), Op. 4
Franz Schubert: First Waltzes, Op. 9, Bk. I
The same: *Deutsche Tänze*, Op. 33

"And now play, Zilia! I wish to duck myself quite under in the harmonies and only occasionally to poke out my head in order that you may not think me drowned from melancholy; for dance music makes one sad and lax, just as church music, quite the other way, makes one joyful and active—me at least." Thus spake Florestan, as Zilia was already floating through the first Kessler

33. Joseph Christoph Kessler, concert pianist and composer for the piano, piano teacher in Lem-berg, Warsaw, Breslau, and Vienna.
34. Sigismund Thalberg, composer for the piano and concert pianist of the first rank, Liszt's chief rival, toured the United States in 1857 together with Vieuxtemps.
35. Pupil of Czerny, concert pianist, toured the United States from 1845 to 1847 and again in 1867 and 1868.

polonaise. "Indeed it would be lovely," he continued, half-listening, half-speaking, "if a dozen lady-Davidsbündler were to make the evening memorable and would embrace each other in a festival of the Graces. Jean Paul has already remarked that girls ought really to dance only with girls (though this would lead, indeed, to there being some weddings fewer); men (I add) ought never to dance at all."

"Should they do so none the less," Eusebius interrupted, "when they come to the trio, he ought to say to his partner-Davidsbündler, 'How simple and how kind you are!' and, in the second part, it would be well if she were to drop her bouquet, to be picked up in flying past and rewarded with a grateful glance."

All this, however, was expressed more in Euseb's bearing and in the music than in anything he actually said. Florestan only tossed his head from time to time, especially at the third polonaise, most brilliant and filled with sounds of horn and violin.

"Now something livelier, and do you play the Thalberg, Euseb; Zilia's fingers are too delicate for it," said Florestan, who soon interrupted to ask that the sections be not repeated, since the waltzes were too transparent—particularly the ninth, which remained on one level, indeed on one measure—"and eternally tonic and dominant, dominant and tonic. Still, it's good enough for those whose ears are in their feet." But, at the end, the one who stood at the foot (a student) called out "Da capo!" in all seriousness, and everyone was obliged to laugh at Florestan's fury at this and at the way he shouted him down, telling him that he might be on his way, that he should interrupt with no further encouragements of this sort or he would silence him with an hour-long trill in thirds, and so forth.

"By a lady, then?" a reviewer might begin, seeing the *Valses romantiques.* "Well, well! Here we shan't need to hunt long for fifths and for the melody!"

Zilia held out four short moonlit harmonies. All listened intently. But on the piano there lay a sprig of roses—Florestan always had vases of flowers in place of the candelabras—and, shaken by the vibration, this had gradually slid down onto the keys. Reaching out for a note in the bass, Zilia struck against this too violently and left off playing, for her finger bled. Florestan asked what the matter was. "Nothing," said Zilia; "as in these waltzes, there is as yet no great pain, only a drop of blood charmed forth by roses." And may she who said this know no other.

A moment later, Florestan plunged into the midst of the brilliant countesses and ambassadresses of the Meyer *salon.* How soothing this is—wealth and beauty, the height of rank and style, with music at the summit; every one speaks and no one listens, for the music drowns all out in waves! "For this," Florestan blurted out, "one really needs an instrument with an extra octave to the right and left, so that one can properly spread out and celebrate." You can have no idea of how Florestan plays this sort of thing and of how he storms away, carrying you along with him. The Davidsbündler, too, were quite worked up, calling in their excitement (musical excitement is insatiable) for "more and more," till Serpentin[36] suggested choosing between the Schubert waltzes and the Chopin boleros. "If, throwing myself at the keyboard from here," Florestan shouted, placing himself in a corner away from the piano, "I can hit the first chord of the last movement of the D Minor Symphony,[37] Schubert wins." He hit it, of course. Zilia played the waltzes by heart.

First waltzes by Franz Schubert. Tiny sprites, ye who hover no higher above the ground than, say, the height of a flower—to be sure, I don't care for the *Sehnsuchtswalzer*, in which a hundred girlish emotions have already bathed, or for the last three either, an aesthetic blemish on the whole for which I can't forgive the author—but the way in which the others turn about these, weaving them in, more or less, with fragrant threads, and the way in which there runs through all of them a so fanciful thoughtlessness that one becomes part of it oneself and believes at the last that one is still playing in the first—this is really first-rate.

In the *Deutsche Tänze*, on the other hand, there dances, to be sure, a whole carnival. "'Twould be fine," Florestan shouted in Fritz Friedrich's[38] ear, "if you would get your magic lantern and follow the masquerade in shadows on the wall." Exit and reenter the latter, jubilant.

The group that follows is one of the most charming. The room dimly lighted—Zilia at the piano, the wounding rose in her hair—Eusebius in his black velvet coat, leaning over her chair—Florestan (ditto), standing on the table and ciceronizing—Serpentin, his legs twined round Walt's[39] neck, sometimes riding back and forth—the painter à la Hamlet, parading his shadow figures through the bull's-eye, some spider-legged ones even running off the wall on to the ceiling. Zilia began, and Florestan may have spoken substantially to this effect, though at much greater length:

"No. 1. In A major. Masks milling about. Kettledrums. Trumpets. The lights go down. Perruquier: 'Everything seems to be going very well.' No. 2. Comic character, scratching himself behind the ears and continually calling out 'Pst, pst!' Exit. No. 3. Harlequin, arms akimbo. Out the door, head over heels. No. 4. Two stiff and elegant masks, dancing and scarcely speaking to one another. No. 5. Slim cavalier, chasing a mask: 'At last I've caught you, lovely zither player!' 'Let me go!' She escapes. No. 6. Hussar at attention, with plume and sabretache. No. 7. Two harvesters, waltzing together blissfully. He, softly: 'Is it thou?' They recognize each other. No. 8. Tenant farmer from the country, getting ready to dance. No. 9. The great doors swing open. Splendid procession of knights and noble ladies. No. 10. Spaniard to an Ursuline: 'Speak at least, since you may not love!' She: 'I would rather not speak, and be understood!' . . ."

But in the midst of the waltz Florestan sprang from the table and out the

36. Carl Banck, music critic and composer of songs.
37. See above, p. 104.
38. The deaf painter. [Au.] The painter J. P. Lyser.
39. The pianist Louis Rakemann, who emigrated to America in 1839.

door. One was used to this in him. Zilia, too, soon left off, and the others scattered in one direction and another.

Florestan, you know, has a habit of often breaking off in the very moment when his enjoyment is at its height, perhaps in order to impress it in all its freshness and fullness on the memory. And this time he had his way—for whenever his friends speak to each other of their happiest evenings, they always recall the twenty-eighth of December, 18— . . .

NEW PATHS
(1853)

Years have passed—nearly as many as I devoted to the former editorship of this journal, namely ten—since last I raised my voice within these covers, so rich in memories. Often, despite my intense creative activity, I have felt myself stimulated; many a new and significant talent has appeared; a new musical force has seemed to be announcing itself—as has been made evident by many of the aspiring artists of recent years, even though their productions are chiefly familiar to a limited circle.[40] Following the paths of these chosen ones with the utmost interest, it has seemed to me that, after such a preparation, there would and must suddenly appear some day one man who would be singled out to make articulate in an ideal way the highest expression of our time, one man who would bring us mastery, not as the result of a gradual development, but as Minerva, springing fully armed from the head of Cronus. And he is come, a young creature over whose cradle graces and heroes stood guard. His name is *Johannes Brahms,* and he comes from Hamburg where he has been working in silent obscurity, trained in the most difficult theses of his art by an excellent teacher who sends me enthusiastic reports of him,[41] recommended to me recently by a well-known and respected master. Even outwardly, he bore in his person all the marks that announce to us a chosen man. Seated at the piano, he at once discovered to us wondrous regions. We were drawn into a circle whose magic grew on us more and more. To this was added an altogether inspired style of playing which made of the piano an orchestra of lamenting and exultant voices. There were sonatas—veiled symphonies, rather; lieder, whose poetry one could understand without knowing the words, although a deep vocal melody ran through them all; single piano pieces, in part of a demonic nature, most attractive in form; then sonatas for violin and piano; string quartets—and every work so distinct from any other that each seemed to flow from a different source. And then it seemed as though, roaring along like a river, he united them all as in a waterfall, bearing aloft a peaceful rainbow

40. Here I have in mind Joseph Joachim, Ernst Naumann, Ludwig Norman, Woldemar Bargiel, Theodor Kirchner, Julius Schäffer, Albert Dietrich, not to forget that profoundly thoughtful student of the great in art, the sacred composer C. F. Wisling. As their valiant advance guard I might also mention Niels Wilhelm Gade, C. F. Mangold, Robert Franz, and Stephen Heller. [Au.]

41. Eduard Marxsen, in Hamburg. [Au.]

above the plunging waters below, surrounded at the shore by playful butterflies and borne along by the calls of nightingales.

Later, if he will wave with his magic wand to where massed forces, in the chorus and orchestra, lend their strength, there lie before us still more wondrous glimpses into the secrets of the spirit world. May the highest genius strengthen him for what expectation warrants, for there is also latent in him another genius—that of modesty. His comrades greet him on his first entrance into the world, where there await him wounds, perhaps, but also palms and laurels; we welcome him as a valiant warrior.

In every time, there reigns a secret league of kindred spirits. Tighten the circle, you who belong to it, in order that the truth in art may shine forth more and more brightly, everywhere spreading joy and peace.

R. S.

158 Franz Liszt and Carolyne von Sayn-Wittgenstein

On November 17, 1852, Hector Berlioz's fourteen-year-old *Benvenuto Cellini,* which had not been heard since its dismal failure at the Paris Opéra in 1838 and 1839, was brilliantly revived in Weimar under Franz Liszt's direction. This was neither the first nor the last of Liszt's generous gestures on behalf of his old friend. Years earlier, in Paris, Liszt had been one of Berlioz's most zealous and most effective partisans. In February 1855 he was to arrange a second "Berlioz Week" in Weimar, and at this time the essay on Berlioz's *Harold,* and old project, began to take definite shape. A third series of concerts, in January 1856, led indirectly to the writing and composition of *Les Troyens.*

For some time now, controversy has reigned about the role taken by Liszt in the production of his prose works, as opposed to roles that may have been played by Countess Marie d'Agoult and Princess Carolyne von Sayn-Wittgenstein. Unfortunately, the scholarly debate has been conducted in an oddly polarized manner, one school insisting that Liszt plagiarized the work in its entirety from the two women, the other rescuing the composer from this charge by arguing that neither woman contributed anything beyond secretarial services and ill-advised interference. Although it is clear that each piece of writing must be evaluated individually, the truth in general seems to lie somewhere between the two extremes, in a collaborative effort of some sort.

Carolyne von Sayn-Wittgenstein, a woman of unusually broad education and of intellectual bent, was Liszt's companion during the years he lived in Weimar and his close friend afterward. That it was she who first suggested the essay on Berlioz is clear from the published correspondence, from which, however, it is also clear that Liszt was to provide sketches for her to "develop." The correspondence shows further that Liszt spoke out when "developments" of this kind displeased him, that in the case of the essay on Berlioz he corrected a proof of the first installment, and that the Princess was obliged to consult him before she could cancel a trifling change that he had made in her wording of the title.

FROM *Berlioz and His* *"Harold" Symphony*
(1855)

[PART 1]

In the realm of ideas there are internal wars, like those of the Athenians, during which everyone is declared traitor to his fatherland who does not publicly take one side or the other and remains an idle spectator of the evil to which the struggle leads. Persuaded of the justice of this procedure, which, if rigorously observed, can only help to put an end to differences and to hasten the victory of those destined for future leadership, we have never concealed our lively and sympathetic admiration for the genius whom we intend to examine today, for the master to whom the art of our time is so decidedly indebted.

All the pros and cons of the noisy quarrel that has sprung up since the appearance of his first works can be reduced to one main point, to suggest which will suffice to show that the consequences inherent in his example go far beyond the pronouncements of those who consider themselves infallible arbitrators in these matters. The blunt antipathies, the accusations of musical high treason, the banishments for life which have been imposed on Berlioz since his first appearance—these have their explanation (why deceive ourselves about it?) in the holy horror, in the pious astonishment which came over musical authorities at the principle implicit in all his works, a principle that can be briefly stated in this form: *The artist may pursue the beautiful outside the rules of the school without fear that, as a result of this, it will elude him.* His opponents may assert that he has abandoned the ways of the old masters; this is easy—who wishes to persuade them of the contrary? His adherents may give themselves the greatest pains to prove that his way is neither always nor yet

TEXT: "Berlioz und seine Haroldsymphonie." *Neue Zeitschrift für Musik* 43 (1855): 25–26, 42–43, 45–46, 49–50, 51–52, 77–79. The essay was published in five installments; the present abridged translation includes the beginning of the first installment, portions of the second and third, and the beginning of the fourth. As printed in 1855, the text is a translation into German, by Richard Pohl, from the French original of Liszt and the Princess Wittgenstein. The later German "translation," by Lina Ramann (*Gesammelte Schriften*, vol. 4 (Leipzig, 1882), 1–102) is simply a fussy revision of the earlier one. Translation by Oliver Strunk.

wholly and completely different from that to which one was formerly used; what do they gain thereby? Both parties remain convinced that Berlioz adheres no less firmly to the creed which we have just pronounced, whether this is demonstrated in fact by one or by one hundred corroborating circumstances. And for the authorities who have arrogated to themselves the privileges of orthodoxy this is a more than sufficient proof of his heresy. Yet since in art no sect maintains a dogma on the basis of revelation and only tradition is authoritative; since music in particular does not, like painting and sculpture, recognize or adhere to an absolute model; the deciding of disputes between orthodox and heresiarchs depends not only on the court of past and present science, but also on the sense for art and for the reasonable in the coming generation. Only after a considerable lapse of time can a final decision be handed down, for what verdict of the present will be acceptable on the one hand to the older generation,[1] which has borne from youth the easy yoke of habit, and on the other hand to the younger generation, who gather belligerently under any banner and love a fight for its own sake? Old and young must then entrust the solution of problems of this sort to a more or less distant future. To this future is alone reserved the complete or partial acceptance of those *violations of certain rules of art and habits of hearing* with which Berlioz is reproached. One point, however, is now already beyond all question. The representatives of the development to come will entertain a quite special respect for works exhibiting such enormous powers of conception and thought and will find themselves obliged to study them intensively, just as even now contemporaries approach them *nolens volens* step by step, their admiration only too often delayed by idle astonishment. Even though these works violate the rules, in that they destroy the hallowed frame which has devolved upon the symphony; even though they offend the ear, in that in the expression of their content they do not remain within the prescribed musical dikes; it will be none the less impossible to ignore them later on as one ignores them now, with the apparent intention of exempting oneself from tribute, from homage, toward a contemporary.

•   •   •   •   •

[PART 2]

Who has the temerity to deny to our inspired art the supreme power of self-sufficiency? But need making oneself master of a new form mean forever renouncing the hereditary and historically inculcated one? Does one forswear

---

1. "The majority would like to see themselves benefited but do not wish their cherished ways of living disturbed, just as the sick man would gladly regain his health but gives up unwillingly that which has made him sick. . . . When an original work appears, demanding that the listener assimilate its ideas instead of appraising its new spirit in the light of traditional concepts and that he adopt the new concept absolutely essential to new ideas, the majority, in the midst of their fervent longings for the 'new,' shrink from the difficulty and find consolation in the warmed-over old, persuading themselves, wherever possible, that it is new."—Marx, *Die Musik des 19. Jahrhunderts* (2d ed., Leipzig, 1873), pp. 154–55. [Au.]

one's mother tongue when one acquires a new branch of eloquence? Because there are works that demand a simultaneous bringing into play of feeling and thought, shall on this account the pure instrumental style lose its magic for those works that prefer to expend themselves and their entire emotional wealth in music alone without being hindered by a definite object in their freedom of feeling? Would it not amount to a lack of confidence in the vitality of the pure instrumental style were one to anticipate its complete decay simply because there arose at its side a new species, distinct from drama, oratorio, and cantata, but having none the less in common with these the poetic basis?

The dwellers in the antipodes of this new artistic hemisphere will perhaps think to advance a telling argument against it by saying that program music, through its apparent reconciliation of various subspecies, surrenders its own individual character and may not for this reason lay claim to independent existence within the art. They will hold that our art attains its purest expression in instrumental music and that it has in this form arrived at its highest perfection and power, revealed itself in its most kingly majesty, and asserted its direct character most impressively; that music, on the other hand, has from time immemorial taken possession of the word with a view to lending it, through song, the charm and force of its expression and has in consequence always developed in two forms as instrumental and vocal; that these two forms are equally indigenous, equally normal; and that the inventive creator, when he wishes to apply music to definite situations and actual persons, can find sufficient motives in the lyric and dramatic vocal forms; so that there can accordingly be no advantage or necessity for him to cause the peculiar properties of that form of music which exists for its own sake and lives its own life to meet and continue on the same path with the development of that other form which identifies itself with the poetic structure of the drama, with the sung and spoken word.

These objections would be well taken if in art two distinct forms could be *combined,* but not *united.* It is obvious that such a combination may be an unharmonious one, and that the work will then be misshapen and the awkward mixture offensive to good taste. This, however, will be due to a fault of execution, not a basic error. Are not the arts in general, and the several arts in particular, quite as rich in variously formed and dissimilar phenomena as nature is in the vicissitudes of her principal kingdoms and their divisions? Art, like nature, is made up of gradual transitions, which link together the remotest classes and the most dissimilar species and which are necessary and natural, hence also entitled to live.

Just as there are in nature no gaps, just as the human soul consists not alone in contrasts, so between the mountain peaks of art there yawn no steep abysses and in the wondrous chain of its great whole no ring is ever missing. In nature, in the human soul, and in art, the extremes, opposites, and high points are bound one to another by a continuous series of various varieties of *being,* in which modifications bring about differences and at the same time maintain similarities. The human soul, that middle ground between nature and art, finds prospects in nature which correspond to all the shadings and modulations of feeling which it experiences before it rests on the steep and solitary peaks of contradictory passions which it climbs only at rare intervals; these prospects found in nature it carries over into art. Art, like nature, weds related or contradictory forms and impressions corresponding to the affections of the human soul; these often arise from cross currents of diverse impulses which, now uniting, now opposing, bring about a divided condition in the soul which we can call neither pure sorrow nor pure joy, neither perfect love nor thorough egoism, neither complete relaxation nor positive energy, neither extreme satisfaction nor absolute despair, forming through such mixtures of various tonalities a harmony, an individuality, or an artistic species which does not stand entirely on its own feet, yet is at the same time different from any other. Art, regarded generally and in the position it occupies in the history of mankind, would not only be impotent, it would remain incomplete, if, poorer and more dependent than nature, it were unable to offer each movement of the human soul the sympathetic sound, the proper shade of color, the indispensable form. Art and nature are so changeable in their progeny that we can neither define nor predict their boundaries; both comprise a host of heterogeneous or intimately related basic elements; both consist in material, substance, and endlessly diverse forms, each of them in turn conditioned by limits of expansion and force; both exercise through the medium of our senses an influence on our souls that is as real as it is indefinable.

An element, through contact with another, acquires new properties in losing old ones; exercising another influence in an altered environment, it adopts a new name. A change in the relative proportions of the mixture is sufficient to make the resultant phenomenon a new one. The amalgamation of forms distinct in their origins will result, in art as in nature, either in phenomena of quite new beauty or in monstrosities, depending on whether a harmonious *union* or a disagreeable *combination* promotes a homogeneous whole or a distressing absurdity.

The more we persuade ourselves of the diverse unity which governs the All in the midst of which man is situated and of that other unity which rules his very life and history, the more we will recognize the diverse unity which reveals itself in the destiny of art, the more we will seek to rid ourselves of our vicious inclination to carp at and curb it, like gardeners who hem in the vegetation in order to grow hedges in a row or who cripple the healthy tree for the sake of artificial shapes. Never do we find in *living* natural phenomena geometrical or mathematical figures; why do we try to impose them on art, who do we try to subject art to a rectilinear system? Why do we not admire its luxurious, unfettered growth, as we admire the oak, whose gnarled and tangled branches appeal in a more lively way to our imaginations than does the yew, distorted into the shape of a pyramid or mandarin's hat? Why all this desire to stunt and control natural and artistic impulses? Vain effort! The first time the little garden-artist mislays his shears, everything grows as it should and must.

Man stands in inverse relations to art and to nature; nature he rules as its capstone, its final flower, its noblest creature; art he creates as a second nature, so to speak, making of it, in relation to himself, that which he himself is to nature.[2] For all this, he can proceed, in creating art, only according to the laws which nature lays down for him, for it is from nature that he takes the materials for his work, aiming to give them then a life superior to that which, in nature's plan, would fall to their lot. These laws carry with them the ineradicable mark of their origin in the similarity they bear to the laws of nature, and consequently, for all that it is the creature of man, the fruit of his will, the expression of his feeling, the result of his reflection, art has none the less an existence not determined by man's intention, the successive phases of which follow a course independent of his deciding and predicting. It exists and flowers in various ways in conformity with basic conditions whose inner origin remains just as much hidden as does the force which holds the world in its course, and, like the world, it is impelled toward an unpredicted and unpredictable final goal in perpetual transformations that can be made subject to no external power. Assuredly, the scholarly investigator can follow up the traces of its past; he cannot, however, foresee the final purpose toward which future revolutions may direct it. The stars in the heavens come and go and the species inhabiting our earth appear and disappear in accordance with conditions which, in the fruitful and perpetual course of time, bring on and again remove the centuries. Thus it is also with art. The fecundating and life-giving suns of its realm gradually lose their brilliance and warmth, and there appear on its horizon new planets, proud, ardent, and radiant with youth. Whole arts die out, their former life in time recognizable only from the skeletons they leave behind, which, like those of antediluvian races, fill us with astonished surprise; through crossbreeding and blending new and hitherto unknown arts spring up, which, as a result of their expansion and intermingling, will perhaps someday be impelled toward their end, just as in the animal and vegetable kingdoms whole species have been replaced by others. Art, proceeding from man as he himself proceeds, it appears, from nature, man's masterpiece as he himself is nature's masterpiece, provided by man with thought and feeling—art cannot escape the inevitable change common to all that time begets. Coexistent with that of mankind, its life principle, like the life principle of nature, does not remain for long in possession of the same forms, going from one to another in an eternal cycle and driving man to create new forms in the same measure as he leaves faded and antiquated ones behind.

· · · · ·

From this variety in the tempo of artistic development proceeds the difficulty of recognizing it in its portents and precursors. One must have taken a step

---

2. Compare Richard Wagner, *The Artwork of the Future,* chap. 1, sec.1 (p. 55 above).

forward before one can recognize as such the progress one has made. As long as this progress remains remote, like an anchorage toward which we sail, only a sort of clairvoyance will enable us to assert positively that we are getting ahead as we approach it. We border here so closely on optical illusion that for skeptics, who regard what others take for progress as retrogressive movement, there can be no demonstrations *a priori*. At the same time it would be idle to wish to deny or dispute an upward tendency in the psychological development of the human mind, which, embodying itself in constantly nobler arts and forms, strives after constantly wider radiation, after a brighter light, after an infinite exaltation.[3] And it would be equally idle to consign an art or the least of its forms to the class of immovable objects by seeking to demolish the new forms in which it manifests itself or to destroy the shoots that spring from the seeds of ripened fruit. These can never be stunted; no profane hand can restrain their seasonal impulse.

Strange contradiction! Nothing human stands still; cult, custom, law, government, science, taste, and mode of enjoyment—all change, all are constantly coming and passing away, without rest, without respite; no country is quite like any other, and no century ends in the same atmosphere with which it began; the endeavors, tendencies, improvements, and ideals of each generation plow up the hereditary fields in order to experiment with a new kind of crop. Yet in the midst of all these ferments, in this tempest of time, in this eternal world-rejuvenation, resembling the transformations of nature, if not in majesty then at least in universality, among all the paths of progress is one alone to remain untrodden—among all the manifestations of the human spirit is the development of the purest and most brilliant one to be forbidden, its mobility forever

3. "One cannot reflect on the deeper significance of the three great (so to speak) cardinal arts—plastics, painting, and music—without being constantly reminded of the history of the three great (so to speak) cardinal senses—touch, sight, and hearing. Then quite unsought there come to light most remarkable relations between the evolution of these senses in the animate world of the planets and the evolution of these forces in the history of mankind. Just as touch is the first and altogether most indispensable means by which the living creature orientates itself, so some form of plastics is the first and most essential art of peoples, the earliest to attain to full development. Sight, that miraculous perception of the most delicate light-effects, appears for the first time at a higher level in the animal kingdom, exhibiting, moreover, a certain inconstancy, seating itself now in a single eye, now in thousands of eyes, again on occasion degenerating altogether, even in the highest animal forms. The flowering of painting falls accordingly in mankind's middle period, assuming the most varied forms, coming to the fore and on occasion retreating suddenly into the background. Still later, indeed last of all, hearing develops, merely prefiguring itself in the higher mollusks and only from the fishes on becoming a permanent property of the animal world, seating itself now with greater constancy and symmetry in two organs, no more, no less, a right one and a left one, and from henceforth never again wanting. In similar measure, genuine music appears only in the last centuries; firm in its basic laws, at the same time developing itself and only holding to these as though riding at anchor, capable of the most delicate and most inspired variation, it thus becomes the mystery in which, free from all imitation of the world of actuality, the spiritualized world of feeling is reflected. If those other arts have long since passed the high point in their development, the full flowering of the tonal world falls in most recent times, and here, hidden under a thin shell, there are still latent many secrets, ready assuredly to reveal themselves to the right rhabdomancer."—Carus. [Au.]

held in check? Among all the virtual forces, is it proposed to deny precisely to this force, to the supreme force, the possibility of perfection that spirit inspires in matter, which possibility, an echo of that first command of creation, forms, with its "Become!", a harmonious All from the reorganized elements of an embryonic chaos? Wondrous power, noblest sacred gift of existence! Where else but in art canst thou be found? However man employs himself on any path of life, however he discovers, invents, collects, analyzes, and combines— he *creates* only in the artwork; only here can he out of free will embody feeling and thought in a sensual mold that will preserve and communicate their sense and content. Is art alone, from a given moment on, to remain unaffected by the ebb and flow of its soul, unmoved by the fluctuations of its hopes, unresponsive to all the changing of its dreams, to all the budding and weaving of its ideas? No, certainly not! Art, in general and in particular, sails with mankind down the stream of life, never to mount again to its source. Even when it appears to stand still momentarily, the tides which bear man and his life continue to remain its element. Art moves, strides on, increases and develops, obeying unknown laws, in cycles whose dissimilar return, recurring like the appearance of certain comets, at unpredictable intervals, does not permit the positive assertion that they will not again pass overhead in all their splendor or having passed will not return once more. Only it is not given us to foresee its unawaited reappearance or the undreamed-of glory in which it will then come forward.

．　．　．　．　．

When the hour of progress strikes for art, the genius is always found in the breach; he fulfills the need of the times, whether it be to bring a discovery from out a misty limbo fully and completely into the light or whether it be to combine single syllables, childishly strung together, into a sonorous word of magical power. It sometimes happens that art blossoms like the plant which gradually unfolds its leaves and that its successive representatives complement one another in equal proportion, so that each master takes only a single step beyond what his teacher has transmitted to him. In such cases, the masses, to whom this slow progress allows ample time, whose *niveau* is only gradually elevated, are enabled to follow the quest for more perfect procedures and higher inspiration. In other cases, the genius leaps ahead of his time and climbs, with one powerful swing, several rungs of the mystic ladder. Then time must elapse until, struggling after him, the general intellectual consciousness attains his point of view; before this happens it is not understood and cannot be judged. In literature, as also in music, this has often been the case. Neither Shakespeare nor Milton, neither Cervantes nor Camoëns, neither Dante nor Tasso, neither Bach nor Mozart, neither Gluck nor Beethoven (to cite only these glorious names) was recognized by his own time in such measure as he was later. In music, which is perpetually in a formative state (and which in our time, developing at a rapid tempo, no sooner accomplishes the ascent of one peak than it begins to climb another), the peculiarity of the genius is that he enriches the art with unused materials as well as with original manipulations of traditional ones, and one can say of music that examples of artists who have, as it were, leaped with both feet into a future time, are here to be found in greatest abundance. How could their anticipation of the style which they recognized as destined for supremacy fail to be offensive to their contemporaries, who had not sufficient strength to tear themselves loose, as they had done, from the comfortable familiarity of traditional forms? Yet, though the crowd turn its back on them, though envious rivals revile them, though pupils desert them, though, depreciated by the stupid and damned by the ignorant, they lead a tortured, hunted life, at death they leave behind their works, like a salutary blessing. These prophetic works transmit their style and their beauty to one after another of those who follow. It often happens that talents little capable of recognizing their significance are the very first to find ways of utilizing certain of their poetic intentions or technical procedures, whose value they estimate according to their lights. These are soon imitated again and thus forced to approach more closely to what was at first misunderstood, until, in the fumbling inherent in such imitations and tentative approaches, there is finally attained the understanding and glorification of the genius who, in his lifetime, demanded recognition in vain. Not until it has become used to admiring works analogous to his, but of lesser value, does the public receive his precious bequest with complete respect and jubilant applause. The old forms, thus made obscure, soon fall into neglect and are finally forgotten by the younger generation that has grown up with the new ones and finds these more acceptable to its poetic ideal. In this way the gap between the genius, gifted with wings, and the public which follows him, snail-like and circumspect, is gradually filled out.

·   ·   ·   ·   ·

[PART 3]

The poetic solution of instrumental music contained in the program seems to us rather one of the various steps forward which the art has still to take, a necessary result of the development of our time, than a symptom of its exhaustion and decadence, for we cannot presume that it is now already obliged to resign itself to the subtleties and aberrations of *raffinement* in order that, after having drained all its auxiliary sources and worn out all its means, it may cover up the impotence of its declining years. If hitherto unused forms arise and, through the magic they exert, win acceptance for themselves with thoughtful artists and with the public, in that the former makes use of them while the latter shows its receptivity toward them, it is not easy to demonstrate their advantages and inconveniences in advance so exhaustively that one can strike an average on the basis of which to establish their expectation of longevity and the nature of their future influence. None the less it would be petty and uncharitable to abstain from inquiry into their origin, significance, bearing, and aim in order to treat works of genius with a disdain of which one may later have reason to be ashamed, in order to withhold due recognition to a widening of the field of art, stamping it, on the contrary and without further ado, as the excrescence of a degenerate period.

We shall forgo deriving advantage from a pronouncement of Hegel's if we can be convinced that great minds (those before whose Herculean intellectual labors every head is bowed, quite apart from sympathy for their doctrines) can characterize precisely those forms as desirable which reveal themselves as sickly and contributory to the downfall of art. Hegel appears to foresee the stimulation which the program can give to instrumental music by increasing the number of those understanding and enjoying it when he says, at the end of the chapter on music in his *Aesthetics,* the intuitive correctness of which as a general survey cannot be prejudiced by certain erroneous conceptions, such as its time brought with it:

> The connoisseur, to whom the inner relationships of sounds and instruments are accessible, enjoys in instrumental music its artistic use of harmonies, interwoven melodies, and changing forms; he is wholly absorbed by the music itself and takes a further interest in comparing what he hears with the rules and precepts which he knows in order to appraise and enjoy the accomplishment to the full, though here the ingenuity of the artist in inventing the new can often embarrass even the connoisseur, to whom precisely this or that progression, transition, etc., is unfamiliar. So complete an absorption is seldom the privilege of the amateur, to whom there comes at once a desire to fill out this apparently meaningless outpour of sound and to find intellectual footholds for its progress and, in general, more definite ideas and a more precise content for that which penetrates into his soul. In this respect, music becomes symbolic for him, yet, in his attempts to overtake its meaning, he is confronted by abstruse problems, rapidly rushing by, which do not always lend themselves to solution and which are altogether capable of the most varied interpretations.

We would modify Hegel's opinion only to state it in a more absolute form, for we cannot concede that the *artist* is satisfied with forms that are too dry for the *amateur.* We assert, on the contrary, that the artist, even more insistently than the amateur, must demand emotional content in the formal container. Only when it is filled with the former does the latter have significance for him. The artist and the connoisseur who, in creating and judging, seek only the ingenious construction, the artfully woven pattern, the complex workmanship, the *kaleidoscopic* multiplicity of mathematical calculation and intertwining lines, drive music toward the dead letter and are to be compared with those who look at the luxuriant poetry of India and Persia only from the point of view of grammar and language, who admire only sonority and symmetrical versification, and do not regard the meaning and wealth of thought and image in its expression, its poetic continuity, not to mention the subject which it celebrates or its historical content. We do not deny the usefulness of philological and geological investigations, chemical analyses, grammatical commentaries—but they are the affair of science, not of art. Every art is the delicate blossom which the solid tree of a science bears at the tips of its leafy branches; the roots ought to remain hidden by a concealing coverlet. The necessity and utility of separating the material and substance in which art embodies itself into their component parts with a view to learning to know and to use their properties do not justify the confusing of science and art, of the study of the one with the practice of the other. Man must investigate art and nature; this is however not the goal of his relation to them—it is essentially a preparatory—if likewise important—moment in them. Both are given him primarily for his *enjoyment;* he is to absorb the divine harmonies of nature, to breathe out in art the melodies of his heart and the sighs of his soul. A work which offers only clever manipulation of its materials will always lay claim to the interest of the immediately concerned—of the artist, student, and connoisseur—but, despite this, it will be unable to cross the threshold of the artistic kingdom. Without carrying in itself the divine spark, without being a living poem, it will be ignored by society as though it did not exist at all, and no people will ever accept it as a leaf in the breviary of the cult of the beautiful. It will retain its value only as long as the art remains in a given state; as soon as art moves on to a new horizon and through experience learns improved methods, it will lose all significance save the historic and will be filed away among the archaeological documents of the past. Poetic art works, on the other hand, live for all time and survive all formal revolution, thanks to the indestructible life principle which the human soul has embodied in them.

·   ·   ·   ·   ·

The specifically musical composer, who attaches importance to the consumption of the material alone, is not capable of deriving new forms from it, of breathing into it new strength, for no intellectual necessity urges him—nor does any burning passion, demanding to be revealed, oblige him—to discover new means. To enrich the form, to enlarge it and make it serviceable, is granted, then, precisely to those who make use of it only as one of the means of expression, as one of the languages which they employ in accordance with the dictates of the ideas to be expressed; the formalists can do nothing better or more intelligent than to use, to popularize, to subdivide, and on occasion to rework what the tone poets have won.

The program asks only acknowledgment for the possibility of precise definition of the psychological moment which prompts the composer to create his work and of the thought to which he gives outward form. If it is on the one hand childish, idle, sometimes even mistaken, to outline programs after the event, and thus to dispel the magic, to profane the feeling, and to tear to pieces with words the soul's most delicate web, in an attempt to *explain* the feeling of an instrumental poem which took this shape precisely because its content could not be expressed in words, images, and ideas; so on the other hand the master is also master of his work and can create it under the influence of definite impressions which he wishes to bring to full and complete realization in the listener. The specifically musical symphonist carries his listeners with him into ideal regions, whose shaping and ornamenting he relinquishes to their individual imaginations; in such cases it is extremely dangerous to wish to impose on one's neighbor the same scenes or successions of ideas into which our imagination feels itself transported. The painter-symphonist, however, setting himself the task of reproducing with equal clarity a picture clearly present in his mind, of developing a series of emotional states which are unequivocally and definitely latent in his consciousness—why may he not, through a program, strive to make himself fully intelligible?

* * *

If music is not on the decline, if its rapid progress since Palestrina and the brilliant development which has fallen to its lot since the end of the last century are not the preordained limits of its course, then it seems to us probable that the programmatic symphony is destined to gain firm footing in the present art period and to attain an importance comparable to that of the oratorio and cantata—in many respects to realize in a modern sense the meaning of these two species. Since the time when many masters brought the oratorio and cantata style to its highest brilliance, to its final perfection, its successful treatment has become difficult; for other reasons too, whose discussion would here be out of place, the two species no longer arouse the same interest as at the time when Handel animated them with the breath of the winged steed. Oratorio and cantata appear to resemble drama in their impersonation and dialogue. But these are after all external similarities, and close examination reveals at once that undeniable differences of constitution prevail. Conflicts of passions, delineations of characters, unexpected peripetias, and continuous action are in them even more noticeably absent than actual representation; indeed we do not for one moment hesitate to deny a close relation here and are on the contrary persuaded that in this form music approaches rather the antique *epos,* whose essential features it can thus best reproduce. Aside from dialogue, held together by a certain continuity in the action it presents, oratorio and cantata have no more in common with the stage than has the epos; through their leaning toward the descriptive, instrumentation lends them a similar frame. Episode and apostrophe play almost the same role in them, and the effect of the whole is that of the solemn recital of a memorable event, the glory of which falls undivided on the head of a single hero. If we were asked which musical form corresponded most closely to the poetic epos, we should doubt whether better examples could be brought forward than the *Israel, Samson, Judas Maccabaeus, Messiah,* and *Alexander* of Handel, the Passion of Bach, the *Creation* of Haydn, the *St. Paul* and *Elijah* of Mendelssohn.

The program can lend to instrumental music characteristics corresponding almost exactly to the various poetic forms; it can give it the character of the ode, of the dithyramb, of the elegy, in a word, of any form of lyric poetry. If all along it has been expressing the moods proper to these various species, it can by defining its subject draw new and undreamed-of advantages from the approximation of certain ideas, the affinity of certain figures, the separation or combination, juxtaposition or fusion of certain poetic images and perorations. What is more, the program can make feasible for music the equivalent of a kind of poetry unknown to antiquity and owing its existence to a characteristically modern way of feeling—the poem ordinarily written in dialogue form which adapts itself even less readily than the epos to dramatic performance.

•   •   •   •   •

Would perhaps the specifically musical symphony be better suited to such subjects? We doubt it. The conflict between its independent style and the one forced on it by the subject would affect us disagreeably, being without evident or intelligible cause. The composer would cease to conduct our imagination into the regions of an ideal common to all mankind and, without definitely announcing the particular path he wishes to choose, would only lead the listener astray. With the help of a program, however, he indicates the direction of his ideas, the point of view from which he grasps a given subject. The function of the program then becomes indispensable, and its entrance into the highest spheres of art appears justified. Surely we have no wish to question the capacity of music to represent characters similar to those the poet princes of our time have drawn. For the rest, we see music arrived at such a point in its relations of dependence on and correspondence with literature, we see at the same time all human feeling and thinking, aim and endeavor, so overwhelmingly directed toward profound inquiry into the sources of our sufferings and errors, we see all other arts, vying one with another in their efforts to satisfy the taste and needs of our time, consumed so specifically by the desire to give expression to this urge, that we consider the introduction of the program into the concert hall to be just as inevitable as the declamatory style is to the opera. Despite all handicaps and setbacks, these two trends will prove their strength in the triumphant course of their development. They are imperative necessities of a moment in our social life, in our ethical training, and as such will sooner or later clear a path for themselves. The custom of providing instrumental pieces with a program has already found such acceptance with the public that musicians cease to struggle against it, regarding it as one of those inevitable facts which politicians call *faits accomplis*. The words of an author previously cited will serve as proof of this.

> Fine instrumental music must reckon with a much smaller number of competent listeners than opera; to enjoy it fully requires genuine artistic insight and a more active and experienced sensitivity. With the large audience, coloring will always pass as expression, for unless it consist of individuals capable of forming an abstract ideal—something not to be expected of a whole auditorium, no matter how select it may be—it will never listen to a symphony, quartet, or other composition of this order without outlining a program for itself during the performance, according to the grandiose, lively, impetuous, serenely soothing, or melancholy character of the music. By means of this trick, listeners identify most concerts of instrumental music

with the expression of certain passionate feelings; they imagine an action differing from those imagined by others as individuals differ among themselves. I speak here of the most cultivated, since for many, frequently for the majority, instrumental music is only a sensual pleasure, if not indeed a tiresome enigma. For them, instrumental music has neither coloring nor expression, and I simply do not know what they look for in it.[4]

Is it not evident from this that it is merely a question of officially recognizing an already existing power with a view to allowing it greater freedom of action and assisting it in the removal of its liabilities, so that henceforward it may work toward its future, toward its fame, not secretly, but in the deliberate repose that comes with an established success?

•   •   •   •   •

[PART 4]

Through song there have always been *combinations* of music with literary or quasi-literary works; the present time seeks a *union* of the two which promises to become a more intimate one than any that have offered themselves thus far. Music in its masterpieces tends more and more to appropriate the master-pieces of literature. What harm can come to music, at the height to which it has grown since the beginning of the modern era, if it attach itself to a species that has sprung precisely from an undeniably modern way of feeling? Why should music, once so inseparably bound to the tragedy of Sophocles and the ode of Pindar, hesitate to unite itself in a different yet more adequate way with works born of an inspiration unknown to antiquity, to identify itself with such names as Dante and Shakespeare? Rich shafts of ore lie here awaiting the bold miner, but they are guarded by mountain spirits who breathe fire and smoke into the faces of those who approach their entrance and, like Slander, whom Voltaire compares to coals, blacken what they do not burn, threatening those lusting after the treasure with blindness, suffocation, and utter destruction.

To our regret we must admit that a secretly smoldering but irreconcilable quarrel has broken out between *vocational* and *professional* musicians. The latter, like the Pharisees of the Old Law, cling to the letter of the command-ment, even at the risk of killing its spirit. They have no understanding of the love revealed in the New Testament, for the thirst after the eternal, the dream of the ideal, the search for the poetically beautiful in every form. They live only in fear, grasp only fear, preach only fear; for them, fear (not precisely the fear of the Lord, however) is the beginning and end of all wisdom; they hang on the language of the law with the pettiness of those whose hearts have not taught them that the fulfillment of the prophecy lies in the abolition of the sacrifice, in the rending of the veil of the temple; their wisdom consists in dogmatic disputes, in sterile and idle speculation on subtleties of the rules. They deny that one may show greater honor to the old masters by seeking out

---

4. Fétis. [Au].

the germs of artistic development which they embedded in their works than by servilely and thoughtlessly tracing the empty forms whose entire content of air and light they drained themselves in their own day. On the other hand the *vocational* musicians hold that to honor these patriarchs one must regard the forms they used as exhausted and look on imitations of them as mere copies of slight value. They do not hope to glean further harvests from fields sown by giants and believe that they cannot continue the work already begun unless, as the patriarchs did in their time, they create new forms for new ideas, put new wine into new bottles.

To Berlioz and his successes has been opposed from the beginning, like an insurmountable dam, that academic aversion to every art product which, instead of following the beaten path, is formed in accordance with an unaccustomed ideal or called up by incantations foreign to the old rite. But with or without the magisterial permission of the titulary and nontitulary professors—even without that of the illustrious director of the Paris Conservatoire, who visited Berlioz's concerts quite regularly in order, as he put it, "to learn how not to do it"—everyone who would keep up with contemporary art must study the scores of this master, precisely to see what is being done today and "to learn how to do it." And in truth, the so-called classicists themselves are not above making use of overheard and stolen ideas and effects and even, in exceptional cases, of conceding that Berlioz does after all show talent for instrumentation and skill in combining, since he is one of those artists, previously mentioned, who through the wider expression of their feelings and the freer unfolding of their individuality expand and enrich the form and make it serviceable. In the last analysis, however, the hypocrisy of his envious opponents consists in refusing to pay him the tuition they owe and have on their conscience while they publicly tread into the mire everything of his which they are not and never will be capable of imitating and privately pull out all feathers of his which they can use as ornaments themselves. We could name many who rise up against Berlioz, though their best works would be disfigured were one to take from them everything for which they are obliged to him. We repeat, therefore, that unusual treatment of form is not the supreme unpardonable error of which Berlioz is accused; his opponents will indeed concede, perhaps, that he has done art a service in discovering new inflections. What they will never forgive is that form has for him an importance subordinate to idea, that he does not, as they do, cultivate form for form's sake; they will never forgive him for being a thinker and a poet.

Strangely enough, that *union* of music and literature of which we have already spoken, constantly increasing in intimacy, developing itself with surprising rapidity, is gaining firm footing despite the equally lively opposition of *professional* musicians and men of letters. Both parties set themselves against it with the same vigor, with the same obstinacy. The latter, looking askance, see their property being taken over into a sphere where, apart from the value *they* placed on it, it acquires new significance; the former are horrified at a violation of their territory by elements with which they do not know how to deal. The tone poets have hence to contend with a double enmity; they find themselves between two fires. But the strength of their cause compensates for the weakness of their position. Whether one recognizes it or not, the fact remains that both arts, more than ever before, feel themselves mutually attracted and are striving for inner union.

Through the endless variety of its forms, art reproduces the endless variety of constitutions and impressions. There are characters and feelings which can attain full development only in the dramatic; there are others which in no wise tolerate the limitations and restrictions of the stage. Berlioz recognized this. From the church, where it was for so many centuries exclusively domiciled and from whence its masterpieces scarcely reached the outer world, musical art moved by degrees into the theater, setting up there a sort of general headquarters or open house where anyone might exhibit his inspirations in any genre he chose. For a while it would scarcely have entered the head of any musician to regard himself as incapable of composing dramatic works. It seemed as though, on admission to the musical guild or brotherhood, one also acquired and accepted the ability, sanction, and duty to supply a certain number of operas, large or small, romantic or comic, *serie* or *buffe*. All hastened to the contest in this arena, hospitably open to everyone. When the terrain of the boards proved slippery, later on, some crept and others danced on the tightrope; many provided themselves with hammers instead of balancing poles and, when their neighbors struggled to keep their balance, hit them over the head. Some bound golden skates to their feet and with their aid left way behind them a train of poor devils, panting to no avail; certain ones, like messengers of the gods, had at their head and heels the wings given them at birth by genius, by means of which, if they did not precisely make rapid progress, they were able at least to fly on occasion to the summit. And, for all that these last remained, here as elsewhere, very much in the minority, they none the less imposed on their successors so great an obligation to surpass their accomplishment that a moment seems to have arrived which should cause many to ask themselves whether the sense of duty which urges them to join in this turmoil is not a prepossession. Those, indeed, who expect more of fame than a draft to be discounted by the present, more than a gilt-paper crown to be snatched at by fabricators of artificial flowers—let them ask themselves whether they were really born to expend their energies in this field, to course and tourney in these narrow lists; whether their temperament does not impel them toward more ideal regions; whether their abilities might not take a higher flight in a realm governed by fewer constraining laws; whether their freer fantasy might not then discover one of the those Atlantides, blissful isles, or unknown constellations for which all students of the earth and sky are seeking. We for our part are persuaded that not every genius can limit his flight within the narrow confines of the stage and that he who cannot is thus forced to form for himself a new *habitaculum*.

To seek to import a foreign element into instrumental music and to domesticate it there by encroaching upon the independence of feeling through definite subjects offered to the intelligence in advance, by forcing upon a composer a concept to be literally represented or poetically formulated, by directing the attention of the listener, not only to the woven pattern of the music, but also to the ideas communicated by its contours and successions—this seems to many an absurd, if not a sacrilegious undertaking. Small wonder that before Berlioz they cover their heads and let their beards grow—before him who carries this beginning so far that, by symbolizing its presence, he causes the human voice to be heard in the hitherto wholly impersonal symphony; before him who undertakes to impart to the symphony a new interest, to enliven it with an entirely new element; before him who—not content to pour out in the symphony the lament of a common woe, to cause to sound forth in it the hopes of all and to stream forth from its focus the affections and shocks, sorrows and ardors, which pulse in the heart of mankind—takes possession of its powers in order to employ them in the expression of the sufferings and emotions of a specific, exceptional individual! Since the pleasure of listening to orchestral works has always been an altogether subjective one for those who followed the poetic content along with the musical, it seems to many a distortion, a violence done to its character, that the imagination is to be forced to adapt completely outlined pictures to that which is heard, to behold and accept figures in precisely the way the author wills. The hitherto usual effect of pure instrumental music on poetic temperaments may perhaps be compared to that which antique sculpture produces in them; in their eyes, these works also represent passions and forms, generating certain movements of the affections, rather than the specific and particular individuals whose names they bear—names, moreover, which are for the most part again allegorical representations of ideas. For them, Niobe is not this or that woman stricken by this or that misfortune; she is the most exalted expression of supreme suffering. In Polyhymnia they see, not a specific person engaged in specific speech or action, but the visible representation of the beauty, harmony, charm, and magic of that compelling, yet soft and placid persuasion whose eloquence can be concentrated in a single glance. Minerva, for them, is not only the divine, blue-eyed mentor of Ulysses, she is also the noblest symbol of that gift of our spirit which simultaneously judges and divines; who, provided with all the attributes of force, armed with all the weapons of war, is still a friend of peace; who, bearing lance and breastplate, causes her most beautiful gift, the olive tree, to sprout, promising peace; who, possessor of the terrifying aegis, loses nothing of the kindliness and attraction of her smile, of the slowly sinking cadence of her movements.

159 John Sullivan Dwight

New Englanders in the nineteenth century were well-nigh obsessed with the cultural development and social "progress" of their still artistically young civilization. Boston, with a highly educated population and an atmosphere significantly influenced by idealist philosophy (in its peculiarly American form, transcendentalism), experienced a new kind of dialogue between the transcendent aesthetic and intellectual values of this movement and the older, more acerbic Puritan culture that had marked the city in earlier times.

John Sullivan Dwight (1813–1893), with his genteel background and his degrees from Harvard College and Harvard Divinity School, aptly symbolizes this moment in New England's cultural history. His years spent living in the transcendentalists' utopian community, Brook Farm, deeply impressed him with a sense of connection between aesthetic ideas and social values; thereafter he devoted his life to music criticism, which he saw as a crucial part of the moral education of Boston and of the country in general.

In 1852 he founded *Dwight's Journal of Music: A Paper of Art and Literature,* which appeared under his direction, first weekly and then biweekly, until 1881. It reprinted articles from the major music journals of Europe, carried reports from musical correspondents in other American cities and abroad, kept its readers informed about musical current events, and, most notably, served as the principal vehicle for Dwight's own writing.

Dwight's aesthetic and moral values leap from every page. He was optimistic about the chances that genuine culture would emerge among Americans, despite what he thought of as their excessive utilitarianism and suspicion of "idle" aesthetic activities. All his life he preached that good music education was the only route to this development. He wholeheartedly undertook what was widely considered the obligation of the cultured to suppress "low" and improper music. By the end of his life his tastes were conservative and narrow, but his basically fair-minded nature led him to devote space in many an essay to the fine points of discerning, as he would put it, which music is genuinely Art.

The National Peace Jubilee

(1869)

To-day our columns are entirely occupied with this remarkable project, the dream, the one life purpose, for two years, of Mr. PATRICK S. GILMORE,[1] and

TEXT: *Dwight's Journal of Music* (July 3, 1869): 60–64.

1. Patrick S. Gilmore (1829–1892), Irish bandmaster, composer, and impresario, active in the United States. He was known especially for mounting gigantic concerts.

with its still more remarkable fulfillment in this city on the five days which an Irishman might call the next to "the top of the year," crowning the slope that leads right up to Midsummer, June 15th to 19th inclusive, making the dreamer famous, a popular hero in his way. Indeed we fear such stars as Mendelssohn just now, or Mozart, if they lived among us, would "pale their ineffectual fires" before such Calcine effulgence. The Jubilee has been the all-absorbing topic for the last month. As we have been silent about it during the preparation of the mighty work; and since, with all the extravagances of the plan, it has been pushed forward with such faith and energy that the imagination of the People, the "popular heart," perhaps we should even say the good genius of our People, fired and filled with it, has adopted it and made it its own, transforming it as it were into its own likeness; since it has been crowned with such unique success, we can do no less than gather together what we can of its history, weigh its results from our own point of view, and note the impression it has made on others.

·　　·　　·　　·　　·

For ourselves, as our readers know, we came to it sceptically, little disposed to trust or countenance a musical project making such enormous claims, and so unblushingly heralded after the manner of things as uncongenial as possible to the whole sphere of Art. The following letters, which we transfer from the *New York Tribune* of Saturday and Monday last, describe our position candidly, before and since the feast, though not as briefly or concisely as we could have wished. It was due to a very large class of the most sincere, enlightened, earnest friends of music and of culture, who, as far as any public expression was concerned, were entirely silent and unrepresented from the first, to state the way the thing looked to them from the outset, even at the risk of some seeming harshness or unfairness now that the plan is generally counted a success, a great event in some important senses, if not all. As for Mr. Gilmore, he has fairly earned all the reward which a grateful people appear eager to bestow. If the laudations of the newspapers do not turn his head—and so far we know he takes it sanely, modestly and simply—it is infinitely to his credit. So was his behavior during the last days of the Jubilee, in keeping himself and his own peculiar element of "Anvil Choruses," &c., resolutely in the background, rather than spoil the classical programme of the fourth day, or rudely break the fairy spell of the school children's festival.

THE PEACE JUBILEE SUMMED UP

·　　·　　·　　·　　·

I. How the Plan Looked at First, and How It Was Worked up

At first sight, certainly, the project was vain-glorious. The whole style of the announcement was such as to commend it more to the noisy and spread-eagle class of patriots than to still, thoughtful lovers of their country and of peace; while, in respect to music, its enormous promise, its ambition to achieve "the greatest," to "thrust" greatness upon us by sheer force of numbers, and so eclipse the musical triumphs of the world by saying: "Go to now, let us do ten times the *biggest* thing that ever yet was done"—this, and the extra-musical *effects,* the clap-trap novelties, grotesquely mingled in its programmes, chilled the sympathies of the real, the enlightened, the disinterested music-lovers, who, feeling for the honor and the modesty of Art, two qualities as inseparable in the artistic character as they are in woman, inevitably shrank from such grandiloquent pretension, as much as they inflamed the imagination the ignorant or only sentimentally and vaguely musical. "Twenty thousand voices!" Why will you have so many, when even the grandest of Handelian Choruses are better-sung by 1,000? And then will "50,000 people" under one roof hear, or let hear, as well as audiences in smaller halls? But it shall be "the Greatest Feast of Sublime and Inspiring Harmony ever heard in any part of the World!" (*sic*). This is calculating greatness upon a mere material scale of numbers; this makes your physical giant a greater man than Shakespeare; this confounds the *grand homme* with the *homme grand.* Shall quantity compete with quality? Shall great in mass be measured against great in kind? We are making musical progress in America; in popular musical education, as well as in the support of high-toned concerts, in some of our cities, we have really something to boast of; but does any one believe that we are yet so musical that we can produce a musical festival as great in quality, in kind, in spirit, as the best of the Old World? To a true musical character, which were the rarer godsend (to *hear,* at least, if not to see): a greatest Jubilee like this, or say some festival at Düsseldorf, with seven or eight hundred performers, but with Mendelssohn for a conductor, and such an orchestra as only can be found in Germany, and such a programme (not only Handel Oratorios, but *Passion Music* or *Magnificat* of Bach, and, as it was at this last Whitsuntide, with a Joachim to play Beethoven's Concerto, instead of an Ole Bull with "Mother's Prayer"); and above all, with such a *spirit* of sincere, true art and poetry and piety pervading the whole feast, to the exclusion of all heterogeneous nonsense, all flattering of vanities, catering to all tastes and no taste, startling *ad captandum* clap-trap, substitution of *effect* for meaning, to which add decent self-respecting abstinence from the "swell" style of advertisement? Or, not to look so far, compare it with our own best efforts here, with the last Handel and Haydn Festival in Boston Music Hall, where audiences of 3,000 people heard three or four great Oratorios entire, with Choral Symphony of Beethoven, and admirable symphony concerts besides, all in one week, impressively performed by an orchestra of hardly more than 100 instruments and chorus of 800 voices: was not that, musically, greater?

Mind, we are putting the case as it looked, as it must have looked, to really musical and sensible persons at the outset; as it would certainly have looked to Mendelssohn, had he been living then and here.

The idea and the authorship presented the same aspect. That the projector, master-spirit, brain, and central organizing force of the "greatest musical festival in all the ages" should be, not a Mendelssohn, a Handel, or great musical man of any sort, or hardly one who fellowshipped with artists, but a Gilmore, a clever leader of a local band, an Irishman by birth, but zealous for the land of his adoption, zealous for freedom in a truer than an Irish sense; a man of common education, singularly good natured and, we doubt not, generous; an enthusiast of rather a sentimental type; chiefly known as caterer in music to the popular street taste, dispenser of military and of patriotic airs, exceedingly fond of demonstrations, restless getter up of "monster concerts," in which classical works of genius were pressed into damaging promiscuity with musical *mix pickel* for the million; bountiful in advertising patronage (sure road to favor with the press): one of the glibbest, most sonorous and voluminous in all the wordy ways of "stunning" and sensational announcement:—that such a man should be the breather of the breath of life into the great feast of song to which "all that have life and breath" are summoned; that the grandest conceivable of all musical demonstrations should be in its spirit like unto his spirit; that our whole musical world, with all the musical resources of the nation, should be set revolving round a musician of that stamp, and that at such a bugle's blast all the makers of sweet sounds in all the land should rally to a Jubilee of Peace with him, in his way, was something too much for the common, unsophisticated intellect, musical or not, to take in at once, unless one took it in the nature of a colossal joke. How any sound mind at that time could conceive it possible for a thing so started to succeed as this has done, is inconceivable to this day, after the great success. Now, indeed, the lorgnette is turned round, and, looking through the small instead of the great end, cause and effect may not appear entirely incommensurate.

But Gilmore was in earnest. His "fixed idea" had vital marrow in it, and he knew how to magnetize other efficient people to like earnestness. His great devotion to that fixed idea saw only the shining end, pressed onward gazing steadily into the sun, using for means whatever came most readily to hand— chiefly that cardinal lever of all modern business enterprise, unscrupulous advertising, meant innocently in this case, no doubt, though questionable to squeamish folk like you and me, dear Tribune! And had he not the example of the whole business world to tempt him? And here, too, the swell mob style, the returned Californian digger garb and heavy watch-chain air, with which the thing presented itself, was not particularly inviting to sincere music-lovers, jealous, as we have said, for both the honor and the modesty of art. The finer instincts are the more suspicious of whatever is most loudly advertised. The quiet gentleman we trust, but from the loud-mouthed quack we turn away. Not so, however, with the simple masses; high-spiced advertisement does its perfect work with them. To draw an audience of 50,000, a whole community must by some means or other first become infatuated. Never was such advertising, in editorial even more than business columns, as this same Jubilee has had.

Shrewd dodges, too! Innocent Bostonian, calm and unsuspecting, opens his daily paper one fine morning, and is coolly informed that he—that all musical Boston—is in a great state of excitement about something of which he never heard a hint before! Our neighbor, in *his* (Democratic) newspaper, has read the same; and so through all the party shades of journalism—all agreed for once! Day by day, beginning with mysterious hints, do they the tale unfold foreshadowing the great event. Day by day, in ceaseless round, all vieing with each other, all the newspapers keep lifting corner after corner of the curtain that conceals the miracle too bright for mortal eyes; kindly provide us with smoked glasses too that we may bear the revelation when the great day comes. Count Cagliostro never conjured more adroitly. Biggest, best-drilled orchestra in all creation? That surely was the Press, which unseen fingers played upon, ever one theme with endless variations, as upon the keys of a piano. The whole expression, publicly, was of one side; the advocates of Jubilee, they only had a hearing. And with a *tutti crescendo* of amazing confidence, new wonder upon wonder was proclaimed, not as a thing suggested, but as *fait accompli*, with a: Resolved unanimously, it is to be! No reason to the contrary, no doubt might dare to peep; no uninvaded nook in newspaperdom where any "still, small voice" might seek to be heard. Pence Jubilee had stolen a march upon us in the night and forestalled every channel of communication.

This ringing confidence of the whole Boston Press, this ceaseless roaring deluge of exalting prophesy, was meant to convey the impression to surrounding populations and to distant States that all Boston, with one mind—Boston, famed for music and fine culture—was thoroughly in sympathy with Gilmore, and committed to the project. We were all made ostensibly responsible for the extravagance of the plan, and all the braggadocio with which it was written up. This representation was by no means just or true. There was a vast discrepancy between this newspaper flourish and the private sentiment and conversation in cultivated circles, particularly among those who had the cause of pure musical taste the most at heart; those who, in a sincere and quiet way, it might be, found their best life in the best music. Unconvinced as they were of either the practicability or the desirableness of a musical festival upon so vast a scale, instinctively averse to clap trap, to startlingly "big things," to the whole spirit of the "monster" concert system, mortified, indignant at the boastful attitude in which they found themselves all placed against their will, against their very nature, these were without representation in any public form whatever, except in the exulting taunts of those who had it all their own way. Mr. Gilmore and his early coadjutators doubtless had a host of obstacles to contend with, and it was often up-hill work with them; we honor the faith and perseverance worthy of the Saints, which overcame so signally; but "*these* little ones," who felt, believed another way, and firmly set themselves against the tide, rather than give in ignominiously to what they could not see to be good, had much the harder trial of their faith, their courage, their integrity.

Meanwhile there had been skillful procuring of indorsements of the project;

letters from influential citizens who, not musical themselves, were readily persuaded to a festival of Peace, and not unwilling to have Boston beat the world
in the grand scale of its music; letters, too, from prominent musicians who
would naturally be the ones to take the lead in practical performance. There
was shrewd calculation shown in the order in which individuals were
approached, and their adhesion won and published; the prime mover knew his
men. Indeed, the thing was worked up with consummate tact; and here lay,
probably, the "genius" which has been so freely ascribed to the Projector; for
surely the conception, the idea itself, did not require creative imagination, nor
invention, until it came to the details of execution, and here, with money, business talent was the one thing needful. And at the critical moment Business
stepped in to the rescue; Business, with the money guaranty, with organizing
skill, with ready way of rushing its big enterprises through. The application of
Dry Goods and Railroad methods saved the whole. The work was well laid out
among responsible committees. The word went forth that now the enterprise
was on its feet. Conversions became numerous; subscriptions, too; whole business streets were canvassed, and it demanded courage in the unbeliever to say
no. The huge Coliseum went up as by magic. The invitation flew abroad to all
the singers; 10,000 wanted; New England—Massachusetts, even—was good
for nearly the amount, could honor the draft at sight. By choral societies, clubs,
choirs, groups who had sung in Conventions, they poured in. Many new societies sprang up for the occasion: musical instruction in the public schools had
silently been feeding all these fountains. They came together with enthusiasm;
it waxed warmer and brighter with rehearsals; the sense of participating, and
feeling like singing particles in the live fragments of the great whole soon to be
fused into *one* conscious life, the mutual magnetism, the sense of pride, of
progress, of coöperation, while the grand culmination loomed beyond—this
was inspiring and uplifting, was a great good in itself, almost enough to offset
the brag, the claptrap and the humbug of the earlier stages, even should the
consummation fail. As for the grand orchestra (1,000 instruments), it was simply a matter of business and money to bring the elements of that together.

The success of the Jubilee in some shape having become a forgone conclusion, those who now took it in hand to draw the actual working plans soon
found it necessary to reduce its scale somewhat to bring it within practicable
dimensions. Instead of 20,000 singers, the limit was set at 10,000; the Coliseum, instead of 50,000, was to hold less than 30,000 hearers—say 37,000,
counting stage and auditorium together. Large enough, in all conscience. With
every such redaction the plan gained in the opinion of really musical persons.
One by one many of these gave in, accepted part in the management or in the
performance, saying: Since its success is certain, let us try to make it worthy of
success; let us mould its character, as far as possible, to some consistency of
true artistic end and outline—make it musical in the best sense we can, eliminate some nonsense wholly, keep guns and anvils within reasonable bounds,
and give the highest music a fair chance. Hence a considerable modification of

the programmes. The 20,000 school children, reduced to 7,000, were to have their own day, sweet and peaceful, set apart, and not be huddled in with the general medley of noisy cannonading choruses and all the boisterous excitement sure to go therewith. The Ninth Symphony was wisely voted quite impracticable. The duration of the Festival, having been increased from three to five days, gave room for two programmes almost exclusively of classical selections. The five programmes as definitely settled were pointed to as miracles of skill and "genius." Yet what was good in them was common, the most familiar choruses of well-known oratorios, &c.; what was uncommon was of questionable taste, as guns and anvils for a sublime occasion. And these incongruous elements were queerly mingled. Which was the ruling element? Which set the key and mainly dominated? Plainly, the pieces which the unmusical many like the best, the national airs, &c., with the anvils. The classical selections had, we must confess, the look of being put in apologetically, in order to conciliate the higher taste. (The "sop to Cerberus" reversed). But we shall see.

II. A Few Notes on the Programmes & Performance

The first day's programme was ceremonial, inaugural, sensational, patriotic. Prayer and addresses, were unheard, while that vast multitude, 12,000 facing 11,000, gazed in wonder on itself, and felt the inspiration of a scene the grandeur and beauty of which were unimaginable before. That spectacle needed no speech, no music even, to make its eloquence sublime and irresistible. That was the secret of the *great* impression throughout all the days: so many beings met and held together there in full sight of each other, and in perfect order. What but music could secure such order? Prayer and speech were brief; but, even could they have been heard, they were superfluous. What fitter prayer than that religious Luther Choral: *"Ein feste Burg,"* which followed? Full, rich, solemn, grand, the chords rolled forth from 10,000 voices, supported by the great orchestra, but even more by that most powerful organ (small, but built for power), which really seemed the backbone of the chorus. We could wish it had been harmonized by Bach, instead of Nicolai, if only that Bach might have had some recognition among the other mighty masters. Two things were proved at once: that there was no increase of loudness at all proportioned to the number of voices; and that, even if the farthest voices reached the ear a fragment of a second later than the nearest, the ear was not aware of it, while many individual imperfections, even false notes, possibly, were swallowed up in the great volume and momentum of the mass. The same held good of the other pieces of plain choral harmony: Keller's "American Hymn," and the concluding "God Save the Queen" (which one of our Psalm Kings, Psalmanazar I., we dare say, has nicknamed "America") sung to "My Country," with all the spread-eagle accompaniments of drums, guns, bells, &c. The Mozart "Gloria" was a good selection for a day of Peace, and, though it moved unsteadily, yet by its animation and its clear intention made most hearers deaf to faults. Wagner's

Tannhäuser Overture did not prove a fortunate selection for that great orchestra, nor had it any special fitness for the occasion, except as a piece of stirring effect music. In few parts of the vast space could much of it be heard; the violins and brass told well; the reeds, intrusted with the theme at times, were lost. The Overture to "Tell" fared somewhat better, at least in the spirited finale, though the opening, so beautiful with violoncellos (60 of them,) was dumb show to all but the nearest. One envied the singers their places round the rim of the great seething instrumental maelstrom, looking down into it as well as hearing. The "Ave Maria" solo, built by Gounod upon a prelude of Bach, was notable for the rich *obligato* unison of the 200 violins (though all there was of Bach about it, the arpeggio modulation, complete in itself, and used by Gounod for accompaniment, was covered up so as to be imperceptible), and for the clearness with which Mme. Rosa's[2] voice penetrated the whole space, although it sounded far off and in miniature, as if heard through the wrong end of an opera glass. In the *Inflammatus* her triumph was more signal, while the great choral climaxes look like the grander summits in the memory of mountain scenery. The rest was sensational: "Star-Spangled Banner," glorified by such broad treatment, with artillery and bells beside—a signal, as it were, to all the world outside that Jubilee had reached its highest moment— and with the melody so divided between deeper and higher voices as to overcome the difficulty for average singers of its great compass. That indeed was thrilling! March from "The Prophet," by full band of one thousand—business enough for all their throats of brass. And Verdi's "Anvil Chorus," causing wildest excitement—not precisely a legitimate effect of music, not the kind of excitement or emotion which musical people seek; fatal to that mood and temper of an audience in which music as such can be felt. Such effects are *extra* musical; the spectacle, the hundred scarlet firemen, &c., had much to do with it. Besides, the hundred anvils had a queer and toy-like sound, jingle of sleigh bells rather than the honest Vulcan *ring*. This was Mr. Gilmore's day, and he conducted all the patriotic pieces, including the opening Choral, in which he realized a good *pianissimo,* one of the finest effects of a vast multiple of voices. Mr. Eichberg[3] conducted in the *Tannhäuser* overture, and "Coronation March;" Mr. Zerrahn[4] in the solos and the *Gloria.*

The second was a great day of excitement. Added to the *eclat* of the Festival, now in full tide of success, was the visit of the President rather disturbing the conditions precedent for the "Grand Classical Programme," which had been much relied on for the conversion or conviction of the musically cultivated. The crowd was enormous—double that of the day before; curiosity, hero-worship, swelling heart of patriotism, doubtless drew more than music did. Of course

2. Euphrosyne Parepa-Rosa (1836–1874), Scottish soprano who toured extensively in the United States.

3. Julius Eichberg (1824–1893), German-American violinist, composer, and teacher.

4. Carl Zerrahn (1829–1909), flutist and conductor of many ensembles including the Handel and Haydn Society and the Harvard Musical Association orchestra.

not the best sort of audience either to hear or let hear. Well, the selections were all excellent; though we would except, perhaps, the opening Festival Overture by Nicolai on Luther's Choral. The plain Choral, to our mind, was grander, than with that orchestral counterpoint and trivial episodical theme between the stanzas; not being great work in that kind, like Bach's, it weakens the impression. Of three Handel Choruses, "See the conquering hero" was the most effective; "And the Glory of the Lord," was taken so slow as to make it hard to sing—a necessity, real or fancied, in conducting so vast a multitude through any labyrinthine movement. We were surprised that we could hear Miss Phillipps's[5] voice so well; there is a weight in her rich tones that carries far and quietly pervades. The piece, one of the best for her, and one of her best efforts, Mozart's "*Non piu di fiori,*" was too good for the crowd, not heard by some on account of restless noise, and not appreciated by the majority. Such a crowd contributes nothing on its own part to music, does not truly listen, but waits to be smitten and carried away. "He watching over Israel," the gentle, softly swelling chorus from *Elijah,* strange to say, proved one of the most successful of all the choruses that week; like a broad Amazon the stream moved steadily and evenly within bounds, and the round, full, smooth quality of the collective tone is something memorable. "Let the bright Seraphim" was just the perfect selection for Parepa-Rosa in that place, and was the chiefest triumph of her voice. With Arbuckle's[6] trumpet obligato (one longs for the real crackling old-fashioned *trumpet* though) it made great effect, by no means so great as it would be in a smaller hall; but the half-musical, which is by far the larger part of any such great audience, always need the *personal element* to interest them in music, and go the full half-way to meet a solo. The intermission was of course filled with the Hero-President. Then came Part II., the great Schubert Symphony in C, Mr. Zerrahn's capital selection for his grand orchestra; great hopes had been placed on that, for what symphonic work can bear such magnified presentment, if not that work? Alas! the Tantalus cup was rudely snatched away. The Symphony was to be sacrificed; the other element, fasting from native noise and anvils and free swing of hurrah boys, had grown irrepressible. To the brave President all music is alike, they say, and how easy for some one of the irrepressibles to prompt him to express a wish for good Spread-Eagle Scream with anvils! So into the programme, unannounced, and right before the Symphony, were thrust bodily "Star Spangled Banner" and "Anvil Chorus," once and again, until the building shook with thunder of applause; all mood for finer music was destroyed, all fine conditions broken up, Prospero Schubert's wand tossed under feet. The Symphony was killed ! knocked on the head by anvils! The wand, however, was picked up and waved for form's sake. But it had grown late; people were weary, restless, moving about, or starting homeward, talking aloud, in no mood to listen or let others hear; so the first move-

---

5. Adelaide Phillipps (1833–1882) English singer and actress, student of Manuel Garcia.
6. Matthew Arbuckle (1828–1883), Scottish-American bandmaster and cornetist.

ment and the Scherzo were omitted; the beautiful Andante (of the "heavenly length") was scarcely heard, and never did the impetuous sublime finale, with the thunder thumps of double basses (think of 70 or 80 of them!) sound so feebly. Were we right in the suspicion that the "classical" programmes were apologetic, meant to be like the "off nights" in a theatre, a compliment to musical taste, while the substantial meal was for the fire-eaters, the sensationalists who go forth "seeking a sign?" Good Mr. Zerrahn's best opportunity was frustrated; he could not try the effect of monster orchestra on this the chosen symphony. How much more satisfactory it may have been in the rehearsal, we do not know. Poor chance after this for Haydn choruses: "The Marvelous Work," and "The Heavens are telling;" for, sing as they might to an audience preoccupied, it still went: "The *anvils* are telling." The selected trio of a dozen solo singers on each part was very pleasing when it could be heard; but there was much floundering in the great chorus, and what was most "telling," as was just said, was retrospective and subjective: the chords those hammers set to vibrating were still undamped.

Third day, like the last, but more so. I was not there, and should have had to be dragged there after that fatigue. It was the 17th of June—of course, the chief day in the anvil calendar. That should have been the President's day; so the two kinds could have been kept distinct, one day for music and one day for glory.

Fourth day, Friday, best of all. The one really *musical* occasion, when the programme, choice in itself, was preserved in its purity. I had the fortune to sit very near the stage, and found it by far the best place for hearing. Even the orchestra became appreciable. Mr. Eichberg led Weber's "Jubilee" Overture, which perhaps went best of all the orchestral pieces in the festival. Mr. Zerrahn led all the rest. The glorious old C minor Symphony of Beethoven, the one of all others the best known among us, and most sure of close attention, was cut short, needlessly, as there was time enough, and the vast audience was calm; the chance at last seemed offered. But no, the experience of Wednesday had unnerved the valor and faith for Symphonies in that place; there was not courage left to risk it. So the first movement ("Fate knocking at 'he door") was left out; so, too, was the Scherzo—the curiosity to hear 80 double basses execute their scramble went ungratified; and, though the glorious March Finale sounded very well (and the Andante, too), yet robbed of its prelude, out of which it grows so marvelously, it lost half its effect, while the return of the three-four Scherzo rhythm in the middle of the march was meaningless. This was the only misdemeanor of the concert. Miss Philipps sang that large and simple aria of Handel, "*Lascia,*" &c., in her noblest style, and with incredible effect for that vast place. The ten thousand singers had grown more at home in their work, more blended and assimilated by common effort and enthusiasm, now burning at something like white heat, and almost everything went better than before with them. Best of all, the grave and solid chorals from St. Paul— that with the startling trumpet interlude, "Sleepers, awake," especially. It is the

solid, ponderous swing of the great mass of sound in plain, long chords like
these, sound equally diffused and oceanic, yet, like the wide waste of waters,
smooth and unobtrusive, that dwells in the mind as the best, the true effect of
choral force so   multiplied. Yet all must own that that more rapid graphic,
difficult, exciting chorus of Mendelssohn, the great Rain chorus from "Elijah"
was, on the whole, the choral achievement of the whole Festival, which most
signally rewarded effort. It was electrifying. Zerrahn, wisely, would not risk a
repetition. The down rush through the scale of those two hundred violins was
a thing to thank God for, like the rain. The Haydn chorus, the "Inflammatus,"
this time with eight choice soprani for the solo, the Prayer from "Moses," and
the Mozart *Gloria* again, made good impression, though faults might be found
had one the impression present. The *Gloria* past, the Handel *Hallelujah* alone
remains, and we await it strong in the peace and security of a pure musical
communion so far unbroken. But think not that "the other element" has all this
time been sitting quite so patiently. Creditable it was, indeed, to musical taste
and culture here, that the vast audience had not shrunk perceptibly before a
programme altogether classical; but think not that *all* those 20,000 people came
there without some inward assurance that the Anvil Chorus would appear and
take its throne, as matter of course, by divine right of its own, divine right of
disorder! Loud was the clamor for it. Fortunately, the means and men for it
were absent: or rather, thanks and all honor to Mr. Gilmore, who modestly
yielded the command that day, and absolutely refused to have the programme
interrupted. Yet the *Hallelujah* suffered after the confusion; singers had grown
weary, nervous too, perhaps, and the effect of the great chorus, even with all
those means was not so overwhelming as it has been on more ordinary occasions. It was on the whole a noble concert, heartily enjoyed by all so placed
that they could listen, and a comparison of this with Wednesday's concert gives
a capital illustration of a great point in the art of programme-making—the
importance, namely, of keeping incongruous elements distinct.

It was on Saturday morning, the School Children's day, that we were touched
and made to *feel* for once. The charming scene, the innocent, pure spirit of the
whole, the fresh, sweet, silvery voices of the 7,000 children, admirably true and
blended in three-part song and unison, their own expressions of delight, their
waving of handkerchiefs, and silvery shouts of applause, the kaleidoscopic unity
of movement in their physical and vocal gymnastic exercises, all combined to
make an exquisite impression. It was good to be there. It meant much for the
future and for culture. It was not an art occasion, to be sure, and did not
pretend to be. It was unique, a side of the Festival entirely by itself; the most
genuine and sincere of all, and, in many respects, the most interesting. The
beauty of it was that it did not pretend or strive to be anything but just what it
was. But when the exercises came to measured breathing, then to the first
utterance of a pure tone, swelling and dying away with the most beautiful
crescendo and *diminuendo* that we ever heard, and finally to the blended tones
of the Trichord, purity itself, like the white ray of "holy light" divided by the

prism, we were fain to call that just the most exquisite moment of the whole week's Festival. Simple, but divine; impersonal, but alive; without conscious meaning, but implying all! And, after such an illustration as the whole Jubilee had given of the musical resources of our people, was it not worth the while to see the nursery where the seeds thereof are sown?

III. The Net Results

As an *occasion*, of a new kind, of unexampled magnitude (unless in semi-barbarous times or Oriental countries)—whatever may have been musically—the Jubilee was a success. All acknowledge it, not without joy, even though at times it may come over some of us again in the character it wore from the first, as a strange overshadowing apparition, a vast work of willfulness, which had intrinsically, ideally, no right to be. As a man eminent in letters and in public life remarked to me yesterday, the amount of it is this: "A ridiculous plan redeemed by a magnificent success." Its friends had a perfect right to be wild over it. Many an unbeliever has been wholly or in great part converted, or at least reconciled to it. It has become a splendid Fact, which has to be accepted. If the projector and his fellow architects were wrong, attempting the impossible, in many points of view the undesirable, they "builded better than they knew." It seems as if—the ball once set in motion, or, rather, the vigorous first twist once given at the heart and centre of the revolving and soon formidably expanding maelstrom—as the dream and the intense will of one, magnetizing a few, then many, passed by degrees into a popular movement, assuming almost national dimensions, until the very air was full of it—soon every particle and feature of it, as it were, underwent "a sea change" in the tempering, transforming, vitalizing, and idealizing element of the new, best life and genius of a great, free People; having adopted it almost before they knew it, and hardly knowing what it was, they meant that it should be American in some sense which they could be proud of, and that the biggest gathering and musical array in human history, in spite of its extravagances, should still denote us truly, and be an earnest to the world of what an ambition for the true glory of a great nation, what a sleepless ideal of an ever higher type of Citizenship and of Society, what an energy and wealth of means, what a zeal for culture, what a principle of order and deep love of harmony are in us, spite of our diversities and the wide space over which we spread. And so it came to pass. And New England, Boston was the place for it. We need not attempt to show what has been so universally acknowledged, that such a feast could have succeeded nowhere else but here.

Musically, the Jubilee had its chief triumphs in precisely those selections which were the least purely musical, of no account as Art, no interest to earnest music-lovers. The parts that were addressed to these were certainly not great successes, and yet more successful than they for the most part had anticipated.

Reasons *a priori* were against great success, and the results do not disprove their soundness.

Consider, in the first place, the mingling of incongruous, internecine elements in the programmes, as we have seen; an incongruity involved in the *mixed motives* of the plan. There lay the knot of the difficulty: the project was ambiguous; music needs a simple *motive*. To fire the imaginations of 50,000 people and bring them all together, something other than good music had to be held up to them; a pure feast of high Art could not do it, nor could the genius of high Art do otherwise than run away and hide its face from such publicity as that. On the other hand, when it came to the ambitious promise of combining all the vocal and orchestral resources of the land, conductors of high standing, artists schooled in Philharmonic concerts, accustomed to the interpretation of the great masters, how could *their* coöperation be had without giving them fit work to do, making the occasion worthy of them? You can have them for Mozart, Beethoven, and Schubert, but not for Anvil Choruses and "Yankee Doodle" only. The pride of their profession, and what there is select, superior in it, has to be respected. They must appear to work for Art, else will they come? Now, the question was not simply of a Musical Festival, but also of a Peace Jubilee. Doubtless, in Mr. Gilmore's mind, the desire to display the musical resources of the land combined in one collective effort found sincere opportunity in the return of Peace. Monster Concerts were his passion; Peace and Country, also, were no strangers to his heart. Glorious and sublime it seemed to him to make the two ends meet; what an electric chain of sparks, brightness unspeakable, shot through his brain at the bringing of those two poles together! Then, again, as the circle widened, less ideal motives came in: the Jubilee would give Boston "such an advertisement as it never had;" trade would flow to us, &c., (though many burnt their fingers). These motives were most openly avowed, and the appeal to hundreds of subscribers was mainly put upon these grounds. All very well; but not for Music. Symphonies were promised to conciliate the musical; guns and anvils, national airs, &c., to draw the million and make no huge a project practicable. We have seen how the two got on together; how the anvils killed the Symphony, and how hard was abstinence from anvils when a classical programme was for once allowed its course.—
There could not be a better illustration of the law in programme-making, to which we have alluded: that elements incongruous be kept apart, as damaging, if not destructive, to each other. Each piece for its effect is much dependent on what goes before and after; sensational pieces, sure to be encored, rob all that follow of all fair chance for attention or effect. It is the art of picture-hanging as applied to music. We are far from saying that all the good things were lost: not a few of them were highly enjoyable to thousands favorably placed, some of the noble choruses, no doubt, to all. One cheering sign, too, could be read in all this, in the mere indication, spite of imperfect realization, of so many good things: it showed how strong and deeply seated, how wide-

spread the love of the highest kinds of music has become in our community, since it was found essential to conciliate it and defer to it so largely in these programmes.

· · · · ·

But I must hasten to a close. Whether the Festival considered musically, were very good or not, it musically *did* good. At any rate to all those singers and performers. It was a great experience for them. It has given them a new impulse, a new consciousness of strength, a new taste of the joy of unity of effort, a new love of cooperation, and a deeper sense of the divine significance and power of music than they ever had. It has caused hundreds of choral societies to spring into existence for the time being, many of which will certainly prove permanent; and their first bond of union has been the practice of *good* music, of master-works of Handel, Haydn, Mozart, Mendelssohn, which, having tasted once in such deep draughts, they will not readily abandon for weak trash. Education must come out of it. It has *planted,* well and widely, for the future.

Was it not good to be there, too, as listener, as looker-on, as sympathetic part and parcel of it? Who would willingly have been left out of such a grand occasion? The greatest assemblage of human beings under one roof ever known! A scene so overwhelming, so sublime, so beautiful from every point of view! An almost boundless sea of live humanity; and all so cheerful, all so happy, full of kindness, rejoicing in the sense of Country and of Brotherhood! Tens on tens of thousands, yet such admirable *Order!* Could any object, any influence but Music, hold such countless restless atoms in such order?

Finally, in a still wider way it has done good. It has given to tens of thousands of all classes (save, unfortunately, the poorest), who were there to hear, and, through them, to thousands more, to whole communities, a new belief in Music: a new conviction of its social worth; above all, of its importance as a pervading, educational and fusing element in our whole democratic life; a heavenly influence which shall go far to correct the crudities, tone down, subdue and harmonize the loud, self-asserting individualities, relieve the glaring and forthputting egotism of our too boisterous and boastful nationality. Thousands now have faith in Music, who never did have much before; thousands for the first time respect it as a high and holy influence, who very likely looked upon it as at the best an innocent, if not a dissipating, idle pleasure. Public opinion, henceforth, will count it among the essentials of that "liberal education," which is the birthright of a free American, and no longer as a superfluous refinement of an over-delicate and fashionable few. We shall no longer have to plead against such odds to claim, that Music have her permanent, her honored seat among the "humanities" of learning and of general culture. We begin to see how Music is to teach a people manners, mutual deference, and, without outward cold authority, without appeal to fear, but freely and divinely from within, inspire the instinct of respect, of fond and childlike reverence for something still above us, be we where we may,—and this is real Self-respect. So far as the Jubilee has wrought this conversion among unbelieving or indifferent thousands, it has done incalculable good; and if, for this alone, we cannot be too grateful to the men who (whatever our mistrust of motives and of methods once) have given us a great experience.

Boston, June 25, 1869

MUSICAL MEANING AND EXPRESSION

160 E. T. A. Hoffmann

A standard-bearer of German romanticism, E. T. A. Hoffmann was born in 1776 in Königsberg and died in 1822 in Berlin. His talents were manifold: he was a poet, a critic, a composer, a theater manager, a draftsman, and a public servant. Best remembered for his fantastic novels, Hoffmann was deeply devoted to music and for some time made music his profession. Among his works for the stage the most important is the opera *Undine* (1813–14). Hoffmann was one of the fathers of modern musical journalism and in this field opened the way to Robert Schumann and Richard Wagner. His literary works testify to the deeply musical nature of his poetic inspiration. In turn, Hoffmann's poetic visions have inspired musical works of the most disparate character. Schumann's *Kreisleriana,* Jacques Offenbach's *Les Contes d'Hoffmann,* Ferruccio Busoni's *Die Brautwahl* are cases in point.

Beethoven's Instrumental Music
(1813)

When we speak of music as an independent art, should we not always restrict our meaning to instrumental music, which, scorning every aid, every admixture of another art (the art of poetry), gives pure expression to music's specific nature, recognizable in this form alone? It is the most romantic of all the arts—one might almost say, the only genuinely romantic one—for its sole subject is the infinite. The lyre of Orpheus opened the portals of Orcus—music discloses to man an unknown realm, a world that has nothing in common with the external sensual world that surrounds him, a world in which he leaves behind him all definite feelings to surrender himself to an inexpressible longing.

Have you even so much as suspected this specific nature, you miserable composers of instrumental music, you who have laboriously strained yourselves to represent definite emotions, even definite events? How can it ever have occurred to you to treat after the fashion of the plastic arts the art diametrically opposed to plastic? Your sunrises, your tempests, your *Batailles des trois Empereurs,*[1] and the rest, these, after all, were surely quite laughable aberrations, and they have been punished as they well deserved by being wholly forgotten.

TEXT: "Beethovens Instrumental-Musik." *Sämtliche Werke,* ed. C. G. von Maassen, vol. 1 (Munich and Leipzig, 1908) pp. 55–58, 60–61, 62–64. As published in 1814 among the "Kreisleriana" of the *Fantasiestücke in Callot's Manier* (and earlier, anonymously, in the *Zeitung für die elegante Welt* for December 1813), this essay combines and condenses two reviews published anonymously in the *Allgemeine musikalische Zeitung* (Leipzig) for July 1810 and March 1813. Translation by Oliver Strunk.

1. Perhaps Hoffmann is thinking of Louis Jadin's "La grande bataille d'Austerlitz," published in an arrangement for the piano by Kühnel of Leipzig in 1807 or earlier.

In song, where poetry, by means of words, suggests definite emotions, the magic power of music acts as does the wondrous elixir of the wise, a few drops of which make any drink more palatable and more lordly. Every passion—love, hatred, anger, despair, and so forth, just as the opera gives them to us—is clothed by music with the purple luster of romanticism, and even what we have undergone in life guides us out of life into the realm of the infinite.

As strong as this is music's magic, and, growing stronger and stronger, it had to break each chain that bound it to another art.

That gifted composers have raised instrumental music to its present high estate is due, we may be sure, less to the more readily handled means of expression (the greater perfection of the instruments, the greater virtuosity of the players) than to the more profound, more intimate recognition of music's specific nature.

Mozart and Haydn, the creators of our present instrumental music, were the first to show us the art in its full glory; the man who then looked on it with all his love and penetrated its innermost being is—Beethoven! The instrumental compositions of these three masters breathe a similar romantic spirit—this is due to their similar intimate understanding of the specific nature of the art; in the character of their compositions there is none the less a marked difference.

In Haydn's writing there prevails the expression of a serene and childlike personality. His symphonies lead us into vast green woodlands, into a merry, gaily colored throng of happy mortals. Youths and maidens float past in a circling dance; laughing children, peering out from behind the trees, from behind the rose bushes, pelt one another playfully with flowers. A life of love, of bliss like that before the Fall, of eternal youth; no sorrow, no suffering, only a sweet melancholy yearning for the beloved object that floats along, far away, in the glow of the sunset and comes no nearer and does not disappear—nor does night fall while it is there, for it is itself the sunset in which hill and valley are aglow.

Mozart leads us into the heart of the spirit realm. Fear takes us in its grasp, but without torturing us, so that it is more an intimation of the infinite. Love and melancholy call to us with lovely spirit voices; night comes on with a bright purple luster, and with inexpressible longing we follow those figures which, waving us familiarly into their train, soar through the clouds in eternal dances of the spheres.[2]

Thus Beethoven's instrumental music opens up to us also the realm of the monstrous and the immeasurable. Burning flashes of light shoot through the deep night of this realm, and we become aware of giant shadows that surge back and forth, driving us into narrower and narrower confines until they destroy *us*—but not the pain of that endless longing in which each joy that has climbed aloft in jubilant song sinks back and is swallowed up, and it is only in this pain, which consumes love, hope, and happiness but does not destroy

2. Mozart's Symphony in E-flat Major, known as the "Swan Song." [Au.]

them, which seeks to burst our breasts with a many-voiced consonance of all
the passions, that we live on, enchanted beholders of the supernatural!

Romantic taste is rare, romantic talent still rarer, and this is doubtless why
there are so few to strike that lyre whose sound discloses the wondrous realm
of the romantic.

Haydn grasps romantically what is human in human life; he is more com-
mensurable, more comprehensible for the majority.

Mozart calls rather for the superhuman, the wondrous element that abides
in inner being.

Beethoven's music sets in motion the lever of fear, of awe, of horror, of
suffering, and wakens just that infinite longing which is the essence of romanticism. He is accordingly a completely romantic composer, and is not this perhaps the reason why he has less success with vocal music, which excludes the
character of indefinite longing, merely representing emotions defined by words
as emotions experienced in the realm of the infinite?

The musical rabble is oppressed by Beethoven's powerful genius; it seeks in
vain to oppose it. But knowing critics, looking about them with a superior air,
assure us that we may take their word for it as men of great intellect and deep
insight that, while the excellent Beethoven can scarcely be denied a very fertile
and lively imagination, he does not know how to bridle it! Thus, they say, he
no longer bothers at all to select or to shape his ideas, but, following the so-
called daemonic method, he dashes everything off exactly as his ardently active
imagination dictates it to him. Yet how does the matter stand if it is *your* feeble
observation alone that the deep inner continuity of Beethoven's every composition eludes? If it is *your* fault alone that you do not understand the master's
language as the initiated understand it, that the portals of the innermost sanctuary remain closed to you? The truth is that, as regards self-possession, Beethoven stands quite on a par with Haydn and Mozart and that, separating his ego
from the inner realm of harmony, he rules over it as an absolute monarch. In
Shakespeare, our knights of the aesthetic measuring rod have often bewailed
the utter lack of inner unity and inner continuity, although for those who look
more deeply there springs forth, issuing from a single bud, a beautiful tree,
with leaves, flowers, and fruit; thus, with Beethoven, it is only after a searching
investigation of his instrumental music that the high self-possession inseparable
from true genius and nourished by the study of the art stands revealed.

Can there be any work of Beethoven's that confirms all this to a higher
degree than his indescribably profound, magnificent symphony in C minor?
How this wonderful composition, in a climax that climbs on and on, leads the
listener imperiously forward into the spirit world of the infinite! . . . No doubt
the whole rushes like an ingenious rhapsody past many a man, but the soul of
each thoughtful listener is assuredly stirred, deeply and intimately, by a feeling
that is none other than that unutterable portentous longing, and until the final
chord—indeed, even in the moments that follow it—he will be powerless to
step out of that wondrous spirit realm where grief and joy embrace him in the

form of sound. The internal structure of the movements, their execution, their instrumentation, the way in which they follow one another—everything contributes to a single end; above all, it is the intimate interrelationship among the themes that engenders that unity which alone has the power to hold the listener firmly in a single mood. This relationship is sometimes clear to the listener when he overhears it in the connecting of two movements or discovers it in the fundamental bass they have in common; a deeper relationship which does not reveal itself in this way speaks at other times only from mind to mind, and it is precisely this relationship that prevails between sections of the two Allegros and the Minuet and which imperiously proclaims the self-possession of the master's genius.

How deeply thy magnificent compositions for the piano have impressed themselves upon my soul, thou sublime master; how shallow and insignificant now all seems to me that is not thine, or by the gifted Mozart or that mighty genius, Sebastian Bach! With what joy I received thy seventieth work, the two glorious trios, for I knew full well that after a little practice I should soon hear them in truly splendid style. And in truth, this evening things went so well with me that even now, like a man who wanders in the mazes of a fantastic park, woven about with all manner of exotic trees and plants and marvelous flowers, and who is drawn further and further in, I am powerless to find my way out of the marvelous turns and windings of thy trios. The lovely siren voices of these movements of thine, resplendent in their many-hued variety, lure me on and on. The gifted lady who indeed honored me, Capellmeister Kreisler,[3] by playing today the first trio in such splendid style, the gifted lady before whose piano I still sit and write, has made me realize quite clearly that only what the mind produces calls for respect and that all else is out of place.

Just now I have repeated at the piano from memory certain striking transitions from the two trios.

•   •   •   •   •

How well the master has understood the specific character of the instrument and fostered it in the way best suited to it!

A simple but fruitful theme, songlike, susceptible to the most varied contrapuntal treatments, curtailments, and so forth, forms the basis of each movement; all remaining subsidiary themes and figures are intimately related to the main idea in such a way that the details all interweave, arranging themselves among the instruments in highest unity. Such is the structure of the whole, yet in this artful structure there alternate in restless flight the most marvelous pictures in which joy and grief, melancholy and ecstasy, come side by side or intermingled to the fore. Strange figures begin a merry dance, now floating off

3. The eccentric, half-mad musician from whose literary remains Hoffmann pretends to have taken his "Kreisleriana." Schumann borrows the title of his Opus 16 from these sketches of Hoffmann's (published in two groups as a part of his *Fantasiestücke in Callot's Manier*).

into a point of light, now splitting apart, flashing and sparkling, evading and pursuing one another in various combinations, and at the center of the spirit realm thus disclosed the intoxicated soul gives ear to the unfamiliar language and understands the most mysterious premonitions that have stirred it.

That composer alone has truly mastered the secrets of harmony who knows how, by their means, to work upon the human soul; for him, numerical proportions, which to the dull grammarian are no more than cold, lifeless problems in arithmetic, become magical compounds from which to conjure up a magic world.

Despite the good nature that prevails, especially in the first trio, not even excepting the melancholy Largo, Beethoven's genius is in the last analysis serious and solemn. It is as though the master thought that, in speaking of deep mysterious things—even when the spirit, intimately familiar with them, feels itself joyously and gladly uplifted—one may not use an ordinary language, only a sublime and glorious one; the dance of the priests of Isis can be only an exultant hymn. Where instrumental music is to produce its effect simply through itself as music and is by no means to serve a definite dramatic purpose, it must avoid all trivial facetiousness, all frivolous *lazzi* [gags]. A deep temperament seeks, for the intimations of that joy which, an import from an unknown land, more glorious and more beautiful than here in our constricted world, enkindles an inner, blissful life within our breasts, a higher expression than can be given to it by mere words, proper only to our circumscribed earthly air. This seriousness, in all of Beethoven's works for instruments and for the piano, is in itself enough to forbid all those breakneck passages up and down for the two hands which fill our piano music in the latest style, all the queer leaps, the farcical capriccios, the notes towering high above the staff on their five- and six-line scaffolds.

On the side of mere digital dexterity, Beethoven's compositions for the piano really present no special difficulty, for every player must be presumed to have in his fingers the few runs, triplet figures, and whatever else is called for; nevertheless, their performance is on the whole quite difficult. Many a so-called virtuoso condemns this music, objecting that it is "very difficult" and into the bargain "very ungrateful."

Now, as regards difficulty, the correct and fitting performance of a work of Beethoven's asks nothing more than that one should understand him, that one should enter deeply into his being, that—conscious of one's own consecration—one should boldly dare to step into the circle of the magical phenomena that his powerful spell has evoked. He who is not conscious of this consecration, who regards sacred Music as a mere game, as a mere entertainment for an idle hour, as a momentary stimulus for dull ears, or as a means of self-ostentation—let him leave Beethoven's music alone. Only to such a man, moreover, does the objection "most ungrateful" apply. The true artist lives only in the work that he has understood as the composer meant it and that he then performs. He is above putting his own personality forward in any way, and all his endeavors are directed toward a single end—that all the wonderful enchanting pictures and apparitions that the composer has sealed into his work with magic power may be called into active life, shining in a thousand colors, and that they may surround mankind in luminous sparkling circles and, enkindling its imagination, its innermost soul, may bear it in rapid flight into the faraway spirit realm of sound.[4]

4. Hoffmann's essay was brought to Beethoven's attention in February or March 1820 by someone who wrote, during a conversation with him: "In the *Fantasiestücke* of Hoffmann there is much talk about you. Hoffmann used to be the music-director in Bromberg; now he is a state counsellor. They give operas by him in Berlin." On the strength of this, evidently, Beethoven wrote the following letter to Hoffman on March 23, 1820:

> Through Herr ———, I seize this opportunity of approaching a man of your intellectual attainments. You have even written about my humble self, and our Herr ——— showed me in his album some lines of yours about me. I must assume, then, that you take a certain interest in me. Permit me to say that, from a man like yourself, gifted with such distinguished qualities, this is very gratifying to me. I wish you the best of everything and remain, sir.
>
> Your devoted and respectful
Beethoven

161 Marc-André Souchay and Felix Mendelssohn

Instrumental music of the Romantic period has long inspired curiosity and controversy as to the possible meanings and references it might hold. Many pieces seem virtually to invite such speculation with suggestive poetic titles or other programmatic glimmers, and many contemporary commentators felt free to explicate compositions in apparently extramusical terms. Mendelssohn's famous *Songs without Words* would surely be ripe for poetic interpretation— why "songs," otherwise?—were it not for a well-known 1842 letter in which the composer seems to reject summarily any such possibility.*

Mendelssohn's explanation of his discomfort is interesting for his assertion that music's import, far from being too vague, is rather too *definite* for verbal translation. But even more fascinating is his corollary and surprisingly modernist

---

* Current scholarship suggests, however, that his attitude was rather more nuanced. See R. Larry Todd, " 'Gerade das Lied wie es dasteht': On Text and Meaning in Mendelssohn's *Lieder ohne Worte*," in *Musical Humanism and Its Legacy: Essays in Honor of Claude Palisca*, ed. Nancy Kovaleff Baker and Barbara Russano Hanning (Stuyvesant, N.Y.: Pendragon Press, 1992), pp. 355–79; and especially John Michael Cooper, "Words without Songs? Of Texts, Titles, and Mendelssohn's *Lieder ohne Worte*," in *Musik als Text: Bericht über den 19. Kongress der Gesellschaft für Musikforschung, Freiburg im Breisgau 1993*, ed. Hermann Danuser (forthcoming).

insistence that words themselves are too ambiguous for accurate communication to be taken for granted.

Until now, it has not been known exactly what question about his *Songs* Mendelssohn was answering in his famous letter. We are pleased to include that query here for the first time, unearthed in the Bodleian Library by John Michael Cooper. Marc-André Souchay, Jr. (1796–1868) was a distant cousin of Cécile Jeanrenaud, Mendelssohn's wife; his devoted attachment to Mendelssohn's music is evident in his heartfelt efforts to make their meaning his own.

An Exchange of Letters
(1842)

Most noble sir,

Please do not think badly of me if my great enthusiasm for your compositions finally wins over my sense of propriety, and I dare to burden you with some few lines from my pen.

Even some time ago I would not have denied myself the joy of asking you, noble sir, for advice and opinions concerning certain circumstances; but I was always prevented from doing so by a sense of modesty, for I feared that it might be understood as mere audacity and impudence. But recently the great hospitality demonstrated by you, noble sir, toward Messrs. Heilß and Lieber, whose acquaintance I made here in Kassel, has emboldened me to set my long-standing wish down in words, since perhaps I too might succeed in receiving a few kind words from you, noble sir, in response.

First of all, I must give you my warmest thanks for the kindness you showed to me through my father last winter. According to your advice, I came to Kassel to receive instruction in theory from Court Chamber-musician Hauptmann; in him I found not only an outstanding teacher, but also an equally fatherly friend. I shall never forget the half-year I spent with him, nor the extraordinary kindness with which he always received me. [But] even more than for his fine instruction and friendship I am indebted to him for his openness, for it is at his suggestion that I have decided (partly from lack of talent, partly because of my poor health) not to continue my *study* of music. He was able, through his frank, well-intentioned judgments, to help me more than did years of pretending from my dear father and other friends. Although it is with heavy heart that I have now given up this study, in which most of the happiness in my life

TEXT: Music Division, Bodleian Library, Oxford: MS. M. Deneke Mendelssohn c. 42, No. 69 (incoming correspondence, "Mendelssohn Green Books") and MS. M. Deneke Mendelssohn c. 32, fols. 56–57; the latter is the most authoritative source of Mendelssohn's letter available since the original, in private hands, is inaccessible. Transcriptions and translations by John Michael Cooper. We are grateful to Peter Ward Jones of the Bodleian Library for permission to publish the translations here.

seemed to reside, music will still continue to bring to me the most beautiful of times and the noblest and most sublime joy; and even under present circumstances it can bring me only the greatest joy to have dedicated myself completely to music for some time, for because of it I am now in a position to bring pleasure and enjoyment to myself as a dilettante.

The most wonderful piano pieces that I know have for years been your *Songs without Words*. Even when I was still a child, I found in them such distinctive feeling and penetrating emotion that they became my favorite of all piano pieces. But this deep feeling, which emerged long ago, has become ever greater, and now that I have formulated for myself a definite idea for each of these masterful works—now they give me twice the pleasure; my earlier love and fondness for them have become complete enthusiasm.

Of course, I have often been laughed at for my fantastic ideas, even by people whom I had to acknowledge and honor as practicing musicians—for example, my current teacher here, the Court Chamber-musician Deichert, who will hear nothing of ideas, but only of notes! But that cannot be correct; I cannot imagine that there is no poem behind these masterful paintings. I beg you, noble sir, not to take it as arrogance if I dare to share my opinion openly with you, but rather to seek the reason for my daring in my extraordinary veneration for you and in my eagerness. I believe it would not be incorrect to say that the various meanings of the songs could perhaps be the following: *Vol. 1:* no. 1, resignation; no. 2, melancholy; no. 3, scene of a *par-force* hunt[1], no. 4, praise of the goodness of God; no. 6, Venetian gondolier-song. *Vol. 2:* no. 1, depiction of a devout and thankful person who has been sought after; no. 2, hunting scene; no. 4, strong desire to go out into the world; no. 5, lullaby; no. 6, Venetian gondolier-song. *Vol. 3:* no. 1, boundless but unrequited love, which therefore often turns into longing, pain, sadness, and despair, but always becomes peaceful again; no. 2, anxious expectation (alternating longing, anxiety, and pain); no. 3, love song; no. 4, contentment; no. 5, despair; no. 6, duet. *Vol. 4:* no. 2, longing; no. 3, despair; no. 5, warlike folk-song.

For the pieces left out I have thus far been unable to formulate any ideas. That many of the songs can be interpreted in very different ways, and that the style of performance always depends upon the interpretation, is certain. The judgment of Herr Hilf, who so often heard these pieces played by you yourself in Leipzig, made me very happy: he said that I play them in pretty much the same fashion as you. I think that these pieces, which are after all supposed to be songs, must be performed like songs for singing, and that, especially in some emotional ones, one does not need to hold to a strict tempo as with other compositions—indeed, often, should not, for the emotion would fade into apathy.

You would make me unspeakably happy with a few words concerning these

1. Originally, a royal hunt, at which the attendance of the king's retainers was required; later, an organized hunting party.

ideas—I would never forget your goodness and humility in doing so, honorable Doctor, and even if my entire point of view is wrong I would be proud to have received a correction from you. . . .

> Your most obedient servant,
> M. A. Souchay
> of Lübeck
> Kassel, October 12, 1842 . . .

. . . There is so much talk about music, and so little is said. I believe that words are not at all up to it, and if I should find that they were adequate I would stop making music altogether. People usually complain that music is so ambiguous, and what they are supposed to think when they hear it is so unclear, while words are understood by everyone. But for me it is exactly the opposite—and not just with entire discourses, but also with individual words; these, too, seem to be so ambiguous, so indefinite, in comparison with good music, which fills one's soul with a thousand better things than words. What the music I love expresses to me are thoughts not too *indefinite* for words, but rather too *definite*.

Thus, I find in all attempts to put these thoughts into words something correct, but also always something insufficient, something not universal; and this is also how I feel about your suggestions. This is not your fault, but rather the fault of the words, which simply cannot do any better. So if you ask me what I was thinking of, I will say: just the song as it stands there. And if I happen to have had a specific word or specific words in mind for one or another of these songs, I can never divulge them to anyone, because the same word means one thing to one person and something else to another, because only the song can say the same thing, can arouse the same feelings in one person as in another— a feeling which is not, however, expressed by the same words.

Resignation, melancholy, praise of God, a *par-force* hunt: one person does not think of these in the same way as someone else. What for one person is resignation is melancholy for another; to a third person, neither suggests anything truly vivid. Indeed, if one were by nature an enthusiastic hunter, for him the *par-force* hunt and the praise of God could come down pretty much to the same thing, and for the latter the sound of horns would truly be the proper way to praise God. We [on the other hand] would hear nothing but the *par-force* hunt, and if we were to debate with him about it we would get absolutely nowhere. The words remain ambiguous, but we both understand the music properly.

Will you accept this as my answer to your question? It is at any rate the only one I know how to give—though these, too, are nothing but ambiguous words. . . .

> Felix Mendelssohn Bartholdy
> Berlin, October 15, 1842

162 Eduard Hanslick

Eduard Hanslick (1825–1904) enjoyed a successful career as a music critic, one of the first to make a profession of it, after a brief stint as a civil servant. Hanslick spent most of his life in Vienna, at the heart of musical current events. Through his regular criticism, he gradually became known as a supporter of Brahms and a polemicist against the Wagnerian school of modern music. His best known piece of writing is surely his brief treatise, *Vom Musikalisch-Schönen (On the Musically Beautiful)*, which was first published in 1854 and went through ten editions within its author's lifetime.

For a brief and quite clearly written book, *On the Musically Beautiful* has given rise to a surprisingly extensive literature of debate. In some quarters, Hanslick is best known for opinions he did not hold; he is often accused, for instance, of advocating a heartless formalism, as though music were a kind of audible calculus.

Not so. Hanslick argued that music is a primarily sensuous art, one of "specifically musical" beauty rather than of conceptual, quasi-literary content. While he made it his principal business to discredit the then-current notion that the primary function of music is to represent emotion, he does not deny that music frequently arouses feelings, nor even that we can aptly characterize much music by analogy with our emotional life. But he wants us to understand that those feelings come, through technical means, from particular patterns within the music and not by some alchemy directly from the soul of the composer. "The artist is inscrutable," he tells us, "but the artwork is not."

Hanslick's goal, therefore, is a scientific musical aesthetics, and another nuance often overlooked is his insistence upon the specificity of this topic. He distinguishes clearly between art-historical questions and aesthetic ones; far from forbidding "intentional" or "contextual" investigations for their own sake, he simply insists that their findings are not relevant to an aesthetic evaluation of the work at hand.

FROM *Vom Musikalisch-Schönen*

(1891)

So far we have proceeded negatively and have sought merely to refute the erroneous assumption that the beauty of music has its being in the representa-

---

TEXT: *On the Musically Beautiful: A Contribution towards the Revision of the Aesthetics of Music*, trans. and ed. Geoffrey Payzant [from the eighth edition (1891) of *Vom Musikalisch-Schönen*] (Indianapolis: Hackett, 1986), chap. 3, pp. 32–35, 38–44. Used by permission. Editorial notes are Payzant's.

tion of feeling. To that sketch, we now have to fill in the positive content. This we shall do by answering the question: What kind of beauty is the beauty of a musical composition?

It is a specifically musical kind of beauty. By this we understand a beauty that is self-contained and in no need of content from outside itself, that consists simply and solely of tones and their artistic combination.

• • • • •

Nothing could be more misguided and prevalent than the view which distinguishes between beautiful music which possesses ideal content and beautiful music which does not. This view has a much too narrow conception of the beautiful in music, representing both the elaborately constructed form and the ideal content with which the form is filled as self-subsistent. Consequently this view divides all compositions into two categories, the full and the empty, like champagne bottles. Musical champagne, however, has the peculiarity that it grows along with the bottle.

One particular musical conception is, taken by itself, witty; another is banal. A particular final cadence is impressive; change two notes, and it becomes insipid. Quite rightly we describe a musical theme as majestic, graceful, tender, dull, hackneyed, but all these expressions describe the musical character of the passage. To characterize this musical expressiveness of a motive, we often choose terms from the vocabulary of our emotional life: arrogant, peevish, tender, spirited, yearning. We can also take our descriptions from other realms of appearance, however, and speak of fragrant, vernal, hazy, chilly music. Feelings are thus, for the description of musical characteristics, only one source among others which offer similarities. We may use such epithets to describe music (indeed we cannot do without them), provided we never lose sight of the fact that we are using them only figuratively and take care not to say such things as "This music portrays arrogance," etc.

Detailed examination of all the musical determinations of a theme convinces us, however, that, despite the inscrutableness of the ultimate ontological grounds, there is a multitude of proximate causes with which the ideal expression of a piece of music is in precise correlation. Each individual musical element (i.e., each interval, tone-color, chord, rhythmic figure, etc) has its own characteristic physiognomy, its specific mode of action. The artist is inscrutable, but the artwork is not.

One and the same melody will not sound the same when accompanied by a triad as when accompanied by a chord of the sixth. A melodic interval of a seventh is wholly unlike a sixth. The accompanying rhythm of a motive, whether loud or soft, on whatever kind of musical instrument, modifies the motive's specific coloration. In brief, each individual factor in a musical passage necessarily contributes to its taking on its own unique ideal expression and having its effect upon the listener in this way and no other. What makes

Halévy's music bizarre and Auber's charming, what brings about the peculiarities by which we at once recognize Mendelssohn and Spohr, can be traced to purely musical factors without reference to the obscurities of the feelings.

Why Mendelssohn's numerous six-five chords and narrow diatonic themes, Spohr's chromaticisms and enharmonic relations, Auber's short, bipartite rhythms, etc., produce just these specific, unequivocal impressions: These questions, of course, neither psychology nor physiology can answer.

If, however, we are asking about proximate causes (and this is a matter of importance especially in connection with the arts), the powerful effect of a theme comes not from the supposed augmentation of anguish in the composer but from this or that augmented interval, not from the trembling of his soul but from the drumstrokes, not from his yearning but from the chromaticism. The correlation of the two we shall not ignore; on the contrary, we shall soon examine it more closely. We should keep in mind, however, that scientific examination of the effect of a theme can only be done with those aforementioned invariable and objective data, never with the supposed state of mind which the composer externalizes by means of them. If we want to reason from that state of mind directly to the effects of the work or to explain the latter in terms of the former, we might perhaps arrive at a correct conclusion but will have omitted the most important thing, the middle term of the syllogism, namely, the music itself.

The proficient composer possesses a working knowledge, be it more by instinct or by deliberation, of the character of every musical element. Nevertheless, a theoretical knowledge of these characters, from their most elaborate constructions to the least discriminable element, is required for scientific explanation of the various musical effects and impressions. The particular feature by which a melody has its power over us is not merely some kind of obscure miracle of which we can have no more than an inkling. It is rather the inevitable result of musical factors which are at work in the melody as a particular combination of those factors. Tight or broad rhythm, diatonic or chromatic progression, each has its characteristic feature and its own kind of appeal. That is why a trained musician, from a printed account of an unfamiliar composition, will get a much better idea of it if he reads, for example, that diminished sevenths and tremolos predominate, than from the most poetical description of the emotional crisis through which the reviewer went as a result of listening to it.

Investigation of the nature of each separate musical element and its connection with a specific impression (just of the facts of the matter, not of the ultimate principles) and finally the reduction of these detailed observations to general laws: that would be the philosophical foundation of music for which so many authors are yearning (without, incidentally, telling us what they really understand by the expression "philosophical foundation of music"). The psychological and physical effect of each chord, each rhythm, each interval, however, is by no means explained by saying that this is red, the other green, this is hope, the other discontent, but only by subsuming the particular musical qualities under general aesthetical categories and these in turn under a supreme principle. If, in the former manner, the separate factors were explained in their isolation, it would then have to be shown how they determine and modify each other in their various combinations. Most musically learned people have granted to harmony and contrapuntal accompaniment the pre-eminent position as the ideal content of a composition. In making this claim, however, they have proceeded much too superficially and atomistically. Some people have settled upon melody as the prompting of genius, as the vehicle for sensuousness and feeling (the Italians are famous for this); harmony has been cast opposite melody in the role of vehicle for the genuine content, being learn-able and the product of deliberation. It is curious the way people keep going along with such a superficial way of looking at things. There is basic truth in both claims, but neither at this level of generality nor in isolation do they carry weight. The mind is a unity, and so is the musical creation of an artist. A theme emerges fully armed with its melody and its harmony, together, out of the head of the composer. Neither the principle of subordination nor that of opposition applies to the essence of the relation of harmony to melody. Both can in one place pursue their own lines of development and in another place readily sub-ordinate one to the other. In either case, the highest degree of ideal beauty can be achieved. Is it perhaps the (very sketchy) harmony in the principal themes of Beethoven's "Coriolanus" overture and Mendelssohn's "Hebrides" which confers upon them the expression of brooding melancholy? Would Rossini's "Oh, Matilda" or a Neapolitan folksong achieve more spirit if a basso continuo or a complicated chord sequence replaced the sparse harmonic background? Each melody must be thought up along with its own particular harmony, with its own rhythm and sonority. The ideal content is due only to the conjunction of them all; mutilation of any one part damages also the expression of the remainder. That melody or harmony or rhythm should be able to predominate is to the advantage of all, and to consider on the one hand all genius to be in chords, and on the other all triviality to be in the lack of them, is sheer ped-antry. The camellia blooms without scent; the lily, without color; the rose delights us with both color and scent. These qualities cannot be transferred from one to another, yet each of the blossoms is beautiful.

So the "philosophical foundation of music" would have to try first of all to find out which necessary ideal determinants are connected with each musical element, and in what manner they are connected. The double requirement of a strictly scientific framework and the most elaborate casuistics makes the task a very formidable but not quite insurmountable one: to strive for the ideal of an "exact" science of music after the model of chemistry or of physiology.

•　　•　　•　　•　　•

It is only recently that people have begun looking at artworks in relation to the ideas and events of the times which produced them. In all likelihood this undeniable connection also applies to music. Being a manifestation of the human mind, it must, of course, also stand in interrelation with the other activities of mind: with contemporaneous productions of the literary and visual arts, the poetic, social, scientific conditions of its time, and ultimately with the individual experiences and convictions of the composer. The examination and demonstration of this interrelation are therefore warranted with regard to individual composers and works, and they are truly profitable. Yet we must always keep in mind that drawing such a parallel between artistic matters and special historical circumstances is an art-historical and not at all an aesthetical procedure. While the connection between art history and aesthetics seems necessary from the methodological point of view, yet each of these two sciences must preserve unadulterated its own unique essence in the face of unavoidable confusion of one with the other. The historian, interpreting an artistic phenomenon in its wider context, might see in Spontini the expression of the French Empire period, in Rossini the political restoration. The aesthetician, however, has to limit himself exclusively to the works of these men, to inquire what in these works is beautiful and why. Aesthetical inquiry does not and should not know anything about the personal circumstances and historical background of the composer; it hears and believes only what the artwork itself has to say. It will accordingly discover in Beethoven's symphonies (the identity and biography of the composer being unknown) turbulence, striving, unappeasable longing, vigorous defiance; but that the composer had republican sympathies, was unmarried and becoming deaf, and all the other features which the art historian digs up as illuminating it will by no means glean from the works and may not be used for the evaluation of them. To compare differences in world view between Bach, Mozart, and Haydn and then go back to the differences between their compositions may count as a very attractive and meritorious exercise, yet it is infinitely complicated and will be the more prone to fallacies, the stricter the causal connection it seeks to establish. The danger of exaggeration as a result of accepting this principle is extraordinarily great. We can all too easily interpret the most incidental contemporary influence as a matter of inherent necessity and interpret the perpetually untranslatable language of music any way we like. It is purely on account of quick-witted delivery that the same paradox spoken by a clever person sounds like wisdom but, spoken by a simple person, sounds like nonsense.

Even Hegel, in discussing music, often misled in that he tacitly confused his predominantly art-historical point of view with the purely aesthetical and identified in music certainties which music itself never possessed. Of course there is a connection between the character of every piece of music and that of its author, but for the aesthetician this is not open to view. The idea of necessary connection between all phenomena can in its actual application be exaggerated to the point of caricature. Nowadays it takes real heroism to declare, in opposition to this pleasantly stimulating and ingeniously represented trend, that historical comprehension and aesthetical judgment are two different things.[1] It is objectively certain, first, that the variety of impressions of the various works and schools is based upon crucially dissimilar arrangements of the musical elements, and second, that what rightly pleases in a composition, be it the strictest fugue of Bach or the dreamiest nocturne of Chopin, is *musically* beautiful.

Even less than with the classical can the musically beautiful be equated with the architectonic, which includes the musically beautiful as one of its branches. The rigid grandeur of superimposed towering figurations, the elaborate entwining of many voices, of which none is free and independent, because all of them are—these have their own ageless rightness. Yet those marvellously sombre vocal pyramids of the old Italians and Netherlanders are just one small part of the realm of the musically beautiful, just as are the many exquisitely wrought saltcellars and silver candelabra of the venerable Sebastian Bach.

Many aestheticians consider that musical enjoyment can be adequately explained in terms of regularity and symmetry. But no beauty, least of all musical beauty, has ever consisted entirely in these. The most insipid theme can be constructed with perfect symmetry. *Symmetry* is merely a relational concept; it leaves open the question: What is it, then, that appears symmetrical? Orderly structure may be detected among the trivial, shabby fragments of even the most pathetic compositions. The musical sense of the word demands always new symmetrical creations.[2]

Most recently Oersted has expounded this Platonic view in connection with

---

1. If we mention in this connection *Musikalischen Charakterköpfe* by [W. H.] Riehl [Stuttgart and Tübingen, 1853], it is with grateful acknowledgment of this brilliant and stimulating book. [Au.]
2. I permit myself to quote here from my book *Die Moderne Oper* by way of illustration.

The well-known saying that the "truly beautiful" can never lose its charm, even after a long time, is for music little more than a pretty figure of speech. (And anyway, who is to be the judge of what is "truly beautiful"?) Music is like nature, which every autumn lets a whole world of flowers fall into decay, out of which arise new flowerings. All music is the work of humans, product of a particular individuality, time, culture, and is for this reason permeated with mortal elements of various life-expectancies. Among the great musical forms, opera is the most complex and conventional and therefore the most transitory. It may be saddening that even the most excellent and brilliant new operas (such as those of Spohr and Spontini) are already beginning to disappear from the theatres. But reality is indefeasible, and the process cannot be halted by blaming the evil spirit of the time, as people have always done. Time is itself a spirit, and it produces its own embodiment. In contrast to the study place of the silent score-reader, the operatic stage is the forum for the actual demands of the public. The stage symbolizes the life of drama, and the struggle for its possession is drama's struggle for existence. In this struggle, a trifling work quite frequently overcomes its betters if it conveys to us the breath of our time, the heartbeat of our sentiments and desires. The public, like the artist, has a legitimate inclination toward the new in music, and criticism which has admiration only for the old and not also the courage to recognize the new undermines artistic production. We must renounce our belief in the deathlessness of the beautiful. Has not every age proclaimed with the same misguided confidence the imperishability of its best operas? Yet Adam Hiller declared in Leipzig that if ever the operas of Hasse ceased to delight, general anarchy must ensue. And yet Schubart, the music-aesthetician from Hohenasperg, assured us concerning Jomelli that it unthinkable that this composer could ever fall into oblivion. And who today ever heard of Hasse and Jomelli? (Preface.) [Au.]

music by means of the example of the circle, for which he claims positive beauty.[3] We may suppose that he had no firsthand experience of such an atrocity as an entirely circular composition.

Perhaps more out of caution than from need, we may add in conclusion that the musically beautiful has nothing to do with mathematics. This notion, which laymen (sensitive authors among them) cherish concerning the role of mathematics in music, is a remarkably vague one. Not content that the vibrations of tones, the spacing of intervals, and consonances and dissonances can be traced back to mathematical proportions, they are also convinced that the beauty of a musical work is based on number. The study of harmony and counterpoint is considered a kind of cabala which teaches compositional calculus.

Even though mathematics provides an indispensable key for the investigation of the physical aspects of musical art, its importance with regard to completed musical works ought not to be overrated. In a musical composition, be it the most beautiful or the ugliest, nothing at all is mathematically worked out. The creations of the imagination are not sums. All monochord experiments, acoustic figures, proportions of intervals, and the like, are irrelevant: The domain of aesthetics begins where these elementary relationships, however important, have left off. Mathematics merely puts in order the rudimentary material for artistic treatment and operates secretly in the simplest relations. Musical thought comes to light without it, however. I confess that I do not understand it when Oersted asks: "Would the lifetime of several mathematicians be enough to calculate all the beauties of a Mozart symphony?"[4] What is there that should or can be calculated? Perhaps the ratio of the vibrations of each tone with those of the next or the lengths of individual phrases or sections with relation to each other? What makes a piece of music a work of art and raises it above the level of physical experiment is something spontaneous, spiritual, and therefore incalculable. In the musical artwork, mathematics has just as small or great a share as in the productions of the other arts. For ultimately mathematics must also guide the hand of the painter and sculptor; mathematics is involved in the measures of verses, in the structures of the architect, and in the figures of the dancer. In every precise study, the application of mathematics, as a function of reason, must find a place. Only we must not grant it an actual, positive, creative power, as so many musicians and aesthetical conservatives would cheerfully have it. Mathematics is in a way like the production of

---

Eduard Hanslick, *Die Moderne Oper* (Berlin, 1875), pp. vi–viii. Regarding Hiller on Hasse: perhaps Hanslick refers to a review of the latter by the former in *Wöchentliche Nachrichten und Anmerkungen die Musik betreffend* (14 April 1767), p. 326. Regarding Schubart on Jomelli: C. F. D. Schubart, *Ideen zu einer Ästhetik der Tonkunst* (reprint ed. Leipzig: Reclam, 1977), p. 68.

3. H. C. Oersted, trans. K. L. Kannegießer, *Neue Beiträge zu dem Geist in der Natur* (Leipzig, 1850), pp. 17–21; trans. L. & J. B. Horner, *The Soul in Nature* (London, 1852), pp. 334–41.

4. *Geist in der Natur*, vol. 3, German by Kannegießer, p. 32. [Au.] Oersted, *Geist*, p. 32; *Soul*, p. 347.

feelings in the listener: It occurs in all the arts, but only in the case of music is a big fuss made about it.

Likewise some people have frequently drawn a parallel between speech and music and have tried to lay down the laws of the former as the laws of the latter. The kinship of song with speech is close enough that one might go along with the similarity of physiological conditions or with their common characteristics as revealing the inner self through the human voice. The analogical relationships are so striking that there is no need for us to go into the matter here. So we would just grant explicitly that, wherever music actually deals just with the subjective revealing of an inner longing, the laws governing speech will in fact to some extent be decisive for song.

That the person who gets into a rage raises the pitch of his voice, while the voice of a speaker who is recovering his composure descends; that sentences of particular gravity will be spoken slowly, and casual ones quickly: These and their like the composer of songs, particularly of dramatic songs, ignores at his peril. However, some people have not been content with these limited analogies but consider music itself to be a kind of language (though more unspecific or more refined), and now they want to abstract the laws of its beauty from the nature of language and trace back every attribute and effect of music to its affinity with language. We take the view that, where the specifics of an art are concerned, their differences with regard to respective domains are more important than their similarities. Such analogies are often enticing but are not at all appropriate to the actual essence of music. Undistracted by them, aesthetical research must push unrelentingly on to the point where language and music part irreconcilably. Only from this point will the art of music be able to germinate truly fruitful aesthetical principles. The essential difference is that in speech the sound[5] is only a sign, that is, a means to an end which is entirely distinct from that means, while in music the sound is an object, i.e., it appears to us as an end in itself. The autonomous beauty of tone-forms in music and the absolute supremacy of thought over sound as merely a means of expression in spoken language are so exclusively opposed that a combination of the two is a logical impossibility.

The essential center of gravity thus lies entirely differently in language and music, and around these centers all other characteristics arrange themselves. All specifically musical laws will hinge upon the autonomous meaning and beauty of the tones, and all linguistic laws upon the correct adaptation of sound to the requirements of expression.

The most harmful and confused views have arisen from the attempt to understand music as a kind of language; we see the practical consequences every day. Above all, it must seem appropriate to composers of not much creative power to regard autonomous musical beauty (which to them is inaccessi-

---

5. In this sentence *sound* translates the German word *Ton*, here used in its general, nonmusical sense.

ble) as a false, materialistic principle and to opt for the programmatic significance of music. Quite apart from Richard Wagner's operas, we often come across interruptions in the melodic flow of even the most insignificant instrumental pieces, due to disconnected cadences, recitatives, and the like. These startle the hearer and behave as if they signify something special, but in fact they signify nothing but ugliness. Some people have taken to praising modern compositions which keep breaking up the overall rhythm and developing inexplicable bumps and heaped-up contrasts. Thus they would have music strive to burst forth from its narrow limits and elevate itself to speech. To us this kind of commendation has always seemed equivocal. The limits of music are by no means narrow, but they are very precisely drawn. Music can never be "elevated" to the level of speech (strictly speaking, from the musical standpoint, one must say "lowered"), since music obviously would have to be an elevated kind of speech.[6]

6. It will not have gone unnoticed that one of the most original and magnificent works of all time has, by virtue of its splendor, contributed to the well-beloved fiction of modern music criticism about "the craving of music's inner self for the definiteness of verbal speech" and "the casting aside of the fetters of the harmonic proportions in sound." We refer to Beethoven's Ninth Symphony. It is one of those spiritual watersheds which interpose themselves insuperably between opposing currents of conviction.

    For some musicians, the grandeur of "intention," the spiritual significance of the abstract purpose, comes ahead of everything else. Such musicians place the Ninth Symphony at the summit of all music, while the few who, clinging to the unfashionable view of beauty, struggle on behalf of purely aesthetical claims, are a bit restrained in their admiration. As may be guessed, the problem is mainly with the Finale, since, concerning the sublime (though not flawless) beauty of the first three movements, little disagreement will arise among attentive and competent listeners. In this last movement, we have never been able to see more than the vast shadow of a titanic body. That from lonely despair a soul is brought in joy to reconciliation is a thought whose immensity a person could understand perfectly while yet finding the music of the last movement (for all its brilliance) unbeautiful. We know all too well the universal disapprobation which attaches to so heterodox a view. One of the most gifted and versatile of German scholars, who in the "A. Allgemeine Zeitung" (1853) undertook to challenge the formal analysis of the Ninth Symphony, acknowledged for this reason the comical necessity of identifying himself in the title as a "numbskull." He directed attention to the aesthetical monstrosity involved in having a multimovement instrumental work end with a chorus and compared Beethoven to a sculptor who carved the legs, torso, and arms of a figure out of colorless marble and then colored the head. Presumably at the entry of the human voices every sensitive listener must be overcome by the same discomfort, "since here the work shifts its center of gravity with a jolt, and thereby threatens to knock the listener down." Almost a decade later, to our delight, the "numbskull" was unmasked and turned out to be David Strauss. ["Musikalische Briefe von einem beschränkten Kopfe." *Allgemeine Zeitung* (Augsburg), No. 217 (August 15, 1853), pp. 3465–66. Reprinted in D. F. Strauss, *Kleine Schriften* (Leipzig, 1862), p. 418.]

    On the other hand, the estimable Dr. Becher, who may here be considered the representative of a whole school of thought, said, concerning the fourth movement, in an essay about the Ninth Symphony published in 1843: "With regard to originality of form, as well as magnificence of composition and the bold sweep of individual conceptions, it is a product of Beethoven's genius not at all to be compared with any other existing musical work." He declares that for him this movement, "with Shakespeare's *King Lear* and perhaps a dozen other manifestations of the human spirit, towers in its immense poetical power above those other artistic peaks like a Dhaulāgiri among the Himalayas." Like almost all his kindred spirits, Becher gives a detailed account of the meaning of the "content" of each of the four movements and their deep symbolism,

Even our singers forget this, who in deeply moving passages bellow words, indeed phrases, as if speaking them, and believe they have thereby demonstrated the highest degree of intensification of music. They fail to notice that the transition from singing to speaking is always a descent, so that the highest normal tone in speech sounds even deeper than the deepest sung tone of the same voice. Just as bad as these practical consequences, indeed worse, because they cannot be experimentally refuted, are theories which would foist upon music the laws of development and construction of speech, as had been attempted in earlier times by Rousseau and Rameau and more recently by the disciples of R. Wagner. The true heart of music, the formal beauty which gratifies in itself, would thereby be pierced through, and the chimera of "meaning" pursued. An aesthetics of musical art must therefore take as its most important task to set forth unrelentingly the basic distinction between the essence of music and that of language and in all deductions hold fast to the principle that, where the specifically musical is concerned, the analogy with language does not apply.

---

but of the music, he has nothing to say [A. J. Becher, "Filharmonische Akademie" (review). *Sonntagsblätter* No. 13 (1843), pp. 297, 295. See Geoffrey Payzant, "Eduard Hanslick and the 'Geistreich' Dr. Alfred Julius Becher," *The Music Review* 44 (1983): 104–15.]. This is utterly characteristic of a whole school of music criticism which, in reply to the question of whether the music is beautiful or not, prefers to sidestep into a solemn disquisition about some great thing the music is supposed to mean. [Au.]

163 Edmund Gurney

Edmund Gurney (1847–1888) was a passionate lover of music born, however, without sufficient talent to make it his profession. His education at Trinity College, Cambridge, was followed by abortive attempts at careers in both medicine and law. Ultimately, he devoted his life to the psychological investigation of music and other phenomena and to parapsychological studies.

In *The Power of Sound*, Gurney explores the origins and nature of music in ways characteristic of his time and place. He enters into scientific dialogue with the likes of James Sully, Herbert Spencer, and Charles Darwin, as well as several continental contemporaries interested in similar questions. Like Eduard Hanslick, Gurney argues that music's power is not referential or representational, but he parts company with his Viennese predecessor in his insistence that it *is* primarily a matter of emotion. This assertion is not romantic, however, but is made within the new scientific spirit of the late nineteenth century. Like his colleagues in science, Gurney is searching not only for a scientific basis of judgment and criticism, but for the evolutionary foundation of the emotions as well.

Along with its evident commitment to evolutionary ideas, Gurney's book also partakes of the efforts to turn the new discipline of psychology away from philosophical speculation and make it an empirical science. For a long time the discipline found itself limited to the experimental method known as introspection, or the examination of the experimenter's own responses. As Gurney notes, "such descriptions . . . can only be arrived at by considerable attention to one's own sensations: I can but hope that as they represent my own experience truly, however inadequately, others may find them to correspond in some degree with theirs."

FROM *The Power of Sound*
(1880)

MUSIC AS IMPRESSIVE AND MUSIC AS EXPRESSIVE

We now pass on to quite a new branch of our enquiry. So far we have been considering Music almost entirely as a means of *im*pression, as a presentation of impressive (or, as too often happens, unimpressive) phenomena. We have now to distinguish this aspect of it from another, its aspect as a means of *ex*pression, of creating in us a consciousness of images, or of ideas, or of feelings, which are known to us in regions outside Music, and which therefore Music, so far as it summons them up within us, may be fairly said to *express*. The chief difficulty in getting a clear view of this part of the subject lies in the vagueness and looseness of thought which is apt to run in the track of general and abstract terms: and this being so, I can only make my argument clear by insisting on the clear separation of the sets of conceptions which come under the heads of *im*pression and *ex*pression respectively, or at any rate may be justifiably so classified after due definition.

The distinction is made very simple by considering that expression involves *two* things, one of which is expressed by the other. The expression may take the form of imitation, as when an appearance or a movement of anything is purposely suggested by some aspect or movement given to something else. Or the thing expressed may be an idea, as when a fine idea is expressed by a metaphor; or a feeling, as when suffering is expressed by tears; or a quality, as when pride is expressed by a person's face or demeanour. As regards expression of qualities, some preliminary explanation is necessary. When a quality is so permanent and general and familiar an attribute of anything that our idea of the thing comprises the quality, the latter does not seem separable enough for us to conceive of it as expressed; and thus we should not naturally say that a tree expressed greenness, or a dark night darkness, or a church-steeple height. In a word, a thing is expressive of *occasional* attributes, not of the essential

TEXT: *The Power of Sound* (London, 1880), chap. 14, pp. 312–18, 347–48.

attributes of its class. There is a doubtful region where such phrases might be used even of very general qualities with reference to some special idea in the speaker's mind: thus a Platonist might say that the face of nature expressed beauty, conceiving of beauty as a single principle, which is one thing; capable of manifesting itself in this or that form, which is another thing: but we should not, in an ordinary way, say that a flower expresses beauty, or a lion strength, but that the flower *is* beautiful and the lion strong. So with respect to musical forms or motions; they are so familiarly conceived as aiming at being beautiful and vigorous, such qualities are so identified with our idea of their function, that we do not naturally think of them as *expressing* beauty and vigour. So with qualities identified with the most general effects of impressive sound on the organism; we do not conceive of any sounds, musical or non-musical, as expressing soothingness or excitingness. But we do not quarrel with the description of music as having a romantic or passionate or sentimental expression, even though the analogy of the effect to modes of feeling known outside Music may be of the dimmest and most intangible kind; and when some more special and distinctive quality appears, such as agitation or melancholy, when a particular feeling in ourselves is identified with a particular character in a particular bit of music, then we say without hesitation that such a particular bit *expresses* the quality or feeling.[1]

It is true that there is a very important method of using words like *expressive* in relation to Music, in the absence of particular describable qualities or particular suggestions of any sort; a usage which has been more than once adopted in this book, and which it seems to me impossible to forego. Thus we often call music which stirs us more *expressive* than music which does not; and we call great music *significant*, or talk of its *import*, in contrast to poor music, which seems meaningless and insignificant; without being able, or dreaming we are able, to connect these general terms with anything *expressed* or *signified*. This usage was explained, at the end of the sixth chapter, as due to the inevitable association of music with utterance, and of utterance with something external to itself which is to be expressed,[2] as our ideas are external to the sounds in

---

1. The necessary connection of quality and feeling should be noted: for there being no personality in music, the qualities it can be in itself expressive of must be identified with some affection of ourselves. Thus we should not say that quick or slow music expressed such impersonal qualities as speed or slowness, but possibly hilarity or solemnity. Music may present even decided qualities which are not suggestive of any special and occasional mode of feeling in ourselves. Thus a melody may be *simple*, but as it does not make us feel simple, and as we have no definite mode of feeling identified with the contemplation of so general a quality, we should not naturally say that it *expressed* simplicity; unless there were some simplicity external to it, in some words or person associated with it. The feeling in ourselves need not necessarily be the *same* as the quality attributed to the music: the special feeling corresponding to melancholy music is melancholy, but the special feeling corresponding to capricious or humorous music is not capriciousness or humorousness, but surprise or amusement: clearly, however, this mode of feeling is sufficiently identified with the contemplation of the quality. [Au.]

2. Quite apart from the notion of such a something to be expressed, our habitual projection either of the composer's or of the performer's or of some imaginary personality behind the music we

which we utter them. But even those who take the transcendental view that something *is* so expressed or signified by all beautiful music—whether the something be the 'Will of the World,' as Schopenhauer taught, or any other supposed fundamental reality to which our present conceptions are inadequate—may still perfectly well accept the following proposition: that there is a difference between music which is expressive in the sense of definitely suggesting or inspiring images, ideas, qualities, or feelings belonging to the region of the *known* outside music, and music which is *not* so expressive, and in reference to which terms of expression and significance, however intuitive and habitual, could only be logically pressed by taking them in a quite peculiar sense, and postulating an *unknown* something behind phenomena, which the phenomena are held to reveal or signify, or, according to Schopenhauer, to 'objectify.'

The distinction as thus stated does not altogether coincide with that conveyed by the words *expressive* and *impressive;* since there is nothing to prevent music which is *expressive* in the former and tangible sense from being also *impressive* by its beauty. As the true distinction involved in the words is between two different *aspects* of Music, both of these may naturally be presented by the same specimen; and indeed we shall find that no music is really expressive in any valuable way which does not also impress us as having the essential character of musical beauty; an unpleasing tune may be lugubrious but not melancholy. But the great point, which is often strangely ignored and for the sake of which the distinction has been thus pedantically emphasised, is that *expressiveness* of the literal and tangible sort is either *absent or only slightly present*[3] in an immense amount of *impressive* music; that to suggest describable images, qualities, or feelings, known in connection with other experiences, however frequent a characteristic of Music, makes up no inseparable or essential part of its function; and that this is not a matter of opinion, or of theory as to what should be, but of definite everyday fact.

The immense importance of this truth, and of its relation to the facts of

---

hear may naturally lead to such phrases as that some one expresses himself or expresses his personality or expresses his soul in the music; in the same sense, *e.g.,* as a theist may hold the Creator to express himself in the beauties of Nature: such a use need not at all confuse the distinction in the text. The word expression, again, in such a general phrase as 'playing with expression' does not mean the signification of any thought or feeling external to the music, but merely the making the utmost, the literal squeezing out, of all the beauty which is there *in* the music. [Au.]

3. It is hard to word this so as to obviate all possible objections. In modern music it may perhaps be the case, more often than not, that some one out of the category of descriptive adjectives may seem at any rate more appropriate than most others: words like energetic, peaceful, solemn, and so on, may be made to cover an immense amount of ground. But the qualities may be said to be slightly expressed if they excite no special remark; if one's impression, if it runs at all into words, is far more vividly 'how beautiful,' or 'how indescribable, how utterly a musical experience,' than 'how extraordinarily solemn,' or 'how exceptionally peaceful.' [Au.]

expression, will further appear when expression has been separately considered; but this independent impressiveness is so entirely at the foundation of the argument that it will be best to start by briefly recalling its root and groundwork. We found these, it will be remembered, in the fusion and sublimation of those strongest elementary passions and emotions which, according to Mr. Darwin's view[4] were associated with the primeval exercise of the musical faculty, the primeval habit of following tones and rhythm with pleasure; and in the light of generally admitted principles of hereditary association, we found no extraordinary difficulty in connecting what are now some of the most profound stirrings of our emotional nature with those crude elements which were yet the most profound emotional stirrings possible to our progenitors. In this connection it is well worth noting that at every stage which comes under our observation, Music seems capable of stirring up the strongest excitement that a being who musically typifies that stage can experience. This enjoyment to the utmost of the best that can be got is exemplified equally in the case of singing-birds, and of the gibbon, moved with rapture at his own performance of the chromatic scale, and of the savage repeating over for hours his few monotonous strains and maddened by the rhythmic beat of the drum, and of the ancient Greek spellbound by performances for the like of which we should probably tell a street-performer to pass on, and of a circle of Arabs sobbing and laughing by turns in ecstasies of passion at the sound of their native melodies, and of the English child to whom some simple tune of Mozart's reveals the unguessed springs of musical feeling, or of the adult in his loftiest communings with the most inspired utterances of Beethoven.[5] And it is all-important to observe that these emotional experiences are essentially connected, throughout the whole long course of development, with the distinctly *melodic* principle, with the presentation of a succession of single sound-units; such series being exemplified in the percussive drummings of the spider and in the song of the gibbon, as well as in the distinguishable lines of tune indispensable to the emotional character of modern composition. So that our general theory entirely bears out the view which in the fifth chapter was deduced from simple musical experi-

4. The comments of Darwin to which Gurney refers are principally found in *The Expression of the Emotions in Men and Animals* (1872), although there are also occasional references to musical sound as an aspect of sexual selection in *The Descent of Man* (1871). Darwin's observations, in their turn, often respond to the ideas of Herbert Spencer in "The Origin and Function of Music" (1858).

5. What is said here may be connected with what was said in the tenth chapter as to the rapid obsolescence of music. The newer and apparently more original kinds of Ideal Motion often make older music seem tame and trite. But it would certainly be most unfair to think of comparing, as regards amount of enjoyment, our own musical experiences with those of a person in the middle of the last century, by comparing the pleasure *we* derive from Beethoven with that which *we* derive from, *e.g.*, the earlier works of Haydn. Evidence entirely confirms what *a priori* we might have guessed, that that earlier music stirred its hearers to the very depths, in a manner which we can only realise by recalling some of the strains which have had a similar effect on ourselves in childhood. [Au.]

ence, that the ground for the essential effects of the art must be sought, not in any considerations connected with large or elaborate structure, or with rich complexity of parts, or splendid masses of tone, but in the facts of mere note-after-note melodic motion.

And while the theory, in its invocation of the strongest of all primitive passions, as germs for the marvellously sublimated emotions of developed Music, seems not only adequate but unique in its adequacy to account generally for the power of those emotions, it further connects itself in the most remarkable manner with that more special peculiarity of independent impressiveness which is now under review; with the fact which attentive examination of musical experience more and more brings home to us, that Music is perpetually felt as strongly emotional while defying all attempts to analyse the experience or to define it even in the most general way in terms of definite emotions. If we press close, so to speak, and try to force our feelings into declaring themselves in definite terms, a score of them may seem pent up and mingled together and shooting across each other—triumph and tenderness, surprise and certainty, yearning and fulfilment; but all the while the essential magic seems to lie at an infinite distance behind them all, and the presentation to be not a subjective jumble but a perfectly distinct object, productive (in a thousand minds it may be at once) of a perfectly distinct though unique and undefinable affection. This is precisely what is explained, if we trace the strong undefinable affection to a gradual fusion and transfiguration of such overmastering and pervading passions as the ardours and desires of primitive loves; and it is in reference to these passions of all others, both through their own possessing nature and from the extreme antiquity which they permit us to assign to their associative influence, that a theory of fusion and transfiguration in connection with a special range of phenomena seems possible and plausible. The problem is indeed a staggering one, by what alchemy abstract forms of sound, however unique and definite and however enhanced in effect by the watching of their evolution moment by moment, are capable of transformation into phenomena charged with feeling, and yet in whose most characteristic impressiveness separate feelings seem as fused and lost as the colours in a ray of white light: but at any rate the suggested theory of association is less oppressive to the speculative mind than the everyday facts of musical experience would be in the absence of such a far-reaching explanation of them.

The more serious difficulty, we found, came later. When we merely ask why are melodic forms emotionally impressive, and why are they emotionally impressive after a fashion which defies analysis or description, the association-theory comes to our assistance. But the further question, why one melodic form is felt as emotionally impressive and another not, reveals in a moment how much any such general theory leaves unaccounted for; and our further examination of melodic forms showed that the faculty of discernment, the faculty in which the cognisance of them is wholly vested, is one whose nature and action have to be accepted as unique and ultimate facts, and whose judgments are absolute, unreasoning, and unquestionable.[6] It is not necessary to repeat what has been said in the preceding chapters as to this extraordinary and independent faculty of co-ordinating a series of time- and pitch-relations into forms or notions, and of deriving various degrees of satisfaction or dissatisfaction from the proportions so progressively contemplated; nor as to the somewhat difficult but still warrantable supposition that the *satisfactory* action of the faculty, the concentration of it on such proportions as give it adequate scope and exercise, is the only mode whereby the flood-gates of emotion from the associational region are opened, and the perception of the form transfused and transfigured; the transfusion *ipso facto* preventing our knowing what the mere perception, the simple musical impression as it might be if the informing associational elements were non-existent, would in itself amount to.

But we now come to the consideration of certain points in musical forms and in the exercise of the musical faculty which are new; these being specially connected with Music in its *expressive* aspect. As long as Music is regarded only as a means of *impression,* as productive of a sort of emotion which, however definite and crude may have been its unfused and undeveloped germs, has been for ages so differentiated as to convey no suggestion of its origin, and is unknown outside the region of musical phenomena—as long as the forms, however various and individual to the musical sense, still present a musical character undistinguished and unpervaded by any particular definable feeling of joy, gloom, triumph, pathos, &c.—no examination of their structure from outside (as we abundantly saw in the seventh and following chapters) throws the slightest light on that musical character and its varieties: no rules can be framed which will not be so general as to include the bad as well as the good. The exercise of the musical faculty on such and such a form is found pleasurable and emotional, its exercise on such and such another is found neutral, or unsatisfactory and irritating; and that is all: a mode of perception which is unique defies illustration, and on this ground the only answer to the questions which present themselves is the showing why they are unanswerable. But when we come to the *expressive* aspect of Music, to the definite suggestion or portrayal of certain special and describable things known outside Music, whether images of objects or ideas or qualities or feelings, we should naturally expect to be able to trace in some degree the connection of any special suggestion or shade of character with some special point or points in the musical form and the process by which we follow it: and we have now to examine the various modes in which such connections may present themselves. None of them, it will now be evident, can be held accountable for any musical *beauty* which may be present: a tune is no more constituted beautiful by an expression, *e.g.,* of mournfulness or of capriciousness than a face is. The impressiveness which we call beauty resides in the unique musical experience whose nature and

6. Absolute and unquestionable, not of course as final or competent judgments of merit or anything else, but in reference to the power of a particular bit of music to affect a particular individual at a particular time. [Au.]

history have just been summarised: but in proportion as the beauty assumes a special and definable character or aspect, it does so in virtue of features in the musical form which are also special and definable.

It will be convenient to consider first the expression of qualities and feelings; the suggestion by music of objects and ideas being of a much more external and accidental kind. In our ordinary experience the natural mode in which qualities and feelings are expressed otherwise than by speech[7] is of course physical movement of some kind; thus human beings express confidence and good spirits by rapid and decisive movements, solemnity by measured movements, agitation by spasmodic movements, and so on. Now the Ideal Motion of Music gives us an aspect of physical movement ready made; the aspect, namely, of pace and rhythm; which can be presented without any sound at all by movements in space, and the correspondence of which with movements in space we perpetually exemplify in our own persons, as we follow and in any way keep time with Music. Moreover the Ideal Motion regarded in its completeness, without such particular reference to the rhythmic element, will be found to present certain faint affinities to external movement and gesture. But while it is naturally in motion that we should look for the signs of definite emotional states, or, as we commonly say, the *expression* of such states, in Music there are three other features connected with expression, two of which belong especially to the tone- or pitch-element apart from peculiarities of motion; the use, namely, of the major or the minor 'mode,' and of occasional noticeable harmonies; the other being *timbre* or sound-colour.

$$\cdot \quad \cdot \quad \cdot \quad \cdot \quad \cdot$$

In conclusion, I can imagine that a reader who has given assent to the various propositions and arguments which have been presented in this chapter, may still feel that, after all, there is a sense in which Music may be truly considered a reflection of the inner life. I am far from denying that such is the case: the error is in not seeing that so far as the idea has any sort of generality of application, the reflection itself must be of the most general and indefinite kind; very different from the definable expression, with its dubious and fragmentary appearances, which we have been discussing. Characters far too wide to be regarded, without absurdity, as what the pieces were written to express, or as what their merit and individuality consist in their expressing, may still make a sort of undefined human atmosphere under which the distinct musical forms are revealed and the distinct musical impressions received. Moreover, if the following and realising of music be regarded as itself *one complete domain* of inner life, we may then perceive that it is large and various enough, full enough

7. The relation of Music to Speech will be discussed in succeeding chapters, with results which will supplement without otherwise affecting the arguments in the present chapter. The emotional elements which music may gain by association with definite words and scenes will also be subsequently treated of; and certain extensions of the senses in which Music can be considered expressive will present themselves in connection with Song and Opera. [Au.]

of change and crisis and contrast, of expectation, memory, and comparison, of general forms of perception which have been employed in other connections by the same mind, for the course of musical experience, as felt under these most abstract aspects and relations, to present a dim affinity to the external course of emotional life. In this way we may feel, at the end of a musical movement, that we have been living an engrossing piece of life which, in the variety and relations of its parts, has certain qualities belonging to any series of full and changing emotions: and this feeling may impress us with much more of reality than any attempted ranking of the several parts and phases of the music under particular heads of expression. It is easy to distinguish general affinities of this kind from anything referable to the more definite categories. Such qualities, *e.g.*, as evenness and continuity, or interruptedness and variability, of musical movement, may suffice to suggest a sort of kinship between musical and other trains of feeling, while far too abstract to define or guarantee the character of the pieces where they occur, and able equally to cover the most various content: the slowness and sustainedness of an *adagio* movement, for instance, often described as typical of a peaceful flow of consciousness, we have found to be as compatible with the undefinable stirrings of musical passion as with the definable expression of calm. Another instance of abstract relationship, equally remote from definite suggestion and expression, may be found in the faint analogy of mingling currents of music to that mingling of various strains of feeling and idea which is so frequent a feature of our ordinary life: it would be absurd in the vast majority of such cases to attempt to represent each musical current as typifying some distinguishable train of known feeling, so that here the quality common to the musical and the extra-musical experience seems so abstract as to be little more than harmonious concomitance of several elements in each: yet this mere parallelism of complexity seems enough to open up in Music faint tracts of association with extra-musical life. A similar affinity has been attributed to the predominance of a single melodic theme in relation to its accompaniment; where the mere relation may possibly suggest our general experience of prominent strains of feeling as standing out from the general stream of consciousness, whose other elements make for it a sort of dimly-felt background.

And Music condenses a very large amount of inner life, of the sort of experience which might lend itself to such general associations, into a very brief space of actual time. The successions of intensity and relaxation, the expectation perpetually bred and perpetually satisfied, the constant direction of the motion to new points, and constant evolution of part from part, comprise an immense amount of alternations of posture and of active adjustment of the will. We may perhaps even extend the suggestions of the last paragraph so far as to imagine that this ever-changing adjustment of the will, subtle and swift in Music beyond all sort of parallel, may project on the mind faint intangible images of extra-musical impulse and endeavour; and that the ease and spontaneity of the motions, the certainty with which a thing known or dimly divined as about to happen *does* happen, creating a half-illusion that the notes are obeying the controlling force of one's own desire, may similarly open up vague channels of association with other moments of satisfaction and attainment. But these affinities are at any rate of the most absolutely general kind; and whatever their importance may be, they seem to me to lie in a region where thought and language struggle in vain to penetrate.

MUSIC THEORY
AND PEDAGOGY

164 Adolf Bernhard Marx

FROM *The Theory of Musical Composition*
(1868)

SONATA FORM

The loose concatenation of various themes and transitions appeared as a character trait of the rondo forms. In the rondo, at first only one theme, the main theme, was important enough to be repeated; it thus stood as the single fixed part of the whole, and for precisely that reason it always had to be brought back in essentially the same manner and in the same key. Thus it provided an element of constancy; but at the same time, the frequent returns to the same point kept the modulations from developing more freely and energetically, limiting them almost exclusively to the spaces between main and subsidiary themes.

The fourth, and especially the fifth, rondo forms went beyond this confining cycle. Because they combine main and subsidiary themes into a more unified whole, especially in the third part, where they bring them back (with the closing theme, if there is one) closely bound together by the main key, one recognizes in these forms another, and higher, orientation: the *separate* themes no longer matter in *isolation;* rather, the intimate union of individual themes in a whole—the *whole* in its inner *unity*—becomes the main concern. In such a

TEXT: *Die Lehre von der musikalischen Komposition,* 4th ed. (Leipzig, 1868), vol. 3 (*Die angewandte Kompositionslehre*), bk. 6 (*Die Komposition für selbständige Instrumente*), pp. 201–2, 220–26, 228–32, 244–51. Translation and notes by Scott Burnham. Throughout, references to musical examples given elsewhere in the book are omitted from the text.

Immediately preceding the excerpted discussion, Marx surveys the rondo forms, presenting them as an evolving series crowned by the sonata form. For Marx, the distinguishing feature of this family of forms is the motion-oriented alternation of thematic utterance (*Satz*) and transitional passage (*Gang*). Marx represents the rondo forms schematically as follows (MT: main theme [*Hauptsatz*] ST: subsidiary theme [*Seitensatz*] CT: closing theme [*Schlusssatz*] Tr: transition [*Gang*]);

First Rondo Form	MT Tr MT
Second Rondo Form	MT ST (Tr) MT
Third Rondo Form	MT ST1 Tr MT ST2 Tr MT
Fourth Rondo Form	MT ST1 Tr MT ST2 Tr MT ST1
Fifth Rondo Form	MT ST1 Tr CT ST2 Tr MT ST1 Tr CT

Satz is a wonderfully flexible term that Marx uses to refer to any closed structure, from the level of a phrase to that of an entire movement. Its diametrical opposite is *Gang*, an open-ended, often transitional, passage. In the present translation *Satz* is usually rendered "theme," as this is the level on which Marx most frequently uses the word. *Gang* is rendered "transition."

whole the isolated theme begins to lose its fixity; no longer there merely for itself, it need not hold to its place, self-contained: it now moves (at least the first subsidiary theme moves) from its original spot to another position (from the dominant or relative key to the main key), and it does so for the sake of the whole, which now wants to close with greater unity and with more material in the main key.

·   ·   ·   ·   ·

The *sonata form*[1] completes what the fourth and fifth rondo forms have begun. Generally speaking, it does this in a twofold manner. First, it gives up the foreign element (the second subsidiary theme) that the fifth rondo form still maintains between the first and third parts, and keeps only those two parts themselves, now more unified internally. This results in the *small sonata form,* or *sonatina form.* Next, it forms a new second, or middle, part—one unified with the first part and indeed made from the same material. This results in *sonata form proper.*[2]

Both forms, or rather, both manners of the one sonata form are used for fast as well as slow movements. We will study it first in fast movements, since it is here, where motion from one section to another predominates along with the liveliness of the sections themselves, that the nature of the form is most clearly revealed.[3]

·   ·   ·   ·   ·

SECTION THREE: SONATA FORM

It immediately becomes apparent that sonatina form is one of those transitional configurations that are certainly justified and necessary both intrinsically and in the sequence of all art forms, but in which a distinct formal concept has not yet reached full ripeness.

The sonatina strove beyond the rondo forms to a more intimate unity of content; but it achieved this by sacrificing a section of the content of those earlier forms—the second subsidiary theme—with a consequent lessening of significance. And, then again, it was inclined to insert a transitional or bridge passage in place of the omitted part; this proves that the rejected second part

1. As is well known, *sonata* means . . . a musical work for one (or two) instruments, made by joining several separate movements together, for instance, Allegro, Adagio, Scherzo, and Finale. Lacking another name already in currency, however, we designate with the name *sonata form* the wholly determinate form of a single movement. The name "allegro" or "allegro form," which is used now and again, is unsuitable because the sonata form is frequently used for slow movements as well. [Au.]

2. Marx's temporal language ("first" the sonatina form, "next" sonata form) in this paragraph and elsewhere reflects his understanding of sonata as a teleologically emerging realization of the spirit of form.

3. Sections One and Two, on sonatina form, are omitted here. Marx presents the small form first in order, as he says, to prepare the ground for the study of the larger.

had its own justification. But what is inserted in its place cannot truly replace it; thus this form is good only for cursory constructions.

This observation leads directly to sonata form itself and its essential character trait: sonata form cannot dispense with a *middle section;* it must assume a *three-part* form. But this middle, or second, part may not introduce *foreign* material—a second subsidiary theme—as in the rondo forms, for this would disrupt the unity whose complete attainment is in fact the task of the sonata. Consequently, the second part[4] of sonata form must hold to the content of the first part, either *exclusively,* or at least *primarily.*

Thus the main features of the new form are arranged as follows:

Part 1	Part 2	Part 3
MT ST Tr CT	————	MT ST Tr CT

One recognizes immediately that the first and last parts, broadly speaking, are familiar from the fifth rondo form and the sonatina form; only the middle part is essentially new.

Before turning to this new part, the most important object of this stage of our study, we note several considerations that follow from our view of the form so far.

First. Let us imagine a piece of music that persists in its main and subsidiary themes through *three* parts: we must acknowledge a deeper meaning in such persistent content than was the case with sonatina form. Or, in other words, the composer must be more compelled by these themes, he must feel predisposed to work with them more intently. Thus themes that are indeed well suited for that slighter form appear too inconsequential for the higher sonata form.

Second. The mere act of repeating a theme already reveals the inclination to grasp it as if it were a possession. Thus in the rondo forms the main theme especially served as a mainstay of the whole, to which one returned to repeat it again and again. A higher interest is manifest in the sonata form. No longer satisfied to bring back such a theme as if it were a dead possession, it enlivens

---

4. According to customary usage, *only two parts* are recognized in those pieces written in sonata form. The first part, which is usually repeated and is conspicuously isolated by the repeat sign, is treated as such; everything else, that is *the second and third parts together,* are treated as a single second part—this is often the case with the fifth rondo form also. But the distinction between the second and third parts, as we already know, is so essential that we cannot ignore it without distorting our perception of the form and losing sight of its rationale. In fact, this has been recognized before now, for within the so-called second part (the combined second and third parts) the return of the main theme and everything after it has been called the *reprise,* while that which precedes the reprise was called the *working-through (Durcharbeitung).* This would indeed mean *three* parts with an essential distinction of the third from the second! Yet the names seem less than exact (the third part is in no way a mere reprise or repetition, and working-through takes place in all sections and, moreover, in many other art forms as well), and this practice—an impediment to study—lumps together in the second part things that then only have to be differentiated again. [Au.]

it instead, lets it undergo variation and be repeated in different manners and with different destinations: it transforms the theme into *an Other,* which is nonetheless recognized as the offspring of the first theme and which stands in for it. The rondo cannot entertain essential alterations of its themes, but only peripheral changes (whereas the sonata form can embrace these as well).

In these transformations, obviously, lies the power to stimulate a more varied and intensified interest in the theme. Thus it is possible, in this larger form, to elevate a theme that is in itself of little significance to the status of a worthy and satisfying subject. Indeed, the power of the form and of the composer not infrequently shows itself to great advantage precisely with those beginnings that appear less important at first blush—although it seems *inartistic* to search out such a theme deliberately, just to show off one's talent, and *negligent* to take up the first good idea that comes along and go to work on it without feeling called to it or excited about it. One of the most successful examples of this sort is offered by the first movement of Beethoven's G major sonata, Op. 31. The main theme, spilling over with ingenious humor, has this as its germ:

Were this to stand for itself, alone and unvaried, one could certainly deem it full of energy but not of significance. Yet under its stimulus the spirit of the artist rings upon it the most ingenious changes, in wonderful succession; they take hold of us ever more profoundly, finally offering even milder harmonies to our unexpectedly moved souls. To assume that the master chose his theme for such a play of technical facility would be to award him paltry praise befitting a schoolboy. There was no question of technique here: for the artist there is no technique. What the artistic spirit seizes becomes its own—under the sway of fervent love it becomes a precious and living witness to that spirit. This process can be recognized and demonstrated with this Beethovenian theme, as with every artwork, and every artist knows it. Technique—outward skill or, worse, vainglorious play—has nothing to do with such artistic love.

Third. That light and capricious, even superficial, manner in which the sonatina form jumps from the half cadence of its main theme into the subsidiary theme and its key center can no longer suffice in the higher sonata form, where the whole is thoroughly permeated and informed by the urge for a unified, powerful sense of forward and progressive motion. A real transition is now necessary, one that will lead us unequivocally from the realm of the main theme into that of the subsidiary theme, and then establish it firmly.

To this end, and in accordance with long recognized precepts, there is a modulation *in the First Part* from the main theme and its key to the dominant of the dominant, and from there back to the dominant. In minor-key movements, as also has long been known, the modulation ordinarily goes not to the dominant but to the relative major.

From these easily settled points we now turn to the most important one, the construction of the second part, which demands separate consideration.

SECTION FOUR: THE SECOND PART OF SONATA FORM

As has already been established, the second part of a sonata form contains in essence no new content. As a consequence it must concern itself principally with the content of the first part—that is, with the main theme, with the subsidiary theme, and even with the closing theme—and specifically, it may deal with only one theme, with two, or even with all of them. But this involvement is in no way just a matter of repetition, as in the handling of the main theme in the rondo. Rather, the recurring themes are *chosen, ordered and connected,* and *varied,* in ways suitable to each different stage of the composition.

Thus it is clear that the second part manifests itself primarily as the locus of variety and motion, and once again we see the original antithesis, the fundamental law of all musical structure now revealed in the three parts of the sonata form: *rest—motion—rest.* The impulse for greater variety in the ordering and disposition of the material lies in the character of the second (or motion-oriented) part. Its general task is as follows: to lead, with material selected from the first part, from the conclusion of the first part to the pedal point on the dominant of the main key, and then to the entrance of the third part. But variety is chiefly found in the linkage *(Anknüpfung),* the way one leads on from the first part, and then in the carrying-through *(Durchführung)*[5] of content that is wholly or at least primarily borrowed from the first part.

It would hardly be possible or necessary to enumerate, much less to begin sketching out, all the typical and unusual procedures that may be used in the

---

5. This term tries to capture both the sense of leading-through and the sense of carrying out, or executing; both senses were implied in the term *Durchführung* before it simply became the equivalent of our musico-formal designation "development."

second part of sonata form; we must limit ourselves to the most important, those which illustrate the main tendencies.[6]

•   •   •   •   •

If we look back for a moment to the rondo forms, we see that it is the first gesture of the second part that most unequivocally distinguishes the sonata form from them and is the mark of the sonata form's characteristic energy and heightened unity. Here too the main theme appears for a second time, as it does in the third and fourth rondo forms, and it will appear again, perhaps unaltered, in the third part. But it has become something else, and not just in peripheral aspects of accompaniment but indeed in its essential features (even in mode).[7] We may indeed deem these changes essential, for, as has been shown, they are called for by the very conditions under which the main theme is constrained to reappear. It was already determined that the main theme has to avoid its initial key here as assiduously as it had to maintain it in the rondo forms; the principle of motion, of progress, was thereby elevated over the subordinate principle of stability that was manifest in the rondo forms.

•   •   •   •   •

It is hoped that these examples—only a few of countless possible ones—will suffice here too to open the door to progress for the student who has gone thus far with us. Here, as always, it is *of utmost importance* that he convince himself that there are inexhaustible ways and means available to the experienced; then that he make them all his own through reflection, steadfast work, and study of the masters (this latter, however, only when he has mastered these lessons to the point of fluency in his own works, so that he will never imitate but always create by his own power); and last, that he ensure, through uninterrupted attention to a work once begun and undisturbed submersion in its atmosphere and ideas, the completion of the work in a unified fashion true to its initial impetus.

•   •   •   •   •

SECTION SEVEN: SUPPLEMENTARY REMARKS ON THE WORKING OUT OF THE SECOND PART

Since the manner of introducing the second part forms an integral whole with the way the rest of it is realized, we have treated its further continuation

6. Here and in the next two sections (not included), Marx discusses, with many homemade musical examples, different ways of beginning the second part: with an immediate return to the main theme (sec. IV), with an entirely new theme (sec. V), with a closing theme that refers back to the main theme or an independent closing theme, or with a "transition-like" introduction (sec. VI).

7. Having considered above which tonalities are suitable for use when starting the second part with the main theme, Marx concludes that, since one cannot use the dominant or the tonic, the tonic minor or the relative minor of the dominant would work best.

simultaneously with the various ways of beginning it, in accordance with the practical bent and method of this entire book. But we had to direct our attention primarily to the introduction, covering the rest in the shortest and simplest way, in order to attain an overview of the second part and to do so repeatedly, even if the full range of its possible configurations could not be illustrated.

Under these circumstances several supplementary hints on the working out of the second part are now called for, which will require but few words.

1. To begin with, it goes without saying that all the important features of the second part that we have demonstrated may appear in greater profusion and at greater length than shown in this textbook, where for the sake of space the tersest exposition—only enough to shed some light—must have priority over a richer and more extensive treatment.

In particular, the transitions and pedal points will usually need further realization. It is hoped that our examples will suffice, since by now it should be clear that nothing is easier than the continuation of a transitional passage or a pedal point once it has been initiated; how much farther one ought to go must be decided in accordance with the particular tendency of each case.

The only general advice we can give is that one would do well—if particular considerations of content and mood do not demand otherwise—to give a certain proportion or equipoise to the various sections, such that the second part is *approximately* as long as the first, the returning main or subsidiary theme groups *approximately* match the preceding or subsequent transitional material, and so forth. This balanced structure expresses the evenhanded and sympathetic scrutiny that the composer should extend to all the sections of his creation, and it calls forth the pleasant feeling of a just and secure control in the listener as well, even if the latter is not equipped to keep tally of such things and is perhaps not even entirely aware of the whole organism that so pleases and benefits him. But the urge to achieve such proportion must never degenerate into an anxious *tallying* and *counting* of measures, above all during composition; this would be the death of any artistic impulse. Even back in [our discussion of] song form, a much more limited and easily surveyable territory, we moved beyond exact proportion to a general sense of proportion, and became convinced that the former was not necessary to achieve the pleasant and rational effect of the latter. If we allowed ourselves even there to answer four bars with five or six, and so forth, then a few bars more or less matter still less here, in compositions so much larger and more complex.

2. We know already from our treatment of polyphony that transitions and themes can be formed or continued polyphonically as well as homophonically. Thus it is obvious that in the sonata form as well, and particularly in the carrying-through of preexisting themes and transitional motives that forms the second part, one can make extensive use of polyphony. As is well known, polyphony enables us to give a whole new meaning to a theme, especially by means of the types of inversion, to gain an entirely new perspective on a famil-

iar theme, and to lend the whole, even in the midst of all these configural changes, a unity and solidity hardly possible in larger realizations except through the use of polyphonic techniques. . . .

3. Thus it follows that one can even make use of fugue in carrying out the second part. It is clear, however, that no actual, freestanding fugue can occur here but merely the use of fugal technique for some part of the section.

Neither the main nor the subsidiary themes can serve as the subject of the fugue; it must be formed from motives taken from these themes, usually from their beginnings. In most cases the choice would have to fall on the main theme, since, for reasons already known, it tends to have the most energetic and thus most promising configuration for fugal working-out *(Fugenarbeit)*. But we can form no rule from this; very often the subsidiary theme is better suited for the construction of a fugue subject, or better fits the mood of the composition as the second part progresses.

•   •   •   •   •

4. Finally, one must mention that sometimes the second part not only begins with the continuation of the closing theme but is exclusively dedicated to the carrying-through *(Durchführung)* of this theme. This occurs whenever the closing theme is the most compelling to the composer, and the main and subsidiary themes are less in need of any further working through because of their makeup—if, for example, they contain a much-repeated germinal theme and therefore their original appearance itself provided sufficient variety. . . . Anyone who understands in general how to develop a theme . . . will be indifferent as to whether the theme to be developed was originally a closing theme or some other.

However, one must regard this situation as exceptional, since it places the center of gravity on a secondary theme instead of on one of the primary (main or subsidiary) ones.

Section Eight: The Third Part of Sonata Form

Concerning the formation of the third part of sonata form there is little to add to what was said in the section on the fifth rondo form, since the third part is essentially shaped just like the third part of that rondo form. It begins with the main theme repeated in its entirety, even altered at some especially suitable point, and perhaps—especially if the second part dealt more with the subsidiary or closing themes—further realized.

The subsidiary theme follows the main theme, as we know, and of course in the main key; touching on the keys of the subdominant and dominant serves to make the main key's establishment here all the more decisive. The allusion to the first of these keys can be easily dispatched, or even completely omitted, if this key was heavily stressed in the second part. This modulation is fashioned differently according to the particular circumstances of each individual piece.

In most cases it takes place within the main theme, by leading it onward as a transition.

At times, when the main theme is firmly closed, a special transitional passage or a chain of phrases *(Satzkette)* will be appended, and the modulation to the subdominant is achieved just as the modulation to the dominant of the dominant was in the first part.

Sometimes it may seem appropriate to introduce the subsidiary theme simply at first, but then to modulate with it to the subdominant and from there through the dominant back again to the main key. . . . At other times, this spot can be used—like a kind of supplement to the second part—for another working out of the main theme or its motives, if the main theme seems especially momentous or fertile, or if it has not been treated in the second part.

•   •   •   •   •

Finally, the closing theme, too, or the transition that precedes it, can be expanded or an extension may be added that brings the main theme to the fore once again. All such expansions do not belong to the essence of the form and are not necessary, so they can easily become a nuisance. One must surely weigh every single case to determine whether there is a call for such enlargements, whether the themes need and are worthy of more frequent treatment—and whether such reiterations in the third part are sufficiently important to justify their presence.

165 Hermann Helmholtz

Hermann Helmholtz (1821–1894) was one of the greatest scientists of the nineteenth century, a polymath whose talents encompassed mathematics, optics, electrodynamics, physiology, and even meteorology. In the scientific world he is best remembered for a famous lecture in 1847 in which he formulated the law of the conservation of energy. Fortunately for the world of music, his was an empiricism heavily tinged with his own love of the aesthetic, and musical acoustics occupied his attention for a time. We are fortunate as well that Alexander J. Ellis, an English scientist of equal distinction in the field of acoustics, undertook to translate Helmholtz's great book on the subject.

Helmholtz was determined to refute romantic "Nature philosophy" and the vestiges of "vital force" theory in contemporary biology, to free scientific investigation from its remaining metaphysical fetters. He argued that all natural phenomena could be explained empirically, including beauty's effects on us. In his optics studies and in *On the Sensations of Tone* (first published in 1863), he searched for the scientific basis of these effects and investigated the reliability of the senses—highly complex and often imperfect in design—as conduits of information from the external world.

His search for the physical scientific basis of musical phenomena is not unusual for his time, in which the empirical spirit reigned. Nonetheless, Helmholtz never attempted to attribute the full experience of music to nature—as simpler minds were determined to do—but acknowledged the preeminent role of artistic invention and human creativity even in the structure of scales and tuning systems. The following excerpt is taken from the very end of the book; Helmholtz's ruminations on "the wonders of great works of art" provide an especially interesting conclusion to a treatise on physiological acoustics.

FROM *On the Sensations of Tone*
(1877)

ESTHETICAL RELATIONS

•　　•　　•　　•　　•

In the last part of my book, I have endeavoured to shew that the construction of scales and of harmonic tissue is a product of artistic invention, and by no means furnished by the natural formation or natural function of our ear, as it has been hitherto most generally asserted. Of course the laws of the natural function of our ear play a great and influential part in this result; these laws are, as it were, the building stones with which the edifice of our musical system has been erected, and the necessity of accurately understanding the nature of these materials in order to understand the construction of the edifice itself, has been clearly shewn by the course of our investigations upon this very subject. But just as people with differently directed tastes can erect extremely different kinds of buildings with the same stones, so also the history of music shews us that the same properties of the human ear could serve as the foundation of very different musical systems. Consequently it seems to me that we cannot doubt, that not merely the composition of perfect musical works of art, but even the construction of our system of scales, keys, chords, in short of all that is usually comprehended in a treatise on Thorough Bass, is the work of artistic invention, and hence must be subject to the laws of artistic beauty. In point of fact, mankind has been at work on the diatonic system for more than 2500 years since the days of Terpander and Pythagoras, and in many cases we are still able to determine that the progressive changes made in the tonal system have been due to the most distinguished composers themselves, partly through

TEXT: *On the Sensations of Tone as a Physiological Basis for the Theory of Music,* translated by Alexander J. Ellis from the fourth (1877) edition of *Lehre von dem Tonempfindungen;* second English edition, 1885, pp. 365–71.

their own independent inventions, and partly through the sanction which they gave to the inventions of others, by employing them artistically.

The esthetic analysis of complete musical works of art, and the comprehension of the reasons of their beauty, encounter apparently invincible obstacles at almost every point. But in the field of elementary musical art we have now gained so much insight into its internal connection that we are able to bring the results of our investigations to bear on the views which have been formed and in modern times nearly universally accepted respecting the cause and character of artistic beauty in general. It is, in fact, not difficult to discover a close connection and agreement between them; nay, there are probably fewer examples more suitable than the theory of musical scales and harmony, to illustrate the darkest and most difficult points of general esthetics. Hence I feel that I should not be justified in passing over these considerations, more especially as they are closely connected with the theory of sensual perception, and hence with physiology in general.

No doubt is now entertained that beauty is subject to laws and rules dependent on the nature of human intelligence. The difficulty consists in the fact that these laws and rules, on whose fulfilment beauty depends and by which it must be judged, are not consciously present to the mind, either of the artist who creates the work, or the observer who contemplates it. Art works with design, but the work of art ought to have the appearance of being undesigned, and must be judged on that ground. Art creates as imagination pictures, regularly without conscious law, designedly without conscious aim. A work, known and acknowledged as the product of mere intelligence, will never be accepted as a work of art, however perfect be its adaptation to its end. Whenever we see that conscious reflection has acted in the arrangement of the whole, we find it poor.

> Man fühlt die Absicht, und man wird verstimmt.
> (We feel the purpose, and it jars upon us.)[1]

And yet we require every work of art to be reasonable, and we shew this by subjecting it to a critical examination, and by seeking to enhance our enjoyment and our interest in it by tracing out the suitability, connection, and equilibrium of all its separate parts. The more we succeed in making the harmony and beauty of all its peculiarities clear and distinct, the richer we find it, and we even regard as the principal characteristic of a great work of art that deeper thought, reiterated observation, and continued reflection shew us more and more clearly the reasonableness of all its individual parts. Our endeavour to comprehend the beauty of such a work by critical examination, in which we partly succeed, shews that we assume a certain adaptation to reason in works of art, which may possibly rise to a conscious understanding, although such understanding is neither necessary for the invention nor for the enjoyment of the beautiful. For what is esthetically beautiful is recognised by the immediate

---

1. Actually, *So fühlt man Absicht und man ist verstimmt.* Goethe, *Torquato Tasso,* Act 2, scene 1.

judgment of a cultivated taste, which declares it pleasing or displeasing, without any comparison whatever with law or conception.

But that we do not accept delight in the beautiful as something individual, but rather hold it to be in regular accordance with the nature of mind in general, appears by our expecting and requiring from every other healthy human intellect the same homage that we ourselves pay to what we call beautiful. At most we allow that national or individual peculiarities of taste incline to this or that artistic ideal, and are most easily moved by it, precisely in the same way that a certain amount of education and practice in the contemplation of fine works of art is undeniably necessary for penetration into their deeper meaning.

The principal difficulty in pursuing this object, is to understand how regularity can be apprehended by intuition without being consciously felt to exist. And this unconsciousness of regularity is not a mere accident in the effect of the beautiful on our mind, which may indifferently exist or not; it is, on the contrary, most clearly, prominently, and essentially important. For through apprehending everywhere traces of regularity, connection, and order, without being able to grasp the law and plan of the whole, there arises in our mind a feeling that the work of art which we are contemplating is the product of a design which far exceeds anything we can conceive at the moment, and which hence partakes of the character of the illimitable. Remembering the poet's words:

> Du gleichst dem Geist, den du begreifst
> (Thou'rt like the spirit thou conceivest),[2]

we feel that those intellectual powers which were at work in the artist, are far above our conscious mental action, and that were it even possible at all, infinite time, meditation, and labour would have been necessary to attain by conscious thought that degree of order, connection, and equilibrium of all parts and all internal relations, which the artist has accomplished under the sole guidance of tact and taste, and which we have in turn to appreciate and comprehend by our own tact and taste, long before we begin a critical analysis of the work.

It is clear that all high appreciation of the artist and his work reposes essentially on this feeling. In the first we honour a genius, a spark of divine creative fire, which far transcends the limits of our intelligent and conscious forecast. And yet the artist is a man as we are, in whom work the same mental powers as in ourselves, only in their own peculiar direction, purer, brighter, steadier; and by the greater or less readiness and completeness with which we grasp the artist's language we measure our own share of those powers which produced the wonder.

Herein is manifestly the cause of that moral elevation and feeling of ecstatic satisfaction which is called forth by thorough absorption in genuine and lofty works of art. We learn from them to feel that even in the obscure depths of a healthy and harmoniously developed human mind, which are at least for the

2. Goethe, *Faust*, Pt 1, l. 511.

present inaccessible to analysis by conscious thought, there slumbers a germ of order that is capable of rich intellectual cultivation, and we learn to recognise and admire in the work of art, though draughted in unimportant material, the picture of a similar arrangement of the universe, governed by law and reason in all its parts. The contemplation of a real work of art awakens our confidence in the originally healthy nature of the human mind, when uncribbed, unharassed, unobscured, and unfalsified.

But for all this it is an essential condition that the whole extent of the regularity and design of a work of art should *not* be apprehended consciously. It is precisely from that part of its regular subjection to reason, which escapes our conscious apprehension, that a work of art exalts and delights us, and that the chief effects of the artistically beautiful proceed, *not* from the part which we are able fully to analyse.

If we now apply these considerations to the system of musical tones and harmony, we see of course that these are objects belonging to an entirely subordinate and elementary domain, but nevertheless they, too, are slowly matured inventions of the artistic taste of musicians, and consequently they, too, must be governed by the general rules of artistic beauty. Precisely because we are here still treading the lower walks of art, and are not dealing with the expression of deep psychological problems, we are able to discover a comparatively simple and transparent solution of that fundamental enigma of esthetics.

The whole of the last part of this book has explained how musicians gradually discovered the relationships between tones and chords, and how the invention of harmonic music rendered these relationships closer, and clearer, and richer. We have been able to deduce the whole system of rules which constitute Thorough Bass, from an endeavour to introduce a clearly sensible connection into the series of tones which form a piece of music.

A feeling for the melodic relationship of consecutive tones, was first developed, commencing with Octave and Fifth and advancing to the Third. We have taken pains to prove that this feeling of relationship was founded on the perception of identical partial tones in the corresponding compound tones. Now these partial tones are of course present in the sensations excited in our auditory apparatus, and yet they are not generally the subject of conscious perception as independent sensations. The conscious perception of everyday life is limited to the apprehension of the tone compounded of these partials, as a whole, just as we apprehend the taste of a very compound dish as a whole, without clearly feeling how much of it is due to the salt, or the pepper, or other spices and condiments. A critical examination of our auditory sensations as such was required before we could discover the existence of upper partial tones. Hence the real reason of the melodic relationship of two tones (with the exception of a few more or less clearly expressed conjectures, as, for example, by Rameau and d'Alembert) remained so long undiscovered, or at least was not in any respect clearly and definitely formulated. I believe that I have been able to furnish the required explanation, and hence clearly to exhibit the whole connection of the phenomena. The esthetic problem is thus referred to the common property of all sensual perceptions, namely, the apprehension of compound aggregates of sensations as sensible symbols of simple external objects, without analysing them. In our usual observations on external nature our attention is so thoroughly engaged by external objects that we are entirely unpractised in taking for the subjects of conscious observation, any properties of our sensations themselves, which we do not already know as the sensible expression of some individual external object or event.

After musicians had long been content with the melodic relationship of tones, they began in the middle ages to make use of harmonic relationship as shewn in consonance. The effects of various combinations of tones also depend partly on the identity or difference of two of their different partial tones, but they likewise partly depend on their combinational tones. Whereas, however, in melodic relationship the equality of the upper partial tones can only be perceived by *remembering* the preceding compound tone, in harmonic relationship it is determined by *immediate sensation*, by the presence or absence of beats. Hence in harmonic combinations of tone, tonal relationship is felt with that greater liveliness due to a present sensation as compared with the recollection of a past sensation. The wealth of clearly perceptible relations grows with the number of tones combined. Beats are easy to recognise as such when they occur slowly; but those which characterise dissonances are, almost without exception, very rapid, and are partly covered by sustained tones which do not beat, so that a careful comparison of slower and quicker beats is necessary to gain the conviction that the essence of dissonance consists precisely in rapid beats. Slow beats do not create the feeling of dissonance, which does not arise till the rapidity of the beats confuses the ear and makes it unable to distinguish them. In this case also the ear feels the difference between the undisturbed combination of sound in the case of two consonant tones, and the disturbed rough combination resulting from a dissonance. But, as a general rule, the hearer is then perfectly unconscious of the cause to which the disturbance and roughness are due.

The development of harmony gave rise to a much richer opening out of musical art than was previously possible, because the far clearer characterisation of related combinations of tones by means of chords and chordal sequences, allowed of the use of much more distant relationships than were previously available, by modulating into different keys. In this way the means of expression greatly increased as well as the rapidity of the melodic and harmonic transitions which could now be introduced without destroying the musical connection.

As the independent significance of chords came to be appreciated in the fifteenth and sixteenth centuries, a feeling arose for the relationship of chords to one another and to the tonic chord, in accordance with the same law which had long ago unconsciously regulated the relationship of compound tones. The relationship of compound tones depended on the identity of two or more partial tones, that of chords on the identity of two or more notes. For the musician, of course, the law of the relationship of chords and keys is much more intelligible than that of compound tones. He readily hears the identical tones, or sees them in the notes before him. But the unprejudiced and uninstructed hearer is as little conscious of the reason of the connection of a clear and agreeable series of fluent chords, as he is of the reason of a well-connected melody. He is startled by a false cadence and feels its unexpectedness, but is not at all necessarily conscious of the reason of its unexpectedness.

Then, again, we have seen that the reason why a chord in music appears to be the chord of a determinate root, depends as before upon the analysis of a compound tone into its partial tones, that is, as before upon those elements of a sensation which cannot readily become subjects of conscious perception. This relation between chords is of great importance, both in the relation of the tonic chord to the tonic tone, and in the sequence of chords.

The recognition of these resemblances between compound tones and between chords, reminds us of other exactly analogous circumstances which we must have often experienced. We recognise the resemblance between the faces of two near relations, without being at all able to say in what the resemblance consists, especially when age and sex are different, and the coarser outlines of the features consequently present striking differences. And yet notwithstanding these differences—notwithstanding that we are unable to fix upon a single point in the two countenances which is absolutely alike—the resemblance is often so extraordinarily striking and convincing, that we have not a moment's doubt about it. Precisely the same thing occurs in recognising the relationship between two compound tones.

Again, we are often able to assert with perfect certainty, that a passage not previously heard is due to a particular author or composer whose other works we know. Occasionally, but by no means always, individual mannerisms in verbal or musical phrases determine our judgment, but as a rule we are mostly unable to fix upon the exact points of resemblance between the new piece and the known works of the author or composer.

The analogy of these different cases may be even carried farther. When a father and daughter are strikingly alike in some well-marked feature, as the nose or forehead, we observe it at once, and think no more about it. But if the resemblance is so enigmatically concealed that we cannot detect it, we are fascinated, and cannot help continuing to compare their countenances. And if a painter drew two such heads having, say, a somewhat different expression of character combined with a predominant and striking, though indefinable, resemblance, we should undoubtedly value it as one of the principal beauties of his painting. Our admiration would certainly not be due merely to his technical skill; we should rather look upon his painting as evidencing an unusually delicate feeling for the significance of the human countenance, and find in this the artistic justification of his work.

Now the case is similar for musical intervals. The resemblance of an Octave to its root is so great and striking that the dullest ear perceives it; the Octave seems to be almost a pure repetition of the root, as it, in fact, merely repeats a part of the compound tone of its root, without adding anything new. Hence the esthetical effect of an Octave is that of a perfectly simple, but little attractive interval. The most attractive of the intervals, melodically and harmonically, are clearly the Thirds and Sixths,—the intervals which lie at the very boundary of those that the ear can grasp. The major Third and the major Sixth cannot be properly appreciated unless the first five partial tones are audible. These are present in good musical qualities of tone. The minor Third and the minor Sixth are for the most part justifiable only as inversions of the former intervals. The more complicated intervals in the scale cease to have any direct or easily intelligible relationship. They have no longer the charm of the Thirds.

Moreover, it is by no means a merely external indifferent regularity which the employment of diatonic scales, founded on the relationship of compound tones, has introduced into the tonal material of music, as, for instance, rhythm introduced some such external arrangement into the words of poetry. I have shewn, on the contrary, in Chapter XIV., that this construction of the scale furnished a means of measuring the intervals of their tones, so that the equality of two intervals lying in different sections of the scale would be recognised by immediate sensation. Thus the melodic step of a Fifth is always characterised by having the second partial tone of the second note identical with the third of the first. This produces a definiteness and certainty in the measurement of intervals for our sensation, such as might be looked for in vain in the system of colours, otherwise so similar, or in the estimation of mere differences of intensity in our various sensual perceptions.

Upon this reposes also the characteristic resemblance between the relations of the musical scale and of space, a resemblance which appears to me of vital importance for the peculiar effects of music. It is an essential character of space that at every position within it like bodies can be placed, and like motions can occur. Everything that is possible to happen in one part of space is equally possible in every other part of space and is perceived by us in precisely the same way. This is the case also with the musical scale. Every melodic phrase, every chord, which can be executed at any pitch, can be also executed at any other pitch in such a way that we immediately perceive the characteristic marks of their similarity. On the other hand, also, different voices, executing the same or different melodic phrases, can move at the same time within the compass of the scale, like two bodies in space, and, provided they are consonant in the accented parts of bars, without creating any musical disturbances. Such a close analogy consequently exists in all essential relations between the musical scale and space, that even alteration of pitch has a readily recognised and unmistakable resemblance to motion in space, and is often metaphorically termed the ascending or descending *motion* or *progression* of a part. Hence, again, it becomes possible for motion in music to imitate the peculiar characteristics of motive forces in space, that is, to form an image of the various impulses and forces which lie at the root of motion. And on this, as I believe, essentially depends the power of music to picture emotion.

It is not my intention to deny that music in its initial state and simplest forms may have been originally an artistic imitation of the instinctive modulations of the voice that correspond to various conditions of the feelings. But I cannot think that this is opposed to the above explanation; for a great part of the natural means of vocal expression may be reduced to such facts as the following: its rhythm and accentuation are an immediate expression of the rapidity or force of the corresponding psychical motives—all effort drives the voice up—a desire to make a pleasant impression on another mind leads to selecting a softer, pleasanter quality of tone—and so forth. An endeavour to imitate the involuntary modulations of the voice and make its recitation richer and more expressive, may therefore very possibly have led our ancestors to the discovery of the first means of musical expression, just as the imitation of weeping, shouting, or sobbing, and other musical delineations may play a part in even cultivated music, (as in operas), although such modifications of the voice are not confined to the action of free mental motives, but embrace really mechanical and even involuntary muscular contractions. But it is quite clear that every completely developed melody goes far beyond an imitation of nature, even if we include the cases of the most varied alteration of voice under the influence of passion. Nay, the very fact that music introduces progression by fixed degrees both in rhythm and in the scale, renders even an approximatively correct representation of nature simply impossible, for most of the passionate affections of the voice are characterised by a gliding transition in pitch. The imitation of nature is thus rendered as imperfect as the imitation of a picture by embroidery on a canvas with separate little squares for each shade of colour. Music, too, departed still further from nature when it introduced the greater compass, the mobility, and the strange qualities of tone belonging to musical instruments, by which the field of attainable musical effects has become so much wider than it was or could be when the human voice alone was employed.

Hence though it is probably correct to say that mankind, in historical development, first learned the means of musical expression from the human voice, it can hardly be denied that these same means of expressing melodic progression act, in artistically developed music, without the slightest reference to the application made of them in the modulations of the human voice, and have a more general significance than any that can be attributed to innate instinctive cries. That this is the case appears above all in the modern development of instrumental music, which possesses an effective power and artistic justification that need not be gainsaid, although we may not yet be able to explain it in all its details.

· · ·

Here I close my work. It appears to me that I have carried it as far as the physiological properties of the sensation of hearing exercise a direct influence on the construction of a musical system, that is, as far as the work especially belongs to natural philosophy. For even if I could not avoid mixing up esthetic problems with physical, the former were comparatively simple, and the latter much more complicated. This relation would necessarily become inverted if I attempted to proceed further into the esthetics of music, and to enter on the theory of rhythm, forms of composition, and means of musical expression. In all these fields the properties of sensual perception would of course have an influence at times, but only in a very subordinate degree. The real difficulty would lie in the development of the psychical motives which here assert themselves. Certainly this is the point where the more interesting part of musical esthetics begins, the aim being to explain the wonders of great works of art, and to learn the utterances and actions of the various affections of the mind. But, however alluring such an aim may be, I prefer leaving others to carry out such investigations, in which I should feel myself too much of an amateur, while I myself remain on the safe ground of natural philosophy, in which I am at home.

166 Amy Fay

Amy Fay was a celebrated American concert pianist as well as a lecturer and teacher. She lived for a time in each of three major musical centers, Boston, Chicago, and New York, and became active in organizations to promote women's participation, such as the Amateur Music Club and the New York Women's Philharmonic Society (which she also served as president).

Fay was born in Louisiana in 1844. At the age of twenty-five she traveled to Germany to continue her musical studies and remained there for six years. Her vivid and perceptive letters home, describing her studies and other musical adventures, were edited for publication by her sister, Melusina Fay Peirce (feminist writer on the reform of domestic architecture and first wife of the philosopher Charles Sanders Peirce). The resulting little book enjoyed great popularity, appearing in twenty-five editions in the United States alone, in several English editions, and in French and German translations.

Women were admitted into European conservatories as performance students in large numbers during the nineteenth century, but many restrictions were placed upon them: instruction was usually segregated by gender, as Amy Fay describes here; the curriculum for women was often a truncated version of that offered to men; and it was not until late in the century that women were admitted as composition students, or that their professional aspirations were taken seriously. Boston composer Mabel Daniels also wrote a memoir, *An American Girl in Munich*, describing her conservatory study a few decades later than Fay's.

FROM *Music-Study in Germany*
(1880)

Berlin, February 8, 1870

$\bullet$　$\bullet$　$\bullet$　$\bullet$　$\bullet$

The day after Tausig's concert I went, as usual, to hear him give the lesson to his best class of girls. I got there a little before the hour, and the girls were in the dressing-room waiting for the young men to be through with their lesson. They were talking about the concert. "Was it not beautiful?" said little Timanoff, to me; "I did not sleep the whole night after it!"—a touch of sentiment that quite surprised me in that small personage, and made me feel some compunctions, as I had slept soundly myself. "I have practiced five hours to-day already," she added. Just then the young men came out of the class-room and we passed into it. Tausig was standing by the piano. "Begin!" said he, to Timanoff, more shortly even than usual; "I trust you have brought me a study *this* time." He always insists upon a study in addition to the piece. Timanoff replied in the affirmative, and proceeded to open Chopin's *Etudes.* She played the great A minor "Winter Wind" study, and most magnificently, too, starting off with the greatest brilliancy and "go." I was perfectly amazed at such a feat from such a child, and expected that Tausig would exclaim with admiration. Not so that Rhadamanthus. He heard it through without comment or correction, and when Timanoff had finished, simply remarked very composedly, "So! Have you taken the *next* Etude, also?" as if the great A minor were not enough for one meal! It is eight pages long to begin with, and there is no let up to the difficulty all the way through. Afterward, however, he told the young men that he "could not have done it better" himself.

Tausig is so hasty and impatient that to be in his classes must be a fearful ordeal. He will not bear the slightest fault. The last time I went into his class to hear him teach he was dreadful. Fräulein H. began, and she has remarkable talent, and is far beyond me. She would not play *piano* enough to suit him, and finally he stamped his foot at her, snatched her hand from the piano, and said: "*Will* you play *piano* or not, for if not we will go no farther?" The second girl sat down and played a few lines. He made her begin over again several times, and finally came up and took her music away and slapped it down on the piano,—"You have been studying this for weeks and you can't play a note of it; practice it for a month and then you can bring it to me again," he said.

The third was Fräulein Timanoff, who is a little genius, I think. She brought a Sonata by Schubert—the one, I believe, in A—and by the way he behaved Tausig must have a particular feeling about that particular Sonata. Timanoff

TEXT: *Music-Study in Germany, from the Home Correspondence of Amy Fay* (Chicago, 1880), pp. 39–42, 163–68, 210–14.

began running it off in her usual nimble style, having practiced it evidently every minute of the time when she was not asleep, since the last lesson. She had not proceeded far down the first page when he stopped her, and began to fuss over the expression. She began again, but this time with no better luck. A third time, but still he was dissatisfied, though he suffered her to go on a little farther. He kept stopping her every moment in the most tantalizing and exasperating manner. If it had been I, I should have cried, but Timanoff was well broken, and only flushed deeply to the very tips of her small ears. From an apple blossom she changed to a carnation. Tausig grew more and more savage, and made her skip whole pages in his impatience. "Play here!" he would say, in the most imperative tone, pointing to a half or whole page farther on. "This I cannot hear!—Go on farther!—It is too bad to be listened to!" Finally, he struck the music with the back of his hand, and exclaimed, in a despairing way, "*Kind, es liegt eine Seele darin. Weisst du nicht es liegt eine* Seele *darin?* (Child, there's a soul in the piece. Don't you know there is a *soul* in it?)" To the little Timanoff, who has no soul, and who is not sufficiently experienced to counterfeit one, this speech evidently conveyed no particular idea. She ran on as glibly as ever till Tausig could endure no more, and shut up the music. I was much disappointed, as it was new to me, and I like to hear Timanoff's little fingers tinkle over the keys, "seele" or no "seele." She has a most accurate and dainty way of doing everything, and somehow, in her healthy little brain I hardly wish for *Seele!*

Last of all Fräulein L. played, and she alone suited Tausig. She is a Swede, and is the best scholar he has, but she has such frightfully ugly hands, and holds them so terribly, that when I look at her I cannot enjoy her playing. Tausig always praises her very much, and she is tremendously ambitious.

Tausig has a charming face, full of expression and very sensitive. He is extremely sharp-sighted, and has eyes in the back of his head, I believe. He is far too small and too despotic to be fascinating, however, though he has a sort of captivating way with him when he is in a good humor.

•   •   •   •   •

Berlin, February 10, 1872

A week ago last Monday I went to Dresden with J. L. to visit B. H. . . . B. did everything in her power to amuse us, and she is the soul of amiability. She kept inviting people to meet us, and had several tea-parties, and when we had no company she took us to the theatre or the opera. She invited Marie Wieck (the sister of Clara Schumann) to tea one night. I was very glad to meet her, for she is an exquisite artist herself, and plays in Clara Schumann's style, though her conception is not so remarkable. Her touch is perfect. At B.'s request she tried to play for us, but the action of B.'s piano did not suit her, and she presently got up, saying that she could do nothing on that instrument, but that if we would come to *her,* she would play for us with pleasure.

I was in high glee at that proposal, for I was very anxious to see the famous

Wieck, the trainer of so many generations of musicians. Fräulein Wieck appointed Saturday evening, and we accordingly went. B. had instructed us how to act, for the old man is quite a character, and has to be dealt with after his own fashion. She said we must walk in (having first laid off our things) as if we had been members of the family all our lives, and say, "Good-evening, Papa Wieck,"—(everybody calls him Papa). Then we were to seat ourselves, and if we had some knitting or sewing with us it would be well. At any rate we must have the apparent intention of spending several hours, for nothing provokes him so as to have people come in simply to call. "What!" he will say, "do you expect to know a celebrated man like me in half an hour?" then (very sarcastically), "perhaps you want my autograph!" He hates to give his autograph.

Well, we went through the prescribed programme. We were ushered into a large room, much longer than it was broad. At either end stood a grand piano. Otherwise the room was furnished with the greatest simplicity. My impression is that the floor was a plain yellow painted one, with a rug or two here and there. A few portraits and bas-reliefs hung upon the walls. The pianos were of course fine. Frau Wieck and "Papa" received us graciously. We began by taking tea, but soon the old man became impatient, and said, "Come! the ladies wish to perform (*vortragen*) something before me, and if we don't begin we shan't accomplish anything." He *lives* entirely in music, and has a class of girls whom he instructs every evening for nothing. Five of these young girls were there. He is very deaf, but strange to say, he is as sensitive as ever to every musical sound, and the same is the case with Clara Schumann. Fräulein Wieck then opened the ball. She is about forty, I should think, and a stout, phlegmatic-looking woman. However, she played superbly, and her touch is one of the most delicious possible. After hearing her, one is not surprised that the Wiecks think nobody can teach touch but themselves. She began with a nocturne by Chopin, in F major. I forgot to say that the old Herr sits in his chair with the air of being on a throne, and announces beforehand each piece that is to be played, following it with some comment: *e.g.*, "This nocturne I allowed my daughter Clara to play in Berlin forty years ago, and afterward the principal newspaper in criticising her performance, remarked: 'This young girl seems to have much talent; it is only a pity that she is in the hands of a father whose head seems stuck full of queer new-fangled notions,'—so new was Chopin to the public at that time." That is the way he goes on.

After Fräulein Wieck had finished the nocturne, I asked for something by Bach, which I'm told she plays remarkably. She said that at the moment she had nothing in practice by Bach, but she would play me a *gigue* by a composer of Bach's time,—Haesler, I think she said, but cannot remember, as it was a name entirely unknown to me. It was very brilliant, and she executed it beautifully. Afterward she played the last movement of Beethoven's Sonata in E flat major, but I wasn't particularly struck with her conception of that. Then we had a pause, and she urged me to play. I refused, for as I had been in Dresden a week and had not practiced, I did not wish to sit down and not do myself justice. My hand is so stiff, that as Tausig said of himself (though of him I can hardly believe it), "When I haven't practiced for fourteen days I can't do anything." The old Herr then said, "Now we'll have something else;" and got up and went to the piano, and called the young girls. He made three of them sing, one after the other, and they sang very charmingly indeed. One of them he made improvise a *cadenza*, and a second sang the alto to it without accompaniment. He was very proud of that. He exercises his pupils in all sorts of ways, trains them to sing any given tone, and "to skip up and down the ladder," as they call the scale.

After the master had finished with the singing, Fräulein Wieck played three more pieces, one of which was an exquisite arrangement by Liszt of that song by Schumann, *"Du meine Seele."* She ended with a *gavotte* by Gluck, or as Papa Wieck would say, "This is a gavotte from one of Gluck's operas, arranged by Brahms for the piano. To the superficial observer the second movement will appear very easy, but in *my* opinion it is a very hard task to hit it exactly." I happened to know just how the thing ought to be played, for I had heard it three times from Clara Schumann herself. Fräulein Wieck didn't please me at all in it, for she took the second movement twice as quickly as the first. "Your sister plays the second movement much slower," said I. "*So?*" said she, "I've never heard it from her." She then asked, "So slow?" playing it slower. "Still slower?" said she, beginning a third time, at my continual disapproval. "*Streng im Tempo* (in strict time)," said I, nodding my head oracularly. "*Väterchen.*" called she to the old Herr, "Miss Fay says that Clara plays the second movement *so* slow," showing him. I don't know whether this correction made an impression, but he was then *determined* that I should play, and on my continued refusal he finally said that he found it very strange that a young lady who had studied more than two years in Tausig's and Kullak's conservatories shouldn't have *one* piece that she could play before people. This little fling provoked me, so up I jumped, and saying to myself, "*Kopf in die Höhe, Brust heraus—vorwärts!*" (one of the military orders here), I marched to the piano and played the fugue at the end of Beethoven's A flat Sonata, Op. 110. They all sat round the room as still as so many statues while I played, and you cannot imagine how dreadfully nervous I was. I thought fifty times I would have to stop, for, like all fugues, it is such a piece that if you once get out you never can get in again, and Bülow himself got mixed up on the last part of it the other night in his concert. But I got well through, notwithstanding, and the old master was good enough to commend me warmly. He told me I must have studied a great deal, and asked me if I hadn't played a great many *Etuden.* I informed him in polite German "He'd better believe I had!"

•   •   •   •   •

Weimar, May 21, 1873

Liszt is so *besieged* by people and so tormented with applications, that I fear I should only have been sent away if I had come without the Baroness von S.'s letter of introduction, for he admires her extremely, and I judge that she has much influence with him. He says "people fly in his face by dozens," and seem to think he is "only there to give lessons." He gives *no* paid lessons whatever, as he is much too grand for that, but if one has talent enough, or pleases him, he lets one come to him and play to him. I go to him every other day, but I don't play more than twice a week, as I cannot prepare so much, but I listen to the others. Up to this point there have been only four in the class besides myself, and I am the only new one. From four to six P. M. is the time when he receives his scholars. The first time I went I did not play to him, but listened to the rest. Urspruch and Leitert, the two young men who I met the other night, have studied with Liszt a long time, and both play superbly. Fräulein Schultz and Miss Gaul (of Baltimore), are also most gifted creatures.

As I entered Liszt's salon, Urspruch was performing Schumann's Symphonic Studies—an immense composition, and one that it took at least half an hour to get through. He played so splendidly that my heart sank down into the very depths. I thought I should never get on *there!* Liszt came forward and greeted me in a very friendly manner as I entered. He was in very good humour that day, and made some little witticisms. Urspruch asked him what title he should give to a piece he was composing. *"Per aspera ad astra,"* said Liszt. This was such a good hit that I began to laugh, and he seemed to enjoy my appreciation of his little sarcasm. I did not play that time, as my piano had only just come, and I was not prepared to do so, but I went home and practiced tremendously for several days on Chopin's B minor sonata. It is a great composition, and one of his last works. When I thought I could play it, I went to Liszt, though with a trembling heart. I cannot tell you what it has cost me every time I have ascended his stairs. I can scarcely summon up courage to go there, and generally stand on the steps awhile before I can make up my mind to open the door and go in!

This day it was particularly trying, as it was really my first serious performance before him, and he speaks so very indistinctly that I feared I shouldn't understand his corrections, and that he would get out of patience with me, for he cannot bear to explain. I think he hates the trouble of speaking German, for he mutters his words and does not half finish his sentences. Yesterday when I was there he spoke to me in French all the time, and to the others in German,—one of his funny whims, I suppose.

Well, on this day the artists Leitert and Urspruch, and the young composer Metzdorf, who is always hanging about Liszt, were in the room when I came. They had probably been playing. At first Liszt took no notice of me beyond a greeting, till Metzdorf said to him, "Herr Doctor, Miss Fay has brought a sonata." "Ah, well, let us hear it," said Liszt. Just then he left the room for a minute, and I told the three gentlemen that they ought to go away and let me play to Liszt alone, for I felt nervous about playing before them. They all laughed at me and said they would not budge an inch. When Liszt came back they said to him, "Only think, Herr Doctor, Miss Fay proposes to send us all home." I said I could not play before such great artists. "Oh, that is healthy for you," said Liszt, with a smile, and added, "you have a very choice audience, now." I don't know whether he appreciated how nervous I was, but instead of walking up and down the room as he often does, he sat down by me like any other teacher, and heard me play the first movement. It was frightfully hard, but I had studied it so much that I managed to get through with it pretty successfully. Nothing could exceed Liszt's amiability, or the trouble he gave himself, and instead of frightening me, he inspired me. Never was there such a delightful teacher! and he is the first sympathetic one I've had. You feel so *free* with him, and he develops the very spirit of music in you. He doesn't keep nagging at you all the time, but he leaves you your own conception. Now and then he will make a criticism, or play a passage, and with a few words give you enough to think of all the rest of your life. There is a delicate *point* to everything he says, as subtle as he is himself. He doesn't tell you anything about the technique. That you must work out for yourself. When I had finished the first movement of the sonata, Liszt said "Bravo!" Taking my seat, he made some little criticisms, and then told me to go on and play the rest of it.

Now, I only half knew the other movements, for the first one was so extremely difficult that it cost me all the labour I could give to prepare that. But playing to Liszt reminds me of trying to feed the elephant in the Zoological Garden with lumps of sugar. He disposes of whole movements as if they were nothing, and stretches out gravely for more! One of my fingers fortunately began to bleed, for I had practiced the skin off, and that gave me a good excuse for stopping. Whether he was pleased at this proof of industry, I know not; but after looking at my finger and saying, "Oh!" very compassionately, he sat down and played the whole three last movements himself. That was a great deal, and showed off all his powers. It was the first time I had heard him, and I don't know which was the most extraordinary,—the Scherzo, with its wonderful lightness and swiftness, the Adagio with its depth and pathos, or the last movement, where the whole keyboard seemed to *"donnern und blitzen* (thunder and lighten)." There is such a vividness about everything he plays that it does not seem as if it were mere music you were listening to, but it is as if he had called up a real, living *form,* and you saw it breathing before your face and eyes. It gives *me* almost a ghostly feeling to hear him, and it seems as if the air were peopled with spirits. Oh, he is a perfect wizard! It is as interesting to see him as it is to hear him, for his face changes with every modulation of the piece, and he looks exactly as he is playing. He has one element that is most captivating, and that is, a sort of delicate and fitful mirth that keeps peering out at you here and there! It is most peculiar, and when he plays that way, the most bewitching little expression comes over his face. It seems as if a little spirit of joy were playing hide and go seek with you.

MUSICAL
ENCOUNTERS

167 Antonín Dvořák

Jeannette Thurber, founder of the National Conservatory of Music in New York, invited Dvořák to become its director. He agreed, arriving in New York in the fall of 1892 and staying in the United States for nearly three years before returning to Prague.

The celebrated Czech composer was a firm believer in national musics, and he took up residence in the United States at least partly in the hope of helping young American composers find their way to a genuinely "American" sound. A number of his own compositions written during his American sojourn may also have been conceived in this spirit, among them a string quartet and string quintet each called "the American" and his most familiar work, Symphony No. 9, "From the New World." He had undertaken, one New York reporter wrote, "a serious study of the national music of this continent as exemplified in the native melodies of the negro and Indian races" (see note 2 below).

Dvořák's impressions of the music of African-Americans and of American Indians, and his understanding of their role in American urban culture, may seem quixotic today, as will his essentialist confusion of a national population with a "race." But there is no question that he took an earnest and energetic interest in the search for a national musical identity which occupied many American composers at the time.

Music in America
(1895)

It is a difficult task at best for a foreigner to give a correct verdict of the affairs of another country. With the United States of America this is more than usually difficult, because they cover such a vast area of land that it would take many years to become properly acquainted with the various localities, separated by great distances, that would have to be considered when rendering a judgment concerning them all. It would ill become me, therefore, to express my views on so general and all-embracing a subject as music in America, were I not pressed to do so, for I have neither travelled extensively, nor have I been here long enough to gain an intimate knowledge of American affairs. I can only judge of it from what I have observed during my limited experience as a musician and teacher in America, and from what those whom I know here tell me about their own country. Many of my impressions therefore are those of a foreigner who has not been here long enough to overcome the feeling of strangeness and bewildered astonishment which must fill all European visitors upon their first arrival.

The two American traits which most impress the foreign observer, I find,

Text: *Harper's New Monthly Magazine* 90 (1895): 429–34.

are the unbounded patriotism and capacity for enthusiasm of most Americans. Unlike the more diffident inhabitants of other countries, who do not "wear their hearts upon their sleeves," the citizens of America are always patriotic, and no occasion seems to be too serious or too slight for them to give expression to this feeling. Thus nothing better pleases the average American, especially the American youth, than to be able to say that this or that building, this or that new patent appliance, is the finest or grandest in the world. This, of course, is due to that other trait—enthusiasm. The enthusiasm of most Americans for all things new is apparently without limit. It is the essence of what is called "push"—American push. Every day I meet with this quality in my pupils. They are unwilling to stop at anything. In the matters relating to their art they are inquisitive to a degree that they want to go to the bottom of all things at once. It is as if a boy wished to dive before he could swim.

At first, when my American pupils were new to me, this trait annoyed me, and I wished them to give more attention to the one matter in hand rather than to everything at once. But now I like it; for I have come to the conclusion that this youthful enthusiasm and eagerness to take up everything is the best promise for music in America. The same opinion, I remember, was expressed by the director of the new conservatory in Berlin, who, from his experience with American students of music, predicted that America within twenty or thirty years would become the first musical country.

Only when the people in general, however, begin to take as lively an interest in music and art as they now take in more material matters will the arts come into their own. Let the enthusiasm of the people once be excited, and patriotic gifts and bequests must surely follow.

It is a matter of surprise to me that all this has not come long ago. When I see how much is done in every other field by public-spirited men in America— how schools, universities, libraries, museums, hospitals, and parks spring up out of the ground and are maintained by generous gifts—I can only marvel that so little has been done for music. After two hundred years of almost unbroken prosperity and expansion, the net results for music are a number of public concert-halls of most recent growth; several musical societies with orchestras of noted excellence, such as the Philharmonic Society in New York, the orchestras of Mr. Thomas and Mr. Seidl, and the superb orchestra supported by a public spirited citizen of Boston; one opera company, which only the upper classes can hear or understand; and a national conservatory which owes its existence to the generous forethought of one indefatigable woman.

It is true that music is the youngest of the arts, and must therefore be expected to be treated as Cinderella, but is it not time that she were lifted from the ashes and given a seat among the equally youthful sister arts in this land of youth, until the coming of the fairy godmother and the prince of the crystal slipper?

Art, of course, must always go a-begging, but why should this country alone, which is so justly famed for the generosity and public spirit of its citizens, close its door to the poor beggar? In the Old World this is not so. Since the days of Palestrina, the three-hundredth anniversary of whose death was celebrated in Rome a few weeks ago, princes and prelates have vied with each other in extending a generous hand to music. Since the days of Pope Gregory the Church has made music one of her own chosen arts. In Germany and Austria princes like Esterhazy, Lobkowitz, and Harrach, who supported Haydn and Beethoven, or the late King of Bavaria, who did so much for Wagner, with many others have helped to create a demand for good music, which has since become universal, while in France all governments, be they monarchies, empires, or republics, have done their best to carry on the noble work that was begun by Louis the Fourteenth. Even the little republic of Switzerland annually sets aside a budget for the furtherance of literature, music, and the arts.

A few months ago only we saw how such a question of art as whether the operas sung in Hungary's capital should be of a national or foreign character could provoke a ministerial crisis. Such is the interest in music and art taken by the governments and people of other countries.

The great American republic alone, in its national government as well as in the several governments of the States, suffers art and music to go without encouragement. Trades and commerce are protected, funds are voted away for the unemployed, schools and colleges are endowed, but music must go unaided, and be content if she can get the support of a few private individuals like Mrs. Jeannette M. Thurber and Mr. H. L. Higginson.

Not long ago a young man came to me and showed me his compositions. His talent seemed so promising that I at once offered him a scholarship in our school; but he sorrowfully confessed that he could not afford to become my pupil, because he had to earn his living by keeping books in Brooklyn. Even if he came on but two afternoons in the week, or on Saturday afternoon only, he said, he would lose his employment, on which he and others had to depend. I urged him to arrange the matter with his employer, but he only received the answer: "If you want to play, you can't keep books. You will have to drop one or the other." He dropped his music.

In any other country the state would have made some provision for such a deserving scholar, so that he could have pursued his natural calling without having to starve. With us in Bohemia the Diet each year votes a special sum of money for just such purposes, and the imperial government in Vienna on occasion furnishes other funds for talented artists. Had it not been for such support I should not have been able to pursue my studies when I was a young man. Owing to the fact that, upon the kind recommendation of such men as Brahms, Hanslick, and Herbeck, the Minister of Public Education in Vienna on five successive years sent me sums ranging from four to six hundred florins, I was able to pursue my work and to get my compositions published, so that at the end of that time I was able to stand on my own feet. This has filled me with lasting gratitude towards my country.

Such an attitude of the state towards deserving artists is not only a kind but a wise one. For it cannot be emphasized too strongly that art, as such, does not "pay," to use an American expression—at least, not in the beginning—and that the art that has to pay its own way is apt to become vitiated and cheap.

It is one of the anomalies of this country that the principle of protection is upheld for all enterprises but art. By protection I do not mean the exclusion of foreign art. That, of course, is absurd. But just as the State here provides for its poor industrial scholars and university students, so should it help the would-be students of music and art. As it is now, the poor musician not only cannot get his necessary instruction, in the first place, but if by any chance he has acquired it, he has small prospects of making his chosen calling support him in the end. Why is this? Simply because the orchestras in which first-class players could find a place in this country can be counted on one hand; while of opera companies where native singers can be heard, and where the English tongue is sung, there are none at all. Another thing which discourages the student of music is the unwillingness of publishers to take anything but light and trashy music. European publishers are bad enough in that respect, but the American publishers are worse. Thus, when one of my pupils last year produced a very creditable work, and a thoroughly American composition at that, he could not get it published in America, but had to send it to Germany, where it was at once accepted. The same is true of my own compositions on American subjects, each of which hitherto has had to be published abroad.

No wonder American composers and musicians grow discouraged, and regard the more promising condition of music in other countries with envy! Such a state of affairs should be a source of mortification to all truly patriotic Americans. Yet it can be easily remedied. What was the situation in England but a short while ago? Then they had to procure all their players from abroad, while their own musicians went to the Continent to study. Now that they have two standard academies of music in London, like those of Berlin, Paris, and other cities, the national feeling for music seems to have been awakened, and the majority of orchestras are composed of native Englishmen, who play as well as the others did before. A single institution can make such a change, just as a single genius can bestow an art upon his country that before was lying in unheeded slumber.

Our musical conservatory in Prague was founded but three generations ago, when a few nobles and patrons of music subscribed five thousand florins, which was then the annual cost of maintaining the school. Yet that little school flour-ished and grew, so that now more than sixfold that amount is annually expended. Only lately a school for organ music has been added to the conserva-tory, so that the organists of our churches can learn to play their instruments at home, without having to go to other cities. Thus a school benefits the com-munity in which it is. The citizens of Prague in return have shown their appreciation of the fact by building the "Rudolfinum" as a magnificent home for all the arts. It is jointly occupied by the conservatory and the Academy of Arts, and besides that contains large and small concert-halls and rooms for picture-galleries. In the proper maintenance of this building the whole community takes an interest. It is supported, as it was founded, by the stockholders of the Bohemian Bank of Deposit, and yearly gifts and bequests are made to the institution by private citizens.

If a school of art can grow so in a country of but six million inhabitants, what much brighter prospects should it not have in a land of seventy millions? The important thing is to make a beginning, and in this the State should set an example.

They tell me that this cannot be done. I ask, why can't it be done? If the old commonwealths of Greece and Italy, and the modern republics of France and Switzerland, have been able to do this, why cannot America follow their example? The money certainly is not lacking. Constantly we see great sums of money spent for the material pleasures of the few, which, if devoted to the purposes of art, might give pleasure to thousands. If schools, art museums, and libraries can be maintained at the public expense, why should not musical conservatories and playhouses? The function of the drama, with or without music, is not only to amuse, but to elevate and instruct while giving pleasure. Is it not in the interest of the State that this should be done in the most approved manner, so as to benefit all of its citizens? Let the owners of private playhouses give their performances for diversion only, let those who may, import singers who sing in foreign tongues, but let there be at least one intelligent power that will see to it that the people can hear and see what is best, and what can be understood by them, no matter how small the demand.

That such a system of performing classic plays and operas pleases the people was shown by the attitude of the populace in Prague. There the people collected money and raised subscriptions for over fifty years to build a national playhouse. In 1880 they at last had a sufficient amount, and the "National Theatre" was accordingly built. It had scarcely been built when it was burned to the ground. But the people were not to be discouraged. Everybody helped, and before a fortnight was over more than a million had been collected, and the house was at once built up again, more magnificent than it was before.

In answer to such arguments I am told that there is no popular demand for good music in America. That is not so. Every concert in New York, Boston, Philadelphia, Chicago, or Washington, and most other cities, no doubt, disproves such a statement. American concert-halls are as well filled as those of Europe, and, as a rule, the listeners—to judge them by their attentive conduct and subsequent expression of pleasure—are not a whit less appreciative. How it would be with opera I cannot judge, since American opera audiences, as the opera is conducted at present, are in no sense representative of the people at large. I have no doubt, however, that if the Americans had a chance to hear grand opera sung in their own language they would enjoy it as well and appreciate it as highly as the opera-goers of Vienna, Paris, or Munich enjoy theirs. The change from Italian and French to English will scarcely have an injurious effect on the present good voices of the singers, while it may have the effect of improving the voices of American singers, bringing out more clearly the beauty and strength of the *timbre,* while giving an intelligent conception of the work that enables singers to use a pure diction, which cannot be obtained in a foreign tongue.

The American voice, so far as I can judge, is a good one. When I first arrived in this country I was startled by the strength and the depth of the voices in the boys who sell papers on the street, and I am still constantly amazed at its penetrating quality.

In a sense, of course, it is true that there is less of a demand for music in America than in certain other countries. Our common folk in Bohemia know this. When they come here they leave their fiddles and other instruments at home, and none of the itinerant musicians with whom our country abounds would ever think of trying their luck over here. Occasionally when I have met one of my countrymen whom I knew to be musical in this city of New York or in the West, and have asked him why he did not become a professional musician, I have usually received the answer, "Oh, music is not wanted in this land." This I can scarcely believe. Music is wanted wherever good people are, as the German poet has sung.[1] It only rests with the leaders of the people to make a right beginning.

When this beginning is made, and when those who have musical talent find it worth their while to stay in America, and to study and exercise their art as the business of their life, the music of America will soon become more national in its character. This, my conviction, I know is not shared by many who can justly claim to know this country better than I do. Because the population of the United States is composed of many different races, in which the Teutonic element predominates, and because, owing to the improved methods of transmission of the present day, the music of all the world is quickly absorbed by this country, they argue that nothing specially original or national can come forth. According to that view, all other countries which are but the results of a conglomeration of peoples and races, as, for instance, Italy, could not have produced a national literature or a national music.

A while ago I suggested that inspiration for truly national music might be derived from the negro melodies or Indian chants.[2] I was led to take this view partly by the fact that the so-called plantation songs are indeed the most striking and appealing melodies that have yet been found on this side of the water, but largely by the observation that this seems to be recognized, though often unconsciously, by most Americans. All races have their distinctively national songs, which they at once recognize as their own, even if they have never heard them before. When a Tsech, a Pole, or a Magyar in this country suddenly hears

---

1. A German saying apparently paraphrased from the poem "Gesänge" (1804) by Georg Seume; the original line reads "Bösewichter haben keine Lieder" ("villains have no songs"). I am grateful to Jocelyne Kolb for locating the source.
2. In an interview in the *New York Herald* (December 15, 1893); reprinted in *I.S.A.M. Newsletter* 14 (November 1987): 4.

one of his folk-songs or dances, no matter if it is for the first time in his life, his eye lights up at once, and his heart within him responds, and claims that music as its own. So it is with those of Teutonic or Celtic blood, or any other men, indeed, whose first lullaby mayhap was a song wrung from the heart of the people.

It is a proper question to ask, what songs, then, belong to the American and appeal more strongly to him than any others? What melody could stop him on the street if he were in a strange land and make the home feeling well up within him, no matter how hardened he might be or how wretchedly the tune were played? Their number, to be sure, seems to be limited. The most potent as well as the most beautiful among them, according to my estimation, are certain of the so-called plantation melodies and slave songs, all of which are distinguished by unusual and subtle harmonies, the like of which I have found in no other songs but those of old Scotland and Ireland. The point has been urged that many of these touching songs, like those of Foster, have not been composed by the negroes themselves, but are the work of white men, while others did not originate on the plantation, but were imported from Africa. It seems to me that this matters but little. One might as well condemn the Hungarian Rhapsody because Liszt could not speak Hungarian. The important thing is that the inspiration for such music should come from the right source, and that the music itself should be a true expression of the people's real feelings. To read the right meaning the composer need not necessarily be of the same blood, though that, of course, makes it easier for him. Schubert was a thorough German, but when he wrote Hungarian music, as in the second movement of the C-Major Symphony, or in some of his piano pieces, like the Hungarian Divertissement, he struck the true Magyar note, to which all Magyar hearts, and with them our own, must forever respond. This is not a *tour de force,* but only an instance of how much can be comprehended by a sympathetic genius. The white composers who wrote the touching negro songs which dimmed Thackeray's spectacles so that he exclaimed, "Behold, a vagabond with a corked face and a banjo sings a little song, strikes a wild note, which sets the whole heart thrilling with happy pity!" had a similarly sympathetic comprehension of the deep pathos of slave life. If, as I have been informed they were, these songs were adopted by the negroes on the plantations, they thus became true negro songs. Whether the original songs which must have inspired the composers came from Africa or originated on the plantations matters as little as whether Shakespeare invented his own plots or borrowed them from others. The thing to rejoice over is that such lovely songs exist and are sung at the present day. I, for one, am delighted by them. Just so it matters little whether the inspiration for the coming folk-songs of America is derived from the negro melodies, the songs of the creoles, the red man's chant, or the plaintive ditties of the homesick German or Norwegian. Undoubtedly the germs for the best of music lie hidden among all the races that are commingled in this great country. The music of the people is like a rare and lovely flower growing amidst encroaching weeds. Thousands pass it, while others trample it under foot, and thus the chances are that it will perish before it is seen by the one discriminating spirit who will prize it above all else. The fact that no one has as yet arisen to make the most of it does not prove that nothing is there.

Not so many years ago Slavic music was not known to the men of other races. A few men like Chopin, Glinka, Moniuszko, Smetana, Rubinstein, and Tschaikowski, with a few others, were able to create a Slavic school of music. Chopin alone caused the music of Poland to be known and prized by all lovers of music. Smetana did the same for us Bohemians. Such national music, I repeat, is not created out of nothing. It is discovered and clothed in new beauty, just as the myths and the legends of a people are brought to light and crystallized in undying verse by the master poets. All that is needed is a delicate ear, a retentive memory, and the power to weld the fragments of former ages together in one harmonious whole. Only the other day I read in a newspaper that Brahms himself admitted that he had taken existing folk-songs for the themes of his new book of songs, and had arranged them for piano music. I have not heard nor seen the songs, and do not know if this be so; but if it were, it would in no wise reflect discredit upon the composer. Liszt in his rhapsodies and Berlioz in his *Faust* did the same thing with existing Hungarian strains, as, for instance, the Racokzy March; and Schumann and Wagner made a similar use of the Marseillaise for their songs of the "Two Grenadiers." Thus, also, Balfe, the Irishman, used one of our most national airs, a Hussite song, in his opera, the *Bohemian Girl,* though how he came by it nobody has as yet explained. So the music of the people, sooner or later, will command attention and creep into the books of composers.

An American reporter once told me that the most valuable talent a journalist could possess was a "nose for news." Just so the musician must prick his ear for music. Nothing must be too low or too insignificant for the musician. When he walks he should listen to every whistling boy, every street singer or blind organ-grinder. I myself am often so fascinated by these people that I can scarcely tear myself away, for every now and then I catch a strain or hear the fragments of a recurring melodic theme that sound like the voice of the people. These things are worth preserving, and no one should be above making a lavish use of all such suggestions. It is a sign of barrenness, indeed, when such characteristic bits of music exist and are not heeded by the learned musicians of the age.

I know that it is still an open question whether the inspiration derived from a few scattering melodies and folk-songs can be sufficient to give a national character to higher forms of music, just as it is an open question whether national music, as such, is preferable. I myself, as I have always declared, believe firmly that the music that is most characteristic of the nation whence it springs is entitled to the highest consideration. The part of Beethoven's Ninth Symphony that appeals most strongly to all is the melody of the last movement, and that is also the most German. Weber's best opera, according to the popular estimate, is *Der Freischütz*. Why? Because it is the most German. His inspiration there clearly came from the thoroughly German scenes and situations of the story, and hence his music assumed that distinctly national character which has endeared it to the German nation as a whole. Yet he himself spent far more pains on his opera *Euryanthe,* and persisted to the end in regarding it as his best work. But the people, we see, claim their own; and, after all, it is for the people that we strive.

An interesting essay could be written on the subject how much the external frame-work of an opera—that is, the words, the characters of the personages, and the general *mise en scène*—contributes towards the inspiration of the composer. If Weber was inspired to produce his masterpiece by so congenial a theme as the story of *Der Freischütz,* Rossini was undoubtedly similarly inspired by the Swiss surroundings of William Tell. Thus one might almost suspect that some of the charming melodies of that opera are more the product and property of Switzerland than of the Italian composer. It is to be noticed that all of Wagner's operas, with the exception of his earliest work, *Rienzi,* are inspired by German subjects. The most German of them all is that of *Die Meistersinger,* that opera of operas, which should be an example to all who distrust the potency of their own national topics.

Of course, as I have indicated before, it is possible for certain composers to project their spirit into that of another race and country. Verdi partially succeeded in striking Oriental chords in his *Aïda,* while Bizet was able to produce so thoroughly Spanish strains and measures as those of *Carmen.* Thus inspiration can be drawn from the depths as well as from the heights, although that is not my conception of the true mission of music. Our mission should be to give pure pleasure, and to uphold the ideals of our race. Our mission as teachers is to show the right way to those who come after us.

My own duty as a teacher, I conceive, is not so much to interpret Beethoven, Wagner, or other masters of the past, but to give what encouragement I can to the young musicians of America. I must give full expression to my firm conviction, and to the hope that just as this nation has already surpassed so many others in marvellous inventions and feats of engineering and commerce, and has made an honorable place for itself in literature in one short century, so it must assert itself in the other arts, and especially in the art of music. Already there are enough public-spirited lovers of music striving for the advancement of this their chosen art to give rise to the hope that the United States of America will soon emulate the older countries in smoothing the thorny path of the artist and musician. When that beginning has been made, when no large city is without its public opera-house and concert hall, and without its school of music and endowed orchestra, where native musicians can be heard and judged, then those who hitherto have had no opportunity to reveal their talent will come forth and compete with one another, till a real genius emerges from their number, who will be as thoroughly representative of his country as Wagner and Weber are of Germany, or Chopin of Poland.

To bring about this result we must trust to the ever-youthful enthusiasm and patriotism of this country. When it is accomplished, and when music has been established as one of the reigning arts of the land, another wreath of fame and glory will be added to the country which earned its name, the "Land of Freedom," by unshackling her slaves at the price of her own blood.[3]

3. The author acknowledges the co-operation of Mr. Edwin Emerson, Jr., in the preparation of this article. [Au.]

168 Frederick Douglass

Frederick Bailey, born into slavery in Maryland in 1817, became a writer and orator of renowned eloquence against all forms of human bondage. He was taught the rudiments of reading by the kindhearted mistress of one household he lived in, and developed the rest of his extraordinary skills on his own. After his escape to New York in 1838, his presence was much in demand at Northern antislavery rallies, where he adopted the surname Douglass in order to avoid recapture until he had raised sufficient money to purchase his freedom.

In addition to extensive travel around the United States, Douglass spent two years on a speaking tour of Great Britain and Ireland, where he lectured on Irish home rule as well as on abolition and met "the liberator," Daniel O'Connell, with whom he found much in common. Douglass served as an advisor to President Lincoln during the Civil War, and after Reconstruction held a variety of government posts until his death in 1895.

Douglass's brief comments about the songs of the slaves, recalled from his own experience, provide a bracing corrective to the more sentimental descriptions by some contemporary white observers.

FROM *My Bondage and My Freedom*
(1885)

Slaves are generally expected to sing as well as to work. A silent slave is not liked by masters or overseers. *"Make a noise," "make a noise,"* and *"bear a hand,"* are the words usually addressed to the slaves when there is silence amongst them. This may account for the almost constant singing heard in the

TEXT: *My Bondage and My Freedom* (New York, 1855), pp. 97–100, 252–53, 278–79. Douglass retold his life story several times; these passages occur in somewhat different form in *Narrative of the Life of Frederick Douglass* (1845) and in *Life and Times of Frederick Douglass* (1893).

southern states. There was, generally, more or less singing among the team-
sters, as it was one means of letting the overseer know where they were, and
that they were moving on with the work. But, on allowance day, those who
visited the great house farm were peculiarly excited and noisy. While on their
way, they would make the dense old woods, for miles around, reverberate with
their wild notes. These were not always merry because they were wild. On the
contrary, they were mostly of a plaintive cast, and told a tale of grief and sorrow.
In the most boisterous outbursts of rapturous sentiment, there was ever a tinge
of deep melancholy. I have never heard any songs like those anywhere since I
left slavery, except when in Ireland. There I heard the same *wailing notes,* and
was much affected by them. It was during the famine of 1845–6. In all the
songs of the slaves, there was ever some expression in praise of the great house
farm; something which would flatter the pride of the owner, and, possibly, draw
a favorable glance from him.

> I am going away to the great house farm,
>   O yea! O yea! O yea!
> My old master is a good old master,
>   Oh yea! O yea! O yea!

This they would sing, with other words of their own improvising—jargon to
others, but full of meaning to themselves. I have sometimes thought, that the
mere hearing of those songs would do more to impress truly spiritual-minded
men and women with the soul-crushing and death-dealing character of slavery,
than the reading of whole volumes of its mere physical cruelties. They speak
to the heart and to the soul of the thoughtful. I cannot better express my sense
of them now, than ten years ago, when, in sketching my life, I thus spoke of
this feature of my plantation experience:

> I did not, when a slave, understand the deep meanings of those rude, and appar-
> ently incoherent songs. I was myself within the circle, so that I neither saw nor heard
> as those without might see and hear. They told a tale which was then altogether
> beyond my feeble comprehension; they were tones, loud, long and deep, breathing
> the prayer and complaint of souls boiling over with the bitterest anguish. Every tone
> was a testimony against slavery, and a prayer to God for deliverance from chains. The
> hearing of those wild notes always depressed my spirits, and filled my heart with
> ineffable sadness. The mere recurrence, even now, afflicts my spirit, and while I am
> writing these lines, my tears are falling. To those songs I trace my first glimmering
> conceptions of the dehumanizing character of slavery. I can never get rid of that
> conception. Those songs still follow me, to deepen my hatred of slavery, and quicken
> my sympathies for my brethren in bonds. If any one wishes to be impressed with a
> sense of the soul-killing power of slavery, let him go to Col. Lloyd's plantation, and,
> on allowance day, place himself in the deep, pine woods, and there let him, in silence,
> thoughtfully analyze the sounds that shall pass through the chambers of his soul, and
> if he is not thus impressed, it will only be because 'there is no flesh in his obdurate
> heart.'

The remark is not unfrequently made, that slaves are the most contented
and happy laborers in the world. They dance and sing, and make all manner of

joyful noises—so they do; but it is a great mistake to suppose them happy because they sing. The songs of the slave represent the sorrows, rather than the joys, of his heart; and he is relieved by them, only as an aching heart is relieved by its tears. Such is the constitution of the human mind, that, when pressed to extremes, it often avails itself of the most opposite methods. Extremes meet in mind as in matter. When the slaves on board of the "Pearl" were overtaken, arrested, and carried to prison—their hopes for freedom blasted—as they marched in chains they sang, and found (as Emily Edmunson tells us) a melancholy relief in singing. The singing of a man cast away on a desolate island, might be as appropriately considered an evidence of his contentment and happiness, as the singing of a slave. Sorrow and desolation have their songs, as well as joy and peace. Slaves sing more to *make* themselves happy, than to express their happiness.

•   •   •   •   •

The fiddling, dancing and *"jubilee beating,"* was going on in all directions [during the Christmas holidays]. This latter performance is strictly southern. It supplies the place of a violin, or of other musical instruments, and is played so easily, that almost every farm has its "Juba" beater.[1] The performer improvises as he beats, and sings his merry songs, so ordering the words as to have them fall pat with the movement of his hands. Among a mass of nonsense and wild frolic, once in a while a sharp hit is given to the meanness of slaveholders. Take the following, for an example:

> We raise de wheat,
> Dey gib us de corn;
> We bake de bread,
> Dey gib us de cruss;
> We sif de meal,
> Dey gib us de huss;
> We peal de meat,
> Dey gib us de skin,
> And dat's de way
> Dey takes us in.
> We skim de pot,
> Dey gib us the liquor,
> And say dat's good enough for nigger.
>> Walk over! walk over!
>> Tom butter and de fat;
>> Poor nigger you can't get over dat;
>>> Walk over!

This is not a bad summary of the palpable injustice and fraud of slavery, giving—as it does—to the lazy and idle, the comforts which God designed should be given solely to the honest laborer. But to the holidays.

1. Juba is the practice of elaborate patterns of hand-clapping and body-slapping as accompaniment to dancing and singing.

Judging from my own observation and experience, I believe these holidays to be among the most effective means, in the hands of slaveholders, of keeping down the spirit of insurrection among the slaves.

．　　．　　．　　．　　．

But with all our caution and studied reserve, I am not sure that Mr. Freeland did not suspect that all was not right with us. It *did* seem that he watched us more narrowly, after the plan of escape had been conceived and discussed amongst us. Men seldom see themselves as others see them; and while, to ourselves, everything connected with our contemplated escape appeared concealed, Mr. Freeland may have, with the peculiar prescience of a slaveholder, mastered the huge thought which was disturbing our peace in slavery.

I am the more inclined to think that he suspected us, because, prudent as we were, as I now look back, I can see that we did many silly things, very well calculated to awaken suspicion. We were, at times, remarkably buoyant, singing hymns and making joyous exclamations, almost as triumphant in their tone as if we had reached a land of freedom and safety. A keen observer might have detected in our repeated singing of

> O Canaan, sweet Canaan,
> I am bound for the land of Canaan,

something more than a hope of reaching heaven. We meant to reach the *north*— and the north was our Canaan.

> I thought I heard them say,
> There were lions in the way,
> I don't expect to stay
> 　Much longer here.
> Run to Jesus—shun the danger—
> I don't expect to stay
> 　Much longer here,

was a favorite air, and had a double meaning. In the lips of some, it meant the expectation of a speedy summons to a world of spirits; but, in the lips of *our* company, it simply meant, a speedy pilgrimage toward a free state, and deliverance from all the evils and dangers of slavery.

169 Richard Wallaschek

Richard Wallaschek (1860–1917) was an Austrian professor of the aesthetics and psychology of music. In the late nineteenth century's flurry of speculation about the origins of music, Wallaschek argued in favor of dance and rhythm as music's sources and against the theory of speech origins put forward by Herbert Spencer. A published controversy between them, incorporating the views of several others as well, appeared in the journal *Mind* between 1890 and 1892.

Considered now as one of the founding generation of comparative musicologists, Wallaschek's work exhibits the scientific orientation characteristic of that school. In *Primitive Music,* written in English during his five-year stay in London, Wallaschek engaged actively with ongoing controversies about the ramifications of evolutionary theory in various spheres of culture.

In common with most of his ethnological contemporaries, Wallaschek regarded living communities of nonliterate peoples as "contemporary ancestors," conflating the passage of historical time with a notional evolutionary scale. In his preface to *Primitive Music,* for instance, he remarks that "it has been my aim to deal with the music of savage races only, while the music of ancient civilisation has merely been glanced at whenever it was necessary to indicate the connecting links between the most primitive and the comparatively advanced culture"—conceptually, that is, his living informants *precede* ancient cultures.

FROM *Primitive Music*

(1893)

HEREDITY AND DEVELOPMENT

. . . . .

I know well that the validity of Darwin's law[1] has been denied for the domain of ethics and art (including, of course, music). This opposition has proceeded from men whose epoch-making importance in the field of natural science imposes upon me the duty of the greatest respect, while at the same time it necessitates my weighing my conclusions with the utmost scrupulousness. In the following I confine myself entirely to the domain of music, and I consider myself the more justified in doing this since the historical facts with which ethnology furnishes us could scarcely be taken into consideration sufficiently,

---

TEXT: *Primitive Music: An Inquiry into the Origin and Development of Music, Songs, Instruments, Dances, and Pantomimes of Savage Races* (London, 1893), chap. 10, pp. 277–89.

1. That is, natural selection.

a connected treatment of the same not existing. Alfred Russell Wallace, in discussing the development of our musical faculties, has made use of the material as furnished by the *English Cyclopædia,* which in my opinion is not quite satisfactory. He says: "Among the lower savages music, as we understand it, hardly exists, though they all delight in rude musical sounds, as of drums, tom-toms, or gongs; and they also sing in monotonous chants. Almost exactly as they advance in general intellect and in the arts of social life, their appreciation of music appears to rise in proportion; and we find among them rude stringed instruments and whistles, till, in Java, we have regular bands of skilled performers, probably the successors of Hindoo musicians of the age before the Mohammedan Conquest. The Egyptians are believed to have been the earliest musicians, and from them the Jews and the Greeks no doubt derived their knowledge of the art, but it seems to be admitted that neither the latter nor the Romans knew anything of harmony or of the essential features of modern music."[2]

I believe that my whole book forms a contradiction to the above statements, and in consequence the conclusions would also have to be changed. In reference to the latter I would like to make one more remark. Wallace says: "The musical ability is undoubtedly, in its lower forms, less uncommon than the artistic or mathematical faculty, but it still differs essentially from the necessary or useful faculties in that it is almost entirely wanting in one-half even of civilised man."[3] To be sure musical activity is *to-day* distributed very unevenly among mankind; but originally it was not the same thing as to-day, in the climax of its development. In fact the whole tribe participates in the musical choral-dance and mimic representation among savages; we have never heard that certain individuals had to be excluded from it through lack of talent. If any one should prove awkward in these dances, some tribes, as we have heard, cut matters short by killing him. Purely musical composition also is much more general than to-day. "Among the Andamans every one composes songs. A man or woman would be thought very little of who could not do so. Even small children compose their own songs."[4] With primitive man music, and painting and sculpture probably as well, are not purely æsthetic occupations in the modern sense, they are most intimately bound up with practical life-preserving and life-continuing activities,[5] and receive only gradually their present more abstract form. And therefore a law like that of "natural selection" has original validity here as well, while it is less easily comprehensible in connection with the music of the present time whose conditions of existence have become too

2. Alfred Russell Wallace, *Darwinism* (London, 1889), pp. 467, 468. [Au.]

3. *Ibid.,* p. 471. [Au.]

4. M. V. Portman, "Andamanese Music," *Journal of the Royal Asiatic Society,* new series 20 (1888), pp. 184, 185. [Au.]

5. I mention this because L. Morgan has said: "Natural selection, which deals with practical life-preserving and life-continuing activities, has little to say to the aesthetic activities, music, painting, sculpture and the like" [C. Lloyd Morgan, *Animal Life and Intelligence* (London, 1890–91), p. 501]. If only music, painting, etc., were aesthetic activities among primitive man! [Au.]

complicated. But after we have recognised the full scope of the law, the spiritual life of man has been brought closer to that of the animals, and in regard to the continuity of both, I would like to add a few more words. Wallace has destroyed the bridge between the spiritual life of man and the animals; a deep cleft separates the two. Darwin attempted to construct the same by trying to trace a number of the psychological traits of man in the animal kingdom; I fear that some of his adherents go too far in this, and that they approach too closely upon anthropomorphism. The hypothetic character of those arguments has been so successfully shown by Prof. Morgan that it is quite sufficient simply to refer to them; but he has also shown that one is not on that account compelled to relinquish the connection between the spiritual life of man and the animals. It is therefore my opinion that it is much easier to show that primitive man still is, in reference to his mental state, an animal. For this view at least we have a more trustworthy collection of empiric facts than for the opinion that the animal is already man, or that there is no connection between the spiritual life of both. To furnish this proof for the whole domain of psychic activity will be one of the tasks of ethnology.

The sense of beauty, in the higher meaning of the term, is an abstract sensation which animals do not possess, just as little as primitive man; how it is nevertheless developed in man in the course of time, is a thing amply illustrated by a mass of reliable observations. For this development the theory of Galton and Weismann[6] seems, in my eyes, to furnish the most satisfactory explanation, especially in the domain of music. To be sure I have not (as I have before mentioned) the impression that music is to be considered an effect of the sense of hearing, and that it is a secondary effect not originally intended by nature; the further development, however, is, in my eyes, only explicable as direct imitation and tradition. Under such conditions it is in no way unlikely (what Weismann also presumed) that we civilised nations, and, for example, the negroes, receive the same degree of musical ability by birth and yet accomplish such different ends. Quite apart from the training of our individuality, they lack examples and the social necessity of coming up to their level. Neither of these can be artificially ingrafted upon their social status, and therefore they are pretty well lost to musical, and probably any other form of, culture.

The average child of civilised parents does not necessarily come into the world with a higher mental equipment than the little savage, as Mr. Nisbet[7] thinks. Nevertheless, it is not obliged to work out everything *de novo* because it comes into *another* world, into a world with a settled tradition. Into this the child gradually grows, and out of it its individuality is formed, while a negro boy will always have the impression that the European world is something

6. Francis Galton, Darwin's cousin and the originator of the science of genetics, and the German evolutionist August Friedrich Weismann both studied mechanisms of heredity, especially the inheritance of talent—though along separate lines and not, as Wallaschek's text suggests, in association.

7. J. F. Nisbet, *Marriage and Heredity* (London, 1889), p. viii. [Au.]

strange to him, not made by his equal. His very colour, if not the general behaviour of his white "friends," will soon convince him of this. All mental progress seems to be traceable in the object rather, while the individuals have remained stationary. More highly gifted individuals are the outcome of sudden favourable combinations, not the climax of a continual line leading up to them.

When primitive music has advanced beyond the first purely rhythmical stage, when an invention of melody takes place which is retained in memory, it has often been observed that these short musical phrases impress just as much to-day as they do among the savages. The advantage we have over primitive man in regard to music is simply that we are able to work up, develop, any given theme, while the former spins out a theme, however short it may be, into a lengthy piece simply through endless repetitions. This art of working up a given theme must be acquired by each individual afresh; the capacity for it is not a whit greater in the present generation than during former times. To be sure it is probable that we learn quicker, but only because we have more numerous and better patterns, and because in our study we save ourselves the trouble of scholastic by-ways, in learning which past generations have, through want of experience, wasted unnecessary time and energy.

On the other hand, those of the savage tribes which are really musical comprehend our music, at least that of a simple character; that means, to the same degree that our peasants do. It is also astonishing how quickly Negro Hottentot and Malay orchestras grasp European dance music and play it immediately, by hearing, in the orchestra.

In the drawings done by savages one can trace exactly the same mistakes and peculiarities as with our children.[8] I do not doubt that this will in time be proved by ethnology more completely than I am able to do within the limits of this abstract. But I might mention that we are able to observe the same in the compositions of children, or more properly in the musical invention of children, even up to the time of boyhood or girlhood, and all this in spite of the fact that the child unconsciously undergoes even in tender youth the influence of modern music.

The origin and development of painting seems also to come under the influence of natural selection. Thus the most important and most original products of Dyaks' painting are the bizarre decorations of their shields. They were bizarre and grotesque in order to frighten the enemy against whom they were held. (The ancient Greek painting of the Gorgo Medusa head originally had the same meaning, *viz.*, to frighten the deity.) The fantastic demons of the Dyaks were the result of a competition in the struggle for life, which sought to constantly increase by new decorations the dread of the defending shields.

---

8. With perfect justice Hirth has expressly not traced the lack of perspective in the disposition of a child's drawing to atavism, but has designated it as a peculiarity of the spirit of the nursery [Georg Hirth, *Aufgaben der Kunstphysiologie,* 2 vols. (Munich and Leipzig, 1891), vol. 2, p. 583]. Examples of savage drawings in Richard Andree, *Ethnographische Parallelen* 1878, Neue Folge (Leipzig, 1889), p. 56. [Au.]

Other ornaments were originally signs of property, and thus the whole branch of ornamental art owed its origin to the struggle for life.[9]

We also have the best of reasons to suppose that among the "faculties" of the human mind the so-called musical faculty at least has not been heightened in course of time, and that all progress has simply been brought about by objective heredity. Long before this could take place the practice of music was so intimately connected with life-continuing and life-preserving activities that the law of natural selection held good even in the domain of music.

A mere psychological consideration of the case will lead us to a similar result. I venture to say that the old doctrine of separate powers, capabilities (Vermögen, as the German psychologists formerly used to call it) in the human mind has generally been abandoned by modern psychologists. There is no such thing as an independent musical ability, or musical sense, distinctly separable from other faculties. If this is so, it is impossible to say that a special musical faculty is developed under a special law. The human mind is one whole, equally subject to one and the same natural influences. More than that, mind and body are one whole. Where is the physiologist or physicist who could draw a distinct line between a mere physical movement, a reflex action, and an intelligent will? Who can say up to what point the mere corporal faculty extends, and from where the mental one begins? How can we say then that our brain is subject to the natural law of natural selection and our ideas to supernatural or any other influence? How can we venture to apply to this one whole of human being different influences and say, for instance, that one part is developed under natural laws, another under supernatural, again another under direct divine agency? how can we say that the one is a primary effect, the other a secondary one, and that among all there is a special compartment somewhere in the brain carefully locked up and called the musical faculty, which is preserved under the particular care of—we do not know what?

As there is no special musical faculty (the term faculty has always been used like the term soul for the shortness of expression) we must again remember that we said it was not the musical talent alone which made the composer. The artist is the man whose total energy, interest, and labour, whose feelings and ambition are entirely given up to the one artistic object, whatever it may be. If this has happened we speak of a peculiar faculty for this object in a certain man, but this so-called "faculty" is nothing but the resulting tendency of our mind as a whole which turns in a certain direction under certain favourable circumstances. And so the "musical faculty" too is the end of a certain disposition of our mind, towards which all the so-called faculties tend, not a separate starting-point from which they arise. Of course, some organic structures may be more favourable to a certain end, under certain external circumstances, but we shall never be able to find a unique source for any artistic disposition. So it

9. Alois Raimund Hein, "Malerei und Technische Künste der Dayaks," *Annalen des K. K. Naturhistorischen Hofmuseums*, Bd. 14, p. 203. [Au.]

may happen that the mental disposition, say of a great politician, would have been much more favourable to artistic development, than that of many actual artists, had he been placed under the most appropriate external conditions. This would not be possible if there were such a thing as a peculiar artistic faculty. It is mental strength in general which characterises the great man of the future, and nobody knows in which direction it will concentrate itself at last. Thus the German poet Victor Scheffel intended to become a painter at first, until one day, quite accidentally, his talent for poetry was discovered by a lady friend and then turned to account by himself. The painter Fritz Uhde felt himself so entirely in the wrong place when he first frequented the painting academy in Dresden that he left it and became an officer. Only later on he took up his former profession again, recognising it, at the same time, as the most appropriate to his talent. Rousseau considered himself a composer only, and wrote his philosophical and educational works, merely occasionally, as an occupation of secondary importance. Had not his opera "Devin du Village" had such an immense success, he would probably have devoted himself entirely to philosophy, and we should not know anything of his compositions. And to what did he owe this success—to favourable circumstances or to the merits of the compositions? Merits? The present generation knows Rousseau as philosopher only, and I dare say there will be many people who never knew that Rousseau composed at all. Goethe once seriously thought of becoming a painter. Zelter, his contemporary, was destined to become a bricklayer like his father, and devoted himself to music comparatively late.

These examples tend to show that general strength and greatness of mind assumes that peculiar shape which in course of time proves itself as the most effective in the outside world and the most appropriate to the circumstances, or as the naturalist would say in plainer language, it assumes the form most *useful* to the individual. This view is not at all in opposition to the fact that great characters assert themselves in spite of their disregarding entirely all the surroundings they have to live in. Thus one may say Richard Wagner would have been more successful in the beginning of his career if he had written in the customary easy-going style of the Italian opera, and with the pomposity of Meyerbeer, in favour with the masses. Precisely so. In the beginning he would have been more successful, but he knew that musical development ought to turn in quite another direction which he pretended to foresee in the future; and with regard to this future of music, which would then prove still more favourable to him than the success of the ordinary musician of his time he wrote what he actually called "Zukunftsmusik." In his earlier days, however, when his operas "Das Liebesverbot" and "Die Feen" had proved failures, he did write in accordance with the taste of the masses, like Meyerbeer, and brought out his "Rienzi." But by this time there happened to be too many competitors in this domain, so he remained unnoticed, and as there was nothing to be hoped from the present he wrote for the future.

Thus it is just the example of Wagner which at first sight seems to tell against the theory of usefulness in art, but which at bottom is eloquent in favour of it. By this theory I do not mean to degrade the action of the artist. The word "use" can be taken in a very ideal sense. He who pretends to despise use is himself too low to conceive a higher meaning of it. If to some friendship is more useful than gain, if the law of usefulness has produced all the beauty in the world, the grandeur of the sky as well as the tender blossoms of the earth, then it will also be effective enough to form the highest artistic ideals the human mind is capable of.

Which artistic direction will be the most useful for a great mind to take is difficult to predict. It depends upon custom, countries, times, even upon the fashion. There have been centuries of poets, of painters, sculptors, architects, while we ourselves seem to live in the century of musicians, I mean of poetical, intelligent musicians of the pattern of Wagner. How such changes in artistic tendency are brought about, how they are felt at once by millions of people on different continents, and why they are responded to, I cannot say. But that they are most effective everybody seems to be aware of.

So much of the past. But how will future events shape themselves? This question has frequently been broached by musicians, especially when they found themselves face to face with a phenomenon so singular and unexpected as Wagner. In their complete surprise and passionate enthusiasm, which can easily be comprehended, they have confessed as their sincere opinion that in him not only music but the whole world in general had reached its climax. From this height all things were expected to decline, and nothing perfectly new could in their opinion be created. This truly Chinese view has, however, hindered the development of music on countless occasions, and has caused such severe struggles as have accompanied the appearance of original geniuses like Berlioz and Wagner. The less are *their* adherents in their turn justified in adopting the same principle, which in the case of the "conservatives" they justly censured. None but the uninitiated could arrive at the above conclusion (and they will probably continue to do so), for any one knowing the prospects of music in the future would already be half a composer; to *theoretically* expound what this future of music may be none, not even the artist, is able to do; the product of his genius, the work of art, alone can and will reveal it. Reasoning in regard to the future of art is futile, but imagination has for a period of five thousand years continued to produce new works of art, and there is no reason why all this should have come to an end in the year 1883. On the contrary, this assumption seems to my mind both narrow-minded and unfounded. Unfounded because there is no absolute standard of beauty, for we, with our purely subjective and individual conception of art, should never make the preposterous assertion that in this way and no other can art attain to absolute perfection. A work of art is made *for* us and is consequently subject to all changes *in* and *through* us.

An experience of my own has always been to me an appropriate example of how opinion may change in course of time. My teacher of counterpoint once took up Bach's mass in B minor and said: "In this work is comprehended all musical wisdom, beyond it we can never go." From the point of view of musical labour and polish, or of the art exercised in execution, he was no doubt right. But there is still another point of view, that of colouring and emotional element, and this has found grander and more eloquent expression in Wagner than in any other composer. Incidentally I may mention that this constitutes, in my opinion, Wagner's supreme mastership. Nobody can say which point of view coming generations will take, for we are not the coming generation, and only in the divinely inspired artist will it be anticipated.

The above negative decision in regard to the future of art is not, however, free from a certain narrowness of view which has excluded the consideration of the long evolution of music, and especially of dramatic music. What a length of time has not elapsed since the first attempt to represent the events of chase and war before the assembled company in order to induce it to participate in common action. How long a time did not elapse before these primitive dances and animal pantomimes could have become customary, and before their old stereotyped form could at last lead to innovations and improvements. Let us not forget that those dances occurred among people who in every other respect have not advanced beyond the civilisation of the stone period. In comparison with them a dramatic festival as advanced and accomplished as the corrobberree or the kuri-dance in Australia represents an epoch in literature, an artistic advancement of centuries. And how simple, how childish this drama appears when compared with the ancient Indian drama, of which we are told that only in later stages was the customary song replaced by spoken words. The tropic glow, the fiery passion of a Sakuntala designate a height of perfection which again is separated by centuries from the epoch of the corrobberree. And still, what is this when compared with the drama of Pericles' time, or of the Roman theatre, both of which have so many characteristics in common with modern dramatic art. But this is the period with which in so many cases our historical investigations used to commence, while for the times preceding we had merely a geological interest. What changes had not occurred in the drama up to the Roman period, and what changes were still to come. Lost in the mental darkness of the middle ages, it nevertheless at last found the saving path from the grimacing, immoral derivations of the old mysteries to the bright splendour of the artistic stage, from mysterious choirs and disreputable cloister-alleys to the open and unreserved tribunal of the people, to those boards that represent the world, a free play, inspired as once before by love of mankind and taken from its varying fates. Now the first oratorios appeared, now the first operas were produced, small in the beginning and diffident, but soon centres of interest for the entire spiritual life of society. On their account parties were formed, on their account the whole of Paris was once roused to passionate enthusiasm and fierce hatred; indeed, in the days of Gluck and Piccini even politics were forgotten for a time, so entirely absorbed were the parties in the musical questions of the day.

But these miracles know no limits. The stage is animated with new characters; the figure of stone appears in the gloom of night; in dungeons deep a prisoner awaits the blessed hour of liberty; elves flit through the air; the spirit of the earth leaves with aching heart the deceitful love-phantom of human life; the Italian carnival crosses the stage in wanton revelry; till at last the daughters of the Rhine rise from the depths of the holy river, Sigfried's horn resounds, and Walhall, the resplendent seat of the gods, shines in sublime grandeur.

This is for the present the last stage in the long line of evolution, more varied and more eloquent in the history of the musical drama than in any other domain of human accomplishments. A review of this domain of our mental activity betrays as much vital creative power as it reveals the prospect of new and glorious blossoms, and an insatiable desire on our part to enjoy them in their full splendour and their eternal youth.

Such at least is the conclusion to which the theoretical observer may come; to everything else the creative artist will return answer.

VII

THE TWENTIETH CENTURY

Edited by ROBERT P. MORGAN

INTRODUCTION

$\mathcal{T}$he richness and complexity of twentieth-century musical culture stems from many factors, the foremost being the volume and variety of the music itself. But another significant feature is the unusually large number of written documents available to us that relate to this music. In no previous epoch have we approached the copiousness of twentieth-century writing about music. All this material—whether its focus be current or past music, concert, vernacular, or folk music, and whether its perspective be analytical, historical, sociological, political, or reportorial—contributes to the music history of our age. The range and diversity of these writings mirror the range and diversity of the era's compositional styles and technical approaches. These two aspects join to create an overall image of both considerable vitality and considerable uncertainty. Whatever one thinks of twentieth-century musical culture as a whole (and it does not present a particularly neat picture), the very multiplicity of its compositional and critical artifacts gives expression to one of its most telling attributes: a deep-seated self-consciousness about what music is, to whom it should be addressed, and its proper role within the contemporary world.

The editor of a collection such as this, confronted with difficult decisions at every turn, must be relentlessly selective. I have generally, if not exclusively, favored writings by active participants in the musical developments of the time rather than by observers. More particularly, my choices reflect the tendency—noticeable in the nineteenth century but typifying the twentieth—of composers to write about their own work, the work of others, and music and musical life in general. Inevitably, significant areas of interest remain neglected. Especially regrettable is the limited representation of academic musical scholarship, whose impressive growth marks the period, and in particular the fields of music theory and analysis, whose characteristic documents are too technical and specialized for this collection.

The music of the twentieth century is stamped by two closely interconnected features. One is the pervasive interest among composers in creating music that is "new," which fosters an unprecedented emphasis on innovation and experimentation. This tendency, though generally characteristic of Western music, became so dominant as to assume an ideologically central position. The other, a direct outcome of the first, is the extraordinary diversity mentioned above—both of compositional styles and techniques and of attitudes about music and its range of uses. Entire musical cultures now coexist temporally and geographically, often in shifting alliances with one another, forming a vibrant whole to which a sizable portion of the world's population has almost immediate access.

This diversity helps account for the unusually large number of entries included here. The original intent—consistent with Oliver Strunk's own policy—was to present relatively long, essentially complete selections. It quickly became evident, however, that in order to give some sense of the scope of twentieth-century musical writing, it would be necessary to select many more items, and significantly shorter ones, than this policy allowed. Though I have chosen a core group of reasonably substantial readings, other entries, some no longer than a single page in length, have been included to indicate the range of issues encompassed during the period and the wealth of different, frequently opposing voices that have articulated them.

Diversity and multiplicity have raised issues of organization as well. After considerable experimentation I have settled on seven conceptual categories under which to order the readings. Inevitably, these disregard other important realms of interest, such as changing conceptions of musical genre, conflicting approaches to performance practice, and interactions between concert music and popular and vernacular musics. Moreover, the categories accommodate only uncomfortably certain entries that could easily fit under two or more headings. Nevertheless, such a framework is useful and even necessary for giving shape to these diverse contents.

The first and perhaps most basic category addresses changes in musical esthetics. During the first quarter of the century, in one of those epoch-defining shifts that have occasionally punctuated Western music history, the predominant nineteenth-century view of music as a spiritual, subjective, and highly individualized art gradually lost ground to a more materialist and objective one emphasizing craftsmanship and social function over transcendence and personal expression. Like all such changes, this one did not take place at once, nor did it coincide neatly with the turn of the century. The inherited view, a legacy of musical Romanticism, prevailed at least until World War I, though not without considerable modification, as in the esthetics of musical impressionism and expressionism, represented here by Claude Debussy and Arnold Schoenberg; and now in conjunction with significant countercurrents, such as the anti-esthetic position of Erik Satie. Even when the older view began rapidly losing favor in the years around the end of World War I, it did not entirely disappear but persisted side by side with the new one. Indeed, the relative merits of the two continued to be debated down to the end of the century, with the "Romantic" view even seeming to regain some momentum in the position of a composer such as George Rochberg.

The basic argument is mapped out in the first three readings. Schoenberg, writing before the onset of World War I, espouses an esthetic of unbridled intuitive creation and expression. Jean Cocteau and Igor Stravinsky, writing after the war, endorse a new kind of music more suitable to the modern age, distinguished by wit, detachment, and restraint. Something of the subsequent dialectic spun out of this opposition can be traced in the views of John Cage, Milton Babbitt, and Evan Ziporyn, who expand and further complicate the confrontation by introducing issues touching upon indeterminacy, integral serialism, and the idea of "world music."

A third significant esthetic position, formalism—the idea that musical significance derives primarily from internal compositional relationships rather than specific external reference—applies equally to both of these views. Though usually associated with the twentieth century, formalism was in fact originally linked with Romanticism, both conceptually and historically;[1] and it can be detected here in such diverse figures as Ferruccio Busoni and the early Schoenberg on one side, and Stravinsky and Babbitt on the other. Though formalism, linked to Romanticism, encouraged a belief in the "purification" of music through withdrawal from its social context (as Busoni seems to hold), it could equally foster tendencies toward social functionalism when associated with an objectivist-materialist position (as in Kurt Weill), thereby edging music back toward its pre-Romantic, contextual condition.[2]

Given their foundational nature, these esthetic matters are inseparable from questions of musical style and language. The abandonment by many composers of the relatively codified principles of common-practice (harmonic) tonality—tonal centricity, dominant-tonic cadential structure, triadic harmony, and the like—that had governed Western music for some two hundred years, drastically affected the way composers went about—and thought about—writing music. Traditional Western tonality, despite the very substantial differences in composers of dissimilar tastes, geographical regions, and cultural backgrounds, retained a central core of relationships throughout the nineteenth century. It represented a shared language that could be internalized by both composers and listeners, seeming thereby to become part of their very mental structure. This internalization fostered and, perhaps, even provided a necessary precondition for the Romantic belief that music resided in the human interior where it possessed the power to project humanity's innermost beliefs and deepest feelings.

When that common language was seriously called into question—as it was in the early years of the new century—without another compositional language emerging as a widely accepted alternative, the musical situation was fundamentally altered. Previously untapped areas of musical experience were suddenly made accessible and were actively explored. Although most composers in the

1. Even later, when nineteenth-century formalist thinking takes on a more rigorous and "scientific" tone (most notably in the writing of Eduard Hanslick), it departs from Romanticism not by rejecting musical "expressivity," or the idea that music is a "spiritual language," but by restricting what music expresses to strictly musical ideas, excluding emotions.

2. The importance of formalistic thinking in twentieth-century music is evident in many of the readings in this volume: from Stravinsky, Babbitt, and Stockhausen at one extreme to Xenakis, Ligeti, and Reich at the other. Even Cage could be included, since he believed that one way composers can allow sounds to "be themselves" is by ruling out human choice through the injunction of purely formal procedures, such as throwing dice or consulting the *I Ching*.

earlier years restricted themselves to using new kinds of nontriadic harmony and nonmetrical (additive) rhythm, the implications of the change were far more fundamental and far-reaching. Once the superstructure of traditional tonality had been compromised, its underlying foundation—the scalar system of twelve-tone equal tuning—was placed in jeopardy as well. As a consequence, not only could the familiar organizational principles associated with musical material be reconfigured, the very nature of that material became subject to reexamination.

The result, addressed in the second group of readings, was an unprecedented and ongoing expansion of sonic resources, which characterized the entire century from its outset. Busoni, writing in 1907, already proposes an augmentation of the basic pitch repertory through microtonal scale divisions and the use of new scalar types. From there it is but a short step to Luigi Russolo's 1913 manifesto calling for the adoption of a new type of sound material altogether: noise, rather than pure pitch. By the beginning of World War I the frontiers of music had thus been vastly extended, so that for many it must have appeared that the art was being transformed into something essentially different, providing a largely uncharted terrain of novel creative possibilities.

An ongoing challenge for composers was to cultivate and extend this newly acquired territory. Charles Ives responds by viewing musical relationships in a more "sculptural" or spatial mode and considers how sounds are altered by distance and direction. Both Edgard Varèse and Pierre Boulez, with the growing confidence produced by advances in science and technology, develop an idea introduced by Busoni: the invention and creative exploitation of new sound-producing instruments. For them, composers will achieve true liberation only when relieved of the limitations of traditional instruments, intended for older music and thus unsuited for the new. By mid-century Boulez even envisions machines capable of producing virtually any sound, a possibility that would at least partly be realized with developments in computer-generated sound, sampling, and sound modification.

The reevaluation of sound materials went hand in hand with a similarly fundamental exploration of compositional method, the third category in this collection. Confronted with the prospect of bringing order to these possibilities, composers sought new musical languages suitable for a greatly expanded sonic universe. It is symptomatic of the scope of this undertaking that, despite the utopian cast of Busoni's and Russolo's early appeals, no serious attempt was made during the first half of the century to formulate a synoptic method for ordering nonpitch sound as a central compositional ingredient. Even proposals for the systematic control of microtonal pitch divisions were rare and had little impact until later in the century. Within the framework of tempered tuning, however, systematic reformulations appeared relatively early, most notably in Schoenberg's twelve-tone system. Schoenberg provided a method for treating the total chromatic as a set of equally weighted elements placed in an ordered sequence and manipulated by serial transformations, a procedure completely bypassing the hierarchical structure that traditional tonality imposed on this material. Karlheinz Stockhausen, writing after the century's midpoint, further generalizes the serial principle, extending it to other components of sound, including duration, timbre, and amplitude, which he sees as emanating from a common physical source, the soundwave. Similar tendencies toward generalization are also expressed by Iannis Xenakis and György Ligeti, who shift emphasis away from the individual sonic components entirely and focus instead on large masses of sound intended to be perceived as global composites. Steve Reich, by comparison, seeking an alternative to the enormous complexity typifying post-tonal musical structures, suggests reducing the sound material to a minimum, thereby achieving a sort of tonal revolution in reverse.

Since these matters of compositional structure, sound material, and esthetic intent are critical elements in determining what makes twentieth-century music unique, they receive generous treatment here. Yet they cannot be considered in a vacuum, as if music were sealed off from the world at large. The erosion of harmonic tonality and its esthetic counterpart, expressive individualism, undermined the essential support for the Romantic view of music as "a world apart," located beyond the realm of everyday problems and concerns. Once music was no longer considered "pure," that is, constituted of an ephemeral material and framed by transcendent relationships handed down by nature (or God), it could be conceived more readily as a normal component of life— a human product capable of assuming social, political, and other practical functions.

This demystification of music, its rerooting in more common soil, is addressed in the fourth section, "Music, Society, Politics." It is most evident in efforts to exploit the social potential of music itself, either as an active agent of political regeneration, as envisioned by Kurt Weill, Cornelius Cardew, and— less openly—Sergey Prokofiev, or as a medium to be manipulated for oppressive control, as evinced in the Joseph Goebbels speech, the *Pravda* review, and Dmitri Shostakovich's description of the Soviet crackdown on composition. But the political face of twentieth-century music is no less recognizable in efforts to transform musical life—to democratize its institutions and practices, rendering them more accessible to previously excluded groups. Ethel Smyth details the benefits that would accrue if women achieved a more active role in performance organizations, and Eva Rieger argues for the unique qualities that women bring to musical composition. Marian Anderson tells of prejudices encountered and overcome by a black performer in mid-century America, and the black composers William Grant Still and Olly Wilson discuss the special challenges confronted by members of an ethnic minority in finding an authentic compositional voice.

The tendency toward inclusiveness in musical life is apparent not only in these extramusical domains but in music itself. A recurring feature in twentieth-century musical thought, considered in the fifth group of readings, is the conviction that Western music has reached a state of exhaustion and requires revitalization from without. The range of suggested sources is impressive: Claude Debussy recommends techniques borrowed from cinema and the music of non-Western cultures, Béla Bartók champions native folk music, Wanda Landowska turns to music from the past, and Harry Partch incorporates the microtonal pitch inflections of non-Western musical cultures. Darius Milhaud, rejecting all pretensions to transcendentalism, proposes a music so ordinary that one should not even notice it at all. And the scholar Bruno Nettl undertakes to interpret the Western musical enterprise from the perspective of an outsider, a detached observer who attempts to make sense of some of its most cherished—and thus least examined—beliefs.

The sixth section documents how concert life and the musical experience of listeners have been altered during the century, both by specifically musical issues—not least the great complexity of so many contemporary compositions—and by changing social and economic conditions. Alban Berg's description of Schoenberg's Vienna concert series for new music vividly betrays that music's isolation, its propensity to address a limited and specialized audience. Theodor W. Adorno analyzes the ways mass communication and commercialization affect musical culture and reception, a point that Lawrence Gilman's radio address serves to exemplify. Roland Barthes examines how the restructuring of musical experience has transmuted the listener from an active participant into a passive consumer, while Steven Connor argues that developments in audio and visual technology have blurred distinctions between musical "presentation" on the one hand and musical "reproduction" or "representation" on the other.

The final group of readings in this collection addresses the most definitive feature of current musical culture: its unparalleled variety, diversity, and culturally pluralistic makeup. Three earlier stages in the development of this state are documented here: Erik Satie lampoons the notion of the artist as prophetic genius, repudiating by implication the belief in a single privileged understanding of the art; Nadia Boulanger is concerned with cultivating the music of a non-European country; and Constant Lambert describes the fashion between the two world wars for creating new works out of simulations of older ones.

Leonard B. Meyer, viewing the matter in the 1960s, finds stylistic plurality so deeply ingrained in the musical culture of the time that he sees it as a permanent condition, allowing different styles to interact freely with one another without any definite sense of direction. For Umberto Eco plurality and instability also inhabit the individual work in much twentieth-century art, which sacrifices traditionally sanctioned qualities of self-sufficiency and closure for an open structure that is tolerant of multiple realizations. George Rochberg, viewing pluralism as a composer, articulates what is at once its cause and consequence: the impossibility of forging a stylistically unified language in an age in which the musical past is just as much with us as the musical present and thus becomes an essential component of the present.

Finally, Carl Dahlhaus addresses the single most encompassing question raised by the current state of music: in the midst of such multiplicity and frag-mentation, can one still speak of something called music at all in a fully inclu-sive sense, accommodating all of the myriad manifestations of today's musical world? His response provides a fitting close to these introductory comments: "One remains true to the idea of 'music' (in the singular) by relinquishing it as a concept of substance in order to reinstate it as a regulative principle of mutual understanding."

* * *

The original 1950 edition of Strunk's *Source Readings in Music History* had no section devoted to the twentieth century. Professor Strunk, whom I knew and greatly admired as a graduate student, did not even find it necessary to explain this omission in his preface: twentieth-century music was, in the view of most musicologists of the time, simply not considered an appropriate topic for serious scholarly work. That attitude has changed dramatically in the intervening years, to a point where twentieth-century studies may well com-mand the field in the coming decades the way nineteenth-century studies have during the previous ones.

Deciding what should be included in this collection thus takes on special importance. That process, at once so stimulating and so frustrating, was greatly facilitated by discussion and correspondence with friends and colleagues, with-out whose counsel and sympathy I would not have undertaken the project. Although I am unable to acknowledge all, I especially want to mention Joseph Auner, Michael Beckerman, Peter Burkholder, Reinhold Brinkmann, Tom DeLio, Christopher Hailey, Charles Hamm, Joseph Horowitz, Jeffrey Kalberg, David Lewin, Karen Painter, Andrew Porter, Sally Reid, Lee Rothfarb, Michael Tenzer, Judith Tick, and Gary Tomlinson. Ruth Solie, editor of the nineteenth-century readings, was especially helpful; and my former colleague Stephen Hinton, in addition to discussing various aspects of the project with me from the beginning, provided translations for the Weill and Dahlhaus entries. Philip Rupprecht and Julia Hubbert performed valuable service as successive research assistants, advising on shape and content as well as tracking down numerous details of fact and bibliography. Finally, Leo Treitler has overseen this project from its inception with care and understanding, providing stimulat-ing suggestions at every stage of the way. Although the result surely differs from a twentieth-century reader he himself might have compiled, it is very much the fruit of a most pleasant and beneficial collaboration.

ESTHETIC
POSITIONS

170 Arnold Schoenberg

The Austrian composer Arnold Schoenberg (1874–1951) was among the most influential figures in twentieth-century music. These excerpts are from letters written to Ferruccio Busoni in 1909, after Busoni, a renowned composer, pianist, and conductor, had sent his younger colleague a transcription of one of Schoenberg's piano pieces, Op. 11, No. 2, intended to render the composition more "pianistic." Schoenberg not only rejects Busoni's notion of pianism as inappropriate to his own work but offers an impassioned statement describing the highly intuitive approach to artistic creation that he favored at the time. This compositional esthetic, a holdover from the nineteenth century, reached its most extreme formulation just as these letters were written—at the moment Schoenberg was breaking away from the tonally centric and harmonically triadic basis of traditional Western music.

Two Letters to Ferruccio Busoni
(1909)

Steinakirchen am Forst [August 1909]

•　　•　　•　　•　　•

I am writing in such detail because I want to declare my intentions (encouraged by your comment: my music affects you because you envisage something of the kind as the goal of our immediate developments).
I strive for: complete liberation from all forms
from all symbols
of cohesion and
of logic.
　　Thus:
away with "motivic working out."
Away with harmony as
cement or bricks of a building.
Harmony is *expression*
and nothing else.
　　Then:
Away with Pathos!
Away with protracted ten-ton scores, from erected or constructed
towers, rocks, and other massive claptrap.
My music must be
brief.

TEXT: *Ferruccio Busoni. Selected Letters*, ed. and trans. by Antony Beaumont (London: Faber & Faber, 1987), pp. 389, 392–97.

Concise! In two notes: not built, but *"expressed"*!!

And the results I wish for:

no stylized and sterile protracted emotion.

People are not like that:

it is *impossible* for a person to have only *one* sensation at a time.

One has *thousands* simultaneously. And these thousands can no more readily be added together than an apple and a pear. They to their own ways.

And this variegation, this multifariousness, this *illogicality* which our senses demonstrate, the illogicality presented by their interactions, set forth by some mounting rush of blood, by some reaction of the senses or the nerves, this I should like to have in my music.

It should be an expression of feeling,[1] as our feelings, which bring us in contact with our subconscious, really are, and no false child of feelings and "conscious logic."

Now I have made my confession and they can burn me. You will not number amongst those who burn me: that I know.

•   •   •   •   •

Steinakirchen am Forst, August 24, 1909

•   •   •   •   •

You must consider the following: it is impossible for me to publish my piece together with a transcription which shows how I could have done it *better*. Which thus indicates that my piece is *imperfect*. And it is impossible to try to make the public believe that my piece is *good*, if I simultaneously indicate that it is *not good*.

I could not do this—out of my instinct for self-preservation—even if I believed it. In this case I would either have to destroy my piece or *rework* it *myself*.

But now—please forgive my unrestrained frankness, just as I do not take yours amiss—*I simply don't believe it*. I firmly believe you are making the same mistake as every *imaginative* critic: you do not wish to put yourself in the writer's place but seek rather, in the work of another, yourself, *only yourself*. And that just isn't possible. An art which is at one and the same time its creator's and its appraiser's cannot exist. One of these has to give way, and I believe this must be the appraiser.

And your reasoning seems to me quite unsound, when you say that I shall become different but no richer by pointlessly doing without what is already established.

I do not believe in putting *new wine* into old bottles. In the history of art I have made the following antipodal observations:

1. Orig. "Sie soll Ausdruck der Empfindung sein." Allusion to Beethoven's comment about his "Pastoral" Symphony, "Mehr Ausdruck der Empfindung als Malerei" = more an expression of feeling than painting. [Tr.]

Bach's contrapuntal art vanishes when Beethoven's melodic homophony begins.

Beethoven's formal art is abandoned when Wagner introduces his expressive art.

Unity of design, richness of coloring, working out of minutest details, painstaking formation, priming and varnishing, use of perspective and all the other constituents of older painting simply die out when the Impressionists begin to paint things as they *appear* and not as they *are*.

Yes indeed, when a new art seeks and finds new means of expression, almost all earlier techniques go hang: seemingly, at any rate; for actually they are retained; but in a different way. (To discuss this would lead me too far.)

And now: I must say that I actually dispensed with more than just piano sound when I began to follow my instincts and compose *such* music. I find that, when renouncing an *art of form,* the architecture of the leading voice, the polyphonic art that Brahms, Wagner, and others brought to a high degree of perfection in the past decades—the little bit of piano sound seems a mere trifle. And I maintain: one must have grasped, admired, and marveled at the mysterious wonders of our tonal harmony, the unbelievably delicate balance of its architectural values and its cabbalistic mathematics as *I* have, in order to feel, when one no longer has need of them, that one requires new means. Questions of sonority, whose attraction ranks scarcely so high amongst the eternal values, are by comparison trivial.

Nevertheless, I take a standpoint in this question from which it is absolutely unnecessary to consider me a renouncer, a loser. Were you to see my new orchestral pieces, you would be able to observe how clearly I turn away from the full "God and Superman" sound of the Wagner orchestra. How everything becomes sweeter, finer. How refracted shades of color replace the former brilliant hues. How my entire orchestral technique takes a path which seems to be leading in quite the opposite direction to anything previously taken. I find this to be the natural reaction. We have had enough of Wagner's full, lush sonorities, to the point of satiation: "Nun laßt uns andere Töne anstimmen . . ."[2]

And now I must add that I feel myself justified in believing (I must repeat this) that my piano writing is *novel*. Not only do my feelings tell me so. Friends and pupils express the opinion that the sonorities of my piano writing are completely novel.

For me the matter is as follows:

I do not consider my piano texture the result of any sort of *incompetence,* but rather the expression of *firm resolve, distinct preferences and palpably clear feelings.*

What it *does not* do is not what it *cannot,* rather what it *will* not.

2. Intended as a quotation from Beethoven's Symphony No. 9. The actual words are: "O Freunde, nicht diese Töne! Sondern laßt uns angenehmere anstimmen . . ." ["O friends, not these sounds! Instead let us strike up more pleasing ones . . ."]. Schoenberg's words mean: now let us strike up other sounds. [Tr.]

What it does is not something which could have turned out differently, rather what it *had* to do.

Therefore it is distinctive, stylish, and organic.

$$\bullet \quad \bullet \quad \bullet \quad \bullet \quad \bullet$$

I fear that a transcription, on the other hand, would either

introduce what I avoid, either fundamentally or according to my preferences;

add what I myself—within the limits of my personality—would never have devised, thus what is foreign or unattainable to me;

omit what I would find necessary, or

improve where I am, and must remain, imperfect.

Thus a transcription would be bound to do me violence: whether it helps or hinders my work.

In your pamphlet, which gives me uncommon pleasure and truly proves how the same thoughts can occur to different people at once, you write about transcription. I particularly agree with your thesis that all notation is transcription.[3] I argued similarly some years ago when Mahler was publicly attacked for changing Beethoven's orchestration. But again: whether one improves upon Beethoven's undoubtedly *old-fashioned* treatment of instruments and orchestration on account of undoubtedly superior *newer* instrumental techniques, or whether one improves upon my piano style with older techniques or, at any rate, techniques whose greater appropriateness has today not yet been established, there is no doubt at all that these are two different matters.

I can at present say this without your having to take it as any harsh criticism, because I have not yet seen your transcription. After all, your arrangement could always prove that I am mistaken. But also, apart from that, I am sure you will not take my vehemence amiss, I am certain, because your opinion of my work was otherwise neither harsh nor unfavorable.

Another point occurs to me which seems a suitable argument against you.

Do you really set such infinite store by perfection? Do you really consider it attainable? Do you really think that works of art are, or should be, perfect?

I do not think so. I find even God's works of art, those of nature, highly imperfect.

But I find perfection only in the work of carpenters, gardeners, pastry-cooks, and hairdressers. Only they produce that smoothness and symmetry which I have so often wished to the Devil. Only they fulfill every requirement one can expect of them, but otherwise nothing human or godlike in the world.

And if

Notation = Transcription = *Imperfection*

then also

---

3. Schoenberg's reference is apparently to the following statement from Busoni's *Sketch of a New Esthetic of Music*, trans. Theodore Baker (New York, 1911), as reprinted in *Three Classics in the Aesthetics of Music* (New York: Dover), p. 84: "Notation, the writing down of musical compositions, is above all an ingenious aid for pinning down an improvisation so that it can be brought to life again."

Transcription = Notation = *Imperfection*.
For if a = b and b = c, then also
   a = c.

Why then replace one imperfection with another?

Why eliminate that which perhaps contributes to the appeal of a work and substitute something added by a foreign hand?

Don't the characteristics of a man's personality also include his defects? Do these not have an effect, even if unbeautiful, then at least as contrast, like the basic color upon which the other shades are superimposed?

I have often thought that one should give Schumann's symphonies (which I believe you have greatly underestimated[4] and which I rate *far above* those of Brahms) a helping hand by improving the orchestration. The theoretical aspects were quite clear to me. This summer I spent a little time on this and— lost courage. For I can see exactly that wherever things misfire, something highly original was intended, and I lack the courage to replace an *interesting idea*, which has not been quite successfully carried out, with a *"reliable"* sonority. And with a true work of art, the imagination of an outsider can achieve no more than this! —

From a purely technical angle, I would like to ask you if you have perhaps taken too slow a tempo. That could make a great difference. Or too *little* rubato. I never stay in time! Never in tempo! —

Your "Outline for a New Esthetic of Music" gave me uncommon pleasure, above all on account of its audacity. Particularly at the beginning, there are a few powerful sentences, of compulsive logic and superlative acuteness of observation. I have also thought a lot about your idea of thirds of tones, though in a different way. But I had been thinking of quarter tones, am however now of the opinion that it will depend less on the construction than on other things. Moreover, one of my pupils[5] calculated, at my suggestion, that the next division of the octave with similar properties to our twelve semitone division would have to introduce 53 notes. If you adopt 18 thirds of tones, that would be approximately equal, for $3 \times 18 = 54$. But then the semitones would disappear completely.

Earlier I thought out the following method of notating quarter tones:

$$c - \tfrac{1}{4} \qquad c \qquad c + \tfrac{1}{4}$$

< and > are
mathematical symbols.

---

4. In the *Sketch of a New Esthetic of Music* Busoni writes: "In general, composers have drawn nearest the true nature of music in preparatory and intermediary passages . . . " The passage is included in the Busoni excerpt found on p. 53.

5. This was the philosopher Dr. Robert Neumann, who studied with Schoenberg from 1907 to 1909. [Tr.]

However, I scarcely think that such attempts at notation will catch on; for I confidently hope that the notation of the future will be—how can I say: "wire-lesser."[6]

I also think differently about tonality—my music shows that. I believe: everything one can do with 113 keys[7] can also be done with 2 or 3 or 4: major-minor, whole-tone, and chromatic. Anyway, I have long been occupied with the removal of all shackles of tonality. And my harmony allows no chords or melodies with tonal implications any more.

Now to your questions.

To what extent I realize my intentions? Not as far as I would like to. Not one piece has yet satisfied me entirely. I would like to achieve even greater variegation of motifs and figures without melodic character; I would like to be freer and less constrained in rhythm and time signature; freer from repetition of motifs and spinning out of thoughts in the manner of a melody. This is my vision: this is how I imagine music before I notate = transcribe it. And I am unable to force this upon myself; I must wait until a piece comes out of its own accord in the way I have envisaged.

And thus I come to answer your other question: how much is intentional and how much instinctive.

My only intention is

to have *no* intentions!

No formal, architectural, or other artistic intentions (except perhaps of capturing the mood of a poem), no esthetic intentions—none of any kind; at most this:

to place nothing inhibiting in the stream of my unconscious sensations. But to allow anything to infiltrate which may be invoked either by intelligence or consciousness.

If you knew how I have developed, you would have no doubts. But I have prepared myself for this question and am thus able to answer it. I knew one would question the naturalness of my intentions, precisely because they are natural. That one would find them formalized for the very reason that I avoid anything formal.

But when one sees how I have developed in stages, how I was long ago approaching a form of expression to which I now adhere freely and unreservedly, one would understand that nothing unorganic, no "cheap aestheticism,"[8] is involved, but that *compulsion* has produced these results.

As I am now fairly clear about the theoretical side, only those can scoff who

---

6. Orig. "drahtloser." Schoenberg presumably means that the communication should be more like a "wireless"—that is, as immediate and instantaneous as possible, and thus independent of any material connection (i.e., the "wire").

7. In the *Sketch of a New Esthetic of Music* Busoni writes: "I have made an attempt to find all the possibilities of arranging the seven-tone scale and have succeeded, by lowering and raising the intervals, in producing 113 different scales." See p. 56.

8. Orig. "nichts 'Verschmockt-Aesthetisches.' " [Tr.]

imagine the unconsciously creating artist to be a sort of half-cretin; and who cannot grasp that after unconscious creativity follows a period of *quiet clear-sightedness,* in which one renders account of one's situation.

As for the third piece,[9] which you do not care for at present, as can be inferred from your caustic criticism, I find it goes a considerable way beyond what was successful in the other two. At any rate, as far as the above-mentioned variegation is concerned. But also in the "harmony"—if one can speak so archi-tecturally here—there seems to be something novel in it. In particular: something more slender, more linear.[10] But I also consider it unjust to expect that one can revolutionize music in three *different* ways in three little piano pieces. Does it not seem permissible, having departed so far from convention, to pause for a moment's breath, to gather new strength, before one rushes on? And is it not unjust to describe laconicism as a mannerism? Is formalism just as much a manner as pointillism or impressionism? Must one build? Is music then a sav-ings bank? Does one get more when it is longer?

If I was wrong *there* to be brief, I have *amply* compensated for it in this *letter!* But there were indeed several things I wanted to say—that I could not express them more concisely can be blamed upon my technical shortcomings.

And finally: I hope my frankness does not annoy you, and that you maintain your interest in me.

Maybe you will find a formula, an explanation, through which I shall be able to publish my piece in your series.

Or perhaps you could publish all three and your paraphrase, with an explana-tion some other time??

In any case, I hope not to lose your good will if I now ask you to tell me whether you wish to play the pieces. For, clearly this would mean an enormous amount to me.

One other curious thing, to close: before composing these piano pieces, I had wanted to contact you—knowing of your predilection for transcriptions—to ask if you would take one of my chamber or orchestral works into your repertoire, transcribed for piano solo.

Curious: now we come into contact again through a transcription! Was I misunderstanding a message from my subconscious, which made me think of you in the context of a transcription?

This has just occurred to me!

9. Schoenberg had completed only the first two of the Three Piano Pieces Op. 11 when he originally sent them to Busoni. The third was sent later, shortly before this letter was written.
10. Orig. "manches dünnere, zweistimmigere." [Tr.]

171 Jean Cocteau

The French writer and filmmaker Jean Cocteau (1889–1963) was a leading figure in *l'esprit nouveau*, "the new spirit" that emerged in French art and culture
at the close of World War I. Erik Satie's 1917 ballet *Parade,* for which Cocteau
supplied the story, Picasso the costumes and sets, and Leonid Massine the choreography, played a major role in defining that spirit; and Cocteau's essay "Cock
and Harlequin," published in 1918, was written while still under the influence
of this collaboration. To replace the intuitive, subjective, and individualistic
esthetic of Romanticism, which in his view was equally present in the music of
both Wagner and Debussy, Cocteau argues for something more in tune with his
idea of French culture: a simpler and more popular, "everyday" music, inspired
by the music hall, cabaret, café concert, and circus. Cocteau's aphoristic writing
style—curt, crisp, hard-edged, and without transition—perfectly mirrors that
new esthetic, so strikingly different from the one expressed by Schoenberg in
the previous entry.

FROM Cock and Harlequin
(1918)

The bad music which superior folk despise is agreeable enough. What is
disagreeable is their good music.

Beware of the paint, say certain placards. I add: Beware of music.

Look out! Be on your guard, because alone of all the arts, music moves all
around you.

Musicians ought to cure music of its convolutions, its dodges and its tricks,
and force it as far as possible to keep *in front of the hearer.*

A POET ALWAYS HAS TOO MANY WORDS IN HIS VOCABULARY, A
PAINTER TOO MANY COLORS ON HIS PALETTE, AND A MUSICIAN
TOO MANY NOTES ON HIS KEYBOARD.

ONE MUST SIT DOWN FIRST; ONE THINKS AFTERWARDS.

This axiom must not serve as an excuse to those who are always sitting down.
A true artist is always on the move.

Picturesqueness, and especially exoticism, are a handicap to musicians, and
cause them to be misunderstood.

•   •   •   •   •

TEXT: *Cock and Harlequin,* trans. by Rollo H. Myers (London: Faber & Gwyer, 1926), pp. 11, 15–
17, 18–26, 32–33.

SATIE VERSUS SATIE. The cult of Satie is difficult because one of Satie's charms is that he offers so little encouragement to deification.

One often wonders why Satie saddles his finest works with grotesque titles which mislead the least hostile sections of the public. Apart from the fact that these titles protect his works from persons obsessed by the sublime, and provide an excuse for the laughter of those who do not realize their value, they can be explained by the Debussy-ist abuse of "precious" titles. No doubt they are meant as a good-humored piece of ill-humor, and maliciously directed against "Lunes descendant sur le temple qui fut," "Terrasses des audiences du Clair de lune" and "Cathédrales englouties."[1]

The public is shocked at the charming absurdity of Satie's titles and system of notation, but respects the ponderous absurdity of the libretto of *Parsifal*.

The same public accepts the most ridiculous titles of François Couperin: "Le ti-toc choc ou les Maillotins" "Les Culbutes Ixcxbxnxs" "Les coucous bénévoles," "Les Calotins et Calotines ou la pièce à trétous," "Les vieux galants et les Trésorières surannées."[2]

The impressionist composers cut a pear into twelve pieces and gave each piece the title of a poem. Then Satie composed twelve poems and entitled the whole "Morceaux en forme de poire."

Satie acquired a distaste for Wagner in Wagnerian circles, in the very heart of the "Rose-Croix."[3] He warned Debussy against Wagner. "Be on your guard," he said. "A scenery tree is not upset because somebody comes on to the stage." That is the whole aesthetic of *Pelléas*.

Debussy missed his way because he fell from the German frying pan into the Russian fire. Once again the pedal blurs rhythm and creates a kind of fluid atmosphere congenial to *short-sighted* ears. Satie remains intact. Hear his *Gymnopédies* so clear in their form and melancholy feeling. Debussy orchestrates them, confuses them, and wraps their exquisite architecture in a cloud. Debussy moves further and further away from Satie's starting point and makes everybody follow in his steps. The thick lightning-pierced fog of Bayreuth becomes a thin snowy mist flecked with impressionist sunshine. Satie speaks of Ingres: Debussy transposes Claude Monet *à la Russe*.

---

1. Cocteau refers to titles of three of Debussy's piano pieces: "Et la lune descend sur le temple qui fût" ("And the Moon Descends on the Temple that was"), "La terrasse des audiences du clair de lune" ("The Terrace of Audiences by the Light of the Moon"), and "La cathédrale engloutie" ("The Sunken Cathedral").

2. Couperin's titles might be translated as: "The Tick-Tock Shock, or the Maillotins" (there is uncertainty as to who the "Maillotins" were); "The Somersaults of the Jxcxbxnxs" (Jxcxbxnxs = Jacobines); "The Complacent Cuckolds"; "The Calotins and Calotines, or the Piece for Buffoons" (the "Calotins" were members of a satirical institution founded at Versailles in 1702 by courtiers and young officers to mock the solemn atmosphere of the court; the humorous pamphlets they issued were called "calotines"); "Aging Suitors and Fading Charmers."

3. A mystical religious sect, modeled on the secret societies of the Middles Ages, which Satie joined in 1891.

•   •   •   •   •

Satie teaches what, in our age, is the greatest audacity, simplicity. Has he not proved that he could refine better than anyone? But he clears, simplifies, and strips rhythm naked. Is this once more the music on which, as Nietzsche said, "the spirit dances," as compared with the music "in which the spirit swims"?

Not music one swims in, nor music one dances on; MUSIC ON WHICH ONE WALKS.

•   •   •   •   •

The Impressionists feared bareness, emptiness, silence. Silence is not necessarily a hole; you must use silence and not a stop gap of vague noises.

BLACK SHADOW. Black silence. Not *violet* silence, interspersed with *violet shadows.*

YOUTHFULNESS. Nothing is so enervating as to lie and soak for a long time in a warm bath. Enough of music in which one lies and soaks.

Enough of clouds, waves, aquariums, watersprites, and nocturnal scents; what we need is a music of the earth, every day music.

Enough of hammocks, garlands, and gondolas; I want someone to build me music I can live in, like a house.

A friend tells me that, after New York, Paris houses seem as if you could take them in your hands. "Your Paris" he added "is beautiful because she is built to fit men." Our music must also be built to fit men.

Music is not all the time a gondola, or a race horse, or a tightrope. It is sometimes a chair as well.

A Holy Family is not necessarily a holy family; it may also consist of a pipe, a pint of beer, a pack of cards, and a pouch of tobacco.

In the midst of the perturbation of French taste and exoticism, the café-concert remains intact in spite of Anglo-American influence. It preserves a certain tradition which, however crapulous, is none the less racial. It is here, no doubt, that a young musician might pick up the lost thread.

•   •   •   •   •

The music hall, the circus, and American Negro bands, all these things fertilize an artist just as life does. To turn to one's own account the emotions aroused by this sort of entertainment is not to derive art from art. These entertainments are not art. They stimulate in the same way as machinery, animals, natural scenery, or danger.

•   •   •   •   •

CONCERNING A CERTAIN ACROBATIC TENDENCY. Our musicians have avoided the Wagnerian torrent on a tightrope, but a tightrope cannot be considered, any more than a torrent, as a respectable mode of locomotion.

MUSICAL BREAD is what we want.

For the last years Chardin, Ingres, Manet, and Cézanne have dominated European painting, and the foreigner comes to us to put his racial gifts to school with them. Now I declare that French music is going to influence the world.

In *Parade* I attempted to do good work, but whatever comes into contact with the theater is corrupted. The luxurious setting characteristic of the only European impresario who was sufficiently courageous and sufficiently interested to accept our work, circumstances in general, and fatigue, made me unable to realize my piece which remains, as it stands, in my opinion, an open window through which may be had a glimpse of what the modern theater ought to be.

The score of *Parade* was meant to supply a musical background to suggestive noises, e.g., of sirens, typewriters, airplanes, and dynamos, placed there like what Georges Braque so aptly calls "facts." Material difficulties and hurried rehearsals prevented these noises from materializing. We suppressed them nearly all. In other words, the piece was played incomplete and without its principle *clou*.

    •   •   •   •   •

Sick to death of flabbiness, fluidity, superfluity, frills, and all the modern sleight-of-hand, though often tempted by a technique of which he knows the ultimate resources, Satie voluntarily abstained, in order to "model in the block" and remain simple, clear, and luminous. But the public hates candor.

Each of Satie's works is an example of renunciation.

The opposition put forward by Erik Satie consists in a return to simplicity. Moreover, that is the only possible kind of opposition in an age of extreme refinement. The good faith of the critics of *Parade,* who thought that the orchestral part was a mere din, can only be explained by the phenomenon of *suggestion.* The word "cubism," wrongly applied, *suggested* an orchestra to them.

The Impressionist musicians thought the orchestra in *Parade* poor, because it had no sauce.

    •   •   •   •   •

Impressionism has fired its last fine fireworks at the end of a long fête. It is up to us to set the rockets for another fête.

One does not blame an epoch; one congratulates oneself on not having belonged to it.

To be on one's guard against a decadent movement is not to deny the individual value of its artists.

Impressionism is a reaction from Wagner. The last reverberation of the storm.

The impressionist school substitutes sunshine for light, and sonority for rhythm.

Debussy played in French, but used the Russian pedal.

"What a crowd of false disciples there is around a Picasso, a Braque, a Stravinsky, or a Satie, who discredit them!" Such is the opinion of the impressionist.
No doubt he forgets the Autumn Salon, and Mélisande's hair splitting.

Pelléas is another example of music to be listened to with one's face in one's
hands. All music which has to be listened to through the hands is suspect.
Wagner is typically music which is listened to through the hands.

One cannot get lost in a Debussy mist as one can in a Wagner fog, but it is
not good for one.

172 Igor Stravinsky

Although the Russian composer Igor Stravinsky (1882–1971) had already established a major reputation before World War I, he significantly redefined his
style, adopting a manner after the war that came to be known as "neoclassicism." Partly influenced by contemporary trends in French music (compare the
previous essay by Jean Cocteau), Stravinsky began cultivating objectivity and
restraint, distinctly departing from the flamboyance shown in much of his earlier
work. The following excerpts from a series of lectures delivered at Harvard University in 1946 address a number of esthetic and technical matters relevant to
his new approach: preference for what Stravinsky here calls "ontological" time
over the dynamic, "psychological" time of musical Romanticism; the redefini-
tion, as opposed to the rejection, of tonal centricity; an emphasis on technique
over inspiration; and the need to set limits.

FROM *Poetics of Music*
(1946)

More complex and really fundamental is the specific problem of musical
time, of the *chronos* of music. This problem has recently been made the object
of a particularly interesting study by Mr. Pierre Souvtchinsky, a Russian philos-
opher-friend of mine. His thinking is so closely akin to mine that I can do no
better than to summarize his thesis here.

Musical creation appears to him an innate complex of intuitions and possibil-

TEXT: *Poetics of Music,* trans. by Arthur Knodel and Ingolf Dahl (Cambridge, Mass.: Harvard
University Press, 1947), pp. 29–32, 34–38, 50–51, 63–65. Reprinted by permission of the publisher.

ities based primarily upon an exclusively musical experiencing of time—*chronos*, of which the musical work merely gives us the functional realization.

Everyone knows that time passes at a rate which varies according to the inner dispositions of the subject and to the events that come to affect his consciousness. Expectation, boredom, anguish, pleasure and pain, contemplation—all of these thus come to appear as different categories in the midst of which our life unfolds, and each of these determines a special psychological process, a particular tempo. These variations in psychological time are perceptible only as they are related to the primary sensation—whether conscious or unconscious—of real time, ontological time.

What gives the concept of musical time its special stamp is that this concept is born and develops as well outside of the categories of psychological time as it does simultaneously with them. All music, whether it submits to the normal flow of time, or whether it disassociates itself therefrom, establishes a particular relationship, a sort of counterpoint between the passing of time, the music's own duration, and the material and technical means through which the music is made manifest.

Mr. Souvtchinsky thus presents us with two kinds of music: one which evolves parallel to the process of ontological time, embracing and penetrating it, inducing in the mind of the listener a feeling of euphoria and, so to speak, of "dynamic calm." The other kind runs ahead of, or counter to, this process. It is not self-contained in each momentary tonal unit. It dislocates the centers of attraction and gravity and sets itself up in the unstable; and this fact makes it particularly adaptable to the translation of the composer's emotive impulses. All music in which the will to expression is dominant belongs to the second type.

This problem of time in the art of music is of capital importance. I have thought it wise to dwell on the problem because the considerations that it involves may help us to understand the different creative types which will concern us in our fourth lesson.

Music that is based on ontological time is generally dominated by the principle of similarity. The music that adheres to psychological time likes to proceed by contrast. To these two principles which dominate the creative process correspond the fundamental concepts of variety and unity.

All the arts have recourse to this principle. The methods of polychromatics and monochromatics in the plastic arts correspond respectively to variety and unity. For myself, I have always considered that in general it is more satisfactory to proceed by similarity rather than by contrast. Music thus gains strength in the measure that it does not succumb to the seductions of variety. What it loses in questionable riches it gains in true solidity.

Contrast produces an immediate effect. Similarity satisfies us only in the long run. Contrast is an element of variety, but it divides our attention. Similarity is born of a striving for unity. The need to seek variety is perfectly legitimate, but we should not forget that the One precedes the Many. Moreover, the coexistence of both is constantly necessary, and all the problems of art, like all possible problems for that matter, including the problem of knowledge and of Being, revolve ineluctably about this question, with Parmenides on one side denying the possibility of the Many, and Heraclitus on the other denying the existence of the One. Mere common sense, as well as supreme wisdom, invite us to affirm both the one and the other. All the same, the best attitude for a composer in this case will be the attitude of a man who is conscious of the hierarchy of values and who must make a choice. Variety is valid only as a means of attaining similarity. Variety surrounds me on every hand. So I need not fear that I shall be lacking in it, since I am constantly confronted by it. Contrast is everywhere. One has only to take note of it. Similarity is hidden; it must be sought out, and it is found only after the most exhaustive efforts. When variety tempts me, I am uneasy about the facile solutions it offers me. Similarity, on the other hand, poses more difficult problems but also offers results that are more solid and hence more valuable to me.

· · · · ·

Consonance, says the dictionary, is the combination of several tones into an harmonic unit. Dissonance results from the deranging of this harmony by the addition of tones foreign to it. One must admit that all this is not clear. Ever since it appeared in our vocabulary, the word dissonance has carried with it a certain odor of sinfulness.

Let us light our lantern: in textbook language, dissonance is an element of transition, a complex or interval of tones which is not complete in itself and which must be resolved to the ear's satisfaction into a perfect consonance.

But just as the eye completes the lines of a drawing which the painter has knowingly left incomplete, just so the ear may be called upon to complete a chord and coöperate in its resolution, which has not actually been realized in the work. Dissonance, in this instance, plays the part of an allusion.

Either case applies to a style where the use of dissonance demands the necessity of a resolution. But nothing forces us to be looking constantly for satisfaction that resides only in repose. And for over a century music has provided repeated examples of a style in which dissonance has emancipated itself. It is no longer tied down to its former function. Having become an entity in itself, it frequently happens that dissonance neither prepares nor anticipates anything. Dissonance is thus no more an agent of disorder than consonance is a guarantee of security. The music of yesterday and of today unhesitatingly unites parallel dissonant chords that thereby lose their functional value, and our ear quite naturally accepts their juxtaposition.

Of course, the instruction and education of the public have not kept pace with the evolution of technique. The use of dissonance, for ears ill-prepared to accept it, has not failed to confuse their reaction, bringing about a state of debility in which the dissonant is no longer distinguished from the consonant.

We thus no longer find ourselves in the framework of classic tonality in the scholastic sense of the word. It is not we who have created this state of affairs, and it is not our fault if we find ourselves confronted with a new logic of music that would have appeared unthinkable to the masters of the past. And this new logic has opened our eyes to riches whose existence we never suspected.

Having reached this point, it is no less indispensable to obey, not new idols, but the eternal necessity of affirming the axis of our music and to recognize the existence of certain poles of attraction. Diatonic tonality is only one means of orienting music towards these poles. The function of tonality is completely subordinated to the force of attraction of the pole of sonority. All music is nothing more than a succession of impulses that converge towards a definite point of repose. That is as true of Gregorian chant as it is of a Bach fugue, as true of Brahms's music as it is of Debussy's.

This general law of attraction is satisfied in only a limited way by the traditional diatonic system, for that system possesses no absolute value.

There are few present-day musicians who are not aware of this state of affairs. But the fact remains that it is still impossible to lay down the rules that govern this new technique. Nor is this at all surprising. Harmony as it is taught today in the schools dictates rules that were not fixed until long after the publication of the works upon which they were based, rules which were unknown to the composers of these works. In this manner our harmonic treatises take as their point of departure Mozart and Haydn, neither of whom ever heard of harmonic treatises.

So our chief concern is not so much what is known as tonality as what one might term the polar attraction of sound, of an interval, or even of a complex of tones. The sounding tone constitutes in a way the essential axis of music. Musical form would be unimaginable in the absence of elements of attraction which make up every musical organism and which are bound up with its psychology. The articulations of musical discourse betray a hidden correlation between the *tempo* and the interplay of tones. All music being nothing but a succession of impulses and repose, it is easy to see that the drawing together and separation of poles of attraction in a way determine the respiration of music.

In view of the fact that our poles of attraction are no longer within the closed system which was the diatonic system, we can bring the poles together without being compelled to conform to the exigencies of tonality. For we no longer believe in the absolute value of the major-minor system based on the entity which musicologists call the *c*-scale.

The tuning of an instrument, of a piano for example, requires that the entire musical range available to the instrument should be ordered according to chromatic steps. Such tuning prompts us to observe that all these sounds converge towards a center which is the *a* above middle *c*. Composing, for me, is putting into an order a certain number of these sounds according to certain interval-relationships. This activity leads to a search for the center upon which the series of sounds involved in my undertaking should converge. Thus, if a center is given, I shall have to find a combination that converges upon it. If, on the other hand, an as yet unoriented combination has been found, I shall have to determine the center towards which it should lead. The discovery of this center suggests to me the solution of my problem. It is thus that I satisfy my very marked taste for such a kind of musical topography.

The superannuated system of classic tonality, which has served as the basis for musical constructions of compelling interest, has had the authority of law among musicians for only a short period of time—a period much shorter than is usually imagined, extending only from the middle of the seventeenth century to the middle of the nineteenth. From the moment when chords no longer serve to fulfill merely the functions assigned to them by the interplay of tones but, instead, throw off all constraint to become new entities free of all ties— from that moment on one may say that the process is completed: the diatonic system has lived out its life cycle. The work of the Renaissance polyphonists had not yet entered into this system, and we have seen that the music of our time abides by it no longer. A parallel progression of ninth-chords would suffice as proof. It was here that the gates opened upon what has been labeled with the abusive term: *atonality*.

The expression is fashionable. But that doesn't mean that it is very clear. And I should like to know just what those persons who use the term mean by it. The negating prefix *a* indicates a state of indifference in regard to the term, negating without entirely renouncing it. Understood in this way, the word *atonality* hardly corresponds to what those who use it have in mind. If it were said that my music is atonal, that would be tantamount to saying that I had become deaf to tonality. Now it well may be that I remain for a considerable time within the bounds of the strict order of tonality, even though I may quite consciously break up this order for the purposes of establishing a new one. In that case I am not *a*tonal, but *anti*tonal. I am not trying to argue pointlessly over words: it is essential to know what we deny and what we affirm.

·   ·   ·   ·   ·

Most music-lovers believe that what sets the composer's creative imagination in motion is a certain emotive disturbance generally designated by the name of *inspiration*.

I have no thought of denying to inspiration the outstanding role that has devolved upon it in the generative process we are studying; I simply maintain that inspiration is in no way a prescribed condition of the creative act, but rather a manifestation that is chronologically secondary.

Inspiration, art, artist—so many words, hazy at least, that keep us from seeing clearly in a field where everything is balance and calculation through which the breath of the speculative spirit blows. It is afterwards, and only afterwards, that the emotive disturbance which is at the root of inspiration may arise—an emotive disturbance about which people talk so indelicately by conferring upon it a meaning that is shocking to us and that compromises the term itself. Is it not clear that this emotion is merely a reaction on the part of the creator grappling with that unknown entity which is still only the object of his creating and which is to become a work of art? Step by step, link by link, it will be granted him to discover the work. It is this chain of discoveries, as well as each individual discovery, that give rise to the emotion—an almost physiological reflex, like that of the appetite causing a flow of saliva—this emotion which invariably follows closely the phases of the creative process.

All creation presupposes at its origin a sort of appetite that is brought on by the foretaste of discovery. This foretaste of the creative act accompanies the intuitive grasp of an unknown entity already possessed but not yet intelligible, an entity that will not take definite shape except by the action of a constantly vigilant technique.

This appetite that is aroused in me at the mere thought of putting in order musical elements that have attracted my attention is not at all a fortuitous thing like inspiration, but as habitual and periodic, if not as constant, as a natural need.

·   ·   ·   ·   ·

Let us understand each other in regard to [the] word fantasy. We are not using the word in the sense in which it is connected with a definite musical form, but in the acceptation which presupposes an abandonment of one's self to the caprices of imagination. And this presupposes that the composer's will is voluntarily paralyzed. For imagination is not only the mother of caprice but the servant and handmaiden of the creative will as well.

The creator's function is to sift the elements he receives from her, for human activity must impose limits upon itself. The more art is controlled, limited, worked over, the more it is free.

As for myself, I experience a sort of terror when, at the moment of setting to work and finding myself before the infinitude of possibilities that present themselves, I have the feeling that everything is permissible to me. If everything is permissible to me, the best and the worst; if nothing offers me any resistance, then any effort is inconceivable, and I cannot use anything as a basis, and consequently every undertaking becomes futile.

Will I then have to lose myself in this abyss of freedom? To what shall I cling in order to escape the dizziness that seizes me before the virtuality of this infinitude? However, I shall not succumb. I shall overcome my terror and shall be reassured by the thought that I have the seven notes of the scale and its chromatic intervals at my disposal, that strong and weak accents are within my reach, and that in all of these I possess solid and concrete elements which offer me a field of experience just as vast as the upsetting and dizzy infinitude that had just frightened me. It is into this field that I shall sink my roots, fully convinced that combinations which have at their disposal twelve sounds in each octave and all possible rhythmic varieties promise me riches that all the activity of human genius will never exhaust.

What delivers me from the anguish into which an unrestricted freedom plunges me is the fact that I am always able to turn immediately to the concrete things that are here in question. I have no use for a theoretic freedom. Let me have something finite, definite—matter that can lend itself to my operation only insofar as it is commensurate with my possibilities. And such matter presents itself to me together with its limitations. I must in turn impose mine upon it. So here we are, whether we like it or not, in the realm of necessity. And yet which of us has ever heard talk of art as other than a realm of freedom? This sort of heresy is uniformly widespread because it is imagined that art is outside the bounds of ordinary activity. Well, in art as in everything else, one can build only upon a resisting foundation: whatever constantly gives way to pressure, constantly renders movement impossible.

My freedom thus consists in my moving about within the narrow frame that I have assigned myself for each one of my undertakings.

I shall go even further: my freedom will be so much the greater and more meaningful the more narrowly I limit my field of action and the more I surround myself with obstacles. Whatever diminishes constraint, diminishes strength. The more constraints one imposes, the more one frees one's self of the chains that shackle the spirit.

To the voice that commands me to create I first respond with fright; then I reassure myself by taking up as weapons those things participating in creation but as yet outside of it; and the arbitrariness of the constraint serves only to obtain precision of execution.

From all this we shall conclude the necessity of dogmatizing on pain of missing our goal. If these words annoy us and seem harsh, we can abstain from pronouncing them. For all that, they nonetheless contain the secret of salvation: "It is evident," writes Baudelaire, "that rhetorics and prosodies are not arbitrarily invented tyrannies, but a collection of rules demanded by the very organization of the spiritual being, and never have prosodies and rhetorics kept originality from fully manifesting itself. The contrary, that is to say, that they have aided the flowering of originality, would be infinitely more true."

173 John Cage

The American composer John Cage (1912–1993) was not only the most controversial composer of the latter part of the twentieth century but arguably the most influential. This essay, written as a lecture in 1957, represents his position after he fully adopted indeterminacy in his work during the early 1950s. He discusses several ideas essential to his work: his belief that sounds are to be enjoyed for their own sake and, to the extent possible, should be left to "be themselves," unaltered by human intervention; the importance of the tape recorder, not so much to allow sounds to be stored but to encourage an entirely new way of thinking about compositional material; his conviction that sound forms an unbroken continuum, encompassing complete silence at one extreme; and his refusal to acknowledge that there are sounds that do not belong to music.

Experimental Music
(1957)

Formerly, whenever anyone said the music I presented was experimental, I objected. It seemed to me that composers knew what they were doing, and that the experiments that had been made had taken place prior to the finished works, just as sketches are made before paintings and rehearsals precede performances. But, giving the matter further thought, I realized that there is ordinarily an essential difference between making a piece of music and hearing one. A composer knows his work as a woodsman knows a path he has traced and retraced, while a listener is confronted by the same work as one is in the woods by a plant he has never seen before.

Now, on the other hand, times have changed; music has changed; and I no longer object to the word "experimental." I use it in fact to describe all the music that especially interests me and to which I am devoted, whether someone else wrote it or I myself did. What has happened is that I have become a listener and the music has become something to hear. Many people, of course, have given up saying "experimental" about this new music. Instead, they either move to a halfway point and say "controversial" or depart to a greater distance and question whether this "music" is music at all.

For in this new music nothing takes place but sounds: those that are notated and those that are not. Those that are not notated appear in the written music as silences, opening the doors of the music to the sounds that happen to be in the environment. This openness exists in the fields of modern sculpture and architecture. The glass houses of Mies van der Rohe reflect their environment, presenting to the eye images of clouds, trees, or grass, according to the situation. And while looking at the constructions in wire of the sculptor Richard Lippold, it is inevitable that one will see other things, and people too, if they happen to be there at the same time, through the network of wires. There is no such thing as an empty space or an empty time. There is always something to see, something to hear. In fact, try as we may to make a silence, we cannot. For certain engineering purposes, it is desirable to have as silent a situation as possible. Such a room is called an anechoic chamber, its six walls made of

TEXT: *Silence* (Middletown: Wesleyan University Press, 1973), pp. 7–12. Reprinted by permission of University Press of New England.

special material, a room without echoes. I entered one at Harvard University several years ago and heard two sounds, one high and one low. When I described them to the engineer in charge, he informed me that the high one was my nervous system in operation, the low one my blood in circulation. Until I die there will be sounds. And they will continue following my death. One need not fear about the future of music.

But this fearlessness only follows if, at the parting of the ways, where it is realized that sounds occur whether intended or not, one turns in the direction of those he does not intend. This turning is psychological and seems at first to be a giving up of everything that belongs to humanity—for a musician, the giving up of music. This psychological turning leads to the world of nature, where, gradually or suddenly, one sees that humanity and nature, not separate, are in this world together; that nothing was lost when everything was given away. In fact, everything is gained. In musical terms, any sounds may occur in any combination and in any continuity.

And it is a striking coincidence that just now the technical means to produce such a free-ranging music are available. When the Allies entered Germany towards the end of World War II, it was discovered that improvements had been made in recording sounds magnetically such that tape had become suitable for the high-fidelity recording of music. First in France with the work of Pierre Schaeffer, later here, in Germany, in Italy, in Japan, and perhaps, without my knowing it, in other places, magnetic tape was used not simply to record performances of music but to make a new music that was possible only because of it. Given a minimum of two tape recorders and a disk recorder, the following processes are possible: 1) a single recording of any sound may be made; 2) a rerecording may be made, in the course of which, by means of filters and circuits, any or all of the physical characteristics of a given recorded sound may be altered; 3) electronic mixing (combining on a third machine sounds issuing from two others) permits the presentation of any number of sounds in combination; 4) ordinary splicing permits the juxtaposition of any sounds, and when it includes unconventional cuts, it, like rerecording, brings about alterations of any or all of the original physical characteristics. The situation made available by these means is essentially a total sound-space, the limits of which are ear-determined only, the position of a particular sound in this space being the result of five determinants: frequency or pitch, amplitude or loudness, overtone structure or timbre, duration, and morphology (how the sound begins, goes on, and dies away). By the alteration of any one of these determinants, the position of the sound in sound-space changes. Any sound at any point in this total sound-space can move to become a sound at any other point. But advantage can be taken of these possibilities only if one is willing to change one's musical habits radically. That is, one may take advantage of the appearance of images without visible transition in distant places, which is a way of saying "television," if one is willing to stay at home instead of going to a theatre. Or one may fly if one is willing to give up walking.

Musical habits include scales, modes, theories of counterpoint and harmony, and the study of the timbres, singly and in combination of a limited number of sound-producing mechanisms. In mathematical terms these all concern discrete steps. They resemble walking—in the case of pitches, on steppingstones twelve in number. This cautious stepping is not characteristic of the possibilities of magnetic tape, which is revealing to us that musical action or existence can occur at any point or along any line or curve or what have you in total sound-space; that we are, in fact, technically equipped to transform our contemporary awareness of nature's manner of operation into art.

Again there is a parting of the ways. One has a choice. If he does not wish to give up his attempts to control sound, he may complicate his musical technique towards an approximation of the new possibilities and awareness. (I use the word "approximation" because a measuring mind can never finally measure nature.) Or, as before, one may give up the desire to control sound, clear his mind of music, and set about discovering means to let sounds be themselves rather than vehicles for man-made theories or expressions of human sentiments.

This project will seem fearsome to many, but on examination it gives no cause for alarm. Hearing sounds which are just sounds immediately sets the theorizing mind to theorizing, and the emotions of human beings are continually aroused by encounters with nature. Does not a mountain unintentionally evoke in us a sense of wonder? otters along a stream a sense of mirth? night in the woods a sense of fear? Do not rain falling and mists rising up suggest the love binding heaven and earth? Is not decaying flesh loathsome? Does not the death of someone we love bring sorrow? And is there a greater hero than the least plant that grows? What is more angry than the flash of lightning and the sound of thunder? These responses to nature are mine and will not necessarily correspond with another's. Emotion takes place in the person who has it. And sounds, when allowed to be themselves, do not require that those who hear them do so unfeelingly. The opposite is what is meant by response ability.

New music: new listening. Not an attempt to understand something that is being said, for, if something were being said, the sounds would be given the shapes of words. Just an attention to the activity of sounds.

Those involved with the composition of experimental music find ways and means to remove themselves from the activities of the sounds they make. Some employ chance operations, derived from sources as ancient as the Chinese *Book of Changes,* or as modern as the tables of random numbers used also by physicists in research. Or, analogous to the Rorschach tests of psychology, the interpretation of imperfections in the paper upon which one is writing may provide a music free from one's memory and imagination. Geometrical means employing spatial superimpositions at variance with the ultimate performance in time may be used. The total field of possibilities may be roughly divided and the actual sounds within these divisions may be indicated as to number but left to the performer or to the splicer to choose. In this latter case, the composer resembles the maker of a camera who allows someone else to take the picture.

Whether one uses tape or writes for conventional instruments, the present musical situation has changed from what it was before tape came into being. This also need not arouse alarm, for the coming into being of something new does not by that fact deprive what was of its proper place. Each thing has its own place, never takes the place of something else; and the more things there are, as is said, the merrier.

But several effects of tape on experimental music may be mentioned. Since so many inches of tape equal so many seconds of time, it has become more and more usual that notation is in space rather than in symbols of quarter, half, and sixteenth notes and so on. Thus where on a page a note appears will correspond to when in time it is to occur. A stop watch is used to facilitate a performance; and a rhythm results which is a far cry from horse's hoofs and other regular beats.

Also it has been impossible with the playing of several separate tapes at once to achieve perfect synchronization. This fact has led some towards the manufacture of multiple-tracked tapes and machines with a corresponding number of heads; while others—those who have accepted the sounds they do not intend—now realize that the score, the requiring that many parts be played in a particular togetherness, is not an accurate representation of how things are. These now compose parts but not scores, and the parts may be combined in any unthought ways. This means that each performance of such a piece of music is unique, as interesting to its composer as to others listening. It is easy to see again the parallel with nature, for even with leaves of the same tree, no two are exactly alike. The parallel in art is the sculpture with moving parts, the mobile.

It goes without saying that dissonances and noises are welcome in this new music. But so is the dominant seventh chord if it happens to put in an appearance.

Rehearsals have shown that this new music, whether for tape or for instruments, is more clearly heard when the several loud-speakers or performers are separated in space rather than grouped closely together. For this music is not concerned with harmoniousness as generally understood, where the quality of harmony results from a blending of several elements. Here we are concerned with the coexistence of dissimilars, and the central points where fusion occurs are many: the ears of the listeners wherever they are. This disharmony, to paraphrase Bergson's statement about disorder, is simply a harmony to which many are unaccustomed.

Where do we go from here? Towards theatre. That art more than music resembles nature. We have eyes as well as ears, and it is our business while we are alive to use them.

And what is the purpose of writing music? One is, of course, not dealing with purposes but dealing with sounds. Or the answer must take the form of paradox: a purposeful purposelessness or a purposeless play. This play, however, is an affirmation of life—not an attempt to bring order out of chaos nor to suggest improvements in creation, but simply a way of waking up to the very life we're living, which is so excellent once one gets one's mind and one's desires out of its way and lets it act of its own accord.

174 Milton Babbitt

Milton Babbitt (b. 1916) represents the kind of rational, intellectually oriented, and technologically sophisticated musician that typified the first generation of composers to reach artistic maturity following World War II. This much-cited 1958 article first appeared in a journal for record enthusiasts, whose editor, discarding Babbitt's original title "The Composer as Specialist," gave it the considerably more inflammatory "Who Cares if You Listen?" by which it subsequently became known. Acknowledging the "musical and societal isolation" of contemporary music as an inevitable consequence of its increasing complexity, Babbitt recommends that composers simply accept this condition as a fact and act accordingly. This leads him to view serious music as an art that is necessarily conceived for a small and elite public and that, like a pure science, requires institutional support in order to flourish.

Who Cares if You Listen?
(1958)

This article might have been entitled "The Composer as Specialist" or, alternatively, and perhaps less contentiously, "The Composer as Anachronism." For I am concerned with stating an attitude towards the indisputable facts of the status and condition of the composer of what we will, for the moment, designate as "serious," "advanced," contemporary music. This composer expends an enormous amount of time and energy—and, usually, considerable money—on the creation of a commodity which has little, no, or negative commodity value. He is, in essence, a "vanity" composer. The general public is largely unaware of and uninterested in his music. The majority of performers shun it and resent it. Consequently, the music is little performed, and then primarily at poorly attended concerts before an audience consisting in the main of fellow professionals. At best, the music would appear to be for, of, and by specialists.

Text: "Who Cares if You Listen?" *High Fidelity*, vol. 8, no. 2 (February, 1958), pp. 38–40. Copyright © Hachette Filipacchi Magazines, Inc. All rights reserved. Reprinted with permission.

Towards this condition of musical and societal "isolation," a variety of attitudes has been expressed, usually with the purpose of assigning blame, often to the music itself, occasionally to critics or performers, and very occasionally to the public. But to assign blame is to imply that this isolation is unnecessary and undesirable. It is my contention that, on the contrary, this condition is not only inevitable, but potentially advantageous for the composer and his music. From my point of view, the composer would do well to consider means of realizing, consolidating, and extending the advantages.

The unprecedented divergence between contemporary serious music and its listeners, on the one hand, and traditional music and its following, on the other, is not accidental and—most probably—not transitory. Rather, it is a result of a half-century of revolution in musical thought, a revolution whose nature and consequences can be compared only with, and in many respects are closely analogous to, those of the mid-nineteenth-century revolution in theoretical physics. The immediate and profound effect has been the necessity for the informed musician to reexamine and probe the very foundations of his art. He has been obliged to recognize the possibility, and actuality, of alternatives to what were once regarded as musical absolutes. He lives no longer in a unitary musical universe of "common practice," but in a variety of universes of diverse practice.

This fall from musical innocence is, understandably, as disquieting to some as it is challenging to others, but in any event the process is irreversible; and the music that reflects the full impact of this revolution is, in many significant respects, a truly "new" music. Apart from the often highly sophisticated and complex constructive methods of any one composition, or group of compositions, the very minimal properties characterizing this body of music are the sources of its "difficulty," "unintelligibility," and—isolation. In indicating the most general of these properties, I shall make reference to no specific works, since I wish to avoid the independent issue of evaluation. The reader is at liberty to supply his own instances; if he cannot (and, granted the condition under discussion, this is a very real possibility), let him be assured that such music does exist.

First. This music employs a tonal vocabulary which is more "efficient" than that of the music of the past, or its derivatives. This is not necessarily a virtue in itself, but it does make possible a greatly increased number of pitch simultaneities, successions, and relationships. This increase in efficiency necessarily reduces the "redundancy" of the language, and as a result the intelligible communication of the work demands increased accuracy from the transmitter (the performer) and activity from the receiver (the listener). Incidentally, it is this circumstance, among many others, that has created the need for purely electronic media of "performance." More importantly for us, it makes ever heavier demands upon the training of the listener's perceptual capacities.

Second. Along with this increase of meaningful pitch materials, the number of functions associated with each component of the musical event also has been multiplied. In the simplest possible terms, each such "atomic" event is located in a five-dimensional musical space determined by pitch-class, register, dynamic, duration, and timbre. These five components not only together define the single event, but, in the course of a work, the successive values of each component create an individually coherent structure, frequently in parallel with the corresponding structures created by each of the other components. Inability to perceive and remember precisely the values of any of these components results in a dislocation of the event in the work's musical space, an alternation of its relation to all other events in the work, and—thus—a falsification of the composition's total structure. For example, an incorrectly performed or perceived dynamic value results in destruction of the work's dynamic pattern, but also in false identification of other components of the event (of which this dynamic value is a part) with corresponding components of other events, so creating incorrect pitch, registral, timbral, and durational associations. It is this high degree of "determinancy" that most strikingly differentiates such music from, for example, a popular song. A popular song is only very partially determined, since it would appear to retain its germane characteristics under considerable alteration of register, rhythmic texture, dynamics, harmonic structure, timbre, and other qualities.

The preliminary differentiation of musical categories by means of this reasonable and usable criterion of "degree of determinacy" offends those who take it to be a definition of qualitative categories, which—of course—it need not always be. Curiously, their demurrers usually take the familiar form of some such "democratic" counterdefinition as: "There is no such thing as 'serious' and 'popular' music. There is only 'good' and 'bad' music." As a public service, let me offer those who still patiently await the revelation of the criteria of Absolute Good an alternative criterion which possesses, at least, the virtue of immediate and irrefutable applicability: "There is no such thing as 'serious' and 'popular' music. There is only music whose title begins with the letter 'X,' and music whose title does not."

Third. Musical compositions of the kind under discussion possess a high degree of contextuality and autonomy. That is, the structural characteristics of a given work are less representative of a general class of characteristics than they are unique to the individual work itself. Particularly, principles of relatedness, upon which depends immediate coherence of continuity, are more likely to evolve in the course of the work than to be derived from generalized assumptions. Here again greater and new demands are made upon the perceptual and conceptual abilities of the listener.

Fourth, and finally. Although in many fundamental respects this music is "new," it often also represents a vast extension of the methods of other musics, derived from a considered and extensive knowledge of their dynamic principles. For, concomitant with the "revolution in music," perhaps even an integral aspect thereof, has been the development of analytical theory, concerned with the systematic formulation of such principles to the end of greater efficiency, economy, and understanding. Compositions so rooted necessarily ask comparable knowledge and experience from the listener. Like all communication, this music presupposes a suitably equipped receptor. I am aware that "tradition" has it that the lay listener, by virtue of some undefined, transcendental faculty, always is able to arrive at a musical judgment absolute in its wisdom if not always permanent in its validity. I regret my inability to accord this declaration of faith the respect due its advanced age.

Deviation from this tradition is bound to dismiss the contemporary music of which I have been talking into "isolation." Nor do I see how or why the situation should be otherwise. Why should the layman be other than bored and puzzled by what he is unable to understand, music or anything else? It is only the translation of this boredom and puzzlement into resentment and denunciation that seems to me indefensible. After all, the public does have its own music, its ubiquitous music: music to eat by, to read by, to dance by, and to be impressed by. Why refuse to recognize the possibility that contemporary music has reached a stage long since attained by other forms of activity? The time has passed when the normally well-educated man without special preparation could understand the most advanced work in, for example, mathematics, philosophy, and physics. Advanced music, to the extent that it reflects the knowledge and originality of the informed composer, scarcely can be expected to appear more intelligible than these arts and sciences to the person whose musical education usually has been even less extensive than his background in other fields. But to this, a double standard is invoked, with the words "music is music," implying also that "music is *just* music." Why not, then, equate the activities of the radio repairman with those of the theoretical physicist, on the basis of the dictum that "physics is physics"? It is not difficult to find statements like the following, from the *New York Times* of September 8, 1957: "The scientific level of the conference is so high ... that there are in the world only 120 mathematicians specializing in the field who could contribute." Specialized music on the other hand, far from signifying "height" of musical level, has been charged with "decadence," even as evidence of an insidious "conspiracy."

It often has been remarked that only in politics and the "arts" does the layman regard himself as an expert, with the right to have his opinion heard. In the realm of politics he knows that this right, in the form of a vote, is guaranteed by fiat. Comparably, in the realm of public music, the concertgoer is secure in the knowledge that the amenities of concert going protect his firmly stated "I didn't like it" from further scrutiny. Imagine, if you can, a layman chancing upon a lecture on "Pointwise Periodic Homeomorphisms." At the conclusion, he announces: "I didn't like it." Social conventions being what they are in such circles, someone might dare inquire: "Why not?" Under duress, our layman discloses precise reasons for his failure to enjoy himself; he found the hall chilly, the lecturer's voice unpleasant, and he was suffering the digestive aftermath of a poor dinner. His interlocutor understandably disqualifies these reasons as irrelevant to the content and value of the lecture, and the development of mathematics is left undisturbed. If the concertgoer is at all versed in the ways of musical lifesmanship, he also will offer reasons for his "I didn't like it"—in the form of assertions that the work in question is "inexpressive," "undramatic," "lacking in poetry," etc., etc., tapping that store of vacuous equivalents hallowed by time for: "I don't like it, and I cannot or will not state why." The concertgoer's critical authority is established beyond the possibility of further inquiry. Certainly he is not responsible for the circumstance that musical discourse is a never-never land of semantic confusion, the last resting place of all those verbal and formal fallacies, those hoary dualisms that have been banished from rational discourse. Perhaps he has read, in a widely consulted and respected book on the history of music, the following: "to call him (Tchaikovsky) the 'modern Russian Beethoven' is footless, Beethoven being patently neither modern nor Russian. . . ." Or, the following, by an eminent "nonanalytic" philosopher: "The music of Lourié is an ontological music. . . . It is born in the singular roots of being, the nearest possible juncture of the soul and the spirit. . . ." How unexceptionable the verbal peccadilloes of the average concertgoer appear beside these masterful models. Or, perhaps, in search of "real" authority, he has acquired his critical vocabulary from the pronouncements of officially "eminent" composers, whose eminence, in turn, is founded largely upon just such assertions as the concertgoer has learned to regurgitate. This cycle is of slight moment in a world where circularity is one of the norms of criticism. Composers (and performers), wittingly or unwittingly assuming the character of "talented children" and "inspired idiots" generally ascribed to them, are singularly adept at the conversion of personal tastes into general principles. Music they do not like is "not music," composers whose music they do not like are "not composers."

In search of what to think and how to say it, the layman may turn to newspapers and magazines. Here he finds conclusive evidence for the proposition that "music is music." The science editor of such publications contents himself with straightforward reporting, usually news of the "factual" sciences; books and articles not intended for popular consumption are not reviewed. Whatever the reason, such matters are left to professional journals. The music critic admits no comparable differentiation. He may feel, with some justice, that music which presents itself in the market place of the concert hall automatically offers itself to public approval or disapproval. He may feel, again with some justice, that to omit the expected criticism of the "advanced" work would be to do the composer an injustice in his assumed quest for, if nothing else, public notice and "professional recognition." The critic, at least to this extent, is himself a victim of the leveling of categories.

Here, then, are some of the factors determining the climate of the public world of music. Perhaps we should not have overlooked those pockets of "power" where prizes, awards, and commissions are dispensed, where music is adjudged guilty, not only without the right to be confronted by its accuser, but without the right to be confronted by the accusations. Or those well-meaning souls who exhort the public "just to *listen* to more contemporary music," apparently on the theory that familiarity breeds passive acceptance. Or those, often the same well-meaning souls, who remind the composer of his "obligation to the public," while the public's obligation to the composer is fulfilled, manifestly, by mere physical presence in the concert hall or before a loudspeaker or—more authoritatively—by committing to memory the numbers of phonograph records and amplifier models. Or the intricate social world within this musical world, where the salon becomes bazaar, and music itself becomes an ingredient of verbal canapés for cocktail conversation.

I say all this not to present a picture of a virtuous music in a sinful world, but to point up the problems of a special music in an alien and inapposite world. And so, I dare suggest that the composer would do himself and his music an immediate and eventual service by total, resolute, and voluntary withdrawal from this public world to one of private performance and electronic media, with its very real possibility of complete elimination of the public and social aspects of musical composition. By so doing, the separation between the domains would be defined beyond any possibility of confusion of categories, and the composer would be free to pursue a private life of professional achievement, as opposed to a public life of unprofessional compromise and exhibitionism.

But how, it may be asked, will this serve to secure the means of survival for the composer and his music? One answer is that after all such a private life is what the university provides the scholar and the scientist. It is only proper that the university, which—significantly—has provided so many contemporary composers with their professional training and general education, should provide a home for the "complex," "difficult," and "problematical" in music. Indeed, the process has begun; and if it appears to proceed too slowly, I take consolation in the knowledge that in this respect, too, music seems to be in historically retarded parallel with now sacrosanct fields of endeavor. In E. T. Bell's *Men of Mathematics*, we read: "In the eighteenth century the universities were not the principal centers of research in Europe. They might have become such sooner than they did but for the classical tradition and its understandable hostility to science. Mathematics was close enough to antiquity to be respectable, but physics, being more recent, was suspect. Further, a mathematician in a university of the time would have been expected to put much of his effort on elementary teaching; his research, if any, would have been an unprofitable luxury. . . ." A simple substitution of "musical composition" for "research," of "academic" for "classical," of "music" for "physics," and of "composer" for "mathematician," provides a strikingly accurate picture of the current situation. And as long as the confusion I have described continues to exist, how can the university and its community assume other than that the composer welcomes and courts public competition with the historically certified products of the past, and the commercially certified products of the present?

Perhaps for the same reason, the various institutes of advanced research and the large majority of foundations have disregarded this music's need for means of survival. I do not wish to appear to obscure the obvious differences between musical composition and scholarly research, although it can be contended that these differences are no more fundamental than the differences among the various fields of study. I do question whether these differences, by their nature, justify the denial to music's development of assistance granted these other fields. Immediate "practical" applicability (which may be said to have its musical analogue in "immediate extensibility of a compositional technique") is certainly not a necessary condition for the support of scientific research. And if it be contended that such research is so supported because in the past it has yielded eventual applications, one can counter with, for example, the music of Anton Webern, which during the composer's lifetime was regarded (to the very limited extent that it was regarded at all) as the ultimate in hermetic, specialized, and idiosyncratic composition; today, some dozen years after the composer's death, his complete works have been recorded by a major record company, primarily—I suspect—as a result of the enormous influence this music has had on the postwar, nonpopular, musical world. I doubt that scientific research is any more secure against predictions of ultimate significance than is musical composition. Finally, if it be contended that research, even in its least "practical" phases, contributes to the sum of knowledge in the particular realm, what possibly can contribute more to our knowledge of music than a genuinely original composition?

Granting to music the position accorded other arts and sciences promises the sole substantial means of survival for the music I have been describing. Admittedly, if this music is not supported, the whistling repertory of the man in the street will be little affected, the concert-going activity of the conspicuous consumer of musical culture will be little disturbed. But music will cease to evolve, and, in that important sense, will cease to live.

175 Evan Ziporyn

Evan Ziporyn (b. 1959) is an American composer who has been influenced by a wide variety of music, including both non-Western (especially Balinese) art music and Western popular and vernacular musics. This 1991 article, whose title plays upon "Who Cares if You Listen?," the title assigned by an editor to the previous essay by Milton Babbitt, argues for a more open conception of musical composition consistent with contemporary cultural pluralism. Noting the power of digital technology to "refashion everything under the sun," Ziporyn questions whether the individual compositional voice still has any validity and whether compositions can represent personal "property." This line of thinking leads him to envision a breaking down of old boundaries through creative interactions among previously unrelated musical traditions, spawned by composers who are "rootless cosmopolitans . . . , endlessly wandering in search of a community, an aesthetic, a musical life."

Who Listens if You Care?
(1991)

In 1977, Chris Maher, composer and massage artist, articulated his vision of what he termed "Marxist music." His idea was simple: no musical material could be owned—all music makers should be able to take whatever they want from whomever they want and use it as they see fit. "Material" could range from a melody, a sound, a formal principle, to an entire piece of music (as in Maher's "New Improved Morton Feldman," in which Feldman's spare sonic world is "enhanced" through the use of digital delay). Maher contended that only in this way could music—rather than an individual's musical career—grow and develop freely. By invading and destroying the notion of musical "property," the scope of musical possibilities would be infinitely expanded. An individual's "piece" would still exist and could still be valued, in any and every sense, but, more importantly, his or her ideas—or, more precisely, any real or imagined musical ideas that could be construed from his or her piece—could be built upon, taken in unexpected directions, used by all.

We were young then, and despite the well-known historical precedents for this position—famous borrowers such as Handel (melodies), Barry Manilow (chord progressions), and Webern (formal principles)—I remember that we found the idea somewhat scandalous and terrifying. This was tied into the seeming impossibility of making careers for ourselves as composers: the task seemed to be "finding a voice" or coming up with some kind of original or innovative structural idea. This daunting task was achieved through "the work" one put into one's music—not simply time or deep thought but some ineffable blend of the two, of quantity and quality. This work was what ultimately mattered: our pieces—the product—would be perfect reflections of it, and, in the course of time, this work—if we but had the strength to persevere tirelessly—would be recognized, lauded, rewarded. Our dedication would magically be transformed into stunning, creative work, and from there glory and achievement would be ours. There was a hidden, mystical equation: talent ("quality") times work ("quantity") divided by fate would equal good fortune, fame, success.

The inevitable disillusionment from our naive faith did not result from any

TEXT: *New Observations*, no. 86 (November / December, 1991), pp. 25–28.

inherent failing in this equation. Most of us ultimately were able to do what we wanted to a greater or lesser degree, and the fact that various bozos managed to get famous on a gimmick didn't seem very irksome once we got used to it (none of us lost much sleep over the Milli Vanilli thing, for example).[1] What caused the destruction of this Calvinistic world-view was rather that Maher's dream became reality, in a far more encompassing way than even he could have imagined. For, as we now all know, the need for new products to market and sell has combined with the digital ability to refashion everything under the sun, and this very un-Marxist combination of consumerism and technology has led to the fulfillment of Chris's dream.

In a deeper way than ever before, all music is available to all people, all the time. In the West, this simple and delightful fact has been patently obvious since Karlheinz Stockhausen's 1966 *Telemusik*, a musique concrète piece for which the source material is traditional music from dozens of cultures, all of whom, the composer asserts, "wanted to participate in *Telemusik* . . . not 'my' music, but a music of the whole world, of all countries and all races." But this early harbinger of things to come, like Brian Eno and David Byrne's 1980 *My Life in the Bush of Ghosts,* a pop version of the same thing, has turned out to be a relatively primitive form of musical imperialism compared to the present state of musical multi-nationalism. Across the globe musicians are begging, borrowing, and stealing from each other at a rapacious pace. Brazilian muzenza ensembles are singing praise songs to Bob Marley, Gambian koro players are rushing to finish commissions for the Kronos Quartet, and hordes of rock icons are scurrying around searching for newer, hipper even more undiscovered grooves.

In the West, this process has involved the merging of every concept of musical "otherness": exotica has been annexed, declared null and void. Up until now, the maintenance of any mainstream—be it the standard concert repertoire, top-40 radio, swing, academic modernism, etc.—included a notion of its opposite, the "out there." This is what allowed Cab Calloway to describe bebop as "Chinese music," or Pierre Boulez to pronounce that "the non-serialist composer is useless." Such statements help define a genre, to alert people to accept no substitutes.

The boundaries of any particular mainstream are by nature always in flux, shifting and indeterminate. Even so, such defining gestures—this is music, that is not—are possible and necessary. Territory can expand, but a line has to be drawn somewhere: language must be employed to corral, tame, and ultimately include or exclude the new sound under scrutiny. One can appeal to nature (as does Rameau in justifying his use of chromaticism in "L'Enharmonique"), to

1. The pop-rap group Milli Vanilli, consisting of Robert Pilatus and Fabrice Morvan, won the 1990 Grammy award for best new artist. Rumors soon surfaced that the group's debut album was actually the work of three backup singers and that the duo had not sung a single note. Upon confirmation, the National Academy of Recording Arts and Sciences requested for the first time in its 33-year history that the Grammy be returned.

morals (saying, for example, that certain types of music are "corrupting" or "degenerate"), to common sense ("My 3-year-old could do better than that"), or to taste and sheer willfulness ("I don't know much about music, but I know what I like").

Nowadays such posturing is less viable, because the very notion of "otherness" has become a marketable commodity, incorporated into the aesthetic. Before, depending on who you were and where you stood, the "other" could be a lot of things: non-Western music, early music, computer music, etc. Now all these things have merged, and a typical "new age" recording might use synthesizers imitating Shona mbiras, Balinese genggong imitating synthesizers, all in the service of evoking a fictional Druidic ritual. As critic Joshua Kosman points out, the "authentic performance" movement has caught on partially because it can be recorded digitally and marketed as the "latest thing." People don't give a shit where the music they like comes from, when it was written, for what purpose, by whom, or how it's played. It's the end of history, in a way Francis Fukuyama could never have anticipated. A sampled mbira is as good as a real one—we know what it's trying to sound like, so what possible difference could it make. There's no point in asking if it's live or Memorex anymore. "Otherness" in Western music is now nothing more than a quality of sound to be lifted and used as quickly as possible.

This point is brought home by the obvious irrelevance of today's copyright laws. The musical material most likely to be borrowed is clearly not protectable—a quality of sound, a rhythm, an inflected phrase. If worse comes to worst, give your music away (just keep the nude, transsexual pictures of rock stars off your CD cover and the industry will probably never even notice).

Whether one's motivation is fun or profit, the end result is the same: an imperialistic groove, under which any and every form of music past or present can be subsumed. "The groove" can be defined in a number of ways—as a steady 4 / 4 disco beat, suitable for DJ mix-and-matching, as a new age wash of sound, suitable for the inducement of bliss and calm, or anything else that feels good. Music thus becomes a service industry, providing listeners with a pleasurable, regulated, and non-threatening surface wash of sound. This results in another Marxian quandary: the byproduct of Maherian/Marxist music is that the listener is now completely cut off from the "means of production," and basically couldn't care less—if I hear the Harmonic Choir on the radio, it is at this point completely irrelevant to me whether David Hykes does it acoustically, electronically or whether it's him doing it at all. And why should I care—such issues are of anecdotal value only, useful in building a reputation, adding to a resume, writing a feature article in *Ear* Magazine.

The traditional boundaries of genre, intended audience, "culture," have been so thoroughly crossed that even when you try it's impossible to take a cohesive stance toward any particular piece of music. One can only applaud when Public Enemy's Chuck D. says that his group's goal is to be a "musician's nightmare," but how is one to respond to David Byrne's use of Cuban rhythms and musicians to sing a song about rent control? Is it exploitative and neo-colonial? Who the hell knows—the beat is good, the words are compelling, and you can dance to it. These are important things. It's catchy, it seems to have vision and imagination. But how does that feeling come about? How much of the power of the music is derived from evocations of other things, from Eddie Palmieri to Ricky Ricardo? (Again, these confusions cut across cultural borders: in 1988 Indonesia's biggest pop star was named Ricki Ricardo, and the biggest hit single was a rock song using traditional gamelan instruments called "Bring Back the Old Bali"). Even if we wanted to, how could we determine what taboos are left to break, what boundaries left to cross?

This situation has had a number of extremely positive effects. Even fifteen years ago, the lack of respect accorded non-Western music (and other "others") seemed somehow unjust. The availability of every form of music to anyone with a record player or a college radio station in the vicinity was an accomplished fact, and yet most college music departments continued to pretend that you could teach "music" as if the term meant something that had existed only in Europe, subsisting until the birth of Bach, flowering until the beginning of this century, and currently experiencing ongoing and agonizing death throes. It seemed important to argue for opening things up, recognizing other vital traditions, talking about musical hybridization, etc.

Now fortunately everything has been turned on its head: cultural critics crawl all over themselves to explain the influence of talking drums on hip-hop; Greg Sandow, composer and critic, once an ardent defender of David Del Tredici and Charles Wuorinen (two ideological enemies currently to be found side by side in the same rubbish heap of history, the "New Music" bin at Tower Records), can now boldly state that "most [!] heavy metal guitarists are influenced by Bach solo violin suites"; Peter Gabriel, a platinum-selling rock star, releases a hit album of "source material" sampled for use in his own work. And even within the academy, the College Music Society issues urgent calls to teach non-Western music, and—luckily—conservative academic trendsetters like Allan Bloom and E. D. Hirsch either don't know enough about music or care enough to target it.

In other words, I'm not complaining: how can I in an era when Boulez' neo-fascist post-war pronouncements seem like medieval schisms, or oracles from another planet? Non-western music doesn't have to fight for respect anymore, and that's an amazing turn of events.

It is also of course true that, here and around the globe, there are still lots of traditional musical uses and users, not just your average Balinese villager (who may have a Michael Jackson poster on his wall), but the classical music lover (for whom Schoenberg is noise), or the academic computer musician (for whom all 19th-century music sounds alike), etc. I am merely asserting that there now exists a large number of us for whom musical boundaries have lost their former meanings. I am talking about people for whom an average day's listening might include the Monroe Brothers, Japanese muzak, Bugandan horns, Sibelius symphonies, and any and everything else, a list more resembling a Borgesian encyclopedia than a radio playlist or concert program. We are the rootless cosmopolitans of music, endlessly wandering in search of a community, an aesthetic, a musical life.

It is difficult for us, faced with this onslaught, to know how to proceed, either pragmatically or philosophically. If we are composers, what instruments to write for? If we teach, what subjects? What set of musical values, technical and aesthetic, are we to subscribe to? Why are we doing it anyway? Even attention and money aren't sufficient motivators, for as Robert Moore puts it, "You can now do whatever you want, because no one will care in any case." What then are we to do?

The answer, I believe, can be found by re-examining the troublesome analogy between music and language. Is music a language at all? Is it a "universal" one? For people who are still able to divide music into traditions, genres, etc., music is like language in that humans do it for other humans (presumably) to hear it, and they do it following spoken or unspoken structural rules that are shared and make sense to various groups of people. Particular musics are associated with particular cultures—your average Balinese, for example, can distinguish between "Balinese music" and everything else in the world. As long as music is defined in this way, as a cultural byproduct or sign system, it's easy to keep our bearings. Music is a code, by definition comprehensible to people within a cultural group. Unfortunately, this also means that any particular music is by definition misunderstood by everyone else in the world, no matter how carefully they listen. In other words, any Ghanaian's subjective hearing of Ghanaian drumming is automatically valid, "authentic"; any non-Ghanaian's invalid, albeit useful, enjoyable, etc. When things are couched in these terms, it becomes clear how inappropriate such distinctions have become, how ridiculous it is to assert the relative validity of anybody's response to any music.

One solution to this is to redefine music as "organized sound," as any collection of noise that is deemed "music" by anybody. Viewed in this light, music is still a sign system, a language, but it's one in which any ordering of "phonemes" is automatically intelligible. (A "musical phoneme" can be defined as any subjectively discerned unit of sound, or as the equivalent of a "syllable" in language.) "Organized sound" might as well mean "sound," since the listener does the organizing—this means everything we hear and don't hear, any combination of sound and silence, and . . . my God! What does sound have to do with music!!!

Phonemically transferable music (music as organized sound) is thus both inherently "universal" and inherently incomprehensible, a sign system in which everyone in the world has their own code book, a language in which no two of us speak a mutually intelligible dialect. We are faced then with an awful choice: a Babel of conflicting tongues or an endless outpouring of gibberish. Either way we're in trouble—either way communication seems impossible.

If music is sound and sound only, then nothing we can do can be more or less understood than anything else. If, on the other hand, music consists of myriad discrete languages, a native speaker confronted with "the other" in any form can do a number of things, among them: 1) ignore it and stick to the purity of the mother tongue (this can be done either as a Boulezian progressive or as a Rochbergian reactionary); 2) exploit it by subsuming it into your own, grander music *(My Life in the Bush of Ghosts, Telemusik);* 3) learn to speak the other like a native (Lou Harrison, Joseph Conrad); 4) respect it and come to terms with it, either by creating self-conscious hybrids *(Finnegans Wake,* Harry Partch), or ones which are designed to have mutually exclusive meanings for different listeners (these are the hardest examples to find—but this was the intention of my own collaboration with Balinese composer Nyoman Windha in *Kekembangan,* a piece for gamelan and saxophone quartet. Malinowski's inclusion of uninterpreted myths in *Argonauts of the Western Pacific* can also be viewed in this way).

Acting linguistically, speaking and writing, all of the above stances can be taken with a clear attitude toward comprehensibility. To be understood, one must subscribe to the hierarchical relationship between languages; in other words, speak one of them at a time. Creating artificial languages—hybrid or synthetic—is possible, but by definition produces incomprehension. But the mere possibility of "phonemic transference," which renders every cultural distinction potentially relative and ephemeral, makes it impossible to honestly assert that this same structure, this same test of understandability, applies to music. Please understand me: it is not our ability to articulate a definition of music as organized sound that creates this relativity, but rather that the experience of "useful misunderstanding," of a meaningful "inauthentic hearing," forces us to consider such a definition. As soon as we have heard the music from another culture in "the wrong way"—listened to West African drumming in 3/4 instead of 12/8, misconstrued the emotional meaning of a praise song, etc.—then we understand how pointless it is to insist that music operates as cultural language only. Despite the rigidity of the language/sound dichotomy, we seem to know that we can make sense of music without thinking of it as a system of signs or sounds. We don't need it to be a symbol of anything at all. And our problems have nothing to do with music, but only with our need to talk about it, to explain music in any way whatsoever.

Our lost youthful vision, that mystical combination of work, integrity, etc., long abandoned, was essentially a Platonic one. We wanted to dig deep within ourselves, to excavate beneath our petty experiences, ideas, etc. in search of the cool and the weird. Making good music meant simply stumbling across that nameless quality that we prayed was in there somewhere. (Our response was, in retrospect, the only reasonable one available to us as products of a system that glorifies individualism. For even if each person is now a society unto himself, with a personal background, interests—and this is the implicit goal of the individualistic project—then the only values can be individual ones, and the search for quality can only be an internal one.)

Plato would have banned music altogether, it being too unwieldy and uncapturable to be controlled by a rational state. And Plato was right, because to talk about music, to categorize it, define it, explain it, is to attach linguistic constructs, rational states, to phenomena that only resemble linear thought in the sense that they move uni-directionally through time. The only way to get around this, outside of banning music, is to separate music from linguistic thought, to stop searching for so much meaning. I'm not suggesting that we stop talking about music, stop trying to figure it out, but simply that we get rid of the notion that the value of music is in this incessant chatter, rather than in the music itself. Viewed in this way, what Maher's Marxist music seeks to dispense with is not "musical property," but the ability to even articulate the phrase. Once we stop believing that our descriptions and analyses enhance, encapsulate and embody the music in any intrinsic way, then issues of musical ownership will become irrelevant and will simply wither away.

We must begin to listen only to our inner voices, whatever their source, to insist that the Platonic ideal doesn't need a name, a language, a category. We must rid ourselves of the notion that a piece of music can or cannot be politically correct, exploitative, collaborative, traditional, iconoclastic, whatever. We must stop trying to explain music, stop caring whether it's a sign system, a random or deliberate collection of sounds, or a symbol of anything other than itself. We must—we must—oh, shut up and listen, will you?

EXPANDED SONIC RESOURCES

176 Ferruccio Busoni

Ferruccio Busoni (1866–1924) was one of the most prominent musicians of the early twentieth century, widely recognized as a composer, pianist, and conductor. His *Sketch of a New Esthetic of Music,* first published in 1907, is the earliest general statement by a major figure to express fully the belief that twentieth-century composers must move beyond the traditional materials of Western music in search of previously untapped compositional possibilities. Though still expressing himself largely within the esthetic categories of Romanticism, emphasizing freedom, individuality, and originality, Busoni argues for the liberation of music from the limited rhythmic and formal structures and tone systems of "hallowed tradition" and from the rules imposed by self-appointed "lawgivers." He exhorts modern composers to embrace novel compositional materials such as "artificial" scales, microtonal divisions, and electro-mechanical instruments, as well as new systems of musical notation.

FROM *Sketch of a New Esthetic of Music*
(1907)

Music as an art, our so-called Western music, is barely four hundred years old. It is in a condition of development, perhaps in the earliest stage of a yet unforeseeable development. Yet we speak of classics and holy traditions.[1] Someone like Cherubini already speaks in his counterpoint textbook of "the ancients."

We have formulated rules, set out principles, and prescribed laws—we apply the maxims of adults to a child who does not yet understand responsibility!

As young as this child is, it already has one radiant characteristic that sets it off from all its older comrades. The lawgivers refuse to recognize this wonderful attribute, for their laws would then be rejected. This child—it floats on air! It does not touch the ground, is not subject to gravity. It is almost incorporeal, its material transparent. It is sonorous air. It is almost nature herself. It is free.

But freedom is something that humans have never fully understood, never completely experienced. They neither recognize it nor acknowledge it.

They deny the destiny of this child and enchain it. This soaring creature is required to walk properly, to conform to the rules of correct behavior, as if it were an ordinary being. It is barely permitted to leap, though it would like to follow the curve of the rainbow and, with the clouds, break apart the rays of the sun.

TEXT: *Entwurf einer neuen Ästhetik der Tonkunst,* 2nd ed. (Leipzig: Insel Verlag, 1916), pp. 7–11, 31, 33, 36–46. Translation by Robert P. Morgan.

1. Tradition is a plaster mask taken from life that, in passing through the course of many years and through the hands of many laborers, retains little resemblance to the original. [Au.]

The art of music was born free and its destiny is to win again its freedom. It will be the most complete of all nature's manifestations, thanks to the limitlessness of its immateriality. Even the poetic word lags behind it in incorporeality. Music can gather into itself and flow outward, can be a motionless calm or a tempestuous storm. It provides the most extreme heights perceptible to humans—what other art does that?—and its perception touches the human breast with an intensity independent of "concepts."

It reproduces an emotion without describing it, through the movement of the soul and the liveliness of continuous moments. The painter or sculptor, on the other hand, presents only one facet, one moment, a "situation"; and the poet must communicate an emotion and its stirrings laboriously, through successive words.

Hence representation and description do not constitute the essence of music. We thus reject program music and move on to consider the goals of music.

Absolute music! What the lawgivers mean thereby is perhaps furthest removed from the true absolute in music. "Absolute music" is a play of forms without a poetic program, the form fulfilling the most important role. True absolute music, however, stands precisely in opposition to form. It has the God-given attribute of floating on air and being free of all material conditions. In a picture, the representation of a sunset ends with the frame. A rectangular boundary is imposed upon the unbounded natural phenomenon; the fixed depiction of a cloud remains forever unchanging. Music can grow brighter, darker, shift position, and finally fade away like the glow of the sunset itself. Instinct leads the creative musician to use just those tones that press the same key, and awaken the same response, in the human heart as does the natural event.

Absolute music, on the other hand, is something quite sober, bringing to mind carefully ordered music stands, relationships of tonic to dominant, or developments to codas.

Now I hear the second violinist laboriously imitate the more adept first violinist a fourth lower; I hear an unnecessary battle being waged so that one can start again at the beginning. Such music should be called architectonic music, or symmetrical music, or sectional music, the result of the way certain composers poured their spirit and emotion into this type of form because it was most natural to them or their time. The lawgivers then identified spirit, emotion, the individuality of those composers, and the character of their time with symmetrical music; and when finally composers could no longer bring forth the spirit or the emotion, nor reproduce the character of that time, the lawgivers retained the form as a symbol, elevating it to a sort of sign, or article of faith. The older composers explored this form and found in it the most suitable means for communicating their thoughts. When they passed on, the lawgivers discovered the garments they left behind on earth and preserved them. . . .

Is it not strange that one demands originality of composers in all things, yet forbids it in matters of form? No wonder that one complains of formlessness when composers become truly original. Mozart! We marvel at and honor the seeker, the discoverer, the great man with a childish heart; not his tonics and dominants, his developments and codas.

Beethoven, the Romantic revolutionary, so longed for freedom that he succeeded in bringing music one small step back toward its higher nature—a small step in the overall task, a large one in his own individual development. Though he failed to achieve fully absolute music, he came close in certain moments, such as the introduction to the fugue of the *Hammerklavier* Sonata. In general, composers have approached nearest the true nature of music in preparatory and intermediary passages (preludes and transitions), where they felt they could ignore symmetrical proportions and, as if unconsciously, breathe more freely. Even a lesser talent like Schumann grasps in such passages something of the boundlessness of this pan-art—one thinks of the transition to the last movement of the D-minor Symphony. And one could say the same of Brahms in the introduction to the finale of his First Symphony.

But as soon as they cross the threshold to the principal subject, composers become stiff and conventional, like someone who has stepped into a business office.

·   ·   ·   ·   ·

Creators should not accept on blind faith any rule that has been handed down to them, forcing them from the outset to consider their own creation as an exception thereto. They must seek and find their own appropriate rule for their own particular case and, after applying it successfully, reject it again in order not to repeat themselves in their next work.

The task of the creator should be to set up rules, not to follow rules. Whoever follows prescribed rules ceases to be a creator.

The power of creation is more easily recognized the more it is able to make itself independent of tradition. But deliberateness in the treatment of rules cannot simulate the power of creation, much less produce it.

True creators strive only for perfection. And by bringing this perfection into harmony with their own individuality, a new rule results quite unintentionally.

·   ·   ·   ·   ·

Our tonal range has become so narrow, its form of expression so stereotypical, that there is now no known motive which cannot be joined with another known motive so that the two can be played simultaneously. In order not to lose myself in games,[2] I will refrain from offering examples.

2. I played such a game once with a friend in order to determine how many of the best-known compositions were constructed according to the formal scheme of the second theme of the Adagio of the Ninth Symphony. In a few moments we had collected some fifteen samples from the most varied genres, including some of a quite primitive sort. And they included Beethoven himself. Is the theme from the Finale of the Fifth Symphony different from the theme that

•   •   •   •   •

What comes closest to the true nature of the art in today's music is the rest and the fermata. Great performing artists, improvisors, know how to give this means of expression its full value. The suspenseful silence between two passages, which is itself also music in this context, provokes us more to presentiment than the more definite, but thus less malleable, sound.

What we today call our "tone system" is nothing but a system of "signs," an ingenious aid in holding fast something of that eternal harmony, a poor pocket edition of that encyclopedic work. Artificial light instead of the sun. Have you noticed how people open their mouths in wonder at the brilliant lighting of a concert hall? They never do so for the midday sunshine, a million times stronger.

And in music too, signs have become more important than what they are supposed to mean, but can only suggest.

How important, after all, are the "third," the "fifth," the "octave"? How strictly do we distinguish "consonances" from "dissonances"—and in a context where there actually can be no dissonances?

We have divided the octave in twelve steps equally separated from one another, because we must somehow make things easier for ourselves. And we have so constructed our instruments that we can never go above, below, or between them. In particular keyboard instruments have thoroughly trained our ears so that we are no longer capable of hearing anything [outside the chromatic octave] except as impurity. And nature created an infinite gradation—infinite! who realizes it today?[3]

And within this twelve-partitioned octave we have marked off yet another succession of particular distances, seven in number, and have constructed our entire tonal art thereon. Did I say one succession? There are two, the major and minor scales. If we construct the same succession of distances starting on one of the other twelve degrees, then there is a new key, and moreover a foreign one. One can read in the rule books what a profoundly limited system this has created:[4] we do not want to repeat it here.

---

begins the Allegro of the Second? Or from the main theme of the Third Piano Concerto, only in minor? [Au.]

3. "Twelve-tone equal temperament, already mentioned theoretically by c. 1500 but not fully formulated until shortly before 1700 (by Andreas Werkmeister), divides the octave into twelve equal divisions (semitones: hence the "twelve-semitone system") and thus produces only average values, enabling no interval to be purely intoned but all to become reasonably serviceable." (Riemann, *Musiklexikon.*) [Au.]

And thus thanks to Andreas Werkmeister, this master workman of art, we have attained the "twelve-semitone system" with many impure yet reasonably serviceable intervals. But what is pure and what impure? Our ear hears as impure an "out-of-tune" piano on which, perhaps, "pure and serviceable" intervals can be heard. The diplomatic twelve-semitone system is an aid born of necessity; yet we take great pains to preserve its imperfections. [Au.]

4. It is called the "theory of harmony." [Au.]

We teach twenty-four keys, twelve each for both types of seven-note scales; yet in fact we make use of only two: the major key and the minor key. The others are simply transpositions. One says that the individual transpositions produce different characters: but that is an illusion. In England, where high voices predominate, the most well-known works are performed a half tone higher than notated, without altering the effect. Singers transpose their arias to suit themselves, yet leave untransposed what precedes and follows them.

Composers of songs often publish their work in three different ranges; the pieces remain in all three entirely the same.

When a familiar face is seen through a window, it is the same whether it looks out from the second or fourth story.

If one could raise or lower a landscape by one hundred meters, as far as the eye could see, it would neither lose nor gain in appearance.

We have created our entire tonal art out of the two seven-note scales, the major and the minor—one limitation requires the other.

We have attributed to each of them a particular character, have taught and learned to hear them as opposite; and they have gradually acquired a symbolic meaning—major and minor, *maggiore e minore,* satisfaction and dissatisfaction, joy and sadness, light and shade. Harmonic symbolism has fenced off musical expression from Bach to Wagner and on to the present day. Minor is used for the same purpose and has the same effect as it had two hundred years ago. Today one can no longer "compose" a funeral march, for it is already eternally at hand. Even the most uneducated amateur knows what is in store as soon as a funeral march—whichever one!—is about to begin. Even the amateur senses in advance the difference between a major and a minor symphony.

It is strange that one experiences major and minor as opposites. They both have the same face, at times lighter and at times more serious; and a small stroke of the pen is sufficient to transform one into the other. The transition from one to the other occurs imperceptibly and without difficulty—and if it occurs quickly enough, the two seem to flow unnoticeably in and out of one another. But if we acknowledge that major and minor form a whole with double meaning, and that the "twenty-four keys" represent merely an elevenfold transposition of the first pair, we recognize immediately the unity of our key system. The notions of related and foreign dissolve—and with them the whole evolved theory of scale degrees and scale relationships. We have a single key, but it is of a very meager sort.

"Unity of key."

—"Perhaps you mean that "key" represents the sunshine while "keys" represent its dispersal into colors?"

No, I do not mean that. For in the heaven of "eternal harmony" our entire key and key system in its totality is but a small fraction of that dispersed radiance of the sun we call "music."

However deeply humankind is tied to habit and inactivity, energy and opposition to the existing order are characteristics of all life. "Nature has her devices" and wins over those who are against progress and change. She moves continuously forward and changes ceaselessly, but in such an unbroken and imperceptible motion that humans can see only stasis. Only when they look back from a more distant perspective are they surprised to discover that they have been deceived.

Reformers thus irritate people of all epochs, because their changes are too unmediated and, above all, too perceptible. Reformers are—in comparison with nature—undiplomatic. And their changes thus become accepted only when the abrupt leaps are imperceptibly blended back into time's advance. Yet in some instances the reformer moves in step with time, while all others fall behind. And then one must forcefully whip these others to leap across the intervening gap. I believe that the major and minor key system with its transpositions, those of the "twelve-semitone system," now constitutes such a lagging behind.

One already finds in certain passages in Liszt and in advanced contemporary music clear examples of such things as different orderings (gradations) of the seven-tone scale. These give expression to a definite urge and desire, to a gifted instinct. But it seems to me that one has yet to form a conscious and systematic conception of such heightened means of expression.

I have made an attempt to find all the possibilities of arranging the seven-tone scale and have succeeded, by lowering and raising the intervals, in producing 113 different scales. These 113 scales (within the octave C–C) not only comprise the greater part of our familiar "twenty-four keys" but also a series of new keys of unusual character. And this does not exhaust the possibilities, as transposition of each of these 113 keys is also possible; and also the inter-mixture of two such keys (and why not still more?) in the harmony and melody.

The scale C–D♭–E♭–F♭–G♭–A♭–B♭–C sounds quite different from the D♭-minor scale if one takes C as its first scale degree. And if one adds a C-major triad as harmony beneath it, a new harmonic effect results. But if one hears the same scale supported by alternating A-minor, E♭-major, and C-major triads, one cannot resist the most pleasant surprise over this strange yet good sound.

And how would a lawgiver classify the scales C–D♭–E♭–F♭–G–A–B–C, C–D♭–E♭–F–G♭–A–B–C, C–D–E♭–F♭–G♭–A–B–C, C–D♭–E–F–G♭–A–B♭–C, or even C–D–E♭–F♭–G–A♯–B–C, C–D–E♭–F♭–G♯–A–B–C, C–D♭–E♭–F♯–G♯–A–B♭–C?

What riches of harmonic and melodic expression this will make available to our ears is not easily foreseen. But one knows without a doubt, and at a glance, that there are a very large number of new possibilities.

With this discussion the unity of all keys should be considered definitively articulated and grounded. A kaleidoscopic shaking up and mixing of all twelve semitones in the three-mirrored chamber of taste, invention and intention: that is the essence of today's harmony.

But only today's harmony, and not for much longer: for everything suggests there will be a revolution, a further step in the direction of "eternal harmony." Let us recall again that in the eternal harmony the division of the octave is infinite, and then try to approach a bit nearer to infinity. The third tone has already been knocking at our door for some time, yet we have failed to answer it. Whoever experiments, as I have done, however modestly, by inserting two equally distant intervals between a whole tone—whether with the voice or with a violin—and trains the ear and practices their technique, will realize that third tones are completely independent intervals of distinct character, not to be confused with out-of-tune half tones. This offers a more refined chromaticism, which for the moment appears to be based on the whole-tone scale. But if we introduce third tones without mediation, we will lose the half tone, the "minor third," and "perfect fifth"; and that loss would be felt to be greater than the relative gain of an "eighteen-tone third-tone system."

But there is no reason why one must give up half tones because of this new system. If we retain within every whole tone a half tone, then we acquire a second succession of whole tones a half step higher than the first. And if we divide this second succession of whole tones into third tones, then every third tone in the lower succession would have a corresponding third tone in the upper one.

A sixth-tone system is actually created thereby; and we may be assured that at some point there will actually be talk of sixth tones. But the tone system that I have sketched should first train the ear to hear third tones, without giving up half tones.

To sum up: Either we construct two successions of third tones a half tone apart, or three successions of the normal half-tone scale, a third tone apart.

Let us take C as the first tone, in order to distinguish it in some way, and C♯ and D♭ as the two next third tones, (small) c as the first half tone, and (small) c♯ and d♭ as the subsequent third divisions. The following table gives the overall result:

	C	C♯	D♭	D	D♯	E♭	E	E♯	F♭	F	F♯	G♭	G	G♯	A♭	A	A♯	B♭	etc.

The question of notation seems secondary to me. The question of how the tones are to be produced, on the other hand, is important and pressing. As a happy coincidence, while working on this essay I received an authentic item of news direct from America, which solves the problem in a simple manner. It reports of an invention by Dr. Thaddeus Cahill.[5] This man has constructed a

5. Ray Stannard Baker, "New Music for an Old World. Dr. Thaddeus Cahill's Dynamaphone, an Extraordinary Electrical Invention for Producing Scientifically Perfect Music." *McClure's Magazine*, vol. 28, no. 3 (July, 1906). [Au.]

sizable apparatus which enables one to transform an electrical current into a precisely determined, fixed number of vibrations. Since pitch depends upon the number of vibrations, and the apparatus can be "adjusted" to any desired number, the infinite division of the octave becomes simply the work of a lever, corresponding to the pointer of a quadrant.

Only long and careful experimentation and progressive education of the ear will render this unfamiliar material useful for the coming generation, and for art.

What wonderful hopes and fantastic ideas will become available! Who has not at some time "floated" in a dream, and believed firmly that the dream was real? Let us undertake to return music to its original essence. Let us free it from architectonic, acoustic, and aesthetic dogmas. Let us allow it to be pure invention and experience in harmonies, forms, and tone colors (since invention and experience are not exclusively the provenance of melody). Let us allow it to follow the curve of the rainbow and compete with the clouds in breaking up the rays of the sun. Music is nothing other than nature mirrored in and reflected back by the human soul. It is sounding air, reaching out beyond the air; and it resides just as universally and fully in humanity itself as in all creation. For it can gather into itself and flow outward without losing intensity.

177 Luigi Russolo

Luigi Russolo (1885–1947) was a prominent painter in the early years of the Italian Futurist movement, who gave up painting for music in 1913 when he issued this manifesto. His vision of a new kind of music responsive to modern technology, based on noise rather than pitched sound, far outstripped the recommendations of his Futurist forerunner and dedicatee Balilla Pratella (himself author of two previous manifestos on music), or of Ferruccio Busoni (see the previous entry). Though the noises used were to be produced by specially designed instruments, allowing them to be manipulated and controlled, Russolo argued that they would bring music closer to life itself, a view that placed him in direct opposition to the Romantic ideal of music as "a world apart." Though compositions written by Russolo for noise instruments appeared within a year of this essay, they had little impact on contemporary musical developments. His manifesto nevertheless offers a striking indication of the radical, virtually instantaneous redrawing of musical boundaries that followed the abandonment of traditional tonality in the early years of the century.

The Art of Noises
Futurist Manifesto
(1913)

MY DEAR BALILLA PRATELLA, GREAT FUTURIST COMPOSER:
   In the crowded Costanzi Theater, in Rome, while I was listening with my
futurist friends Marinetti, Boccioni, and Balla to the orchestral performance of
your overwhelming MUSICA FUTURISTA, there came to my mind the idea of a
new art: the Art of Noises, a logical consequence of your marvelous innovations.
   Life in ancient times was silent. In the nineteenth century, with the invention of machines, Noise was born. Today Noise is triumphant, and reigns
supreme over the senses of men. For many centuries life evolved in silence, or,
at the most, with but a muted sound. The loudest noises that interrupted this
silence were neither violent nor prolonged nor varied, since—if we overlook
such exceptional phenomena as hurricanes, tempests, avalanches, waterfalls—
nature is silent.
   Noises being so scarce, the first *musical sounds* which man succeeded in
drawing from a hollow reed or from a stretched string were a new, astonishing,
miraculous discovery. By primitive peoples musical sound was ascribed to the
gods, regarded as holy, and entrusted to the sole care of the priests, who made
use of it to enrich their rites with mystery. Thus was born the conception of
musical sound as a thing having an independent existence, a thing different
from life and unconnected with it. From this conception resulted an idea of
music as a world of fantasy superimposed upon reality, a world inviolate and
sacred. It will be readily understood how this idea of music must inevitably
have impeded its progress, as compared with that of the other arts. The Greeks
themselves—with their theory of music (systematized mathematically by
Pythagoras) which permitted the use of a few consonant intervals only—greatly
limited music's scope and excluded all possibility of harmony, of which they
knew nothing.
   The Middle Ages, with their modifications of the Greek tetrachord system,
with their Gregorian chants and their folk songs, enriched the art of music. Yet
they continued to regard music from the point of view of *linear development
in time*—a narrow view of the art which lasted several centuries and which
persists in the more complicated polyphony of the Flemish contrapuntists. The
chord did not exist: the flow of the individual parts was never subordinated to
the agreeable effect produced at any given moment by the ensemble of those
parts. In a word, the medieval conception of music was horizontal, not vertical.

TEXT: Nicholas Slonimsky, *Music Since 1900*, 4th ed. (New York: Charles Scribner's Sons, 1971),
pp. 1298–1302. Translation by Stephen Somervell. Reprinted with permission of Schirmer Books,
an imprint of Macmillan Publishing Company.

An interest in the simultaneous union of different sounds, that is, in the chord as a complex sound, developed gradually, passing from the perfect consonance, with a few passing dissonances, to the complicated and persistent dissonances which characterize the music of today.

The art of music at first sought and achieved purity and sweetness of sound; later, it blended diverse sounds, but always with intent to caress the ear with suave harmonics. Today, growing ever more complicated, it seeks those combinations of sounds that fall most dissonantly, strangely, and harshly upon the ear. We thus approach nearer and nearer to the *music of noise.*

This musical evolution parallels the growing multiplicity of machines, which everywhere are assisting mankind. Not only amid the clamor of great cities but even in the countryside, which until yesterday was ordinarily quiet, the machine today has created so many varieties and combinations of noise that pure musical sound—with its poverty and its monotony—no longer awakens any emotion in the hearer.

To excite and exalt our senses, music continued to develop toward the most complex polyphony and the greatest variety of orchestral timbres, or colors, devising the most complicated successions of dissonant chords and preparing in a general way for the creation of MUSICAL NOISE. This evolution toward noise was hitherto impossible. An eighteenth-century ear could not have endured the dissonant intensity of certain chords produced by our modern orchestras—triple the size of the orchestras of that day. But our own ears—trained as they are by the modern world, so rich in variegated noises—not only enjoy these dissonances but demand more and more violent acoustic emotions.

Moreover, musical sound is too limited in qualitative variety of timbre. The most complicated of orchestras reduce themselves to four or five classes of instruments differing in timbre: instruments played with the bow, plucked instruments, brass winds, wood winds, and percussion instruments. So that modern music, in its attempts to produce new kinds of timbre, struggles vainly within this little circle.

We must break out of this narrow circle of pure musical sounds, and conquer the infinite variety of noise-sounds.

Everyone will recognize that every musical sound carries with it an incrustation of familiar and stale sense associations, which predispose the hearer to boredom, despite all the efforts of innovating musicians. We futurists have all deeply loved the music of the great composers. Beethoven and Wagner for many years wrung our hearts. But now we are satiated with them and derive much greater pleasure from ideally combining the noises of street-cars, internal-combustion engines, automobiles, and busy crowds than from re-hearing, for example, the "Eroica" or the "Pastorale."

We cannot see the immense apparatus of the modern orchestra without being profoundly disappointed by its feeble acoustic achievements. Is there anything more absurd than to see twenty men breaking their necks to multiply the meowling of a violin? All this will naturally infuriate the musicomaniacs and perhaps disturb the somnolent atmosphere of our concert halls. Let us enter, as futurists, into one of these institutions for musical anemia. The first measure assails your ear with the boredom of the already-heard and causes you to anticipate the boredom of the measure to come. Thus we sip, from measure to measure, two or three different sorts of boredom, while we await an unusual emotion that never arrives. Meanwhile we are revolted by the monotony of the sensations experienced, combined with the idiotic religious excitement of the listeners, Buddhistically intoxicated by the thousandth repetition of their hypocritical and artificial ecstasy. Away! Let us be gone, since we shall not much longer succeed in restraining a desire to create a new musical realism by a generous distribution of sonorous blows and slaps, leaping nimbly over violins, pianofortes, contrabasses, and groaning organs. Away!

The objection cannot be raised that all noise is loud and disagreeable. I need scarcely enumerate all the small and delicate noises which are pleasing to the ear. To be convinced of their surprising variety one need only think of the rumbling of thunder, the howling of the wind, the roar of a waterfall, the gurgling of a brook, the rustling of leaves, the receding clatter of a horse's hoofs, the bumping of a wagon over cobblestones, and the deep, solemn breathing of a city at night, all the noises made by wild and domesticated animals, and all those that the human mouth can produce, apart from speaking or singing.

Let us wander through a great modern city with our ears more attentive than our eyes, and distinguish the sounds of water, air, or gas in metal pipes, the purring of motors (which breathe and pulsate with an indubitable animalism), the throbbing of valves, the pounding of pistons, the screeching of gears, the clatter of streetcars on their rails, the cracking of whips, the flapping of awnings and flags. We shall amuse ourselves by orchestrating in our minds the noise of the metal shutters of store windows, the slamming of doors, the bustle and shuffle of crowds, the multitudinous uproar of railroad stations, forges, mills, printing presses, power stations, and underground railways.

Nor should the new noises of modern warfare be forgotten. Recently the poet Marinetti, in a letter from the trenches of Adrianopolis, described to me in admirably unfettered language the orchestra of a great battle:

> *"every 5 seconds siege guns splitting the belly of space with a* TZANG-TUMB-TUU-UMB *chord revolt of 500 echos to tear it to shreds and scatter it to infinity In the center of these* TZANG-TUMB-TUUUMB *spied out breadth 50 square kilometers leap reports knife-thrusts rapid-fire batteries Violence ferocity regularity this deep bass ascending the strange agitated insane high-pitched notes of battle Fury panting breath eyes ears nostrils open! watching! straining! what joy to see hear smell everything everything taratatata of the machine guns frantically screaming amid bites blows traak-traak whipcracks pic-pac pum-tumb strange goings-on leaps height 200 meters of the infantry Down down at the bottom of the orchestra stirring up pools oxen buffaloes goads wagons pluff plaff rearing of horses flic flac tzing tzing shaak hilarious neighing iiiiiii stamping clanking 3 Bulgarian battalions on the march*

croooc-craaac (lento) *Shumi Maritza or Kárvavena* TZANG-TUMB-TUUUMB *toc-toctoctoc* (rapidissimo) *crooc-craac* (lento) *officers' yells resounding like sheets of brass bang here crack there* BOOM *ching chak* (presto) *chacha-cha-cha-chak up down back forth all around above look out for your head chak good shot! Flames flames flames flames flames collapse of the forts over behind the smoke Shukri Pasha talks to 27 forts over the telephone in Turkish in German Hallo! Ibrahim!! Rudolf! Hallo! Hallo, actors playlists echos prompters scenarios of smoke forests applause smell of hay mud dung my feet are frozen numb smell of saltpeter smell of putrefaction Timpani flutes clarinets everywhere low high birds chirping beatitudes shade cheep-cheep-cheep breezes verdure herds dong-dang-dong-ding-baaaa the lunatics are assaulting the musicians of the orchestra the latter soundly thrashed play on Great uproar don't cancel the concert more precision dividing into smaller more minute sounds fragments of echos in the theater area 300 square kilometers Rivers Maritza Tundja stretch out Rudopi Mountains standing up erect boxes balconies 2000 shrapnel spraying exploding snow-white handkerchiefs full of gold srrrrrrr-TUMB-TUMB 2000 hand-grenades hurled shearing off black-haired heads with their splinters TZANG-srrrrrr-TUMB-TZANG-TUMB-TUUUMB the orchestra of the noises of war swells beneath a long-held note of silence in high heaven gilded spherical balloon which surveys the shooting , , ."*

We must fix the pitch and regulate the harmonies and rhythms of these extraordinarily varied sounds. To fix the pitch of noises does not mean to take away from them all the irregularity of tempo and intensity that characterizes their vibrations, but rather to give definite gradation or pitch to the stronger and more predominant of these vibrations. Indeed, noise is differentiated from musical sound merely in that the vibrations that produce it are confused and irregular, both in tempo and in intensity. Every noise has a note—sometimes even a chord—that predominates in the ensemble of its irregular vibrations. Because of this characteristic note it becomes possible to fix the pitch of a given noise, that is, to give it not a single pitch but a variety of pitches, without losing its characteristic quality—its distinguishing timbre. Thus certain noises produced by rotary motion may offer a complete ascending or descending chromatic scale by merely increasing or decreasing the speed of the motion.

Every manifestation of life is accompanied by noise. Noise is therefore familiar to our ears and has the power to remind us immediately of life itself. Musical sound, a thing extraneous to life and independent of it, an occasional and unnecessary adjunct, has become for our ears what a too familiar face is to our eyes. Noise, on the other hand, which comes to us confused and irregular as life itself, never reveals itself wholly but reserves for us innumerable surprises. We are convinced, therefore, that by selecting, co-ordinating, and controlling noises we shall enrich mankind with a new and unsuspected source of pleasure. Despite the fact that it is characteristic of sound to remind us brutally of life, the Art of Noises must not limit itself to reproductive imitation. It will reach its greatest emotional power through the purely acoustic enjoyment which the inspiration of the artist will contrive to evoke from combinations of noises.

These are the futurist orchestra's six families of noises, which we shall soon produce mechanically:

1	2	3	4	5	6
Booms	Whistles	Whispers	Screams	Noises	Voices of
Thunder-	Hisses	Murmurs	Screeches	obtained	animals
claps	Snorts	Mutter-	Rustlings	by per-	and
Explo-		ings	Buzzes	cussion	men:
sions		Bustling	Cracklings	on	Shouts
Crashes		noises	Sounds ob-	metals,	Shrieks
Splashes		Gurgles	tained by	wood,	Groans
Roars			friction	stone,	Howls
				terra-	Laughs
				cotta,	Wheezes
				etc.	Sobs

In this list we have included the most characteristic fundamental noises; the others are but combinations of these.

The rhythmic movements within a single noise are of infinite variety. There is always, as in a musical note, a predominant rhythm, but around this may be perceived numerous secondary rhythms.

CONCLUSIONS

1.—Futurist musicians must constantly broaden and enrich the field of sound. This is a need of our senses. Indeed, we note in present-day composers of genius a tendency toward the most complex dissonances. Moving further and further away from pure musical sound, they have almost reached the *noise-sound*. This need and this tendency can only be satisfied *by the supplementary use of noise and its substitution for musical sounds.*

2.—Futurist musicians must substitute for the limited variety of timbres of the orchestral instruments of the day the infinite variety of the timbres of noises, reproduced by suitable mechanisms.

3.—The musician's sensibility, liberating itself from facile, traditional rhythm, must find in noises the way to amplify and renew itself, since each noise offers a union of the most diverse rhythms, in addition to the predominant rhythm.

4.—Since every noise has in its irregular vibrations a general, predominating tone, it will be easy to obtain, in constructing the instruments which imitate it, a sufficiently wide variety of tones, semitones, and quarter-tones. This variety of tones will not deprive any single noise of its characteristic timbre but will merely increase its tessitura, or extension.

5.—The practical difficulties in the construction of these instruments are not serious. Once the mechanical principle producing a given noise is found, one may vary its pitch by applying the general laws of acoustics. For example, in instruments employing rotary motion the speed of rotation will be increased or diminished; in others, the size or tension of the sounding parts will be varied.

6.—Not by means of a succession of noises imitating those of real life, but through a fanciful blending of these varied timbres and rhythms, will the new orchestra obtain the most complex and novel sound effects. Hence every instrument must be capable of varying its pitch and must have a fairly extensive range.

7.—There is an infinite variety of noises. If, today, with perhaps a thousand different kinds of machines, we can distinguish a thousand different noises, tomorrow, as the number of new machines is multiplied, we shall be able to distinguish ten, twenty, or thirty thousand different noises, not merely to be imitated but to be combined as our fancy dictates.

8.—Let us therefore invite young musicians of genius and audacity to listen attentively to all noises, so that they may understand the varied rhythms of which they are composed, their principal tone, and their secondary tones. Then, comparing the varied timbres of noises with those of musical tones, they will be convinced how much more numerous are the former than the latter. Out of this will come not merely an understanding of noises, but even a taste and an enthusiasm for them. Our increased perceptivity, which has already acquired futurist eyes, will then have futurist ears. Thus the motors and machines of our industrial cities may some day be intelligently pitched, so as to make of every factory an intoxicating orchestra of noises.

I submit these statements, my dear Pratella, to your futuristic genius, and invite you to discuss them with me. I am not a professional musician; I have therefore no acoustic prejudices and no works to defend. I am a futurist painter projecting into an art he loves and has studied his desire to renovate all things. Being therefore more audacious than a professional musician could be, caring nought for my seeming incompetence, and convinced that audacity makes all things lawful and all things possible, I have imagined a great renovation of music through the Art of Noises.

Milan, March 11, 1913

178 Charles Ives

Though Charles Ives (1874–1954) was the earliest American composer to acquire widespread international recognition, his fame did not come until after his death. During the first half of the century Ives was almost totally unknown, earning his living outside music as a very successful insurance executive. Yet this professional independence undoubtedly helped foster Ives's remarkable musical daring, allowing him to fuse a style out of apparent contradictions: complexity and simplicity, innovation and conservatism, radical experimentation along with quotation of popular tunes and hymns. This essay was originally conceived as a long footnote to the second movement of Ives's Fourth Symphony, written for its first publication in 1929. The movement features multi-orchestral textures made up of dense strands of contrasting materials combining different keys and tempos in an extraordinarily rich tapestry. Addressing problems raised by the work, Ives discusses spatial separation as an aid for the ear in sorting out simultaneous musical layers. He also considers the effect of distance on sound and the importance of active listening for the comprehension of new music. Above all, Ives advocates exploring possibilities rather than setting down fixed principles: the future of music, in his view, lies "in the way it encourages and extends, rather than limits."

Music and Its Future
(1929)

To give the various instrumental parts of the orchestra in their intended relations is, at times, as conductors and players know, more difficult than it may seem to the casual listener. After a certain point it is a matter which seems to pass beyond the control of any conductor or player into the field of acoustics. In this connection, a distribution of instruments or group of instruments or an arrangement of them at varying distances from the audience is a matter of some interest; as is also the consideration as to the extent it may be advisable and practicable to devise plans in any combination of over two players so that the distance sounds shall travel from the sounding body to the listener's ear may be a favorable element in interpretation. It is difficult to reproduce the sounds and feeling that distance gives to sound wholly by reducing or increasing the number of instruments or by varying their intensities. A brass band playing *pianissimo* across the street is a different-sounding thing from the same band, playing the same piece *forte,* a block or so away. Experiments, even on a limited scale, as when a conductor separates a chorus from the orchestra or places a choir off the stage or in a remote part of the hall, seem to indicate that there are possibilities in this matter that may benefit the presentation of music, not only from the standpoint of clarifying the harmonic, rhythmic, thematic material, etc., but of bringing the inner content to a deeper realization (assuming, for argument's sake, that there is an inner content). Thoreau found a deeper import even in the symphonies of the Concord church bell when its sounds were rarefied through the distant air. "A melody, as it were, imported into the wilderness. . . . at a distance over the woods the sound acquires a cer-

TEXT: *American Composers on American Music,* ed. by Henry Cowell (Palo Alto: Stanford University Press, 1933), pp. 191–98. Copyright renewed 1961 by Henry Cowell. Reprinted with permission of the publishers.

tain vibratory hum as if the pine needles in the horizon were the strings of a harp which it swept. . . . a vibration of the universal lyre, just as the intervening atmosphere makes a distant ridge of earth interesting to the eye by the azure tint it imparts."

A horn over a lake gives a quality of sound and feeling that it is hard to produce in any other way. It has been asked if the radio might not help in this matter. But it functions in a different way. It has little of the ethereal quality. It is but a photographing process which seems only to hand over the fore-ground or parts of it in a clump.

The writer remembers hearing, when a boy, the music of a band in which the players were arranged in two or three groups around the town square. The main group in the bandstand at the center usually played the main themes, while the others, from the neighboring roofs and verandas, played the varia-tions, refrains, and so forth. The piece remembered was a kind of paraphrase of "Jerusalem the Golden," a rather elaborate tone-poem for those days. The bandmaster told of a man who, living nearer the variations, insisted that they were the real music and it was more beautiful to hear the hymn come sifting through them than the other way around. Others, walking around the square, were surprised at the different and interesting effects they got as they changed position. It was said also that many thought the music lost in effect when the piece was played by the band all together, though, I think, the town vote was about even. The writer remembers, as a deep impression, the echo parts from the roofs played by a chorus of violins and voices.

Somewhat similar effects may be obtained indoors by partially inclosing the sounding body. For instance, in a piece of music which is based, on its rhythmic side, principally on a primary and wider rhythmic phrase and a secondary one of shorter span, played mostly simultaneously—the first by a grand piano in a larger room which opens into a smaller one in which there is an upright piano playing the secondary part—if the listener stands in the larger room about equidistant from both pianos but not in a direct line between them (the door between the rooms being partially closed), the contrasting rhythms will be more readily felt by the listener than if the pianos are in the same room. The foregoing suggests something in the way of listening that may have a bearing on the interpretation of certain kinds of music.

In the illustration described above, the listener may choose which of these two rhythms he wishes to hold in his mind as primal. If it is the shorter-spaced one and it is played after the longer has had prominence, and the listener stands in the room with the piano playing this, the music may react in a differ-ent way, not enough to change its character, but enough to show possibilities in this way of listening. As the eye, in looking at a view, may focus on the sky, clouds, or distant outlines, yet sense the color and form of the foreground, and then, by observing the foreground, may sense the distant outlines and color, so, in some similar way, the listener can choose to arrange in his mind the relation of the rhythmic, harmonic, and other material. In other words, in music the ear may play a rôle similar to the eye in the foregoing instance.

Some method similar to that of the inclosed parts of a pipe organ played by the choir or swell manuals might be adopted in some way for an orchestra. That similar plans, as suggested, have been tried by conductors and musicians is quite certain, but the writer knows only of the ways mentioned in the instances above.

When one tries to use an analogy between the arts as an illustration, especially of some technical matter, he is liable to get it wrong. But the general aim of the plans under discussion is to bring various parts of the music to the ear in their relation to each other, as the perspective of a picture brings each object to the eye. The distant hills, in a landscape, range upon range, merge at length into the horizon; and there may be something corresponding to this in the presentation of music. Music seems too often all foreground, even if played by a master of dynamics.

Among the physical difficulties to be encountered are those of retarded sounds that may affect the rhythmic plan unfavorably and of sounds that are canceled as far as some of the players are concerned, though the audience in general may better hear the various groups in their intended relationships. Another difficulty, probably less serious, is suggested by the occasional impression, in hearing sounds from a distance, that the pitch is changed to some extent. That pitch is not changed by the distance a sound travels unless the sounding body is moving at a high velocity is an axiom of acoustics; that is, the number of the vibrations of the fundamental is constant; but the effect does not always sound so—at least to the writer—perhaps because, as the overtones become less acute, the pitch seems to sag a little. There are also difficulties transcending those of acoustics. The cost of trial rehearsals, of duplicate players, and of locations or halls suitably arranged and acoustically favorable is very high nowadays.

The matter of placement is only one of the many things which, if properly examined, might strengthen the means and functions of interpretation, and so forth. The means to examine seem more lacking than the will to examine. Money may travel faster than sound in some directions, but not in the direction of musical experimentation or extension. If only one one-hundredth part of the funds that are expended in this country for the elaborate production of opera, spectacular or otherwise, or of the money invested in soft-headed movies with their music resultants, or in the manufacture of artless substitutes for the soul of man, putting many a true artist in straitened circumstances—if only a small part of these funds could be directed to more of the unsensational but important fields of musical activity, music in general would be the gainer.

Most of the research and other work of extending and distributing new premises, either by the presentation of new works or by other means, has been done by societies and individuals against trying obstacles. Organizations like the Pro-Musica Society, with its chapters throughout this and foreign countries, the League of Composers, the Friends of Music (in its work of uncovering neglected premises of the past), and similar societies in the cities of this and other countries, are working with little or no aid from the larger institutions and foundations which could well afford to help them in their cause. The same may be said of individual workers—writers, lecturers, and artists who take upon themselves unremunerative subjects and unremunerative programs for the cause, or, at least, for one of the causes they believe in; the pianist and teacher who, failing to interest any of the larger piano companies in building a quarter-tone piano for the sake of further study in that field, after a hard day's work in the conservatory, takes off his coat and builds the piano with his own hands; the self-effacing singing teacher who, by her genius, character, and unconscious influence, puts a new note of radiance into the life of a shop-girl; the open-minded editor of musical literature and the courageous and unselfish editor of new music quarterlies who choose their subject-matter with the commercial eye closed.

Individual creative work is probably more harmed than helped by artificial stimulants, such as contests, prizes, commissions, and subsidies; but some material aid in better organizing the medium through which the work is done and through which it is interpreted will be of some benefit to music as a whole.

In closing, and to go still farther afield, it may be suggested that in any music based to some extent on more than one or two rhythmic, melodic, harmonic schemes, the hearer has a rather active part to play. Conductors, players, and composers (as a rule or at least some) do the best they can and for that reason get more out of music and, incidentally, more out of life, though, perhaps, not more in their pockets. Many hearers do the same. But there is a type of auditor who will not meet the performers halfway by projecting himself, as it were, into the premises as best he can, and who will furnish nothing more than a ticket and a receptive inertia which may be induced by predilections or static ear habits, a condition perhaps accounting for the fact that some who consider themselves unmusical will get the "gist of" and sometimes get "all set up" by many modern pieces, which those who call themselves musical (this is not saying they're not)—probably because of long acquaintance solely with certain consonances, single tonalities, monorhythms, formal progressions, and struc-ture—do not like. Some hearers of the latter type seem to require pretty con-stantly something, desirable at times, which may be called a kind of ear-easing, and under a limited prescription; if they get it, they put the music down as beautiful; if they don't get it, they put it down and out—to them it is bad, ugly, or "awful from beginning to end." It may or may not be all of this; but whatever its shortcomings, they are not those given by the man who does not listen to what he hears.

"Nature cannot be so easily disposed of," says Emerson. "All of the virtues are not final"—neither are the vices.

The hope of all music—of the future, of the past, to say nothing of the present—will not lie with the partialist who raves about an ultra-modern opera (if there is such a thing) but despises Schubert, or with the party man who viciously maintains the opposite assumption. Nor will it lie in any cult or any idiom or in any artist or any composer. "All things in their variety are of one essence and are limited only by themselves."

The future of music may not lie entirely with music itself, but rather in the way it encourages and extends, rather than limits, the aspirations and ideals of the people, in the way it makes itself a part with the finer things that humanity does and dreams of. Or to put it the other way around, what music is and is to be may lie somewhere in the belief of an unknown philosopher of half a century ago who said: "How can there be any bad music? All music is from heaven. If there is anything bad in it, I put it there—by my implications and limitations. Nature builds the mountains and meadows and man puts in the fences and labels." He may have been nearer right than we think.

179 Edgard Varèse

The French-born composer Edgard Varèse (1883–1965) lived primarily in the United States after 1915, eventually acquiring American citizenship. Epitomizing a new type of twentieth-century composer, Varèse was deeply influenced by his scientific background and committed to exploiting new technology for compositional purposes. The following excerpts were taken from three lectures—the first two dating from the late 1930s, the third from 1959—that were assembled for publication by Varèse's former student Chou Wen-chung. They reflect his belief in the need for artists and scientists to collaborate in expanding the realm of musical sound, his recognition of the close links between creativity and experimentation, his fascination with sound-producing machines, and his new conception of musical form as the interaction of "attractive and repulsive forces."

The Liberation of Sound

I dream of instruments obedient to my thought and which with their contribution of a whole new world of unsuspected sounds, will lend themselves to the exigencies of my inner rhythm.[1]

TEXT: *Contemporary Composers on Contemporary Music,* ed. by Elliott Schwartz and Barney Childs (New York: Holt, Rinehart and Winston, 1967), pp. 196–204. The Varèse entry was compiled and edited by Chou Wen-chung; the first part is from a lecture given at Mary Austin House, Santa Fe, in 1936, the second from a lecture given at the University of Southern California in 1939, and the third from a lecture given at Princeton University in 1959.

1. From *391* (periodical), no. 5 (June, 1917); trans. from the French by Louise Varèse.

NEW INSTRUMENTS AND NEW MUSIC
(1936)

At a time when the very newness of the mechanism of life is forcing our activities and our forms of human association to break with the traditions and the methods of the past in the effort to adapt themselves to circumstances, the urgent choices which we have to make are concerned not with the past but with the future. We cannot, even if we would, live much longer by tradition. The world is changing, and we change with it. The more we allow our minds the romantic luxury of treasuring the past in memory, the less able we become to face the future and to determine the new values which can be created in it.

Art's function is not to prove a formula or an esthetic dogma. Our academic rules were taken out of the living works of former masters. As Debussy has said, *works of art make rules but rules do not make works of art*. Art exists only as a medium of expression.

The emotional impulse that moves a composer to write his scores contains the same element of poetry that incites the scientist to his discoveries. There is solidarity between scientific development and the progress of music. Throwing new light on nature, science permits music to progress—or rather to grow and change with changing times—by revealing to our senses harmonies and sensations before unfelt. On the threshold of beauty science and art collaborate. John Redfield voices the opinion of many when he says: "There should be at least one laboratory in the world where the fundamental facts of music could be investigated under conditions reasonably conducive to success. The interest in music is so widespread and intense, its appeal so intimate and poignant, and its significance for mankind so potent and profound, that it becomes unwise not to devote some portion of the enormous outlay for music to research in its fundamental questions."[2]

When new instruments will allow me to write music as I conceive it, the movement of sound-masses, of shifting planes, will be clearly perceived in my work, taking the place of the linear counterpoint. When these sound-masses collide, the phenomena of penetration or repulsion will seem to occur. Certain transmutations taking place on certain planes will seem to be projected onto other planes, moving at different speeds and at different angles. There will no longer be the old conception of melody or interplay of melodies. The entire work will be a melodic totality. The entire work will flow as a river flows.

We have actually three dimensions in music: horizontal, vertical, and dynamic swelling or decreasing. I shall add a fourth, sound projection—that feeling that sound is leaving us with no hope of being reflected back, a feeling akin to that aroused by beams of light sent forth by a powerful searchlight—for the ear as for the eye, that sense of projection, of a journey into space.

Today with the technical means that exist and are easily adaptable, the differentiation of the various masses and different planes as well as these beams of

2. John Redfield, *Music, a Science and an Art* (New York, 1928). [Chou]

sound, could be made discernible to the listener by means of certain acoustical arrangements. Moreover, such an acoustical arrangement would permit the delimitation of what I call "zones of intensities." These zones would be differentiated by various timbres or colors and different loudnesses. Through such a physical process these zones would appear of different colors and of different magnitude, in different perspectives for our perception. The role of color or timbre would be completely changed from being incidental, anecdotal, sensual or picturesque; it would become an agent of delineation, like the different colors on a map separating different areas, and an integral part of form. These zones would be felt as isolated, and the hitherto unobtainable non-blending (or at least the sensation of non-blending) would become possible.

In the moving masses you would be conscious of their transmutations when they pass over different layers, when they penetrate certain opacities, or are dilated in certain rarefactions. Moreover, the new musical apparatus I envisage, able to emit sounds of any number of frequencies, will extend the limits of the lowest and highest registers, hence new organizations of the vertical resultants: chords, their arrangements, their spacings—that is, their oxygenation. Not only will the harmonic possibilities of the overtones be revealed in all their splendor, but the use of certain interferences created by the partials will represent an appreciable contribution. The never-before-thought-of use of the inferior resultants and of the differential and additional sounds may also be expected. An entirely new magic of sound!

I am sure that the time will come when the composer, after he has graphically realized his score, will see this score automatically put on a machine that will faithfully transmit the musical content to the listener. As frequencies and new rhythms will have to be indicated on the score, our actual notation will be inadequate. The new notation will probably be seismographic. And here it is curious to note that at the beginning of two eras, the Mediaeval primitive and our own primitive era (for we are at a new primitive stage in music today), we are faced with an identical problem: the problem of finding graphic symbols for the transposition of the composer's thought into sound. At a distance of more than a thousand years we have this analogy: our still primitive electrical instruments find it necessary to abandon staff notation and to use a kind of seismographic writing much like the early ideographic writing originally used for the voice before the development of staff notation. Formerly the curves of the musical line indicated the melodic fluctuations of the voice; today the machine-instrument requires precise design indications.

MUSIC AS AN ART-SCIENCE
(1939)

The philosophers of the Middle Ages separated the liberal arts into two branches: the *trivium,* or the Arts of Reason as applied to language—grammar, rhetoric and dialectic—and the *quadrivium,* or the Arts of Pure Reason, which today we would call the Sciences, and among which music has its place in the company of mathematics, geometry and astronomy.

Today, music is more apt to be rated with the arts of the *trivium*. At least, it seems to me that too much emphasis is placed on what might be called the grammar of music.

At different times and in different places music has been considered either as an Art or as a Science. In reality music partakes of both. Hoëne Wronsky and Camille Durutte,[3] in their treatise on harmony in the middle of the last century, were obliged to coin new words when they assigned music its place as an "Art-Science," and defined it as "the corporealization of the intelligence that is in sounds." Most people rather think of music solely as an art. But when you listen to music do you ever stop to realize that you are being subjected to a physical phenomenon? Not until the air between the listener's ear and the instrument has been disturbed does music occur. Do you realize that every time a printed score is brought to life it has to be re-created through the different sound machines, called musical instruments, that make up our orchestras [and] are subject to the same laws of physics as any other machine? In order to anticipate the result, a composer must understand the mechanics of the instruments and must know just as much as possible about acoustics. Music must live in sound. On the other hand, the possession of a perfectly pitched ear is only of a relative importance to a composer. What a composer must have, must have been born with, is what I call the "inner ear," the ear of imagination. The inner ear is the composer's Pole Star! Let us look at music as it is more popularly considered—as an Art—and inquire: what is composition?

Brahms has said that composition is the *organizing of disparate elements.* But what is the situation of the would-be creator today, shaken by the powerful impulses and rhythms of this age? How is he to accomplish this "organizing" in order to express himself and his epoch? Where is he to find those "disparate elements"? Are they to be found in the books he studies in his various courses in harmony, composition, and orchestration? Are they in the great works of the great masters that he pores over with love and admiration and, with all his might, means to emulate? Unfortunately too many composers have been led to believe that these elements can be found as easily as that.[4]

Eric Temple Bell, in a book called *The Search for Truth*, says: "Reverence for the past no doubt is a virtue that has had its uses, but if we are to go forward the reverent approach to old difficulties is the wrong one!" I should say that in music the "reverent approach" has done a great deal of harm: it has kept would-

---

3. Hoëne Wronsky (1778–1853), also known as Joseph Marie Wronsky, was a Polish philosopher and mathematician, known for his system of *Messianism*. Camille Durutte (1803–1881), in his *Technie Harmonique* (1876), a treatise on "musical mathematics," quoted extensively from the writings of Wronsky. [Chou]

4. This, Varèse said in the same lecture, "undoubtedly accounts for one of the most deplorable trends of music today—the impotent return to the formulas of the past that has been called neo-Classicism." [Chou]

be appreciators from really appreciating! And it has created the music critic! The very basis of creative work is irreverence! The very basis of creative work is experimentation—bold experimentation. You have only to turn to the revered past for the corroboration of my contention. The links in the chain of tradition are formed by men who have all been revolutionists! To the student of music I should say that the great examples of the past should serve as spring-boards from which he may leap free, into his own future.

In every domain of art, a work that corresponds to the need of its day carries a message of social and cultural value. Preceding ages show us that changes in art occur because societies and artists have new needs. New aspirations ema-nate from every epoch. The artist, being always of his own time, is influenced by it and, in turn, is an influence. It is the artist who crystallizes his age—who fixes his age in history. Contrary to general notion, the artist is never ahead of his own time, but is simply the only one who is not way behind.

Now let me come back to the subject of music as an Art-Science. The raw material of music is sound. That is what the "reverent approach" has made most people forget—even composers. Today, when science is equipped to help the composer realize what was never before possible—all that Beethoven dreamed, all that Berlioz gropingly imagined possible—the composer contin-ues to be obsessed by the traditions that are nothing but the limitations of his predecessors. Composers, like everyone else today, are delighted to use the many gadgets continually put on the market for our daily comfort. But when they hear sounds that no violins, no woodwind or percussion instruments of the orchestra can produce, it does not occur to them to demand those sounds of science. Yet science is even now equipped to give them everything they may require.

Personally, for my conceptions, I need an entirely new medium of expres-sion: a sound-*producing* machine (not a sound-*reproducing* one). Today it is possible to build such a machine with only a certain amount of added research.

If you are curious to know what such a machine could do that the orchestra with its man-powered instruments cannot do, I shall try briefly to tell you: whatever I write, whatever my message, it will reach the listener unadulterated by "interpretation." It will work something like this: after a composer has set down his score on paper by means of a new graphic notation, he will then, with the collaboration of a sound engineer, transfer the score directly to this electric machine. After that, anyone will be able to press a button to release the music exactly as the composer wrote it—exactly like opening a book.

And here are the advantages I anticipate from such a machine: liberation from the arbitrary, paralyzing tempered system; the possibility of obtaining any number of cycles or, if still desired, subdivisions of the octave, and conse-quently the formation of any desired scale; unsuspected range in low and high registers; new harmonic splendors obtainable from the use of sub-harmonic combinations now impossible; the possibility of obtaining any differentiation of timbre, of sound-combinations; new dynamics far beyond the present human-powered orchestra; a sense of sound-projection in space by means of the emission of sound in any part or in many parts of the hall, as may be required by the score; cross-rhythms unrelated to each other, treated simultaneously, or, to use the old word, "contrapuntally," since the machine would be able to beat any number of desired notes, any subdivision of them, omission or fraction of them—all these in a given unit of measure or time that is humanly impossible to attain.

In conclusion, let me read to you something that Romain Rolland said in his *Jean Christophe* and which remains pertinent today. Jean Christophe, the hero of his novel, was a prototype of the modern composer and was modeled on different composers whom Romain Rolland knew—among others, myself.

> The difficulty began when he tried to cast his ideas in the ordinary musical forms: he made the discovery that none of the ancient molds were suited to them; if he wished to fix his visions with fidelity he had to begin by forgetting all the music he had heard, all that he had written, to make a clean slate of all the formalism he had learned, of traditional technique, to throw away those crutches of impotency, that bed, all prepared for the laziness of those who, fleeing the fatigue of thinking for themselves, lie down in other men's thoughts.[5]

RHYTHM, FORM AND CONTENT
(1959)

Because for so many years I crusaded for new instruments[6] with what may have seemed fanatical zeal, I have been accused of desiring nothing less than the destruction of all musical instruments and even of all performers. This is, to say the least, an exaggeration. Our new liberating medium—the electronic—is not meant to replace the old musical instruments, which composers, including myself, will continue to use. Electronics is an additive, not a destructive, factor in the art and science of music. It is because new instruments have been constantly added to the old ones that Western music has such a rich and varied patrimony.

Grateful as we must be for the new medium, we should not expect miracles from machines. The machine can give out only what we put into it. The musical principles remain the same whether a composer writes for orchestra or tape. Rhythm and form are still his most important problems and the two elements in music most generally misunderstood.

Rhythm is too often confused with metrics. Cadence or the regular succes-

---

5. Romain Rolland (1866–1944), *Jean Christophe* (1904–12); published in English as *John Christopher* (G. Cannan, 1910–13). [Chou]
6. As early as 1916, Varèse was quoted in the New York *Morning Telegraph* as saying: "Our musical alphabet must be enriched. We also need new instruments very badly. . . . In my own works I have always felt the need of new mediums of expression . . . which can lend themselves to every expression of thought and can keep up with thought." And in the *Christian Science Monitor*, in 1922: "The composer and the electrician will have to labor together to get it." [Chou]

sion of beats and accents has little to do with the rhythm of a composition. Rhythm is the element in music that gives life to the work and holds it together. It is the element of stability, the generator of form. In my own works, for instance, rhythm derives from the simultaneous interplay of unrelated elements that intervene at calculated, but not regular, time-lapses. This corresponds more nearly to the definition of rhythm in physics and philosophy as "a succession of alternate and opposite or correlative states."

As for form, Busoni once wrote: "Is it not singular to demand of a composer originality in all things and to forbid it as regards form? No wonder that once he becomes original, he is accused of formlessness."[7]

The misunderstanding has come from thinking of form as a point of departure, a pattern to be followed, a mold to be filled. Form is a result—the result of a process. Each of my works discovers its own form. I could never have fitted them into any of the historical containers. If you want to fill a rigid box of a definite shape, you must have something to put into it that is the same shape and size or that is elastic or soft enough to be made to fit in. But if you try to force into it something of a different shape and harder substance, even if its volume and size are the same, it will break the box. My music cannot be made to fit into any of the traditional music boxes.

Conceiving musical form as a *resultant*—the result of a process—I was struck by what seemed to me an analogy between the formation of my compositions and the phenomenon of crystallization. Let me quote the crystallographic description given me by Nathaniel Arbiter, professor of minerology at Columbia University:

> The crystal is characterized by both a definite external form and a definite internal structure. The internal structure is based on the unit of crystal which is the smallest grouping of the atoms that has the order and composition of the substance. The extension of the unit into space forms the whole crystal. But in spite of the relatively limited variety of internal structures, the external forms of crystals are limitless.

Then Mr. Arbiter added in his own words:

> Crystal form itself is a *resultant* [the very word I have always used in reference to musical form] rather than a primary attribute. Crystal form is the consequence of the interaction of attractive and repulsive forces and the ordered packing of the atom.

This, I believe, suggests, better than any explanation I could give, the way my works are formed. There is an idea, the basis of an internal structure, expanded and split into different shapes or groups of sound constantly changing in shape, direction, and speed, attracted and repulsed by various forces. The form of the work is the consequence of this interaction. Possible musical forms are as limitless as the exterior forms of crystals.

Connected with this contentious subject of form in music is the really futile

---

7. Ferruccio Busoni, *Sketch of a New Esthetic of Music,* trans. by Dr. Theodore Baker (New York, 1911), reprinted in *Three Classics in the Aesthetics of Music* (New York, Dover Publications, 1962), p. 79. [Chou] See also this collection, pp. 1322–23.

question of the difference between form and content. There is no difference. Form and content are one. Take away form, and there is no content, and if there is no content, there is only a rearrangement of musical patterns, but no form. Some people go so far as to suppose that the content of what is called program music is the subject described. This subject is only the ostensible motive I have spoken of, which in program music the composer chooses to reveal. The content is still only music. The same senseless bickering goes on over style and content in poetry. We could very well transfer to the question of music what Samuel Beckett has said of Proust: "For Proust the quality of language is more important than any system of ethics or esthetics. Indeed he makes no attempt to dissociate form from content. The one is the concretion of the other—the revelation of a world."[8] To reveal a new world is the function of creation in all the arts, but the act of creation defies analysis. A composer knows about as little as anyone else about where the substance of his work comes from.

As an epigraph to his book,[9] Busoni uses this verse from a poem by the Danish poet Oelenschläger:

> What seek you? Say! And what do you expect?
> I know not what; the Unknown I would have!
> What's known to me is endless; I would go
> Beyond the known: The last word still is wanting.
>
> (*Der mächtige Zauberer*)

And so it is for any artist.

8. Samuel Beckett, *Proust* (1957).
9. Busoni, *Sketch*, p. 75.

180 Pierre Boulez

As both composer and conductor, Pierre Boulez (b. 1926) has occupied an important position in music of the second half of the twentieth century. In this essay, published in 1957 but based on material dating to the early 1950s, Boulez echoes ideas voiced by Edgard Varèse in the previous essay, but they are now delivered within the context of a rapidly emerging new technology that seems to make the possibilities for future sonic development virtually unlimited. Boulez interprets earlier twentieth-century music in essentially negative terms, as destroying an old language and thus providing the necessary groundwork for the creation of a new and less restricted one. The music of his own day, on the other hand, he sees as poised on "the brink of an undreamt-of sound world," which he feels can be fully realized only through serial control and electro-acoustical extensions. These ideas would assume more concrete form in 1976 when Boulez founded the Institute for Research and Electro-acoustical Coordination (IRCAM) in Paris, dedicated to bringing together scientists and musicians in joint creative enterprises.

Tendencies in Recent Music
(1957)

When one considers what has happened to the language of music, it is obvious that we are at present in a period of stocktaking and reorganization, which has been preceded by a period of destructive experiment in which tonality and regular metre have been abolished. There has also come about a curious phenomenon of dissociation in the evolution of music.

On the one hand, Stravinsky developed rhythm on entirely new structural principles, based on the dissymmetry, independence, and development of rhythmic cells, but remaining trapped, linguistically, in what one could call an impasse (since we know it ended up as one) but which I prefer to call a survival, and even a reinforced survival where the processes of aggregation round very elementary poles give the vocabulary unaccustomed force.

On the other hand, in Vienna at the same time a new language was being formulated, patiently and by stages; first, the dissolution of tonal attraction—the opposite step to the one taken by Stravinsky—then functional ultra-thematicization, which was to lead to the discovery of serialism, a method used in quite different ways by Schoenberg, Berg, and Webern. The only one, in truth, who was conscious of a new dimension in sound, of the abolition of the horizontal–vertical opposition in favour of a view of the series as simply a way of giving structure, or *texture,* to musical space, was Webern, who arrived at this position, when all is said and done, by specious means which in some transitional works I find disturbing; by trying, on the basis of regular canonic forms, to use the series as a contrapuntal device with harmonic controls. Later on, he adopted a functional distribution of intervals which, in my opinion, marks a crucial moment in the history of the language. On the other hand, the rhythmic element has no connection at all with the serial technique.

It should perhaps be pointed out that this phenomenon of dissociation applied to both aspects of the language. For his rhythmic discoveries, Stravinsky needed a simpler and more malleable material with which to experiment. In the same way, Webern could only concentrate on a proper morphology by, to a considerable extent, ignoring rhythmic structure.

Admittedly this is a little too schematic to be completely accurate. Which is why, to test it, I should like to follow a less well-worn path and start by playing truant with the music of Varèse, that lone ranger whose conception of music has happily never fitted into any orthodoxy. This music, it has to be recognized,

TEXT: *Stocktakings from an Apprenticeship,* ed. by Paule Thévenin, trans. by Stephen Walsh (Oxford: Clarendon Press, 1991), pp. 173–79.

is essentially concerned with the physical phenomenon of sound itself; I imagine Varèse preoccupied constantly with the effect of chords as objects; chord function no longer has anything to do with traditional harmony, but becomes a property of the whole body of sound, calculated as a function of natural harmonics, inferior resonances, and the various tensions necessary to the vitality of such a body. Hence the remarkable dynamic qualities so often observed in the music of Varèse. One may notice the flat rejection of anything that could be called expressive nuance, in the pejorative sense (a constraint inherited from certain aspects of *fin-de-siècle* romanticism); dynamics here play the role of tensor, an essential factor for the optimum rendering of a note-aggregate, and a far more highly evolved role than usual, since, instead of remaining at the purely affective level, they participate in the actual harmonic structure, from which they cannot be detached without completely destroying the equilibrium of the music thus composed. These two points—the abolition of the traditional function of chords in favour of their intrinsic quality as sound, and the incorporation of dynamics as an element of structure—can be combined into a single overriding preoccupation of Varèse: acoustics.

Taking acoustics as the basis of all sound relationships, Varèse set himself to discover in what way they could control a musical construction. This led him—as an isolated experiment—to write for percussion alone *(Ionisation)*.

We should finally note of Varèse—for the moment only in passing—his profound rejection of equal temperament, which he called 'the octave's cheese-wire'.[1] It is well known that equal temperament is the most artificial thing possible, and that it was adopted in the eighteenth century merely as a convenience. If it was temperament that enabled the full flowering of western music—which it is hardly possible to forget—it must be admitted that it remains a purely western phenomenon, and that in other musical civilizations there has never been any question of temperament, just as there has never been any question of disallowing any unit interval other than the semitone. For Varèse, with his acoustical attitude to musical structure, temperament was obviously pure nonsense. Recently he has even spoken of non-octave-based scales, which reproduce on a *spiral* principle or, to put it more clearly, a principle by which the transposition of pitch scales no longer works in octaves, but according to different intervallic functions.

In the next generation an American musician, John Cage, came to believe that, if it was such an effort to avoid the clichés of tonal music, this was largely the fault of our instruments, which were specifically designed to meet the needs of tonality. He thus turned, like Varèse, to percussion, with its world of unpitched sounds, in which rhythm is the only architectonic element of sufficient power to allow a valid non-improvised structure—apart, obviously, from the timbre and acoustical relations which exist between the different categories of such instruments (skin, wood, or metal).

1. Orig. "le fil à couper l'octave." [Tr.]

At the opposite pole to this music which deliberately does not concern itself with pitch or registral relations, stands the work of Webern, whose main preoccupation was, on the contrary, to find a new way of structuring pitch. Certainly the most important figure of our time, and the threshold to contemporary music, in the sense that he rethought the whole notion of polyphonic music in serial terms (terms which he himself established through his own music by assigning an increasingly primary role to interval as such, and even to the sound in isolation): such is Webern. Throughout his work one senses an urge to reduce the articulation of the discourse as far as possible to pure serial functions. In his view, the purity and rigour of the experiment had to be preserved at all costs. Increasingly he enlarged his field of musical possibilities, without thereby losing any of his fanatical intransigence. And from this moment there irrupt into the acquired sensibility the first rudiments of a musical mentality that cannot be reduced to the basic schemas of previous sound-worlds. Here it really seems a question of an upheaval comparable to what the passage from monody to polyphony may have been, that is a radically new conception of the available sound-space. But, while melody remained the fundamental element at the heart of polyphony, one can say that in the serial method as conceived by Webern it is polyphony itself which becomes the basic element: and that is how his way of thinking comes to transcend the notions of vertical and horizontal. So the significance of Webern's work, its historical *raison d'être*—quite apart from its indisputable intrinsic value—is to have introduced a new mode of musical *being*.

This mode lacks, however, the rigour necessary to its complete fulfilment. While Webern concentrated on pitch structure—eminently a western problem—matters of rhythm interested him much less, as did dynamics, even though dynamics do play a certain structural role in his music.

Recently, Olivier Messiaen has crystallized these scattered preoccupations of valid contemporary music in his *Mode de valeurs et d'intensités*, in which the idea of global—in this case modal—organization is applied not only to register, but equally to duration (that is to say, the rhythmic organization of music time), dynamics (that is, the amplitude of the sound) and attack (or the initial profile of the sound). With Varèse, remember, dynamics played a structural role by virtue of his preoccupation with acoustics; here, in Messiaen, dynamics, like duration and pitch, are organized as an actual compositional function, which is to say that, over and above acoustics as such, there is a concern to integrate all sound elements into a study of form.

The one area still needing to be explored is the world of non-tempered sound. Why indeed should one regard as inviolate a decision which has rendered immense service but has no further *raison d'être*, since the tonal organization which required such standardization is now practically destroyed? Admittedly the question of instruments is a by no means negligible obstacle to the development of a musical thought based on non-tempered intervals and concerned with such things as complex tones and sound-complexes. All the acoustical approximations which have gradually accumulated in the course of western musical evolution ought to disappear, since they are no longer needed; but how, for the moment, do we get round the problem of sound-production?

•   •   •

The prepared piano of John Cage provides an artisan solution, embryonic, but none the less plausible. At least the prepared piano has the great virtue of making already tangible a sound universe which we would have for the time being to renounce, given its difficulty of realization. The piano thus becomes an instrument capable, by means of an artisan tablature, of yielding complex frequency patterns: artisan tablature since, to prepare the piano, objects of various materials such as metal, wood, or rubber are inserted between the strings at certain critical points along their length, materials which modify the four characteristics of the sound produced by a vibrating string: duration, amplitude, frequency, and timbre. If we bear in mind that, for much of the piano, any given key has three corresponding strings, and if we then imagine these various modifying materials at critical points on these three strings, we can get an idea of the variety and complexity of the sounds produced by such means. The route is marked out from here towards a future evolution of music in which, with the help of increasingly perfected tablatures, instruments will be able to assist in the creation of a new sound-world which needs and demands them.

If now, after this excursion into a region where Webern never ventured, we return to his work, we will find in it an extraordinary preoccupation with timbre and with new ways of using it. The musical evidence, of which I spoke earlier, is by no means neglected at this level. Orchestration no longer has a purely decorative value, but participates in the actual structure, providing a particularly effective way of relating and synthesizing pitch, duration and dynamics. To such an extent that, with Webern, we are no longer talking about the historical orchestra, but must seek out new and essential orchestral functions.

•   •   •

We can now see how urgent it is to gather up our various investigations, generalize our discoveries, and expand the resources of this now known technique, which, having hitherto been largely an instrument of destruction—and hence bound up with what it wanted to destroy—has now to be given its autonomy, by linking rhythmic to serial structures through a common organization which embraces not only duration, but also timbre and dynamics. It is easy to imagine the bewildering range of discoveries waiting to be made through constructive research. The development of musical thought is called upon to fling itself powerfully in Webern's wake, since it is possible to justify an entire musical organization in terms of the serial principle, from the tiniest component up to the complete structure.

Such serial thinking can at last escape the number twelve, in which it has been imprisoned for so long and with such good reason, since it was precisely the twelve notes, that is the chromatic scale, which allowed the transition from the increasingly feeble structure of tonality to that of serialism. But in the end it is not the twelve notes that are paramount, so much as the serial idea itself, the idea, that is, of a sound universe, specific to each work, derived from a phenomenon that is undifferentiated until the moment the series is chosen, at which point it becomes unique and essential. The permutations thereby defined on the basis of the original permutation can be generalized into whatever sound-space is given as material, which is why we should speak of series of non-tempered intervals, even of frequency characteristics, and with no predetermined number, leading eventually to defining intervals other than the octave. (And this brings us back to Varèse.) There is then no longer anything incompatible between micro-intervals, non-tempered intervals, and the familiar twelve semitones.

Similarly with rhythm, one can envisage not only rational divisions of the unit, but also irrational fractions which would mainly be used within the basic unit. If we want to break the unit down into fractions—a necessity we face, for example, when superimposing series of units and series of durations, which makes performance virtually impossible and notation unrealizable except by recourse to a scale of the unit and its fractions—if, then, we want to introduce a concept of total rhythmic freedom, what can we do except turn to the machine?

We are here on the brink of an undreamt-of sound-world, rich in possibilities and still practically unexplored, whose implications we are only now beginning to perceive. We may notice one happy coincidence in the present state of musical thinking (but perhaps it is not mere chance: certainly we should not be surprised that the musicians in different countries who take most interest in these developments are the ones who unite a certain body of opinion): this coincidence lies in the need for certain means of realization having arisen at the very moment when electro-acoustic techniques are in a position to supply them. In effect, there are two ways of producing a sound: either with a natural sounding body or through artificial production by electronics. Or, in between the two, the electro-acoustical transformation of a sound produced by a natural sounding body. In the two extreme cases, the procedure envisaged is radically different; the sounding body produces sounds whose essential definition is timbre, duration, register, and the limits of its dynamic range; if we make use of a natural sounding body, we must first take account of the possibilities it offers, since the only possible modifications are in dynamics and variations in attack and decay: we therefore need an ensemble of sounding bodies each with a different set of characteristics. These characteristics exist in a virtual state in the sounding body, within precise and well-understood limits. But if we think of the domain of electronics, it is pretty obvious that we are dealing initially with a non-limitation of possibilities, whether of timbre, of register, of dynamics, or of duration; we thus create the characteristics of each sound, characteristics which depend on the overall structure; the sound is reciprocally linked to the work as the work is linked to the sound. The far end of the serial perspective which was already proposing a universe peculiar to each work, but solely from the point of view of serialized frequencies, thus brings us into the domain of sound itself, and the actual interior of the sound.

Rarely, in the whole history of music, could we have assisted at a more radical development, or one which confronts the musician with a more unfamiliar requirement: the choice of sound material, not merely for decorative effect or for the musical evidence—a banal version of the problem of orchestration or instrumentation—but the real choice of material for its intrinsic structural properties. The composer becomes performer, in a field where performance and realization have an enhanced importance, and like a painter he acts directly on the quality of the realization.

Moreover, questions of tempered or non-tempered, vertical or horizontal, no longer have any meaning: we arrive instead at the "sound-figure," which is the most general object that presents itself to the composer's imagination: sound-figure, or even, with the new techniques, sound-object. If in fact we extend the notion of series to the way the basic temporal unfolding acts upon the organizational differences between these objects—if, that is, we expand it to include the modifications that can be made to such objects—we shall have established a category of works free at last from all constraint outside what is specific to themselves. Quite an abrupt transformation, when one considers that previously music was a collection of codified possibilities applicable to any work indifferently.

These observations are nevertheless still premature; we are merely on the road to such a music. The crucial research into the intrinsic qualities of sound has yet to be undertaken; the perfected and manageable equipment necessary to the composition of such works has yet to be built. All the same, the ideas are not so utopian that we can ignore them; it is even probable that the growing interest aroused by the epiphany of this unfamiliar and undreamt-of sound-world will only hasten their solution. We may modestly hope to be the first practitioners.

COMPOSITIONAL APPROACHES

181 Arnold Schoenberg

Mirroring the general esthetic transformations in Western music following the First World War, Arnold Schoenberg moved away from the extreme "intuitive" approach he favored in the prewar years (see pp. 1283–89, passim). In this excerpt from a lecture dating from 1934 (that achieved final form in 1941), Schoenberg retains his earlier belief in creation as "inspiration and perfection" but now stresses clarity, communication, and the hard work required to bring a compositional vision to realization. And looking back on the music he composed during the early years of the century, written as he was breaking away from traditional tonality, he finds limitations stemming from the absence of the constructive force of traditional tonality: either the pieces were short or they required texts to provide large-scale coherence. Schoenberg justifies his twelve-tone system, developed in the early postwar years, as having been a necessary response to the need for "conscious control" over the new chromatic material, providing post-tonal music with a resource "comparable to the regularity and logic of the earlier harmony."

FROM Composition with Twelve Tones
(1941)

I

To understand the very nature of creation one must acknowledge that there was no light before the Lord said: "Let there be Light." And since there was not yet light, the Lord's omniscience embraced a vision of it which only His omnipotence could call forth.

We poor human beings, when we refer to one of the better minds among us as a creator, should never forget what a creator is in reality.

A creator has a vision of something which has not existed before this vision.

And a creator has the power to bring his vision to life, the power to realize it.

In fact, the concept of creator and creation should be formed in harmony with the Divine Model; inspiration and perfection, wish and fulfilment, will and accomplishment coincide spontaneously and simultaneously. In Divine Creation there were no details to be carried out later; 'There was Light' at once and in its ultimate perfection.

Alas, human creators, if they be granted a vision, must travel the long path between vision and accomplishment; a hard road where, driven out of Paradise, even geniuses must reap their harvest in the sweat of their brows.

TEXT: *Style and Idea*, ed. by Leonard Stein, trans. by Leo Black (Berkeley: University of California Press, 1975), pp. 214–26.

Alas, it is one thing to envision in a creative instant of inspiration and it is another thing to materialize one's vision by painstakingly connecting details until they fuse into a kind of organism.

Alas, suppose it becomes an organism, a homunculus or a robot, and possesses some of the spontaneity of a vision; it remains yet another thing to organize this form so that it becomes a comprehensible message "to whom it may concern."

II

Form in the arts, and especially in music, aims primarily at comprehensibility. The relaxation which a satisfied listener experiences when he can follow an idea, its development, and the reasons for such development is closely related, psychologically speaking, to a feeling of beauty. Thus, artistic value demands comprehensibility, not only for intellectual, but also for emotional satisfaction. However, the creator's *idea* has to be presented, whatever the *mood* he is impelled to evoke.

Composition with twelve tones has no other aim than comprehensibility. In view of certain events in recent musical history, this might seem astonishing, for works written in this style have failed to gain understanding in spite of the new medium of organization. Thus, should one forget that contemporaries are not final judges, but are generally overruled by history, one might consider this method doomed. But, though it seems to increase the listener's difficulties, it compensates for this deficiency by penalizing the composer. For composing thus does not become easier, but rather ten times more difficult. Only the better-prepared composer can compose for the better-prepared music lover.

III

The method of composing with twelve tones grew out of a necessity.

In the last hundred years, the concept of harmony has changed tremendously through the development of chromaticism. The idea that one basic tone, the root, dominated the construction of chords and regulated their succession—the concept of *tonality*—had to develop first into the concept of *extended tonality*. Very soon it became doubtful whether such a root still remained the center to which every harmony and harmonic succession must be referred. Furthermore, it became doubtful whether a tonic appearing at the beginning, at the end, or at any other point really had a constructive meaning. Richard Wagner's harmony had promoted a change in the logic and constructive power of harmony. One of its consequences was the so-called impressionistic use of harmonies, especially practised by Debussy. His harmonies, without constructive meaning, often served the coloristic purpose of expressing moods and pictures. Moods and pictures, though extra-musical, thus became constructive elements, incorporated in the musical functions; they produced a sort of emotional comprehensibility. In this way, tonality was already dethroned in practice, if not in theory. This alone would perhaps not have caused a radical change in compositional technique. However, such a change became necessary when there occurred simultaneously a development which ended in what I call the *emancipation of the dissonance.*

The ear had gradually become acquainted with a great number of dissonances, and so had lost the fear of their "sense-interrupting" effect. One no longer expected preparations of Wagner's dissonances or resolutions of Strauss's discords; one was not disturbed by Debussy's non-functional harmonies, or by the harsh counterpoint of later composers. This state of affairs led to a freer use of dissonances comparable to classic composers' treatment of diminished seventh chords, which could precede and follow any other harmony, consonant or dissonant, as if there were no dissonance at all.

What distinguishes dissonances from consonances is not a greater or lesser degree of beauty, but a greater or lesser degree of *comprehensibility.* In my *Harmonielehre* I presented the theory that dissonant tones appear later among the overtones, for which reason the ear is less intimately acquainted with them. This phenomenon does not justify such sharply contradictory terms as concord and discord. Closer acquaintance with the more remote consonances—the dissonances, that is—gradually eliminated the difficulty of comprehension and finally admitted not only the emancipation of dominant and other seventh chords, diminished sevenths and augmented triads, but also the emancipation of Wagner's, Strauss's, Moussorgsky's, Debussy's, Mahler's, Puccini's, and Reger's more remote dissonances.

The term *emancipation of the dissonance* refers to its comprehensibility, which is considered equivalent to the consonance's comprehensibility. A style based on this premise treats dissonances like consonances and renounces a tonal centre. By avoiding the establishment of a key modulation is excluded, since modulation means leaving an established tonality and establishing *another* tonality.

The first compositions in this new style were written by me around 1908 and, soon afterwards, by my pupils, Anton von Webern and Alban Berg. From the very beginning such compositions differed from all preceding music, not only harmonically but also melodically, thematically, and motivically. But the foremost characteristics of these pieces *in statu nascendi* were their extreme expressiveness and their extraordinary brevity. At that time, neither I nor my pupils were conscious of the reasons for these features. Later I discovered that our sense of form was right when it forced us to counterbalance extreme emotionality with extraordinary shortness. Thus, subconsciously, consequences were drawn from an innovation which, like every innovation, destroys while it produces. New colourful harmony was offered; but much was lost.

Formerly the harmony had served not only as a source of beauty, but, more important, as a means of distinguishing the features of the form. For instance, only a consonance was considered suitable for an ending. Establishing functions demanded different successions of harmonies than roving functions; a bridge, a transition, demanded other successions than a codetta; harmonic variation could be executed intelligently and logically only with due consideration of the fundamental meaning of the harmonies. Fulfilment of all these functions—comparable to the effect of punctuation in the construction of sentences, of subdivision into paragraphs, and of fusion into chapters—could scarcely be assured with chords whose constructive values had not as yet been explored. Hence, it seemed at first impossible to compose pieces of complicated organization or of great length.

A little later I discovered how to construct larger forms by following a text or a poem. The differences in size and shape of its parts and the change in character and mood were mirrored in the shape and size of the composition, in its dynamics and tempo, figuration and accentuation, instrumentation and orchestration. Thus the parts were differentiated as clearly as they had formerly been by the tonal and structural functions of harmony.

IV

Formerly the use of the fundamental harmony had been theoretically regulated through recognition of the effects of root progressions. This practice had grown into a subconsciously functioning *sense of form* which gave a real composer an almost somnambulistic sense of security in creating, with utmost precision, the most delicate distinctions of formal elements.

Whether one calls oneself conservative or revolutionary, whether one composes in a conventional or progressive manner, whether one tries to imitate old styles or is destined to express new ideas—whether one is a good composer or not—one must be convinced of the infallibility of one's own fantasy and one must believe in one's own inspiration. Nevertheless, the desire for a conscious control of the new means and forms will arise in every artist's mind; and he will wish to know *consciously* the laws and rules which govern the forms which he has conceived "as in a dream." Strongly convincing as this dream may have been, the conviction that these new sounds obey the laws of nature and of our manner of thinking—the conviction that order, logic, comprehensibility and form cannot be present without obedience to such laws—forces the composer along the road of exploration. He must find, if not laws or rules, at least ways to justify the dissonant character of these harmonies and their successions.

V

After many unsuccessful attempts during a period of approximately twelve years, I laid the foundations for a new procedure in musical construction which seemed fitted to replace those structural differentiations provided formerly by tonal harmonies.

I called this procedure *Method of Composing with Twelve Tones Which are Related Only with One Another.*

This method consists primarily of the constant and exclusive use of a set of twelve different tones. This means, of course, that no tone is repeated within the series and that it uses all twelve tones of the chromatic scale, though in a different order. It is in no way identical with the chromatic scale.[1]

Ex. 1

Example 1 shows that such a basic set (BS) consists of various intervals. It should never be called a scale, although it is invented to substitute for some of the unifying and formative advantages of scale and tonality. The scale is the source of many figurations, parts of melodies and melodies themselves, ascending and descending passages, and even broken chords. In approximately the same manner the tones of the basic set produce similar elements. Of course, cadences produced by the distinction between principal and subsidiary harmonies will scarcely be derived from the basic set. But something different and more important is derived from it with a regularity comparable to the regularity and logic of the earlier harmony; the association of tones into harmonies and their successions is regulated (as will be shown later) by the order of these tones. The basic set functions in the manner of a motive. This explains why such a basic set has to be invented anew for every piece. It has to be the first creative thought. It does not make much difference whether or not the set appears in the composition at once like a theme or a melody, whether or not it is characterized as such by features of rhythm, phrasing, construction, character, etc.

Why such a set should consist of twelve different tones, why none of these tones should be repeated too soon, why, accordingly, only one set should be used in one composition—the answers to all these questions came to me gradually.

1. Curiously and wrongly, most people speak of the "system" of the chromatic scale. Mine is no system but only a method, which means a *modus* of applying regularly a preconceived formula. *A method can, but need not,* be one of the consequences of a system. I am also not the inventor of the chromatic scale; somebody else must have occupied himself with this task long ago. [Au.]

Discussing such problems in my *Harmonielehre* (1911), I recommended the avoidance of octave doublings.[2] To double is to emphasize, and an emphasized tone could be interpreted as a root, or even as a tonic; the consequences of such an interpretation must be avoided. Even a slight reminiscence of the former tonal harmony would be disturbing, because it would create false expectations of consequences and continuations. The use of a tonic is deceiving if it is not based on *all* the relationships of tonality.

The use of more than one set was excluded because in every following set one or more tones would have been repeated too soon. Again there would arise the danger of interpreting the repeated tone as a tonic. Besides, the effect of unity would be lessened.

Justified already by historical development, the method of composing with twelve tones is also not without esthetic and theoretical support. On the contrary, it is just this support which advances it from a mere technical device to the rank and importance of a scientific theory.

Music is not merely another kind of amusement, but a musical poet's, a musical thinker's representation of musical ideas; these musical ideas must correspond to the laws of human logic; they are a part of what man can apperceive, reason and express. Proceeding from these assumptions, I arrived at the following conclusions:

THE TWO-OR-MORE-DIMENSIONAL SPACE IN WHICH MUSICAL IDEAS ARE PRESENTED IS A UNIT. Though the elements of these ideas appear separate and independent to the eye and the ear, they reveal their true meaning only through their co-operation, even as no single word alone can express a thought without relation to other words. All that happens at any point of this musical space has more than a local effect. It functions not only in its own plane, but also in all other directions and planes, and is not without influence even at remote points. For instance, the effect of progressive rhythmical subdivision, through what I call "the tendency of the shortest notes" to multiply themselves, can be observed in every classic composition.

A musical idea, accordingly, though consisting of melody, rhythm, and harmony, is neither the one nor the other alone, but all three together. The elements of a musical idea are partly incorporated in the horizontal plane as successive sounds, and partly in the vertical plane as simultaneous sounds. The mutual relation of tones regulates the succession of intervals as well as their association into harmonies; the rhythm regulates the succession of tones as well as the succession of harmonies and organizes phrasing. And this explains why, as will be shown later, a basic set of twelve tones (BS) can be used in either dimension, as a whole or in parts.

The basic set is used in diverse mirror forms. The composers of the last century had not employed such mirror forms as much as the masters of contrapuntal times; at least, they seldom did so consciously. Nevertheless, there exist

2. Still sometimes occurring in my first compositions in this style. [Au.]

examples, of which I want to mention only one from Beethoven's last String Quartet, Op. 135, in F major:

EX. 2: BEETHOVEN, STRING QUARTET, OP. 135, 4TH MOVEMENT, INTRODUCTION

The original form, *a*, "Muss es sein," appears in *b* inverted and in the major; *c* shows the retrograde form of this inversion, which, now reinverted in *d* and filled out with passing notes in *e*, results in the second phrase of the main theme.

Whether or not this device was used consciously by Beethoven does not matter at all. From my own experience I know that it can also be a subconsciously received gift from the Supreme Commander.

EX. 3: KAMMERSYMPHONIE, OP. 9, E MAJOR

The two principal themes of my *Kammersymphonie* (Chamber Symphony) can be seen in Example 3 under *a* and *b*. After I had completed the work I worried very much about the apparent absence of any relationship between the two themes. Directed only by my sense of form and the stream of ideas, I had not asked such questions while composing; but, as usual with me, doubts arose as soon as I had finished. They went so far that I had already raised the sword for the kill, taken the red pencil of the censor to cross out the theme *b*. Fortunately, I stood by my inspiration and ignored these mental tortures. About twenty years later I saw the true relationship. It is of such a complicated nature that I doubt whether any composer would have cared deliberately to construct a theme in this way; but our subconscious does it involuntarily. In *c* the true principal tones of the theme are marked, and *d* shows that all the intervals ascend. Their correct inversion *e* produces the first phrase *f* of the theme *b*.

It should be mentioned that the last century considered such a procedure cerebral, and thus inconsistent with the dignity of genius. The very fact that there exist classical examples proves the foolishness of such an opinion. But the validity of this form of thinking is also demonstrated by the previously stated law of the unity of musical space, best formulated as follows: *the unity of musical space demands an absolute and unitary perception.* In this space, as in Swedenborg's heaven (described in Balzac's *Seraphita*) there is no absolute down, no right or left, forward or backward. Every musical configuration, every movement of tones has to be comprehended primarily as a mutual relation of sounds, of oscillatory vibrations, appearing at different places and times. To the imaginative and creative faculty, relations in the material sphere are as independent from directions or planes as material objects are, in their sphere, to our perceptive faculties. Just as our mind always recognizes, for instance, a knife, a bottle or a watch, regardless of its position, and can reproduce it in the imagination in every possible position, even so a musical creator's mind can operate subconsciously with a row of tones, regardless of their direction, regardless of the way in which a mirror might show the mutual relations, which remain a given quality.

VI

The introduction of my method of composing with twelve tones does not facilitate composing; on the contrary, it makes it more difficult. Modernistically-minded beginners often think they should try it before having acquired the necessary technical equipment. This is a great mistake. The restrictions imposed on a composer by the obligation to use only one set in a composition are so severe that they can only be overcome by an imagination which has survived a tremendous number of adventures. Nothing is given by this method; but much is taken away.

It has been mentioned that for every new composition a special set of twelve tones has to be invented. Sometimes a set will not fit every condition an experienced composer can foresee, especially in those ideal cases where the set appears at once in the form, character, and phrasing of a theme. Rectifications in the order of tones may then become necessary.

In the first works in which I employed this method, I was not yet convinced that the exclusive use of one set would not result in monotony. Would it allow the creation of a sufficient number of characteristically differentiated themes, phrases, motives, sentences, and other forms? At this time, I used complicated devices to assure variety. But soon I discovered that my fear was unfounded; I could even base a whole opera, *Moses and Aron*, solely on one set; and I found that, on the contrary, the more familiar I became with this set the more easily I could draw themes from it. Thus, the truth of my first prediction had received splendid proof. One has to follow the basic set; but, nevertheless, one composes as freely as before.

VII

It has been mentioned that the basic set is used in mirror forms.

Ex. 4

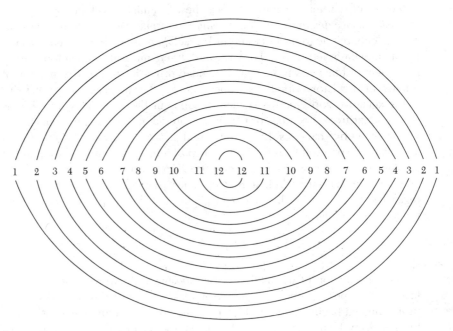

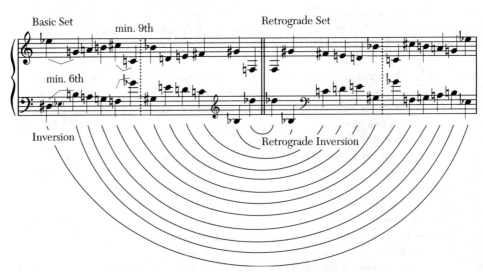

BS means Basic Set; INV means inversion of the Basic Set; INV 8, INV 5, INV 3, INV 6 means inversion at the 8ve, 5th, minor 3rd, or major 6th from the beginning tone.

From the basic set, three additional sets are automatically derived: (1) the inversion; (2) the retrograde; and (3) the retrograde inversion. The employment of these mirror forms corresponds to the principle of *the absolute and unitary perception of musical space*. The set of Example 4 is taken from the Wind Quintet Op. 26, one of my first compositions in this style.

Later, especially in larger works, I changed my original idea, if necessary, to fit the following conditions: the inversion a fifth below of the first six tones, the antecedent, should not produce a repetition of one of these six tones, but should bring forth the hitherto unused six tones of the chromatic scale. Thus, the consequent of the basic set, the tones 7 to 12, comprises the tones of this inversion, but, of course, in a different order.

·   ·   ·   ·   ·

VIII

In every composition preceding the method of composing with twelve tones, all the thematic and harmonic material is primarily derived from three sources: the tonality, the *basic motive* which in turn is a derivative of the tonality, and the *rhythm*, which is included in the basic motive. A composer's whole thinking was bound to remain in an intelligible manner around the central root. A composition which failed to obey these demands was considered "amateurish"; but a composition which adhered to it rigorously was never called "cerebral." On the contrary, the capacity to obey the principle instinctively was considered a natural condition of a talent.[3]

The time will come when the ability to draw thematic material from a basic set of twelve tones will be an unconditional prerequisite for obtaining admission into the composition class of a conservatory.

IX

The possibilities of evolving the formal elements of music—melodies, themes, phrases, motives, figures, and chords—out of a basic set are unlimited. In the following pages, a number of examples from my own works will be analysed to reveal some of these possibilities. It will be observed that the succession of the tones according to their order in the set has always been strictly observed. One could perhaps tolerate a slight digression from this order (according to the same principle which allowed a remote variant in former styles)[4] in the later part of a work, when the set had already become familiar to the ear. However, one would not thus digress at the beginning of a piece.

3. There are scores of mathematical geniuses who can square and cube in their minds. There are scores of chess players who play blindfolded, and every chess player has to work out in his mind the possibilities of the next five moves. There must not be many who can exceed ten moves, but only to them should one compare the imaginative capacity of a real musical mind. [Au.]
4. As, for instance, in the fourth of the Diabelli Variations, Beethoven omits, in an inexplicable manner, one measure. [Au.]

The set is often divided into groups; for example, into two groups of six tones, or three groups of four, or four groups of three tones. This grouping serves primarily to provide a regularity in the distribution of the tones. The tones used in the melody are thereby separated from those to be used as accompaniment, as harmonies or as chords and voices demanded by the nature of the instrumentation, by the instrument, or by the character and other circumstances of a piece. The distribution may be varied or developed according to circumstances, in a manner comparable to the changes of what I call the "Motive of the Accompaniment."

•   •   •   •   •

182 Karlheinz Stockhausen

Karlheinz Stockhausen (b. 1926) was a leading figure in the development of "integral serialism," one of the two principal compositional esthetics to emerge in the early years following World War II (the other was indeterminacy). Reacting against the neoclassicism evident in European music since the end of World War I, the serialists aspired to develop a completely integrated structural approach to composition, as independent of traditional conceptions as possible. Ideally, even traditional instruments should be discarded, since they necessarily bring "preformed" material into the compositional mix. This article, written during the early 1960s and drawing upon the advantages of the electronic medium, proposes that the entire sonic structure be understood as a unified phenomenon: that all of its individual components—timbre, pitch, intensity, and duration—represent different manifestations of a single event, "the temporal structure of sound waves," which can thus be placed under the control of a "single principle of ordering."

FROM The Concept of Unity in Electronic Music

(1962)

On several previous occasions, when I have been asked to explain the composition of electronic music, I have described four characteristics that seem

TEXT: *Perspectives of New Music* 1 (Fall 1962): 39–43. Translation by Elaine Barkin.

important to me for electronic composition as distinguished from the composition of instrumental music:

1) the correlation of the coloristic, harmonic-melodic, and metric-rhythmic aspects of composition
2) the composition and de-composition of timbres
3) the characteristic differentiation among degrees of intensity
4) the ordered relationships between sound and noise

Here, I would like to discuss only the correlation of timbre, pitch, intensity, and duration. In the past, it has been customary to regard these correlative properties of sound as mutually independent, as belonging to fundamentally distinct spheres. They have appeared increasingly separate as our acoustical perception developed along such lines.

Similarly, the means employed for the production of sound, as well as the compositional process itself, were consequent upon this conceptual separation. To generate sound-events having single perceptible pitches, we used the so-called sine tone, square-wave, or saw-tooth generators, which produce periodic oscillations. Sound-events of indeterminate pitch, those that are more or less noise-like, were produced by means of noise generators.

We varied such sound- or noise-colors by means of electrical filters, with which one can strengthen, attenuate, or suppress entirely individual partials or whole frequency-bands—the so-called formants, or bands of noise—of the spectra.

Intensity was controlled by regulating, with the aid of a voltmeter, the voltages recorded on tape (whereby the spectrum itself automatically varied with the variations in intensity), whereas duration was determined simply by the length of tape on which a sound was recorded.

Compositionally, in terms of the production and manipulation of sound, these individual sound-properties had to be dealt with separately. But, on the other hand, we perceive a sound-event as a homogeneous phenomenon rather than as a composite of four separate properties. At a relatively early stage of my work in electronic composition, I had already considered the possibility of equating this unity of perception with an analogous unity in composition itself. In the preparatory work for my composition *Kontakte,* I found, for the first time, ways to bring all properties under a single control. I deduced that all differences of acoustic perception can be traced to differences in the temporal structure of sound waves. These temporal relations enable us to distinguish the many different manifestations of pitch, timbre, simultaneity, sound-mixture, and noise: their speed of oscillation, their particular intervals—either equal and regular or more or less irregular—their density, and the frequency with which pulsations reach the ear. It seemed to me that the differences in intensity among sounds ultimately derive from the latter property: when pulsations of equal value follow one another in closer temporal succession, the over-all intensity increases; to effect this, the density would, in fact, have to be so great that the individual pulses were no longer conveyed as a succession of equal perturbations of the atmosphere but rather as mutually interfering sound-waves: the particles of air agitated by the initial pulses would thus be reactivated by further pulses before they have become quiescent and are, so to speak, "shaken up," so that the impression given is of an increase in over-all intensity. The total complex thus appears as a *single* greater wave rather than *several* smaller ones. The faster the succession of pulses, the stronger will be the appearance of the resultant wave.

A periodic sound wave, such as a simple tone, fluctuating regularly in intensity, would thus be the result of a succession of pulses that alternately accelerate and decelerate within each period. The difference between the fastest and slowest rates of speed of the pulses in each period would define the direction of its intensity (its "intensity envelope") and its amplitude. The distance between periodically recurring equal rates of speed would determine the pitch.

Ex. 1

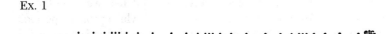

If a succession of pulses of this kind were to be accelerated so that between the periodic recurrences of the highest speed there were a time interval of, say, 1/440 sec., one would hear a simple tone with the pitch of A-440.

If the rate of speed of the pulse-succession did not fluctuate regularly (‿‿‿) but consisted instead of periods of several unequal parts within each equal time-span (as, for example, ⌇⌇⌇), the so-called "color" of a steady sound would vary according to the wave crests. A "period" divided into two parts would be represented as follows:

Ex. 2

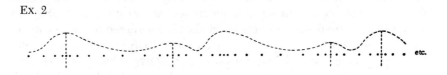

In a more or less noiselike sound-event the periods would no longer be regular; i.e. the time intervals between recurrences of equal rates of speed would not remain constant but would vary irregularly between a given fastest and slowest speed. These extremes determine the limits of a frequency band, a so-called "colored noise" band. If the rate of speed of the pulse succession were so widely varied that the smallest interval between pulses were ca. 1/16,000 sec., and the longest ca. 1/20 sec., occurring at regular time-intervals, and everything between these extremes occurred in a highly aperiodic fashion (in a manner that one might term "aleatoric") the result would be "white noise."

For most musicians, these considerations may seem specifically related to acoustics rather than to music. Actually, however, a musical composition is no more than a temporal ordering of sound events, just as each sound event in a composition is a temporal ordering of pulses. It is only a question of the point at which composition begins: in composing for instruments whose sounds are predetermined, a composer need not be concerned with these problems. On the other hand, in electronic music, one can either compose each sound directly in terms of its wave succession, or, finally, each individual sound wave may be determined in terms of its actual vibration, by an ordering of the succession of pulses.

If, in fact, all of the experiential properties of sound could be traced to a single principle of ordering—such temporally composed successions of pulses—compositional thought would have to be radically reoriented. The distinction between the "acoustical prearrangement" *within* the material and "musical ordering" *using* this material would now have to be discarded. The prevailing additive, or "synthetic" compositional procedure, in which the different properties are bound together, would now be expanded through a proto-generative and more unified approach. One would not proceed from sound properties that had already been experienced and then allow these to determine temporal variations; instead, one would compose the temporal arrangements of pulses themselves, and discover their resultant sound properties experimentally.

After my first, relatively simple, attempt at such a procedure, I was able to predict roughly the particular temporal orderings of the pulses. I then proceeded to record fixed successions of pulses on tape within a relatively low speed range (using pulsation intervals of between 1/16 and 16 secs.) and then increased the speed until I arrived at the "field" of frequencies and color that I desired. This was done by means of a pulse generator with which the speed of the pulse succession was regulated by hand. Thus, for example, if I wished to generate a periodic wave—that is, a sound of constant pitch—from a succession of pulses lasting eight seconds whose speed variations are fixed, I would have to accelerate the rhythmized eight-second succession 1,024 times, that is, transpose it ten octaves upwards, reducing its duration from eight to 1/128 sec. In order to sustain this pitch of 128 cps. for 10 sec., I would have to re-record the original succession 128×10, or 1,280 times, which can easily be done by means of a tape loop. The "color" of the resulting sound would be determined by the variations of speed among the pulses of the original succession, which are now determined by the periodic duplications and accelerations of the wave form within each time span—i.e. the "intensity envelope."

With such a compositional procedure, then, one must proceed from a basic concept of a *single, unified musical time;* and the different perceptual categories, such as color, harmony and melody, meter and rhythm, dynamics, and "form," must be regarded as corresponding to the different *components* of this unified time, as follows:

1. Harmony and melody correspond to periodic waves (that is, to sound-events of constant pitch) whose individual periods should not be greater than ca. 1/16 or less than ca. 1/6,000 sec. because beyond these limits they are no longer audible as "pitches."

2. The color of harmonic spectra corresponds to the whole number fractions which, as "fundamentals," refer to periods of between ca. 1/13,000 and ca. 1/16 sec.; the color of nonharmonic or noiselike spectra corresponds to more or less aperiodic successions of periods.

3. Between ca. 1/30 and 1/16 sec. our perception of duration gradually changes into perception of meter and rhythm; i.e., *periodic* periods may then be considered as *meters,* and the *internal intervallic relationships* of the distances between pulses within any given meter—that which determines the tone color for periods shorter than ca. 1/16 sec.—may here be considered as "rhythm."

Aperiodic relationships of periods, which are considered *"noises"* in the sphere of color, correspond, when the periods are longer than ca. 1/16 sec. to *aperiodic rhythms* having no recognizable meters—i.e. no recognizable periodicity (just as a deviation from simple periodicity in the sphere of frequency—*"dissonance"*—corresponds, in the sphere of duration, to *syncopation*).

Although many of the new compositions have been criticized for their alleged "lack of rhythm," they may actually be considered to have "pure rhythm" without meter. This objection, moreover, is exactly analogous to that directed against the use of aperiodic sound waves, i.e. against "noises."

4. Meter and rhythm correspond to the time intervals whose order of magnitude is between ca. 1/8 and ca. 8 secs. At about 8 secs. our ability to distinguish durational relationships gradually breaks down. With values of greater length we are no longer able to remember the exact lengths of durations or perceive their proportions as accurately as we can those that lie between ca. 1/8 and ca. 8 secs.

"Form" in a special sense—the time relationships of longer events—corresponds to durations of the order of magnitude of from several seconds to about 15–60 minutes (for "movements" or whole "compositions").

The transitions and overlappings between all the time spheres are quite flexible, but this is especially so with reference to "form," which is most obviously an approximation (in the literature of music, of course, the durations of "movements" or *continuous* works vary from several minutes to ca. one hour).

•　　•　　•

183 Iannis Xenakis

Like Edgard Varèse, Iannis Xenakis (b. 1925) was trained as a scientist; and even more than his predecessor, he has applied the ideas and methods of mathematics and science to develop a new conception of musical structure and compositional process. Xenakis views both earlier Western music in general and integral serialism in particular as inconsistent with modern scientific views of the nature of reality, since he sees both as based upon assumptions of absolute causality and determinism. During the early 1950s he thus began introducing the concept of indeterminacy into his work—not the absolute indeterminacy of a John Cage, which he finds equally unscientific, but the indeterminacy of probability theory and polyvalent logic, consistent with modern physics. Rejecting the "linear category" characteristic of Western musical thought up to his time, Xenakis proposes that music be reconceived in terms of "mass events," as an interaction of complex multitudes of sound that can be experienced and understood only as totalities. This conception will enable composers to mediate between the unmanageable extremes of complete order on the one hand and complete disorder on the other. Originally published in 1960, the following article provides a nontechnical introduction to this radically new approach.

Free Stochastic Music
(1960)

Art, and above all, music has a fundamental function, which is to catalyze the sublimation that it can bring about through all means of expression. It must aim through fixations which are landmarks to draw towards a total exaltation in which the individual mingles, losing his consciousness in a truth immediate, rare, enormous, and perfect. If a work of art succeeds in this undertaking even for a single moment, it attains its goal. This tremendous truth is not made of objects, emotions, or sensations; it is beyond these, as Beethoven's Seventh Symphony is beyond music. This is why art can lead to realms that religion still occupies for some people.

But this transmutation of every-day artistic material which transforms trivial products into meta-art is a secret. The "possessed" reach it without knowing its "mechanisms." The others struggle in the ideological and technical mainstream of their epoch which constitutes the perishable "climate" and the stylistic fashion. Keeping our eyes fixed on this supreme meta-artistic goal, we shall attempt to define in a more modest manner the paths which can lead to it from our

TEXT: *Formalized Music,* rev. ed. (Stuyvesant, NY: Pendragon Press, 1992); pp. 3–5, 8–10, 264.

point of departure, which is the magma of contradictions in present music.

There exists a historical parallel between European music and the successive attempts to explain the world by reason. The music of antiquity, causal and deterministic, was already strongly influenced by the schools of Pythagoras and Plato. Plato insisted on the principle of causality, "for it is impossible for anything, to come into being without cause" (Timaeus). Strict causality lasted until the nineteenth century when it underwent a brutal and fertile transformation as a result of statistical theories in physics. Since antiquity the concepts of chance (tyche), disorder (ataxia), and disorganization were considered as the opposite and negation of reason (logos), order (taxis), and organization (systasis). It is only recently that knowledge has been able to penetrate chance and has discovered how to separate its degrees—in other words to rationalize it progressively, without, however, succeeding in a definitive and total explanation of the problem of "pure chance."

After a time lag of several decades, atonal music broke up the tonal function and opened up a new path parallel to that of the physical sciences, but at the same time constricted by the virtually absolute determinism of serial music.

It is therefore not surprising that the presence or absence of the principle of causality, first in philosophy and then in the sciences, might influence musical composition. It caused it to follow paths that appeared to be divergent, but which, in fact, coalesced in probability theory and finally in polyvalent logic, which are kinds of generalization and enrichments of the principle of causality. The explanation of the world, and consequently of the sonic phenomena which surround us or which may be created, necessitated and profited from the enlargement of the principle of causality, the basis of which enlargement is formed by the law of large numbers. This law implies an asymptotic evolution towards a stable state, towards a kind of goal, of stochos, whence comes the adjective "stochastic."

But everything in pure determinism or in less pure indeterminism is subjected to the fundamental operational laws of logic, which were disentangled by mathematical thought under the title of general algebra. These laws operate on isolated states or on sets of elements with the aid of operations, the most primitive of which are the union, notated $\cup$, the intersection, notated $\cap$, and the negation. Equivalence, implication, and quantifications are elementary relations from which all current science can be constructed.

Music, then, may be defined as an organization of these elementary operations and relations between sonic entities or between functions of sonic entities. We understand the first-rate position which is occupied by set theory, not only for the construction of new works, but also for analysis and better comprehension of the works of the past. In the same way a stochastic construction or an investigation of history with the help of stochastics cannot be carried through without the help of logic—the queen of the sciences, and I would even venture to suggest, of the arts—or its mathematical form algebra. For everything that is said here on the subject is also valid for all forms of art (painting, sculpture, architecture, films, etc.).

From this very general, fundamental point of view, from which we wish to examine and *make* music, primary time appears as a wax or clay on which operations and relations can be inscribed and engraved, first for the purposes of work, and then for communication with a third person. On this level, the asymmetric, noncommutative character of time is used (B after $A \neq A$ after B, i.e., lexicographic order). Commutative, metric time (symmetrical) is subjected to the same logical laws and can therefore also aid organizational speculations. What is remarkable is that these fundamental notions, which are necessary for construction, are found in man from his tenderest age, and it is fascinating to follow their evolution as Jean Piaget[1] has done.

After this short preamble on generalities we shall enter into the details of an approach to musical composition which I have developed over several years. I call it "stochastic," in honor of probability theory, which has served as a logical framework and as a method of resolving the conflicts and knots encountered.

The first task is to construct an abstraction from all inherited conventions and to exercise a fundamental critique of acts of thought and their materialization. What, in fact, does a musical composition offer strictly on the construction level? It offers a collection of sequences which it wishes to be causal. When, for simplification, the major scale implied its hierarchy of tonal functions—tonics, dominants, and subdominants—around which the other notes gravitated, it constructed, in a highly deterministic manner, linear processes, or melodies on the one hand, and simultaneous events, or chords, on the other. Then the serialists of the Vienna school, not having known how to master logically the indeterminism of atonality, returned to an organization which was extremely causal in the strictest sense, more abstract than that of tonality; however, this abstraction was their great contribution. Messiaen generalized this process and took a great step in systematizing the abstraction of all the variables of instrumental music. What is paradoxical is that he did this in the modal field. He created a multimodal music which immediately found imitators in serial music. At the outset Messiaen's abstract systematization found its most justifiable embodiment in a multiserial music. It is from here that the postwar neoserialists have drawn their inspiration. They could now, following the Vienna school and Messiaen, with some occasional borrowing from Stravinsky and Debussy, walk on with ears shut and proclaim a truth greater than the others. Other movements were growing stronger; chief among them was the systematic exploration of sonic entities, new instruments, and "noises." Varèse was the pioneer in this field, and electromagnetic music has been the beneficiary (electronic music being a branch of instrumental music). However, in electro-

---

1. Jean Piaget, *Le Développement de la notion de temps chez l'enfant* (Paris: Presses Universitaires de France, 1946). [Au.]

magnetic music, problems of construction and of morphology were not faced conscientiously. Multiserial music, a fusion of the multimodality of Messiaen and the Viennese school, remained, nevertheless, at the heart of the fundamental problem of music.

But by 1954 it was already in the process of deflation, for the completely deterministic complexity of the operations of composition and of the works themselves produced an auditory and ideological nonsense. I described the inevitable conclusion in "The Crisis of Serial Music":

> Linear polyphony destroys itself by its very complexity; what one hears is in reality nothing but a mass of notes in various registers. The enormous complexity prevents the audience from following the intertwining of the lines and has as its macroscopic effect an irrational and fortuitous dispersion of sounds over the whole extent of the sonic spectrum. There is consequently a contradiction between the polyphonic linear system and the heard result, which is surface or mass. This contradiction inherent in polyphony will disappear when the independence of sounds is total. In fact, when linear combinations and their polyphonic superpositions no longer operate, what will count will be the statistical mean of isolated states and of transformations of sonic components at a given moment. The macroscopic effect can then be controlled by the mean of the movements of elements which we select. The result is the introduction of the notion of probability, which implies, in this particular case, combinatory calculus. Here, in a few words, is the possible escape route from the "linear category" in musical thought.[2]

This article served as a bridge to my introduction of mathematics in music. For if, thanks to complexity, the strict, deterministic causality which the neoserialists postulated was lost, then it was necessary to replace it by a more general causality, by a probabilistic logic which would contain strict serial causality as a particular case. This is the function of stochastic science. "Stochastics" studies and formulates the law of large numbers, which has already been mentioned, the laws of rare events, the different aleatory procedures, etc. As a result of the impasse in serial music, as well as other causes, I originated in 1954 a music constructed from the principle of indeterminism; two years later I named it "Stochastic Music." The laws of the calculus of probabilities entered composition through musical necessity.

But other paths also led to the same stochastic crossroads—first of all, natural events such as the collision of hail or rain with hard surfaces, or the song of cicadas in a summer field. These sonic events are made out of thousands of isolated sounds; this multitude of sounds, seen as a totality, is a new sonic event. This mass event is articulated and forms a plastic mold of time, which itself follows aleatory and stochastic laws. If one then wishes to form a large mass of point-notes, such as string pizzicati, one must know these mathematical laws, which, in any case, are no more than a tight and concise expression of a chain of logical reasoning. Everyone has observed the sonic phenomena of a political crowd of dozens or hundreds of thousands of people. The human river shouts a slogan in a uniform rhythm. Then another slogan springs from the head of

---

2. I. Xenakis, *Gravesaner Blätter*, no. 1 (1955). [Au.]

the demonstration; it spreads towards the tail, replacing the first. A wave of transition thus passes from the head to the tail. The clamor fills the city, and the inhibiting force of voice and rhythm reaches a climax. It is an event of great power and beauty in its ferocity. Then the impact between the demonstrators and the enemy occurs. The perfect rhythm of the last slogan breaks up in a huge cluster of chaotic shouts, which also spreads to the tail. Imagine, in addition, the reports of dozens of machine guns and the whistle of bullets adding their punctuations to this total disorder. The crowd is then rapidly dispersed, and after sonic and visual hell follows a detonating calm, full of despair, dust, and death. The statistical laws of these events, separated from their political or moral context, are the same as those of the cicadas or the rain. They are the laws of the passage from complete order to total disorder in a continuous or explosive manner. They are stochastic laws.

Here we touch on one of the great problems that have haunted human intelligence since antiquity: continuous or discontinuous transformation. The sophisms of movement (e.g., Achilles and the tortoise) or of definition (e.g., baldness), especially the latter, are solved by statistical definition; that is to say, by stochastics. One may produce continuity with either continuous or discontinuous elements. A multitude of short glissandi on strings can give the impression of continuity, and so can a multitude of pizzicati. Passages from a discontinuous state to a continuous state are controllable with the aid of probability theory. For some time now I have been conducting these fascinating experiments in instrumental works; but the mathematical character of this music has frightened musicians and has made the approach especially difficult.

Here is another direction that converges on indeterminism. The study of the variation of rhythm poses the problem of knowing what the limit of total asymmetry is, and of the consequent complete disruption of causality among durations. The sounds of a Geiger counter in the proximity of a radioactive source give an impressive idea of this. Stochastics provides the necessary laws.

Before ending this short inspection tour of events rich in the new logic, which were closed to the understanding until recently, I would like to include a short parenthesis. If glissandi are long and sufficiently interlaced, we obtain sonic spaces of continuous evolution. It is possible to produce ruled surfaces by drawing the glissandi as straight lines. I performed this experiment with *Metastasis* (this work had its premiere in 1955 at Donaueschingen). Several years later, when the architect Le Corbusier, whose collaborator I was, asked me to suggest a design for the architecture of the Philips Pavilion in Brussels, my inspiration was pin-pointed by the experiment with *Metastasis*. Thus I believe that on this occasion music and architecture found an intimate connection.[3]

• • • • •

3. I. Xenakis, *Revue technique Philips*, vol. 20, no. 1 (1958), and Le Corbusier, *Modulor 2* (Boulogne-Seine: Architecture d'Aujourd'hui, 1955). [Au.]

184 György Ligeti

György Ligeti (b. 1926) left his native Hungary following the 1956 Revolution there and settled in Western Europe, where he became closely associated with Karlheinz Stockhausen and other composers of the integral serialist movement. This article dates from 1960, when the serialists were beginning to move in new directions, bringing them somewhat closer to such composers as Iannis Xenakis and John Cage. Ligeti discusses the emergence of a "general new feeling for musical form," less beholden to determinacy and automatism. He sees this development as following inevitably from the negative effects of serialism itself, such as its tendencies to neutralize musical content, subvert hierarchical connections, undermine metrical regularity, and increase "entropy," thereby lowering the degree of perceptible contrast. Ligeti notes that serial composers are consequently turning away from their earlier obsession with matters of detail to focus more on issues of overall musical structure and perceptible effect. Though strict determinacy is not entirely abandoned, it is applied to "global categories" and general planning, leaving the composers more freedom in working out individual details.

FROM Metamorphoses of Musical Form
(1960)

A general new feeling for musical form seems to be emerging, despite the not inconsiderable idiomatic differences in the works of the various "serial" composers. It is irrelevant to consider whether this is the result of research into the serial ordering of the musical material, or whether the serial manipulations are themselves the consequence of the new idea of form. Technique and imagination influence one another in a constant interchange. Every artistic innovation in the craft of composition ferments the whole spiritual edifice, and every change in this edifice demands constant revision of compositional procedure.

Relations of this sort have always urged us on to metamorphoses in the way we work. The modifications of pitch, once seemingly insignificant, in the modal framework—at first a mere sharpening of individual leading-notes—led to the formation of functional harmony, together with the whole architecture of periodic forms and their specific world of expression. In the craft of com-

TEXT: *Die Reihe*, ed. by Karlheinz Stockhausen and Herbert Eimert, trans. Cornelius Cardew (Bryn Mawr: Theodore Presser, 1965) 7, pp. 5–11. This reference and all others below to *Die Reihe* pertain to the English-language edition. © copyright 1965 by Universal Edition A. G. Wien. © copyright renewed. All Rights Reserved. Used by permission of European American Music Distributors Corporation, Sole U. S. and Canadian agent for Universal Edition A. G. Wien.

position this process led to techniques of modulation and development that undermined and finally ruined the periodic forms themselves, and the leading note—which had spawned the tonal system—then condemned it to extinction by annexing to itself more and more of the harmonic and melodic activity.

But the newly installed chromatic republic stood in need of its own legislation. The which having been supplied by Schönberg's "composition with twelve notes related only to one another," the serial principle—originally set up only for the dimension of pitches—sought to spread itself over the totality of form. This led to the discrete quantification of all parameters, and the music became a product of superpositions of prefabricated arrangements. In this way the musical structure acquired a "pointillistic" character.

Hard on the heels of the serial organization of durations, intensities and timbres, came the expansion of the method to cover more global categories like relationships of register and density, distribution of various types of movement and structure, and also the proportionalization of the whole formal sequence. Considerable adjustments in compositional planning now came into play: as the larger form-categories came under serial control, the serial ordering of the elementary parameters became looser and looser. A strict determination of these took second place in the total composition, and this again put a new complexion on the form: the concept of "pointillism" was extended to embrace "statistical fields."[1]

The serial arrangement of pitches, which had initiated the whole process, was the first thing sacrificed in this shift of emphasis.[2] Disintegration had set in here even before the "statistical" phase of serial technique, in fact during the period of composition with series of fixed elements.

Within this disintegration we can distinguish various "destruction-types," as follows:

1. The individual character of the various serial arrangements fades as a result of the superposition of several horizontal series, in which, wherever possible, common notes occur at the same pitch. Such interweaving obscures the single serial threads (especially when all the parts are played on one instrument), and the resulting intervals have little or nothing to do with the original arrangement. Where such a procedure is coupled with series of durations the composer can hardly even retain an influence over the intervals that are to result, let alone determine them. They follow automatically from the type of procedure. In this way the pitch series loses its last remnant of function, paralysed by the emerging complex. This situation is especially typical for the early

1. Cf. K. Stockhausen ". . . how time passes . . ." *Die Reihe* 3, p. 10. [Au.]
2. Cf. Luciano Berio: "Aspetti di artigianato formale," *Incontri Musicali* 1 (Milan 1956), p. 62. Berio writes expressly of the "superamento della sensazione di serie di altezze focali e di intervallo a favore di una sensazione di qualità sonore e di registro, considerando questi ultimi gli elementi attivi e determinanti della struttura formale." [Au.] The Italian quote reads: "the supression of a sensation of discrete scale degrees and intervals in favor of a sensation of sonic quality and register, these last two being considered the active and determining elements of the formal structure."

stages of integral-serial composition, particularly for the case of composers—Boulez amongst others—who tend to think in terms of horizontal layers.[3]

Self-propagating automatisms of this kind evince a relation of indeterminacy, and the structural contexts are of necessity subject to this. For the degree of indeterminacy of the structure increases in proportion to the number of directives that are issued, and vice versa: in proportion as a composer worries about determining the result, he finds he can determine less and less about the order and relationships of the elements. It is essential to recognize this contradiction, if one is not to be entirely at the mercy of the arbitrary dictates of compositional "craftsmanship," for it has its roots deep in the peculiar nature of the serial conception of musical material. When this is recognized, it is of course a personal matter for the composer how he regards the situation: should he allow the form to follow from pre-stabilized elements and schemes of organization, fully aware of the risk he runs of virtually allowing the result to slip through his fingers? Or should he take the other path and progress from a total vision into particularities, accepting as part of the bargain the fact that he will have to sacrifice any number of attractive and, in themselves, logically developed details?

2. The character of pitch-series is weakened by the increasing preference for homogeneous sequences of intervals, particularly the chromatic scale. Stockhausen in his "Klavierstück 2," for example, instead of a fixed 12-note series, uses various permutations of the notes of sections of the chromatic scale.[4] The basis of Nono's "Il canto sospeso" is the series A, B-flat, A-flat, B, G, C, F-sharp, C-sharp, F, D, E, E-flat. At first glance this poses as an all-interval series, but it can be seen to consist of an interpolation of two sequences of semitones in contrary motion.[5] Finally, in his "Cori di Didone," Nono has chosen the chromatic scale itself for his raw material; this is really no longer a series but simply a regulator to ensure an even distribution of the 12 notes. The vertical disposition of this material results in a piling up of neighbouring tones. It is no longer primarily the intervals that constitute the structure but relations of density, distribution of registers and various displacements in the building up and breaking down of the vertical complexes. From the point of view of "traditional" 12-note composition, this technique would doubtless be regarded as an impoverishment. But seen in the light of the requirements of integral-serial composition, this accusation misses fire. Nono's attention is concentrated mainly on the construction and dismantling of piles of layers (which represents in a way a macroscopic projection of attack and decay processes that are not usually analysable by the human ear), and in this context a pitch-series, however artfully constructed, would have been no use to him at all—it would have gone astray and succumbed in a network of structures such as these.

3. Cf. G. Ligeti: "Pierre Boulez—Decision and Automatism in Structure Ia," *Die Reihe* 4, p. 36ff. [Au.]

4. See L. Nono: "Zur Entwicklung der Serientechnik," *Gravesaner Blätter,* vol . 4 (1956), pp. 17–18. [Au.]

5. Cf. U. Unger: "Luigi Nono," *Die Reihe* 4, p. 12. A transposition of the same series serves as the basis of the "Varianti." (Cf. R. Kolisch: "Nono's 'Varianti,'" *Melos,* October 1957, p. 292ff.) [Au.]

3. The succession of notes becomes subject to a higher ruling, which has the prerogative of altering—to a greater or lesser degree—the original series of pitches. This state of affairs can be observed in Stockhausen's "Gruppen für drei Orchester." In this composition, the individual groups are characterized in various ways, among others by the specific ambitus of the sounds involved. The limits of the ambitus in each case are determined by a higher order series. The ambitus is a feature of the group as a whole, whereas the succession of pitches is executed discretely with the entry of each note; consequently the requirements of the pitch series are compelled to accommodate themselves to the larger, more comprehensive order. If the ambitus in question covers an octave or some larger span, the 12-note series is of course not threatened, because only the registers of the notes are influenced. But if a group is required to fit into a span of less than an octave, then the series suffers a compression; its elements tend towards identity with each other in proportion as the span is narrower. The original series can, it is true, be retained in its proportions if electronic means of sound-production are employed, or if intervals smaller than a semitone are available (as they are with instruments of the string family). But with even temperament (the division of the octave into twelve equal parts) the original series is inevitably destroyed.

4. The function of the pitch-series is grafted on to other parameters. For example, in Pousseur's Quintet for clarinet, bass clarinet, piano, violin, and cello, the basic 12-note series—borrowed from Webern's Saxophone quartet Op 22 in homage—is shorn of its function simply by filling out each interval chromatically. The pitch-series has been transformed into a series of densities.[6]

5. Any pre-formation of pitches is completely abandoned in favour of serial depositions of a higher order. Among other things, this step enables us to re-assert our sovereignty over intervallic relationships. This can be observed in Koenig's Wind Quintet, for instance. However paradoxical this state of affairs may seem, it is logical: the 12-note method, created for the purpose of allowing a compositional control over the intervals, has to be liquidated in order that the same control can be exercised in the changed situation.

Taken as a whole, this tendency (outlined in the above points) leads to an erosion of any intervallic profile. (The possibility mentioned in point 5 is an exception). Sequences of notes and vertical complexes of notes are for the most part indifferent in respect of the intervals of which they are composed. Concepts of "consonance" and "dissonance" can no longer be applied: tension and relaxation are surrendered to the statistical properties of form, e.g. relationships of register, the density and weave of the structure.[7]

Pousseur documents the growing impediment of the intervallic function by regarding major sevenths and minor ninths not as fixed relationships of pitch

6. See H. Pousseur: "Outline of a Method," *Die Reihe* 3, p. 50ff. [Au.]

7. The tendency towards melodic and harmonic indifference has its roots firmly planted in "traditional" twelve-note composition. See T. W. Adorno: *Philosophie der neuen Musik* (Tübingen, 1949), p. 49ff. [Au.]

but as "impure octaves."[8] Note that the octave is taken as the comparative measure.[9] In the midst of the general erosion this interval seems the least affected. In any case, our sensibility regarding the octave is rather negative; the interval is generally shunned—a well-developed idiosyncrasy even in the days of traditional twelve-note composition.[10] There are several reasons for this: on the one hand, the discrepancy between the melodic breadth and reach of the octave and its high degree of harmonic fusibility—i.e. its lack of harmonic tension—is disturbing, and on the other hand the octave's overt relationship of overtone to fundamental advertises too plainly a tonal and hierarchical connection, and this makes it appear a foreign body in a context that is not tonal.[11]

Sensitiveness on this point leads to the practice of fixing the register of individual recurring tones, and preferring unisons to octaves. Despite its close relationship to the octave, the prime position (unison) has completely different properties: it is free of the contradiction we mentioned between the harmonic and melodic dimension, and is free of tension in both directions; and because in itself the unison presents no overtone-relationships—apart from the spectra necessarily produced by specific instruments—it cannot be suspected of defaulting back into the tonal sphere.

In dense textures we are not so allergic to the octave; progressively less so as the texture becomes more and more difficult to "hear through" (in the sense undergrowth is difficult to "see through"). In a particularly complex pile-up it is hardly possible to distinguish the individual intervals; octaves cannot be recognized as an individual shape, and consequently no longer disturb us. This explains the use of octaves in the denser passages of Stockhausen's "Gruppen," to take a familiar example.

Our decreasing sensitivity to intervals gives rise to a condition which, for want of a better word, we may call "permeability." This means that structures of different textures can run concurrently, penetrate each other and even merge into one another completely, whereby the horizontal and vertical density-relationships are altered, it is true, but it is a matter of indifference which intervals coincide in the thick of the fray.

Permeability has not in the past exerted any great influence on form; nevertheless it was not entirely unknown in earlier musical styles.

Palestrina's music had perhaps the lowest degree of permeability; simultaneous parts had to fit into each other in a manner prescribed by unequivocal laws. The high-degree determination of the various possibilities of combining intervals would not tolerate the slightest confusion in the structure, and as a

8. Cf. Pousseur, loc. cit., p. 54, and G. M. Koenig: "Henri Pousseur," *Die Reihe* 4, p. 23f. [Au.]

9. The octave performs this special role already in Webern's music. H. Eimert points out that "Webern achieves spatial tension by, so to speak, knocking in his acoustic objects right at the edge of the octave-gaps." ("A Change of Focus," *Die Reihe* 2, p. 34.) [Au.]

10. See H. Jelinek: *Anleitung zur Zwölftonkomposition* I (Vienna 1952), p. 47ff. [Au.]

11. Works in which the octave plays an important part in the construction, as in *Nones* by Berio, do not weaken this assertion. The use of octaves is legitimized by overemphasizing their role (Cf. P. Santi: "Luciano Berio," *Die Reihe* 4, p. 99.) [Au.]

consequence of this the handling of consonance and dissonance was most sensitive in that school.[12]

The tonal music following this was also fairly impermeable, although much less than the harmony books intended for school use would have us believe. It is well known that the hierarchy of functional harmony permitted a certain freedom in the treatment of passing notes and suspensions occurring simultaneously since, as a consequence of cadential connexions, the attention was directed more towards the role of these subsidiary notes in relation to the harmony notes. Particularly where simultaneous parts are strongly contrasted in timbre—as voices and instruments, strings and wind, solo instrument and accompaniment—the music can well tolerate small harmonic impurities, and slight delays and anticipations in time. In such cases the intervals relinquish some of their sensitivity about conflicting with each other; the higher order regulator is more important, i.e. the functional progression of the harmony. This permeability increases considerably in more complex structures; there are places in Bach—in the Brandenburgs, notably the first Brandenburg, and in many choral works with instrumental accompaniment that is rich in figuration—where the functional interval-relationships are retained, but where the individuality of many single intervals is lost in the general harmonic field of the complex figurative texture.

This is only one of many historical examples. Similar points could be made with reference to the medieval motet composers, the heterophonic folk music of certain areas, the music of non-European cultures, the music of Debussy, and many other spheres.

Of necessity, serial structures possess a different sort of permeability; the historical state of the material is after all a different one. Statistical-serial regulation is however slightly reminiscent of traditional systems of control, as for instance the system of figured basses.

The high degree of permeability of many serial structures has decisive formal consequences:

1. It makes possible the mobility of individual shapes—this mobility is in direct proportion to the size of the field in question—and this effects a loosening of the temporal flow. For its part, this loosening now permits the simultaneous control of activity in various different tempi, as in Stockhausen's "Zeitmasse" for five wind instruments.

2. The interpenetration of different structures gave rise to those specific forms that are concerned with the superposition of several layers that are different in quality. In electronic compositions such a method of construction is inspired by the technical conditions of the process of realization, i.e. the necessary procedure of producing individual contexts first and later synchronizing them. However, even the instrumental works of almost all serial composers show a tendency towards "layer-composition". The overlapping groups in

---

12. See K. Jeppesen: *The Style of Palestrina and the Dissonance* (2nd ed., London, 1946). [Au.]

Stockhausen's cited work for three orchestras[13] and many of Pousseur's methods[14] are examples chosen at random from a varied host. Koenig's 'Zwei Klavierstücke' are an example of the purest layer-composition; the form is completely ruled by this procedure. Separate layers of various different types of configuration are pressed together into a simultaneous activity, smelted together as it were by the uniform timbre of the piano. The final form is thus a product of interferences amongst the originally heterogeneous shapes. This method of work is related to that of weaving simultaneous series together, as, for example, in Boulez's "Structures." In this latter case, however, the individual layers were simply single horizontal threads of notes, whereas in the Koenig piece it is a matter of complex prefabricated textures, folded into each other according to a higher order plan.

High permeability and insensibility to intervals are even more essential features of the music of Cage and his circle, although this music proceeds from quite different points of departure. Cage has written pieces which can be played either on their own or together with other pieces. The separate pieces of music thus become layers of a larger whole, which, though more dense than its constituent parts, is yet not different in principle. The indifference of such structures—which are the result of chance manipulations—is closely related to the indifference of the automatic products of early serial music.

This indifference shows a tendency to spread beyond interval relationships to other musical dimensions. Now that hierarchical connections have been destroyed, regular metrical pulsations dispensed with, and durations, degrees of loudness, and timbres have been turned over to the tender mercies of serial distribution, it becomes increasingly difficult to achieve contrast. A flattening-out process has begun to absorb the whole musical form. The more integral the preformation of serial connections, the greater the entropy of the resulting structures; for—in accordance with the relation of indeterminacy mentioned earlier—the result of knitting together separate chains of connexions falls victim to automatism, in proportion to the degree of predetermination.

Let us take an illuminating analogy: playing with plasticine. The distinct lumps of the various colors gradually become dispersed the more you knead the stuff; the result is a conglomeration in which patches of the colors can still be distinguished, whereas the whole is characterized by lack of contrast. Knead on, and the little patches of color disappear in their turn, and give place to a uniform gray. This flattening-out process cannot be reversed. Similar symptoms can be discerned in elementary serial compositions. The postulation of series means, here, that each element should be used with equal frequency and should be given equal importance. This leads irresistably to an increase of entropy. The finer the network of operations with pre-ordered material, the

---

13. Cf. Stockhausen, loc. cit., p. 24. [Au.]
14. The reader's attention is drawn to Pousseur's remarks (in the article already quoted) about "Polyphonic density" as one of the compositional parameters. His *Quintett* is conceived almost entirely in layers. (Cf. loc. cit., p. 52.) [Au.]

higher the degree of levelling-out in the result. Total, consistent application of the serial principle negates, in the end, serialism itself. There is really no basic difference between the results of automatism and the products of chance; total determinacy comes to be identical with total indeterminacy. This is the place to seek the parallelism (mentioned earlier) between integral-serial music and music governed by chance (John Cage). The following is characteristic of both types: pause—event—pause—event—pause, etc.;[15] naturally the events are variously structured and the pauses have different durations but the more differentiated the individual events and caesuras, the more evident becomes the levelling-out process in the result. This is a consequence of the fact that increased differentiation in the separate moments is only possible at the expense of the differentiation of the whole.

At the same time however there are tendencies at work in opposition to the levelling-out process that we have been describing. They result from the dissolution of the elementary serial organizations, which stands in direct and mutual relation to the levelling-out process. The primitive stage to which composition is relegated by automatism will only be supported by musicians who succumb to the fetish of total integration, and debase musical form to a simple arithmetical game, thus preparing the way for an imitative academicism that is certainly no better than the traditional sort. Adorno's negative diagnosis may well apply to such musicians (but not to the élite who pursue their thoughts further).[16]

It is only possible to take adequate measures against the levelling-out process when predetermination and chance are kept within bounds, i.e. when the highest possible degree of order is sought by means of decisions made by the composer in the process of composition. This is the only way in which a composer can work out individual, unconfused characters, and write music that is not content with the cheap function of being a more or less pleasant wallpaper-pattern in sound.

The possibilities of organizing such an order and defining such musical characters are available where the weight of serial composition has been shifted onto the global categories that we mentioned earlier. The total form is serially guided, but the individual moments are, within given limits, left to the composer's discretion.[17] "Musical office-work"[18] is thus thrust back into its proper place, where it fulfils its function in general planning. It ensures a control of the emerging form in its general shape, but raises no claims to being the work

15. However it is perhaps noteworthy that the pauses in Cage's music are generally longer than those in serial structures. [Au.]

16. See Adorno, "Das Altern der Neuen Musik" (The aging of new music), which appeared in the book *Dissonanzen* (Göttingen, 1956), p. 102ff. [Au.]

17. Several composers have given expression to these ideas in their theoretical articles, and despite their differences in orientation, they show remarkable unanimity. See the quoted articles by Stockhausen and Pousseur in *Die Reihe* 3, and also "Alea" by Boulez, which appeared in the *Darmstädter Beiträger zur neuen Musik* (Mainz, 1958), p. 44ff. [Au.]

18. We are indebted to Antoine Goléa for this term. [Au.]

itself. The formal function of this sort of serial "programming"[19] corresponds approximately to the modulations, cadential progressions and connected methods of articulation in tonal music. But here the planning is non-centralized and non-hierarchical (as opposed to the case of tonal music) and the controlling directives enjoy equal rights and even distribution in the determination of the form. The network of serial connections stands in the same relation to the form as do the genes in the chromosomes to the emerging organism.

When such a procedure is adopted, the compositional labor divides into two successive phases:

1. Serial preformation of the global determining factors.
2. Filling out by detailed decisions the network of possibilities that is the result of the first phase.[20] The desired characters can be worked out by postulating or avoiding certain specific constellations.[21]

A form conceived in this way, free of the rigid static quality of automatic products, can be handled with great flexibility, and this makes possible the composition of transitions. An example: in his "Gruppen" Stockhausen was in a position to compose, besides passages of homogeneous instrumentation— passages for strings alone, brass alone, percussion alone—passages of various degrees and mixtures, in which the transition from one dominant timbre to another was never a linear transition but always a transition proceeding by serial dosages. Stockhausen succeeded—with his specific ranges or ambituses, his statistical mobility-resultants and his group-densities—in typically characterizing the individual regions of his composition. These typical characteristics counteracted the otherwise general effect of the pulverization of the durations and thus maintained and articulated the form.

•   •   •   •   •

19. H. Eimert, "The composer's freedom of choice," *Die Reihe* 3, p. 7. [Au.]
20. Cf. Pousseur, loc. cit., p. 67, second paragraph. [Au.]
21. This idea is similar to one developed by Boulez in his article "Alea." However I cannot agree with his intention of making the network of possibilities submit to a method of "guided chance." Any latitude achieved by the loosening of the network should not be thrown open to chance but submitted to further ordered decisions, as I said before, with the aim of reducing the entropy of the structure to a relative minimum. It is a deceptive fallacy that the design of the resulting form can be left to the interpreter in the form of "freedom"—as is the case for example in Stockhausen's "Klavierstück XI" and Boulez's Third Piano Sonata. The interpreter is given a set of more or less finished building blocks and finds himself in a confusing position: he is supposed to be helping with the composition, but cannot escape from the circle of possible permutations that has been circumscribed by the composer. All possible "interpretations" have in fact been envisaged by the composer—and if not, then so much the worse for the overall form. In any case there is no genuine freedom of interpretation, simply a manifold *ossia* form (however much Boulez would like to defend himself against this view in his article). [Au.]

185 Steve Reich

Steve Reich (b. 1934) was a pioneer in the minimalist movement, which began in the 1960s. Minimalism marked a departure not only from the extremes of integral serialism and indeterminacy, but also from the sort of compositional complexities associated with composers such as Iannis Xenakis; and it proved to be greatly influential on subsequent musical developments. In the first of these two articles, which were written in 1968 and 1973, Reich advocates a process-oriented music that proceeds, like serial music, more or less automatically once it is set in motion while limiting itself to processes that transform the materials (in Reich's case, relatively simple diatonic patterns) in easily perceptible ways. The second essay reveals Reich's discomfort with contemporary musical specialization. Reflecting upon his dual status as composer and performer, he discusses the relationship of his work to the small ensemble for which it was then written and in which he himself performed, and to his fellow musicians, who played such a vital role in shaping that music.

FROM *Writings about Music*

MUSIC AS A GRADUAL PROCESS
(1968)

I do not mean the process of composition, but rather pieces of music that are, literally, processes.

The distinctive thing about musical processes is that they determine all the note-to-note (sound-to-sound) details and the over all form simultaneously. (Think of a round or infinite canon.)

I am interested in perceptible processes. I want to be able to hear the process happening throughout the sounding music.

To facilitate closely detailed listening a musical process should happen extremely gradually.

Performing and listening to a gradual musical process resembles:

> pulling back a swing, releasing it, and observing it gradually come to rest;
> turning over an hour glass and watching the sand slowly run through to the bottom;
> placing your feet in the sand by the ocean's edge and watching, feeling, and listening to the waves gradually bury them.

TEXT: *Writings about Music* (New York: New York University Press, 1974), pp. 9–11, 45–48.

Though I may have the pleasure of discovering musical processes and composing the musical material to run through them, once the process is set up and loaded it runs by itself.

Material may suggest what sort of process it should be run through (content suggests form), and processes may suggest what sort of material should be run through them (form suggests content). If the shoe fits, wear it.

As to whether a musical process is realized through live human performance or through some electro-mechanical means is not finally the main issue. One of the most beautiful concerts I ever heard consisted of four composers playing their tapes in a dark hall. (A tape is interesting when it's an interesting tape.)

It is quite natural to think about musical processes if one is frequently working with electro-mechanical sound equipment. All music turns out to be ethnic music.

Musical processes can give one a direct contact with the impersonal and also a kind of complete control, and one doesn't always think of the impersonal and complete control as going together. By "a kind" of complete control I mean that by running this material through this process I completely control all that results, but also that I accept all that results without changes.

John Cage has used processes and has certainly accepted their results, but the processes he used were compositional ones that could not be heard when the piece was performed. The process of using the *I Ching* or imperfections in a sheet of paper to determine musical parameters can't be heard when listening to music composed that way. The compositional processes and the sounding music have no audible connection. Similarly in serial music, the series itself is seldom audible. (This is a basic difference between serial (basically European) music and serial (basically American) art, where the perceived series is usually the focal point of the work.)

What I'm interested in is a compositional process and a sounding music that are one and the same thing.

James Tenney said in conversation, "then the composer isn't privy to anything." I don't know any secrets of structure that you can't hear. We all listen to the process together since it's quite audible, and one of the reasons it's quite audible is, because it's happening extremely gradually.

The use of hidden structural devices in music never appealed to me. Even when all the cards are on the table and everyone hears what is gradually happening in a musical process, there are still enough mysteries to satisfy all. These mysteries are the impersonal, unintended, psycho-acoustic by-products of the intended process. These might include sub-melodies heard within repeated melodic patterns, stereophonic effects due to listener location, slight irregularities in performance, harmonics, difference tones, etc.

Listening to an extremely gradual musical process opens my ears to *it,* but *it* always extends farther than I can hear, and that makes it interesting to listen to that musical process again. That area of every gradual (completely controlled) musical process, where one hears the details of the sound moving out away from intentions, occuring for their own acoustic reasons, is *it*.

I begin to perceive these minute details when I can sustain close attention and a gradual process invites my sustained attention. By "gradual" I mean extremely gradual; a process happening so slowly and gradually that listening to it resembles watching a minute hand on a watch—you can perceive it moving after you stay with it a little while.

Several currently popular modal musics like Indian classical and drug oriented rock and roll may make us aware of minute sound details because in being modal (constant key center, hypnotically droning and repetitious) they naturally focus on these details rather than on key modulation, counterpoint and other peculiarly Western devices. Nevertheless, these modal musics remain more or less strict frameworks for improvisation. They are not processes.

The distinctive thing about musical processes is that they determine all the note-to-note details and the over all form simultaneously. One can't improvise in a musical process—the concepts are mutually exclusive.

While performing and listening to gradual musical processes one can participate in a particular liberating and impersonal kind of ritual. Focusing in on the musical process makes possible that shift of attention away from *he* and *she* and *you* and *me* outwards towards *it*.

NOTES ON THE ENSEMBLE
(1973)

Since late in 1966 I have been rehearsing and performing my music with my own ensemble.

In 1963 I first decided that despite my limitations as a performer I had to play in all my compositions. It seemed clear that a healthy musical situation would only result when the functions of composer and performer were united.

In San Francisco in 1963 I formed my first ensemble which was devoted to free, and sometimes controlled, improvisation. This quintet met at least once a week for about six months, but because we were improvising on nothing but spur of the moment reactions I felt there was not any musical growth except when I brought in what I called *Pitch Charts*, which gave all players the same notes to play at the same time, but with free rhythm. Even with these charts the musical growth was much too limited, and the group was disbanded.

In the fall of 1965 I returned to New York, and by late in 1966 I had formed a group of three musicians; pianist Art Murphy, woodwind player Jon Gibson, and myself playing piano. This ensemble was able to perform *Piano Phase* for two pianos; *Improvisations on a Watermelon* for two pianos (later discarded); *Reed Phase* for soprano saxophone and tape (later discarded), and several tape pieces. This trio remained intact with occasional additions, notably that of composer/pianist James Tenney in 1967 to play a four piano version of *Piano Phase* and other pieces, until 1970 when the composition of *Phase Patterns* for four electric organs, and *Four Organs* for four electric organs and maracas created the need for a quintet adding pianist Steve Chambers and occasionally, composer/performer Phil Glass. In 1971, with the composition of *Drumming,* the ensemble underwent a significant expansion to twelve musicians and singers. At this time I sought out and found a number of fine percussionists, the most outstanding of whom, Russ Hartenberger and James Preiss, continue to play in the present ensemble. Also, and for the first time, I had to find singers who had the sense of time, intonation, and timbre necessary to blend in with the sound of the marimbas in *Drumming.* Joan LaBarbara and Jay Clayton proved to be perfectly suited to this new vocal style. It was in 1971 that the name of the ensemble, *Steve Reich and Musicians,* was first adopted.

I have thus become a composer with a repertory ensemble. Each new composition is added to the repertoire and our concerts present a selection of new and/or older works.

The question often arises as to what contribution the performers make to the music. The answer is that they select the resulting patterns in all compositions that have resulting patterns, and that certain details of the music are worked out by members of the ensemble during rehearsals. Resulting patterns are melodic patterns that result from the combination of two or more identical instruments playing the same repeating melodic pattern one or more beats out of phase with each other. During the selection of resulting patterns to be sung in the second section of *Drumming,* Joan LaBarbara, Jay Clayton, Judy Sherman and I all contributed various patterns we heard resulting from the combination of the three marimbas. These patterns were selected, and an order for singing them worked out, with the help of tape loops of the various marimba combinations played over and over again at my studio during rehearsals held throughout the summer of 1971. Similarly, in the resulting patterns for *Six Pianos,* Steve Chambers, James Preiss and I worked out the resulting patterns and the order in which to play them during rehearsals at the Baldwin Piano store during the fall and winter of 1972–73.

During the summer of 1973 in Seattle I worked with different singers in the marimba section of *Drumming* who heard and sang very different resulting patterns from the singers in New York. When I returned to New York I showed the new resulting patterns to Jay Clayton and Joan LaBarbara who decided to incorporate some of these patterns into their own version. The details of the music changed when the performers changed.

Selecting resulting patterns is not improvising; it is actually filling in the details of the composition itself. It offers the performer the opportunity to listen to minute details and to sing or play the ones he or she finds most musical.

There's a certain idea that's been in the air, particularly since the 1960's, and it's been used by choreographers as well as composers and I think it is an extremely misleading idea. It is that the only pleasure a performer (be it musician or dancer) could get was to improvise, or in some way be free to express his or her momentary state of mind. If anybody gave them a fixed musical score or specific instructions to work with this was equated with political control and it meant the performer was going to be unhappy about it. John Cage has said that a composer is somebody who tells other people what to do, and that it is not a good social situation to do that. But if you know and work with musicians you will see that what gives them joy is playing music they love, or at least find musically interesting, and whether that music is improvised or completely worked out is really not the main issue. The main issue is what's happening *musically;* is this beautiful, is this sending chills up and down my spine, or isn't it?

The musicians play in this ensemble, usually for periods of three to five years or more, because, presumably, they like playing the music, or at least because they find it of some musical interest. They do not make all their income from playing in this ensemble. Some are Doctoral candidates in the study of African, Indonesian and Indian music, some teach percussion, and all perform professionally in a variety of musical ensembles including orchestras, chamber groups, Medieval music ensembles, South Indian, African and Indonesian classical ensembles, free improvisation and jazz groups. It is precisely the sort of musician who starts with a strong Western classical background and then later gravitates towards these other types of music that I find ideally suited for this ensemble.

The presence of musicians who play certain instruments or sing encourages me to write more music for those instruments or voices. The percussionists and singers I began working with in *Drumming* encouraged me to write more percussion and vocal music. *Music for Mallet Instruments, Voices and Organ* is one of the results. Since the keyboard music I write involves up and down movements of the hands exclusively, instead of conventional keyboard technique, percussionists are better suited to play pieces like *Six Pianos* than most pianists are. Most of the musicians in my ensemble are therefore percussionists who double on the keyboard.

These musicians are also my first and most important critics. During early rehearsals when a first version of a new piece is being tried out, the reactions of the players will often tell me whether the new composition really works, or not. Not only direct verbal comments during or after rehearsal, but an appreciative laugh or an embarrassed averted glance may be enough to let me know I am on the right or wrong track. This was particularly the case in the early fall of 1972 when the reactions of James Preiss, Russell Hartenberger and Steve Chambers were enough to make me throw away several attempts at multiple piano pieces that preceded the finished version of *Six Pianos.*

There is also the question of frequency of rehearsals. Most new pieces of about 20 minutes in length will be rehearsed once or twice a week for two or three months. *Drumming,* which lasts about an hour and twenty minutes took almost a year of weekly rehearsals. This amount of rehearsing allows for many small compositional changes while the work is in progress and at the same time builds a kind of ensemble solidity that makes playing together a joy.

MUSIC, SOCIETY, POLITICS

186 Kurt Weill

The changes in musical language that occurred in the early years of the twentieth century also raised basic questions about the social responsibilities of music: for whom and what purpose was new music to be written? This became particularly evident in the period following the First World War. One of the first "classical" composers who attempted to address a larger and more diverse public was the German Kurt Weill (1900–1950). In the 1920s he abandoned the more traditionally modernist approach of his younger years to write theater works of social commitment that drew heavily upon popular and vernacular traditions. In this article, written in 1927, he stresses the need for music to assume a social function, urging composers to address larger audiences and explore outlets extending beyond the traditional concert hall. Turning from the "individualistic principle" of previous Western art music, Weill considers modes of artistic collaboration and the possibility of developing an epic form of music better able to affect public opinion.

Shifts in Musical Production
(1927)

If I am to address the question of the current musical situation from the point of view of the creative musician, then I must restrict myself to considering that situation as it relates to the state of development in my own production.

The development of music in recent years has chiefly been an aesthetic one. The emancipation from the 19th century, the opposition to extra-musical influences (programme music, symbolism, realism), the return to absolute music, the hard-won acquisition of new expressive means (the enrichment of harmonic language, the cultivation of a new linearity) or an expansion of the old means—these were the ideas which claimed musicians' attention. Today we have come a step further. A clear split is becoming apparent between, on the one hand, those musicians who, full of disdain for their audience, continue as it were by shutting out the public sphere to work on the solution to aesthetic problems and, on the other, those who enter into contact with some sort of audience, integrating their work into some sort of larger concern, because they see that above the artistic there is also a common human attitude that springs from some sense of communal belonging and which has to be the determining factor behind the genesis of a work of art.

It is clear that this withdrawal from the individualistic principle of art, observable everywhere, has nowhere emerged with such eruptive force as in

TEXT: *Musik und Theater: Gesammelte Schriften*, ed. by Stephen Hinton and Jürgen Schebera (Berlin: Hemschelverlag, 1990), pp. 45–47. Translation by Stephen Hinton. Used by permission of the Kurt Weill Foundation.

Germany, where the foregoing development (the influence of the 19th century and the violent emancipation from it) was much more intense. While the search for a community is, for us, by no means to be confused with any concession to public taste, a large number of musicians from Latin countries are thoroughly attuned to a very cultivated type of *Gebrauchsmusik*. (Rieti, Poulenc, Auric, etc.) The serious musicians in search of new expressive means are apparently much more isolated and receive much less public attention there than in Germany. Yet precisely in Paris, among a budding generation of musicians, a rejuvenation of Catholicism, which originates from literature, seems to be leading to a new sense of community. Moreover, a ritualistic tendency, untypical for French art and finding expression in a preference for themes from antiquity, is characteristic of the current situation. (Stravinsky's *Oedipus Rex*, Milhaud's minute operas.) As far as they are known to us, however, the Russian musicians seem to have little affinity for communal art, although it is from them that one would most expect it. A conspicuous dependence on Scriabin among many Russian musicians would seem to preclude a 'revolutionary' attitude.

In Germany, then, there are the clearest signs that musical production must find a new justification for its existence. Here a restructuring of the public is clearly observable. The arts engendered by established society, originating as they do from another age and another aesthetic, are increasingly losing ground. The new orchestral and chamber music, for which a genuine demand used to exist on the part of the public, nowadays relies almost exclusively on music societies and organizations devoted to the cultivation of new music whose patrons are themselves mainly musicians. That is why music is seeking a rapprochement with the interests of a wider public since only in this way will it retain its viability. It does so, first of all, by utilizing the lightness and musical facility [*Musizierfreudigkeit*] acquired in recent years, in order to create a worthwhile *Gebrauchsmusik*. The whole area of mechanical music and film music should no longer be the sole preserve of a cheap, everyday commodity. Rather, a young generation of musicians has set about cultivating this area of musical life, for which the public at large also displays an interest. It now depends on the resolve of the appropriate 'industry' to lure the most talented young musicians and to provide them with the basis for a new development, which by no means needs to involve trivialization of any kind.

In addition, we find attempts to attract an audience specifically for the appreciation and cultivation of New Music. Of decisively symptomatic significance in this connection is the activity of a number of musicians within the Amateur Musicians' Guild [*Musikantengilde*] (Hindemith, Ludwig Weber), though it remains to be seen whether this youth movement is not too restricted to certain circles really to create the basis for the renewal of our musical culture or even for the creation of a people's art. More important than these endeavours is, for me, the fact that a large number of musicians whose merit is beyond doubt are again considering the possibility of speaking immediately to a wider public. This much is certain: the clarity of language, the precision of expression and the simplicity of emotion, which new music has regained by pursuing a straight line of development, form together the secure aesthetic foundation for a wider dissemination of this art.

The current situation is most clearly evinced in the field of music theatre. For opera today no longer represents a discrete musical genre (as in the 19th century) but has again taken its rightful place (starting, say, with Busoni's *Doktor Faust*) in the whole area of absolute music. It will also represent a most decisive factor in the development whereby music is no longer accorded the role of an art form engendered by established society but rather that of a socially regenerative or promoting force. Hence it cannot restrict itself either to a purely aesthetic renaissance, which allows principles of musical style to be the sole determinants, or to representing matters of merely superficial, topical relevance which are valid only for the briefest period of the work's genesis. I believe, above all, that musicians ought first to overcome their fear of truly equal collaborators. It has proved to be quite possible, working closely with representatives of equal stature in the sister arts, to set about creating the kind of music theatre that can provide an untopical [*unaktuelle*], unique and definitive representation of our age. I am also convinced, thanks to the newly attained inner and outer uncomplicatedness of subject matter and means of expression, that a branch of opera is developing into a new epic form such as I have employed with Brecht in the *Mahagonny* Songspiel.[1] True, this form of music theatre presupposes a basically theatrical type of music. Yet it also makes it possible to give opera a structure that is absolutely musical, even instrumental.

In this and in other areas of contemporary opera it is quite evident that the development of music is receiving new impulses from stage works produced for the cinema [*Theaterfilm*].

1. "Songspiel" is a term coined by Weill that he retained in English.

187 Joseph Goebbels

This is a shortened version of an address Joseph Goebbels, the German Minister of Enlightenment and Propaganda during the Third Reich, delivered in May 1938 at a music festival in Düsseldorf. An exhibition titled "Degenerate Music" was held in connection with this festival, modeled on the much more expansive and widely publicized exhibition of "degenerate visual art" held in Munich the previous summer. The cover of the guide for the music exhibition featured a caricature of a black man playing a saxophone and wearing a Star of David, joining in one image an expression of racial, religious, and musical hatred.

Speech for the Düsseldorf Music Festival
(1938)

The decline of German spiritual and artistic life in the years 1918 to 1933 did not spare music. The great sins of the time were also evident there and produced the most fruitful destruction in the domain of an art that until then had been seen throughout the world as the most German of all. A certain period of transition was thus required to remove the errors, failures, and manifestations of decline through systematic reform and the removal of the causes and symptoms of illness, and through the cultivation of the true artistic strengths of our German music. In a five-year plan of reconstruction we have attempted to overcome the severe crisis and gradually secure a firm new hold.

In the year 1933 German music life was in a truly desperate state. A threatening spiritual and artistic disintegration was imminent. The dissolution of all inner value, something that in Germany's past music had enabled it to achieve predominance throughout the entire world, seemed almost inevitable. The German masters, who with true artistic command had created immortal works of German tonal art, were suppressed by the flagrantly commercial elements of international Jewry. The so-called music that the latter produced and propagated inevitably led in time to the total constriction of public musical life.

It thus seemed like an impossible task to produce change and to direct the creative powers of the time back again to their own roots and to the strength-dispensing foundation of the German People. Here one could not prescribe, decree, or implement through force. The damage that had been produced had to be gradually alleviated through systematic cultivation of all the valuable strengths of German music. And good will alone would not suffice; time was necessary.

National Socialism has produced change. In a great burst it has swept away the pathological products of Jewish musical intellectualism. The power of Jewry is now broken in the realm of German music; German musical life is now cleansed of the last traces of Jewish arrogance and predominance. Our classical masters again appear before the public in pure and untarnished form. They will be brought before the broad masses of the People in large-scale concerts. In place of pure construction and desolate atonal expressionism, artistic intuition will again step forward as the source of musical creation. Perhaps this represents more than merely a work of national reform. Perhaps it is the beginning of the delivery of all Western music from a threatening decline.

TEXT: Joseph Wulf, *Musik im Dritten Reich: eine Dokumentation* (Gütersloh: Sigbert Mohn Verlag, 1963), pp. 416–17. Translation by Robert P. Morgan.

188 *Pravda*

Dmitri Shostakovich's opera *Lady Macbeth of the Mtsensk District* was reviewed in the official Soviet Party newspaper *Pravda* in January 1936. The opera, completed in 1932, had already been performed with considerable critical and public success both within Russia and abroad, but after ninety-seven performances in Moscow, it was chosen as the vehicle for announcing a new official policy of musical and artistic repression, delivered in the form of this review. Though the Soviets had tolerated considerable experimentation and innovation in the arts in the early years following the Revolution, this liberal attitude had been under attack for some time, especially since the full consolidation of Stalin's power in the early 1930s. The *Lady Macbeth* review marked an important milestone, signaling the onset of an extended period of severe artistic repression: never before had a Soviet composer been so ruthlessly and publicly denounced.

Chaos Instead of Music
(1936)

With the general cultural development of our country there grew also the necessity for good music. At no time and in no other place has the composer had a more appreciative audience. The people expect good songs, but also good instrumental works, and good operas.

Certain theaters are presenting to the new culturally mature Soviet public Shostakovich's opera *Lady Macbeth* as an innovation and an achievement. Musical criticism, always ready to serve, has praised the opera to the skies and given it resounding glory. The young composer, instead of hearing serious business-like criticism, which could have helped him in his future work, hears only enthusiastic compliments.

From the first minute, the listener is shocked by deliberate dissonance, by a confused stream of sounds. Snatches of melody, the beginnings of a musical phrase, are drowned, emerge again, and disappear in a grinding and squealing roar. To follow this "music" is most difficult; to remember it, impossible.

Thus it goes practically throughout the entire opera. The singing on the stage is replaced by shrieks. If the composer chances to come on the path of a clear and simple melody, then immediately, as though frightened at this misfortune, he throws himself back into a wilderness of musical chaos—in places becoming cacophony. The expression which the listener demands is supplanted by wild rhythm. Passion is here supposed to be expressed by musical noise. All this is

TEXT: Victor Seroff, *Dimitri Shostakovich: the Life and Background of a Soviet Composer* (New York: Alfred A. Knopf, 1943), pp. 204–7. Reprint permission granted by Ayer Company Publishers.

not due to lack of talent, or to lack of ability to depict simple and strong emotions in music. Here is music turned deliberately inside out in order that nothing will be reminiscent of classical opera, or have anything in common with symphonic music or with simple and popular musical language accessible to all. This music is built on the basis of rejecting opera—the same basis on which leftist[1] art rejects in the theater simplicity, realism, clarity of image, and the unaffected spoken word—which carries into the theater and into music the most negative features of "Meyerholdism"[2] infinitely multiplied. Here we have leftist confusion instead of natural, human music. The power of good music to infect the masses has been sacrificed to a petty-bourgeois, "formalist" attempt to create originality through cheap clowning. It is a game of clever ingenuity that may end very badly.

The danger of this trend to Soviet music is clear. Leftist distortion in opera stems from the same source as the leftist distortion in painting, poetry, teaching, and science. Petty-bourgeois "innovations" lead to a break with real art, real science, and real literature.

The author of *Lady Macbeth* was forced to borrow from jazz its nervous, convulsive, and spasmodic music in order to lend "passion" to his characters. While our music critics swear by the name of socialist realism, the stage serves us, in Shostakovich's creation, the coarsest kind of naturalism. He reveals[3] the merchants and the people monotonously and bestially. The predatory merchant woman who scrambles into possession of wealth through murder is pictured as some kind of "victim" of bourgeois society. The story of Leskov has been given a significance it does not possess.

And all this is coarse, primitive, and vulgar. The music quacks, grunts, and growls, and suffocates itself, in order to express the amatory scenes as naturalistically as possible. And "love" is smeared all over the opera in the most vulgar manner. The merchant's double bed occupies the central position on the stage. On it all "problems" are solved. In the same coarse, naturalistic style is shown the death from poisoning and the flogging—both practically on stage.

The composer apparently never considered the problem of what the Soviet audience expects and looks for in music. As though deliberately, he scribbles down his music, confusing all the sounds in such a way that his music would reach only the effete "formalists" who had lost their wholesome taste. He ignored the demand of Soviet culture that all coarseness and wildness be abolished from every corner of Soviet life. Some critics call this glorification of merchants' lust a satire. But there is no question of satire here. The author has

1. V. I. Lenin occasionally used the word "left" in his writings to characterize negatively the extreme "petty-bourgeois," "semi-anarchist," and "anti-Marxist" branch of the Russian revolutionary movement. See for example his article " 'Left-Wing' Communism—An Infantile Disorder," in Lenin, *Selected Writings* (Moscow: Progress Publishers, 1968), esp. p. 521.
2. Vsevolod Emilievich Meyerhold (1874–1942) was head of theater in the postrevolutionary U.S.S.R.; his progressive theatrical productions came under increasing criticism during the 1930s, ending in his arrest and disappearance in 1939.
3. "Reveals" presumably means "depicts" here—i.e., "depicts the merchants [on the stage]."

tried, with all the musical and dramatic means at his command, to arouse the sympathy of the spectators for the coarse and vulgar leanings and behavior of the merchant woman, Katerina Ismailova.

Lady Macbeth is having great success with bourgeois audiences abroad. Is it not because the opera is absolutely unpolitical and confusing that they praise it? Is it not explained by the fact that it tickles the perverted tastes of the bourgeoisie with its fidgety, screaming, neurotic music?

Our theaters have expended a great deal of labor on giving Shostakovich's opera a thorough presentation. The actors have shown exceptional talent in dominating the noise, the screaming, and the roar of the orchestra. With their dramatic action they tried to reinforce the weakness of melodic content. Unfortunately, this served only to bring out the opera's vulgar features more vividly. The talented acting earns gratitude; the wasted efforts, regrets.

189 Sergey Prokofiev

The relationship between Soviet composers and the official government policy toward the arts was complex and shifting. In order to function professionally, composers had to follow the party line, but just what that was could vary, especially in the earlier years. In its broad outlines, moreover, Soviet artistic policy was not so different from that promulgated by many non-Soviets during the years between the wars, and even the major Russian figures could often agree with it, at least in general. Certainly the following excerpts from writings by Sergey Prokofiev (1891–1953), the first and third dating from the late 1930s, the second from 1951, express views that seem in themselves innocuous enough: that music should appeal to large audiences without "playing down" to them; that it should be "clear" and "straightforward" in construction; and that composers should have a sense of social responsibility. Precisely how these recommendations were to be interpreted, however, or carried through, was another matter; and one is no doubt justified in reading Prokofiev's statements with some misgiving, considering the conditions of artistic repression and censorship that prevailed after the 1930s and the extent to which this composer himself suffered from them.

Three Commentaries

THE MASSES WANT GREAT MUSIC

The time is past when music was written for a handful of esthetes. Today vast crowds of people have come face to face with serious music and are waiting with eager impatience. Composers: take heed of this if you repel these crowds they will turn away from you to jazz or vulgar music. But if you can hold them you will win an audience such as the world has never before seen. But this does not mean that you must pander to this audience. Pandering always has an element of insincerity about it and nothing good ever came of that. The masses want great music, great events, great love, lively dances. They understand far more than some composers think, and they want to deepen their understanding.

I ADHERE TO THE CONVICTION . . .
(1951)

In America and Western Europe much is said about the mission of an artist and the freedom of his creativity. Indeed, can an artist stand aloof from life? Can he lock himself in an ephemeral "tower," circumscribe the circle of his creativity with subjective emotions, or should he be there where he is needed, where his word, his music, his chisel can help the people live a better and more interesting life?

Let us recall the creative paths of Beethoven and Shakespeare, Mozart and Tolstoy, Tchaikovsky and Dickens—those titans of the human intellect. Does not their greatness lie precisely in the fact that they, by their own will, by the call of duty and their souls, gave their mighty talents to the service of mankind? Are not their immortal works noted first and foremost for this trait?

When I was in the United States and in England I often heard people discuss the following questions: whom should music serve, what should a composer write about, and what should direct his creativity? I adhere to the conviction that a composer just as a poet, sculptor or painter is called upon to serve man and his people. He should beautify man's life and defend it. He is obligated, above all, to be a citizen in his art and to glorify man's life and lead man to a bright future. From my point of view, such is the firm code of art.

TEXT: *Materials, Articles, Interviews,* compiled by Vladimir Blok (Moscow: Progress Publishers, 1978), pp. 42, 52. *Autobiography, Articles, Reminiscences,* ed. by S. Shlifstein, trans. by Rose Prokofieva (Moscow, 1960), pp. 101–2. "The Masses Want Great Music" comes from a 1937 notebook, "I Adhere to the Conviction . . ." from the article "Music and Life," *Novosti,* No. 10, 1951, and "Flourishing of Art" from notes probably for the main points of an article or speech.

FLOURISHING OF ART

The search for a musical idiom in keeping with the epoch of socialism is a worthy, but difficult task for the composer. Music in our country has become the heritage of vast masses of people. Their artistic taste and demands are growing with amazing speed. And this is something the Soviet composer must take into account in each new work.

It is something like shooting at a moving target: only by aiming ahead, at tomorrow, will you avoid being left behind at the level of yesterday's needs. That is why I consider it a mistake for a composer to strive for simplification. Any attempt to "play down" to the listener is a subconscious underestimation of his cultural maturity and the development of his tastes; such an attempt has an element of insincerity. And music that is insincere cannot be enduring.

In my own work written in this fruitful year, I have striven for clarity and melodiousness. At the same time I have scrupulously avoided palming off familiar harmonies and tunes.

That is where the difficulty of composing clear, straightforward music lies: the clarity must be new, not old.

My main work this year has been a large cantata dedicated to the 20th anniversary of October. Its principal themes are the Great October Socialist Revolution, victory, industrialization and the Constitution.

The cantata is written for two choruses, professional and amateur, and four orchestras—symphony, military, percussion and accordion bands. No less than 500 people are required for its performance.

It gave me great pleasure to write this cantata. The complex events reflected in it demanded a complex musical idiom. But I trust that the passion and sincerity of the music will make it accessible to our audiences.[1]

Another large work just completed is a suite for chorus, soloists and orchestra which I intend to entitle *Songs of Our Days*. It will be performed for the first time on January 5 in the Large Hall of the Moscow Conservatory. It is written to words by Lebedev-Kumach, Marshak and other texts translated from Ukrainian and Byelorussian folk-lore and published in *Pravda*. My melodies here are written in the style of the given nationality. I hope they will be easily understood and remembered.

I have also composed several marches for military band, some mass songs and romances to Pushkin's verse on the occasion of the centenary of his death. Unfortunately, the theatres have not made use of the incidental music I wrote for a number of Pushkin productions.[2]

1. This cantata was never performed. Part of the musical material was used for the *Ode on the End of the War*. [Shlifstein]
2. Reference to music for the projected productions of *Boris Godunov* and *Eugene Onegin* and for the film *The Queen of Spades*. Part of this music was used in other compositions; some of it went into the opera *War and Peace* (scene in Hélène's house) and the Fifth Symphony (*Adagio*). [Shlifstein]

190 Dmitri Shostakovich

Dmitri Shostakovich (1906–1975) was one of the two most prominent Russian composers of the Soviet period (the other was Sergey Prokofiev). Like those of his compatriot, all of Shostakovich's writings published during his lifetime closely hewed to the Communist Party line. Following the composer's death, however, the Russian music critic Solomon Volkov, who emigrated to the United States in 1976, published *Testimony,* a book of memoirs based on material dictated to him by the composer in the early 1970s. Though efforts have been made to discredit this work, most Shostakovich scholars accept the material as authentic. Certainly it offers a view of Soviet musical life much different from and more critical than anything officially published in the U.S.S.R. The excerpt included here recounts the events surrounding one of the two most wide-reaching Soviet crackdowns on progressive music (the other being the 1936 review of Shostakovich's own *Lady Macbeth of the Mtsensk District,* see No. 19): the notorious 1948 attack on Vano Ilyich Muradeli's opera *The Great Friendship.* In a manner at once humorous yet bitterly sarcastic, Shostakovich tells of Muradeli's desperate efforts to regain status after his sudden fall from official favor.

FROM *Testimony*

One of the disgruntled was Muradeli,[1] a fact that is now forgotten. After the historic resolution "On the Opera *The Great Friendship,*" Muradeli seemed to walk among the victims, but actually Muradeli was never a victim, and he was planning to warm his hands on his *Great Friendship.*

And he wanted more than just personal glory, he hoped to pull formalism out by the roots from music. His subsequently infamous opera was accepted for production in 1947 by almost twenty opera companies, and most important, the Bolshoi was doing it, and they were planning it for an important occasion—the thirtieth anniversary of the October Revolution. They were going to open at the Bolshoi on November 7, with Stalin attending.

Muradeli walked around and blustered, "He Himself will invite me into his box! I'll tell him everything! I'll tell him the formalists have been blocking

TEXT: *Testimony: the Memoirs of Dmitri Shostakovich,* as related to and edited by Solomon Volkov, trans. by Antonina W. Bouis (New York: HarperCollins Publishers, Inc., 1979), pp. 142–47. Reprinted by permission of HarperCollins Publishers, Inc.

1. Vano Ilyich Muradeli (1908–1970), a composer whose place in the history of Russian music is assured because he was grouped with Shostakovich and Prokofiev as a "formalist." Of course Muradeli does have his own musical "record": a singing Lenin makes his first appearance in his opera *October* (1964). (A talking Lenin appeared in Soviet opera in 1939, in Khrennikov's *Into the Storm.*) [Volkov]

my way. Something has to be done!" Everything seemed to augur success for Muradeli. The plot had ideology, from the lives of the Georgians and Ossetians. The Georgian Commissar Ordzhonikidze was a character in the opera, he was cleaning up the Caucasus. The composer was also of Caucasian descent. What more could you ask?

But Muradeli had miscalculated terribly. Stalin disliked the opera. First of all, he didn't like the plot, he found a major political error in it. According to the plot, Ordzhonikidze convinces the Georgians and Ossetians not to fight with the Russians. Stalin, as you know, was an Ossetian himself (and not a Georgian, as is usually thought). He took offense on behalf of the Ossetians. Stalin had his own view of the matter. He despised the Chechens and Ingush, who were just then being moved out of the Caucasus. That was a simple thing to do in Stalin's day. They loaded two nations into wagons and took them away to the devil. So Muradeli should have blamed all the evildoing on the Chechens and Ingush, but he didn't display the necessary mental nimbleness.

And then there was Ordzhonikidze. Muradeli showed his naïveté once more. He thought that it would be a good idea to have Ordzhonikidze in the opera, he didn't think that reminding Stalin of him was like stepping on a corn. At the time, the country had been informed that Ordzhonikidze had died from a heart attack. Actually, Ordzhonikidze shot himself. Stalin drove him to it.

But the main problem was with the *lezghinka*.[2] The opera was based on life in the Caucasus, so Muradeli crammed it full of native songs and dances. Stalin expected to hear his native songs, but instead he heard Muradeli's own *lezghinka*, which he had composed in a fit of forgetfulness. And it was that original *lezghinka* that angered Stalin the most.

There were black clouds, a storm was brewing. It just lacked an excuse, the lightning needed an oak to strike, or at least a blockhead. Muradeli played the part of the blockhead.

But in the end, Muradeli didn't get burned by the historic resolution "On the Opera *The Great Friendship*."[3] He was a clever man and he managed to profit even from the historic resolution.

As you know, the resolution drew heated interest among the toiling masses. Meetings and gatherings were held everywhere, in factories, communal farms, industrial cartels, and places of public food consumption. And the workers discussed the document with enthusiasm, since, as it turned out, the document

2. In the Stalin years, the sounds of the *lezghinka*, a national Georgian folk dance, as well as the melody "Suliko," Stalin's favorite Georgian folk song, were familiar to millions of Soviet people. [Volkov]

3. "The year 1948 is a historical, watershed year in the history of Soviet and world musical culture. The 'Resolution of the Central Committee of All-Union Communist Party (Bolshevik) of February 10, 1948, On the Opera *The Great Friendship* by V. Muradeli,' harshly condemning the anti-people formalist tendency in Soviet music, broke the decadent fetters that hobbled for so many years the creativity of many Soviet composers; for many years ahead the only correct path for the development of musical art in the U.S.S.R. has been determined." (From a collective work published in 1948 by the Composers' Union.) [Volkov]

echoed the spiritual needs of millions of people. These millions were united in their rejection of Shostakovich and other formalists. And so Muradeli added his babble to satisfy the spiritual interests of the workers ... for money, of course.

Muradeli began making appearances at various organizations. He came to the people and repented. I was a so-and-so, a formalist and cosmopolite. I wrote the wrong *lezghinka,* but the Party showed me the way in time. And now I, the former formalist and cosmopolite Muradeli, have stepped onto the righteous road of progressive realistic creativity. And in the future I'm determined to write *lezghinkas* that are worthy of our great epoch.

Muradeli said all this in an agitated manner, with Caucasian temperament. The only thing he didn't do was dance the *lezghinka.* And then he sat at the piano and played excerpts from his future, yet-to-be-written works, worthy of our great epoch. The excerpts were melodious and harmonious, quite like the harmony exercises from the conservatory textbook.

Everyone was satisfied, the workers saw a live formalist, they had something to tell their friends and neighbors. Muradeli earned good money and met the Composers' Union's plan on self-criticism.

Why am I spending so much time on Muradeli? In a musical sense he was a rather pathetic figure and as a man he was extremely malignant. An excess of temperament might lead Muradeli to perform a good deed, but only by accident. For instance, once he got the wild idea of reconciling Prokofiev and me. He decided that if Prokofiev and I sat down at a table and started drinking Georgian wines and eating shashlik, we would become great friends. We had to, for who could resist Georgian wines and shashlik? Naturally, nothing came of that idea.

However, Muradeli played an important role in the business with formalism, albeit an extremely deplorable one. This was the situation. There was Shostakovich, who needed to be put in his place, and there was Muradeli, whose opera *The Great Friendship* displeased Stalin. But the problem of formalism in music did not yet exist, the horrible picture of a formalist conspiracy had not yet formed. They could hit Shostakovich and hit Muradeli and be finished. Stalin might not have even taken aim at all of Soviet music.[4] The impetus to start a broadly based destruction of Soviet music came from Muradeli and him alone.

After the unhappy presentation of *The Great Friendship,* a meeting was called at the Bolshoi Theater, and at that meeting Muradeli repented and came up with the following theory: that he loved melody and understood melody and

---

4. In order to appreciate Shostakovich's commentaries, one must picture the ubiquity of the "discussions" of formalism in music instituted in 1948. Unlike the "antiformalist" campaign of 1936, which had struck at many victims but then paled before the mass repressions, the "formalism" theme of 1948 became the most important issue in the public life of the times and dominated every conversation. [Volkov]

he would be more than happy to write melody alone, including melodious and harmonious *lezghinkas,* but it seems that he was kept from writing melodious *lezghinkas* because the formalist conspirators were everywhere—in the conservatories, in the publishing houses, in the press. Everywhere. And they forced poor Muradeli to write a formalist *lezghinka* instead of a melodious and harmonious one. Muradeli's *lezghinka* was the direct result of a conspiracy of enemies of the people, formalists, and toadies to the West.

And this version from Muradeli interested Stalin, who was always interested in conspiracies, an unhealthy interest that always had unpleasant consequences. The unpleasant consequences were quick to follow in this instance as well. One provocateur—Muradeli—had been found. But that wasn't enough. They gathered the composers, who began hanging one another. It was a pathetic sight that I would rather not recall. Of course, almost nothing surprises me, but this is one thing that's too repugnant to think about. Stalin designated to Zhdanov the task of compiling a list of the "main offenders." Zhdanov worked like an experienced torturer—he set one composer against the other.

Of course, Zhdanov didn't have to work too hard; the composers chewed one another up with glee. No one wanted to be on the list, it wasn't a list for prizes but for possible extermination. Everything had significance here—your position on the list, for instance. If you were first, consider yourself gone. Last—there was still hope. And the citizen composers knocked themselves out to avoid the list and did everything they could to get their comrades on it.[5] They were real criminals, whose philosophy was: you die today, and I'll go tomorrow.

Well, they worked and worked on the list. They put some names on, crossed others off. Only two names had the top spots sewn up. My name was number one, and Prokofiev's number two. The meeting was over, and the historic resolution appeared. And after that . . .

Meeting upon meeting, conference upon conference. The whole country was in a fever, the composers more than anyone. It was like a dam breaking and a flood of murky, dirty water rushing in. Everyone seemed to go mad and anyone who felt like it expressed an opinion on music.

Zhdanov announced, "The Central Committee of Bolsheviks demands beauty and refinement from music." And he added that the goal of music was to give pleasure, while our music was crude and vulgar, and listening to it undoubtedly destroyed the psychological and physical balance of a man, for example a man like Zhdanov.

Stalin was no longer considered a man. He was a god and all this did not

---

5. The reference is in part to the desperate attempt by Dmitri Borisovich Kabalevsky (1904–1987) to replace his name in a blacklist, prepared by Zhdanov, of composers "who held formalistic, anti-People tendencies" with that of Gavriil Nikolayevich Popov (1904–1972). The attempt was successful. The final text of the Party's "historic resolution" does not mention Kabalevsky. The talented Popov eventually drank himself to death. [Volkov]

concern him. He was above it all. The leader and teacher washed his hands of it, and I think he did so consciously. He was being smart. But I only realized this later. At the time it seemed as though my end had come. Sheet music was reprocessed; why burn it? That was wasteful. But by recycling all the caco-phonic symphonies and quartets, they could save on paper. They destroyed tapes at the radio stations. And Khrennikov said, "There, it's gone forever. The formalist snake will never rear its head again."

All the papers printed letters from the workers, who all thanked the Party for sparing them the torture of listening to the symphonies of Shostakovich. The censors met the wishes of the workers and put out a blacklist, which named those symphonies of Shostakovich's that were being taken out of circula-tion. Thus I stopped personally offending Asafiev, that leading figure of musical scholarship, who complained, "I take the Ninth Symphony as a personal insult."

From now unto forever, music had to be refined, harmonious, and melodi-ous. They wanted particular attention devoted to singing with words, since singing without words satisfied only the perverted tastes of a few aesthetes and individualists.

Altogether this was called: The Party has saved music from liquidation. It turned out that Shostakovich and Prokofiev had wanted to liquidate music, and Stalin and Zhdanov didn't let them. Stalin could be happy. The whole country, instead of thinking about its squalid life, was entering mortal combat with for-malist composers.

191 Marian Anderson

The contralto Marian Anderson (1897–1993) was one of the first African-Ameri-can artists to be recognized as a major performer of Western concert music. After completing her training in the United States, Anderson began concertizing and won a major New York Philharmonic competition in 1925; but only after successful concert tours in Europe in the early 1930s did she begin to receive full recognition at home. Indeed, Anderson's Metropolitan Opera debut did not take place until 1955, when she was past her prime. In this passage from her 1956 autobiography, Anderson recounts the most famous and politically charged event of her career: the refusal by officials at Constitution Hall in Wash-ington, D.C. to allow her to perform there in 1939 (supposedly on orders from the Daughters of the American Revolution, the hall's owners) and the legendary free outdoor concert she presented at the Lincoln Memorial instead.

FROM *My Lord, What a Morning*
(1956)

The excitement over the denial of Constitution Hall to me did not die down. It seemed to increase and to follow me wherever I went. I felt about the affair as about an election campaign; whatever the outcome, there is bound to be unpleasantness and embarrassment. I could not escape it, of course. My friends wanted to discuss it, and even strangers went out of their way to express their strong feelings of sympathy and support.

What were my own feelings? I was saddened and ashamed. I was sorry for the people who had precipitated the affair. I felt that their behavior stemmed from a lack of understanding. They were not persecuting me personally or as a representative of my people so much as they were doing something that was neither sensible nor good. Could I have erased the bitterness, I would have done so gladly. I do not mean that I would have been prepared to say that I was not entitled to appear in Constitution Hall as might any other performer. But the unpleasantness disturbed me, and if it had been up to me alone I would have sought a way to wipe it out. I cannot say that such a way out suggested itself to me at the time, or that I thought of one after the event. But I have been in this world long enough to know that there are all kinds of people, all suited by their own natures for different tasks. It would be fooling myself to think that I was meant to be a fearless fighter; I was not, just as I was not meant to be a soprano instead of a contralto.

Then the time came when it was decided that I would sing in Washington on Easter Sunday. The invitation to appear in the open, singing from the Lincoln Memorial before as many people as would care to come, without charge, was made formally by Harold L. Ickes, Secretary of the Interior. It was duly reported, and the weight of the Washington affair bore in on me.

•　　•　　•　　•　　•

I studied my conscience. In principle the idea was sound, but it could not be comfortable to me as an individual. As I thought further, I could see that my significance as an individual was small in this affair. I had become, whether I liked it or not, a symbol, representing my people. I had to appear.

I discussed the problem with Mother, of course. Her comment was characteristic: "It is an important decision to make. You are in this work. You intend to stay in it. You know what your aspirations are. I think you should make your own decision."

Mother knew what the decision would be. In my heart I also knew. I could not run away from this situation. If I had anything to offer, I would have to do so now. It would be misleading, however, to say that once the decision was made I was without doubts.

•   •   •   •   •

We reached Washington early that Easter morning and went to the home of Gifford Pinchot, who had been Governor of Pennsylvania. The Pinchots had been kind enough to offer their hospitality, and it was needed because the hotels would not take us. Then we drove over to the Lincoln Memorial. Kosti was well enough to play,[1] and we tried out the piano and examined the public-address system, which had six microphones, meant not only for the people who were present but also for a radio audience.

When we returned that afternoon I had sensations unlike any I had experienced before. The only comparable emotion I could recall was the feeling I had had when Maestro Toscanini had appeared in the artist's room in Salzburg. My heart leaped wildly, and I could not talk. I even wondered whether I would be able to sing.

The murmur of the vast assemblage quickened my pulse beat. There were policemen waiting at the car, and they led us through a passageway that other officers kept open in the throng. We entered the monument and were taken to a small room. We were introduced to Mr. Ickes, whom we had not met before. He outlined the program. Then came the signal to go out before the public.

If I did not consult contemporary reports I could not recall who was there. My head and heart were in such turmoil that I looked and hardly saw, I listened and hardly heard. I was led to the platform by Representative Caroline O'Day of New York, who had been born in Georgia, and Oscar Chapman, Assistant Secretary of the Interior, who was a Virginian. On the platform behind me sat Secretary Ickes, Secretary of the Treasury [Henry] Morgenthau [Jr.], Supreme Court Justice [Hugo] Black, Senators [Robert] Wagner, [James] Mead, [Alben] Barkley, [D. Worth] Clark, [Joseph] Guffey, and [Arthur] Capper, and many Representatives, including Representative Arthur W. Mitchell of Illinois, a Negro. Mother was there, as were people from Howard University and from churches in Washington and other cities. So was Walter White, then secretary of the National Association for the Advancement of Colored People. It was Mr. White who at one point stepped to the microphone and appealed to the crowd, probably averting serious accidents when my own people tried to reach me.

I report these things now because I have looked them up. All I knew then as I stepped forward was the overwhelming impact of that vast multitude. There seemed to be people as far as the eye could see. The crowd stretched in a great semicircle from the Lincoln Memorial around the reflecting pool on to the shaft of the Washington Monument. I had a feeling that a great wave of good will poured out from these people, almost engulfing me. And when I

1. Kosti Vehanen, Anderson's Finnish accompanist.

stood up to sing our National Anthem I felt for a moment as though I were choking. For a desperate second I thought that the words, well as I know them, would not come.

I sang, I don't know how. There must have been the help of professionalism I had accumulated over the years. Without it I could not have gone through the program. I sang—and again I know because I consulted a newspaper clipping—"America," the aria "O mio Fernando," Schubert's "Ave Maria," and three spirituals—"Gospel Train," "Trampin'," and "My Soul Is Anchored in the Lord."

192 Cornelius Cardew

During the 1960s, the English composer Cornelius Cardew (1936–1981), like many other young composers of the time, began focusing his energies on developing a more explicit social role for music, especially the "possibilities for political music-making." In 1969 he cofounded the Scratch Orchestra, a cooperative organization consisting of both professional and amateur musicians "willing and eager to engage in experimental performance activities." Players, both skilled and unskilled, participated on equal terms; and all musical decisions regarding what was to be played and how were determined by mutual agreement. Though the Scratch Orchestra had a brief and turbulent history and was plagued by considerable internal strife, it came to typify efforts of the time to rethink the entire musical project in more socially activist terms. This excerpt from the orchestra's "draft constitution" contains a definition, a statement of intent, and descriptions of four of the five repertory categories (the draft also includes a fifth, called "Research Project," and four "appendices" listing compositions, improvisations, and special projects).

FROM A Scratch Orchestra: Draft Constitution

(1969)

Definition: A Scratch Orchestra is a large number of enthusiasts pooling their resources (not primarily material resources) and assembling for action (music-making, performance, edification).

TEXT: *Scratch Music,* ed. by Cornelius Cardew (Cambridge: MIT Press, 1972), p. 10.

Note: The word music and its derivatives are here not understood to refer exclusively to sound and related phenomena (hearing, *etc*). What they do refer to is flexible and depends entirely on the members of the Scratch Orchestra.

The Scratch Orchestra intends to function in the public sphere, and this function will be expressed in the form of—for lack of a better word—concerts. In rotation (starting with the youngest) each member will have the option of designing a concert. If the option is taken up, all details of that concert are in the hands of that person or his delegates; if the option is waived the details of the concert will be determined by random methods, or by voting (a vote determines which of these two). The material of these concerts may be drawn, in part or wholly, from the basic repertory categories outlined below.

1 SCRATCH MUSIC

Each member of the orchestra provides himself with a notebook (or Scratchbook) in which he notates a number of accompaniments, performable continuously for indefinite periods. The number of accompaniments in each book should be equal to or greater than the current number of members of the orchestra. An accompaniment is defined as music that allows a solo (in the event of one occurring) to be appreciated as such. The notation may be accomplished using any means—verbal, graphic, musical, collage, *etc*—and should be regarded as a period of training: never notate more than one accompaniment in a day. If many ideas arise on one day they may all be incorporated in one accompaniment. The last accompaniment in the list has the status of a solo and if used should only be used as such. On the addition of further items, what was previously a solo is relegated to the status of an accompaniment, so that at any time each player has only one solo and that his most recent. The sole differentiation between a solo and an accompaniment is in the mode of playing.

The performance of this music can be entitled *Scratch Overture, Scratch Interlude* or *Scratch Finale* depending on its position in the concert.

2 POPULAR CLASSICS

Only such works as are familiar to several members are eligible for this category. Particles of the selected works will be gathered in Appendix 1. A particle could be: a page of score, a page or more of the part for one instrument or voice, a page of an arrangement, a thematic analysis, a gramophone record, *etc*.

The technique of performance is as follows: a qualified member plays the given particle, while the remaining players join in as best they can, playing along, contributing whatever they can recall of the work in question, filling the gaps of memory with improvised variational material.

As is appropriate to the classics, avoid losing touch with the reading player (who may terminate the piece at his discretion), and strive to act concertedly rather than independently. These works should be programmed under their original titles.

3 IMPROVISATION RITES

A selection of the rites in *Nature Study Notes* will be available in Appendix 2. Members should constantly bear in mind the possibility of contributing new rites. An improvisation rite is not a musical composition; it does not attempt to influence the music that will be played; at most it may establish a community of feeling, or a communal starting-point, through ritual. Any suggested rite will be given a trial run and thereafter left to look after itself. Successful rites may well take on aspects of folklore, acquire nicknames, *etc.*

Free improvisation may also be indulged in from time to time.

4 COMPOSITIONS

Appendix 3 will contain a list of compositions performable by the orchestra. Any composition submitted by a member of the orchestra will be given a trial run in which all terms of the composition will be adhered to as closely as possible. Unless emphatically rejected, such compositions will probably remain as compositions in Appendix 3. If such a composition is repeatedly acclaimed it may qualify for inclusion in the Popular Classics, where it would be represented by a particle only, and adherence to the original terms of the composition would be waived.

· · · · · ·

193 Ethel Smyth

Against seemingly insurmountable odds, Ethel Smyth (1858–1944) established herself as a composer and critical writer of considerable importance in late nineteenth- and early twentieth-century England, a time when professional opportunities were largely barred to women in the field of music. Smyth, who was also active in the women's suffrage movement, wrote sharp-penned prose that met with considerable critical and popular success. The following excerpt is from an article written shortly after World War I, a time when women, having recently acquired new freedom and mobility during the war, were suddenly thrust back into their former positions of subservience. Smyth argues for a resuscitation of the moribund postwar English orchestral life through an influx of feminine vitality, which she believes would bring a new richness and more robust spirit to performances. And as she also observes, taking this step would help create a musical atmosphere in which women musicians, including composers, would be able to compete on a more equal professional footing with men.

FROM *Streaks of Life*
(1921)

AN OPEN SECRET

I know few places more depressing nowadays than concert rooms, apart from their being too often half empty when the free list is suspended. Programme after programme is reeled off with scarce a semblance of fervour (even the critics, the least critical beings in the world, are beginning to notice it), and judging by appearances the audience are derelicts putting in time till something more interesting happens—a tea-party perhaps, or, if it is an evening concert, bed. Of course there are exceptions, but as a rule this is the situation.

It may be partly owing to war fatigue, and I fancy another factor is the disappearance of the Germans and German Jews who, whatever their faults, really do love music and disseminated an attitude towards it that counteracted our own fundamental indifference. But I also believe that the commercial principles we carry into everything, and which result in as many performances and as little rehearsing as possible, bring their own Nemesis. Spiritual aridity, the mead of all who industrialize sacred things, has overtaken languid performer and bored listener, and people who once cherished illusions on this subject are beginning to ask themselves whether we are a musical people—in the sense that we certainly are a sporting and an adventurous people. The exterior equipment, perhaps a heritage of the past, is there still—beautiful voices, exquisitely fine ears, and great natural technical facility; but the fire within burns low and capriciously.

The one element of hope lies, I think, in the gradual interpenetration of the life musical by women. I say this in no fanatical feminist spirit, but in all calmness, as the result of quiet and, I trust, sane observation of things in general, and of what is going on under my nose in particular. What is more, many thoughtful, knowledgeable men I know are saying the same; not openly, for moral courage is, I think, the rarest virtue in the world, but in corners!

Generally speaking I find women more capable of enthusiasm and devotion, readier to spend and be spent emotionally than men—as I noticed in my deal-

TEXT: *The Memoirs of Ethel Smyth*, abridged and introduced by Ronald Crichton (New York: Viking Penguin, Inc., 1987), pp. 339–42. Reprinted by permission of David Higham Associates.

ings with stage choruses long before the war. Their nerves, too, seem nearer the surface, more responsive to appeal, less deeply buried under that habitual resistance to the emotional appeal which is surely a post-Elizabethan trait. I cannot conceive of music being an Englishman's religion—that is, a thing pure of financial taint—but in the case of an Englishwoman I can conceive it. At this moment, too, women are the keener, the harder-working sex. All the world over men seem disinclined to put their backs into the job—war-weariness, it is called—and the responsible statesmen of Europe are unanimous in ascribing the slackness of trade in large measure to the slackness of the workers. But during the war woman *found out her powers,* glories in them now, and only asks to go on using them.

During the war it became impossible to carry on without admitting women into the orchestras, and few things more deeply impressed such as were capable of dispassionate judgement than the increased brilliance and warmth of tone. A new and refreshing spirit, too, was perceptible—in part the result, no doubt, of sex rivalry of the right sort. Well do I remember the transfiguration of a certain elderly violinist who seldom used more than half his bow, and who now was making it bite into the strings as it had not bitten for years in honour of the extremely capable maiden who was sharing his desk. But I think the main gain was the infusion of un-war-wearied feminine vitality, the "go" of keen young talents for the first time allowed scope.

It was generous-minded Sir Henry Wood, I think, who first started mixed bathing in the sea of music, and so successful was the innovation that many other orchestras followed suit. True, the London Symphony Orchestra, much to its disadvantage, in my opinion, still remained an all-male body, except of course as regards the harp (an immemorial concession, I imagine, to aesthetic promptings . . . this solitary, daintily clad, white-armed sample of womanhood among the black coats, as it might be a flower on a coal dump). One hoped however that in time the LSO would come to see the error of its ways and that one more selfish monopoly was a thing of the past.

But now, a bolt from the blue: it appears that the Hallé orchestra at Manchester, true to its Hun origin I suppose, has suddenly sacked its women members. Not in order to make way for fighting men whose places they had been occupying—no woman that breathes but gives way gladly in such case—but merely because of their sex!

Asked to justify this proceeding, the Committee give two reasons that remind one of the wonderful excuses put forward for opposing female Suffrage—excuses so feeble, so transparently bogus, that one almost pities the gentlemen who, unequal to higher flights of invention, imagine that this sort of thing will do!

The first excuse is that when on tour it is not always easy to find suitable hotel accommodation for "the ladies." Very sad—yet dramatic companies have not yet reverted to the Elizabethan practice of entrusting women's roles to men on that account!

But the second excuse is the supreme effort—as fine an instance of solemn pretentious humbug, in other words cant, as I have ever come across. It is in the interests of "Unity of Style," we are told, that the women have been shown the door!

Now will anyone bind a wet towel round his head (yes, *his* head, for only a man can expound the deeper workings of the male mind) and tell us what on earth this means? What, pray, is "unity of style" in this sense? When Joachim and Lady Hallé played the Double Concerto in the very town whence issues this precious pronouncement, did the fathers and uncles of the members of that Committee hand in their resignation? Did Bach turn in his grave with horror (although it is his own fault for not mentioning the sex question in his score)? Do the soprani and alti interfere with the "unity of style" in a chorus? Does the English Quartet, that is led by Miss Hayward, lack it?

No! You can talk of unity of style between static things, such as Italian violins, verses of a poem, houses in a street, bank clerks, priests, etc., but not in the case of a fluid force. Sex will not give it to forty men of different talent, temperament, habit, digestions and schools; that is the conductor's office. And two first-class artists of different sexes who respond subtly to his intention can more easily be welded by him into the "unity" he wants than a first-rate and fourth-rate male.

But a truce to poking about in the unsavoury dust-heap of man's disingenuous reasons for doing an ugly action. Let us rather see what that action leads to.

Apart from the more spiritual element which I know women will bring, as performers, to the making of music, their admission on equal terms with men to our orchestras has another aspect. As I am never weary of pointing out, orchestral playing is the finest training a young composer can have, and the cheapest. The whole of musical literature passes across your desk; you are learning form and instrumentation automatically; and even though much of your time be spent in what must be the hateful work of giving lessons, you are on the crest of the wave of music, where strong breezes refresh your spirit and keep it buoyant.

Finally, to wind up with a consideration of a practical order, once you are member of a well-known orchestra, you are entitled to ask good fees for private lessons.

All this was hitherto denied to woman; no wonder the sacred flame that burned in her bosom throughout her student years too often flickered out. I have always maintained that until we are in the rough and tumble of musical life as men are, there cannot possibly be many women composers worth talking about. Competition, environment, and the sort of chance you get all round, are to talent what sunshine and the less poetical activities of the gardener are to a flower. In a word, the general level of human circumstance determines what stature one particularly gifted being can be expected to attain, and if you have to hurl yourself upwards from the sea-level you may become a Tenerife, but improbably a Mount Everest.

Bullying and cowardice, meanness and jealousy, are not pretty qualities, and I wonder if men have a notion with what contempt women view these attempts to prevent them from earning their livelihood in any sphere for which they can prove themselves fitted? Meanwhile, as finishing touch, a certain group of young intellectuals are busy shedding crocodile's tears in any newspaper that will act as blotting paper over the paucity of female stars of the first magnitude, *the equality of their chances with men notwithstanding!* . . .

194 Eva Rieger

The participation of women in professional musical life has grown dramatically in the second half of the twentieth century and has encompassed all areas, including performance, composition, scholarship, and teaching. This growth has been achieved, however, only with considerable struggle, and since full equity is far from attained, that struggle continues. While many have argued for more active professional participation by women simply on the principle of equal opportunity for all, others have maintained that such participation is desirable because women bring unique qualities to the art, enhancing and enriching it. The latter, so-called essentialist, position is represented in this 1992 article (here somewhat condensed) by the Dutch musicologist Eva Rieger. Noting that "sex role is one of the most important determinants of human behavior," Rieger identifies and discusses characteristics she finds typical of much music composed by women.

"I Recycle Sounds": Do Women
Compose Differently?
(1992)

No one would get worked up if one decided to study ethnological differences in music of people living in various geographical places, but when one suggests studying differences in music by people of opposed sex, musicologists get

TEXT: *Journal of the International League of Women Composers*, March 1992, pp. 22–25. The present text is a shortened version of the original, made with the author's approval.

extremely touchy. Yet sociologists teach us that gender is one of the most important determinants of human behavior. In our Western culture men and women have had different cultural fields assigned to them, and this tradition prevails in our thoughts and emotions. Pedagogical research has shown that girls prefer different musical instruments than boys, their musical preferences differ, and a German research project on children's drawings revealed that boys mostly draw instrumentalists standing on their own, whereas girls show them playing in a group. Yet the question whether women compose differently than men has been posed mainly by the feminist scene up to now. It is usually assumed that the musical style and development is something confined solely to aesthetic issues and has nothing to do with gender.

When discussing the subject of women aesthetics, someone is bound to protest and say "oh, but I know a male composer who composes exactly that way," or "I know a female composer who composes exactly opposite." This level of argument leads nowhere, as it is confined to personal experience. Yet my assumptions are also based on listening experience. Should I therefore bury the subject? I admit that it is well-nigh impossible to prove my points; they remain hypothetical. Yet if we on the other hand wanted to come to scientifically proven results we would have to study hundreds of pieces of music by women and just as many by men. We would have to take their age, their nationality, their opinions, their development just as much into account as their sex. Such a research project would need enormous personal and financial resources, and even then we would not really come to fixed results. Nevertheless, I am aware that one day such research will have to be undertaken in order to put the subject on a more reliable level. This paper serves only to spark a discussion on the subject.

I am not determined to prove by all means that women compose differently. That would be ideological. I am just taking the before-mentioned assumption seriously that sex role is one of the most important determinants of human behavior. In consequence it seems to me sensible to ask whether gender influences music, especially since other disciplines like the visual arts, film and literature have been posing these questions for years.

Although we must distinguish between the *theoretical* constructions of male and female, as can be found in ideologies and which have led to a distorted picture of women, and the *real* differences, I believe that the real differences, which are based on different biological, social, psychological and aesthetic experiences of women and men in patriarchal culture, are to an extent influenced by the theoretical constructions of female. By suggesting that women have adopted certain traits because of their roles, I do not intend to push them back to the confinement of the past. However, the more I realize that women cannot rid themselves of their traditions by a sheer act of will-power (our past is too much a part of our present), the question arises as to whether they should not redefine some of these traditions and derive strength from them, instead of ignoring or condemning them.

In the past women acquiesced to the male-defining music system, and their creations were absorbed into the masculine tradition, which resulted for instance in Clara Schumann speaking disparagingly of her own music. I do not agree with Elaine Showalter, who in her book *Feminist Criticism in the Wilderness* maintains that a woman's culture existed in the past. I doubt whether we can find an independent counter-tradition, but there are signs that women in the past had a different approach to music, and that some mutual bonds between women composers exist. If we compare Clara Schumann's piano variations on a theme by Robert Schumann with the variations of Johannes Brahms on the same theme, we find that whereas Clara Schumann's variations are closely connected with the original theme, Brahms creates a well-nigh new piece of work. He departs from the original theme and turns his music into Brahms' music. It seems to me typical for a woman of the nineteenth century that Clara Schumann was thinking more of Robert than of herself. But our culture will always define Brahms' variations as the more valuable, because in our aesthetic hierarchy the innovative effect is ranked highest of all.

It would be ridiculous to maintain that all women compose similarly or in a specific style. Women composers cannot be judged all on the same scale—they differ by age, nationality, talents, places of residence, state of maturity, experience, etc. All sorts of music ranging from uncritical adaptation and assimilation up to the search for specifically female modes of expression can be found. Yet when listening to music composed by women in the twentieth century I have very often found what seem to me remarkable similarities. I have not just listed them—that would be arbitrary—but have attempted to trace them back to specific social-historical conditions and facts. I shall state and discuss seven points which I find typical for a great deal of music written by women.

1. Many women have a special ability to create a maximum amount out of a minimum of material, a sort of "restricted aesthetics."

Although women have composed in all forms and genres, ranging from small piano pieces to the mass and the symphony, they were in the nineteenth century confined mainly to parlor music on account of their social status. (This of course led to the well-known prejudice that women were unable to compose large forms.) They are skilled in writing music which can be performed easily and are less experienced in writing music for its own sake. This tradition prevails: songs, piano and chamber music predominate in music written by women. It is difficult to judge whether women are struggling with a negative burden or whether their ability to make the most of limited circumstances can also be a specific talent which is linked to their social character. The striving of composers like Pauline Oliveros, Annea Lockwood, Anne Gillis, Joan La Barbara and others to intensify the act of listening by limiting the material should be seen in this light.

2. Many have a special preference for functional music.

Women were also allotted to the fields of church music, music for educational purposes and music for amateurs. This has to do with the jobs women could get in the nineteenth century; the main field open for them was the so-called "social mothering," meaning jobs as teachers, governesses and nurses.

Even today a large amount of music written by women is functional music, and once more we must ask whether women prefer this branch because they are particularly skilled, or because they have not rid themselves of the constraints of tradition. Whatever the reason may be, women have written excellent functional music. German composers like Erna Woll and Felicitas Kukuck are known for the high quality of their church and pedagogic music.

3. Communication is of primary concern to them.

A while ago the German feminist magazine EMMA organized a competition for female journalists. The jury announced later: "When women write, they don't ramble. They have a message to transmit." This attitude can often be found in many women composers. They often compose music that alludes to something or someone; they like to tell stories. They write music that can be played, performed, and understood and the contact to the audience is of primary concern to many of them. Sofia Gubaidulina has for instance written hardly any music without a title, a text, a ritual or some kind of instrumental "action."

The traditional view of the male gender role in Western societies emphasizes power, strength, aggressiveness, competitiveness and logic, while the female role involves nurturing, cooperativeness and emotion. The role of women as mothers has taught them to harmonize conflicts, to negotiate in family problems, to unite instead of separate. This has consequences for their artistic output. For instance, they often have the performers in mind while composing, prefer to talk to the instrumentalists beforehand and get acquainted with their way of handling their instruments, and this influences them when composing.

4. Women composers are more interested in constituent substance than in compulsive innovation.

The male desire for narcissistic self-celebration is frequently missing in women, so that they do not feel the impulse to create sensations with hitherto unheard-of music. Many male composers seem to have their careers foremost in mind when composing. They aspire to become famous, and their music is often a novelty which aims at publicity, possible notoriety. It is quite possible that women might one day imitate men's burning desire for becoming famous, but for women today it has not the same importance. This has to do with the tradition of the nineteenth century when no jobs were offered them and they composed for their own pleasure (amateur status vs. professional status). This is why they do not find the craze for novelty and uniqueness as important as men, and it may explain why composers like Louise Farrenc, Louisa Adolpha Le Beau or Emilie Mayer in the nineteenth century, or Ethel Smyth, Grazyna Bacewicz and others in the twentieth century did not crave to develop a new language but rather leaned back on tradition. I am certainly not suggesting that women have difficulties in creating novelties, but rather that they do not find it important to be novel just for novelty's sake. They stress the content more than the aspect of material development. The German Canadian composer Hildegard Westerkamp uses background music from the radio as material, and she says of herself: "I recycle sounds."

5. They often strive to overcome binary contrasts.

Myriam Marbe firmly believes there is no such thing as past and present, but rather that times melt into each other. We often find women composers or performers attempting to combine various traditions, as for instance Ushio Torikai or Jin Him Kim who integrates into her work elements that she has assimilated from traditional Korean music. Eliane Radigue converted to Tibetan Buddhism and writes music in a semi-religious style which is intended to slow down the listeners. This aptitude to turn back instead of straight ahead can be seen as a more cyclic preference, contrary to the dynamic straight-forward line preferred by many men.

6. The aspect of "Ganzheitlichkeit" [the quality of being complete] means that they wish to combine various fields of art, but also the whole of human being, body and soul, Mankind (or Womankind) and Nature.

This probably has to do with women's preference to combine rather than to tear apart, which again can be attributed to women's role in society for many centuries. Women musicians like the Japanese Ushio Torikai or Meredith Monk often include other arts such as theatre, dance and performance in their music. They find it adequate to express themselves by taking fragments of the cultural diversity surrounding them and moulding these fragments into a unity. The wish to combine music and the visual arts is also strong. In the USA Performance Art has been developed mainly by women. Women composers often express the wish to be at harmony with nature. The American composer and singer Candace Natvig has studied bird's singing and tries to prove that music of old societies is influenced by the sounds of nature.

7. They relate closely to their own bodies and the human voice.

Men are physically nonproductive, whereas the creative powers of women are experienced in their own bodies. They did not experience the rigid borderline between body and spirit as did men. The confinement of women to the home also led to their composing innumerable songs in the nineteenth century. This tradition has led to a close relationship of the woman composer with the human voice, and especially to the female voice. This voice tradition is very alive today. Contemporary composers like Meredith Monk, Pauline Oliveros, Laurie Anderson, Connie Beckley and others trod new ground with their voice experiments. Joan LaBarbara is renowned for her exploration of vocal techniques inspired by musical traditions throughout the world. She has developed a vocabulary of new techniques including multiphonics, circular breathing and guttural sounds.

Sometimes these points unite in one composer, as for instance in the case of Oliveros or Gubaidulina. Pauline Oliveros need not be mentioned in detail as her striving to intensify the experience of listening, to abolish the linear structure of Western music and to unite many disparate elements in her music is well known. Sofia Gubaidulina is not interested in feminism, yet she composes as if she were a feminist: she is open towards all material. She is not stylistically bound, but concentrates on the contents of music. For her religion and music are just as much a unity as music and language, music and scenes. She combines folkloristic instruments like the bajan with classical instruments (violoncello); she is concerned with improvisation, is not interested in originality for its own sake, wishes to convert her audience from their "staccato" life style to a more meditative attitude, and she often stresses the unity of mankind with nature.

When one listens to music one cannot judge whether it has been written by a man or woman, one can only guess. It is possible, however, to trace female mentality and experience in the music of women. This is easy for instance in music of someone like Ruth Anderson, who in her piece, *I come out of your sleep,* uses electronic music to create the sound of breathing, which has a soothing effect on her listeners. On the other hand you will find that someone as rational-minded as Elisabeth Lutyens prefers to change time signatures, as she feels rhythm is more akin to breathing and spontaneous movement than to the military march. The music styles of Anderson and Lutyens differ hugely and prove that it would be useless to define a feminine aesthetic in the same sense of similarity; but we can trace their convictions back to their female experience.

I believe that women composers should get involved with women's traditions because they could then derive power and energy from them instead of ignoring or negating them. As to theorists and feminists, we should not forget that our Western culture is made to fit male requirements. If we continue to evaluate music written by women by male standards, we would have to define much of it as "deficient." As long as symphonic music is looked upon as more prestigious than chamber music, as long as functional music counts less than absolute (abstract) music, as long as the product is looked on as more valuable than the act of production, as long as music is defined by qualities such as loudness, virtuosity and greatest input instead of emphasizing heightened awareness and sensibility, as long as binary contrast such as body/soul, pop music/classical music, tradition/progression, functional music/absolute music etc. persist, music written by men will be looked on as superior. It will be necessary to attack conventional hierarchies and search for other values in which women can be represented. This can only be done satisfactorily, of course, if women's role is put on an equal basis with men's in society. In the meantime there are signs that male composers are changing their attitudes towards the role of music in society, and that they are taking over "feminine" traits in their music. So the challenge goes to both sexes, and it looks as if some exciting music is in store for us in the future.

195 William Grant Still

William Grant Still (1895–1978) was the first black composer to gain widespread recognition as a writer of American concert music. After receiving a degree in music from Oberlin College, Still moved to New York, where he studied privately with Edgard Varèse and became a leading figure in the Harlem Renaissance Movement of the 1920s. Still's pioneering role in American music is reflected in numerous accomplishments: he was the first African-American to write a symphony and have it performed by a major orchestra, the first to conduct a major symphony orchestra, the first to compose an opera produced by a major American company, and the first to produce music for radio, film, and television. In this autobiographical passage from an address delivered at UCLA in 1957, Still discusses the diverse influences he encountered as a young black composer and speaks of his wish—contrary to the advice of those advocating a more traditional concert style or more emphasis on ethnic and vernacular materials—to remain receptive to all of them.

FROM Horizons Unlimited
(1957)

I speak as a composer who has, in a very real sense, been through the mill. In my early days, I studied at Conservatories with Conservatory-trained teachers. There I learned the traditions of music and acquired the basic tools of the trade. If I had stopped there, the sort of music I later composed might have been quite different. But necessity forced me to earn a living, so I turned to the field of commercial music.

Back in the days when America became aware of the "Blues," I worked with W. C. Handy in his office on Beale Street in Memphis. This certainly would not seem to be an occupation nor a place where anything of real musical value could be gained. Nor would nearby Gayoso Street, which was then a somewhat disreputable section. But, in searching for musical experiences that might later help me, I found there an undeniable color and a musical atmosphere that stemmed directly from the folk.

Any alert musician could learn something, even in that sordid atmosphere. W. C. Handy listened and learned—and what he learned profited him financially and in other ways in the succeeding years. He, of course, belongs in the popular field of music. But if a popular composer could profit by such contacts with folk music, why couldn't a serious composer? Instead of having a feeling

TEXT: *William Grant Still and the Fusion of Cultures in American Music*, ed. by Robert Bartlett Haas (Los Angeles: Black Sparrow Press, 1975), pp. 114–16. Reprinted by permission of William Grant Still Music.

of condescension, I tried to keep my ears open so that I could absorb and make mental notes of things that might be valuable later.

As the years went on, and I went from one commercial job to another, there were always people who tried to make me believe that the commercial field was an end in itself, and who argued that I should not waste my time on what is now often called "long-hair" music. In this, I disagreed. I felt that I was learning something valuable, but only insofar as I could use it to serve a larger purpose.

The next important step was my study with Edgard Varèse. He might be classed as one of the most extreme of the ultramodernists. He took for himself, and encouraged in others, absolute freedom in composing. Inevitably, while I was studying with him, I began to think as he did and to compose music which was performed; music which was applauded by the avant-garde, such as were found in the International Composers' Guild. As a matter of fact, I was so intrigued by what I learned from Mr. Varèse that I let it get the better of me. I became its servant, not its master. It followed as a matter of course that, after freeing me from the limitation of tradition, it too began to limit me.

It took me a little while to realize that it *was* limiting me, and that the ultra-modern style alone (that is to say, in its unmodified form) did not allow me to express myself as I wished. I sought then to develop a style that debarred neither the ultra-modern nor the conventional.

Certain people thought this decision was unwise, and tried to persuade me to stay strictly in the ultra-modern fold. I didn't do it, but at the same time, the things I learned from Mr. Varèse—let us call them the horizons he opened up to me—have had a profound effect on the music I have written since then. The experience I gained was thus most valuable even though it did not have the result that might have been expected.

After this period, I felt that I wanted for a while to devote myself to writing racial music. And here, because of my own racial background, a great many people decided that I ought to confine myself to that sort of music. In that too, I disagreed. I was glad to write Negro music then, and I still do it when I feel so inclined, for I have a great love and respect for the idiom. But it has certainly not been the *only* musical idiom to attract me.

Fortunately for me, nobody tried to talk me out of the two things that strikingly influenced my musical leanings, possibly because those influences were not the sort which make themselves known to outsiders as readily as others. The first was my love for grand opera, born around 1911 when my stepfather bought many of the early Red Seal recordings for our home record library. I knew then that I would be happy only if someday I could compose operatic music, and I have definitely leaned toward a lyric style for that reason.

The second influence had to do with writing for the symphony orchestra, something which has deeply interested me from the very start of my musical life. Many years ago, I began to evolve theories pertaining to orchestration, and to experiment with them from time to time. Applying those theories has tended to modify, perhaps even to curtail, the development of a contrapuntal style as it is known today. However, their use has enabled me to better achieve the result I sought.

Today the music I write stems in some degree from all of my experiences, but it is what *I* would like to write, not what others have insisted that I write. Some people have been kind enough to say that I have developed a distinctly personal style of musical expression. I hope they are right, and if they are, I'm sure it has come from keeping an open mind, meanwhile making an effort to select what is valuable and to reject what is unimportant, in my estimation.

196 Olly Wilson

In contrast to the relatively conciliatory tone taken by William Grant Still regarding his relationship to American music at large (see pp. 1421–22), Olly Wilson (b. 1937), some forty years younger and writing in 1972 at the height of the civil rights movement, adopts a more aggressive, even accusatory manner. Traditionally trained, with degrees in music from major universities, and holding a professorship at the University of California at Berkeley, Wilson puts forward a somewhat bifurcated position. On the one hand, he responds to the historical suppression of black culture through racism with an essentialist stance (compare the essay by Eva Rieger, pp. 1415–20), arguing that the black composer has a unique voice shaped by sources that lie "deeply embedded in the collective consciousness of his people" (Wilson himself studied music in Africa during 1971 and 1972). On the other hand, he eschews parochialism, encouraging black composers to make use of all the technical resources they have available in order to write music that, while culturally specific, is universal in reach.

The Black American Composer
(1972)

At a time when the collective consciousness of black people has been raised to a renewed awareness of the power and significance of their culture, the black composer finds himself in a vital though demanding position. The role of any artist is to reinterpret human existence by means of the conscious transformation of his experience. He does this by ordering the media that he has chosen in such a manner that his fellow men gain new perspectives on their shared

TEXT: *Readings in Black American Music*, 2nd ed., compiled and edited by Eileen Southern (New York: W. W. Norton, 1983), pp. 327–32.

experiences; that they realize new dimensions of perception and expression and thereby broaden the scope of their existence.

The black composer (or any black artist) is unique because, unlike his white counterpart, his cultural history has been plagued by an exploitive racism as damnable as any ever to exist in the history of mankind. This obviously has a profound effect on the way he reinterprets the world; his reality is different from that of someone who has not had his experience. He sees the world from a unique point of view.

To paraphrase something that Leroi Jones wrote several years ago (in his set of essays entitled *Home*), the view from the top of the hill is significantly different from that of the bottom, and in most cases each viewer is unaware of the existence of another perspective. The latter part of that statement is particularly important because all too often one's concept of reality is held to be absolute. Thus positions that do not conform to that reality are seen as incorrect. People whose world view is different from that of Blacks, for example, frequently see such concepts as black music, black art, black theater, or black anything—where the emphasis is on black as a distinctive factor—as an aberrant or distorted concept. The usual rejoinder to the claims of a special world view is that there is no such thing as black art or black music—there is simply music and art.

I call your attention to a recent review of a recording by the black pianist Natalie Hinderas. The recording, entitled *Natalie Hinderas Plays Compositions by Black Composers,* was reviewed by Irving Kolodin in the *Saturday Review* magazine. Kolodin took exception to the idea of a recording by black composers on the grounds that he could not define what constituted black music. Since he could not determine what constituted black music, he felt there was not a meaningful distinction to be made. In his view, therefore, the notion of black music was an absurdity. It was absurd because his perspective was devoid of anything which would allow him to be aware of those unique elements which united all of those pieces. Because his frame of reference did not include those elements, he assumed they did not exist.

Kolodin's attitude very frequently has been manifest historically in the white American psyche. One of its most dramatic exhibitions occurred in the pseudo-scholarly investigations of the origin of the Negro Spirituals. As others before him, but without the trappings of scholarship, George P. Jackson (a white musicologist) developed a theory that the Negro spiritual was in fact derived from southern white Gospel songs. Briefly, his basic proposition was that in view of the fact that many Negro spirituals have text and notated melodies similar to those of white gospel songs, the Negro Spiritual must have been derived from the gospel song.

It was outside his range of possibilities that the African exiles and their progeny brought with them a sophisticated musical tradition, which flourished in this country in adapted forms both as religious and secular music. It was outside his range of possibilities because he subscribed to the conventional wisdom of the time which held that there was no significant African musical tradition. Therefore, he was incapable of dealing adequately with black music because of his limited perspective—limited in the same sense as was Kolodin's. In both cases there was no recognition of a black music because the scope of the viewer was blurred by both ignorance and cultural bias.

The black composer, on the other hand, approaches his task from a different perspective—a perspective from which he is consciously aware of the black music tradition. In transforming his experience, he draws upon a wide spectrum of musical expression which includes much not normally regarded as a part of the Euro-American tradition. Paradoxically, much of that Euro-American tradition itself was derived from the Afro-American tradition. It is this black tradition and the black composer's individual interpretation of it that makes his work unique. It is this special tradition that enables him to project human experience in a unique and meaningful manner.

At the same time it must be recognized that the universality of his work is not diminished. Universality in art does not stem from a denial of individual differences. It is not based upon a universal homogeneity of expression. It stems, rather, from the recognition of the similarity of the human condition which transcends important differences between cultures. The form and character of the work itself, however, is derived from strong cultural bases. The source of Verdi's music, for example, lies deeply imbedded in the collective sensibilities of the Italian people. It is deeply infected with the love of drama, with passionate emotions, surface clarity, and disarming candor.

The source of the black composer's music lies deeply embedded in the collective consciousness of his people. Along with a heightened sensitivity to motion, qualitative rhythm, and immediateness of expression, it includes a dimension which encompasses the wordless moans of a mid-week poorly attended prayer meeting, the Saturday-night ecstatic shrieks of a James Brown, the relentless intensity of the modal excursions of a John Coltrane, and the tonal word-songs of the teenage brothers "rapping" on the corner, full of the pride of new-found self respect.

The means by which the black composer brings these things to bear on his music are of individual concern. These means are as diverse as are the composers. In the work of many black composers, for example, the elements easily identified with the black experience are features of the foreground of their music. That is, they are clearly distinguishable since they form the external as well as internal aspects of the musical events shaped by the composer.

In other works these factors may be more subtle, but nonetheless are equally as important. They are used to determine internal factors, such as pacing, intensity, and formal development. In the works of such composers as T. J. Anderson, David Baker, and Wendell Logan may be found examples of this.

In this regard, it may be instructive to cite the work of the contemporary black painter Romare Bearden. Superficially, Bearden's work appears to have been influenced by the cubists (who, paradoxically, were strongly influenced by African sculpture). But a closer examination of Bearden's work reveals a sense of ritual, a sense of color, and a sense of motion which I do not detect in the works of most cubists. I attribute my response to factors which reside in Bearden's singular conception.

Nevertheless, I also sense some of these feelings when listening to the work of the above-named fellow composers. In short, the black composer brings with him cultural baggage, just as his African ancestors did. It is my contention that this cultural baggage will be manifest if the artist honestly follows the dictates of his musical imagination. The manifestation may take different forms and may not always be immediately obvious, but it will always exist.

It should not be deduced from what I have said that the black American composer is uninfluenced by music that comes from non-black traditions. Nothing could be further from the truth. The black composer is like any contemporary composer who is constantly stimulated by a bombardment of diverse musical sources. As a matter of fact, one of the general characteristics of twentieth-century music of any type is the pervasiveness of cross-cultural influences. This has led one observer of contemporary music to refer to this eclectic period as one in which the norm was one of constant stylistic diversity—or a period of "fluctuating stasis." There is no such thing in the world of today as complete cultural isolation. One need only turn on the radio to hear the mixtures of various musical cultures. Aretha Franklin is "big" in Japan, Indian ragas are popular on American college campuses, the Edwin Hawkins singers were a smashing success in Europe.

Nevertheless, the many influences that bear upon a black composer are so adapted as to project his personal conception from a black perspective. Any compositional technique or instrumental innovation may be used as long as the composer is controlling it. As long as he is shaping it, it will reflect him. A few years ago I began using the electronic media in some of my compositions. Some of my associates accused me of copping out, of using a white man's machine to try to express my black humanity—an endeavor which they felt was intrinsically contradictory.

My response, in some despair, was to point out to my brothers that for several hundred years now since our forefathers' involuntary departure from the homeland, black people have been adapting machines in the American environment to suit their purposes. Everything from food and dress to language and religion has been adapted to conform to an essentially African way of doing things. Nowhere has this adaptation been truer than in music. After all the Belgian Adolph Sax invented the saxophone and Jimmie Smith's last name was not Hammond. The point here is that, as in African Bantu philosophy, a thing is given meaning only by the will of a human being. The media is a vehicle of expression, not the substance of expression. Since the substance stems from the well springs of the individual, the media may be derived therefore from any source.

My approach to the electronic media is similar to my approach to any musical media. I use it as a means of projecting the musical idea I am trying to convey in a particular piece. It is as illogical to assume that different composers using the same media will produce similar works, as it is to assume that different artists using the same plastic media will produce works that look alike. Both Scott Joplin and Arnold Schoenberg wrote pieces for the piano about the same time, but there any similarity ends. Each man was expressing something out of his personal experience, and those experiences were culturally light-years apart. Nevertheless, each man created something that was universal in that it reflected universal sentiments from a discernible cultural perspective. My approach to electronic media, like my approach to the orchestra or any instrument, carries with it the sensibilities of a black man in the latter half of the twentieth century.

The attitude I hold toward media is also applicable to my approach to compositional techniques. I will use any technique or device which will enable me to project my musical ideas. It is debilitating to limit oneself a priori to any one system or style. For me, questions of musical technique are meaningless outside the context of a specific piece and should not limit one's appreciation of the musical ideas. A response to any music ultimately must be on the basis of the communicability of that music. One should ask himself, "Does this affect me in a meaningful way?," not "Does it use this or that technique?"

In conclusion, I would like to make a final statement on the role of the black composer in the struggle for Black Liberation. I am sometimes asked by students and others how I am able to justify my activity as a composer at this crucial historical moment. The question betrays a fundamental lack of understanding of the role of music in the traditional black community, both in the United States and in Africa. In traditional West African cultures music is not an abstraction, separate from life, a distillation of experience. It is, rather, a force by which man communicates with other men, the gods, and nature. In this sense it is obligatory and vital to existence.

The ideal I strive toward as a composer is to approach music as it is approached in traditional African cultures. In that sense my music is directly related to the struggle in that it aspires to inform, motivate, and humanize my fellow men in their aspirations.

EXTENDING WESTERN MUSIC'S BOUNDARIES

197 Claude Debussy

Claude Debussy (1862–1918) is considered by many the most important composer of the early twentieth century in establishing an esthetic orientation independent of Romanticism. Employed as a writer and critic throughout much of his career, Debussy actively espoused the need for widespread renewal in music. The first of these three pieces, dating from 1902, responds to a question posed in the first issue of a new periodical, *Musica:* "Is it possible to predict where the music of tomorrow will be?" The second and third, both written in 1913 for a prominent French music journal, *La revue musicale S.I.M.,* cover a broad spectrum of ideas. Collectively, these writings articulate many of Debussy's principal esthetic positions: that traditional training leads to standardization; that music should not slavishly imitate nature but evoke its fluidity, freedom, and mystery; that composers should adopt innovative approaches, such as techniques borrowed from cinematography; and that they should seek inspiration in music by earlier composers, such as François Couperin, and in music beyond the Western tradition, such as that of Java and Indochina.

Three Articles for Music Journals

[I]
(1902)

The best thing one could wish for French music would be to see the study of harmony abolished as it is practiced in the conservatories. It is the most ridiculous way of arranging notes. Furthermore, it has the severe disadvantage of standardizing composition to such a degree that every composer, except for a few, harmonizes in the same way. We can be sure that old Bach, the essence of all music, scorned harmonic formulae. He preferred the free play of sonorities whose curves, whether flowing in parallel or contrary motion, would result in an undreamed of flowering, so that even the least of his countless manuscripts bears an indelible stamp of beauty.

That was the age of the "wonderful arabesque," when music was subject to laws of beauty inscribed in the movements of Nature herself. Rather will our time be remembered as the era of the "age of veneer"—although here I am speaking generally and not forgetting the isolated genius of certain of my colleagues.

Contemporary dramatic music, however, embraces everything from Wagnerian metaphysics to the trivialities of the Italians—not a particularly French orientation. Perhaps in the end we will see the light and achieve conciseness of expression and form (the fundamental qualities of French genius). Will we

TEXT: *Debussy on Music*, ed. by François Lesure, trans. and ed. by Richard Langham Smith (New York: Alfred A. Knopf, 1977), pp. 84–85, 277–79, 295–98. Reprinted by permission of Alfred A. Knopf, Inc.

rediscover that abundant fantasy of which music alone is capable? It seems to have been forgotten under the pretext of research, which at first sight makes it seem as if the days of music are numbered.

Art is the most beautiful deception of all! And although people try to incorporate the everyday events of life in it, we must hope that it will remain a deception lest it become a utilitarian thing, sad as a factory. Ordinary people, as well as the élite, come to music to seek oblivion: is that not also a form of deception? The Mona Lisa's smile probably never existed in real life, yet her charm is eternal. Let us not disillusion anyone by bringing too much reality into the dream. . . . Let us content ourselves with more consoling ways: such music can contain an everlasting expression of beauty.

[II]
(1913)

Our symphonic painters do not pay nearly enough attention to the beauty of the seasons. Their studies of Nature show her dressed in unpleasantly artificial clothes, the rocks made of cardboard and the leaves of painted gauze. Music is the art that is in fact the closest to Nature, although it is also the one that contains the most subtle pitfalls. Despite their claims to be true representationalists, the painters and sculptors can only present us with the beauty of the universe in their own free, somewhat fragmentary interpretation. They can capture only one of its aspects at a time, preserve only one moment. It is the musicians alone who have the privilege of being able to convey all the poetry of night and day, of earth and sky. Only they can re-create Nature's atmosphere and give rhythm to her heaving breast. . . . We know that it is a privilege they do not abuse. It is a rare thing when Nature wrings from them one of those sincere love cries of the kind that make certain pages of *Der Freischütz* so wonderful; usually her passion is somewhat tamed because they portray her green beauty in such a lifeless way. It comes out like pressed leaves festering in dreary old books. Berlioz made do with such an approach all his life; otherwise sweet delights were soured because he insisted on patronizing artificial flower shops.

The music of our time has learned how to free itself from the romantic fancies of this literary view of things, but other weaknesses remain. During the past few years we have seen it tending toward an indulgence in the mechanical harshness of certain combinations of landscape. We can certainly do without the naïve aesthetics of Jean-Jacques Rousseau, but all the same we can learn great things from the past. We should think about the example Couperin's harpsichord pieces set us: they are marvelous models of grace and innocence long past. Nothing could ever make us forget the subtly voluptuous perfume, so delicately perverse, that so innocently hovers over the *Barricades mystérieuses*.

Let us be frank: those who really know the art of expressing themselves symphonically are those who have never learned how to do it. There is no conservatoire or music school that holds the secret. The theater offers a happy

alternative, however, in its resources of gesture, dramatic cries, and movements; they come to the aid of many a perplexed musician. Pure music offers
no such easy way out: one should either have a natural gift for evocation or
give up the struggle. And in any case, where did the symphonic music of our
country come from? Who are those ancestors who urge us toward this form of
expression? . . . First of all, our musicians willingly allowed themselves to be
inspired by the symphonic poems of Liszt and of Richard Strauss. And note,
furthermore, that any attempts at emancipation were soon forcibly quelled.
Each time anyone tried to break free from this inherited tradition he was
brought to order, crushed beneath the weight of the more illustrious examples.
Beethoven—who ought really be permitted to take a well-earned rest from
criticism—was brought to the rescue. Those severe old critics passed judgment
and threatened terrible punishments for breach of the classical rules whose
construction—they should have realized—was nothing less than mechanical.
Did they not realize that no one could ever go further than Bach, one of their
judges, toward freedom and fantasy in both composition and form?

Why, furthermore, did they not so much as try to understand that it really
would not be worthwhile having so many centuries of music behind us, having
benefited from the magnificent intellectual heritage it has bequeathed us, and
trying childishly to rewrite history? Is it not our duty, on the contrary, to try
and find the symphonic formulae best suited to the audacious discoveries of
our modern times, so committed to progress? The century of aeroplanes has a
right to a music of its own. Let those who support our art not be left to waste
away in the lowest ranks of our army of inventors, let them not be outdone by
the genius of engineers!

Dramatic music is also directly involved in this change in symphonic ideals;
its fate is governed by that of pure music. If it is suffering at the moment it is
because it has wrongly interpreted the Wagnerian ideal and tried to find in it a
formula. Such a formula could never be in tune with the French spirit. Wagner
was not a good teacher of French.

Let us purify our music! Let us try to relieve its congestion, to find a less
cluttered kind of music. And let us be careful that we do not stifle all feeling
beneath a mass of superimposed designs and motives: how can we hope to
preserve our finesse, our spirit, if we insist on being preoccupied with so many
details of composition? We are attempting the impossible in trying to organize
a braying pack of tiny themes, all pushing and jostling each other for the sake
of a bite out of the poor old sentiment! If they are not careful the sentiment
will depart altogether, in an attempt to save its skin. As a general rule, every
time someone tries to complicate an art form or a sentiment, it is simply
because they are unsure of what they want to say.

But we must first understand that our fellow countrymen have no love of
music. Composers are therefore discouraged from doing battle or starting
afresh. Music is simply not liked in France; if you doubt this, just listen to the
tone in which the critics speak of her. How obvious it is that they feel no love
for her at all! They always seem to be taking it out on the poor unfortunate

creature, assuaging some nasty deep-seated hatred. Such a feeling is not peculiar to our own time. Beauty has always been taken by some as a secret insult. People instinctively feel they need to take their revenge on her, defiling the ideal that humiliates them. We should be grateful to those few critics who do not hate her: for the scrupulous severity of Sainte-Beuve, who himself cared passionately for literature, and for Baudelaire, who was not only a critic with a unique understanding but a fine artist as well.

There remains but one way of reviving the taste for symphonic music among our contemporaries: to apply to pure music the techniques of cinematography. It is the film—the Ariadne's thread—that will show us the way out of this disquieting labyrinth. M. Léon Moreau and Henry Février have just supplied the proof of this with great success.[1] Those hordes of listeners who find themselves bored stiff by a performance of a Bach *Passion,* or even Beethoven's *Missa Solemnis,* would find themselves brought to attention if the screen were to take pity on their distress. One could even provide a film of what the composer was doing while composing the piece.

How many misunderstandings would thus be avoided! The spectator is not always to be blamed for his mistakes! He cannot always prepare for each new piece he listens to as if he were engaged on a piece of research, for the normal routine of an ordinary citizen is not well suited to include matters of aesthetics. In this way the author would no longer be betrayed; we would be free from any false interpretations. At last we would know the truth with certainty—the truth, the whole truth, and nothing but the truth!

Unfortunately we are too set in our ways. We are reluctant to renounce the boring! On we go in the same old way, imitating one another.

What a pity Mozart was not French. He would have really been worth imitating!

[III]
(1913)

In these times, when we are so preoccupied with trying out various different ways of educating people, we are gradually losing our sense of the mysterious. The true meaning of the word "taste" is also bound to be lost.

In the last century, having "taste" was merely a convenient way of defending one's opinions. Today the word has come to mean much more than that: it is now used in many different ways. It generally signifies something that involves the kind of argument usually settled with knuckle-dusters; one makes one's point, but in a way somewhat lacking in elegance. The natural decline of a "taste" concerned with nuance and delicacy has given way to this "bad taste," in which colors and forms fight each other. . . . But then perhaps these reflections are rather too general, for here I am only supposed to be concerned with music—a difficult enough task in itself.

1. Debussy refers to a film directed by Louis Feuillade, *L'Agonie de Byzance.* [Tr.]

Geniuses can evidently do without taste: take the case of Beethoven, for example. But on the other hand there was Mozart, to whose genius was added a measure of the most delicate "good taste." And if we look at the works of J. S. Bach—a benevolent God to whom all musicians should offer a prayer before commencing work, to defend themselves from mediocrity—on each new page of his innumerable works we discover things we thought were born only yesterday—from delightful arabesques to an overflowing of religious feeling greater than anything we have since discovered. And in his works we will search in vain for anything the least lacking in "good taste."

Portia in *The Merchant of Venice* speaks of a music that everyone has within them: "The man that hath no music in himself . . . let no such man be trusted." Those people who are only preoccupied with the formula that will yield them the best results, without ever having listened to the still small voice of music within themselves, would do well to think on these words. And so would those who most ingeniously juggle around with bars, as if they were no more than pathetic little squares of paper. That is the kind of music that smells of the writing desk, or of carpet slippers. (I mean that in the special sense used by mechanics who, when trying out a badly assembled machine, say, "That smells of oil.") We should distrust the *writing* of music: it is an occupation for moles, and it ends up by reducing the vibrant beauty of sound itself to a dreadful system where two and two make four. Music has known for a long time what the mathematicians call "the folly of numbers."

Above all, let us beware of systems that are designed as dilettante traps.

There used to be—indeed, despite the troubles that civilization has brought, there still are—some wonderful peoples who learn music as easily as one learns to breathe. Their school consists of the eternal rhythm of the sea, the wind in the leaves, and a thousand other tiny noises, which they listen to with great care, without ever having consulted any of those dubious treatises. Their traditions are preserved only in ancient songs, sometimes involving dance, to which each individual adds his own contribution century by century. Thus Javanese music obeys laws of counterpoint that make Palestrina seem like child's play. And if one listens to it without being prejudiced by one's European ears, one will find a percussive charm that forces one to admit that our own music is not much more than a barbarous kind of noise more fit for a traveling circus.

The Indochinese have a kind of embryonic opera, influenced by the Chinese, in which we can recognize the roots of the *Ring*. Only there are rather more gods and rather less scenery! A frenetic little clarinet is in charge of the emotional effects, a tam-tam invokes terror—and that is all there is to it. No special theater is required, and no hidden orchestra. All that is needed is an instinctive desire for the artistic, a desire that is satisfied in the most ingenious ways and without the slightest hints of "bad taste." And to say that none of those concerned ever so much as dreamed of going to Munich to find their formulae—what could they have been thinking of?

Was it not the professionals who spoiled the civilized countries? And the accusation that the public likes only simple music (implying bad music)—is that not somewhat misguided?

The truth is that real music is never "difficult." That is merely an umbrella term that is used to hide the poverty of bad music. There is only one kind of music: music whose claim to existence is justified by what it actually is, whether it is just another piece in waltz time (for example, the music of the *café-concert*) or whether it takes the imposing form of the symphony. Why do we not admit that, of these two cases, it is very often the waltz that is in better taste? The symphony can often only be unraveled with great difficulty—a pompous web of mediocrity.

Let us not persist in exalting this commonplace invention, as stupid as it is famous: taste and color should be beyond mention. On the other hand, let us discuss, rediscover our own taste; it is not as if we have completely lost it, but we have stifled it beneath our northern eiderdowns. That would be a step forward in the fight against the barbarians, who have become much worse since they started parting their hair in the center. . . .

We should constantly be reminding ourselves that the beauty of a work of art is something that will always remain mysterious; that is to say one can never find out exactly "how it is done." At all costs let us preserve this element of magic peculiar to music. By its very nature music is more likely to contain something of the magical than any other art.

After the god Pan had put together the seven pipes of the syrinx, he was at first only able to imitate the long, melancholy note of the toad wailing in the moonlight. Later he was able to compete with the singing of the birds, and it was probably at this time that the birds increased their repertoire.

These are sacred enough origins, and music can be proud of them and preserve a part of their mystery. In the name of all the gods, let us not rid it of this heritage by trying to "explain" it. . . . Let it be enhanced by delicately preserving our "good taste," the guardian of all that is secret.

198 Béla Bartók

In addition to being a leading composer of the first half of the twentieth century, Béla Bartók (1881–1945) was a pioneer in the study of folk music, helping establish the discipline now known as ethnomusicology. The two aspects of his professional life were intimately connected, as Bartók drew upon his knowledge of native music for both technical and expressive enrichment of his own work. In the following two articles, Bartók considers relationships between folk music and twentieth-century concert music. In the first, dating from 1931, he discusses the use of folk music as an aid to breaking away from traditional musical conceptions and the different ways such music can be incorporated into contemporary works: through quotation, imitation, or—most ideally—total stylistic absorption. In the second, written a decade earlier, Bartók expresses his disdain for the use of folk materials merely to provide an "exotic" effect—covering the surface of a traditional substance with "foreign" color—thus destroying the essential nature of the borrowed materials.

FROM Two Articles on the Influence of Folk Music

THE INFLUENCE OF PEASANT MUSIC ON MODERN MUSIC
(1931)

There have always been folk music influences on the higher types of art music. In order not to go back too far into hardly known ages, let us begin by referring to the pastorals and musettes of the seventeenth and eighteenth centuries, which are nothing but copies of the folk music of that time performed on the bagpipe or the hurdy-gurdy.

It is a well-known fact the Viennese classical composers were influenced to a considerable extent by folk music. In Beethoven's Pastoral Symphony, for instance, the main motive of the first movement is a Yugoslav dance melody. Beethoven obviously heard this theme from bagpipers, perhaps even in Western Hungary; the *ostinato*-like repetition of one of the measures, at the beginning of the movement, points to such an association.

But it was only a number of so-called "national" composers who yielded deliberately and methodically to folk music influences, such as Liszt (Hungarian Rhapsodies) and Chopin (Polonaises and other works with Polish characteristics). Grieg, Smetana, Dvořák, and the late nineteenth-century composers continued in that vein, stressing even more distinctly the racial character in their works. In fact, Moussorgsky is the only composer among the latter to yield completely and exclusively to the influence of peasant music, thereby forestalling his age—as it is said. For it seems that the popular art music of the eastern and northern countries provided enough impulse to the other "blatantly nationalistic" composers of the nineteenth century, with very few exceptions. There is no doubt that such music also contained quite a number of peculiarities missing till then in the higher types of Western art music, but it was mixed—as I have said previously—with Western hackneyed patterns and Romantic sentimentality.

TEXT: *Béla Bartók Essays*, ed. by Benjamin Suchoff (London: Faber & Faber, 1976), pp. 322–23, 340–44. Reprinted by permission of Faber & Faber Ltd. and the University of Nebraska Press.

At the beginning of the twentieth century there was a turning point in the history of modern music.

The excesses of the Romanticists began to be unbearable for many. There were composers who felt: "this road does not lead us anywhere; there is no other solution but a complete break with the nineteenth century."

Invaluable help was given to this change (or let us rather call it rejuvenation) by a kind of peasant music unknown till then.

The right type of peasant music is most varied and perfect in its forms. Its expressive power is amazing, and at the same time it is devoid of all sentimentality and superfluous ornaments. It is simple, sometimes primitive, but never silly. It is the ideal starting point for a musical renaissance, and a composer in search of new ways cannot be led by a better master. What is the best way for a composer to reap the full benefits of his studies in peasant music? It is to assimilate the idiom of peasant music so completely that he is able to forget all about it and use it as his musical mother tongue.

In order to achieve this, Hungarian composers went into the country and made their collections there. It may be that the Russian Stravinsky and the Spaniard Falla did not go on journeys of collection, and mainly drew their material from the collections of others, but they too, I feel sure, must have studied not only books and museums but the living music of their countries.

In my opinion, the effects of peasant music cannot be deep and permanent unless this music is studied in the country as part of a life shared with the peasants. It is not enough to study it as it is stored up in museums. It is the character of peasant music, indescribable in words, that must find its way into our music. It must be pervaded by the very atmosphere of peasant culture. Peasant motives (or imitations of such motives) will only lend our music some new ornaments; nothing more.

Some twenty to twenty-five years ago well-disposed people often marvelled at our enthusiasm. How was it possible, they asked, that trained musicians, fit to give concerts, took upon themselves the "subaltern" task of going into the country and studying the music of the people on the spot. What a pity, they said, that this task was not carried out by people unsuitable for a higher type of musical work. Many thought our perseverance in our work was due to some crazy idea that had got hold of us.

Little did they know how much this work meant to us. We went into the country and obtained first-hand knowledge of a music that opened up new ways to us.

The question is, what are the ways in which peasant music is taken over and becomes transmuted into modern music?

We may, for instance, take over a peasant melody unchanged or only slightly varied, write an accompaniment to it and possibly some opening and concluding phrases. This kind of work would show a certain analogy with Bach's treatment of chorales.

Two main types can be distinguished among works of this character.

In the one case accompaniment, introductory and concluding phrases are of secondary importance, and they only serve as an ornamental setting for the precious stone: the peasant melody.

It is the other way round in the second case: the melody only serves as a 'motto' while that which is built round it is of real importance.

All shades of transition are possible between these two extremes and sometimes it is not even possible to decide which of the elements is predominant in any given case. But in every case it is of the greatest importance that the musical qualities of the setting should be derived from the musical qualities of the melody, from such characteristics as are contained in it openly or covertly, so that melody and all additions create the impression of complete unity.

At this point I have to mention a strange notion widespread some thirty or forty years ago. Most trained and good musicians then believed that only simple harmonizations were well suited to folk melodies. And even worse, by simple harmonies they meant a succession of triads of tonic, dominant and possibly subdominant.

How can we account for this strange belief? What kind of folk songs did these musicians know? Mostly new German and Western European songs and so-called folk songs made up by popular composers. The melody of such songs usually moves along the triad of tonic and dominant; the main melody consists of a breaking up of these chords into single notes, for example, the opening measures of "O du lieber Augustin" and "Kutya, kutya tarka." It is obvious that melodies of this description do not go well with a more complex harmonization.

But our musicians wanted to apply the theory derived from this type of song to an entirely different type of Hungarian song built up on pentatonic scales.

It may sound odd, but I do not hesitate to say: the simpler the melody the more complex and strange may be the harmonization and accompaniment that go well with it. Let us for instance take a melody that moves on two successive notes only (there are many such melodies in Arab peasant music). It is obvious that we are much freer in the invention of an accompaniment than in the case of a melody of a more complex character. These primitive melodies moreover, show no trace of the stereotyped joining of triads. That again means greater freedom for us in the treatment of the melody. It allows us to bring out the melody most clearly by building round it harmonies of the widest range varying along different keynotes. I might almost say that the traces of polytonality in modern Hungarian music and in Stravinsky's music are to be explained by this possibility.

Similarly, the strange turnings of melodies in our Eastern European peasant music showed us new ways of harmonization. For instance the new chord of the seventh which we use as a concord may be traced back to the fact that in our folk melodies of a pentatonic character the seventh appears as an interval of equal importance with the third and the fifth. We so often heard these intervals as of equal value in the succession, that nothing was more natural than that we should try to make them sound of equal importance when used simultaneously. We sounded the four notes together in a setting which made us feel it not necessary to break them up. In other words: the four notes were made to form a concord.

The frequent use of fourth-intervals in our old melodies suggested to us the use of fourth chords. Here again what we heard in succession we tried to build up in a simultaneous chord.

Another method by which peasant music becomes transmuted into modern music is the following: the composer does not make use of a real peasant melody but invents his own imitation of such melodies. There is no true difference between this method and the one described above.

Stravinsky never mentions the sources of his themes. Neither in his titles nor in footnotes does he ever allude to whether a theme of his is his own invention or whether it is taken over from folk music. In the same way the old composers never gave any data: let me simply mention the beginning of the Pastoral Symphony. Stravinsky apparently takes this course deliberately. He wants to demonstrate that it does not matter a jot whether a composer invents his own themes or uses themes from elsewhere. He has a right to use musical material taken from all sources. What he has judged suitable for his purpose has become through this very use his mental property. In the same manner Molière is reported to have replied to a charge of plagiarism: "Je prends mon bien où je le trouve." In maintaining that the question of the origin of a theme is completely unimportant from the artist's point of view, Stravinsky is right. The question of origins can only be interesting from the point of view of musical documentation.

Lacking any data I am unable to tell which themes of Stravinsky's in his so-called "Russian" period are his own inventions and which are borrowed from folk music. This much is certain, that if among the thematic material of Stravinsky's there are some of his own invention (and who can doubt that there are) these are the most faithful and clever imitations of folk songs. It is also notable that during his "Russian" period, from Le Sacre du Printemps onward, he seldom uses melodies of a closed form consisting of three or four lines, but short motives of two or three measures, and repeats them "à la ostinato." These short recurring primitive motives are very characteristic of Russian music of a certain category. This type of construction occurs in some of our old music for wind instruments and also in Arab peasant dances.

This primitive construction of the thematic material may partly account for the strange mosaic-like character of Stravinsky's work during his early period.

The steady repetition of primitive motives creates an air of strange feverish excitement even in the sort of folk music where it occurs. The effect is increased a hundredfold if a master of Stravinsky's supreme skill and his precise knowledge of dynamic effects employs these rapidly chasing sets of motives.

There is yet a third way in which the influence of peasant music can be traced in a composer's work. Neither peasant melodies nor imitations of peasant melodies can be found in his music, but it is pervaded by the atmosphere of peasant music. In this case we may say, he has completely absorbed the idiom of peasant music which has become his musical mother tongue. He masters it as completely as a poet masters his mother tongue.

In Hungarian music the best example of this kind can be found in Kodály's work. It is enough to mention *Psalmus Hungaricus,* which would not have been written without Hungarian peasant music. (Neither, of course, would it have been written without Kodály.)

THE RELATION OF FOLK SONG TO THE DEVELOPMENT OF THE ART MUSIC OF OUR TIME
(1921)

* * * * *

Peasant music, in the strict sense of the word, must be regarded as a natural phenomenon; the forms in which it manifests itself are due to the instinctive *transforming power* of a community entirely devoid of erudition. It is just as much a natural phenomenon as, for instance, the various manifestations of Nature in fauna and flora. Correspondingly it has in its individual parts an absolute artistic perfection, a perfection in miniature forms which—one might say—is equal to the perfection of a musical masterpiece of the largest proportions. It is the classical model of how to express an idea musically in the most concise form, with the greatest simplicity of means, with freshness and life, briefly yet completely and properly proportioned. This is quite sufficient to account for the fact that peasant music, in the strict sense of the word, is not generally understood by the average musician. He finds it empty and inexpressive; popular art music suits his taste much better. This latter derives from individual composers, known or unknown, who possess a certain musical erudition. With us in Eastern Europe, it comes from amateurs of gentle birth who satisfy the creative impulse of their slender musical talents by the composition of more or less simple tunes. Their music is partly made up of elements of Western European art music—a jumble of commonplaces in this respect—but it also bears traces of the peasant music of their own country. This is what lends their music a certain exotic flavour by which even men like Liszt, Brahms, and Chopin felt themselves attracted. Nevertheless the outcome of this mixture of exoticism and banality is something imperfect, inartistic, in marked contrast to the clarity of real peasant music with which it compares most unfavourably. At all events it is a noteworthy fact that artistic perfection can only be achieved by one of the two extremes: on the one hand by peasant folk in the mass, completely devoid of the culture of the town-dweller, on the other by creative power of an individual genius. The creative impulse of anyone who has the misfortune to be born somewhere between these two extremes leads only to barren, pointless and misshapen works. When peasants or the peasant classes lose their naïvety and their artless ignorance, as a result of the conventional culture, or more accurately half-culture, of the town-dwelling folk, they lose at the same time all their artistic transforming power. So that in western countries it is a long while since there was any real peasant music in the strict sense of the word.

In Eastern Europe about a hundred years ago or even earlier many popular art melodies were appropriated by the peasant classes, who, by means of alterations, in a greater or lesser degree, have given them a new lease of life in a new *milieu;* but these tunes have not led to the formation of a new style of peasant music, nor indeed have they contributed anything towards it. The greater the alteration, or rather the more complete the process of perfection that they have undergone at the hands of their peasant appropriators has been, the more nearly do they approximate to the true style of peasant music; at the same time it is impossible to regard them as representative peasant melodies.

• • • • •

199 Darius Milhaud

Of the diverse ways in which twentieth-century composers reacted against the perceived pretensions of Romanticism, none was more characteristic than the turn from a view of the art as a deeply "spiritual," even quasi-religious phenomenon to one with a more "materialistic," ordinary perspective. This tendency took many different forms, two of which are found in this brief autobiographical passage by Darius Milhaud (1892–1974), a member of *Les Six,* a group of French composers closely linked with Erik Satie at the end of World War I. Milhaud first recounts a joint attempt with Satie to create a truly "everyday" music (compare the entry by Cocteau, pp. 20–24), indeed a music so ordinary that it would not—or so Milhaud and Satie hoped—be "listened to" at all: what they called *musique d'ameublement,* or "furniture music." He then discusses two notorious instances of anti-Romantic "objectivity" evident in text setting: his own two song cycles based on unadorned listings of items chosen from commercial catalogues.

FROM *Notes without Music*
(1949)

MUSIQUE D'AMEUBLEMENT AND CATALOGUE MUSIC

Just as one's field of vision embraces objects and forms, such as the pattern on the wallpaper, the cornice of the ceiling, or the frame of the mirror, which the eye sees but to which it pays no attention, though they are undoubtedly

TEXT: *Notes without Music* (New York: Alfred A. Knopf, 1953), pp. 122–24.

there, Satie thought that it would be amusing to have music that would not be listened to, *"musique d'ameublement,"* or background music that would vary like the furniture of the rooms in which it was played. Auric and Poulenc disapproved of this suggestion, but it tickled my fancy so much that I experimented with it, in cooperation with Satie, at a concert given in the Galerie Barbazange. During the program, Marcelle Meyer played music by Les Six, and Bertin presented a play by Max Jacob called *Un Figurant au théâtre de Nantes,* which required the services of a trombone. He also sang Stravinsky's *Berceuses du chat* to the accompaniment of three clarinets, so Satie and I scored our music for the instruments used in the course of these various items on the program. In order that the music might seem to come from all sides at once, we posted the clarinets in three different corners of the theater, the pianist in the fourth, and the trombone in a box on the balcony floor. A program note warned the audience that it was not to pay any more attention to the ritornellos that would be played during the intermissions than to the candelabra, the seats, or the balcony. Contrary to our expectations, however, as soon as the music started up, the audience began to stream back to their seats. It was no use for Satie to shout: "Go on talking! Walk about! Don't listen!" They listened without speaking. The whole effect was spoiled. Satie had not counted on the charm of his own music. This was our one and only public experiment with this sort of music. Nevertheless Satie wrote another *"ritournelle d'ameublement"* for Mrs. Eugene Meyer, of Washington, when she asked him, through me, to give her an autograph. But for this *Musique pour un cabinet préfectoral* to have its full meaning, she should have had it recorded and played over and over again, thus forming part of the furniture of her beautiful library in Crescent Place, adorning it for the ear in the same way as the still life by Manet adorned it for the eye. In any case, the future was to prove that Satie was right: nowadays, children and housewives fill their homes with unheeded music, reading and working to the sound of the radio. And in all public places, large stores and restaurants the customers are drenched in an unending flood of music. In America cafeterias are equipped with a sufficient number of machines for each client to be able, for the modest sum of five cents, to furnish his own solitude with music or supply a background for his conversation with his guest. Is this not *"musique d'ameublement,"* heard, but not listened to?

We frequently gave concerts in picture galleries. At Poiret's, Auric and I gave the first performance of Debussy's *Épigraphes antiques* for piano duet. At the Galerie la Boétie, Honegger played his violin sonatas with Vaurabourg, and the pianist André Salomon pieces by his friend Satie. Delgrange conducted my *Machines agricoles.*

I had written musical settings for descriptions of machinery taken from a catalogue that I had brought back from an exhibition of agricultural machinery which I had visited in company with Mme de B. and Mlle de S., who wanted to choose a reaper for their estate in the Bordeaux area. I had been so impressed by the beauty of these great multicolored metal insects, magnificent modern brothers to the plow and the scythe, that the idea came to me of celebrating them in music. I had put away in a drawer a number of catalogues, that I came across in 1919. I then composed a little suite for singer and seven solo instruments in the style of my little symphonies; the titles were *"La Faucheuse"* (reaper), *"La Lieuse"* (binder), *"La Déchaumeuse-Semeuse-Enfouisseuse"* (harrow, seeder, and burier), *"La Moissonneuse Espigadora"* (harvester), *"La Fouilleuse-Draineuse"* (subsoil and draining plow), *"La Faneuse"* (tedder). A few months later I used the same group of instruments for settings to some delightful poems by Lucien Daudet inspired by a florist's catalogue: *Catalogue de fleurs*.

Not a single critic understood what had impelled me to compose these works, or that they had been written in the same spirit as had in the past led composers to sing the praises of harvest-time, the grape harvest, or the "happy plowman," or Honegger to glorify a locomotive, and Fernand Leger to exalt machinery. Every time anyone wanted to prove my predilection for leg-pulling and eccentricity he cited *Les Machines agricoles*. I have never been able to fathom why sensible beings should imagine that any artist would spend his time working, with all the agonizing passion that goes into the process of creation, with the sole purpose of making fools of a few of them.

200 Wanda Landowska

Although the nineteenth century experienced a growing sense of historical consciousness, as evident in music as in other areas, when compositions of the more distant past were performed, they were normally transcribed so as to be rendered more acceptable to contemporary taste. During the course of the twentieth century, however, performers tried increasingly to approach earlier music on its own terms. The Polish harpsichordist Wanda Landowska (1879–1959) took a leading role in this development in the early years of the century, playing Bach's keyboard works on the harpsichord rather than the piano, which had by then become the long-preferred medium for this music. This excerpt from her groundbreaking 1909 book *Music of the Past*, here as condensed and revised for a subsequent publication, speaks for the importance of older music and for its capacity to enrich contemporary musical life. The so-called early music movement, which Landowska helped pioneer and which in recent years has attained truly remarkable currency, represents one of numerous efforts in the present century to establish a more encompassing conception of musical culture.

The Return to the Music of the Past
(1909)

I have insisted on the fallacy of progress in music because I consider it to be the principal cause of ignorance about our past and of most errors in the interpretation of our ancient masters. Because of this prejudice, blown up almost to the importance of a religion, the true beauties of music—as numerous as those of other arts—are still very poorly revealed. We remain deaf to these miracles of beauty, so marvelously remote; yet they should uplift the soul by their melodious echo, and, from century to century, they should link sympathetic hearts with a divine tie.

If sometimes we tire of grandiosity and if we lack air in the thick atmosphere of exaggerated romanticism, we need only to open wide the windows on our magnificent past; it will refresh our soul. We wish to participate in all emotions, in all ecstasies at the whim of our fancy. No longer shall we believe that while all the arts flourished marvelously in the past, music alone, although admired, was like a frail and sickly plant that could hardly break through the ground. Even supposing that music was in its cradle, we may be as sensitive to the charm of a prattling child as to the most skillful speech of a seasoned orator. If, on the contrary, music is afflicted with old age, we know how to admire the beauty of a lined face. No, the genius of the composers of the past was not a mere flash in the pan; it is an eternal flame, softly warming. It will never perish.

Yes, but one must go along with one's own time. Let new beauties be created, and we shall like them; but, at the same time, let us not relegate to darkness the works of the masters who were our models. They are not wolves; they will not, as Gounod said, devour the new masterpieces.

And in the name of what prejudice shall we continue to be suspended from the tiny spot we occupy in space instead of extending our view afar, instead of being contemporaries of all men? Only when we are strong enough to withstand that prejudice shall we really belong to our epoch. The great merit of the last half of the nineteenth century was that it awakened a taste for retrospection, a sense of comparison, and made us delight in that which is old, an "old" that is often newer than the new. A passion has been kindled in us; it does not encompass superior civilizations alone, but also those that our computer of taste had rated childish, decadent, or barbaric.

There is an evergrowing interest in the music of the past. But this would prove little in itself, since at all times the greatest musicians bowed before the works of the geniuses that preceded them. "We are not recapturing the

TEXT: *Landowska on Music*, ed. and trans. by Denise Restout and Robert Hawkins (New York: Stein and Day, 1964), pp. 159–60. Reprinted with permission of Denise Restout.

masterpieces," said Jules Janin; "the masterpieces themselves are recapturing us." Sooner or later, everyone will understand that a work of Josquin des Prés is well worth a Breughel. People of refined taste will feel that a Magnificat of Pachelbel, a chanson of Jannequin, a cantata of Bach, and a motet of Palestrina are worth more than the songs of modern sirens and of all the machines of speed. Then they will help us to erect a museum where we shall be able to hear and admire all our Titians, our Velasquezes, and our Raphaels, just as painters are able to admire theirs. And then we shall be able to enhance our lives with the memory of times that are gone.

201 Harry Partch

Not only did the traditional system of Western harmonic tonality come into question during the twentieth century, so did its underlying basis in equal temperament. In this 1940 article, originally intended (though later discarded) as an introduction for his book *A Genesis of Music,* the American composer Harry Partch (1901–1976) argues for a more flexible and subtly modulated tone system encompassing microtonal divisions. For Partch this proposal formed an essential part of his lifelong effort to undermine the rationalistic foundations of Western art in order to create an alternative, more ritualistically conceived music incorporating theater, dance, and costume, as well as specially constructed instruments that themselves took on the function of theatrical sets.

Patterns of Music
(1940)

He is an artist. Before him is a scale of colors, and in his mind he approaches the reds. For his brush's immediate use he sees a carmine, a vermilion, a scarlet, a crimson, a cerise, a garnet, a ruby, and verging off into other color values are an orchid and a magenta, a nasturtium and an orange, and a sienna, a rust, and an ochre.

He ponders leisurely. No, the exact shade he envisions—despite the great variety at hand—isn't here. With the assurance born of a life spent in being able to get what he wants, he then mixes—in just the right proportions—a bit of white, rust, and cerise to his vermilion, and—there! He has it!

TEXT: *Bitter Music,* ed. by Thomas McGeary (Urbana: University of Illinois Press, 1991), pp. 159–61.

Consider the writer of music. Before him is also a scale. It holds seven white keys and five black ones. In his mind he approaches C-sharp, one of the five blacks. He approaches it, and he lands on it. His action is direct, simple, predetermined.

There are no shades of C-sharp, no shades of red, for him. The one shade that his gods will allow him to use is before him. He is taught that that is enough; it is good, traditional, and proper, and he feels a vague sense of immorality in even wondering about those possible bastard C-sharps.

The present-day musician might observe: "If he doesn't like C-sharp he has D," which paraphrases: "He has yellow; why must he be so difficult as to also want vermilion?"

With the disquietude born of a life getting substitutes for nearly everything he really wants, the composer yearns for the streaking shades of sunset. He gets red. He longs for geranium, and gets red. He dreams of tomato, but he gets red. He doesn't want red at all, but he gets red, and is presumed to like it. But does he?

Another picture. It is that of a poet in torment over a line, and—to particularize—let us conjure a vision of Hart Crane laboring over the handful of words which, referring to the ocean, end: "Her undinal vast belly moonward bends."

There is no intention here to divine the thought processes of Crane in coming at last to this particular beauty of word cadence. But—were Hart Crane a composer of music—it would be exceedingly easy to unravel his processes, and, because his medium wouldn't allow him subtle and unusual shadings, he would never, never arrive at—"Her undinal vast belly moonward bends."

He would tentatively write: "The deep blue ocean moonward bends—"

Or: "With the moon rolls the boundless deep—"

Or, if he wanted to be modern: "Mooncalls sea-ocean bluedeep rolling—"

"Deep blue ocean" was and is used to excess by every writer of music since Palestrina. "The boundless deep" dates from Schubert and John Field, and is still widely used, and the last version is a fair literary paraphrase of most modern tonality—a cliché hash.

Before he ever writes a note the most brilliant composer is doomed to a system that is not capable of growth at his hands—or even of elasticity—and thus to a weary sea of worn-out forms, phrases, progressions, cadences, and chords.

Perhaps better than in any other way the two pictures above explain the reason for my musical heresy. The wayward trail began eighteen years ago, and, having traveled it all—inch by inch—I would not recommend it to others too heartily.

The great cathedral of modern music, erected in trial and labor and pain through most of the Christian era, is a safe and beautiful sanctuary. Its one sad aspect is that it seems to be finished—there is so little, if anything, that is significant that can be added to it. On the other hand, in the wild, little-known country of subtle tones beyond the safe cathedral, the trails are old and dim, they disappear completely, and there are many hazards.

The zealot driving into this wilderness should have more than one life to give: one to create instruments within the tyranny of the five-fingered hand, to play the tones he finds; one that will wrestle with notation and theory, so that he can make a record of what he finds, and give it understandable exposition; still another that will create and re-create significant music for his new-old instruments and in his new-old media; and, finally, another that will perform it, give it—as a revelation—to the general wealth of human culture.

It is not so simple as the few minutes' work of dabbing colors together from the already rich language of color. It is not so simple as combining a few choice words from the already rich language of words. It is the long, painful process of making less poor the pathetically impoverished language of tone.

The present book shows how the bonds of the composer might be, and are being, burst—how that which is too limited is being delimited. It is not a new trail in itself. It is only a survey—but a survey of all trails, both old and projected, and of one particular new trail.

Hence, *Patterns of Music.*

202 Bruno Nettl

Aided by developments in communication and transportation, the boundaries of Western musical culture have been extended dramatically in recent years, embracing music and musical practices from all parts of the globe. One result of this development toward "multiculturalism" has been an interest in reexamining Western musical culture from a more detached, "non-native" point of view: to pry beneath its surface manifestations (particular compositions, stylistic groupings, performers, best-selling records, and the like) in search of its ideological foundations. At first evident mainly in the work of feminist writers and of socially, politically, and gender-oriented critics, the tendency has subsequently had a considerable impact on music studies in general. The field of ethnomusicology is especially interesting in this connection, as its practitioners are by nature concerned with the role of music in its larger socio-ideological framework. Historically, the discipline has been applied almost exclusively to non-Western cultures, a tradition that is broken in this 1992 article by the American scholar Bruno Nettl (b. 1930).

FROM Mozart and the Ethnomusicological Study of Western Culture

An Essay in Four Movements
(1992)

In works such as this, it is common to begin by defining ethnomusicology. I shall give three definitions and use them all: the comparative study of musical systems and cultures; the study of music in or as culture; the study of a musical culture from an outsider's perspective. None of these excludes the art-music culture of Western society, but few ethnomusicological studies have actually been devoted to it. I would like to deal with this topic, speaking at times as an American ethnomusicologist, at other times pretending to be an outsider, and sometimes acting as the native informant of this study. For comparative perspective I shall turn to one or two other societies with whose musical cultures I have become acquainted. I doubt that this essay states anything new. It is intended to provide food for thought, but it is also—by implication, at least—a critique of ethnomusicological approaches.

I. ADAGIO: WE BEGIN IN MONTANA

GUIDING PRINCIPLES

As this paper is also presented in homage to Mozart, the most special of composers, it follows, in its attempt to establish interplay of ideas and cultures, the form of an eighteenth-century symphony. And as the first movement may begin with an introduction quite removed, at least on the surface, from the main subject matter of the movement, I take the liberty of beginning an essay about Mozart with an excursion to the Blackfoot people of Montana.

After working with them for a time, I came to believe—influenced by a series of recent musical ethnographies published in the wake of significant works by Alan Merriam[1]—that the system of ideas about music held in each society, however small, is complex but coherent and that it informs importantly about both music and culture. It became clear to me, for example, that the principal unit of musical thought in Blackfoot culture is the song, an indivisible unit which is thought by Blackfoot people not to undergo change or variation and which is identified by use and secondarily by persons and events with which it is associated. The musical universe of the Blackfoot is capable of infinite expansion, as new songs can always come into existence although their

TEXT: *Disciplining Music: Musicology and its Canons*, ed. by Katherine Bergeron and Philip V. Bohlman (Chicago: University of Chicago Press, 1992), pp. 137–45.

1. Alan P. Merriam, *The Anthropology of Music* (Evanston: Northwestern University Press, 1964) and *Ethnomusicology of the Flathead Indians* (Chicago: Aldine, 1967).

style may not be new. One melody dreamed separately by two seekers of visions is in certain respects considered to be two songs. The concepts of composition and learning are closely related, as new songs are seen as extant musical units learned from an outside source. Most important, songs are significant mediators among groups of beings—between groups of humans and between humans and supernatural forces.

It became clear also that in Blackfoot culture, certain things about music and not others are evaluated. A person may say that he likes or dislikes genres of song, such as gambling songs or Grass Dance songs, and a singer or a singing group may be praised for the totality of their performance. But most individual songs, and individual performances, are not verbally evaluated. People say, "I like hand-game songs," "That's a good singing group," and "He's a good singer," but not "That is a fine song" or "I like the way they sang that particular song." And they do not say things like "That group is good because they work so hard" or "I like this group of songs because it must have taken a long time to make them."[2]

ALLEGRO ASSAI: ETHNOGRAPHY OF THE MUSIC BUILDING

FIRST THEME: A VISITOR FROM MARS

This summary may be a guide to the kinds of things that a perfect stranger in Western art music culture might note and investigate. When I teach courses in the anthropology of music, one of my favorite figures is an "ethnomusicologist from Mars" who has the task of discerning the basics of Western art music culture as manifested by the community of denizens of a fictitious (well, maybe not so fictitious) Music Building. Would the visitor's experiences be a bit like mine in a Blackfoot community? We can imagine him or her (or it?) on arrival looking in the windows of the little practice rooms, seeing people playing on various instruments to themselves, and being told by a bystander, "He's a very talented young man, practicing Mozart, but until recently he used to play only bluegrass." A woman turns on the radio, there is music, and she says, "Aha, it's Mozart" (or Brahms, maybe; but not, for instance, "Aha, it's piano music" or "It's Heifetz," or "Thank heavens, a rondo!"). The Martian is told that he simply *must* hear the symphony orchestra that evening, or the opera—but he is confused when he is told that he shouldn't bother with the day's soap operas or the evening TV's "Grand Ole Opry." He is urged to go to a concert of student compositions, told that what he may hear will surely be wonderfully new and experimental, even though it actually might sound quite awful.

Walking around the Music Building, he sees names engraved in stone around the top: Bach, Beethoven, Haydn, Palestrina (on Smith Memorial Hall

---

2. For explanations in more detail, see Bruno Nettl, *Blackfoot Musical Thought: Comparative Perspectives* (Kent, Ohio: Kent State University Press, 1989).

in Urbana); or a more hierarchical, much longer list clearly featuring Beethoven, Mozart, Bach, Haydn, and Wagner (in Bloomington). No names are found on the English Building, and no Franz Boas or Claude Lévi-Strauss or Margaret Mead at Social Sciences. And he hears of no music buildings with "Concerto," "Symphony," "Oratorio." Seeking a score at the library, he must look under "Mozart." "Symphony," "long pieces," "loud pieces," "sad" or "meditative," "C minor" and "Dorian" won't do.

There is no need to belabor the impact that the initial experiences may have on any newcomer to a culture. Confronting the Music Building, one is quickly exposed to a number of guiding principles of Western art music.[3] Importantly, they include the concept of hierarchy—among musical systems and repertories and, within art music, among types of ensembles and composers. There is a pyramid, at the top one of two or three composers. There is the preeminence of large ensembles and grand performances, and their metaphorical extensions to other grand, dramatic events in life. Talent and practicing go together in a way, but they are also opposing forces, the one both practically and philosophically a possible complement for the other. There is the great value placed on innovation, but it is the old and trusted, the music of the great masters of the past, that is most respected. In particular, our visitor is struck by the enormous significance of the concept of the master composer, a concept of which the figure of W. A. Mozart is paradigmatic.

SECOND THEME: AMADEUS

In his stay, our Martian friend runs into the concept of Mozart in many guises; and having read Merriam,[4] Steven Feld,[5] Lorraine Sakata,[6] and others, he realizes that one way to do good fieldwork is to pursue a concept wherever it leads you. What he pursues, of course, is the Mozart of today; and so he is doing—and I want to do—something quite different from what is done by the many scholars (prominent among whom was my father) who have studied the Mozart who lived in the eighteenth century. The two are closely related and depend on each other, but they are not identical. In suggesting that the study of today's Mozart may be a task for ethnomusicology, I must add that what I say here is at best suggestive, that I have not really done much research and have little hard data. My claim to authority is really that I am speaking as the Martian's native informant in the culture.

So far he has been confronted by Mozart as a composer or, perhaps more properly, Mozart as a group of pieces. A second, perhaps relatively minor form

3. For anthropological studies of schools of music, see Catherine Cameron, "Dialectics of the Arts" (Ph.D. diss., University of Illinois, 1982) and Henry Kingsbury, *Music, Talent, Performance: A Conservatory Cultural System* (Philadelphia: Temple University Press, 1988).
4. See note 1 above.
5. Steven Feld, *Sound and Sentiment: Birds, Weeping, Poetics, and Song in Kaluli Expression* (Philadelphia: University of Pennsylvania Press, 1983).
6. Hiromi Lorraine Sakata, *Music in the Mind* (Kent, Ohio: Kent State University Press, 1983).

of Mozart is the composer as a person. Denizens of the Music Building think of a composer in these two forms, forms that are partly congruent but that sometimes also conflict. It is in this context that the ethnomusicologist encounters the play *Amadeus* by Peter Shaffer.[7]

Let me now leave our imaginary colleague and talk about musicologists. The literary and dramatic merits of the play have been widely debated, and I can surely not contribute to this discussion. But musicologists have, in writing but in talking even more, taken an essentially critical position. The point is this, I believe: *Amadeus* involves the depiction of Mozart as a thoroughly ludicrous figure who is nevertheless able to compose incredible music—although only his enemy, the composer Antonio Salieri, recognizes it. Obviously, the play is not about the historical Mozart but uses him as a metaphor for the concept of the genius, the man loved by God; and Salieri for the hardworking, competent musician who is not a genius and therefore feels betrayed by God. Some musicologists who were put off by the play said that history was falsified, but there are other works of fiction about Mozart,[8] partly about the mystery of his death, and they are not usually the subject of heated criticism. The critical view of *Amadeus* has, I suggest, other bases. Mozart was made to look ridiculous, the kind of person who could not possibly be taken seriously as a great master of music. The response was similarly heated when Beethoven, in a psychoanalytical study, was made to look weak, impotent, petty.[9] The Music Building denizens are concerned about the *kinds* of persons to whom they have accorded the great-master status, but they have not resolved certain dilemmas. Are great composers great souls, and does the music come from divine inspiration, or are they just excellent technicians? Is it better to be a genius who comes to his accomplishments effortlessly or someone who achieves by the sweat of his brow? Who should properly be loved by God? In some societies the matter has been resolved. In Madras I was told, "Tyagaraja was such a great composer *because* he was such a holy man;" and a Blackfoot composer received his songs directly from the supernatural, a source above criticism.

DEVELOPMENT AND RECAPITULATION: THE GREAT MASTERS

In real life, these two themes are mixed and intertwined; let me briefly develop and eventually recapitulate them, returning to the ethnography of the Music Building and the centrality of the "great masters"—a dozen or so figures who are the deities of the culture. As geniuses, they exist on a different plane from other musicians. In the symphonic and chamber repertory, their works

---

7. Peter Shaffer, *Amadeus* (New York: Harper & Row, 1981).

8. For example, Eduard Friedrich Mörike, *Mozart auf der Reise nach Prag* (Vienna: Schroll, 1855), Alexander Pushkin, *Mozart and Salieri*, trans. R. M. Hewitt (Nottingham: University College, 1938; originally published as *Motsart i Salieri,* 1831), and Marcia Davenport, *Mozart* (New York: Charles Scribner's Sons, 1932).

9. Edith Sterba and Richard Sterba, *Beethoven and His Nephew* (New York: Pantheon, 1954).

occupy some 65 percent of performance time, a bit less in piano and choral concerts. An elite within a segment of musical culture already elite, they stand out because they wrote only great music, and when they did not, it must be explained. Beethoven's works are accorded universal status as masterworks, and when a *Wellington's Victory* appears, special excuses have to be made: He didn't mean it, was playing games, composed the work only for money. Although there are borderline composers, for those individuals not in this group, one or two major works are regarded as masterworks while the rest are essentially ignored.

The great masters wrote great music, but opinion is sometimes divided on the basis of their personalities. The music of Richard Wagner, a man with tremendous ego and little regard for his fellow humans, so one is given to understand, is disliked by many for precisely that reason. Richard Strauss, an occasional Nazi sympathizer, was widely ignored as a composer. J. S. Bach's obviously profamily attitude has helped his music to be extolled, while Chopin's slightly outré lifestyle, Tchaikovsky's homosexuality, and Schumann's psychiatric history have lowered their status a bit. To the denizens of the Music Building, music lives in their conception of the principal units of musical thought—the persons of the great composers.

In musicology as well, the selection of research topics often revolves about a person; one is a "Mozart scholar," "Bach scholar," "Liszt scholar." Successful research on a minor composer depends to a considerable extent on the scholar's ability to show relationship to or influence from or upon a member of the great-master elite. The coherence of the corpus of creations by a composer is a paramount issue to scholars. To know the person who composed a piece is to know the most important thing about it. To find a new piece by a great master can give you the musicological equivalent of the Nobel Prize. To learn that a piece "by" Beethoven is actually by Friedrich Witt would today get you on the front pages of the *New York Times.* Such a piece, a bit like the song dreamed by two Blackfoot visionaries, is somehow no longer the same piece if Beethoven did not write it. And that it be truly a *piece* on its own terms, without excessive relationship to others, represents another value of the Music Building: the great importance of innovation.

The Music Building is in North America, but its denizens don't worry that the great masters are not Americans but, indeed, largely ethnic Germans. Their concept of art music is supranational, more so perhaps than in the case of visual art or literature. The emblem of this concept is the use of a single notation system which enables musicians who cannot speak to each other to play in the same orchestra. (This is not so everywhere; note the many systems operative in Japanese traditional music.) Furthermore, there is a universal terminology, derived from Italian, which has only recently begun to give way to national vernaculars. Why it should be Italian, in a repertory dominated by Germans, moves us to another guiding principle of Western art music, that of the musician as stranger. Deep in the roots of European culture is an ambivalence about music, suspicion of it, a belief that somehow the musician, often a strangely behaving person who can perform incredible feats, is in league with the devil. The musician is permitted, even required, to be a strange, unconventional person, wear his hair long, speak with an accent, be absent minded. The mad, inexplicable genius, perhaps; but he may also be thought to have a deviant lifestyle, to be a habitual drunkard, drug addict, debtor, homosexual, womanizer, but then also a foreigner. It is, I suggest, the idea of keeping music at arm's length that results in a foreign terminology for music, motivates denizens of the Music Building to be so much attracted to foreign teachers, and causes orchestras to seek foreign conductors (while never promoting, say, the first clarinettist to that post).

And so, while Austrians make much of *their* Mozart, and Germans of Beethoven, nations throughout the world, including some where their works have rarely if ever been heard, put their likenesses on postage stamps.

II. ANDANTE: MYTHOLOGICAL VARIATIONS

THEME: THE MYTH OF BEAVER

Our Martian observer has noted a number of guiding principles, foremost among which are hierarchies headed by a pantheon of great masters. If they are the deities, their character may be explained by myths widely told, if not rationally believed. Can one gain important insights into musical culture from the reading of myths? It is an approach well established in anthropology, and ethnomusicologists have begun to join it. Steven Feld, in *Sound and Sentiment* (1983), builds the interpretation of an entire musical culture on a single central myth about a boy who became a bird. Could one show the Music Building's system of ideas about music as the function of a mythic duel between Mozart and Beethoven? Let me show you what I mean by recalling an important myth of the Blackfoot people.

It concerns the interaction of a human family and the figure of the beaver, who is a kind of lord of the part of the world below the surface of the water, a sort of underworld. A great human hunter has killed a specimen of each animal and bird, and their dressed skins decorate his tent. While he is hunting, a beaver comes to visit his wife and seduces her, and she follows him into the water. After four days she returns to her husband, and in time gives birth to a beaver child. In Blackfoot society, such an affair would have been severely punished, but the hunter continues to be kind to his wife and particularly to the child. One day the beaver visits the wife again and, expressing pleasure at the way his child is treated, says that he wants to give the hunter some of his supernatural power as a reward. He asks for certain ritual preparations to be made and then visits the hunter. They smoke together and then the beaver begins to sing, song after song, each song containing a request for a particular bird or animal skin. The hunter gives the skin and in return receives the song. At the end, the hunter has received the songs of the beaver and their supernatural power—and with them the principal ritual of Blackfoot religion.[10]

This myth imparts many important things about Blackfoot music. Here is a brief summary. Songs come to humans and exist as whole units, and they are learned in one hearing. They are objects that can be traded, as it were, for physical objects. The musical system reflects the cultural system, as each being in the environment has its song. Music reflects and contains supernatural power. It is something which only men use and perform, but women are instrumental in bringing its existence about. Music is given to a human who acts morally, gently, in a civilized manner. It is the result of a period of dwelling with the supernatural, after which a major aspect of culture is brought, so in a way it symbolizes humanness and Blackfootness, a role that music has in some other Native American myths. Music has specific roles and functions and is used in a prescribed ritual. There is more, despite the fact that this is not specifically a myth of the origins of music.

Two Variations: Myths of Mozart and Beethoven

The mythology of the Music Building has more characters, and facts and fancy are intertwined in its stories. Yet they are myths in the sense that they explain complex reality to the ignorant and the young. We now hear a native consultant telling about his childhood in a family of denizens of the Music Building, though on another continent. He hears an attractive piece of music and is told it "is" Mozart, and, in bits of pieces, learns this: Mozart was a young boy with incredible talent and ability; no one could explain his feats. He composed without much in the way of lessons. His father took him to show him off to the royalty of Europe, but he seemed not to appreciate these advantages and eventually got along badly with his father. Later he tried to make his living as a composer but was always poor. He was not appreciated in his own city of Salzburg, and also not very much in Vienna; only in the somewhat foreign city of Prague was he understood. Very important: He could compose without trying, his music came full-blown into his mind and had only to be written down. He could hear a piece of music and play it back unerringly by ear, and he was a superb improviser. He had a ribald sense of humor. He was disliked by his rival Salieri and died very young, a mysterious death. When he was terminally ill, someone came to ask him to write a requiem, and he had the notion that it was for his own funeral but died before he could finish it. His accomplishments were the result of some kind of supernatural power; thus the great attention to his mysterious death. He was born a genius—a traditional European notion, related to social immobility and the belief in elites. (And indeed, Mozart is, I

10. For a more detailed account, see John Ewers, *The Blackfeet, Raiders on the Northwestern Plains* (Norman, Okla.: University of Oklahoma Press, 1958).

think, held in even higher esteem in Europe than in North America, as his kind of life fits better into the older, European notion of the relationship of art and life.)

Mozart, a composer whom a child could understand. But there is a second variation, as the informant soon hears about another composer, his music better for older people: Beethoven. He was a different kind of person; like his music, difficult, hard to get along with. In various ways, he was quite the opposite of Mozart. As Mozart had a mystery about his death, Beethoven had one about his birth; was he Dutch, German, maybe exotic, and was he aristocratic or lower class? He had a dark and brooding look. He suffered greatly, was frequently disappointed, never found the right woman, and of course there was the tragedy of his deafness. His music didn't come easily, you could tell he had to work hard to write it, you had to work hard to listen to it. His humor was ponderous. But he is said to be the man who "freed music" (from the likes of Mozart?). He had no children, but a nephew on whom he doted but who disappointed him.

For adults, the myth is elaborated: Beethoven, the master of serious music, had a hard life; his deafness dominates our idea of him. He worked hard, sketched his works for years before getting them right, is seen as a struggler against many kinds of bonds—musical, social, political, moral, personal. He is thought to have seen himself as a kind of high priest, giving up much for the spiritual aspects of his music. He was a genius, but he had to work hard to become and be one. It is perhaps no coincidence that he has been, to Americans, the quintessential great master of music—for this is, after all, the culture in which hard work was once prized above all, labor rewarded; the culture in which you weren't born to greatness but were supposed to struggle to achieve it.

These are the myths that this native informant pieced together in early years; they correspond, I believe, in general nature if not in detail to those perceived by that part of society that is involved with this music, the denizens of the Music Building. The two composers represent complementary values, they are the opposites in a Lévi-Straussian diagram, and they reflect the tensions that are the subject of the debates airing the most general issues of art and life.

Of course, speaking now as a musicology professor, I know that these two men were not all that different in their work habits, that Mozart was a workaholic and an innovator and did some sketching, while Beethoven was not just a grind and a firebrand. The point is that in looking at the popular conceptions of a population of musicians, ferreting out myths from various sources, we can learn about the relationship of the musical system to the rest of culture.

And so, as the Blackfoot beaver myth shows us important things about the way Blackfoot people conceive of their songs, the ideas we—today—have about Mozart and Beethoven reveal some of the values of our musical culture. Genius must suffer. There is conflict between inspiration and labor and between consistency and innovation. The great composer has supernatural connections or is a stranger. Music is mysterious; its great practitioners come, in some sense, from outside the culture. The "composers" are the main units of musical thought and recognition. Their configuration illuminates major structural principles of Western music and society such as hierarchy and duality.

·   ·   ·   ·   ·

CONCERT LIFE, RECEPTION, AND THE CULTURE INDUSTRY

203 Alban Berg

Arnold Schoenberg's Society of Private Musical Performances, founded in Vienna in 1918, offers a pointed early indication of twentieth-century music's separation from general concert life and thus of its isolation from the greater musical public. In this statement of aims, written by Schoenberg's former pupil Alban Berg shortly after the organization's founding, we can see the extraordinary efforts made to avoid normal concert trappings in order to allow the music that was performed to be experienced as "purely" as possible. No publicity, no critics, and no applause were permitted, and no names of pieces were announced in advance. Consistent with the society's "semi-pedagogical" purpose, emphasis was placed upon well-rehearsed renderings so as to make the music as "comprehensible" as possible. One notes the society's self-proclaimed "private"—today one might say "elitist"—character: only members and out-of-town guests were welcome at the concerts.

FROM Society for Private Music Performances in Vienna
A Statement of Aims

(1919)

The Society was founded in November, 1918, for the purpose of enabling Arnold Schoenberg to carry out his plan to give artists and music-lovers a real and exact knowledge of modern music.

The attitude of the public toward modern music is affected to an immense degree by the circumstance that the impression it receives from that music is inevitably one of obscurity. Aim, tendency, intention, scope and manner of expression, value, essence, and goal, all are obscure; most performances of it lack clarity; and specially lacking in lucidity is the public's consciousness of its own needs and wishes. All works are therefore valued, considered, judged, and lauded, or else misjudged, attacked, and rejected, exclusively upon the basis of one effect which all convey equally—that of obscurity.

This situation can in the long run satisfy no one whose opinion is worthy of consideration, neither the serious composer nor the thoughtful member of an audience. To bring light into this darkness and thus fulfill a justifiable need and desire was one of the motives that led Arnold Schoenberg to found this society.

To attain this goal three things are necessary:

1. Clear, well-rehearsed performances.

TEXT: Nicolas Slonimsky, *Music Since 1900*, 4th ed. (New York: Charles Scribner's Sons, 1971), pp. 1307–1308. Trans. by Stephen Somervell. Reprinted with permission of Schirmer Books, an imprint of Macmillan Publishing Company.

2. Frequent repetitions.

3. The performances must be removed from the corrupting influence of publicity; that is, they must not be directed toward the winning of competitions and must be unaccompanied by applause, or demonstrations of disapproval.

Herein lies the essential difference revealed by a comparison of the Society's aims with those of the everyday concert world, from which it is quite distinct in principle. Although it may be possible, in preparing a work for performance, to get along with the strictly limited and always insufficient number of rehearsals hitherto available, for better or worse (usually the latter), yet for the Society the number of rehearsals allotted to works to be performed will be limited only by the attainment of the greatest possible clarity and by the fulfillment of all the composer's intentions as revealed in his work. And if the attainment of these minimum requirements for good performance should necessitate a number of rehearsals that cannot be afforded (as was the case, for example, with a symphony of Mahler, which received its first performance after twelve four-hour rehearsals and was repeated after two more), then the work concerned should not, and will not, be performed by the Society.

In the rehearsal of new works, the performers will be chosen preferably from among the younger and less well-known artists, who place themselves at the Society's disposal out of interest in the cause; artists of high-priced reputation will be used only so far as the music demands and permits; and moreover that kind of virtuosity will be shunned which makes of the work to be performed not the end in itself but merely a means to an end which is not the Society's, namely, the display of irrelevant virtuosity and individuality, and the attainment of a purely personal success. Such things will be rendered automatically impossible by the exclusion (already mentioned) of all demonstrations of applause, disapproval, and thanks. The only success that an artist can have here is that (which should be most important to him) of having made the work, and therewith its composer, intelligible.

While such thoroughly rehearsed performances are a guarantee that each work will be enabled to make itself rightly understood, an even more effective means to this end is given to the Society through the innovation of weekly meetings[1] and by frequent repetitions of every work. Moreover, to ensure equal attendance at each meeting, the program will not be made known beforehand.

Only through the fulfillment of these two requirements—thorough preparation and frequent repetition—can clarity take the place of the obscurity which used to be the only impression remaining after a solitary performance; only thus can an audience establish an attitude towards a modern work that bears any relation to its composer's intention, completely absorb its style and idiom, and achieve that intimacy that is to be gained only through direct study—an

---

1. At that time, every Sunday morning from 10 to 12, in the Society's small concert hall. [Slonimsky]

intimacy with which the concert-going public can be credited only with respect to the most frequently performed classics.

The third condition for the attainment of the aims of the Society is that the performances shall be in all respects private; that guests (foreign visitors excepted) shall not be admitted, and that members shall be obligated to abstain from giving any public report of the performances and other activities of the Society, and especially to write or inspire no criticisms, notices, or discussions of them in periodicals.

This rule, that the sessions shall not be publicized, is made necessary by the semipedagogic activities of the Society and is in harmony with its tendency to benefit musical works solely through good performance and thus simply through the good effect made by the music itself. Propaganda for works and their composers is not the aim of the Society.

For this reason no school shall receive preference and only the worthless shall be excluded; for the rest, all modern music—from that of Mahler and Strauss to the newest, which practically never, or, at most, rarely, is to be heard—will be performed.

In general the Society strives to choose for performance such works as show their composers' most characteristic and, if possible, most pleasing sides. In addition to songs, pianoforte pieces, chamber music, and short choral pieces, even orchestral works will be considered, although the latter—since the Society has not yet the means to perform them in their original form—can be given only in good and well-rehearsed 4-hand and 8-hand arrangements. But the necessity becomes a virtue. In this manner it is possible to hear and judge a modern orchestral work divested of all the sound-effects and other sensuous aids that only an orchestra can furnish. Thus the old reproach is robbed of its force—that this music owes its power to its more or less opulent and effective instrumentation and lacks the qualities that were hitherto considered characteristic of good music—melody, richness of harmony, polyphony, perfection of form, architecture, etc.

A second advantage of this manner of music-making lies in the concert style of the performance of these arrangements. Since there is no question of a substitute for the orchestra but of so rearranging the orchestral work for the piano that it may be regarded, and should in fact be listened to, as an independent work and as a pianoforte composition, all the characteristic qualities and individualities of the piano are used, all the pianistic possibilities exploited. And it happens that in this reproduction—with different tone quality—of orchestral music, almost nothing is lost. Indeed, these very works, through the sureness of their instrumentation, the aptness of their instinctively chosen tone-colors, are best able to elicit from the piano tonal effects that far exceed its usual expressive possibilities.

·   ·   ·   ·   ·

204 Theodor W. Adorno

Theodor W. Adorno (1903–1969) was a leading German philosopher and social critic who devoted a significant portion of his work to music, most notably his book *Philosophy of New Music*. Trained as a composer under Alban Berg, Adorno was especially concerned with how music reflects and is influenced by larger social and intellectual issues. In this essay, written in 1945 when he was a refugee in the United States, Adorno examines the effects of mass media—specifically radio—on music and the musical experience. While openly betraying the exclusively "high-art" orientation of his thought (evident in his contemptuous dismissal of popular music and jazz), Adorno raises issues that continue to be seriously debated: the growing commodification and standardization of music, the detrimental effect of electronic transmission on listening (in particular the tendency toward "atomization"—dwelling on the part rather than the whole)—and the power of mass media to instill its audiences with a sense of "smugness and self-satisfaction."

FROM A Social Critique of Radio Music
(1945)

Some would approach the problem of radio by formulating questions of this type: If we confront such and such a sector of the population with such and such a type of music, what reactions may we expect? How can these reactions be measured and expressed statistically? Or: How many sectors of the population have been brought into contact with music and how do they respond to it?

What intention lies behind such questions? This approach falls into two major operations:

(a) We subject some groups to a number of different treatments and see how they react to each.

(b) We select and recommend the procedure which produces the effect we desire.

The aim itself, the tool by which we achieve it, and the persons upon whom it works are generally taken for granted in this procedure. The guiding interest behind such investigations is basically one of *administrative* technique: how to manipulate the masses. The pattern is that of market analysis even if it appears to be completely remote from any selling purpose. It might be research of an *exploitive* character, i.e. guided by the desire to induce as large a section of the

TEXT: *The Kenyon Review,* vol. 7 (Spring 1945), pp. 208–15.

population as possible to buy a certain commodity. Or it may be what Paul F. Lazarsfeld calls *benevolent* administrative research, putting questions such as, "How can we bring good music to as large a number of listeners as possible?"

I would like to suggest an approach that is antagonistic to exploitive and at least supplementary to benevolent administrative research. It abandons the form of question indicated by a sentence like: How can we, under given conditions, best further certain aims? On the contrary, this approach in some cases questions the aims and in all cases the successful accomplishment of these aims under the given conditions. Let us examine the question: how can good music be conveyed to the largest possible audience?

What is "good music"? Is it just the music which is given out and accepted as "good" according to current standards, say the programs of the Toscanini concerts? We cannot pass it as "good" simply on the basis of the names of great composers or performers, that is, by social convention. Furthermore, is the goodness of music invariant, or is it something that may change in the course of history with the technique at our disposal? For instance, let us take it for granted—as I do—that Beethoven really is good music. Is it not possible that this music, by the very problems it sets for itself, is far away from our own situation? That by constant repetition it has deteriorated so much that it has ceased to be the living force it was and has become a museum piece which no longer possesses the power to speak to the millions to whom it is brought? Or, even if this is not so, and if Beethoven in a musically young country like America is still as fresh as on the first day, is radio actually an adequate means of communication? Does a symphony played on the air remain a symphony? Are the changes it undergoes by wireless transmission merely slight and negligible modifications or do those changes affect the very essence of the music? Are not the stations in such a case bringing the masses in contact with something totally different from what it is supposed to be, thus also exercising an influence quite different from the one intended? And as to the large numbers of people who listen to "good music": *how* do they listen to it? Do they listen to a Beethoven symphony in a concentrated mood? Can they do so even if they want to? Is there not a strong likelihood that they listen to it as they would to a Tchaikovsky symphony, that is to say, simply listen to some neat tunes or exciting harmonic stimuli? Or do they listen to it as they do to jazz, waiting in the introduction of the finale of Brahms's First Symphony for the solo of the French horn, as they would for Benny Goodman's solo clarinet chorus? Would not such a type of listening make the high cultural ideal of bringing good music to large numbers of people altogether illusory?

These questions have arisen out of the consideration of so simple a phrase as "bringing good music to as large an audience as possible." None of these or similar questions can be wholly solved in terms of even the most benevolent research of the administrative type. One should not study the attitude of listeners without considering how far these attitudes reflect broader social behavior patterns and, even more, how far they are conditioned by the structure of society as a whole. This leads directly to the problem of a social critique of radio music, that of discovering social position and function. We first state certain axioms.

(a) We live in a society of commodities—that is, a society in which production of goods is taking place, not primarily to satisfy human wants and needs, but for profit. Human needs are satisfied only incidentally as it were. This basic condition of production affects the form of the product as well as the human interrelationships.

(b) In our commodity society there exists a general trend toward a heavy concentration of capital which makes for a shrinking of the free market in favor of monopolized mass production of standardized goods; this holds true particularly of the communications industry.

(c) The more the difficulties of contemporary society increase as it seeks its own continuance, the stronger becomes the general tendency to maintain, by all means available, the existing conditions of power and property relations against the threats which they themselves breed. Whereas on the one hand standardization necessarily follows from the conditions of contemporary economy, it becomes, on the other hand, one of the means of preserving a commodity society at a stage in which, according to the level of the productive forces, it has already lost its justification.

(d) Since in our society the forces of production are highly developed, and, at the same time, the relations of production fetter those productive forces, it is full of antagonisms. These antagonisms are not limited to the economic sphere where they are universally recognized, but dominate also the cultural sphere where they are less easily recognized.

How did music become, as our first axiom asserts it to be, a commodity? After music lost its feudal protectors during the latter part of the 18th Century it had to go to the market. The market left its imprint on it either because it was manufactured with a view to its selling chances, or because it was produced in conscious and violent reaction against the market requirements. What seems significant, however, in the present situation, and what is certainly deeply connected with the trend to standardization and mass production, is that *today the commodity character of music tends radically to alter it.* Bach in his day was considered, and considered himself, an artisan, although his music functioned as art. Today music is considered ethereal and sublime, although it actually functions as a commodity. Today the terms ethereal and sublime have become trademarks. Music has become a means instead of an end, a fetish. That is to say, music has ceased to be a human force and is consumed like other consumers' goods. This produces "commodity listening," a listening whose ideal it is to dispense as far as possible with any effort on the part of the recipient—even if such an effort on the part of the recipient is the necessary condition of grasping the sense of the music. It is the ideal of Aunt Jemima's ready-mix for pancakes extended to the field of music. The listener suspends all intellectual activity when dealing with music and is content with consuming and evaluating its gustatory qualities—just as if the music which tasted best were also the best music possible.

Famous master violins may serve as a drastic illustration of musical fetishism. Whereas only the expert is able to distinguish a "Strad" from a good modern fiddle, and whereas he is often least preoccupied with the tone quality of the fiddles, the layman, induced to treat these instruments as commodities, gives them a disproportionate attention and even a sort of adoration. One radio company went so far as to arrange a cycle of broadcasts looking, not primarily to the music played, nor even to the performance, but to what might be called an acoustic exhibition of famous instruments such as Paganini's violin and Chopin's piano. This shows how far the commodity attitude in radio music goes, though under a cloak of culture and erudition.

Our second axiom—increasing standardization—is bound up with the commodity character of music. There is, first of all, the haunting similarity between most musical programs, except for the few non-conformist stations which use recorded material of serious music; and also the standardization of orchestral performance, despite the musical trademark of an individual orchestra. And there is, above all, that whole sphere of music whose lifeblood is standardization: popular music, jazz, be it hot, sweet, or hybrid.

The third point of our social critique of radio concerns its ideological effect. Radio music's ideological tendencies realize themselves regardless of the intent of radio functionaries. There need be nothing intentionally malicious in the maintenance of vested interests. Nonetheless, music under present radio auspices serves to keep listeners from criticizing social realities; in short, it has a soporific effect upon social consciousness. The illusion is furthered that the best is just good enough for the man in the street. The ruined farmer is consoled by the radio-instilled belief that Toscanini is playing for him and for him alone, and that an order of things that allows him to hear Toscanini compensates for low market prices for farm products; even though he is ploughing cotton under, radio is giving him culture. Radio music is calling back to its broad bosom all the prodigal sons and daughters whom the harsh father has expelled from the door. In this respect radio music offers a new function not inherent in music as an art—the function of creating smugness and self-satisfaction.

The last group of problems in a social critique of radio would be those pertaining to social antagonisms. While radio marks a tremendous technical advance, it has proved an impetus to progress neither in music itself nor in musical listening. Radio is an essentially new technique of musical reproduction. But it does not broadcast, to any considerable extent, serious modern music. It limits itself to music created under pre-radio conditions. Nor has it, itself, thus far evoked any music really adequate to its technical conditions.

The most important antagonisms arise in the field of so-called musical mass-

culture. Does the mass distribution of music really mean a rise of musical culture? Are the masses actually brought into contact with the kind of music
which, from broader social considerations, may be regarded as desirable? Are
the masses really participating in music culture or are they merely forced consumers of musical commodities? What is the role that music actually, not verbally, plays for them?

Under the aegis of radio there has set in a retrogression of listening. In
spite of and even because of the quantitative increase in musical delivery, the
psychological effects of this listening are very much akin to those of the motion
picture and sport spectatoritis which promotes a retrogressive and sometimes
even infantile type of person. "Retrogressive" is meant here in a psychological
and not a purely musical sense.

An illustration: A symphony of the Beethoven type, so-called classical, is one
of the most highly integrated musical forms. The whole is everything; the part,
that is to say, what the layman calls the melody, is relatively unimportant. Retrogressive listening to a symphony is listening which, instead of grasping that
whole, dwells upon those melodies, just as if the symphony were structurally
the same as a ballad. There exists today a tendency to listen to Beethoven's
Fifth as if it were a set of quotations from Beethoven's Fifth. We have developed a larger framework of concepts such as atomistic listening and quotation
listening, which lead us to the hypothesis that something like a musical children's language is taking shape.

As today a much larger number of people listen to music than in pre-radio
days, it is difficult to compare today's mass-listening with what could be called
the elite listening of the past. Even if we restrict ourselves, however to select
groups of today's listeners (say, those who listen to the Philharmonics in New
York and Boston), one suspects that the Philharmonic listener of today listens
in radio terms. A clear indication is the relation to serious advanced modern
music. In the Wagnerian period, the elite listener was eager to follow the most
daring musical exploits. Today the corresponding group is the firmest bulwark
against musical progress and feels happy only if it is fed Beethoven's Seventh
Symphony again and again.

In analyzing the fan mail of an educational station in a rural section in the
Middle West, which has been emphasizing serious music at regular hours with
a highly skilled and resourceful announcer, one is struck by the apparent enthusiasm of the listeners' reception, by the vast response, and by the belief in the
highly progressive social function that this program was fulfilling. I have read
all of those letters and cards very carefully. They are exuberant indeed. But
they are enthusiastic in a manner that makes one feel uncomfortable. It is what
might be called standardized enthusiasm. The communications are almost literally identical: "Dear X, Your Music Shop is swell. It widens my musical horizon and gives me an ever deeper feeling for the profound qualities of our great
music. I can no longer bear the trashy jazz which we usually have to listen to.
Continue with your grand work and let us have more of it." No musical item

was mentioned, no specific reference to any particular feature was made, no criticism was offered, although the programs were amateurish and planless.

It would do little good to explain these standard responses by reference to the difficulty in verbalizing musical experience: for anybody who has had profound musical experiences and finds it hard to verbalize them may stammer and use awkward expressions, but he would be reluctant, even if he knew no other, to cloak them in rubber stamp phrases. I am forced to another explanation. The listeners were strongly under the spell of the announcer as the personified voice of radio as a social institution, and they responded to his call to prove one's cultural level and education by appreciating this good music. But they actually failed to achieve that very appreciation which stamped them as cultured. They took refuge in repeating, often literally, the announcer's speeches in behalf of culture. Their behavior might be compared with that of the fanatical radio listener entering a bakery and asking for "that delicious, golden crispy Bond Bread."

· · · · ·

205 Lawrence Gilman

The commercialization of music referred to by Theodor Adorno in the previous entry is reflected in this talk by the American music writer Lawrence Gilman (1878–1939), presented during the intermission of Arturo Toscanini's final radio broadcast with the NBC Symphony on April 26, 1938. Gilman, music critic for the *New York Tribune* (later *Herald-Tribune*) from 1923 until his death, was a pioneering author in the field later known as "music appreciation." Among his books were *Stories of Symphonic Music* (New York, 1907), *Aspects of Modern Opera* (New York, 1909), and *Nature in Music and Other Studies* (New York, 1914). In this address Gilman praises Toscanini as being no less than "vicar of the Immortals" and "music-lover *in excelsis*." Such adulation helped shape the "star system" that has become so characteristic of twentieth-century concert life and that provides one essential component of the packaging of music for mass consumption. The following excerpts present the opening and closing portions of Gilman's address.

FROM Intermission Talk for Toscanini's Final Radio Concert

(1938)

Today's concert is Mr. Toscanini's farewell to the radio audience. Many of you have sent him letters of gratitude and appreciation with the thought of letting him know what his leadership of these concerts has meant to you, and I should like to add my own inadequate tribute to those that he has already received from you.

I have been wondering what it is about Toscanini that makes him unique as an artist; and I think the answer probably is that he represents with peculiar completeness the perfect type and example of the music-lover.

Of all the musicians I have known and observed as interpretive artists, I have never known one who loved music with the concentrated, fanatical, devastating intensity that is characteristic of Toscanini. As Shelley, one might say, is the perfect type of the poet, the poet *in excelsis,* and Mozart the music-maker *in excelsis,* and Napoleon the military genius *in excelsis,* so Toscanini will be known, I think, as the music-lover *in excelsis.*

Toscanini has many great qualities as an interpretive musician. But the one that transcends and animates them all is a passion for music so imperious and ungovernable that it will not let him rest until he has shared with us, through the medium of the instruments that he commands and inspires, his image of the ideal beauty that possesses him.

A great scholastic philosopher of an earlier century said that the influence of inspired men is to be explained in several ways. First, he said, because they have an undistorted vision of reality. Second, because they are receptacles of light; third, because they know, and make us know, that the reality which they see is identical with beauty. Fourth, because they are distinguished by what he called "an excess of love." They have in themselves, he concluded, "an inextinguishable light, illuminating others."

I think that this describes all men, all artists, who are vehicles of what we call, for want of a better name, inspiration. Their perception is undistorted; they receive and shed illumination; they see beauty as the supreme reality of the spirit; and their love of it is boundless, unquenchable, and creative.

•   •   •   •   •

Toscanini is leaving us; and we who have listened to him discerningly, season after season, are well aware of what we are about to lose. But we must face the fact with all possible fortitude and philosophy. We are confronted, as an Ameri-

TEXT: Typescript, New York Public Library, Library and Museum of the Performing Arts at Lincoln Center, NBC Archives, Toscanini Clipping Files.

can statesman once observed, with a condition and not a theory. Mr. Toscanini, vicar of the Immortals, is bound by mortal laws. He has served the Immortals long and gloriously, and with incomparable devotion; and now he would lighten his burden. He is sixty-nine years old. He would conduct when he chooses—not when conducting becomes burdensome and exhausting. And so we must do without him.

To minimize his loss would be an act of treachery toward our assumed allegiance to that ideal of lofty and self-effacing service which this great artist has exemplified. It would be an act of gross ingratitude to an interpreter who has re-created the music of the masters with unforgettable beauty and fidelity.

206 Roland Barthes

The literary and cultural critic Roland Barthes (1915–1980) was a leading figure in both the structuralist and poststructuralist schools of late twentieth-century French literary and philosophical thought. In this essay, written in 1970 and one of a number Barthes devoted to music, he considers certain features of contemporary musical life. He notes the replacement of the traditional "amateur," who recreated music "manually" and "muscularly" at a piano or some other instrument, by listeners who respond "passively" and "receptively" to music heard in concert, on record, and over the radio. For Barthes this transformation is tied to musical specialization, particularly to the development of the performing technician, who "relieves the listener of all activity." Yet Barthes closes by considering changes in the reception of Beethoven's works that reflect this same process more positively, fostering a response to music that requires "writing it anew." This idea of what he elsewhere terms the "readerly" text, which must be reconstructed actively by the reader/listener to be adequately comprehended (and which is especially characteristic of contemporary art), is of central importance to Barthes' later literary criticism.

Musica Practica
(1970)

There are two musics (at least so I have always thought): the music one listens to, the music one plays. These two musics are two totally different arts, each with its own history, its own sociology, its own esthetics, its own erotic;

TEXT: *Image, Music, Text,* ed. and trans. by Stephen Heath (New York: Hill and Wang, 1977), pp. 149–54. Reprinted by permission of Hill and Wang, a division of Farrar, Straus, & Giroux, Inc.

the same composer can be minor if you listen to him, tremendous if you play him (even badly)—such is Schumann.

The music one plays comes from an activity that is very little auditory, being above all manual (and thus in a way much more sensual). It is the music which you or I can play, alone or among friends, with no other audience than its participants (that is, with all risk of theater, all temptation of hysteria removed); a muscular music in which the part taken by the sense of hearing is one only of ratification, as though the body were hearing—and not "the soul"; a music which is not played "by heart": seated at the keyboard or the music stand, the body controls, conducts, coordinates, having itself to transcribe what it reads, making sound and meaning, the body as inscriber and not just transmitter, simple receiver. This music has disappeared; initially the province of the idle (aristocratic) class, it lapsed into an insipid social rite with the coming of the democracy of the bourgeoisie (the piano, the young lady, the drawing room, the nocturne) and then faded out altogether (who plays the piano today?). To find practical music in the West, one has now to look to another public, another repertoire, another instrument (the young generation, vocal music, the guitar). Concurrently, passive, receptive music, sound music, has become *the* music (that of concert, festival, record, radio): playing has ceased to exist; musical activity is no longer manual, muscular, kneadingly physical, but merely liquid, effusive, "lubrificating," to take up a word from Balzac. So too has the performer changed. The amateur, a role defined much more by a style than by a technical imperfection, is no longer anywhere to be found; the professionals, pure specialists whose training remains entirely esoteric for the public (who is there who is still acquainted with the problems of musical education?), never offer that style of the perfect amateur the great value of which could still be recognized in a Lipati or a Panzera, touching off in us not satisfaction but desire, the desire to *make* that music. In short, there was first the actor of music, then the interpreter (the grand Romantic voice), then finally the technician, who relieves the listener of all activity, even by procuration, and abolishes in the sphere of music the very notion of *doing*.

The work of Beethoven seems to me bound up with this historical problem, not as the straightforward expression of a particular moment (the transition from amateur to interpreter) but as the powerful germ of a disturbance of civilization, Beethoven at once bringing together its elements and sketching out its solution; an ambiguity which is that of Beethoven's two historical roles: the mythical role which he was made to play by the whole of the nineteenth century and the modern role which our own century is beginning to accord him (I refer here to Boucourechliev's study).[1]

For the nineteenth century, leaving aside a few stupid representations, such as the one given by Vincent d'Indy who just about makes of Beethoven a kind of reactionary and anti-Semitic hypocrite, Beethoven was the first man of music

---

1. André Boucourechliev, *Beethoven* (Paris: 1969). [Au.]

to be *free*. Now for the first time the fact of having several successive *manners* was held to the glory of an artist; he was acknowledged the right of metamorphosis, he could be dissatisfied with himself or, more profoundly, with his language, he could change his codes as he went through life (this is what is expressed by Lenz's naive and enthusiastic image of Beethoven's three different manners).[2] From this moment that the work becomes the trace of a movement, of a journey, it appeals to the idea of fate. The artist is in search of his "truth" and this quest forms an order in itself, a message that can be read, in spite of the variations in its content, over all the work or, at least, whose readability feeds on a sort of totality of the artist: his career, his loves, his ideas, his character, his words become traits of meaning; a Beethovian biography is born (one ought to be able to say a bio-mythology), the artist is brought forward as a complete hero, endowed with a discourse (a rare occurrence for a musician), a legend (a good ten or so anecdotes), an iconography, a race (that of the Titans of Art: Michelangelo, Balzac) and a fatal malady (the deafness of he who creates for the pleasure of our ears). Into this system of meaning that is the Romantic Beethoven are incorporated truly structural features (features which are ambiguous, at once musical and psychological): the paroxysmal development of contrasts in intensity (the signifying opposition of the *piano* and the *forte,* an opposition the historical importance of which is perhaps not very clearly recognized, it characterizing after all only a tiny portion of the music of the world and corresponding to the invention of an instrument whose name is indicative enough, the *piano-forte*), the shattering of the melody, taken as the symbol of restlessness and the seething agitation of creativeness, the emphatic redundancy of moments of excitement and termination (a naive image of fate dealing its blows), the experience of limits (the abolition or the inversion of the traditional parts of musical speech), the production of musical chimera (the voice rising out of the symphony)—and all this, which could easily be transformed metaphorically into pseudo-philosophical values, nonetheless musically acceptable since always deployed under the authority of the fundamental code of the West, tonality.

Further, this romantic image (the meaning of which finally is a certain *discord*) creates a problem of performance: the amateur is unable to master Beethoven's music, not so much by reason of the technical difficulties as by the very breakdown of the code of the former *musica practica*. According to this code, the fantasmatic (that is to say corporal) image which guided the performer was that of a song ("spun out" inwardly); with Beethoven, the mimetic impulse (does not musical fantasy consist in giving oneself a place, as subject, in the scenario of the performance?) becomes orchestral, thus escaping from the fetishism of a single element (voice or rhythm). The body strives to be total, and so the idea of an intimist or familial activity is destroyed: *to want* to play

2. Barthes refers to Wilhelm von Lenz (1809–1883), a Russian official of German descent, whose study *Beethoven et ses trois styles* (*Beethoven and his Three Styles*) appeared in 1852.

Beethoven is to see oneself as the conductor of an orchestra (the dream of how many children? the tautological dream of how many conductors, a prey in their conducting to all the signs of the panic of possession?). Beethoven's work forsakes the amateur and seems, in an initial moment, to call on the new Romantic deity, the interpreter. Yet here again we are disappointed: who (what soloist, what pianist?) can play Beethoven well? It is as though this music offers only the choice between a "role" and its absence, the illusion of demiurgy and the prudence of platitude, sublimated as "renunciation."

The truth is perhaps that Beethoven's music has in it something *inaudible* (something for which hearing is not the *exact* locality), and this brings us to the second Beethoven. It is not possible that a musician be deaf by pure contingency or poignant destiny (they are the same thing). Beethoven's deafness designates the lack wherein resides all signification; it appeals to a music that is not abstract or inward, but that is endowed, if one may put it like this, with a tangible intelligibility, with the intelligible as tangible. Such a category is truly revolutionary, unthinkable in the terms of the old esthetics; the work that complies with it cannot be received on the basis of pure sensuality, which is always cultural, nor on that of an intelligible order of (rhetorical, thematic) development, and without it neither the modern text nor contemporary music can be accepted. As we know since Boucourechliev's analyses, this Beethoven is exemplarily the Beethoven of the *Diabelli Variations* and the operation by which we can grasp this Beethoven (and the category he initiates) can no longer be either performance or hearing, but reading. This is not to say that one has to sit with a Beethoven score and get from it an inner recital (which would still remain dependent on the old animistic fantasy); it means that with respect to this music one must put oneself in the position or, better, in the activity of an operator, who knows how to displace, assemble, combine, fit together; in a word (if it is not too worn out), who knows how to structure (very different from constructing or reconstructing in the classic sense). Just as the reading of the modern text (such at least as it may be postulated) consists not in receiving, in knowing or in feeling that text, but in writing it anew, in crossing its writing with a fresh inscription, so too reading this Beethoven is *to operate* his music, to draw it (it is willing to be drawn) into an unknown *praxis*.

In this way may be rediscovered, modified according to the movement of the historical dialectic, a certain *musica practica*. What is the use of composing if it is to confine the product within the precinct of the concert or the solitude of listening to the radio? To compose, at least by propensity, is *to give to do*, not to give to hear but to give to write. The modern location for music is not the concert hall, but the stage on which the musicians pass, in what is often a dazzling display, from one source of sound to another. It is we who are playing, though still it is true by proxy; but one can imagine the concert—later on?—as exclusively a workshop, from which nothing spills over—no dream, no imaginary, in short, no "soul" and where all the musical art is absorbed in a praxis *with no remainder*. Such is the utopia that a certain Beethoven, who is not played, teaches us to formulate—which is why it is possible now to feel in him a musician with a future.

207 Steven Connor

In this excerpt from his book *Postmodernist Culture* (1989), the English cultural critic Steven Connor examines the nature of live performance in an age dominated by new technologies of representation. Though Connor develops his argument mainly in connection with rock music, it applies equally to many aspects of music in general. Connor is particularly interested in the way such "reproductive" innovations as film, recordings, and television have increased the public's desire for face-to-face contact. He also discusses the related pull between the producers of commercial music interested in supplying a marketable object and the public searching for a kind of immediate experience that is by nature ephemeral. Connor explores the tensions inherent in the notion of "presence" in a mass-media context, evident in efforts to package "live" experience itself (suitably enhanced through technological extensions), and suggests that the line between the "real" and the "representational" has been rendered largely illusory.

FROM *Postmodernist Culture*

(1989)

• • • • •

The dread of being frozen into a commodity brings about the contradictory response described by Henry Sayre as the 'mythology of presence' with which performance and such things as the oral poetry movement have surrounded themselves.[1] To highlight the fugitive intensity of the 'liberated' performance is to deny and downgrade any attempt to provide documentary records of such performances in galleries, museums and books, even as it simultaneously creates an ever more intense desire for such records (and opportunities for different kinds of packaging and display, in tapes, photographs and archives of

TEXT: *Postmodernist Culture: An Introduction to Theories of the Contemporary* (Cambridge: Basil Blackwell, 1989), pp. 148–55.

1. Henry Sayre, "The Object of Performance: Aesthetics in the Seventies," *Georgia Review* 37:1 (1983): 177. [Au.]

performance). Sayre is right to emphasize as he does the parasitic relationship between free performance and exploitable commodity, for it is in fact never possible to abstract one pole of the opposition and simply set it against the other, to insist on performance against text. For our intuition of the immediacy of performance is always a second-degree intuition, itself formed within a context of habits and expectations. What is more, the desire for noncommodifiable immediacy, for free theatrical experience, is no more immune from the operations of commodification than practices which yield an obvious object. In fact, the fixation of much postmodern performance theory upon the opposition of the commodity and of free experience draws, in an oddly anachronistic way, upon the language and concepts more appropriate to an earlier period in the development of capitalism. Late capitalism, organized in new ways around vastly enhanced networks of information, communication and reproduction, seems effectively to have dissolved the simple opposition of dead commodity-as-thing and live performance-as-process. The problem may then be not so much that performance always risks falling into the dead residue of objecthood in reproduction (photographs, audio- and video-recordings) as that performance and reproduction have become intertwined in complex ways.

This can best be exemplified, not in the more restricted field of avant-garde drama and performance, but in the much larger and culturally more pervasive area of rock music.[2] (This is not to deny the significant forms of connection between the two realms in the work of artists like Andy Warhol, Peter Gabriel and Laurie Anderson, of course.) Rock music, with its recurrent display of the values enshrined in performance, along with its extraordinary generation of new reproductive technologies, instances in a particularly powerful way the mutations undergone by those conceptual opposites, performance and text. The late 1970s and 1980s have seen a return in rock music to the "primitive" value and vitality of "live" performance, after the retreat of the largest and most influential bands like The Beatles and Pink Floyd into the technological delights of the studio. It is striking that the most powerful and successful artists over the last ten years have all felt obliged to demonstrate their capacity to engage with audiences in the direct contact of live performance as well as via albums and video recordings—the most familiar examples being Bruce Springsteen, Dire Straits and Michael Jackson. It is perhaps Springsteen whose career projects most unassailably the values associated with live performance, and because of this, the Springsteen mythology provides the most useful and interesting place to begin analysing the problematic status of the concept of the 'live' in postmodern mass culture. It needs to be said at this point that not many people would be inclined to see Bruce Springsteen's work as

2. I use the term "rock music" to distinguish the popular music of the 1960s onwards from the larger field of popular music in this century; the former would begin with rock and roll, Elvis Presley and the Beatles, the latter would include artists like Bing Crosby and Frank Sinatra and would extend back at least until the 1920s. [Au.]

itself postmodernist in style or expressive content; but, the ways in which his work is taken up, dispersed and distributed provide a way of understanding the contemporary conditions with which a theory of postmodern culture has to deal.

The most important part of the Springsteen mythology has always been his reputation as a live performer, one who works hard to give himself with energy and enthusiasm to his enormous audiences. To see Springsteen live is to be in the presence of a mythical figure, to enjoy a certain erotic closeness. Springsteen is most authentically "himself" when he is on stage, and the ecstasy generated by the sudden shrinking of distance between fan and star is at its most extreme in live performance. This ecstasy of desired identification is a comparatively recent phenomenon in mass culture and turns out to depend oddly upon the technology of mass reproduction and communication; for it is only when the means exist to provide audiences with various kinds of substitute for the presence of the star—films, records, tapes, pictures—that this ecstatic yield of pleasure can be obtained from being in his actual presence. In fact, the success of the rock industry, which has taken over from the film industry in the business of star-manufacture, depends upon the kinds of desire that high fidelity reproduction stimulates, the itch for more, for more faithful reproductions of the "real thing," the yearning to move ever closer to the "original."

There is a drama of possession and control acted out through this. To own a record is, in a limited sense, to be able to control the music that it encodes, for, with certain exclusions, one purchases with the record the freedom to reproduce and replay it wherever and whenever one wishes, at home, in the street, in the car. This repeatability is what seems to guarantee the consumer's possession and control of the commodity; but it also encloses a hidden deficiency. If recorded music is infinitely repeatable, then this is precisely because it is a form of copy, which must always stand at one remove from its original. So paradoxically, at the moment of its greatest yielding, the commodity always holds something back; the more the record is played, the more it confirms the possession and control of the consumer, the more it displays its failure to be the real thing. What guarantees the possibility of the consumer's control is an intrinsic shortfall in the commodity, the fact that it can never be the original of itself.

These factors connect with the more general issues which have been the subject of intensified debate within postmodern cultural theory in recent years. As Deleuze, Derrida and others have argued, we continue to depend upon an opposition between things which are felt to be immediate, original and "real" on the one hand, and the representations of those things, which we conceive of as secondary, derived and therefore "false" on the other. Repetition plays a crucial part in sustaining our sense of the real, since repetition is always, as Deleuze argues, tied to the conception of a return of the Same, and the threat posed by repetition and replication to the authority of original and universal ideas is only ever a temporary threat, which customarily reverts to the service of origins.[3]

In the light of the fantastic proliferation of processes for the replication of products, texts and information, many cultural theorists, from Walter Benjamin to Jean Baudrillard, have seen a diminution in the authority of ideas of originality, Benjamin arguing that the "aura" of the original work of art is lost with the predominance of mechanical reproduction, and Baudrillard proclaiming that the very opposition between original and copy has been lost in an age of simulacra, or repetitions without originals.[4] At the same time, it is possible to see how the proliferation of reproductions actually intensifies the desire for origin, even if that origin is increasingly sensed as an erotic lack rather than a tangible and satisfying presence. In Baudrillard's terms, the real is ceaselessly manufactured as an intensified version of itself, as hyperreality.

For the rock fan, it is above all the live show which seems to offer this unfalsifiably real corporeal presence, for here—apparently—are to be found life, music, the body themselves, naked and unignorable, unobscured by barriers of reproduction or representation. But what kind of live experience characterizes contemporary rock music? In the case of Bruce Springsteen it is an experience of manufactured mass closeness. Whereas audiences at the great pop festivals of the 1970s had to make do with the sight of tiny figures performing inconsequentially on a stage half a mile away ("Is that Dylan in the hat?"), and a sound system that worked efficiently only with a following wind, Springsteen's appearances on his world tour in 1985, which were rarely to fewer than 50,000 people, made sure that no member of the vast audience could escape the slightest nuance of music or voice. Behind him, an enormous video screen projected claustrophobically every detail of his agonized facial expressions in a close-up which at one and the same time abolished and re-emphasized the actual distance between him and his audience.

Intimacy and immediacy on this scale can only be achieved by massively conspicuous acts of representation. Enormous amplification, hugely expanded images; these are the forms which reproduction takes in the context of the live. Sound and image are simultaneous with the "real" music that is being performed (although, of course, in the case of most contemporary music the "original" sound is usually itself only an amplified derivation from an initiating signal), even if it remains obvious that what is most real about the event is precisely the fact that it is being projected as mass experience. The normal condition for Springsteen's performances is an ecstatic, somatic excess that spills over into and is constituted by an excess of representations at the very heart of the live experience.

3. See Giles Deleuze, *Différence et répétition* (Paris: Presses Universitaires de France, 1968). [Au.]
4. Walter Benjamin, "The Work of Art in the Age of Mechanical Reproduction," in *Illuminations,* trans. Harry Zohn (London: Fontana, 1970), pp. 219–54; Jean Baudrillard, "The Precession of Simulacra," in *Simulations,* trans. Paul Foss, Paul Patton, and Philip Bleitchman (New York: Semiotext(e), 1983), pp. 1–80. [Au.]

It is for this reason that audiences of 80,000 or more now regularly attend concerts to watch videos, albeit "live" videos; the ecstasy of experience is turned into what Baudrillard calls an "ecstasy of communication," a fantastic, barely-controllable excess of images and representations.[5] This was well borne out during the Live Aid concerts in 1985 when Phil Collins, after playing in London, absurdly travelled across the Atlantic on Concorde in order to play in Philadelphia later that day, during the same global transmission of the concert, in a monstrously inflated version of the prank in which a schoolchild runs from one end to the other of a serial school photograph in order to be photographed in two places. But Phil Collins travelled 3,000 miles not in order to be visible in the flesh, but to provide an image to be projected on to the video-screen which projected close-up images of him to the audience in the stadium and round the world.

During the Live Aid concerts, video screens allowed the easy incorporation of other, recorded material into the live spectacle. David Bowie and Mick Jagger had originally planned to sing "Dancing in the Street" simultaneously in Philadelphia and London, but the unavoidable half-second delay in transmission made this impossible; so they came together in a video recording which was fitted seamlessly into the experience of the live concerts—and the fact that the song and the dance routines in the video exemplified the theme of spontaneous, *en plein air* celebration only added ironic piquancy to the blending of the real and the represented. The audience were also closely involved in this process of willed simulation. Often, the viewer of the spectacle at home was shown the audience watching an image of themselves on the giant video screen, so that when we subsequently saw shots of the audience at home, we were not sure whether it was the audience itself that we were seeing, or the image of the audience projected on to the video-screen at the event—whether we were watching them, in other words, or watching them watching themselves.

What emerges from all this is not so much the abolition of the desire for originality and presence in the performing instant, as the inversion of the structural dependence of copies upon originals. In the case of the "live" performance, the desire for originality is a secondary effect of various forms of reproduction. The intense "reality" of the performance is not something that lies behind the particulars of the setting, the technology and the audience; its reality consists in all of that apparatus of representation.

We should not be surprised, therefore, at the success of that postmodernist oxymoron, the "live recording." Of course many of the protocols of live performance derive from the familiarity of audience and performer alike with representations of other live performances. This is confirmed by the aesthetic conventions that determine the ways in which live recordings, in that evocative

---

5. "The Ecstasy of Communication," in *Postmodern Culture*, ed. Hal Foster (London and Sydney: Pluto Press, 1985), pp. 126–34. [Au.]

contemporary term, are "produced." After recording a live album, most artists have to spend considerable amounts of time in the studio, reworking sections, altering the balance, overdubbing vocals, adding instruments, correcting mistakes and, indeed, sometimes, roughing up a sound that may be too smooth in actual performance. (Once this becomes known, it can produce a primitivist reflex, as with Dire Straits' *Alchemy* album, which made a selling point of the fact that the 'original' sound had not been tampered with in any way.)

Increasingly, then, the experience of the "live" is itself being commodified, "produced" as a strategic category of the semiotic, even though its function *within* semiotic systems may be to embody that which remains authentically and dangerously outside the distortions of the commodity and of signification itself. The live is always in a sense the quotation of itself—never the live, always the "live." Paradoxically, the desire for original and authentic experience exists alongside the recognition that there can never be any such thing, at least in contemporary rock music. The increasing sophistication of studio technology, and the consequent multiplication of versions of a single song, in remixes and extended twelve-inch versions, combined more recently with the cult of "sampling," or the appropriation and re-editing of snatches of music from other songs, means the loss of a sense that there can be such a thing as an original version of a song. Nowadays, the title of a song names a diverse and theoretically endless range of embodiments and performances, or versions of performances, since one performance may be mixed and reassembled in any number of ways. This means that the opposition between the live and the reproduced which is sustained within studio recordings themselves—promotional videos often show the studio as a sort of substitute scene of the "live," discovering in the instant of recording a kind of immediacy which the technology of recording disseminates—is jeopardized. This recalls Walter Benjamin's argument that the abandonment of "real time" continuity in film-making with the chopping up of the narrative into discontinuous segments for the purpose of filming, results in a loss of "aura," since the narrative that is eventually synthesized has never been acted out anywhere all at once. Something similar happens in the modern studio recording, which assembles a performance which has never had any existence all at once anywhere except on the producer's console.

These points may be considerably generalized. Everywhere the world of the mass media holds out the possibility and desirability of "live" experience, and embraces "process" while discrediting fixity of definition. The economics of mass culture, far from requiring the freezing of freely contingent human experiences into commodifiable forms, consciously promotes these forms of transient intensity, since it is, in the end, much easier to control and stimulate demand for experiences which are spontaneously (nothing of the kind, of course) sensed as outside representation. From rock music to tourism to television and even education, advertising imperatives and consumer demand are no longer for goods, but for experiences.

Here, as elsewhere, postmodern theory has a complicated and ambivalent relationship to this process. Postmodern theories of performance, whether inversive (asserting the presence of performance against the inauthenticity of representation) or deconstructive (examining the mutual implications of performance and text) simultaneously stand aside from and form part of this semiotic terrain. In the attempt to think through the complexities of performance, and the ways in which it reproduces authoritative structures of thought, postmodern theory aligns itself with what it describes, and perhaps secretly designates itself in its descriptions of the subversive mission of avant-garde art. But, at the same time, it can function as an imaginative and institutional filtering of its own vision of the subversive sublime of pure performance. The more successful the intellectual paradigm of postmodern performance becomes, the tighter is the circuit of exchange between the self-acknowledging and unmistakable energies of performance and the exemplary or demonstrative function that such free energies perform for the paradigm. The freedom of performance, of the "live," is mortgaged to the theory and, of course, the cultural codes and assumptions, which accredit it in advance *as* freedom. The postmodern theory of a performance that escapes the museum, the script, or the recording, is the discursive form which precisely legislates the conditions of that escape.

PLURALISM

208 Erik Satie

No composer of the early twentieth century did more than the Frenchman Erik Satie (1866–1925) to deflate the artistic pretensions of the immediate past, something he accomplished with a detached, ironic tone that was itself an important aspect of his new esthetic. The stark simplicity of Satie's music, his humorous indications to the performer ("very seriously silent"), and the absurd titles of his works ("Three Pieces in the Form of a Pear") all mock the expressive and programmatic excesses of the nineteenth century. These three brief prose pieces, originally written between 1912 and 1914, for the French periodical *La revue musicale S.I.M.* and later collected in the characteristically titled "Memoirs of an Amnesiac," brilliantly display the proto-surrealistic quality of Satie's mind, revealing his delight in satirizing the artistic enterprise and his refusal to take even himself too seriously.

FROM Memoirs of an Amnesiac

WHAT I AM
(1912)

Everyone will tell you that I am not a musician. That is correct.

From the very beginning of my career I classed myself as a phonometrographer. My work is completely phonometrical. Take my *Fils des étoiles*, or my *Morceaux en forme de poire*, my *En habit de cheval* or my *Sarabandes*—it is evident that musical ideas played no part whatsoever in their composition. Science is the dominating factor.

Besides, I enjoy measuring a sound much more than hearing it. With my phonometer in my hand, I work happily and with confidence.

What haven't I weighed or measured? I've done all Beethoven, all Verdi, etc. It's fascinating.

The first time I used a phonoscope, I examined a B-flat of medium size. I can assure you that I have never seen anything so revolting. I called in my man to show it to him.

On my phono-scales a common or garden F-sharp registered 93 kilos. It came out of a fat tenor whom I also weighed.

Do you know how to clean sounds? It's a filthy business. Stretching them out is cleaner; indexing them is a meticulous task and needs good eyesight. Here, we are in the realm of phonotechnique.

On the question of sound explosions, which can often be so unpleasant, some

TEXT: *The Writings of Erik Satie*, ed. and trans. by Nigel Wilkins (London: Eulenburg Books, 1980), pp. 58–59, 62. Reprinted by permission of Nigel Wilkins.

cotton-wool in the ears can deaden their effect quite satisfactorily. Here, we are in the realm of pyrophony.

To write my *Pièces froides,* I used a caleidophone recorder. It took seven minutes. I called in my man to let him hear them.

I think I can say that phonology is superior to music. There's more variety in it. The financial return is greater, too. I owe my fortune to it.

At all events, with a motodynamophone, even a rather inexperienced phono-metrologist can easily note down more sounds than the most skilled musician in the same time, using the same amount of effort. This is how I have been able to write so much.

And so the future lies with philophony.

THE MUSICIAN'S DAY
(1913)

An artist must organize his life.

Here is the exact timetable of my daily activities:

Get up: 7.18 am; be inspired: 10.23 to 11.47 am. I take lunch at 12.11 pm and leave the table at 12.14 pm.

Healthy horse-riding, out in my grounds: 1.19 to 2.53 pm. More inspiration: 3.12 to 4.07 pm.

Various activities (fencing, reflection, immobility, visits, contemplation, swimming, etc. . . .): 4.21 to 6.47 pm.

Dinner is served at 7.16 and ends at 7.20 pm. Then come symphonic readings, out loud: 8.09 to 9.59 pm.

I go to bed regularly at 10.37 pm. Once a week (on Tuesdays) I wake up with a start at 3.19 am.

I eat only white foodstuffs: eggs, sugar, scraped bones; fat from dead animals; veal, salt, coconuts, chicken cooked in white water; mouldy fruit, rice, turnips; camphorated sausage, things like spaghetti, cheese (white), cotton salad and certain fish (minus their skins).

I boil my wine and drink it cold mixed with fuchsia juice. I have a good appetite, but never talk while eating, for fear of strangling myself.

I breathe carefully (a little at a time). I very rarely dance. When I walk, I hold my sides and look rigidly behind me.

Serious in appearance, if I laugh it is not on purpose. I always apologize about it nicely.

My sleep is deep, but I keep one eye open. My bed is round, with a hole cut out to let my head through. Once every hour a servant takes my temperature and gives me another.

I have long subscribed to a fashion magazine. I wear a white bonnet, white stockings and a white waistcoat.

My doctor has always told me to smoke. Part of his advice runs:

—Smoke away, my dear chap: if you don't, someone else will.

PERFECT SURROUNDINGS
(1914)

Living in the midst of wonderful Works of Art is one of the greatest joys anyone can know. Among the precious monuments to human thought which my limited fortune has obliged me to choose as my life companions, I would single out a magnificent fake Rembrandt, wide and deep, so good to press with one's eyes, like a fat but unripe fruit.

You could also see, in my study, a canvas of undeniable beauty, a unique object of admiration: the delicious "Portrait attributed to an Unknown Artist."

Have I told you about my imitation Téniers? It's adorable, a lovely thing and a real rarity.

Aren't those divine, those gems mounted in hardwood? Aren't they?

And yet, there is something which surpasses these masterly works; which crushes them beneath the colossal weight of its majestic genius; which makes them grow pale with its dazzling radiance—it is a forged Beethoven manuscript (a sublime apocryphal Symphony by the Master) piously purchased by myself ten years ago, I think.

Of all the works of this grandiose composer, this 10th Symphony, which nobody knows, is one of the most sumptuous. Its proportions are on a palatial scale; its ideas are fresh and plentiful; the developments are exact and appropriate.

This Symphony had to exist: the number 9 just wouldn't suit Beethoven. He liked the decimal system: "I have ten fingers," he used to explain.

Certain admirers who came dutifully to take in this masterpiece with thoughtful and attentive ears, quite wrongly felt it to be one of Beethoven's inferior works and went so far as to say so. They even went further than that.

In no way can Beethoven be inferior to himself. His form and technique are always portentous, even in his slightest works. In his case the word rudimentary cannot be used. As an artist he can easily stand up to any counterfeit attributed to him.

Would you think that an athlete, who had been famous for years and whose skill and strength had been acknowledged in many a public triumph, was made any the less worthy because he was easily able to carry a bouquet of mixed tulips and jasmine? Would he be any less admirable if a child helped him as well?

Of course not.

209 Nadia Boulanger

The Frenchwoman Nadia Boulanger (1887–1979) had an important influence on the development of American music during the first half of the century. Though a composer, conductor, and keyboard player of considerable accomplishment, Boulanger was best known as a brilliant and demanding teacher of composition and musicianship. Many of the leading American composers of the generation that reached maturity between the two world wars—among them Aaron Copland, Roy Harris, Virgil Thomson, and Elliott Carter—studied with her. Closely associated with Stravinsky and the neoclassical movement, and conscious of the special burden of working in an era in which "everything is in question," Boulanger emphasized discipline and the establishment of compositional limits. In these two excerpts from interviews conducted near the end of her life, she focuses upon matters with which she was particularly concerned: teaching composition and the development of American musicians.

FROM Two Interviews

(1970s)

A MENTOR

Do you know that text of Valéry's: "In the past, one imitated mastery, today one searches for singularity."

It is cruel, for one is singular because one cannot be like everyone else. One isn't singular by choice.

I desperately try to make a pupil understand that he must express what he wants; I don't mind whether he agrees with me or not, so long as he can tell me: "This is what I want to say, this is what I love, this is what I'm looking for." Today, we are at a fascinating point because everything is in question. Those who provide an answer are those who find a new language which isn't to be discussed, or approved, or rejected: it simply exists. We know already that there are some who make themselves understood and others who seek to do so, and others who haven't much to say and are looking for something to say. But that has been the case in the past, too. The difference is that previously there was such an established style that if the music was trivial, it was nevertheless intelligible; whereas in a time of experiment, when language is handled by people

TEXT: *Mademoiselle: Conversations with Nadia Boulanger*, ed. by Bruno Monsaingeon, trans. by Robyn Marsack (Boston: Northeastern University Press, 1988), pp. 60–62, 72–73. Reprint by permission of Carcanet Press Limited.

who don't know what they're doing, it makes for the vague, the uncertain in the uncertain.

When my students compose, I prefer them to be mistaken if they must make mistakes, but to remain natural and free rather than wishing to appear other than what they are. I remember a day when Stravinsky was dining here. He took his neighbor at the table by the lapels, violently! His neighbor, crushed, said to him; "But Monsieur Stravinsky, I don't know why we're talking like this, I agree with you." And Stravinsky exclaimed furiously, "Yes, but not for the right reasons, so you are wrong."

You can have good or bad reasons for searching. If you search in order to hide your inadequacy, you're wrong. If you are looking in order to say what you really want to say, you're right. And so it's very important for a teacher first of all to let his pupil play as he wishes, write as he wishes; and then to be ruthless on questions of discipline.

The student who has completely assimilated Hindemith's book, *Elementary Training for Musicians*—a pedagogical masterpiece—cannot be stumped by any question of rhythm, harmony or counterpoint. It is a book of pure theory, indispensable to all musicians and containing remarkable exercises. Hindemith knew about music in such an amazing way that sometimes it is difficult to distinguish the composer from the teacher. The whole of his work is made up of very beautiful writing and the most exquisite combinations. But despite his very curious and analytic mind, I wonder whether his teaching hasn't influenced his work as a composer. Certainly there is a difference between the Hindemith of *Mathis der Maler* and that of *Marienleben,* but the development isn't very marked. The second version of *Marienleben* seems to me, in some of the pieces that I love deeply, a betrayal of his original thought. I say this in all humility.

He himself said of his educational books that they had led to bad Hindemith being written by many young composers, and sometimes by himself. On the necessity and danger of convention: without conventions, you don't have a framework, and without a framework you're lost, you lose your balance. But you fall over too if you abandon yourself to convention or to fashion.

A great work, I believe, is made out of a combination of obedience and liberty. Such a work satisfies the mind, together with that curious thing which is artistic emotion. Stravinsky said, "If I were permitted everything, I would be lost in the abyss of liberty." On the one hand he knew the limits, on the other he ceaselessly extended them.

If we look at the history of human production we note that there is a kind of tacit and profound accord between what has been achieved and what has been transcended. Take a work of the importance of Bach's *Well-Tempered Clavier;* the obedience is such that when Bach makes a decision, it always corresponds to a rule, to a convention that can be explained in clear terms. Thus he begins by obeying. But within that obedience, he is absolutely free. He doesn't submit to obedience, he chooses it.

PUPILS FROM THE NEW WORLD

I have had a lot of American pupils, that's true. It's easy to forget that fifty years ago, no one knew of American music, it wasn't an expression you used. There's been an enormous change since then, and today Mr. Copland comes to conduct in London, in Rome, in Paris; Mr. Bernstein conducts, and his works are played all over the world.

The term "American musician" is no longer unusual. It was unknown before for specific reasons: a number of foreign musicians had settled in America, but no musicians had been trained entirely there. This situation was linked to polit- ical, religious and racial questions; the artistic culture of America developed relatively late. The amalgam of these elements seems to have been achieved first in America through popular music, supplied by black men who had a particular talent for music but were hardly American in origin.

Of course, very few of us are pure French for generations back without any dilution; most of us are descended from parents of diverse origins, there's a mixture. But this mixing has gone on for such a long time that, as a wine that's quite old is more itself, more recognizable than an absolutely new wine, we can easily assert our identity. A tree has roots that establish themselves deep in the earth and the process requires time. The musical heritage of black Ameri- cans still constitutes an essential compost. Beginning from that, and little by little, American musicians have created an entirely new concept by using old methods. America has managed to generate a very advanced civilization with- out roots; it had to create simultaneously the fruit and the root; it has, I believe, succeeded to a very great extent.

210 Constant Lambert

Though well known in his day as a composer and conductor, the Englishman Constant Lambert (1905–1951) is perhaps now best remembered as the author of a brilliant and opinionated 1934 book on early twentieth-century music, *Music Ho! A Study of Music in Decline*. Here Lambert takes a jaundiced view of the whole modern compositional scene, letting fly with his own quirky yet stimulating views on whatever happens to have come across his field of hearing. In the following section he examines a characteristic feature of the period fol- lowing World War I: the tendency to create new compositions based on stylistic simulations of older music. For Lambert this practice reflects an age that has lost faith in its own voice: the first era in which the music of the past is deemed superior to that of the present. He decries the use of "pastiche"—the making of something new out of fragments of borrowed material—not simply as a "curiosity" but "as a chosen medium for self-expression" (though he takes no account of similar practices in medieval and Renaissance music).

FROM *Music Ho!*

(1934)

THE AGE OF PASTICHE

To describe the present age in music as one of pastiche may seem a sweeping generalization but, like the description of the Impressionist period as one of disruption, it is a generalization with a strong basis in fact. There are many contemporary composers of note who stand to some extent outside this classification, just as there were many composers who stood outside the Impressionism of the pre-war period, but the dominant characteristic of post-war music is either pastiche or an attempted consolidation that achieves only pastiche.

Pastiche has existed in music for many years, but it is only since the war that it has taken the place of development and experiment. In the nineteenth century a number of minor composers turned out their suites in the olden style, but these mild pièces d'occasion[1] no more affected the main course of music than an Olde Worlde Bunne Shoppe affects the architectural experiments of Corbusier and Mallet-Stevens. Apart from these studio pieces, pastiche has always existed in the form of stage decoration as, for example, the Mozartean divertissement in Tchaikovsky's *Queen of Spades,* or the music off stage in the second act of Puccini's *Tosca.* It need hardly be pointed out, though, that these touches of dramatic colour indicated no change of heart on the part of the composer. Tchaikovsky did not write symphonies modelled on Haydn any more than Puccini set out to imitate Rossini or Mercadante.

The deliberate and serious use of pastiche, not as a curiosity or as a pièce d'occasion but as a chosen medium for self-expression, is the property of the post-war period alone.

The idea that music of an earlier age can be better than the music of one's own is an essentially modern attitude. The Elizabethans did not tire of their conceits and go back to the sweet simplicity of Hucbald, any more than the late Caroline composers deserted the new and airy Italian style for the grave fantasias of Dowland. Burney's *History of Music* is an astonishing example of the complete satisfaction with its own period so typical of the eighteenth century. To him the earlier composers were only of interest as stepping-stones to the glorious and unassailable music of his own day. Passages in the earlier

TEXT: *Music Ho! A Study of Music in Decline* (London: Faber & Faber, 1966), pp. 66–71.

1. "Occasional pieces," here implying "light music."

music which do not display the smoothness of texture that the eighteenth century looked on as technical perfection were dismissed as crudities due to lack of taste and skill.

The nineteenth century was to carry this smug attitude one stage further. The eighteenth-century masters were admired not so much for their own sake as for being precursors of the romantic school which through its sheer position in time was naturally an improvement. Once Beethoven's Symphonies were accepted they were considered as being superior to Mozart's in the way that a six-cylinder car is preferred to a four-cylinder car, or a talking to a silent film. Schumann, it is true, admired Scarlatti, but with a touch of the patronage displayed by a Lady Bountiful visiting the village, and Clara Schumann simply could not understand how Brahms could take any interest in composers earlier than Bach. Wagner's followers did not look upon *The Ring* as a way of writing operas that was different from Bellini's, but as a way that clearly was a much better one.

Even in the early twentieth century, when the attitude towards music of a past age was broader and more cultured, showing at times a certain humility, the direction taken, not only by composers but by the public and critics, was progressive in the mechanical sense of the word. Those who were swept off their feet by Strauss and, later, by Scriabin—and they included some of our most levelheaded critics—thought nothing of referring to Mozart as a snuffbox composer in comparison with these cosmic masters; and it is clear that the more fervent admirers of Debussy and Stravinsky regarded their music as not only a reaction against Wagner, but as the death of Wagner.

That is not to say that music until the present has proceeded in a mechanical series of reactions. It is not until Stravinsky that a new movement in music is held to have automatically wiped out all traces of the preceding one (of which the wretched followers, like Babylonian courtiers, are forcibly immolated on the tomb of their master). The new music from Italy undoubtedly changed the course of Purcell's musical thought, but the Elizabethan spirit and technique displayed in his early string fantasias is not entirely banished from his later work, which, though experimental to a degree, and in no way reactionary, yet has a distinct connection with the work of previous generations.

Revolutionary, in fact, is an unsuitable word with which to describe the experimental periods of past ages. The revolutionaries of the seventeenth century were hardy pioneers who struck out boldly across undiscovered plains and cultivated the virgin soil. The revolutionaries of today are no more hardy than the man who takes a ticket on the Inner Circle, and is at liberty to travel in either direction, knowing that eventually he will arrive at the station which the fashion of the day has decreed to be the centre of the town. The modern musical revolutions are revolutions in the meanest sense of the word—the mere turning of a stationary wheel.

A great deal of pre-war music may have sounded, to use a dear old phrase, "like nothing on earth," but that at least is a negative merit from the revolutionaries' point of view. Most music of today sounds only too reminiscent of something that has previously been in existence.

Comparison to an earlier composer, at one time a well-known form of musician-baiting, is now come to be a delicate compliment. If you had told Wagner that you admired his operas because they were "like'" Cimarosa he would probably have kicked you out of the house, and I doubt if Liszt would have been pleased if you had said that his *Études transcendentales* were charming because they were "like" Couperin.

But today every composer's overcoat has its corresponding hook in the cloak-room of the past. Stravinsky's concertos (we have it on the composer's own authority) are "like" Bach and Mozart; Sauguet's music is admired because "c'est dans le vrai tradition de Gounod";[2] another composer's score is praised because in it "se retrouvent les graces étincellantes de Scarlatti."[3] The composer can no longer pride himself on being true to himself—he can only receive the pale reflected glory of being true to whichever past composer is credited at the moment with having possessed the Elixir of Life.

It would be a mistake, I think, to put this attitude down to a spiritual humility comparable to the quite natural inferiority complex a modern sculptor might feel in the presence of some early Chinese carving. It is more in the nature of a last refuge, comparable to the maudlin religiosity of a satiated rake. After the debauches of the Impressionist period nothing is left to the modern composer in the way of a new *frisson* save a fashionable repentance.

Unlike the experimental period of the seventeenth century the pre-war period has led to a psychological cul-de-sac. There are many explanations of this, of which the most convincing is a simple and practical one. By 1913 music had already reached the absolute limit of complication allowed by the capacity of composers, players, listeners and instrument makers. With very few exceptions in detail—such as the piano writing of Sorabji, the polytonal choral writing of Milhaud and the quarter-tone writing of Aloys Haba—there is nothing in present-day music more complicated from any point of view than what we find in the music of twenty years ago. The composer is now faced, not with further experiment but with the more difficult task of consolidating the experiments of this vertiginous period. He is like a man in a high-powered motor-car that has got out of control. He must either steer it away from the cliff's edge back to the road or leap out of it altogether. Most modern composers have chosen the latter plan, remarking, as they dexterously save their precious lives: "I think motor-cars are a little *vieux jeu*[4]—don't you?"

There is an obvious end to the amount of purely physical experiment in music, just as there is an obvious end to geographical exploration. Wyndham Lewis has pointed out that when speed and familiarity have reduced travelling in space to the level of the humdrum those in search of the exotic will have to

2. I.e., "it is in the true tradition of Gounod."
3. I.e., in it "are found the glittering graces of Scarlatti."
4. I.e., "old hat."

travel in time, and this is what has already happened in music. The Impression-ist composers vastly speeded up the facilities for space travel in music, explor-ing the remotest jungles and treating uncharted seas as though they were the Serpentine. Stravinsky, at one time the globe trotter par excellence, can no longer thrill us with his traveller's tales of the primitive steppe and has, quite logically, taken to time travelling instead. He reminds one of the character in a play by Evreinoff who lives half in the eighteenth century, half in the present.

The advantages of time travelling are obvious. The pioneer work has been done for you already and, owing to the increased facilites for moving from one century or decade to another, you can always be in the right decade at the right time, whereas in space travelling you may be delayed by a month or two, or even find that the intellectual world has gone on to the next port.

211 Leonard B. Meyer

The pluralism that was already evident in the post–World War I period, dis-cussed by Constant Lambert in the previous reading, became even more charac-teristic of music composed during the second half of the century. In this excerpt from his book *Music, the Arts, and Ideas,* the music theorist and cultural histo-rian Leonard B. Meyer (b. 1918) argues that the condition of stylistic plurality in contemporary art is not just a passing phase but will remain a permanent attri-bute, at least into the foreseeable future. Music will exist within a state of con-stant change and fluctuation, without any single compositional orientation gaining an upper hand, except perhaps for a relatively brief period. With this view Meyer was among the first to develop a theory of the "postmodern," although the term had not been coined when his book appeared in 1967. Time, moreover, seems to have supported Meyer's hypothesis, at least to date: musical developments of the subsequent quarter century have done little to refute it.

FROM *Music, the Arts, and Ideas*
(1967)

THE AESTHETICS OF STABILITY

> *And therefore I have sailed and come*
> *To the holy city of Byzantium.*
> —W. B. Yeats

INTRODUCTION

. . . . .

The present seems to be aberrant, uncertain, and baffling because the prevalent view of style change—involving notions of progress and teleology, *Zeitgeist* and cultural coherence, necessity and organic development, or some combination of these—posits the eventual establishment of a single common style in each, or even in all, of the arts. As a result, composers as well as critics and historians have come to expect that one dominant style would emerge in the arts—whether as the result of radically new developments, an accommodation of prevailing styles to one another, or the "triumph" of some existing style. Thus Winthrop Sargeant, commenting upon the works of composers who employ quite different styles, says, "The astonishing thing is that these composers all exist at the same time, and the inference to be drawn from this fact is that none of the revolutions has been definitive."[1] And, though composing in an idiom anathema to Mr. Sargeant, Boulez also tacitly assumes a monolithic model of style development, asserting, "Anyone who has not felt . . . the necessity of the 12-tone language is SUPERFLUOUS. For everything he writes will fall short of the imperatives of our time."[2]

But suppose that the paradigm which posits cumulative change and the discovery of a common style is no longer pertinent and viable? Perhaps none of the "revolutions" will be definitive; then astonishment would disappear. Suppose, too, that there are no "imperatives" of the sort that Boulez assumes (Whose imperatives? What is "our time" but the totality of actions, including art works, that take place in it?), and, consequently, that no style is necessarily superfluous. Suppose, in short, that the present pluralism of coexisting styles (each with its particular premises and even its attendant ideology) represents not an anomalous, transient state of affairs, but a relatively stable and enduring one.

I am suggesting not only that such a hypothesis is neither theoretically absurd

TEXT: *Music, the Arts, and Ideas* (Chicago: University of Chicago Press, 1967), pp. 171–75.

1. "Twin Bill," *The New Yorker* 42 (May 28, 1966), p. 88. [Au.]
2. Harold C. Schonberg, "Very Big Man of Avant-Garde," *New York Times,* May 9, 1965, sec. 2, p. 11. [Au.]

nor empirically impossible but that, once it is adopted, seemingly incompatible pieces of the puzzling present begin to form an intelligible pattern. If our time appears to be one of "crisis," it does so largely because we have misunderstood the present situation and its possible consequences. Because a past paradigm has led us to expect a monolithic, all-encompassing style, the cultural situation has seemed bizarre and perplexing. The "crisis" dissolves when the possibility of a continuing stylistic coexistence is recognized and the delights of diversity are admitted. The question then becomes not is this style going to be THE STYLE, but is this particular work well-made, challenging, and enjoyable.

THE PROFILE OF PLURALISM
THE DYNAMICS OF FLUCTUATION

What the proposed hypothesis, then, envisages is the persistence over a considerable period of time of a fluctuating stasis—a steady-state in which an indefinite number of styles and idioms, techniques and movements, will coexist in each of the arts.[3] There will be no central, common practice in the arts, no stylistic "victory." In music, for instance, tonal and non-tonal styles, aleatoric and serialized techniques, electronic and improvised means will all continue to be employed. Similarly in the visual arts, current styles and movements—abstract expressionism and surrealism, representational and Op art, kinetic sculpture and magic realism, Pop and non-objective art—will all find partisans and supporters. Though schools and techniques are less clearly defined in literature, present attitudes and tendencies—the "objective" novel, the theater of the absurd, as well as more traditional manners and means—will, I suspect, persist.

Though new methods and directions may be developed in any or in all of the arts, these will not displace existing styles. The new will simply be additions to the already existing spectrum of styles. Interaction and accommodation among different traditions of music, art, or literature may from time to time produce hybrid combinations or composites, but the possibility of radical innovation seems very remote. As will be suggested, however, the abrupt juxtaposition of markedly unlike styles—perhaps from different epochs and traditions—within a single work may not be uncommon.

Though a spectrum of styles will coexist in what is essentially a steady-state, this does not mean that in a given art all methods and idioms will be equally favored at a particular time. In music, for example, one or possibly two of the stylistic options available to composers may for a number of years prove especially attractive; and activity will be most intense in those parts of the stylistic spectrum. But this will not indicate that other traditions and idioms are no longer viable or are declining. For subsequently, fascinated by different prob-

3. Pluralism is by no means confined to the arts. Diversity and heterogeneity characterize most disciplines and subjects. Often disparate paradigms or conceptual schemes coexist within a single field. [Au.]

lems or swayed by different attitudes, composers will, by and large, turn to other traditions and other styles.

Such a succession of wavelike fluctuations may make it appear as though one style has followed or replaced another. But what will in fact have happened is that one style—or perhaps a group of related styles—will, so to speak, have "crested," becoming for a time particularly conspicuous. And at the very time most composers are riding the crest of the stylistic wave, others will have continued to follow ways and procedures temporarily less popular.

Fluctuation of this sort has, it seems to me, been characteristic of the history of the arts during the past fifty years. Various musical styles have appeared to succeed one another—late romanticism (serial as well as tonal), primitivism, neo-classicism, aleatoric and totally ordered music; but almost all have continued, in one form or another, as ways of making music. Some—for instance, serialism—have already "crested" more than once; none has really disappeared or been replaced. In the plastic arts, where learning a syntax is not involved and the resistance of performers to novelty is not a consideration, fluctuation has been both more rapid and more patent. After a long sequence of styles and movements, beginning with those that followed World War I and continuing through abstract expressionism, action-painting, Pop, Op, and so on, many painters are "returning" to more or less traditional forms of representation, to surrealism and the like. Not that the latter styles were ever really abandoned— only that for a time the majority of artists found them less provocative and exciting than other means and modes.

Though a fluctuating stasis may well be characteristic of present and future changes in the arts, I do not wish to suggest that the rate, direction, or kind of changes exhibited by them will be concurrent or congruent. Sometimes style changes in two or more arts may be simultaneous. In such a case, if the arts in question move in a similar direction—say, toward greater freedom from traditional norms or toward a more meticulous control of means—some common ideological-aesthetic tendency may be involved. At other times, such concurrent changes may simply happen by chance. More often than not, however, each of the arts will probably exhibit its own peculiar pattern of style fluctuation.

The continuing existence of a spectrum of styles is also indicated by the fact that a number of composers, artists, and writers have found it possible to move easily from one practice or tradition to another—according to their interest, taste, or humor. Thus, after developing and writing a number of works in the twelve-tone method, Schönberg found it interesting and not inconsistent occasionally to compose in the idiom of tonal music. In like manner, Picasso has from time to time returned to a neo-classicism which he first employed quite early in his career. If the repertory of available styles grows, as I believe it will, to include many of the styles of earlier Western art[4] and even some from non-

---

4. When the term "art" or "work of art" is used, it will generally mean all the arts. Similarly, when the term "artists" is used alone, it will refer to plastic artists, musicians, writers, and so on. [Au.]

Western civilizations, such shifts in style from one work to another will become more common.

This does not imply that all artists, or even a majority of them, will be stylistically polylingual. Many will cultivate only one of the many styles available. (Generally these will, I suspect, be the "Traditionalists" for whom art is a form of personal expression, and whose motto must, accordingly, be: One Man, One Style.) Frequently, too, there will be deep and irreconcilable differences between artists working in different traditions or espousing different ideologies.[5]

Which styles or traditions are preferred by any considerable number of artists at a particular time—and for how long—will depend upon a number of different factors. The ability of one outstanding composer—or perhaps even a group of composers—to write convincing, effective, and interesting music in a particular idiom will be important in attracting others to the style. The challenge and fascination of particular compositional methods and problems may also serve to stimulate a wave of activity in a particular part of the stylistic spectrum. Related to this is the real possibility that one style may be abandoned and another adopted simply because the composer no longer finds the problems and procedures of the first style interesting. At times a conceptual model of order (or disorder), developed in connection with some other art or one of the sciences, may also influence the direction of style change. Nor, as recent history indicates, should one underestimate the role played by theory and criticism in shaping stylistic interests and tendencies. Finally, the power of patrons, particularly institutional ones—foundations, universities, symphony orchestras, museums, and the like—to encourage or discourage stylistic movements and tendencies may be of considerable importance.

Because they may not necessarily exhibit any consistent direction or pattern, such successive waves of stylistic activity may seem little more than a series of fashions. Possibly so; but the implied value judgment is not warranted. For since in the coming years the criteria of aesthetic value will, according to the present hypothesis, be those of skill and elegance, rather than those of imitation, expression, or social relevance as they have been in the past, style fluctuations occasioned by problems to be solved would not be capricious or merely modish. Just as the scientists, for instance, tend to direct their energies toward sets of problems where developments in one field have made exciting advances and elegant solutions possible (perhaps in a different field)—yesterday in nuclear physics, today in genetics and molecular biology—so, for the composers, musical problems broached or solutions proposed in one segment of the stylistic spectrum may make elegant and fruitful activity in some other segment possible and attractive.

•　　•　　•　　•　　•

5. See Harold Rosenberg, *The Tradition of the New* (New York: Horizon Press, 1959), pp. 54–55. [Au.]

212 Umberto Eco

The Italian Umberto Eco (b. 1932), one the most prominent and versatile thinkers of the later twentieth century, has produced major work in such diverse
fields as semiology, literary criticism, cultural theory, and creative writing. (His
novel *The Name of the Rose* even achieved bestseller status.) The influential
essay from which this reading is taken appeared in the 1960s, when indeterminacy was a particularly prominent feature in artistic activities. Eco uses examples drawn from music of the time (he was then closely associated with the
Italian composer Luciano Berio) to develop his notion of the "open" work,
which, like a "construction kit," allows itself to be assembled in different forms,
producing multiple final shapes, none of which can be considered the "work
proper." Eco also questions why such structures, based upon artistic assumptions so markedly contrary to tradition, appeal so strongly to contemporary artists, noting analogies between these "works in movement" and certain
developments in modern science.

FROM The Poetics of the Open Work
(1962)

A number of recent pieces of instrumental music are linked by a common
feature: the considerable autonomy left to the individual performer in the way
he chooses to play the work. Thus, he is not merely free to interpret the composer's instructions following his own discretion (which in fact happens in traditional music), but he must impose his judgment on the form of the piece, as
when he decides how long to hold a note or in what order to group the sounds:
all this amounts to an act of improvised creation. Here are some of the best-
known examples of the process.

1. In *Klavierstück XI*, by Karlheinz Stockhausen, the composer presents the
performer a single large sheet of music paper with a series of note groupings.
The performer then has to choose among these groupings, first for the one to
start the piece and, next, for the successive units in the order in which he
elects to weld them together. In this type of performance, the instrumentalist's
freedom is a function of the "narrative" structure of the piece, which allows
him to "mount" the sequence of musical units in the order he chooses.

2. In Luciano Berio's *Sequenza for Solo Flute*, the composer presents the
performer a text which predetermines the sequence and intensity of the sounds

TEXT: *The Open Work*, trans. by Anna Concogni (Cambridge, Mass.: Harvard University Press, 1989), pp. 1–5, 17–20. Reprinted by permission of the publishers.

to be played. But the performer is free to choose how long to hold a note inside the fixed framework imposed on him, which in turn is established by the fixed pattern of the metronome's beat.

3. Henri Pousseur has offered the following description of his piece *Scambi:*

> *Scambi* is not so much a musical composition as a *field of possibilities,* an explicit invitation to exercise choice. It is made up of sixteen sections. Each of these can be linked to any two others, without weakening the logical continuity of the musical process. Two of its sections, for example, are introduced by similar motifs (after which they evolve in divergent patterns); another pair of sections, on the contrary, tends to develop towards the same climax. Since the performer can start or finish with any one section, a considerable number of sequential permutations are made available to him. Furthermore, the two sections which begin on the same motif can be played simultaneously, so as to present a more complex structural polyphony. It is not out of the question that we conceive these formal notations as a marketable product: if they were tape-recorded and the purchaser had a sufficiently sophisticated reception apparatus, then the general public would be in a position to develop a private musical construct of its own and a new collective sensibility in matters of musical presentation and duration could emerge.

4. In Pierre Boulez's *Third Sonata for Piano,* the first section (*Antiphonie, Formant 1*) is made up of ten different pieces on ten corresponding sheets of music paper. These can be arranged in different sequences like a stack of filing cards, though not all possible permutations are permissible. The second part (*Formant 2, Trope*) is made up of four parts with an internal circularity, so that the performer can commence with any one of them, linking it successively to the others until he comes round full circle. No major interpretative variants are permitted inside the various sections, but one of them, *Parenthèse,* opens with a prescribed time beat, which is followed by extensive pauses in which the beat is left to the player's discretion. A further prescriptive note is evinced by the composer's instructions on the manner of linking one piece to the next (for example, *sans retenir, enchaîner sans interruption,* and so on).

What is immediately striking in such cases is the macroscopic divergence between these forms of musical communication and the time-honored tradition of the classics. This difference can be formulated in elementary terms as follows: a classical composition, whether it be a Bach fugue, Verdi's *Aïda,* or Stravinsky's *Rite of Spring,* posits an assemblage of sound units which the composer arranged in a closed, well-defined manner before presenting it to the listener. He converted his idea into conventional symbols which more or less oblige the eventual performer to reproduce the format devised by the composer himself, whereas the new musical works referred to above reject the definitive, concluded message and multiply the formal possibilities of the distribution of their elements. They appeal to the initiative of the individual performer, and hence they offer themselves not as finite works which prescribe specific repetition along given structural coordinates but as "open" works, which are brought to their conclusion by the performer at the same time as he experiences them on an esthetic plane.[1]

To avoid any confusion in terminology, it is important to specify that here the definition of the "open work," despite its relevance in formulating a fresh dialectics between the work of art and its performer, still requires to be separated from other conventional applications of this term. Esthetic theorists, for example, often have recourse to the notions of "completeness" and "openness" in connection with a given work of art. These two expressions refer to a standard situation of which we are all aware in our reception of a work of art: we see it as the end product of an author's effort to arrange a sequence of communicative effects in such a way that each individual addressee can refashion the original composition devised by the author. The addressee is bound to enter into an interplay of stimulus and response which depends on his unique capacity for sensitive reception of the piece. In this sense the author presents a finished product with the intention that this particular composition should be appreciated and received in the same form as he devised it. As he reacts to the play of stimuli and his own response to their patterning, the individual addressee is bound to supply his own existential credentials, the sense conditioning which is peculiarly his own, a defined culture, a set of tastes, personal inclinations, and prejudices. Thus, his comprehension of the original artifact is always modified by his particular and individual perspective. In fact, the form of the work of art gains its esthetic validity precisely in proportion to the number of different perspectives from which it can be viewed and understood. These give it a wealth of different resonances and echoes without impairing its original essence; a road traffic sign, on the other hand, can be viewed in only one sense, and, if it is transfigured into some fantastic meaning by an imaginative driver, it merely ceases to be *that* particular traffic sign with that particular meaning. A work of art, therefore, is a complete and *closed* form in its uniqueness as a balanced organic whole, while at the same time constituting an *open* product on account of its susceptibility to countless different interpretations which do not impinge on its unadulterable specificity. Hence, every reception of a work of art is both an *interpretation* and a *performance* of it, because in every reception the work takes on a fresh perspective for itself.

Nonetheless, it is obvious that works like those of Berio and Stockhausen are "open" in a far more tangible sense. In primitive terms we can say that they are quite literally "unfinished": the author seems to hand them on to the perfor-

---

1. Here we must eliminate a possible misunderstanding straightaway: the practical intervention of a "performer" (the instrumentalist who plays a piece of music or the actor who recites a passage) is different from that of an interpreter in the sense of consumer (somebody who looks at a picture, silently reads a poem, or listens to a musical composition performed by someone else). For the purposes of esthetic analysis, however, both cases can be seen as different manifestations of the same interpretative attitude. Every "reading," "contemplation," or "enjoyment" of a work of art represents a tacit or private form of "performance." [Au.]

mer more or less like the components of a construction kit. He seems to be unconcerned about the manner of their eventual deployment. This is a loose and paradoxical interpretation of the phenomenon, but the most immediately striking aspect of these musical forms can lead to this kind of uncertainty, although the very fact of our uncertainty is itself a positive feature: it invites us to consider *why* the contemporary artist feels the need to work in this kind of direction, to try to work out what historical evolution of esthetic sensibility led up to it and which factors in modern culture reinforced it. We are then in a position to surmise how these experiences should be viewed in the spectrum of a theoretical esthetics.

Pousseur has observed that the poetics of the "open" work tends to encourage "acts of conscious freedom" on the part of the performer and place him at the focal point of a network of limitless interrelations, among which he chooses to set up his own form without being influenced by an external *necessity* which definitively prescribes the organization of the work in hand.[2] At this point one could object (with reference to the wider meaning of "openness" already introduced in this essay) that any work of art, even if it is not passed on to the addressee in an unfinished state, demands a free, inventive response, if only because it cannot really be appreciated unless the performer somehow reinvents it in psychological collaboration with the author himself. Yet this remark represents the theoretical perception of contemporary esthetics, achieved only after painstaking consideration of the function of artistic performance; certainly an artist of a few centuries ago was far from being aware of these issues. Instead nowadays it is primarily the artist who is aware of its implications. In fact, rather than submit to the "openness" as an inescapable element of artistic interpretation, he subsumes it into a positive aspect of his production, recasting the work so as to expose it to the maximum possible "opening."

•   •   •   •   •

It would be quite natural for us to think that this flight away from the old, solid concept of necessity and the tendency toward the ambiguous and the indeterminate reflect a crisis of contemporary civilization. On the other hand, we might see these poetical systems, in harmony with modern science, as expressing the positive possibility of thought and action made available to an individual who is open to the continuous renewal of his life patterns and cognitive processes. Such an individual is productively committed to the development of his own mental faculties and experiential horizons. This contrast is too facile and Manichaean. Our main intent has been to pick out a number of analogies which reveal a reciprocal play of problems in the most disparate areas of contemporary culture and which point to the common elements in a new way of looking at the world.

2. Henri Pousseur, "La nuova sensibilità musicale," *Incontri musicali* 2 (May, 1958), p. 25. [Au.]

What is at stake is a convergence of new canons and requirements which the forms of art reflect by way of what we could term *structural homologies*. This need not commit us to assembling a rigorous parallelism—it is simply a case of phenomena like the "work in movement" simultaneously reflecting mutually contrasted epistemological situations, as yet contradictory and not satisfactorily reconciled. Thus, the concepts of "openness" and dynamism may recall the terminology of quantum physics: indeterminacy and discontinuity. But at the same time they also exemplify a number of situations in Einsteinian physics.

The multiple polarity of a serial composition in music, where the listener is not faced by an absolute conditioning center of reference, requires him to constitute his own system of auditory relationships.[3] He must allow such a center to emerge from the sound continuum. Here are no privileged points of view, and all available perspectives are equally valid and rich in potential. Now, this multiple polarity is extremely close to the spatiotemporal conception of the universe which we owe to Einstein. The thing which distinguishes the Einsteinian concept of the universe from quantum epistemology is precisely this faith in the totality of the universe, a universe in which discontinuity and indeterminacy can admittedly upset us with their surprise apparitions, but in fact, to use Einstein's words, presuppose not a God playing random games with dice but the Divinity of Spinoza, who rules the world according to perfectly regulated laws. In this kind of universe, relativity means the infinite variability of experience as well as the infinite multiplication of possible ways of measuring things and viewing their position. But the objective side of the whole system can be found in the invariance of the simple formal descriptions (of the differential equations) which establish once and for all the relativity of empirical measurement.

• • •

This is not the place to pass judgment on the scientific validity of the metaphysical construct implied by Einstein's system. But there is a striking analogy between his universe and the universe of the work in movement. The God in Spinoza, who is made into an untestable hypothesis by Einsteinian metaphysics, becomes a cogent reality for the work of art and matches the organizing impulse of its creator.

The *possibilities* which the work's openness makes available always work within a given *field of relations*. As in the Einsteinian universe, in the "work in movement" we may well deny that there is a single prescribed point of view. But this does not mean complete chaos in its internal relations. What it does imply is an organizing rule which governs these relations. Therefore, to sum up, we can say that the "work in movement" is the possibility of numerous different personal interventions, but it is not an amorphous invitation to indis-

---

3. On the "éclatement multidirectionnel des structures," see A. Boucourechliev, "Problèmes de la musique moderne," *Nouvelle revue française* (December–January, 1960–61). [Au.]

criminate participation. The invitation offers the performer the opportunity for an oriented insertion into something which always remains the world intended by the author.

In other words, the author offers the interpreter, the performer, the addressee a work *to be completed.* He does not know the exact fashion in which his work will be concluded, but he is aware that once completed the work in question will still be his own. It will not be a different work, and, at the end of the interpretative dialogue, a form which is *his* form will have been organized, even though it may have been assembled by an outside party in a particular way that he could not have foreseen. The author is the one who proposed a number of possibilities which had already been rationally organized, oriented, and endowed with specifications for proper development.

Berio's *Sequenza,* which is played by different flutists, Stockhausen's *Klavier-stück XI,* or Pousseur's *Mobiles,* which are played by different pianists (or performed twice over by the same pianists), will never be quite the same on different occasions. Yet they will never be gratuitously different. They are to be seen as the actualization of a series of consequences whose premises are firmly rooted in the original data provided by the author.

This happens in the musical works which we have already examined, and it happens also in the plastic artifacts we considered. The common factor is a mutability which is always deployed within the specific limits of a given taste, or of predetermined formal tendencies, and is authorized by the concrete pliability of the material offered for the performer's manipulation. Brecht's plays appear to elicit free and arbitrary response on the part of the audience. Yet they are also rhetorically constructed in such a way as to elicit a reaction oriented toward, and ultimately anticipating, a Marxist dialectic logic as the basis for the whole field of possible responses.

All these examples of "open" works and "works in movement" have this latent characteristic, which guarantees that they will always be seen as "works" and not just as a conglomeration of random components ready to emerge from the chaos in which they previously stood and permitted to assume any form whatsoever.

213 George Rochberg

Stylistic pluralism, discussed by Constant Lambert in connection with post–World War I music (see pp. 220–24) and Leonard Meyer in a more general esthetic context (pp. 224–28), became particularly prominent during the 1960s, when composers started not only evoking and parodying earlier music but actually quoting large segments of it, often constructing entire compositions by reworking preexistent material. At the same time there was a widespread move in both Europe and the Americas to "return to tonality," not merely by quotation but through reassimilation of the techniques and gestures of Western common-practice music. The Third String Quartet by the American George Rochberg (b. 1922), a leading figure in advancing both quotation and simulation, played a major role in this development, attracting considerable controversy when it first appeared in 1965. Though there is no actual quotation in the quartet, there is one lengthy movement of an almost purely Beethovenian character, along with others that combine segments sounding like Mahler and Bartók with what is presumably Rochberg's "own" contemporary style.

On the Third String Quartet
(1965)

When I wrote my Third String Quartet I had no idea it would call forth the quantity and kinds of critical comment that followed its first performances and recording. Some critics rejected the work out of hand on the grounds that its combination of tonal and nontonal musics simply did not add up to being "contemporary." Some seemed fascinated but still puzzled by the phenomenon of structural fusion of past and present. The majority of writers, however, welcomed it even though they were uncertain whether the direction that the quartet pointed to could or would be followed up.

The acceptability of such a work hinges no doubt on whether one is able to reconcile a juxtaposition of musically opposite styles. In order to effect such a reconciliation, one has to be persuaded, first, that the idea of history as "progress" is no longer viable and, second, that the radical avant-garde of recent years has proved to be bankrupt. Both conditions lay behind the impulse that generated my quartet. Both were determining factors in my choice of ideas, levels of musical action, and the structure of the work itself. Far from seeing tonality and atonality as opposite "styles," I viewed them as significant aspects of an enlarged language of musical expression with branching subdivisions of what I like to call "dialects"—a particular way of stressing or inflecting parts of the whole spectrum of Western musical language. These dialects can be presented singly or in combination depending on what one wants to say and the particular size, shape, and character of the work one wants to say it in. In the quartet the dialects range widely from diatonic, key-centered tonality to forms of chromaticism which veer toward nineteenth-century or early-twentieth-century practices (but still structurally tonal) to a more atonally oriented chromaticism; from predictable to unpredictable periodicities of phrase structure; from simple to complex metric pulsation; and from continuous to noncontinuous gestural relationships between phrases, sections, and movements.

TEXT: *The Aesthetic of Survival*, ed. by William Bolcom (Ann Arbor: University of Michigan Press, 1984), pp. 239–42. Used by permission.

By embracing the earlier traditions of tonality and combining them with the more recently developed atonality, I found it possible to release my music from the overintense, expressionistic manner inherent in a purely serially organized, constant chromaticism, and from the inhibition of physical pulse and rhythm which has enervated so much recent music. With the enlargement of this spectrum of possible means came an enlargement of perspective which potentially placed the entire past at my disposal. I was freed of the conventional perceptions which ascribe some goal-directed, teleological function to that past, insisting that each definable historical development supersedes the one that has just taken place either by incorporating or nullifying it.

In this view, the invention of classical twelve-tone methodology—and later total serialism—not only superseded everything that came before it but literally declared it null and void. Obviously, I rejected this view—though not without great discomfort and difficulty, because I had acquired it, along with a number of similar notions, as a seemingly inevitable condition of the twentieth-century culture in which I had grown up. The demanding effort to evolve and maintain a personal kind of transcendentalism still occupies me; but that effort has resulted in being able to compose whatever kind of music I feel deeply and intensely.

I am not aware that anyone has yet attempted a full-scale answer to the questions my quartet seems to have raised. Perhaps wisely—because I believe the issues involved are complex beyond imagining, and therefore certainly not susceptible to the kind of either/or, binary thinking so characteristic of the contemporary mind. To live with paradox and contradiction is not and has not been our cultural or intellectual way. I suspect that what my quartet suggests to others, and what I began to accept for myself at least fifteen years ago, is that we can no longer live with monolithic ideas about art and how it is produced. Nor can we take as artistic gospel the categorical imperatives laid down by cultural messiahs or their self-appointed apologists and followers of whatever persuasion.

On the contrary, the twentieth century has pointed—however reluctant we may be to accept it in all areas of life, social as well as political, cultural as well as intellectual—toward a difficult-to-define pluralism, a world of new mixtures and combinations of everything we have inherited from the past and whatever we individually or collectively value in the inventions of our own present, replete with juxtapositions of opposites (or seeming opposites) and contraries. In other words, not the narrow, pat, plus/minus, monoview of the rational-minded, but the web of living ideas which combine in strange and unexpected ways much as the stuff of biological matter does; not the self-conscious aesthetic or morality which excludes so much for the sake of "purity," but the sensed (if not quite yet articulate) notion that stretches to embrace everything possible to one's taste and experience, regardless of its time or place of origin. This not only makes it mandatory to see the "past" as continuously viable and alive in our "present" but also to be able to perceive large chunks of time as

unities which create a vast physical-mental-spiritual web enfolding our individual lives, actions, and feelings.

I believe we are the filaments of a universal mind which transcends our
individual egos and histories. The degree to which we partake of that universal
mind is the degree to which we identify with the collective imagery, fate, wisdom, and tragedy of our still struggling species. By ourselves we are virtually
nothing—but by opening ourselves to the transcendent collectivity of mankind
and its experiences, we share in a totality which, however mysterious its
sources, dimensions, and ultimate fate, sustains us.

Pluralism, as I understand it, does not mean a simplistic array of different
things somehow stuck together in arbitrary fashion but a way of seeing new
possibilities of relationships; of discovering and uncovering hidden connections
and working with them structurally; of joining antipodes without boiling out
their tensions; of resolving the natural tensions of contradictory terms on new
symbiotic hierarchic levels—more than all of the above, a way of preserving
the uncertainty of the artistic enterprise which itself demands that, out of the
tensions and anxieties attendant upon it, we struggle for clarity and order, to
gain not a permanent certainty (which is not possible anyhow) but a momentary
insight into how it is possible to resolve the chaos of existence into a shape or
form which takes on beauty, perhaps meaning, certainly strength. Art is a way
of fighting the encroachment of the forces which diminish us. Through art we
are all Don Quixotes battling Time and Death.

Granting pluralism, how is a composer to deal with it? From the inside out,
i.e., from the internal psychic imagery which becomes the musical gesture to
its artistic manifestation. Gesture, singly or in combination, successive or simultaneous, is the determining factor—not style, language, system, or method.

Given the very strong possibility that music is rooted in our biological structure—as are spoken language and mathematics—the gestures of music can
only proceed authentically from one direction: from inside. That is where they
get their energy, their power, their immediacy. The conscious effort to give
voice to the vast range of these gestures becomes the act of composing, and
inevitably demands not only freedom of choice but freedom of combination. If
Beethoven, for example, had not felt this way, we would not have the late
quartets—those glories of our civilization. There is surely no logic to a movement such as the "Heiliger Dankgesang" of Op. 132, with its combination of
alternating Baroque chorale variations and eighteenth/nineteenth-century idealized dance which hides vestiges of the old courtly minuet; or to the insertion
of a German folk dance in the more metaphysical surroundings of Op. 130
which Beethoven capped with the grandest fugue of them all. There's no rational way to understand Ives's placing a diatonic fugue in C major cheek by jowl
with the layered musics of the other movements of his Fourth Symphony; or
his juxtaposition and overlay of chromatic on diatonic, diatonic on chromatic,
in his two gems, "The Unanswered Question" and "Central Park in the Dark."
(Consider the juxtaposition of the intensely chromatic fugue and essentially

pandiatonic last movement in Bartók's *Music for Strings, Percussion and Celesta.*)

The determination to write the Third Quartet the way I did (and other works similar in nature but cast differently, because of different gestural needs, balances, and projections) stems from my personal way of understanding composers like Beethoven, Bartók, and Ives, but is not limited to them. If, in the need to expand our sources—pluralism of gesture, language, and style—we lay ourselves open to the charge of eclecticism, we need not concern ourselves. Other and earlier forms of eclecticism may also be charged to medieval music or to early classical music or to Bach or to Mozart (who seemed thoroughly eclectic to his contemporaries), or to Stravinsky.

Some of the critics who have commented on my quartet have wondered out loud whether the work would "last." How can anyone tell? It is not important. Culture is not the additive product of a series of discrete, specific events or works. It is, like the biology that it rests on, a self-renewing, self-sustaining organism that proliferates, spreads, unites, subdivides, reunites, dies individually but lives collectively. The cultural mechanism for continuity (posterity; immortality) resides in human memory and the preservation of what is authentic and has, therefore, captured a piece of human wit or wisdom (as possible in music as in painting, as in literature). The cultural mechanism for renewal resides in the courage to use human passion and energy in the direction of what is authentic again and again. The ring of authenticity is more important than the clang of originality. Whatever is authentic about the twentieth century will be preserved, and we need not worry about it. Given that certainty, we can safely leave it alone and get back to the business of writing music without falsely institutionalizing the means we use to produce it. But we must be sure that it *is* music; i.e., that we write what we believe in, write it consummately well and that we intend it at least for the delectation and edification of the human ear and heart—beyond that, if possible, for the purification of the mind.

To quote from my notes to the recording of the Third Quartet: "I am turning away from what I consider the cultural pathology of my own time toward what can only be called a *possibility:* that music can be renewed by regaining contact with the tradition and means of the past, to re-emerge as a spiritual force with reactivated powers of melodic thought, rhythmic pulse, and large-scale structure."

214 Carl Dahlhaus

The German Carl Dahlhaus (1928–1989), one of the most far-ranging thinkers in twentieth-century musicology, wrote extensively on such diverse topics as music historiography, the evolution of harmonic tonality, the history of nineteenth-century music, the music of Schoenberg, and music theory and esthetics. In this essay, the final chapter of his book *What is Music?* (1985), Dahlhaus discusses the ways in which even our most basic ideas about music have been affected by the changes the art has experienced in the twentieth century. Dahlhaus is particularly interested in the strains placed upon a unified concept of music in an age characterized by constant contact with the musics of other peoples and cultures. Such modern Western distinctions as those between "the musical" and "the extramusical," "serious" and "entertainment" music, and even "music" and "noise," become difficult to maintain in a world filled with such diversities. Relating the question of "music" (in the singular) to the more encompassing one of "humanity" (also in the singular), Dahlhaus concludes that "according to twentieth-century criteria . . . , humanity consists less in making the heterogeneous more homogenous than in mutual acceptance, even where differences may appear unbridgeable."

Music—or Musics?

(1985)

The idea of a world history of music—an idea behind a UNESCO project which the organizers seem disinclined to abandon despite mounting difficulties of an intrinsic and extrinsic nature—carries a double burden: the vagueness of the concept "music" and the ideological implications of the notion of a "world history." And the one difficulty is closely related to the other: the problem of whether "music," in the singular, actually exists cannot even be defined (at any rate, not in a way that invites a foreseeable solution) without a clear idea of whether and in what sense "history," in the singular, is a reality or a mere figment of the imagination.

TEXT: "Gibt es 'die' Musik," in Carl Dahlhaus and Hans Heinrich Eggebrecht, *Was ist Musik?*, ed. by R. Schaal, Taschenbücher zur Musikwissenschaft 100 (Wilhelmshaven: Heinrichshofen Verlag, 1985), pp. 9–17. Translation by Stephen Hinton.
Translated word for word, the title should read: "Does 'the' music exist?" The use of articles, both definite and indefinite, before the singular form of nouns differs between German and English. Nor is it consistent. When the definite article is used, as here, it not only lays stress on the singular but can also imply oneness. Yet German-speaking people may well wonder whether the unity of *die Musik* (at once emphasized and questioned by the quotation marks) is essential or accidental, as Carl Dahlhaus's text makes apparent. The increasingly widespread use in English of the plural "musics" seems to confirm the thrust of Dahlhaus's observations. [Tr.]

The linguistic convention that proscribes making a plural from the word "music" has been increasingly ignored in recent years, owing to difficulties that arise when one clings to the singular, although the attendant stylistic discomfort, which is also discomfort about substance, still lingers. The naïvety with which the nineteenth century either dismissed the musical "other" as undeveloped or unconsciously assimilated it has disappeared or at least diminished, and as a result (a) social, (b) ethnic, and (c) historical differences prove so huge that one feels forced to abandon a unified concept of music.

(a) For several decades a controversy has been conducted, with unvarying arguments, about the dichotomy between classical music and light music,[1] and the terminological issues associated with that socio-esthetic division are so closely bound up with notions and decisions that directly impinge on social practice as to make those issues seem like a theoretical reflection of that practice. The quarrel about the social functions and esthetic criteria of classical music and light music would not be possible if the sonic phenomena, kept separate from one another through their respective labels, were not at the same time bracketed together by the umbrella term "music." Yet it is by no means obvious that a pop song and a twelve-tone composition belong to the same category, as a comparison with other fields shows. No one describes newspapers as "literature," though since a newspaper is printed language, such an application of the term, albeit unusual, would hardly be absurd from an etymological point of view. (The linguistic umbrella term linking journalism and poetry, "text types" [*Textsorten*], has not become common parlance.) And linguistic convention is both cause and effect of the fact that it is not customary to compare the social functions and esthetic criteria of newspapers and poems. Yet twelve-tone compositions are forced to compete with products of the musical entertainment industry via listener statistics, from which practical consequences are drawn. The "spell cast by language" [*Verhexung durch die Sprache*] (Ludwig Wittgenstein)[2]—in this case, by the precarious and questionable singular "music"—precludes a differentiation that seems quite natural in the case of the printed word. (The term "text types," which has pretensions toward neutrality and is supposed to render such differentiations ideologically suspect, is itself underpinned by a "counter-ideology": commensurability instead of incommensurability.) The dissimilarity in the categorization of language and music can be explained pragmatically. Since there is no musical

---

1. Dahlhaus uses the conceptual pair "E-Musik" (*ernste Musik:* "serious music") and U-Musik (*Unterhaltungsmusik:* "entertainment music"), which carries more terminological weight than the various English equivalents ("classical vs. light," "serious vs. pop," "high vs. low," etc.). Not only have the terms been institutionalized, the large radio stations in Germany have two music departments, and music royalties are paid on two scales, with a distinction being drawn in each case between "E-Musik" and "U-Musik." The terms have also served as the basis for countless esthetic debates. [Tr.]

2. The Austrian philosopher Ludwig Wittgenstein, in his *Philosophical Investigations* (Oxford: Basil Blackwell, 1958), §109, describes philosophy as "a battle against the bewitchment of our intelligence by means of language."

language that serves as an everyday tool of communication, like a vernacular, pop song and twelve-tone composition, both equally removed from everyday reality, are instinctively subsumed under the same category. The convention of talking about "music" in both cases may thus be explained in historical and socio-psychological terms, but such an explanation can hardly be construed as an esthetic justification. Although it might still give one pause, the plural "musics" would be more realistic.

(b) If the consequences arising from the collective singular impinge in a direct and far-reaching way on musico-social reality—a reality defined by the dichotomy between classical and light music, whereby the neutralizing word "music" represents a more serious problem than the controversial adjectives "classical" and "light"—in the case of ethnic and regional differences, the questionable consequences of a universal and neutralizing concept of music are apparent less in practice than in scholarly debate. Sonic phenomena for which a European observer reserves the term "music"—a word for which a linguistic equivalent is often missing in non-European cultures—lose their original meaning if they are divorced from their "extra-musical" context. Strictly speaking, the context of which they are an inextricable part is neither "musical" nor "extra-musical." The former expression [that is, "musical"] stretches the concept of music, a concept of European origin, to such an extent that it can no longer correspond with European reality, while the latter ["extra-musical"] presupposes a concept of music that is not only European but specifically modern. This latter concept of music, which, in a strict sense, dates only from the eighteenth century, crudely distorts non-European musical reality—a reality not just of sonic facts but also of the consciousness of those facts.

If it is true that the category "music" (which supplies criteria for isolating certain "specifically musical"[3] features in complex cultural processes) is an abstraction made only in certain cultures and not in others, then one is faced with an unfortunate alternative: either to reinterpret and expand the European concept of music to the point of alienating it from its origins, or to exclude the sonic creations of a number of non-European cultures from the concept of music. Deciding one way would be precarious in terms of the history of ideas. Deciding the other way would invite the charge of being Eurocentric (as a rule most Africans, even when they emphasize the *négritude* of their culture, do not wish to relinquish "music" as a label of prestige). And a way out of the dilemma is to be found only by considering the ethnological problems in relation to the historical ones; by attempting to solve any difficulties by first increasing them.

(c) The differences between the epochs of European music history, however substantial they may have been, left the inner unity of the concept of music essentially intact as long as the tradition of the ancient world obtained: a tradi-

---

3. "Spezifisch musikalisch" is a phrase used by Eduard Hanslick in *Vom Musikalisch-Schönen* (Leipzig: Rudolph Weigel, 1854), p. 31. [Tr.]

tion whose essential ingredient was the principle of an unchanging tonal system [*Tonsystem*],[4] constituted by direct and indirect relations of consonance, that underpinned a multiplicity of styles. (The principle may not be specifically European, but that does not alter the fact that it formed the essential link in the chain of historical continuity from Antiquity via the Middle Ages through the Modern Age. What is specific—contrary to a prejudice fostered by the method of determination by demarcation—is not always what is essential.)

It was electronic music and "sound-composition" [*Klangkomposition*] inspired by John Cage that first provoked the question whether sonic phenomena that renounce the tonal system can still be considered music according to the European tradition. At the same time, a response to the question seemed plausible: electronic music perpetuated that tradition insofar as the issues it addressed continued a line of historical development. It is indeed possible to interpret the idea of "composing" tone colors (assembling them from sine tones or filtering them out of white noise) as an extreme manifestation of the tendency toward rationalization which Max Weber believed to be the law governing the development of European music: the tendency toward the control of nature, toward giving the compositorial subject unlimited power over its sonic material [*Tonstoff*] or, put in Hanslick's terms, toward making "spirit" [*Geist*] the undisputed master of that "matter which is capable of spirituality" [*geistfähiges Material*].[5] And guided at the outset by the axioms of serialism, one was able to establish a direct connection with the current state of development reached by avant-garde composition. That is why electronic music indubitably became a matter for composers rather than for physicists and engineers. Hence it could still be subsumed under the category of music as this is understood in modern Europe: a historically changeable category that is defined and continually redefined by the work of composers.

The social, ethnic, and historical disparities that appear to force an abandonment of the concept of music seem scarcely reconcilable. If one nonetheless refrains from completely relinquishing the idea expressed or intimated by the collective singular, then a plausible premise for "rescuing" it could be that the idea of "music" in the singular was ultimately grounded in Hegel's conception of world history: a world history which began in the Near East and made its way via Greece and Rome to the Romance and Germanic nations. Hegel's construction undoubtedly suffers from being Eurocentric; yet to make the charge 150 years later is as futile as it is easy. More germane than this manifest shortcoming is the less obvious fact that the anthropological idea which informs

---

4. "Tonal system" is used here in the broadest sense. It is not restricted to "functional tonality" but covers all musical systems—from Antiquity to the present day—that are organized on the basis of "an arrangement of intervals" (see Carl Dahlhaus's entry on "Tonsysteme," *Musik in Geschichte und Gegenwart*, vol. 13 (Kassel, 1966), cols. 533–47. [Tr.]

5. The word *Geist* is ultimately untranslatable. The word's usage embraces the Latin expressions *spiritus, anima, mens,* and *genius*. The original phrase alluded to here is: "Das Componieren ist ein Arbeiten des Geistes in geistfähigem Material" (Eduard Hanslick, *Vom Musikalisch-Schönen*, p. 35). [Tr.]

Hegel's Philosophy of History [*geschichtsphilosophische Konzeption*] is by no means obsolete: the idea that a culture—even a musical culture—of remote epochs or parts of the world "belongs to world history" to the extent that it participates in "education toward humanity," as that development was commonly called around 1800. The concept of history (in the singular) or world history—a rigorously selective category which excludes from "history proper" the greater part of what occurred in former times as mere detritus—is plausible only when one realizes that it was guided by the classical idea of humanity (in precarious rivalry to the development of science, technology, and industry, which similarly constitutes "a" history—in the singular—regardless of ethnic and social differences).

The concept of world history, at least with regard to earlier epochs, can scarcely be justified in pragmatic terms: the Japanese, Indian, and West European cultures of the fourteenth century scarcely permit the construction either of an external, empirical framework or of a unifying *Zeitgeist*. Their "simultaneity" was chronologically abstract, not historically concrete. Only in the twentieth century have the continents grown together, thanks to economic, technological, and political interdependence, to form a single world whose structure makes it historiographically viable to write world history in the pragmatic sense of the word: a history which also includes the history of music, since the external connection between cultures has become irrefutable, even though any intrinsic one is often questionable, as illustrated by the fad for Indian music.

On the other hand, the idealistic concept of world history need not be relinquished, as long as it is radically modified. It is no longer possible to determine in a dogmatic fashion what a step in the direction of "education toward humanity" should be—from the perspective, that is, of a "cosmopolite" of the early 1800s, who turns out to be an enlightened bourgeois masquerading as the ideal of humanity. "Humanity" in the singular no more exists than "history" in the singular. What remains is the patient effort of understanding, which not only tolerates the "other" precisely on account of its initially disconcerting otherness (tolerance can imply disparagement) but actually respects it.

According to twentieth-century criteria, which are probably not immutable, humanity consists less in making the heterogeneous more homogenous than in mutual acceptance, even where differences may appear unbridgeable. If so, the search in music esthetics (as a derivation of the idea of humanity) for an underlying foundation common to the sonic phenomena of all ages and continents is less important than an awareness and mutual recognition of utterly different principles of formation: the elements and basic patterns are less crucial than the consequences and differentiations. It may be that the principle of consonance and alternating rhythm are "innate ideas" which are merely being forever "transformed," as some historians and ethnomusicologists believe. Or perhaps one can accept as independent, irreducible, and equally valid principles the measurement of interval size alongside relations of consonance, and additive or quantitative rhythm alongside alternating [or qualitative] rhythm [*i.e.*, a succession of *arsis* and *thesis* or strong and weak beats]. Either way, such questions are less important than the appreciation of a substantial dissimilarity of formations or "transformations" [*"Überformungen"*], whether these are constructed on common or differing foundations. To ground the concept of "music" (in the singular) as some "natural given," whether as a musically objective or an anthropological structure, is a difficult and probably pointless enterprise, unless one misuses the concept of "transformation" by invoking it without naming the criteria that allow one to distinguish between "transformations" of common but unrecognizable "deep structures" on the one hand and incoherent diversity on the other. (Moreover, rather than opposing nature and history, one should adopt Fernand Braudel's suggestion and draw a distinction between structures of long, medium, and short duration.)

The driving force behind the idea of "music" (in the singular)—itself a result of "history" (in the singular)—was the classical utopia of humanity that, in Kant's *Critique of Judgment* [*Kritik der Urteilskraft*], formed the basis of an esthetics in which judgments of taste are "subjective" but nevertheless "universal," to the extent that subjectivities strive to converge in a *sensus communis,* a "common sense." If, however, humanity finds expression less in the discovery of a common substance than in the principle of respecting untranscendable difference, one remains true to the idea of "music" (in the singular) by relinquishing it as a concept of substance in order to reinstate it as a regulative principle of mutual understanding.

INDEX

Note: Numbers in boldface refer to pages where definitions for a term are found, or to the source reading passages themselves.